CENSUS OF INDIA 1911

Owing to the antiquity and rarity of this book, certain pages are regrettably absent, and readability is compromised due to the blurring of the original text. If you possess any insights regarding the availability of these missing sections, kindly inform us. Your assistance is crucial in ensuring the completion of this significant work for the benefit of future generations.

CENSUS OF INDIA, 1911

VOLUME - XXII

RAJPUTANA AND AJMER-MERWARA

PART II - TABLES

E. H. KEALY

GYAN

Published by

Gyan Publishing House
5, Ansari Road
Daryaganj, New Delhi-110002
Phone: 011-47034999, 9811692060
E-mail: books@gyanbooks.com

Distribution Network
gyanbooks.com
India, USA, Canada, UK, Australia

ISBN: 978-81-212-7127-1 (Set) 23 Vols. In 41 Bindings

ISBN: 978-81-212-7421-0 (PB) Vol. XXII, Pt. II

First Published, 1913

2nd Impression 2024

Printed at: Gyan Press, Delhi.

CENSUS OF INDIA 1911

CENSUS OF INDIA, 1911

VOLUME XXII

RAJPUTANA

AND

AJMER-MERWARA

PART II

TABLES

Agents for the Sale of Books published by the Superintendent of Government Printing, India, Calcutta.

In United Kingdom.

P. S. King & Son, 2 and 4, Great Smith Street, Westminster, London, S.W.
Kegan Paul, Trench, Trübner & Co., 68—74, Carter Lane, London, E.C.
Bernard Quaritch, 11, Grafton Street, New Bond Street, London, W.
H. S. King & Co., 65, Cornhill, and 9, Pall Mall, London.
Grindlay & Co., 54, Parliament Street, London, S.W.
T. Fisher Unwin, 1, Adelphi Terrace, London, W.C.
W. Thacker & Co., 2, Creed Lane, London, E.C.
Luzac & Co., 46, Great Russell Street, London, W.C.
Oliver & Boyd, Tweeddale Court, Edinburgh.
Constable & Co., 10, Orange Street, Leicester Square, London, W.C.
B. H. Blackwell, 50 and 51, Broad Street, Oxford.
Deighton Bell & Co., Cambridge.
E. Ponsonby, Ld., 116, Grafton Street, Dublin.

On the Continent.

R. Friedländer & Sohn, Berlin, W. N. Carlstrasse, 11.
Otto Harrassowitz, Leipzig, Germany.
Karl W. Hiersemann, Leipzig. Germany.
Ernest Leroux, 28, Rue Bonaparte, Paris, France.
Martinus Nijhoff, The Hague, Holland.

In India.

Thacker, Spink & Co., Calcutta and Simla.
Newman & Co., Calcutta.
R. Cambray & Co., Calcutta.
S. K. Lahiri & Co., Calcutta.
B. Banerjee & Co., Calcutta.
The Calcutta School Book and Useful Literature Society, 309, Bow Bazar Street, Calcutta.
Butterworth & Co. (India), Ld., Calcutta.
The Weldon Library, 18-5, Chowringhee, Calcutta.
Higginbotham & Co., Madras.
V. Kalyanarama Iyer & Co., Madras.
G. A. Natesan & Co., Madras.
S. Murthy & Co., Madras.
Thompson & Co., Madras.
Temple & Co., Madras.
Combridge & Co., Madras.
P. R. Rama Iyer & Co., Madras.
Thacker & Co., Ld., Bombay.
D. B. Taraporevala, Sons & Co., Bombay.
A. J. Combridge & Co., Bombay.
Radhabai Atmaram Sagoon, Bombay.
Sundur Pandurang, Bombay.
Gopal Narayan & Co., Bombay.
Ram Chandra Govind & Son, Kalbadevi, Bombay.
N. B. Mathur, Superintendent, Nazair-Kanun Hind Press, Allahabad.
Rai Sahib M. Gulab Singh & Sons, Mufid-i-Am Press, Lahore and Calcutta.
A. Chand & Co., Punjab, Lahore.
Superintendent, American Baptist Mission Press, Rangoon.
A. M. & J. Ferguson, Colombo, Ceylon.
S. C. Talukdar, Proprietor, Students and Company, Cooch Behar.

CENSUS OF INDIA, 1911

VOLUME XXII

RAJPUTANA

AND

AJMER-MERWARA

PART II
TABLES

BY

E. H. KEALY, M.A., I.C.S.,

Superintendent Census Operations, Rajputana and Ajmer-Merwara

CALCUTTA
SUPERINTENDENT GOVERNMENT PRINTING, INDIA
1912

TABLE OF CONTENTS.

PAGE.

INTRODUCTORY NOTE. 1

Imperial Tables.

Provincial Tables.

INTRODUCTORY NOTE.

The census, the statistics of which are embodied in this volume, was taken on March 10th, 1911.

At previous censuses the Sironj, Chhabra, and Pirawa Parganas of Tonk State, though included in the Provincial Tables, were excluded from all the Imperial Tables. But having been transferred in 1910 from the Central India to the Rajputana Agency they are included now in the Tonk figures in the Imperial Tables.

The figures for the detached tracts of Central India, namely Nandwas, belonging to Indore State, and Gangapur, belonging to Gwalior State, which are situated in the Mewar Agency, are included, as before, in the statistics of Mewar State in the Imperial Tables, and excluded from the Provincial Tables.

The figures for Nimrol village, situated in the Central India Agency, have been excluded from Dholpur State in the Imperial Tables and included in the Provincial Tables.

The figures for the pargana of Sambhar, held jointly by the Jaipur and Marwar Darbars, have been divided between the two States in the Imperial and Provincial Tables.

The figures for areas under British administration in Rajputana are included, in the Imperial and Provincial Tables, in the statistics of the States in which they are situated.

At previous censuses the figures for the Province of Ajmer-Merwara were published in separate volumes. They are printed now with the Rajputana figures throughout the Tables.

The 21 inhabited villages belonging to the Marwar Darbar, and the 92 belonging to the Mewar Darbar, which are all situated in the Merwara District of Ajmer-Merwara and administered, on certain conditions, by the British Government, have been excluded from the Ajmer-Merwara figures in the Provincial Tables and included in the statistics for the two States in question, and *vice versâ* in the Imperial Tables. At previous censuses they were incorporated in the Ajmer-Merwara figures.

The optional Tables, XV-C and XV-D, prescribed by the Government of India, have not been compiled for Rajputana and Ajmer-Merwara; and Table XVI has been prepared only for Europeans and allied races, Armenians, and Anglo-Indians.

Detailed statistics of area, houses, population, religion, and literacy, for the various administrative units (*i.e.*, Parganas, Tahsils, etc.) in the States and Districts, will be found in the Provincial Tables I and II at the end of this volume.

TABLE I.

Area, Houses and Population.

Explanatory Note.

The States in Rajputana are arranged in this Table in three groups, corresponding to the main natural divisions of Rajputana. Within the divisional group they are arranged alphabetically.

The increase of 1,446 square miles in the area of Rajputana, compared with 1901, is explained as follows :—

State.	Increase.	Cause.
Bikaner	+4	Transfer of two villages, Ratakhera and Babalwas, from the Punjab.
Mewar	+3	Gained from Idar State as result of boundary settlement.
Tonk	+1,439	Transfer of Chhabra, Pirawa, and Sironj Parganas from the Central India to the Rajputana Agency.

The areas and populations of the places under British administration in Rajputana are as follows :—

	State.	Area.	Population.		
			Total.	Males.	Females.
Kherwara . . .	Mewar . .	1 square mile .	2,016	1,295	721
Kotra	Mewar . .	Ditto .	746	461	285
Erinpura	Sirohi . .	Ditto . .	3,033	1,856	1,177
Mount Abu . . .	Sirohi . .	·83 square miles .	3,286	2,083	1,203

They have been included in the Tables in the figures of the States in which they are situated.

In Lawa, Mewar, Partabgarh, and Shahpura, hamlets have been counted as separate villages in column 4. In all other cases they have been included in the main village.

TABLE I.—AREA, HOUSES AND POPULATION.

Province and State or District.	Area in square miles.	Inhabited towns.	Inhabited villages.	OCCUPIED HOUSES.			POPULATION.								
				Total.	In towns.	In villages.	PERSONS.			MALES.			FEMALES.		
							Total.	Urban.	Rural.	Total.	Urban.	Rural.	Total.	Urban.	Rural.
1	2	3	4	5	6	7	8	9	10	11	12	13	14	15	16
Rajputana	128,987	133	32,271	2,438,346	337,125	2,101,221	10,530,432	1,343,095	9,187,337	5,515,275	688,936	4,826,339	5,015,157	654,159	4,360,998
Western Division	*74,340*	*35½*	*6,716*	*635,013*	*93,336*	*511,677*	*2,846,847*	*387,765*	*2,459,082*	*1,495,258*	*195,505*	*1,299,753*	*1,351,589*	*192,260*	*1,159,329*
Bikaner	23,315	9	2,177	152,773	28,710	124,063	700,983	127,482	573,501	371,489	63,245	308,244	329,494	64,237	265,257
Jaisalmer	16,062	1	472	20,937	2,068	18,869	88,311	7,420	80,891	48,500	3,667	44,833	39,811	3,753	36,058
*Marwar	34,963	25½	4,067	461,303	62,558	398,745	2,057,553	252,863	1,804,690	1,075,269	128,593	946,676	982,284	124,270	858,014
Southern Division	*18,999*	*25*	*10,386*	*464,995*	*41,930*	*423,065*	*1,892,267*	*151,407*	*1,740,860*	*972,455*	*78,294*	*894,161*	*919,812*	*73,113*	*846,699*
Banswara	1,606	1	1,070	37,648	2,104	35,544	165,463	7,665	157,798	81,620	3,729	77,891	83,843	3,936	79,907
Dungarpur	1,447	3	713	38,100	3,523	34,577	159,192	14,883	144,309	79,105	7,190	71,915	80,087	7,693	72,394
Kushalgarh (Chiefship)	340	1	285	4,636	696	3,040	22,005	2,594	19,411	10,956	1,276	9,680	11,049	1,318	9,731
†Mewar	12,756	14	7,292	322,140	26,318	295,822	1,293,776	93,812	1,199,964	670,750	48,807	621,943	623,026	45,005	578,021
Partabgarh	880	1	617	16,087	2,342	13,745	62,704	8,329	54,375	31,735	4,186	27,549	30,969	4,143	26,826
Sirohi	1,964	5	409	46,384	6,947	39,437	189,127	24,124	165,003	98,289	13,106	85,183	90,838	11,018	79,820
Eastern Division	*35,648*	*72½*	*15,169*	*1,338,338*	*201,859*	*1,136,479*	*5,791,318*	*803,923*	*4,987,395*	*3,047,562*	*415,137*	*2,632,425*	*2,743,756*	*388,786*	*2,354,970*
Alwar	3,141	7	1,765	176,494	19,380	157,114	791,688	74,604	717,084	413,659	39,185	374,474	378,029	35,419	342,610
Bharatpur	1,982	7	1,285	134,268	20,480	113,788	558,785	77,520	481,265	302,254	42,069	260,185	256,531	35,451	221,080
Bundi	2,220	2	796	50,822	6,508	44,314	218,730	24,558	194,172	113,211	12,314	100,897	105,519	12,244	93,275
Dholpur	1,155	3	519	56,695	8,648	48,047	263,188	37,713	225,475	144,244	20,065	124,179	118,944	17,648	101,296
‡Jaipur	15,579	37½	5,765	598,333	97,333	501,000	2,636,647	411,757	2,224,890	1,385,750	210,890	1,174,860	1,250,897	200,867	1,050,030
Jhalawar	810	2	408	23,765	5,755	18,010	96,271	18,664	77,607	50,034	9,144	40,890	46,237	9,520	36,717
Karauli	1,242	1	439	36,005	5,312	30,693	146,587	19,803	126,784	80,081	10,548	69,533	66,506	9,255	57,251
Kishangarh	858	3	226	21,334	5,051	16,283	87,191	17,824	69,367	45,718	9,180	36,538	41,473	8,644	32,829
Kotah	5,684	4	2,554	157,136	15,659	141,477	639,089	52,592	586,497	330,324	27,118	303,206	308,765	25,474	283,291
Lawa (Estate)	19	..	7	647	..	647	2,564	..	2,564	1,302	..	1,302	1,262	..	1,262
Shahpura (Chiefship)	405	1	133	11,291	2,163	9,128	47,397	7,929	39,468	24,595	4,074	20,521	22,802	3,855	18,947
Tonk	2,553	5	1,273	71,548	15,570	55,078	303,181	60,959	242,222	156,390	30,550	125,840	146,791	30,409	116,382
Ajmer-Merwara	2,711	5	743	122,832	37,712	85,120	501,395	140,394	361,001	266,198	77,177	189,021	235,197	63,217	171,980
Ajmer	2,070	4	425	93,562	31,585	61,977	380,384	117,594	262,790	201,911	64,849	137,062	178,473	52,745	125,728
§Merwara	641	1	318	29,270	6,127	23,143	121,011	22,800	98,211	64,287	12,328	51,959	56,724	10,472	46,252

* Marwar includes half Sambhar as follows:—

Column 5	1,978	Column 6	1,498	Column 7	480
" 8	7,468	" 9	5,443	" 10	2,025
" 11	3,994	" 12	2,918	" 13	1,076
" 14	3,474	" 15	2,525	" 16	949

† Mewar includes Nandwas Pargana of Indore and Gangapur Pargana of Gwalior as follows:—

Column 2—62; Column 4—43 Columns 6 and 7—2,678
Columns 8 and 10—12,492, Columns 11 and 13—6,463 Columns 14 and 16—6,029

‡ Jaipur includes half Sambhar as follows:—

Column 5	1,970	Column 6	1,490	Column 7	480
" 8	7,468	" 9	5,444	" 10	2,024
" 11	3,995	" 12	2,919	" 13	1,076
" 14	3,473	" 15	2,525	" 16	948

§ Merwara District includes the following:—

	Column 4.	Columns 5 and 7.	Columns 8 and 10.	Columns 11 and 13.	Columns 14 and 16.
Mewar villages	92	9,489	39,516	20,932	18,584
Marwar villages	21	1,711	7,209	3,893	3,316
TOTAL NON-BRITISH villages.	113	11,200	46,725	24,825	21,900

Corrigendum.

In the Explanatory Note to Table II on page 5 against Sirohi, *for* "Unenumerated Grassias" *read* "Unenumerated Bhils and Grassias of the Bhakar Tahsil."

TABLE II.

Variation in Population since 1881.

Explanatory Note.

No Census was taken in Rajputana in 1872. This Table, therefore, cannot be carried back beyond 1881.

In Ajmer-Merwara a Census was taken in 1872, but as it was considered untrustworthy another count was held in 1876. The figures in connection with it were as follows :—

Province and District.	Persons.	Males.	Females.	Variation 1876 to 1881.	Net variation 1876 to 1911.
Ajmer-Merwara	396,331	212,265	184,066	+64,391	+105,064
Ajmer	309,914	164,510	145,404	+49,374	+70,470
Merwara	86,417	47,755	38,662	+15,017	+34,594

The figures for Rajputana for 1881 do not agree with the corresponding figures in the volume of India Tables, as the former include 167,850 persons of the 3 parganas of the Tonk State, Chhabra, Pirawa, and Sironj, which were situated in 1881 in the Central India Agency but were omitted in the India Tables from the totals for that Agency, figures being given for Central India States only.

The States are arranged in three groups, corresponding to the main natural divisions of Rajputana. Within the divisional group they are arranged alphabetically.

Bikaner.—All columns include figures for villages of Babalwas and Ratakhera, transferred from Hissar District, Punjab, between 1901 and 1911.

Marwar.—All columns include figures for half Sambhar.

Banswara.—Columns 5, 9, 13 exclude unenumerated Bhils.

Dungarpur.—Columns 4, 5, 8, 9, 12, 13 exclude unenumerated Bhils.

Kushalgarh.—(i) columns 4, 8, 12 exclude unenumerated Bhils. (ii) Columns 5, 9, 13, population not enumerated in 1881. (iii) Columns 16 and 17 ; this difference is hypothetical as figures for 1881 are not available.

Mewar.—(i) Columns 4, 5, 8, 9, 12, 13, exclude unenumerated Bhils. (ii) The 1881 figure do not include the population of the detached districts of Nandwas of Indore and Gangapur of Gwalior, as no census was taken there in 1881.

Partabgarh.—Columns 5, 9, 13, exclude unenumerated Bhils.

Sirohi.—Columns 4, 8, 12, 15, 16, exclude unenumerated Grassias.

Dholpur.—All columns exclude figures for Nimrol.

Jaipur.—All columns include figures for half Sambhar.

Jhalawar.—Figures in columns 4, 5, 8, 9, 12, 13, 15, 16, 17, have been adjusted in connection with transfer of territory to Kotah in 1899.

Kotah.—Figures in columns 4, 5, 8, 9, 12, 13, 15, 16, 17, have been adjusted in connection with transfer of territory from Jhalawar in 1899.

Tonk.—All columns include the population of the parganas of Sironj, Pirawa, and Chhabra, formerly situated in the Central India Agency, but transferred in 1910 to the Rajputana Agency.

TABLE II.—VARIATION IN POPULATION SINCE 1881.

Province; and State or District.	Persons.				Males.				Females.				Variation; Increase (+) Decrease (−).			Net variation in period, 1881-1911.
	1911.	1901.	1891.	1881.	1911.	1901.	1891.	1881.	1911.	1901.	1891.	1881.	1901 to 1911.	1891 to 1901.	1881 to 1891.	
1	2	3	4	5	6	7	8	9	10	11	12	13	14	15	16	17
Rajputana	10,530,432	9,853,366	12,171,749	10,102,105	5,515,275	5,171,519	6,436,856	5,461,527	5,015,157	4,681,847	5,734,893	4,640,578	+677,066	−2,318,383	+2,069,644	+428,327
Western Division	*2,846,847*	*2,593,690*	*3,475,944*	*2,374,638*	*1,495,258*	*1,361,882*	*1,832,291*	*1,327,876*	*1,351,599*	*1,232,308*	*1,643,653*	*1,046,962*	*+253,167*	*− 882,254*	*+ 1,101,106*	*+472,009*
Bikaner	700,983	584,755	832,065	509,077	371,489	306,462	440,114	293,684	329,494	278,293	391,951	215,393	+116,228	− 247,310	+ 322,988	+191,906
Jaisalmer	88,311	73,370	115,701	108,143	48,500	39,389	62,699	61,127	39,811	33,981	53,002	47,016	+ 14,941	− 42,331	+ 7,558	− 19,832
Marwar	2,057,553	1,935,565	2,528,178	1,757,618	1,075,269	1,015,531	1,329,478	973,065	982,284	920,034	1,198,700	784,553	+121,988	− 592,613	+ 770,560	+299,935
Southern Division	*1,892,267*	*1,502,234*	*2,289,139*	*1,855,774*	*972,455*	*777,201*	*1,193,656*	*968,001*	*919,812*	*725,033*	*1,095,483*	*867,773*	*+390,033*	*− 786,905*	*+ 433,365*	*+ 36,493*
Banswara	165,463	149,128	180,268	104,000	81,620	73,553	92,540	53,498	83,843	75,575	87,728	50,502	+ 16,335	− 31,140	+ 76,268	+ 61,463
Dungarpur	159,192	100,103	98,448	86,429	79,105	50,050	49,444	44,568	80,087	50,053	49,004	41,861	+ 59,089	+ 1,655	+ 12,019	+ 72,763
Kushalgarh (Chiefship)	22,005	16,222	5,775	not available	10,956	8,229	2,920	not available	11,049	7,993	2,855	not available	+ 5,783	+ 10,447	+ 5,775	+ 22,005
Mewar	1,293,776	1,030,212	1,728,097	1,443,144	670,750	537,913	904,288	772,685	623,026	492,299	824,409	670,459	+263,564	− 698,485	+ 285,553	−149,368
Partabgarh	62,704	52,025	87,975	79,296	31,735	26,036	45,842	41,118	30,969	25,989	42,133	38,180	+ 10,679	− 35,950	+ 8,677	− 16,594
Sirohi	189,127	154,544	187,976	142,903	98,289	81,420	98,622	76,132	90,838	73,124	89,354	66,771	+ 34,583	− 33,432	+ 45,073	+ 46,224
Eastern Division	*5,791,318*	*5,757,442*	*6,406,666*	*5,871,493*	*3,047,562*	*3,032,936*	*3,410,909*	*3,145,650*	*2,743,756*	*2,724,506*	*2,995,757*	*2,725,843*	*+ 33,876*	*− 649,224*	*+ 535,173*	*− 80,175*
Alwar	791,688	828,487	767,786	682,926	413,659	431,035	403,898	360,384	378,029	397,452	363,888	322,542	− 36,799	+ 60,701	+ 84,860	+108,762
Bharatpur	558,785	626,665	640,303	645,540	302,254	335,156	347,830	350,475	256,531	291,509	292,473	295,065	− 67,880	− 13,638	− 5,237	− 86,755
Bundi	218,730	171,227	295,675	254,701	113,211	88,731	156,033	133,103	105,519	82,496	139,642	121,598	+ 47,503	− 124,448	+ 40,974	− 35,971
Dholpur	263,188	270,073	279,890	249,657	144,244	147,601	157,123	138,342	118,944	123,372	122,767	111,315	− 7,785	− 8,917	+ 30,233	+ 13,531
Jaipur	2,636,647	2,658,666	2,823,966	2,527,142	1,385,750	1,405,458	1,505,765	1,365,194	1,250,897	1,253,208	1,318,201	1,161,948	− 22,019	− 165,300	+ 296,824	+109,505
Jhalawar	96,271	90,175	151,097	150,361	50,034	46,737	80,389	81,708	46,237	43,438	70,708	68,653	+ 6,096	− 60,922	+ 736	− 54,090
Karauli	146,587	156,786	156,587	148,670	80,081	85,356	84,555	80,645	66,506	71,430	72,032	68,025	− 10,199	+ 199	+ 7,917	− 2,083
Kishangarh	87,191	90,970	125,516	112,633	45,718	47,475	65,038	59,098	41,473	43,495	60,478	53,535	− 3,779	− 34,546	+ 12,883	− 25,442
Kotah	639,089	544,879	718,771	707,402	330,324	280,912	375,210	371,255	308,765	263,967	343,561	336,147	+ 94,210	− 173,892	+ 11,369	− 68,313
Lawa (Estate)	2,564	2,671	3,360	2,082	1,302	1,326	1,728	1,360	1,262	1,345	1,632	1,322	− 107	− 689	+ 678	− 118
Shahpura (Chiefship)	47,397	42,676	63,646	51,750	24,595	22,221	33,243	27,217	22,802	20,455	30,403	24,533	+ 4,721	− 20,970	+ 11,896	− 4,353
Tonk	303,181	273,267	380,069	338,029	156,390	140,928	200,097	176,869	146,791	132,339	179,972	161,160	+ 29,914	− 106,802	+ 42,040	− 34,848
Ajmer-Merwara	501,395	476,912	542,358	460,722	266,198	251,026	288,325	248,844	235,197	225,886	254,033	211,878	+24,483	−65,446	+81,636	+40,673
Ajmer	380,384	367,453	422,359	359,288	201,911	193,384	223,547	192,669	178,473	174,069	198,812	166,619	+ 12,931	− 54,906	+ 63,071	+ 21,096
Merwara	121,011	109,459	119,999	101,434	64,287	57,642	64,778	56,175	56,724	51,817	55,221	45,259	+ 11,552	− 10,540	+ 18,565	+ 19,577

TABLE III.

Towns and Villages Classified by Population.

Explanatory Note.

The States in Rajputana have been arranged in natural divisions, and alphabetically within the divisions.

Travellers by railway, and the population enumerated in encampments and fairs, have been shown separately in column 22, instead of being included, as in 1901, in the places at which they were enumerated. Out of 7,985 in Rajputana 4,101 persons, and in Ajmer-Merwara all the population i n this column, were travellers by railway.

Except in Lawa, Partabgarh, Mewar, and Shahpura, hamlets have been included in the villages to which they belong.

There is an apparent increase of 2,375 or 7·9 per cent. in the number of towns and villages in Rajputana, compared with 1901. The increase is most marked in the following three States :—

State.	*Actual increase.*	*Percentage of increase.*	*Explanation.*
Mewar . . .	+ 1,223	+ 20·1	Reckoning hamlets as separate villages instead of including them in the parent villages as in 1901, and the re-inhabiting of villages lying deserted in 1901.
Partabgarh . .	+ 205	+ 49·6	Reckoning hamlets as separate villages instead of including them in the parent villages as in 1901.
Tonk . . .	+ 734	+ 134·9	Inclusion of 752 villages of Chhabra, Pirawa and Sironj Parganas, recently transferred from the Central India to the Rajputana Agency.

TABLE III.

TOWNS AND VILLAGES CLASSIFIED BY POPULATION.

TABLE III.—TOWNS AND VILLAGES CLASSIFIED BY POPULATION.

PROVINCE; AND STATE OR DISTRICT.	Total number of inhabited towns and villages.	POPULATION.	TOWNS AND VILLAGES WITH A POPULATION OF :— UNDER 500. Number.	Population.	500—999. Number.	Population.	1,000—1,999. Number.	Population.	2,000—4,999. Number.	Population.	5,000—9,999. Number.	Population.	10,000—19,999. Number.	Population.	20,000—49,999. Number.	Population.	50,000—99,999. Number.	Population.	100,000 AND OVER. Number.	Population.	Railway travellers, and population enumerated in encampments and fairs.
1	2	3	4	5	6	7	8	9	10	11	12	13	14	15	16	17	18	19	20	21	22
Rajputana	*32,404*	*10,530,432*	**27,472**	**4,419,741**	**3,326**	**2,262,582**	**1,129**	**1,539,432**	**378**	**1,089,106**	**64**	**423,815**	**25**	**318,762**	**7**	**217,226**	**2**	**114,924**	**1**	**136,859**	**7,985**
Western Division	*6,751½*	*2,846,847*	**5,282**	**1,030,625**	**1,004**	**690,124**	**328**	**451,260**	**105**	**296,357**	**19½**	**127,823**	**10**	**112,955**	**1**	**20,270**	**2**	**114,924**	...	...	**2,509**
Bikaner	*2,186*	*700,983*	1,900	332,274	219	143,722	40	66,465	10	32,415	3	16,496	4	53,233	...	...	1	55,662	...	...	716
Jaisalmer	*473*	*88,311*	442	54,872	21	14,402	9	11,617	...	...	1	7,420	...	...	...	...	...	...	...	...	...
Marwar	*4,092½*	*2,057,553*	2,940	643,479	764	532,000	270	373,178	95	263,942	15½	103,907	6	59,722	1	20,270	1	59,262	...	...	1,793
Southern Division	*10,411*	*1,892,267*	**9,684**	**1,097,281**	**503**	**323,776**	**161**	**214,593**	**53**	**159,069**	**9**	**62,598**	...	...	**1**	**33,229**	...	...	...	...	**1,721**
Banswara	*1,071*	*165,463*	1,018	111,630	36	23,190	15	20,801	1	2,177	1	7,065	...	...	...	...	...	...	...	...	...
Dungarpur	*716*	*159,192*	654	97,300	46	30,651	13	16,298	2	8,413	1	6,470	...	...	...	...	...	...	...	...	...
Kushalgarh (Chiefship).	*286*	*22,005*	285	19,411	...	...	...	...	1	2,594	...	...	...	...	...	...	...	...	...	...	...
Mewar	*7,306*	*1,293,776*	6,831	775,085	331	206,511	101	137,578	38	114,108	4	26,662	...	...	1	33,229	...	...	...	...	603
Partabgarh	*613*	*62,704*	601	42,404	11	6,686	5	5,285	...	...	1	8,329	...	...	...	...	...	...	...	...	...
Sirohi	*414*	*189,127*	205	51,391	79	56,738	27	34,631	11	31,777	2	13,472	...	...	...	...	...	...	...	...	1,118
Eastern Division	*15,241½*	*5,791,318*	**12,506**	**2,291,835**	**1,819**	**1,248,682**	**640**	**873,579**	**220**	**633,680**	**35½**	**233,394**	**15**	**205,807**	**5**	**163,727**	...	...	**1**	**136,859**	**3,755**
Alwar	*1,772*	*791,688*	1,334	297,639	304	207,337	97	133,562	32	85,045	4	26,706	...	...	1	41,185	...	...	...	...	214
Bharatpur	*1,292*	*558,785*	988	206,370	226	155,794	53	70,885	19	50,451	4	26,146	1	13,147	1	33,735	...	...	...	...	257
Bundi	*797*	*218,730*	708	107,924	58	39,261	23	30,472	7	21,399	...	...	1	19,598	...	...	...	...	...	...	76
Dholpur	*522*	*263,188*	373	83,767	102	72,002	39	54,789	5	14,800	1	6,390	2	31,323	...	...	...	...	...	...	117
Jaipur	*5,802½*	*2,636,647*	4,545	910,687	733	537,512	317	433,999	127	367,235	21½	137,819	7	88,638	1	22,317	...	...	1	136,859	1,631
Jhalawar	*410*	*96,271*	383	54,923	21	13,128	1	1,020	3	8,491	1	7,190	1	11,474	...	...	...	...	...	...	45
Karauli	*440*	*146,587*	366	62,944	55	38,243	16	20,928	2	4,067	...	...	1	19,189	...	...	...	...	...	...	616
Kishangarh	*229*	*87,191*	189	36,552	27	18,493	9	12,202	3	9,526	...	...	1	10,347	...	...	...	...	...	...	71
Kotah	*2,558*	*639,089*	2,327	346,077	147	98,679	63	87,294	18	58,700	2	15,050	...	...	1	32,626	...	...	...	...	663
Lawa (Estate)	*7*	*2,564*	6	453	...	...	...	...	1	2,111	...	...	...	...	...	...	...	...	...	...	...
Shahpura (Chiefship).	*134*	*47,397*	109	17,820	18	12,408	5	6,760	1	2,480	1	7,929	...	...	...	...	...	...	...	...	...
Tonk	*1,278*	*303,181*	1,178	104,729	78	55,825	17	21,668	2	8,775	1	6,164	1	18,091	1	33,864	...	...	...	...	65
Ajmer-Merwara	*748*	*501,395*	**521**	**113,025**	**139**	**96,144**	**56**	**74,658**	**27**	**76,990**	**2**	**11,131**	...	...	**2**	**42,761**	**1**	**85,471**	...	...	**1,215**
Ajmer	*429*	*386,384*	253	67,075	107	74,947	44	59,718	21	60,889	2	11,131	...	...	1	20,208	1	85,471	...	...	945
Merwara	*319*	*121,011*	268	45,950	32	21,197	12	14,940	6	16,101	...	...	...	...	1	22,553	...	...	...	...	270

NOTE.—The half town in columns 2 and 12 refers to Sambhar Town which is divided between the Jaipur and Marwar States.

TABLE IV.

Towns Classified by Population with Variation since 1881.

Explanatory Note.

This Table shows the population of all cities and towns.

No census was taken in Rajputana before 1881. The Table, therefore, cannot be carried back beyond 1881. In Ajmer-Merwara a census was taken in 1876. The figures in connection with it for the towns in Ajmer-Merwara were as follows :—

Towns.	District.	Population. 1876.	Increase. 1876 to 1881.	Variation. 1876 to 1911.
Ajmer	Ajmer	35,111	13,624	51,111
Beawar	Merwara	12,308	3,631	10,492
Deoli	Ajmer	(Figures not available.)		
Kekri	Ajmer	4,885	1,234	1,041
Nasirabad	Ajmer	20,097	1,223	144

As in 1901, a city means (*i*) every town containing not less than 100,000 inhabitants, (*ii*) any other town treated by the Provincial Census Superintendent, with the sanction of the Local Government, as a city for census purposes. Only one city, Jaipur, falls within the former category. The remaining seven Rajputana cities and Ajmer have again been included in the latter category, as in 1901. No new cities have come into existence since 1901.

There has been a decrease in Kotah city, due to the separation of Chhaoni, and an increase in the area of Alwar. Their adjusted populations for 1901 are as follows:—

	Persons.	Males.	Females.
Alwar	58,113	30,269	27,844
Kotah	32,146	16,832	15,314

A town was defined in the Imperial Census Code as including (1) every Municipality, (2) all civil lines not included within Municipal limits, (3) every Cantonment, (4) every other continuous collection of houses inhabited by not less than 5,000 persons, treated by the Provincial Census Superintendent as a town for census purposes. But the numerical limit in the case of category (4) has been relaxed in Rajputana so as to admit certain places having urban characteristics, which had been treated as towns in 1901.

Towns have been arranged in four classes, and alphabetically within the class. The number of towns in each class is as follows :—

Class.	Number of towns in Rajputana.	Number of towns in Ajmer-Merwara.
I. 20,000 and over	2	2
II. 10,000—20,000	24	...
III. 5,000—10,000	59	2
IV. Under 5,000	40	...
Total	125	4

The following seven places have been included as towns for the first time :—

Towns.	1911 : total population.	State or District.	Reasons for inclusion.
Chhabra	6,164	Tonk	Transfer from Central India Agency.
Deoli	5,205	Ajmer	Cantonment.
Galiakot	3,914	Dungarpur	Municipality.
Kushalgarh	2,594	Kushalgarh	Municipality.
Pirawa	4,562	Tonk	Transfer from Central India Agency.
Sagwara	4,499	Dungarpur	Municipality.
Sironj	12,091	Tonk	Transfer from Central India Agency.
	39,029		

Kuchera, which had a population of only 3,488, and was treated as a town in 1901, has been omitted this time at the request of the Marwar Durbar, having lost its urban characteristics.

There has been a slight increase in the areas of two towns in Ajmer-Merwara, Beawar (·392 square miles), and Kekri (·23 square miles). But as it has not been possible to ascertain the previous population of the new areas the adjusted 1901 population cannot be given.

As far as possible the population of suburbs has been shown separately.

The figures for Sambhar town, which is in the joint jurisdiction of the Jaipur and Marwar Durbars, have been divided between the two States.

Unlike Table III travellers by railway, and persons enumerated in encampments and fairs, are included in the population of the towns in whose limits they were enumerated. This has not, however, affected the classification of any town as compared with that in Table III.

TABLE IV.—Towns Classified by Population, with Variation since 1881.

Province and Town.	State or District.	Municipality, Suburbs, Cantonment.	Population. 1911.	Population. 1901.	Population. 1891.	Population. 1881.	Variation. Increase (+) Decrease (−). 1901–1911.	Variation. 1891–1901.	Variation. 1881–1891.	Variation in period 1881–1911. Increase (+) Decrease (−).	Males. 1911.	Males. 1901.	Males. 1891.	Females. 1911.	Females. 1901.	Females. 1891.
1	2	3	4	5	6	7	8	9	10	11	12	13	14	15	16	17
Rajputana	**Urban Population.**	...	**1,343,095**	**1,437,477**	**1,549,709**	**1,348,392**	**−94,382**	**−112,232**	**+201,317**	**−5,297**	**688,936**	**736,480**	**803,548**	**654,159**	**700,997**	**746,161**
Cities	**8 cities**	**Total**	427,255	492,443	521,298	468,183	−65,188	−28,855	+53,115	−40,928	220,775	253,909	273,848	206,480	238,534	247,450
1. Alwar	Alwar	M.	24,617	44,867	...	...	−20,250	..		...	12,280	22,429	...	12,329	22,438	...
		S.	16,688	11,904	...		+4,784	...	...	...	9,065	7,146	..	6,723	4,759	...
		Total	**41,305**	**56,771**	**51,427**	**49,867**	**−15,466**	**+5,344**	**+1,560**	**−8,562**	**22,254**	**29,574**	**27,764**	**19,051**	**27,197**	**23,663**
2. Bharatpur	Bharatpur	M.	33,918	43,601	67,555	66,163	−9,683	−23,954	+1,392	−32,245	18,803	23,703	37,330	15,115	19,898	30,216
3. Bikaner	Bikaner	M.	55,714	52,775	50,040	33,063	+2,939	+2,735	+16,977	+22,651	28,200	26,466	24,712	27,506	26,309	25,337
		S.	112	300	464	91	−188	−164	+373	+21	66	143	267	46	157	197
		Total	**55,826**	**53,075**	**50,513**	**33,154**	**+2,751**	**+2,562**	**+17,359**	**+22,672**	**28,275**	**26,709**	**24,979**	**27,551**	**26,366**	**25,574**
4. Jaipur	Jaipur	M.	112,281	132,091	132,421	125,785	−19,810	−330	+6,636	−13,504	56,734	67,237	68,167	55,547	64,854	64,254
		S.	24,817	28,076	26,366	16,793	−3,259	+1,710	+9,573	+8,024	14,112	16,617	15,837	10,705	11,459	10,529
		Total	**137,098**	**160,167**	**158,787**	**142,578**	**−23,069**	**+1,380**	**+16,209**	**−5,480**	**70,846**	**83,854**	**84,024**	**66,252**	**76,313**	**74,763**
5. Jodhpur	Marwar	M.	50,262	60,437	61,759	57,211	−10,175	−1,322	+4,548	+2,051	29,351	30,043	31,063	20,911	30,394	30,006
6. Kotah	Kotah	M.	32,753	33,657	38,620	40,270	−904	−4,963	−1,650	−7,517	16,940	17,188	20,003	15,804	16,669	18,617
7. Tonk	Tonk	...	33,864	38,759	45,944	40,726	−4,895	−7,185	+5,218	−6,862	16,837	18,986	23,203	17,027	19,774	22,741
8. Udaipur	Mewar	...	33,230	45,976	46,693	38,214	−12,747	−717	+8,479	−4,985	17,400	23,463	24,873	15,760	22,523	21,820
Towns	**125 Towns**	**Total**	915,840	945,034	1,028,411	880,209	−29,194	−83,377	+148,202	+35,031	468,161	482,571	529,700	447,679	462,463	498,711
Class I	*(20,000 and over).*	*Total*	*42,811*	*40,195*	*38,543*	*23,857*	*+2,616*	*+1,652*	*+14,686*	*+18,954*	*23,991*	*22,832*	*22,288*	*18,820*	*17,363*	*16,255*
9. Jodhpur	Marwar	...	20,404	18,672	18,646	6,118	+1,822	+26	+12,528	+14,286	12,397	11,459	11,064	8,007	7,213	6,982
10. Sikar	Jaipur	...	22,317	21,523	19,897	17,739	+794	+1,626	+2,158	+4,578	11,504	11,873	10,624	10,813	10,150	9,273
Class II.	*(10,000–20,000).*	*Total*	*319,860*	*318,670*	*342,962*	*300,384*	*+1,190*	*−24,292*	*+42,578*	*+19,476*	*160,770*	*160,150*	*174,026*	*159,090*	*158,520*	*168,936*
11. Bari	Dholpur	...	11,401	11,603	12,092	11,547	−202	−489	+545	−146	5,755	5,975	6,273	5,646	5,728	5,819
12. Bundi	Bundi	...	19,598	19,313	22,544	20,744	+285	−3,231	+1,800	−1,146	9,805	9,637	11,960	9,793	9,676	10,584
13. Chhaoni Jhalrapatan.	Jhalawar	M.	11,474	14,315	23,363	20,303	−2,841	−9,048	+3,060	−8,829	5,597	7,046	12,126	5,877	7,269	11,237
14. Churu	Bikaner	M.	16,038	15,657	14,014	10,666	+381	+1,643	+3,348	+5,372	7,703	7,723	6,910	8,245	7,934	7,104
15. Dholpur	Dholpur	...	19,922	19,310	17,028	15,833	+612	+2,282	+1,195	+4,089	10,783	10,079	8,900	9,139	9,231	8,128
16. Didwana	Marwar	...	10,122	9,410	11,376	6,617	+712	−1,966	+4,759	+3,505	5,438	4,910	5,708	4,684	4,401	5,606
17. Dig	Bharatpur	M.	13,147	15,409	15,166	15,828	−2,262	+243	−662	−2,681	7,076	8,150	8,223	6,071	7,253	6,943
18. Fatehpur	Jaipur	...	17,204	16,303	16,580	14,731	+901	−187	+1,849	+2,563	8,280	7,730	7,932	9,014	8,563	8,648
19. Hindaun	Jaipur	...	10,640	11,938	12,996	12,701	−1,298	−1,058	+235	−2,121	5,737	6,200	6,780	4,903	5,738	6,216
20. Jhunjhunu	Jaipur	...	13,266	12,279	12,267	9,538	+987	+12	+2,729	+3,728	6,575	6,168	6,297	6,691	6,111	5,690
21. Karauli	Karauli	M.	19,803	23,482	23,124	25,607	−3,679	+358	−2,483	−5,804	10,548	12,725	11,769	9,255	10,757	11,356
22. Kishangarh	Kishangarh	M.	10,418	12,663	15,457	14,824	−2,245	−2,794	+633	−4,406	5,443	6,656	8,072	4,975	6,005	7,438
23. Lachhmangarh	Jaipur	..	10,828	10,176	9,507	8,713	+652	+669	+794	+2,115	5,024	4,942	4,656	5,804	5,234	4,851
24. Nagaur	Marwar	...	12,960	13,377	17,191	14,067	−417	−3,814	+3,124	−1,107	6,442	6,541	9,418	6,518	6,836	8,772
25. Nawalgarh	Jaipur	...	14,059	12,315	12,567	10,032	+1,744	−252	+2,535	+4,027	6,874	6,113	6,267	7,185	6,202	6,300

TABLE IV.—Towns Classified by Population, with Variation since 1881—(*continued*).

Province and Town.	State or District.	Municipality, Suburbs, Cantonment.	Population. 1911.	1901.	1891.	1881.	Variation. Increase (+) Decrease (–). 1901–1911.	1891–1901.	1881–1891.	Variation in period 1881–1911. Increase (+) Decrease (–).	Males. 1911.	1901.	1891.	Females. 1911.	1901.	1891.
1	2	3	4	5	6	7	8	9	10	11	12	13	14	15	16	17
26. Pali	Marwar	...	12,939	12,673	17,166	13,346	+ 266	– 4,477	+ 3,805	– 406	6,580	6,501	8,536	6,359	6,172	8,615
27. Phalodi	Marwar	...	13,825	13,924	10,497	9,448	– 99	+ 3,427	+ 1,049	+ 4,377	6,375	6,600	4,811	7,450	7,324	5,686
28. Ramgarh	Jaipur	...	11,556	11,023	12,197	11,313	+ 533	– 1,174	+ 884	+ 243	5,657	5,299	5,980	5,899	5,724	6,217
29. Ratangarh	Bikaner	M.	12,803	11,744	10,536	7,580	+ 1,059	+ 1,208	+ 2,956	+ 5,223	6,078	5,606	5,123	6,725	6,138	5,413
30. Sardar Shahr	Bikaner	M.	12,375	10,052	9,196	5,824	+ 2,323	+ 856	+ 3,372	+ 6,551	6,008	4,874	4,463	6,367	5,178	4,733
31. Sawai Madhopur.	Jaipur	...	11,166	10,328	13,972	14,075	+ 838	– 3,644	– 103	– 2,909	5,900	5,499	7,143	5,266	4,829	6,829
32. Sironj	Tonk	...	12,091	10,417	11,737	11,356	+ 1,674	– 1,320	+ 381	+ 735	6,083	5,291	6,676	6,008	5,126	5,061
33. Sojat	Marwar	...	10,049	11,107	12,624	10,394	– 1,058	– 1,517	+ 2,230	– 345	4,971	5,243	6,060	5,078	5,864	6,564
34. Sujangarh	Bikaner	M.	12,086	9,762	9,781	5,238	+ 2,324	– 19	+ 4,543	+ 6,848	5,948	4,723	4,824	6,138	5,039	4,957
Class III	*(5,000—10,000)*	*Total*	*397,958*	*416,871*	*454,834*	*394,799*	*– 18,913*	*– 37,963*	*+ 60,035*	*+ 3,159*	*203,248*	*212,429*	*233,362*	*194,710*	*204,442*	*221,472*
35. Bairat	Jaipur	...	5,273	5,637	5,748	5,649	– 364	– 111	+ 99	– 376	2,549	2,806	2,912	2,724	2,831	2,836
36. Bali	Marwar	...	5,593	5,186	5,354	4,438	+ 407	– 168	+ 916	+ 1,155	2,732	2,644	2,617	2,861	2,542	2,737
37. Balotra	Marwar	...	5,408	5,118	5,435	...	+ 290	– 317	+ 5,435	+ 5,408	2,802	2,680	2,762	2,606	2,438	2,673
38. Banswara	Banswara	M	7,655	7,028	8,224	7,898	+ 627	– 1,196	+ 326	– 243	3,720	3,376	3,988	3,935	3,652	4,236
39. Baran	Kotah	M	8,607	7,592	6,867	7,714	+ 1,015	+ 825	– 847	+ 1,703	4,073	3,994	3,303	4,534	3,598	3,564
40. Barmer	Marwar	...	6,380	6,064	5,610	...	+ 316	+ 454	+ 5,610	+ 6,380	3,285	3,200	2,801	3,095	2,864	2,809
41. Baswa	Jaipur	...	5,532	5,908	6,117	5,791	– 376	– 209	+ 326	– 259	2,820	3,058	3,230	2,712	2,850	2,887
42. Bayana	Bharatpur	...	7,029	6,867	8,085	8,758	+ 162	– 1,218	– 673	– 1,729	3,714	3,446	4,154	3,315	3,421	3,931
43. Behror	Alwar	...	5,253	5,540	5,719	5,533	– 287	– 179	+ 186	– 280	2,685	2,715	2,810	2,568	2,825	2,909
44. Bhilwara	Mewar	...	8,763	10,346	10,343	8,175	– 1,583	+ 3	+ 2,168	+ 588	4,613	5,446	5,485	4,150	4,900	4,858
45. Bhinmal	Marwar	...	5,214	4,354	5,736	5,224	+ 860	– 1,101	+ 512	– 10	2,398	2,295	2,906	2,816	2,059	2,830
46. Bilara	Marwar	...	8,606	8,695	11,384	7,699	– 89	– 2,689	+ 3,685	+ 907	4,453	4,464	5,996	4,153	4,231	5,388
47. Riasau	Jaipur	...	6,838	7,726	8,041	6,546	– 888	– 315	+ 1,495	+ 292	3,203	3,716	4,047	3,635	4,010	3,994
48. Chaumu	Jaipur	...	6,497	9,300	8,570	3,928	– 2,803	+ 730	+ 4,642	+ 2,569	3,225	4,631	4,351	3,272	4,669	4,219
49. Chhabra	Tonk	...	6,164	6,724	7,426	8,040	– 560	– 702	– 614	– 1,876	3,108	3,615	3,730	3,056	3,109	3,696
50. Chirawa	Jaipur	...	7,979	7,065	6,701	5,489	+ 914	+ 364	+ 1,212	+ 2,490	3,911	3,603	3,382	4,068	3,462	3,319
51. Chitorgarh	Mewar	...	7,332	7,593	9,354	6,931	– 261	– 1,761	+ 2,423	+ 401	3,939	4,122	4,955	3,393	3,471	4,399
52. Daosa	Jaipur	...	5,191	7,540	8,416	7,384	– 2,349	– 876	+ 1,032	– 2,193	2,572	3,836	4,518	2,619	3,704	3,898
53. Deogarh	Mewar	...	5,461	5,384	7,400	6,846	+ 77	– 2,016	+ 554	– 1,385	2,638	2,807	3,635	2,823	2,577	3,765
54. Dungarpur	Dungarpur	M	6,470	6,094	6,431	6,449	+ 376	– 337	– 18	+ 21	3,116	2,870	3,003	3,354	3,224	3,428
55. Gangapur	Jaipur	...	5,780	5,155	5,880	5,880	+ 625	– 725	...	– 100	3,199	2,700	3,106	2,581	2,446	2,773
56. Jaisalmer	Jaisalmer	...	7,420	7,137	10,509	10,965	+ 283	– 3,372	– 456	– 3,545	3,667	3,575	5,015	3,753	3,562	5,494
57. Jalor	Marwar	...	7,624	7,443	9,656	6,394	+ 181	– 2,213	+ 3,262	+ 1,230	3,791	3,675	4,788	3,833	3,768	4,868
58. Kaman	Bharatpur	...	8,912	12,083	11,417	13,199	– 3,171	+ 666	– 1,782	– 4,287	4,867	6,252	5,951	4,045	5,831	5,466
59. Khandela	Jaipur	...	8,206	9,156	10,067	7,949	– 950	– 911	+ 2,118	+ 257	3,995	4,444	4,980	4,211	4,712	5,087
60. Kharari (Abu Road).	Sirohi	...	7,180	6,661	4,438	...	+ 519	+ 2,223	+ 4,438	+ 7,180	4,007	3,801	2,465	3,173	2,860	1,973
61. Khetri	Jaipur	...	7,125	8,537	8,418	5,283	– 1,412	+ 119	+ 3,135	+ 1,842	3,718	4,479	4,420	3,407	4,058	3,998
62. Kot Putli	Jaipur	...	6,879	8,439	7,589	8,084	– 1,560	+ 850	– 495	– 1,205	3,443	4,152	3,796	3,436	4,287	3,793
63. Kuchaman	Marwar	...	9,605	10,749	12,816	13,052	– 1,144	– 2,067	– 236	– 3,447	4,754	5,361	6,527	4,851	5,388	6,289
64. Kumher	Bharatpur	...	5,075	6,240	6,661	7,306	– 1,165	– 421	– 645	– 2,231	2,679	3,240	3,443	2,396	3,000	3,218
65. Ladnun	Marwar	...	9,685	8,064	7,404	5,183	+ 1,621	+ 660	+ 2,221	+ 4,502	4,574	3,718	3,482	5,111	4,346	3,922
66. Lalsot	Jaipur	...	6,697	8,131	8,163	8,743	– 1,434	– 32	– 580	– 2,046	3,390	4,031	4,021	3,307	4,100	4,142
67. Malpura	Jaipur	...	6,140	6,503	8,345	8,212	– 363	– 1,842	+ 133	– 2,072	3,230	3,368	4,336	2,910	3,135	4,009
68. Maudawa	Jaipur	...	5,536	5,165	4,942	4,409	+ 371	+ 223	+ 533	+ 1,127	2,754	2,532	2,479	2,782	2,633	2,463
69. Mundwa	Marwar	...	5,027	5,121	5,213	4,265	– 94	– 92	+ 948	+ 762	2,473	2,554	2,602	2,554	2,567	2,611
70. Naraina	Jaipur	...	5,190	5,260	5,071	4,974	– 70	+ 195	+ 97	+ 216	3,255	3,289	2,668	1,935	1,977	2,403
71. Nathdwara	Mewar	...	5,424	8,591	9,331	8,458	– 3,167	– 740	+ 873	– 3,034	2,906	4,461	4,877	2,518	4,130	4,454

TABLE IV.—Towns Classified by Population, with Variation since 1881—(*continued*).

Province and Town.	State or District.	Municipality, Suburbs, Cantonment.	Population. 1911.	Population. 1901.	Population. 1891.	Population. 1881.	Variation. Increase (+) Decrease (−). 1901–1911.	Variation. 1891–1901.	Variation. 1881–1891.	Variation in period 1881–1911. Increase (+) Decrease (−).	Males. 1911.	Males. 1901.	Males. 1891.	Females. 1911.	Females. 1901.	Females. 1891.
1	2	3	4	5	6	7	8	9	10	11	12	13	14	15	16	17
72. Nawa	Marwar	...	5,657	5,640	5,126	4,142	+ 17	+ 514	+ 984	+ 1,515	2,963	3,001	2,742	2,694	2,639	2,384
73. Nimaj	Marwar	...	5,015	4,104	5,744	4,371	+ 911	− 1,640	+ 1,373	+ 644	2,520	3,058	2,928	2,495	1,046	2,816
74. Nimka Thana	Jaipur	...	5,946	6,741	5,733	2,711	− 795	+ 1,008	+ 3,022	+ 3,235	3,291	3,726	3,323	2,655	3,015	2,410
75. Nohar	Bikaner	M	5,133	4,698	5,655	3,784	+ 435	− 957	+ 1,871	+ 1,349	2,518	2,275	2,904	2,615	2,423	2,751
76. Partabgarh	Partabgarh	M	8,329	9,819	14,819	12,439	− 1,490	− 5,000	+ 2,380	− 4,110	4,186	4,759	7,906	4,143	5,060	6,913
77. Patan	Jhalawar	M	7,190	7,955	10,783	11,469	− 765	− 2,828	− 686	− 4,279	3,547	4,089	5,680	3,643	3,866	5,103
78. Pipar	Marwar	...	7,556	6,785	8,153	6,608	+ 771	− 1,368	+ 1,545	+ 948	3,796	3,239	3,924	3,760	3,546	4,229
79. Pokaran	Marwar	...	5,814	7,125	7,895	6,467	− 1,311	− 770	+ 1,428	− 653	2,863	3,519	3,893	2,951	3,606	4,002
80. Rajakhera	Dholpur	...	6,390	6,609	6,786	6,274	− 219	− 177	+ 512	+ 116	3,527	3,608	3,731	2,863	3,001	3,055
81. Rajgarh	Alwar	M	9,865	11,008	10,302	9,749	− 1,143	+ 706	+ 553	+ 116	4,954	5,582	5,084	4,911	5,426	5,218
82. Reni	Bikaner	M	5,904	5,745	6,653	5,198	+ 159	− 908	+ 1,455	+ 706	2,873	2,781	3,349	3,031	2,964	3,304
83. ½Sambhar	Jaipur	...	5,548	5,437	6,181	5,397	+ 111	− 744	+ 784	+ 151	2,997	2,834	3,401	2,551	2,603	2,780
½ Sambhar	Marwar	...	5,546	5,436	6,181	5,397	+ 110	− 745	+ 784	+ 149	2,995	2,832	3,401	2,551	2,604	2,780
84. Sangod	Kotah	M	5,543	4,369	6,046	5,006	+ 1,174	− 677	+ 40	+ 537	2,767	3,108	3,547	2,776	2,261	2,499
85. Shahpura	Shahpura	..	7,929	8,974	11,718	10,647	− 1,045	− 2,744	+ 1,071	− 2,718	4,074	4,707	5,930	3,855	4,267	5,788
86. Singhana	Jaipur	...	5,268	5,176	5,901	5,259	+ 92	− 725	+ 642	+ 9	2,422	2,432	2,770	2,846	2,744	3,131
87. Sirohi	Sirohi	...	6,615	5,651	6,207	5,699	+ 964	− 556	+ 508	+ 916	3,272	2,722	3,075	3,343	2,929	3,132
88. Sri Madhopur	Jaipur	...	6,738	6,892	6,130	6,847	− 154	+ 762	− 717	− 109	3,367	3,519	3,004	3,371	3,373	3,126
89. Surajgarh	Jaipur	...	5,992	5,243	5,561	5,250	+ 749	− 318	+ 311	+ 742	2,962	2,531	2,761	3,030	2,712	2,800
90. Tijara	Alwar	M	6,561	7,784	7,049	7,723	− 1,223	+ 735	− 674	− 1,162	3,341	3,927	3,543	3,220	3,857	3,506
91. Toda Bhim	Jaipur	...	6,886	6,629	7,063	7,142	+ 257	− 434	− 79	− 256	3,519	3,422	3,692	3,367	3,207	3,371
92. Udaipur	Jaipur	...	7,743	8,638	10,343	9,161	− 895	− 1,705	+ 1,182	− 1,418	4,459	4,793	6,562	3,284	3,845	3,781
93. Wer	Bharatpur	...	5,130	5,711	6,824	7,210	− 581	− 1,113	− 386	− 2,080	2,678	3,015	3,509	2,452	2,696	3,315
Class IV	*(Under 5,000)*	*Total*	*155,211*	*169,298*	*192,072*	*161,169*	− *14,087*	− *22,774*	+ *30,903*	− *5,958*	*80,152*	*87,160*	*100,024*	*75,059*	*82,138*	*92,048*
94. Bahadurpur	Alwar	M	4,236	4,087	4,254	4,171	+ 149	− 167	+ 83	+ 65	2,098	1,996	2,114	2,138	2,091	2,140
95. Bamanwas	Jaipur	...	4,292	5,294	5,806	6,125	− 1,002	− 512	− 319	− 1,833	2,229	2,863	3,014	2,063	2,431	2,792
96. Banera	Mewar	...	4,335	4,261	5,760	4,718	+ 74	− 1,499	− 1,042	− 383	2,144	2,125	2,886	2,191	2,136	2,874
97. Begun	Mewar	...	4,385	3,625	5,882	5,641	+ 760	− 2,257	+ 241	− 1,256	2,204	1,767	2,988	2,181	1,858	2,894
98. Bhusawar	Bharatpur	...	4,309	6,690	7,419	6,480	− 2,381	− 729	+ 939	− 2,171	2,252	3,416	3,778	2,057	3,274	3,641
99. Bhindar	Mewar	..	4,630	5,172	6,790	6,532	− 542	− 1,618	+ 258	− 1,902	2,345	2,569	3,434	2,285	2,603	3,356
100. Chaksu	Jaipur	...	3,940	4,903	7,870	6,219	− 963	− 2,967	+ 1,651	− 2,279	2,090	2,704	4,589	1,850	2,199	3,281
101. Chhoti Sadri	Mewar	...	4,576	5,050	5,368	4,521	− 474	− 318	+ 847	+ 55	2,344	2,520	2,709	2,232	2,530	2,659
102. Erinpura	Sirohi	C	3,033	3,206	3,466	...	− 173	− 260	+ 3,466	+ 3,033	1,856	1,830	2,098	1,177	1,376	1,368
103. Galiakot	Dungarpur	M	3,914	1,989	1,479	1,504	+ 1,925	+ 510	− 25	+ 2,410	1,965	982	716	1,949	1,007	763
104. Govindgarh	Alwar	M	3,879	4,932	5,243	4,989	− 1,053	− 311	+ 254	− 1,110	1,993	2,506	2,688	1,886	2,426	2,555
105. Jahazpur	Mewar	...	3,986	3,399	5,106	4,676	+ 587	− 1,707	+ 430	− 690	2,105	1,761	2,665	1,881	1,638	2,441
106. Jaitaran	Marwar	...	4,371	4,033	...	...	+ 338	+ 4,033	...	+ 4,371	2,108	2,010	...	2,263	2,023	...
107. Kherwara	Mewar	C	2,016	2,289	848	...	− 273	+ 1,441	+ 848	+ 2,016	1,295	1,523	788	721	766	60
108. Kotra	Mewar	C	746	903	150	...	− 157	+ 753	+ 150	+ 746	461	487	147	285	416	3
109. Kushalgarh	Kushalgarh	M	2,594	2,938	2,819	2,990	− 344	+ 119	− 171	− 396	1,276	1,414	1,391	1,318	1,524	1,428
110. Lohawat	Marwar	...	4,814	5,322	5,366	2,479	− 508	− 44	+ 2,887	+ 2,335	2,472	2,793	2,802	2,342	2,529	2,564
111. Mangrol	Kotah	M	4,789	5,156	5,714	5,906	− 367	− 558	− 192	− 1,117	2,429	2,637	2,937	2,360	2,519	2,777
112. Manoharpur	Jaipur	...	2,094	5,032	4,644	3,570	− 2,938	+ 388	+ 1,074	− 1,476	1,084	2,540	2,425	1,010	2,492	2,219
113. Merta	Marwar	...	4,397	4,361	7,135	6,682	+ 36	− 2,774	+ 453	− 2,285	2,283	2,270	3,654	2,114	2,091	3,481
114. Mt. Abu—Bazar	Sirohi	M	1,675	1,954	1,280	...	− 279	+ 674	+ 1,280	+ 1,675	995	1,084	768	680	870	512
Civil Station.		M	1,158	1,339	1,213	...	− 181	+ 126	+ 1,213	+ 1,158	753	865	821	405	474	392
Military limits.		M	453	195	92	...	+ 258	+ 103	+ 92	+ 453	335	116	56	118	79	36
		Total	3,286	3,488	2,585	...	− 202	+ 903	+ 2,585	+ 3,286	2,083	2,065	1,645	1,203	1,423	940

TABLE IV.—Towns Classified by Population, with Variation since 1881—(concluded).

Province and Town.	State or District.	Municipality, Suburbs, Cantonment.	Population. 1911.	Population. 1901.	Population. 1891.	Population. 1881.	Variation. Increase (+) Decrease (−). 1901—1911.	1891—1901.	1881—1891.	Variation in period 1881—1911. Increase (+) Decrease (—).	Males. 1911.	Males. 1901.	Males. 1891.	Females. 1911.	Females. 1901.	Females. 1891.
1	2	3	4	5	6	7	8	9	10	11	12	13	14	15	16	17
115. Naenwa . .	Bundi . .	...	4,960	4,501	5,063	5,254	+ 459	− 1,502	+ 830	− 294	2,500	3,277	3,148	2,461	3,224	2,945
116. Nawai . .	Jaipur . .	...	4,730	4,432	5,832	4,501	+ 298	− 1,400	+ 1,331	+ 229	2,851	2,677	3,569	1,879	1,755	2,263
117. Nimbahera .	Tonk . .	...	4,278	5,446	5,482	6,289	− 1,168	− 36	− 807	− 2,011	2,260	3,047	2,818	2,018	2,400	2,664
118. Pachbhadra .	Marwar . .	...	2,158	3,194	5,125	4,271	− 1,036	− 1,931	+ 854	− 2,113	1,098	1,583	2,656	1,060	1,611	2,469
119. Pirawa . .	Tonk . .	...	4,562	4,771	5,627	5,681	− 209	− 856	− 54	− 1,119	2,262	2,415	2,819	2,300	2,356	2,808
120. Pur . .	Mewar . .	...	4,423	4,498	6,800	5,757	− 75	− 2,302	+ 1,043	− 1,334	2,209	2,296	3,450	2,214	2,202	3,350
121. Rajgarh . .	Bikaner . .	M	4,536	4,136	4,677	3,726	+ 400	− 541	+ 951	+ 810	2,282	2,041	2,346	2,254	2,095	2,331
122. Ramgarh .	Alwar . .	M	3,505	5,179	5,099	5,101	− 1,674	+ 80	− 2	− 1,596	1,860	2,675	2,640	1,645	2,504	2,460
123. Rupnagar .	Kishangarh .	M	2,388	3,676	5,011	5,665	− 1,288	− 1,335	− 654	− 3,277	1,219	1,809	2,496	1,169	1,867	2,525
124. Sadri . .	Marwar . .	...	4,742	6,621	7,596	3,640	− 1,879	− 975	+ 3,956	+ 1,102	2,389	3,137	3,656	2,353	3,484	3,940
125. Sagwara .	Dungarpur .	M	4,400	4,034	4,085	3,665	+ 466	− 51	+ 420	+ 834	2,100	1,902	2,094	2,300	2,132	1,601
126. Salumbar .	Mewar . .	...	4,506	4,692	6,029	5,574	− 186	− 1,337	+ 455	− 1,068	2,144	2,254	2,952	2,362	2,438	3,077
127. Samod . .	Jaipur . .	...	2,806	3,257	6,582	3,670	− 451	− 3,325	+ 2,906	− 870	1,381	1,060	3,386	1,425	1,597	3,196
128. Sarwar . .	Kishangarh .	M	4,418	4,520	5,904	5,361	− 102	− 1,384	+ 543	− 943	2,218	2,343	3,030	2,200	2,177	2,876
129. Shahpura .	Jaipur . .	...	3,633	5,245	4,590	3,758	− 1,612	+ 655	+ 832	− 125	1,904	2,681	2,396	1,729	2,564	2,194
130. Sheoganj .	Sirohi . .	...	4,010	4,361	...	...	− 351	+ 4,361	...	+ 4,010	1,888	2,077	...	2,122	2,284	...
131. Suratgarh .	Bikaner . .	M	2,791	2,398	2,659	1,831	+ 393	− 261	+ 828	+ 960	1,490	1,318	1,453	1,301	1,080	1,206
132. Toda Rai Singh	Jaipur . .	...	4,432	3,847	5,649	5,546	+ 585	− 1,802	+ 103	− 1,114	2,321	1,974	2,927	2,111	1,873	2,722
133. Uniara . .	Jaipur . .	...	4,613	4,461	5,728	4,680	+ 152	− 1,267	+ 1,048	− 67	2,353	2,307	2,920	2,260	2,154	2,808
Ajmer-Merwara.	**Urban population.**	..	**140,394**	**129,411**	**123,915**	**92,003**	**+ 10,983**	**+ 5,496**	**+ 31,912**	**+ 48,391**	**77,177**	**68,394**	**67,667**	**63,217**	**61,017**	**56,248**
Cities . .																
1. Ajmer . .	Ajmer . .	M	86,222	73,839	68,843	48,735	+ 12,383	+ 4,996	+ 20,108	+ 37,487	47,354	39,467	37,985	38,868	34,372	30,858
Towns . .	**4 Towns** .	**Total** .	54,172	55,572	55,072	43,208	− 1,400	+ 500	+ 11,804	+ 10,904	29,823	28,927	29,682	24,349	26,645	25,390
Class I. .	*(20,000 and over)*	*Total*	*43,041*	*44,429*	*42,688*	*37,149*	*− 1,381*	*+ 1,734*	*+ 5,539*	*+ 5,892*	*23,626*	*23,038*	*22,731*	*19,415*	*21,384*	*19,957*
2. Beawar . .	Merwara . .	M	22,800	21,928	20,978	15,829	+ 872	+ 950	+ 5,149	+ 6,971	12,328	11,146	11,446	10,472	10,782	9,532
3. Nasirabad .	Ajmer . .	C	20,241	22,491	21,710	21,330	− 2,250	+ 781	+ 380	− 1,089	11,298	11,892	11,285	8,943	10,602	10,425
Class III .	*(5,000-10,000)*	*Total* .	*11,131*	*11,150*	*12,384*	*6,119*	*− 19*	*− 1,234*	*+ 6,265*	*+ 5,012*	*6,197*	*5,889*	*6,951*	*4,934*	*5,261*	*5,433*
4. Deoli* . .	Ajmer . .	C	5,205	4,097	5,284	...	+ 1,108	− 1,187	+ 5,284	+ 5,205	3,071	2,248	3,201	2,134	1,849	2,083
5. Kekri . .	Ajmer . .	M	5,926	7,063	7,100	6,119	− 1,137	− 37	+ 981	− 193	3,126	3,641	3,750	2,800	3,412	3,350

* Including Sadar and Agency Bazars.

TABLE V.

Towns arranged Territorially with Population by Religion.

Explanatory Note.

In this Table towns are arranged territorially. The capital town of the State is placed at the top of each group, and the remaining towns are arranged in alphabetical order.

Hinduism and the followers of its allied religions, Arya Samajists, Jains, and Sikhs, have been grouped under the common head "Indo-Aryan." The group "Hindu Brahmanic" represents those styled Hindus in the more restricted religious sense of the term. The remaining religions are arranged in numerical order.

The group "Animist" includes all those who returned no recognised religion but only their caste name in the religion column in the schedules. The majority of them are forest or aboriginal tribes, such as Bhils, Minas, Bauris, and Grassias, who follow primitive forms of belief. The border line between Animism and Hinduism is, however, a thin one, and many of those who were classed as Animists in 1901 have been returned as Hindus at this Census, and *vice versâ.*

The columns for "others" include the following :—

State or District.	Towns, etc.		Persons.	Males.	Females.
Alwar	Alwar city (suburbs)	Parsi	3	2	1
Banswara	Banswara town	Parsi	4	4	...
Bharatpur	Bharatpur city	Parsi	7	3	4
	Kaman town	Brahmo	8	3	5
Bikaner	Bikaner city	Parsi	4	1	3
Bundi	Bundi	Parsi	6	4	2
	Naenwa	Parsi	2	2	...
Dholpur	Dholpur town	Brahmo	4	2	2
		Parsi	6	3	3
Jaipur	Jaipur city	Parsi	19	10	9
	Gangapur	Parsi	1	1	...
	Hindaun	Parsi	2	1	1
	Sawai Madhopur	Parsi	1	1	...
	Sikar	Parsi	4	2	2
Jhalawar	Patan	Parsi	1	1	...
Kotah	Kotah city	Buddhist	1	1	...
	Kotah suburbs	Jewish	1	1	...
	Baran	Parsi	6	3	3
Kishangarh	Kishangarh	Parsi	7	4	3
Marwar	Jodhpur city	Parsi	1	1	...
	Jodhpur town	Jewish	1	1	...
		Parsi	65	37	28
Mewar	Udaipur city	Parsi	15	7	8
	Chitor	Parsi	2	2	...
Partabgarh	Partabgarh town	Parsi	5	4	1
Shahpura	Shahpura town	Parsi	2	2	...
Sirohi	Erinpura Cantonment	Jewish	5	3	2
	Kharari (Abu Road)	Jewish	9	5	4
		Parsi	80	50	30
	Mount Abu Bazar	Parsi	35	13	22
	Mount Abu, Civil Station	Buddhist	1	1	...
		Jewish	10	4	6
		Parsi	18	11	7
	Sirohi town	Parsi	2	1	1
Tonk	Nimbahera town	Brahmo	59	32	27
Ajmer	Ajmer city	Jewish	25	12	13
		Parsi	181	94	87
	Kekri town	Parsi	1	1	...
	Nasirabad Cantonment	Jewish	2	2	...
		Parsi	63	32	31
Merwara	Beawar town	Parsi	16	6	10

TABLE V.

TOWNS BY RELIGION.

TABLE V.—Towns arranged Territorially

Serial number.	Province; State or District; and Town.	Municipality, Cantonment.	Urban Population. Persons.	Urban Population. Males.	Urban Population. Females.	Indo-Aryan. Hindu (Brahmanic). Persons.	Hindu (Brahmanic). Males.	Hindu (Brahmanic). Females.	Hindu (Arya). Persons.	Hindu (Arya). Males.	Hindu (Arya). Females.	Sikh. Persons.	Sikh. Males.	Sikh. Females.
	1	2	3	4	5	6	7	8	9	10	11	12	13	14
1	**Rajputana**		**1,343,095**	**688,936**	**654,159**	**933,224**	**482,146**	**451,078**	**1,032**	**585**	**447**	**661**	**443**	**218**
2	*Alwar*		*74,604*	*39,185*	*35,419*	*52,630*	*27,713*	*24,917*	*14*	*6*	*8*	*20*	*11*	*9*
3	Alwar city	M.	24,617	12,289	12,328	16,292	8,121	8,171	6	3	3	7	3	4
4	" suburbs	...	16,688	9,965	6,723	12,952	7,590	5,362	2	1	1	8	4	4
5	*Total*		*41,305*	*22,254*	*19,051*	*29,244*	*15,711*	*13,533*	*8*	*4*	*4*	*15*	*7*	*8*
6	Bahadurpur	M.	4,236	2,098	2,138	2,499	1,267	1,232	...	...	...	...	...	...
7	Behror	M.	5,253	2,685	2,568	4,053	2,096	1,957	5	1	4	...	...	...
8	Govindgarh	M.	3,879	1,993	1,886	2,590	1,343	1,247	1	1	...	...	...	...
9	Rajgarh	M.	9,865	4,954	4,911	8,087	4,092	3,995	...	...	...	...	...	...
10	Ramgarh	M.	3,505	1,860	1,645	2,544	1,346	1,198	...	...	...	2	2	...
11	Tijara	M.	6,561	3,341	3,220	3,613	1,858	1,755	...	...	...	3	2	1
	Banswara													
12	Banswara	M.	7,665	3,729	3,936	4,251	2,061	2,100	3	2	1	1	1	...
13	*Bharatpur*		*77,520*	*42,069*	*35,451*	*56,963*	*31,081*	*25,882*	*207*	*116*	*91*	*42*	*22*	*20*
14	Bharatpur city	M.	33,918	18,803	15,115	22,798	12,784	10,014	178	100	78	36	19	17
15	Bhasawar	...	4,309	2,252	2,057	3,063	1,625	1,438	8	3	5	2	1	1
16	Bayana	...	7,029	3,714	3,315	5,276	2,806	2,470	7	3	4	...	...	...
17	Dig	M.	13,147	7,076	6,071	10,552	5,660	4,892	14	10	4	...	...	...
18	Kaman	...	8,912	4,867	4,045	7,376	4,067	3,309	...	...	...	...	...	...
19	Kumher	...	6,075	3,679	2,396	3,867	2,038	1,829	...	...	...	4	2	2
20	Wer	...	5,130	2,678	2,452	4,031	2,101	1,930	...	...	...	...	...	...
21	*Bikaner*		*127,482*	*63,245*	*64,237*	*89,115*	*44,594*	*44,521*	*112*	*68*	*44*	*181*	*151*	*30*
22	Bikaner city	M.	55,826	28,275	27,551	40,471	20,522	19,949	38	27	11	168	141	27
23	Churu	M.	16,038	7,793	8,245	10,707	5,269	5,438	26	15	11	2	2	...
24	Nohar	M.	5,133	2,518	2,615	3,687	1,803	1,884	5	2	3	3	2	1
25	Rajgarh	M.	4,526	2,262	2,264	2,434	1,262	1,172	...	...	...	1	1	...
26	Ratangarh	M.	12,803	6,078	6,725	9,849	4,649	5,200	1	1	...	2	2	...
27	Reni	M.	5,904	2,873	3,031	4,313	2,151	2,162	7	4	3	1	1	...
28	Sardar-Shahr	M.	12,375	6,008	6,367	7,318	3,740	3,578	1	1	...	3	1	2
29	Sujangarh	M.	12,086	5,948	6,139	8,048	4,004	4,044	34	18	16	...	...	...
30	Suratgarh	M.	2,701	1,400	1,301	2,288	1,194	1,094	...	...	...	1	1	...
31	*Bundi*		*24,558*	*12,314*	*12,244*	*17,313*	*8,706*	*8,607*	...	...	...	...	...	...
32	Bundi	...	19,598	9,805	9,793	13,831	6,940	6,891	...	...	...	...	...	...
33	Naenwa	...	4,960	2,509	2,451	3,482	1,766	1,716	...	...	...	...	...	...
34	*Dholpur*		*37,713*	*20,065*	*17,648*	*26,869*	*14,552*	*12,317*	*10*	*5*	*5*	*87*	*51*	*36*
35	Dholpur	...	19,922	10,783	9,139	13,581	7,428	6,153	9	4	5	87	51	36
36	Bari	...	11,401	5,755	5,646	7,940	4,167	3,773	1	1	...	...	...	...
37	Raja-khera	...	6,390	3,527	2,863	5,348	2,957	2,391	...	...	...	...	...	...
38	*Dungarpur*		*14,883*	*7,190*	*7,693*	*6,553*	*3,185*	*3,368*	*8*	*4*	*4*	*5*	*3*	*2*
39	Dungarpur	M.	6,470	3,116	3,354	3,495	1,694	1,801	...	...	...	5	3	2
40	Galia Kot	M.	3,914	1,965	1,949	960	491	469	...	...	...	...	...	...
41	Sagwara	M.	4,499	2,109	2,390	2,098	1,000	1,098	8	4	4	...	...	...
42	*Jaipur*		*411,757*	*210,890*	*200,867*	*299,946*	*154,211*	*145,735*	*120*	*67*	*53*	*149*	*83*	*66*
43	Jaipur city	M.	137,098	70,846	66,252	91,470	46,962	44,508	82	39	43	118	60	58
44	Bairat	...	5,273	2,549	2,724	4,083	2,004	2,079	...	...	...	...	...	...
45	Bamanwas	...	4,292	2,229	2,063	4,061	2,105	1,956	...	...	...	...	...	...
46	Baswa	...	5,532	2,820	2,712	4,993	2,560	2,433	...	...	...	...	...	...
47	Bissau	...	6,838	3,203	3,635	4,681	2,180	2,501	...	...	...	...	...	...
48	Chaksu	...	3,949	2,099	1,850	3,009	1,628	1,381	2	1	1	8	7	1
49	Chaumu	...	6,497	3,225	3,272	5,458	2,735	2,723	...	...	...	...	...	...
50	Chirawa	...	7,979	3,891	4,088	6,798	3,282	3,516	...	...	...	...	...	...
51	Daosa	...	5,191	2,672	2,519	4,114	2,151	1,963	...	...	...	...	...	...
52	Fatehpur	...	17,294	8,280	9,014	11,825	5,667	6,158	9	7	2	...	...	...
53	Gangapur	...	5,780	3,199	2,581	4,638	2,527	2,111	1	1	...	...	...	...
54	Hindaun	...	10,640	5,737	4,903	8,300	4,517	3,783	2	1	1	...	...	...
55	Jhunjhunu	...	13,266	6,575	6,691	7,369	3,770	3,599	2	2	...	...	...	...
56	Khandela	...	8,206	3,995	4,211	6,734	3,865	2,869	7	7	...	...	...	...
57	Khetri	...	7,125	3,718	3,407	5,236	2,751	2,485	13	8	5	...	...	...
58	Kot-putli	...	6,879	3,443	3,436	5,480	2,759	2,721	...	...	...	...	...	...
59	Lachhmangarh	...	10,828	5,024	5,804	8,880	4,070	4,810	...	...	...	...	...	...
60	Lalsot	...	6,697	3,300	3,397	6,153	3,019	3,134	...	...	...	...	...	...
61	Malpura	...	6,140	3,230	2,910	4,287	2,244	2,043	...	...	...	...	...	...
62	Mandawa	...	5,546	2,764	2,782	4,695	2,328	2,367	...	...	...	...	...	...
63	Manoharpur	...	2,094	1,084	1,010	1,732	917	815	...	...	...	...	...	...
64	Naraina	...	5,190	3,255	1,935	4,273	2,763	1,510	...	...	...	...	...	...
65	Nawai	...	4,730	2,851	1,879	3,861	2,371	1,490	...	...	...	...	...	...
66	Nawalgarh	...	14,059	6,874	7,185	11,673	5,704	5,969	...	...	...	...	...	...
67	Nim-ka-thana	...	5,946	3,291	2,655	5,105	2,803	2,302	...	...	...	...	...	...
68	Ramgarh	...	11,556	5,657	5,899	8,788	4,354	4,434	1	...	1	...	...	...
69	Sambhar	...	5,548	2,897	2,651	3,700	1,989	1,711	...	...	...	...	...	...
70	Samod	...	2,806	1,381	1,425	2,959	1,703	1,256	...	...	...	...	...	...
71	Sawai-Madhopur	...	11,166	5,900	5,266	7,935	4,246	3,689	...	...	...	11	11	...
72	Shahpura	...	3,633	1,904	1,729	3,211	1,677	1,534	...	...	...	...	...	...
73	Sikar	...	22,317	11,504	10,813	12,679	6,716	5,963	1	1	...	7	3	4
74	Singhana	...	5,268	2,422	2,846	2,877	1,412	1,465	...	...	...	...	...	...
75	Sri Madhopur	...	6,738	3,367	3,371	5,964	2,958	3,006	...	...	...	5	2	3
76	Surajgarh	...	5,992	2,962	3,030	4,690	2,318	2,372	...	...	...	...	...	...
77	Toda Bhim	...	6,886	3,519	3,367	5,755	2,980	2,775	...	...	...	...	...	...
78	Toda-Rai Singh	...	4,432	2,321	2,111	3,359	1,750	1,609	...	...	...	...	...	...
79	Udaipur	...	7,743	4,479	3,264	6,077	4,055	2,022	...	...	...	...	...	...
80	Uniara	...	4,613	2,353	2,260	3,646	1,872	1,774	...	...	...	...	...	...
	Jaisalmer													
81	Jaisalmer	...	7,420	3,667	3,753	6,015	2,963	3,052	...	...	...	...	...	...
82	*Jhalawar*		*18,664*	*9,144*	*9,520*	*12,542*	*6,163*	*6,379*	*48*	*30*	*18*	*38*	*22*	*16*
83	Chhaoni Jhalrapatan	M.	11,474	5,597	5,877	7,466	3,649	3,817	48	30	18	38	22	16
84	Patan	M.	7,190	3,547	3,643	5,076	2,514	2,562	...	...	...	...	...	...
	Karauli													
85	Karauli	M.	19,803	10,548	9,255	15,011	8,102	6,909	7	4	3	...	...	...
86	*Kotah*		*52,592*	*27,118*	*25,474*	*36,800*	*19,126*	*17,674*	*87*	*49*	*38*	*22*	*12*	*10*
87	Kotah city	M.	24,844	12,643	12,201	15,375	7,882	7,493	43	23	20	10	7	3
88	" suburbs	...	7,909	4,306	3,603	6,461	3,507	2,954	21	13	8	12	5	7
89	*Total*		*32,753*	*16,949*	*15,804*	*21,836*	*11,389*	*10,447*	*64*	*36*	*28*	*22*	*12*	*10*

INDO-ARYAN—*contd.* Jain.			Musalman.			Animist.			Christian.			Others.			
Persons.	Males.	Females.	Persons.	Males.	Females.	Persons.	Males.	Females.	Persons.	Males.	Females.	Persons.	Males.	Females.	Serial number.
15	16	17	18	19	20	21	22	23	24	25	26	27	28	29	
77,977	37,010	40,967	318,755	162,251	156,504	8,374	4,709	3,665	2,666	1,569	1,097	406	223	183	1
1,378	*751*	*627*	*20,437*	*10,663*	*9,774*	*1*	*1*	...	*71*	*38*	*33*	*3*	*2*	*1*	2
457	273	184	7,840	3,882	3,958	...	...	...	15	7	8	...	...	...	3
31	16	15	3,644	2,325	1,319	1	1	...	47	26	21	3	2	1	4
488	*289*	*199*	*11,484*	*6,207*	*5,277*	*1*	*1*	...	*62*	*33*	*29*	*3*	*2*	*1*	5
23	13	10	1,714	818	896	...	...	...	...	...	...	...	...	...	6
101	51	50	1,094	537	557	...	...	...	...	...	...	...	...	...	7
107	52	55	1,181	597	584	...	...	...	...	...	...	...	...	...	8
115	67	48	1,652	768	884	...	...	...	9	5	4	...	...	...	9
184	97	87	777	417	360	...	...	...	...	...	...	...	...	...	10
360	182	178	2,585	1,200	1,286	...	...	...	...	...	...	...	...	...	11
268	141	127	2,227	1,041	1,186	911	479	432	...	...	...	4	4	...	12
1,259	*694*	*565*	*18,501*	*9,858*	*8,643*	...	...	...	*533*	*292*	*241*	*15*	*6*	*9*	13
837	208	229	9,868	5,328	4,540	...	...	...	404	271	133	7	3	4	14
3	2	1	1,233	621	612	...	...	...	...	...	...	...	...	...	15
179	95	84	1,567	810	757	...	...	...	...	...	...	...	...	...	16
229	127	102	2,340	1,273	1,067	...	...	...	12	6	6	...	...	...	17
179	94	85	1,349	703	646	...	...	...	...	...	...	8	3	5	18
63	35	28	1,114	589	525	...	...	...	27	15	12	...	...	...	19
69	43	26	1,030	534	496	...	...	...	...	...	...	...	...	...	20
10,097	*4,447*	*6,450*	*27,001*	*13,893*	*13,108*	...	...	...	*149*	*91*	*51*	*4*	*1*	*3*	21
3,810	1,610	2,200	11,190	5,887	5,313	...	...	...	136	87	49	4	1	3	22
804	398	406	4,408	2,108	2,300	...	...	...	1	1	...	...	...	...	23
243	96	147	1,195	615	580	...	...	...	...	...	...	...	...	...	24
342	149	193	1,740	850	890	...	...	...	...	...	...	...	...	...	25
537	198	339	2,414	1,228	1,186	...	...	...	...	...	...	...	...	...	26
533	218	315	1,050	499	551	...	...	...	...	...	...	...	...	...	27
2,930	1,122	1,808	2,123	1,144	979	...	...	...	...	...	...	...	...	...	28
1,615	644	971	2,389	1,282	1,107	...	...	...	...	...	...	...	...	...	29
23	12	11	474	280	194	...	...	...	5	3	2	...	...	...	30
1,644	*843*	*801*	*5,459*	*2,685*	*2,774*	*134*	*74*	*60*	...	...	...	*8*	*6*	*2*	31
894	470	424	4,733	2,317	2,416	134	74	60	...	...	...	6	4	2	32
750	373	377	726	368	358	...	...	...	...	...	...	2	2	...	33
500	*287*	*213*	*10,198*	*5,140*	*5,058*	...	...	...	*39*	*25*	*14*	*10*	*5*	*5*	34
47	30	17	6,151	3,242	2,909	...	...	...	37	23	14	10	5	5	35
11	5	6	3,448	1,581	1,867	...	...	...	1	1	...	...	...	...	36
442	252	190	599	317	282	...	...	...	1	1	...	...	...	...	37
1,296	*639*	*657*	*5,081*	*2,368*	*2,713*	*1,938*	*990*	*948*	*2*	*1*	*1*	...	...	...	38
654	325	329	1,796	821	975	520	273	247	...	...	...	...	...	...	39
234	110	124	2,285	1,115	1,170	433	248	185	2	1	1	...	...	...	40
408	204	204	1,000	432	568	985	469	516	...	...	...	...	...	...	41
13,151	*6,665*	*6,486*	*97,851*	*49,562*	*48,289*	*63*	*35*	*28*	*450*	*252*	*198*	*27*	*15*	*12*	42
7,503	3,863	3,640	37,664	19,773	17,891	...	...	...	242	139	103	19	10	9	43
392	182	210	798	363	435	...	...	...	...	...	...	...	...	...	44
55	30	25	176	94	82	...	...	...	...	...	...	...	...	...	45
103	50	53	433	209	224	...	...	...	3	1	2	...	...	...	46
23	12	11	2,134	1,011	1,123	...	...	...	...	...	...	...	...	...	47
147	80	67	783	383	400	...	...	...	...	...	...	...	...	...	48
133	68	65	906	422	484	...	...	...	...	...	...	...	...	...	49
14	6	8	1,167	603	564	...	...	...	...	...	...	...	...	...	50
72	43	29	1,005	478	527	...	...	...	...	...	...	...	...	...	51
591	263	328	4,863	2,343	2,520	...	...	...	...	...	...	...	...	...	52
59	33	26	994	618	376	1	...	1	146	79	67	1	1	...	53
128	68	60	2,199	1,146	1,053	...	...	...	9	4	5	2	1	1	54
177	76	101	5,099	2,715	2,384	19	12	7	...	...	...	...	...	...	55
132	64	68	2,333	1,059	1,274	...	...	...	...	...	...	...	...	...	56
22	10	12	1,854	949	905	...	...	...	...	...	...	...	...	...	57
...	...	...	1,309	594	715	...	...	...	...	...	...	...	...	...	58
44	24	20	1,904	930	974	...	...	...	...	...	...	...	...	...	59
82	43	39	462	238	224	...	...	...	...	...	...	...	...	...	60
325	183	142	1,499	790	709	29	13	16	...	...	...	...	...	...	61
7	5	2	834	421	413	...	...	...	...	...	...	...	...	...	62
...	...	...	362	167	195	...	...	...	...	...	...	...	...	...	63
125	64	61	786	425	361	...	...	...	6	3	3	...	...	...	64
430	224	206	439	256	183	...	...	...	...	...	...	...	...	...	65
43	23	20	2,343	1,147	1,196	...	...	...	...	...	...	...	...	...	66
23	12	11	818	476	342	...	...	...	...	...	...	...	...	...	67
111	50	61	2,685	1,283	1,402	...	...	...	1	...	1	...	...	...	68
71	40	31	1,746	1,040	706	...	...	...	31	20	11	...	...	...	69
6	4	2	342	175	167	...	...	...	...	...	...	...	...	...	70
640	332	308	2,578	1,309	1,269	...	...	...	1	1	...	1	1	...	71
...	...	...	422	227	195	...	...	...	...	...	...	...	...	...	72
838	384	454	8,698	4,397	4,301	...	...	...	1	1	...	4	2	2	73
18	7	11	2,373	1,003	1,370	...	...	...	...	...	...	...	...	...	74
44	21	23	715	382	333	...	...	...	10	4	6	...	...	...	75
2	2	...	1,300	642	658	...	...	...	...	...	...	...	...	...	76
35	20	15	1,096	519	577	...	...	...	...	...	...	...	...	...	77
426	214	212	633	347	286	14	10	4	...	...	...	...	...	...	78
5	2	3	752	402	350	...	...	...	...	...	...	...	...	...	79
325	163	162	642	318	324	...	...	...	...	...	...	...	...	...	80
181	60	121	992	518	474	232	126	106	...	...	...	...	...	...	81
713	*353*	*360*	*5,284*	*2,549*	*2,735*	*13*	*9*	*4*	*25*	*17*	*8*	*1*	*1*	...	82
172	88	84	3,713	1,783	1,930	12	8	4	25	17	8	...	...	...	83
541	265	276	1,571	768	803	1	1	...	...	...	...	1	1	...	84
284	152	132	4,474	2,275	2,199	2	2	...	25	13	12	...	...	...	85
1,455	*788*	*667*	*14,109*	*7,087*	*7,022*	*32*	*18*	*14*	*79*	*33*	*46*	*8*	*5*	*3*	86
894	473	421	8,467	4,234	4,233	14	7	7	40	16	24	1	1	...	87
83	44	39	1,276	708	568	17	11	6	39	17	22	1	1	...	88
976	*517*	*459*	*9,743*	*4,942*	*4,801*	*31*	*18*	*13*	*79*	*33*	*46*	*2*	*2*	...	89

TABLE V.

TOWNS BY RELIGION.

TABLE V.—Towns arranged Territorially

Serial number.	Province; State or District; and Town.	Municipality, Cantonment.	Urban Population.			Indo-Aryan. Hindu (Brahmanic).			Hindu (Arya).			Sikh.		
			Persons.	Males.	Females.	Persons.	Males.	Females.	Persons.	Males.	Females.	Persons.	Males.	Females.
	1	2	3	4	5	6	7	8	9	10	11	12	13	14
90	Baran	M.	9,507	4,873	4,634	7,004	3,745	3,340	14	9	5	...	...	...
91	Mangrol	M.	4,789	2,429	2,360	3,443	1,769	1,674	9	4	5	...	...	...
92	Sangod	M.	5,543	2,767	2,776	4,437	2,223	2,201	...	...	...	...	...	...
93	*Kishangarh*		*17,824*	*9,180*	*8,644*	*12,009*	*6,324*	*5,875*	*19*	*11*	*8*	*4*	*4*	...
94	Kishangarh	M.	10,418	5,443	4,075	6,765	3,510	3,255	19	11	8	4	4	...
95	Rupnagar	M.	3,068	1,510	1,460	2,207	1,123	1,084	...	...	...	...	...	...
96	Sarwar	M.	4,419	2,218	2,200	3,127	1,601	1,536	...	...	...	...	...	...
	Kushalgarh													
97	Kushalgarh	M.	2,594	1,276	1,318	1,282	616	666	...	...	...	...	...	...
98	*Marwar*		*253,863*	*128,593*	*124,970*	*173,511*	*89,532*	*83,979*	*265*	*144*	*121*	*28*	*17*	*11*
99	Jodhpur city	M.	59,262	29,351	20,911	30,633	10,512	20,121	62	39	23	12	6	6
100	Bali	...	5,503	2,732	2,561	3,387	1,771	1,616	...	...	...	...	...	...
101	Balotra	...	5,408	2,802	2,606	3,800	2,016	1,784	...	...	...	3	1	2
102	Barmer	...	6,380	3,285	3,035	4,561	2,398	2,163	13	6	7	...	...	...
103	Bhinmal	...	5,214	2,598	2,616	3,076	1,585	1,401	1	1	...	...	...	...
104	Bilara	...	8,606	4,453	4,153	7,389	3,837	3,552	...	...	...	...	...	...
105	Didwana	...	10,122	5,438	4,684	7,146	4,006	3,140	...	...	...	...	...	...
106	Jaitaran	...	4,371	2,108	2,263	2,986	1,481	1,505	...	...	...	...	...	...
107	Jalor	...	7,624	3,791	3,833	4,927	2,572	2,355	...	...	...	...	...	...
108	Jodhpur	...	20,494	12,487	8,007	16,365	10,088	6,277	124	65	59	9	7	2
109	Kuchawan	...	9,605	4,754	4,851	7,123	3,548	3,575	...	...	...	...	...	...
110	Ladnun	...	9,685	4,574	5,111	4,684	2,309	2,375	...	...	...	...	...	...
111	Lohawat	...	4,814	2,472	2,342	3,874	2,030	1,784	...	...	...	...	...	...
112	Merta	...	4,397	2,283	2,114	2,924	1,515	1,409	...	...	...	...	...	...
113	Mundwa	...	6,027	3,473	2,554	4,231	2,105	2,185	...	...	...	...	...	...
114	Nagaur	...	13,900	6,412	6,518	7,106	3,483	3,623	12	6	6	4	3	1
115	Nawa	...	5,657	2,963	2,694	4,228	2,233	1,995	8	2	6	...	...	...
116	Nimaj	...	5,015	2,520	2,495	4,203	2,129	2,074	...	...	...	...	...	...
117	Pachbhadra	...	2,158	1,038	1,030	1,355	721	634	...	...	...	...	...	...
118	Pali	...	12,939	6,580	6,359	6,834	3,478	3,356	...	...	...	...	...	...
119	Phalodi	...	13,825	6,375	7,450	9,634	4,431	5,173	...	...	...	...	...	...
120	Pipar	...	7,556	3,796	3,760	4,848	2,401	2,357	10	5	5	...	...	...
121	Pokaran	...	5,814	2,863	2,951	4,054	2,248	2,406	...	...	...	...	...	...
122	Sadri	...	4,742	2,389	2,353	3,837	1,047	1,890	6	4	2	...	...	...
123	½ Sambhar	...	5,546	2,995	2,551	3,699	1,988	1,711	...	...	...	...	...	...
124	Sojat	...	10,049	4,071	5,078	6,917	3,489	3,428	29	16	13	...	...	...
125	*Mewar*	...	*93,812*	*48,807*	*45,005*	*64,528*	*33,329*	*31,199*	*2*	*1*	*1*	*3*	*2*	*1*
126	Udaipur city	...	33,229	17,460	15,769	20,137	10,401	9,736	2	1	1	1	1	...
127	Banera	...	4,335	2,144	2,191	3,351	1,644	1,707	...	...	...	...	...	...
128	Begun	...	4,385	2,204	2,181	3,157	1,571	1,586	...	...	...	...	...	...
129	Bhilwara	...	8,763	4,613	4,150	6,481	3,363	3,069	...	...	...	...	...	...
130	Bhindar	...	4,630	2,345	2,285	3,188	1,566	1,622	...	...	...	...	...	...
131	Chhoti Sadri		4,576	2,344	2,233	3,342	1,722	1,620	...	...	...	...	...	...
132	Chitor	...	7,332	3,939	3,333	5,225	2,781	2,444	...	...	...	...	...	...
133	Deogarh	...	5,461	2,638	2,823	3,758	1,827	1,931	...	...	...	...	...	...
134	Jahazpur	...	3,066	2,165	1,881	2,872	1,540	1,332	...	...	...	...	...	...
135	Kherwara	C.	2,016	1,205	721	1,578	1,047	531	...	...	...	...	...	...
136	Kotra	C.	743	461	283	298	161	137	...	...	...	3	1	1
137	Nathdwara	...	5,424	2,906	2,318	4,752	2,533	2,219	...	...	...	...	...	...
138	Pur	...	4,423	2,209	2,214	3,368	1,687	1,681	...	...	...	...	...	...
139	Salumbar	...	4,506	2,144	2,362	3,071	1,489	1,585	...	...	...	...	...	...
	Partabgarh													
140	Partabgarh	M.	8,329	4,186	4,143	4,358	2,180	2,100	8	5	3	2	1	1
	Shahpura													
141	Shahpura	...	7,929	4,074	3,855	5,770	2,964	2,803	119	70	49	...	...	...
142	*Sirohi*		*24,124*	*13,106*	*11,018*	*16,160*	*8,304*	*7,856*	*2*	*2*	...	*76*	*63*	*13*
143	Sirohi	...	6,615	3,272	3,343	4,071	2,497	2,474	...	...	...	1	1	...
144	Erinpura	C.	3,033	1,856	1,177	2,135	1,250	885	...	...	...	70	58	12
145	Kharari (Abu Road)	...	7,180	4,007	3,173	4,610	2,598	2,012	...	...	...	2	2	...
146	Mt. Abu (Bazar)	M.	1,675	995	680	1,230	736	494	...	...	...	3	2	1
147	" (Civil Station).		1,159	758	403	604	379	225	2	2	...	...	...	...
148	" (Military limits).		453	335	118	197	153	44	...	...	...	...	...	...
149	*Total*	...	*3,284*	*2,083*	*1,203*	*2,031*	*1,268*	*763*	*2*	*2*	...	*3*	*2*	*1*
150	Sheoganj	...	4,010	1,888	2,122	2,413	1,191	1,222	...	...	...	...	...	...
151	*Tonk*	..	*60,939*	*30,550*	*30,409*	*31,478*	*16,031*	*15,447*	*1*	*1*	...	*3*	...	*3*
152	Tonk city	...	33,864	16,837	17,027	14,800	7,580	7,310	1	1	...	3	...	3
153	Chhabra	...	6,164	3,109	3,056	4,479	2,280	2,193	...	...	...	...	...	...
154	Nimbahera	...	4,278	2,260	2,018	3,532	1,310	1,222	...	...	...	...	...	...
155	Pirawa	...	4,562	2,263	2,300	2,266	1,128	1,138	...	...	...	...	...	...
156	Sironj	...	12,031	6,083	6,008	7,302	3,724	3,578	...	...	...	...	...	...
157	**Ajmer-Merwara**		**140,394**	**77,177**	**63,217**	**85,196**	**46,560**	**38,636**	**836**	**495**	**341**	**904**	**774**	**130**
158	*Ajmer*		*117,594*	*64,849*	*52,745*	*69,663*	*38,163*	*31,500*	*711*	*428*	*283*	*903*	*773*	*130*
159	Ajmer city	M.	86,232	47,354	38,868	49,208	27,187	22,021	683	414	269	87	61	26
160	*Deoli	C.	5,205	3,071	2,134	4,203	2,467	1,736	1	1	...	115	86	29
161	Kekri	M.	5,926	3,126	2,800	4,431	2,280	2,151	...	...	...	...	...	...
162	Nasirabad	C.	20,241	11,238	8,943	11,831	6,229	5,602	27	13	14	701	626	75
	Merwara													
163	Beawar	M.	22,800	12,328	10,472	15,533	8,397	7,136	125	67	58	1	1	...

* Including Sadar and Agency Bazars.

WITH POPULATION BY RELIGION—*continued.*

TABLE V.

TOWNS BY RELIGION.

INDO-ARYAN—*contd.* Jain.			Musalman.			Animist.			Christian.			Others.			Serial number.
Persons.	Males.	Females.	Persons.	Males.	Females.	Persons.	Males.	Females.	Persons.	Males.	Females.	Persons.	Males.	Females.	
15	16	17	18	19	20	21	22	23	24	25	26	27	28	29	
261	156	105	2,132	1,060	1,072	...	...	...	...	...	...	6	3	3	90
92	50	42	1,245	606	630	...	...	...	...	...	...	...	...	...	91
126	65	61	989	479	510	1	...	1	...	...	...	...	...	...	92
1,361	*687*	*674*	*4,183*	*2,178*	*2,004*	*139*	*64*	*65*	*23*	*8*	*15*	*7*	*4*	*3*	93
840	443	407	2,741	1,459	1,282	14	7	7	19	6	13	7	4	3	94
255	121	134	522	273	240	...	...	...	4	2	2	...	...	...	95
257	124	133	919	446	473	115	57	58	...	...	...	...	...	...	96
407	258	239	404	203	201	411	199	212	...	...	...	...	...	...	97
26,360	*11,884*	*14,476*	*50,975*	*26,083*	*24,892*	*1,351*	*732*	*619*	*306*	*162*	*144*	*67*	*39*	*28*	98
4,164	2,087	2,077	15,310	7,647	7,663	11	7	4	39	22	17	1	1	...	99
1,606	655	951	600	306	294	...	...	...	...	...	...	...	...	...	100
903	413	490	700	371	329	...	...	...	3	2	1	...	...	...	101
995	471	524	790	401	389	12	9	3	...	...	...	...	...	...	102
1,473	627	846	248	147	101	416	238	178	...	...	...	...	...	...	103
578	288	290	639	328	311	...	...	...	...	...	...	...	...	...	104
195	81	114	2,765	1,343	1,422	...	...	...	16	8	8	...	...	...	105
535	235	300	830	372	458	...	...	...	...	...	...	...	...	...	106
1,552	664	888	796	371	425	340	184	156	...	...	...	...	...	...	107
431	223	208	3,269	1,953	1,316	39	17	22	191	96	95	66	38	28	108
536	242	294	1,945	963	982	...	...	...	1	1	...	...	...	...	109
2,112	819	1,293	2,889	1,446	1,443	...	...	...	...	...	...	...	...	...	110
803	307	496	80	48	32	57	27	30	...	...	...	...	...	...	111
226	118	108	1,247	650	597	...	...	...	...	...	...	...	...	...	112
40	22	18	694	345	349	...	...	...	2	...	2	...	...	...	113
1,274	596	678	4,559	2,350	2,209	...	...	...	5	4	1	...	...	...	114
283	129	154	1,119	590	529	...	...	...	19	9	10	...	...	...	115
318	150	168	494	241	253	...	...	...	...	...	...	...	...	...	116
630	290	340	40	21	19	133	66	67	...	...	...	...	...	...	117
2,146	1,047	1,099	3,932	2,031	1,901	7	4	3	...	...	...	...	...	...	118
2,205	857	1,348	1,844	984	860	142	73	69	...	...	...	...	...	...	119
990	460	530	1,699	831	868	...	...	...	...	...	...	...	...	...	120
65	30	35	930	490	440	165	95	70	...	...	...	...	...	...	121
732	340	392	147	86	61	20	12	8	...	...	...	...	...	...	122
71	40	31	1,746	947	799	...	...	...	30	20	10	...	...	...	123
1,489	685	804	1,614	781	833	...	...	...	...	...	...	...	...	...	124
8,713	*4,470*	*4,243*	*17,582*	*9,106*	*8,476*	*2,789*	*1,769*	*1,020*	*178*	*121*	*57*	*17*	*9*	*8*	125
3,572	1,883	1,689	7,594	3,931	3,663	1,801	1,167	634	107	69	38	15	7	8	126
236	125	111	748	375	373	...	...	...	...	...	...	...	...	...	127
392	188	204	832	443	389	4	2	2	...	...	...	...	...	...	128
687	350	337	1,028	689	339	14	10	4	3	1	2	...	...	...	129
671	359	312	744	402	342	27	18	9	...	...	...	...	...	...	130
496	254	242	732	366	366	6	2	4	...	...	...	...	...	...	131
538	290	248	1,401	792	609	91	63	28	16	11	4	2	2	...	132
991	493	498	642	282	360	70	36	34	...	...	...	...	...	...	133
25	18	7	1,073	531	542	16	16	...	...	...	...	...	...	...	134
14	10	4	379	204	175	...	...	...	43	33	10	...	...	...	135
12	5	7	96	57	39	338	236	102	2	2	...	...	...	...	136
98	61	37	384	214	170	182	93	89	8	5	3	...	...	...	137
546	257	289	478	248	230	31	17	14	...	...	...	...	...	...	138
435	177	258	791	372	419	209	109	100	...	...	...	...	...	...	139
2,177	1,100	1,077	1,707	859	848	42	28	14	...	...	...	5	4	1	140
476	265	211	1,474	726	748	87	46	41	1	1	...	2	2	...	141
2,509	*1,072*	*1,437*	*4,227*	*2,452*	*1,775*	*201*	*116*	*85*	*780*	*509*	*271*	*169*	*88*	*81*	142
1,098	447	651	529	316	213	...	...	...	14	10	4	2	1	1	143
24	13	11	764	506	258	8	7	1	27	19	8	5	3	2	144
178	104	74	1,697	1,040	657	24	13	11	332	186	146	98	55	43	145
37	27	10	357	210	147	...	...	...	13	7	6	35	13	22	146
...	...	...	199	143	56	145	81	64	179	132	47	29	16	13	147
...	...	...	18	13	5	23	14	9	215	155	60	...	...	...	148
37	*27*	*10*	*574*	*366*	*208*	*153*	*80*	*73*	*407*	*294*	*113*	*64*	*29*	*35*	149
1,172	481	691	424	215	209	1	1	...	...	...	...	...	...	...	150
2,828	*1,454*	*1,374*	*26,540*	*13,005*	*13,535*	*38*	*21*	*17*	*12*	*6*	*6*	*59*	*32*	*27*	151
1,009	520	489	17,898	8,680	9,218	2	1	1	12	6	6	...	...	...	152
251	132	119	1,433	695	738	1	1	...	...	...	...	...	...	...	153
470	254	216	1,182	645	537	35	19	16	...	...	...	59	32	27	154
747	355	392	1,540	770	770	...	...	...	...	...	...	...	...	...	155
351	193	158	4,438	2,166	2,272	...	...	...	...	...	...	...	...	...	156
5,737	3,060	2,677	42,421	23,066	19,355	273	155	118	4,739	2,920	1,819	288	147	141	157
3,371	*1,824*	*1,547*	*38,074*	*20,649*	*17,425*	*260*	*147*	*113*	*4,340*	*2,724*	*1,616*	*272*	*141*	*131*	158
2,692	1,440	1,252	30,654	16,635	14,019	101	52	49	2,591	1,459	1,132	206	106	100	159
44	29	15	785	449	336	1	1	...	56	38	18	...	...	...	160
365	204	162	1,122	637	485	...	...	...	6	4	2	1	1	...	161
269	151	118	5,513	2,928	2,585	158	94	64	1,687	1,223	464	65	34	31	162
2,366	1,236	1,130	4,347	2,417	1,930	13	8	5	309	106	203	16	6	10	163

TABLE VI.

Religions.

Explanatory Note.

Hinduism and the followers of its allied religions—Arya Samajists, Brahmo Samajists, Jains, and Sikhs—have been grouped under the common head "Indo-Aryan." The group "Hindu Brahmanic" represents those styled Hindus in the more restricted religious sense of the term.

The remaining religions are arranged in numerical order.

The group "Animist" includes all those who returned no recognized religion but only their caste name in the religion column in the schedules. The majority of them are forest or aboriginal tribes, such as Bhils, Minas, Bauris, and Grassias, who follow primitive forms of belief. The border line between Animism and Hinduism is, however, a thin one, and many of those who were classed as Animists in 1901 have been returned as Hindus at this Census, and *vice versâ*.

TABLE VI.—Population by Religions.

Province ; and State or District.	Population.			Indo-Aryan.											
				Hindu (Brahmanic).			Hindu (Arya).			Hindu (Brahmo).			Jain.		
	Persons.	Males.	Females.	Persons.	Males.	Females.	Persons.	Males.	Females.	Persons.	Males.	Females.	Persons.	Males.	Females.
1	2	3	4	5	6	7	8	9	10	11	12	13	14	15	16
Rajputana	**10,530,432***	**5,515,275***	**5,015,157**	**8,752,045**	**4,600,170**	**4,151,875**	**1,792**	**1,032**	**760**	**82**	**42**	**40**	**332,397**	**161,856**	**170,541**
Western Division	*2,846,847*	*1,495,258*	*1,351,589*	*2,346,648*	*1,239,491*	*1,107,157*	*638*	*351*	*287*	*5*	*2*	*3*	*157,950*	*72,118*	*85,832*
Bikaner	700,983	371,480	329,494	575,699	306,050	209,040	128	76	52	...	...	...	24,858	10,255	14,603
Jaisalmer	88,311	48,500	39,811	60,951	33,198	27,753	...	...	...	...	...	...	1,102	549	553
Marwar	2,057,553	1,075,269	982,284	1,709,998	899,634	810,364	510	275	235	5	2	3	131,990	61,314	70,676
Southern Division	*1,892,267*†	*972,455*†	*919,812*	*1,351,874*	*697,908*	*653,966*	*87*	*46*	*41*	..	..	...	*98,429*	*49,359*	*49,070*
Banswara	165,463	81,620	83,843	60,339	29,611	30,728	3	2	1	...	...	...	4,396	2,196	2,200
Dungarpur	159,192	79,105	80,087	72,681	35,540	37,132	9	5	4	...	...	...	5,510	2,703	2,807
Kushalgarh (Chiefship)	22,005	10,956	11,049	3,694	1,848	1,846	...	...	...	...	...	...	513	270	243
Mewar	1,293,776	670,750	623,026	1,021,906	529,936	491,970	51	28	23	...	...	..	66,704	34,641	32,063
Partabgarh	62,704	31,735	30,969	33,848	17,077	16,771	21	8	13	...	...	...	4,318	2,259	2,059
Sirohi	189,127†	98,289†	90,838	159,406	83,887	75,519	3	3	...	...	...	...	16,988	7,290	9,698
Eastern Division	*5,791,318*†	*3,047,562*†	*2,743,756*	*5,053,523*	*2,662,771*	*2,390,752*	*1,067*	*635*	*432*	*77*	*40*	*37*	*76,018*	*40,879*	*35,639*
Alwar	791,688	413,659	378,029	588,230	307,425	280,805	43	19	24	...	...	...	4,111	2,158	1,953
Bharatpur	558,785	302,254	256,531	452,730	245,735	206,995	253	146	107	8	3	5	2,720	1,474	1,246
Bundi	218,730	113,211	105,519	196,919	102,040	94,879	...	...	...	...	...	...	6,614	3,475	3,139
Dholpur	263,188	144,244	118,944	242,734	133,416	109,318	15	6	9	4	2	2	2,031	1,175	856
Jaipur	2,636,647	1,385,750	1,250,897	2,398,880	1,262,280	1,136,600	298	196	102	6	3	3	38,408	20,295	18,113
Jhalawar	96,271	50,034	46,237	84,585	44,137	40,448	72	40	32	...	...	...	2,488	1,312	1,176
Karauli	146,587	80,081	66,506	137,989	75,485	62,504	8	5	3	...	...	...	394	225	169
Kishangarh	87,191	45,718	41,473	76,642	40,171	36,471	19	11	8	...	...	...	3,176	1,680	1,496
Kotah	639,089†	330,324†	308,765	584,137	301,657	282,480	151	91	60	...	...	...	6,412	3,460	2,952
Lawa (Estate)	2,564	1,302	1,262	2,282	1,143	1,139	1	1	...	...	...	...	142	75	67
Shahpura (Chiefship)	47,397	24,505	22,802	41,249	21,381	19,868	167	101	66	...	...	...	1,619	885	734
Tonk	303,181	156,390	146,791	247,146	127,901	119,245	40	19	21	59	32	27	7,903	4,165	3,738
Ajmer-Merwara	**501,395**	**266,198**	**235,197**	**388,552**	**204,856**	**183,696**	**884**	**524**	**360**	...	...	...	**20,302**	**10,809**	**9,493**
Ajmer	380,384	201,911	178,473	296,076	155,993	140,083	753	454	299	...	...	...	14,313	7,654	6,659
Merwara	121,011	64,287	56,724	92,476	48,863	43,613	131	70	61	...	...	...	5,989	3,155	2,834

* Includes 2 Buddhist males.

† Includes 1 Buddhist male.

TABLE VI.—POPULATION BY RELIGIONS—*continued.*

Province; and State or District.	INDO-ARYAN—*contd.* Sikh. Persons.	Males.	Females.	MUSALMAN. Persons.	Males.	Females.	ANIMIST. Persons.	Males.	Females.	CHRISTIAN. Persons.	Males.	Females.	ZOROASTRIAN (PARSI). Persons.	Males.	Females.	JEWISH. Persons.	Males.	Females.
1	17	18	19	20	21	22	23	24	25	26	27	28	29	30	31	32	33	34
Rajputana	**8,958**	**5,489**	**3,469**	**985,825**	**517,560**	**468,265**	**444,702**	**226,508**	**218,194**	**4,256**	**2,409**	**1,847**	**342**	**191**	**151**	**31**	**16**	**15**
Western Division	*8,253*	*5,079*	*3,174*	*279,573*	*149,342*	*130,231*	*53,115*	*28,500*	*24,615*	*591*	*332*	*259*	*73*	*42*	*31*	*1*	*1*	...
Bikaner	8,214	5,054	3,160	91,929	49,347	42,582	...	...	...	151	97	54	4	1	3	...	...	...
Jaisalmer	1	1	...	22,099	12,506	9,593	4,158	2,246	1,912	...	...	...	...	...	...	...	...	...
Marwar	38	24	14	165,545	87,489	78,056	48,957	26,254	22,703	440	235	205	69	41	28	1	1	...
Southern Division	*95*	*75*	*20*	*68,859*	*36,312*	*32,547*	*371,669*	*187,966*	*183,703*	*1,043*	*675*	*368*	*186*	*101*	*85*	*24*	*12*	*12*
Banswara	1	1	...	4,886	2,483	2,403	95,834	47,323	48,511	...	...	...	4	4	...	...	...	...
Dungarpur	6	4	2	6,703	3,320	3,383	74,281	37,523	36,758	2	1	1	...	...	...	...	...	...
Kushalgarh (Chiefship)	...	...	...	697	349	348	17,100	8,488	8,612	...	...	...	1	1	...	...	...	...
Mewar	10	6	4	45,752	24,180	21,572	159,094	81,794	77,300	237	152	85	22	13	9	...	...	...
Partabgarh	2	1	1	3,581	1,856	1,725	20,929	10,530	10,399	...	...	...	5	4	1	...	...	...
Sirohi	76	63	13	7,240	4,124	3,116	4,431	2,308	2,123	804	522	282	154	79	75	24	12	12
Eastern Division	*610*	*335*	*275*	*637,393*	*331,906*	*305,487*	*19,918*	*10,042*	*9,876*	*2,622*	*1,402*	*1,220*	*83*	*48*	*35*	*6*	*3*	*3*
Alwar	29	16	13	199,149	103,972	95,177	31	17	14	92	50	42	3	2	1	...	...	...
Bharatpur	52	28	24	102,449	54,550	47,899	...	...	...	566	315	251	7	3	4	...	...	...
Bundi	1	1	...	10,656	5,414	5,242	4,532	2,275	2,257	...	...	...	8	6	2	...	...	...
Dholpur	95	56	39	18,262	9,560	8,702	...	...	...	41	26	15	6	3	3	...	...	...
Jaipur	157	89	68	195,760	101,225	94,535	1,779	955	824	1,326	689	637	28	16	12	5	2	3
Jhalawar	53	32	21	8,625	4,265	4,360	420	228	192	26	18	8	2	2	...	...	...	...
Karauli	...	...	...	8,160	4,345	3,815	8	6	2	28	15	13	...	...	...	...	...	...
Kishangarh	4	4	...	6,785	3,577	3,208	535	263	272	23	8	15	7	4	3	...	...	...
Kotah	216	109	107	44,569	23,163	21,406	3,075	1,558	1,517	507	274	233	20	10	10	1	1	...
Lawa (Estate)	...	...	...	139	83	56	...	...	...	...	...	...	...	...	...	...	...	...
Shahpura (Chiefship)	...	...	...	2,407	1,236	1,171	1,953	989	963	1	1	...	2	2	...	...	...	...
Tonk	3	...	3	40,432	20,516	19,916	7,586	3,751	3,835	12	6	6	...	...	...	...	...	...
Ajmer-Merwara	**922**	**783**	**139**	**81,035**	**43,833**	**37,202**	**3,979**	**1,987**	**1,992**	**5,432**	**3,258**	**2,174**	**262**	**134**	**128**	**27**	**14**	**13**
Ajmer	916	779	137	60,465	32,585	27,880	2,678	1,308	1,370	4,910	2,996	1,914	246	128	118	27	14	13
Merwara	6	4	2	20,570	11,248	9,322	1,301	679	622	522	262	260	16	6	10	...	...	...

TABLE VII.

Age, Sex, and Civil Condition.

Explanatory Note.

The Table is divided into four parts, each showing the distribution of the population by age, sex, and civil condition.

Part A.—Shows, for each Province as a whole, the distribution of the total population (all religions) and of each religion.

Part B.—Shows, for States and Districts, the distribution of the total population (all religions).

Part C.—Shows, for States and Districts, the distribution of the population of each main religion (Animist, Christian, Hindu, Jain, Musalman, Sikh).

Part D.—Shows, for each City, the distribution of the total population (all religions).

In Parts B, C, and D the age periods are given in less detail than in Part A, those for the individual years 1, 2, 3, 4 being omitted, and those from 20 onwards being compressed into 3 periods, 20—39, 40—59 and 60 and over.

The ages of the people recorded in the Census schedules represented the actual number of completed years on the day of the Census, not the current year of age. Divorced persons were included in the heading " widowed," provided that they were not remarried.

TABLE VII.—A.
RAJPUTANA.

TABLE VII.—Age, Sex, and Civil Condition

(I). RAJ

Age and Religion.	Population.			Unmarried.			Married.			Widowed.		
	Persons.	Males.	Females.	Persons.	Males.	Females.	Persons.	Males.	Females.	Persons.	Males.	Females.
1	2	3	4	5	6	7	8	9	10	11	12	13
ALL RELIGIONS	**10,530,432**	**5,515,275**	**5,015,157**	**4,314,278**	**2,723,755**	**1,590,523**	**4,931,468**	**2,418,819**	**2,512,649**	**1,284,686**	**372,701**	**911,985**
0	408,016	205,088	202,928	407,825	205,034	202,791	187	52	135	4	2	2
1	157,664	77,956	79,708	157,466	77,918	79,548	190	33	157	8	5	3
2	309,229	152,439	156,790	308,266	152,219	156,047	938	206	732	25	14	11
3	351,175	172,961	178,214	349,111	172,409	176,702	2,016	534	1,482	48	18	30
4	295,831	150,418	145,413	292,928	149,634	143,294	2,794	746	2,048	109	38	71
Total 0—4	*1,521,915*	*758,862*	*763,053*	*1,515,596*	*757,214*	*758,382*	*6,125*	*1,571*	*4,554*	*194*	*77*	*117*
5—9	1,263,376	668,685	594,691	1,210,476	655,242	555,234	51,265	12,349	38,916	1,635	594	1,041
10—14	936,507	536,201	400,306	699,452	476,160	223,292	231,009	57,816	173,193	6,046	2,225	3,821
15—19	904,837	509,037	395,800	380,434	344,487	35,947	504,973	157,489	347,484	19,430	7,061	12,369
20—24	994,864	495,995	498,869	209,138	202,775	6,363	740,952	276,765	464,187	44,774	16,455	28,319
25—29	1,000,180	527,560	472,620	117,823	114,896	2,927	813,305	386,032	427,273	69,052	26,632	42,420
30—34	1,006,639	522,519	484,120	67,416	64,448	2,968	821,351	420,532	400,819	117,872	37,539	80,333
35—39	576,283	313,514	262,769	27,987	26,832	1,155	459,734	258,783	200,951	88,562	27,899	60,663
40—44	786,742	396,186	390,556	31,225	29,483	1,742	543,104	315,484	227,620	212,413	51,219	161,194
45—49	337,797	184,652	153,145	13,433	12,918	515	221,582	141,788	79,794	102,782	29,946	72,836
50—54	576,769	294,396	282,373	20,742	19,852	890	299,956	208,582	91,374	256,071	65,971	190,100
55—59	145,169	81,263	63,906	5,609	5,434	175	75,015	53,629	21,386	64,545	22,200	42,345
60—64	324,732	150,526	174,226	9,800	9,226	574	116,521	89,724	26,797	198,431	51,576	146,855
65—69	51,383	27,627	23,756	1,801	1,707	94	18,983	15,210	3,773	30,599	10,710	19,889
70 and over	103,219	48,252	54,967	3,346	3,090	256	27,593	22,565	5,028	72,280	22,597	49,683
ANIMIST	**444,702**	**226,508**	**218,194**	**214,551**	**121,138**	**93,413**	**201,617**	**98,708**	**102,909**	**28,534**	**6,662**	**21,872**
0	22,411	11,065	11,346	22,408	11,064	11,344	3	1	2	..	..	..
1	10,137	4,919	5,218	10,130	4,918	5,212	7	1	6	..	..	..
2	20,493	9,854	10,639	20,469	9,847	10,622	24	7	17	..	..	..
3	24,541	11,803	12,738	24,495	11,786	12,709	44	16	28	2	1	1
4	19,706	10,044	9,662	19,652	10,028	9,624	52	15	37	2	1	1
Total 0—4	*97,288*	*47,685*	*49,603*	*97,154*	*47,643*	*49,511*	*130*	*40*	*90*	*4*	*2*	*2*
5—9	63,600	33,644	29,956	62,878	33,453	29,425	690	172	518	32	19	13
10—14	29,054	16,302	12,752	25,162	15,405	9,757	3,825	862	2,963	67	35	32
15—19	30,987	16,661	14,326	15,660	12,552	3,108	15,049	3,959	11,090	278	150	128
20—24	40,539	18,695	21,844	8,036	7,361	675	31,730	10,875	20,855	773	459	314
25—29	47,259	23,341	23,918	3,325	3,037	288	42,515	19,530	22,985	1,419	774	645
30—34	45,194	23,757	21,437	1,234	985	249	41,433	21,749	19,684	2,527	1,023	1,504
35—39	24,631	13,241	11,390	407	280	127	22,281	12,363	9,918	1,943	598	1,345
40—44	28,142	14,745	13,397	358	220	138	22,070	13,577	8,493	5,714	948	4,766
45—49	9,760	5,153	4,606	92	57	35	7,284	4,692	2,592	2,393	414	1,979
50—54	15,929	7,813	8,116	141	89	52	9,207	6,704	2,503	6,581	1,020	5,561
55—59	2,782	1,392	1,390	21	15	6	1,700	1,183	517	1,061	194	867
60—64	7,291	3,060	4,231	50	20	30	2,865	2,322	543	4,376	718	3,658
65—69	782	350	432	9	6	3	333	263	70	440	81	359
70 and over	1,455	659	796	24	15	9	505	417	88	926	227	699
ARYA	**1,792**	**1,032**	**760**	**790**	**527**	**263**	**826**	**444**	**382**	**176**	**61**	**115**
0	59	28	31	59	28	31	..	..	..	..	..	..
1	19	10	9	19	10	9	..	..	..	..	..	..
2	55	27	28	55	27	28	..	..	..	..	..	..
3	43	19	24	43	19	24	..	..	..	..	..	..
4	39	22	17	39	22	17	..	..	..	..	..	..
Total 0—4	*215*	*106*	*109*	*215*	*106*	*109*	..	..	..	..	..	..
5—9	208	116	92	206	116	90	2	..	2	..	..	..
10—14	237	160	77	200	146	54	37	14	23	..	..	..
15—19	205	128	77	99	91	8	99	35	64	7	2	5
20—24	173	95	78	28	26	2	139	67	72	6	2	4
25—29	162	89	73	19	19	..	133	67	66	10	3	7
30—34	141	80	61	4	4	..	118	64	54	19	12	7
35—39	109	66	43	6	6	..	92	55	37	11	5	6
40—44	106	56	50	6	6	..	72	44	28	28	6	22
45—49	76	52	24	3	3	..	55	42	13	18	7	11
50—54	76	46	30	2	2	..	46	33	13	28	11	17
55—59	24	14	10	..	..	..	12	7	5	12	7	5
60—64	37	15	22	1	1	..	16	11	5	20	3	17
65—69	16	8	8	1	1	..	5	5	..	10	2	8
70 and over	7	1	6	..	..	..	..	..	..	7	1	6
BRAHMO	**82**	**42**	**40**	**25**	**14**	**11**	**48**	**25**	**23**	**9**	**3**	**6**
0	1	..	1	1	..	1	..	..	..	..	..	..
1	2	2	..	2	2	..	..	..	..	..	..	..
2	2	..	2	2	..	2	..	..	..	..	..	..
3	1	..	1	1	..	1	..	..	..	..	..	..
4	4	2	2	4	2	2	..	..	..	..	..	..
Total 0—4	*10*	*4*	*6*	*10*	*4*	*6*	..	..	..	..	..	..
5—9	7	3	4	7	3	4	..	..	..	..	..	..
10—14	7	5	2	6	5	1	1	..	1	..	..	..
15—19	5	..	5	..	..	..	5	..	5	..	..	..
20—24	9	3	6	1	1	..	7	1	6	1	1	..
25—29	8	5	3	..	..	..	6	5	1	2	..	2
30—34	10	7	3	..	..	..	10	7	3	..	..	..
35—39	5	3	2	1	1	..	3	2	1	1	..	1
40—44	7	2	5	..	..	..	6	2	4	1	..	1
45—49	4	3	1	..	..	..	4	3	1	..	..	..
50—54	3	2	1	..	..	..	2	1	1	1	1	..
55—59	..	..	..	..	..	..	..	..	..	..	..	..
60—64	5	4	1	..	..	..	3	3	..	2	1	1
65—69	2	1	1	..	..	..	1	1	..	1	..	1
70 and over	..	..	..	..	..	..	..	..	..	..	..	..

PART A.—PROVINCIAL SUMMARY.

TABLE VII.—A.

PUTANA. RAJPUTANA.

Age and Religion.	Population.			Unmarried.			Married.			Widowed.		
	Persons.	Males.	Females.	Persons.	Males.	Females.	Persons.	Males.	Females.	Persons.	Males.	Females.
1	2	3	4	5	6	7	8	9	10	11	12	13
BUDDHIST	**2**	**2**	..	**1**	**1**	..	**1**	**1**	..	..	..	..
25—29	1	1	..	1	1	..	..	..	..	..	..	..
45—49	1	1	..	..	..	..	1	1	..	..	..	..
CHRISTIAN	**4,256**	**2,409**	**1,847**	**2,274**	**1,403**	**871**	**1,758**	**933**	**825**	**224**	**73**	**151**
0	169	79	90	169	79	90	..	..	..	..	..	..
1	96	45	51	96	45	51	..	..	..	..	..	..
2	132	63	69	132	63	69	..	..	..	..	..	..
3	119	52	67	119	52	67	..	..	..	..	..	..
4	93	51	42	93	51	42	..	..	..	..	..	..
Total 0—4	*609*	*290*	*319*	*609*	*290*	*319*	..	..	..	..	..	..
5—9	434	250	184	430	249	181	4	1	3	..	..	..
10—14	384	270	114	371	265	106	10	5	5	3	..	3
15—19	431	226	205	331	211	120	95	12	83	5	3	2
20—24	578	300	269	259	199	61	309	104	205	10	7	3
25—29	496	292	204	121	87	34	360	194	166	15	11	4
30—34	408	227	181	72	50	22	318	168	150	18	9	9
35—39	267	162	105	36	28	8	217	132	85	14	2	12
40—44	224	138	86	20	9	11	160	118	56	35	16	19
45—49	130	83	47	7	4	3	104	76	28	19	3	16
50—54	142	81	61	11	8	3	92	61	31	39	12	27
55—59	58	40	18	..	..	..	44	38	6	14	2	12
60—64	56	27	29	4	3	1	25	19	6	27	5	22
65—69	14	5	9	2	..	2	5	4	1	7	1	6
70 and over	25	9	16	1	1	..	6	6	..	18	2	16
HINDU	**8,752,045**	**4,600,170**	**4,151,875**	**3,540,565**	**2,259,610**	**1,280,955**	**4,122,556**	**2,023,352**	**2,099,204**	**1,088,924**	**317,208**	**771,716**
0	334,345	168,183	166,162	334,172	168,135	166,037	169	46	123	4	2	2
1	127,345	63,143	64,202	127,169	63,111	64,058	171	29	142	5	3	2
2	252,752	124,774	127,978	251,884	124,577	127,307	849	186	663	19	11	8
3	286,603	141,353	145,250	281,722	140,858	140,864	1,839	479	1,360	42	16	26
4	241,807	123,101	118,706	239,214	122,399	116,815	2,501	671	1,830	92	31	61
Total 0—4	*1,242,852*	*620,554*	*622,298*	*1,237,161*	*619,080*	*618,081*	*5,529*	*1,411*	*4,118*	*162*	*63*	*99*
5—9	1,037,134	550,244	486,890	990,209	538,434	451,775	45,516	11,321	34,195	1,409	489	920
10—14	774,378	446,299	328,079	567,582	393,832	173,750	201,574	50,565	151,009	5,222	1,902	3320
15—19	755,732	428,219	327,513	312,726	287,722	25,004	426,283	134,411	291,872	16,723	6,086	10,637
20—24	827,586	415,318	412,268	174,862	170,606	4,256	614,969	230,817	384,143	37,764	13,895	23,869
25—29	833,066	442,302	390,764	100,688	98,628	2,060	674,265	321,019	353,246	58,113	22,655	35,458
30—34	843,033	439,238	403,795	58,023	55,834	2,189	684,982	351,298	333,684	100,028	32,106	67,922
35—39	480,550	261,992	218,558	24,207	23,383	824	381,067	214,958	166,709	74,676	23,651	51,025
40—44	662,839	331,313	328,526	27,112	25,876	1,236	434,677	264,530	190,147	181,050	43,907	137,143
45—49	283,287	154,933	128,354	11,570	11,207	363	184,919	118,359	66,560	86,798	25,367	61,431
50—54	487,258	249,082	238,176	18,327	17,681	646	251,080	174,847	76,233	217,851	56,554	161,297
55—59	121,645	68,060	53,585	4,987	4,866	121	62,214	44,446	17,768	54,444	18,748	35,696
60—64	274,308	127,087	147,221	8,653	8,256	397	97,034	74,754	22,280	168,621	44,077	124,544
65—69	42,735	22,808	19,927	1,563	1,499	64	15,513	12,375	3,138	25,659	8,934	16,725
70 and over	85,642	39,721	45,921	2,895	2,706	189	22,343	18,241	4,102	60,404	18,774	41,630
JAIN	**332,397**	**161,856**	**170,541**	**135,012**	**83,542**	**51,470**	**135,836**	**63,325**	**72,511**	**61,549**	**14,969**	**46,580**
0	12,606	6,358	6,248	12,604	6,358	6,246	2	..	2	..	..	..
1	4,006	1,949	2,057	4,003	1,946	2,057	2	2	..	1	1	..
2	9,007	4,533	4,474	8,991	4,529	4,462	13	4	9	3	..	3
3	9,191	4,588	4,603	9,173	4,580	4,593	18	8	10	..	..	..
4	7,827	3,930	3,897	7,803	3,921	3,882	17	6	11	7	3	4
Total 0—4	*42,637*	*21,358*	*21,279*	*42,574*	*21,334*	*21,240*	*52*	*20*	*32*	*11*	*4*	*7*
5—9	39,160	19,984	19,176	38,826	19,888	18,938	301	79	222	33	17	16
10—14	28,805	14,940	13,865	23,889	14,113	9,776	4,747	787	3,960	169	40	129
15—19	27,088	13,565	13,523	10,470	9,433	1,037	15,757	4,008	11,749	861	124	737
20—24	32,141	14,821	17,320	6,486	6,327	159	22,998	8,006	14,992	2,657	488	2,169
25—29	31,880	15,393	16,487	4,159	4,087	72	23,200	10,433	12,767	4,521	873	3,648
30—34	29,722	14,159	15,563	2,600	2,529	71	20,491	10,340	10,151	6,631	1,290	5,341
35—39	21,081	10,717	10,364	1,487	1,460	27	14,040	7,919	6,121	5,554	1,338	4,216
40—44	23,689	10,591	13,098	1,502	1,462	40	12,697	7,084	5,613	9,490	2,045	7,445
45—49	14,489	7,359	7,130	913	890	23	7,559	4,741	2,818	6,017	1,728	4,289
50—54	19,187	8,750	10,437	1,111	1,075	36	7,427	5,004	2,423	10,649	2,671	7,978
55—59	6,808	3,580	3,228	336	327	9	2,728	1,940	788	3,744	1,313	2,431
60—64	10,080	4,087	5,993	434	413	21	2,598	1,948	650	7,048	1,726	5,322
65—69	2,579	1,298	1,281	109	97	12	707	578	129	1,763	623	1,140
70 and over	3,051	1,254	1,797	116	107	9	534	438	96	2,401	709	1,692

TABLE VII.—AGE, SEX, AND CIVIL CONDITION.

(I). RAJPUTANA—*concluded.*

Age and Religion.	Population.			Unmarried.			Married.			Widowed.		
	Persons.	Males.	Females.	Persons.	Males.	Females.	Persons.	Males.	Females.	Persons.	Males.	Females.
1	2	3	4	5	6	7	8	9	10	11	12	13
JEWISH	**31**	**16**	**15**	**17**	**8**	**9**	**14**	**8**	**6**	..	..	..
0	..	..	..	..	..	..	..	..	..	..	..	..
1	2	2	..	2	2	..	..	..	..	..	..	..
2	..	..	..	..	..	..	..	..	..	..	..	..
3	1	1	..	1	1	..	..	..	..	..	..	..
4	2	..	2	2	..	2	..	..	..	..	..	..
Total 0—4	*5*	*3*	*2*	*5*	*3*	*2*	..	..	..	..	..	..
5—9	6	1	5	6	1	5	..	..	..	..	..	..
10—14	4	1	3	3	1	2	1	..	1	..	..	..
15—19	3	2	1	1	1	..	2	1	1	..	..	..
20—24	2	1	1	1	1	..	1	..	1	..	..	..
25—29	4	3	1	..	..	..	4	3	1	..	..	..
30—34	1	..	1	..	..	..	1	..	1	..	..	..
35—39	2	1	1	1	1	..	1	..	1	..	..	..
40—44	1	1	..	..	..	..	1	1	..	..	..	..
45—49	1	1	..	..	..	..	1	1	..	..	..	..
50—54	1	1	..	..	..	..	1	1	..	..	..	..
55—59	..	..	..	..	..	..	..	..	..	..	..	..
60—64	1	1	..	..	..	..	1	1	..	..	..	..
65—69	..	..	..	..	..	..	..	..	..	..	..	..
70 and over	..	..	..	..	..	..	..	..	..	..	..	..
MUSALMAN	**985,825**	**517,560**	**468,265**	**416,291**	**254,316**	**161,975**	**464,849**	**229,838**	**235,011**	**104,685**	**33,406**	**71,279**
0	38,062	19,189	18,873	38,049	19,184	18,865	13	5	8	..	..	..
1	15,895	7,802	8,093	15,883	7,800	8,083	10	1	9	2	1	1
2	26,503	13,050	13,453	26,448	13,038	13,410	52	9	43	3	3	..
3	30,376	14,980	15,396	30,258	14,948	15,310	114	31	83	4	1	3
4	26,110	13,140	12,970	25,878	13,083	12,795	224	64	170	8	3	5
Total 0—4	*136,946*	*68,161*	*68,785*	*136,516*	*68,053*	*68,463*	*413*	*100*	*313*	*17*	*8*	*9*
5—9	121,682	63,808	57,874	116,796	62,474	54,322	4,725	1,265	3,460	161	69	92
10—14	102,642	57,559	45,083	81,303	51,753	29,550	20,755	5,558	15,197	584	248	336
15—19	89,448	49,598	39,850	40,523	33,947	6,576	47,372	14,956	32,416	1,553	695	858
20—24	92,867	46,119	46,748	19,082	17,887	1,195	70,240	26,644	43,596	3,545	1,588	1,957
25—29	86,445	45,612	40,833	9,338	8,869	469	72,167	34,448	37,719	4,940	2,295	2,645
30—34	87,390	44,619	42,771	5,427	4,990	437	73,356	36,552	36,804	8,607	3,077	5,530
35—39	49,187	27,061	22,126	1,809	1,642	167	41,054	23,139	17,915	6,324	2,280	4,044
40—44	71,150	35,975	35,175	2,196	1,879	317	52,924	29,836	23,088	16,030	4,260	11,770
45—49	29,743	16,858	12,885	838	747	91	21,412	13,707	7,705	7,493	2,404	5,089
50—54	53,762	28,353	25,409	1,127	965	162	31,804	21,728	10,076	20,831	5,660	15,171
55—59	13,713	8,087	5,626	259	220	39	8,230	5,953	2,277	5,224	1,914	3,310
60—64	32,717	16,084	16,633	652	527	125	13,846	10,566	3,280	18,219	4,991	13,228
65—69	5,203	3,121	2,082	117	104	13	2,386	1,956	430	2,700	1,061	1,639
70 and over	12,930	6,545	6,385	308	259	49	4,165	3,430	735	8,457	2,856	5,601
PARSI	**342**	**191**	**151**	**184**	**103**	**81**	**140**	**79**	**61**	**18**	**9**	**9**
0	5	3	2	5	3	2	..	..	..	..	..	..
1	3	3	..	3	3	..	..	..	..	..	..	..
2	3	2	1	3	2	1	..	..	..	..	..	..
3	5	4	1	5	4	1	..	..	..	..	..	..
4	10	3	7	10	3	7	..	..	..	..	..	..
Total 0—4	*26*	*15*	*11*	*26*	*15*	*11*	..	..	..	..	..	..
5—9	40	18	22	40	18	22	..	..	..	..	..	..
10—14	39	19	20	38	19	19	1	..	1	..	..	..
15—19	36	10	26	29	10	19	7	..	7	..	..	..
20—24	44	23	21	27	18	9	16	4	12	1	1	..
25—29	28	18	10	14	13	1	14	5	9	..	..	..
30—34	30	21	9	7	7	..	23	14	9	..	..	..
35—39	15	13	2	1	1	..	12	11	1	2	1	1
40—44	22	13	9	..	..	..	20	12	8	2	1	1
45—49	20	14	6	1	1	..	17	12	5	2	1	1
50—54	14	10	4	1	1	..	10	7	3	3	2	1
55—59	10	6	4	..	..	..	8	6	2	2	..	2
60—64	8	5	3	..	..	..	5	3	2	3	2	1
65—69	6	4	2	..	..	..	5	3	2	1	1	..
70 and over	4	2	2	..	..	..	2	2	..	2	..	2
SIKH	**8,958**	**5,489**	**3,469**	**4,568**	**3,093**	**1,475**	**3,823**	**2,106**	**1,717**	**567**	**290**	**277**
0	358	183	175	358	183	175	..	..	..	..	..	..
1	159	81	78	159	81	78	..	..	..	..	..	..
2	282	136	146	282	136	146	..	..	..	..	..	..
3	295	161	134	294	161	133	1	..	1	..	..	..
4	233	125	108	233	125	108	..	..	..	..	..	..
Total 0—4	*1,327*	*686*	*641*	*1,326*	*686*	*640*	*1*	..	*1*	..	..	..
5—9	1,103	617	488	1,078	606	472	27	11	16	..	..	..
10—14	957	646	311	898	621	277	58	25	33	1	..	1
15—19	902	628	274	595	520	75	304	107	197	3	1	2
20—24	925	611	314	356	350	6	552	247	305	17	14	3
25—29	831	504	327	158	155	3	641	328	313	32	21	11
30—34	710	411	299	49	49	..	619	340	279	42	22	20
35—39	436	258	178	32	30	2	367	204	163	37	24	13
40—44	562	352	210	31	31	..	468	285	183	63	36	27
45—49	277	185	92	9	9	..	226	154	72	42	22	20
50—54	397	258	139	22	22	..	287	196	91	88	40	48
55—59	129	84	45	6	6	..	79	56	23	44	22	22
60—64	249	156	93	6	6	..	128	97	31	115	53	62
65—69	46	32	14	..	..	..	28	25	3	18	7	11
70 and over	105	61	44	2	2	..	38	31	7	65	28	37

PART A.—PROVINCIAL SUMMARY—*continued.*

TABLE VII.—A.

(II). AJMER-MERWARA.

AJMER-MERWARA.

Age and Religion.	Population.			Unmarried.			Married.			Widowed.		
	Persons.	Males.	Females.	Persons.	Males.	Females.	Persons.	Males.	Females.	Persons.	Males.	Females.
1	2	3	4	5	6	7	8	9	10	11	12	13
ALL RELIGIONS	**501,395**	**266,198**	**235,197**	**198,345**	**125,606**	**72,739**	**240,914**	**120,869**	**120,045**	**62,136**	**19,723**	**42,413**
0	20,761	10,387	10,374	20,750	10,386	10,364	11	1	10	..	..	..
1	7,850	3,888	3,962	7,834	3,887	3,947	16	1	15	..	..	..
2	15,144	7,596	7,548	15,059	7,585	7,474	83	10	73	2	1	1
3	16,889	8,385	8,504	16,691	8,344	8,347	196	40	156	2	1	1
4	13,124	6,825	6,299	12,851	6,745	6,106	262	78	184	11	2	9
Total 0—4	*73,768*	*37,081*	*36,687*	*73,185*	*36,947*	*36,238*	*568*	*130*	*438*	*15*	*4*	*11*
5—9	56,572	29,871	26,701	53,343	28,851	24,492	3,093	955	2,138	136	65	71
10—14	37,689	21,771	15,918	27,961	19,064	8,897	9,360	2,520	6,840	359	178	181
15—19	41,363	22,965	18,398	17,529	15,659	1,870	22,807	6,806	16,001	1,027	500	527
20—24	53,195	27,540	25,655	12,053	11,612	441	38,578	14,723	23,855	2,564	1,205	1,359
25—29	52,692	28,842	23,850	6,784	6,559	225	42,078	20,353	21,725	3,830	1,930	1,900
30—34	50,530	26,982	23,548	3,498	3,305	193	41,139	21,396	19,743	3,893	2,281	1,612
35—39	28,714	16,313	12,401	1,070	1,005	65	22,985	13,617	9,368	4,659	1,691	2,968
40—44	35,671	18,011	17,660	1,078	938	140	24,972	14,625	10,347	9,621	2,448	7,173
45—49	16,290	9,065	7,225	448	410	38	10,833	7,210	3,623	5,009	1,445	3,564
50—54	27,240	14,097	13,143	713	647	66	14,170	10,242	3,928	12,357	3,208	9,149
55—59	6,808	3,928	2,880	171	161	10	3,514	2,669	845	3,123	1,098	2,025
60—64	14,612	6,756	7,856	352	316	36	4,979	4,075	904	9,281	2,365	6,916
65—69	2,175	1,108	1,067	59	54	5	710	594	116	1,406	460	946
70 and over	4,076	1,868	2,208	101	78	23	1,119	945	174	2,856	845	2,011
ANIMIST	**3,879**	**1,887**	**1,992**	**1,620**	**917**	**703**	**2,005**	**961**	**1,044**	**354**	**109**	**245**
0	193	97	96	193	97	96	..	..	..	..	..	..
1	90	40	50	90	40	50	..	..	..	..	..	..
2	137	56	81	137	56	81	..	..	..	..	..	..
3	176	79	97	176	79	97	..	..	..	..	..	..
4	131	58	73	129	57	72	2	1	1	..	..	..
Total 0—4	*727*	*330*	*397*	*725*	*329*	*396*	*2*	*1*	*1*	..	..	..
5—9	524	266	258	504	262	242	20	4	16	..	..	..
10—14	225	133	92	168	119	47	55	14	41	4	..	4
15—19	299	141	158	115	105	10	179	32	147	5	4	1
20—24	430	202	228	72	66	6	346	130	216	12	6	6
25—29	449	230	219	21	20	1	409	194	215	19	16	3
30—34	421	226	195	8	8	..	385	200	185	28	18	10
35—39	212	126	86	4	3	1	190	111	79	18	12	6
40—44	249	128	121	3	3	..	195	116	79	51	9	42
45—49	85	38	47	..	..	..	56	33	23	29	5	24
50—54	191	84	107	1	1	..	96	70	26	94	13	81
55—59	34	18	16	..	..	..	21	14	7	13	4	9
60—64	94	44	50	..	..	..	35	29	6	39	15	24
65—69	11	2	9	..	..	..	3	1	2	8	1	7
70 and over	28	19	9	1	1	..	13	12	1	14	6	8
ARYA	**884**	**524**	**360**	**413**	**271**	**142**	**403**	**233**	**170**	**68**	**20**	**48**
0	22	9	13	22	9	13	..	..	..	..	..	..
1	14	7	7	14	7	7	..	..	..	..	..	..
2	21	12	9	21	12	9	..	..	..	..	..	..
3	30	14	16	30	14	16	..	..	..	..	..	..
4	12	5	7	12	5	7	..	..	..	..	..	..
Total 0—4	*99*	*47*	*52*	*99*	*47*	*52*	..	..	..	..	..	..
5—9	103	56	47	101	55	46	2	1	1	..	..	..
10—14	126	85	41	109	80	29	16	4	12	1	1	..
15—19	132	86	46	71	56	15	60	29	31	1	1	..
20—24	87	52	35	18	18	..	69	34	35	..	..	..
25—29	66	44	22	5	5	..	59	38	21	2	1	1
30—34	69	36	33	2	2	..	58	31	27	9	3	6
35—39	54	32	22	2	2	..	45	28	17	7	2	5
40—44	50	31	19	2	2	..	39	26	13	9	3	6
45—49	39	24	15	1	1	..	29	22	7	9	1	8
50—54	28	17	11	2	2	..	14	10	4	12	5	7
55—59	10	6	4	..	..	..	5	4	1	5	2	3
60—64	6	2	4	..	..	..	3	2	1	3	..	3
65—69	6	1	5	..	..	..	1	1	..	5	..	5
70 and over	9	5	4	1	1	..	3	3	..	5	1	4
CHRISTIAN	**5,432**	**3,258**	**2,174**	**3,593**	**2,342**	**1,251**	**1,612**	**836**	**776**	**227**	**80**	**147**
0	153	87	66	153	87	66	..	..	..	..	..	..
1	73	40	33	73	40	33	..	..	..	..	..	..
2	93	43	50	93	43	50	..	..	..	..	..	..
3	116	48	68	116	48	68	..	..	..	..	..	..
4	106	57	49	106	57	49	..	..	..	..	..	..
Total 0—4	*541*	*275*	*266*	*541*	*275*	*266*	..	..	..	..	..	..
5—9	448	194	254	447	194	253	1	..	1	..	..	..
10—14	430	233	197	419	230	189	11	3	8	..	..	..
15—19	762	328	434	638	314	324	122	13	109	2	1	1
20—24	1,210	907	303	889	795	94	310	111	199	11	1	10
25—29	773	563	210	434	376	58	320	178	142	19	9	10
30—34	354	223	131	108	90	18	229	126	103	17	7	10
35—39	233	153	80	44	33	11	171	114	57	18	6	12
40—44	206	102	104	30	16	14	145	80	65	31	6	25
45—49	150	86	64	13	7	6	117	69	48	20	10	10
50—54	142	84	58	14	4	10	97	72	25	31	8	23
55—59	68	48	20	5	3	2	46	37	9	17	8	9
60—64	62	31	31	6	3	3	19	16	3	37	12	25
65—69	19	10	9	1	1	..	7	3	4	11	6	5
70 and over	34	21	13	4	1	3	17	14	3	13	6	7

TABLE VII.—A.

AJMER-MERWARA.

TABLE VII.—Age, Sex, and Civil Condition.

(II). AJMER-

Age and Religion.	Population.			Unmarried.			Married.			Widowed.		
	Persons.	Males.	Females.	Persons.	Males.	Females.	Persons.	Males.	Females.	Persons.	Males.	Females.
1	2	3	4	5	6	7	8	9	10	11	12	13
HINDU	**388,552**	**204,856**	**183,696**	**149,791**	**94,775**	**55,016**	**189,771**	**94,715**	**95,056**	**48,990**	**15,366**	**33,624**
0	16,293	8,052	8,241	16,286	8,052	8,234	7	..	7	..	..	..
1	6,177	3,061	3,116	6,162	3,060	3,102	15	1	14	..	..	..
2	12,010	6,041	5,969	11,935	6,031	5,904	73	9	64	2	1	1
3	13,380	6,621	6,759	13,199	6,582	6,617	179	38	141	2	1	1
4	10,345	5,411	4,934	10,090	5,335	4,755	244	74	170	11	2	9
Total 0—4	*58,205*	*29,186*	*29,019*	*57,672*	*29,060*	*28,612*	*518*	*122*	*396*	*15*	*4*	*11*
5—9	43,647	23,064	20,583	40,861	22,189	18,672	2,673	819	1,854	113	56	57
10—14	27,950	16,156	11,794	20,136	13,952	6,184	7,535	2,066	5,469	279	138	141
15—19	31,430	17,434	13,996	12,507	11,519	988	18,086	5,496	12,590	837	419	418
20—24	38,400	18,453	19,947	6,278	6,081	197	30,152	11,431	18,721	1,970	941	1,029
25—29	41,338	22,384	18,954	4,909	4,815	94	33,445	16,041	17,404	2,984	1,528	1,456
30—34	40,088	21,336	18,752	2,647	2,561	86	32,778	16,961	15,817	4,663	1,814	2,849
35—39	22,451	12,670	9,781	738	706	32	18,108	10,683	7,425	3,605	1,281	2,324
40—44	27,939	14,061	13,878	735	669	66	19,587	11,499	8,088	7,617	1,893	5,724
45—49	12,603	6,952	5,651	297	280	17	8,359	5,575	2,784	3,947	1,097	2,850
50—54	21,369	10,948	10,421	522	491	31	10,918	7,921	2,997	9,929	2,536	7,393
55—59	5,113	2,908	2,205	123	119	4	2,569	1,946	623	2,421	843	1,578
60—64	11,522	5,241	6,281	260	238	22	3,818	3,125	693	7,444	1,878	5,566
65—69	1,596	798	798	44	43	1	491	411	80	1,061	344	717
70 and over	2,901	1,265	1,636	62	52	10	734	619	115	2,105	594	1,511
JAIN	**20,302**	**10,809**	**9,493**	**8,187**	**5,547**	**2,640**	**8,240**	**4,108**	**4,132**	**3,875**	**1,154**	**2,721**
0	673	340	333	673	340	333	..	..	..	..	..	..
1	280	144	136	280	144	136	..	..	..	..	..	..
2	528	269	259	528	269	259	..	..	..	..	..	..
3	513	261	252	511	260	251	2	1	1	..	..	..
4	439	230	209	437	230	207	2	..	2	..	..	..
Total 0—4	*2,433*	*1,244*	*1,189*	*2,429*	*1,243*	*1,186*	*4*	*1*	*3*	..	..	..
5—9	2,109	1,113	996	2,094	1,108	986	13	4	9	2	1	1
10—14	1,533	905	628	1,251	853	398	269	49	220	13	3	10
15—19	1,718	1,004	714	779	738	41	891	258	633	48	8	40
20—24	2,252	1,166	1,086	564	553	11	1,509	570	939	179	43	136
25—29	2,155	1,195	960	344	339	5	1,527	778	749	284	78	206
30—34	1,951	1,023	928	247	242	5	1,242	652	590	462	129	333
35—39	1,403	798	605	128	127	1	835	514	321	440	157	283
40—44	1,501	728	773	116	115	1	768	445	323	617	168	449
45—49	943	524	419	75	75	..	467	301	166	401	148	253
50—54	1,138	558	580	87	84	3	404	286	118	647	188	459
55—59	401	234	167	29	28	1	161	127	34	211	79	132
60—64	506	208	298	34	32	2	103	82	21	369	94	275
65—69	118	55	63	4	4	..	23	21	2	91	30	61
70 and over	141	54	87	6	6	..	24	20	4	111	28	83
JEWISH	**27**	**14**	**13**	**15**	**10**	**5**	**10**	**4**	**6**	**2**	..	**2**
0	2	1	1	2	1	1	..	..	..	..	..	..
1	..	..	..	..	..	..	..	..	..	..	..	..
2	..	..	..	..	..	..	..	..	..	..	..	..
3	1	..	1	1	..	1	..	..	..	..	..	..
4	..	..	..	..	..	..	..	..	..	..	..	..
Total 0—4	*3*	*1*	*2*	*3*	*1*	*2*	..	..	..	..	..	..
5—9	4	1	3	4	1	3	..	..	..	..	..	..
10—14	1	1	..	1	1	..	..	..	..	..	..	..
15—19	4	3	1	3	3	..	1	..	1	..	..	..
20—24	3	3	..	3	3	..	..	..	..	..	..	..
25—29	2	1	1	1	1	..	1	..	1	..	..	..
30—34	2	..	2	..	..	..	2	..	2	..	..	..
35—39	4	2	2	..	..	..	3	2	1	1	..	1
40—44	1	..	1	..	..	..	1	..	1	..	..	..
45—49	..	..	..	..	..	..	..	..	..	..	..	..
50—54	1	1	..	..	..	..	1	1	..	..	..	..
55—59	1	1	..	..	..	..	1	1	..	..	..	..
60—64	..	..	..	..	..	..	..	..	..	..	..	..
65—69	1	..	1	..	..	..	..	..	..	1	..	1
70 and over	..	..	..	..	..	..	..	..	..	..	..	..

PART A.—PROVINCIAL SUMMARY—*concluded.*

TABLE VII.—A.

MERWARA—*concluded.*

AJMER-MERWARA.

Age and Religion.	Population.			Unmarried.			Married.			Widowed.		
	Persons.	Males.	Females.	Persons.	Males.	Females.	Persons.	Males.	Females.	Persons.	Males.	Females.
1	2	3	4	5	6	7	8	9	10	11	12	13
MUSALMAN	81,035	43,833	37,202	34,060	21,190	12,870	38,414	19,692	18,722	8,561	2,951	5,610
0	3,401	1,786	1,615	3,397	1,785	1,612	4	1	3	..	..	..
1	1,203	590	612	1,201	590	611	1	..	1	..	..	..
2	2,337	1,168	1,169	2,327	1,167	1,160	10	1	9	..	..	..
3	2,654	1,352	1,302	2,639	1,351	1,288	15	1	14	..	..	..
4	2,079	1,057	1,022	2,065	1,054	1,011	14	3	11	..	..	..
Total 0—4	*11,673*	*5,953*	*5,720*	*11,639*	*5,947*	*5,682*	*44*	*6*	*38*	..	..	..
5—9	9,677	5,145	4,532	9,272	5,010	4,262	384	127	257	21	8	13
10—14	7,374	4,225	3,149	5,834	3,800	2,034	1,478	389	1,089	62	36	26
15—19	6,855	3,834	3,021	3,283	2,809	474	3,441	961	2,480	131	64	67
20—24	8,472	4,463	4,009	2,019	1,892	127	6,071	2,366	3,705	382	205	177
25—29	7,745	4,282	3,463	987	922	65	6,245	3,071	3,174	513	289	224
30—34	7,531	4,062	3,469	456	372	84	6,369	3,387	2,982	706	303	403
35—39	4,273	2,460	1,813	143	123	20	3,563	2,107	1,456	567	230	337
40—44	5,670	2,920	2,750	187	128	59	4,193	2,426	1,767	1,290	366	924
45—49	2,444	1,418	1,026	60	45	15	1,784	1,190	594	600	183	417
50—54	4,354	2,395	1,959	87	65	22	2,629	1,875	754	1,638	455	1,183
55—59	1,176	712	464	14	11	3	708	539	169	454	162	292
60—64	2,410	1,222	1,188	52	43	9	994	815	179	1,364	364	1,000
65—69	421	241	180	10	6	4	183	156	27	228	79	149
70 and over	960	501	459	27	17	10	328	277	51	605	207	398
PARSI	262	134	128	146	75	71	104	57	47	12	2	10
0	8	6	2	8	6	2	..	..	..	..	..	..
1	5	3	2	5	3	2	..	..	..	..	..	..
2	10	4	6	10	4	6	..	..	..	..	..	..
3	7	3	4	7	3	4	..	..	..	..	..	..
4	4	2	2	4	2	2	..	..	..	..	..	..
Total 0—4	*34*	*18*	*16*	*34*	*18*	*16*	..	..	..	..	..	..
5—9	30	14	16	30	14	16	..	..	..	..	..	..
10—14	24	11	13	24	11	13	..	..	..	..	..	..
15—19	29	11	18	29	11	18	..	..	..	..	..	..
20—24	24	9	15	15	9	6	9	..	9	..	..	..
25—29	17	11	6	7	5	2	10	6	4	..	..	..
30—34	25	13	12	4	4	..	21	9	12	..	..	..
35—39	27	18	9	3	3	..	24	15	9	..	..	..
40—44	20	11	9	..	..	..	16	10	6	4	1	3
45—49	11	8	3	..	..	..	9	8	1	2	..	2
50—54	6	3	3	..	..	..	5	3	2	1	..	1
55—59	4	1	3	..	..	..	3	1	2	1	..	1
60—64	7	4	3	..	..	..	5	4	1	2	..	2
65—69	3	1	2	..	..	..	2	1	1	1	..	1
70 and over	1	1	..	..	..	..	..	..	..	1	1	..
SIKH	922	783	139	520	479	41	355	263	92	47	41	6
0	16	9	7	16	9	7	..	..	..	..	..	..
1	9	3	6	9	3	6	..	..	..	..	..	..
2	8	3	5	8	3	5	..	..	..	..	..	..
3	12	7	5	12	7	5	..	..	..	..	..	..
4	8	5	3	8	5	3	..	..	..	..	..	..
Total 0—4	*53*	*27*	*26*	*53*	*27*	*26*	..	..	..	..	..	..
5—9	30	18	12	30	18	12	..	..	..	..	..	..
10—14	26	22	4	21	18	3	5	4	1	..	..	..
15—19	134	124	10	104	104	..	27	17	10	3	3	..
20—24	317	283	32	193	195	..	112	81	31	10	9	1
25—29	147	132	15	76	76	..	62	47	15	9	9	..
30—34	89	63	26	26	26	..	55	30	25	8	7	1
35—39	57	54	3	8	8	..	46	43	3	3	3	..
40—44	35	30	5	5	5	..	28	23	5	2	2	..
45—49	15	15	..	2	2	..	12	12	..	1	1	..
50—54	11	7	4	..	..	..	6	4	2	5	3	2
55—59	1	..	1	..	..	..	..	..	..	1	..	1
60—64	5	4	1	..	..	..	2	2	..	3	2	1
65—69	..	..	..	..	..	..	..	..	..	..	..	..
70 and over	2	2	..	..	..	..	..	..	..	2	2	..

TABLE VII.

PART B.

BY STATES OR DISTRICTS.

ALL RELIGIONS.

TABLE VII.—B.

ALL RELIGIONS.

TABLE VII.—Age, Sex and Civil Condition.

Age; and State or District.	Population.			Unmarried.			Married.			Widowed.		
	Persons.	Males.	Females.	Persons.	Males.	Females.	Persons.	Males.	Females.	Persons.	Males.	Females.
1	2	3	4	5	6	7	8	9	10	11	12	13
RAJPUTANA												
ALWAR	*791,688*	*413,659*	*378,029*	*331,187*	*202,820*	*128,367*	*368,292*	*179,587*	*188,705*	*92,209*	*31,252*	*60,957*
0—4	103,714	51,261	52,453	103,652	51,243	52,409	60	18	42	2	..	2
5—9	97,081	50,622	46,459	94,924	50,000	44,304	2,078	536	1,542	79	26	53
10—14	91,483	51,092	40,391	71,808	46,249	25,559	19,205	4,660	14,546	469	183	286
15—19	77,913	43,429	34,484	31,920	27,409	4,511	44,405	15,376	29,029	1,588	644	944
20—39	237,339	121,199	116,139	21,670	20,938	732	195,728	92,801	102,927	19,940	7,460	12,480
40—59	139,932	73,000	66,932	5,715	5,500	215	90,325	58,626	36,689	43,892	13,864	30,028
60 and over	44,227	23,056	21,171	1,498	1,421	77	16,490	12,560	3,930	26,239	9,075	17,164
BANSWARA	*165,463*	*81,620*	*83,843*	*78,853*	*44,388*	*34,465*	*71,011*	*34,415*	*36,596*	*15,599*	*2,817*	*12,782*
0—4	33,912	16,700	17,212	33,905	16,700	17,205	7	..	7	..	..	..
5—9	22,423	11,504	10,919	22,165	11,451	10,714	255	53	202	3	..	3
10—14	11,983	6,402	5,581	10,132	5,987	4,145	1,821	408	1,413	30	7	23
15—19	13,047	6,819	6,228	6,626	5,073	1,553	6,318	1,712	4,606	103	34	69
20—39	58,225	28,743	29,482	5,586	4,921	665	48,657	22,808	25,849	3,982	1,014	2,968
40—59	22,084	10,188	11,896	383	229	154	12,979	8,606	4,373	8,722	1,353	7,369
60 and over	3,789	1,264	2,525	56	27	29	974	828	146	2,759	409	2,350
BHARATPUR	*558,785*	*302,254*	*256,531*	*210,586*	*136,407*	*74,179*	*270,178*	*135,260*	*134,918*	*78,021*	*30,587*	*47,434*
0—4	61,225	31,220	30,005	61,211	31,215	29,996	14	5	9	..	..	..
5—9	67,181	35,674	31,507	63,748	34,822	28,926	3,316	807	2,509	117	45	72
10—14	65,500	38,434	27,066	44,890	31,807	13,083	19,797	6,251	13,546	813	376	487
15—19	54,472	31,109	23,363	18,806	17,070	1,736	33,689	13,100	20,589	1,977	939	1,038
20—39	182,767	97,732	85,035	17,583	17,205	378	144,216	71,166	73,050	20,968	9,361	11,607
40—59	101,784	54,607	47,177	3,748	3,705	43	60,518	37,247	23,271	37,518	13,055	23,803
60 and over	25,856	13,478	12,378	600	583	17	8,628	6,084	1,044	16,628	6,211	10,417
BIKANER	*700,983*	*371,489*	*329,494*	*302,400*	*196,710*	*105,690*	*308,033*	*149,094*	*158,939*	*90,550*	*25,685*	*64,865*
0—4	99,046	50,119	48,927	98,844	50,063	48,781	198	54	144	4	2	2
5—9	82,590	43,495	39,095	80,269	43,058	37,211	2,250	427	1,823	71	10	61
10—14	63,335	35,585	27,750	49,132	32,789	16,348	13,854	2,724	11,130	349	72	277
15—19	64,973	37,524	27,449	30,366	27,883	2,484	33,117	9,332	23,785	1,490	310	1,169
20—39	233,165	123,921	109,244	36,817	36,125	692	173,605	81,335	92,270	22,743	6,461	16,282
40—59	123,466	65,181	58,325	5,789	5,648	141	73,663	46,727	26,936	44,004	12,756	31,248
60 and over	34,418	15,714	18,704	1,183	1,145	38	11,346	8,495	2,851	21,889	6,074	15,815
BUNDI	*218,730*	*113,211*	*105,519*	*90,767*	*55,793*	*34,974*	*103,751*	*50,907*	*52,844*	*24,212*	*6,511*	*17,701*
0—4	36,077	17,462	18,615	36,077	17,462	18,615	..	..	..	..	..	..
5—9	27,685	14,526	13,159	26,647	14,308	12,339	988	200	788	50	18	32
10—14	13,380	7,733	5,647	10,032	7,152	2,880	3,268	548	2,720	80	33	47
15—19	14,963	8,303	6,660	6,358	5,918	440	8,352	2,285	6,067	253	100	153
20—39	79,116	40,719	38,397	9,766	9,248	518	63,359	29,374	33,985	5,991	2,097	3,894
40—59	38,823	20,354	18,469	1,576	1,426	150	24,674	16,026	8,648	12,573	2,902	9,671
60 and over	8,686	4,114	4,572	311	279	32	3,110	2,474	636	5,265	1,361	3,904
DHOLPUR	*263,188*	*144,244*	*118,944*	*102,293*	*67,906*	*34,387*	*128,062*	*63,935*	*64,127*	*32,833*	*12,403*	*20,430*
0—4	30,013	15,415	14,598	30,013	15,415	14,598	..	..	..	..	..	..
5—9	33,642	18,015	15,627	31,619	17,550	14,069	1,983	442	1,541	40	23	17
10—14	29,990	17,694	12,296	18,862	14,280	4,582	10,869	3,318	7,551	259	96	163
15—19	25,037	14,322	10,715	8,033	7,607	426	16,364	6,426	9,938	640	289	351
20—39	84,072	45,816	38,256	10,286	9,829	457	65,551	32,350	33,201	8,235	3,637	4,598
40—59	47,269	26,078	21,191	2,929	2,752	177	28,618	17,719	10,899	15,722	5,607	10,115
60 and over	13,165	6,904	6,261	551	473	78	4,677	3,680	997	7,937	2,751	5,186
DUNGARPUR	*159,192*	*79,105*	*80,087*	*71,772*	*41,293*	*30,479*	*71,390*	*34,852*	*36,538*	*16,030*	*2,960*	*13,070*
0—4	31,575	15,487	16,088	31,528	15,475	16,053	45	12	33	2	..	2
5—9	19,900	10,441	9,459	19,503	10,360	9,143	393	79	314	4	2	2
10—14	10,836	5,806	5,030	8,577	5,309	3,268	2,220	489	1,731	39	8	31
15—19	12,588	6,704	5,884	5,768	4,732	1,036	6,686	1,933	4,753	134	39	95
20—39	58,800	29,014	29,786	5,788	5,030	758	48,275	22,881	25,394	4,737	1,103	3,634
40—59	22,220	10,466	11,754	530	333	197	12,849	8,717	4,132	8,841	1,416	7,425
60 and over	3,273	1,187	2,086	78	54	24	922	741	181	2,273	392	1,881
JAIPUR	*2,636,647*	*1,385,750*	*1,250,897*	*1,033,805*	*668,268*	*365,537*	*1,381,894*	*624,652*	*657,242*	*320,948*	*92,830*	*228,118*
0—4	332,123	165,446	166,677	331,537	165,284	166,253	566	159	407	20	3	17
5—9	307,578	162,967	144,611	296,435	160,757	135,678	10,858	2,135	8,723	285	75	210
10—14	253,865	146,688	107,177	184,342	130,503	53,839	68,114	15,722	52,392	1,409	463	946
15—19	232,765	131,964	100,801	92,627	86,520	6,107	135,713	44,012	91,701	4,425	1,432	2,993
20—39	866,597	446,722	419,875	99,944	97,245	2,699	695,879	327,135	368,744	70,774	22,342	48,432
40—59	501,694	263,743	237,951	23,668	22,943	725	320,524	197,053	123,471	157,502	43,747	113,755
60 and over	142,025	68,220	73,805	5,252	5,016	236	50,240	38,436	11,804	86,538	24,768	61,765

PART B.—BY STATES OR DISTRICTS. ALL RELIGIONS.

TABLE VII—B.
ALL RELIGIONS.

Age; and State or District.	Population.			Unmarried.			Married.			Widowed.		
	Persons.	Males.	Females.	Persons.	Males.	Females.	Persons.	Males.	Females.	Persons.	Males.	Females.
1	2	3	4	5	6	7	8	9	10	11	12	13
RAJPUTANA—contd.												
JAISALMER	*88,311*	*48,500*	*30,811*	*43,119*	*29,310*	*13,809*	*33,247*	*16,097*	*17,150*	*11,945*	*3,093*	*8,852*
0—4	12,452	6,497	5,955	12,408	6,489	5,919	43	7	36	1	1	..
5—9	10,589	6,040	4,549	10,420	6,007	4,413	163	31	132	6	2	4
10—14	9,711	5,933	3,778	8,400	5,685	2,715	1,248	234	1,014	63	14	49
15—19	8,009	4,593	3,416	4,479	3,953	526	3,280	600	2,680	250	40	210
20—39	20,235	15,843	13,392	6,560	6,366	194	19,279	8,733	10,546	3,396	744	2,652
40—59	14,758	7,932	6,826	714	679	35	8,197	5,614	2,583	5,847	1,639	4,208
60 and over	3,557	1,662	1,895	138	131	7	1,037	878	159	2,382	653	1,729
JHALAWAR	*96,271*	*50,034*	*46,237*	*35,968*	*23,416*	*12,552*	*46,231*	*22,788*	*23,443*	*14,072*	*3,830*	*10,242*
0—4	13,729	6,761	6,968	13,639	6,746	6,893	90	15	75	..	..	..
5—9	11,158	5,790	5,368	10,002	5,579	4,423	1,133	197	936	23	14	9
10—14	6,400	3,663	2,737	4,085	3,147	938	2,253	507	1,746	62	9	53
15—19	7,037	4,188	3,449	2,935	2,785	150	4,460	1,340	3,120	242	63	179
20—39	36,172	18,600	17,572	4,595	4,487	108	27,223	12,878	14,345	4,354	1,235	3,119
40—59	17,107	8,900	8,207	607	570	37	9,652	6,635	3,017	6,848	1,695	5,153
60 and over	4,068	2,132	1,936	105	102	3	1,420	1,216	204	2,543	814	1,729
KARAULI	*146,587*	*80,081*	*66,506*	*59,216*	*30,128*	*20,088*	*69,204*	*34,483*	*34,719*	*18,167*	*6,468*	*11,699*
0—4	17,870	9,203	8,667	17,870	9,203	8,667	..	..	..	..	..	..
5—9	18,160	9,824	8,336	17,366	9,667	7,699	787	154	633	7	3	4
10—14	15,761	9,220	6,541	10,895	7,911	2,984	4,762	1,271	3,491	104	38	66
15—19	13,337	7,734	5,608	5,232	4,836	396	7,815	2,772	5,043	290	126	164
20—39	49,712	27,084	22,628	6,421	6,150	271	38,655	19,003	19,652	4,636	1,931	2,705
40—59	25,042	13,548	11,494	1,209	1,159	50	14,864	9,409	5,455	8,969	2,930	5,989
60 and over	6,705	3,468	3,237	223	202	21	2,321	1,876	445	4,161	1,390	2,771
KISHANGARH	*87,191*	*45,718*	*41,473*	*32,206*	*20,803*	*11,403*	*42,013*	*20,754*	*21,259*	*12,972*	*4,161*	*8,811*
0—4	11,915	5,887	6,028	11,718	5,836	5,882	187	44	143	10	7	3
5—9	9,987	5,376	4,611	9,078	5,109	3,969	869	247	622	40	20	20
10—14	6,743	3,950	2,793	4,465	3,263	1,202	2,175	640	1,535	103	47	56
15—19	7,261	4,028	3,233	2,607	2,471	136	4,381	1,421	2,960	273	136	137
20—39	32,456	17,173	15,283	3,498	3,387	111	25,023	12,234	12,789	3,935	1,552	2,383
40—59	15,424	7,822	7,602	702	633	69	8,442	5,423	3,019	6,280	1,766	4,514
60 and over	3,405	1,482	1,923	138	104	34	936	745	191	2,331	633	1,698
KOTAH	*639,089*	*330,324*	*308,765*	*252,936*	*155,062*	*97,874*	*310,363*	*154,025*	*156,338*	*75,790*	*21,237*	*54,553*
0—4	100,096	49,120	50,976	100,062	49,095	50,967	34	25	9	..	..	..
5—9	75,187	38,495	36,692	72,565	37,878	34,692	2,557	597	1,960	65	25	40
10—14	45,293	25,756	19,537	33,250	23,086	10,164	11,858	2,604	9,254	185	66	119
15—19	48,294	25,908	22,386	18,897	17,644	1,253	28,609	8,018	20,591	788	246	542
20—39	236,065	121,891	114,174	24,487	23,856	631	191,861	91,309	100,552	19,717	6,726	12,991
40—59	108,560	56,215	52,345	3,006	2,882	124	66,382	43,889	22,493	39,172	9,444	29,728
60 and over	25,594	12,939	12,655	669	626	43	9,062	7,583	1,479	15,863	4,730	11,133
KUSHALGARH	*22,005*	*10,956*	*11,049*	*11,381*	*6,290*	*5,091*	*8,964*	*4,370*	*4,594*	*1,660*	*296*	*1,364*
0—4	4,181	2,026	2,155	4,181	2,026	2,155	..	..	..	..	..	..
5—9	3,419	1,790	1,629	3,404	1,786	1,618	15	4	11	..	..	..
10—14	1,812	929	883	1,677	899	778	132	30	102	3	..	3
15—19	1,683	918	715	1,050	745	305	569	169	400	14	4	10
20—39	7,403	3,615	3,788	986	780	206	6,041	2,728	3,313	376	107	269
40—59	3,027	1,500	1,527	74	50	24	2,056	1,316	740	897	134	763
60 and over	530	178	352	9	4	5	151	123	28	370	51	319
LAWA	*2,564*	*1,309*	*1,369*	*938*	*574*	*364*	*1,234*	*609*	*639*	*393*	*190*	*266*
0—4	355	155	200	354	155	199	1	..	1	..	..	..
5—9	286	140	146	263	135	128	23	5	18	..	..	..
10—14	205	124	81	143	114	29	60	9	51	2	1	1
15—19	222	115	107	76	68	8	138	42	96	8	5	3
20—39	942	479	463	87	87	..	748	358	388	109	34	75
40—59	447	230	217	14	14	..	237	161	76	196	55	141
60 and over	107	59	48	1	1	..	29	27	2	77	31	46
MARWAR	*2,057,553*	*1,075,269*	*982,284*	*871,037*	*554,618*	*316,419*	*931,116*	*452,732*	*478,384*	*255,400*	*67,919*	*187,481*
0—4	307,796	155,713	152,083	304,400	154,888	149,518	3,299	780	2,519	91	45	46
5—9	242,887	129,177	113,710	227,364	124,235	103,129	14,967	4,721	10,246	556	221	335
10—14	187,408	105,567	81,841	145,776	93,775	52,001	40,381	11,290	29,082	1,251	436	758
15—19	176,669	99,517	77,152	82,116	72,929	9,187	90,880	25,481	65,449	3,673	1,137	2,516
20—39	695,306	362,051	333,255	95,676	93,719	1,957	536,206	249,489	286,717	63,424	18,843	44,581
40—59	351,002	180,163	170,839	12,814	12,298	516	214,502	136,719	77,783	123,686	31,146	92,540
60 and over	96,485	43,081	53,404	2,885	2,774	111	30,681	24,293	6,588	62,719	16,014	46,705

TABLE VII.—B.
ALL RELIGIONS.

TABLE VII.—Age, Sex and Civil Condition. Part B.—By States or Districts. All Religions.—*continued.*

Age; and State or District.	Population. Persons.	Population. Males.	Population. Females.	Unmarried. Persons.	Unmarried. Males.	Unmarried. Females.	Married. Persons.	Married. Males.	Married. Females.	Widowed. Persons.	Widowed. Males.	Widowed. Females.
1	2	3	4	5	6	7	8	9	10	11	12	13
RAJPUTANA—*concld.*												
MEWAR	*1,293,776*	*670,750*	*623,026*	*538,680*	*330,103*	*208,317*	*599,940*	*298,119*	*301,821*	*155,156*	*42,538*	*112,628*
0—4	226,364	111,463	114,901	225,668	111,244	114,424	666	212	454	30	7	23
5—9	159,909	85,741	73,868	154,547	84,356	70,191	4,874	1,306	3,568	188	79	109
10—14	77,945	45,471	32,474	59,130	40,913	18,217	18,286	4,349	13,937	529	209	320
15—19	99,996	56,650	43,346	43,123	39,486	3,637	54,476	16,013	38,463	2,397	1,151	1,246
20—39	476,726	249,318	227,408	50,484	48,766	1,718	381,371	183,036	198,335	44,871	17,516	27,355
40—59	214,427	105,898	108,529	5,038	4,705	333	128,206	83,454	44,752	81,183	17,739	63,444
60 and over	38,709	16,209	22,500	690	633	57	12,061	9,749	2,312	25,958	3,827	20,131
PARTABGARH	*62,704*	*31,735*	*30,969*	*25,853*	*15,488*	*10,365*	*28,954*	*14,278*	*14,676*	*7,897*	*1,969*	*5,928*
0—4	11,191	5,511	5,680	11,093	5,485	5,608	97	26	71	1	..	1
5—9	7,497	4,002	3,495	7,132	3,914	3,218	360	88	272	5	..	5
10—14	4,198	2,372	1,826	3,138	2,124	1,014	1,031	240	791	29	8	21
15—19	4,748	2,499	2,249	2,026	1,742	284	2,607	716	1,891	115	41	74
20—39	24,162	12,091	12,071	2,205	2,018	187	19,286	9,220	10,066	2,671	853	1,818
40—59	9,358	4,608	4,750	227	183	44	5,126	3,610	1,516	4,005	815	3,190
60 and over	1,550	652	898	32	22	10	447	378	69	1,071	252	819
SHAHPURA	*47,397*	*24,595*	*22,802*	*18,457*	*11,424*	*7,033*	*22,960*	*11,374*	*11,586*	*5,980*	*1,797*	*4,183*
0—4	7,654	3,788	3,866	7,592	3,774	3,818	62	14	48	..	..	..
5—9	5,760	2,968	2,792	5,424	2,872	2,552	329	91	238	7	5	2
10—14	2,721	1,595	1,126	1,932	1,385	547	770	201	569	19	9	10
15—19	3,469	1,962	1,507	1,322	1,256	66	2,059	665	1,394	88	41	47
20—39	17,696	9,329	8,369	1,800	1,765	35	14,261	6,825	7,436	1,637	739	898
40—59	8,357	4,236	4,121	313	301	12	4,993	3,194	1,799	3,051	741	2,310
60 and over	1,738	717	1,021	71	71	3	486	384	102	1,178	262	916
SIROHI	*189,197*	*98,359*	*90,838*	*83,237*	*50,610*	*32,627*	*87,222*	*43,487*	*43,735*	*18,668*	*4,193*	*14,476*
0—4	32,599	16,214	16,385	32,249	16,143	16,106	343	70	273	7	1	6
5—9	24,297	13,037	11,260	23,338	12,786	10,552	937	243	694	22	8	14
10—14	15,921	9,464	6,457	13,446	8,751	4,695	2,398	677	1,719	79	36	43
15—19	14,820	8,335	6,485	7,094	6,257	837	7,494	1,988	5,506	232	90	142
20—39	63,150	32,037	31,113	6,502	6,182	320	52,307	24,572	27,735	4,341	1,283	3,058
40—59	30,323	15,668	14,655	194	107	87	20,754	13,537	7,217	9,075	1,724	7,351
60 and over	8,017	3,531	4,486	114	84	30	2,991	2,400	591	4,912	1,050	3,862
TONK	*303,181*	*156,390*	*146,791*	*119,587*	*73,344*	*46,243*	*147,409*	*73,006*	*74,403*	*36,185*	*10,040*	*26,145*
0—4	48,028	23,414	24,614	47,589	23,273	24,316	413	130	283	26	11	15
5—9	36,460	19,061	17,399	34,263	18,557	15,706	2,130	486	1,644	67	18	49
10—14	22,017	12,723	9,294	15,340	11,031	4,309	6,508	1,635	4,873	169	57	112
15—19	22,984	12,416	10,568	8,973	8,104	869	13,561	4,138	9,423	450	174	276
20—39	108,859	56,211	52,648	11,623	10,847	776	87,813	41,877	45,936	9,423	3,487	5,936
40—59	51,383	26,210	25,173	1,459	1,261	198	32,096	20,791	11,305	17,828	4,158	13,670
60 and over	13,450	6,355	7,095	340	271	69	4,888	3,949	939	8,322	2,135	6,187
AJMER-MERWARA—												
AJMER	*380,384*	*201,911*	*178,473*	*145,998*	*92,545*	*53,453*	*184,852*	*93,359*	*91,493*	*49,534*	*16,007*	*33,527*
0—4	53,451	26,856	26,595	52,947	26,754	26,193	489	98	391	15	4	11
5—9	42,237	22,175	20,062	39,462	21,302	18,160	2,652	815	1,837	123	58	65
10—14	29,784	17,189	12,595	21,471	14,777	6,694	7,992	2,246	5,746	321	166	155
15—19	32,129	17,707	14,422	12,922	11,452	1,470	18,319	5,815	12,504	888	440	448
20—39	141,409	76,480	64,929	16,831	16,130	701	110,469	54,404	56,065	14,109	5,946	8,163
40—59	65,876	34,350	31,526	1,949	1,761	188	40,074	26,004	14,070	23,853	6,585	17,268
60 and over	15,498	7,154	8,344	416	369	47	4,857	3,977	880	10,225	2,808	7,417
MERWARA	*121,011*	*64,287*	*56,724*	*52,347*	*33,061*	*19,286*	*56,062*	*27,510*	*28,552*	*12,602*	*3,716*	*8,886*
0—4	20,317	10,225	10,092	20,238	10,193	10,045	79	32	47	..	..	..
5—9	14,335	7,696	6,639	13,881	7,549	6,332	441	140	301	13	7	6
10—14	7,905	4,582	3,323	6,490	4,287	2,203	1,377	283	1,094	38	12	26
15—19	9,234	5,258	3,976	4,607	4,207	400	4,488	991	3,497	139	60	79
20—39	43,722	23,197	20,525	6,574	6,351	223	34,311	15,685	18,626	2,837	1,161	1,676
40—59	20,133	10,751	9,382	461	395	66	13,415	8,742	4,673	6,257	1,314	4,943
60 and over	5,365	2,578	2,787	96	79	17	1,951	1,637	314	3,318	862	2,456

TABLE VII.

Part C.

BY STATES OR DISTRICTS.

ANIMISTS.

TABLE VII.—C.

ANIMISTS.

Age; and State or District.	Population.			Unmarried.			Married.			Widowed.		
	Persons.	Males.	Females.	Persons.	Males.	Females.	Persons.	Males.	Females.	Persons.	Males.	Females.
1	2	3	4	5	6	7	8	9	10	11	12	13
RAJPUTANA—												
ALWAR	*31*	*17*	*14*	*21*	*13*	*8*	*9*	*4*	*5*	*1*	..	*1*
0—4	3	3	..	3	3	..	..	..	..	..	..	..
5—9	11	3	8	9	3	6	2	..	2	..	..	..
10—14	4	4	..	4	4	..	..	..	..	..	..	..
15—19	1	1	..	1	1	..	..	..	..	..	..	..
20—39	8	3	5	4	2	2	3	1	2	1	..	1
40—59	3	2	1	..	..	..	3	2	1	..	..	..
60 and over	1	1	..	..	..	..	1	1	..	..	..	..
BANSWARA	*95,834*	*47,323*	*48,511*	*49,266*	*26,800*	*22,466*	*40,685*	*19,502*	*21,183*	*5,883*	*1,021*	*4,862*
0—4	22,056	10,868	11,188	22,055	10,868	11,187	1	..	1	..	..	..
5—9	14,351	7,343	7,008	14,306	7,325	6,981	45	18	27	..	..	..
10—14	6,629	3,470	3,159	5,929	3,279	2,650	693	186	507	7	5	2
15—19	7,144	3,720	3,424	4,015	2,833	1,182	3,102	873	2,229	27	14	13
20—39	32,869	16,078	16,791	2,831	2,446	385	28,836	13,185	15,651	1,202	447	735
40—59	10,987	5,257	5,730	112	43	69	7,455	4,789	2,666	3,420	425	2,995
60 and over	1,798	587	1,211	18	6	12	553	451	102	1,227	130	1,097
BUNDI	*4,632*	*2,375*	*2,257*	*2,108*	*1,160*	*948*	*2,149*	*1,051*	*1,098*	*275*	*64*	*211*
0—4	1,106	529	577	1,106	529	577	..	..	..	..	..	..
5—9	688	369	319	677	369	308	9	..	9	2	..	2
10—14	172	98	74	123	98	25	44	5	39	..	..	..
15—19	235	104	131	78	66	12	154	37	117	3	1	2
20—39	1,643	796	847	107	96	11	1,451	661	790	85	39	46
40—59	603	340	263	9	5	4	456	318	138	138	17	121
60 and over	85	39	46	3	2	1	35	30	5	47	7	40
DUNGARPUR	*74,281*	*37,523*	*36,758*	*36,767*	*20,108*	*16,659*	*33,412*	*16,431*	*16,981*	*4,102*	*984*	*3,118*
0—4	17,394	8,498	8,896	17,386	8,494	8,892	8	4	4	..	..	..
5—9	10,514	5,542	4,972	10,440	5,517	4,923	73	24	49	1	1	..
10—14	4,601	2,459	2,142	4,025	2,322	1,703	567	132	435	9	5	4
15—19	5,363	2,824	2,539	2,660	1,099	661	2,680	809	1,871	23	16	7
20—39	26,629	13,245	13,?84	2,089	1,707	382	23,582	11,124	12,458	958	414	544
40—59	8,575	4,496	4,079	151	64	87	6,080	4,015	2,065	2,344	417	1,927
60 and over	1,205	459	746	16	5	11	422	323	99	767	131	636
JAIPUR	*1,779*	*955*	*824*	*766*	*453*	*313*	*874*	*455*	*419*	*139*	*47*	*92*
0—4	319	145	174	318	144	174	1	1	..	..	..	..
5—9	212	118	94	204	116	88	8	2	6	..	..	..
10—14	122	73	49	97	68	29	25	5	20	..	..	..
15—19	149	82	67	66	57	9	82	25	57	1	..	1
20—39	640	349	291	73	62	11	531	268	263	36	19	17
40—59	275	148	127	8	6	2	192	124	68	75	18	57
60 and over	62	40	22	..	..	..	35	30	5	27	10	17
JAISALMER	*4,158*	*2,246*	*1,912*	*2,095*	*1,291*	*804*	*1,761*	*865*	*896*	*302*	*90*	*212*
0—4	709	344	365	706	343	363	3	1	2	..	..	..
5—9	633	362	271	626	360	266	7	2	5	..	..	..
10—14	503	320	183	456	306	150	45	13	32	2	1	1
15—19	339	186	153	173	151	22	159	34	125	7	1	6
20—39	1,238	605	633	125	122	3	1,041	462	579	72	21	51
40—59	587	343	244	8	8	..	434	292	142	145	43	102
60 and over	149	86	63	1	1	..	72	61	11	76	24	52

PART C.—BY STATES OR DISTRICTS. MAIN RELIGIONS.

TABLE VII.—C.

ANIMISTS.

Age; and State or District.	Population.			Unmarried.			Married.			Widowed.		
	Persons.	Males.	Females.	Persons.	Males.	Females.	Persons.	Males.	Females.	Persons.	Males.	Females.
1	2	3	4	5	6	7	8	9	10	11	12	13
RAJPUTANA—*contd.*												
JHALAWAR .	***430***	***238***	***192***	***198***	***124***	***74***	***196***	***95***	***101***	***36***	***9***	***27***
0—4 . .	75	44	31	75	44	31	..	..	..	..	..	..
5—9 . .	59	30	29	57	30	27	2	..	2	..	..	..
10—14 . .	37	25	12	29	21	8	8	4	4	..	..	..
15—19 . .	29	14	15	15	10	5	14	4	10	..	..	..
20—39 . .	133	63	70	22	19	3	107	43	64	4	1	3
40—59 . .	71	42	29	..	..	..	56	37	19	15	5	10
60 and over .	16	10	6	..	..	..	9	7	2	7	3	4
KARAULI . .	***8***	***6***	***2***	***4***	***3***	***1***	***4***	***3***	***1***	..	..	..
0—4 . .	1	..	1	1	..	1	..	..	..	..	..	..
5—9 . .	1	1	..	1	1	..	..	..	..	..	..	..
10—14 . .	1	1	..	1	1	..	..	..	..	..	..	..
15—19 . .	1	1	..	1	1	..	..	..	..	..	..	..
20—39 . .	1	1	..	..	..	..	1	1	..	..	..	..
40—59 . .	3	2	1	..	..	..	3	2	1	..	..	..
60 and over .	..	..	..	..	..	..	..	..	..	..	..	..
KISHANGARH .	***535***	***263***	***272***	***220***	***122***	***98***	***282***	***131***	***151***	***33***	***10***	***23***
0—4 . .	113	53	60	110	53	57	3	..	3	..	..	..
5—9 . .	68	31	37	65	31	34	3	..	3	..	..	..
10—14 . .	30	15	15	20	15	5	10	..	10	..	..	..
15—19 . .	38	19	19	10	9	1	28	10	18	..	..	..
20—39 . .	200	104	96	13	13	..	178	85	93	9	6	3
40—59 . .	70	35	35	2	1	1	52	30	22	16	4	12
60 and over .	16	6	10	..	..	..	6	6	2	8	..	8
KOTAH . .	***3,075***	***1,558***	***1,517***	***1,348***	***772***	***576***	***1,507***	***742***	***765***	***220***	***44***	***176***
0—4 . .	661	328	333	661	328	333	..	..	..	..	..	..
5—9 . .	410	223	187	409	223	186	1	..	1	..	..	..
10—14 . .	191	106	85	149	102	47	41	4	37	1	..	1
15—19 . .	200	86	114	70	65	5	127	20	107	3	1	2
20—39 . .	1,107	563	544	57	52	5	992	489	503	58	22	36
40—59 . .	414	206	208	2	2	..	303	190	113	109	14	95
60 and over .	92	46	46	..	..	..	43	39	4	49	7	42
KUSHALGARH .	***17,100***	***8,488***	***8,612***	***9,116***	***4,928***	***4,188***	***7,002***	***3,399***	***3,603***	***982***	***161***	***821***
0—4 . .	3,456	1,679	1,777	3,456	1,679	1,777	..	..	..	..	..	..
5—9 . .	2,773	1,436	1,337	2,763	1,432	1,331	10	4	6	..	..	..
10—14 . .	1,401	709	692	1,321	686	635	79	23	56	1	..	1
15—19 . .	1,230	689	541	808	551	257	415	135	280	7	3	4
20—39 . .	5,627	2,722	2,905	725	556	169	4,734	2,110	2,624	168	56	112
40—59 . .	2,233	1,122	1,111	36	21	15	1,643	1,030	613	554	71	483
60 and over .	380	131	249	7	3	4	121	97	24	252	31	221
MARWAR . .	***48,957***	***26,254***	***22,703***	***23,759***	***14,613***	***9,146***	***21,735***	***10,779***	***10,956***	***3,463***	***862***	***2,601***
0—4 . .	9,309	4,627	4,682	9,265	4,612	4,653	42	13	29	2	2	..
5—9 . .	6,316	3,445	2,871	6,191	3,409	2,782	118	31	87	7	5	2
10—14 . .	4,623	2,771	1,852	4,067	2,651	1,416	540	112	428	16	8	8
15—19 . .	3,984	2,303	1,681	2,186	1,966	220	1,775	328	1,447	23	9	14
20—39 . .	15,826	8,352	7,474	1,967	1,905	62	13,171	6,226	6,945	688	221	467
40—59 . .	7,101	3,825	3,276	71	61	10	5,294	3,401	1,893	1,736	363	1,373
60 and over .	1,798	931	867	12	9	3	795	668	127	991	254	737

TABLE VII.—C.
ANIMISTS.

TABLE VII.—Age, Sex and Civil Condition. Part C.—By States or Districts. Main Religions.—*continued.*

Age; and State or District.	Population.			Unmarried.			Married.			Widowed.		
	Persons.	Males.	Females.	Persons.	Males.	Females.	Persons.	Males.	Females.	Persons.	Males.	Females.
1	2	3	4	5	6	7	8	9	10	11	12	13
RAJPUTANA— *contd.*												
MEWAR	***159,094***	***81,794***	***77,300***	***73,235***	***41,836***	***31,399***	***75,321***	***37,141***	***38,180***	***10,538***	***2,817***	***7,721***
0—4	34,650	16,911	17,739	34,592	16,892	17,700	56	19	37	2	..	2
5—9	22,832	12,271	10,561	22,525	12,195	10,330	288	64	224	19	12	7
10—14	8,580	5,025	3,555	7,199	4,734	2,465	1,357	277	1,080	24	14	10
15—19	10,010	5,412	4,598	4,550	3,943	607	5,295	1,372	3,923	165	97	68
20—30	58,759	29,866	28,893	4,190	3,929	261	51,886	24,574	27,312	2,683	1,363	1,320
40—59	21,116	10,906	10,210	163	132	31	15,143	9,796	5,347	5,810	978	4,832
60 and over	3,147	1,403	1,744	16	11	5	1,296	1,039	257	1,835	353	1,482
PARTABGARH	***20,929***	***10,530***	***10,399***	***9,635***	***5,480***	***4,155***	***9,776***	***4,725***	***5,051***	***1,518***	***395***	***1,193***
0—4	4,503	2,234	2,269	4,501	2,234	2,267	2	..	2	..	..	..
5—9	2,924	1,523	1,401	2,880	1,517	1,363	44	6	38	..	..	..
10—14	1,300	733	567	1,078	682	396	219	51	168	3	..	3
15—19	1,341	733	608	660	565	95	675	166	509	6	2	4
20—39	7,873	3,798	4,075	486	461	25	6,936	3,175	3,761	451	162	289
40—59	2,585	1,359	1,226	26	20	6	1,751	1,211	540	808	128	680
60 and over	403	150	253	4	1	3	149	116	33	250	33	217
SHAHPURA	***1,952***	***989***	***963***	***809***	***451***	***351***	***1,035***	***503***	***532***	***125***	***35***	***90***
0—4	434	220	214	432	220	212	2	..	2	..	..	..
5—9	279	140	139	255	134	121	23	5	18	1	1	..
10—14	101	59	42	65	50	15	36	9	27	..	..	..
15—19	118	56	62	28	26	2	89	29	60	1	1	..
20—39	699	345	354	20	19	1	649	311	338	30	15	15
40—59	273	142	131	2	2	..	206	132	74	65	8	57
60 and over	48	27	21	..	..	..	20	17	3	28	10	18
SIROHI	***4,431***	***2,308***	***2,123***	***2,034***	***1,204***	***830***	***2,108***	***1,040***	***1,068***	***289***	***64***	***225***
0—4	909	434	475	903	433	470	6	1	5	..	..	..
5—9	565	319	246	549	310	239	15	9	6	1	..	1
10—14	368	219	149	304	205	99	64	14	50	..	..	..
15—19	361	205	159	172	159	13	189	45	144	3	1	2
20—39	1,451	727	724	96	91	5	1,304	612	692	51	24	27
40—59	636	340	296	8	6	2	467	309	158	161	25	136
60 and over	138	64	74	2	..	2	63	50	13	73	14	59
TONK	***7,586***	***3,751***	***3,835***	***3,177***	***1,780***	***1,397***	***3,771***	***1,842***	***1,929***	***638***	***129***	***509***
0—4	1,590	768	822	1,584	767	817	6	1	5	..	..	..
5—9	964	488	476	921	481	440	42	7	35	1	..	1
10—14	391	215	176	290	186	104	97	27	70	4	2	2
15—19	441	226	215	167	150	17	265	72	193	9	4	5
20—39	2,920	1,417	1,503	197	183	14	2,557	1,190	1,367	166	44	122
40—59	1,090	548	542	14	10	4	723	478	245	353	60	293
60 and over	190	89	101	4	3	1	81	67	14	105	19	86
AJMER-MERWARA—												
AJMER	***2,678***	***1,308***	***1,370***	***1,063***	***568***	***495***	***1,398***	***675***	***723***	***217***	***65***	***152***
0—4	488	208	280	486	207	279	2	1	1	..	..	..
5—9	361	177	184	345	174	171	16	3	13	..	..	..
10—14	154	92	62	113	80	33	40	12	28	1	..	1
15—19	197	83	114	62	56	6	131	24	107	4	3	1
20—39	1,051	533	518	55	49	6	948	455	493	48	29	19
40—59	356	179	177	2	2	..	234	156	78	120	21	99
60 and over	71	36	35	..	..	..	27	24	3	44	12	32
MERWARA	***1,301***	***679***	***622***	***557***	***349***	***208***	***607***	***286***	***321***	***137***	***44***	***93***
0—4	239	122	117	239	122	117	..	..	..	..	..	..
5—9	163	89	74	159	88	71	4	1	3	..	..	..
10—14	71	41	30	53	39	14	15	2	13	3	..	3
15—19	102	58	44	53	49	4	48	8	40	1	1	..
20—39	461	251	210	50	48	2	382	180	202	29	23	6
40—59	203	89	114	2	2	..	134	77	57	67	10	57
60 and over	62	29	33	1	1	..	24	18	6	37	10	27

N.B.—Bharatpur, Bikaner, Dholpur, and Lawa, which contain no Animists, have not been shewn.

TABLE VII.

PART C.

BY STATES OR DISTRICTS.

CHRISTIANS.

TABLE VII.—C.
CHRISTIANS.

TABLE VII.—AGE, SEX AND CIVIL CONDITION.

Age; and State or District.	Population.			Unmarried.			Married.			Widowed.		
	Persons.	Males.	Females.	Persons.	Males.	Females.	Persons.	Males.	Females.	Persons.	Males.	Females.
1	2	3	4	5	6	7	8	9	10	11	12	13
RAJPUTANA—												
ALWAR . .	*92*	*50*	*42*	*41*	*20*	*21*	*43*	*24*	*19*	*8*	*6*	*2*
0—4 . .	11	4	7	11	4	7	..	..	..	..	..	..
5—9 . .	7	3	4	7	3	4	..	..	..	..	..	..
10—14 . .	9	4	5	9	4	5	..	..	..	..	..	..
15—19 . .	5	2	3	4	2	2	1	..	1	..	..	..
20—39 . .	36	20	16	8	7	1	27	12	15	1	1	..
40—59 . .	17	12	5	1	..	1	12	9	3	4	3	1
60 and over .	7	5	2	1	..	1	3	3	..	3	2	1
BHARATPUR .	*566*	*315*	*251*	*250*	*157*	*93*	*253*	*130*	*123*	*63*	*28*	*35*
0—4 . .	80	43	37	80	43	37	..	..	..	..	..	..
5—9 . .	73	46	27	71	46	25	2	..	2	..	..	..
10—14 . .	42	27	15	38	26	12	3	1	2	1	..	1
15—19 . .	54	30	24	26	19	7	23	8	15	5	3	2
20—39 . .	204	110	94	31	23	8	159	77	82	14	10	4
40—59 . .	101	55	46	4	..	4	63	41	22	34	14	20
60 and over .	12	4	8	..	..	..	3	3	..	9	1	8
BIKANER . .	*151*	*97*	*54*	*70*	*48*	*22*	*69*	*45*	*24*	*12*	*4*	*8*
0—4 . .	19	9	10	19	9	10	..	..	..	..	..	..
5—9 . .	14	9	5	14	9	5	..	..	..	..	..	..
10—14 . .	7	5	2	6	4	2	1	1	..	..	..	..
15—19 . .	11	10	1	10	10	..	1	..	1	..	..	..
20—39 . .	70	42	28	18	13	5	48	28	20	4	1	3
40—59 . .	24	19	5	3	3	..	16	14	2	5	2	3
60 and over .	6	3	3	..	..	..	3	2	1	3	1	2
DHOLPUR . .	*41*	*26*	*15*	*18*	*13*	*5*	*23*	*13*	*10*	..	..	..
0—4 . .	5	3	2	5	3	2	..	..	..	..	..	..
5—9 . .	3	3	..	3	3	..	..	..	..	..	..	..
10—14 . .	3	3	..	3	3	..	..	..	..	..	..	..
15—39 . .	3	1	2	1	1	..	2	..	2	..	..	..
20—39 . .	20	10	10	6	3	3	14	7	7	..	..	..
40—59 . .	6	5	1	..	..	..	6	5	1	..	..	..
60 and over .	1	1	..	..	..	..	1	1	..	..	..	..
DUNGARPUR .	*2*	*1*	*1*	..	..	..	*2*	*1*	*1*	..	..	..
0—4 . .	..	..	..	..	..	..	..	..	..	..	..	..
5—9 . .	..	..	..	..	..	..	..	..	..	..	..	..
10—14 . .	..	..	..	..	..	..	..	..	..	..	..	..
15—19 . .	1	..	1	..	..	..	1	..	1	..	..	..
20—39 . .	1	1	..	..	..	..	1	1	..	..	..	..
40—59 . .	..	..	..	..	..	..	..	..	..	..	..	..
60 and over .	..	..	..	..	..	..	..	..	..	..	..	..
JAIPUR . .	*1,326*	*689*	*637*	*769*	*426*	*343*	*476*	*244*	*232*	*81*	*19*	*62*
0—4 . .	187	87	100	187	87	100	..	..	..	..	..	..
5—9 . .	136	82	54	136	82	54	..	..	..	..	..	..
10—14 . .	149	100	49	144	100	44	3	..	3	2	..	2
15—19 . .	142	48	94	125	48	77	17	..	17	..	..	..
20—39 . .	513	261	252	167	102	65	324	151	173	22	8	14
40—50 . .	160	97	63	7	6	1	119	83	36	34	8	26
60 and over .	39	14	25	3	1	2	13	10	3	23	3	20

Part C.—By States or Districts. Main Religions—*continued.*

TABLE VII.—C.
CHRISTIANS.

Age; and State or District.	Population.			Unmarried.			Married.			Widowed.		
	Persons.	Males.	Females.	Persons.	Males.	Females.	Persons.	Males.	Females.	Persons.	Males.	Females.
1	2	3	4	5	6	7	8	9	10	11	12	13
RAJPUTANA—*contd.*												
JHALAWAR	***26***	***18***	***8***	***13***	***10***	***3***	***13***	***8***	***5***	..	..	..
0—4	1	1	..	1	1	..	..	..	..	..	..	..
5—9	1	1	..	1	1	..	..	..	..	..	..	..
10—14	..	..	..	..	..	..	..	..	..	..	..	..
15—19	3	1	2	1	1	..	2	..	2	..	..	..
20—39	12	8	4	7	4	3	5	4	1	..	..	..
40—59	7	5	2	2	2	..	5	3	2	..	..	..
60 and over	2	2	..	1	1	..	1	1	..	..	..	..
KARAULI	***28***	***15***	***13***	***14***	***7***	***7***	***11***	***7***	***4***	***3***	***1***	***2***
0—4	1	1	..	1	1	..	..	..	..	..	..	..
5—9	3	1	2	3	1	2	..	..	..	..	..	..
10—14	5	2	3	5	2	3	..	..	..	..	..	..
15—19	3	1	2	2	1	1	1	..	1	..	..	..
20—39	11	6	5	3	2	1	7	4	3	1	..	1
40—59	4	3	1	..	..	..	2	2	..	2	1	1
60 and over	1	1	..	..	..	..	1	1	..	..	..	..
KISHANGARH	***23***	***8***	***15***	***10***	***3***	***7***	***11***	***5***	***6***	***2***	..	***2***
0—4	3	..	3	3	..	3	..	..	..	..	..	..
5—9	1	..	1	1	..	1	..	..	..	..	..	..
10—14	1	..	1	1	..	1	..	..	..	..	..	..
15—19	4	3	1	3	3	..	1	..	1	..	..	..
20—39	10	4	6	2	..	2	7	4	3	1	..	1
40—59	4	1	3	..	..	..	3	1	2	1	..	1
60 and over	..	..	..	..	..	..	..	..	..	..	..	..
KOTAH	***507***	***274***	***233***	***239***	***143***	***96***	***259***	***130***	***129***	***9***	***1***	***8***
0—4	124	48	76	124	48	76	..	..	..	..	..	..
5—9	18	5	13	18	5	13	..	..	..	..	..	..
10—14	21	18	3	21	18	3	..	..	..	..	..	..
15—19	62	46	16	44	43	1	18	3	15	..	..	..
20—39	247	138	109	29	27	2	216	110	106	2	1	1
40—50	32	17	15	3	2	1	23	15	8	6	..	6
60 and over	3	2	1	..	..	..	2	2	..	1	..	1
MARWAR	***440***	***235***	***205***	***207***	***117***	***90***	***211***	***114***	***97***	***22***	***4***	***18***
0—4	59	24	35	59	24	35	..	..	..	..	..	..
5—9	49	22	27	49	22	27	..	..	..	..	..	..
10—14	19	15	4	17	13	4	2	2	..	..	..	..
15—19	42	18	24	27	18	9	15	..	15	..	..	..
20—39	183	103	80	47	34	13	131	66	65	5	3	2
40—59	79	53	26	8	6	2	62	46	16	9	1	8
60 and over	9	..	9	..	..	..	1	..	1	8	..	8
MEWAR	***237***	***152***	***85***	***120***	***89***	***31***	***114***	***62***	***52***	***3***	***1***	***2***
0—4	32	18	14	32	18	14	..	..	..	..	..	..
5—9	17	8	9	16	8	8	1	..	1	..	..	..
10—14	21	18	3	20	17	3	1	1	..	..	..	..
15—19	38	28	10	29	27	2	9	1	8	..	..	..
20—39	95	67	28	23	19	4	71	37	34	1	1	..
40—59	30	20	10	..	..	..	29	20	9	1	..	1
60 and over	4	3	1	..	..	..	3	3	..	1	..	1

TABLE VII.—AGE, SEX AND CIVIL CONDITION. PART C.—BY STATES OR DISTRICTS. MAIN RELIGIONS—*continued*.

Age ; and State or District.	Population.			Unmarried.			Married.			Widowed.		
	Persons.	Males.	Females.	Persons.	Males.	Females.	Persons.	Males.	Females.	Persons.	Males.	Females.
1	2	3	4	5	6	7	8	9	10	11	12	13
RAJPUTANA—*concld.*												
SHAHPURA	*1*	*1*	..	..	..	..	*1*	*1*	..	..	..	..
0—4	..	..	..	..	..	..	..	..	..	..	..	..
5—9	..	..	..	..	..	..	..	..	..	..	..	..
10—14	..	..	..	..	..	..	..	..	..	..	..	..
15—19	..	..	..	..	..	..	..	..	..	..	..	..
20—39	..	..	..	..	..	..	..	..	..	..	..	..
40—59	1	1	..	..	..	..	1	1	..	..	..	..
60 and over	..	..	..	..	..	..	..	..	..	..	..	..
SIROHI	*804*	*522*	*282*	*517*	*369*	*148*	*266*	*144*	*122*	*21*	*9*	*12*
0—4	87	52	35	87	52	35	..	..	..	..	..	..
5—9	111	70	41	110	69	41	1	1	..	..	..	..
10—14	106	78	28	106	78	28	..	..	..	..	..	..
15—19	61	38	23	57	38	19	4	..	4	..	..	..
20—39	340	225	115	145	128	17	189	93	96	6	4	2
40—59	88	53	35	10	2	8	67	47	20	11	4	7
60 and over	11	6	5	2	2	..	5	3	2	4	1	3
TONK	*12*	*6*	*6*	*6*	*1*	*5*	*6*	*5*	*1*	..	..	..
0—4	..	..	..	..	..	..	..	..	..	..	..	..
5—9	1	..	1	1	..	1	..	..	..	..	..	..
10—14	1	..	1	1	..	1	..	..	..	..	..	..
15—19	2	..	2	2	..	2	..	..	..	..	..	..
20—39	7	5	2	2	1	1	5	4	1	..	..	..
40—59	1	1	..	..	..	..	1	1	..	..	..	..
60 and over	..	..	..	..	..	..	..	..	..	..	..	..
AJMER-MERWARA—												
AJMER	*4,910*	*2,996*	*1,914*	*3,276*	*2,183*	*1,093*	*1,424*	*741*	*683*	*210*	*72*	*138*
0—4	480	249	231	480	249	231	..	..	..	..	..	..
5—9	400	174	226	399	174	225	1	..	1	..	..	..
10—14	388	194	194	379	192	187	9	2	7	..	..	..
15—19	679	270	409	577	258	319	100	11	89	2	1	1
20—39	2,369	1,770	599	1,389	1,277	112	917	471	446	63	22	41
40—59	492	282	210	45	28	17	356	226	130	91	28	63
60 and over	102	57	45	7	5	2	41	31	10	54	21	33
MERWARA	*522*	*262*	*260*	*317*	*159*	*158*	*188*	*95*	*93*	*17*	*8*	*9*
0—4	61	26	35	61	26	35	..	..	..	..	..	..
5—9	48	20	28	48	20	28	..	..	..	..	..	..
10—14	42	39	3	40	38	2	2	1	1	..	..	..
15—19	83	58	25	61	56	5	22	2	20	..	..	..
20—39	201	76	125	86	17	69	113	58	55	2	1	1
40—59	74	38	36	17	2	15	49	32	17	8	4	4
60 and over	13	5	8	4	..	4	2	2	..	7	3	4

N. B.—Banswara, Bundi. Jaisalmer, Kushalgarh, Lawa, and Partabgarh, which contain no Christians, have not been shown.

TABLE VII.

PART C.

BY STATES OR DISTRICTS.

HINDUS.

TABLE VII.—C
HINDUS.

TABLE VII.—Age, Sex and Civil Condition.

Age; and State or District.	Population.			Unmarried.			Married.			Widowed.		
	Persons.	Males.	Females.	Persons.	Males.	Females.	Persons.	Males.	Females.	Persons.	Males.	Females.
1	2	3	4	5	6	7	8	9	10	11	12	13
RAJPUTANA.												
ALWAR . .	*588,230*	*307,425*	*280,805*	*243,257*	*150,356*	*92,901*	*273,546*	*133,224*	*140,322*	*71,427*	*23,845*	*47,582*
0—4 . .	76,295	37,682	38,613	76,230	37,671	38,579	44	11	33	1	..	1
5—9 . .	71,364	37,162	34,202	69,831	36,804	33,027	1,484	343	1,141	49	15	34
10—14 . .	66,214	37,126	29,088	51,118	33,459	17,659	14,750	3,540	11,210	346	127	219
15—19 . .	56,929	31,638	25,291	22,726	19,720	3,006	32,988	11,468	21,520	1,215	450	765
20—39 . .	178,460	91,357	87,103	17,065	16,612	453	145,966	69,240	76,726	15,429	5,505	9,924
40—59 . .	105,763	55,338	50,425	4,970	4,847	123	66,604	39,678	26,926	34,189	10,813	23,376
60 and over .	33,205	17,122	16,083	1,297	1,243	54	11,710	8,944	2,766	20,198	6,935	13,263
BANSWARA .	*60,339*	*29,611*	*30,728*	*25,734*	*15,247*	*10,487*	*26,276*	*12,885*	*13,391*	*8,329*	*1,479*	*6,850*
0—4 . .	10,516	5,176	5,340	10,511	5,176	5,335	5	..	5	..	..	..
5—9 . .	7,098	3,665	3,433	6,902	3,634	3,268	193	31	162	3	..	3
10—14 . .	4,533	2,511	2,022	3,498	2,303	1,195	1,014	206	808	21	2	19
15—19 . .	5,090	2,702	2,388	2,255	1,932	323	2,771	752	2,019	64	18	46
20—39 . .	21,861	10,812	11,049	2,303	2,035	268	17,197	8,314	8,883	2,361	463	1,898
40—59 . .	9,580	4,196	5,384	231	150	81	4,761	3,282	1,479	4,588	764	3,824
60 and over .	1,661	549	1,112	34	17	17	335	300	35	1,292	232	1,060
BHARATPUR	*452,730*	*243,735*	*206,995*	*167,221*	*109,587*	*57,634*	*219,877*	*110,209*	*109,668*	*65,632*	*25,939*	*39,693*
0—4 . .	48,753	24,907	23,846	48,742	24,903	23,839	11	4	7	..	..	..
5—9 . .	54,348	28,963	25,385	51,243	28,184	23,059	3,005	743	2,262	100	36	64
10—14 . .	52,359	30,822	21,537	34,490	25,028	9,462	17,157	5,467	11,690	712	327	385
15—19 . .	43,657	25,062	18,595	14,238	13,213	1,025	27,695	11,039	16,656	1,724	810	914
20—39 . .	148,697	79,982	68,715	14,641	14,414	227	116,334	57,656	58,678	17,722	7,912	9,810
40—59 . .	83,621	44,953	38,668	3,350	3,333	17	48,787	29,995	18,792	31,484	11,625	19,859
60 and over .	21,295	11,046	10,249	517	512	5	6,888	5,305	1,583	13,890	5,229	8,661
BIKANER . .	*575,699*	*306,659*	*269,040*	*245,748*	*162,034*	*83,714*	*259,749*	*129,391*	*130,358*	*77,202*	*22,234*	*54,968*
0—4 . .	80,187	40,520	39,667	80,041	40,475	39,566	143	43	100	3	2	1
5—9 . .	66,212	34,919	31,293	64,438	34,621	29,817	1,714	293	1,421	60	5	55
10—14 . .	50,130	28,424	21,706	38,505	26,288	12,277	11,262	2,079	9,183	303	57	246
15—19 . .	53,405	31,322	22,083	25,070	23,501	1,569	27,068	7,551	19,517	1,267	270	997
20—39 . .	194,404	104,173	90,231	31,577	31,194	383	143,278	67,307	75,971	19,549	5,672	13,877
40—59 . .	103,032	54,511	48,521	5,027	4,947	80	60,273	38,409	21,864	37,732	11,155	26,577
60 and over .	28,329	12,790	15,530	1,030	1,008	22	9,011	6,709	2,302	18,288	5,073	13,215
BUNDI . .	*196,919*	*102,040*	*94,879*	*81,921*	*50,477*	*31,444*	*93,391*	*45,817*	*47,574*	*21,607*	*5,746*	*15,861*
0—4 . .	32,572	15,801	16,771	32,572	15,801	16,771	..	..	..	..	..	..
5—9 . .	24,994	13,149	11,845	24,033	12,947	11,096	916	185	731	45	17	28
10—14 . .	12,068	6,995	5,073	9,068	6,480	2,588	2,927	487	2,440	73	28	45
15—19 . .	13,499	7,519	5,980	5,773	5,396	377	7,499	2,031	5,468	227	92	135
20—39 . .	71,171	36,668	34,503	8,835	8,375	460	57,031	26,454	30,577	5,305	1,839	3,466
40—59 . .	34,924	18,266	16,658	1,370	1,234	136	22,268	14,463	7,805	11,286	2,569	8,717
60 and over .	7,691	3,642	4,049	270	244	26	2,750	2,197	553	4,671	1,201	3,470
DHOLPUR . .	*242,734*	*133,416*	*109,318*	*94,084*	*62,778*	*31,306*	*118,230*	*59,045*	*59,185*	*30,420*	*11,593*	*18,827*
0—4 . .	27,692	14,221	13,471	27,692	14,221	13,471	..	..	..	..	..	..
5—9 . .	31,071	16,673	14,398	29,147	16,227	12,920	1,888	426	1,462	36	20	16
10—14 . .	27,696	16,378	11,318	17,227	13,147	4,080	10,228	3,140	7,088	241	91	150
15—19 . .	23,154	13,292	9,862	7,290	6,967	323	15,268	6,060	9,208	596	265	331
20—39 . .	77,664	42,443	35,221	9,496	9,152	344	60,428	29,867	30,561	7,740	3,424	4,316
40—59 . .	43,485	24,075	19,410	2,730	2,610	120	26,193	16,226	9,967	14,562	5,239	9,323
60 and over .	11,972	6,334	5,638	502	454	48	4,225	3,326	899	7,245	2,554	4,691
DUNGARPUR .	*72,681*	*35,540*	*37,139*	*30,200*	*18,233*	*11,967*	*32,386*	*15,693*	*16,693*	*10,095*	*1,623*	*8,472*
0—4 . .	12,386	6,106	6,280	12,356	6,101	6,255	30	7	23	2	..	2
5—9 . .	8,101	4,224	3,877	7,850	4,190	3,660	249	34	215	2	..	2
10—14 . .	5,237	2,809	2,428	3,789	2,503	1,286	1,427	304	1,123	21	2	19
15—19 . .	6,234	3,387	2,847	2,700	2,385	315	3,434	982	2,452	100	20	80
20—39 . .	27,480	13,479	14,001	3,155	2,822	333	21,188	10,092	11,096	3,137	565	2,572
40—59 . .	11,530	4,961	6,569	301	194	107	5,683	3,962	1,721	5,566	825	4,741
60 and over .	1,691	561	1,130	49	38	11	375	312	63	1,267	211	1,056
JAIPUR . .	*2,398,880*	*1,262,280*	*1,136,600*	*940,612*	*610,236*	*330,376*	*1,166,123*	*568,030*	*598,093*	*292,145*	*84,014*	*208,131*
0—4 . .	301,559	150,371	151,188	301,086	150,235	150,851	457	134	323	16	2	14
5—9 . .	279,152	148,161	130,991	269,571	146,358	123,213	9,339	1,741	7,598	242	62	180
10—14 . .	230,976	133,755	97,221	167,715	119,296	48,419	62,022	14,054	47,968	1,239	405	834
15—19 . .	212,460	120,836	91,624	84,452	79,376	5,076	123,976	40,179	83,797	4,032	1,281	2,751
20—39 . .	789,825	407,790	382,035	91,069	88,957	2,112	634,420	298,693	335,728	64,336	20,141	44,195
40—59 . .	457,291	240,300	216,991	21,857	21,354	583	291,211	179,075	112,136	144,193	39,871	104,322
60 and over .	127,617	61,067	66,550	4,832	4,660	172	44,698	34,155	10,543	78,087	22,252	55,835

PART C.—BY STATES OR DISTRICTS. MAIN RELIGIONS—*continued.*

TABLE VII.—C

HINDUS.

Age; and State or District.	Population.			Unmarried.			Married.			Widowed.		
	Persons.	Males.	Females.	Persons.	Males.	Females.	Persons.	Males.	Females.	Persons.	Males.	Females.
1	2	3	4	5	6	7	8	9	10	11	12	13
RAJPUTANA—*contd.*												
JAISALMER	*60,951*	*33,198*	*27,753*	*29,107*	*20,036*	*9,071*	*22,844*	*10,971*	*11,873*	*9,000*	*2,191*	*6,809*
0—4	8,501	4,405	4,096	8,467	4,399	4,068	33	5	28	1	1	..
5—9	6,857	3,897	2,960	6,733	3,873	2,860	119	22	97	5	2	3
10—14	6,727	4,102	2,625	5,686	3,906	1,780	985	184	801	56	12	44
15—19	5,742	3,297	2,445	3,104	2,835	269	2,423	430	1,993	215	32	183
20—39	20,783	11,270	9,513	4,551	4,476	75	13,501	6,234	7,267	2,731	560	2,171
40—59	10,099	5,242	4,857	482	465	17	5,196	3,589	1,607	4,421	1,188	3,233
60 and over	2,242	985	1,257	84	82	2	587	507	80	1,571	396	1,175
JHALAWAR	*84,585*	*44,137*	*40,448*	*31,473*	*20,621*	*10,852*	*40,747*	*20,139*	*20,608*	*12,365*	*3,377*	*8,988*
0—4	12,180	5,966	6,214	12,098	5,954	6,142	84	12	72	..	..	..
5—9	9,789	5,099	4,690	8,673	4,898	3,775	1,094	188	906	22	13	9
10—14	5,509	3,156	2,353	3,410	2,675	735	2,044	473	1,571	55	8	47
15—19	6,699	3,709	2,990	2,548	2,446	102	3,925	1,206	2,719	226	57	169
20—39	32,189	16,689	15,500	4,146	4,073	73	24,097	11,487	12,610	3,946	1,129	2,817
40—59	14,829	7,742	7,087	511	487	24	8,354	5,783	2,571	5,964	1,472	4,492
60 and over	3,390	1,776	1,614	89	88	1	1,149	990	159	2,152	698	1,454
KARAULI	*137,989*	*75,485*	*62,504*	*55,771*	*36,978*	*18,793*	*65,110*	*32,362*	*32,748*	*17,108*	*6,145*	*10,963*
0—4	16,853	8,715	8,138	16,853	8,715	8,138	..	..	..	..	..	..
5—9	17,173	9,319	7,854	16,407	9,170	7,237	759	146	613	7	3	4
10—14	14,934	8,763	6,171	10,266	7,488	2,778	4,568	1,240	3,328	100	35	65
15—19	12,570	7,276	5,294	4,869	4,519	350	7,435	2,646	4,789	266	111	155
20—39	46,742	25,453	21,289	6,041	5,812	229	36,290	17,801	18,489	4,411	1,840	2,571
40—59	23,461	12,702	10,759	1,129	1,086	43	13,899	8,790	5,109	8,433	2,826	5,607
60 and over	6,256	3,257	2,999	206	188	18	2,159	1,739	420	3,891	1,330	2,561
KISHANGARH	*76,649*	*40,171*	*36,478*	*28,224*	*18,191*	*10,033*	*37,132*	*18,322*	*18,810*	*11,286*	*3,658*	*7,628*
0—4	10,614	5,237	5,377	10,438	5,191	5,247	167	39	128	9	7	2
5—9	8,807	4,743	4,064	7,956	4,489	3,467	814	235	579	37	19	18
10—14	5,920	3,475	2,445	3,842	2,829	1,013	1,986	603	1,383	92	43	49
15—19	6,313	3,495	2,818	2,225	2,111	114	3,839	1,260	2,579	249	124	125
20—39	28,553	15,108	13,445	3,021	2,920	101	22,151	10,826	11,325	3,381	1,362	2,019
40—59	13,462	6,819	6,643	615	558	57	7,388	4,724	2,659	5,464	1,537	3,927
60 and over	2,973	1,294	1,679	127	93	34	792	635	157	2,054	566	1,488
KOTAH	*584,137*	*301,657*	*282,480*	*231,141*	*141,571*	*89,570*	*283,936*	*140,795*	*143,141*	*69,060*	*19,291*	*49,769*
0—4	92,183	45,187	46,996	92,152	45,164	46,988	31	23	8	..	..	..
5—9	68,894	35,255	33,639	66,425	34,657	31,768	2,410	574	1,836	59	24	35
10—14	41,123	23,366	17,757	29,952	20,859	9,093	10,999	2,446	8,553	172	61	111
15—19	48,852	28,579	20,273	17,042	15,981	1,061	26,102	7,376	18,726	708	222	486
20—39	216,059	111,408	104,651	22,241	21,718	523	175,784	83,540	92,244	18,034	6,150	11,884
40—59	99,018	51,239	47,779	2,716	2,615	101	60,486	40,041	20,445	35,816	8,583	27,232
60 and over	23,008	11,623	11,385	613	577	36	8,124	6,795	1,329	14,271	4,251	10,020
KUSHALGARH	*3,694*	*1,848*	*1,846*	*1,710*	*1,024*	*686*	*1,459*	*724*	*735*	*525*	*100*	*425*
0—4	536	252	284	536	252	284	..	..	..	..	..	..
5—9	498	274	224	493	274	219	5	..	5	..	..	..
10—14	299	161	138	257	155	102	40	6	34	2	..	2
15—19	294	167	127	181	141	40	110	25	85	3	1	2
20—39	1,339	679	660	213	181	32	964	458	506	162	40	122
40—59	619	288	331	29	21	8	321	219	102	269	48	221
60 and over	109	27	82	1	..	1	19	16	3	89	11	78
LAWA	*2,282*	*1,143*	*1,139*	*843*	*507*	*336*	*1,109*	*535*	*574*	*330*	*101*	*229*
0—4	320	138	182	320	138	182	..	..	..	..	..	..
5—9	259	122	137	237	117	120	22	5	17	..	..	..
10—14	180	108	72	127	101	26	51	6	45	2	1	1
15—19	205	107	98	73	65	8	124	37	87	8	5	3
20—39	822	415	407	74	74	..	667	315	352	81	26	55
40—59	398	201	197	11	11	..	217	146	71	170	44	126
60 and over	98	52	46	1	1	..	28	26	2	69	25	44
MARWAR	*1,709,998*	*899,634*	*810,364*	*717,021*	*460,739*	*256,282*	*782,327*	*381,902*	*400,425*	*210,650*	*56,993*	*153,657*
0—4	255,699	129,549	126,150	252,513	128,783	123,730	3,108	729	2,379	78	37	41
5—9	198,901	106,110	92,791	184,662	101,576	83,086	13,744	4,351	9,393	495	183	312
10—14	153,553	87,326	66,227	117,141	76,806	40,335	35,326	10,094	25,232	1,086	426	660
15—19	147,792	84,201	63,591	68,536	61,428	7,108	76,151	21,715	54,436	3,105	1,058	2,047
20—39	581,749	305,924	275,825	81,062	79,526	1,536	449,355	210,255	239,100	51,332	16,143	35,189
40—59	291,901	150,704	141,197	10,646	10,238	408	179,052	114,604	64,449	102,202	25,862	76,340
60 and over	80,403	35,820	44,583	2,461	2,382	79	25,590	20,154	5,436	52,352	13,284	39,068

TABLE VII.—C. HINDUS.

TABLE VII.—AGE, SEX AND CIVIL CONDITION. PART C.—BY STATES OR DISTRICTS. MAIN RELIGIONS—*continued.*

Age ; and State or District.	POPULATION.			UNMARRIED.			MARRIED.			WIDOWED.		
	Persons.	Males.	Females.	Persons.	Males.	Females.	Persons.	Males.	Females.	Persons.	Males.	Females.
1	2	3	4	5	6	7	8	9	10	11	12	13
RAJPUTANA—*concld.*												
MEWAR	*1,021,906*	*529,936*	*491,970*	*420,318*	*260,065*	*160,253*	*473,892*	*235,217*	*238,675*	*127,696*	*34,654*	*93,042*
0—4	175,657	86,727	88,930	175,050	86,535	88,515	581	186	395	26	6	20
5—9	124,250	67,009	57,241	119,761	65,774	53,987	4,328	1,172	3,156	161	63	98
10—14	61,497	36,015	25,482	45,580	32,073	13,507	15,469	3,765	11,704	448	177	271
15—19	80,845	46,089	34,756	34,521	31,858	2,663	44,332	13,262	31,070	1,992	969	1,023
20—39	375,485	196,892	178,593	40,755	39,492	1,263	297,831	142,956	154,875	36,899	14,444	22,455
40—59	172,566	84,247	88,319	4,083	3,810	273	101,708	66,112	35,596	66,775	14,325	52,450
60 and over	31,606	12,957	18,649	568	523	45	9,643	7,764	1,879	21,395	4,670	16,725
PARTABGARH	*33,848*	*17,077*	*16,771*	*13,043*	*8,026*	*5,019*	*15,689*	*7,783*	*7,906*	*5,114*	*1,268*	*3,846*
0—4	5,573	2,747	2,826	5,480	2,721	2,759	92	26	66	1	..	1
5—9	3,795	2,057	1,738	3,499	1,977	1,522	292	80	212	4	..	4
10—14	2,230	1,281	949	1,518	1,102	416	688	171	517	24	8	16
15—19	2,731	1,432	1,299	1,061	928	133	1,581	471	1,110	89	33	56
20—39	13,265	6,675	6,590	1,317	1,170	147	10,164	4,945	5,219	1,784	560	1,224
40—59	5,357	2,516	2,841	152	115	37	2,645	1,897	748	2,560	504	2,056
60 and over	897	369	528	18	13	5	227	193	34	652	163	489
SHAHPURA	*41,249*	*21,381*	*19,868*	*16,023*	*9,936*	*6,087*	*19,991*	*9,893*	*10,098*	*5,235*	*1,552*	*3,683*
0—4	6,606	3,259	3,347	6,552	3,245	3,307	54	14	40	..	..	..
5—9	5,007	2,576	2,431	4,704	2,492	2,212	297	80	217	6	4	2
10—14	2,366	1,373	993	1,658	1,186	472	693	181	512	15	6	9
15—19	3,066	1,746	1,320	1,168	1,109	59	1,821	601	1,220	77	36	41
20—39	15,427	8,178	7,249	1,609	1,581	28	12,388	5,939	6,449	1,430	658	772
40—59	7,274	3,648	3,626	264	255	9	4,322	2,752	1,570	2,688	641	2,047
60 and over	1,503	601	902	68	68	..	416	326	90	1,019	207	812
SIROHI	*159,406*	*83,887*	*75,519*	*70,622*	*43,379*	*27,243*	*74,118*	*37,117*	*37,001*	*14,666*	*3,391*	*11,275*
0—4	28,156	14,032	14,124	27,820	13,965	13,855	329	66	263	7	1	6
5—9	20,630	11,169	9,461	19,722	10,940	8,782	887	221	666	21	8	13
10—14	13,196	8,039	5,157	11,004	7,389	3,615	2,119	616	1,503	73	34	39
15—19	12,452	7,159	5,293	6,076	5,425	651	6,188	1,653	4,535	188	81	107
20—39	53,079	27,266	25,813	5,542	5,293	249	44,332	20,899	23,433	3,205	1,074	2,131
40—59	25,335	13,331	12,004	372	306	66	17,754	11,644	6,110	7,209	1,381	5,828
60 and over	6,558	2,891	3,667	86	61	25	2,509	2,018	491	3,963	812	3,151
TONK	*247,146*	*127,901*	*119,245*	*96,490*	*59,589*	*36,901*	*121,624*	*60,298*	*61,326*	*29,032*	*8,014*	*21,018*
0—4	40,012	19,554	20,458	39,634	19,435	20,199	360	112	248	18	7	11
5—9	29,934	15,698	14,236	27,922	15,232	12,690	1,957	451	1,506	55	15	40
10—14	17,631	10,314	7,317	11,671	8,759	2,912	5,819	1,503	4,316	141	52	89
15—19	18,743	10,204	8,539	6,818	6,386	432	11,553	3,667	7,886	372	151	221
20—39	89,181	46,189	42,992	9,067	8,574	493	72,508	34,815	37,693	7,606	2,800	4,806
40—59	41,464	21,089	20,375	1,120	994	126	25,772	16,791	8,981	14,572	3,304	11,268
60 and over	10,181	4,853	5,328	258	209	49	3,655	2,959	696	6,268	1,685	4,583
AJMER-MERWARA—												
AJMER	*296,076*	*155,993*	*140,083*	*110,253*	*69,862*	*40,391*	*146,363*	*73,554*	*72,809*	*39,460*	*12,577*	*26,883*
0—4	42,367	21,256	21,111	41,908	21,162	20,746	444	90	354	15	4	11
5—9	32,850	17,308	15,542	30,438	16,548	13,890	2,310	709	1,601	102	51	51
10—14	22,226	12,836	9,390	15,495	10,856	4,639	6,479	1,851	4,628	252	129	123
15—19	24,572	13,587	10,985	9,181	8,468	713	14,661	4,749	9,912	730	370	360
20—39	110,699	59,096	51,603	11,560	11,257	303	87,942	43,140	44,802	11,197	4,699	6,498
40—59	51,550	26,602	24,948	1,371	1,293	78	31,020	20,149	10,871	19,159	5,160	13,999
60 and over	11,312	5,308	6,504	300	278	22	3,507	2,866	641	8,005	2,164	5,841
MERWARA	*92,476*	*48,863*	*43,613*	*39,538*	*24,913*	*14,625*	*43,408*	*21,161*	*22,247*	*9,530*	*2,789*	*6,741*
0—4	15,838	7,930	7,908	15,764	7,898	7,866	74	32	42	..	..	..
5—9	10,797	5,756	5,041	10,423	5,641	4,782	363	110	253	11	5	6
10—14	5,724	3,320	2,404	4,641	3,096	1,545	1,056	215	841	27	9	13
15—19	6,858	3,847	3,011	3,326	3,051	275	3,425	747	2,678	107	49	58
20—39	33,578	17,747	15,831	5,012	4,906	106	26,541	11,976	14,565	2,025	865	1,160
40—59	15,474	8,267	7,207	306	246	40	10,413	6,792	3,621	4,755	1,209	3,546
60 and over	4,207	1,996	2,211	66	55	11	1,536	1,289	247	2,605	852	1,953

TABLE VII.

Part C.

BY STATES OR DISTRICTS.

JAINS.

TABLE VII.—C.

JAINS.

TABLE VII.—Age, Sex and Civil Condition.

Age; and State or District.	Population.			Unmarried.			Married.			Widowed.		
	Persons.	Males.	Females.	Persons.	Males.	Females.	Persons.	Males.	Females.	Persons.	Males.	Females.
1	2	3	4	5	6	7	8	9	10	11	12	13
RAJPUTANA—												
ALWAR	*4,111*	*2,158*	*1,953*	*1,655*	*1,033*	*622*	*1,735*	*826*	*909*	*721*	*299*	*422*
0—4	485	232	253	485	232	253	..	..	..	..	..	..
5—9	465	231	234	457	230	227	8	1	7	..	..	..
10—14	416	221	195	326	195	131	87	26	61	3	..	3
15—19	366	203	163	135	129	6	218	70	148	13	4	9
20—39	1,252	646	606	159	156	3	909	418	491	184	72	112
40—59	870	484	386	75	73	2	441	256	185	354	155	199
60 and over	257	141	116	18	18	..	72	55	17	167	68	99
BANSWARA	*4396*	*2,196*	*2,200*	*1,769*	*1,134*	*635*	*1,694*	*838*	*856*	*933*	*224*	*709*
0—4	576	293	283	576	293	283	..	..	..	..	..	..
5—9	395	199	196	392	199	193	3	..	3	..	..	..
10—14	353	176	177	310	171	139	42	5	37	1	..	1
15—19	407	195	212	176	157	19	223	37	186	8	1	7
20—39	1,711	931	780	288	287	1	1,112	578	534	311	66	245
40—59	792	348	444	25	25	..	290	196	94	477	127	350
60 and over	162	54	108	2	2	..	24	22	2	136	30	106
BHARATPUR	*2,720*	*1,474*	*1,246*	*1,055*	*721*	*334*	*1,093*	*534*	*559*	*573*	*219*	*353*
0—4	248	128	120	248	128	120	..	..	..	..	..	..
5—9	283	143	140	278	142	136	5	1	4	..	..	..
10—14	312	185	127	247	172	75	62	12	50	3	1	2
15—19	289	146	143	87	84	3	181	57	124	21	5	16
20—39	908	492	416	139	139	..	592	295	297	177	58	119
40—59	575	323	252	53	53	..	233	153	80	289	117	172
60 and over	105	57	48	3	3	..	20	16	4	82	38	44
BIKANER	*24,858*	*10,255*	*14,603*	*9,957*	*5,733*	*4,224*	*10,333*	*3,869*	*6,464*	*4,568*	*653*	*3,915*
0—4	3,547	1,835	1,712	3,541	1,834	1,707	5	1	4	1	..	1
5—9	3,479	1,745	1,734	3,451	1,743	1,708	24	1	23	4	1	3
10—14	2,524	1,174	1,350	1,768	1,054	714	742	116	626	14	4	10
15—19	2,071	741	1,330	407	383	24	1,555	347	1,208	109	11	98
20—39	7,176	2,533	4,643	528	496	32	5,331	1,920	3,411	1,317	117	1,200
40—59	4,664	1,714	2,950	211	182	29	2,302	1,207	1,095	2,151	325	1,826
60 and over	1,397	513	884	51	41	10	374	277	97	972	195	777
BUNDI	*6,614*	*3,475*	*3,139*	*2,510*	*1,685*	*825*	*2,912*	*1,409*	*1,503*	*1,192*	*381*	*811*
0—4	777	379	398	777	379	398	..	..	..	..	..	..
5—9	712	344	368	690	340	350	20	4	16	2	..	2
10—14	395	234	161	270	208	62	121	23	98	4	3	1
15—19	471	263	208	172	168	4	285	91	194	14	4	10
20—39	2,546	1,367	1,179	430	423	7	1,768	830	938	348	114	234
40—59	1,298	729	669	149	146	3	631	395	236	618	188	430
60 and over	315	159	156	22	21	1	87	66	21	206	72	134
DHOLPUR	*2,031*	*1,175*	*856*	*807*	*569*	*238*	*930*	*466*	*464*	*294*	*140*	*154*
0—4	221	129	92	221	129	92	..	..	..	..	..	..
5—9	239	118	121	234	117	117	5	1	4	..	..	..
10—14	234	138	96	130	103	27	103	35	68	1	..	1
15—19	170	98	72	49	47	2	115	48	67	6	3	3
20—39	676	396	280	124	124	..	479	233	246	73	39	34
40—59	384	232	152	40	40	..	198	125	73	146	67	79
60 and over	107	64	43	9	9	..	30	24	6	68	31	37
DUNGARPUR	*5,510*	*2,703*	*2,807*	*2,026*	*1,337*	*689*	*2,193*	*1,107*	*1,086*	*1,291*	*259*	*1,032*
0—4	682	334	348	681	334	347	1	..	1	..	..	..
5—9	456	247	209	453	246	207	3	1	2	..	..	..
10—14	360	198	162	298	191	107	60	7	53	2	..	2
15—19	422	230	192	188	170	18	226	59	167	8	1	7
20—39	2,334	1,154	1,180	340	331	9	1,490	729	761	504	94	410
40—59	1,077	478	599	59	59	..	385	284	101	633	135	498
60 and over	179	62	117	7	6	1	28	27	1	144	29	115
JAIPUR	*38,408*	*20,295*	*18,113*	*14,704*	*10,163*	*4,541*	*16,307*	*7,933*	*8,374*	*7,397*	*2,199*	*5,198*
0—4	3,973	1,936	2,037	3,969	1,935	2,034	4	1	3	..	..	..
5—9	3,897	2,046	1,851	3,854	2,037	1,817	38	8	30	5	1	4
10—14	3,226	1,862	1,364	2,353	1,711	642	843	146	697	30	5	25
15—19	3,099	1,721	1,378	1,144	1,118	26	1,867	586	1,281	88	17	71
20—39	13,363	7,070	6,293	2,323	2,309	14	8,945	4,215	4,730	2,095	546	1,549
40—59	8,505	4,548	3,957	896	891	5	4,055	2,540	1,515	3,554	1,117	2,437
60 and over	2,345	1,112	1,233	165	162	3	555	437	118	1,625	513	1,112

PART C.—BY STATES OR DISTRICTS. MAIN RELIGIONS—*continued.*

TABLE VII.—C.

JAINS.

Age; and State or District.	Population.			Unmarried.			Married.			Widowed.		
	Persons.	Males.	Females.	Persons.	Males.	Females.	Persons.	Males.	Females.	Persons.	Males.	Females.
1	2	3	4	5	6	7	8	9	10	11	12	13
RAJPUTANA—*contd.*												
JAISALMER	*1,102*	*549*	*553*	*523*	*329*	*194*	*387*	*180*	*207*	*192*	*40*	*152*
0—4	157	76	81	157	76	81	..	..	..	..	..	..
5—9	155	77	78	152	77	75	3	..	3	..	..	..
10—14	101	60	41	90	58	32	11	2	9	..	..	..
15—19	100	48	52	44	38	6	53	10	43	3	..	3
20—39	346	180	166	63	63	..	230	108	122	53	9	44
40—59	194	87	107	11	11	..	81	53	28	102	23	79
60 and over	49	21	28	6	6	..	9	7	2	34	8	26
JHALAWAR	*2,488*	*1,312*	*1,176*	*932*	*663*	*269*	*1,036*	*503*	*533*	*530*	*146*	*384*
0—4	249	127	122	248	127	121	1	..	1	..	..	..
5—9	237	115	122	231	113	118	6	2	4	..	..	..
10—14	177	115	62	137	111	26	38	4	34	2	..	2
15—19	227	128	99	91	89	2	132	37	95	4	2	2
20—39	922	485	437	160	158	2	619	293	326	153	34	119
40—59	546	285	261	55	55	..	213	150	63	278	80	198
60 and over	130	57	73	10	10	..	27	17	10	93	30	63
KARAULI	*394*	*225*	*169*	*152*	*109*	*43*	*169*	*88*	*81*	*73*	*28*	*45*
0—4	36	16	20	36	16	20	..	..	..	..	..	..
5—9	35	20	15	35	20	15	..	..	..	..	..	..
10—14	35	19	16	27	19	8	8	..	8	..	..	..
15—19	40	25	15	16	16	..	21	8	13	3	1	2
20—39	143	86	57	27	27	..	93	49	44	23	10	13
40—59	79	44	35	10	10	..	37	23	14	32	11	21
60 and over	26	15	11	1	1	..	10	8	2	15	6	9
KISHANGARH	*3,176*	*1,680*	*1,496*	*1,282*	*899*	*383*	*1,200*	*586*	*614*	*694*	*195*	*499*
0—4	305	161	144	305	161	144	..	..	..	..	..	..
5—9	365	199	166	359	198	161	6	1	5	..	..	..
10—14	274	149	125	213	142	71	58	5	53	3	2	1
15—19	259	159	100	113	112	1	138	45	93	8	2	6
20—39	1,272	674	598	234	230	4	758	371	387	280	73	207
40—59	600	291	309	52	50	2	216	145	71	332	96	236
60 and over	101	47	54	6	6	..	24	19	5	71	22	49
KOTAH	*6,412*	*3,460*	*2,952*	*2,304*	*1,606*	*698*	*2,848*	*1,454*	*1,394*	*1,260*	*400*	*860*
0—4	682	339	343	682	339	343	..	..	..	..	..	..
5—9	604	311	293	592	311	281	12	..	12	..	..	..
10—14	437	235	202	291	219	72	145	16	129	1	..	1
15—19	525	289	236	168	167	1	344	121	223	13	1	12
20—39	2,520	1,402	1,118	434	434	..	1,704	865	839	382	103	279
40—59	1,323	728	595	124	123	1	562	382	180	637	223	414
60 and over	321	156	165	13	13	..	81	70	11	227	73	154
KUSHALGARH	*513*	*270*	*243*	*233*	*151*	*82*	*189*	*97*	*92*	*91*	*22*	*69*
0—4	69	39	30	69	39	30	..	..	..	..	..	..
5—9	64	35	29	64	35	29	..	..	..	..	..	..
10—14	53	28	25	46	27	19	7	1	6	..	..	..
15—19	46	24	22	22	18	4	21	6	15	3	..	3
20—39	179	96	83	26	26	..	128	63	65	25	7	18
40—59	87	43	44	6	6	..	31	25	6	50	12	38
60 and over	15	5	10	..	..	..	2	2	..	13	3	10
LAWA	*142*	*75*	*67*	*45*	*31*	*14*	*58*	*31*	*27*	*39*	*13*	*26*
0—4	17	9	8	17	9	8	..	..	..	..	..	..
5—9	12	7	5	12	7	5	..	..	..	..	..	..
10—14	9	5	4	5	4	1	4	1	3	..	..	..
15—19	9	3	6	1	1	..	8	2	6	..	..	..
20—39	63	33	30	8	8	..	36	21	15	19	4	15
40—59	28	15	13	2	2	..	10	7	3	16	6	10
60 and over	4	3	1	..	..	..	..	..	..	4	3	1
MARWAR	*131,990*	*61,314*	*70,676*	*55,265*	*32,421*	*22,844*	*52,596*	*23,760*	*28,836*	*24,099*	*5,133*	*18,966*
0—4	17,321	8,799	8,522	17,297	8,788	8,509	18	10	8	6	1	5
5—9	16,909	8,619	8,290	16,808	8,574	8,234	85	33	52	16	12	4
10—14	12,718	6,221	6,497	11,263	5,966	5,297	1,397	241	1,156	58	14	44
15—19	10,634	4,964	5,670	4,149	3,549	600	6,137	1,387	4,750	318	28	290
20—39	43,092	19,007	24,085	4,335	4,192	143	31,179	13,616	17,563	7,578	1,199	6,379
40—59	24,764	11,081	13,683	1,177	1,136	41	12,132	7,244	4,888	11,455	2,701	8,754
60 and over	6,552	2,623	3,929	236	216	20	1,648	1,229	419	4,668	1,178	3,490

TABLE VII.—Age, Sex and Civil Condition. Part C.—By States or Districts. Main Religions—*continued*.

Age; and State or District.	Population. Persons.	Population. Males.	Population. Females.	Unmarried. Persons.	Unmarried. Males.	Unmarried. Females.	Married. Persons.	Married. Males.	Married. Females.	Widowed. Persons.	Widowed. Males.	Widowed. Females.
1	2	3	4	5	6	7	8	9	10	11	12	13
RAJPUTANA—*concld.*												
MEWAR	*66,704*	*34,641*	*32,063*	*27,418*	*17,621*	*9,797*	*27,290*	*13,633*	*13,637*	*11,996*	*3,367*	*8,629*
0—4	9,089	4,470	4,619	9,078	4,465	4,613	10	4	6	1	1	..
5—9	7,276	3,715	3,561	7,226	3,696	3,530	47	17	30	3	2	1
10—14	4,540	2,559	1,981	3,826	2,452	1,374	681	99	582	33	8	25
15—19	5,540	3,170	2,370	2,558	2,378	180	2,833	758	2,075	149	34	115
20—39	25,573	13,603	11,970	4,000	3,917	83	17,523	8,583	8,940	4,050	1,103	2,947
40—59	12,550	6,234	6,316	657	642	15	5,757	3,827	1,930	6,136	1,765	4,371
60 and over	2,138	890	1,248	73	71	2	439	365	74	1,624	454	1,170
PARTABGARH	*4,318*	*2,259*	*2,059*	*1,753*	*1,156*	*597*	*1,759*	*871*	*888*	*806*	*232*	*574*
0—4	551	276	275	551	276	275	..	..	..	..	..	..
5—9	404	233	171	399	233	166	4	..	4	1	..	1
10—14	368	195	173	308	190	118	58	5	53	2	..	2
15—19	396	190	206	184	150	34	198	37	161	14	3	11
20—39	1,675	911	764	267	264	3	1,107	568	539	301	79	222
40—59	799	390	409	37	37	..	364	234	130	398	119	279
60 and over	125	64	61	7	6	1	28	27	1	90	31	59
SHAHPURA	*1,619*	*883*	*734*	*654*	*443*	*209*	*670*	*338*	*332*	*395*	*202*	*193*
0—4	201	103	98	200	103	97	1	..	1	..	..	..
5—9	175	89	86	173	87	86	2	2	..	..	..	..
10—14	89	58	31	82	58	24	7	..	7	..	..	..
15—19	114	75	39	57	57	..	50	16	34	7	2	5
20—39	656	350	306	101	101	..	459	218	241	96	31	65
40—59	319	181	138	39	38	1	136	90	46	144	53	91
60 and over	65	29	36	2	1	1	15	12	3	48	16	32
SIROHI	*16,988*	*7,290*	*9,698*	*6,910*	*3,718*	*3,192*	*6,976*	*3,060*	*3,916*	*3,103*	*513*	*2,590*
0—4	2,446	1,206	1,240	2,442	1,204	1,238	4	2	2	..	..	..
5—9	2,144	1,046	1,098	2,136	1,042	1,094	8	4	4	..	..	..
10—14	1,593	758	835	1,470	737	733	118	20	98	5	1	4
15—19	1,285	530	755	464	363	101	791	164	627	30	3	27
20—39	5,468	2,128	3,340	314	296	18	4,198	1,727	2,471	956	105	851
40—59	3,081	1,236	1,845	68	62	6	1,591	940	651	1,422	234	1,188
60 and over	971	386	585	16	14	2	266	203	63	689	169	520
TONK	*7,903*	*4,165*	*3,738*	*3,058*	*2,018*	*1,040*	*3,471*	*1,722*	*1,749*	*1,374*	*425*	*949*
0—4	1,005	471	534	994	467	527	8	2	6	3	2	1
5—9	854	445	409	830	441	389	22	3	19	2	1	1
10—14	591	350	241	429	325	104	155	23	132	7	2	5
15—19	618	363	255	245	239	6	361	122	239	12	2	10
20—39	2,949	1,546	1,403	432	422	10	2,079	998	1,081	438	126	312
40—59	1,538	809	729	116	113	3	746	493	253	676	203	473
60 and over	348	181	167	12	11	1	100	81	19	236	89	147
AJMER-MERWARA—												
AJMER	*14,313*	*7,654*	*6,659*	*5,754*	*3,923*	*1,831*	*5,827*	*2,892*	*2,935*	*2,732*	*839*	*1,893*
0—4	1,700	863	837	1,697	862	835	3	1	2	..	..	..
5—9	1,533	826	707	1,518	821	697	13	4	9	2	1	1
10—14	1,105	662	443	868	616	252	225	43	182	12	3	9
15—19	1,210	696	514	512	485	27	660	204	456	38	7	31
20—39	5,407	2,918	2,489	894	879	15	3,538	1,732	1,806	975	307	668
40—59	2,830	1,475	1,355	232	220	3	1,280	819	461	1,318	427	891
60 and over	528	214	314	33	31	2	108	89	19	387	94	293
MERWARA	*3,989*	*3,155*	*2,834*	*2,433*	*1,624*	*809*	*2,413*	*1,216*	*1,197*	*1,143*	*315*	*828*
0—4	733	381	352	732	381	351	1	..	1	..	..	..
5—9	576	287	289	576	287	289	..	..	..	..	..	..
10—14	428	243	185	383	237	146	44	6	38	1	..	1
15—19	508	308	200	267	253	14	231	54	177	10	1	9
20—39	2,354	1,264	1,090	389	382	7	1,575	782	793	390	100	290
40—59	1,153	569	584	75	73	2	520	340	180	558	150	403
60 and over	237	103	134	11	11	..	42	34	8	184	58	126

TABLE VII.

Part C.

BY STATES OR DISTRICTS.

MUSALMANS.

TABLE VII.—C.
MUSALMANS.

TABLE VII.—Age, Sex and Civil Condition.

Age; and State or District.	Population.			Unmarried.			Married.			Widowed.		
	Persons.	Males.	Females.	Persons.	Males.	Females.	Persons.	Males.	Females.	Persons.	Males.	Females.
1	2	3	4	5	6	7	8	9	10	11	12	13
RAJPUTANA—												
ALWAR	*199,149*	*103,972*	*95,177*	*86,180*	*51,380*	*34,800*	*92,920*	*45,490*	*47,430*	*20,049*	*7,102*	*12,947*
0—4	26,908	13,334	13,574	26,891	13,327	13,564	16	7	9	1	..	1
5—9	25,228	13,220	12,008	24,614	13,017	11,597	584	192	392	30	11	19
10—14	24,828	13,731	11,097	20,340	12,582	7,758	4,368	1,093	3,275	120	56	64
15—19	20,609	11,584	9,025	9,053	7,556	1,497	11,196	3,838	7,358	360	190	170
20—39	57,556	29,160	28,396	4,431	4,158	273	48,801	23,120	25,681	4,324	1,882	2,442
40—59	33,265	17,157	16,108	669	580	89	23,253	13,684	9,569	9,343	2,893	6,450
60 and over	10,755	5,786	4,969	182	160	22	4,702	3,556	1,146	5,871	2,070	3,801
BANSWARA	*4,886*	*2,483*	*2,403*	*2,083*	*1,206*	*877*	*2,350*	*1,185*	*1,165*	*453*	*92*	*361*
0—4	763	362	401	762	362	400	1	..	1	..	..	..
5—9	579	297	282	565	293	272	14	4	10	..	..	..
10—14	468	245	223	395	234	161	72	11	61	1	..	1
15—19	406	202	204	180	151	29	222	50	172	4	1	3
20—39	1,778	917	861	164	153	11	1,507	727	780	107	37	70
40—59	724	386	338	15	11	4	472	338	134	237	37	200
60 and over	168	74	94	2	2	..	62	55	7	104	17	87
BHARATPUR	*102,449*	*54,550*	*47,899*	*41,923*	*25,859*	*16,064*	*48,801*	*24,307*	*24,494*	*11,725*	*4,384*	*7,341*
0—4	12,102	6,119	5,983	12,099	6,118	5,981	3	1	2	..	..	..
5—9	12,439	6,506	5,933	12,118	6,434	5,684	304	63	241	17	9	8
10—14	12,750	7,378	5,372	10,085	6,561	3,524	2,568	769	1,799	97	48	49
15—19	10,438	5,850	4,588	4,437	3,739	698	5,777	1,991	3,786	224	120	104
20—39	32,849	17,090	15,759	2,765	2,622	143	27,035	13,091	13,944	3,049	1,377	1,672
40—59	17,435	9,241	8,194	339	317	22	11,401	7,035	4,366	5,695	1,889	3,806
60 and over	4,436	2,366	2,070	80	68	12	1,713	1,357	356	2,643	941	1,702
BIKANER	*91,929*	*49,347*	*42,582*	*42,288*	*25,953*	*16,335*	*41,365*	*20,857*	*20,508*	*8,276*	*2,537*	*5,739*
0—4	14,038	7,110	6,928	13,989	7,100	6,889	49	10	39	..	..	..
5—9	11,837	6,229	5,608	11,342	6,102	5,240	488	123	365	7	4	3
10—14	9,752	5,352	4,400	7,925	4,837	3,088	1,796	504	1,292	31	11	20
15—19	8,636	4,858	3,778	4,316	3,497	819	4,208	1,332	2,876	112	29	83
20—39	28,870	15,546	13,324	4,137	3,876	261	22,972	11,069	11,903	1,761	601	1,160
40—59	14,475	8,071	6,404	484	452	32	10,078	6,456	3,622	3,913	1,163	2,750
60 and over	4,321	2,181	2,140	95	89	6	1,774	1,363	411	2,452	729	1,723
BUNDI	*10,656*	*5,414*	*5,242*	*4,222*	*2,467*	*1,755*	*5,297*	*2,628*	*2,669*	*1,137*	*319*	*818*
0—4	1,622	753	869	1,622	753	869	..	..	..	..	..	..
5—9	1,290	664	626	1,246	652	594	43	11	32	1	1	..
10—14	743	405	338	564	370	194	176	33	143	3	2	1
15—19	757	416	341	334	287	47	414	126	288	9	3	6
20—39	3,753	1,885	1,868	393	353	40	3,107	1,427	1,680	253	105	148
40—59	1,396	1,017	379	47	40	7	1,319	850	469	530	127	403
60 and over	595	274	321	16	12	4	238	181	57	341	81	260
DHOLPUR	*18,263*	*9,560*	*8,703*	*7,338*	*4,518*	*2,820*	*8,813*	*4,376*	*4,437*	*2,111*	*666*	*1,445*
0—4	2,076	1,053	1,023	2,076	1,053	1,023	..	..	..	..	..	..
5—9	2,318	1,215	1,103	2,224	1,197	1,027	90	15	75	4	3	1
10—14	2,048	1,169	879	1,494	1,021	473	537	143	394	17	5	12
15—19	1,698	924	774	687	587	100	973	316	657	38	21	17
20—39	5,670	2,946	2,724	658	548	110	4,592	2,225	2,367	420	173	247
40—59	3,370	1,749	1,621	150	102	57	2,200	1,348	852	1,011	299	712
60 and over	1,082	504	578	40	10	30	421	329	92	621	165	456
DUNGARPUR	*6,703*	*3,320*	*3,383*	*2,771*	*1,610*	*1,161*	*3,391*	*1,617*	*1,774*	*541*	*93*	*448*
0—4	1,108	546	562	1,102	545	557	6	1	5	..	..	..
5—9	826	425	401	757	404	353	68	20	48	1	1	..
10—14	636	340	296	464	293	171	165	46	119	7	1	6
15—19	568	263	305	220	178	42	345	83	262	3	2	1
20—39	2,349	1,130	1,219	203	169	34	2,009	932	1,077	137	29	108
40—59	1,018	511	507	19	16	3	701	456	245	298	39	259
60 and over	198	105	93	6	5	1	97	79	18	95	21	74
JAIPUR	*195,760*	*101,225*	*94,535*	*76,734*	*46,832*	*29,902*	*97,896*	*47,862*	*50,034*	*21,130*	*6,531*	*14,599*
0—4	26,050	12,893	13,157	25,942	12,869	13,073	104	23	81	4	1	3
5—9	24,137	12,537	11,600	22,627	12,141	10,486	1,472	384	1,088	38	12	26
10—14	19,298	10,829	8,469	13,950	9,264	4,686	5,210	1,512	3,698	138	53	85
15—19	16,865	9,236	7,629	6,810	5,892	918	9,752	3,211	6,541	303	133	170
20—39	62,090	31,153	30,937	6,286	5,790	496	51,532	23,739	27,793	4,272	1,624	2,648
40—59	35,387	18,602	16,785	867	683	184	24,804	15,104	9,700	9,626	2,725	6,901
60 and over	11,933	5,975	5,958	252	193	59	4,932	3,799	1,133	6,749	1,983	4,766

PART C.—BY STATES OR DISTRICTS. MAIN RELIGIONS—*continued.*

TABLE VII.—C.

MUSALMANS.

Age; and State or District.	POPULATION.			UNMARRIED.			MARRIED.			WIDOWED.		
	Persons.	Males.	Females.	Persons.	Males.	Females.	Persons.	Males.	Females.	Persons.	Males.	Females.
1	2	3	4	5	6	7	8	9	10	11	12	13
RAJPUTANA—*contd.*												
JAISALMER	*22,099*	*12,506*	*9,593*	*11,393*	*7,653*	*3,740*	*8,255*	*4,081*	*4,174*	*2,451*	*772*	*1,679*
0—4	3,085	1,672	1,413	3,078	1,671	1,407	7	1	6	..	..	..
5—9	2,944	1,704	1,240	2,909	1,697	1,212	34	7	27	1	..	1
10—14	2,380	1,451	929	2,168	1,415	753	207	35	172	5	1	4
15—19	1,828	1,062	766	1,158	929	229	645	126	519	25	7	18
20—39	6,867	3,787	3,080	1,820	1,704	116	4,507	1,929	2,578	540	154	386
40—59	3,878	2,260	1,618	213	195	18	2,486	1,680	806	1,179	385	794
60 and over	1,117	570	547	47	42	5	369	303	66	701	225	476
JHALAWAR	*8,625*	*4,265*	*4,360*	*3,304*	*1,972*	*1,332*	*4,188*	*2,008*	*2,180*	*1,133*	*285*	*848*
0—4	1,211	617	594	1,206	614	592	5	3	2	..	..	..
5—9	1,055	537	518	1,023	529	494	31	7	24	1	1	..
10—14	667	364	303	501	337	164	161	26	135	5	1	4
15—19	666	327	339	275	235	40	380	89	291	11	3	8
20—39	2,877	1,330	1,547	257	230	27	2,374	1,034	1,340	246	66	180
40—59	1,629	812	817	38	25	13	1,010	654	356	581	133	448
60 and over	520	278	242	4	2	2	227	195	32	289	81	208
KARAULI	*8,160*	*4,345*	*3,815*	*3,273*	*2,030*	*1,243*	*3,905*	*2,021*	*1,884*	*982*	*294*	*688*
0—4	977	470	507	977	470	507	..	..	..	..	..	..
5—9	948	483	465	920	475	445	28	8	20	..	..	..
10—14	786	435	351	596	401	195	186	31	155	4	3	1
15—19	723	431	292	344	299	45	358	118	240	21	14	7
20—39	2,811	1,535	1,276	350	309	41	2,260	1,145	1,115	201	81	120
40—59	1,493	796	697	70	63	7	922	591	331	501	142	359
60 and over	422	195	227	16	13	3	151	128	23	255	54	201
KISHANGARH	*6,785*	*3,577*	*3,208*	*2,461*	*1,581*	*880*	*3,372*	*1,700*	*1,672*	*952*	*296*	*656*
0—4	879	436	443	861	431	430	17	5	12	1	..	1
5—9	745	403	342	696	391	305	46	11	35	3	1	2
10—14	517	310	207	388	276	112	121	32	89	8	2	6
15—19	642	349	293	254	234	20	372	105	267	16	10	6
20—39	2,406	1,272	1,134	224	220	4	1,920	942	978	262	110	152
40—59	1,282	672	610	33	24	9	784	520	264	465	128	337
60 and over	314	135	179	5	5	..	112	85	27	197	45	152
KOTAH	*44,569*	*23,163*	*21,406*	*17,745*	*10,869*	*6,876*	*21,634*	*10,808*	*10,826*	*5,190*	*1,486*	*3,704*
0—4	6,388	3,189	3,199	6,385	3,187	3,198	3	2	1	..	..	..
5—9	5,221	2,682	2,539	5,082	2,659	2,423	133	22	111	6	1	5
10—14	3,494	2,010	1,484	2,815	1,870	945	668	135	533	11	5	6
15—19	3,626	1,891	1,735	1,559	1,376	183	2,003	493	1,510	64	22	42
20—39	15,982	8,297	7,685	1,701	1,602	99	13,052	6,251	6,801	1,229	444	785
40—59	7,708	3,990	3,718	160	139	21	4,968	3,233	1,735	2,575	618	1,957
60 and over	2,155	1,104	1,051	43	36	7	807	672	135	1,305	396	909
KUSHALGARH	*697*	*349*	*348*	*322*	*187*	*135*	*313*	*149*	*164*	*62*	*13*	*49*
0—4	120	56	64	120	56	64	..	..	..	..	..	..
5—9	84	45	39	84	45	39	..	..	..	..	..	..
10—14	59	31	28	53	31	22	6	..	6	..	..	..
15—19	63	38	25	39	35	4	23	3	20	1	..	1
20—39	257	117	140	22	17	5	214	96	118	21	4	17
40—59	88	47	41	3	2	1	61	42	19	24	3	21
60 and over	26	15	11	1	1	..	9	8	1	16	6	10
LAWA	*139*	*83*	*56*	*49*	*35*	*14*	*67*	*36*	*31*	*23*	*12*	*11*
0—4	18	8	10	17	8	9	1	..	1	..	..	..
5—9	15	11	4	14	11	3	1	..	1	..	..	..
10—14	16	11	5	11	9	2	5	2	3	..	..	..
15—19	8	5	3	2	2	..	6	3	3	..	..	..
20—39	57	31	26	5	5	..	43	22	21	9	4	5
40—59	20	13	7	..	..	..	10	8	2	10	5	5
60 and over	5	4	1	..	..	..	1	1	..	4	3	1
MARWAR	*165,545*	*87,489*	*78,056*	*74,508*	*46,545*	*27,963*	*73,962*	*36,034*	*37,928*	*17,075*	*4,910*	*12,165*
0—4	25,340	12,676	12,664	25,204	12,643	12,561	131	28	103	5	5	..
5—9	20,629	10,933	9,696	19,574	10,606	8,968	1,017	306	711	38	21	17
10—14	16,431	9,202	7,229	13,233	8,308	4,925	3,107	849	2,258	91	45	46
15—19	14,136	7,993	6,143	7,178	5,936	1,242	6,763	1,995	4,768	195	62	133
20—39	54,254	28,550	25,704	8,235	8,032	203	42,211	19,248	22,963	3,808	1,272	2,536
40—59	27,050	14,430	12,620	910	855	55	17,892	11,372	6,520	8,257	2,212	6,045
60 and over	7,696	3,696	4,000	174	165	9	2,841	2,238	603	4,681	1,293	3,388

TABLE VII.—C.
MUSALMANS.

TABLE VII.—Age, Sex and Civil Condition. Part C.—By States or Districts. Main Religions—*continued.*

Age; and State or District.	Population.			Unmarried.			Married.			Widowed.		
	Persons.	Males.	Females.	Persons.	Males.	Females.	Persons.	Males.	Females.	Persons.	Males.	Females.
1	2	3	4	5	6	7	8	9	10	11	12	13
RAJPUTANA—contd.												
MEWAR	*45,752*	*24,180*	*21,572*	*17,555*	*10,474*	*7,081*	*23,284*	*12,021*	*11,263*	*4,913*	*1,685*	*3,228*
0—4	6,928	3,333	3,595	6,908	3,330	3,578	19	3	16	1	..	1
5—9	5,227	2,735	2,492	5,012	2,680	2,332	210	53	157	5	2	3
10—14	3,297	1,850	1,447	2,496	1,633	863	777	207	570	24	10	14
15—19	3,559	1,950	1,609	1,465	1,280	185	2,004	619	1,385	90	51	39
20—39	16,784	8,882	7,902	1,508	1,404	104	14,040	6,875	7,165	1,236	603	633
40—59	8,145	4,477	3,668	133	119	14	5,556	3,688	1,868	2,456	670	1,786
60 and over	1,812	953	859	33	28	5	678	576	102	1,101	349	752
PARTABGARH	*3,581*	*1,856*	*1,725*	*1,409*	*820*	*589*	*1,716*	*893*	*824*	*456*	*144*	*312*
0—4	561	252	309	558	252	306	3	..	3	..	..	..
5—9	372	189	183	352	187	165	20	2	18	..	..	..
10—14	299	163	136	233	150	83	66	13	53	..	..	..
15—19	278	144	134	121	99	22	151	42	109	6	3	3
20—39	1,335	699	636	131	120	11	1,071	527	544	133	52	81
40—59	612	341	271	11	10	1	363	267	96	238	64	174
60 and over	124	68	56	3	2	1	42	41	1	79	25	54
SHAHPURA	*2,407*	*1,236*	*1,171*	*900*	*537*	*363*	*1,190*	*592*	*598*	*317*	*107*	*210*
0—4	382	190	192	377	190	187	5	..	5	..	..	..
5—9	277	147	130	270	143	127	7	4	3	..	..	..
10—14	148	90	58	114	79	35	30	8	22	4	3	1
15—19	151	76	75	63	59	4	85	15	70	3	2	1
20—39	864	426	438	65	59	6	719	333	386	80	34	46
40—59	464	248	216	7	5	2	310	204	106	147	39	108
60 and over	121	59	62	4	2	2	34	28	6	83	29	54
SIROHI	*7,240*	*4,124*	*3,116*	*3,013*	*1,851*	*1,162*	*3,649*	*2,063*	*1,586*	*578*	*210*	*368*
0—4	979	474	505	975	473	502	4	1	3	..	..	..
5—9	816	420	396	790	412	378	26	8	18	..	..	..
10—14	632	355	277	537	327	210	94	27	67	1	1	..
15—19	618	378	240	289	249	40	318	124	194	11	5	6
20—39	2,719	1,628	1,091	380	354	26	2,220	1,201	1,019	119	73	46
40—59	1,149	688	461	34	29	5	848	582	266	267	77	190
60 and over	327	181	146	8	7	1	139	120	19	180	54	126
TONK	*40,432*	*20,516*	*19,916*	*16,820*	*9,937*	*6,883*	*18,481*	*9,111*	*9,370*	*5,131*	*1,468*	*3,663*
0—4	5,411	2,618	2,793	5,367	2,601	2,766	39	15	24	5	2	3
5—9	4,695	2,426	2,269	4,577	2,399	2,178	109	25	84	9	2	7
10—14	3,393	1,838	1,555	2,941	1,755	1,186	435	82	353	17	1	16
15—19	3,173	1,621	1,552	1,739	1,327	412	1,377	277	1,100	57	17	40
20—39	13,761	7,030	6,731	1,921	1,663	258	10,631	4,852	5,779	1,209	515	694
40—59	7,276	3,756	3,520	209	144	65	4,842	3,022	1,820	2,225	590	1,635
60 and over	2,723	1,227	1,496	66	48	18	1,048	838	210	1,609	341	1,268
AJMER-MERWARA—												
AJMER	*60,465*	*32,585*	*27,880*	*24,621*	*15,207*	*9,414*	*29,049*	*14,986*	*14,063*	*6,795*	*2,392*	*4,403*
0—4	8,248	4,197	4,051	8,208	4,191	4,017	40	6	34	..	..	..
5—9	6,940	3,606	3,334	6,611	3,502	3,109	310	98	212	19	6	13
10—14	5,749	3,291	2,458	4,473	2,927	1,546	1,221	331	890	55	33	22
15—19	5,197	2,859	2,338	2,393	2,020	373	2,694	784	1,910	110	55	55
20—39	20,948	11,443	9,505	2,574	2,316	258	16,595	8,271	8,324	1,779	856	923
40—59	10,433	5,668	4,765	287	197	90	7,029	4,540	2,489	3,117	931	2,186
60 and over	2,950	1,521	1,429	75	54	21	1,160	956	204	1,715	511	1,204
MERWARA	*20,570*	*11,248*	*9,322*	*9,430*	*5,983*	*3,456*	*9,365*	*4,706*	*4,659*	*1,766*	*559*	*1,207*
0—4	3,425	1,756	1,669	3,421	1,756	1,665	4	..	4	..	..	..
5—9	2,737	1,539	1,198	2,661	1,508	1,153	74	29	45	2	2	..
10—14	1,625	934	691	1,361	873	488	257	58	199	7	3	4
15—19	1,658	975	683	890	789	101	747	177	570	21	9	12
20—39	7,073	3,824	3,249	1,031	993	38	5,653	2,660	2,993	389	171	218
40—59	3,211	1,777	1,434	61	52	9	2,285	1,490	795	865	235	630
60 and over	841	443	398	14	12	2	345	292	53	482	139	343

TABLE VII.

PART C.

BY STATES OR DISTRICTS.

SIKHS.

TABLE VII.—C.
SIKHS.

TABLE VII.—Age, Sex and Civil Condition

Age; and State or District.	Population.			Unmarried.			Married.			Widowed.		
	Persons.	Males.	Females.	Persons.	Males.	Females.	Persons.	Males.	Females.	Persons.	Males.	Females.
1	2	3	4	5	6	7	8	9	10	11	12	13
RAJPUTANA—												
ALWAR . .	*29*	*16*	*13*	*13*	*8*	*5*	*15*	*8*	*7*	*1*	..	*1*
0—4 . .	6	2	4	6	2	4	..	..	..	..	..	..
5—9 . .	2	2	..	2	2	..	..	..	..	..	..	..
10—14 . .	3	2	1	3	2	1	..	..	..	..	..	..
15—19 . .	..	..	..	..	..	..	..	..	..	..	..	..
20—39 . .	11	7	4	2	2	..	9	5	4	..	..	..
40—59 . .	6	2	4	..	..	..	5	2	3	1	..	1
60 and over .	1	1	..	..	..	..	1	1	..	..	..	..
BANSWARA .	*1*	*1*	..	..	..	..	..	..	..	*1*	*1*	..
0—4 . .	..	..	..	..	..	..	..	..	..	..	..	..
5—9 . .	..	..	..	..	..	..	..	..	..	..	..	..
10—14 . .	..	..	..	..	..	..	..	..	..	..	..	..
15—19 . .	..	..	..	..	..	..	..	..	..	..	..	..
20—39 . .	1	1	..	..	..	..	..	..	..	1	1	..
40—59 . .	..	..	..	..	..	..	..	..	..	..	..	..
60 and over .	..	..	..	..	..	..	..	..	..	..	..	..
BHARATPUR .	*52*	*28*	*24*	*22*	*12*	*10*	*29*	*15*	*14*	*1*	*1*	..
0—4 . .	6	3	3	6	3	3	..	..	..	..	..	..
5—9 . .	7	2	5	7	2	5	..	..	..	..	..	..
10—14 . .	4	2	2	4	2	2	..	..	..	..	..	..
15—19 .	6	3	3	3	3	..	3	..	3	..	..	..
20—39 . .	18	10	8	1	1	..	17	9	6	..	..	..
40—59 . .	11	8	3	1	1	..	9	6	3	1	1	..
60 and over .	..	..	..	..	..	..	..	..	..	..	..	..
BIKANER . .	*8,214*	*5,054*	*3,160*	*4,275*	*2,902*	*1,373*	*3,457*	*1,899*	*1,558*	*482*	*253*	*229*
0—4 . .	1,233	638	595	1,232	638	594	1	..	1	..	..	..
5—9 . .	1,040	588	452	1,016	578	438	24	10	14	..	..	..
10—14 . .	906	619	287	854	595	259	51	24	27	1	..	1
15—19 . .	834	581	253	556	484	72	276	97	179	2	..	2
20—39 . .	2,603	1,600	1,003	548	538	10	1,945	993	952	110	69	41
40—59 . .	1,235	803	432	62	62	..	978	633	345	195	108	87
60 and over .	363	225	138	7	7	..	182	142	40	174	76	98
BUNDI . .	*1*	*1*	..	*1*	*1*	..	..	..	..	..	..	..
0—4 . .	..	..	..	..	..	..	..	..	..	..	..	..
5—9 . .	..	..	..	..	..	..	..	..	..	..	..	..
10—14 . .	..	..	..	..	..	..	..	..	..	..	..	..
15—19 . .	..	..	..	..	..	..	..	..	..	..	..	..
20—39 . .	..	..	..	..	..	..	..	..	..	..	..	..
40—59 . .	1	1	..	1	1	..	..	..	..	..	..	..
60 and over .	..	..	..	..	..	..	..	..	..	..	..	..
DHOLPUR .	*95*	*56*	*39*	*38*	*26*	*12*	*50*	*26*	*24*	*7*	*4*	*3*
0—4 . .	16	8	8	16	8	8	..	..	..	..	..	..
5—9 . .	9	6	3	9	6	3	..	..	..	..	..	..
10—14 . .	7	6	1	7	6	1	..	..	..	..	..	..
15—19 . .	10	6	4	4	4	..	6	2	4	..	..	..
20—39 . .	32	17	16	2	2	..	30	14	16	1	1	..
40—59 . .	17	12	5	..	..	..	14	10	4	3	2	1
60 and over .	3	1	2	..	..	..	..	..	..	3	1	2

SIKHS.

Age ; and State or District.	Population.			Unmarried.			Married.			Widowed.		
	Persons.	Males.	Females.	Persons.	Males.	Females.	Persons.	Males.	Females.	Persons.	Males.	Females.
1	2	3	4	5	6	7	8	9	10	11	12	13
RAJPUTANA—*contd.*												
DUNGARPUR .	*6*	*4*	*2*	*4*	*3*	*1*	*2*	*1*	*1*	..	..	..
0—4 . .	1	1	..	1	1	..	..	..	..	..	..	..
5—9 . .	1	1	..	1	1	..	..	..	..	..	..	..
10—14 . .	1	..	1	1	..	1	..	..	..	..	..	..
15—19 . .	..	..	..	..	..	..	..	..	..	..	..	..
20—39 . .	3	2	1	1	1	..	2	1	1	..	..	..
40—59 . .	..	..	..	..	..	..	..	..	..	..	..	..
60 and over .	..	..	..	..	..	..	..	..	..	..	..	..
JAIPUR . .	*157*	*89*	*68*	*58*	*37*	*21*	*71*	*40*	*31*	*28*	*12*	*16*
0—4 . .	12	6	6	12	6	6	..	..	..	..	..	..
5—9 . .	9	4	5	9	4	5	..	..	..	..	..	..
10—14 . .	18	6	12	15	6	9	3	..	3	..	..	..
15—19 . .	11	9	2	5	5	..	5	3	2	1	1	..
20—39 . .	69	43	26	17	16	1	44	24	20	8	3	5
40—59 . .	24	13	11	..	..	..	16	11	5	8	2	6
60 and over .	14	8	6	..	..	..	3	2	1	11	6	5
JAISALMER .	*1*	*1*	..	*1*	*1*	..	..	..	..	..	..	..
0—4 . .	..	..	..	..	..	..	..	..	..	..	..	..
5—9 . .	..	..	..	..	..	..	..	..	..	..	..	..
10—14 . .	..	..	..	..	..	..	..	..	..	..	..	..
15—19 . .	..	..	..	..	..	..	..	..	..	..	..	..
20—39 . .	1	1	..	1	1	..	..	..	..	..	..	..
40—59 . .	..	..	..	..	..	..	..	..	..	..	..	..
60 and over .	..	..	..	..	..	..	..	..	..	..	..	..
JHALAWAR .	*53*	*32*	*21*	*21*	*11*	*10*	*23*	*15*	*8*	*9*	*6*	*3*
0—4 . .	8	4	4	8	4	4	..	..	..	..	..	..
5—9 . .	8	3	5	8	3	5	..	..	..	..	..	..
10—14 . .	2	1	1	2	1	1	..	..	..	..	..	..
15—19 . .	..	..	..	..	..	..	..	..	..	..	..	..
20—39 . .	18	11	7	1	1	..	15	8	7	2	2	..
40—59 . .	11	7	4	1	1	..	5	4	1	5	2	3
60 and over .	6	6	..	1	1	..	3	3	..	2	2	..
KISHANGARH .	*4*	*4*	..	*2*	*2*	..	*1*	*1*	..	*1*	*1*	..
0—4 . .	..	..	..	..	..	..	..	..	..	..	..	..
5—9 . .	..	..	..	..	..	..	..	..	..	..	..	..
10—14 . .	..	..	..	..	..	..	..	..	..	..	..	..
15—19 . .	..	..	..	..	..	..	..	..	..	..	..	..
20—39 . .	4	4	..	2	2	..	1	1	..	1	1	..
40—59 . .	..	..	..	..	..	..	..	..	..	..	..	..
60 and over .	..	..	..	..	..	..	..	..	..	..	..	..
KOTAH . .	*216*	*109*	*107*	*83*	*52*	*31*	*101*	*49*	*52*	*32*	*8*	*24*
0—4 . .	38	20	18	38	20	18	..	..	..	..	..	..
5—9 . .	19	8	11	18	7	11	1	1	..	..	..	..
10—14 . .	10	7	3	7	6	1	3	1	2	..	..	..
15—19 . .	19	9	10	7	6	1	12	3	9	..	..	..
20—39 . .	76	39	37	12	12	..	61	25	36	3	2	1
40—59 . .	43	20	23	1	1	..	21	16	5	21	3	18
60 and over .	11	6	5	..	..	..	3	3	..	8	3	5

TABLE VII.—AGE, SEX AND CIVIL CONDITION. PART C.—BY STATES OR DISTRICTS. MAIN RELIGIONS—*continued.*

Age; and State or District.	Population.			Unmarried.			Married.			Widowed.		
	Persons.	Males.	Females.	Persons.	Males.	Females.	Persons.	Males.	Females.	Persons.	Males.	Females.
1	2	3	4	5	6	7	8	9	10	11	12	13
RAJPUTANA—*concld.*												
MARWAR	*38*	*24*	*14*	*10*	*5*	*5*	*26*	*17*	*9*	*2*	*2*	..
0—4	2	2	..	2	2	..	..	..	..	..	..	..
5—9	6	2	4	4	2	2	2	..	2	..	..	..
10—14	2	..	2	2	..	2	..	..	..	..	..	..
15—19	3	2	1	2	1	1	1	1	..	..	..	..
20—39	16	11	5	..	..	..	15	10	5	1	1	..
40—59	9	7	2	..	..	..	8	6	2	1	1	..
60 and over	..	..	..	..	..	..	..	..	..	..	..	..
MEWAR	*10*	*6*	*4*	*3*	*2*	*1*	*6*	*4*	*2*	*1*	..	*1*
0—4	1	..	1	1	..	1	..	..	..	..	..	..
5—9	..	..	..	..	..	..	..	..	..	..	..	..
10—14	..	..	..	..	..	..	..	..	..	..	..	..
15—19	..	..	..	..	..	..	..	..	..	..	..	..
20—39	3	1	2	..	..	..	3	1	2	..	..	..
40—59	4	3	1	2	2	..	1	1	..	1	..	1
60 and over	2	2	..	..	..	..	2	2	..	..	..	..
PARTABGARH	*2*	*1*	*1*	..	..	..	*2*	*1*	*1*	..	..	..
0—4	..	..	..	..	..	..	..	..	..	..	..	..
5—9	..	..	..	..	..	..	..	..	..	..	..	..
10—14	..	..	..	..	..	..	..	..	..	..	..	..
15—19	..	..	..	..	..	..	..	..	..	..	..	..
20—39	2	1	1	..	..	..	2	1	1	..	..	..
40—59	..	..	..	..	..	..	..	..	..	..	..	..
60 and over	..	..	..	..	..	..	..	..	..	..	..	..
SIROHI	*76*	*63*	*13*	*37*	*31*	*6*	*37*	*30*	*7*	*2*	*2*	..
0—4	4	2	2	4	2	2	..	..	..	..	..	..
5—9	4	1	3	4	1	3	..	..	..	..	..	..
10—14	3	3	..	3	3	..	..	..	..	..	..	..
15—19	19	18	1	18	17	1	1	1	..	..	..	..
20—39	43	36	7	8	8	..	34	27	7	1	1	..
40—59	3	3	..	..	..	..	2	2	..	1	1	..
60 and over	..	..	..	..	..	..	..	..	..	..	..	..
TONK	*3*	..	*3*	..	..	..	*3*	..	*3*	..	..	..
0—4	..	..	..	..	..	..	..	..	..	..	..	..
5—9	..	..	..	..	..	..	..	..	..	..	..	..
10—14	1	..	1	..	..	..	1	..	1	..	..	..
15—19	..	..	..	..	..	..	..	..	..	..	..	..
20—39	1	..	1	..	..	..	1	..	1	..	..	..
40—59	1	..	1	..	..	..	1	..	1	..	..	..
60 and over	..	..	..	..	..	..	..	..	..	..	..	..
AJMER-MERWARA—												
AJMER	*916*	*779*	*137*	*517*	*477*	*40*	*359*	*261*	*98*	*47*	*41*	*6*
0—4	51	26	25	51	26	25	..	..	..	..	..	..
5—9	29	17	12	29	17	12	..	..	..	..	..	..
10—14	26	22	4	21	18	3	5	4	1	..	..	..
15—19	134	124	10	104	104	..	27	17	10	3	3	..
20—39	607	532	75	305	305	..	272	199	73	30	28	2
40—59	62	52	10	7	7	..	46	39	7	9	6	3
60 and over	7	6	1	..	..	..	2	2	..	5	4	1
MERWARA	*6*	*4*	*2*	*3*	*2*	*1*	*3*	*2*	*1*	..	..	..
0—4	2	1	1	2	1	1	..	..	..	..	..	..
5—9	1	1	..	1	1	..	..	..	..	..	..	..
10—14	..	..	..	..	..	..	..	..	..	..	..	..
15—19	..	..	..	..	..	..	..	..	..	..	..	..
20—39	3	2	1	..	..	..	3	2	1	..	..	..
40—59	..	..	..	..	..	..	..	..	..	..	..	..
60 and over	..	..	..	..	..	..	..	..	..	..	..	..

N.B.—Karauli, Kushalgarh, Lawa, and Shahpura, which contain no Sikhs, have not been shown.

TABLE VII.

Part D.

BY CITIES.

ALL RELIGIONS.

TABLE VII.—D.
ALL RELIGIONS.

TABLE VII.—AGE, SEX AND CIVIL CONDITIONS. PART D.—BY CITIES.
ALL RELIGIONS.

Age ; and City.	POPULATION.			UNMARRIED.			MARRIED.			WIDOWED.		
	Persons.	Males.	Females.	Persons.	Males.	Females.	Persons.	Males.	Females.	Persons.	Males.	Females.
1	2	3	4	5	6	7	8	9	10	11	12	13
RAJPUTANA—												
ALWAR	*41,305*	*22,254*	*19,051*	*14,854*	*9,286*	*5,568*	*20,191*	*10,597*	*9,594*	*6,260*	*2,871*	*3,389*
0—4	4,494	2,152	2,342	4,493	2,151	2,342	1	1	..	..	..	..
5—9	3,756	1,872	1,884	3,664	1,849	1,815	90	22	68	2	1	1
10—14	3,667	1,071	1,696	2,911	1,768	1,143	723	191	532	33	12	21
15—19	3,609	1,987	1,622	1,392	1,214	178	2,096	720	1,376	121	53	68
20—39	13,419	7,483	5,936	1,154	1,102	52	10,914	5,716	5,198	1,351	665	686
40—59	8,997	5,061	3,936	929	905	24	5,340	3,182	2,158	2,728	974	1,754
60 and over	3,363	1,728	1,635	311	297	14	1,027	765	262	2,025	666	1,359
BHARATPUR	*33,918*	*18,803*	*15,115*	*11,413*	*7,637*	*3,776*	*16,800*	*8,968*	*7,832*	*5,705*	*2,198*	*3,507*
0—4	3,214	1,643	1,571	3,211	1,643	1,568	3	..	3	..	..	..
5—9	3,092	1,661	1,431	2,969	1,626	1,343	119	31	88	4	4	..
10—14	3,697	2,193	1,504	2,577	1,862	715	1,074	310	764	46	21	25
15—19	3,730	2,085	1,625	1,277	1,183	94	2,288	833	1,455	145	69	76
20—39	12,295	6,973	5,322	1,130	1,096	34	9,418	5,058	4,355	1,752	819	933
40—59	6,568	3,591	2,977	216	202	14	3,553	2,436	1,117	2,799	953	1,846
60 and over	1,342	657	685	33	25	8	350	300	50	959	332	627
BIKANER	*55,836*	*28,275*	*27,561*	*19,550*	*12,690*	*6,860*	*27,536*	*13,804*	*13,732*	*8,750*	*1,781*	*6,969*
0—4	6,478	3,226	3,252	6,474	3,226	3,248	4	..	4	..	..	..
5—9	5,762	2,982	2,780	5,509	2,941	2,568	248	41	207	5	..	5
10—14	4,736	2,612	2,124	3,018	2,202	816	1,683	407	1,276	35	3	32
15—19	5,256	2,737	2,519	1,671	1,595	76	3,418	1,106	2,312	167	36	131
20—39	19,917	10,495	9,422	2,343	2,249	94	15,253	7,758	7,495	2,321	488	1,833
40—59	10,457	4,989	5,468	435	392	43	6,022	3,800	2,222	4,000	797	3,203
60 and over	3,220	1,234	1,986	100	85	15	898	692	206	2,222	457	1,765
JAIPUR	*137,098*	*70,846*	*66,252*	*41,470*	*26,686*	*14,784*	*71,948*	*36,769*	*35,179*	*23,680*	*7,391*	*16,289*
0—4	12,740	6,300	6,440	12,713	6,292	6,421	27	8	19	..	..	..
5—9	12,253	6,323	5,930	11,736	6,220	5,516	497	99	398	20	4	16
10—14	10,923	6,235	4,688	7,422	5,347	2,075	3,368	835	2,533	133	53	80
15—19	11,938	6,284	5,654	3,726	3,448	278	7,758	2,661	5,097	454	175	279
20—39	48,563	25,013	23,550	4,500	4,170	330	38,317	18,715	19,602	5,746	2,128	3,618
40—59	30,456	15,836	14,620	1,108	987	121	18,623	11,789	6,834	10,725	3,060	7,665
60 and over	10,225	4,855	5,370	265	222	43	3,358	2,662	696	6,602	1,971	4,631
*JODHPUR	*79,756*	*41,838*	*37,918*	*29,338*	*19,289*	*10,049*	*39,130*	*19,933*	*19,197*	*11,288*	*2,616*	*8,672*
0—4	8,315	4,231	4,084	8,262	4,217	4,045	52	14	38	1	..	1
5—9	8,762	4,439	4,323	8,259	4,304	3,955	494	130	364	9	5	4
10—14	7,557	4,238	3,319	5,176	3,638	1,538	2,318	580	1,738	63	20	43
15—19	7,902	4,391	3,511	3,013	2,764	249	4,684	1,574	3,110	205	53	152
20—39	29,377	16,134	13,243	3,834	3,665	169	22,459	11,604	10,855	3,084	865	2,219
40—59	14,105	6,929	7,176	647	569	78	8,045	5,217	2,828	5,413	1,143	4,270
60 and over	3,738	1,476	2,262	147	132	15	1,078	814	264	2,513	530	1,983
KOTAH	*32,753*	*16,949*	*15,804*	*10,876*	*7,064*	*3,812*	*16,209*	*8,317*	*7,892*	*5,668*	*1,568*	*4,100*
0—4	3,631	1,779	1,852	3,630	1,779	1,851	1	..	1	..	..	..
5—9	2,781	1,362	1,419	2,685	1,346	1,339	93	16	77	3	..	3
10—14	2,074	1,210	864	1,518	1,111	407	543	98	445	13	1	12
15—19	2,888	1,502	1,386	1,144	1,057	87	1,674	430	1,244	70	15	55
20—39	13,546	7,212	6,334	1,632	1,551	81	10,151	5,073	5,078	1,763	588	1,175
40—59	6,416	3,215	3,201	230	189	41	3,322	2,322	1,000	2,864	704	2,160
60 and over	1,417	669	748	37	31	6	425	378	47	955	260	695
TONK	*33,864*	*16,837*	*17,027*	*12,523*	*7,426*	*5,097*	*15,899*	*7,720*	*8,179*	*5,442*	*1,691*	*3,751*
0—4	4,136	1,987	2,149	4,085	1,963	2,122	41	18	23	10	6	4
5—9	3,519	1,807	1,712	3,420	1,779	1,641	91	25	66	8	3	5
10—14	2,503	1,373	1,130	2,033	1,273	760	437	89	348	33	11	22
15—19	2,834	1,404	1,430	1,334	1,019	315	1,409	348	1,061	91	37	54
20—39	11,607	5,862	5,745	1,408	1,216	192	8,816	4,027	4,789	1,383	619	764
40—59	6,712	3,252	3,460	193	140	53	4,171	2,473	1,698	2,348	639	1,709
60 and over	2,553	1,152	1,401	50	36	14	934	740	194	1,569	376	1,193
UDAIPUR	*33,229*	*17,460*	*15,769*	*11,063*	*7,118*	*3,945*	*17,075*	*8,768*	*8,307*	*5,091*	*1,574*	*3,517*
0—4	3,760	1,874	1,886	3,755	1,874	1,881	4	..	4	1	..	1
5—9	3,197	1,681	1,516	3,067	1,651	1,416	122	27	95	8	3	5
10—14	2,148	1,259	889	1,572	1,127	445	540	112	428	36	20	16
15—19	2,722	1,458	1,264	997	918	79	1,614	490	1,124	111	50	61
20—39	13,780	7,383	6,397	1,465	1,368	97	10,755	5,432	5,323	1,560	583	977
40—59	6,284	3,188	3,096	165	143	22	3,625	2,366	1,259	2,494	679	1,815
60 and over	1,338	617	721	42	37	5	415	341	74	881	239	642
AJMER-MERWARA—												
AJMER	*86,222*	*47,354*	*38,868*	*32,631*	*21,070*	*11,561*	*43,160*	*22,688*	*20,472*	*10,431*	*3,596*	*6,835*
0—4	9,894	4,966	4,928	9,890	4,963	4,927	4	3	1	..	..	..
5—9	8,463	4,338	4,125	8,072	4,240	3,832	368	92	276	23	6	17
10—14	7,944	4,555	3,389	5,818	4,012	1,806	2,050	507	1,543	76	36	40
15—19	8,677	4,807	3,870	3,548	3,064	484	4,911	1,629	3,282	218	94	124
20—39	32,103	18,275	13,828	4,710	4,321	389	24,501	12,661	11,840	2,892	1,293	1,599
40—59	15,243	8,458	6,785	476	358	118	9,914	6,627	3,287	4,853	1,473	3,380
60 and over	3,898	1,955	1,943	117	92	25	1,412	1,169	243	2,369	694	1,675

*Including Jodhpur suburbs which have been shewn in Table IV and V under the name of "Jodhpur town."

TABLE VIII.

Education.

Explanatory Note.

This Table is divided into four Parts, corresponding to those adopted for Table VII.

Part A shows the extent of literacy in each of the Provinces as a whole, and by each religion.

Part B gives similar details for each State or District for its population as a whole.

Part C gives similar details for each State or District by main religions (Animist, Christian, Hindu, Jain, Musalman, Sikh).

Part D shows the extent of literacy in each City.

Literacy was defined, for the purpose of this Census, as the ability to read *and* write a letter. The Table gives separate details of literacy in English in columns 11 to 13, which show both those whose only language of literacy was English and those literate in English as well as some other language. Persons shown in these columns, however, are included also in the main "Literate" columns, 5 to 7. The totals in columns 2 to 4 thus represent the aggregates of columns 5 to 10 only.

In Part A Christians have been sub-divided into (*a*) Indians and (*b*) "others" to illustrate the extent of literacy among Indian Christians.

TABLE VIII.—A.
PROVINCIAL SUMMARY.

TABLE VIII.—EDUCATION. PART A.—

Age, Province and Religion.	Population. Total. Persons.	Population. Total. Males.	Population. Total. Females.	Population. Literate. Persons.	Population. Literate. Males.	Population. Literate. Females.	Population. Illiterate. Persons.	Population. Illiterate. Males.	Population. Illiterate. Females.	Literate in English. Persons.	Literate in English. Males.	Literate in English. Females.
1	2	3	4	5	6	7	8	9	10	11	12	13
RAJPUTANA.												
ALL RELIGIONS	*10,530,432*	*5,515,275*	*5,015,157*	*340,470*	*327,960*	*12,510*	*10,189,962*	*5,187,315*	*5,002,647*	*12,257*	*11,437*	*820*
0—9 . .	2,765,291	1,427,547	1,337,744	4,400	3,952	448	2,780,891	1,423,595	1,357,296	223	149	74
10—14 . .	936,507	536,201	400,306	22,817	21,856	961	913,690	514,345	399,345	893	808	85
15—19 . .	904,837	509,037	395,800	37,130	35,612	1,518	867,707	473,425	394,282	1,807	1,721	86
20 and over .	5,903,797	3,042,490	2,861,307	276,123	266,540	9,583	5,627,674	2,775,950	2,851,724	9,334	8,759	575
ANIMIST . .	*444,702*	*226,508*	*218,194*	*74*	*74*	..	*444,628*	*226,434*	*218,194*	..	..	..
0—9 . .	160,888	81,329	79,559	1	1	..	160,887	81,328	79,559	..	..	..
10—14 . .	29,054	16,302	12,752	..	..	..	29,054	16,302	12,752	..	..	..
15—19 . .	30,987	16,661	14,326	..	..	..	30,987	16,661	14,326	..	..	..
20 and over .	223,773	112,216	111,557	73	73	..	223,700	112,143	111,557	..	..	..
ARYA . .	*1,792*	*1,032*	*760*	*757*	*607*	*150*	*1,035*	*425*	*610*	*250*	*246*	*4*
0—9 . .	423	222	201	39	22	17	384	200	184	..	..	..
10—14 . .	237	160	77	124	104	20	113	56	57	41	41	..
15—19 . .	205	128	77	111	88	23	94	40	54	42	40	2
20 and over .	927	522	405	483	393	90	444	129	315	167	165	2
BRAHMO . .	*82*	*42*	*40*	*35*	*29*	*6*	*47*	*13*	*34*	*4*	*4*	..
0—9 . .	17	7	10	1	..	1	16	7	9	..	..	..
10—14 . .	7	5	2	2	2	..	5	3	2	..	..	..
15—19 . .	5	..	5	2	..	2	3	..	3	..	..	..
20 and over .	53	30	23	30	27	3	23	3	20	4	4	..
BUDDHIST . .	*2*	*2*	..	*2*	*2*	..	..	..	..	*2*	*2*	..
20 and over .	2	2	..	2	2	..	..	..	..	2	2	..
CHRISTIAN . .	*4,256*	*2,409*	*1,847*	*2,504*	*1,596*	*908*	*1,752*	*903*	*849*	*1,712*	*1,045*	*667*
(a) Indians .	**2,548**	**1,429**	**1,119**	**1,118**	**691**	**427**	**1,430**	**738**	**692**	**349**	**242**	**107**
0—9 . .	612	308	304	32	18	14	580	290	290	8	3	5
10—14 . .	215	160	55	135	112	23	80	48	32	27	17	10
15—19 . .	328	179	149	204	104	100	124	75	49	36	19	17
20 and over .	1,393	782	611	747	457	290	646	325	321	278	203	75
(b) Others . .	**1,708**	**980**	**728**	**1,386**	**815**	**571**	**322**	**165**	**157**	**1,363**	**803**	**560**
0—9 . .	431	232	199	163	100	63	268	132	136	160	98	62
10—14 . .	169	110	59	145	92	53	24	18	6	144	91	53
15—19 . .	103	47	56	92	47	45	11	..	11	90	45	45
20 and over .	1,005	591	414	986	576	410	19	15	4	969	569	400
HINDU . .	*8,752,015*	*4,600,170*	*4,151,845*	*228,672*	*220,829*	*7,843*	*8,523,373*	*4,379,341*	*4,144,032*	*7,624*	*7,324*	*300*
0—9 . .	2,270,986	1,170,798	1,100,188	2,599	2,368	231	2,277,387	1,168,430	1,108,957	42	37	5
10—14 . .	774,378	446,299	328,079	14,876	14,287	589	759,502	432,012	327,490	492	480	12
15—19 . .	755,732	428,219	327,513	25,115	24,224	921	730,587	403,995	326,592	1,224	1,206	18
20 and over .	4,941,949	2,554,854	2,387,095	186,052	179,950	6,102	4,755,897	2,374,904	2,380,993	5,866	5,801	65

TABLE VIII.—A.
PROVINCIAL SUMMARY.

Age, Province, and Religion.	POPULATION.									LITERATE IN ENGLISH.		
	TOTAL.			LITERATE.			ILLITERATE.					
	Persons.	Males.	Females.	Persons.	Males.	Females.	Persons.	Males.	Females.	Persons.	Males.	Females.
1	2	3	4	5	6	7	8	9	10	11	12	13
RAJPUTANA— *concld.*												
JAIN . .	*332,307*	*161,856*	*170,541*	*83,543*	*81,408*	*2,137*	*248,832*	*80,448*	*168,404*	*849*	*845*	*4*
0—9 . .	81,797	41,342	40,455	1,252	1,188	64	80,545	40,154	40,391	3	3	..
10—14 . .	28,805	14,940	13,865	6,052	5,918	134	22,753	9,022	13,731	71	70	1
15—19 . .	27,088	13,565	13,523	9,058	8,842	216	18,030	4,723	13,307	172	171	1
20 and over .	194,707	92,009	102,698	67,183	65,460	1,723	127,524	26,549	100,975	603	601	2
JEWISH .	*31*	*16*	*15*	*21*	*13*	*8*	*10*	*3*	*7*	*14*	*10*	*4*
0—9 . .	11	4	7	2	1	1	9	3	6	..	..	..
10—14 . .	4	1	3	4	1	3	..	..	..	2	..	2
15—19 . .	3	2	1	3	2	1	..	..	..	1	1	..
20 and over .	13	9	4	12	9	3	1	..	1	11	9	2
MUSALMAN .	*985,825*	*517,560*	*468,265*	*24,108*	*22,889*	*1,219*	*961,717*	*494,671*	*467,046*	*1,602*	*1,582*	*20*
0—9 . .	258,628	131,969	126,659	282	241	41	258,346	131,728	126,618	10	8	2
10—14 . .	102,642	57,559	45,083	1,422	1,302	120	101,220	56,257	44,963	97	96	1
15—19 . .	89,448	49,598	39,850	2,429	2,245	184	87,019	47,353	39,666	226	225	1
20 and over .	535,107	278,434	256,673	19,975	19,101	874	515,132	259,333	255,799	1,269	1,253	16
PARSI . .	*342*	*191*	*151*	*272*	*161*	*111*	*70*	*30*	*40*	*133*	*112*	*21*
0—9 . .	66	33	33	22	9	13	44	24	20	..	..	..
10—14 . .	39	19	20	34	18	16	5	1	4	15	9	6
15—19 . .	36	10	26	28	9	19	8	1	7	5	3	2
20 and over .	201	129	72	188	125	63	13	4	9	113	100	13
SIKH . .	*8,958*	*5,489*	*3,469*	*480*	*442*	*38*	*8,478*	*5,047*	*3,431*	*67*	*67*	..
0—9 . .	2,432	1,303	1,129	7	4	3	2,425	1,299	1,126	..	..	..
10—14 . .	957	646	311	23	20	3	934	626	308	4	4	..
15—19 . .	902	628	274	58	51	7	844	577	267	11	11	..
20 and over .	4,667	2,912	1,755	392	367	25	4,275	2,545	1,730	52	52	..
AJMER-MERWARA.												
ALL RELIGIONS	*501,395*	*266,198*	*235,197*	*36,209*	*33,037*	*3,172*	*465,186*	*233,161*	*232,025*	*6,881*	*6,164*	*717*
0—9 . .	130,340	66,952	63,388	748	538	210	129,592	66,414	63,178	134	75	59
10—14 . .	37,689	21,771	15,918	2,793	2,434	359	34,896	19,337	15,559	416	359	57
15—19 . .	41,363	22,965	18,398	4,338	3,665	673	37,025	19,300	17,725	956	842	114
20 and over .	292,003	154,510	137,493	28,330	26,400	1,930	263,673	128,110	135,563	5,375	4,888	487
ANIMIST .	*3,979*	*1,987*	*1,992*	*4*	*4*	..	*3,975*	*1,983*	*1,992*	..	..	..
0—9 . .	1,251	596	655	..	..	..	1,251	596	655	..	..	..
10—14 . .	225	133	92	..	..	..	225	133	92	..	..	..
15—19 . .	299	141	158	..	..	..	299	141	158	..	..	..
20 and over .	2,204	1,117	1,087	4	4	..	2,200	1,113	1,087	..	..	..
ARYA . .	*884*	*524*	*360*	*447*	*359*	*88*	*437*	*165*	*272*	*137*	*137*	..
0—9 . .	202	108	99	23	19	4	179	84	95	1	1	..
10—14 . .	126	85	41	81	65	16	45	20	25	9	9	..
15—19 . .	132	86	46	97	74	23	35	12	23	28	28	..
20 and over .	424	250	174	246	201	45	178	49	129	99	99	..

TABLE VIII.—A.
PROVINCIAL SUMMARY.

TABLE VIII.—EDUCATION. PART A—PROVINCIAL SUMMARY—*continued.*

Age, Province and Religion.	Population.									Literate in English.		
	Total.			Literate.			Illiterate.					
	Persons.	Males.	Females.	Persons.	Males.	Females.	Persons.	Males.	Females.	Persons.	Males.	Females.
1	2	3	4	5	6	7	8	9	10	11	12	13
AJMER-MERWARA—*concld.*												
CHRISTIAN	*5,432*	*3,258*	*2,174*	*3,971*	*2,544*	*1,427*	*1,461*	*714*	*747*	*2,634*	*2,002*	*632*
(a) **Indians**	**2,967**	**1,477**	**1,490**	**1,840**	**928**	**912**	**1,127**	**549**	**578**	**526**	**398**	**128**
0—9	612	281	331	114	38	76	498	243	255	8	5	3
10—14	339	181	158	250	119	131	89	62	27	44	31	13
15—19	643	263	380	556	209	347	87	54	33	150	102	48
20 and over	1,373	752	621	920	562	358	453	190	263	324	260	64
(b) **Others**	**2,465**	**1,781**	**684**	**2,131**	**1,616**	**515**	**334**	**165**	**169**	**2,108**	**1,604**	**504**
0—9	377	188	189	97	46	51	280	142	138	96	45	51
10—14	91	52	39	77	45	32	14	7	7	76	45	31
15—19	119	65	54	103	52	51	16	13	3	100	51	49
20 and over	1,878	1,476	402	1,854	1,473	381	24	3	21	1,836	1,463	373
HINDU	*388,552*	*204,856*	*183,696*	*19,805*	*18,652*	*1,153*	*368,747*	*186,204*	*182,543*	*2,983*	*2,932*	*51*
0—9	101,852	52,250	49,602	312	256	56	101,540	51,994	49,546	24	20	4
10—14	27,950	16,156	11,794	1,532	1,399	133	26,418	14,757	11,661	203	195	8
15—19	31,430	17,434	13,996	2,281	2,109	172	29,149	15,325	13,824	499	491	8
20 and over	227,320	119,016	108,304	15,686	14,984	702	211,640	104,128	107,512	2,257	2,226	31
JAIN	*20,302*	*10,809*	*9,493*	*7,132*	*6,933*	*199*	*13,170*	*3,876*	*9,294*	*168*	*167*	*1*
0—9	4,542	2,357	2,185	133	124	9	4,409	2,233	2,176	..	..	..
10—14	1,533	905	628	529	512	17	1,004	393	611	12	12	..
15—19	1,718	1,004	714	832	804	28	886	200	686	38	38	..
20 and over	12,509	6,543	5,966	5,638	5,495	143	6,871	1,050	5,821	118	117	1
JEWISH	*27*	*14*	*13*	*9*	*8*	*1*	*18*	*6*	*12*	*6*	*6*	..
0—9	7	2	5	..	..	..	7	2	5	..	..	..
10—14	1	1	..	1	1	..	..	..	..	1	1	..
15—19	4	3	1	..	..	..	4	3	1	..	..	..
20 and over	15	8	7	8	7	1	7	1	6	5	5	..
MUSALMAN	*81,035*	*43,833*	*37,202*	*4,388*	*4,160*	*228*	*76,647*	*39,673*	*36,974*	*818*	*814*	*4*
0—9	21,350	11,098	10,252	63	53	10	21,287	11,045	10,242	4	4	..
10—14	7,374	4,225	3,149	299	276	23	7,075	3,949	3,126	58	57	1
15—19	6,855	3,834	3,021	415	383	32	6,440	3,451	2,989	121	120	1
20 and over	45,456	24,676	20,780	3,611	3,448	163	41,845	21,228	20,617	635	633	2
PARSI	*262*	*134*	*128*	*166*	*99*	*67*	*96*	*35*	*61*	*111*	*83*	*29*
0—9	64	32	32	4	1	3	60	31	29	1	..	1
10—14	24	11	13	18	11	7	6	..	6	10	6	4
15—19	29	11	18	26	10	16	3	1	2	15	7	8
20 and over	145	80	65	118	77	41	27	3	24	85	69	16
SIKH	*922*	*783*	*139*	*287*	*278*	*9*	*635*	*505*	*130*	*24*	*24*	..
0—9	83	45	38	2	1	1	81	44	37	..	..	..
10—14	26	22	4	6	6	..	20	16	4	3	3	..
15—19	134	124	10	28	24	4	106	100	6	5	5	..
20 and over	679	592	87	251	247	4	428	345	83	16	16	..

TABLE VIII.—PART B

EDUCATION.

STATES OR DISTRICTS.

ALL RELIGIONS.

TABLE VIII.—B.
ALL RELIGIONS.

TABLE VIII.—EDUCATION. PART B.—

Age, Province, and State or District.	POPULATION.									LITERATE IN ENGLISH.		
	TOTAL.			LITERATE.			ILLITERATE.					
	Persons.	Males.	Females.	Persons.	Males.	Females.	Persons.	Males.	Females.	Persons.	Males.	Females.
1	2	3	4	5	6	7	8	9	10	11	12	13
RAJPUTANA.												
ALWAR . .	*791,688*	*413,639*	*378,029*	*20,769*	*20,253*	*510*	*770,936*	*393,407*	*377,519*	*875*	*849*	*33*
0—9 . .	200,793	101,883	98,912	295	272	23	200,500	101,611	98,889	2	1	1
10—14 . .	91,488	51,092	40,391	1,368	1,320	48	90,117	49,772	40,345	27	21	6
15—19 . .	77,918	43,429	34,484	2,048	1,991	57	75,865	41,438	34,427	80	77	3
20 and over .	421,497	217,255	204,242	17,053	16,669	384	404,444	200,586	203,858	766	743	23
BANSWARA .	*165,463*	*81,690*	*83,843*	*3,984*	*3,788*	*196*	*161,479*	*77,839*	*83,647*	*50*	*48*	*2*
0—9 . .	56,335	28,204	28,131	30	27	3	56,305	28,177	28,128	..	..	..
10—14 . .	11,983	6,402	5,581	210	204	6	11,773	6,198	5,575	3	3	..
15—19 . .	13,047	6,819	6,228	420	400	20	12,627	6,419	6,208	2	2	..
20 and over .	84,098	40,195	43,903	3,324	3,157	167	80,774	37,038	43,736	45	43	2
BHARATPUR .	*558,785*	*302,254*	*256,531*	*18,061*	*17,263*	*798*	*540,724*	*284,991*	*255,733*	*916*	*871*	*45*
0—9 . .	128,406	66,894	61,512	253	218	35	128,153	66,676	61,477	7	6	1
10—14 . .	65,500	38,434	27,066	2,035	1,928	107	63,465	36,506	26,959	87	86	1
15—19 . .	54,472	31,109	23,363	2,964	2,831	133	51,508	28,278	23,230	195	188	7
20 and over .	310,407	165,817	144,590	12,809	12,286	523	297,598	153,531	144,067	627	591	36
BIKANER .	*700,983*	*371,489*	*329,494*	*20,568*	*19,760*	*808*	*680,415*	*351,729*	*328,686*	*881*	*865*	*16*
0—9 . .	181,636	93,614	88,022	170	156	14	181,466	93,458	88,008	3	2	1
10—14 . .	63,335	35,585	27,750	1,357	1,312	45	61,978	34,273	27,705	65	64	1
15—19 . .	64,973	37,524	27,449	2,426	2,332	94	62,547	35,192	27,355	178	178	..
20 and over .	391,039	204,766	186,273	16,615	15,960	655	374,424	188,806	185,618	635	621	14
BUNDI . .	*218,730*	*113,211*	*105,519*	*5,130*	*4,982*	*148*	*213,600*	*208,239*	*105,371*	*94*	*93*	*1*
0—9 . .	63,762	31,988	31,774	29	28	1	63,733	31,960	31,773	..	..	..
10—14 . .	13,380	7,733	5,647	194	183	11	13,186	7,550	5,636	6	6	..
15—19 . .	14,963	8,306	6,660	393	380	13	14,570	7,923	6,647	23	22	1
20 and over .	126,625	65,187	61,438	4,514	4,391	123	122,111	60,796	61,315	65	65	..
DHOLPUR .	*263,188*	*144,244*	*118,944*	*5,463*	*5,183*	*280*	*257,725*	*139,061*	*118,664*	*418*	*403*	*15*
0—9 . .	63,635	33,430	30,225	103	94	9	63,552	33,336	30,216	3	3	..
10—14 . .	29,990	17,694	12,296	558	522	36	29,432	17,172	12,260	22	20	2
15—19 . .	25,037	14,322	10,715	664	613	51	24,373	13,709	10,664	78	75	3
20 and over .	144,506	78,798	65,708	4,138	3,954	184	140,368	74,844	65,524	305	295	10
DUNGARPUR .	*159,193*	*79,105*	*80,087*	*4,339*	*4,129*	*210*	*154,853*	*74,976*	*79,877*	*49*	*47*	*2*
0—9 . .	51,475	25,928	25,547	53	46	7	51,422	25,882	25,540	..	..	..
10—14 . .	10,886	5,806	5,080	245	228	17	10,691	5,578	5,013	2	2	..
15—19 . .	12,588	6,704	5,884	434	399	35	12,154	6,305	5,849	7	6	1
20 and over .	84,293	40,667	43,626	3,807	3,456	251	80,686	37,211	43,475	40	39	1
JAIPUR . .	*2,636,647*	*1,385,750*	*1,250,897*	*87,704*	*84,651*	*3,053*	*2,548,943*	*1,301,099*	*1,247,844*	*3,382*	*3,083*	*298*
0—9 . .	639,701	328,413	311,288	1,052	938	114	638,649	327,475	311,174	92	63	29
10—14 . .	253,865	146,688	107,177	5,689	5,463	226	248,176	141,225	106,951	310	276	34
15—19 . .	232,765	131,964	100,801	9,686	9,310	376	223,079	122,654	100,425	512	491	21
20 and over .	1,510,316	778,685	731,631	71,277	68,940	2,337	1,439,039	709,745	729,294	-2,467	2,258	214

TABLE VIII.—B.
ALL RELIGIONS.

Age, Province, and State or District.	POPULATION.									LITERATE IN ENGLISH.		
	TOTAL.			LITERATE.			ILLITERATE.					
	Persons.	Males.	Females.	Persons.	Males.	Females.	Persons.	Males.	Females.	Persons.	Males.	Females.
1	2	3	4	5	6	7	8	9	10	11	12	13
RAJPUTANA—contd.												
JAISALMER.	*88,311*	*48,500*	*39,811*	*2,825*	*2,727*	*98*	*85,486*	*45,773*	*39,713*	*42*	*41*	*1*
0—9	23,041	12,537	10,504	45	45	..	22,996	12,492	10,504	..	..	..
10—14	9,711	5,933	3,778	208	205	3	9,503	5,728	3,775	5	5	..
15—19	8,009	4,593	3,416	307	297	10	7,702	4,296	3,406	9	8	1
20 and over	47,550	25,437	22,113	2,265	2,180	85	45,285	23,257	22,028	28	28	..
JHALAWAR	*96,271*	*50,034*	*46,237*	*3,714*	*3,456*	*258*	*92,557*	*46,578*	*45,979*	*159*	*153*	*6*
0—9	24,887	12,551	12,336	42	35	7	24,845	12,516	12,329	..	..	..
10—14	6,400	3,663	2,737	258	233	25	6,142	3,430	2,712	2	2	..
15—19	7,637	4,188	3,449	409	378	31	7,228	3,810	3,418	20	20	..
20 and over	57,347	29,632	27,715	3,005	2,810	195	54,342	26,822	27,520	137	131	6
KARAULI.	*146,587*	*80,081*	*66,506*	*3,918*	*3,772*	*146*	*142,669*	*76,309*	*66,360*	*96*	*96*	..
0—9	36,030	19,027	17,003	65	59	6	35,965	18,968	16,997	..	..	..
10—14	15,761	9,220	6,541	219	203	16	15,542	9,017	6,525	8	8	..
15—19	13,337	7,734	5,603	375	357	18	12,962	7,377	5,585	12	12	..
20 and over	81,459	44,100	37,359	3,259	3,153	106	78,200	40,947	37,253	76	76	..
KISHANGARH	*87,191*	*45,718*	*41,473*	*3,965*	*3,766*	*199*	*83,226*	*41,952*	*41,274*	*141*	*132*	*9*
0—9	21,902	11,263	10,639	74	70	4	21,828	11,193	10,635	..	..	..
10—14	6,743	3,950	2,793	291	277	14	6,452	3,673	2,779	12	11	1
15—19	7,261	4,028	3,233	454	424	30	6,807	3,604	3,203	15	13	2
20 and over	51,285	26,477	24,808	3,146	2,995	151	48,139	23,482	24,657	114	108	6
KOTAH	*639,089*	*330,324*	*308,765*	*18,927*	*18,133*	*794*	*620,162*	*312,191*	*307,971*	*681*	*649*	*32*
0—9	175,283	87,615	87,668	211	183	28	175,072	87,432	87,640	4	2	2
10—14	45,293	25,756	19,537	1,184	1,120	64	44,109	24,636	19,473	33	31	2
15—19	48,294	25,908	22,386	1,934	1,828	106	46,360	24,080	22,280	77	74	3
20 and over	370,219	191,045	179,174	15,598	15,002	596	354,621	176,043	178,578	567	542	25
KUSHALGARH	*22,005*	*10,956*	*11,049*	*519*	*486*	*33*	*21,486*	*10,470*	*11,016*	*7*	*7*	..
0—9	7,600	3,816	3,784	23	23	..	7,577	3,793	3,784	..	..	..
10—14	1,812	929	883	58	55	3	1,754	874	880	..	..	..
15—19	1,633	918	715	54	51	3	1,579	867	712	..	..	..
20 and over	10,960	5,293	5,667	384	357	27	10,576	4,936	5,640	7	7	..
LAWA	*2,564*	*1,302*	*1,262*	*104*	*90*	*14*	*2,460*	*1,212*	*1,248*	*1*	*1*	..
0—9	641	295	346	1	..	1	640	295	345	..	..	..
10—14	205	124	81	2	2	..	203	122	81	..	..	..
15—19	222	115	107	7	6	1	215	109	106	..	..	..
20 and over	1,496	768	728	94	82	12	1,402	686	716	1	1	..
MARWAR	*2,057,553*	*1,075,269*	*982,284*	*78,172*	*75,374*	*2,798*	*1,979,381*	*999,895*	*979,486*	*2,384*	*2,286*	*98*
0—9	550,683	284,890	265,793	1,200	1,102	98	549,483	283,788	265,695	28	18	10
10—14	187,408	105,567	81,841	5,696	5,522	174	181,712	100,045	81,667	138	132	6
15—19	176,669	99,517	77,152	8,565	8,278	287	168,104	91,239	76,865	356	343	13
20 and over	1,142,793	585,295	557,498	62,711	60,472	2,239	1,080,082	524,823	555,259	1,862	1,793	69

TABLE VIII.—B. **TABLE VIII.—EDUCATION. PART B—BY STATES OR DISTRICTS.**
ALL RELIGIONS. ALL RELIGIONS—*continued.*

Age, Province, and State or District.	POPULATION.									LITERATE IN ENGLISH.		
	TOTAL.			LITERATE.			ILLITERATE.					
	Persons.	Males.	Females.	Persons.	Males.	Females.	Persons.	Males.	Females.	Persons.	Males.	Females.
1	2	3	4	5	6	7	8	9	10	11	12	13
RAJPUTANA—concld.												
MEWAR	**1,293,776**	**670,750**	**693,026**	**41,197**	**39,999**	**1,198**	**1,252,579**	**630,751**	**621,828**	**653**	**620**	**33**
0—9	383,973	197,204	188,769	317	291	26	385,656	196,913	188,743	1	..	1
10—14	77,945	45,471	32,474	1,778	1,706	72	76,167	43,765	32,402	24	20	4
15—19	99,996	56,650	43,346	3,866	3,728	138	96,130	52,922	43,208	81	77	4
20 and over	729,862	371,425	358,437	35,236	34,274	962	694,626	337,151	357,475	547	623	24
PARTABGARH	**62.704**	**31.733**	**30.969**	**2,882**	**2,761**	**121**	**59,822**	**28,974**	**30,848**	**64**	**64**	..
0—9	18,688	9,513	9,175	27	23	4	18,661	9,490	9,171	..	..	..
10—14	4,198	2,372	1,826	177	171	6	4,021	2,201	1,820	2	2	..
15—19	4,748	2,499	2,249	304	288	16	4,444	2,211	2,233	11	11	..
20 and over	35,070	17,351	17,719	2,374	2,279	95	32,696	15,072	17,024	51	51	..
SHAHPURA	**47.397**	**24,505**	**22,809**	**2,258**	**2,181**	**77**	**45,139**	**22,414**	**22,725**	**76**	**75**	**1**
0—9	13,414	6,756	6,658	23	20	3	13,391	6,736	6,655	..	..	..
10—14	2,721	1,505	1,126	116	108	8	2,605	1,487	1,118	9	9	..
15—19	3,469	1,962	1,507	227	221	6	3,242	1,741	1,501	12	11	1
20 and over	27,793	14,282	13,511	1,892	1,832	60	25,901	12,450	13,451	55	55	..
SIROHI	**189.127**	**98,289**	**90.838**	**9,826**	**9,185**	**641**	**179,301**	**89,104**	**90,197**	**1,108**	**894**	**214**
0—9	56,896	29,251	27,645	352	296	56	56,544	28,955	27,589	81	54	27
10—14	15,921	9,464	6,457	928	857	71	14,993	8,607	6,386	121	93	28
15—19	14,820	8,335	6,485	1,036	960	76	13,784	7,375	6,409	109	85	24
20 and over	101,490	51,239	50,251	7,510	7,072	438	93,980	44,167	49,813	797	662	135
TONK	**303,181**	**156,390**	**146,791**	**6,152**	**6,022**	**130**	**297,029**	**150,368**	**146,661**	**181**	**167**	**14**
0—9	84,488	42,475	42,013	35	26	9	84,453	42,449	42,004	2	..	2
10—14	22,017	12,723	9,294	248	237	11	21,769	12,486	9,283	7	7	..
15—19	22,984	12,416	10,568	557	540	17	22,427	11,876	10,551	30	28	2
20 and over	173,692	88,776	84,916	5,312	5,219	93	168,380	83,557	84,823	142	132	10
AJMER-MERWARA.												
AJMER	**380,384**	**201,911**	**178,473**	**30,012**	**27,199**	**2,813**	**350,372**	**174,712**	**175,660**	**6,530**	**5,825**	**705**
0—9	95,688	49,031	46,657	676	484	192	95,012	48,547	46,465	133	74	59
10—14	29,784	17,189	12,595	2,305	2,063	332	27,389	15,126	12,263	410	353	57
15—19	32,129	17,707	14,422	3,592	2,972	620	28,537	14,735	13,802	902	788	114
20 and over	222,783	117,984	104,709	23,340	21,680	1,669	199,434	96,304	103,130	5,085	4,610	475
MERWARA	**121,011**	**64.287**	**56,724**	**6,197**	**5.838**	**359**	**114,814**	**58,449**	**56,365**	**351**	**339**	**12**
0—9	34,652	17,921	16,731	72	54	18	34,580	17,867	16,713	1	1	..
10—14	7,905	4,582	3,323	398	371	27	7,507	4,211	3,296	6	6	..
15—19	9,234	5,258	3,976	746	693	53	8,488	4,565	3,923	54	54	..
20 and over	69,220	36,526	32,694	4,981	4,720	261	64,239	31,806	32,433	290	278	12

TABLE VIII.—PART C.

EDUCATION.

STATES OR DISTRICTS.

ANIMISTS.

TABLE VIII.—C.
ANIMISTS.

TABLE VIII.—EDUCATION. PART C.—BY

Age, Province, and State or District.	POPULATION.									LITERATE IN ENGLISH.		
	TOTAL.			LITERATE.			ILLITERATE.					
	Persons.	Males.	Females.	Persons.	Males.	Females.	Persons.	Males.	Females.	Persons.	Males.	Females.
1	2	3	4	5	6	7	8	9	10	11	12	13
RAJPUTANA.												
ALWAR	*31*	*17*	*14*	*1*	*1*	..	*30*	*16*	*14*	..	..	..
0—9	14	6	8	..	..	..	14	6	8	..	..	..
10—14	4	4	..	..	..	..	4	4	..	..	..	..
15—19	1	1	..	..	..	..	1	1	..	..	..	..
20 and over	12	6	6	1	1	..	11	5	6	..	..	..
BANSWARA	*95,834*	*47,323*	*48,511*	*7*	*7*	..	*95,827*	*47,316*	*48,511*	..	..	..
0—9	36,407	18,211	18,196	..	..	..	36,407	18,211	18,196	..	..	..
10—14	6,629	3,470	3,159	..	..	..	6,629	3,470	3,159	..	..	..
15—19	7,144	3,720	3,424	..	..	..	7,144	3,720	3,424	..	..	..
20 and over	45,654	21,922	23,732	7	7	..	45,647	21,915	23,732	..	..	..
BUNDI	*4,532*	*2,275*	*2,257*	..	..	..	*4,532*	*2,275*	*2,257*	..	..	..
0—9	1,794	898	896	..	..	..	1,794	898	896	..	..	..
10—14	172	98	74	..	..	..	172	98	74	..	..	..
15—19	235	104	131	..	..	..	235	104	131	..	..	..
20 and over	2,331	1,175	1,156	..	..	..	2,331	1,175	1,156	..	..	..
DUNGARPUR	*74,281*	*37,523*	*36,758*	*11*	*11*	..	*74,270*	*37,512*	*36,758*	..	..	..
0—9	27,908	14,040	13,868	..	..	..	27,908	14,040	13,868	..	..	..
10—14	4,601	2,459	2,142	..	..	..	4,601	2,459	2,142	..	..	..
15—19	5,363	2,824	2,539	..	..	..	5,363	2,824	2,539	..	..	..
20 and over	36,409	18,200	18,209	11	11	..	36,398	18,189	18,209	..	..	..
JAIPUR	*1,779*	*955*	*824*	..	..	..	*1,779*	*955*	*824*	..	..	..
0—9	531	263	268	..	..	..	531	263	268	..	..	..
10—14	122	73	49	..	..	..	122	73	49	..	..	..
15—19	149	82	67	..	..	..	149	82	67	..	..	..
20 and over	977	537	440	..	..	..	977	537	440	..	..	..
JAISALMER	*4,158*	*2,246*	*1,912*	..	..	..	*4,158*	*2,246*	*1,912*	..	..	..
0—9	1,342	706	636	..	..	..	1,342	706	636	..	..	..
10—14	503	320	183	..	..	..	503	320	183	..	..	..
15—19	339	186	153	..	..	..	339	186	153	..	..	..
20 and over	1,974	1,034	940	..	..	..	1,974	1,034	940	..	..	..

ANIMISTS.

Age, Province, and State or District.	POPULATION.									LITERATE IN ENGLISH.		
	TOTAL.			LITERATE.			ILLITERATE.					
	Persons.	Males.	Females.	Persons.	Males.	Females.	Persons.	Males.	Females.	Persons.	Males.	Females.
1	2	3	4	5	6	7	8	9	10	11	12	13
RAJPUTANA— *contd.*												
JHALAWAR .	*430*	*238*	*192*	..	..	..	*430*	*238*	*192*	..	..	..
0—9 . .	134	74	60	..	..	..	134	74	60	..	..	..
10—14 . .	37	25	12	..	..	..	37	25	12	..	..	..
15—19 . .	29	14	15	..	..	..	29	14	15	..	..	..
20 and over .	220	115	105	..	..	..	220	115	105	..	..	..
KARAULI .	*8*	*6*	*2*	..	..	..	*8*	*6*	*2*	..	..	..
0—9 . .	2	1	1	..	..	..	2	1	1	..	..	..
10—14 . .	1	1	..	..	..	..	1	1	..	..	..	..
15—19 . .	1	1	..	..	..	..	1	1	..	..	..	..
20 and over .	4	3	1	..	..	..	4	3	1	..	..	..
KISHANGARH .	*535*	*263*	*272*	..	..	..	*535*	*263*	*272*	..	..	..
0—9 . .	181	84	97	..	..	..	181	84	97	..	..	..
10—14 . .	30	15	15	..	..	..	30	15	15	..	..	..
15—19 . .	38	19	19	..	..	..	38	19	19	..	..	..
20 and over .	286	145	141	..	..	..	286	145	141	..	..	..
KOTAH . .	*3,075*	*1,558*	*1,517*	..	..	..	*3,075*	*1,558*	*1,517*	..	..	..
0—9 . .	1,071	551	520	..	..	..	1,071	551	520	..	..	..
10—14 . .	191	106	85	..	..	..	191	106	85	..	..	..
15—19 . .	200	86	114	..	..	..	200	86	114	..	..	..
20 and over .	1,613	815	798	..	..	..	1,613	815	798	..	..	..
KUSHALGARH .	*17,100*	*8,488*	*8,612*	..	..	..	*17,100*	*8,488*	*8,612*	..	..	..
0—9 . .	6,229	3,115	3,114	..	..	..	6,229	3,115	3,114	..	..	..
10—14 . .	1,401	709	692	..	..	..	1,401	709	692	..	..	..
15—19 . .	1,230	689	541	..	..	..	1,230	689	541	..	..	..
20 and over .	8,240	3,975	4,265	..	..	..	8,240	3,975	4,265	..	..	..
MARWAR .	*48,957*	*26,254*	*22,703*	..	..	..	*48,957*	*26,254*	*22,703*	..	..	..
0—9 . .	15,625	8,072	7,553	..	..	..	15,625	8,072	7,553	..	..	..
10—14 . .	4,623	2,771	1,852	..	..	..	4,623	2,771	1,852	..	..	..
15—19 . .	3,984	2,303	1,681	..	..	..	3,984	2,303	1,681	..	..	..
20 and over .	24,725	13,108	11,617	..	..	..	24,725	13,108	11,617	..	..	..

TABLE VIII.—C.
ANIMISTS.

TABLE VIII.—EDUCATION. PART C.—BY STATES OR DISTRICTS.
MAIN RELIGIONS—*continued.*

Age, Province, and State or District.	POPULATION.									LITERATE IN ENGLISH.		
	TOTAL.			LITERATE.			ILLITERATE.					
	Persons.	Males.	Females.	Persons.	Males.	Females.	Persons.	Males.	Females.	Persons.	Males.	Females.
1	2	3	4	5	6	7	8	9	10	11	12	13
RAJPUTANA—*concld.*												
MEWAR	*159,094*	*81,794*	*77,300*	*52*	*52*	..	*159,042*	*81,742*	*77,300*	..	..	..
0—9	57,482	29,182	28,300	..	..	..	57,482	29,182	28,300	..	..	..
10—14	8,580	5,025	3,555	..	..	..	8,580	5,025	3,555	..	..	..
15—19	10,010	5,412	4,598	..	..	..	10,010	5,412	4,598	..	..	..
20 and over	83,022	42,175	40,847	52	52	..	82,970	42,123	40,847	..	..	..
PARTABGARH	*20,929*	*10,530*	*10,399*	*1*	*1*	..	*20,928*	*10,529*	*10,399*	..	..	..
0—9	7,427	3,757	3,670	..	..	..	7,427	3,757	3,670	..	..	..
10—14	1,300	733	567	..	..	..	1,300	733	567	..	..	..
15—19	1,341	733	608	..	..	..	1,341	733	608	..	..	..
20 and over	10,861	5,307	5,554	1	1	..	10,860	5,306	5,554	..	..	..
SHAHPURA	*1,952*	*989*	*963*	..	..	..	*1,952*	*989*	*963*	..	..	..
0—9	713	360	358	..	..	..	713	360	353	..	..	..
10—14	101	59	42	..	..	..	101	59	42	..	..	..
15—19	118	56	62	..	..	..	118	56	62	..	..	..
20 and over	1,020	514	506	..	..	..	1,020	514	506	..	..	..
SIROHI	*4,431*	*2,308*	*2,123*	*2*	*2*	..	*4,429*	*2,306*	*2,123*	..	..	..
0—9	1,474	753	721	1	1	..	1,473	752	721	..	..	..
10—14	368	219	149	..	..	..	368	219	149	..	..	..
15—19	364	205	169	..	..	..	364	205	159	..	..	..
20 and over	2,225	1,131	1,094	1	1	..	2,224	1,130	1,094	..	..	..
TONK	*7,586*	*3,751*	*3,835*	..	..	..	*7,586*	*3,751*	*3,835*	..	..	..
0—9	2,554	1,256	1,298	..	..	..	2,554	1,256	1,298	..	..	..
10—14	391	215	176	..	..	..	391	215	176	..	..	..
15—19	441	226	215	..	..	..	441	226	215	..	..	..
20 and over	4,200	2,054	2,146	..	..	..	4,200	2,054	2,146	..	..	..
AJMER-MERWARA.												
AJMER	*2,678*	*1,308*	*1,370*	*3*	*3*	..	*2,675*	*1,305*	*1,370*	..	..	..
0—9	849	385	464	..	..	..	849	385	464	..	..	..
10—14	154	92	62	..	..	..	154	92	62	..	..	..
15—19	197	83	114	..	..	..	197	83	114	..	..	..
20 and over	1,478	748	730	3	3	..	1,475	745	730	..	..	..
MERWARA	*1,301*	*679*	*622*	*1*	*1*	..	*1,300*	*678*	*622*	..	..	..
0—9	402	211	191	..	..	..	402	211	191	..	..	..
10—14	71	41	30	..	..	..	71	41	30	..	..	..
15—19	102	58	44	..	..	..	102	58	44	..	..	..
20 and over	726	369	357	1	1	..	725	368	357	..	..	..

N.B.—Bharatpur, Bikaner, Dholpur, and Lawa, which contain no Animists, have not been shown.

TABLE VIII.—PART C.

EDUCATION.

STATES OR DISTRICTS

CHRISTIANS.

TABLE VIII.—C.
CHRISTIANS.

TABLE VIII.— EDUCATION PART C.—

Age, Province, and State or District.	POPULATION.									LITERATE IN ENGLISH.		
	TOTAL.			LITERATE.			ILLITERATE.					
	Persons.	Males.	Females.	Persons.	Males.	Females.	Persons.	Males.	Females.	Persons.	Males.	Females.
1	2	3	4	5	6	7	8	9	10	11	12	13
RAJPUTANA—												
ALWAR . .	*93*	*50*	*43*	*72*	*44*	*28*	*20*	*6*	*14*	*64*	*39*	*25*
0—9 .	18	7	11	1	1	..	17	6	11	..	..	..
10—14 . .	9	4	5	9	4	5	..	..	..	9	4	5
15—19 . .	5	2	3	4	2	2	1	..	1	2	..	2
20 and over .	60	37	23	58	37	21	2	..	2	53	35	18
BHARATPUR .	*566*	*315*	*251*	*97*	*52*	*45*	*469*	*263*	*206*	*68*	*34*	*34*
0—9 . .	153	89	64	8	5	3	145	84	61	3	2	1
10—14 . .	42	27	15	1	1	..	41	26	15	1	1	..
15—19 . .	54	30	24	7	2	5	47	28	19	6	1	5
20 and over .	317	169	148	81	44	37	236	125	111	58	30	28
BIKANER .	*151*	*97*	*54*	*53*	*39*	*14*	*98*	*58*	*40*	*30*	*20*	*10*
0—9 . .	33	18	15	..	..	..	33	18	15	..	..	..
10—14 . .	7	5	2	1	1	..	6	4	2	1	1	..
15—19 . .	11	10	1	..	..	..	11	10	1	..	..	..
20 and over .	100	64	36	52	38	14	48	26	22	29	19	10
DHOLPUR .	*41*	*26*	*15*	*23*	*13*	*10*	*18*	*13*	*5*	*20*	*12*	*8*
0—9 . .	8	6	2	..	..	..	8	6	2	..	..	..
10—14 . .	3	3	..	2	2	..	1	1	..	2	2	..
15—19 . .	3	1	2	2	1	1	1	..	1	2	1	1
20 and over .	27	16	11	19	10	9	8	6	2	16	9	7
DUNGARPUR .	*2*	*1*	*1*	*2*	*1*	*1*	..	..	..	*2*	*1*	*1*
0—9 . .	..	..	..	..	..	..	..	..	..	..	..	..
10—14 . .	..	..	..	..	..	..	..	..	..	..	..	..
15—19 . .	1	..	1	1	..	1	..	..	..	1	..	1
20 and over .	1	1	..	1	1	..	..	..	..	1	1	..
JAIPUR .	*1,326*	*689*	*637*	*884*	*479*	*405*	*442*	*210*	*232*	*581*	*334*	*247*
0—9 . .	323	169	154	80	50	30	243	119	124	67	40	27
10—14 . .	149	100	49	129	90	39	20	10	10	54	26	28
15—19 . .	142	48	94	113	34	79	29	14	15	28	12	16
20 and over .	712	372	340	562	305	257	150	67	83	432	256	176

Age, Province, and State or District.	POPULATION.									LITERATE IN ENGLISH.		
	TOTAL.			LITERATE.			ILLITERATE.					
	Persons.	Males.	Females.	Persons.	Males.	Females.	Persons.	Males.	Females.	Persons.	Males.	Females.
1	2	3	4	5	6	7	8	9	10	11	12	13
RAJPUTANA—*contd.*												
JHALAWAR	*26*	*18*	*8*	*15*	*10*	*5*	*11*	*8*	*3*	*14*	*9*	*5*
0—9	2	2	..	..	..	..	2	2	..	..	..	..
10—14	..	..	..	..	..	..	..	..	..	..	..	..
15—19	3	1	2	..	..	..	3	1	2	..	..	..
20 and over	21	15	6	15	10	5	6	5	1	14	9	5
KARAULI	*28*	*15*	*13*	*13*	*10*	*3*	*15*	*5*	*10*	*6*	*6*	..
0—9	4	2	2	..	..	..	4	2	2	..	..	..
10—14	5	2	3	1	..	1	4	2	2	..	..	..
15—19	3	1	2	1	..	1	2	1	1	..	..	..
20 and over	16	10	6	11	10	1	5	..	5	6	6	..
KISHANGARH	*23*	*8*	*15*	*19*	*8*	*11*	*4*	..	*4*	*13*	*6*	*7*
0—9	4	..	4	1	..	1	3	..	3	..	..	..
10—14	1	..	1	1	..	1	..	..	..	1	..	1
15—19	4	3	1	4	3	1	..	..	..	3	2	1
20 and over	14	5	9	13	5	8	1	..	1	9	4	5
KOTAH	*507*	*274*	*233*	*306*	*182*	*124*	*201*	*92*	*109*	*61*	*38*	*23*
0—9	142	53	89	2	..	2	140	53	87	1	..	1
10—14	21	18	3	17	15	2	4	3	1	3	1	2
15—19	62	46	16	50	37	13	12	9	3	5	4	1
20 and over	282	157	125	237	130	107	45	27	18	52	33	19
MARWAR	*440*	*235*	*205*	*250*	*151*	*99*	*190*	*84*	*106*	*187*	*107*	*80*
0—9	108	46	62	17	6	11	91	40	51	14	5	9
10—14	19	15	4	8	5	3	11	10	1	4	2	2
15—19	42	18	24	27	14	13	15	4	11	17	7	10
20 and over	271	156	115	198	126	72	73	30	43	152	93	59
MEWAR	*237*	*152*	*85*	*138*	*98*	*40*	*99*	*54*	*45*	*63*	*40*	*23*
0—9	49	26	23	3	2	1	46	24	22	1	..	1
10—14	21	18	3	14	13	1	7	5	2	1	..	1
15—19	38	28	10	31	24	7	7	4	3	7	4	3
20 and over	129	80	49	90	59	31	39	21	18	54	36	18

TABLE VIII.—C.
CHRISTIANS.

TABLE VIII.—Education. Part C.—By States or Districts—Main Religions—*continued.*

Age, Province, and State or District.	POPULATION.									Literate in English.		
	Total.			Literate.			Illiterate.					
	Persons.	Males.	Females.	Persons.	Males.	Females.	Persons.	Males.	Females.	Persons.	Males.	Females.
1	2	3	4	5	6	7	8	9	10	11	12	13
RAJPUTANA—*concld.*												
SHAHPURA	*1*	*1*	..	*1*	*1*	..	..	..	..	*1*	*1*	..
0—9	..	..	..	..	..	..	..	..	..	..	..	..
10—14	..	..	..	..	..	..	..	..	..	..	..	..
15—19	..	..	..	..	..	..	..	..	..	..	..	..
20 and over	1	1	..	1	1	..	..	..	..	1	1	..
SIROHI	*804*	*522*	*282*	*623*	*414*	*209*	*181*	*108*	*73*	*594*	*394*	*200*
0—9	198	122	76	82	64	28	116	68	48	81	54	27
10—14	106	78	28	97	73	24	9	5	4	95	71	24
15—19	61	38	23	55	34	21	6	4	2	54	33	21
20 and over	439	284	155	380	252	136	50	31	19	364	236	128
TONK	*12*	*6*	*6*	*8*	*4*	*4*	*4*	*2*	*2*	*8*	*4*	*4*
0—9	1	..	1	1	..	1	..	..	..	1	..	1
10—14	1	..	1	..	..	..	1	..	1	..	..	..
15—19	2	..	2	1	..	1	1	..	1	1	..	1
20 and over	8	6	2	6	4	2	2	2	..	6	4	2
AJMER-MERWARA.												
AJMER	*4,910*	*2,996*	*1,914*	*3,651*	*2,355*	*1,296*	*1,259*	*641*	*618*	*2,577*	*1,954*	*623*
0—9	880	423	457	197	79	118	683	344	339	103	49	54
10—14	388	194	194	291	130	161	97	64	33	118	74	44
15—19	679	270	409	583	207	376	96	63	33	237	140	97
20 and over	2,963	2,109	854	2,580	1,939	641	383	170	213	2,119	1,691	428
MERWARA	*522*	*262*	*260*	*330*	*189*	*131*	*202*	*73*	*129*	*57*	*48*	*9*
0—9	109	46	63	14	5	9	95	41	54	1	1	..
10—14	42	39	3	36	34	2	6	5	1	2	2	..
15—19	83	58	25	76	54	22	7	4	3	13	13	..
20 and over	288	119	169	194	96	98	94	23	71	41	32	9

N.B.—Banswara, Bundi, Jaisalmer, Kushalgarh, Lawa, and Partabgarh, which contain no Christians, have not been shewn.

TABLE VIII.—PART C.

EDUCATION.

STATES OR DISTRICTS.

HINDUS.

TABLE VIII.—C.
HINDUS.

TABLE VIII.—Education. Part C.—By

Age, Province, and State or District.	Population.									Literate in English.		
	Total.			Literate.			Illiterate.					
	Persons.	Males.	Females.	Persons.	Males.	Females.	Persons.	Males.	Females.	Persons.	Males.	Females.
1	2	3	4	5	6	7	8	9	10	11	12	13
RAJPUTANA—												
ALWAR . .	*588,230*	*307,425*	*280,805*	*18,181*	*17,756*	*425*	*570,049*	*289,669*	*280,380*	*716*	*710*	*6*
0—9 . .	147,659	74,844	72,815	265	247	18	147,394	74,597	72,797	1	..	1
10—14 . .	66.214	37.126	29,088	1,240	1,203	37	64,974	35,923	29,051	16	15	1
15—19 . .	56,929	31.638	25,291	1,852	1,802	50	55,077	29,836	25,241	68	67	1
20 and over .	317,428	163,817	153,611	14,824	14,504	320	302,604	149,313	153,291	631	628	3
BANSWARA .	*60,339*	*29,611*	*30,728*	*2,128*	*1,961*	*167*	*58,211*	*27,650*	*30,561*	*38*	*36*	*2*
0—9 . .	17,614	8,841	8,773	17	16	1	17,597	8,825	8,772	..	..	..
10—14 . .	4,533	2,511	2,022	125	120	5	4,408	2,391	2,017	2	2	..
15—19 . .	5,090	2,702	2,388	221	205	16	4,869	2,497	2,372	1	1	..
20 and over .	33,102	15,557	17,545	1,765	1,620	145	31,337	13,937	17,400	35	33	2
BHARATPUR .	*452,730*	*245,735*	*206,995*	*14,679*	*14,185*	*494*	*438,051*	*231,550*	*206,501*	*563*	*556*	*7*
0—9 . .	103,101	53.870	49,231	193	173	20	102,908	53,697	49,211	4	4	..
10—14 . .	52,359	30,822	21,537	1,710	1,640	70	50,649	29,182	21,467	70	69	1
15—19 . .	43,657	25,062	18,595	2,487	2,413	74	41,170	22,649	18,521	128	128	..
20 and over .	253,613	135,981	117,632	10,289	9,959	330	243,324	126,022	117,302	361	355	6
BIKANER .	*575,699*	*306,659*	*269,040*	*14,957*	*14,455*	*502*	*560,742*	*292,204*	*268,538*	*618*	*613*	*5*
0—9 . .	146,399	75,439	70,960	108	101	7	146,291	75,338	70,953	3	2	1
10—14 . .	50,130	28,424	21,706	954	919	35	49,176	27,505	21,671	47	46	1
15—19 . .	53,405	31,322	22,083	1,756	1,088	68	51,649	29,634	22,015	128	128	..
20 and over .	323,765	171,474	154,291	12,130	11,747	392	313,620	159,727	153,899	440	437	3
BUNDI . .	*196,919*	*102,040*	*94,879*	*3,578*	*3,461*	*117*	*193,341*	*98,579*	*94,762*	*75*	*74*	*1*
0—9 . .	57,566	28,950	28,616	18	18	..	57,548	28,932	28,616	..	..	..
10—14 . .	12,068	6,995	5,073	139	130	9	11,929	6,865	5,064	5	5	..
15—19 . .	13,499	7,519	5,980	271	260	11	13,228	7,259	5,969	21	20	1
20 and over .	113,786	58,576	55,210	3,150	3,053	97	110,636	55,523	55.113	49	40	..
DHOLPUR .	*242,734*	*133,416*	*109,318*	*4,585*	*4,398*	*187*	*238,149*	*129,018*	*109,131*	*302*	*297*	*5*
0—9 . .	58,763	30,894	27,869	91	86	5	58,672	30,808	27,864	3	3	..
10—14 . .	27,696	16,378	11,318	478	451	27	27,218	15,927	11,291	25	24	1
15—19 . .	23,154	13,292	9.862	545	519	26	22.609	12,773	9,836	59	58	1
20 and over .	133,121	72,852	60.269	3,471	3,342	129	129,650	69,510	60,140	215	212	3
DUNGARPUR .	*72,681*	*35,549*	*37.132*	*1,792*	*1,696*	*96*	*70,889*	*33,853*	*37,036*	*28*	*27*	*1*
0—9 . .	20,489	10,332	10,157	23	18	5	20,466	10,314	10,152	..	..	..
10—14 . .	5,237	2,809	2,428	95	89	6	5,142	2,720	2,422	..	..	..
15—19 . .	6,234	3,387	2,847	195	182	13	6,039	3,205	2,834	5	5	..
20 and over .	40,721	19,021	21,700	1,479	1,407	72	39,242	17,614	21,628	23	22	1
JAIPUR . .	*2,398,880*	*1,262,280*	*1,136,600*	*71,166*	*69.020*	*2,146*	*2,327,714*	*1,193,260*	*1,134,454*	*1,992*	*1,947*	*45*
0—9 . .	580,711	298,532	282,179	761	695	66	579,950	297,837	282,113	19	17	2
10—14 . .	230,976	133,755	97,221	4,516	4,374	142	226,460	129,381	97,079	161	155	6
15—19 .	212.460	120,836	91,624	7,964	7,724	240	204,496	113,112	91,384	345	340	5
20 and over .	1,374,733	709,157	665,576	57,925	56,227	1,698	1,316,808	652,930	663,878	1,467	1,435	32

Age, Province, and State or District.	POPULATION.									LITERATE IN ENGLISH.		
	TOTAL.			LITERATE.			ILLITERATE.					
	Persons.	Males.	Females.	Persons.	Males.	Females.	Persons.	Males.	Females.	Persons.	Males.	Females.
1	2	3	4	5	6	7	8	9	10	11	12	13
RAJPUTANA—*contd.*												
JAISALMER .	*60,951*	*33,198*	*27,753*	*2,491*	*2,408*	*83*	*58,460*	*30,790*	*27,670*	*41*	*40*	*1*
0—9 . .	15,358	8,302	7,056	44	44	..	15,314	8,258	7,056	..	..	..
10—14 . .	6,727	4,102	2,625	192	189	3	6,535	3,913	2,622	5	5	..
15—19 . .	5,742	3,297	2,445	277	267	10	5,465	3,030	2,435	8	7	1
20 and over .	33,124	17,497	15,627	1,978	1,908	70	31,146	15,589	15,557	28	28	..
JHALAWAR .	*84,585*	*44,137*	*40,448*	*2,440*	*2,269*	*171*	*82,145*	*41,868*	*40,277*	*94*	*93*	*1*
0—9 . .	21,969	11,065	10,904	31	26	5	21,938	11,039	10,899	..	..	..
10—14 . .	5,509	3,156	2,353	168	150	18	5,341	3,006	2,335	2	2	..
15—19 . .	6,699	3,709	2,990	259	244	15	6,440	3,465	2,975	14	14	..
20 and over .	50,408	26,207	24,201	1,982	1,849	133	48,426	24,358	24,068	78	77	1
KARAULI .	*137,989*	*75,485*	*62,504*	*3,440*	*3,303*	*137*	*134,549*	*72,182*	*62,367*	*76*	*76*	..
0—9 . .	34,026	18,034	15,992	43	37	6	33,983	17,997	15,986	..	..	..
10—14 . .	14,934	8,763	6,171	176	162	14	14,758	8,601	6,157	6	6	..
15—19 . .	12,570	7,276	5,294	324	307	17	12,246	6,969	5,277	10	10	..
20 and over .	78,459	41,412	35,047	2,897	2,797	100	73,562	38,615	34,947	60	60	..
KISHANGARH	*76,643*	*40,172*	*36,471*	*2,577*	*2,456*	*121*	*74,065*	*37,715*	*36,350*	*86*	*84*	*2*
0—9 . .	19,421	9,980	9,441	40	38	2	19,381	9,942	9,439	..	..	..
10—14 . .	5,920	3,475	2,445	179	171	8	5,741	3,304	2,437	4	4	..
15—19 . .	6,313	3,495	2,818	283	265	18	6,030	3,230	2,800	9	8	1
20 and over .	44,988	23,221	21,767	2,075	1,982	93	42,913	21,239	21,674	73	72	1
KOTAH . .	*584,137*	*301,657*	*282,480*	*14,690*	*14,214*	*476*	*569,447*	*287,443*	*282,004*	*467*	*461*	*6*
0—9 . .	161,077	80,442	80,635	160	142	18	160,917	80,300	80,617	2	1	1
10—14 . .	41,123	23,366	17,757	925	884	41	40,198	22,482	17,716	23	23	..
15—19 . .	43,852	23,579	20,273	1,497	1,423	74	42,355	22,156	20,199	54	52	2
20 and over .	338,085	174,270	163,815	12,108	11,765	343	325,977	162,505	163,472	388	385	3
KUSHALGARH .	*3,694*	*1,848*	*1,846*	*267*	*251*	*16*	*3,427*	*1,597*	*1,830*	*6*	*6*	..
0—9 . .	1,034	526	508	17	17	..	1,017	509	508	..	..	..
10—14 . .	299	161	138	30	30	..	269	131	138	..	..	..
15—19 . .	294	167	127	22	22	..	272	145	127	..	..	..
20 and over .	2,067	994	1,073	198	182	16	1,869	812	1,057	6	6	..
LAWA . .	*2,282*	*1,143*	*1,139*	*64*	*52*	*12*	*2,218*	*1,091*	*1,127*	*1*	*1*	..
0—9 . .	579	260	319	1	..	1	578	260	318	..	..	..
10—14 . .	180	108	72	..	..	..	180	108	72	..	..	..
15—19 . .	205	107	98	5	4	1	200	103	97	..	..	..
20 and over .	1,318	668	650	58	48	10	1,260	620	640	1	1	..
MARWAR .	*1,709,998*	*899,634*	*810,364*	*40,342*	*38,695*	*1,647*	*1,669,656*	*860,939*	*808,717*	*1,624*	*1,614*	*10*
0—9 . .	454,600	235,659	218,941	500	452	48	454,100	235,207	218,893	10	10	..
10—14 . .	153,553	87,326	66,227	2,529	2,428	101	151,024	84,898	66,126	94	93	1
15—19 . .	147,792	84,201	63,591	4,310	4,138	172	143,482	80,063	63,419	259	256	3
20 and over .	954,053	492,448	461,605	33,003	31,677	1,326	921,050	460,771	460,279	1,261	1,255	6

TABLE VIII.—Education. Part C.—By States or Districts. Main Religions—*continued*.

Age, Province, and State or District.	POPULATION.									Literate in English.		
	Total.			Literate.			Illiterate.					
	Persons.	Males.	Females.	Persons.	Males.	Females.	Persons.	Males.	Females.	Persons.	Males.	Females.
1	2	3	4	5	6	7	8	9	10	11	12	13
RAJPUTANA— *concld.*												
MEWAR	*1,031,906*	*539,936*	*491,970*	*31,937*	*31,226*	*711*	*999,969*	*508,710*	*491,259*	*423*	*419*	*4*
0—9	299,907	153,736	146,171	151	136	15	299,756	153,600	146,156	..	..	..
10—14	61,497	36,015	25,482	875	837	38	60,622	35,178	25,444	14	13	1
15—19	80,845	46,089	34,756	1,921	1,849	72	78,924	44,240	34,684	48	47	1
20 and over	579,657	294,096	285,561	18,990	18,404	586	560,667	275,692	284,975	361	359	2
PARTABGARH	*33,848*	*17,077*	*16,771*	*1,280*	*1,214*	*66*	*32,568*	*15,863*	*16,705*	*30*	*30*	..
0—9	9,368	4,804	4,564	9	7	2	9,359	4,797	4,562	..	..	..
10—14	2,230	1,281	949	73	68	5	2,157	1,213	944	1	1	..
15—19	2,731	1,432	1,299	132	123	9	2,599	1,309	1,290	5	5	..
20 and over	19,519	9,560	9,959	1,066	1,016	50	18,453	8,544	9,909	24	24	..
SHAHPURA	*41,249*	*21,381*	*19,868*	*1,547*	*1,499*	*48*	*39,702*	*19,882*	*19,820*	*27*	*27*	..
0—9	11,613	5,835	5,778	6	6	..	11,607	5,829	5,778	..	..	..
10—14	2,366	1,373	993	68	63	5	2,298	1,310	988	..	..	..
15—19	3,066	1,746	1,320	152	149	3	2,914	1,597	1,317	6	6	..
20 and over	24,204	12,427	11,777	1,321	1,281	40	22,883	11,146	11,737	21	21	..
SIROHI	*159,406*	*83,887*	*75,519*	*3,791*	*3,605*	*186*	*155,615*	*80,282*	*75,333*	*347*	*343*	*4*
0—9	48,786	25,201	23,585	109	97	12	48,677	25,104	23,573	..	..	..
10—14	13,196	8,039	5,157	286	265	21	12,910	7,774	5,136	15	15	..
15—19	12,452	7,159	5,293	429	402	27	12,023	6,757	5,266	43	41	2
20 and over	84,972	43,488	41,484	2,967	2,841	126	82,005	40,647	41,358	289	287	2
TONK	*247,146*	*127,901*	*119,245*	*2,740*	*2,705*	*35*	*244,406*	*125,196*	*119,210*	*70*	*70*	..
0—9	69,946	35,252	34,694	12	12	..	69,934	35,240	34,694	..	..	..
10—14	17,631	10,314	7,317	118	114	4	17,513	10,200	7,313	2	2	..
15—19	18,743	10,204	8,539	243	238	5	18,500	9,966	8,534	13	13	..
20 and over	140,826	72,131	68,695	2,367	2,341	26	138,459	69,790	68,669	55	55	..
AJMER-MERWARA—												
AJMER	*296,076*	*155,993*	*140,083*	*16,699*	*15,673*	*1,026*	*279,377*	*140,320*	*139,057*	*2,773*	*2,724*	*49*
0—9	75,217	38,564	36,653	288	236	52	74,929	38,328	36,601	24	20	4
10—14	22,226	12,836	9,390	1,336	1,222	114	20,890	11,614	9,276	201	193	8
15—19	24,572	13,587	10,985	1,937	1,783	154	22,635	11,804	10,831	464	456	8
20 and over	174,061	91,006	83,055	13,138	12,432	706	160,923	78,574	82,349	2,084	2,055	29
MERWARA	*92,476*	*48,863*	*43,613*	*3,106*	*2,979*	*127*	*89,370*	*45,884*	*43,486*	*210*	*208*	*2*
0—9	26,635	13,686	12,949	24	20	4	26,611	13,666	12,945	..	..	..
10—14	5,724	3,320	2,404	196	177	19	5,528	3,143	2,385	2	2	..
15—19	6,858	3,847	3,011	344	326	18	6,514	3,521	2,993	35	35	..
20 and over	53,259	28,010	25,249	2,542	2,456	86	50,717	25,554	25,163	173	171	2

TABLE VIII.—PART C.

EDUCATION.

STATES OR DISTRICTS.

JAINS.

TABLE VIII.—C.

JAINS.

TABLE VIII.—EDUCATION. PART C.—

Age, Province, and State or District.	POPULATION.									LITERATE IN ENGLISH.		
	TOTAL.			LITERATE.			ILLITERATE.					
	Persons.	Males.	Females.	Persons.	Males.	Females.	Persons.	Males.	Females.	Persons.	Males.	Females.
1	2	3	4	5	6	7	8	9	10	11	12	13
RAJPUTANA.												
ALWAR . .	*4,111*	*2,158*	*1,953*	*1,010*	*992*	*18*	*3,101*	*1,166*	*1,935*	*13*	*13*	..
0—9 . .	950	463	487	14	11	3	936	452	484	..	..	..
10—14 . .	416	221	195	57	56	1	359	165	194	1	1	..
15—19 . .	366	203	163	89	88	1	277	115	162	1	1	..
20 and over .	2,379	1,271	1,108	850	837	13	1,529	434	1,095	11	11	..
BANSWARA .	*4,396*	*2,196*	*2,200*	*1,421*	*1,401*	*20*	*2,975*	*795*	*2,180*	*2*	*2*	..
0—9 . .	971	492	479	10	9	1	961	483	478	..	..	..
10—14 . .	353	176	177	65	64	1	288	112	176	1	1	..
15—19 . .	407	195	212	154	152	2	253	43	210	..	..	..
20 and over .	2,665	1,333	1,332	1,192	1,176	16	1,473	157	1,316	2	2	..
BHARATPUR .	*2,720*	*1,474*	*1,246*	*884*	*846*	*38*	*1,836*	*628*	*1,208*	*43*	*42*	*1*
0—9 . .	531	271	260	11	11	..	520	260	260	..	..	..
10—14 . .	312	185	127	98	92	6	214	93	121	3	3	..
15—19 . .	289	146	143	111	99	12	178	47	131	8	7	1
20 and over .	1,588	872	716	664	644	20	924	228	696	32	32	..
BIKANER .	*24,858*	*10,255*	*14,603*	*4,111*	*3,876*	*235*	*20,747*	*6,379*	*14,368*	*107*	*107*	..
0—9 . .	7,026	3,580	3,446	51	46	5	6,975	3,534	3,441	..	..	..
10—14 . .	2,524	1,174	1,350	328	320	8	2,196	854	1,342	12	12	..
15—19 . .	2,071	741	1,330	497	483	14	1,574	258	1,316	24	24	..
20 and over .	13,237	4,760	8,477	3,235	3,027	208	10,002	1,733	8,269	71	71	..
BUNDI . .	*6,614*	*3,475*	*3,139*	*1,319*	*1,299*	*20*	*5,295*	*2,176*	*3,119*	*6*	*6*	..
0—9 . .	1,489	723	766	10	10	..	1,479	713	766	..	..	..
10—14 . .	395	234	161	46	46	..	349	188	161	..	..	..
15—19 . .	471	263	208	104	103	1	367	160	207	1	1	..
20 and over .	4,259	2,255	2,004	1,159	1.140	19	3,100	1,115	1,985	5	5	..
DHOLPUR .	*2,031*	*1,175*	*856*	*165*	*156*	*9*	*1,866*	*1,019*	*847*	*5*	*5*	..
0—9 . .	460	247	213	4	3	1	456	244	212	..	..	..
10—14 . .	234	138	96	24	23	1	210	115	95	..	..	..
15—19 . .	170	98	72	20	18	2	150	80	70	2	2	..
20 and over .	1,167	692	475	117	112	5	1,050	580	470	3	3	..
DUNGARPUR .	*5,510*	*2,703*	*2,807*	*1,647*	*1,630*	*17*	*3,863*	*1,073*	*2,790*	*6*	*6*	..
0—9 . .	1,138	581	557	22	21	1	1,116	560	556	..	..	..
10—14 . .	360	198	162	100	98	2	260	100	160	1	1	..
15—19 . .	422	230	192	151	149	2	271	81	190	..	..	..
20 and over .	3,590	1,694	1,896	1,374	1,362	12	2,216	332	1,884	5	5	..
JAIPUR . .	*38,408*	*20,295*	*18,113*	*10,538*	*10,306*	*232*	*27,870*	*9,989*	*17,881*	*251*	*250*	*1*
0—9 . .	7,870	3,982	3,888	133	122	11	7,737	3,860	3,877	2	2	..
10—14 . .	3,226	1,862	1,364	721	693	28	2,505	1,169	1,336	24	24	..
15—19 . .	3,099	1,721	1,378	1,108	1,080	28	1,991	641	1,350	55	55	..
20 and over .	24,213	12,730	11,483	8,576	8,411	165	15,637	4,319	11,318	170	169	1

By States or Districts. Main Religions—*continued.*

TABLE VIII.—C.

JAINS.

Age, Province, and State or District.	POPULATION.									Literate in English.		
	Total.			Literate.			Illiterate.					
	Persons.	Males.	Females.	Persons.	Males.	Females.	Persons.	Males.	Females.	Persons.	Males.	Females.
1	2	3	4	5	6	7	8	9	10	11	12	13
RAJPUTANA—*contd.*												
JAISALMER .	*1,109*	*549*	*553*	*266*	*253*	*13*	*836*	*296*	*540*	..	..	..
0—9 . .	312	153	159	1	1	..	311	152	159	..	..	..
10—14 . .	101	60	41	13	13	..	88	47	41	..	..	..
15—19 . .	100	48	52	25	25	..	75	23	52	..	..	..
20 and over .	589	288	301	227	214	13	362	74	288	..	..	..
JHALAWAR .	*2,488*	*1,312*	*1,176*	*638*	*605*	*33*	*1,850*	*707*	*1,143*	*13*	*13*	..
0—9 . .	486	242	244	5	3	2	481	239	242	..	..	..
10—14 . .	177	115	62	50	50	..	127	65	62	..	..	..
15—19 . .	227	128	99	72	67	5	155	61	94	3	3	..
20 and over .	1,598	827	771	511	485	26	1,087	342	745	10	10	..
KARAULI .	*394*	*225*	*169*	*158*	*158*	..	*236*	*67*	*169*	*3*	*3*	..
0—9 . .	71	36	35	3	3	..	68	33	35	..	..	..
10—14 . .	35	19	16	10	10	..	25	9	16	2	2	..
15—19 . .	40	25	15	24	24	..	16	1	15	..	..	..
20 and over .	248	145	103	121	121	..	127	24	103	1	1	..
KISHANGARH .	*3,176*	*1,680*	*1,496*	*1,051*	*1,007*	*44*	*2,125*	*673*	*1,452*	*14*	*14*	..
0—9 . .	670	360	310	30	30	..	640	330	310	..	..	..
10—14 . .	274	149	125	80	77	3	194	72	122	3	3	..
15—19 . .	259	159	100	128	121	7	131	38	93	2	2	..
20 and over .	1,973	1,012	961	813	779	34	1,160	233	927	9	9	..
KOTAH . .	*6,419*	*3,460*	*2,959*	*1,788*	*1,730*	*58*	*4,634*	*1,730*	*2,894*	*12*	*12*	..
0—9 . .	1,286	650	636	26	25	1	1,260	625	635	..	..	..
10—14 . .	437	235	202	97	89	8	340	146	194	1	1	..
15—19 . .	525	289	236	174	169	5	351	120	231	..	..	..
20 and over .	4,164	2,286	1,878	1,491	1,447	44	2,673	839	1,834	11	11	..
KUSHALGARH .	*513*	*270*	*243*	*165*	*165*	..	*348*	*105*	*243*	..	..	..
0—9 . .	133	74	59	6	6	..	127	68	59	..	..	..
10—14 . .	53	28	25	18	18	..	35	10	25	..	..	..
15—19 . .	46	24	22	22	22	..	24	2	22	..	..	..
20 and over .	281	144	137	119	119	..	162	25	137	..	..	..
LAWA . .	*149*	*75*	*67*	*39*	*37*	*2*	*103*	*38*	*65*	..	..	..
0—9 . .	29	16	13	..	..	..	29	16	13	..	..	..
10—14 . .	9	5	4	2	2	..	7	3	4	..	..	..
15—19 . .	9	3	6	2	2	..	7	1	6	..	..	..
20 and over .	95	51	44	35	33	2	60	18	42	..	..	..
MARWAR .	*131,990*	*61,314*	*70,676*	*34,331*	*33,456*	*875*	*97,659*	*27,858*	*69,801*	*209*	*208*	*1*
0—9 . .	34,230	17,418	16,812	619	597	22	33,611	16,821	16,790	1	1	..
10—14 . .	12,718	6,221	6,457	2,940	2,902	38	9,778	3,319	6,459	16	16	..
15—19 . .	10,634	4,964	5,670	3,915	3,837	78	6,719	1,127	5,592	44	44	..
20 and over .	74,408	32,711	41,697	26,857	26,120	737	47,551	6,591	40,960	148	147	1

TABLE VIII. —Education. Part C.—By States or Districts.
Main Religions—*continued.*

Age, Province, and State or District.	POPULATION.									Literate in English.		
	Total.			Literate.			Illiterate.					
	Persons.	Males.	Females.	Persons.	Males.	Females.	Persons.	Males.	Females.	Persons.	Males.	Females.
1	2	3	4	5	6	7	8	9	10	11	12	13
RAJPUTANA—*concld.*												
MEWAR . .	*66,704*	*34,641*	*32,063*	*16,243*	*15,913*	*330*	*50,461*	*18,728*	*31,733*	*77*	*77*	..
0—9 . .	16,365	8,185	8,180	144	137	7	16,221	8,048	8,173	..	..	..
10—14 . .	4,540	2,559	1,981	748	729	19	3,792	1,830	1,962	3	3	..
15—19 . .	5,540	3,170	2,370	1,668	1,624	44	3,872	1,546	2,326	17	17	..
20 and over .	40,259	20,727	19,532	13,683	13,423	260	26,576	7,304	19,272	57	57	..
PARTABGARH .	*4,318*	*2,359*	*2,039*	*1,294*	*1,273*	*21*	*3,094*	*986*	*2,038*	*21*	*21*	..
0—9 . .	955	509	446	15	14	1	940	495	445	..	..	..
10—14 . .	368	195	173	91	91	..	277	104	173	..	..	..
15—19 . .	396	196	200	146	142	4	250	48	202	5	5	..
20 and over .	2,599	1,365	1,234	1,042	1,020	16	1,557	339	1,218	16	16	..
SHAHPURA .	*1,619*	*885*	*734*	*562*	*545*	*17*	*1,057*	*340*	*717*	*18*	*18*	..
0—9 . .	376	192	184	9	8	1	367	184	183	..	..	..
10—14 . .	89	58	31	27	25	2	62	33	29	1	1	..
15—19 . .	114	75	39	64	63	1	50	12	38	2	2	..
20 and over .	1,040	560	480	462	449	13	578	111	467	15	15	..
SIROHI . .	*16,988*	*7,290*	*9,698*	*4,389*	*4,248*	*141*	*12,599*	*3,042*	*9,557*	*44*	*43*	*1*
0—9 . .	4,590	2,252	2,338	134	127	7	4,456	2,125	2,331	..	..	..
10—14 . .	1,593	758	835	479	465	14	1,114	293	821	3	2	1
15—19 . .	1,285	530	755	435	425	10	850	105	745	6	6	..
20 and over .	9,520	3,750	5,770	3,341	3,231	110	6,179	519	5,660	35	35	..
TONK . .	*7,903*	*4,165*	*3,738*	*1,526*	*1,512*	*14*	*6,377*	*2,653*	*3,724*	*4*	*4*	..
0—9 . .	1,859	916	943	5	4	1	1,854	912	942	..	..	..
10—14 . .	591	350	241	58	55	3	533	295	238	..	..	..
15—19 . .	618	363	255	149	149	..	469	214	255	2	2	..
20 and over .	4,835	2,536	2,299	1,314	1,304	10	3,521	1,232	2,289	2	2	..
AJMER-MERWARA—												
AJMER . .	*14,313*	*7,654*	*6,659*	*5,032*	*4,896*	*136*	*9,281*	*2,758*	*6,523*	*156*	*156*	..
0—9 . .	3,233	1,689	1,544	107	100	7	3,126	1,589	1,537	..	..	..
10—14 . .	1,105	662	443	397	383	14	708	279	429	12	12	..
15—19 . .	1,210	696	514	570	547	23	640	149	491	38	38	..
20 and over .	8,765	4,607	4,158	3,958	3,866	92	4,807	741	4,066	106	106	..
MERWARA .	*5,989*	*3,155*	*2,834*	*2,100*	*2,037*	*63*	*3,889*	*1,118*	*2,771*	*12*	*11*	*1*
0—9 . .	1,309	668	641	26	24	2	1,283	644	639	..	..	..
10—14 . .	428	243	185	132	129	3	296	114	182	..	..	..
15—19 . .	508	308	200	262	257	5	246	51	195	..	..	..
20 and over .	3,744	1,936	1,808	1,680	1,627	53	2,064	309	1,755	12	11	1

TABLE VIII.—PART C.

EDUCATION.

STATES OR DISTRICTS.

MUSALMANS.

TABLE VIII.—C.
MUSALMANS.

TABLE VIII.—Education. Part C.—

Age, Province, and State or District.	POPULATION.									LITERATE IN ENGLISH.		
	Total.			Literate.			Illiterate.					
	Persons.	Males.	Females.	Persons.	Males.	Females.	Persons.	Males.	Females.	Persons.	Males.	Females.
1	2	3	4	5	6	7	8	9	10	11	12	13
RAJPUTANA—												
ALWAR	*109,140*	*103,073*	*95,177*	*1,473*	*1,436*	*36*	*197,677*	*102,536*	*95,141*	*74*	*73*	*1*
0—9	52,136	26,554	25,582	14	12	2	52,122	26,542	25,580	1	1	..
10—14	24,828	13,731	11,097	56	53	3	24,772	13,678	11,094	1	1	..
15—19	20,609	11,584	9,025	101	98	3	20,508	11,486	9,022	9	9	..
20 and over	101,576	52,103	49,473	1,301	1,273	28	100,275	50,830	49,445	63	62	1
BANSWARA	*4,886*	*2,483*	*2,403*	*433*	*414*	*9*	*4,463*	*2,069*	*2,394*	*6*	*6*	..
0—9	1,342	659	683	3	2	1	1,339	657	682	..	..	..
10—14	468	245	223	20	20	..	448	225	223	..	..	..
15—19	406	202	204	45	43	2	361	159	202	1	1	..
20 and over	2,670	1,377	1,293	355	349	6	2,315	1,028	1,287	5	5	..
BHARATPUR	*109,449*	*54,550*	*47,899*	*2,331*	*2,063*	*168*	*100,318*	*52,487*	*47,731*	*186*	*185*	*1*
0—9	24,541	12,625	11,916	31	25	6	24,510	12,600	11,910	..	..	..
10—14	12,750	7,378	5,372	206	184	22	12,544	7,194	5,350	11	11	..
15—19	10,438	5,850	4,588	334	300	34	10,104	5,550	4,554	44	44	..
20 and over	54,720	28,697	26,023	1,660	1,554	106	53,060	27,143	25,917	131	130	1
BIKANER	*91,929*	*49,347*	*43,582*	*1,175*	*1,137*	*38*	*90,754*	*48,210*	*42,544*	*96*	*96*	..
0—9	25,875	13,339	12,536	9	9	..	25,866	13,330	12,536	..	..	..
10—14	9,752	5,352	4,400	67	65	2	9,685	5,287	4,398	5	5	..
15—19	8,636	4,858	3,778	142	133	9	8,494	4,725	3,769	18	18	..
20 and over	47,666	25,798	21,868	957	930	27	46,709	24,868	21,841	73	73	..
BUNDI	*10,656*	*5,414*	*5,242*	*225*	*216*	*9*	*10,431*	*5,198*	*5,233*	*9*	*9*	..
0—9	2,912	1,417	1,495	..	..	..	2,912	1,417	1,495	..	..	..
10—14	743	405	338	7	6	1	736	399	337	..	..	..
15—19	757	416	341	17	16	1	740	400	340	..	..	..
20 and over	6,244	3,176	3,068	201	194	7	6,043	2,982	3,061	9	9	..
DHOLPUR	*18,262*	*9,560*	*8,702*	*620*	*565*	*55*	*17,642*	*8,995*	*8,647*	*66*	*66*	..
0—9	4,394	2,268	2,126	5	4	1	4,389	2,264	2,125	..	..	..
10—14	2,048	1,169	879	46	41	5	2,002	1,128	874	2	2	..
15—19	1,698	924	774	87	68	19	1,611	856	755	12	12	..
20 and over	10,122	5,199	4,923	482	452	30	9,640	4,747	4,893	52	52	..
DUNGARPUR	*6,703*	*3,320*	*3,383*	*877*	*785*	*92*	*5,826*	*2,535*	*3,291*	*11*	*11*	..
0—9	1,934	971	963	7	6	1	1,927	965	962	..	..	..
10—14	636	340	296	48	41	7	588	299	289	1	1	..
15—19	568	263	305	87	68	19	481	195	286	1	1	..
20 and over	3,565	1,746	1,819	735	670	65	2,830	1,076	1,754	9	9	..
JAIPUR	*195,760*	*101,225*	*94,535*	*4,870*	*4,633*	*237*	*190,890*	*96,592*	*94,298*	*446*	*442*	*4*
0—9	50,187	25,430	24,757	67	63	4	50,120	25,367	24,753	4	4	..
10—14	19,298	10,829	8,469	266	251	15	19,032	10,578	8,454	38	38	..
15—19	16,865	9,236	7,629	467	442	25	16,398	8,794	7,604	63	63	..
20 and over	109,410	55,730	53,680	4,070	3,877	193	105,340	51,853	53,487	341	337	4

Age, Province, and State or District.	POPULATION.									LITERATE IN ENGLISH.		
	TOTAL.			LITERATE.			ILLITERATE.					
	Persons.	Males.	Females.	Persons.	Males.	Females.	Persons.	Males.	Females.	Persons.	Males.	Females.
1	2	3	4	5	6	7	8	9	10	11	12	13
RAJPUTANA— *contd.*												
JAISALMER .	*22,099*	*12,506*	*9,593*	*68*	*66*	*2*	*22,031*	*12,440*	*9,591*	*1*	*1*	..
0—9 . .	6,029	3,376	2,653	..	..	..	6,029	3,376	2,653	..	..	..
10—14 . .	2,380	1,451	929	3	3	..	2,377	1,448	929	..	..	..
15—19 . .	1,828	1,062	766	5	5	..	1,823	1,057	766	1	1	..
20 and over .	11,862	6,617	5,245	60	58	2	11,802	6,559	5,243	..	..	..
JHALAWAR .	*8,625*	*4,265*	*4,360*	*575*	*534*	*41*	*8,050*	*3,731*	*4,319*	*28*	*28*	..
0—9 . .	2,266	1,154	1,112	5	5	..	2,261	1,149	1,112	..	..	..
10—14 . .	667	364	303	35	31	4	632	333	299	..	..	..
15—19 . .	666	327	339	69	60	9	597	267	330	3	3	..
20 and over .	5,026	2,420	2,606	466	438	28	4,560	1,982	2,578	25	25	..
KARAULI .	*8,160*	*4,345*	*3,815*	*301*	*297*	*4*	*7,859*	*4,048*	*3,811*	*8*	*8*	..
0—9 . .	1,925	953	972	19	19	..	1,906	934	972	..	..	..
10—14 . .	786	435	351	32	31	1	754	404	350	..	..	..
15—19 . .	723	431	292	26	26	..	697	405	292	2	2	..
20 and over .	4,726	2,526	2,200	224	221	3	4,502	2,305	2,197	6	6	..
KISHANGARH .	*6,785*	*3,577*	*3,208*	*296*	*280*	*16*	*6,489*	*3,297*	*3,192*	*22*	*22*	..
0—9 . .	1,624	839	785	2	2	..	1,622	837	785	..	..	..
10—14 . .	517	310	207	30	28	2	487	282	205	4	4	..
15—19 . .	642	349	293	34	32	2	608	317	291	1	1	..
20 and over .	4,002	2,079	1,923	230	218	12	3,772	1,861	1,911	17	17	..
KOTAH . .	*44,569*	*23,163*	*21,406*	*2,006*	*1,892*	*114*	*42,563*	*21,271*	*21,292*	*114*	*113*	*1*
0—9 . .	11,609	5,871	5,738	17	14	3	11,592	5,857	5,735	1	1	..
10—14 . .	3,494	2,010	1,484	133	121	12	3,361	1,889	1,472	6	6	..
15—19 . .	3,626	1,891	1,735	204	190	14	3,422	1,701	1,721	16	16	..
20 and over .	25,840	13,391	12,449	1,652	1,567	85	24,188	11,824	12,364	91	90	1
KUSHALGARH .	*697*	*349*	*348*	*86*	*69*	*17*	*611*	*280*	*331*	..	..	..
0—9 . .	204	101	103	..	..	..	204	101	103	..	..	..
10—14 . .	59	31	28	10	7	3	49	24	25	..	..	..
15—19 . .	63	38	25	10	7	3	53	31	22	..	..	..
20 and over .	371	179	192	66	55	11	305	124	181	..	..	..
LAWA . .	*139*	*83*	*56*	..	..	..	*139*	*83*	*56*	..	..	..
0—9 . .	33	19	14	..	..	..	33	19	14	..	..	..
10—14 . .	16	11	5	..	..	..	16	11	5	..	..	..
15—19 . .	8	5	3	..	..	..	8	5	3	..	..	..
20 and over .	82	48	34	..	..	..	82	48	34	..	..	..
MARWAR .	*165,545*	*87,489*	*78,056*	*3,061*	*2,922*	*139*	*162,484*	*84,567*	*77,917*	*294*	*291*	*3*
0—9 . .	45,969	23,609	22,360	57	42	15	45,912	23,567	22,345	3	2	1
10—14 . .	16,431	9,202	7,229	196	171	25	16,235	9,031	7,204	20	19	1
15—19 . .	14,136	7,993	6,143	285	271	14	13,851	7,722	6,129	28	28	..
20 and over . .	89,009	46,685	42,324	2,523	2,438	85	86,486	44,247	42,239	243	242	1

TABLE VIII.—C.
MUSALMANS.

TABLE VIII.—Education. Part C.—By States or Districts. Main Religions—*continued*.

Age, Province, and State or District.	POPULATION.									LITERATE IN ENGLISH.		
	Total.			Literate.			Illiterate.					
	Persons.	Males.	Females.	Persons.	Males.	Females.	Persons.	Males.	Females.	Persons.	Males.	Females.
1	2	3	4	5	6	7	8	9	10	11	12	13
RAJPUTANA— *concld.*												
MEWAR . .	*45,752*	*24,180*	*21,572*	*2,784*	*2,681*	*103*	*42,968*	*21,499*	*21,469*	*69*	*69*	..
0—9 . .	12,155	6,068	6,087	18	16	2	12,137	6,052	6,085	..	..	..
10—14 . .	3,297	1,850	1,447	133	123	10	3,164	1,727	1,437	1	1	..
15—19 . .	3,559	1,950	1,609	244	230	14	3,315	1,720	1,595	9	9	..
20 and over .	26,741	14,312	12,429	2,389	2,312	77	24,352	12,000	12,352	59	59	..
PARTABGARH	*3,581*	*1,856*	*1,725*	*293*	*264*	*29*	*3,288*	*1,592*	*1,696*	*7*	*7*	..
0—9 . .	933	441	492	3	2	1	930	439	491	..	..	..
10—14 . .	299	163	136	12	12	..	287	151	136	1	1	..
15—19 . .	278	144	134	25	23	2	253	121	132	1	1	..
20 and over .	2,071	1,108	963	253	227	26	1,818	881	937	5	5	..
SHAHPURA .	*2,407*	*1,236*	*1,171*	*71*	*69*	*2*	*2,336*	*1,167*	*1,169*	*9*	*9*	..
0—9 .	659	337	322	1	1	..	658	336	322	..	..	..
10—14 . .	148	90	58	5	5	..	143	85	58	2	2	..
15—19 . .	151	76	75	1	1	..	150	75	75	1	1	..
20 and over .	1,449	733	716	64	62	2	1,385	671	714	6	6	..
SIROHI . .	*7,240*	*4,124*	*3,116*	*835*	*797*	*38*	*6,405*	*3,327*	*3,078*	*63*	*63*	..
0—9 . .	1,795	894	901	9	9	..	1,786	885	901	..	..	..
10—14 . .	632	355	277	47	42	5	585	313	272	..	..	..
15—19 . .	618	378	240	84	79	5	534	290	235	2	2	..
20 and over .	4,195	2,497	1,698	695	667	28	3,500	1,830	1,670	61	61	..
TONK . .	*40,432*	*20,516*	*19,916*	*1,839*	*1,769*	*70*	*38,593*	*18,747*	*19,846*	*93*	*83*	*10*
0—9 . .	10,106	5,044	5,062	15	10	5	10,091	5,034	5,057	1	..	1
10—14 . .	3,393	1,838	1,555	70	67	3	3,323	1,771	1,552	5	5	..
15—19 . .	3,173	1,621	1,552	162	153	9	3,011	1,468	1,543	14	13	1
20 and over .	23,760	12,013	11,747	1,592	1,539	53	22,168	10,474	11,694	73	65	8
AJMER-MERWARA—												
AJMER . .	*60,465*	*32,585*	*27,880*	*3,798*	*3,589*	*209*	*56,667*	*28,996*	*27,671*	*768*	*764*	*4*
0—9 . .	15,188	7,803	7,385	59	51	8	15,129	7,752	7,377	4	4	..
10—14 . .	5,749	3,291	2,458	270	248	22	5,479	3,043	2,436	56	55	1
15—19 . .	5,197	2,859	2,338	368	338	30	4,829	2,521	2,308	116	115	1
20 and over .	34,331	18,632	15,699	3,101	2,952	149	31,230	15,680	15,550	592	590	2
MERWARA . .	*20,570*	*11,248*	*9,322*	*590*	*571*	*19*	*19,980*	*10,677*	*9,303*	*50*	*50*	..
0—9 .	6,162	3,295	2,867	4	2	2	6,158	3,293	2,865	..	..	..
10—14 . .	1,625	934	691	29	28	1	1,596	906	690	2	2	..
15—19	1,658	975	683	47	45	2	1,611	930	681	5	5	..
20 and over .	11,125	6,044	5,081	510	496	14	10,615	5,548	5,067	43	43	..

TABLE VIII.—PART C.

EDUCATION.

STATES OR DISTRICTS.

SIKHS.

TABLE VIII.—C.
SIKHS.

TABLE VIII.—Education. Part C.—By

Age, Province, and State or District.	POPULATION.									Literate in English.		
	Total.			Literate.			Illiterate.					
	Persons.	Males.	Females.	Persons.	Males.	Females.	Persons.	Males.	Females.	Persons.	Males.	Females.
1	2	3	4	5	6	7	8	9	10	11	12	13
RAJPUTANA.												
ALWAR . .	*29*	*16*	*13*	*10*	*10*	..	*19*	*6*	*13*	*3*	*3*	..
0—9 . .	8	4	4	1	1	..	7	3	4	..	..	..
10—14 . .	3	2	1	1	1	..	2	1	1	..	..	..
15—19 . .	..	..	..	..	..	..	..	..	..	..	..	..
20 and over .	18	10	8	8	8	..	10	2	8	3	3	..
BANSWARA .	*1*	*1*	..	..	..	..	*1*	*1*	..	..	..	..
0—9 . .	..	..	..	..	..	..	..	..	..	..	..	..
10—14 . .	..	..	..	..	..	..	..	..	..	..	..	..
15—19 . .	..	..	..	..	..	..	..	..	..	..	..	..
20 and over .	1	1	..	..	..	..	1	1	..	..	..	..
BHARATPUR .	*52*	*28*	*24*	*26*	*17*	*9*	*26*	*11*	*15*	*11*	*11*	..
0—9 . .	13	5	8	2	..	2	11	5	6	..	..	..
10—14 . .	4	2	2	2	1	1	2	1	1	1	1	..
15—19 . .	6	3	3	5	3	2	1	..	1	3	3	..
20 and over .	29	18	11	17	13	4	12	5	7	7	7	..
BIKANER. .	*8,314*	*5,054*	*3,260*	*216*	*208*	*8*	*7,998*	*4,846*	*3,152*	*17*	*17*	..
0—9 . .	2,273	1,226	1,047	1	..	1	2,272	1,226	1,046	..	..	..
10—14 . .	906	619	287	6	6	..	900	613	287	..	..	..
15—19 . .	834	581	253	20	19	1	814	562	252	4	4	..
20 and over .	4,201	2,628	1,573	189	183	6	4,012	2,445	1,567	13	13	..
BUNDI . .	*1*	*1*	..	..	..	..	*1*	*1*	..	..	..	..
0—9 . .	..	..	..	..	..	..	..	..	..	..	..	..
10—14 . .	..	..	..	..	..	..	..	..	..	..	..	..
15—19 . .	..	..	..	..	..	..	..	..	..	..	..	..
20 and over .	1	1	..	..	..	..	1	1	..	..	..	..
DHOLPUR .	*95*	*56*	*39*	*52*	*41*	*11*	*43*	*15*	*28*	*16*	*16*	..
0—9 .	25	14	11	1	1	..	24	13	11	..	..	..
10—14 . .	7	6	1	6	5	1	1	1	..	2	2	..
15—19 . .	10	6	4	8	6	2	2	..	2	1	1	..
20 and over .	53	30	23	37	29	8	16	1	15	13	13	..

States or Districts. Main Religions—*continued*.

SIKHS.

Age, Province, and State or District.	Population.									Literate in English.		
	Total.			Literate.			Illiterate.					
	Persons.	Males.	Females.	Persons.	Males.	Females.	Persons.	Males.	Females.	Persons.	Males.	Females.
1	2	3	4	5	6	7	8	9	10	11	12	13
RAJPUTANA—*contd.*												
DUNGARPUR .	*6*	*4*	*2*	*5*	*3*	*2*	*1*	*1*	..	*1*	*1*	..
0—9 . .	2	2	..	1	1	..	1	1	..	..	..	..
10—14 . .	1	..	1	1	..	1	..	..	..	..	..	..
15—19 . .	..	..	..	..	..	..	..	..	..	..	..	..
20 and over .	3	2	1	3	2	1	..	..	..	1	1	..
JAIPUR . .	*157*	*89*	*68*	*43*	*43*	..	*114*	*46*	*68*	*3*	*3*	..
0—9 . .	21	10	11	1	1	..	20	9	11	..	..	..
10—14 . .	18	6	12	1	1	..	17	5	12	..	..	..
15—19 . .	11	9	2	3	3	..	8	6	2	..	..	..
20 and over .	107	64	43	38	38	..	69	26	43	3	3	..
JAISALMER .	*1*	*1*	..	..	..	..	*1*	*1*	..	..	..	..
0—9 . .	..	..	..	..	..	..	..	..	..	..	..	..
10—14 . .	..	..	..	..	..	..	..	..	..	..	..	..
15—19 . .	..	..	..	..	..	..	..	..	..	..	..	..
20 and over .	1	1	..	..	..	..	1	1	..	..	..	..
JHALAWAR .	*53*	*32*	*21*	*7*	*7*	..	*46*	*25*	*21*	*1*	*1*	..
0—9 . .	16	7	9	..	..	..	16	7	9	..	..	..
10—14 . .	2	1	1	..	..	..	2	1	1	..	..	..
15—19 . .	..	..	..	..	..	..	..	..	..	..	..	..
20 and over .	35	24	11	7	7	..	28	17	11	1	1	..
KISHANGARH .	*4*	*4*	..	*1*	*1*	..	*3*	*3*	..	..	..	..
0—9 . .	..	..	..	..	..	..	..	..	..	..	..	..
10—14 . .	..	..	..	..	..	..	..	..	..	..	..	..
15—19 . .	..	..	..	..	..	..	..	..	..	..	..	..
20 and over .	4	4	..	1	1	..	3	3	..	..	..	..
KOTAH .	*216*	*109*	*107*	*52*	*50*	*2*	*164*	*59*	*105*	*3*	*3*	..
0—9 .	57	28	29	..	..	..	57	28	29	..	..	..
10—14 . .	10	7	3	5	5	..	5	2	3	..	..	..
15—19 .	19	9	10	4	4	..	15	5	10	..	..	..
20 and over .	130	65	65	43	41	2	87	24	63	3	3	..

TABLE VIII.—C.
SIKHS.

TABLE VIII.—Education. Part C.—By States or Districts.
Main Religions—*concluded.*

Age, Province, and State or District.	POPULATION.									Literate in English.		
	Total.			Literate.			Illiterate.					
	Persons.	Males.	Females.	Persons.	Males.	Females.	Persons.	Males.	Females.	Persons.	Males.	Females.
1	2	3	4	5	6	7	8	9	10	11	12	13
RAJPUTANA— *concld.*												
MARWAR .	*38*	*24*	*14*	*19*	*15*	*4*	*19*	*9*	*10*	*5*	*5*	..
0—9 . .	8	4	4	..	..	..	8	4	4	..	..	..
10—14 . .	2	..	2	..	..	..	2	..	2	..	..	..
15—19 . .	3	2	1	3	2	1	..	..	..	1	1	..
20 and over .	25	18	7	16	13	3	9	5	4	4	4	..
MEWAR . .	*10*	*6*	*4*	*3*	*3*	..	*7*	*3*	*4*	..	..	..
0—9 . .	1	..	1	..	..	..	1	..	1	..	..	..
10—14 . .	..	..	..	..	..	..	..	..	..	..	..	..
15—19 . .	..	..	..	..	..	..	..	..	..	..	..	..
20 and over .	9	6	3	3	3	..	6	3	3	..	..	..
PARTABGARH .	*2*	*1*	*1*	..	..	..	*2*	*1*	*1*	..	..	..
0—9 . .	..	..	..	..	..	..	..	..	..	..	..	..
10—14 . .	..	..	..	..	..	..	..	..	..	..	..	..
15—19 . .	..	..	..	..	..	..	..	..	..	..	..	..
20 and over .	2	1	1	..	..	..	2	1	1	..	..	..
SIROHI . .	*76*	*63*	*13*	*46*	*44*	*2*	*30*	*19*	*11*	*7*	*7*	..
0—9 . .	8	3	5	..	..	..	8	3	5	..	..	..
10—14 . .	3	3	..	1	1	..	2	2	..	1	1	..
15—19 . .	19	18	1	15	14	1	4	4	..	2	2	..
20 and over .	46	39	7	30	29	1	16	10	6	4	4	..
TONK . .	*3*	..	*3*	..	..	..	*3*	..	*3*	..	..	..
0—9 . .	..	..	..	..	..	..	..	..	..	..	..	..
10—14 . .	1	..	1	..	..	..	1	..	1	..	..	..
15—19 . .	..	..	..	..	..	..	..	..	..	..	..	..
20 and over .	2	..	2	..	..	..	2	..	2	..	..	..
AJMER-MERWARA—												
AJMER . .	*916*	*779*	*137*	*283*	*275*	*8*	*633*	*504*	*129*	*23*	*23*	..
0—9 . .	80	43	37	1	..	1	79	43	36	..	..	..
10—14 . .	26	22	4	6	6	..	20	16	4	3	3	..
15—19 . .	134	124	10	28	24	4	106	100	6	5	5	..
20 and over .	676	590	86	248	245	3	428	345	83	15	15	..
MERWARA .	*6*	*4*	*2*	*4*	*3*	*1*	*2*	*1*	*1*	*1*	*1*	..
0—9 . .	3	2	1	1	1	..	2	1	1	..	..	..
10—14 . .	..	..	..	..	..	..	..	..	..	..	..	..
15—19 . .	..	..	..	..	..	..	..	..	..	..	..	..
20 and over .	3	2	1	3	2	1	..	..	..	1	1	..

N.B.—Kushalgarh, Lawa, Karauli, and Shahpura, which contain no Sikhs have not been shown.

TABLE VIII.—PART D.

EDUCATION.

CITIES.

ALL RELIGIONS.

TABLE VIII.—Education by Religion and Age. Part D.—For Cities. All Religions.

Age, Province, and City.	Population. Total.			Population. Total Literate.			Population. Illiterate.			Literate in English.		
	Persons.	Males.	Females.	Persons.	Males.	Females.	Persons.	Males.	Females.	Persons.	Males.	Females.
1	2	3	4	5	6	7	8	9	10	11	12	13
RAJPUTANA—												
ALWAR . .	41,305	22,254	19,051	3,520	3,409	111	37,785	18,845	18,940	570	547	23
0—9 . .	8,250	4,024	4,226	39	35	4	8,211	3,989	4,222	1	1	..
10—14 . .	3,667	1,971	1,696	126	114	12	3,541	1,857	1,684	10	5	5
15—19 . .	3,609	1,987	1,622	193	189	4	3,416	1,798	1,618	47	45	2
20 and over .	25,779	14,272	11,507	3,162	3,071	91	22,617	11,201	11,416	512	496	16
BHARATPUR .	33,918	18,803	15,115	4,074	3,659	[illegible]	29,844	15,151	14,693	537	496	41
0—9 . .	6,306	3,304	3,002	85	62	23	6,221	3,242	2,979	6	5	1
10—14 . .	3,697	2,193	1,504	394	332	62	3,303	1,861	1,442	40	46	1
15—19 . .	3,710	2,085	1,625	517	451	66	3,103	1,634	1,559	94	87	7
20 and over .	20,205	11,221	8,984	3,078	2,807	271	17,127	8,414	8,713	388	356	32
BIKANER .	55,826	28,275	27,551	6,414	6,044	370	49,412	22,231	27,181	561	547	14
0—9 . .	12,240	6,208	6,032	62	54	8	12,178	6,154	6,024	1	..	1
10—14 . .	4,736	2,612	2,124	404	387	17	4,332	2,225	2,107	58	57	1
15—19 . .	5,256	2,737	2,519	734	683	51	4,522	2,054	2,468	125	125	..
20 and over .	33,594	16,718	16,876	5,214	4,920	294	28,380	11,798	16,582	377	365	12
JAIPUR .	137,098	70,846	66,252	14,351	13,469	882	122,747	57,378	65,369	1,646	1,569	77
0—9 . .	24,993	12,623	12,370	256	210	46	24,737	12,413	12,324	32	27	5
10—14 . .	10,923	6,235	4,688	917	834	83	10,006	5,401	4,605	155	150	5
15—19 . .	11,938	6,284	5,654	1,547	1,423	124	10,391	4,861	5,530	328	322	6
20 and over .	89,244	45,704	43,540	11,631	11,002	629	77,613	34,703	42,910	1,131	1,070	61
* JODHPUR .	79,756	41,838	37,918	11,121	10,511	610	68,635	31,327	37,308	1,297	1,243	54
0—9 . .	17,077	8,670	8,407	247	203	44	16,830	8,467	8,363	23	18	5
10—14 . .	7,557	4,238	3,319	793	747	46	6,764	3,491	3,273	90	86	4
15—19 . .	7,902	4,391	3,511	1,264	1,198	66	6,638	3,193	3,445	228	224	4
20 and over .	47,220	24,539	22,681	8,817	8,363	454	38,403	16,176	22,227	956	915	41
KOTAH . .	32,753	16,949	15,804	3,620	3,333	287	29,133	13,616	15,517	292	280	12
0—9 . .	6,412	3,141	3,271	34	29	5	6,378	3,112	3,266	2	1	1
10—14 . .	2,074	1,210	864	228	198	30	1,846	1,012	834	13	13	..
15—19 . .	2,888	1,502	1,386	430	385	45	2,458	1,117	1,341	50	48	2
20 and over .	21,379	11,096	10,283	2,928	2,721	207	18,454	8,375	10,076	227	218	9
TONK . .	33,864	16,837	17,027	1,904	1,832	72	31,960	15,005	16,955	121	107	14
0—9 . .	7,655	3,794	3,861	18	11	7	7,637	3,783	3,854	2	..	2
10—14 . .	2,503	1,373	1,130	72	60	3	2,431	1,304	1,127	6	6	..
15—19 . .	2,834	1,404	1,430	196	184	12	2,638	1,220	1,418	21	19	2
20 and over .	20,872	10,266	10,606	1,618	1,568	50	19,254	8,698	10,556	92	82	10
UDAIPUR .	33,229	17,460	15,769	4,055	3,923	132	29,174	13,537	15,637	220	203	17
0—9 . .	6,957	3,555	3,402	12	10	2	6,945	3,545	3,400	..	..	..
10—14 . .	2,148	1,259	889	137	130	7	2,011	1,129	882	8	6	2
15—19 . .	2,722	1,458	1,264	431	410	21	2,291	1,048	1,243	35	33	2
20 and over .	21,402	11,188	10,214	3,475	3,373	102	17,927	7,815	10,112	177	164	13
AJMER-MERWARA—												
AJMER . .	86,222	47,354	38,868	12,996	11,259	1,737	73,226	36,095	37,131	4,710	4,157	553
0—9 . .	18,357	9,304	9,053	324	196	128	18,033	9,108	8,925	112	60	52
10—14 . .	7,944	4,555	3,389	1,168	972	196	6,776	3,583	3,193	366	320	46
15—19 . .	8,677	4,807	3,870	1,759	1,442	317	6,918	3,365	3,553	750	678	72
20 and over .	51,244	28,688	22,556	9,745	8,649	1,096	41,499	20,039	21,460	3,482	3,099	383

* Including Jodhpur suburbs which have been shown in Tables IV and V under the name of "Jodhpur Town".

TABLE IX.

Education by Selected Castes, Tribes, and Races.

Explanatory Note.

The castes selected for this Table are those—

(*a*) numbering, in the two Provinces combined, 40,000 and over, or about 3¼ per mille of the combined population, except Gadri, Jogi, Kunbi, and Sirvi;

(*b*) numbering 15,000 and over of any one religion other than Hindu, except Bhishti, Julaha, Mirasi, and Pinjara;

(*c*) numbering 3,000 and over in Ajmer-Merwara alone, except Dholi and Kahar;

(*d*) of particular local or general interest, such as Chakar, Golapurab, Merat, Prohit, Sevag, and Goanese, Jew, Kayastha, Parsi, respectively.

The castes noted above as excepted were not sorted for the Table in the first instance as they were comparatively small in 1901.

For the purpose of this Table Christians (excluding Goanese) have been treated as a separate race, and have been subdivided into "Indians" and "Others." But the figures do not agree exactly with those for Christians in Tables VI, VII, VIII, and XVII, as the latter include Goanese who are shewn separately in this Table, and a Jewess by race who returned her religion as Christian.

The figures for Jews in this Table likewise differ from those for the Jewish religion in Tables VI, VII, and VIII, as the latter include individuals who were returned as Jewish by religion but were not Jews by race.

The figures in columns 3, 4, 5, will not always agree with the corresponding ones in Table XIII as in some cases, subsequent to the compilation of this Table, amalgamation of castes has been made in Table XIII.

Regarding the figures for literacy in English a reference to the Explanatory Note to Table VIII should be made.

TABLE IX.

EDUCATION BY SELECTED CASTES.

TABLE IX.—EDUCATION BY SELECTED

[In Col. 2 A=Animist, Ar=Arya, Br=Brahmo, C=Christian,

RAJPUTANA.

Caste, tribe, or race.	Religion.	POPULATION.									LITERATE IN ENGLISH.		
		TOTAL.			LITERATE.			ILLITERATE.					
		Persons.	Males.	Females.	Persons.	Males.	Females.	Persons.	Males.	Females.	Persons.	Males.	Females.
1	2	3	4	5	6	7	8	9	10	11	12	13	14
Ahir	**Total**	**169,110**	**91,159**	**77,951**	**796**	**769**	**27**	**168,314**	**90,390**	**77,924**	**45**	**45**	...
	H.	169,097	91,150	77,947	795	769	26	168,302	90,381	77,921	45	45	...
	M.	13	9	4	1	...	1	12	9	3	...	...	...
Bairagi	**Total**	**54,339**	**29,433**	**24,906**	**1,391**	**1,373**	**18**	**52,948**	**28,060**	**24,888**	**12**	**12**	...
	A.	5	1	4	...	...	...	5	1	4	...	...	...
	H.	54,332	29,432	24,900	1,391	1,373	18	52,941	28,059	24,882	12	12	...
	J.	2	...	2	...	...	...	2	...	2	...	...	...
Balai	**Total**	**197,489**	**101,065**	**96,424**	**124**	**124**	...	**197,365**	**100,941**	**96,424**	**3**	**3**	...
	H.	197,469	101,048	96,421	124	124	...	197,345	100,924	96,421	3	3	...
	M	20	17	3	...	...	...	20	17	3	...	...	...
Bambhi	H.	**133,826**	**69,940**	**63,886**	**28**	**27**	**1**	**133,798**	**69,913**	**63,885**	...	...	...
Bhangi	**Total**	**82,808**	**42,432**	**40,376**	**53**	**50**	**3**	**82,755**	**42,382**	**40,373**	**1**	**1**	...
	H.	81,937	41,980	39,957	52	49	3	81,885	41,931	39,954	1	1	...
	M.	609	318	291	...	...	...	609	318	291	...	...	...
	S.	262	134	128	1	1	...	261	133	128	...	...	...
Bhil	**Total**	**448,835**	**229,223**	**219,612**	**231**	**229**	**2**	**448,604**	**228,994**	**219,610**	**1**	**1**	...
	A.	385,903	196,242	180,601	69	69	...	385,834	196,173	189,661	...	...	...
	H.	62,929	32,979	29,950	162	160	2	62,767	32,819	29,948	1	1	...
	M.	3	2	1	...	...	...	3	2	1	...	...	...
Bishnoi	H.	**52,877**	**28,491**	**24,386**	**131**	**130**	**1**	**52,746**	**28,361**	**24,385**	**4**	**4**	...
Brahman	**Total**	**920,286**	**474,623**	**445,664**	**76,437**	**74,210**	**2,227**	**843,849**	**400,412**	**443,437**	**3,108**	**3,068**	**40**
	Ar.	448	248	200	207	168	39	241	80	161	71	70	1
	H.	919,805	474,352	445,453	76,213	74,026	2,187	843,592	400,326	443,266	3,036	2,997	39
	J.	18	10	8	7	7	...	11	3	8	...	...	...
	S.	15	12	3	10	9	1	5	3	2	1	1	...
Chakar	**Total**	**34,837**	**16,679**	**18,158**	**465**	**420**	**45**	**34,372**	**16,259**	**18,113**	**11**	**11**	...
	Ar.	23	13	10	7	7	...	16	6	10	1	1	...
	H.	34,702	16,616	18,086	451	407	44	34,251	16,209	18,042	10	10	...
	J.	42	16	26	5	4	1	37	12	25	...	...	...
	M.	70	34	36	2	2	...	68	32	36	...	...	...
Chamar	**Total**	**725,052**	**373,301**	**351,751**	**280**	**275**	**5**	**724,772**	**373,026**	**351,746**	**9**	**9**	...
	H.	724,865	373,205	351,660	280	275	5	724,585	372,930	351,655	9	9	...
	M.	99	46	53	...	...	...	99	46	53	...	...	...
	S.	88	50	38	...	...	...	88	50	38	...	...	...
Chhipa	**Total**	**37,914**	**19,623**	**18,291**	**1,119**	**1,110**	**9**	**36,795**	**18,513**	**18,282**	**13**	**13**	...
	H.	30,898	15,923	14,975	791	786	5	30,107	15,137	14,970	8	8	...
	J.	1	1	...	...	...	...	1	1	...	...	...	...
	M.	7,015	3,699	3,316	328	324	4	6,687	3,375	3,312	5	5	...
Christian	**Total**	**4,092**	**2,288**	**1,804**	**2,432**	**1,446**	**986**	**1,660**	**842**	**818**	**1,667**	**1,008**	**659**
(a) Indians	C.	2,385	1,308	1,077	1,047	631	416	1,338	677	661	305	205	100
(b) Others	C.	1,707	980	727	1,385	815	570	322	165	157	1,362	803	559
Darogah	**Total**	**110,434**	**53,573**	**56,861**	**1,088**	**1,029**	**59**	**109,346**	**52,544**	**56,802**	**29**	**29**	...
	Ar.	19	11	8	...	...	...	19	11	8	...	...	...
	H.	110,412	53,560	56,852	1,087	1,028	59	109,325	52,532	56,793	29	29	...
	J	3	2	1	1	1	...	2	1	1	...	...	...

CASTES, TRIBES, OR RACES.

H=Hindu, J=Jain, M=Musalman, S=Sikh.]

TABLE IX.

EDUCATION BY SELECTED CASTES.

AJMER-MERWARA.

Caste, tribe or race.	Religion.	POPULATION.									LITERATE IN ENGLISH.		
		TOTAL.			LITERATE.			ILLITERATE.					
		Persons.	Males.	Females.	Persons.	Males.	Females.	Persons.	Males.	Females.	Persons.	Males.	Females.
1	2	3	4	5	6	7	8	9	10	11	12	13	14
Ahir . . .	Total .	**1,755**	**999**	**756**	**99**	**94**	**5**	**1,656**	**905**	**751**	**31**	**28**	**3**
	H.	1,752	997	755	99	94	5	1,653	903	750	31	28	3
	M.	3	2	1	...	...	...	3	2	1	...	...	...
Bairagi . .	H.	**487**	**224**	**263**	**11**	**11**	...	**476**	**213**	**263**	...	...	...
Balai . . .	Total .	**23,773**	**12,234**	**11,539**	**160**	**159**	**1**	**23,613**	**12,075**	**11,538**	**4**	**4**	...
	H.	23,759	12,224	11,535	160	159	1	23,599	12,065	11,534	4	4	...
	M.	14	10	4	...	...	...	14	10	4	...	...	...
Bambhi . .	H.	**2,550**	**1,305**	**1,245**	**15**	**15**	...	**2,535**	**1,290**	**1,245**	**1**	**1**	...
Bhangi . .	Total .	**5,098**	**2,697**	**2,401**	**59**	**58**	**1**	**5,039**	**2,639**	**2,400**	**12**	**12**	...
	H.	5,070	2,671	2,399	59	58	1	5,011	2,613	2,398	12	12	...
	M.	28	26	2	...	...	...	28	26	2	...	...	...
Bhil . . .	Total .	**6,504**	**3,287**	**3,217**	**7**	**7**	...	**6,497**	**3,280**	**3,217**	...	...	...
	A.	3,339	1,658	1,681	3	3	...	3,336	1,655	1,681	...	...	...
	H.	3,165	1,629	1,536	4	4	...	3,161	1,625	1,536	...	...	...
Bishnoi . .	H.	**2**	**1**	**1**	...	...	...	**2**	**1**	**1**	...	...	...
Brahman . .	Total .	**24,036**	**12,884**	**11,152**	**5,521**	**5,106**	**415**	**18,515**	**7,778**	**10,737**	**1,089**	**1,074**	**15**
	Ar	372	221	151	168	131	37	204	90	114	56	56	...
	H.	23,659	12,659	11,000	5,352	4,974	378	18,307	7,685	10,622	1,033	1,018	15
	S.	5	4	1	1	1	...	4	3	1	...	...	...
Chakar . .	H.	**255**	**122**	**133**	**9**	**9**	...	**246**	**113**	**133**	...	...	...
Chamar . .	Total .	**13,337**	**6,810**	**6,527**	**169**	**168**	**1**	**13,168**	**6,642**	**6,526**	**10**	**10**	...
	H.	13,336	6,809	6,527	168	167	1	13,168	6,642	6,526	10	10	...
	M.	1	1	...	1	1	...	...	...	...	...	...	...
Chhipa . .	Total .	**2,648**	**1,414**	**1,234**	**272**	**268**	**4**	**2,376**	**1,146**	**1,230**	**8**	**8**	...
	H.	1,802	972	830	200	198	2	1,602	774	828	5	5	...
	M.	846	442	404	72	70	2	774	372	402	3	3	...
Christian . .	Total .	**5,195**	**3,090**	**2,105**	**3,852**	**2,446**	**1,406**	**1,343**	**644**	**699**	**2,564**	**1,943**	**621**
(a) Indians .	C.	2,730	1,309	1,421	1,721	830	891	1,009	479	530	456	339	117
(b) Others .	C.	2,465	1,781	684	2,131	1,616	515	334	165	169	2,108	1,604	504
Darogah . .	H.	**8,934**	**4,536**	**4,398**	**310**	**296**	**14**	**8,624**	**4,240**	**4,384**	**12**	**12**	...

TABLE IX.

EDUCATION BY SELECTED CASTES.

TABLE IX.—Education by Selected

RAJPUTANA—*contd.*

[In Col. 2 A=Animist, Ar=Arya, Br=Brahmo, C=Christian,

Caste, tribe, or race.	Religion.	POPULATION. Total. Persons.	Total. Males.	Total. Females.	Literate. Persons.	Literate. Males.	Literate. Females.	Illiterate. Persons.	Illiterate. Males.	Illiterate. Females.	Literate in English. Persons.	Literate in English. Males.	Literate in English. Females.
1	2	3	4	5	6	7	8	9	10	11	12	13	14
Darzi . . .	Total .	**45,200**	**23,068**	**22,132**	**643**	**625**	**18**	**44,557**	**22,443**	**22,114**	**17**	**17**	...
	H.	44,931	22,931	22,000	639	621	18	44,292	22,310	21,982	16	16	...
	M.	269	137	132	4	4	...	265	133	132	1	1	...
Dhakar . . .	Total .	**93,361**	**47,661**	**45,700**	**599**	**596**	**3**	**92,762**	**47,065**	**45,697**	...	...	...
	Ar.	1	1	...	1	1	...	...	...	...	...	...	...
	H	93,360	47,660	45,700	598	595	3	92,762	47,065	45,697	...	...	...
Dhobi . .	Total .	**45,801**	**23,348**	**22,453**	**73**	**67**	**6**	**45,728**	**23,281**	**22,447**	**1**	**1**	...
	H.	39,699	20,305	19,394	58	52	6	39,641	20,253	19,388	1	1	...
	M.	6,102	3,043	3,059	15	15	...	6,087	3,028	3,059	...	...	...
Fakir . .	Total .	**55,208**	**29,024**	**26,184**	**282**	**280**	**2**	**54,926**	**28,744**	**26,182**	...	...	...
	H.	275	159	116	6	6	...	269	153	116	...	...	...
	M.	54,933	28,865	26,068	276	274	2	54,657	28,591	26,066	...	...	...
Goanese . .	C.	**163**	**121**	**42**	**71**	**60**	**11**	**92**	**61**	**31**	**44**	**37**	**7**
Golapurab . .	H.	**11,397**	**5,957**	**5,440**	**126**	**115**	**11**	**11,271**	**5,842**	**5,429**	**1**	**1**	...
Gujar . .	Total .	**498,607**	**270,412**	**228,195**	**1,367**	**1,313**	**54**	**497,240**	**269,099**	**228,141**	**37**	**37**	...
	Ar.	15	10	5	1	1	...	14	9	5	...	...	...
	H.	498,588	270,399	228,189	1,366	1,312	54	497,222	269,087	228,135	37	37	...
	J.	4	3	1	...	...	...	4	3	1	...	...	...
Jat . . .	Total .	**925,391**	**500,001**	**425,390**	**3,467**	**3,365**	**102**	**921,924**	**496,636**	**425,288**	**113**	**112**	**1**
	Ar.	8	6	2	...	...	...	8	6	2	...	...	...
	H.	919,452	496,237	423,215	3,206	3,121	85	916,246	493,116	433,130	85	84	1
	J.	5	4	1	...	...	...	5	4	1	...	...	...
	M.	131	70	61	1	1	...	130	69	61	...	...	...
	S.	5,795	3,684	2,111	260	243	17	5,535	3,441	2,094	28	28	...
Jew . . .	Jewish	**31**	**15**	**16**	**21**	**12**	**9**	**10**	**3**	**7**	**14**	**9**	**5**
Kachhi . .	H.	**60,630**	**31,734**	**28,896**	**76**	**76**	...	**60,554**	**31,658**	**28,896**	**9**	**9**	...
Kaimkhani .	M.	**28,340**	**14,824**	**13,516**	**443**	**436**	**7**	**27,897**	**14,388**	**13,509**	**7**	**7**	...
Kalal . .	Total .	**39,844**	**20,327**	**19,517**	**1,128**	**1,116**	**12**	**38,716**	**19,211**	**19,505**	**34**	**34**	...
	H.	36,364	18,519	17,845	1,084	1,074	10	35,280	17,445	17,835	34	34	...
	M.	3,480	1,808	1,672	44	42	2	3,436	1,766	1,670	...	...	...
Kasai . .	M.	**28,578**	**14,577**	**14,001**	**104**	**100**	**4**	**28,474**	**14,477**	**13,997**	**2**	**2**	...
Kayastha . .	Total .	**23,600**	**12,847**	**10,753**	**8,887**	**8,160**	**727**	**14,713**	**4,687**	**10,026**	**1,500**	**1,480**	**20**
	Ar.	268	156	112	156	113	43	112	43	69	46	44	2
	Br.	77	39	38	32	28	4	45	11	34	3	3	...
	H.	23,249	12,651	10,598	8,698	8,018	680	14,551	4,633	9,918	1,450	1,432	18
	S.	6	1	5	1	1	...	5	...	5	1	1	...
Khati . .	Total .	**134,762**	**69,136**	**65,626**	**794**	**778**	**16**	**133,968**	**68,358**	**65,610**	**37**	**37**	...
	Ar.	31	15	16	1	1	...	30	14	16	...	...	...
	H.	134,696	69,099	65,597	792	776	16	133,904	68,323	65,581	36	36	...
	S.	35	22	13	1	1	...	34	21	13	1	1	...
Khatik . .	H.	**51,259**	**26,370**	**24,889**	**96**	**91**	**5**	**51,163**	**26,279**	**24,884**	**2**	**2**	...
Koli . . .	Total .	**104,047**	**53,499**	**50,548**	**147**	**138**	**9**	**103,900**	**53,361**	**50,539**	**7**	**7**	...
	H.	104,033	53,494	50,539	147	138	9	103,886	53,356	50,530	7	7	...
	M.	14	5	9	...	...	...	14	5	9	...	...	...

CASTES, TRIBES, OR RACES—*continued*.

H=Hindu, J=Jain, M=Musalman, S=Sikh.]

TABLE IX.

EDUCATION BY SELECTED CASTES.

AJMER-MERWARA—*contd.*

Caste, tribe, or race.	Religion.	POPULATION.									LITERATE IN ENGLISH.		
		TOTAL.			LITERATE.			ILLITERATE.					
		Persons.	Males.	Females.	Persons.	Males.	Females.	Persons.	Males.	Females.	Persons.	Males.	Females.
1	2	3	4	5	6	7	8	9	10	11	12	13	14
Darzi . . .	Total .	2,245	1,225	1,020	217	210	7	2,028	1,015	1,013	20	19	1
	H.	2,235	1,217	1,018	217	210	7	2,018	1,007	1,011	20	19	1
	M.	10	8	2	...	...	...	10	8	2	...	...	...
Dhakar . .	H.	626	321	305	3	3	...	623	318	305	1	1	...
Dhobi . .	Total .	2,882	1,479	1,403	13	13	...	2,869	1,466	1,403	...	...	...
	H.	2,475	1,278	1,197	12	12	...	2,463	1,266	1,197	...	..	..
	M	407	201	206	1	1	...	406	200	206	..	...	...
Fakir . . .	Total .	1,751	921	830	32	32	...	1,719	889	830	1	1	...
	H.	32	8	24	...	...	...	33	8	24	...	...	..
	M.	1,719	913	806	32	33	...	1,687	881	806	1	1	...
Goanese . .	C.	237	168	69	119	98	21	118	70	48	70	59	11
Golapurab . .	H.	15	7	8	...	...	...	15	7	8	...	...	...
Gujar . .	H.	34,694	18,415	16,279	198	196	2	34,496	18,219	16,277	21	21	...
Jat . . .	Total .	30,486	16,517	13,969	704	692	12	29,782	15,825	13,957	37	36	1
	H.	29,731	15,850	13,881	465	456	9	29,266	15,394	13,872	29	28	1
	M.	4	3	1	...	...	...	4	3	1	...	...	...
	S.	751	664	87	239	236	3	512	428	84	8	8	...
Jew . . .	Jewish	25	12	13	7	6	1	18	6	12	4	4	...
Kachhi . .	H.	77	41	36	6	4	2	71	37	34	1	1	...
Kaimkhani . .	M.	542	306	236	14	13	1	528	293	235	...	...	...
Kalal . .	Total .	1,341	695	646	108	105	3	1,233	590	643	2	2	...
	H.	1,308	674	634	108	105	3	1,200	569	631	2	2	...
	M.	33	21	12	...	...	...	33	21	12	...	...	...
Kasai . . .	M.	1,088	549	539	18	17	1	1,070	532	538	...	...	...
Kayastha . .	Total .	2,439	1,320	1,119	1,004	896	114	1,435	430	1,005	539	532	7
	Ar.	42	24	18	25	19	6	17	5	12	12	12	...
	H.	2,397	1,296	1,101	979	871	108	1,418	425	993	527	520	7
Khati . . .	H.	6,806	3,601	3,205	265	260	5	6,541	3,341	3,200	36	36	...
Khatik . .	H.	3,543	1,790	1,753	56	53	3	3,487	1,737	1,750	8	7	1
Koli . . .	H.	6,554	3,476	3,078	87	83	4	6,467	3,393	3,074	9	9	...

TABLE IX.

EDUCATION BY SELECTED CASTES.

RAJPUTANA—*contd.*

TABLE IX.—EDUCATION BY SELECTED

[In Col. 2 A=Animist, Ar=Arya, Br=Brahmo,

Caste, tribe, or race.	Religion.	POPULATION.									LITERATE IN ENGLISH.		
		TOTAL.			LITERATE.			ILLITERATE.					
		Persons.	Males.	Females.	Persons.	Males.	Females.	Persons.	Males.	Females.	Persons.	Males.	Females.
1	2	3	4	5	6	7	8	9	10	11	12	13	14
Kumhar	**Total**	**309,228**	**159,672**	**149,556**	**464**	**457**	**7**	**308,764**	**159,215**	**149,549**	**7**	**7**	..
	Ar.	1	1	...	...	...	...	1	1	...	...	...	...
	H.	302,017	155,819	146,198	456	450	6	301,561	155,369	146,192	7	7	...
	J	10	6	4	2	2	...	8	4	4	...	...	...
	M	6,888	3,665	3,223	6	5	1	6,882	3,660	3,222	...	...	...
	S.	312	181	131	...	...	...	312	181	131	...	...	...
Lodha	**Total**	**47,013**	**24,526**	**22,487**	**120**	**117**	**3**	**46,893**	**24,409**	**22,484**	**3**	**3**	...
	H.	47,003	24,520	22,483	120	117	3	46,883	24,403	22,480	3	3	...
	M.	10	6	4	...	...	...	10	6	4	...	...	...
Lohar	**Total**	**80,810**	**41,240**	**39,570**	**389**	**378**	**11**	**80,421**	**40,862**	**39,559**	**21**	**21**	...
	H.	62,665	32,346	30,319	287	281	6	62,378	32,065	30,313	18	18	...
	M.	18,145	8,894	9,251	102	97	5	18,043	8,797	9,246	3	3	...
Mahajan or Baniya	**Total**	**707,404**	**352,999**	**354,405**	**161,695**	**159,010**	**2,685**	**545,709**	**193,989**	**351,720**	**1,989**	**1,977**	**12**
	Ar.	179	111	68	91	73	18	88	38	50	22	22	...
	H.	377,292	192,344	184,948	79,430	78,463	967	207,862	113,881	183.981	1,126	1,117	9
	J.	329,933	160,544	169,389	82,174	80,474	1,700	247,759	80,070	167,689	841	838	3
Mali	**Total**	**336,874**	**174,965**	**161,909**	**1,007**	**957**	**50**	**335,867**	**174,008**	**161,859**	**56**	**56**	..
	Ar.	132	70	62	23	22	1	109	48	61	6	6	...
	H.	336,196	174,636	161,560	974	925	49	335,222	173,711	161,511	49	49	...
	J.	17	8	9	...	...	...	17	8	9	...	...	...
	M.	529	251	278	10	10	...	519	241	278	1	1	...
Meghwal	**Total**	**57,333**	**30,005**	**27,328**	**16**	**16**	...	**57,317**	**29,989**	**27,328**	...	...	...
	H.	57,327	30,001	27,326	16	16	...	57,311	29,985	27,326	...	...	...
	M.	6	4	2	...	...	...	6	4	2	...	...	...
Meo or Mewati	**Total**	**165,689**	**87,346**	**78,343**	**344**	**343**	**1**	**165,345**	**87,003**	**78,342**	**2**	**2**	
	H.	146	73	73	...	...	...	146	73	73	...	...	..
	M.	165,543	87,273	78,270	344	343	1	165,199	86,930	78,269	2	2	..
Mer	**Total**	**13,712**	**7,156**	**6,556**	**165**	**165**	...	**13,547**	**6,991**	**6,556**	**2**	**2**	...
	H.	13,658	7,127	6,531	165	165	...	13,493	6,962	6,531	2	2	...
	M.	54	29	25	...	...	...	54	29	25	...	...	...
Morat	**Total**	**2,142**	**1,190**	**952**	**10**	**10**	...	**2,132**	**1,180**	**952**	..	...	..
(*a*) Gorat	H.	26	16	10	...	...	...	26	16	10	...	...	...
(*b*) Kathat	M.	2,116	1,174	942	10	10	...	2,106	1,164	942	...	...	...
Mina	**Total**	**558,687**	**296,205**	**262,482**	**1,489**	**1,467**	**22**	**557,198**	**294,738**	**262,460**	**7**	**7**	...
	A.	46,044	23,730	22,314	3	3	...	46,041	23,727	22,314	...	...	...
	H.	512,504	272,411	240,093	1,486	1,464	22	511,018	270,947	240,071	7	7	...
	M.	139	64	75	...	...	...	139	64	75	...	...	...
Meghal	M.	**13,999**	**7,406**	**6,593**	**630**	**587**	**43**	**13,369**	**6,819**	**6,550**	**62**	**61**	**1**
Nai	**Total**	**162,235**	**84,751**	**77,484**	**761**	**742**	**19**	**161,474**	**84,009**	**77,465**	**33**	**33**	...
	Ar.	6	3	3	1	1	...	5	2	3	...	...	...
	H.	152,973	80,009	72,964	710	691	19	152,263	79,318	72,945	32	32	...
	M.	9,256	4,739	4,517	50	50	...	9,206	4,689	4,517	1	1	.
Naik or Nayak	**Total**	**42,391**	**22,111**	**20,280**	**58**	**55**	**3**	**42,333**	**22,056**	**20,277**	...	...	...
	H.	42,267	22,041	20,226	52	49	3	42,215	21,992	20,223	...	...	...
	M.	124	70	54	6	6	...	118	64	54	...	...	...

CASTES, TRIBES OR RACES—*continued.*

H=Hindu, J=Jain, M=Musalman, S=Sikh.]

TABLE IX.

EDUCATION BY SELECTED CASTES.

AJMER-MERWARA—*contd.*

Caste, tribe or race.	Religion.	POPULATION.									LITERATE IN ENGLISH.		
		TOTAL.			LITERATE.			ILLITERATE.					
		Persons.	Males.	Females.	Persons.	Males.	Females.	Persons.	Males.	Females.	Persons.	Males.	Females.
1	2	3	4	5	6	7	8	9	10	11	12	13	14
Kumhar	**Total**	**14,106**	**7,206**	**6,900**	**107**	**104**	**3**	**13,999**	**7,102**	**6,897**	**5**	**5**	...
	H.	14,048	7,177	6,871	105	102	3	13,943	7,075	6,868	5	5	...
	J.	1	1	...	...	...	...	1	1	...	...	...	...
	M.	55	26	29	1	1	...	54	25	29	...	...	...
	S.	2	2	...	1	1	...	1	1	...	...	...	...
Lodha	H.	**1,121**	**566**	**555**	**17**	**17**	...	**1,104**	**549**	**555**	**2**	**2**	...
Lohar	**Total**	**4,212**	**2,255**	**1,957**	**102**	**97**	**5**	**4,110**	**2,158**	**1,952**	**8**	**8**	...
	H.	2,477	1,320	1,157	87	82	5	2,390	1,238	1,152	8	8	...
	M.	1,735	935	800	15	15	...	1,720	920	800	...	...	...
Mahajan or Baniya	**Total**	**34,467**	**18,410**	**16,057**	**11,887**	**11,557**	**330**	**22,580**	**6,853**	**15,727**	**648**	**645**	**3**
	Ar.	181	105	76	101	85	16	80	20	60	40	40	...
	H.	14,296	7,646	6,650	4,891	4,745	146	9,405	2,901	6,504	446	443	3
	J.	19,990	10,659	9,331	6,895	6,727	168	13,095	3,932	9,163	162	162	...
Mali	**Total**	**14,328**	**7,492**	**6,836**	**229**	**223**	**6**	**14,099**	**7,269**	**6,830**	**35**	**35**	...
	H.	14,307	7,482	6,825	228	223	5	14,079	7,259	6,820	35	35	...
	J.	1	...	1	1	...	1	...	...	...	...	...	...
	M.	20	10	10	..	...	...	20	10	10	...	...	...
Meghwal	H.	**1**	...	**1**	...	...	...	**1**	...	**1**	...	...	...
Meo or Mewati	**Total**	**173**	**94**	**79**	**6**	**4**	**2**	**167**	**90**	**77**	**1**	**1**	...
	H.	6	2	4	...	...	..	6	2	4	...	...	...
	M.	167	92	75	6	4	2	161	88	73	1	1	...
Mer	**Total**	**21,803**	**11,634**	**10,169**	**235**	**233**	**2**	**21,568**	**11,401**	**10,167**	**4**	**4**	...
	H.	21,774	11,623	10,151	234	232	2	21,540	11,391	10,149	4	4	...
	M.	29	11	18	1	1	...	28	10	18	...	...	...
Merat	**Total**	**5,209**	**3,149**	**2,060**	**102**	**100**	**2**	**5,107**	**3,049**	**2,058**	**4**	**4**	...
(*a*) Gorat	H.	1,945	1,257	688	60	58	2	1,885	1,199	686	2	2	...
(*b*) Kathat	M.	3,264	1,892	1,372	42	42	...	3,222	1,850	1,372	2	2	...
Mina	**Total**	**4,221**	**2,440**	**1,781**	**125**	**125**	...	**4,096**	**2,315**	**1,781**	**1**	**1**	...
	A.	1	1	...	...	...	...	1	1	...	...	...	...
	H.	4,217	2,436	1,781	125	125	...	4,092	2,311	1,781	1	1	...
	M.	3	3	..	...	...	...	3	3	...	...	...	...
Moghal	M.	**1,415**	**778**	**637**	**132**	**127**	**5**	**1,283**	**651**	**632**	**40**	**40**	...
Nai	**Total**	**6,499**	**3,293**	**3,206**	**187**	**184**	**3**	**6,312**	**3,109**	**3,203**	**19**	**19**	...
	Ar.	10	4	6	1	...	1	9	4	5	...	...	...
	H.	6,278	3,181	3,097	182	180	2	6,096	3,001	3,095	19	19	...
	M.	211	108	103	4	4	...	207	104	103	...	...	...
Naik or Nayak	H.	**2,494**	**1,295**	**1,199**	**11**	**10**	**1**	**2,483**	**1,285**	**1,198**	...	...	...

TABLE IX.

EDUCATION BY SELECTED CASTES.

TABLE IX.—EDUCATION BY SELECTED

RAJPUTANA—*concld.*

[In Col. 2 A=Animist, Ar=Arya, Br=Brahmo,

Caste, tribe, or race.	Religion.	POPULATION.									LITERATE IN ENGLISH.		
		TOTAL.			LITERATE.			ILLITERATE.					
		Persons.	Males.	Females.	Persons.	Males.	Females.	Persons.	Males.	Females.	Persons.	Males.	Females.
1	2	3	4	5	6	7	8	9	10	11	12	13	14
Parsi . . .	Parsi.	**342**	**191**	**151**	**272**	**161**	**111**	**70**	**30**	**40**	**130**	**109**	**21**
Patel . .	H.	**55,797**	**27,750**	**28,047**	**57**	**56**	**1**	**55,740**	**27,694**	**28,046**	**14**	**14**	...
Pathan . .	M.	**108,225**	**57,471**	**50,754**	**5,549**	**5,331**	**218**	**102,676**	**52,140**	**50,536**	**379**	**374**	**5**
Prohit . .	**Total** .	**36,942**	**19,130**	**17,812**	**646**	**623**	**23**	**36,296**	**18,507**	**17,789**	**26**	**26**	...
	Ar.	3	2	1	2	1	1	1	1	...	1	1	...
	H.	36,939	19,128	17,811	644	622	22	36,295	18,506	17,789	25	25	...
Raigar . .	**Total** .	**81,568**	**41,626**	**39,942**	**35**	**35**	...	**81,533**	**41,591**	**39,942**	**1**	**1**	...
	H.	81,557	41,622	39,935	35	35	...	81,522	41,587	39,935	1	1	...
	M.	11	4	7	...	...	...	11	4	7	...	...	...
Rajput . .	**Total** .	**663,996**	**372,557**	**291,439**	**17,724**	**15,131**	**2,593**	**646,272**	**357,426**	**288,846**	**726**	**711**	**15**
	Ar.	259	160	99	117	95	22	142	65	77	60	60	...
	Br.	1	1	...	...	...	...	1	1	...	...	...	...
	H.	632,384	355,421	276,963	17,283	14,724	2,559	615,101	340,697	274,404	643	628	15
	J.	28	13	15	4	4	...	24	9	15	...	...	...
	M.	31,190	16,890	14,300	280	271	9	30,910	16,619	14,291	16	16	...
	S.	134	72	62	40	37	3	94	35	59	7	7	...
Rangrez . .	M.	**15,485**	**8,049**	**7,436**	**244**	**240**	**4**	**15,241**	**7,809**	**7,432**	**4**	**4**	...
Rawat . .	**Total** .	**13,697**	**7,544**	**6,153**	**14**	**14**	...	**13,683**	**7,530**	**6,153**	**2**	**2**	...
	A.	15	11	4	...	...	...	15	11	4	...	...	...
	H.	13,676	7,529	6,147	14	14	...	13,662	7,515	6,147	2	2	...
	M.	6	4	2	...	...	...	6	4	2	...	...	...
Rebari . .	**Total** .	**129,917**	**67,759**	**62,158**	**46**	**44**	**2**	**129,871**	**67,715**	**62,156**	...	...	...
	H.	129,911	67,754	62,157	46	44	2	129,865	67,710	62,155	...	...	...
	M.	6	5	1	...	...	...	6	5	1	...	...	...
Sadhu . .	**Total** .	**10,230**	**6,261**	**3,969**	**1,593**	**1,336**	**257**	**8,637**	**4,925**	**3,712**	**8**	**8**	...
	Ar.	4	2	2	2	2	...	2	...	2	...	...	...
	H.	9,636	6,072	3,564	1,219	1,197	22	8,417	4,875	3,542	8	8	...
	J.	575	179	396	369	134	235	206	45	161	...	...	...
	S.	15	8	7	3	3	...	12	5	7	...	...	...
Saiyad . .	M.	**28,954**	**15,242**	**13,712**	**3,793**	**3,494**	**299**	**25,161**	**11,748**	**13,413**	**402**	**397**	**5**
Sevag . .	**Total** .	**10,075**	**4,863**	**5,212**	**1,072**	**1,058**	**14**	**9,003**	**3,805**	**5,198**	**7**	**7**	...
	H.	9,959	4,796	5,163	1,041	1,027	14	8,918	3,769	5,149	7	7	...
	J.	116	67	49	31	31	...	85	36	49	...	...	...
Shekh . .	M.	**181,704**	**96,638**	**85,066**	**6,890**	**6,561**	**329**	**174,814**	**90,077**	**84,737**	**589**	**581**	**8**
Sunar . .	**Total** .	**69,014**	**35,556**	**33,458**	**5,159**	**5,095**	**64**	**63,855**	**30,461**	**33,394**	**42**	**42**	...
	Ar.	10	7	3	4	4	...	6	3	3	...	...	...
	H.	68,961	35,527	33,434	5,154	5,090	64	63,807	30,437	33,370	42	42	...
	J.	12	7	5	...	...	...	12	7	5	...	...	...
	M.	31	15	16	1	1	...	30	14	16	...	...	...
Sutar . . .	**Total** .	**45,933**	**23,688**	**22,245**	**296**	**292**	**4**	**45,637**	**23,396**	**22,241**	**8**	**8**	...
	Ar.	4	...	4	...	...	...	4	...	4	...	...	...
	H.	45,928	23,687	22,241	296	292	4	45,632	23,395	22,237	8	8	...
	J.	1	1	...	...	...	...	1	1	...	...	...	...
Teli . .	**Total** .	**78,427**	**40,628**	**37,799**	**503**	**493**	**10**	**77,924**	**40,135**	**37,789**	**10**	**10**	...
	Ar.	6	3	3	1	1	...	5	2	3	...	...	...
	H.	46,476	24,001	22,477	362	357	5	46,116	23,644	22,472	5	5	...
	M.	31.943	16,024	15,319	140	135	5	31,808	16,489	15,314	5	5	...

CASTES, TRIBES, OR RACES—*concluded.*

TABLE IX.

EDUCATION BY SELECTED CASTES.

H.=Hindus, J=Jain, M=Musalman, S=Sikh.]

AJMER-MERWARA—*concld.*

Caste, tribe, or race.	Religion.	POPULATION. Total. Persons.	Total. Males.	Total. Females.	Literate. Persons.	Literate. Males.	Literate. Females.	Illiterate. Persons.	Illiterate. Males.	Illiterate. Females.	Literate in English. Persons.	Literate in English. Males.	Literate in English. Females.
1	2	3	4	5	6	7	8	9	10	11	12	13	14
Parsi . .	Parsi.	**262**	**134**	**128**	**166**	**99**	**67**	**96**	**35**	**61**	**111**	**82**	**29**
Patel . . .	H.	**6**	**4**	**2**	**1**	**1**	.	**5**	**3**	**2**	...	...	...
Pathan . .	M.	**11,420**	**6,176**	**5,244**	**990**	**967**	**23**	**10,430**	**5,219**	**5,211**	**228**	**228**	...
Prohit . .	H.	**178**	**90**	**88**	**14**	**14**	...	**164**	**76**	**88**	...	...	...
Raigar . .	H.	**19,834**	**10,135**	**9,699**	**54**	**53**	**1**	**19,780**	**10,082**	**9,698**	...	...	...
Rajput . .	Total .	**14,301**	**8,224**	**6,077**	**1,586**	**1,380**	**206**	**12,715**	**6,844**	**5,871**	**259**	**258**	**1**
	Ar.	58	43	15	34	28	6	24	15	9	10	10	...
	H.	14,134	8,006	6,088	1,527	1,328	199	12,607	6,768	5,809	244	243	1
	J.	2	1	1	...	...	...	2	1	1	...	...	...
	M.	100	79	21	20	20	...	80	59	21	2	2	...
	S.	7	5	2	5	4	1	2	1	1	3	3	...
Rangrez . .	M.	**621**	**358**	**263**	**24**	**23**	**1**	**597**	**335**	**262**	**1**	**1**	...
Rawat . . .	Total .	**47,904**	**24,962**	**22,942**	**525**	**522**	**3**	**47,379**	**24,440**	**22,939**	**16**	**16**	...
	H.	47,861	24,953	22,908	525	522	3	47,336	24,431	22,905	16	16	...
	M.	43	9	34	...	...	...	43	9	34	...	...	...
Rebari . .	H.	**2,031**	**1,083**	**948**	...	...	...	**2,031**	**1,083**	**948**	...	...	...
Sadhu . . .	Total .	**4,635**	**2,552**	**2,083**	**449**	**425**	**24**	**4,186**	**2,127**	**2,059**	**12**	**12**	...
	H.	4,581	2,523	2,058	424	409	15	4,157	2,114	2,043	12	12	...
	J.	54	29	25	25	16	9	29	13	16	...	...	...
Saiyad . .	M.	**5,189**	**2,883**	**2,306**	**764**	**720**	**44**	**4,425**	**2,163**	**2,262**	**165**	**165**	...
Sevag . . .	Total .	**254**	**137**	**117**	**58**	**58**	...	**196**	**79**	**117**	**7**	**7**	...
	H.	250	135	115	57	57	...	193	78	115	6	6	...
	J.	4	2	2	1	1	...	3	1	2	1	1	...
Shekh . .	M.	**25,130**	**13,380**	**11,750**	**1,618**	**1,525**	**93**	**23,512**	**11,855**	**11,657**	**334**	**330**	**4**
Sunar . .	Total .	**3,193**	**1,670**	**1,523**	**445**	**433**	**12**	**2,748**	**1,237**	**1,511**	**18**	**17**	**1**
	Ar.	15	7	8	5	4	1	10	3	7	...	...	...
	H.	3,178	1,663	1,515	440	429	11	2,738	1,234	1,504	18	17	1
Sutar . . .	H.	**1**	**1**	...	...	...	...	**1**	**1**	...	...	...	...
Teli . . .	Total .	**4,405**	**2,284**	**2,121**	**79**	**78**	**2**	**4,326**	**2,206**	**2,120**	**4**	**4**	...
	H.	3,935	2,038	1,897	58	57	1	3,877	1,981	1,896	4	4	...
	M.	470	246	224	21	21	...	449	225	224	...	...	...

TABLE X.

Language.

Explanatory Note.

This Table shows the languages ordinarily spoken by the people in their own homes. Infants and dumb persons have been classified as speaking their mother's language.

The languages entered in the Table are those actually returned in the schedules, except that entries, which were obviously either purely local terms, or not languages at all, have been shewn under the languages which, after further enquiry, it was considered were intended. On the last page of the Table will be found an Appendix shewing the most important of such entries, as found in the schedules, and the proper languages in which they have been included.

The Table is divided into four groups :—

A.—Vernaculars of India, commencing with the two most frequently spoken in Rajputana, Rajasthani and Western Hindi, the rest being in alphabetical order.

B.—Vernaculars of Asiatic countries beyond India.

C.—European languages.

D.—Other languages.

Languages of numerical insignificance have been amalgamated under "others" in each group. Their details are as follows :—

Language.		Sex.	State or District.																	
			Alwar.	Banswara.	Bharatpur.	Bikaner.	Bundi.	Dholpur.	Jaipur.	Jaisalmer.	Jhalawar.	Kishangarh.	Kotah.	Marwar.	Mewar.	Shahpura.	Sirohi.	Tonk.	Ajmer.	Merwara.
A.—Vernaculars of India.	Burmese	F.	..	..	..	..	..	..	1	..	..	..	..	..	..	..	..	..	..	..
	Eastern Hindi	M.	..	..	..	..	..	..	..	..	..	..	..	10	7	1	..	..	13	5
		F.	..	..	..	..	..	..	..	..	..	1	..	3	2	1	..	..	5	4
	Eastern Pahari or Nepali.	M.	..	..	..	..	..	..	3	..	..	..	1	2	3	..	..	..	5	..
		F.	..	..	..	..	..	..	..	..	..	..	1	..	56	..	..	..	1	..
	Gondi	M.	..	..	..	..	..	..	..	..	..	..	8	..	..	..	..	..	..	..
	Kanarese	M.	..	..	..	..	..	..	..	..	1	..	15	..	..	..	..	..	1	..
		F.	..	..	..	..	..	..	..	..	..	..	1	..	..	..	..	..	2	..
	Kashmiri	M.	..	1	5	3	..	..	13	..	..	..	..	9	..	..	..	..	6	..
		F.	..	..	6	2	..	..	6	..	..	..	..	6	..	..	..	..	1	..
	Kherwari-Korwa	M.	..	..	..	..	..	..	..	..	..	..	..	..	..	..	2	..	..	..
	Malayalum	M.	..	..	..	..	..	..	..	..	..	1	..	..	..	..	..	..	..	..
	Oriya	M.	..	..	..	..	..	..	..	..	..	..	..	3	..	..	2	..	1	..
	Tamil	M.	1	..	4	..	1	..	11	..	1	1	6	1	5	..	19	1	94	..
		F.	..	..	1	..	3	..	10	..	..	..	3	..	5	..	11	..	64	..
	Telugu	M.	..	..	10	..	..	..	9	..	..	..	1	1	3	..	..	..	13	1
		F.	..	..	9	..	..	..	12	..	..	..	7	1	..	..	1	..	8	..
	Western Pahari	M.	..	..	..	..	..	..	..	..	..	..	..	..	1	..	..	..	..	..
	Western Panjabi	M.	..	..	..	188	..	2	..	..	..	10	1	16	..	..	..	..	128	..
		F.	..	..	..	214	..	..	..	..	..	9	..	13	5	..	..	1	157	2
B.—Vernaculars of Asiatic Countries beyond India.	Chinese	M.	..	..	..	..	..	..	..	..	..	..	1	..	..	..	..	..	..	..
	Hebrew	M.	..	..	..	..	..	..	..	..	..	..	..	..	..	..	1	..	8	..
		F.	..	..	..	..	..	..	..	..	..	..	..	..	..	..	1	..	11	..
	Japanese	M.	..	..	..	..	..	..	..	..	..	..	1	..	..	..	..	..	..	..
	Persian	M.	1	..	..	..	1	3	3	..	..	..	1	2	4	..	5	..	10	..
		F.	..	..	..	..	..	..	2	..	..	..	..	1	1	..	..	..	3	..
	Turkish dialects	M.	..	..	..	..	..	..	1	4	..	..	2	..	..	..	..	..	..	1
C.—European languages.	French	M.	..	..	..	..	..	1	10	..	8	..	..	..	..	..	2	..	21	..
		F.	..	..	..	..	..	1	3	..	1	..	..	1	..	..	2	..	14	..
	German	M.	..	..	..	..	..	..	3	..	..	..	..	..	..	..	1	..	..	..
		F.	..	..	..	..	..	..	2	..	2	..	..	..	..	..	1	..	..	..
	Greek	M.	..	..	..	..	..	..	..	..	..	..	..	..	..	..	..	..	..	1
	Portuguese	M.	8	..	..	..	..	..	6	..	..	..	3	7	2	1	13	..	116	2
		F.	6	..	..	..	..	..	3	..	..	2	..	4	1	..	3	..	57	..
	Russian	M.	..	..	..	..	..	..	..	..	..	..	..	..	..	..	..	..	1	..
	Spanish		..	..	..	..	..	..	..	..	1	..	1	..	..	..	..	..	..	..

So, too, dialects numerically insignificant have been included in the figures for the main language to which they belong (see Appendix at end of Table).

TABLE X.—LANGUAGE.

Province; and State or District.	POPULATION.			A.—VERNACULARS OF INDIA.								
				TOTAL.			RAJASTHANI.					
							Total Rajasthani.			Ajmeri.		
	Persons.	Males.	Females.	Persons.	Males.	Females.	Persons.	Males.	Females.	Persons.	Males.	Females.
1	2	3	4	5	6	7	8	9	10	11	12	13
Rajputana . .	10,530,432	5,515,275	5,015,157	10,528,569	5,514,185	5,014,384	*8,437,064*	*4,396,871*	*4,040,193*	3,199	1,611	1,588
Alwar . . .	791,688	413,659	378,029	791,634	413,628	378,006	*466,196*	*242,171*	*224,025*	2	...	2
Banswara . . .	165,463	81,620	83,843	165,463	81,620	83,843	*68,566*	*33,663*	*34,903*	...	...	...
Bharatpur . . .	558,785	302,254	256,531	558,747	302,240	256,507	*66,019*	*34,854*	*31,165*	1	1	...
Bikaner . . .	700,983	371,489	329,494	700,959	371,475	329,484	*649,271*	*342,418*	*306,853*	47	32	15
Bundi . . .	218,730	113,211	105,519	218,729	113,210	105,519	*217,095*	*112,312*	*104,783*	37	20	17
Dholpur . . .	263,188	144,244	118,944	263,158	144,225	118,933	*372*	*209*	*163*	...	...	...
Dungarpur . . .	159,192	79,105	80,087	159,190	79,103	80,087	*81,408*	*39,738*	*41,670*	1	1	...
Jaipur . . .	2,636,647	1,385,750	1,250,897	2,635,948	1,385,377	1,250,571	*2,387,195*	*1,253,874*	*1,133,321*	486	236	250
Jaisalmer . . .	88,311	48,500	39,811	88,307	48,496	39,811	*79,173*	*43,295*	*35,878*	...	...	...
Jhalawar . . .	96,271	50,034	46,237	96,257	50,025	46,232	*56,039*	*29,544*	*26,495*	...	...	...
Karauli . . .	146,587	80,081	66,506	146,585	80,079	66,506	*204*	*99*	*105*	...	...	...
Kishangarh . . .	87,191	45,718	41,473	87,188	45,718	41,470	*86,466*	*45,251*	*41,215*	600	361	239
Kotah . . .	639,089	330,324	308,765	639,030	330,288	308,742	*618,537*	*319,012*	*299,525*	245	128	117
Kushalgarh (Chiefship)	22,005	10,956	11,049	22,005	10,956	11,049	*2,126*	*1,046*	*1,080*	...	...	...
Lawa (Estate) . .	2,564	1,302	1,262	2,564	1,302	1,262	*2,549*	*1,294*	*1,255*	1	1	...
Marwar . . .	2,057,553	1,075,269	982,284	2,057,381	1,075,179	982,202	*1,989,910*	*1,038,743*	*951,167*	404	237	167
Mewar . . .	1,293,776	670,750	623,026	1,293,727	670,720	623,007	*1,194,813*	*618,584*	*576,229*	1,056	460	506
Partabgarh . . .	62,704	31,735	30,969	62,704	31,735	30,969	*39,411*	*19,882*	*19,529*	15	8	7
Shahpura (Chiefship) .	47,397	24,595	22,802	47,396	24,594	22,802	*47,240*	*24,497*	*22,743*	277	110	167
Sirohi . . .	189,127	98,289	90,838	188,446	97,850	90,596	*159,908*	*82,908*	*77,000*	25	15	10
Tonk . . .	303,181	156,390	146,791	303,149	156,365	146,784	*225,266*	*114,677*	*110,589*	2	1	1
Ajmer-Merwara .	501,395	266,198	235,197	498,628	264,211	234,417	*411,229*	*216,578*	*194,651*	255,488	135,340	120,148
Ajmer . . .	380,384	201,911	178,473	377,646	199,942	177,704	*296,593*	*155,839*	*140,754*	254,854	135,042	119,812
Merwara . . .	121,011	64,287	56,724	120,982	64,269	56,713	*114,636*	*60,739*	*53,897*	634	298	336

TABLE X.—LANGUAGE.—*contd.*

Province; and State or District.	A.—VERNACULARS OF INDIA—*contd.*														
	RAJASTHANI—*contd.*														
	Bagri or Shekhawati.			Dhundari or Jaipuri.			Dhundari-Dadari.			Harauti.			Malvi, Rangri, or Ahiri.		
	Persons.	Males.	Females.	Persons.	Males.	Females.	Persons.	Males.	Females.	Persons.	Males.	Females.	Persons.	Males.	Females.
1	14	15	16	17	18	19	20	21	22	23	24	25	26	27	28
Rajputana	568,184	290,826	277,358	2,137,446	1,127,273	1,010,173	28,662	15,050	13,612	642,966	330,049	312,917	236,970	120,775	116,195
Alwar	208	80	128	326	90	236	...	...	...	3	3	...	...	..	...
Banswara	64,710	31,742	32,968	48	39	9	...	...	...	1	1	...	610	308	302
Bharatpur	...	...	...	191	99	92	...	...	...	1	1	...	2	1	1
Bikaner	34	22	12	1,449	989	460	...	...	...	...	...	...	5	4	1
Bundi	3	...	3	4,369	1,719	2,650	...	...	...	166,086	86,123	79,963	63	20	43
Dholpur	...	...	...	39	19	20	...	...	...	...	...	...	29	7	22
Dungarpur	79,017	38,625	40,392	3	2	1	...	...	...	...	...	...	137	66	91
Jaipur	483,393	219,870	203,523	1,043,076	1,027,409	910,507	...	...	...	1,007	358	640	45	19	26
Jaisalmer	5	4	1	5	5	...	...	...	...	...	...	...	...	...	...
Jhalawar	...	...	..	88	54	34	...	...	...	117	56	61	8,956	4,541	4,415
Karauli	...	...	...	121	48	73	...	...	..	...	...	...	1	1	...
Kishangarh	20	8	12	84,139	44,021	40,118	...	..	...	19	8	11	21	14	10
Kotah	50	38	12	6,046	3,432	2,614	27,680	14,615	13,074	474,326	243,071	231,255	102,721	53,872	48,849
Kushalgarh (Chiefship)	...	...	...	...	...	...	...	...	.	...	...	...	2,080	1,023	1,066
Lawa (Estate)	...	...	...	2,540	1,289	1,251	...	...	...	...	...	...	...	...	...
Marwar	155	90	65	12,434	5,487	6,947	...	...	...	15	10	5	26	11	15
Mewar	162	91	71	1,370	737	633	973	435	538	1,236	319	917	835	399	436
Partabgarh	...	...	...	19	10	9	...	...	...	3	2	1	38,995	19,654	19,341
Shahpura (Chiefship)	11	8	3	207	109	98	...	...	...	94	62	32	76	60	16
Sirohi	411	245	166	1,047	615	432	...	...	...	...	...	...	...	...	...
Tonk	5	3	2	79,029	41,040	37,989	...	...	...	58	35	23	82,336	40,776	41,561
Ajmer-Merwara	395	225	170	9,709	4,814	4,895	...	...	...	357	117	240	141	91	50
Ajmer	304	168	136	7,470	3,502	3,968	...	..	...	357	117	240	125	79	46
Merwara	91	57	34	2,239	1,312	927	...	...	...	...	...	...	16	12	4

TABLE X.—LANGUAGE.—*contd.*

Province; and State or District.	A.—VERNACULARS OF INDIA—*contd.*														
	RAJASTHANI—*contd.*														
	Marwari.			Merwari.			Mewari.			Mewari-Khairari.			Mewati.		
	Persons.	Males.	Females.	Persons.	Males.	Females.	Persons.	Males.	Females.	Persons.	Males.	Females.	Persons.	Males.	Females.
1	29	30	31	32	33	34	35	36	37	38	39	40	41	42	43
Rajputana	2,889,784	1,509,752	1,380,032	1,754	772	982	1,284,893	661,224	618,669	44,104	23,397	20,707	533,820	277,594	256,226
Alwar	252	119	133	...	...	...	1	...	1	...	...	...	465,404	241,879	223,525
Banswara	905	421	484	...	...	...	2,292	1,152	1,140	...	...	...	...	...	...
Bharatpur	289	157	132	1		1	...	...	...	...	...	...	65,534	34,595	30,939
Bikaner	647,696	341,346	306,350	...	.	...	7	4	3	...	...	...	11	8	3
Bundi	1,961	907	1,054	...	...	...	1,795	824	971	42,779	22,698	20,081	2	1	1
Dholpur	299	180	119	...	...	...	...	...	...	.	...	...	5	3	2
Dungarpur	937	439	498	...	...	...	1,293	605	688	...	...	...	...	...	...
Jaipur	13,923	3,521	10,402	...	...	...	877	436	441	1,097	566	531	2,390	899	1,491
Jaisalmer	79,159	43,284	35,875	...	...	...	...	...	...	...	...	...	...	...	...
Jhalawar	227	130	97	...	...	...	100	56	44	...	...	...	5	3	2
Karauli	65	34	31	...	...	...	17	16	1	...	...	...	...	...	...
Kishangarh	1,259	658	601	...	...	...	385	173	212	7	5	2	3	2	...
Kotah	3,253	1,647	1,606	17	1	16	3,485	1,837	1,648	203	121	82	239	89	150
Kushalgarh (Chiefship)	13	6	7	...	...	...	24	17	7	...	...	...	...	...	...
Lawa (Estate)	8	4	4	...	...	...	...	...	...	...	...	...	...	...	...
Marwar	1,975,198	1,032,155	943,043	34	11	23	1,534	691	843	...	...	...	46	19	27
Mewar	5,548	2,795	2,753	1,444	582	862	1,182,056	612,721	569,335	18	7	11	86	32	54
Partabgarh	207	101	106	...	...	...	139	92	47	...	...	...	33	15	18
Shahpura (Chiefship)	204	140	64	5	1	4	46,866	24,007	22,359	...	...	...	...	...	...
Sirohi	157,400	81,103	76,297	238	164	74	35	22	13	...	...	...	51	43	8
Tonk	981	605	376	15	13	2	42,487	21,571	20,916	...	...	...	12	6	6
Ajmer-Merwara	40,678	21,163	19,515	96,011	51,304	44,707	8,240	3,419	4,821	35	9	26	133	60	73
Ajmer	25,730	13,307	12,333	2,127	1,315	812	5,477	2,141	3,336	35	9	26	76	33	43
Merwara	14,948	7,766	7,182	93,884	49,989	43,895	2,763	1,278	1,485	...	...	...	57	27	30

TABLE X.—Language.—*contd.*

Province; and State or District.	A.—VERNACULARS OF INDIA—*contd.*														
	Rajasthani—*concld.*						Western-Hindi.								
	Rajasthani.			Sundwari.			Total Western-Hindi.			Bhadaori.			Braj Bhasha.		
	Persons.	Males.	Females.	Persons.	Males.	Females.	Persons.	Males.	Females.	Persons.	Males.	Females.	Persons.	Males.	Females.
1	44	45	46	47	48	49	50	51	52	53	54	55	56	57	58
Rajputana	121	51	70	67,161	35,497	31,664	*1,624,935*	*874,500*	*750,435*	1,236	1,058	178	260,004	143,927	116,077
Alwar	...	...	...	...	...	...	*325,232*	*171,326*	*153,906*	...	...	...	49	15	34
Banswara	...	...	...	...	...	...	*721*	*405*	*316*	...	...	...	1	1	...
Bharatpur	...	...	...	...	...	...	*492,170*	*267,067*	*225,103*	...	...	...	...	...	...
Bikaner	22	13	9	...	...	...	*3,599*	*2,306*	*1,293*	...	...	...	181	102	79
Bundi	...	...	...	...	...	...	*838*	*459*	*379*	...	...	...	178	90	88
Dholpur	...	...	...	...	...	...	*262,070*	*143,566*	*118,504*	6	4	2	252,591	140,179	112,412
Dungarpur	...	...	...	...	...	...	*426*	*276*	*150*	...	...	...	...	...	...
Jaipur	...	...	...	1	...	1	*245,473*	*130,155*	*115,318*	...	...	...	4,347	2,271	2,076
Jaisalmer	4	2	2	...	...	...	*11*	*7*	*4*	...	...	...	1	...	1
Jhalawar	...	...	...	46,546	24,704	21,842	*38,718*	*19,704*	*19,014*	...	...	...	43	29	14
Karauli	...	...	...	...	...	...	*146,161*	*79,844*	*66,317*	...	...	...	1	1	...
Kishangarh	11	1	10	...	...	...	*310*	*206*	*104*	14	13	1	5	5	...
Kotah	...	...	...	263	161	102	*14,282*	*7,644*	*6,638*	...	...	...	1,729	789	940
Kushalgarh (Chiefship)	...	...	...	...	...	...	*1,020*	*490*	*530*	...	...	...	...	...	...
Lawa (Estate)	...	...	...	...	...	...	*15*	*8*	*7*	6	2	4	...	...	...
Marwar	64	32	32	...	...	...	*4,834*	*2,948*	*1,886*	...	...	...	46	30	16
Mewar	19	2	17	10	4	6	*5,769*	*3,339*	*2,430*	107	23	84	812	404	408
Partabgarh	...	...	...	...	...	...	*1,076*	*583*	*493*	...	...	...	10	7	3
Shahpura (Chiefship)	...	...	...	...	...	...	*56*	*27*	*29*	...	...	...	...	...	...
Sirohi	1	1	...	...	...	...	*5,751*	*3,351*	*2,400*	...	...	...	10	4	6
Tonk	...	...	...	20,341	10,628	9,713	*76,403*	*40,789*	*35,614*	1,103	1,016	87	...	...	...
Ajmer-Merwara	42	36	6	...	...	...	*80,825*	*43,501*	*37,324*	41	26	15	482	272	210
Ajmer	38	36	2	...	...	...	*75,305*	*40,467*	*34,838*	39	24	15	96	63	33
Merwara	4	...	4	...	...	...	*5,520*	*3,034*	*2,486*	2	2	...	386	209	177

TABLE X.—LANGUAGE.—*contd.*

Province ; and State or District.	A.—VERNACULARS OF INDIA—*contd.*														
	WESTERN-HINDI—*concld.*												BALOCH.		
	Dangi.			Hindi.			Urdu.			Western-Hindi.					
	Persons.	Males.	Females.	Persons.	Males.	Females.	Persons.	Males.	Females.	Persons.	Males.	Females.	Persons.	Males.	Females.
1	59	60	61	62	63	64	65	66	67	68	69	70	71	72	73
Rajputana	21,917	12,135	9,782	1,190,083	636,297	553,786	147,257	78,663	68,594	4,438	2,420	2,018	945	519	426
Alwar	1,885	768	1,117	319,090	168,240	150,850	4,114	2,290	1,824	94	13	81	...	...	...
Banswara	...	...	...	69	47	22	650	356	294	1	1	...	2	1	1
Bharatpur	10,035	5,772	4,263	472,158	255,616	216,542	9,971	5,675	4,296	6	4	2	11	11	...
Bikaner	...	...	...	1,803	1,176	627	1,175	781	394	440	247	193	...	...	...
Bundi	...	...	...	211	140	71	442	227	215	7	2	5	...	...	...
Dholpur	...	...	...	7,556	2,428	5,128	1,719	857	862	198	98	100	...	...	...
Dungarpur	...	...	...	239	141	98	187	135	52	...	...	...	7	3	4
Jaipur	302	112	250	212,188	112,765	99,423	28,209	14,802	13,407	367	205	162	2	2	...
Jaisalmer	...	...	...	...	...	...	10	7	3	...	...	...	134	62	72
Jhalawar	...	...	...	34,710	17,716	16,994	3,960	1,957	2,003	5	2	3	...	...	...
Karauli	9,617	5,473	4,144	132,404	72,208	60,196	4,138	2,162	1,976	1	...	1	...	...	...
Kishangarh	...	...	...	29	15	14	176	122	54	86	51	35	...	...	...
Kotah	...	...	...	2,433	1,440	993	9,540	5,120	4,420	580	295	285	2	2	...
Kushalgarh (Chiefship)	13	6	7	1,005	484	521	2	...	2	...	...	...	18	9	9
Lawa (Estate)	...	...	...	4	4	...	5	2	3	...	...	...	...	...	...
Marwar	...	...	...	1,117	730	387	2,888	1,716	1,172	783	472	311	622	334	288
Mewar	...	...	...	2,544	1,631	913	1,801	1,048	753	505	233	272	9	9	...
Partabgarh	...	...	...	188	137	51	874	437	437	4	2	2	9	7	2
Shahpura (Chiefship)	...	...	...	33	15	18	22	11	11	1	1	...	...	...	...
Sirohi	5	4	1	2,136	1,254	882	2,696	1,543	1,153	904	546	358	129	79	50
Tonk	...	...	...	166	110	56	74,678	39,415	35,263	456	248	208	...	...	...
Ajmer-Merwara	...	...	..	49,251	20,311	22,940	30,225	16,427	13,798	826	405	361	...	...	...
Ajmer	...	...	...	48,149	25,668	22,481	26,433	14,380	12,053	588	332	256	...	...	...
Merwara	...	...	...	1,102	643	459	3,792	2,047	1,745	238	183	105	...	...	...

TABLE X.—LANGUAGE.—*contd.*

Province; and State or District.	A.—VERNACULARS OF INDIA—*contd.*																	
	BEHARI.			BENGALI.			CENTRAL PAHARI.			GIPSY LANGUAGES.								
										Total Gipsy Languages.*			Banjari or Labhani.			Beldari.		
	Persons.	Males.	Females.	Persons.	Males.	Females.	Persons.	Males.	Females.	Persons.	Males.	Females.	Persons.	Males.	Females.	Persons.	Males.	Females.
1	74	75	76	77	78	79	80	81	82	83	84	85	86	87	88	89	90	91
Rajputana	3,476	2,092	1,384	619	355	264	530	479	51	*4,778*	*2,636*	*2,142*	4,290	2,308	1,901	363	180	174
Alwar	40	20	20	5	3	2	3	3	...	...	...	...	...	...	...	...	...	...
Banswara	10	6	4	...	...	...	2	2	...	...	...	...	...	...	...	...	...	...
Bharatpur	24	16	8	54	34	20	...	...	...	...	...	...	...	...	...	...	...	...
Bikaner	179	135	44	17	14	3	...	...	...	...	...	...	...	...	...	...	...	...
Bundi	54	35	19	...	...	...	15	14	1	*103*	*61*	*42*	103	61	42	...	...	...
Dholpur	98	56	42	44	19	25	156	128	28	...	...	...	...	...	...	...	...	...
Dungarpur	...	...	...	...	...	...	...	...	...	*1,408*	*697*	*711*	1,408	697	711	...	...	...
Jaipur	788	436	352	310	161	149	85	68	17	*172*	*100*	*72*	149	94	55	...	...	...
Jaisalmer	...	...	...	2	1	1	...	...	...	*207*	*118*	*89*	...	...	...	207	118	89
Jhalawar	127	80	47	1	1	...	2	2	...	*17*	*11*	*6*	17	11	6	...	...	...
Karauli	19	6	13	67	39	28	...	...	...	...	...	...	...	...	...	...	...	...
Kishangarh	126	83	43	2	2	...	11	11	...	...	...	...	...	...	...	...	...	...
Kotah	568	363	205	5	5	...	101	187	4	*1,556*	*907*	*649*	1,556	907	649	...	...	...
Kushalgarh (Chiefship)	1	1	...	...	...	...	...	...	...	*334*	*169*	*165*	334	169	165	...	...	...
Lawa (Estate)	...	...	...	...	...	...	...	...	...	...	...	...	...	...	...	...	...	...
Marwar	400	241	159	50	37	22	...	...	...	...	...	...	...	...	...	...	...	...
Mewar	475	294	181	40	35	11	41	40	1	*96*	*46*	*50*	3	3	...	...	...	...
Partabgarh	57	35	22	...	...	...	4	4	...	*204*	*141*	*63*	161	122	39	43	19	24
Shahpura (Chiefship)	8	6	2	...	...	...	17	17	...	*14*	*6*	*8*	14	6	8	...	...	...
Sirohi	448	241	207	6	3	3	...	...	...	...	...	...	...	...	...	...	...	...
Tonk	54	38	16	1	1	...	3	3	...	*667*	*380*	*287*	554	328	226	113	52	61
Ajmer-Merwara	1,484	847	637	291	132	159	35	35	...	*223*	*109*	*114*	14	11	3	...	...	...
Ajmer	1,240	699	541	287	128	159	35	35	...	*223*	*109*	*114*	14	11	3	...	...	...
Merwara	244	148	96	4	4	...	...	...	...	...	...	...	...	...	...	...	...	...

* Includes also

		Persons.	Males.	Females.
(1) Kanjari	Ajmer-Merwara / Ajmer	69	36	33
(2) Moghia	Rajputana / Mewar	93	43	50
(3) Pardhi	Rajputana / Jaipur	23	6	17
(4) Sansia	Ajmer-Merwara / Ajmer	140	62	78

TABLE X.—LANGUAGE.—*contd.*

Province; and State or District.	A.—VERNACULARS OF INDIA—*contd.* GUJRATI. Total Gujrati.			Bhil Languages. Total Bhil languages.			Bhili.			Gilasiya (Grassia).			Vagdi.			Gujrati.		
	Persons.	Males.	Females.	Persons.	Males.	Females.	Persons.	Males.	Females.	Persons.	Males.	Females.	Persons.	Males.	Females.	Persons.	Males.	Females.
1	92	93	94	95	96	97	98	99	100	101	102	103	104	105	106	107	108	109
Rajputana	*359,649*	*183,152*	*176,497*	341,137	172,997	168,140	313,972	156,377	157,595	7,614	3,885	3,729	19,551	12,735	6,816	18,503	10,154	8,349
Alwar	*46*	*27*	*19*	...	...	...	...	...	...	...	...	...	...	...	...	46	27	19
Banswara	*96,111*	*47,507*	*48,604*	95,834	47,323	48,511	95,834	47,323	48,511	...	...	...	...	...	...	277	184	93
Bharatpur	*301*	*160*	*141*	...	...	...	...	...	...	...	...	...	...	...	...	301	160	141
Bikaner	*82*	*59*	*23*	...	...	...	...	...	...	...	...	...	...	...	...	82	59	23
Bundi	*513*	*264*	*249*	25	17	8	25	17	8	...	...	...	...	...	...	488	247	241
Dholpur	*155*	*80*	*75*	135	68	67	135	68	67	...	...	...	...	...	...	20	12	8
Dungarpur	*75,860*	*38,334*	*37,526*	73,807	37,345	36,562	73,807	37,245	36,562	...	...	...	...	...	...	2,053	1,089	964
Jaipur	*737*	*437*	*300*	96	54	42	96	54	42	...	...	...	...	...	...	641	383	258
Jaisalmer	*81*	*45*	*36*	...	...	...	...	...	...	...	...	...	...	...	...	81	45	36
Jhalawar	*1,236*	*617*	*619*	212	119	93	212	119	93	...	...	...	...	...	...	1,024	498	526
Karauli	*113*	*75*	*38*	...	...	...	...	...	...	...	...	...	...	...	...	113	75	38
Kishangarh	*191*	*109*	*82*	117	58	59	117	58	59	...	...	...	...	...	...	71	51	20
Kotah	*3,138*	*1,697*	*1,441*	1,110	516	594	1,106	516	590	...	...	...	4	...	4	2,028	1,181	847
Kushalgarh (Chiefship)	*18,493*	*9,235*	*9,258*	18,286	9,127	9,159	17,487	8,692	8,795	...	...	...	799	435	364	207	108	99
Lawa (Estate)	...	...	...	...	...	...	...	...	...	...	...	...	...	...	...	...	...	...
Marwar	*25,991*	*13,469*	*12,522*	23,308	11,986	11,322	22,997	11,823	11,174	311	163	148	...	...	...	2,683	1,483	1,200
Mewar	*91,836*	*48,033*	*43,803*	87,166	45,567	41,599	68,475	33,297	35,178	...	...	...	18,691	12,270	6,421	4,664	2,465	2,199
Partabgarh	*21,738*	*10,954*	*10,784*	21,014	10,578	10,436	21,003	10,571	10,432	...	...	...	11	7	4	724	376	348
Shahpura (Chiefship)	*42*	*28*	*14*	...	...	...	...	...	...	...	...	...	...	...	...	42	28	14
Sirohi	*22,343*	*11,613*	*10,730*	19,590	10,123	9,467	12,241	6,378	5,863	7,303	3,722	3,581	46	23	23	2,753	1,490	1,263
Tonk	*642*	*409*	*233*	437	216	221	437	216	221	...	...	...	...	...	...	205	193	12
Ajmer-Merwara	*1,516*	*871*	*645*	302	150	152	302	150	152	...	...	...	...	...	...	1,212	720	492
Ajmer	*1,102*	*630*	*472*	301	150	151	301	150	151	...	...	...	...	...	...	799	479	320
Merwara	*414*	*241*	*173*	1	...	1	1	...	1	...	...	...	...	...	...	413	241	172

TABLE X.—LANGUAGE.—*contd.*

Province and State or District.	A.—VERNACULARS OF INDIA—*contd.*																	
	GUJRATI—*concld.*			MARATHI.												Panjabi.		
	Khandeshi.			Total Marathi.			Dakhini.			Goanese.			Marathi.					
	Persons.	Males.	Females.	Persons.	Males.	Females.	Persons.	Males.	Females.	Persons.	Males.	Females.	Persons.	Males.	Females.	Persons.	Males.	Females.
1	110	111	112	113	114	115	116	117	118	119	120	121	122	123	124	125	126	127
Rajputana	9	1	8	*2,028*	*1,105*	*923*	123	66	57	58	48	10	1,847	991	856	35,081	19,901	15,180
Alwar	...	...	...	*10*	*7*	*3*	...	...	...	2	2	...	8	5	3	86	66	20
Banswara	...	...	...	*16*	*11*	*5*	2	2	...	...	...	...	14	9	5	4	2	2
Bharatpur	...	...	...	*17*	*11*	*6*	1	...	1	6	3	3	10	8	2	105	58	47
Bikaner	...	...	...	*28*	*19*	*9*	...	...	...	6	6	...	22	13	9	31,815	17,897	13,918
Bundi	...	...	...	*104*	*61*	*43*	2	1	1	...	...	...	102	60	42	3	3	...
Dholpur	...	...	...	*62*	*35*	*27*	...	...	...	1	1	...	61	34	27	182	113	69
Dungarpur	...	...	...	*9*	*7*	*2*	...	...	...	...	...	...	9	7	2	7	5	2
Jaipur	...	...	...	*515*	*209*	*306*	21	9	12	11	9	2	483	191	292	567	364	203
Jaisalmer	...	...	...	*1*	...	*1*	...	...	...	...	...	...	1	...	1	1,185	681	504
Jhalawar	...	...	...	*88*	*43*	*45*	15	10	5	3	2	1	70	31	39	21	17	4
Karauli	...	...	...	*1*	...	*1*	1	...	1	...	...	...	...	...	...	19	15	4
Kishangarh	3	...	3	*44*	*30*	*14*	7	6	1	1	...	1	36	24	12	16	14	2
Kotah	...	...	...	*355*	*222*	*133*	6	2	4	2	2	...	347	218	129	304	175	129
Kushalgarh (Chiefship)	...	...	...	...	...	...	...	...	...	...	...	...	...	...	...	...	...	...
Lawa (Estate)	...	...	...	...	...	...	...	...	...	...	...	...	...	...	...	...	...	...
Marwar	...	...	...	*219*	*152*	*67*	34	18	16	2	1	1	183	133	50	354	226	128
Mewar	6	1	5	*260*	*133*	*127*	2	1	1	...	...	...	258	132	126	202	123	79
Partabgarh	...	...	...	*12*	*6*	*6*	...	...	...	...	...	...	12	6	6	3	2	1
Shahpura (Chiefship)	...	...	...	...	...	...	...	...	...	...	...	...	...	...	...	17	12	5
Sirohi	...	...	...	*244*	*137*	*107*	17	9	8	24	22	2	203	106	97	152	112	40
Tonk	...	...	...	*43*	*22*	*21*	15	8	7	...	...	...	28	14	14	39	16	23
Ajmer-Merwara	2	1	1	*688*	*372*	*316*	78	39	39	92	69	23	518	264	254	1,598	1,299	299
Ajmer	2	1	1	*625*	*335*	*290*	73	36	37	92	69	23	400	230	230	1,536	1,261	275
Merwara	...	...	...	*63*	*37*	*26*	5	3	2	...	...	...	58	34	24	62	38	24

TABLE X.—LANGUAGE.—*contd.*

Province; and State or District.	A.—VERNACULARS OF INDIA—*concld.*															B.—VERNACULARS OF ASIATIC COUNTRIES BEYOND INDIA.		
	Pashto.			SINDHI.									OTHERS.*			TOTAL.		
				Total Sindhi.			Kachchhi.			Sindhi.								
	Persons.	Males.	Females.	Persons.	Males.	Females.	Persons.	Males.	Females.	Persons.	Males.	Females.	Persons.	Males.	Females.	Persons.	Males.	Females.
1	128	129	130	131	132	133	134	135	136	137	138	139	140	141	142	143	144	145
Rajputana	572	420	152	*58,118*	*31,772*	*26,346*	153	100	53	57,965	31,672	26,293	774	383	391	76	63	13
Alwar	15	4	11	...	...	...	...	...	...	...	...	...	1	1	...	11	7	4
Banswara	30	22	8	...	...	...	...	...	...	...	...	...	1	1	...	...	...	...
Bharatpur	4	4	...	*7*	*6*	*1*	3	3	...	4	3	1	35	19	16	...	...	...
Bikaner	22	21	1	*15,539*	*8,415*	*7,124*	7	7	...	15,532	8,408	7,124	407	191	216	...	...	...
Bundi	...	...	...	...	...	...	...	...	...	...	...	...	4	1	3	1	1	...
Dholpur	17	17	...	...	...	...	...	...	...	...	...	...	2	2	...	3	3	...
Dungarpur	65	43	22	...	...	...	...	...	...	...	...	...	...	...	...	2	2	...
Jaipur	34	32	2	*5*	*3*	*2*	4	2	2	1	1	...	65	36	29	10	8	2
Jaisalmer	...	...	...	*7,513*	*4,287*	*3,226*	8	3	5	7,505	4,284	3,221	...	...	...	4	4	...
Jhalawar	6	4	2	...	...	...	...	...	...	...	...	...	2	2	...	...	...	...
Karauli	...	...	...	*1*	*1*	...	1	1	...	...	...	...	...	...	...	1	1	...
Kishangarh	...	...	...	...	...	...	...	...	...	...	...	...	22	12	10	...	...	...
Kotah	21	21	...	*27*	*21*	*6*	27	21	6	...	...	...	44	32	12	4	4	...
Kushalgarh (Chiefship)	1	1	...	*12*	*5*	*7*	12	5	7	...	...	...	...	...	...	...	...	...
Lawa (Estate)	...	...	...	...	...	...	...	...	...	...	...	...	...	...	...	...	...	...
Marwar	21	18	3	*34,906*	*18,969*	*15,937*	16	9	7	34,890	18,960	15,930	65	42	23	3	2	1
Mewar	62	48	14	*31*	*17*	*14*	11	8	3	20	9	11	87	19	68	5	4	1
Partabgarh	190	121	69	...	...	...	...	...	...	...	...	...	...	...	...	...	...	...
Shahpura (Chiefship)	...	...	...	...	...	...	...	...	...	...	...	...	2	1	1	...	...	...
Sirohi	56	36	20	*76*	*47*	*29*	63	40	23	13	7	6	35	23	12	7	6	1
Tonk	28	28	...	*1*	*1*	...	1	1	...	...	...	...	2	1	1	25	21	4
Ajmer-Merwara	191	176	15	*43*	*25*	*18*	39	21	18	4	4	...	507	268	239	33	19	14
Ajmer	171	160	11	*37*	*20*	*17*	34	17	17	3	3	...	494	261	233	32	18	14
Merwara	20	16	4	*6*	*5*	*1*	5	4	1	1	1	...	13	7	6	1	1	...

* For details see Title page.

TABLE X.—Language.—*concld.*

Province; and State or District.	B.—Vernaculars of Asiatic Countries beyond India—*concld.* Arabic. Persons.	Arabic. Males.	Arabic. Females.	Others.* Persons.	Others.* Males.	Others.* Females.	C.—European Languages. Total. Persons.	Total. Males.	Total. Females.	English. Persons.	English. Males.	English. Females.	Others.* Persons.	Others.* Males.	Others.* Females.	D.—Other Languages. Wolof (African.) Persons.	Wolof (African.) Males.	Wolof (African.) Females.
1	146	147	148	149	150	151	152	153	154	155	156	157	158	159	160	161	162	163
Rajputana	43	35	8	35	30	5	1,783	1,024	759	1,684	957	727	97	65	32	4	3	1
Alwar	10	6	4	1	1	...	43	24	19	29	16	13	14	8	6	...	...	...
Banswara	...	...	...	...	...	...	...	...	...	...	...	...	...	...	...	...	...	...
Bharatpur	...	...	...	...	...	...	38	14	24	38	14	24	...	...	...	...	...	...
Bikaner	...	...	...	...	...	...	24	14	10	24	14	10	...	...	...	...	...	...
Bundi	...	...	...	1	1	...	...	...	...	...	...	...	...	...	...	...	...	...
Dholpur	...	...	...	3	3	...	23	13	10	21	12	9	2	1	1	4	3	1
Dungarpur	2	2	...	...	...	...	...	...	...	...	...	...	...	...	...	...	...	...
Jaipur	4	4	...	6	4	2	689	365	324	662	346	316	27	19	8	...	...	...
Jaisalmer	...	...	...	4	4	...	...	...	...	...	...	...	...	...	...	...	...	...
Jhalawar	...	...	...	...	...	...	14	9	5	4	2	2	10	7	3	...	...	...
Karauli	1	1	...	...	...	...	1	1	...	1	1	...	...	...	...	...	...	...
Kishangarh	...	...	...	...	...	...	3	...	3	1	...	1	2	...	2	...	...	...
Kotah	1	1	...	5	5	...	55	32	23	49	26	23	4	4	...	...	...	...
Kushalgarh (Chiefship)	...	...	...	...	...	...	...	...	...	...	...	...	...	...	...	...	...	...
Lawa (Estate)	...	...	...	...	...	...	...	...	...	...	...	...	...	...	...	...	...	...
Marwar	...	...	...	3	2	1	169	88	81	157	81	76	12	7	5	...	...	...
Mewar	...	...	...	5	4	1	44	26	18	41	24	17	3	2	1	...	...	...
Partabgarh	...	...	...	...	...	...	...	...	...	...	...	...	...	...	...	...	...	...
Shahpura (Chiefship)	...	...	...	...	...	...	1	1	...	...	...	...	1	1	...	...	...	...
Sirohi	...	...	...	7	6	1	672	433	239	650	417	233	22	16	6	...	...	...
Tonk	25	21	4	.	...	...	7	4	3	7	4	3	...	...	...	...	...	...
Ajmer-Merwara	2	2	...	31	17	14	2,732	1,986	766	2,520	1,825	695	212	141	71	...	...	...
Ajmer	2	2	...	30	16	14	2,704	1,969	735	2,495	1,811	684	209	138	71	...	...	...
Merwara	...	...	...	1	1	...	28	17	11	25	14	11	3	3	...	...	...	...

* For details see Title page.

APPENDIX TO TABLE X.—(See Explanatory Note on Title Page).

Entry in Schedule.	Language in Table in which classified.	Number speaking dialect in column 1.			
		Ajmer-Merwara.		Rajputana.	
		Males.	Females.	Males.	Females.
Ahirwati	Western Hindi	...	...	1	34
Alwari	Western Hindi	46	56	99	70
Bharatpuri	Western Hindi	332	242	167	59
Bikaneri	Rajasthani	32	4	33	36
Braj Bhasha Jadobati	Western Hindi (Braj Bhasha)	...	...	92	115
Bundelkhandi	Western Hindi	4	2	638	678
Chitori	Rajasthani (Mewari)	9	7	4	14
Dangi Dangbhang	Western Hindi (Dangi)	...	...	11,245*	8,407*
Dholpuri	Western Hindi (Braj Bhasha)	2	...	140,113†	112,350†
Dhundari Kathaira	Rajasthani (Jaipuri)	1	...	51	174
Dhundari Kishangarhi	Rajasthani (Jaipuri)	243	292	43,462‡	39,573‡
Dhundari Nagarchal	Rajasthani (Jaipuri)	7	4	168	168
Dhundari Rajwati	Western Hindi (Dangi)	...	...	774	1,119
Fatehpuri	Punjabi	24	17	...	1
Gwaliori	Western Hindi (Bhadaori)	12	14	1,054	172
Hariani	Western Hindi	52	43	954	658
Hindustani	Western Hindi	...	...	499	313
Jangli	Bhili	...	...	184	170
Jodhpuri	Rajasthani (Marwari)	19	121	4	1
Kabuli	Pashto	37	6	18	4
Karauli	Rajasthani (Mewari)	3	...	1,002	746
Kathiawadi	Gujrati	11	5	405	173
Kherwa	Rajasthani (Mewari)	...	...	24	20
Konkani	Marathi	9	3	27	11
Madrasi	Tamil	72	56	35	22
Makrani	Baloch	...	...	129	74
Mewati Kather	Rajasthani (Mewati)	...	...	13,485§	10,416§
Mewati Nahera	Rajasthani (Mewati)	...	...	69,327‖	64,972‖
Mewati Rath	Rajasthani (Mewati)	...	...	71,510¶	67,416¶
Mini	Bhili	...	...	29	28
Multani	Western Punjabi	119	157	211	240
Powadi	Punjabi	...	...	73	18
Purbi	Behari	846	637	2,092	1,384
Rathi	Rajasthani (Marwari)	1	...	2,096**	1,727**
Sapari	Rajasthani (Harauti)	...	...	1,069††	1,014††
Tonki	Western Hindi	12	9	14	114
Udaipuri	Rajasthani (Mewari)	14	269	...	2

	M.	F.		M.	F.		M.	F.
* Bharatpur	5,772	4,263	‡ Kishangarh	43,300	39,344	¶ Alwar	71,497	69,329
* Karauli	5,473	4,144	§ Alwar	13,463	10,414	** All in Bikaner.		
† Dholpur	140,109	112,350	‖ Alwar	69,327	64,971	†† Kotah	1,065	1,008

For the following entries either figures are not available, or those returning them numbered less than 30.

Language in which included.	Entries in Schedules.
Behari	Magdhi.
Central Pahari	Garhwali Tehri.
Eastern Hindi	Allahabadi, Baiswari, Banarsi, Cawnpuri, Lucknowi, Kolahri, Madhdeshi, Nawabganji, Muradabadi, Sultanpuri.
Gujrati	Parsi, Surti.
Gujrati Khandeshi	Khandevi.
Kherwari-Korwa	Singli.
Marathi	Ahmedabadi, Haidarabadi, Nagpuri.
Pashto	Afghani, Pathani.
Punjabi	Dogri.
Rajasthani	Dhati, Jaisalmeri, Jhalawari, Nimari, Partabgarhi.
Rajasthani (Bagri)	Narnauli.
Rajasthani (Harauti)	Bundi, Kotah.
Rajasthani (Jaipuri)	Dhundari-Tonrawati, Jharsai, Pachwari.
Rajasthani (Malwi)	Bhopali, Indori.
Rajasthani (Marwari)	Godwari or Gorwadi, Mahajani, Nagauri, Sambhari, Sirohi.
Rajasthani (Merwari)	Magra, Merati.
Rajasthani (Mewari)	Karveli, Shahpuri.
Rajasthani (Mewati)	Rewari.
Sindhi (Kachchhi)	Bhati.
Tamil	Drawdi or Darawri.
Turkish dialects	Bukhari.
Western Hindi	Agri, Arya Bhasha, Bhilali, Dehli, Farrukhabadi, Hindi-Dhadbar, Jabalpuri, Kanauji, Khundwi, Musalmani, Nagri, Nimbar, Rajgarhi, Rewi, Rohelkhandi, Sanskrit, Shahjahanabadi.
Western Hindi (Bhadaori)	Lashkari.
Western Hindi (Braj Bhasha)	Brajki, Bundhali, Maithuli, Mathuri.
Western Hindi (Dangi)	Dangi Kakachhu.
Western Pasari	Rampuri.
Western Punjabi	Peshawari

TABLE XI.

Birthplace.

Explanatory Note.

This Table shows the birthplaces of persons enumerated in Rajputana and Ajmer-Merwara. It is divided into seven sections :—

A.—India. In this section those born in Rajputana and Ajmer-Merwara are shown first, the remaining provinces being arranged alphabetically. French and Portuguese settlements are printed last.

B.—Asia outside India.

C.—Europe.

D.—Africa.

E.—America.

F.—Australasia.

G.—Born at sea.

The Table also gives separate figures for persons enumerated in cities, but such persons are also included in the State and District figures. Jodhpur City includes Jodhpur suburbs which have been shown in Tables IV and V under the name of Jodhpur Town.

In A, only those Districts or States have been shown separately in which 1,000 or more, in Rajputana and Ajmer-Merwara combined, were born. In the case of cities no details for any States or Districts outside Rajputana and Ajmer-Merwara have been given except for those furnishing 500 or more immigrants to any one city. The remaining Districts or States of each Province have been either amalgamated under "others," or shown simply in the Provincial Totals.

Countries in which less than 20 persons were born have been amalgamated in Sections B and C in "others," and in Sections D and E in the "Total" column. Their details are as follows :—

	Birthplace.	Sex.	State or District of Enumeration.														
			Rajputana total.	Bharatpur.	Dholpur.	Dungarpur.	Jaipur.	Jaisalmer.	Jhalawar.	Kotah.	Marwar.	Mewar.	Sirohi.	Tonk.	Ajmer-Merwara total.	Ajmer.	Merwara.
Asiatic countries outside India.	Bukhara	M.	7	..	..	..	1	4	..	..	2	..	..	..	..	..	..
	China	M.	4	..	..	..	2	..	..	1	..	..	1	..	..	..	..
		F.	4	..	..	..	4	..	..	..	..	..	..	..	1	1	..
	Japan	M.	1	..	..	..	..	..	..	1	..	..	..	..	1	1	..
		F.	..	..	..	..	..	..	..	..	..	..	..	..	1	1	..
	Persia	M.	6	..	1	..	..	2	..	..	..	3	..	..	..	..	..
		F.	1	..	..	..	1	..	..	..	..	..	..	..	1	1	..
	Straits Settlements	M.	2	..	..	..	1	..	..	..	..	..	1	..	..	..	..
	Tibet	M.	2	..	..	..	1	..	..	..	..	..	..	1	1	1	..
		F.	4	..	..	..	4	..	..	..	..	..	..	..	..	..	..
	Turkey in Asia	F.	1	..	..	..	..	..	..	..	..	1	..	..	1	1	..
Europe.	Belgium	M.	2	..	..	..	..	..	..	..	..	..	2	..	..	..	..
	Bulgaria	M.	1	..	..	..	..	..	..	1	..	..	..	..	..	..	..
	Denmark	F.	1	..	..	..	..	..	..	..	1	..	..	..	..	..	..
	Germany	M.	4	..	..	..	2	..	..	..	..	..	2	..	..	..	..
		F.	4	..	..	..	1	..	2	..	..	..	1	..	..	..	..
	Greece	M.	1	..	..	..	..	..	..	..	..	..	1	..	1	..	1
	Italy	M.	2	..	..	..	1	..	..	..	..	1	..	..	..	..	..
		F.	2	..	..	..	..	..	..	..	..	1	1	..	..	..	..
	Norway	M.	..	..	..	..	..	..	..	..	..	..	..	..	1	1	..
	Portugal	M.	..	..	..	..	..	..	..	..	..	..	..	..	4	4	..
		F.	..	..	..	..	..	..	..	..	..	..	..	..	1	1	..
	Russia	M.	1	..	..	..	..	..	..	..	..	..	1	..	1	1	..
		F.	..	..	..	..	..	..	..	..	..	..	..	..	1	1	..
	Spain	M.	1	..	..	..	..	..	1	..	..	..	..	..	1	1	..
		F.	..	..	..	..	..	..	..	..	..	..	..	..	1	1	..
	Sweden	F.	..	..	..	..	..	..	..	..	..	..	..	..	1	1	..
	Switzerland	F.	1	..	..	..	..	..	..	..	1	..	..	..	2	2	..
Africa.	Mauritius	M.	4	3	..	..	..	..	..	..	..	..	1	..	1	1	..
		F.	3	..	..	..	..	..	..	..	1	..	2	..	..	..	..
	Transvaal	F.	2	..	..	..	2	..	..	..	..	..	..	..	..	..	..
	South Africa	M.	1	..	..	..	..	..	..	..	..	..	1	..	1	1	..
	Unspecified	M.	5	..	1	1	2	..	..	..	..	..	..	1	4	4	..
		F.	1	..	..	..	..	..	..	..	..	..	1	..	3	1	2
America.	Argentine Republic	F.	1	..	..	..	..	..	..	1	..	..	..	..	..	..	..
	Bermuda	M.	..	..	..	..	..	..	..	..	..	..	..	..	1	1	..
	Canada	M.	1	..	..	..	1	..	..	..	..	..	..	..	1	1	..
	California	F.	1	..	..	..	1	..	..	..	..	..	..	..	..	..	..
	United States of America	M.	5	..	..	..	3	..	..	..	1	..	1	..	1	1	..
		F.	2	..	..	..	1	..	..	..	..	..	1	..	1	1	..
	Unspecified	M.	4	..	1	..	1	..	..	..	1	..	1	..	1	1	..
		F.	2	..	..	..	1	..	..	..	..	..	1	..	4	4	..

TABLE XI.—Birthplace.

Province; and State, District or City of enumeration.	Total population of Province, State, District, or City of enumeration.			A.—Born in India.														
				Total born in India.			Rajputana.											
							Total Rajputana.			Alwar.			Banswara.			Bharatpur.		
	P.	M.	F.	P.	M.	F.	P.	M.	F.	P.	M.	F.	P.	M.	F.	P.	M.	F.
1	2	3	4	5	6	7	8	9	10	11	12	13	14	15	16	17	18	19
Rajputana	10,530,432	5,515,275	5,015,157	10,529,368	5,514,546	5,014,822	10,226,879	5,398,594	4,828,285	753,224	407,086	346,138	160,514	79,898	80,616	502,952	283,098	219,854
Alwar	791,688	413,659	378,029	791,676	413,652	378,024	763,712	407,717	355,995	717,694	396,266	321,428	3	3	..	13,683	3,747	9,936
Banswara	165,463	81,620	83,843	165,435	81,593	83,842	162,336	80,378	81,958	1	1	..	155,111	78,274	76,837	5	2	3
Bharatpur	558,785	302,254	256,531	558,746	302,228	256,518	513,177	287,977	225,200	16,221	5,447	10,774	..	..	..	478,934	275,854	203,080
Bikaner	700,983	371,489	329,494	700,948	371,460	329,488	665,836	363,083	312,753	356	196	160	..	..	..	41	22	19
Bundi	218,730	113,211	105,519	218,730	113,211	105,519	217,704	112,660	105,044	82	43	39	4	1	3	98	58	40
Dholpur	263,188	144,244	118,944	263,173	144,235	118,938	238,902	137,571	101,331	40	19	21	1	..	1	1,350	411	939
Dungarpur	159,192	79,105	80,087	159,158	79,076	80,082	156,235	77,973	78,262	38	37	1	2,028	376	1,652	3	2	1
Jaipur	2,636,647	1,385,750	1,250,897	2,636,374	1,385,575	1,250,799	2,611,103	1,375,775	1,235,328	16,772	3,943	12,829	3	2	1	5,668	1,444	4,224
Jaisalmer	88,311	48,500	39,811	88,303	48,494	39,809	86,347	47,523	38,824	..	..	..	2	2	..	1	..	1
Jhalawar	96,271	50,034	46,237	96,251	50,021	46,230	82,384	45,406	36,978	69	41	28	3	1	2	158	96	62
Karauli	146,587	80,081	66,506	146,584	80,078	66,506	142,879	79,959	63,920	135	51	84	2	1	1	1,212	364	848
Kishangarh	87,191	45,718	41,473	87,191	45,718	41,473	79,387	43,206	36,181	129	56	73	..	..	..	16	10	6
Kotah	639,089	330,324	308,765	639,033	330,279	308,754	607,146	315,784	291,362	412	247	165	15	3	12	1,157	711	446
Kushalgarh (Chiefship)	22,005	10,956	11,049	22,004	10,955	11,049	20,373	10,293	10,080	..	..	..	851	313	538	..	..	..
Lawa (Estate)	2,564	1,302	1,262	2,564	1,302	1,262	2,533	1,295	1,238	9	2	7	..	..	..	..	..	..
Marwar	2,057,553	1,075,269	982,284	2,057,496	1,075,225	982,271	2,047,099	1,070,086	977,013	430	208	222	5	2	3	144	82	62
Mewar	1,293,776	670,750	623,026	1,293,669	670,711	622,958	1,270,780	659,537	611,243	252	168	84	480	136	344	245	150	95
Partabgarh	62,704	31,735	30,969	62,688	31,723	30,965	55,158	28,958	26,200	4	2	2	1,998	783	1,215	7	6	1
Shahpura (Chiefship)	47,397	24,595	22,802	47,397	24,595	22,802	44,207	23,601	20,606	17	13	4	..	..	..	3	2	1
Sirohi	189,127	98,289	90,838	188,844	98,084	90,760	181,221	93,872	87,349	419	278	141	4	..	4	128	85	43
Tonk	303,181	156,390	146,791	303,104	156,331	146,773	278,260	146,840	131,420	144	68	76	4	1	3	154	107	47
Ajmer-Merwara	501,395	266,198	235,197	499,929	264,902	235,027	72,972	30,144	42,828	2,018	1,236	782	39	37	2	1,514	841	673
Ajmer	380,384	201,911	178,473	378,935	200,628	178,307	57,186	23,253	33,933	1,798	1,097	701	37	35	2	1,254	704	550
Merwara	121,011	64,287	56,724	120,994	64,274	56,720	15,786	6,891	8,895	220	139	81	2	2	..	260	137	123
CITIES.																		
Rajputana	447,749	233,262	214,487	447,508	233,097	214,411	427,661	222,257	205,404	39,739	21,718	18,021	30	13	17	28,155	16,285	11,870
Alwar	41,305	22,254	19,051	41,301	22,251	19,050	39,628	21,496	18,132	38,099	20,837	17,262	..	..	..	265	128	137
Bharatpur	33,918	18,803	15,115	33,899	18,790	15,109	28,882	16,613	12,269	384	186	198	..	..	..	27,436	15,890	11,546
Bikaner	55,826	28,275	27,551	55,804	28,259	27,545	53,899	26,962	26,937	136	84	52	..	..	..	6	4	2
Jaipur	137,098	70,846	66,252	137,033	70,805	66,228	132,951	68,513	64,438	816	432	384	3	2	1	141	71	70
Jodhpur	79,756	41,838	37,918	79,729	41,821	37,908	77,292	40,323	36,969	122	76	46	2	..	2	33	20	13
Kotah	32,753	16,949	15,804	32,726	16,937	15,790	29,823	15,335	14,488	98	58	40	14	2	12	219	134	85
Tonk	33,864	16,837	17,027	33,815	16,795	17,020	32,899	16,282	16,617	39	14	25	1	1	..	21	14	7
Udaipur	33,229	17,460	15,769	33,201	17,449	15,752	32,187	16,793	15,394	45	31	14	10	8	2	34	24	10
Ajmer-Merwara—																		
Ajmer	86,222	47,354	38,868	85,835	47,067	38,768	22,360	11,904	10,456	1,495	918	577	35	34	1	1,127	724	403

TABLE XI.—BIRTHPLACE—*contd.*

A.—BORN IN INDIA—*contd.*

RAJPUTANA—*contd.*

Province; and State, District, or City of enumeration.	Bikaner. P.	Bikaner. M.	Bikaner. F.	Bundi. P.	Bundi. M.	Bundi. F.	Dholpur. P.	Dholpur. M.	Dholpur. F.	Dungarpur. P.	Dungarpur. M.	Dungarpur. F.	Jaipur. P.	Jaipur. M.	Jaipur. F.	Jaisalmer. P.	Jaisalmer. M.	Jaisalmer. F.
1	20	21	22	23	24	25	26	27	28	29	30	31	32	33	34	35	36	37
Rajputana	**647,216**	**342,846**	**304,370**	**216,912**	**111,541**	**105,371**	**241,361**	**139,046**	**102,315**	**155,146**	**77,720**	**77,426**	**2,681,517**	**1,405,584**	**1,275,933**	**81,725**	**46,819**	**34,906**
Alwar	139	49	90	22	9	13	62	13	49	..	..	..	31,257	7,386	23,871	2	1	1
Banswara	2	1	1	1	1	..	1	1	..	4,336	1,110	3,226	77	58	19	..	..	..
Bharatpur	46	29	17	26	13	13	3,426	1,490	1,936	..	..	..	12,278	4,234	8,044	19	10	9
Bikaner	632,686	339,622	293,064	10	3	7	3	2	1	..	..	..	19,764	8,013	11,751	524	157	367
Bundi	8	4	4	200,116	106,125	93,991	3	1	2	..	..	..	6,115	2,286	3,829	3	2	1
Dholpur	36	21	15	2	..	2	234,702	136,294	98,408	..	..	..	357	168	189	..	..	..
Dungarpur	1	1	..	9	3	6	..	..	..	148,717	75,989	72,728	18	12	6	1	1	..
Jaipur	8,655	1,730	6,925	2,855	494	2,361	263	78	185	..	..	..	2,544,602	1,358,959	1,185,643	40	21	19
Jaisalmer	1,368	363	1,005	1	..	1	..	..	..	6	3	3	51	39	12	79,201	45,908	33,293
Jhalawar	26	15	11	249	99	150	17	12	5	..	..	..	659	374	285	8	5	3
Karauli	9	3	6	30	20	10	2,453	869	1,584	..	..	..	10,413	3,023	7,390	12	5	7
Kishangarh	44	10	34	72	20	52	2	1	1	1	1	..	7,195	1,920	5,275	6	1	5
Kotah	71	38	33	9,548	3,786	5,762	225	143	82	4	3	1	9,870	5,151	4,719	31	20	11
Kushalgarh (Chiefship)	..	..	..	..	..	..	1	1	..	21	13	8	14	6	8	..	..	..
Lawa (Estate)	..	..	..	2	1	1	..	..	..	..	..	..	761	244	517	..	..	..
Marwar	4,004	900	3,104	53	20	33	12	3	9	3	..	3	18,636	6,600	12,036	1,839	673	1,166
Mewar	43	18	25	2,219	545	1,674	78	70	8	1,960	557	1,403	2,878	1,379	1,499	6	2	4
Partabgarh	8	2	6	6	4	2	1	1	..	97	44	53	46	29	17	4	1	3
Shahpura (Chiefship)	5	3	2	76	17	59	1	..	1	..	..	..	534	213	321	..	..	..
Sirohi	31	19	12	5	3	2	10	8	2	..	..	..	2,082	1,215	867	3	1	2
Tonk	34	18	16	1,601	378	1,223	101	59	42	1	..	1	13,890	4,275	9,615	26	11	15
Ajmer-Merwara	**346**	**188**	**158**	**951**	**301**	**650**	**209**	**144**	**65**	**14**	**13**	**1**	**22,611**	**10,325**	**12,286**	**13**	**8**	**5**
Ajmer	317	176	141	925	292	633	199	138	61	14	13	1	20,101	8,882	11,219	10	5	5
Merwara	29	12	17	26	9	17	10	6	4	..	..	..	2,510	1,443	1,067	3	3	..
CITIES.																		
Rajputana	**51,243**	**25,346**	**25,897**	**2,488**	**1,032**	**1,456**	**248**	**115**	**133**	**48**	**28**	**20**	**137,101**	**70,465**	**66,636**	**169**	**94**	**75**
Alwar	14	8	11	8	4	4	14	7	7	..	..	..	984	404	580	1	1	..
Bharatpur	17	12	6	5	3	2	133	50	83	..	..	..	656	348	308	12	6	6
Bikaner	50,922	25,172	25,750	6	1	5	3	2	1	..	..	..	726	506	220	102	54	48
Jaipur	161	85	76	20	10	10	20	5	15	..	..	..	130,083	67,109	63,074	16	9	7
Jodhpur	73	48	25	33	8	25	6	2	4	2	..	2	594	371	223	15	11	4
Kotah	32	16	16	2,253	972	1,281	60	40	20	4	3	1	1,416	815	601	13	9	4
Tonk	11	7	4	150	32	118	5	6	..	..	..	..	2,480	808	1,672	9	3	6
Udaipur	11	3	10	4	2	2	7	4	3	42	25	17	162	104	58	1	1	..
Ajmer-Merwara—																		
Ajmer	192	95	97	65	32	33	173	117	56	14	13	1	9,151	4,934	4,217	6	2	4

TABLE XI.—BIRTHPLACE—*contd.*

Province; and State, District, or City of enumeration.	A.—BORN IN INDIA—*contd.*																				
	RAJPUTANA—*contd.*																				
	Jhalawar.			Karauli.			Kishangarh.			Kotah.			Kushalgarh.			Lawa.			Marwar.		
	P.	M.	F.	P.	M.	F.	P.	M.	F.	P.	M.	F.	P.	M.	F.	P.	M.	F.	P.	M.	F.
1	38	39	40	41	42	43	44	45	46	47	48	49	50	51	52	53	54	55	56	57	58
Rajputana	**83,560**	**46,188**	**37,372**	**140,603**	**78,779**	**61,824**	**71,168**	**41,146**	**30,022**	**587,107**	**304,036**	**283,071**	**19,549**	**9,982**	**9,567**	**1,533**	**995**	**538**	**2,072,896**	**1,079,154**	**993,742**
Alwar	24	10	14	311	62	249	108	36	72	42	21	21	..	..	..	..	..	..	291	109	182
Banswara	7	2	5	2	2	..	..	..	..	9	4	5	115	43	72	..	..	..	36	18	18
Bharatpur	18	11	7	1,761	658	1,103	40	29	11	146	71	75	..	..	..	..	..	..	124	62	62
Bikaner	8	4	4	13	8	5	32	15	17	21	9	12	..	..	..	..	..	..	12,274	4,973	7,301
Bundi	150	38	112	110	50	60	83	30	53	6,519	2,279	4,240	..	..	..	2	2	..	551	263	288
Dholpur	3	1	2	2,250	584	1,666	2	2	..	42	13	29	..	..	..	..	..	..	71	46	25
Dungarpur	14	4	10	1	1	..	12	5	7	4	4	..	..	..	..	..	..	..	24	14	10
Jaipur	233	28	205	5,670	1,609	4,061	2,694	792	1,902	1,168	378	790	8	1	7	52	14	38	14,679	3,633	11,046
Jaisalmer	2	2	..	..	..	..	..	..	..	7	5	2	..	..	..	..	..	..	5,662	1,176	4,486
Jhalawar	74,139	42,199	31,940	213	121	92	48	36	12	4,487	1,582	2,905	..	..	..	..	..	..	185	88	97
Karauli	9	4	5	128,421	74,591	53,830	1	..	1	106	46	62	..	..	..	..	..	..	67	34	33
Kishangarh	12	1	11	14	8	6	66,343	39,554	26,789	26	13	13	..	..	..	..	..	..	4,317	1,278	3,039
Kotah	6,575	3,099	3,476	1,461	857	604	91	60	41	569,770	297,917	271,853	..	..	..	..	..	..	1,309	720	589
Kushalgarh (Chiefship)	..	..	..	..	..	..	..	..	..	2	1	1	19,390	9,925	9,474	..	..	..	17	6	11
Lawa (Estate)	..	..	..	..	..	..	18	3	10	3	1	2	..	..	..	1,472	979	493	9	3	6
Marwar	26	14	12	25	9	16	890	283	607	13	8	5	21	11	10	..	..	..	2,014,831	1,059,337	955,494
Mewar	85	35	50	146	102	44	303	116	187	1,046	341	705	2	1	1	..	..	..	4,123	2,139	1,984
Partabgarh	61	31	30	2	2	..	17	6	11	35	20	15	4	1	3	..	..	..	150	73	77
Shahpura (Chiefship)	58	23	30	8	3	5	397	144	253	56	43	13	..	..	..	..	..	..	219	131	88
Sirohi	7	3	4	4	4	..	37	26	11	27	12	15	..	..	..	..	..	..	12,999	4,625	8,374
Tonk	2,134	679	1,455	191	108	83	57	19	38	3,576	1,268	2,308	..	..	..	7	..	7	958	426	532
Ajmer-Merwara	**83**	**55**	**28**	**206**	**116**	**90**	**7,729**	**2,684**	**5,045**	**569**	**285**	**334**	**2**	**1**	**1**	..	..	..	**21,124**	**8,941**	**12,183**
Ajmer	70	53	26	201	114	87	7,523	2,580	4,943	527	217	310	1	1	..	..	..	..	13,056	5,270	7,786
Merwara	4	2	2	5	2	3	206	104	102	42	18	24	1	..	1	..	..	..	8,068	3,671	4,397
CITIES.																					
Rajputana	**1,361**	**704**	**657**	**750**	**424**	**326**	**313**	**136**	**177**	**23,336**	**11,924**	**11,412**	**1**	**1**	..	**3**	..	**3**	**79,871**	**41,182**	**37,889**
Alwar	17	6	11	45	19	26	82	30	52	17	10	7	..	..	..	..	..	..	45	26	19
Bharatpur	5	4	1	127	62	65	22	14	8	29	15	14	..	..	..	..	..	..	26	12	14
Bikaner	7	3	4	8	4	4	21	10	11	14	6	8	..	..	..	..	..	..	1,889	1,028	861
Jaipur	9	3	6	96	48	48	118	49	69	89	50	39	1	1	..	..	..	..	614	269	345
Jodhpur	1	1	..	13	6	7	12	4	8	2	2	..	..	..	..	..	..	..	76,149	39,647	36,502
Kotah	1,306	680	626	377	237	140	30	18	12	23,097	11,803	11,294	..	..	..	..	..	..	197	107	90
Tonk	6	4	2	24	11	13	15	2	13	78	33	45	..	..	..	3	..	3	81	43	38
Udaipur	10	3	7	60	37	23	13	9	4	10	5	5	..	..	..	..	..	..	70	50	20
Ajmer-Merwara—																					
Ajmer	59	37	22	104	57	47	2,251	1,075	1,176	267	125	142	1	1	..	..	..	..	5,302	2,634	2,668

TABLE XI.—Birthplace—*contd.*

Province; and State, District, or City of enumeration.	A.—BORN IN INDIA—*contd.*																							
	Rajputana—*concld.*																		Ajmer-Merwara.					
	Mewar.			Partabgarh.			Shahpura.			Sirohi.			Tonk.			Rajputana unspecified.			Total Ajmer-Merwara.			Ajmer.		
	P.	M.	F.	P.	M.	F.	P.	M.	F.	P.	M.	F.	P.	M.	F.	P.	M.	F.	P.	M.	F.	P.	M.	F.
1	59	60	61	62	63	64	65	66	67	68	69	70	71	72	73	74	75	76	77	78	79	80	81	82
Rajputana	**1,290,341**	**665,410**	**624,931**	**51,807**	**27,337**	**24,470**	**39,860**	**22,234**	**17,626**	**167,287**	**87,772**	**79,515**	**261,056**	**141,829**	**119,227**	**145**	**94**	**51**	**27,543**	**9,941**	**17,602**	**26,032**	**9,132**	**16,900**
Alwar	77	41	36	..	..	..	2	1	1	6	3	3	39	10	29	..	..	..	*139*	*50*	*89*	133	48	85
Banswara	1,789	639	1,150	824	211	613	..	..	..	8	4	4	12	7	5	..	..	..	*29*	*10*	*19*	29	10	19
Bharatpur	55	25	30	2	2	..	..	..	..	8	6	2	73	36	37	..	..	..	*194*	*106*	*88*	194	106	88
Bikaner	64	37	27	22	13	9	..	..	..	8	4	4	10	5	5	..	..	..	*264*	*166*	*98*	264	166	98
Bundi	2,072	877	1,195	6	3	3	27	10	17	1	..	1	1,687	550	1,137	72	43	29	*160*	*94*	*66*	159	93	66
Dholpur	6	1	5	3	3	..	..	..	..	1	..	1	36	8	28	..	..	..	*23*	*12*	*11*	23	12	11
Dungarpur	5,201	1,453	3,748	121	49	72	..	..	..	40	20	20	3	2	1	..	..	..	*22*	*14*	*8*	21	13	8
Jaipur	1,845	737	1,108	13	7	6	9	6	3	54	26	28	5,813	1,869	3,944	7	4	3	*5,350*	*1,876*	*3,474*	5,330	1,870	3,460
Jaisalmer	15	8	7	..	..	..	..	..	..	31	17	14	..	..	..	..	..	..	*12*	*4*	*8*	9	3	6
Jhalawar	423	198	225	55	17	38	3	..	3	2	1	1	1,639	521	1,118	1	..	1	*67*	*38*	*29*	66	38	28
Karauli	67	37	30	..	..	..	..	..	..	2	1	1	27	8	10	2	2	..	*24*	*13*	*11*	24	13	11
Kishangarh	921	257	664	6	1	5	131	28	103	9	3	6	143	44	99	..	..	..	*7,276*	*2,185*	*5,091*	7,270	2,179	5,091
Kotah	2,860	1,309	1,551	18	8	10	..	..	..	58	84	10	3,616	1,645	1,971	60	43	17	*754*	*409*	*345*	745	407	338
Kushalgarh (Chiefship)	41	22	19	26	6	20	..	..	..	..	..	..	1	..	1	..	..	..	*2*	*2*	..	2	2	..
Lawa (Estate)	3	..	3	..	..	..	..	..	..	..	..	..	261	62	199	..	..	..	*24*	*4*	*20*	24	4	20
Marwar	2,780	1,067	1,713	3	2	1	4	..	4	3,268	822	2,446	92	45	47	..	..	..	*3,046*	*1,069*	*1,977*	2,274	624	1,650
Mewar	1,254,260	652,944	601,316	536	217	319	632	194	438	47	27	20	1,438	395	1,043	1	1	..	*5,831*	*2,267*	*3,551*	5,192	1,955	3,237
Partabgarh	2,559	1,143	1,416	50,078	26,771	23,307	1	1	..	1	1	..	79	37	42	..	..	..	*52*	*27*	*25*	15	8	7
Shahpura (Chiefship)	4,367	1,008	3,359	1	1	..	38,430	21,987	16,443	..	..	..	40	13	27	..	..	..	*2,939*	*846*	*2,093*	2,939	846	2,093
Sirohi	1,687	763	924	10	4	6	..	..	..	163,734	86,802	76,932	33	23	10	1	1	..	*1,069*	*629*	*440*	1,037	612	425
Tonk	9,249	2,844	6,405	83	22	61	21	7	14	14	1	13	240,014	130,549	109,465	1	..	1	*276*	*120*	*156*	264	114	150
Ajmer-Merwara	**12,500**	**3,630**	**8,870**	**115**	**73**	**42**	**682**	**214**	**468**	**362**	**182**	**180**	**1,867**	**908**	**959**	**18**	**12**	**6**	**404,817**	**221,690**	**183,127**	**301,964**	**165,338**	**136,626**
Ajmer	8,243	2,363	5,880	106	64	42	682	214	468	284	146	138	1,811	877	934	18	12	6	*301,439*	*165,427*	*136,012*	290,182	164,164	126,018
Merwara	4,257	1,267	2,990	9	9	..	..	..	..	78	36	42	56	31	25	..	..	..	*103,378*	*56,263*	*47,115*	2,782	1,174	1,608
CITIES.																								
Rajputana	**32,514**	**16,879**	**15,635**	**34**	**19**	**15**	**21**	**8**	**13**	**78**	**51**	**27**	**30,914**	**15,796**	**15,118**	**44**	**37**	**7**	**1,710**	**871**	**839**	**1,690**	**791**	**899**
Alwar	14	12	2	..	..	..	1	1	..	1	1	..	21	7	14	..	..	..	*66*	*20*	*46*	62	19	43
Bharatpur	6	2	4	..	..	..	..	..	..	7	5	2	17	4	13	..	..	..	*111*	*63*	*48*	111	63	48
Bikaner	37	17	20	11	6	5	..	..	..	7	3	4	4	2	2	..	..	..	*208*	*132*	*76*	208	132	76
Jaipur	168	87	81	5	2	3	1	1	..	21	14	7	560	266	294	..	..	..	*292*	*114*	*178*	291	114	177
Jodhpur	160	78	82	..	..	..	3	..	3	33	24	9	39	25	14	..	..	..	*370*	*205*	*165*	278	134	144
Kotah	434	210	215	4	1	3	..	..	..	2	1	1	323	183	140	44	37	7	*403*	*207*	*196*	402	207	195
Tonk	46	17	29	2	2	..	16	6	10	2	1	1	29,910	15,279	14,631	..	..	..	*123*	*48*	*75*	122	47	75
Udaipur	31,649	16,447	15,202	12	8	4	..	..	..	5	2	3	40	30	10	..	..	..	*137*	*82*	*55*	126	75	51
Ajmer-Merwara—																								
Ajmer	851	463	388	84	59	25	82	45	37	205	123	82	800	501	299	6	5	1	*47,332*	*25,897*	*21,435*	45,528	24,750	20,778

TABLE XI.—BIRTHPLACE—*contd.*

Province; and State, District, or City of enumeration.	A.—BORN IN INDIA—*contd.*																							
	Ajmer-Merwara—*contd.*						Assam.									Baluchistan Agency.								
	Merwara.			Ajmer-Merwara unspecified.			Total Assam.			Districts.			States.			Total Baluchistan.			Districts.			States.		
	P.	M.	F.	P.	M.	F.	P.	M.	F.	P.	M.	F.	P.	M.	F.	P.	M.	F.	P.	M.	F.	P.	M.	F.
1	83	84	85	86	87	88	89	90	91	92	93	94	95	96	97	98	99	100	101	102	103	104	105	106
Rajputana	1,461	797	664	39	21	18	105	41	64	102	40	62	3	1	2	210	140	70	119	75	44	91	65	26
Alwar	5	1	4	1	1	..	..	..	..	..	..	..	..	..	..	..	..	..	..	..	..	..	..	..
Banswara	..	..	..	..	..	..	..	..	..	..	..	..	..	..	..	*6*	*5*	*1*	..	..	..	6	5	1
Bharatpur	..	..	..	..	..	..	..	..	..	..	..	..	..	..	..	..	..	..	..	..	..	..	..	..
Bikaner	..	..	..	..	..	..	*75*	*31*	*44*	74	30	44	1	1	..	*3*	*3*	..	3	3	..	..	..	..
Bundi	1	1	..	..	..	..	..	..	..	..	..	..	..	..	..	..	..	..	..	..	..	..	..	..
Dholpur	..	..	..	..	..	..	..	..	..	..	..	..	..	..	..	*3*	*3*	..	..	..	..	3	3	..
Dungarpur	..	..	..	1	1	..	..	..	..	..	..	..	..	..	..	..	..	..	..	..	..	..	..	..
Jaipur	7	4	3	4	2	2	*20*	*6*	*14*	20	6	14	..	..	..	*11*	*11*	..	11	11	..	..	..	..
Jaisalmer	3	1	2	..	..	..	..	..	..	..	..	..	..	..	..	*11*	*5*	*6*	10	4	6	1	1	..
Jhalawar	1	..	1	..	..	..	..	..	..	..	..	..	..	..	..	..	..	..	..	..	..	..	..	..
Karauli	..	..	..	..	..	..	..	..	..	..	..	..	..	..	..	..	..	..	..	..	..	..	..	..
Kishangarh	6	6	..	..	..	..	..	..	..	..	..	..	..	..	..	..	..	..	..	..	..	..	..	..
Kotah	9	2	7	..	..	..	..	..	..	..	..	..	..	..	..	*3*	*3*	..	3	3	..	..	..	..
Kushalgarh (Chiefship)	..	..	..	..	..	..	..	..	..	..	..	..	..	..	..	*16*	*12*	*4*	..	..	..	16	12	4
Lawa (Estate)	..	..	..	..	..	..	..	..	..	..	..	..	..	..	..	..	..	..	..	..	..	..	..	..
Marwar	772	445	327	..	..	..	*3*	*2*	*1*	3	2	1	..	..	..	*76*	*42*	*34*	42	19	23	34	23	11
Mewar	627	311	316	2	1	1	..	..	..	..	..	..	..	..	..	..	..	..	..	..	..	..	..	..
Partabgarh	6	3	3	31	16	15	..	..	..	..	..	..	..	..	..	*2*	*2*	..	..	..	..	2	2	..
Shahpura (Chiefship)	..	..	..	..	..	..	..	..	..	..	..	..	..	..	..	..	..	..	..	..	..	..	..	..
Sirohi	32	17	15	..	..	..	*2*	..	*2*	..	..	..	2	..	2	*79*	*54*	*25*	50	35	15	29	19	10
Tonk	12	6	6	..	..	..	*5*	*2*	*3*	5	2	3	..	..	..	..	..	..	..	..	..	..	..	..
Ajmer-Merwara	102,844	56,345	46,409	9	7	2	6	4	2	6	4	2	..	..	..	23	13	10	23	13	10	..	..	..
Ajmer	2,248	1,256	902	9	7	2	*6*	*4*	2	6	4	2	..	..	..	*21*	*11*	*10*	21	11	10	..	..	..
Merwara	100,596	55,089	45,507	..	..	..	..	..	..	..	..	..	..	..	..	*2*	*2*	..	2	2	..	..	..	..
CITIES.																								
Rajputana	109	79	30	1	1	..	11	6	5	11	6	5	..	..	..	6	2	4	6	2	4	..	..	..
Alwar	3	..	3	1	1	..	..	..	..	..	..	..	..	..	..	..	..	..	..	..	..	..	..	..
Bharatpur	..	..	..	..	..	..	..	..	..	..	..	..	..	..	..	..	..	..	..	..	..	..	..	..
Bikaner	..	..	..	..	..	..	*5*	*3*	*2*	5	3	2	..	..	..	..	..	..	..	..	..	..	..	..
Jaipur	1	..	1	..	..	..	*3*	*1*	*2*	3	1	2	..	..	..	..	..	..	..	..	..	..	..	..
Jodhpur	92	71	21	..	..	..	*1*	..	*1*	1	..	1	..	..	..	*4*	..	*4*	4	..	4	..	..	..
Kotah	1	..	1	..	..	..	..	..	..	..	..	..	..	..	..	*2*	*2*	..	2	2	..	..	..	..
Tonk	1	1	..	..	..	..	*2*	*2*	..	2	2	..	..	..	..	..	..	..	..	..	..	..	..	..
Udaipur	11	7	4	..	..	..	..	..	..	..	..	..	..	..	..	..	..	..	..	..	..	..	..	..
Ajmer-Merwara—																								
Ajmer	1,804	1,147	657	..	..	..	*3*	*3*	..	3	3	..	..	..	..	*21*	*11*	*10*	21	11	10	..	..	..

TABLE XI.—BIRTHPLACE—*contd.*

A.—BORN IN INDIA—*contd.*

Province; and State, District, or City of enumeration.	Baroda State. Total. P.	Baroda State. Total. M.	Baroda State. Total. F.	Behar and Orissa. Total.† P.	Behar and Orissa. Total.† M.	Behar and Orissa. Total.† F.	Bengal. Total.* P.	Bengal. Total.* M.	Bengal. Total.* F.	Bombay. Total Bombay. P.	Bombay. Total Bombay. M.	Bombay. Total Bombay. F.	Bombay. Districts. Total Districts. P.	Bombay. Districts. Total Districts. M.	Bombay. Districts. Total Districts. F.	Bombay. Districts. Ahmedabad. P.	Bombay. Districts. Ahmedabad. M.	Bombay. Districts. Ahmedabad. F.	Bombay. Districts. Bombay City. P.	Bombay. Districts. Bombay City. M.	Bombay. Districts. Bombay City. F.	Bombay. Districts. Panch-mahals. P.	Bombay. Districts. Panch-mahals. M.	Bombay. Districts. Panch-mahals. F.
1	107	108	109	110	111	112	113	114	115	116	117	118	119	120	121	122	123	124	125	126	127	128	129	130
Rajputana	**1,601**	**888**	**713**	**398**	**268**	**130**	**737**	**377**	**360**	**14,558**	**6,472**	**8,086**	**6,624**	**3,279**	**3,345**	**1,060**	**608**	**452**	**1,105**	**569**	**536**	**1,525**	**623**	**902**
Alwar	2	..	2	26	23	3	17	9	8	*57*	*37*	*20*	33	22	11	6	4	2	9	6	3	..	..	..
Banswara	36	24	12	1	1	..	3	1	2	*1,454*	*476*	*978*	831	287	544	20	12	8	9	8	1	776	257	519
Bharatpur	16	11	5	53	44	9	30	5	25	*192*	*116*	*76*	70	54	16	10	3	7	8	7	1	..	..	..
Bikaner	6	3	3	39	18	21	110	54	56	*102*	*72*	*30*	36	24	12	10	6	4	15	8	7	..	..	..
Bundi	4	1	3	1	1	..	2	1	1	*21*	*15*	*6*	13	10	3	..	..	..	8	6	2	1	1	..
Dholpur	2	..	2	11	5	6	36	17	19	*32*	*22*	*10*	31	21	10	2	2	..	4	4	..	..	..	..
Dungarpur	143	62	81	..	..	..	1	1	..	*2,330*	*777*	*1,513*	823	450	373	280	142	147	101	50	51	285	187	98
Jaipur	75	49	26	112	75	37	297	150	147	*531*	*328*	*203*	381	227	154	81	40	41	150	89	61	10	7	3
Jaisalmer	8	3	5	..	..	..	3	1	2	*665*	*228*	*437*	546	177	369	..	..	..	1	1	..	..	..	..
Jhalawar	37	20	17	7	4	3	3	3	..	*72*	*51*	*21*	54	38	16	7	3	4	9	7	2	..	..	..
Karauli	..	..	..	19	8	11	32	11	21	*24*	*22*	*2*	17	15	2	2	1	1	..	..	..	..	..	..
Kishangarh	7	3	4	1	1	..	11	5	6	*103*	*74*	*29*	86	62	24	30	25	5	7	6	1	..	..	..
Kotah	329	160	169	23	16	7	14	12	2	*527*	*347*	*180*	306	178	128	65	44	21	79	38	41	6	3	3
Kushalgarh (Chiefship)	5	..	5	..	..	..	..	..	..	*565*	*219*	*346*	444	170	274	2	1	1	..	..	..	435	162	273
Lawa (Estate)	..	..	..	..	..	..	..	..	..	..	..	..	..	..	..	..	..	..	..	..	..	..	..	..
Marwar	350	230	120	57	45	12	87	50	37	*3,037*	*1,397*	*1,640*	1,445	773	672	207	127	80	240	144	105	1	1	..
Mewar	152	74	78	29	20	9	33	21	12	*1,232*	*569*	*663*	324	191	133	108	68	40	47	24	23	2	1	1
Partabgarh	21	10	11	..	..	..	2	..	2	*26*	*15*	*11*	14	9	5	7	6	1	..	..	..	5	1	4
Shahpura (Chiefship)	1	1	..	..	..	..	2	1	1	*25*	*17*	*8*	13	13	..	1	1	..	..	..	..	..	..	..
Sirohi	408	234	169	15	5	10	45	26	19	*3,546*	*1,674*	*1,572*	1,131	543	588	212	122	90	396	166	230	4	3	1
Tonk	4	3	1	4	2	2	9	9	..	*27*	*16*	*11*	26	15	11	1	1	..	13	5	8	..	..	..
Ajmer-Merwara	**224**	**133**	**91**	**112†**	**89**	**23**	**289**	**137**	**152**	**1,917**	**1,109**	**808**	**1,570**	**926**	**644**	**343**	**200**	**143**	**414**	**239**	**175**	**2**	..	**2**
Ajmer	202	117	85	103	81	22	282	133	149	*1,402*	*818*	*584*	1,223	716	507	162	88	74	340	198	142	..	..	..
Merwara	22	16	6	9	8	1	7	4	3	*515*	*291*	*224*	347	210	137	181	112	69	74	41	33	2	..	2
CITIES.																								
Rajputana	**132**	**76**	**56**	**140**	**109**	**31**	**301**	**173**	**128**	**996**	**651**	**345**	**593**	**410**	**183**	..	..	..	..	..	..	..	..	..
Alwar	..	..	..	20	20	..	8	6	2	*42*	*27*	*15*	24	15	9	..	..	..	..	..	..	..	..	..
Bharatpur	6	3	3	21	15	6	11	3	8	*99*	*65*	*34*	45	36	9	..	..	..	..	..	..	..	..	..
Bikaner	4	1	3	9	5	4	23	16	7	*64*	*45*	*19*	13	8	5	..	..	..	..	..	..	..	..	..
Jaipur	18	15	3	43	31	12	171	88	83	*246*	*171*	*75*	162	117	45	..	..	..	..	..	..	..	..	..
Jodhpur	38	24	14	41	33	8	55	33	22	*295*	*186*	*109*	195	134	61	..	..	..	..	..	..	..	..	..
Kotah	56	27	29	4	4	..	8	8	..	*130*	*82*	*48*	73	43	30	..	..	..	..	..	..	..	..	..
Tonk	2	1	1	2	1	1	9	9	..	*13*	*8*	*5*	13	8	5	..	..	..	..	..	..	..	..	..
Udaipur	8	5	3	..	..	..	16	10	6	*107*	*67*	*40*	68	49	19	..	..	..	..	..	..	..	..	..
Ajmer-Merwara—																								
Ajmer	99	60	39	77	63	14	228	117	111	*1,165*	*668*	*497*	1,009	585	424	..	..	..	..	..	..	..	..	..

† All born in Districts.

* All born in Districts except one male of Bikaner born in Kuch Behar State.

TABLE XI.—BIRTHPLACE—*contd.*

Province; and State, District, or City of enumeration.	A.—BORN IN INDIA—*contd.*																							
	BOMBAY—*contd.*																							
	DISTRICTS—*contd.*						STATES.																	
	Sindh.			Others.			Total States.			Kathiawar.			Mahi-kantha.			Palanpur.			Rewa-kantha.			Others.		
	P.	M.	F.	P.	M.	F.	P.	M.	F.	P.	M.	F.	P.	M.	F.	P.	M.	F.	P.	M.	F.	P.	M.	F.
1	131	132	133	134	135	136	137	138	139	140	141	142	143	144	145	146	147	148	149	150	151	152	153	154
Rajputana	**1,403**	**588**	**815**	**1,531**	**891**	**640**	**7,934**	**3,193**	**4,741**	**1,064**	**663**	**401**	**2,014**	**584**	**1,430**	**3,289**	**1,309**	**1,980**	**1,094**	**284**	**810**	**473**	**263**	**210**
Alwar	9	6	3	9	6	3	24	15	9	23	15	8	..	..	..	..	..	..	..	..	..	1	..	1
Banawara	..	..	..	26	10	16	623	189	434	14	7	7	105	47	58	..	..	..	503	135	368	1	..	1
Bharatpur	14	11	3	38	33	5	122	62	60	73	36	37	..	..	..	..	..	..	..	..	..	49	26	23
Bikaner	5	5	..	6	5	1	66	48	18	48	39	9	..	..	..	..	..	..	..	..	..	18	9	9
Bundi	..	..	..	4	3	1	8	5	3	7	4	3	..	..	..	..	..	..	..	..	..	1	1	..
Dholpur	..	..	..	25	15	10	1	1	..	..	..	..	..	..	..	..	..	..	..	..	..	1	1	..
Dungarpur	..	..	..	148	71	77	1,497	327	1,170	81	48	33	883	164	719	43	13	30	488	100	388	2	2	..
Jaipur	11	5	6	129	86	43	150	101	49	108	72	36	..	..	..	6	5	1	..	..	..	36	24	12
Jaisalmer	540	173	367	5	3	2	119	51	68	2	2	..	..	..	..	4	4	..	..	..	..	113	45	68
Jhalawar	..	..	..	38	28	10	18	13	5	13	9	4	..	..	..	..	..	..	2	1	1	3	3	..
Karauli	1	..	1	14	14	..	7	7	..	..	..	..	..	..	..	1	1	..	..	..	..	6	6	..
Kishangarh	..	..	..	49	31	18	17	12	5	13	10	3	..	..	..	3	2	1	..	..	..	1	..	1
Kotah	9	6	3	147	87	60	221	169	52	180	136	44	..	..	..	1	1	..	..	..	..	40	32	8
Kushalgarh (Chiefship)	..	..	..	7	7	..	121	49	72	8	5	3	34	7	27	..	..	..	77	36	41	2	1	1
Lawa (Estate)	..	..	..	..	..	..	..	..	..	..	..	..	..	..	..	..	..	..	..	..	..	..	..	..
Marwar	765	348	417	223	153	70	1,592	624	968	188	118	70	31	11	20	1,316	469	847	2	2	..	57	26	31
Mewar	12	12	..	155	86	69	908	378	530	157	68	89	686	277	409	14	7	7	..	..	..	51	26	25
Partabgarh	..	..	..	2	2	..	12	6	6	2	2	..	4	1	3	..	..	..	5	3	2	..	..	..
Shahpura (Chiefship)	..	..	..	12	12	..	12	4	8	7	3	4	..	..	..	..	..	..	5	1	4	..	..	..
Sirohi	35	20	15	484	232	252	2,415	1,131	1,284	141	90	51	271	77	194	1,901	897	1,004	11	6	5	91	61	30
Tonk	2	2	..	10	7	3	1	1	..	1	1	..	..	..	..	..	..	..	..	..	..	..	..	..
Ajmer-Merwara	**66**	**29**	**37**	**745**	**458**	**287**	**347**	**183**	**164**	**230**	**119**	**111**	..	..	..	**45**	**29**	**16**	..	..	..	**72**	**35**	**37**
Ajmer	65	28	37	656	402	254	179	102	77	105	51	54	..	..	..	28	23	5	..	..	..	46	28	18
Merwara	1	1	..	89	56	33	168	81	87	125	68	57	..	..	..	17	6	11	..	..	..	26	7	19
CITIES.																								
Rajputana	..	..	..	..	..	..	**403**	**241**	**162**	..	..	..	..	..	..	..	..	..	..	..	..	..	..	..
Alwar	..	..	..	..	..	..	18	12	6	..	..	..	..	..	..	..	..	..	..	..	..	..	..	..
Bharatpur	..	..	..	..	..	..	54	29	25	..	..	..	..	..	..	..	..	..	..	..	..	..	..	..
Bikaner	..	..	..	..	..	..	51	37	14	..	..	..	..	..	..	..	..	..	..	..	..	..	..	..
Jaipur	..	..	..	..	..	..	84	54	30	..	..	..	..	..	..	..	..	..	..	..	..	..	..	..
Jodhpur	..	..	..	..	..	..	100	52	48	..	..	..	..	..	..	..	..	..	..	..	..	..	..	..
Kotah	..	..	..	..	..	..	57	39	18	..	..	..	..	..	..	..	..	..	..	..	..	..	..	..
Tonk	..	..	..	..	..	..	..	..	..	..	..	..	..	..	..	..	..	..	..	..	..	..	..	..
Udaipur	..	..	..	..	..	..	39	18	21	..	..	..	..	..	..	..	..	..	..	..	..	..	..	..
Ajmer-Merwara—																								
Ajmer	..	..	..	..	..	..	156	83	73	..	..	..	..	..	..	..	..	..	..	..	..	..	..	..

TABLE XI.—BIRTHPLACE—*contd.*

Province; and State, District, or City of enumeration.	A.—BORN IN INDIA—*contd.*																										
	BURMA.			CENTRAL INDIA.																							
	Total.*			Total Central India.			Bhopal.			Gwalior.			Indore.			Jaora.			Khilchipur.			Rajgarh.			Rutlam.		
	P.	M.	F.	P.	M.	F.	P.	M.	F.	P.	M.	F.	P.	M.	F.	P.	M.	F.	P	M.	F.	P.	M.	F.	P.	M.	F.
1	155	156	157	158	159	160	161	162	163	164	165	166	167	168	169	170	171	172	173	174	175	176	177	178	179	180	181
Rajputana	**32**	**14**	**18**	**99,329**	**38,291**	**61,038**	**1,499**	**567**	**932**	**66,716**	**25,631**	**41,085**	**17,319**	**6,429**	**10,890**	**1,708**	**621**	**1,087**	**2,156**	**915**	**1,241**	**2,522**	**1,177**	**1,345**	**1,843**	**751**	**1,092**
Alwar	2	2	..	*216*	*78*	*138*	15	3	12	132	44	88	38	15	23	4	3	1	..	..	..	2	2	..	15	6	9
Banswara	..	..	..	*1,370*	*559*	*811*	14	10	4	207	94	113	113	64	49	136	58	80	..	..	..	5	4	1	673	257	416
Bharatpur	1	1	..	*574*	*262*	*312*	21	8	13	475	211	264	36	18	18	5	4	1	..	..	..	..	..	..	7	2	5
Bikaner	15	5	10	*102*	*63*	*39*	2	2	..	63	35	28	21	12	9	..	..	..	1	..	1	..	..	..	4	3	1
Bundi	..	..	..	*546*	*256*	*290*	18	12	6	412	195	217	69	30	39	..	..	..	..	..	..	..	..	..	10	6	4
Dholpur	1	1	..	*7,077*	*1,983*	*5,094*	7	3	4	6,890	1,906	4,984	19	7	12	..	..	..	..	..	..	5	1	4	1	1	..
Dungarpur	..	..	..	*303*	*151*	*152*	3	1	2	110	53	57	48	31	17	23	7	16	..	..	..	..	..	..	46	23	23
Jaipur	8	1	7	*1,621*	*542*	*1,079*	50	22	28	1,348	405	943	138	73	65	9	5	4	..	..	..	24	9	15	24	12	12
Jaisalmer	..	..	..	*99*	*44*	*55*	46	18	28	11	4	7	6	2	4	1	1	..	1	..	1	1	1	..	3	2	1
Jhalawar	..	..	..	*12,871*	*3,966*	*8,905*	24	13	11	5,846	1,784	4,062	5,231	1,558	3,673	233	77	156	91	40	51	33	9	24	32	11	21
Karauli	..	..	..	*2,344*	*543*	*1,801*	4	..	4	2,306	529	1,777	9	2	7	..	..	..	1	..	1	..	..	..	2	1	1
Kishangarh	..	..	..	*122*	*55*	*67*	3	1	2	67	27	40	28	15	13	4	2	2	..	..	..	..	..	..	6	2	4
Kotah	1	1	..	*26,758*	*11,299*	*15,459*	200	99	101	15,721	6,781	8,940	5,421	1,956	3,465	50	26	24	2,043	868	1,175	2,339	1,096	1,243	70	37	33
Kushalgarh (Chiefship)	..	..	..	*1,025*	*417*	*608*	10	8	2	42	18	24	70	25	45	7	3	4	..	..	..	1	..	1	286	120	166
Lawa (Estate)	..	..	..	*4*	*1*	*3*	..	..	..	4	1	3	..	..	..	..	..	..	..	..	..	..	..	..	..	..	..
Marwar	2	1	1	*272*	*132*	*140*	18	10	8	99	52	47	77	29	48	9	5	4	..	..	..	7	5	2	31	14	17
Mewar	1	1	..	*13,458*	*6,793*	*6,665*	31	17	14	10,036	4,927	5,109	3,071	1,692	1,379	82	47	35	..	..	..	2	2	..	84	42	42
Partabgarh	..	..	..	*7,184*	*2,513*	*4,671*	60	24	36	4,095	1,394	2,701	576	227	349	1,035	347	688	..	..	..	1	..	1	496	174	322
Shahpura (Chiefship)	..	..	..	*139*	*77*	*62*	..	..	..	90	51	39	20	16	4	13	6	7	..	..	..	..	..	..	6	3	3
Sirohi	1	1	..	*182*	*99*	*83*	1	..	1	84	40	44	79	44	35	..	..	..	..	..	..	..	..	..	14	13	1
Tonk	..	..	..	*23,062*	*8,458*	*14,604*	972	316	656	18,678	7,080	11,598	2,249	613	1,636	95	32	63	19	7	12	102	48	54	25	13	12
Ajmer-Merwara	**21**	**13**	**8**	**2,046**	**983**	**1,063**	**69**	**40**	**29**	**1,227**	**577**	**650**	**493**	**247**	**246**	**67**	**25**	**42**	..	..	..	**20**	**2**	**18**	**73**	**32**	**41**
Ajmer	21	13	8	*1,830*	*886*	*944*	61	36	25	1,090	518	572	434	217	217	63	25	38	..	..	..	20	2	18	66	29	37
Merwara	..	..	..	*216*	*97*	*119*	8	4	4	137	59	78	59	30	29	4	..	4	..	..	..	..	..	..	7	3	4
CITIES.																											
Rajputana	**3**	**2**	**1**	**1,998**	**1,081**	**917**	..	..	..	**1,360**	**749**	**611**	..	..	..	..	..	..	..	..	..	..	..	..	..	..	..
Alwar	2	2	..	*53*	*22*	*31*	..	..	..	30	14	16	..	..	..	..	..	..	..	..	..	..	..	..	..	..	..
Bharatpur	..	..	..	*149*	*74*	*75*	..	..	..	119	60	59	..	..	..	..	..	..	..	..	..	..	..	..	..	..	..
Bikaner	..	..	..	*73*	*49*	*24*	..	..	..	48	30	18	..	..	..	..	..	..	..	..	..	..	..	..	..	..	..
Jaipur	1	..	1	*243*	*123*	*120*	..	..	..	128	64	64	..	..	..	..	..	..	..	..	..	..	..	..	..	..	..
Jodhpur	..	..	..	*78*	*47*	*31*	..	..	..	23	21	2	..	..	..	..	..	..	..	..	..	..	..	..	..	..	..
Kotah	..	..	..	*1,096*	*591*	*505*	..	..	..	826	460	366	..	..	..	..	..	..	..	..	..	..	..	..	..	..	..
Tonk	..	..	..	*149*	*69*	*80*	..	..	..	89	36	53	..	..	..	..	..	..	..	..	..	..	..	..	..	..	..
Udaipur	..	..	..	*157*	*106*	*51*	..	..	..	97	64	33	..	..	..	..	..	..	..	..	..	..	..	..	..	..	..
Ajmer-Merwara—																											
Ajmer	18	11	7	*1,265*	*638*	*627*	..	..	..	700	340	360	..	..	..	..	..	..	..	..	..	..	..	..	..	..	..

* All born in Districts.

TABLE XI.—BIRTHPLACE—*contd.*

Province; and State, District, or City of enumeration.	A.—BORN IN INDIA—*contd.*																							
	CENTRAL INDIA—*concld.*			CENTRAL PROVINCES AND BERAR.			HYDERABAD STATE.			KASHMIR STATE.			MADRAS.									MYSORE STATE.		
	Others.			*Total.			Total.			Total.			Total Madras.			Districts.			States.			Total.		
	P.	M.	F.	P.	M.	F.	P.	M.	F.	P.	M.	F.	P.	M.	F.	P.	M.	F.	P.	M.	F.	P.	M.	F.
1	182	183	184	185	186	187	188	189	190	191	192	193	194	195	196	197	198	199	200	201	202	203	204	205
Rajputana	5,566	2,200	3,366	936	500	436	321	172	149	90	67	23	290	157	133	283	153	130	7	4	3	67	28	39
Alwar	10	5	5	22	12	10	7	5	2	6	6	..	*1*	*1*	..	1	1	..	..	..	..	..	..	..
Banswara	222	74	148	36	14	22	9	5	4	1	1	..	..	..	..	..	..	..	..	..	..	..	..	..
Bharatpur	30	19	11	30	17	18	9	4	5	8	6	2	*35*	*20*	*15*	37	19	18	1	1	..	..	..	..
Bikaner	11	11	..	55	32	23	11	6	5	7	5	2	*2*	*1*	*1*	2	1	1	..	..	..	..	..	..
Bundi	37	13	24	3	1	2	..	..	..	..	..	..	*4*	*1*	*3*	4	1	3	..	..	..	..	..	..
Dholpur	155	65	90	32	11	21	5	5	..	8	6	2	*2*	*2*	..	2	2	..	..	..	..	9	3	6
Dungarpur	71	36	35	34	20	14	2	1	1	..	..	..	*3*	*2*	*1*	3	2	1	..	..	..	..	..	..
Jaipur	28	16	12	105	58	47	46	30	16	37	27	10	*72*	*38*	*34*	71	37	34	1	1	..	13	7	6
Jaisalmer	30	16	14	80	43	37	1	..	1	..	..	..	..	..	..	..	..	..	..	..	..	..	..	..
Jhalawar	1,381	474	907	18	9	9	2	..	2	..	..	..	*2*	*2*	..	1	1	..	1	1	..	..	..	..
Karauli	22	11	11	27	11	16	4	1	3	1	1	..	*3*	*1*	*2*	3	1	2	..	..	..	..	..	..
Kishangarh	14	8	6	14	7	7	9	7	2	..	..	..	*1*	*1*	..	1	1	..	..	..	..	..	..	..
Kotah	914	436	478	183	109	74	24	12	12	2	1	1	*35*	*12*	*23*	35	12	23	..	..	..	1	1	..
Kushalgarh (Chiefship)	600	234	366	..	..	..	..	..	..	..	..	..	..	..	..	..	..	..	..	..	..	..	..	..
Lawa (Estate)	..	..	..	..	..	..	..	..	..	..	..	..	..	..	..	..	..	..	..	..	..	..	..	..
Marwar	31	17	14	65	42	23	75	37	38	19	14	5	*34*	*24*	*10*	33	24	9	1	..	1	9	1	8
Mewar	152	66	86	41	23	18	75	35	40	..	..	..	*20*	*11*	*9*	19	10	9	1	1	..	..	..	..
Partabgarh	921	347	574	1	1	..	1	1	..	..	..	..	..	..	..	..	..	..	..	..	..	..	..	..
Shahpura (Chiefship)	11	1	10	..	..	..	..	..	..	..	..	..	..	..	..	..	..	..	..	..	..	..	..	..
Sirohi	4	2	2	32	24	8	14	8	6	2	1	1	*69*	*38*	*31*	67	38	29	2	..	2	34	15	19
Tonk	922	349	573	158	66	92	27	15	12	..	..	..	*4*	*3*	*1*	4	3	1	..	..	..	1	1	..
Ajmer-Merwara	97	60	37	341	174	167	247	134	113	35	27	8	224	126	98	218	123	95	6	3	3	64	33	31
Ajmer	96	59	37	327	169	158	228	124	104	34	26	8	*217*	*122*	*95*	211	119	92	6	3	3	60	32	28
Merwara	1	1	..	14	5	9	19	10	9	1	1	..	*7*	*4*	*3*	7	4	3	..	..	..	4	1	3
CITIES.																								
Rajputana	638	332	306	182	104	78	57	31	26	37	31	6	*66*	*33*	*33*	64	37	27	2	1	1	4	3	1
Alwar	23	8	15	4	3	1	1	..	1	4	4	..	..	..	..	..	..	..	..	..	..	..	..	..
Bharatpur	30	14	16	17	10	7	1	..	1	4	4	..	*18*	*10*	*8*	17	9	8	1	1	..	..	..	..
Bikaner	25	19	6	50	30	20	7	3	4	2	2	..	*1*	*1*	..	1	1	..	..	..	..	..	..	..
Jaipur	115	59	56	33	17	16	21	11	10	14	11	3	*20*	*9*	*11*	20	9	11	..	..	..	2	2	..
Jodhpur	55	26	29	38	25	13	7	4	3	13	10	3	*19*	*13*	*6*	18	13	5	1	..	1	1	..	1
Kotah	270	131	139	26	14	12	12	6	6	..	..	..	*3*	..	*3*	3	..	3	..	..	..	..	..	..
Tonk	60	33	27	6	2	4	6	6	..	..	..	..	*1*	*1*	..	1	1	..	..	..	..	1	1	..
Udaipur	60	42	18	8	3	5	2	1	1	..	..	..	*4*	*4*	..	4	4	..	..	..	..	..	..	..
Ajmer-Merwara—																								
Ajmer	565	298	267	245	128	117	172	94	78	31	24	7	*118*	*75*	*73*	143	73	70	5	2	3	30	15	15

* All born in Districts.

TABLE XI.—BIRTHPLACE—*contd.*

Province; and State, District, or City of enumeration.	A.—BORN IN INDIA—*contd.*																			
	NORTH-WEST FRONTIER.									PUNJAB.										
	Total N.-W. F.			Districts.			Political Agencies.			Total Punjab.			DISTRICTS.							
													Total Districts.			Delhi.			Ferozepur.	
	P.	M.	F.	P.	M.	F.	P.	M.	F.	P.	M.	F.	P.	M.	F.	P.	M.	F.	P.	M.	F.
1	206	207	208	209	210	211	212	213	214	215	216	217	218	219	220	221	222	223	224	225	226
Rajputana	507	416	91	504	413	91	3	3	..	85,526	32,047	53,479	63,655	24,590	39,065	2,751	1,387	1,364	11,258	6,472	4,786
Alwar	3	2	1	3	2	1	..	..	..	25,419	4,869	20,550	17,590	3,741	13,849	530	172	358	38	15	23
Banswara	44	38	6	43	37	6	1	1	..	29	24	5	23	19	4	9	7	2	1	1	..
Bharatpur	5	5	..	5	5	..	..	..	..	10,653	3,441	7,212	10,537	3,371	7,166	321	164	157	14	6	8
Bikaner	22	15	7	22	15	7	..	..	..	33,099	17,108	15,991	26,110	13,245	12,865	152	83	69	11,133	6,414	4,719
Bundi	1	1	..	1	1	..	..	..	..	22	15	7	15	11	4	11	7	4	..	..	..
Dholpur	28	23	5	28	23	5	..	..	..	286	169	117	243	139	104	44	17	27	4	2	2
Dungarpur	25	21	4	25	21	4	..	..	..	22	19	3	22	19	3	6	5	1	1	..	1
Jaipur	53	41	12	53	41	12	..	..	..	11,105	3,305	7,800	5,858	1,942	3,916	752	390	362	32	13	19
Jaisalmer	9	3	6	9	3	6	..	..	..	1,028	623	405	20	14	6	1	..	1	..	..	..
Jhalawar	..	..	..	..	..	..	..	..	..	112	79	33	101	70	31	32	17	15	1	..	1
Karauli	1	1	..	1	1	..	..	..	..	94	63	31	74	44	30	33	16	17	..	..	..
Kishangarh	..	..	..	..	..	..	..	..	..	60	45	15	60	45	15	27	16	11	..	..	..
Kotah	14	13	1	14	13	1	..	..	..	617	397	220	559	364	195	129	74	55	4	3	1
Kushalgarh (Chiefship)	..	..	..	..	..	..	..	..	..	4	3	1	4	3	1	4	3	1	..	..	..
Lawa (Estate)	..	..	..	..	..	..	..	..	..	..	..	..	..	..	..	..	..	..	..	..	..
Marwar	47	30	17	47	30	17	..	..	..	1,120	715	405	970	627	343	316	171	145	9	4	5
Mewar	83	74	9	81	72	9	2	2	..	816	502	314	609	385	224	75	56	19	7	4	3
Partabgarh	91	80	11	91	80	11	..	..	..	26	21	5	21	16	5	7	5	2	1	1	..
Shahpura (Chiefship)	..	..	..	..	..	..	..	..	..	23	16	7	22	15	7	2	1	1	..	..	..
Sirohi	25	23	2	25	23	2	..	..	..	778	505	273	617	399	218	202	125	77	11	6	5
Tonk	56	46	10	56	46	10	..	..	..	218	138	80	200	121	79	98	58	40	2	1	1
Ajmer-Merwara	106	84	22	105	84	21	1	..	1	4,111	2,778	1,333	3,496	2,380	1,116	859	500	359	86	59	27
Ajmer	101	79	22	100	79	21	1	..	1	3,710	2,506	1,204	3,160	2,152	1,008	807	467	340	70	50	20
Merwara	5	5	..	5	5	..	..	..	..	401	272	129	336	228	108	52	33	19	16	9	7
CITIES.																					
Rajputana	106	96	10	106	96	10	..	..	..	4,331	2,480	1,851	3,437	1,940	1,497	1,051	527	524	..	..	..
Alwar	2	2	..	2	2	..	..	..	..	936	361	575	818	301	517	254	75	179	..	..	..
Bharatpur	2	2	..	2	2	..	..	..	..	480	287	193	437	260	177	101	51	50	..	..	..
Bikaner	11	8	3	11	8	3	..	..	..	849	631	218	515	395	120	53	36	17	..	..	..
Jaipur	9	8	1	9	8	1	..	..	..	954	527	427	738	395	343	329	179	150	..	..	..
Jodhpur	11	6	5	11	6	5	..	..	..	490	305	185	451	285	166	175	97	78	..	..	..
Kotah	..	..	..	..	..	..	..	..	..	215	137	78	189	126	63	48	31	17	..	..	..
Tonk	26	25	1	26	25	1	..	..	..	116	70	46	109	65	44	58	37	21	..	..	..
Udaipur	45	45	..	45	45	..	..	..	..	293	162	131	180	113	67	33	21	12	..	..	..
Ajmer-Merwara—																					
Ajmer	68	59	9	68	59	9	..	..	..	2,009	1,240	769	1,777	1,114	663	742	431	311	..	..	..

TABLE XI.—BIRTHPLACE—*contd.*

Province; and State, District, or City of enumeration.	A.—BORN IN INDIA—*contd.*																				
	PUNJAB—*contd.*																				
	DISTRICTS—*concld.*												STATES.								
	Gurgaon.			Hissar.			Rohtak.			Others.			Total States.			Bhawalpur.			Nabha.		
	P.	M.	F.	P.	M.	F.	P.	M.	F.	P.	M.	F.	P.	M.	F.	P.	M.	F.	P.	M.	F.
1	227	228	229	230	231	232	233	234	235	236	237	238	239	240	241	242	243	244	245	246	247
Rajputana	29,933	7,644	22,289	14,017	5,887	8,130	1,442	617	825	4,254	2,583	1,671	21,871	7,457	14,414	3,519	2,018	1,501	3,883	960	2,923
Alwar	15,876	3,263	12,613	222	34	188	636	127	509	288	130	158	7,829	1,128	6,701	..	..	..	2,867	478	2,194
Banswara	..	..	..	..	..	..	..	..	..	13	11	2	6	5	1	..	..	..	..	..	..
Bharatpur	9,902	3,003	6,899	24	18	6	89	62	27	187	116	71	116	70	46	..	..	..	45	23	22
Bikaner	312	206	104	13,037	5,594	7,443	230	148	82	1,246	798	448	6,989	3,863	3,126	2,496	1,406	1,090	300	193	107
Bundi	..	..	..	..	..	..	..	..	..	4	4	..	7	4	3	..	..	..	..	..	..
Dholpur	41	32	9	5	4	1	3	1	2	146	83	63	43	30	13	1	1	..	12	9	3
Dungarpur	1	1	..	..	..	..	..	..	..	14	13	1	..	..	..	..	..	..	..	..	..
Jaipur	3,377	853	2,524	637	179	458	233	114	119	827	393	434	5,247	1,363	3,884	5	2	3	729	172	557
Jaisalmer	..	..	..	3	8	..	..	..	..	11	6	5	1,008	609	399	1,003	604	399	..	..	..
Jhalawar	11	6	5	..	..	..	8	5	3	49	42	7	18	9	7	..	..	..	1	..	1
Karauli	4	2	2	..	..	..	1	1	..	36	25	11	10	9	1	..	..	..	..	..	..
Kishangarh	3	3	..	1	..	1	..	..	..	29	26	3	..	..	..	..	..	..	..	..	..
Kotah	63	46	17	20	9	11	30	25	14	304	207	97	58	33	25	1	..	1	12	7	5
Kushalgarh (Chiefship)	..	..	..	..	..	..	..	..	..	..	..	..	..	..	..	..	..	..	..	..	..
Lawa (Estate)	..	..	..	..	..	..	..	..	..	..	..	..	..	..	..	..	..	..	..	..	..
Marwar	103	72	31	43	28	15	43	26	17	456	326	130	150	38	62	2	..	2	10	8	2
Mewar	100	64	36	7	4	3	121	77	44	299	180	119	207	117	90	8	2	6	43	31	13
Partabgarh	..	..	..	1	1	..	..	..	..	12	0	3	5	5	..	..	..	..	..	..	..
Shahpura (Chiefship)	2	1	1	..	..	..	..	..	..	18	13	5	1	1	..	..	..	..	..	..	..
Sirohi	112	71	41	11	8	3	38	30	8	243	159	84	161	106	55	..	..	..	63	43	20
Tonk	26	19	7	1	..	1	1	1	..	72	42	30	18	17	1	3	3	..	1	1	..
Ajmer-Merwara	425	263	162	119	66	53	93	60	33	1,914	1,432	482	615	398	217	9	8	1	61	45	16
Ajmer	332	196	134	80	38	42	59	39	20	1,812	1,360	452	550	354	196	9	8	1	48	36	12
Merwara	93	65	28	39	28	11	34	21	13	102	72	30	65	44	21	..	..	..	13	9	4
CITIES.																					
Rajputana	..	..	..	..	..	..	..	..	..	2,386	1,413	973	894	540	354	..	..	..	..	..	..
Alwar	..	..	..	..	..	..	..	..	..	564	226	338	118	60	58	..	..	..	..	..	..
Bharatpur	..	..	..	..	..	..	..	..	..	336	209	127	43	27	16	..	..	..	..	..	..
Bikaner	..	..	..	..	..	..	..	..	..	462	359	103	334	236	98	..	..	..	..	..	..
Jaipur	..	..	..	..	..	..	..	..	..	409	216	193	216	132	84	..	..	..	..	..	..
Jodhpur	..	..	..	..	..	..	..	..	..	276	188	88	39	20	19	..	..	..	..	..	..
Kotah	..	..	..	..	..	..	..	..	..	141	95	46	26	11	15	..	..	..	..	..	..
Tonk	..	..	..	..	..	..	..	..	..	51	28	23	5	5	..	..	..	..	..	..	..
Udaipur	..	..	..	..	..	..	..	..	..	147	92	55	113	49	64	..	..	..	..	..	..
Ajmer-Merwara—																					
Ajmer	..	..	..	..	..	..	..	..	..	1,035	683	352	232	126	106	..	..	..	..	..	..

TABLE XI.—BIRTHPLACE—*contd.*

Province: and State, District, or City of enumeration.	A.—BORN IN INDIA—*contd.*																				
	PUNJAB—*concld.*						UNITED PROVINCES OF AGRA AND OUDH.														
	STATES—*concld.*						Total United Provinces.			DISTRICTS.											
	Patiala.			Others.						Total Districts.			Agra.			Aligarh.			Allahabad.		
	P.	M.	F.	P.	M.	F.	P.	M.	F.	P.	M.	F.	P.	M.	F.	P.	M.	F.	P.	M.	F.
1	248	249	250	251	252	253	254	255	256	257	258	259	260	261	262	263	264	265	266	267	268
Rajputana	**12,375**	**3,483**	**8,892**	**2,096**	**988**	**1,108**	**70,064**	**26,003**	**44,061**	**69,464**	**25,542**	**43,922**	**36,847**	**11,624**	**25,223**	**2,610**	**976**	**1,634**	**732**	**463**	**269**
Alwar	5,063	633	4,430	99	22	77	*2,040*	*836*	*1,204*	2,026	825	1,201	597	187	410	122	57	65	7	3	4
Banswara	6	5	1	..	..	..	*81*	*57*	*24*	78	55	23	3	2	1	2	1	1	3	3	..
Bharatpur	40	25	15	31	22	9	*33,759*	*10,208*	*23,551*	33,742	10,200	23,542	16,068	5,105	10,963	821	306	515	68	47	21
Bikaner	2,834	1,613	1,221	1,359	651	708	*1,194*	*789*	*405*	1,183	779	404	298	185	113	78	43	35	25	17	8
Bundi	7	4	3	..	..	..	*259*	*165*	*94*	236	146	90	42	21	21	4	3	1	7	4	3
Dholpur	28	18	10	2	2	..	*16,714*	*4,400*	*12,314*	16,699	4,396	12,303	15,343	3,763	11,580	119	44	75	22	14	8
Dungarpur	..	..	..	..	..	..	*48*	*35*	*13*	48	35	13	2	2	..	..	..	..	1	1	..
Jaipur	4,117	1,016	3,101	396	173	223	*5,781*	*3,231*	*2,550*	5,705	3,185	2,520	1,029	84	945	329	188	141	227	139	88
Jaisalmer	4	4	..	1	1	..	*40*	*17*	*23*	40	17	23	1	..	1	9	5	4	..	..	..
Jhalawar	13	7	6	2	2	..	*669*	*441*	*228*	627	412	215	163	114	49	18	8	10	6	4	2
Karauli	10	9	1	..	..	..	*1,042*	*354*	*688*	1,039	351	688	565	154	411	28	22	6	7	4	3
Kishangarh	..	..	..	..	..	..	*198*	*129*	*69*	184	121	63	24	21	13	3	3	..	3	..	3
Kotah	34	20	14	11	6	5	*2,593*	*1,694*	*899*	2,392	1,503	889	478	295	183	100	70	30	47	35	12
Kushalgarh (Chiefship)	..	..	..	..	..	..	*14*	*9*	*5*	14	9	5	..	..	..	4	3	1	..	..	..
Lawa (Estate)	..	..	..	..	..	..	*3*	*2*	*1*	3	2	1	..	..	..	..	..	..	..	..	..
Marwar	106	64	42	32	16	16	*2,075*	*1,296*	*779*	2,064	1,290	774	569	345	224	276	171	105	154	91	63
Mewar	21	15	6	135	69	66	*1,109*	*768*	*341*	1,047	717	330	120	71	49	27	18	9	20	13	7
Partabgarh	1	1	..	4	4	..	*124*	*95*	*29*	109	83	26	14	11	3	2	2	..	1	1	..
Shahpura (Chiefship)	1	1	..	..	..	..	*60*	*35*	*25*	52	27	25	15	5	10	..	..	..	..	..	..
Sirohi	76	45	31	22	18	4	*1,269*	*831*	*438*	1,263	827	436	403	254	149	25	16	9	111	71	40
Tonk	14	13	1	..	..	..	*992*	*611*	*381*	913	562	351	203	105	98	34	16	18	23	16	7
Ajmer-Merwara	**472**	**292**	**180**	**73**	**53**	**20**	**12,115**	**7,042**	**5,073**	**11,981**	**6,958**	**5,023**	**5,530**	**3,115**	**2,415**	**685**	**391**	**294**	**720**	**411**	**309**
Ajmer	443	274	169	50	36	14	*11,509*	*6,640*	*4,869*	11,377	6,557	4,820	5,358	3,010	2,348	639	361	278	715	408	307
Merwara	29	18	11	23	17	6	*606*	*402*	*204*	604	401	203	172	105	67	46	30	16	5	3	2
CITIES.																					
Rajputana	..	..	..	..	..	..	**9,695**	**5,031**	**4,664**	**9,501**	**4,901**	**4,600**	**2,906**	**1,287**	**1,619**	**805**	**439**	**366**	**199**	**120**	**79**
Alwar	..	..	..	..	..	..	*529*	*283*	*246*	524	279	245	139	77	62	41	22	19	4	2	2
Bharatpur	..	..	..	..	..	..	*4,092*	*1,637*	*2,455*	4,083	1,632	2,451	1,791	652	1,139	265	120	145	48	31	17
Bikaner	..	..	..	..	..	..	*593*	*425*	*168*	590	422	168	168	118	50	30	20	10	15	13	2
Jaipur	..	..	..	..	..	..	*1,998*	*1,152*	*846*	1,937	1,115	822	376	186	190	173	101	72	39	18	21
Jodhpur	..	..	..	..	..	..	*955*	*596*	*359*	951	595	356	188	100	74	217	134	83	69	41	28
Kotah	..	..	..	..	..	..	*842*	*508*	*334*	831	497	334	170	98	72	52	32	20	13	11	2
Tonk	..	..	..	..	..	..	*461*	*269*	*192*	406	238	168	54	30	24	23	8	15	11	4	7
Udaipur	..	..	..	..	..	..	*225*	*161*	*64*	179	123	56	25	17	8	4	2	2	..	..	..
Ajmer-Merwara—																					
Ajmer	..	..	..	..	..	..	*10,339*	*5,895*	*4,444*	10,234	5,830	4,404	5,213	2,927	2,286	612	342	270	689	396	293

TABLE XI.—BIRTHPLACE—*contd.*

Province; and State, District, or City of enumeration.	A.—BORN IN INDIA—*contd.* United Provinces of Agra and Oudh—*concld.* Districts—*concld.* Cawnpur. P.	M.	F.	Farrukhabad. P.	M.	F.	Moradabad. P.	M.	F.	Muttra. P.	M.	F.	Others—Agra. P.	M.	F.	Others—Oudh. P.	M.	F.	States. Total. P.	M.	F.	Unspecified—India. P.	M.	F.	French Settlements. Pondicherry. P.	M.	F.
1	269	270	271	272	273	274	275	276	277	278	279	280	281	282	283	284	285	286	287	288	289	290	291	292	293	294	295
Rajputana	1,172	665	500	809	513	296	807	537	270	17,501	5,958	12,533	7,423	4,349	3,074	2,073	1,359	714	600	461	139	5	..	5	2	1	1
Alwar	30	11	19	50	35	15	60	43	17	542	158	384	555	294	261	68	87	25	14	11	3	..	..	..	..	..	..
Banswara	1	1	..	7	6	1	..	..	..	3	3	..	43	28	15	16	11	5	3	2	1	..	..	..	..	..	..
Bharatpur	53	33	20	72	49	23	57	31	26	15,502	4,043	11,459	974	508	468	127	78	49	17	8	9	..	..	..	..	..	..
Bikaner	56	31	25	30	19	11	46	30	16	63	49	13	581	364	167	57	41	16	11	10	1	..	..	..	..	..	..
Bundi	13	9	4	4	3	1	7	4	3	40	26	14	100	61	39	19	15	4	23	19	4	..	..	..	..	..	..
Dholpur	65	30	35	53	28	25	27	12	15	239	95	144	765	374	391	66	36	30	15	4	11	..	..	..	..	..	..
Dungarpur	5	3	2	..	..	..	..	..	..	1	1	..	35	26	9	4	2	2	..	..	..	..	..	..	..	..	..
Jaipur	257	132	125	155	93	62	226	152	74	510	273	237	1,555	896	659	517	325	180	76	46	30	2	..	2	..	..	..
Jaisalmer	2	2	..	..	..	..	3	1	2	9	2	7	16	7	9	..	..	..	..	..	..	..	..	..	..	..	..
Jhalawar	38	25	13	76	51	25	30	24	6	45	29	16	153	91	62	98	66	32	42	29	18	..	..	..	..	..	..
Karauli	66	7	59	15	5	10	10	7	3	71	44	27	246	93	153	31	15	16	3	3	..	..	..	..	..	..	..
Kishangarh	34	19	15	10	7	3	..	..	..	10	2	8	76	57	19	14	12	2	14	8	6	..	..	..	..	..	..
Kotah	165	107	58	142	102	40	84	57	27	248	138	110	835	512	323	284	187	97	201	191	10	..	..	..	..	..	..
Kushalgarh (Chiefship)	1	1	..	7	3	4	..	..	..	1	1	..	1	1	..	..	..	..	..	..	..	..	..	..	..	..	..
Lawa (Estate)	..	..	..	..	..	..	..	..	..	2	1	1	1	1	..	..	..	..	..	..	..	..	..	..	..	..	..
Marwar	154	101	58	72	39	33	69	44	25	114	71	43	464	289	175	103	139	53	11	6	5	1	..	1	..	..	..
Mewar	115	79	36	48	33	15	32	18	14	129	82	47	374	270	104	182	133	49	62	51	11	..	..	..	..	..	..
Partabgarh	5	3	2	1	1	..	4	3	1	4	4	..	42	35	7	36	23	13	15	12	3	..	..	..	..	..	..
Shahpura (Chiefship)	4	2	2	..	..	..	8	5	3	3	..	3	18	14	4	4	1	3	8	8	..	..	..	..	..	..	..
Sirohi	85	53	32	13	9	4	25	21	4	35	24	11	316	226	90	250	153	97	6	4	2	2	..	2	2	1	1
Tonk	23	14	9	54	30	24	110	63	34	21	12	9	323	202	121	113	83	31	79	49	30	..	..	..	..	..	..
Ajmer-Merwara	318	179	139	300	185	115	264	167	97	953	519	434	2,235	1,353	882	976	638	338	184	84	50	13	5	8	3	3	..
Ajmer	275	148	127	263	159	104	255	161	94	923	499	424	2,077	1,245	832	872	566	306	132	83	49	13	5	8	3	3	..
Merwara	43	31	12	37	26	11	9	6	3	30	20	10	158	108	50	104	72	32	2	1	1	..	..	..	..	..	..
CITIES.																											
Rajputana	..	..	..	..	..	..	..	..	..	1,854	770	1,084	3,102	1,878	1,224	636	407	228	194	130	64	..	..	..	..	..	..
Alwar	..	..	..	..	..	..	..	..	..	65	33	32	242	124	118	33	21	12	5	4	1	..	..	..	..	..	..
Bharatpur	..	..	..	..	..	..	..	..	..	1,404	504	900	505	284	221	70	41	29	9	5	4	..	..	..	..	..	..
Bikaner	..	..	..	..	..	..	..	..	..	32	24	8	301	215	86	44	32	12	8	3	..	..	..	..	..	..	..
Jaipur	..	..	..	..	..	..	..	..	..	166	93	73	917	653	364	266	164	102	61	37	24	..	..	..	..	..	..
Jodhpur	..	..	..	..	..	..	..	..	..	56	39	17	359	225	134	67	47	20	4	1	3	..	..	..	..	..	..
Kotah	..	..	..	..	..	..	..	..	..	107	60	47	405	241	164	84	55	29	11	11	..	..	..	..	..	..	..
Tonk	..	..	..	..	..	..	..	..	..	14	9	5	262	159	103	42	28	14	55	31	24	..	..	..	..	..	..
Udaipur	..	..	..	..	..	..	..	..	..	10	8	2	111	77	34	29	19	10	46	38	8	..	..	..	..	..	..
Ajmer-Merwara—																											
Ajmer	..	..	..	..	..	..	..	..	..	872	460	403	2,257	1,323	934	591	373	218	105	65	40	6	3	3	3	3	..

TABLE XI.—BIRTHPLACE—*contd.*

Province; and State, District, or City of enumeration.	A.—BORN IN INDIA—*concld.* Portuguese Settlements. Goa.			B.—BORN IN ASIATIC COUNTRIES OUTSIDE INDIA. Total Asiatic Countries outside India.			Afghanistan.			Arabia.			Ceylon.			Nepal.			Others.*			C.—BORN IN EUROPE. Total Europe.			France.		
	P.	M.	F.	P.	M.	F.	P.	M.	F.	P.	M.	F.	P.	M.	F.	P.	M.	F.	P.	M.	F.	P.	M.	F.	P.	M.	F
1	296	297	298	299	300	301	302	303	304	305	306	307	308	309	310	311	312	313	314	315	316	317	318	319	320	321	322
Rajputana	168	129	39	466	336	130	243	214	29	36	28	8	15	9	6	140	63	77	32	22	10	561	371	190	20	17	3
Alwar	8	6	2	*1*	..	*1*	..	..	..	..	..	..	..	..	..	1	..	1	..	..	..	*11*	*7*	*4*	..	..	..
Banswara	..	..	..	*28*	*27*	*1*	26	25	1	..	..	..	..	..	..	2	2	..	..	..	..	..	..	..	..	..	..
Bharatpur	7	5	2	*28*	*20*	*8*	12	12	..	1	..	1	..	..	..	15	8	7	..	..	..	*8*	*3*	*5*	..	..	..
Bikaner	6	6	..	*25*	*25*	..	19	19	..	1	1	..	..	..	..	5	5	..	..	..	..	*8*	*4*	*4*	..	..	..
Bundi	3	..	3	..	..	..	..	..	..	..	..	..	..	..	..	..	..	..	..	..	..	..	..	..	..	..	..
Dholpur	2	2	..	*3*	*2*	*1*	1	1	..	..	..	..	..	..	..	1	..	1	1	1	..	*10*	*5*	*5*	2	1	1
Dungarpur	..	..	..	*33*	*28*	*5*	33	28	5	..	..	..	..	..	..	..	..	..	..	..	..	..	..	..	..	..	..
Jaipur	32	25	7	*75*	*50*	*25*	21	21	..	4	4	..	6	1	5	30	19	11	14	5	9	*184*	*116*	*68*	6	5	1
Jaisalmer	..	..	..	*8*	*6*	*2*	2	..	2	..	..	..	..	..	..	..	..	..	6	6	..	..	..	..	..	..	..
Jhalawar	2	2	..	*7*	*5*	*2*	6	4	2	..	..	..	..	..	..	1	1	..	..	..	..	*13*	*8*	*5*	7	6	1
Karauli	..	..	..	*2*	*2*	..	..	..	..	1	1	..	..	..	..	1	1	..	..	..	..	*1*	*1*	..	..	..	..
Kishangarh	2	..	2	..	..	..	..	..	..	..	..	..	..	..	..	..	..	..	..	..	..	..	..	..	..	..	..
Kotah	9	9	..	*36*	*34*	*2*	29	28	1	1	1	..	1	1	..	3	2	1	2	2	..	*19*	*11*	*8*	2	2	..
Kushalgarh (Chiefship)	..	..	..	*1*	*1*	..	1	1	..	..	..	..	..	..	..	..	..	..	..	..	..	..	..	..	..	..	..
Lawa (Estate)	..	..	..	..	..	..	..	..	..	..	..	..	..	..	..	..	..	..	..	..	..	..	..	..	..	..	..
Marwar	22	12	10	*26*	*26*	..	11	11	..	..	..	..	1	1	..	12	12	..	2	2	..	*28*	*16*	*12*	2	2	..
Mewar	19	16	3	*94*	*33*	*61*	21	18	3	..	..	..	1	..	1	68	12	56	4	3	1	*13*	*6*	*7*	..	..	..
Partabgarh	..	..	..	*16*	*12*	*4*	16	12	4	..	..	..	..	..	..	..	..	..	..	..	..	..	..	..	..	..	..
Shahpura (Chiefship)	1	1	..	..	..	..	..	..	..	..	..	..	..	..	..	..	..	..	..	..	..	..	..	..	..	..	..
Sirohi	54	44	10	*9*	*9*	..	4	4	..	..	..	..	2	2	..	1	1	..	2	2	..	*264*	*192*	*72*	1	1	..
Tonk	1	1	..	*74*	*56*	*18*	41	30	11	28	21	7	4	4	..	..	..	..	1	1	..	*2*	*2*	..	..	..	..
Ajmer-Merwara	243	181	62	170	150	20	134	124	10	8	7	1	5	4	1	17	13	4	6	2	4	1,266	1,131	135	29	24	5
Ajmer	241	179	62	*160*	*142*	*18*	126	118	8	7	6	1	5	4	1	16	12	4	6	2	4	*1,261*	*1,126*	*135*	29	24	5
Merwara	2	2	..	*10*	*8*	*2*	8	6	2	1	1	..	..	..	..	1	1	..	..	..	..	*5*	*5*	..	..	..	..
CITIES.																											
Rajputana	72	55	17	144	114	30	64	63	1	30	22	8	7	6	1	29	14	15	14	9	5	85	45	40	8	7	1
Alwar	6	5	1	..	..	..	..	..	..	..	..	..	..	..	..	..	..	..	..	..	..	*4*	*3*	*1*	..	..	..
Bharatpur	6	4	2	*12*	*11*	*1*	11	11	..	1	..	1	..	..	..	..	..	..	..	..	..	*7*	*2*	*5*	..	..	..
Bikaner	6	6	..	*13*	*13*	..	11	11	..	1	1	..	..	..	..	1	1	..	..	..	..	*7*	*3*	*4*	..	..	..
Jaipur	14	12	2	*26*	*18*	*8*	12	12	..	1	1	..	..	..	..	5	2	3	8	3	5	*33*	*19*	*14*	6	5	1
Jodhpur	21	11	10	*9*	*9*	..	..	..	..	..	..	..	1	1	..	8	8	..	..	..	..	*16*	*7*	*9*	..	..	..
Kotah	6	6	..	*18*	*17*	*1*	14	14	..	..	..	..	1	1	..	1	..	1	2	2	..	*8*	*5*	*3*	2	2	..
Tonk	1	1	..	*46*	*39*	*7*	14	14	..	27	20	7	4	4	..	..	..	..	1	1	..	*2*	*2*	..	..	..	..
Udaipur	12	10	2	*20*	*7*	*13*	2	1	1	..	..	..	1	..	1	14	3	11	3	3	..	*8*	*4*	*4*	..	..	..
Ajmer-Merwara—																											
Ajmer	216	159	57	*139*	*127*	*12*	114	108	6	7	6	1	5	4	1	9	8	1	4	1	3	*225*	*148*	77	20	15	5

* For details see title page.

TABLE XI.—BIRTHPLACE—*concld.*

Province; and State, District, or City of enumeration.	C.—BORN IN EUROPE—*concld.* United Kingdom. Total United Kingdom. P.	M.	F.	Channel Islands. P.	M.	F.	England and Wales. P.	M.	F.	Ireland. P.	M.	F.	Scotland. P.	M.	F.	Others* P.	M.	F.	D.—BORN IN AFRICA. Total.* P.	M.	F.	E.—BORN IN AMERICA. Total.* P.	M.	F.	F.—BORN IN AUSTRALASIA. Total.† P.	M.	F.	G.—BORN AT SEA. Total. P.	M.	F.
1	323	324	325	326	327	328	329	330	331	332	333	334	335	336	337	338	339	340	341	342	343	344	345	346	347	348	349	350	351	352
Rajputana	521	342	179	1	..	1	367	252	115	41	25	16	112	65	47	20	12	8	16	10	6	16	10	6	4	2	2	1	..	1
Alwar	*11*	*7*	*4*	..	..	..	9	5	4	2	2	..	..	..	..	..	..	..	..	..	..	..	..	..	..	..	..	..	..	..
Banswara	..	..	..	..	..	..	..	..	..	..	..	..	..	..	..	..	..	..	..	..	..	..	..	..	..	..	..	..	..	..
Bharatpur	*8*	*3*	*5*	..	..	..	7	2	5	..	..	..	1	1	..	..	..	..	3	3	..	..	..	..	..	..	..	..	..	..
Bikaner	*8*	*4*	*4*	..	..	..	8	4	4	..	..	..	..	..	..	..	..	..	..	..	..	..	..	..	2	..	2	..	..	..
Bundi	..	..	..	..	..	..	..	..	..	..	..	..	..	..	..	..	..	..	..	..	..	..	..	..	..	..	..	..	..	..
Dholpur	*8*	*4*	*4*	..	..	..	6	3	3	1	1	..	1	..	1	..	..	..	1	1	..	1	1	..	..	..	..	..	..	..
Dungarpur	..	..	..	..	..	..	..	..	..	..	..	..	..	..	..	..	..	..	1	1	..	..	..	..	..	..	..	..	..	..
Jaipur	*174*	*108*	*66*	..	..	..	114	71	43	13	11	2	47	26	21	4	3	1	4	2	2	8	5	3	2	2	..	..	..	..
Jaisalmer	..	..	..	..	..	..	..	..	..	..	..	..	..	..	..	..	..	..	..	..	..	..	..	..	..	..	..	..	..	..
Jhalawar	*3*	*1*	*2*	1	..	1	1	1	..	..	..	..	1	..	1	3	1	2	..	..	..	..	..	..	..	..	..	..	..	..
Karauli	*1*	*1*	..	..	..	..	1	1	..	..	..	..	..	..	..	..	..	..	..	..	..	..	..	..	..	..	..	..	..	..
Kishangarh	..	..	..	..	..	..	..	..	..	..	..	..	..	..	..	..	..	..	..	..	..	..	..	..	..	..	..	..	..	..
Kotah	*16*	*8*	*8*	..	..	..	14	7	7	..	..	..	2	1	1	1	1	..	..	..	..	1	..	1	..	..	..	..	..	..
Kushalgarh (Chiefship)	..	..	..	..	..	..	..	..	..	..	..	..	..	..	..	..	..	..	..	..	..	..	..	..	..	..	..	..	..	..
Lawa (Estate)	..	..	..	..	..	..	..	..	..	..	..	..	..	..	..	..	..	..	..	..	..	..	..	..	..	..	..	..	..	..
Marwar	*24*	*14*	*10*	..	..	..	16	10	6	5	2	3	3	2	1	2	..	2	1	..	1	2	2	..	..	..	..	..	..	..
Mewar	*11*	*5*	*6*	..	..	..	4	2	2	3	2	1	4	1	3	2	1	1	..	..	..	..	..	..	..	..	..	..	..	..
Partabgarh	..	..	..	..	..	..	..	..	..	..	..	..	..	..	..	..	..	..	..	..	..	..	..	..	..	..	..	..	..	..
Shahpura (Chiefship)	..	..	..	..	..	..	..	..	..	..	..	..	..	..	..	..	..	..	..	..	..	..	..	..	..	..	..	..	..	..
Sirohi	*255*	*185*	*70*	..	..	..	185	144	41	17	7	10	53	34	19	8	6	2	5	2	3	4	2	2	..	..	..	1	..	1
Tonk	*2*	*2*	..	..	..	..	2	2	..	..	..	..	..	..	..	..	..	..	1	1	..	..	..	..	..	..	..	..	..	..
Ajmer-Merwara	1,223	1,099	124	..	..	..	1,094	1,013	81	52	36	16	77	50	27	14	8	6	9	6	3	9	4	5	12	5	7	..	..	..
Ajmer	*1,219*	*1,095*	*124*	..	..	..	1,090	1,009	81	52	36	16	77	50	27	13	7	6	7	6	1	9	4	5	12	5	7	..	..	..
Merwara	*4*	*4*	..	..	..	..	4	4	..	..	..	..	..	..	..	1	1	..	2	..	2	..	..	..	..	..	..	..	..	..
CITIES.																														
Rajputana	70	33	37	..	..	..	50	22	28	10	6	4	10	5	5	7	5	2	2	1	1	8	5	3	2	..	2	..	..	..
Alwar	*4*	*3*	*1*	..	..	..	3	2	1	1	1	..	..	..	..	..	..	..	..	..	..	..	..	..	..	..	..	..	..	..
Bharatpur	*7*	*2*	*5*	..	..	..	7	2	5	..	..	..	..	..	..	..	..	..	..	..	..	..	..	..	..	..	..	..	..	..
Bikaner	*7*	*3*	*4*	..	..	..	7	3	4	..	..	..	..	..	..	..	..	..	..	..	..	..	..	..	2	..	2	..	..	..
Jaipur	*23*	*11*	*12*	..	..	..	19	9	10	1	1	..	3	1	2	4	3	1	..	..	..	6	4	2	..	..	..	..	..	..
Jodhpur	*16*	*7*	*9*	..	..	..	8	3	5	5	2	3	3	2	1	..	..	..	1	..	1	1	1	..	..	..	..	..	..	..
Kotah	*5*	*2*	*3*	..	..	..	4	1	3	..	..	..	1	1	..	1	1	..	..	..	..	1	..	1	..	..	..	..	..	..
Tonk	*2*	*2*	..	..	..	..	2	2	..	..	..	..	..	..	..	..	..	..	4	1	..	..	..	..	..	..	..	..	..	..
Udaipur	*6*	*3*	*3*	..	..	..	..	..	..	3	2	1	3	1	2	2	1	1	..	..	..	..	..	..	..	..	..	..	..	..
Ajmer-Merwara—																														
Ajmer	*196*	*129*	*66*	..	..	..	139	97	42	18	10	8	38	22	16	10	4	6	6	5	1	8	3	5	9	4	5	..	..	..

* For details see title page. † All born in Australia except one male of Jaipur born in Sumatra.

TABLE XII.

Infirmities.

Explanatory Note.

The infirmities recorded at the Census were insanity, deaf-mutism from birth, total blindness, and corrosive leprosy.

The Table is divided into two parts. Part I shows the distribution of the afflicted persons according to age for each of the two Provinces, and Part II the distribution according to locality. In Part II the States in Rajputana have been grouped by natural divisions, the States within the divisions being arranged alphabetically.

Persons suffering from more than one infirmity have been shewn under each of such infirmities. Such persons have been counted more than once among the population afflicted, shewn in columns 2, 3, 4.

TABLE XII.—INFIRMITIES. PART I.—DISTRIBUTION BY AGE.

RAJPUTANA.

Age.	Total Infirmities.			Insane.			Deaf-mutes.			Blind.			Lepers.		
	Persons.	Males.	Females.	Persons.	Males.	Females.	Persons.	Males.	Females.	Persons.	Males.	Females.	Persons.	Males.	Females.
1	2	3	4	5	6	7	8	9	10	11	12	13	14	15	16
Total	**27,491**	**13,692**	**13,799**	**1,426**	**973**	**453**	**3,069**	**1,992**	**1,077**	**22,346**	**10,212**	**12,134**	**650**	**515**	**135**
0	44	26	18	...	...	...	1	1	...	43	25	18	...	...	...
1	25	15	10	...	...	...	2	...	2	23	15	8	...	...	...
2	91	58	33	1	..	1	8	5	3	82	53	29	...	...	...
3	158	92	66	9	8	1	27	15	12	122	69	53	...	...	...
4	190	129	61	13	7	6	57	43	14	120	79	41	...	...	...
Total 0–4	***508***	***320***	***188***	***23***	***15***	***8***	***95***	***64***	***31***	***390***	***241***	***149***	...	...	...
5–9	1,092	674	418	70	51	19	358	239	119	657	380	277	7	4	3
10–14	1,144	756	388	104	66	38	358	234	124	664	445	219	18	11	7
15–19	1,231	779	452	142	96	46	301	210	91	763	455	308	25	18	7
20–24	1,499	943	556	175	130	45	346	242	104	942	548	394	36	23	13
25–29	1,510	898	612	158	125	33	299	199	100	1,004	536	468	49	38	11
30–34	2,033	1,060	973	182	129	53	311	204	107	1,454	663	791	86	64	22
35–39	1,280	664	616	98	68	30	164	115	49	968	440	528	50	41	9
40–44	2,458	1,099	1,359	160	90	70	228	128	100	1,940	774	1,166	130	107	23
45–49	1,330	658	672	68	51	17	97	54	43	1,115	511	604	50	42	8
50–54	3,263	1,473	1,790	122	82	40	202	117	85	2,834	1,186	1,648	105	88	17
55–59	1,188	572	616	30	20	10	54	35	19	1,080	494	586	24	23	1
60–64	4,324	1,684	2,640	65	33	32	133	68	65	4,080	1,546	2,534	46	37	9
65–69	1,074	536	538	3	1	2	32	25	7	1,025	500	525	14	10	4
70 and over	3,557	1,576	1,981	26	16	10	91	58	33	3,430	1,493	1,937	10	9	1

TABLE XII.—Infirmities. Part I.—Distribution by Age.

AJMER-MERWARA.

Age.	Total Infirmities.			Insane.			Deaf-mutes.			Blind.			Lepers.		
	Persons.	Males.	Females.	Persons.	Males.	Females.	Persons.	Males.	Females.	Persons.	Males	Females.	Persons.	Males.	Females.
1	2	3	4	5	6	7	8	9	10	11	12	13	14	15	16
Total	**1,558**	**794**	**764**	**95**	**66**	**29**	**82**	**60**	**22**	**1,370**	**661**	**709**	**11**	**7**	**4**
0	5	3	2	...	...	...	...	...	...	5	3	2	...	...	...
1	1	1	...	...	...	...	...	...	...	1	1	...	...	...	...
2	7	2	5	1	...	1	1	...	1	5	2	3	...	...	...
3	9	5	4	...	...	...	2	1	1	7	4	3	...	...	...
4	9	6	3	1	...	1	..	...	...	8	6	2	...	...	...
Total 0–4	***31***	***17***	***14***	***2***	...	***2***	***3***	***1***	***2***	***26***	***16***	***10***	...	...	...
5—9	48	28	20	4	3	1	8	5	3	36	20	16	...	...	...
10—14	43	31	11	5	4	1	15	13	2	21	13	8	1	1	...
15—19	74	55	19	12	9	3	9	7	2	53	39	14	...	...	...
20—24	77	51	26	16	12	4	5	5	...	55	33	22	1	1	...
25—29	92	57	35	13	8	5	10	6	4	68	42	26	1	1	...
30—34	134	77	57	11	9	2	10	7	3	111	60	51	2	1	1
35—39	62	31	31	6	5	1	4	2	2	52	24	28	...	...	...
40—44	150	75	81	5	5	...	9	7	2	140	62	78	2	1	1
45—49	103	49	54	5	3	2	4	3	1	94	43	51	...	...	...
50—54	217	106	111	7	3	4	3	2	1	206	100	106	1	1	...
55—59	69	41	28	1	...	1	...	...	...	68	41	27	...	...	...
60—64	254	97	157	5	3	2	1	1	...	248	93	155	...	...	...
65—69	45	16	29	1	...	1	...	...	...	43	16	27	1	...	1
70 and over	154	63	91	2	2	...	1	1	...	149	59	90	2	1	1

TABLE XII.—Infirmities. Part II.—By States or Districts.

Province; and State or District.	Total Infirmities.			Insane.			Deaf-mutes.			Blind.			Lepers.		
	Persons.	Males.	Females.	Persons.	Males.	Females.	Persons.	Males.	Females.	Persons.	Males.	Females.	Persons.	Males.	Females.
1	2	3	4	5	6	7	8	9	10	11	12	13	14	15	16
Rajputana	**27,491**	**13,692**	**13,799**	**1,426**	**973**	**453**	**3,069**	**1,992**	**1,077**	**22,346**	**10,212**	**12,134**	**650**	**515**	**135**
Western Division	*9,867*	*4,770*	*5,097*	*397*	*275*	*122*	*952*	*625*	*327*	*8,234*	*3,641*	*4,593*	*284*	*229*	*55*
Bikaner	2,935	1,402	1,533	158	106	52	276	181	95	2,427	1,049	1,378	74	66	8
Jaisalmer	266	153	113	25	20	5	52	32	20	187	99	88	2	2	...
Marwar	6,666	3,215	3,451	214	149	65	624	412	212	5,620	2,493	3,127	208	161	47
Southern Division	*2,615*	*1,409*	*1,206*	*221*	*154*	*67*	*408*	*269*	*139*	*1,916*	*934*	*981*	*71*	*52*	*19*
Banswara	350	153	197	35	21	14	72	41	31	231	82	149	12	9	3
Dungarpur	196	91	105	27	16	11	37	20	17	128	53	75	4	2	2
Kushalgarh (Chiefship)	26	18	8	1	1	...	4	3	1	21	14	7	...	...	...
Mewar	1,394	842	552	133	98	35	255	177	78	983	546	437	23	21	2
Partabgarh	114	59	55	6	5	1	15	8	7	71	32	39	22	14	8
Sirohi	535	246	289	19	13	6	25	20	5	481	207	274	10	6	4
Eastern Division	*15,009*	*7,513*	*7,496*	*808*	*544*	*264*	*1,709*	*1,098*	*611*	*12,197*	*5,637*	*6,560*	*295*	*234*	*61*
Alwar	2,526	1,239	1,287	87	63	24	244	160	84	2,162	985	1,177	33	31	2
Bharatpur	1,896	881	1,015	46	33	13	218	152	66	1,608	680	928	24	16	8
Bundi	478	252	226	31	20	11	57	32	25	380	191	189	10	9	1
Dholpur	731	342	389	26	16	10	77	53	24	613	260	353	15	13	2
Jaipur	5,698	2,989	2,709	396	273	123	681	444	237	4,561	2,223	2,338	60	49	11
Jhalawar	162	86	76	19	11	8	26	16	10	103	47	56	14	12	2
Karauli	230	120	110	11	7	4	27	18	9	186	89	97	6	6	...
Kishangarh	289	136	153	21	16	5	22	14	8	246	106	140	...	...	...
Kotah	1,895	921	974	100	97	43	217	127	90	1,484	660	824	85	67	18
Lawa (Estate)	9	3	6	...	...	...	...	...	...	9	3	6	...	...	...
Shahpura (Chiefship)	125	70	55	11	6	5	10	9	1	104	55	49	...	...	...
Tonk	970	474	496	51	32	19	130	73	57	741	338	403	48	31	17
Ajmer-Merwara	**1,558**	**794**	**764**	**95**	**66**	**29**	**82**	**60**	**22**	**1,370**	**661**	**709**	**11**	**7**	**4**
Ajmer	1,195	613	582	75	55	20	67	49	18	1,045	504	541	8	5	3
Merwara	363	181	182	20	11	9	15	11	4	325	157	168	3	2	1

TABLE XII-A.

Infirmities by Selected Castes, Tribes or Races.

The castes chosen for this Table are the same as those for Table IX (*vide* Explanatory Note to that Table) with the following exceptions :—

(*a*) Jews, Goanese, Parsis, Christians ("others") which include all Europeans and allied races and Anglo-Indians, have been excluded, as no infirmities were returned among them.

(*b*) Bhishti, Dakot, Dhanak, Garoda, Gosain, Jogi, Lakhera, Sad, Sausi, Sindhi, Swami have been included.

The total populations of each caste in columns 4, 5, 6 correspond exactly, religion by religion, to those in Table XIII (Caste). But, in any caste, religions containing no infirmities have not been shewn separately, though they have been included in the caste Totals on which the percentages in column 19 have been calculated.

Where a caste in one of the two localities in column 2 has no infirmities and, at the same time, is numerically so small as not to affect materially the percentage of infirmities in the caste as a whole, figures for the more important locality only have been given.

A reference to Table XIII will show how the castes actually returned in the schedules have been amalgamated in this Table also.

In calculating the percentages in column 19, persons suffering from more than one infirmity have been counted more than once, no separate record of such persons having been kept in the abstraction offices.

TABLE XII-A.—INFIRMITIES BY SELECTED CASTES, TRIBES, OR RACES.

[In column 3, A.=Animist. Ar.=Arya. Br.=Brahmo. C=Christian. H=Hindu. J=Jain. M=Musalman. S=Sikh.]

Caste, Tribe, or Race.	Locality.	Religion.	Total population of caste.			Insane.			Deaf-mutes.			Blind.			Lepers.			Percentage of total infirmities to population dealt with.
			Persons.	Males.	Females.	Persons.	Males.	Females.	Persons.	Males.	Females.	Persons.	Males.	Females.	Persons.	Males.	Females.	
1	2	3	4	5	6	7	8	9	10	11	12	13	14	15	16	17	18	19
Ahir	Rajputana	H.	160,008	91,151	77,947	16	10	6	47	34	13	296	147	149	10	8	2	..
	Total	Ar. H. J. M.	169,129	91,171	77,958	16	10	6	47	34	13	296	147	149	10	8	2	·21
	Ajmer-Merwara	H.	1,752	997	755	1	1	..	..	..	..	3	2	1	..	..	..	..
	Total	Ar. H. M.	1,760	1,003	757	1	1	..	..	..	..	3	2	1	..	..	..	·28
Bairagi	Rajputana	H.	57,979	31,365	26,614	6	5	1	21	16	5	162	81	81	2	1	1	..
	Total	A. Ar. H. J. S.	57,991	31,370	26,621	6	5	1	21	16	5	162	81	81	2	1	1	·32
	Ajmer-Merwara	H.	487	224	263	..	..	..	..	..	..	1	1	..	..	..	..	·21
Balai	Rajputana	H.	197,491	101,057	96,434	20	16	4	39	23	16	284	117	167	13	11	2	..
	Total	H. M.	197,511	101,074	96,437	20	16	4	39	23	16	284	117	167	13	11	2	·18
	Ajmer-Merwara	H.	23,750	12,224	11,536	3	1	2	..	..	..	90	36	54	1	..	1	..
	Total	H. M.	23,773	12,234	11,539	3	1	2	..	..	..	90	36	54	1	..	1	·39
Bambhi	Rajputana	H.	133,826	69,940	63,886	7	4	3	22	11	11	296	136	160	8	6	2	·24
	Ajmer-Merwara	H.	2,550	1,305	1,245	..	..	..	..	..	..	2	1	1	..	..	..	·07
Bhangi	Rajputana	H. M.	83,116 835	42,642 437	40,474 398	6 ..	1 ..	5 ..	32 1	17 ..	15 1	253 2	132 2	121 ..	1 ..	.. ..	1 ..	.. ..
	Total	A. H. M. S.	84,960	43,655	41,325	6	1	5	33	17	16	255	134	121	1	..	1	·34
	Ajmer-Merwara	A. H.	243 5,090	130 2,676	113 2,414	.. 2	.. 1	.. 1	1 ..	1 ..	.. ..	.. 13	.. 8	.. 5	.. 1	.. 1	.. ..	.. ..
	Total	A. H. M.	5,361	2,832	2,529	2	1	1	1	1	..	13	8	5	1	1	..	·31
Bhil	Rajputana	A. H.	385,903 63,004	196,242 33,022	189,661 29,982	30 5	23 3	7 2	96 6	63 3	34 3	251 53	104 24	147 29	27 5	23 5	4 ..	.. ..
	Total	A. H. M.	448,910	229,266	219,644	35	26	9	102	65	37	304	128	176	33	28	4	·11
	Ajmer-Merwara	A. H.	3,339 3,165	1,658 1,629	1,681 1,536	1 1	.. 1	1 ..	1 ..	1 ..	.. ..	9 2	5 1	4 1	.. ..	.. ..	.. ..	.. ..
	Total	A. Ar. H.	6,509	3,289	3,220	2	1	1	1	1	..	11	6	5	..	..	..	·21
Bhishti	Rajputana	H. M.	138 24,651	56 12,634	82 12,017	.. 3	.. 3	.. ..	.. 17	.. 12	.. 5	13 55	11 20	2 35	1 ..	1 ..	.. ..	.. ..
	Total	H. M.	24,789	12,690	12,099	3	3	..	17	12	5	68	31	37	1	1	..	·35
	Ajmer-Merwara	M.	754	419	335	..	..	..	..	..	..	1	..	1	..	..	..	..
	Total	H. M.	758	421	337	..	..	..	..	..	..	1	..	1	..	..	..	·13

TABLE XII-A.—INFIRMITIES BY SELECTED CASTES, TRIBES, OR RACES—*contd.*

[In column 3, A=Animist. Ar.=Arya. Br.=Brahmo. C=Christian. H=Hindu. J=Jain. M=Musalman. S=Sikh.]

Caste, Tribe, or Race.	Locality.	Religion.	Total population of caste.			Insane.			Deaf-mutes.			Blind.			Lepers.			Percentage of total infirmities to population dealt with.
			Persons.	Males.	Females.	Persons.	Males.	Females.	Persons.	Males.	Females.	Persons.	Males.	Females.	Persons.	Males.	Females.	
1	2	3	4	5	6	7	8	9	10	11	12	13	14	15	16	17	18	19
Bishnoi	Rajputana	H.	52,877	28,491	24,386	6	5	1	15	10	5	65	30	35	5	3	2	..
	Total	Ar. H.	52,879	28,492	24,387	6	5	1	15	10	5	65	30	35	5	3	2	·17
Brahman	Rajputana	H.	922,318	475,627	446,691	175	110	56	313	213	100	2,851	1,265	1,586	57	47	10	..
		J.	24	11	13	..	..	..	..	..	..	1	..	1	..	..	..	..
	Total	Ar. H. J. M. S.	922,810	475,901	446,909	175	119	56	313	213	100	2,852	1,265	1,587	57	47	10	·36
	Ajmer-Merwara	Ar.	372	221	151	..	..	..	..	..	..	3	2	1	..	..	..	..
		H.	23,659	12,659	11,000	3	2	1	6	4	2	81	42	39	2	1	1	..
	Total	Ar. H. J. S.	24,042	12,887	11,155	3	2	1	6	4	2	84	44	40	2	1	1	·39
Chakar	Rajputana	H.	58,297	28,189	30,108	9	3	6	19	14	5	105	46	59	5	3	2	..
		M.	157	62	95	..	..	..	1	..	1	1	..	1	..	..	..	..
	Total	Ar. H. J. M.	58,606	28,320	30,286	9	3	6	20	14	6	106	46	60	5	3	2	·23
Chamar	Rajputana	H.	733,878	377,898	355,980	69	43	26	167	109	58	1,475	607	868	42	28	14	..
		M.	107	48	59	2	2	..	..	..	..	6	..	6	..	..	..	..
	Total	Ar. H. M. S.	734,110	378,017	356,093	71	45	26	167	109	58	1,481	607	374	42	28	14	·22
	Ajmer-Merwara	H.	13,340	6,817	6,529	1	..	1	2	2	..	35	13	22	..	..	..	..
	Total	Ar. H. M.	13,351	6,822	6,529	1	..	1	2	2	..	35	13	22	..	..	..	·28
Chhipa	Rajputana	H.	30,868	15,912	14,956	5	3	2	11	8	3	96	38	58	4	4	..	..
		M.	7,038	3,714	3,324	1	..	1	..	..	..	27	15	12	1	..	1	..
	Total	H. J. M. S.	37,940	19,645	18,295	6	3	3	11	8	3	123	53	70	5	4	1	·38
	Ajmer-Merwara	H.	1,802	972	830	..	..	..	..	..	..	3	..	3	..	..	..	..
	Total	Ar. H. M. S.	2,652	1,418	1,234	..	..	..	..	..	..	3	..	3	..	..	..	·11
Christian (Indian)	Rajputana	C.	2,384	1,307	1,077	..	..	..	1	1	..	6	5	1	..	..	..	·29
	Ajmer-Merwara	C.	2,730	1,309	1,421	..	..	..	1	1	..	16	7	9	..	..	..	·62
Dakot	Rajputana	H.	20,326	10,166	10,160	5	2	3	7	3	4	59	23	36	1	..	1	·35
Daroga	Rajputana	H.	118,882	57,639	61,243	16	6	10	30	21	9	231	97	134	3	3	..	..
		M.	5	4	1	..	..	..	1	..	1	..	..	..	..	..	..	..
	Total	Ar. H. J. M.	118,914	57,658	61,256	16	6	10	31	21	10	231	97	134	3	3	..	·23
	Ajmer-Merwara	H.	8,934	4,536	4,398	..	..	..	1	1	..	24	12	12	..	..	..	..
	Total	Ar. H. J.	8,952	4,550	4,402	..	..	..	1	1	..	24	12	12	..	..	..	·27

TABLE XII-A.—Infirmities by Selected Castes, Tribes, or Races—*contd.*

[In column 3, A=Animist. Ar.=Arya. B.=Brahmo. C=Christian. H=Hindu. J=Jain. M=Musalman. S=Sikh.]

Caste, Tribe, or Race.	Locality.	Religion.	Total population of caste.			Insane.			Deaf-mutes.			Blind.			Lepers.			Percentage of total infirmities to population dealt with.
			Persons.	Males.	Females.	Persons.	Males.	Females.	Persons.	Males.	Females.	Persons.	Males.	Females.	Persons.	Males.	Females.	
1	2	3	4	5	6	7	8	9	10	11	12	13	14	15	16	17	18	19
Darri . . .	Rajputana . .	H.	44,931	22,931	22,000	8	5	3	10	13	6	138	66	72	2	1	1	..
		M.	269	137	132	..	..	..	..	..	..	5	1	4	..	..	..	..
	Total .	H. J. M.	45,293	23,069	22,134	8	5	3	19	13	6	148	67	76	2	1	1	·38
	Ajmer-Merwara .	H.	2,235	1,217	1,018	1	..	1	..	..	..	18	11	7	..	..	..	..
	Total .	Ar. H. M.	2,250	1,226	1,024	1	..	1	..	..	..	18	11	7	..	..	..	·84
Dhakar . .	Rajputana . .	H.	93,360	47,660	45,700	8	5	3	23	13	10	148	62	86	7	5	2	..
	Total .	Ar. H. M.	93,365	47,662	45,703	8	5	3	23	13	10	148	62	86	7	5	2	·19
Dhanak. . .	Rajputana	H.	25,485	12,799	12,686	7	5	2	10	7	3	80	35	45	1	1	..	..
	Total .	A. H. M.	25,521	12,822	12,699	7	5	2	10	7	3	80	35	45	1	1	..	·38
	Ajmer-Merwara .	H.	1,366	739	627	..	..	..	..	..	..	3	1	2	..	..	..	..
	Total . .	A. H.	1,371	741	630	..	..	..	..	..	..	3	1	2	..	..	..	·21
Dhobi . . .	Rajputana . .	H.	30,690	20,305	19,394	9	5	4	15	9	6	25	27	58	4	3	1	..
		M.	6,102	3,043	3,059	..	..	..	7	5	2	21	6	15	..	..	..	..
	Total .	H. M.	45,801	23,348	22,453	9	5	4	22	14	8	106	33	73	4	3	1	·31
	Ajmer-Merwara .	H.	2,475	1,278	1,197	3	2	1	..	..	..	4	2	2	..	..	..	..
		M.	407	201	206	..	..	..	..	..	..	5	3	2	..	..	..	..
	Total .	H. M.	2,882	1,479	1,403	3	2	1	..	..	..	9	5	4	..	..	..	·41
Fakir . . .	Rajputana . .	H.	275	159	116	2	2	..	..	..	..	2	1	1	..	..	..	..
		M.	54,990	28,895	26,095	14	9	5	17	11	6	181	87	94	1	1	..	..
	Total .	H. M.	55,265	29,054	26,211	16	11	5	17	11	6	183	88	95	1	1	..	·39
	Ajmer-Merwara .	M.	1,719	913	806	2	2	..	..	..	..	10	4	6	..	..	..	..
	Total .	H. M.	1,751	921	830	2	2	..	..	..	..	10	4	6	..	..	..	·68
Garoda . . .	Rajputana . .	H.	10,863	5,755	5,108	..	..	..	3	3	..	38	18	20	..	..	..	·37
Gosain . .	Rajputana . .	H.	27,782	15,409	12,373	1	1	..	13	8	5	91	51	40	2	2	..	..
	Total .	Ar. H. M.	27,806	15,418	12,388	1	1	..	13	8	5	91	51	40	2	2	..	·38
	Ajmer-Merwara .	H.	902	477	425	1	..	1	..	..	..	4	3	1	..	..	..	..
	Total .	H. M.	903	478	425	1	..	1	..	..	..	4	3	1	..	..	..	·55
Gujar . . .	Rajputana . .	H.	500,023	271,172	228,851	46	27	19	111	67	44	721	328	393	17	12	5	..
		J.	4	3	1	1	..	1	..	..	..	1	1	..	..	..	..	..
	Total .	A. Ar. H. J.	500,046	271,188	228,858	47	27	20	111	67	44	722	329	393	17	12	5	·17
	Ajmer-Merwara .	H.	35,046	18,600	16,446	4	..	4	4	2	2	73	24	49	2	1	1	..
	Total .	Ar. H.	35,059	18,609	16,450	4	..	4	4	2	2	73	24	49	2	1	1	·23

TABLE XII-A.—INFIRMITIES BY SELECTED CASTES, TRIBES, OR RACES—*contd.*

[In column 3, A=Animist, Ar.=Arya, Br.=Brahmo, C=Christian, H=Hindu, J=Jain, M.=Musalman, S=Sikh.]

Caste, Tribe, or Race.	Locality.	Religion.	Total population of caste.			Insane.			Deaf-mutes.			Blind.			Lepers.			Percentage of total infirmities to population dealt with.
			Persons.	Males.	Females.	Persons.	Males.	Females.	Persons.	Males.	Females.	Persons.	Males.	Females.	Persons.	Males.	Females.	
1	2	3	4	5	6	7	8	9	10	11	12	13	14	15	16	17	18	19
Jat . . .	Rajputana . .	H.	922,501	497,824	424,677	79	50	29	231	151	80	1,546	672	874	63	46	17	..
		M.	131	70	61	..	..	..	..	..	..	3	1	2	..	..	..	..
		S.	5,809	3,691	2,118	1	1	..	8	2	1	9	4	5	..	..	..	..
	Total .	Ar. H. J. M. S.	928,486	501,616	426,870	80	51	29	234	153	81	1,558	677	881	63	46	17	·21
	Ajmer-Merwara .	H.	29,731	15,850	13,881	2	2	..	2	1	1	67	24	43	..	..	..	..
	Total .	Ar. H. J. M. S.	30,497	16,526	13,971	2	2	..	2	1	1	67	24	43	..	..	..	·23
Jogi . . .	Rajputana .	H.	64,904	34,133	30,771	10	6	4	19	14	5	164	82	82	1	1	..	..
	Total .	A. Ar. H. M.	67,144	35,317	31,827	10	6	4	19	14	5	164	82	82	1	1	..	·28
	Ajmer-Merwara .	H.	2,533	1,380	1,153	1	1	..	..	..	..	8	4	4	..	..	..	..
	Total .	Ar. H.	2,534	1,381	1,153	1	1	..	..	..	..	8	4	4	..	..	..	·35
Kachhi . . .	Rajputana . .	H.	60,630	31,734	28,896	5	1	4	10	7	3	113	52	61	6	5	1	..
	Total .	Ar. H. M.	60,666	31,766	28,900	5	1	4	10	7	3	113	52	61	6	5	1	·22
Kaimkhani . .	Rajputana .	M.	28,340	14,824	13,516	2	2	..	3	3	..	31	17	14	1	1	..	·13
Kalal . . .	Rajputana .	H.	36,364	18,519	17,845	5	2	3	10	7	3	76	36	40	2	1	1	..
		M.	3,480	1,808	1,672	..	..	..	2	2	..	14	9	5	..	..	..	..
	Total .	Ar. H. J. M. S.	39,860	20,334	19,526	5	2	3	12	9	3	90	45	45	2	1	1	·27
	Ajmer-Merwara .	H.	1,308	674	634	..	..	..	..	..	..	6	4	2	..	..	..	..
	Total .	H. M.	1,341	695	646	..	..	..	..	..	..	6	4	2	..	..	..	·44
Kasai . . .	Rajputana .	M.	29,400	15,006	14,394	7	3	4	23	13	10	72	32	40	1	1	..	·35
	Ajmer-Merwara .	M	1,088	549	539	1	1	..	..	..	..	2	..	2	..	..	..	·27
Kayastha . .	Rajputana .	Br.	77	39	38	..	..	..	..	..	..	1	..	1	..	..	..	..
		H.	23,258	12,656	10,602	9	5	4	12	6	6	65	37	28	2	1	1	..
	Total .	Ar. Br. H. S.	23,610	12,853	10,757	9	5	4	12	6	6	66	37	29	2	1	1	·37
	Ajmer-Merwara .	H.	2,397	1,296	1,101	..	..	..	..	..	..	5	3	2	..	..	..	..
	Total .	Ar. H.	2,439	1,320	1,119	..	..	..	..	..	..	5	3	2	..	..	..	·21
Khati . . .	Rajputana .	H.	134,926	69,208	65,718	11	7	4	46	23	23	346	151	195	7	6	1	..
	Total .	Ar. H. S.	134,992	69,245	65,747	11	7	4	46	23	23	346	151	195	7	6	1	·30
	Ajmer-Merwara .	H.	6,806	3,001	3,205	2	1	1	1	1	..	18	10	8	..	..	..	..
	Total .	Ar. H.	6,839	3,620	3,219	2	1	1	1	1	..	18	10	8	..	..	..	·31

TABLE XII-A.—INFIRMITIES BY SELECTED CASTES, TRIBES, OR RACES—*contd.*

[In column 3, A=Animist, Ar.=Arya. Br.=Brahmo. C=Christian. H=Hindu. J=Jain. M=Musalman. S=Sikh.]

Caste, Tribe, or Race.	Locality.	Religion.	Total population of caste.			Insane.			Deaf-mutes.			Blind.			Lepers.			Percentage of total infirmities to population dealt with.
			Persons.	Males.	Females.	Persons.	Males.	Females.	Persons.	Males.	Females.	Persons.	Males.	Females.	Persons.	Males.	Females.	
1	2	3	4	5	6	7	8	9	10	11	12	13	14	15	16	17	18	19
Khatik . . .	Rajputana . .	H.	51,274	26,378	24,896	7	2	5	13	8	5	96	58	38	3	1	2	..
	Total .	Ar. H.	**51,276**	**26,380**	**24,896**	**7**	**2**	**5**	**13**	**8**	**5**	**96**	**58**	**38**	**3**	**1**	**2**	·23
	Ajmer-Merwara .	H.	3,543	1,790	1,753	..	..	..	1	1	..	15	9	6	..	..	..	..
	Total .	A. H.	**3,552**	**1,793**	**1,759**	..	..	..	**1**	**1**	..	**15**	**9**	**6**	..	..	..	·45
Koli . . .	Rajputana . .	H.	104,033	53,494	50,539	12	6	6	26	14	12	264	101	163	3	3	..	..
	Total .	H. M. S.	**104,055**	**53,502**	**50,553**	**12**	**6**	**6**	**26**	**14**	**12**	**264**	**101**	**163**	**3**	**3**	..	·29
	Ajmer-Merwara .	H.	6,554	3,476	3,078	..	..	..	2	2	..	8	6	2	..	..	..	..
	Total .	A. Ar. H.	**6,565**	**3,480**	**3,085**	..	..	..	**2**	**2**	..	**8**	**6**	**2**	..	..	..	·15
Kumhar . .	Rajputana . .	H. M.	302,018 6,891	155,819 3,667	146,199 3,224	29 1	21 1	8 ..	116 2	74 2	42 ..	621 14	239 3	382 11	25 ..	15 ..	10 ..	.. ..
	Total .	A. Ar. H. J. M. S.	**309,234**	**159,676**	**149,558**	**30**	**22**	**8**	**118**	**76**	**42**	**635**	**242**	**393**	**25**	**15**	**10**	·26
	Ajmer-Merwara .	H.	14,048	7,177	6,871	1	1	..	2	1	1	39	18	21	1	1	..	..
	Total .	A. Ar. H. J.M.S.	**14,120**	**7,218**	**6,902**	**1**	**1**	..	**2**	**1**	**1**	**39**	**18**	**21**	**1**	**1**	..	·30
Lakhera . .	Rajputana . .	H.	10,751	5,538	5,213	2	1	1	..	..	..	41	24	17	4	4	..	..
	Total .	H. J.	**10,752**	**5,539**	**5,213**	**2**	**1**	**1**	..	..	..	**41**	**24**	**17**	**4**	**4**	..	·43
	Ajmer-Merwara .	H.	749	375	374	..	..	..	..	..	..	5	2	3	..	..	..	..
	Total .	Ar. H.	**750**	**376**	**374**	..	..	..	..	..	..	**5**	**2**	**3**	..	..	..	·66
Lodha . .	Rajputana . .	H.	47,003	24,520	22,483	13	10	3	11	8	3	84	40	44	11	11	..	..
	Total .	H. M.	**47,013**	**24,526**	**22,487**	**13**	**10**	**3**	**11**	**8**	**3**	**84**	**40**	**44**	**11**	**11**	..	·25
Lohar . . .	Rajputana . .	H. M.	62,668 18,145	32,348 8,894	30,320 9,251	7 5	4 2	3 3	17 6	9 2	8 4	168 46	82 21	86 25	1 1	.. 1	1 ..	.. ..
	Total .	Ar. H. M.	**80,822**	**41,247**	**39,575**	**12**	**6**	**6**	**23**	**11**	**12**	**214**	**103**	**111**	**2**	**1**	**1**	·31
	Ajmer-Merwara .	H. M.	2,477 1,735	1,320 935	1,157 800	.. ..	.. ..	.. ..	2 ..	2 ..	.. ..	9 7	3 3	6 4	.. ..	.. ..	.. ..	.. ..
	Total .	Ar. H. J. M.	**4,214**	**2,256**	**1,958**	..	..	..	**2**	**2**	..	**16**	**6**	**10**	..	..	..	·42
Mahajan or Baniya .	Rajputana . .	H. J.	377,335 330,207	192,370 160,671	184,965 169,536	129 80	110 56	19 24	195 131	138 72	67 59	1,312 1,279	661 641	651 638	33 21	31 19	2 2	.. ..
	Total .	Ar. H. J.	**707,721**	**353,152**	**354,569**	**209**	**166**	**43**	**326**	**210**	**116**	**2,591**	**1,302**	**1,289**	**54**	**50**	**4**	·45
	Ajmer-Merwara .	H. J.	14,296 19,990	7,646 10,659	6,650 9,331	6 ..	6 ..	.. ..	3 11	2 8	1 3	44 91	25 49	19 42	.. ..	.. ..	.. ..	.. ..
	Total .	Ar. H. J. S.	**34,470**	**18,413**	**16,057**	**6**	**6**	..	**14**	**10**	**4**	**135**	**74**	**61**	..	..	..	·44

TABLE XII-A.—INFIRMITIES BY SELECTED CASTES, TRIBES, OR RACES—*contd.*

(In column 3, A=Animist. Ar.=Arya Br.=Brahmo. C=Christian. H=Hindu. J=Jain. M=Musalman. S=Sikh.)

Caste, Tribe, or Race.	Locality.	Religion.	TOTAL POPULATION OF CASTE.			INSANE.			DEAF-MUTES.			BLIND.			LEPERS.			Percentage of total infirmities to population dealt with.
			Persons.	Males.	Females.	Persons.	Males.	Females.	Persons.	Males.	Females.	Persons.	Males.	Females.	Persons.	Males.	Females.	
1	2	3	4	5	6	7	8	9	10	11	12	13	14	15	16	17	18	19
Mali	Rajputana . .	H. J. M.	336,197 17 529	174,636 8 251	161,561 9 278	38	22	16	88 1 ..	50	38 1 ..	551 3 1	226 1 1	325 2 ..	21 1 ..	15 1 ..	6	.. .. ..
	Total .	Ar. H. J. M.	336,876	174,966	161,910	38	22	16	89	50	39	555	228	327	22	16	6	·21
	Ajmer-Merwara .	H.	14,307	7,482	6,825	6	3	3	2	1	1	41	12	29	..	..	..	..
	Total .	Ar. H. J. M.	14,349	7,499	6,841	6	3	3	2	1	1	41	12	29	..	..	..	·34
Meghwal (Megh) .	Rajputana. . .	H.	57,510	30,083	27,427	12	9	3	9	5	4	152	71	81	5	5	..	..
	Total .	H. M.	57,516	30,087	27,429	12	9	3	9	5	4	153	71	81	5	5	..	·31
Meo (Mewati) .	Rajputana . .	H. M.	146 165,543	73 87,273	73 78,270	.. 14	.. 7	.. 7	.. 41	.. 26	.. 15	.. 411	.. 146	.. 265	1 6	1 3	.. 3	.. ..
	Total .	Ar. H. M.	165,690	87,347	78,343	14	7	7	41	26	15	411	146	265	7	4	3	·28
Mer	Rajputana . .	H. M.	13,658 54	7,127 29	6,531 25	2 ..	1 ..	1 ..	2 ..	.. ..	2 ..	39 2	12 2	27 ..	1 ..	.. ..	1 ..	.. ..
	Total .	H. M.	13,712	7,156	6,556	2	1	1	2	..	2	41	14	27	1	..	1	·33
	Ajmer-Merwara .	H. M.	21,774 29	11,623 11	10,151 18	2 1	2 1	.. ..	3 ..	1 ..	2 ..	42 1	19 1	23 ..	.. ..	.. ..	.. ..	.. ..
	Total .	H. M.	21,803	11,634	10,169	3	3	..	3	1	2	43	20	23	..	..	..	·22
Merat Gorat . .	Ajmer-Merwara .	H.	2,025	1,300	725	..	..	..	2	1	1	7	5	2	..	..	..	·44
Merat Kathat .	Rajputana . .	M.	2,250	1,283	967	..	..	..	1	..	1	..	..	..	..	..	..	·04
	Ajmer-Merwara	M.	17,626	9,651	7,975	1	1	..	1	..	1	39	24	15	..	..	..	·23
Mina . .	Rajputana . .	A. H.	46,044 512,506	23,730 272,411	22,314 240,095	.. 49	.. 36	.. 13	1 118	1 82	.. 36	8 641	8 313	.. 328	.. 21	.. 17	.. 4	.. ..
	Total .	A. H. M.	558,689	296,205	262,484	49	36	13	119	83	36	649	321	328	21	17	4	·14
	Ajmer-Merwara .	H.	4,217	2,436	1,781	1	..	1	..	..	..	3	1	2	..	..	..	..
	Total .	A. Ar. H. M.	4,223	2,442	1,781	1	..	1	..	..	..	3	1	2	..	..	..	·09
Moghal . . .	Rajputana .	M.	14,121	7,469	6,652	4	3	1	8	6	2	22	14	8	..	..	..	·24
	Ajmer-Merwara .	M.	1,415	778	637	..	..	..	..	..	..	5	4	1	..	..	..	·35
Nal . . .	Rajputana . .	H. M.	153,117 9,318	80,078 4,767	73,039 4,551	25 4	21 2	4 2	60 3	40 2	20 1	464 18	207 18	257 25	12 2	9 2	3 ..	.. ..
	Total .	Ar. H. J. M. S.	162,463	84,866	77,597	29	23	6	63	42	21	507	225	282	14	11	3	·37
	Ajmer-Merwara .	H. M.	6,278 211	3,181 108	3,097 103	.. ..	.. ..	.. ..	2 ..	1 ..	1 ..	23 1	10 1	13 ..	.. ..	.. ..	.. ..	.. ..
	Total .	Ar H. M S.	6,503	3,297	3,206	..	..	..	2	1	1	24	11	13	..	..	..	·39

TABLE XII-A.—INFIRMITIES BY SELECTED CASTES, TRIBES, OR RACES—*contd.*

[In column 3, A=Animist. Ar.=Arya. Br.=Brahmo. C=Christian. H=Hindu. J=Jain. M=Musalman. S=Sikh.]

Caste, Tribe, or Race.	Locality.	Religion.	Total population of caste. Persons.	Males.	Females.	Insane. Persons.	Males.	Females.	Deaf-mutes. Persons.	Males.	Females.	Blind. Persons.	Males.	Females.	Lepers. Persons.	Males.	Females.	Percentage of total infirmities to population dealt with.
1	2	3	4	5	6	7	8	9	10	11	12	13	14	15	16	17	18	19
Naik (Nayak)	Rajputana	H. M.	42,267 124	22,041 70	20,226 54	5 1	5 1	.. ..	16 ..	9 ..	7 ..	108 ..	47 ..	61 ..	2 ..	1 ..	1 ..	.. ..
	Total	H. M.	42,391	22,111	20,280	6	6	..	16	9	7	108	47	61	2	1	1	·21
	Ajmer-Merwara	H.	2,494	1,295	1,199	..	..	..	..	..	..	8	5	3	..	..	..	..
	Total	A. H.	2,497	1,298	1,199	..	..	..	..	..	..	8	5	3	..	..	..	·32
Patel	Rajputana	H.	55,797	27,750	28,047	9	3	6	23	16	7	71	32	39	3	3	..	..
	Total	H. J.	55,798	27,751	28,047	9	3	6	23	16	7	71	32	39	3	3	..	·18
Pathan	Rajputana	M.	108,291	57,505	50,786	27	20	7	30	22	8	204	100	104	5	3	2	·24
	Ajmer-Merwara	M.	11,420	6,176	5,244	2	2	..	1	1	..	30	15	15	1	..	1	·29
Prohit	Rajputana	H.	36,939	19,128	17,811	8	6	2	10	6	4	140	51	89	5	4	1	..
	Total	Ar. H.	36,942	19,130	17,812	8	6	2	10	6	4	140	51	89	5	4	1	·44
Raigar	Rajputana	H.	81,557	41,622	39,935	9	6	3	13	4	9	165	76	89	3	3	..	..
	Total	H. M.	81,568	41,626	39,942	9	6	3	13	4	9	165	76	89	3	3	..	·23
	Ajmer-Merwara	H.	19,834	10,135	9,699	2	2	..	2	2	..	82	38	44	..	..	..	..
	Total	A. H.	19,858	10,148	9,710	2	2	..	2	2	..	82	38	44	..	..	..	·43
Rajput	Rajputana	H. M.	632,613 54,242	355,559 29,308	277,054 24,934	70 14	56 9	14 5	171 17	120 14	51 3	1,087 99	580 43	507 56	54 2	47 1	7 1	.. ..
	Total	Ar. Br. H. J. M. S.	687,202	385,194	302,168	84	65	19	188	134	54	1,186	623	563	56	48	8	·22
	Ajmer-Merwara	H.	14,134	8,096	6,038	2	2	..	2	2	..	34	22	12	..	..	..	..
	Total	A. H. J. M. S.	14,302	8,225	6,077	2	2	..	2	2	..	34	22	12	..	..	..	·26
Rangres	Rajputana Ajmer-Merwara	M. M.	15,485 631	8,049 368	7,436 263	4 ..	3 ..	1 ..	13 ..	8 ..	5 ..	41 1	18 1	23 ..	.. ..	.. ..	.. ..	·37 ·16
Rawal	Rajputana	H.	13,733	7,565	6,168	..	..	..	4	3	1	9	8	1	..	..	..	..
	Total	A. H. M.	13,754	7,580	6,174	..	..	..	4	3	1	9	8	1	..	..	..	·09
	Ajmer-Merwara	H.	47,861	24,953	22,908	7	5	2	6	5	1	77	34	43	2	2	..	..
	Total	H. J. M.	47,905	24,963	22,942	7	5	2	6	5	1	77	34	43	2	2	..	·19
Rebari	Rajputana	H.	129,911	67,754	62,157	8	2	6	22	15	7	261	88	173	6	5	1	..
	Total	A. H. M.	129,918	67,760	62,158	8	2	6	22	15	7	261	88	173	6	5	1	·22
	Ajmer-Merwara	H.	2,033	1,085	948	1	..	1	..	..	..	16	6	10	..	..	..	·83
Sad	Rajputana	H.	28,452	15,528	12,924	6	4	2	25	15	10	241	162	79	4	4	..	..
	Total	A. Ar. H.	28,544	15,573	12,971	6	4	2	25	15	10	241	162	79	4	4	..	·96

TABLE XII-A.—INFIRMITIES BY SELECTED CASTES, TRIBES, OR RACES—*concld.*

[In column 3, A=Animist. Ar.=Arya. Br.=Brahmo. C=Christian. H=Hindu. J=Jain. M=Musalman. S=Sikh.]

Caste, Tribe, or Race.	Locality.	Religion.	Total population of caste.			Insane.			Deaf-mutes.			Blind.			Lepers.			Percentage of total infirmities to population dealt with.
			Persons.	Males.	Females.	Persons.	Males.	Females.	Persons.	Males.	Females.	Persons.	Males.	Females.	Persons.	Males.	Females.	
1	2	3	4	5	6	7	8	9	10	11	12	13	14	15	16	17	18	19
Sadhu . . .	Rajputana . .	H. J	9,922 576	6,259 180	3,663 396	2 1	2 1	.. ..	3 ..	2 ..	1 ..	25 1	16 ..	9 1	1 ..	1 ..	.. ..	.. ..
	Total .	Ar. H. J. S.	10,519	6,451	4,068	3	3	..	3	2	1	26	16	10	1	1	..	·26
	Ajmer-Merwara .	H.	4,584	2,523	2,061	2	2	..	3	3	..	21	12	9	..	..	..	..
	Total .	H. J.	4,638	2,552	2,086	2	2	..	3	3	..	21	12	9	..	..	..	·56
Saiyad . . .	Rajputana . .	M.	28,954	15,242	13,712	13	12	1	16	13	3	53	25	28	..	..	..	·28
	Ajmer-Merwara .	M.	5,199	2,823	2,376	4	4	..	1	1	..	7	4	3	..	.	..	23
Sansi (Sansri) .	Rajputana . .	H.	4,262	1,993	2,269	..	..	..	..	..	..	7	1	6	..	.	..	..
	Total .	A. H. M.	4,489	2,127	2,362	..	..	..	..	..	..	7	1	6	..	..	..	·15
Sevag . . .	Rajputana . .	H. J.	9,959 116	4,796 67	5,163 49	1 ..	1 ..	.. ..	3 ..	2 ..	1 ..	34 1	15 ..	19 1	1 ..	1 ..	.. ..	.. ..
	Total .	H. J.	10,075	4,863	5,212	1	1	..	3	2	1	35	15	20	1	1	..	·39
Shekh . .	Rajputana . .	M.	182,019	96,788	85,231	56	34	22	70	49	21	356	181	175	5	4	1	·26
	Ajmer-Merwara .	M.	25,139	13,380	11,759	14	9	5	8	6	2	80	48	32	..	..	..	·41
Sindhi . .	Rajputana . .	M.	33,277	17,775	15,502	1	1	..	12	7	5	24	8	16	..	..	..	·11
Sunar . . .	Rajputana . .	H.	68,961	35,527	33,434	22	17	5	21	9	12	201	99	102	6	4	2	..
	Total .	Ar. H. J. M. S.	69,034	35,569	33,465	22	17	5	21	9	12	201	99	102	6	4	2	·36
	Ajmer-Merwara .	H.	3,178	1,663	1,515	2	2	..	.	..	..	12	4	8	..	..	..	..
	Total .	Ar. H. S.	3,206	1,674	1,532	2	2	..	..	..	..	12	4	8	..	..	..	·43
Sutar . . .	Rajputana . .	H.	45,928	23,687	22,241	4	3	1	13	8	5	108	46	62	3	2	1	..
	Total .	Ar. H. J. S.	45,941	23,692	22,249	4	3	1	13	8	5	108	46	62	3	2	1	·27
Swami . . .	Rajputana . .	H.	33,207	19,871	13,336	14	14	..	17	12	5	208	151	57	2	2	..	..
	Total .	H. J.	33,297	19,890	13,407	14	14	..	17	12	5	208	151	57	2	2	..	·72
	Ajmer-Merwara .	H.	332	169	163	..	..	..	..	..	..	1	1	..	..	..	..	·30
Teli . . .	Rajputana . .	H. M.	46,611 31,943	24,071 16,624	22,540 15,319	8 3	5 2	3 1	17 7	6 3	11 4	109 58	48 27	61 31	4 3	3 1	1 2	.. ..
	Total .	Ar. H. M.	78,560	40,698	37,862	11	7	4	24	9	15	167	75	92	7	4	3	·26
	Ajmer-Merwara .	H. M.	3,935 470	2,038 246	1,897 224	.. 1	.. 1	.. ..	.. ..	.. ..	.. ..	13 3	7 ..	6 3	.. ..	.. ..	.. ..	.. ..
	Total .	Ar. H. M.	4,406	2,284	2,122	1	1	..	..	..	..	16	7	9	..	..	..	·38

TABLE XIII.

Caste, Tribe, or Race.

Explanatory Note.

This Table is divided in two parts. Part I contains the figures by Caste, Tribe, or Race, and Sex for each of the two Provinces. Part II gives them in detail by States or Districts and by Religion.

In both parts separate details have been given only for the following castes, etc. :—

(*a*) Those numbering, in the two Provinces combined 7,000 and over, or about ·6 per mille of the combined population ;

(*b*) Those numbering 4,000 and over of any one religion other than Hindus ;

(*c*) All non-Indian races ;

(*d*) Certain castes of particular local or general interest, *viz.*, Goanese, Indian Christians, Khawaswal, Mehtar, Merat Gorat, Moghia, Parsi, Sansi.

The figures for the remaining castes, etc., have been amalgamated under the head " minor castes," which includes those noted below and a few others which were obviously not caste names at all and were unidentifiable. The list is not completely exhaustive as two or three of the States' abstraction offices kept no details of the castes included by them among the minor ones.

*Details of minor castes.**

Castes containing over 2,000.

Caste.	Religion.	Alwar.	Banswara.	Bharatpur.	Bikaner.	Bundi.	Dholpur.	Dungarpur.	Jaipur.	Jaisalmer.	Jhalawar.	Karauli.	Kishangarh.	Kotah.	Kushalgarh.	Marwar.	Mewar.	Partabgarh.	Shahpura.	Sirohi.	Tonk.	Rajputana Total.	Ajmer-Merwara Total.
Baid	...	...	925	...	...	...	...	1,105	3	...	...	...	...	9	...	8	1,101	33	...	..	...	3,304	22
Bari	H. M.	252	10	76	17	73	325	...	901	..	1	...	...	42	...	707	..	..	30	20	...	2,540	...
Bhadbhunja	H. M.	673	60	821	96	39	529	...	1,194	13	23	...	...	109	...	429	...	...	...	25	..	4,031	...
Bisati	H. M.	78	...	32	630	50		...	956	...	...	...	..	19	...	460	...	.	12	...	..	2,246	...
Dom (Sweepers).	H. M.	1,800	...	578	638	2	60	...	970	...	...	...	..	6	...	...	...	..	...	...	...	4,073	3
Gaddi	M.	...	...	2,038	...	74	...	...	671	...	...	...	...	...	...	...	...	...	...	...	...	3,683	...
Gawaria	A.H.M.	266	18	40	289	217	...	...	418	...	12	...	.	201	..	1,029	...	..	28	72	.	2,599	...
Ghosi	M.	175	...	330	513	5	...	...	104	..	98	..	.	868	...	877	...	19	.	237	35	3,241	203
Jaga	...	507	...	70	...	105	86	...	1,150	...	...	334	...	298	...	...	145	..	18	...	30	2,842	365
Khangar	H. M.	28	...	...	...	69	...	...	917	...	...	27	7	701	...	...	450	...	...	1	...	2,199	2
Kharwar	...	89	...	...	53	20	...	...	3,844	...	...	...	...	1,083	...	1,100	381	...	...	70	...	6,630	...
Kumrawat	H. M.	...	...	...	...	283	...	...	...	...	56	...	...	1,378	...	...	1,594	...	1,062	...	201	4,662	44
Lok	...	...	...	...	...	...	...	...	...	...	...	...	...	...	...	...	916	...	...	1,111	...	2,027	...
Patwa	H. M.	201	...	578	4	65	150	...	1,220	...	...	...	...	242	...	3	...	..	...	...	...	2,472	...
Rawal	...	...	...	...	41	...	...	...	63	...	...	...	...	6	...	1,610	...	...	5	3,088	...	4,813	...
Sikligar	H. M.	88	42	144	113	19	47	20	685	..	30	36	6	71	13	125	318	...	69	1	61	2,096	19
Suar	...	...	...	...	...	...	...	...	3	...	...	...	...	...	...	50	...	...	...	2,041	...	2,094	...
Tamboli	H. M.	68	38	1,224	17	597	243	...	830	...	206	...	...	1,443	...	51	3	...	20	30	...	4,385	...

Between 1,000 and 2,000.

Aheri, Babar, Badi, Baloch (M.), Bandhera, Bansfod, Barwa, Bawaria, Bhargava Dusar, Bhand (H. M.), Bhatiara (H. M.), Bhopa, Chadwa (M.), Chobdar (H. M.), Gowar, Jagripatar (H. M.), Kalbelia, Kanjar (H. M.), Kasera (H. M.), KapriKharadi (M.), Mallah, Mohar, Mujawar, Niyaria (H. M.), Rathi, Shikari, Sindhi Sipahi (M.), Taragi, Thathera (H. M.).

Between 500 and 1,000.

Ajna, Bargi, Bediya (H. M.), Bhagat, Bharawa (H. M.), Gadoliya (Gadu Lohar), Ganchha, Hamal (M.), Jati (H. M. J.), Kachara (H. M.), Kazi (M.), Khoja (M.), Machhi (M.), Mahar, Mahawat (M.), Ruwala, Salvi, Satia, Sipahi (M.), Tarkhan (H. M. S.), Tawaif (M.), Turi.

Between 200 and 500.

Arain, Bazigar (H. M.), Chandal, Charwadar (M.), Chitara (H. M.), Chungar (M.), Dabgar (H. M.), Dhanbadari, Dom (Ballad-singers), Garu, Ghasiara (M.), Gujrati, Jasondia, Kalawat (H. M.), Kamnigar (H. M.), Kataiya, Kuchband, Lohona, Makrani (M.), Maratha, Mehra, Mirdha (H. M.), Purbia, Qureshi (M.), Randi (H. M.), Sabugar (M.), Sapera (H. M.), Sarbhangi, Shorgar (M.), Suara, Tirgar (H. M.), Turkia (M.).

Between 100 and 200.

Bedia, Bidhakia, Bodla (M.), Chamta, Charaniya Bambhi, Darugar (M.), Farash (M.), Gatrara (M.), Gayna, Kamar, Kathiyara (M.), Langha (M.), Mahtama (H. J.), Multani (M.), Nanakpanthi, Phadali (M.), Sompara (H. M.), Thakarla, Tirgar.

Under 100.

Aghori, Arab (M.), Arya, Atit, Bachra, Bahelia (H. M.), Bahrupia, Bahti, Bajania, Bandi, Bankor, Barar, Barda, Bargonda, Barmiya, Basumati, Bengali, Beria (H. M.), Bhadwa, Bhanmati, Bhawaiya, Bhirai (M.), Bhubalia, Bhurji (H. M.), Bogdi Sudra, Chabak Sowar (M.), Chadawal (M.), Chakra (M.), Charkata (M.), Chawda, Chirimar (M.), Chita (M.), Dafali, Dakotra (M.), Damor, Dar (M.), Darukuta, Dasundi, Desantri (M.) (Sirohi), Dhangar, Dhanka (Sweepers) (Partabgarh), Dhuldhoya (M.), Dogar (M.), Dogra (S.), Dosad, Gandhi (M.), Gandhrap, Gania, Garmanga, Garwa, Gati, Gawar, Godibad, Gole, Gond, Gori (M.), Guran (J.), Gurao (J.), Gurkha, Guwaria, Habsi (M.), Habura, Halwai, Hijra (H. M.), Hoshiyara (M.), Hurkiya (M.), Jada (H. M.), Jatua (H. M.), Jaiswar, Jaithi, Jeta (M.), Jhinwar (H. M.), Jingar, Joia (M.), Kabirpanthi, Kadia, Kagzi, Kaibatra, Kalandar (M.), Kalhaigar (M.), Kalumbi, Kanchan, Kanjawa, Kashmeri (M.), Kathak, Kathiara (M.), Katwal, Khent, Khichi, Khokhar, Khumra (M.), Kirsora, Kokni, Koria, Kotwal, Lala (H.M.), Langa (M.), Lunia, Machar, Madari (M.), Mallik (M.), Mehta, Modi (H. M.) (except Bikaner), Mohyal, Motisar, Mukhania (M.), Mulla (M.), Murai, Murid (M.), Naga, Nalband (M.), Naomuslim (M.), Naydu, Niwargar (M.), Pachtali, Pannigar, Pardhi, Pasi, Pattidar, Perna, Pirzada (M.), Potgar (M.), Prabhu, Pujari, Puria (grooms), Ranimanga, Rusangi, Sais, Salar Bansi (S.), Sangtarash, Sarwar, Sengupta Siddiki (M.), Singiwala (M.), Someri (M.), Suribas, Surti, Tailangi, Takara, Tarkash (M.), Telagu, Udasi, Vellala, Vilayati (M.).

The heading Mahajan " others " includes the following castes :—

Mahajan Castes. **Over 1,000.** Bagerwal (H. J.), Chitora (H. J.), Jeswal (H. J.), Sungah (H. J.).

Between 500 and 1,000. Mahor, Mehatwal, Narsingpura (H. J.), Tironkhia.

Between 100 and 500. Kharwal, Maretwal, Meghwal, Nagar, Nima (H. J.), Palliwal (H. J.), Pokara, Rustogi.

Under 100. Bhatia, Harsola, Machhar, Mehta, Metwal (H. J.), Mod, Modi (J.), Momia, Nagdalla (J.), Pardhan, Purbi, Sailwal, Sakarwal, Tabi.

As far as possible entries in the schedules which were synonyms, or sub-castes, or mere local equivalents of a true caste, have been amalgamated with the castes to which they appeared to belong after such enquiries, local or otherwise, as it was possible to make. The more important of these are mentioned in the footnotes to the Table. A more exhaustive list of such amalgamations will be found in the Appendix at the end of the Table.

The term " Anglo-Indian " has been substituted for " Eurasian " under the orders of the Government of India. It includes all persons hitherto known as Eurasians and is not confined to those of partially British origin.

Indian Christians who returned their original caste names in the schedules have been included in the head " Christian (Indian)." Details of their former castes, however, will be found in the Report Volume.

All those who returned their caste instead of their religion in the religion column in the schedules have been classified as Animists by religion.

* Where no particular religion has been specified in brackets, the caste includes Hindus only.

TABLE XIII.—Caste, Tribe, or Race.

Part I.—Provincial Summary.

Caste.	Rajputana.			Ajmer-Merwara.		
	Persons.	Males.	Females.	Persons.	Males.	Females.
1	2	3	4	5	6	7
Total	10,530,432	5,515,275	5,015,157	501,395	266,198	235,197
Afghān	362	310	52	9	5	4
Ahir(a)	169,129	91,171	77,958	1,760	1,003	757
American	14	8	6	9	4	5
Anglo-Indian	529	263	266	710	379	331
Armenian	2	..	2	..	..	..
Australian	1	1	..	3	..	3
Bāgri	11,112	5,756	5,356	547	286	261
Bairāgi	57,991	31,370	26,621	487	224	263
Balāi	197,511	101,074	96,437	23,773	12,234	11,539
Bāmbhi	133,826	69,940	63,886	2,550	1,305	1,245
Banjārā	22,103	11,938	10,165	428	214	214
Barhai	9,610	5,125	4,485	23	16	7
Bauri	30,931	16,232	14,699	271	143	128
Belgian	1	1	..	..	..	..
Bhangi	84,980	43,655	41,325	5,361	2,832	2,529
Bhāt	34,533	17,842	16,691	1,004	543	461
Bhil	448,910	229,266	219,644	6,509	3,289	3,220
Bhishti	24,789	12,690	12,099	758	421	337
Bhoi	8,627	4,284	4,343	58	39	19
Bishnoi	52,879	28,492	24,387	3	2	1
Bohrā	11,286	5,916	5,370	60	42	18
Boiā	22,736	11,546	11,190	..	..	..
Brāhman(b)	922,810	475,901	446,909	24,042	12,887	11,155
Bulgarian	1	1	..	..	..	..
Canadian	..	..	..	1	1	..
Chākar(c)	58,606	28,320	30,286	270	129	141
Chamar(d)	734,110	378,017	356,093	13,351	6,822	6,529
Chāran(e)	37,574	19,510	18,064	315	168	147
Chhipā(f)	37,940	19,645	18,295	2,652	1,418	1,234
Chinese	1	1	..	..	..	..
Christian (Indian)	2,384	1,307	1,077	2,730	1,309	1,421
Dādupanthi	7,670	7,517	153	20	16	4
Dākot	20,326	10,166	10,160	580	299	281
Dāngi	38,100	19,557	18,543	1	1	..
Darogā	118,914	57,658	61,256	8,952	4,550	4,402
Darzi	45,203	23,069	22,134	2,250	1,226	1,024
Deswāli	6,869	3,497	3,372	2,449	1,413	1,036
Dhākar	93,365	47,662	45,703	626	321	305
Dhānak (Dhānuk, Dhānkā, or Dhānkiā)	25,521	12,822	12,699	1,371	741	630
Dhed	16,830	8,826	8,004	13	6	7
Dhobi	45,801	23,348	22,453	2,882	1,479	1,403
Dholi(g)	30,906	16,127	14,781	5,378	2,766	2,612
English	788	490	298	1,302	1,107	195
European (unspecified)	30	14	16	145	100	45
Fakir	55,265	29,054	26,211	1,751	921	830
French	35	25	10	33	26	7
Gadariā (Gādri)	65,128	33,743	31,385	38	24	14
Garodā (Garodiā)(h)	10,863	5,755	5,108	91	47	44
German	13	4	9	1	1	..
Ghānchā (Ghānchi, Ghāchhi)	19,352	10,212	9,140	3	1	2
Goanese	163	121	42	237	168	69
Gosāin	27,806	15,418	12,388	903	478	425
Orissiā	17,419	8,918	8,501	..	..	..
Greek	..	..	..	1	1	..
Gujar(i)	500,046	271,188	228,858	35,059	18,609	16,450
Irish	96	64	32	105	70	35
Italian	1	1	..	..	..	..
Japanese	1	1	..	..	..	..
Jat	928,486	501,616	426,870	30,497	16,526	13,971
Jew	31	15	16	25	12	13
Jogi(j)	67,144	35,317	31,827	2,534	1,381	1,153
Julāhā(k)	18,333	9,478	8,855	1,096	568	528
Kāchhi	60,666	31,766	28,900	77	41	36
Kahār	15,164	7,967	7,197	3,043	1,580	1,463
Kāimkhāni	28,340	14,824	13,516	542	306	236
Kalāl	39,860	20,334	19,526	1,341	695	[illegible]
Kanderā (Karerā)(l)	8,629	4,434	4,195	17	9	8
Kassāi(m)	29,400	15,006	14,394	1,088	549	539
Kāyastha	23,610	12,853	10,757	2,439	1,320	1,119
Khānzādā	9,198	4,712	4,486	1	1	..
Khārol(n)	7,861	4,003	3,858	1,702	894	808
Khāti (o)	134,992	69,245	65,747	6,839	3,620	3,219
Khatik	51,276	26,380	24,896	3,552	1,793	1,759
Khatri(p)	10,410	5,441	4,969	1,407	750	657
Khawāswāl	1,203	727	476	..	..	..

(a) Includes Goālā.
(b) Includes Āchāraj, Bohrā Nandwānā, Joshi.
(c) Includes Chelā, Dāvadā, Golāpurab, Gulām, Hazuri, Khānezad, Pasbān (Kotah), Pāswānia (Mewar), Vasir.
(d) Includes Jatiā and Musalman Boiā.
(e) Includes Bārot.
(f) Includes Hindu Niligar and Rangrez.
(g) Includes Hindu Dārhi, Dhādi, Mirāsi.
(h) Includes Garda, Gurrah.
(i) Includes Hindu Ghosi.
(j) Includes Nāth.
(k) Includes Momin.
(l) Includes Hindu Dhuniā, Pinārā, Pinjārā.
(m) Includes Musalman Khatik.
(n) Includes Agar.
(o) Includes Hindu Kherāti.
(p) Includes Korr.

TABLE XIII.—Caste, Tribe, or Race.

Part I.—Provincial Summary.

Caste.	Rajputana.			Ajmer-Merwara.		
	Persons.	Males.	Females.	Persons.	Males.	Females.
1	2	3	4	5	6	7
Kir	21,674	11,237	10,437	974	497	477
Kirār	11,804	6,109	5,695	..	..	..
Koli	104,055	53,502	50,553	6,565	3,480	3,085
Kumhār(a)	309,234	159,676	149,558	14,120	7,218	6,902
Kunbi	48,202	24,910	23,292	412	206	206
Kunjrā	4,251	2,226	2,025	258	145	113
Labhāna	4,591	2,373	2,218	..	..	..
Lakherā(b)	10,752	5,539	5,213	750	376	374
Lodā(c)	7,713	4,105	3,608	..	..	..
Lodhā	47,013	24,526	22,487	1,139	575	564
Lohār	80,822	41,247	39,575	4,214	2,256	1,958
Mahājan or Baniyā (Total)	707,721	353,152	354,569	34,470	18,413	16,057
" *Agarwal*	*199,629*	*101,638*	*97,991*	*8,400*	*4,444*	*3,956*
" *Bijābargi*	*9,879*	*5,115*	*4,764*	*728*	*357*	*371*
" *Hamar or Humbad*	*8,583*	*4,257*	*4,326*	..	..	..
" *Khandelwal*	*63,064*	*33,918*	*29,146*	*1,864*	*902*	*962*
" *Maheri*	*91,106*	*44,597*	*46,509*	*5,414*	*2,924*	*2,490*
" *Mewar or Mahdwar*	*9,753*	*5,052*	*4,701*	..	..	..
" *Oswal*	*209,965*	*100,685*	*109,280*	*14,228*	*7,566*	*6,662*
" *Porwal*	*33,036*	*14,894*	*18,142*	*1*	*1*	..
" *Sarsogi*	*38,041*	*19,835*	*18,206*	*3,223*	*1,858*	*1,365*
" *Others*	*44,665*	*23,161*	*21,504*	*612*	*361*	*251*
Māli(d)	336,876	174,966	161,910	14,340	7,499	6,841
Manihār(e)	8,978	4,672	4,306	93	54	39
Meghwal (Megh)	57,516	30,087	27,429	1	..	1
Mehtar	6,151	3,124	3,027	838	449	389
Meo or Mewāti	165,690	87,347	78,343	173	94	79
Mer	13,712	7,156	6,556	21,803	11,634	10,169
Merāt Gorāt	26	16	10	2,025	1,300	725
Merāt Kathāt	2,250	1,263	987	17,626	9,651	7,975
Minā	558,689	296,205	262,484	4,223	2,442	1,781
Mirāsi(f)	21,729	11,200	10,529	506	252	254
Mochi	15,428	8,101	7,327	1,611	810	801
Moghal	14,121	7,469	6,652	1,415	778	637
Moghiā	4,314	2,211	2,103	..	..	..
Nai	162,463	84,866	77,597	6,503	3,297	3,206
Naik (Nāyak)	42,391	22,111	20,280	2,497	1,298	1,199
Nat	8,447	4,392	4,055	920	479	441
Od (Odh)(g)	7,839	4,159	3,680	343	183	160
Pārsi	342	191	151	262	134	128
Patel	55,798	27,751	28,047	6	4	2
Pathān	108,291	57,505	50,786	11,420	6,176	5,244
Pinārā(h)	14,298	7,288	7,010	1,006	555	451
Portuguese	45	25	20	29	20	9
Prohit	36,942	19,130	17,812	178	90	88
Raigar	81,568	41,626	39,942	19,858	10,148	9,710
Rajput(i)	687,292	385,124	302,168	14,302	9,225	6,077
Rānā	11,808	5,967	5,841	14	9	5
Rangrez(j)	15,485	8,049	7,436	621	358	263
Rāo	12,571	6,335	6,236	324	178	146
Rāwat	13,754	7,580	6,174	47,905	24,963	22,942
Rebāri	129,918	67,760	62,158	2,033	1,085	948
Russian	..	..	..	1	1	..
Sād (k)	28,544	15,573	12,971	..	..	..
Sādhu(l)	10,519	6,451	4,068	4,638	2,552	2,086
Sahar	13,801	6,998	6,803	..	..	..
Saiyad	28,954	15,242	13,712	5,199	2,823	2,376
Sanjogi	9,908	5,327	4,581	..	..	..
Sansi (Sānsia, Sānsri)	4,489	2,127	2,362	325	149	176
Sargarā	26,520	13,865	12,655	824	424	400
Scotch	144	80	64	115	66	49
Sevag(m)	10,075	4,863	5,212	254	137	117
Shekh	182,019	96,788	85,231	25,130	13,380	11,750
Silāwat	7,858	3,922	3,936	..	..	..
Sindhi	33,277	17,775	15,502	..	..	..
Sirvi	50,995	26,651	24,344	10	7	3
Sondhiā	31,693	17,018	14,675	..	..	..
Spaniard	2	1	1	1	1	..
Sunār	69,034	35,569	33,465	3,200	1,674	1,526
Sutār	45,941	23,692	22,249	1	1	..
Swāmi	33,297	19,890	13,407	332	169	163
Swiss	1	..	1	3	..	3
Teli	78,560	40,698	37,862	4,406	2,284	2,122
Thori	28,413	15,167	13,246	39	24	15
Welsh	4	3	1	8	6	2
West African	1	..	1	..	..	..
Minor castes	187,092	96,141	90,951	12,894	6,922	5,973
Unspecified	323	199	124	163	116	47

(a) Includes Rājkumhār.
(b) Includes Manihār.
(c) Includes Lodhā (Kotah).
(d) Includes Bāghbān.
(e) Includes Musalman Churigar and Lakherā.
(f) Includes Musalman Dārhi, Dhādi, Dholi, Nagārchi.
(g) Includes Beldār.
(h) Includes Musalman Dhuniā, Kanderā.
(i) Details of the various Rājput clans will be found in the subsidiary Tables in the Report Volume.
(j) Includes Musalman Nilgar.
(k) Includes Sādh (Bharatpur and Marwar).
(l) Includes Sādh (Bikaner, Jaisalmer, and Sirohi).
(m) Includes Bhojak.

TABLE XIII.—Caste, Tribe, or Race. Part II.—By States or Districts, and Religions.

Province; and State or District.	Population.			Afghān.		Ahir.*										American.		Anglo-Indian.		Armenian.		Australian.		Bāgri.							
				Musalman.		Total.		Arya.		Hindu.		Jain.		Musalman.		Christian.		Christian.		Christian.		Christian.		Total.		Animist.		Hindu.		Musalman.	
	Persons.	Males.	Females.	M.	F.	M.	F.	M.	F.	M.	F.	M.	F.	M.	F.	M.	F.	M.	F.	M.	F.	M.	F.	M.	F.	M.	F.	M.	F.	M.	F.
1	2	3	4	5	6	7	8	9	10	11	12	13	14	15	16	17	18	19	20	21	22	23	24	25	26	27	28	29	30	31	32
Rajputana	**10,530,432**	**5,515,275**	**5,015,157**	*370*	*59*	*91,171*	*77,958*	**9**	**5**	**91,151**	**77,947**	**2**	**2**	**9**	**4**	*8*	*6*	*263*	*266*	..	*2*	*1*	..	*5,756*	*5,356*	**512**	**487**	**5,241**	**4,869**	**3**	..
Alwar	791,688	413,659	378,029	*1*	..	*36,023*	*31,363*	..	..	36,022	31,363	..	..	1	..	..	..	*4*	*3*	..	*1*	..	..	*1*	..	..	..	1	..	..	..
Banswara	165,463	81,620	83,843	..	..	*5*	*8*	..	..	5	8	..	..	..	..	..	..	..	..	..	..	..	..	..	..	..	..	..	..	..	..
Bharatpur	558,785	302,254	256,531	..	..	*2,008*	*1,701*	..	..	2,008	1,701	..	..	..	..	..	..	*12*	*11*	..	..	..	..	*267*	*250*	..	..	267	250	..	..
Bikaner	700,983	371,489	329,494	..	..	*681*	*489*	2	..	671	485	2	1	6	3	..	..	*4*	..	..	..	..	..	..	..	..	..	..	..	..	..
Bundi	218,730	113,211	105,519	..	..	*481*	*430*	..	..	481	430	..	..	..	..	..	..	..	..	..	..	..	..	*102*	*91*	..	..	102	91	..	..
Dholpur	263,188	144,244	118,944	..	..	*351*	*255*	..	..	351	255	..	..	..	..	..	..	*5*	*5*	..	..	..	..	..	..	..	..	..	..	..	..
Dungarpur	159,192	79,105	80,087	..	..	..	..	..	..	..	..	..	..	..	..	..	..	..	..	..	..	..	..	..	..	..	..	..	..	..	..
Jaipur	2,636,647	1,385,750	1,250,897	*307*	*51*	*37,429*	*31,060*	..	..	37,428	31,060	..	..	1	..	*5*	*3*	*128*	*156*	..	..	*1*	..	*618*	*862*	191	187	427	675	..	..
Jaisalmer	88,311	48,500	39,811	..	..	..	..	..	..	..	..	..	..	..	..	..	..	..	..	..	..	..	..	..	..	..	..	..	..	..	..
Jhalawar	96,271	50,034	46,237	..	..	*236*	*212*	6	4	230	208	..	..	..	..	..	..	*1*	..	..	..	..	..	*646*	*574*	..	..	646	574	..	..
Karauli	146,587	80,081	66,506	..	..	*45*	*10*	..	..	45	10	..	..	..	..	..	..	..	..	..	..	..	..	*4*	*2*	4	2	..	..	..	..
Kishangarh	87,191	45,718	41,473	..	..	*187*	*125*	..	..	187	123	..	..	..	..	..	..	..	..	..	..	..	..	*242*	*233*	62	51	180	182	..	..
Kotah	639,089	330,324	308,765	..	..	*4,080*	*3,011*	..	1	4,080	3,010	..	..	..	..	..	..	*8*	*8*	..	..	..	..	*39*	*33*	..	..	39	33	..	..
Kushalgarh (Chiefship)	22,005	10,956	11,049	..	..	*1*	..	..	..	1	..	..	..	..	..	..	..	..	..	..	..	..	..	..	..	..	..	..	..	..	..
Lawa (Estate)	2,564	1,302	1,262	..	..	..	..	..	..	..	..	..	..	..	..	..	..	..	..	..	..	..	..	*4*	*3*	..	..	4	3	..	..
Marwar	2,057,553	1,075,269	982,284	*2*	*1*	*646*	*443*	..	..	646	442	..	..	..	1	*1*	*2*	*31*	*33*	..	..	..	..	*1,507*	*1,265*	26	24	1,481	1,241	..	..
Mewar	1,293,776	670,750	623,026	..	..	*4,497*	*4,214*	..	..	4,496	4,213	..	1	1	..	..	..	*2*	..	..	..	..	..	*431*	*413*	12	5	419	408	..	..
Partabgarh	62,704	31,735	30,969	..	..	*19*	*20*	..	..	19	20	..	..	..	..	..	..	..	..	..	..	..	..	*1*	*1*	..	..	1	1	..	..
Shahpura (Chiefship)	47,397	24,595	22,802	..	..	*20*	*12*	..	..	20	12	..	..	..	..	..	..	..	..	..	..	..	..	*23*	*19*	14	12	9	7	..	..
Sirohi	189,127	98,289	90,838	..	..	*40*	*21*	..	..	40	21	..	..	..	..	*2*	*1*	*63*	*45*	..	1	..	..	*403*	*358*	27	23	373	335	3	..
Tonk	303,161	156,370	146,791	..	..	*4,522*	*3,978*	1	..	4,521	3,978	..	..	..	..	..	..	..	..	..	..	..	..	*1,468*	*1,252*	186	183	1,282	1,069	..	..
Ajmer-Merwara	**501,395**	**266,198**	**235,197**	*5*	*4*	*1,003*	*757*	**4**	**1**	**997**	**755**	..	..	**2**	**1**	*4*	*5*	*379*	*331*	..	..	..	*3*	*286*	*261*	**47**	**51**	**239**	**210**	..	..
Ajmer	380,384	201,911	178,473	*5*	*4*	*868*	*675*	4	1	863	674	..	..	1	..	*4*	*5*	*373*	*325*	..	..	..	3	*279*	*259*	47	51	232	208	..	..
Merwara	121,011	64,287	56,724	..	..	*135*	*82*	..	..	134	81	..	..	1	1	..	..	*6*	*6*	..	..	..	..	*7*	*2*	..	..	7	2	..	..

* Includes Goāla.

TABLE XIII.—Caste, Tribe, or Race. Part II.—By States or Districts, and Religions—*contd.*

Province; and State or District.	Bairāgi. Total. M.	Total. F.	Animist. M.	Animist. F.	Arya. M.	Arya. F.	Hindu. M.	Hindu. F.	Jain. M.	Jain. F.	Sikh. M.	Sikh. F.
1	33	34	35	36	37	38	39	40	41	42	43	44
Rajputana	31,370	26,631	1	4	2	1	31,365	26,614	..	2	2	..
Alwar	574	322	..	..	..	..	574	322	..	..	..	..
Banswara	349	289	..	..	..	..	349	289	..	..	..	..
Bharatpur	2,353	1,729	..	..	..	..	2,353	1,729	..	..	..	..
Bikaner	7,058	5,858	..	..	..	..	7,056	5,858	..	..	2	..
Bundi	1,934	1,666	..	..	..	..	1,934	1,666	..	..	..	..
Dholpur	505	363	..	..	..	..	505	363	..	..	..	..
Dungarpur	291	279	..	..	..	..	291	279	..	..	..	..
Jaipur	1,586	1,192	..	..	..	..	1,586	1,192	..	..	..	..
Jaisalmer	..	..	..	..	..	..	..	..	..	..	..	..
Jhalawar	674	597	..	..	..	..	674	597	..	..	..	..
Karauli	189	57	..	..	..	..	189	57	..	..	..	..
Kishangarh	33	12	..	..	..	..	33	12	..	..	..	..
Kotah	3,816	3,435	..	..	2	1	3,814	3,434	..	..	..	..
Kushalgarh (Chiefship)	20	25	..	..	..	..	20	25	..	..	..	..
Lawa (Estate)	8	1	..	..	..	..	8	1	..	..	..	..
Marwar	27	5	..	..	..	..	27	5	..	..	..	..
Mewar	9,719	8,752	1	4	..	..	9,718	8,746	..	2	..	..
Partabgarh	574	572	..	..	..	..	574	572	..	..	..	..
Shahpura (Chiefship)	290	267	..	..	..	..	290	267	..	..	..	..
Sirohi	49	19	..	..	..	..	49	10	..	..	..	..
Tonk	1,321	1,181	..	..	..	..	1,321	1,181	..	..	..	..
Ajmer-Merwara	224	263	..	..	..	..	224	263	..	..	..	..
Ajmer	215	256	..	..	..	..	215	256	..	..	..	..
Merwara	9	7	..	..	..	..	9	7	..	..	..	..

Province; and State or District.	Balāi. Total. M.	Total. F.	Hindu. M.	Hindu. F.	Musalman. M.	Musalman. F.	Bāmbhi. Hindu. M.	Hindu. F.	Banjārā. Total. M.	Total. F.	Animist. M.	Animist. F.	Arya. M.	Arya. F.	Hindu. M.	Hindu. F.	Jain. M.	Jain. F.	Musalman. M.	Musalman. F.
1	45	46	47	48	49	50	51	52	53	54	55	56	57	58	59	60	61	62	63	64
Rajputana	101,074	96,437	101,057	96,434	17	3	69,940	63,886	11,938	10,165	17	14	..	..	11,438	9,757	..	1	482	393
Alwar	3,274	3,234	3,270	3,233	4	1	..	..	298	166	..	..	..	..	201	114	..	..	97	42
Banswara	1,292	1,304	1,292	1,304	..	..	..	..	1,006	981	..	..	..	..	1,006	981	..	..	..	..
Bharatpur	935	867	935	867	..	..	..	..	798	563	..	..	..	..	751	515	..	..	47	28
Bikaner	1,016	1,014	1,013	1,014	3	..	96	91	22	13	..	..	..	..	20	10	..	..	2	3
Bundi	5,175	5,132	5,175	5,132	..	..	..	..	455	342	..	..	..	..	455	342	..	..	..	..
Dholpur	14	19	14	19	..	..	..	..	70	25	..	..	..	..	70	25	..	..	..	..
Dungarpur	1,133	1,005	1,133	1,005	..	..	5	4	1,082	1,046	..	..	..	..	1,082	1,046	..	..	..	..
Jaipur	37,682	35,680	37,674	35,678	8	2	..	..	1,260	983	..	..	..	..	1,027	742	..	..	233	241
Jaisalmer	..	..	..	..	..	..	..	..	..	..	..	..	..	..	..	..	..	..	..	..
Jhalawar	2,373	2,340	2,373	2,340	..	..	22	20	35	21	17	14	..	..	18	7	..	..	..	..
Karauli	..	..	..	..	..	..	..	..	21	18	..	..	..	..	21	18	..	..	..	..
Kishangarh	2,599	2,387	2,599	2,387	..	..	3	1	65	46	..	..	..	..	41	26	..	..	24	20
Kotah	4,057	3,970	4,057	3,970	..	..	52	76	3,613	2,943	..	..	..	..	3,581	2,919	..	1	32	23
Kushalgarh (Chiefship)	2	..	2	..	..	..	9	6	..	..	..	..	..	..	..	..	..	..	..	..
Lawa (Estate)	12	20	12	20	..	..	..	..	..	..	..	..	..	..	..	..	..	..	..	..
Marwar	9,142	9,123	9,140	9,123	2	..	68,351	62,349	163	158	..	..	..	..	139	140	..	..	24	18
Mewar	29,011	27,119	29,011	27,119	..	..	1,155	1,079	2,496	2,443	..	..	..	..	2,478	2,427	..	..	18	16
Partabgarh	613	625	613	625	..	..	42	50	1	3	..	..	..	..	1	3	..	..	..	..
Shahpura (Chiefship)	720	698	720	698	..	..	..	..	10	14	..	..	..	..	10	14	..	..	..	..
Sirohi	142	119	142	119	..	..	1	1	37	21	..	..	..	..	32	19	..	..	5	2
Tonk	1,882	1,781	1,882	1,781	..	..	204	206	506	409	..	..	..	..	506	409	..	..	..	..
Ajmer-Merwara	12,234	11,539	12,224	11,535	10	4	1,305	1,245	214	214	..	..	1	1	143	128	..	..	70	85
Ajmer	8,985	8,641	8,979	8,638	6	3	465	457	209	207	..	..	1	1	139	122	..	..	69	84
Merwara	3,249	2,898	3,245	2,897	4	1	840	788	5	7	..	..	..	..	4	6	..	..	1	1

TABLE XIII.—CASTE, TRIBE, OR RACE. PART II.—BY STATES OR DISTRICTS, AND RELIGIONS—*contd.*

Province; and State or District.	BARHAI.						BAURI.												BELGIAN.		BHANGI.									
	TOTAL.		ARYA.		HINDU.		TOTAL.		ANIMIST.		ARYA.		HINDU.		MUSALMAN.		SIKH.		CHRISTIAN.		TOTAL.		ANIMIST.		HINDU.		MUSALMAN.		SIKH.	
	M.	F.	M.	F.	M.	F.	M.	F.	M.	F.	M.	F.	M.	F.	M.	F.	M.	F.	M.	F.	M.	F.	M.	F.	M.	F.	M.	F.	M.	F.
1	65	66	67	68	69	70	71	72	73	74	75	76	77	78	79	80	81	82	83	84	85	86	87	88	89	90	91	92	93	94
Rajputana	*5,125*	*4,485*	2	3	5,123	4,482	*16,939*	*14,699*	2,279	2,038	..	..	13,768	12,487	1	..	184	174	*1*	..	*43,655*	*41,335*	5	3	42,642	40,474	437	398	571	450
Alwar	..	..	..	..	..	..	..	..	..	..	..	..	..	..	..	..	..	..	..	..	*6,455*	*6,459*	..	..	6,448	6,452	7	7	..	..
Banswara	..	..	..	..	..	..	..	..	..	..	..	..	..	..	..	..	..	..	..	..	*180*	*185*	..	..	180	185	..	..	..	..
Bharatpur	*982*	*922*	..	..	982	922	*43*	*42*	..	..	..	..	43	42	..	..	..	..	..	..	*4,097*	*3,400*	..	..	4,097	3,400	..	..	..	..
Bikaner	*23*	*23*	..	..	23	23	*1,875*	*1,752*	..	..	..	..	1,691	1,578	..	..	184	174	..	..	*3,216*	*2,848*	..	..	2,445	2,210	200	188	571	450
Bundi	..	..	..	..	..	..	..	..	..	..	..	..	..	..	..	..	..	..	..	..	*898*	*892*	..	..	830	838	68	54	..	..
Dholpur	*2,439*	*2,071*	2	3	2,437	2,068	..	..	..	..	..	..	..	..	..	..	..	..	..	..	*1,118*	*1,030*	..	..	1,118	1,030	..	..	..	..
Dungarpur	..	..	..	..	..	..	..	..	..	..	..	..	..	..	..	..	..	..	..	..	*200*	*218*	..	..	200	218	..	..	..	..
Jaipur	*52*	*59*	..	..	52	59	*761*	*622*	52	50	..	..	708	572	1	..	..	..	..	..	*11,361*	*10,988*	4	3	11,350	10,980	7	5	..	..
Jaisalmer	..	..	..	..	..	..	*13*	*7*	13	7	..	..	..	..	..	..	..	..	..	..	*20*	*20*	..	..	20	20	..	..	..	..
Jhalawar	*759*	*648*	..	..	759	648	..	..	..	..	..	..	..	..	..	..	..	..	..	..	*451*	*456*	..	..	451	456	..	..	..	..
Karauli	*859*	*757*	..	..	859	757	..	..	..	..	..	..	..	..	..	..	..	..	..	..	*835*	*749*	..	..	835	749	..	..	..	..
Kishangarh	..	..	..	..	..	..	*232*	*232*	..	..	..	..	232	232	..	..	..	..	..	..	*240*	*218*	..	..	240	218	..	..	..	..
Kotah	*11*	*5*	..	..	11	5	*21*	*10*	..	..	..	..	21	10	..	..	..	..	..	..	*2,936*	*2,776*	1	..	2,930	2,767	5	9	..	..
Kushalgarh (Chiefship)	..	..	..	..	..	..	..	..	..	..	..	..	..	..	..	..	..	..	..	..	*7*	*9*	..	..	7	9	..	..	..	..
Lawa (Estate)	..	..	..	..	..	..	..	..	..	..	..	..	..	..	..	..	..	..	..	..	*21*	*15*	..	..	21	15	..	..	..	..
Marwar	..	..	..	..	..	..	*12,855*	*11,632*	2,214	1,981	..	..	10,641	9,651	..	..	..	..	..	..	*6,533*	*6,107*	..	..	6,487	6,059	46	48	..	..
Mewar	..	..	..	..	..	..	*235*	*210*	1	..	..	..	234	210	..	..	..	..	..	..	*3,102*	*3,081*	..	..	3,002	2,995	100	86	..	..
Partabgarh	..	..	..	..	..	..	*13*	*14*	..	..	..	..	13	14	..	..	..	..	..	..	*157*	*125*	..	..	154	124	3	1	..	..
Shahpura (Chiefship)	..	..	..	..	..	..	*136*	*118*	..	..	..	..	136	118	..	..	..	..	..	..	*98*	*93*	..	..	98	93	..	..	..	..
Sirohi	..	..	..	..	..	..	..	..	..	..	..	..	..	..	..	..	..	..	*1*	..	*483*	*422*	..	..	482	422	1	..	..	..
Tonk	..	..	..	..	..	..	*49*	*60*	..	..	..	..	49	60	..	..	..	..	..	..	*1,248*	*1,236*	..	..	1,248	1,236	..	..	..	..
Ajmer-Merwara	*16*	*7*	..	..	16	7	*143*	*128*	..	..	..	1	143	127	..	..	..	..	..	..	*2,832*	*2,529*	130	113	2,676	2,414	26	2	..	..
Ajmer	*16*	*7*	..	..	16	7	*92*	*89*	..	..	..	1	92	88	..	..	..	..	..	..	*2,431*	*2,144*	87	72	2,318	2,070	26	2	..	..
Merwara	..	..	..	..	..	..	*51*	*39*	..	..	..	..	51	39	..	..	..	..	..	..	*401*	*385*	43	41	358	344	..	..	..	..

TABLE XIII.—Caste, Tribe, or Race. Part II.—By States or Districts, and Religions—*contd.*

Province; and State or District.	Bhāt.								Bhil.										Bhishti.					
	Total.		Animist.		Hindu.		Musalman.		Total.		Animist.		Arya.		Hindu.		Musalman.		Total.		Hindu.		Musalman.	
	M.	F.	M.	F.	M.	F.	M.	F.	M.	F.	M.	F.	M.	F.	M.	F.	M.	F.	M.	F.	M.	F.	M.	F.
1	95	96	97	98	99	100	101	102	103	104	105	106	107	108	109	110	111	112	113	114	115	116	117	118
Rajputana	17,849	16,691	23	37	17,273	16,024	546	630	229,366	219,644	196,342	189,661	..	..	33,022	29,982	2	1	12,690	12,680	56	63	12,634	12,617
Alwar	88	95	..	..	84	74	4	21	1	..	1	..	..	..	..	..	..	..	4,527	4,361	8	25	4,519	4,336
Banswara	214	213	..	..	214	213	..	..	47,323	48,511	47,322	48,511	..	..	..	..	..	..	18	28	..	..	18	28
Bharatpur	434	408	..	..	427	403	7	5	1	1	..	..	..	..	1	1	..	..	2,237	2,080	..	..	2,237	2,080
Bikaner	1,544	1,227	..	..	1,453	1,152	91	75	3	..	..	..	..	..	3	..	..	..	632	556	1	2	631	554
Bundi	179	175	..	..	179	175	..	..	2,337	2,317	2,257	2,254	..	..	80	63	..	..	182	209	18	18	164	191
Dholpur	345	278	..	..	345	278	..	..	..	..	..	..	..	..	..	..	..	..	307	287	..	..	307	287
Dungarpur	321	313	18	27	303	286	..	..	37,501	36,728	37,501	36,728	..	..	..	..	..	..	8	9	..	..	8	9
Jaipur	1,080	1,193	..	..	996	1,136	84	57	861	751	547	461	..	..	314	290	..	..	2,488	2,406	26	37	2,462	2,369
Jaisalmer	31	11	..	..	31	11	..	..	2,229	1,903	2,229	1,903	..	..	..	..	..	..	..	..	..	..	..	..
Jhalawar	69	62	..	..	69	62	..	..	1,287	1,159	98	76	..	..	1,189	1,083	..	..	193	202	..	..	193	202
Karauli	5	9	..	..	5	9	..	..	..	..	..	..	..	..	..	..	..	..	226	226	..	..	226	226
Kishangarh	236	207	..	..	236	207	..	..	383	368	211	221	..	..	172	147	..	..	34	36	..	..	34	36
Kotah	526	530	..	..	490	494	36	36	9,464	9,193	748	730	..	..	8,716	8,463	..	..	432	434	..	..	432	434
Kushalgarh (Chiefship)	15	12	..	..	15	12	..	..	8,488	8,612	8,488	8,612	..	..	..	..	..	..	..	..	..	..	..	..
Lawa (Estate)	..	..	..	..	..	..	..	..	..	..	..	..	..	..	..	..	..	..	..	..	..	..	..	..
Marwar	9,068	8,484	..	..	8,746	8,049	322	435	26,785	23,057	23,681	20,402	..	..	3,103	2,654	1	1	482	439	..	..	482	439
Mewar	2,003	1,905	5	10	1,998	1,895	..	..	71,696	67,079	57,952	54,845	..	..	13,743	12,234	1	..	350	319	3	..	347	319
Partabgarh	268	266	..	..	268	266	..	..	10,533	10,401	10,530	10,399	..	..	3	2	..	..	16	20	..	..	16	20
Shahpura (Chiefship)	81	75	..	..	81	75	..	..	985	965	975	951	..	..	10	14	..	..	18	17	..	..	18	17
Sirohi	1,194	1,119	..	..	1,192	1,118	2	1	7,420	6,643	1,898	1,782	..	..	5,522	4,861	..	..	83	83	..	..	83	83
Tonk	141	109	..	..	141	109	..	..	1,969	1,956	1,803	1,786	..	..	166	170	..	..	457	378	..	..	457	378
Ajmer-Merwara	543	461	..	..	535	451	8	10	3,289	3,220	1,658	1,681	2	3	1,629	1,536	..	..	421	337	2	2	419	335
Ajmer	393	340	..	..	385	330	8	10	2,452	2,447	1,027	1,107	2	3	1,423	1,337	..	..	381	309	2	2	379	307
Merwara	150	121	..	..	150	121	..	..	837	773	631	374	..	..	206	199	..	..	40	28	..	..	40	28

TABLE XIII.—Caste, Tribe, or Race. Part II.—By States or Districts, and Religions—*contd.*

Province; and State or District.	Bhoi. Total. M.	Bhoi. Total. F.	Bhoi. Hindu. M.	Bhoi. Hindu. F.	Bhoi. Musalman. M.	Bhoi. Musalman. F.	Bishnoi. Total. M.	Bishnoi. Total. F.	Bishnoi. Arya. M.	Bishnoi. Arya. F.	Bishnoi. Hindu. M.	Bishnoi. Hindu. F.	Bohrā. Total. M.	Bohrā. Total. F.	Bohrā. Animist. M.	Bohrā. Animist. F.	Bohrā. Musalman. M.	Bohrā. Musalman. F.	Bolā. Hindu. M.	Bolā. Hindu. F.	Brāhman.* Total. M.	Brāhman.* Total. F.	Brāhman.* Arya. M.	Brāhman.* Arya. F.	Brāhman.* Hindu. M.	Brāhman.* Hindu. F.	Brāhman.* Jain. M.	Brāhman.* Jain. F.
1	119	120	121	122	123	124	125	126	127	128	129	130	131	132	133	134	135	136	137	138	139	140	141	142	143	144	145	146
Rajputana	*4,284*	*4,343*	4,282	4,343	2	..	*28,492*	*24,387*	1	1	28,491	24,386	*5,916*	*5,370*	2	..	5,914	5,370	*11,546*	*11,100*	*475,901*	*446,909*	246	206	475,627	446,691	11	13
Alwar	..	..	..	..	..	..	..	..	..	..	..	..	..	..	..	..	..	..	..	..	*36,821*	*34,281*	2	9	36,919	34,272	..	..
Banswara	*808*	*875*	808	875	..	..	..	..	..	..	..	..	*726*	*615*	..	..	726	615	..	..	*4,443*	*4,881*	2	1	4,441	4,880	..	..
Bharatpur	..	..	..	..	..	..	..	..	..	..	..	..	..	..	..	..	..	..	..	..	*29,778*	*24,696*	31	20	29,746	24,676	..	..
Bikaner	*1*	..	1	..	..	..	*5,761*	*5,029*	..	..	5,761	5,029	..	..	..	..	..	..	..	..	*33,610*	*33,880*	41	41	33,560	33,837	..	2
Bundi	*63*	*42*	63	42	..	..	..	..	..	..	..	..	..	..	..	..	..	..	*2,282*	*2,289*	*9,707*	*9,040*	..	..	9,707	9,040	..	..
Dholpur	*5*	*5*	5	3	..	..	..	..	..	..	..	..	..	..	..	..	..	..	..	..	*18,246*	*14,179*	1	..	18,240	14,174	..	..
Dungarpur	*455*	*454*	455	454	..	..	..	..	..	..	..	..	*1,518*	*1,665*	..	..	1,518	1,665	..	..	*5,586*	*6,321*	..	..	5,586	6,321	..	..
Jaipur	*12*	*9*	10	9	2	..	*2*	..	..	..	2	..	..	..	..	..	..	..	*28*	*1*	*158,733*	*150,239*	53	35	158,680	150,204	..	..
Jaisalmer	..	..	..	..	..	..	*1,813*	*1,483*	..	..	1,813	1,483	..	..	..	..	..	..	..	..	*2,319*	*2,214*	..	..	2,310	2,214	..	..
Jhalawar	*195*	*209*	195	209	..	..	..	..	..	..	..	..	*323*	*377*	..	..	323	377	..	..	*3,260*	*2,957*	9	4	3,251	2,953	..	..
Farauli	..	..	..	..	..	..	..	..	..	..	..	..	..	..	..	..	..	..	..	..	*9,532*	*7,872*	1	..	9,551	7,872	..	..
Kishangarh	..	..	..	..	..	..	..	..	..	..	..	..	..	..	..	..	..	..	..	..	*3,644*	*3,398*	2	3	3,642	3,395	..	..
Kotah	*503*	*500*	503	500	..	..	..	*1*	..	..	..	1	*158*	*86*	2	..	156	86	*735*	*796*	*21,126*	*18,344*	9	9	21,117	18,332	..	3
Kushalgarh (Chiefship)	*56*	*48*	56	48	..	..	..	..	..	..	..	..	*112*	*101*	..	..	112	101	..	..	*207*	*234*	..	..	207	234	..	..
Lawa (Estate)	..	..	..	..	..	..	..	..	..	..	..	..	..	..	..	..	..	..	..	..	*63*	*68*	1	..	62	62	..	..
Marwar	*125*	*110*	125	110	..	..	*20,337*	*17,328*	1	1	20,336	17,327	*128*	*110*	..	..	128	110	..	..	*66,975*	*66,689*	37	31	66,032	66,651	6	7
Mewar	*1,833*	*1,849*	1,833	1,849	..	..	*579*	*546*	..	..	579	546	*2,529*	*2,042*	..	..	2,520	2,042	*8,496*	*8,190*	*63,612*	*60,731*	19	15	63,618	60,715	5	1
Partabgarh	*54*	*68*	54	68	..	..	..	..	..	..	..	..	*263*	*237*	..	..	262	237	..	..	*1,670*	*1,495*	3	1	1,667	1,494	..	..
Shahpura (Chiefship)	..	..	..	..	..	..	..	..	..	..	..	..	..	..	..	..	..	..	*5*	*1*	*1,923*	*1,806*	35	31	1,888	1,775	..	..
Sirohi	*174*	*174*	174	174	..	..	..	..	..	..	..	..	*105*	*86*	..	..	105	86	..	..	*5,900*	*5,981*	1	..	5,899	5,981	..	..
Tonk	..	..	..	..	..	..	..	..	..	..	..	..	*55*	*51*	..	..	53	51	..	..	*8,696*	*7,609*	1	..	8,695	7,600	..	..
Ajmer-Merwara	*39*	*19*	39	19	..	..	*2*	*1*	1	..	1	1	*49*	*18*	..	..	42	18	..	..	*12,887*	*11,155*	221	151	12,659	11,000	3	3
Ajmer	*39*	*19*	39	19	..	..	..	..	..	..	..	..	*29*	*7*	..	..	29	7	..	..	*11,375*	*9,963*	203	136	11,165	9,823	3	3
Merwara	..	..	..	..	..	..	*2*	*1*	1	..	1	1	*13*	*11*	..	..	13	11	..	..	*1,512*	*1,192*	18	15	1,494	1,177	..	..

* Includes Āchāraj, Bohrā Nandwānis, Joshi.

TABLE XIII.—Caste, Tribe, or Race. Part II.—By States or Districts, and Religions—*contd.*

Province; and State or District.	*BRĀHMAN—*concld.* Musalman. M.	Musalman. F.	Sikh. M.	Sikh. F.	BULGARIAN. Jew. M.	Jew. F.	CANADIAN. Christian. M.	Christian. F.	CHĀKAR.† Total. M.	Total. F.	Arya. M.	Arya. F.	Hindu. M.	Hindu. F.	Jain. M.	Jain. F.	Musalman. M.	Musalman. F.	CHAMĀR.‡ Total. M.	Total. F.	Arya. M.	Arya. F.	Hindu. M.	Hindu. F.	Musalman. M.	Musalman. F.	Sikh. M.	Sikh. F.
1	147	148	149	150	151	152	153	154	155	156	157	158	159	160	161	162	163	164	165	166	167	168	169	170	171	172	173	174
Rajputana	1	..	14	5	*1*	..	..	..	*28,320*	*30,286*	13	13	28,189	30,106	23	34	96	131	*378,017*	*356,093*	21	16	377,898	355,960	48	59	50	38
Alwar	..	..	..	..	..	..	..	..	*978*	*1,065*	..	..	971	1,058	..	..	7	10	*43,537*	*41,890*	..	..	43,527	41,855	30	35	..	..
Banswara	..	..	..	..	..	..	..	..	*699*	*1,021*	..	..	699	1,021	..	..	..	..	*2,189*	*2,153*	..	..	2,189	2,158	..	..	..	..
Bharatpur	1	..	..	..	..	..	..	..	..	..	..	..	..	..	..	..	..	..	*48,863*	*44,886*	..	..	48,863	44,886	..	..	..	..
Bikaner	..	..	9	..	..	..	..	..	*2,082*	*2,089*	..	..	2,077	2,081	5	8	..	..	*34,196*	*30,541*	..	..	35,187	30,493	9	10	50	38
Bundi	..	..	..	..	..	..	..	..	..	..	..	..	..	..	..	..	..	..	*7,895*	*7,810*	..	..	7,895	7,840	..	..	..	..
Dholpur	..	..	5	5	..	..	..	..	*3,705*	*2,932*	..	..	3,703	2,932	..	..	..	..	*22,486*	*19,715*	..	..	22,486	19,715	..	..	..	..
Dungarpur	..	..	..	..	..	..	..	..	*2*	..	..	..	2	..	..	..	..	..	*2,402*	*2,375*	..	..	2,402	2,375	..	..	..	..
Jaipur	..	..	..	..	..	..	..	..	*1,523*	*1,460*	..	..	1,517	1,460	..	..	6	..	*115,755*	*109,774*	..	..	115,751	109,771	4	3	..	..
Jaisalmer	..	..	..	..	..	..	..	..	*1,318*	*1,228*	..	..	1,309	1,223	..	..	9	5	*414*	*405*	..	..	414	405	..	..	..	..
Jhalawar	..	..	..	..	..	..	..	..	*311*	*467*	..	..	310	463	1	4	..	..	*4,381*	*4,312*	..	..	4,381	4,312	..	..	..	..
Karauli	..	..	..	..	..	..	..	..	*364*	*604*	..	..	363	602	..	..	1	2	*11,738*	*10,595*	..	..	11,738	10,595	..	..	..	..
Kishangarh	..	..	..	..	..	..	..	..	*153*	*257*	..	..	153	257	..	..	..	..	*1,589*	*1,474*	..	..	1,589	1,474	..	..	..	..
Kotah	..	..	..	..	*1*	..	..	..	*1,465*	*1,950*	..	..	1,463	1,949	2	1	..	0	*34,359*	*33,942*	18	14	34,340	33,927	1	1	..	..
Kushalgarh (Chiefship)	..	..	..	..	..	..	..	..	..	..	..	..	..	..	..	..	..	..	*146*	*114*	..	..	146	144	..	..	..	..
Lawa (Estate)	..	..	..	..	..	..	..	..	..	..	..	..	..	..	..	..	..	..	*130*	*156*	..	..	130	156	..	..	..	..
Marwar	..	..	..	..	..	..	..	..	*1,473*	*1,530*	..	..	1,422	1,462	5	5	46	63	*3,772*	*3,388*	..	..	3,770	3,386	2	2	..	..
Mewar	..	..	..	..	..	..	..	..	*12,277*	*13,653*	1	1	12,246	13,609	9	16	21	32	*19,885*	*19,285*	..	..	19,883	19,279	2	6	..	..
Partabgarh	..	..	..	..	..	..	..	..	*4*	*19*	..	3	..	..	..	..	4	16	*1,546*	*1,543*	..	..	1,546	1,543	..	..	..	..
Shahpura (Chiefship)	..	..	..	..	..	..	..	..	*728*	*798*	12	9	714	786	..	..	2	3	*2,051*	*1,977*	..	..	2,051	1,977	..	..	..	..
Sirohi	..	..	..	..	..	..	..	..	*984*	*898*	..	..	984	898	..	..	..	..	*423*	*366*	..	..	423	364	..	2	..	..
Tonk	..	..	..	..	..	..	..	..	*256*	*307*	..	..	256	307	..	..	..	..	*19,240*	*19,327*	3	2	19,237	19,325	..	..	..	..
Ajmer-Merwara	..	..	4	1	..	..	*1*	..	*130*	*141*	..	..	129	141	..	..	..	..	*6,822*	*6,529*	4	..	6,817	6,529	1	..	..	..
Ajmer	..	..	4	1	..	..	*1*	..	*126*	*139*	..	..	126	139	..	..	..	..	*6,406*	*6,148*	4	..	6,401	6,148	1	..	..	..
Merwara	..	..	..	..	..	..	..	..	*3*	*2*	..	..	3	2	..	..	..	..	*416*	*381*	..	..	416	381	..	..	..	..

* Includes Ācharaj, Bohrā Nandwānis, Joshi. † Includes Chelā, Dāvadā, Golāpurab, Gulām, Hasuri, Khānezād, Pāsbān (Kotah), Pāswānis (Mewar), Vazir. ‡ Includes Jatiā, and Musalman Bols.

TABLE XIII.—Caste, Tribe, or Race. Part II.—By States or Districts, and Religions—*contd.*

Province; and State or District.	CHĀRAN.* Total. M.	Total. F.	Arya. M.	Arya. F.	Hindu. M.	Hindu. F.	Jain. M.	Jain. F.	CHHIPĀ.† Total. M.	Total. F.	Arya. M.	Arya. F.	Hindu. M.	Hindu. F.	Jain. M.	Jain. F.	Musalman. M.	Musalman. F.	Sikh. M.	Sikh. F.	CHINESE. Christian. M.	Christian. F.	CHRISTIAN (INDIAN). M.	CHRISTIAN (INDIAN). F.	DĀDUPANTHI. Hindu. M.	Hindu. F.	DĀKOT. Hindu. M.	Hindu. F.
1	175	176	177	178	179	180	181	182	183	184	185	186	187	188	189	190	191	192	193	194	195	196	197	198	199	200	201	202
Rajputana	*19,510*	*18,064*	10	..	19,499	18,064	1	..	*19,645*	*18,295*	..	..	15,912	14,956	1	..	3,714	3,324	18	15	1	..	*1,307*	*1,077*	*7,517*	*153*	*10,166*	*10,160*
Alwar	*136*	*118*	..	..	136	118	..	..	*1,081*	*980*	..	..	1,081	980	..	..	..	..	..	..	..	..	*21*	*20*	*37*	*3*	*982*	*395*
Banswara	*82*	*88*	..	..	82	88	..	..	*79*	*69*	..	..	79	69	..	..	..	..	..	..	..	..	..	..	..	..	..	..
Bharatpur	..	..	..	..	..	..	..	..	*531*	*467*	..	..	531	467	..	..	..	..	..	..	..	..	*292*	*224*	..	..	..	..
Bikaner	*2,117*	*1,762*	..	..	2,116	1,762	1	..	*2,060*	*1,748*	..	..	1,322	1,136	..	..	719	597	18	15	..	..	*76*	*44*	*48*	*3*	*1,517*	*1,498*
Bundi	*873*	*898*	..	..	873	898	..	..	*535*	*506*	..	..	535	506	..	..	..	..	..	..	..	..	..	..	*107*	*5*	*3*	*3*
Dholpur	..	..	..	..	..	..	..	..	*102*	*63*	..	..	95	57	..	..	7	6	..	..	..	..	*12*	*5*	..	..	..	..
Dungarpur	*93*	*116*	..	..	93	116	..	..	*164*	*171*	..	..	164	170	..	..	..	1	..	..	..	..	*1*	*1*	..	..	..	..
Jaipur	*2,502*	*2,646*	3	..	2,799	2,845	..	..	*5,168*	*4,626*	..	..	5,097	4,567	..	..	71	58	..	..	..	..	*307*	*308*	*6,983*	*68*	*4,017*	*4,161*
Jaisalmer	*482*	*408*	..	..	482	408	..	..	*7*	*8*	..	..	7	7	..	..	..	1	..	..	..	..	..	..	..	..	*135*	*139*
Jhalawar	*92*	*101*	..	..	92	101	..	..	*186*	*168*	..	..	186	168	..	..	..	..	..	..	..	..	*4*	*2*	..	..	*82*	*81*
Karauli	..	..	..	..	..	..	..	..	*308*	*262*	..	..	307	262	..	..	1	..	..	..	..	..	*14*	*13*	*4*	..	..	..
Kishangarh	*228*	*214*	..	..	228	214	..	..	*267*	*227*	..	..	164	144	..	..	103	83	..	..	..	..	*7*	*11*	*10*	*3*	*77*	*107*
Kotah	*2,136*	*2,197*	..	..	2,136	2,197	..	..	*1,926*	*1,806*	..	..	1,924	1,805	..	..	2	..	..	..	2	..	*241*	*211*	*210*	*66*	*62*	*53*
Kushalgarh (Chiefship)	*4*	*4*	..	..	4	4	..	..	*1*	..	..	..	1	..	..	..	..	..	..	..	..	..	..	..	..	..	..	..
Lawa (Estate)	..	..	..	..	..	..	..	..	*9*	*7*	..	..	9	7	..	..	..	..	..	..	..	..	..	..	*6*	..	..	..
Marwar	*8,311*	*7,379*	7	..	8,304	7,379	..	..	*3,614*	*3,307*	..	..	1,452	1,315	..	..	2,162	1 902	..	..	..	..	*154*	*130*	*22*	*1*	*2,118*	*2,128*
Mewar	*1,259*	*1,260*	..	..	1,259	1,260	..	..	*2,435*	*2,297*	..	..	1,654	1,778	1	..	580	519	..	..	..	..	*112*	*65*	*55*	*13*	*1,129*	*1,066*
Partabgarh	*42*	*41*	..	..	42	41	..	..	*15*	*12*	..	..	14	12	..	..	1	..	..	..	..	..	..	..	..	..	*6*	*7*
Shahpura (Chiefship)	*11*	*12*	..	..	11	12	..	..	*206*	*191*	..	..	180	172	..	..	26	19	..	..	..	..	..	..	*1*	..	*14*	*12*
Sirohi	*495*	*489*	..	..	495	489	..	..	*483*	*499*	..	..	455	459	..	..	28	40	..	..	..	..	*63*	*37*	..	..	*3*	*1*
Tonk	*347*	*332*	..	..	347	332	..	..	*468*	*883*	..	..	454	875	..	..	14	8	..	..	..	..	*3*	*6*	*34*	*2*	*21*	*9*
Ajmer-Merwara	*162*	*147*	3	..	164	147	1	..	*1,418*	*1,934*	1	..	972	830	..	..	442	404	3	..	..	..	*1,309*	*1,421*	*16*	*4*	*290*	*281*
Ajmer	*151*	*136*	3	..	147	136	1	..	*1,001*	*857*	1	..	940	811	..	..	57	46	3	..	..	..	*1,064*	*1,173*	*11*	..	*229*	*233*
Merwara	*17*	*11*	..	..	17	11	..	..	*417*	*377*	..	..	32	19	..	..	385	358	..	..	..	..	*245*	*248*	*6*	*4*	*70*	*48*

* Includes Bārot.

† Includes Hindu Nilgar and Rangrez.

TABLE XIII.—Caste, Tribe, or Race. Part II.—By States or Districts, and Religions—*contd.*

Province; and State or District.	Dângi.						Darogâ.										Darzi.										Deswâli.	
	Total.		Arya.		Hindu.		Total.		Arya.		Hindu.		Jain.		Musalman.		Total.		Arya.		Hindu.		Jain.		Musalman.		Musalman.	
	M.	F.	M.	F.	M.	F.	M.	F.	M.	F.	M.	F.	M.	F.	M.	F.	M.	F.	M.	F.	M.	F.	M.	F.	M.	F.	M.	F.
1	203	204	205	206	207	208	209	210	211	212	213	214	215	216	217	218	219	220	221	222	223	224	225	226	227	228	229	230
Rajputana	*19,557*	*18,543*	..	..	19,557	18,543	*57,658*	*61,256*	11	8	57,639	61,243	4	4	4	1	*93,000*	*22,134*	..	..	22,931	22,000	1	2	137	128	*3,497*	*3,372*
Alwar	..	..	..	..	..	..	*2,332*	*2,275*	..	..	2,332	2,274	..	..	..	1	*752*	*666*	..	..	748	662	..	..	4	4	..	..
Banswara	..	..	..	..	..	..	..	..	..	..	..	..	..	..	..	..	*497*	*499*	..	..	495	497	..	..	2	2	..	..
Bharatpur	..	..	..	..	..	..	*11*	*9*	..	..	11	9	..	..	..	..	*478*	*451*	..	..	477	448	..	..	1	3	..	..
Bikaner	..	..	..	..	..	..	*3,507*	*3,305*	..	..	3,501	3,302	2	3	4	..	*1,271*	*1,274*	..	..	1,270	1,274	..	..	1	..	..	..
Bundi	..	..	..	..	..	..	*1,667*	*1,993*	..	..	1,667	1,993	..	..	..	..	*357*	*345*	..	..	351	335	..	..	6	10	*132*	*148*
Dholpur	..	..	..	..	..	..	..	..	..	..	..	..	..	..	..	..	*313*	*256*	..	..	312	255	..	..	1	1	..	..
Dungarpur	..	..	..	..	..	..	..	..	..	..	..	..	..	..	..	..	*661*	*659*	..	..	661	659	..	..	..	..	..	..
Jaipur	*3*	*3*	..	..	3	3	*18,579*	*21,597*	..	..	18,570	21,597	..	..	..	..	*4,412*	*4,278*	..	..	4,354	4,243	..	..	58	35	*749*	*599*
Jaisalmer	..	..	..	..	..	..	..	..	..	..	..	..	..	..	..	..	*442*	*476*	..	..	442	476	..	..	..	..	..	..
Jhalawar	*22*	*20*	..	..	22	20	..	..	..	..	..	..	..	..	..	..	*377*	*352*	..	..	376	350	1	2	..	..	..	..
Karauli	..	..	..	..	..	..	..	..	..	..	..	..	..	..	..	..	*100*	*107*	..	..	43	37	..	..	57	70	..	..
Kishangarh	..	..	..	..	..	..	*974*	*929*	..	..	973	928	1	1	..	..	*197*	*242*	..	..	197	242	..	..	..	..	*391*	*414*
Kotah	*421*	*361*	..	..	421	361	*4*	*32*	..	..	4	32	..	..	..	..	*977*	*864*	..	..	976	864	..	..	1	..	*10*	*19*
Kushalgarh (Chiefship)	..	..	..	..	..	..	..	..	..	..	..	..	..	..	..	..	*35*	*30*	..	..	35	30	..	..	..	..	*7*	*4*
Lawa (Estate)	..	..	..	..	..	..	*68*	*83*	..	..	68	83	..	..	..	..	*5*	*5*	..	..	5	5	..	..	..	..	*4*	*4*
Marwar	..	..	..	..	..	..	*26,640*	*26,918*	11	8	26,629	26,910	..	..	..	..	*7,700*	*7,421*	..	..	7,696	7,415	..	..	4	6	*1,573*	*1,455*
Mewar	*15,509*	*15,000*	..	..	15,509	15,000	*3,852*	*4,086*	..	..	3,851	4,086	1	..	..	..	*3,150*	*2,993*	..	..	3,150	2,993	..	..	..	..	*53*	*58*
Partabgarh	*456*	*435*	..	..	456	435	..	..	..	..	..	..	..	..	..	..	*337*	*349*	..	..	337	340	..	..	..	..	*171*	*172*
Shahpura (Chiefship)	..	..	..	..	..	..	*10*	*16*	..	..	10	16	..	..	..	..	*108*	*98*	..	..	108	98	..	..	..	..	*10*	*7*
Sirohi	*2*	*2*	..	..	2	2	*14*	*13*	..	..	14	13	..	..	..	..	*178*	*127*	..	..	176	126	..	..	2	1	*4*	*4*
Tonk	*3,144*	*2,723*	..	..	3,144	2,722	..	..	..	..	..	..	..	..	..	..	*722*	*642*	..	..	722	642	..	..	..	..	*393*	*438*
Ajmer-Merwara	*2*	..	1	..	..	..	*4,550*	*4,403*	6	3	4,536	4,398	8	1	..	..	*1,226*	*1,024*	1	4	1,217	1,018	..	..	8	2	*1,413*	*1,036*
Ajmer	*1*	..	1	..	..	..	*4,349*	*4,205*	6	3	4,335	4,201	8	1	..	..	*1,032*	*873*	1	4	1,026	867	..	..	5	2	*1,411*	*1,036*
Merwara	..	..	..	..	..	..	*201*	*197*	..	..	201	197	..	..	..	..	*194*	*151*	..	..	191	151	..	..	3	..	*2*	..

TABLE XIII.—Caste, Tribe, or Race. Part II.—By States or Districts, and Religions—*contd.*

Province; and State or District.	DHĀKAR.								DHĀNAK (DHĀNUK, DHĀNKĀ OR DHĀNKIĀ.)								DHED.		DHOBI.					
	Total.		Arya.		Hindu.		Musalman.		Total.		Animist.		Hindu.		Musalman.		Hindu.		Total.		Hindu.		Musalman.	
	M.	F.	M.	F.	M.	F.	M.	F.	M.	F.	M.	F.	M.	F.	M.	F.	M.	F.	M.	F.	M.	F.	M.	F.
1	231	232	233	234	235	236	237	238	239	240	241	242	243	244	245	246	247	248	249	250	251	252	253	254
Rajputana	*47,669*	*45,703*	1	..	47,690	45,700	1	3	*19,822*	*12,699*	3	2	12,780	12,686	20	11	*8,826*	*8,004*	*23,348*	*22,453*	20,305	19,394	3,043	3,059
Alwar	*149*	*137*	..	..	149	137	..	..	*2,497*	*2,674*	..	..	2,485	2,664	12	10	..	..	*2,371*	*2,388*	1,951	1,946	420	442
Banswara	..	..	..	..	..	..	..	..	..	..	..	..	..	..	..	..	..	..	*33*	*34*	33	34	..	..
Bharatpur	*2,505*	*2,386*	..	..	2,505	2,386	..	..	*15*	*18*	..	..	15	18	..	..	..	..	*1,811*	*1,665*	1,492	1,402	319	263
Bikaner	*3*	..	..	..	3	..	..	..	*2,698*	*2,421*	..	..	2,698	2,421	..	..	..	..	*833*	*782*	208	205	625	577
Bundi	*4,025*	*3,932*	..	..	4,025	3,932	..	..	..	..	..	..	..	..	..	..	..	..	*610*	*531*	610	531	..	..
Dholpur	..	..	..	..	..	..	..	..	*109*	*112*	..	..	109	112	..	..	..	..	*1,907*	*1,751*	1,898	1,744	9	7
Dungarpur	..	..	..	..	..	..	..	..	..	..	..	..	..	..	..	..	..	..	*24*	*34*	24	34	..	..
Jaipur	*2,036*	*1,860*	..	..	2,036	1,860	..	..	*7,096*	*7,051*	3	2	7,085	7,048	8	1	*1*	*1*	*6,260*	*6,240*	5,228	5,106	1,032	1,134
Jaisalmer	..	..	..	..	..	..	..	..	..	..	..	..	..	..	..	..	..	..	*68*	*73*	..	..	68	73
Jhalawar	*747*	*691*	..	..	747	691	..	..	*20*	*27*	..	..	20	27	..	..	..	..	*220*	*222*	220	222	..	..
Karauli	*22*	..	..	..	22	..	..	..	*29*	*35*	..	..	29	33	..	..	..	..	*503*	*442*	503	442	..	..
Kishangarh	*474*	*429*	..	..	474	429	..	..	*34*	*19*	..	..	34	19	..	..	..	..	*212*	*185*	212	185	..	..
Kotah	*21,945*	*21,202*	..	..	21,944	21,199	1	3	*6*	*6*	..	..	6	6	..	..	..	*1*	*2,571*	*2,342*	2,564	2,338	7	4
Kushalgarh (Chiefship)	..	..	..	..	..	..	..	..	..	..	..	..	..	..	..	..	..	..	*10*	*16*	10	16	..	..
Lawa (Estate)	..	..	..	..	..	..	..	..	..	..	..	..	..	..	..	..	..	..	*10*	*8*	10	8	..	..
Marwar	..	..	..	..	..	..	..	..	*154*	*177*	..	..	154	177	..	..	*1*	..	*1,748*	*1,683*	1,213	1,147	535	536
Mewar	*12,154*	*11,670*	..	..	12,154	11,670	..	..	*19*	*23*	..	..	19	23	..	..	*123*	*109*	*2,350*	*2,134*	2,346	2,132	4	2
Partabgarh	*101*	*100*	..	..	101	100	..	..	..	..	..	..	..	..	..	..	..	..	*237*	*229*	237	229	..	..
Shahpura (Chiefship)	*186*	*187*	*1*	..	185	187	..	..	*23*	*22*	..	..	23	22	..	..	..	..	*182*	*157*	182	157	..	..
Sirohi	..	..	..	..	..	..	..	..	*43*	*38*	..	..	43	38	..	..	*8,701*	*7,893*	*163*	*137*	152	129	11	8
Tonk	*3,315*	*3,109*	..	..	3,315	3,109	..	..	*79*	*76*	..	..	79	76	..	..	..	..	*1,230*	*1,200*	1,217	1,187	13	13
Ajmer-Merwara	*321*	*305*	..	..	321	305	..	..	*741*	*630*	2	3	739	627	..	..	*6*	*7*	*1,479*	*1,403*	1,278	1,197	201	206
Ajmer	*281*	*266*	..	..	281	266	..	..	*728*	*607*	2	3	726	604	..	..	*6*	*7*	*1,301*	*1,248*	1,106	1,049	195	199
Merwara	*40*	*39*	..	..	40	39	..	..	*13*	*23*	..	..	13	23	..	..	..	..	*178*	*155*	172	148	6	7

TABLE XIII.—Caste, Tribe, or Race. Part II.—By States or Districts, and Religions—*contd.*

Province; and State or District.	Dholi.*						English.						European (unspecified).		Fakir.						French.		Gadaria (Gādri).					
	Total.		Animist.		Hindu.		Total.		Christian.		Jew.		Christian.		Total.		Hindu.		Musalman.		Christian.		Total.		Hindu.		Musalman.	
	M.	F.	M.	F.	M.	F.	M.	F.	M.	F.	M.	F.	M.	F.	M.	F.	M.	F.	M.	F.	M.	F.	M.	F.	M.	F.	M.	F.
1	255	256	257	258	259	260	261	262	263	264	265	266	267	268	269	270	271	272	273	274	275	276	277	278	279	280	281	282
Rajputana	16,127	14,781	4	3	16,123	14,778	490	298	490	298	..	..	14	16	29,045	26,211	150	116	28,895	26,095	25	10	33,743	31,383	33,741	31,396	2	..
Alwar	27	41	..	..	27	41	12	7	12	7	..	..	..	..	9,523	8,665	35	24	9,488	8,641	..	..	51	43	51	43	..	..
Banswara	403	392	..	..	403	392	..	..	..	..	..	..	..	..	66	43	3	2	63	41	..	..	629	671	629	671	..	..
Bharatpur	49	33	..	..	49	33	4	9	4	9	..	..	..	..	4,905	4,332	..	..	4,905	4,332	..	..	2,799	2,361	2,799	2,361	..	..
Bikaner	1,231	1,121	..	..	1,231	1,121	10	10	10	10	..	..	..	..	1,092	970	21	9	1,071	961	..	..	9	3	7	3	2	..
Bundi	51	39	..	..	51	39	..	..	..	..	..	..	..	..	380	366	..	..	380	366	..	..	1	..	1	..	..	..
Dholpur	1	..	..	..	1	..	3	3	3	3	..	..	..	..	346	286	2	6	344	280	1	1	3,501	3,146	3,501	3,146	..	..
Dungarpur	97	86	4	3	93	83	..	..	..	..	..	..	..	..	40	40	..	..	40	40	..	..	173	227	173	227	..	..
Jaipur	1,160	943	..	..	1,160	943	130	100	130	100	..	..	12	13	5,723	5,454	45	40	5,678	5,414	14	6	28	20	28	20	..	..
Jaisalmer	127	103	..	..	127	103	..	..	..	..	..	..	..	..	19	6	..	..	19	6	..	..	..	..	..	..	..	..
Jhalawar	335	310	..	..	335	310	1	1	1	1	..	..	..	..	80	67	..	..	80	67	6	1	112	108	112	108	..	..
Karauli	43	15	..	..	43	15	1	..	1	..	..	..	..	..	500	403	..	1	500	402	..	..	2	1	2	1	..	..
Kishangarh	251	238	..	..	251	238	..	..	..	..	..	..	..	..	161	142	..	..	161	142	..	..	2	..	2	..	..	..
Kotah	158	142	..	..	158	142	10	10	10	10	..	..	2	2	1,702	1,508	6	3	1,696	1,505	..	..	1,271	1,311	1,271	1,311	..	..
Kushalgarh (Chiefship)	32	31	..	..	32	31	..	..	..	..	..	..	..	..	3	3	..	..	3	3	..	..	22	21	22	21	..	..
Lawa (Estate)	1	..	..	..	1	..	..	..	..	..	..	..	..	..	6	4	..	..	6	4	..	..	..	..	..	..	..	..
Marwar	5,577	5,100	..	..	5,577	5,100	27	19	27	19	..	..	..	..	2,375	2,029	29	14	2,346	2,015	2	1	17	15	17	15	..	..
Mewar	5,244	5,008	..	..	5,244	5,008	12	5	12	5	..	..	..	..	1,128	960	7	9	1,121	951	..	..	22,118	20,694	22,118	20,694	..	..
Partabgarh	183	196	..	..	183	196	..	..	..	..	..	..	..	..	44	41	..	..	44	41	..	..	708	694	708	694	..	..
Shahpura (Chiefship)	163	148	..	..	163	148	..	..	..	..	..	..	..	..	113	63	..	..	113	63	..	..	621	570	621	570	..	..
Sirohi	578	489	..	..	578	489	270	134	270	134	..	..	..	1	65	50	1	2	64	48	2	1	10	4	10	4	..	..
Tonk	419	337	..	..	419	337	1	..	1	..	..	..	..	..	780	778	7	6	773	772	..	..	1,669	1,496	1,669	1,496	..	..
Ajmer-Merwara	2,766	2,612	..	..	2,766	2,612	1,107	195	1,105	195	2	..	100	45	921	830	8	24	913	806	26	7	24	14	24	14	..	..
Ajmer	1,720	1,636	..	..	1,720	1,636	1,102	194	1,100	194	2	..	97	41	756	654	1	8	755	646	26	7	23	13	23	13	..	..
Merwara	1,046	976	..	..	1,046	976	5	1	5	1	..	..	3	4	165	176	7	16	158	160	..	..	1	1	1	1	..	..

*Includes Hindu Darhi, Dhadi, Mirasi.

TABLE XIII.—Caste, Tribe, or Race. Part II.—By States or Districts, and Religions—*contd.*

Province; and State or District.	Garodā (Gārodiā.)* Hindu.		German. Christian.		Ghānchā (Ghāchhi, Ghānchi). Total.		Arya.		Hindu.		Jain.		Musalman.		Goanese. Christian.		Gosāin. Total.		Arya.		Hindu.		Musalman.		Grassiā. Total.		Animist.		Hindu.		Greek. Christian.	
	M.	F.	M.	F.	M.	F.	M.	F.	M.	F.	M.	F.	M.	F.	M.	F.	M.	F.	M.	F.	M.	F.	M.	F.	M.	F.	M.	F.	M.	F.	M.	F.
1	283	284	285	286	287	288	289	290	291	292	293	294	295	296	297	298	299	300	301	302	303	304	305	306	307	308	309	310	311	312	313	314
Rajputana	5,735	5,108	4	9	10,212	9,140	2	2	9,727	8,730	1	..	482	408	191	49	15,418	12,388	9	11	15,409	12,373	..	4	8,918	8,301	587	564	8,331	7,937	..	..
Alwar	2	3	..	..	..	..	..	..	..	..	..	..	..	..	4	..	389	352	..	..	389	352	..	..	..	..	..	..	..	..	..	..
Banswara	..	..	..	..	..	..	..	..	..	..	..	..	..	..	..	..	30	33	..	..	30	33	..	..	..	..	..	..	..	..	..	..
Bharatpur	..	..	..	..	..	..	..	..	..	..	..	..	..	..	3	3	191	144	..	..	191	144	..	..	..	..	..	..	..	..	..	..
Bikaner	192	177	..	..	..	..	..	..	..	..	..	..	..	..	7	..	2,079	1,525	..	..	2,079	1,525	..	..	..	..	..	..	..	..	..	..
Bundi	..	..	..	..	..	..	..	..	..	..	..	..	..	..	..	..	279	255	..	..	279	255	..	..	..	..	..	..	..	..	..	..
Dholpur	..	..	..	..	..	..	..	..	..	..	..	..	..	..	1	..	1,486	1,155	..	..	1,486	1,155	..	..	..	..	..	..	..	..	..	..
Dungarpur	..	..	..	..	477	407	..	..	..	..	..	..	477	407	..	..	121	102	..	..	121	102	..	..	..	..	..	..	..	..	..	..
Jaipur	175	146	2	5	1	..	..	..	1	..	..	..	..	..	19	7	2,130	1,572	..	..	2,130	1,568	..	4	..	..	..	..	..	..	..	..
Jaisalmer	263	276	..	..	..	..	..	..	..	..	..	..	..	..	..	..	..	..	..	..	..	..	..	..	..	..	..	..	..	..	..	..
Jhalawar	..	..	..	2	..	..	..	..	..	..	..	..	..	..	5	1	317	289	8	9	300	280	..	..	..	..	..	..	..	..	..	..
Karauli	..	..	..	..	..	..	..	..	..	..	..	..	..	..	..	..	130	69	..	..	130	69	..	..	..	..	..	..	..	..	..	..
Kishangarh	13	7	..	..	..	..	..	..	..	..	..	..	..	..	1	4	167	104	..	..	167	104	..	..	..	..	..	..	..	..	..	..
Kotah	129	84	..	..	..	..	..	..	..	..	..	..	..	..	7	..	1,380	1,114	..	..	1,380	1,114	..	..	..	..	..	..	..	..	..	..
Kushalgarh (Chiefship)	3	2	..	..	..	..	..	..	..	..	..	..	..	..	..	..	6	2	..	..	6	2	..	..	..	..	..	..	..	..	..	..
Lawa (Estate)	..	..	..	..	..	..	..	..	..	..	..	..	..	..	..	..	..	1	..	..	..	1	..	..	..	..	..	..	..	..	..	..
Marwar	3,986	3,499	..	1	6,909	6,318	2	2	6,907	6,316	..	..	..	..	8	5	2,320	1,859	1	2	2,319	1,857	..	..	1,468	1,480	159	140	1,309	1,340	..	..
Mewar	530	518	..	..	185	134	..	..	180	134	..	..	5	..	17	3	3,539	3,071	..	..	3,539	3,071	..	..	1,807	1,669	289	286	1,518	1,373	..	..
Partabgarh	..	..	..	..	..	..	..	..	..	..	..	..	..	..	..	..	86	91	..	..	86	91	..	..	..	..	..	..	..	..	..	..
Shahpura (Chiefship)	2	..	..	..	..	..	..	..	..	..	..	..	..	..	1	..	131	111	..	..	131	111	..	..	..	..	..	..	..	..	..	..
Sirohi	460	396	2	1	2,640	2,281	..	..	2,639	2,280	1	..	..	1	47	19	92	79	..	..	92	79	..	..	5,643	5,362	139	138	5,504	5,224	..	..
Tonk	..	..	..	..	..	..	..	..	..	..	..	..	..	..	1	..	548	460	..	..	542	460	..	..	..	..	..	..	..	..	..	..
Ajmer-Merwara	47	44	1	..	1	3	..	..	1	2	..	..	..	..	168	69	478	425	..	..	477	425	1	..	..	..	..	..	..	..	1	..
Ajmer	47	44	1	..	1	..	..	..	1	..	..	..	..	..	166	69	416	382	..	..	415	382	1	..	..	..	..	..	..	..	..	..
Merwara	..	..	..	..	..	2	..	..	..	2	..	..	..	..	2	..	62	43	..	..	62	43	..	..	..	..	..	..	..	..	1	..

*Includes Gurdā and Gurrāh.

TABLE XIII.—CASTE, TRIBE, OR RACE. PART II.—BY STATES OR DISTRICTS, AND RELIGIONS—*contd.*

Province; and State or District.	GUJAR.* Total. M.	F.	Animist. M.	F.	Arya. M.	F.	Hindu. M.	F.	Jain. M.	F.	IRISH. Christian. M.	F.	ITALIAN. Christian. M.	F.	JAPANESE. Buddhist. M.	F.
1	315	316	317	318	319	320	321	322	323	324	325	326	327	328	329	330
Rajputana	*271,188*	*228,858*	1	1	12	5	271,172	228,851	3	1	*64*	*39*	*1*	..	*1*	..
Alwar	*24,082*	*21,321*	..	..	..	..	24,082	21,321	..	..	3	..	..	..	..	..
Banswara	*179*	*180*	..	..	..	..	179	180	..	..	..	..	..	..	..	..
Bharatpur	*23,899*	*18,784*	..	..	2	..	23,897	18,784	..	..	*1*	..	..	..	..	..
Bikaner	*826*	*592*	..	..	..	..	826	592	..	..	..	..	..	..	..	..
Bundi	*13,170*	*11,553*	..	..	..	..	13,169	11,552	1	1	..	..	..	..	..	..
Dholpur	*11,722*	*8,244*	..	..	..	..	11,722	8,244	..	..	*4*	..	..	..	..	..
Dungarpur	*3*	*1*	..	..	..	..	3	1	..	..	..	..	..	..	..	..
Jaipur	*101,916*	*87,038*	1	1	..	..	101,915	87,037	..	..	*19*	*6*	*1*	..	..	..
Jaisalmer	..	..	..	..	..	..	..	..	..	..	..	..	..	..	..	..
Jhalawar	*1,981*	*1,802*	..	..	..	..	1,981	1,802	..	..	..	..	..	..	..	..
Karauli	*8,588*	*5,788*	..	..	..	..	8,588	5,788	..	..	..	..	..	..	..	..
Kishangarh	*3,624*	*3,112*	..	..	..	..	3,624	3,112	..	..	..	..	..	..	..	..
Kotah	*20,744*	*18,219*	..	..	..	..	20,744	18,219	..	..	..	..	..	..	..	..
Kushalgarh (Chiefship)	..	..	..	..	..	..	..	..	..	..	..	..	..	..	*1*	..
Lawa (Estate)	*122*	*130*	..	..	..	..	122	130	..	..	..	..	..	..	..	..
Marwar	*11,778*	*10,141*	..	..	..	..	11,778	10,141	..	..	*7*	*8*	..	..	..	..
Mewar	*36,060*	*32,348*	..	..	..	..	36,058	32,348	2	..	*5*	*6*	..	..	..	..
Partabgarh	*358*	*369*	..	..	..	..	358	369	..	..	..	..	..	..	..	..
Shahpura (Chiefship)	*2,267*	*2,005*	..	..	10	5	2,257	2,000	..	..	..	..	..	..	..	..
Sirohi	*133*	*98*	..	..	..	..	133	98	..	..	*24*	*12*	..	..	..	..
Tonk	*7,936*	*7,064*	..	..	..	..	7,936	7,064	..	..	*1*	..	..	..	..	..
Ajmer-Merwara	*18,609*	*16,450*	..	..	9	4	18,600	16,446	..	..	*70*	*35*	..	..	..	..
Ajmer	*17,574*	*15,562*	..	..	8	1	17,566	15,561	..	..	*70*	*35*	..	..	..	..
Merwara	*1,035*	*888*	..	..	1	3	1,034	885	..	..	..	..	..	..	..	..

Province; and State or District.	JAT. Total. M.	F.	Arya. M.	F.	Hindu. M.	F.	Jain. M.	F.	Musalman. M.	F.	Sikh. M.	F.	JEW. Total. M.	F.	Christian. M.	F.	Jewish. M.	F.
1	331	332	333	334	335	336	337	338	339	340	341	342	343	344	345	346	347	348
Rajputana	*501,616*	*426,870*	18	8	497,824	424,677	13	6	70	61	3,691	2,118	*15*	*16*	..	1	15	15
Alwar	*18,701*	*15,995*	..	..	18,699	15,994	..	..	..	..	2	1	..	..	..	..	..	..
Banswara	*3*	*2*	..	..	2	2	..	..	..	..	1	..	..	..	..	..	..	..
Bharatpur	*46,199*	*35,643*	10	6	46,165	35,619	..	..	..	..	24	18	..	..	..	..	..	..
Bikaner	*87,293*	*71,451*	..	..	83,761	69,430	9	4	57	53	3,466	1,964	..	..	..	..	..	6
Bundi	*1,140*	*1,002*	..	..	1,139	1,002	..	..	..	..	1	..	..	..	..	..	..	..
Dholpur	*1,590*	*1,100*	..	..	1,576	1,088	..	..	..	..	14	12	..	..	..	..	..	..
Dungarpur	*1*	..	..	..	1	..	..	..	..	..	..	..	..	..	..	..	..	..
Jaipur	*153,407*	*131,564*	..	..	153,402	131,562	..	..	5	2	..	..	*2*	*4*	..	1	2	3
Jaisalmer	*225*	*216*	..	..	225	215	..	..	..	1	..	..	..	..	..	..	..	..
Jhalawar	*218*	*180*	2	..	187	160	..	..	..	..	29	20	..	..	..	..	..	..
Karauli	*445*	*376*	..	..	445	376	..	..	..	..	..	..	..	..	..	..	..	..
Kishangarh	*8,252*	*7,077*	..	..	8,248	7,077	..	..	..	..	4	..	..	..	..	..	..	..
Kotah	*2,191*	*1,845*	..	..	2,110	1,758	..	1	..	..	81	86	..	..	..	..	..	..
Kushalgarh (Chiefship)	*2*	*2*	..	..	2	2	..	..	..	..	..	..	..	..	..	..	..	..
Lawa (Estate)	*189*	*194*	..	..	189	194	..	..	..	..	..	..	..	..	..	..	..	..
Marwar	*138,258*	*119,589*	6	2	138,227	119,577	4	1	8	5	13	4	*1*	..	..	..	1	..
Mewar	*36,297*	*33,972*	..	..	36,294	33,969	..	..	..	..	3	3	..	..	..	..	..	..
Partabgarh	*83*	*85*	..	..	83	85	..	..	..	..	..	..	..	..	..	..	..	..
Shahpura (Chiefship)	*1,984*	*1,906*	..	..	1,984	1,906	..	..	..	..	..	..	..	..	..	..	..	..
Sirohi	*88*	*30*	..	..	35	23	..	..	..	..	53	7	*12*	*12*	..	..	12	12
Tonk	*5,051*	*4,641*	..	..	5,051	4,638	..	..	..	..	..	3	..	..	..	..	..	..
Ajmer-Merwara	*16,526*	*13,971*	7	2	15,850	13,881	2	..	3	1	664	87	*12*	*13*	..	..	12	13
Ajmer	*15,775*	*13,398*	6	2	15,100	13,308	2	..	3	1	664	87	*12*	*13*	..	..	12	13
Merwara	*751*	*573*	1	..	750	573	..	..	..	..	..	..	..	..	..	..	..	..

* Includes Hindu Ghosi.

TABLE XIII.—Caste, Tribe, or Race. Part II.—By States or Districts, and Religions—*contd.*

JOGI.*

Province; and State or District.	Total M.	Total F.	Animist M.	Animist F.	Arya M.	Arya F.	Hindu M.	Hindu F.	Musalman M.	Musalman F.
1	349	350	351	352	353	354	355	356	357	358
Rajputana	*33,317*	*31,827*	5	2	3	2	34,133	30,771	1,176	1,052
Alwar	*4,372*	*4,027*	..	..	3	2	3,525	3,272	844	753
Banswara	*921*	*939*	..	..	..	..	921	939	..	..
Bharatpur	*2,019*	*1,742*	..	..	..	..	1,726	1,484	293	258
Bikaner	*1,384*	*1,096*	..	..	..	..	1,383	1,096	1	..
Bundi	*435*	*465*	..	..	..	..	433	465	..	..
Dholpur	*72*	*50*	..	..	..	..	72	50	..	..
Dungarpur	*779*	*851*	..	..	..	..	779	851	..	..
Jaipur	*12,269*	*10,877*	..	..	..	..	12,240	10,842	20	35
Jaisalmer	*5*	*2*	5	2	..	..	..	..	..	..
Jhalawar	*262*	*212*	..	..	..	..	262	212	..	..
Karauli	*867*	*794*	..	..	..	..	867	794	..	..
Kishangarh	*367*	*335*	..	..	..	..	367	335	..	..
Kotah	*2,654*	*2,435*	..	..	..	..	2,647	2,429	7	6
Kushalgarh (Chiefship)	*12*	*15*	..	..	..	..	12	15	..	..
Lawa (Estate)	*2*	*1*	..	..	..	..	2	1	..	..
Marwar	*4,001*	*3,460*	..	..	..	..	3,999	3,460	2	..
Mewar	*3,765*	*3,457*	..	..	..	..	3,765	3,457	..	..
Partabgarh	*107*	*103*	..	..	..	..	107	103	..	..
Shahpura (Chiefship)	*68*	*70*	..	..	..	..	68	70	..	..
Sirohi	*191*	*168*	..	..	..	..	191	168	..	..
Tonk	*765*	*719*	..	..	..	..	765	719	..	..
Ajmer-Merwara	*1,381*	*1,153*	..	..	1	..	1,380	1,153	..	..
Ajmer	*1,031*	*859*	..	..	1	..	1,030	859	..	..
Merwara	*350*	*294*	..	..	..	..	350	294	..	..

JULĀHĀ.†

Province; and State or District.	Total M.	Total F.	Hindu M.	Hindu F.	Musalman M.	Musalman F.
1	359	360	361	362	363	364
Rajputana	*9,478*	*8,833*	143	93	9,335	8,762
Alwar	*850*	*782*	43	27	807	725
Banswara	..	..	..	..	..	..
Bharatpur	*361*	*334*	9	3	352	331
Bikaner	*123*	*92*	5	2	118	90
Bundi	*791*	*759*	3	1	788	758
Dholpur	*24*	*14*	..	..	24	14
Dungarpur	..	..	..	..	..	..
Jaipur	*1,458*	*1,481*	41	34	1,417	1,447
Jaisalmer	*175*	*164*	..	..	175	164
Jhalawar	*131*	*131*	..	..	131	131
Karauli	*49*	*43*	..	..	49	43
Kishangarh	*106*	*75*	2	1	104	74
Kotah	*3,243*	*3,083*	..	..	3,243	3,083
Kushalgarh (Chiefship)	*5*	*7*	..	..	5	7
Lawa (Estate)	..	..	..	..	..	..
Marwar	*921*	*765*	5	1	916	764
Mewar	*682*	*698*	4	7	678	691
Partabgarh	*3*	*1*	..	..	3	1
Shahpura (Chiefship)	*7*	*7*	..	..	7	7
Sirohi	*117*	*63*	31	16	86	46
Tonk	*432*	*387*	..	1	432	386
Ajmer-Merwara	*568*	*528*	3	2	565	526
Ajmer	*479*	*451*	3	2	476	449
Merwara	*89*	*77*	..	..	89	77

KĀCCHI.

Province; and State or District.	Total M.	Total F.	Arya M.	Arya F.	Hindu M.	Hindu F.	Musalman M.	Musalman F.
1	365	366	367	368	369	370	371	372
Rajputana	*31,766*	*28,900*	5	4	31,734	28,896	27	..
Alwar	*5*	*4*	..	..	5	4	..	..
Banswara	..	..	..	..	..	..	..	..
Bharatpur	*3,342*	*2,896*	..	..	3,342	2,896	..	..
Bikaner	..	..	..	..	..	..	..	..
Bundi	*735*	*737*	..	..	735	737	..	..
Dholpur	*12,960*	*11,354*	..	..	12,960	11,354	..	..
Dungarpur	..	..	..	..	..	..	..	..
Jaipur	*555*	*562*	2	1	553	561	..	..
Jaisalmer	..	..	..	..	..	..	..	..
Jhalawar	*75*	*74*	..	..	75	74	..	..
Karauli	*5,503*	*4,692*	..	..	5,503	4,692	..	..
Kishangarh	*1*	..	..	..	1	..	..	..
Kotah	*4,332*	*4,113*	1	..	4,304	4,113	27	..
Kushalgarh (Chiefship)	..	..	..	..	..	..	..	..
Lawa (Estate)	*1*	*1*	..	..	1	1	..	..
Marwar	*9*	*6*	..	..	9	6	..	..
Mewar	*77*	*60*	..	..	77	60	..	..
Partabgarh	..	..	..	..	..	..	..	..
Shahpura (Chiefship)	..	..	..	..	..	..	..	..
Sirohi	*4*	*2*	..	..	4	2	..	..
Tonk	*4,167*	*4,399*	2	3	4,165	4,396	..	..
Ajmer-Merwara	*41*	*36*	..	..	41	36	..	..
Ajmer	*41*	*36*	..	..	41	36	..	..
Merwara	..	..	..	..	..	..	..	..

KAHĀR.

Province; and State or District.	Total M.	Total F.	Arya M.	Arya F.	Hindu M.	Hindu F.
1	373	374	375	376	377	378
Rajputana	*7,067*	*7,197*	2	..	7,065	7,196
Alwar	*415*	*392*	..	..	415	392
Banswara	..	..	..	..	..	..
Bharatpur	*1,332*	*1,064*	..	..	1,332	1,064
Bikaner	*124*	*125*	1	..	123	125
Bundi	*116*	*152*	..	..	116	152
Dholpur	*1,122*	*1,004*	..	..	1,118	1,003
Dungarpur	..	..	..	..	..	..
Jaipur	*1,116*	*1,032*	1	..	1,115	1,032
Jaisalmer	..	..	..	..	..	..
Jhalawar	*60*	*69*	..	..	60	60
Karauli	*509*	*425*	..	..	509	425
Kishangarh	*5*	*2*	..	..	5	2
Kotah	*1,664*	*1,580*	..	..	1,663	1,580
Kushalgarh (Chiefship)	..	..	..	..	..	..
Lawa (Estate)	*1*	..	..	..	1	..
Marwar	*34*	*11*	..	..	34	11
Mewar	*309*	*356*	..	..	309	356
Partabgarh	..	..	..	..	..	..
Shahpura (Chiefship)	*219*	*199*	..	..	219	199
Sirohi	*16*	*6*	..	..	16	6
Tonk	*925*	*781*	..	..	925	781
Ajmer-Merwara	*1,580*	*1,463*	..	1	1,579	1,462
Ajmer	*1,562*	*1,452*	..	1	1,561	1,451
Merwara	*15*	*11*	..	..	18	11

* Includes Nath. † Includes Momin.

TABLE XIII.—CASTE, TRIBE, OR RACE. PART II.—BY STATES OR DISTRICTS, AND RELIGIONS—*contd.*

Province; and State or District.	KAHĀR—*contd.*				KĀIMKHĀNI		KALĀL.												*KANDERĀ (KARERĀ).		KASĀI†		KĀYASTHA.					
	MUSALMAN.		SIKH.		MUSALMAN.		TOTAL.		ARYA.		HINDU.		JAIN.		MUSALMAN.		SIKH.		HINDU.		MUSALMAN.		TOTAL.		ARYA.		BRAHMO.	
	M.	F.	M.	F.	M.	F.	M.	F.	M.	F.	M.	F.	M.	F.	M.	F.	M.	F.	M.	F.	M.	F.	M.	F.	M.	F.	M.	F.
1	379	380	381	382	383	384	385	386	387	388	389	390	391	392	393	394	395	396	397	398	399	400	401	402	403	404	405	406
Rajputana	1	..	4	1	*14,834*	*13,516*	*20,334*	*19,526*	3	..	18,519	17,845	2	3	1,808	1,672	2	7	*4,434*	*4,195*	*15,006*	*14,394*	*12,853*	*10,757*	157	112	39	38
Alwar	..	..	..	..	*128*	*36*	*1,121*	*1,045*	..	..	1,127	1,044	..	..	..	1	..	..	*324*	*285*	*2,085*	*1,847*	*717*	*621*	1	..	..	..
Banswara	..	..	..	..	..	..	*1,276*	*1,396*	..	..	1,276	1,396	..	..	..	..	..	..	..	..	*3*	*3*	*25*	*18*	..	..	..	..
Bharatpur	..	..	..	..	*3*	*4*	*416*	*376*	3	..	410	376	..	..	3	..	..	..	*838*	*729*	*1,745*	*1,586*	*789*	*640*	44	46	3	5
Bikaner	..	..	..	..	*3,429*	*2,766*	*772*	*663*	..	..	164	136	..	..	606	520	2	7	..	..	*2,295*	*2,063*	*260*	*151*	5	..	..	..
Bundi	..	..	..	..	*5*	*3*	*536*	*522*	..	..	536	522	..	..	..	..	..	..	*134*	*133*	*1*	*1*	*233*	*195*	..	..	..	..
Dholpur	..	..	4	1	..	..	*143*	*121*	..	..	143	121	..	..	..	..	..	..	*474*	*411*	*18*	*17*	*1,327*	*1,030*	1	..	..	..
Dungarpur	..	..	..	..	..	..	*1,231*	*1,290*	..	..	1,225	1,278	..	..	5	12	..	..	..	..	..	..	*8*	*10*	1	..	..	..
Jaipur	..	..	..	..	*7,022*	*6,611*	*3,816*	*2,982*	..	..	2,364	2,144	..	..	851	838	..	..	*1,452*	*1,471*	*4,659*	*4,389*	*3,180*	*3,090*	34	17	3	3
Jaisalmer	..	..	..	..	..	..	*1*	*1*	..	..	1	1	..	..	..	..	..	..	..	..	*29*	*24*	*1*	..	..	..	..	..
Jhalawar	..	..	..	..	..	..	*90*	*97*	..	..	90	97	..	..	..	..	..	..	*2*	*5*	*48*	*54*	*311*	*280*	7	10	..	..
Karauli	..	..	..	..	..	..	*82*	*69*	..	..	82	69	..	..	..	..	..	..	*318*	*266*	*167*	*151*	*92*	*57*	3	3	..	..
Kishangarh	..	..	..	..	*200*	*169*	*172*	*146*	..	..	161	137	..	..	11	9	..	..	*1*	*5*	*5*	*5*	*158*	*134*	1	..	..	..
Kotah	1	..	..	..	*6*	*3*	*2,365*	*2,311*	..	..	2,363	2,309	2	2	..	..	..	..	*738*	*726*	*321*	*324*	*1,068*	*858*	40	23	..	..
Kushalgarh (Chiefship)	..	..	..	..	..	..	*155*	*130*	..	..	155	130	..	..	..	..	..	..	..	..	..	..	*13*	*15*	..	..	..	..
Lawa (Estate)	..	..	..	..	..	..	*2*	*2*	..	..	2	2	..	..	..	..	..	..	..	..	..	..	..	..	..	..	..	..
Marwar	..	..	..	..	*3,299*	*3,245*	*1,988*	*1,759*	..	..	1,656	1,467	..	..	332	292	..	..	..	..	*2,856*	*2,729*	*2,590*	*2,254*	13	10	2	3
Mewar	..	..	..	..	*277*	*240*	*6,035*	*5,905*	..	..	6,035	5,905	..	..	..	..	..	..	*112*	*101*	*37*	*29*	*680*	*640*	..	..	..	..
Partabgarh	..	..	..	..	*1*	..	*242*	*254*	..	..	242	254	..	..	..	..	..	..	..	..	*7*	*7*	*29*	*22*	3	3	..	..
Shahpura (Chiefship)	..	..	..	..	*225*	*234*	*73*	*76*	..	..	73	76	..	..	..	..	..	..	*9*	*11*	*8*	*6*	*29*	*26*	1	..	..	..
Sirohi	..	..	..	..	*74*	*9*	*48*	*48*	..	..	48	48	..	..	..	..	..	..	*2*	*6*	*66*	*72*	*82*	*46*	..	..	..	..
Tonk	..	..	..	..	*155*	*196*	*365*	*333*	..	..	365	333	..	..	..	..	..	..	*56*	*46*	*856*	*352*	*896*	*670*	3	..	31	27
Ajmer-Merwara	1	..	..	..	*306*	*236*	*695*	*646*	..	..	674	634	..	..	21	13	..	..	*9*	*8*	*519*	*539*	*1,320*	*1,119*	24	18	..	..
Ajmer	1	..	..	..	*276*	*218*	*408*	*380*	..	..	387	368	..	..	21	12	..	..	*9*	*8*	*400*	*388*	*1,236*	*1,052*	23	16	..	..
Merwara	..	..	..	..	*30*	*18*	*257*	*266*	..	..	287	266	..	..	..	..	..	..	..	..	*119*	*151*	*84*	*67*	1	2	..	..

*Includes Hindu Dhunia, Pinārā, and Pinjārā. †Includes Musalman Khatik.

TABLE XIII.—CASTE, TRIBE, OR RACE. PART II.—BY STATES OR DISTRICTS, AND RELIGIONS—*contd.*

Province; and State or District.	KĀYASTHA—*concld.* Hindu. M.	Hindu. F.	Sikh. M.	Sikh. F.	KHĀNZADĀ. Musalman. M.	Musalman. F.	KHĀROL.* Hindu. M.	Hindu. F.	KHĀTI.† Total. M.	Total. F.	Arya. M.	Arya. F.	Hindu. M.	Hindu. F.	Sikh. M.	Sikh. F.
1	407	408	409	410	411	412	413	414	415	416	417	418	419	420	421	422
Rajputana	12,656	10,602	1	5	4,719	4,486	4,003	3,858	69,245	65,747	15	16	69,208	65,718	22	13
Alwar	770	621	..	..	3,975	3,762	119	119	7,062	6,916	..	..	7,063	6,910	..	..
Banswara	25	18	..	..	..	..	..	..	6	1	..	..	6	1	..	..
Bharatpur	742	580	..	..	451	417	624	594	3,422	2,757	..	..	3,422	2,757	..	..
Bikaner	255	151	..	..	..	..	..	..	4,239	3,516	..	..	4,217	3,533	22	13
Bundi	233	195	..	..	..	..	152	156	1,725	1,591	..	..	1,725	1,591	..	..
Dholpur	1,325	1,020	1	1	..	..	..	..	26	21	..	..	26	21	..	..
Dungarpur	7	10	..	..	..	..	..	..	8	7	..	..	8	7	..	..
Jaipur	3,443	3,070	..	..	274	305	327	342	24,508	24,494	..	..	24,508	24,494	..	..
Jaisalmer	1	..	..	..	..	..	..	..	..	..	..	..	..	..	..	..
Jhalawar	304	270	..	..	..	..	..	..	..	..	..	..	..	..	..	..
Karauli	89	54	..	..	..	..	..	..	316	260	..	..	316	260	..	..
Kishangarh	157	134	..	..	..	..	213	223	797	730	..	..	797	730	..	..
Kotah	1,028	831	..	4	..	..	33	23	4,362	3,931	..	..	4,362	3,931	..	..
Kushalgarh (Chiefship)	18	15	..	..	..	..	2	2	..	..	..	..	..	..	..	..
Lawa (Estate)	..	..	..	..	..	..	34	25	23	17	..	..	23	17	..	..
Marwar	2,575	2,241	..	..	3	..	405	280	13,534	12,992	14	15	13,520	12,977	..	..
Mewar	680	640	..	..	..	..	1,870	1,843	6,019	5,677	..	..	6,019	5,677	..	..
Partabgarh	26	19	..	..	..	..	40	51	1	..	..	..	1	..	..	..
Shahpura (Chiefship)	28	26	..	..	..	..	184	195	405	419	1	1	404	418	..	..
Sirohi	82	46	..	..	9	2	..	..	83	41	..	..	83	41	..	..
Tonk	862	643	..	..	..	..	..	..	2,709	2,447	..	..	2,709	2,447	..	..
Ajmer-Merwara	1,296	1,101	..	..	1	..	894	808	3,620	3,919	19	14	3,601	3,905	..	..
Ajmer	1,213	1,036	..	..	1	..	871	784	3,108	2,786	19	14	3,089	2,772	..	..
Merwara	83	65	..	..	..	..	23	24	512	433	..	..	512	433	..	..

Province; and State or District.	KHATIK. Total. M.	Total. F.	Animist. M.	Animist. F.	Arya. M.	Arya. F.	Hindu. M.	Hindu. F.	KHATRI.‡ Total. M.	Total. F.	Arya. M.	Arya. F.	Hindu. M.	Hindu. F.
1	423	424	425	426	427	428	429	430	431	432	433	434	435	436
Rajputana	26,380	24,896	..	..	2	..	26,378	24,896	5,441	4,969	39	37	5,218	4,867
Alwar	2,299	2,237	..	..	..	..	2,299	2,237	26	14	..	..	22	10
Banswara	19	21	..	..	..	..	19	21	4	2	..	..	4	2
Bharatpur	1,286	1,149	..	..	2	..	1,284	1,149	96	75	13	11	79	58
Bikaner	392	303	..	..	..	..	392	303	1,492	1,330	3	3	1,362	1,296
Bundi	615	598	..	..	..	..	615	598	144	139	..	..	144	139
Dholpur	720	674	..	..	..	..	720	674	53	42	2	6	34	23
Dungarpur	139	136	..	..	..	..	139	136	..	..	..	..	..	..
Jaipur	9,605	8,970	..	..	..	..	9,605	8,970	418	333	5	6	411	329
Jaisalmer	5	2	..	..	..	..	5	2	235	222	..	..	235	222
Jhalawar	55	57	..	..	..	..	55	57	19	15	..	..	19	15
Karauli	341	293	..	..	..	..	341	293	18	9	1	..	17	9
Kishangarh	505	481	..	..	..	..	505	484	19	27	..	..	19	27
Kotah	1,155	1,152	..	..	..	..	1,155	1,152	216	188	5	4	198	177
Kushalgarh (Chiefship)	..	..	..	..	..	..	..	..	..	..	..	..	..	..
Lawa (Estate)	40	43	..	..	..	..	40	43	1	..	..	..	1	..
Marwar	2,612	2,454	..	..	..	..	2,612	2,454	2,271	2,095	6	5	2,259	2,084
Mewar	5,370	5,221	..	..	..	..	5,370	5,221	299	291	..	..	299	291
Partabgarh	89	71	..	..	..	..	89	71	14	10	..	..	13	9
Shahpura (Chiefship)	192	174	..	..	..	..	192	174	14	13	4	2	10	11
Sirohi	107	95	..	..	..	..	107	95	63	60	..	..	57	58
Tonk	834	762	..	..	..	..	834	762	35	52	..	..	35	52
Ajmer-Merwara	1,793	1,759	3	6	..	..	1,790	1,753	750	657	19	10	712	638
Ajmer	1,485	1,461	3	6	..	..	1,482	1,455	659	576	18	10	622	557
Merwara	308	298	..	..	..	..	308	298	91	81	1	..	90	81

*Includes Āgar. †Includes Hindu Kheràti. ‡Includes Rorā.

TABLE XIII.—Caste, Tribe, or Race. Part II.—By States or Districts, and Religions—*contd.*

Province; and State or District.	Khatri*—contd.						Khawāswāl.						Kir.		Kirār.		Koli.												Kumhār.†			
	Jain.		Musalman.		Sikh.		Total.		Hindu.		Musalman.		Hindu.		Hindu.		Total.		Animist.		Arya.		Hindu.		Musalman.		Sikh.		Total.		Animist.	
	M.	F.	M.	F.	M.	F.	M.	F.	M.	F.	M.	F.	M.	F.	M.	F.	M.	F.	M.	F.	M.	F.	M.	F.	M.	F.	M.	F.	M.	F.	M.	F.
1	437	438	439	440	441	442	443	444	445	446	447	448	449	450	451	452	453	454	455	456	457	458	459	460	461	462	463	464	465	466	467	468
Rajputana	2	1	2	1	180	123	727	476	725	476	2	..	11,237	10,437	6,109	5,695	53,502	50,553	..	..	..	..	53,494	50,539	7	12	1	2	159,676	140,358	1	..
Alwar	..	..	..	..	4	4	720	465	718	465	2	..	662	531	..	..	6,548	6,243	..	..	..	..	6,543	6,234	5	9	..	..	9,321	9,133	..	..
Banswara	..	..	..	..	..	..	..	..	..	..	..	..	64	54	..	..	5	4	..	..	..	..	5	4	..	..	..	..	589	632	..	..
Bharatpur	..	..	..	..	4	6	..	..	..	..	..	..	10	9	18	19	6,958	6,166	..	..	..	..	6,968	6,166	..	..	..	..	6,196	5,575	..	..
Bikaner	..	..	1	..	126	81	..	..	..	..	..	..	..	..	9	4	11	7	..	..	..	..	11	7	..	..	..	..	11,304	9,714	..	..
Bundi	..	..	..	..	..	..	..	..	..	..	..	..	1,362	1,454	144	149	820	818	..	..	..	..	820	818	..	..	..	..	2,736	2,628	..	..
Dholpur	..	..	..	..	16	13	..	..	..	..	..	..	..	..	214	156	4,438	3,920	..	..	..	..	4,438	3,920	..	..	..	..	1,991	1,763	..	..
Dungarpur	..	..	..	..	..	..	..	..	..	..	..	..	19	22	..	..	..	..	..	..	..	..	..	..	..	..	..	..	848	907	..	..
Jaipur	..	..	..	..	2	..	..	..	..	..	..	..	2,98[illegible]	3,676	..	2	20,481	19,788	..	..	..	..	20,480	19,786	..	..	1	2	44,563	43,571	1	..
Jaisalmer	..	..	..	..	..	..	..	..	..	..	..	..	..	..	..	..	..	..	..	..	..	..	..	..	..	..	..	..	1,024	903	..	..
Jhalawar	..	..	..	..	..	..	..	..	..	..	..	..	123	113	1	..	217	212	..	..	..	..	217	212	..	..	..	..	759	753	..	..
Karauli	..	..	..	..	..	..	7	11	7	11	..	..	1	..	5	3	2,512	2,175	..	..	..	..	2,512	2,175	..	..	..	..	1,323	1,320	..	..
Kishangarh	..	..	..	..	..	..	..	..	..	..	..	..	144	145	..	..	40	48	..	..	..	..	40	48	..	..	..	..	1,221	1,054	..	..
Kotah	..	..	..	..	13	7	..	..	..	..	..	..	1,531	1,401	5,718	5,337	4,452	4,323	..	..	..	..	4,450	4,320	2	3	..	..	6,599	6,498	..	..
Kushalgarh (Chiefship)	..	..	..	..	..	..	..	..	..	..	..	..	..	..	..	..	2	..	..	..	..	..	2	..	..	..	..	..	72	60	..	..
Lawa (Estate)	..	..	..	..	..	..	..	..	..	..	..	..	..	..	..	..	64	60	..	..	..	..	64	60	..	..	..	..	19	12	..	..
Marwar	2	1	..	..	4	5	..	..	..	..	..	..	347	300	..	..	462	402	..	..	..	..	462	402	..	..	..	..	39,461	36,463	..	..
Mewar	..	..	..	..	..	..	..	..	..	..	..	..	2,736	2,701	..	23	374	423	..	..	..	..	374	423	..	..	..	..	20,250	19,162	..	..
Partabgarh	..	..	..	..	1	1	..	..	..	..	..	..	94	81	..	..	..	2	..	..	..	..	..	2	..	..	..	..	1,384	1,343	..	..
Shahpura (Chiefship)	..	..	..	..	..	..	..	..	..	..	..	..	244	198	..	..	165	158	..	..	..	..	165	188	..	..	..	..	612	631	..	..
Sirohi	..	..	1	1	10	6	..	..	..	..	..	..	198	92	..	..	2,741	2,511	..	..	..	..	2,744	2,514	..	..	..	..	5,656	5,195	..	..
Tonk	..	..	..	..	..	..	..	..	..	..	..	..	754	655	..	..	3,179	3,260	..	..	..	..	3,170	3,260	..	..	..	..	3,195	3,184	..	..
Ajmer-Merwara	1	..	..	..	18	9	..	..	..	..	..	..	497	477	..	..	3,480	3,083	2	.	2	7	3,476	3,078	..	..	..	..	7,218	6,902	4	..
Ajmer	1	..	..	..	18	9	..	..	..	..	..	..	476	464	..	..	3,418	3,015	2	..	2	7	3,414	3,038	..	..	..	..	5,680	5,400	4	..
Merwara	..	..	..	..	..	..	..	..	..	..	..	..	21	13	..	..	62	40	..	..	..	..	63	40	..	..	..	..	1,538	1,502	..	..

*Includes Rora.

†Includes Rāj Kumhār.

TABLE XIII.—Caste, Tribe, or Race. Part II.—By States or Districts, and Religions—*contd.*

Province and State or District.	Kumhar.*—contd. Arya. M.	Arya. F.	Hindu. M.	Hindu. F.	Jain. M.	Jain. F.	Musalman. M.	Musalman. F.	Sikh. M.	Sikh. F.	Kunbi. Total. M.	Total. F.	Arya. M.	Arya. F.	Hindu. M.	Hindu. F.	Kunjra. Total. M.	Total. F.	Hindu. M.	Hindu. F.	Musalman. M.	Musalman. F.	Labhana. Total. M.	Total. F.	Hindu. M.	Hindu. F.	Musalman. M.	Musalman. F.
1	469	470	471	472	473	474	475	476	477	478	479	480	481	482	483	484	485	486	487	488	489	490	491	492	493	494	495	496
Rajputana	2	..	155,819	146,189	6	4	3,667	3,224	181	131	*24,910*	*23,909*	4	..	24,906	23,909	*2,226*	*2,025*	20	6	2,206	2,019	*2,373*	*2,218*	285	273	2,088	1,945
Alwar	..	..	9,205	9,119	..	..	26	14	..	..	*1*	*2*	..	..	1	2	*515*	*412*	1	..	514	412	..	..	..	..	..	..
Banswara	..	..	589	632	..	..	..	..	..	..	..	..	..	..	..	..	*6*	*5*	..	..	6	5	*285*	*273*	285	273	..	..
Bharatpur	1	..	6,190	5,570	..	..	5	5	..	..	*46*	*44*	..	..	46	44	*280*	*223*	..	..	280	223	..	..	..	..	..	..
Bikaner	..	..	10,396	8,992	2	3	725	588	181	131	*2*	*2*	..	..	2	2	*320*	*314*	5	..	315	314	*2,088*	*1,945*	..	..	2,088	1,945
Bundi	..	..	2,786	2,628	..	..	..	..	..	..	*11*	*11*	..	..	11	11	*4*	*5*	..	..	4	5	..	..	..	..	..	..
Dholpur	..	..	1,991	1,768	..	..	..	..	..	..	*7*	*7*	..	..	7	7	*17*	*14*	..	..	17	14	..	..	..	..	..	..
Dungarpur	..	..	848	907	..	..	..	..	..	..	..	..	..	..	..	..	*6*	*7*	..	..	6	7	..	..	..	..	..	..
Jaipur	..	..	44,521	42,547	..	..	41	24	..	..	*100*	*88*	4	..	96	88	*450*	*432*	14	6	436	426	..	..	..	..	..	..
Jaisalmer	..	..	912	810	..	..	112	93	..	..	..	..	..	..	..	..	..	..	..	..	..	..	..	..	..	..	..	..
Jhalawar	..	..	739	782	..	..	..	..	..	..	*822*	*745*	..	..	822	745	*2*	*1*	..	..	2	1	..	..	..	..	..	..
Karauli	..	..	1,523	1,320	..	..	..	..	..	..	..	..	..	..	..	..	*38*	*43*	..	..	38	43	..	..	..	..	..	..
Kishangarh	..	..	1,223	1,054	..	..	1	..	..	..	*1*	..	..	..	1	..	..	..	..	..	..	..	..	..	..	..	..	..
Kotah	..	..	6,809	6,498	..	..	..	..	..	..	*610*	*553*	..	..	610	553	*108*	*128*	..	..	108	128	..	..	..	..	..	..
Kushalgarh (Chiefship)	..	..	72	60	..	..	..	..	..	..	..	..	..	..	..	..	..	..	..	..	..	..	..	..	..	..	..	..
Lawa (Estate)	..	..	19	12	..	..	..	..	..	..	..	..	..	..	..	..	..	..	..	..	..	..	..	..	..	..	..	..
Marwar	..	..	37,038	34,289	..	..	2,423	2,174	..	..	*14,854*	*14,018*	..	..	14,854	14,018	*75*	*63*	..	..	75	63	..	..	..	..	..	..
Mewar	..	..	20,246	19,159	3	1	1	2	..	..	*1,362*	*1,356*	..	..	1,362	1,356	*200*	*189*	..	..	200	189	..	..	..	..	..	..
Partabgarh	..	..	1,384	1,343	..	..	..	..	..	..	*830*	*752*	..	..	830	752	*49*	*57*	..	..	49	57	..	..	..	..	..	..
Shahpura (Chiefship)	1	..	671	654	..	..	..	..	..	..	..	..	..	..	..	..	*5*	*2*	..	..	5	2	..	..	..	..	..	..
Sirohi	..	..	5,352	4,871	1	..	333	324	..	..	*3,889*	*3,544*	..	..	3,889	3,544	*1*	*1*	..	..	1	1	..	..	..	..	..	..
Tonk	..	..	3,105	3,184	..	..	..	..	..	..	*2,375*	*2,170*	..	..	2,375	2,170	*150*	*129*	..	..	150	129	..	..	..	..	..	..
Ajmer-Merwara	8	2	7,177	6,871	1	..	26	29	2	..	*206*	*206*	..	..	206	206	*145*	*113*	..	..	145	113	..	..	..	..	..	..
Ajmer	8	2	5,650	5,376	..	..	16	22	2	..	*205*	*206*	..	..	205	206	*112*	*76*	..	..	112	76	..	..	..	..	..	..
Merwara	..	..	1,527	1,495	1	..	10	7	..	..	*1*	..	..	..	1	..	*33*	*37*	..	..	33	37	..	..	..	..	..	..

* Includes Rāj Kumhār.

TABLE XIII.—Caste, Tribe, or Race. Part II.—By States or Districts, and Religions—*contd.*

Province; and State or District.	† Lakherā.								Lodā.*		Lodhā.								Lohār.									
	Total.		Arya.		Hindu.		Jain.		Hindu.		Total.		Arya.		Hindu.		Musalman.		Total.		Arya.		Hindu.		Jain.		Musalman.	
	M.	F.	M.	F.	M.	F.	M.	F.	M.	F.	M.	F.	M.	F.	M.	F.	M.	F.	M.	F.	M.	F.	M.	F.	M.	F.	M.	F.
1	497	498	499	500	501	502	503	504	505	506	507	508	509	510	511	512	513	514	515	516	517	518	519	520	521	522	523	524
Rajputana	*5,539*	*5,213*	..	..	5,538	5,213	1	..	*4,105*	*3,608*	*24,536*	*22,487*	..	..	24,520	22,483	6	4	*41,247*	*39,575*	5	4	32,348	30,320	..	..	8,894	9,251
Alwar	*303*	*318*	..	..	303	318	..	..	..	..	*142*	*140*	..	..	142	140	..	..	*1,940*	*1,888*	..	..	1,357	1,346	..	..	583	542
Banswara	*14*	*9*	..	..	14	9	..	..	..	..	..	..	..	..	..	..	..	..	*898*	*894*	..	..	898	894	..	..	..	..
Bharatpur	*61*	*68*	..	..	61	68	..	..	..	..	*3,450*	*2,958*	..	..	3,450	2,958	..	..	*1,739*	*1,466*	..	..	1,502	1,250	..	..	237	216
Bikaner	*187*	*181*	..	..	186	181	1	..	..	..	*2*	..	..	..	2	..	..	..	*1,968*	*1,738*	..	..	1,392	1,254	..	..	576	484
Bundi	*171*	*160*	..	..	171	160	..	..	..	..	*273*	*250*	..	..	273	250	..	..	*1,251*	*1,164*	..	..	1,031	964	..	..	220	200
Dholpur	*13*	*4*	..	..	13	4	..	..	..	..	*5,821*	*5,078*	..	..	5,821	5,078	..	..	*101*	*100*	..	..	99	98	..	..	2	2
Dungarpur	*23*	*23*	..	..	23	23	..	..	..	..	..	..	..	..	..	..	..	..	*1,079*	*1,103*	..	..	1,079	1,103	..	..	..	..
Jaipur	*1,263*	*1,189*	..	..	1,263	1,189	..	..	..	..	*589*	*517*	..	..	587	517	2	..	*4,443*	*4,440*	4	4	2,471	2,235	..	..	1,968	2,201
Jaisalmer	*37*	*38*	..	..	37	38	..	..	..	..	..	..	..	..	..	..	..	..	*111*	*86*	..	..	105	86	..	..	6	..
Jhalawar	*27*	*27*	..	..	27	27	..	..	..	..	*244*	*236*	..	..	244	236	..	..	*534*	*475*	..	..	509	448	..	..	25	27
Karauli	*29*	*26*	..	..	29	26	..	..	..	..	*55*	*48*	..	..	55	48	..	..	*221*	*191*	..	..	189	157	..	..	32	34
Kishangarh	*104*	*83*	..	..	104	83	..	..	..	..	*1*	..	..	..	1	..	..	..	*164*	*155*	..	..	113	108	..	..	51	47
Kotah	*261*	*261*	..	..	261	261	..	..	*4,050*	*3,544*	*11,561*	*10,912*	..	..	11,559	10,909	2	3	*3,146*	*3,006*	1	..	2,909	2,782	..	..	236	224
Kushalgarh (Chiefship)	*5*	*8*	..	..	6	8	..	..	..	..	..	..	..	..	..	..	..	..	*91*	*120*	..	..	91	120	..	..	..	..
Lawa (Estate)	*2*	*3*	..	..	2	3	..	..	..	..	..	..	..	..	..	..	..	..	*13*	*12*	..	..	..	..	..	..	13	12
Marwar	*1,255*	*1,175*	..	..	1,255	1,175	..	..	..	..	..	..	..	..	..	..	..	..	*11,872*	*11,592*	..	..	7,712	7,095	..	..	4,160	4,497
Mewar	*1,384*	*1,249*	..	..	1,384	1,249	..	..	..	2	*310*	*329*	..	..	308	328	2	1	*8,314*	*8,464*	..	..	8,339	8,000	..	..	475	464
Partabgarh	*47*	*38*	..	..	47	38	..	..	*47*	*62*	*10*	*13*	..	..	10	13	..	..	*232*	*271*	..	..	232	271	..	..	..	..
Shahpura (Chiefship)	*73*	*73*	..	..	73	73	..	..	..	..	*104*	*82*	..	..	104	82	..	..	*203*	*203*	..	..	203	203	..	..	..	..
Sirohi	*172*	*164*	..	..	172	164	..	..	..	..	*57*	*56*	..	..	57	56	..	..	*1,322*	*1,207*	..	..	1,224	1,132	..	..	98	75
Tonk	*108*	*116*	..	..	108	116	..	..	..	..	*1,907*	*1,868*	..	..	1,907	1,868	..	..	*1,055*	*1,020*	..	..	843	794	..	..	212	226
Ajmer-Merwara	*376*	*374*	1	..	375	374	..	..	..	..	*575*	*564*	9	9	566	555	..	..	*2,256*	*1,958*	..	1	1,320	1,157	1	..	935	800
Ajmer	*294*	*272*	1	..	293	272	..	..	..	..	*549*	*538*	8	6	541	532	..	..	*1,419*	*1,191*	..	1	829	686	1	..	589	504
Merwara	*82*	*102*	..	..	82	102	..	..	..	..	*26*	*26*	1	3	25	23	..	..	*837*	*767*	..	..	491	471	..	..	346	296

† Includes Manihar. * Includes Lodhā (Kotah).

TABLE XIII.—Caste, Tribe, or Race. Part II.—By States or Districts, and Religions—*contd.*

Province; and State or District.	Mahājan or Baniyā.																											
	Total Mahājan or Baniyā.										Agarwāl.										Bijābargi.							
	Total.		Arya.		Hindu.		Jain.		Sikh.		Total.		Arya.		Hindu.		Jain.		Sikh.		Total.		Arya.		Hindu.		Jain.	
	M.	F.	M.	F.	M.	F.	M.	F.	M.	F.	M.	F.	M.	F.	M.	F.	M.	F.	M.	F.	M.	F.	M.	F.	M.	F.	M.	F.
1	525	526	527	528	529	530	531	532	533	534	535	536	537	538	539	540	541	542	543	544	545	546	547	548	549	550	551	552
Rajputana	*353,152*	*354,569*	**111**	**68**	**192,370**	**184,965**	**160,671**	**160,536**	..	..	*101,638*	*97,991*	**57**	**35**	**95,129**	**91,955**	**6,452**	**6,001**	..	..	*5,115*	*4,764*	**5**	**4**	**5,066**	**4,724**	**45**	**36**
Alwar	*20,548*	*18,704*	1	..	18,391	16,752	2,156	1,952	..	..	*7,232*	*6,429*	..	..	6,653	5,941	579	488	..	..	*594*	*612*	..	..	594	612	..	..
Banswara	*2,658*	*2,620*	..	..	462	420	2,196	2,200	..	..	*19*	*5*	..	..	10	5	..	..	..	..	..	..	..	..	..	..	..	..
Bharatpur	*14,055*	*11,545*	20	14	12,561	10,285	1,474	1,246	..	..	*9,715*	*8,033*	13	12	9,382	7,722	318	299	..	..	*45*	*48*	..	..	41	45	4	3
Bikaner	*25,134*	*32,823*	8	2	15,049	18,393	10,077	14,428	..	..	*7,766*	*8,877*	8	2	7,528	8,603	230	272	..	..	*18*	*22*	..	..	18	22	..	..
Bundi	*6,039*	*5,330*	..	..	2,577	2,195	3,462	3,135	..	..	*931*	*874*	..	..	207	182	724	692	..	..	*97*	*99*	..	..	97	96	..	3
Dholpur	*7,268*	*5,748*	..	..	6,093	4,892	1,175	856	..	..	*4,874*	*3,932*	..	..	4,869	3,931	5	1	..	..	..	..	..	..	..	..	..	..
Dungarpur	*3,119*	*3,241*	3	4	418	430	2,698	2,807	..	..	*12*	*11*	..	..	12	11	..	..	..	..	..	..	..	..	..	..	..	..
Jaipur	*99,853*	*95,721*	36	20	79,571	77,609	20,246	18,092	..	..	*53,020*	*53,745*	11	5	50,538	51,386	2,471	2,354	..	..	*2,044*	*1,819*	..	..	2,010	1,793	34	26
Jaisalmer	*2,454*	*2,302*	..	..	1,917	1,749	537	553	..	..	*2*	..	..	..	2	..	..	..	..	..	..	..	..	..	..	..	..	..
Jhalawar	*2,548*	*2,379*	7	4	1,241	1,218	1,300	1,157	..	..	*318*	*326*	4	3	286	297	28	26	..	..	*39*	*29*	..	..	39	29	..	..
Karauli	*4,764*	*3,814*	..	..	4,544	3,645	220	169	..	..	*4,484*	*3,632*	..	..	4,477	3,625	7	7	..	..	..	..	..	..	..	..	..	..
Kishangarh	*3,201*	*2,836*	1	..	1,525	1,350	1,675	1,486	..	..	*354*	*299*	..	..	316	269	38	30	..	..	*33*	*22*	..	..	31	22	2	..
Kotah	*11,113*	*9,545*	10	7	7,659	6,604	3,444	2,934	..	..	*3,521*	*3,027*	3	..	2,581	2,193	937	834	..	..	*1,105*	*1,038*	5	4	1,095	1,030	5	4
Kushalgarh (Chiefship)	*302*	*257*	..	..	34	19	268	238	..	..	*7*	*3*	..	..	4	..	3	3	..	..	..	..	..	..	..	..	..	..
Lawa (Estate)	*76*	*67*	..	..	1	..	75	67	..	..	*57*	*49*	..	..	..	..	57	49	..	..	*1*	..	..	..	1	..	..	..
Marwar	*80,667*	*91,672*	9	7	19,868	21,470	60,790	70,195	..	..	*4,662*	*4,695*	9	7	4,591	4,644	62	44	..	..	*273*	*244*	..	..	273	244	..	..
Mewar	*49,344*	*45,053*	7	7	14,043	13,201	34,304	31,845	..	..	*1,715*	*1,534*	2	3	1,440	1,283	273	248	..	..	*361*	*385*	..	..	361	385	..	..
Partabgarh	*2,684*	*2,403*	1	..	424	344	2,259	2,059	..	..	..	..	..	..	..	..	..	..	..	..	..	..	..	..	..	..	..	..
Shahpura (Chiefship)	*1,640*	*1,431*	8	3	758	701	874	727	..	..	*83*	*76*	5	3	55	60	23	13	..	..	*2*	*3*	..	..	2	3	..	..
Sirohi	*8,560*	*10,901*	..	..	1,374	1,245	7,186	9,656	..	..	*876*	*777*	..	..	842	739	34	38	..	..	*7*	*12*	..	..	7	12	..	..
Tonk	*7,125*	*6,177*	..	..	2,960	2,441	4,165	3,736	..	..	*1,990*	*1,667*	..	..	1,327	1,064	663	603	..	..	*496*	*431*	..	..	496	431	..	..
Ajmer-Merwara	*18,413*	*16,057*	**105**	**76**	**7,646**	**6,650**	**10,659**	**9,331**	**3**	..	*4,444*	*3,956*	**39**	**26**	**3,658**	**3,286**	**744**	**644**	**3**	..	*357*	*371*	**1**	..	**356**	**371**	..	..
Ajmer	*14,021*	*12,217*	76	52	6,391	5,625	7,551	6,540	3	..	*3,614*	*3,270*	30	22	2,845	2,608	736	640	3	..	*314*	*324*	1	..	313	324	..	..
Merwara	*4,392*	*3,840*	29	24	1,255	1,025	3,108	2,791	..	..	*830*	*686*	9	4	813	678	8	4	..	..	*43*	*47*	..	..	43	47	..	..

TABLE XIII.—CASTE, TRIBE, OR RACE. PART II.—BY STATES OR DISTRICTS, AND RELIGIONS—*contd.*

Province; and State or District.	MAHĀJAN OR BANIYĀ—*contd.*																											
	HAMAR OR HUMBAD.						KHANDELWĀL.								MAHESRI.								MĪWAR OR MAHĪWAR.					
	Total.		Hindu.		Jain.		Total.		Arya.		Hindu.		Jain.		Total.		Arya.		Hindu.		Jain.		Total.		Arya.		Hindu.	
	M.	F.	M.	F.	M.	F.	M.	F.	M.	F.	M.	F.	M.	F.	M.	F.	M.	F.	M.	F.	M.	F.	M.	F.	M.	F.	M.	F.
1	553	554	555	556	557	558	559	560	561	562	563	564	565	566	567	568	569	570	571	572	573	574	575	576	577	578	579	580
Rajputana	*4,257*	*4,326*	12	16	4,245	4,310	*33,918*	*29,146*	3	2	29,762	25,843	4,153	3,301	*44,597*	*46,509*	3	..	44,434	46,381	160	128	*5,053*	*4,701*	2	1	5,050	4,700
Alwar	..	..	..	..	..	..	*5,994*	*5,469*	1	..	5,759	5,272	234	197	*213*	*213*	..	..	213	213	..	..	*4,876*	*4,484*	..	..	4,676	4,484
Banswara	*1,622*	*1,634*	..	..	1,622	1,634	*25*	*7*	..	..	25	7	..	..	*11*	*10*	..	..	11	10	..	..	..	..	..	..	..	..
Bharatpur	..	..	..	..	..	..	*3,117*	*2,479*	..	..	2,794	2,246	323	233	*90*	*81*	..	..	90	81	..	..	*11*	*10*	..	..	11	10
Bikaner	..	..	..	..	..	..	*16*	*23*	..	..	1	3	15	20	*7,080*	*9,427*	..	..	7,080	9,427	..	..	..	..	..	..	..	..
Bundi	..	..	..	..	..	..	*57*	*38*	..	..	29	21	28	17	*1,544*	*1,258*	..	..	1,544	1,257	..	1	..	..	..	..	..	..
Dholpur	..	..	..	..	..	..	*24*	*19*	..	..	17	15	7	4	*5*	*3*	..	..	5	3	..	..	..	..	..	..	..	..
Dungarpur	*1,254*	*1,313*	1	6	1,253	1,307	*7*	*3*	..	..	3	..	4	3	*3*	..	..	..	..	..	3	..	..	..	..	..	..	..
Jaipur	..	..	..	..	..	..	*22,735*	*19,398*	2	2	19,303	16,652	3,430	2,744	*5,014*	*5,154*	1	..	5,010	5,145	3	9	*155*	*204*	..	..	155	204
Jaisalmer	..	..	..	..	..	..	..	..	..	..	..	..	..	..	*1,642*	*1,507*	..	..	1,640	1,506	2	1	..	..	..	..	..	..
Jhalawar	..	..	..	..	..	..	*76*	*60*	..	..	76	60	..	..	*313*	*300*	..	..	280	259	33	41	*2*	*1*	2	1	..	..
Karauli	..	..	..	..	..	..	*33*	*21*	..	..	19	11	14	10	*14*	*4*	..	..	14	4	..	..	..	..	..	..	..	..
Kishangarh	..	..	..	..	..	..	*45*	*42*	..	..	45	42	..	..	*981*	*915*	..	..	981	915	..	..	*2*	..	..	..	2	..
Kotah	..	..	..	..	..	..	*1,046*	*895*	..	..	967	836	79	59	*890*	*713*	..	..	887	710	3	3	..	..	..	..	..	..
Kushalgarh (Chiefship)	*168*	*153*	..	..	168	153	..	..	..	..	..	..	..	..	*6*	*4*	..	..	6	4	..	..	..	..	..	..	..	..
Lawa (Estate)	..	..	..	..	..	..	..	*1*	..	..	..	..	..	1	..	..	..	..	..	..	..	..	..	..	..	..	..	..
Marwar	..	..	..	..	..	..	*257*	*248*	..	..	257	248	..	..	*13,637*	*15,360*	..	..	13,609	15,339	28	21	..	..	..	..	..	..
Mewar	*1,213*	*1,226*	11	10	1,202	1,216	*186*	*189*	..	..	169	177	17	12	*11,876*	*10,431*	..	..	11,828	10,399	53	32	*5*	*2*	..	..	5	2
Partabgarh	..	..	..	..	..	..	..	..	..	..	..	..	..	..	..	..	..	..	..	..	..	..	..	..	..	..	..	..
Shahpura (Chiefship)	..	..	..	..	..	..	..	..	..	..	..	..	..	..	*683*	*623*	2	..	681	623	..	..	*1*	..	..	..	1	..
Sirohi	..	..	..	..	..	..	*11*	*4*	..	..	11	4	..	..	*17*	*8*	..	..	15	7	2	1	..	..	..	..	..	..
Tonk	..	..	..	..	..	..	*289*	*250*	..	..	287	249	2	1	*578*	*498*	..	..	545	479	33	19	..	..	..	..	..	..
Ajmer-Merwara	..	..	..	..	..	..	*909*	*962*	..	..	338	237	569	725	*2,924*	*2,490*	32	22	2,878	2,460	14	8	..	..	..	..	..	..
Ajmer	..	..	..	..	..	..	*799*	*874*	..	..	230	150	569	724	*2,640*	*2,280*	17	9	2,613	2,263	10	8	..	..	..	..	..	..
Merwara	..	..	..	..	..	..	*108*	*88*	..	..	108	87	..	1	*284*	*210*	15	13	265	197	4	..	..	..	..	..	..	..

TABLE XIII.—CASTE, TRIBE, OR RACE. PART II.—BY STATES OR DISTRICTS, AND RELIGIONS—*contd.*

Province; and State or District.	MAHĀJAN OR BANIYĀ—*contd.*																									
	OSWĀL.								PORWĀL.								SARĀOGI.						OTHERS.			
	Total.		Arya.		Hindu.		Jain.		Total.		Arya.		Hindu.		Jain.		Total.		Hindu.		Jain.		Total.		Arya.	
	M.	F.	M.	F.	M.	F.	M.	F.	M.	F.	M.	F.	M.	F.	M.	F.	M.	F.	M.	F.	M.	F.	M.	F.	M.	F.
1	581	582	583	584	585	586	587	588	589	590	591	592	593	594	595	596	597	598	599	600	601	602	603	604	605	606
Rajputana	*100,685*	*109,280*	10	5	2,540	1,953	98,135	107,322	*14,894*	*18,149*	..	2	1,724	1,559	13,170	16,590	*19,835*	*18,306*	104	89	19,731	18,117	*23,161*	*21,504*	31	19
Alwar	*145*	*142*	..	..	36	23	100	119	..	..	..	..	..	..	..	..	*340*	*306*	3	..	337	306	*1,154*	*1,049*	..	..
Banswara	*113*	*105*	..	..	..	..	113	105	*78*	*78*	..	..	..	..	78	78	*1*	..	..	..	1	..	*789*	*781*	..	..
Bharatpur	*148*	*137*	..	..	2	1	146	136	..	..	..	..	..	..	..	..	*113*	*89*	..	..	113	89	*816*	*668*	5	2
Bikaner	*9,830*	*13,937*	..	..	408	313	9,422	13,624	..	..	..	..	..	..	..	..	*410*	*512*	..	2	410	510	*14*	*25*	..	..
Bundi	*200*	*168*	..	..	5	5	195	163	*201*	*151*	..	..	25	11	176	140	*1,242*	*1,060*	9	6	1,233	1,054	*1,767*	*1,682*	..	..
Dholpur	*129*	*71*	..	..	..	..	129	71	..	..	..	..	..	..	..	..	*2*	*2*	..	..	2	2	*2,234*	*1,721*	..	..
Dungarpur	*127*	*108*	..	..	110	102	17	6	*648*	*632*	..	..	34	36	614	596	..	..	..	..	..	..	*1,068*	*1,174*	3	4
Jaipur	*2,458*	*2,238*	2	..	247	152	2,209	2,086	*1,038*	*812*	..	..	203	137	835	705	*10,502*	*9,553*	16	10	10,486	9,543	*2,887*	*2,768*	20	13
Jaisalmer	*661*	*637*	..	..	126	85	535	552	..	..	..	..	..	..	..	..	..	..	..	..	..	..	*149*	*158*	..	..
Jhalawar	*953*	*824*	..	..	67	66	801	758	*367*	*386*	..	..	264	203	103	93	*228*	*225*	..	..	228	225	*247*	*228*	1	..
Karauli	*98*	*71*	..	..	6	..	92	71	..	..	..	..	..	..	..	..	*65*	*43*	..	..	65	43	*70*	*43*	..	..
Kishangarh	*1,157*	*1,029*	..	..	85	54	1,072	975	..	..	..	..	..	..	..	..	*572*	*503*	23	22	549	481	*57*	*26*	1	..
Kotah	*723*	*614*	2	1	69	35	652	578	*1,129*	*985*	..	2	982	852	147	181	*962*	*763*	7	10	955	753	*1,737*	*1,510*	..	..
Kushalgarh (Chiefship)	*94*	*78*	..	..	..	..	94	78	..	..	..	..	..	..	..	..	..	..	..	..	..	..	*27*	*19*	..	..
Laws (Estate)	*3*	*1*	..	..	..	..	3	1	..	..	..	..	..	..	..	..	*15*	*16*	..	..	15	16	..	..	..	..
Marwar	*51,840*	*58,514*	..	..	785	677	51,055	57,837	*6,706*	*9,261*	..	..	46	41	6,660	9,220	*2,985*	*3,072*	20	15	2,965	3,057	*307*	*278*	..	..
Mewar	*26,200*	*23,808*	5	4	533	392	25,662	23,412	*789*	*736*	..	..	31	27	758	709	*1,371*	*1,182*	26	24	1,345	1,158	*5,628*	*5,560*	..	..
Partabgarh	*21*	*19*	..	..	21	19	..	..	..	..	..	..	..	..	..	..	..	..	..	..	..	..	*2,663*	*2,384*	1	..
Shahpura (Chiefship)	*591*	*510*	1	..	..	..	590	510	*19*	*14*	..	..	19	14	..	..	*261*	*204*	..	..	261	204	..	*1*	..	..
Sirohi	*3,807*	*5,084*	..	..	37	27	3,770	5,057	*3,414*	*4,638*	..	..	47	00	3,367	4,548	*1*	*1*	..	..	1	1	*427*	*377*	..	..
Tonk	*1,382*	*1,185*	..	..	3	2	1,379	1,183	*505*	*419*	..	..	73	49	432	370	*765*	*675*	..	..	765	675	*1,120*	*1,052*	..	..
Ajmer-Merwara	*7,566*	*6,663*	22	19	134	82	7,410	6,561	*1*	..	..	..	1	..	..	..	*1,858*	*1,365*	57	31	1,801	1,334	*361*	*251*	11	9
Ajmer	*4,662*	*4,044*	17	12	110	69	4,535	3,963	*1*	..	..	..	1	..	..	..	*1,635*	*1,177*	53	29	1,582	1,148	*356*	*248*	11	9
Merwara	*2,904*	*2,618*	5	7	24	13	2,875	2,598	..	..	..	..	..	..	..	..	*223*	*188*	4	2	219	186	*5*	*3*	..	..

TABLE XIII.—Caste, Tribe, or Race. Part II.—By States or Districts, and Religions—contd.

Province; and State or District.	Mahājan or Baniyā—contd.				Māli.*										Manihār.†		Meghwāl (Megh).					
	Others—contd.				Total.		Arya.		Hindu.		Jain.		Musalman.		Musalman.		Total.		Hindu.		Musalman.	
	Hindu.		Jain.																			
	M.	F.	M.	F.	M.	F.	M.	F.	M.	F.	M.	F.	M.	F.	M.	F.	M.	F.	M.	F.	M.	F.
1	607	608	609	610	611	612	613	614	615	616	617	618	619	620	621	622	623	624	625	626	627	628
Rajputana	8,550	7,754	14,580	13,731	174,966	161,910	71	62	174,636	161,561	8	9	251	278	4,072	4,306	30,087	27,439	30,083	27,437	4	2
Alwar	257	207	897	842	15,753	14,555	..	..	15,621	14,399	..	..	132	156	159	162	..	..	..	..	..	..
Banswara	407	308	382	383	47	55	..	..	47	55	..	..	..	..	116	164	..	..	..	..	..	..
Bharatpur	241	180	570	486	10,238	9,076	..	..	10,232	9,076	..	..	..	..	389	322	..	..	..	..	..	..
Bikaner	14	25	..	..	4,904	4,580	..	..	4,898	4,577	..	..	6	3	630	529	1,440	1,254	1,440	1,254	..	..
Bundi	661	617	1,106	1,065	8,585	8,248	..	..	8,583	8,246	2	2	..	..	44	43	34	29	34	29	..	..
Dholpur	1,202	943	1,032	778	73	65	..	..	73	65	..	..	..	..	120	99	..	..	..	..	..	..
Dungarpur	258	275	807	895	123	126	..	..	123	126	..	..	..	..	76	75	..	..	..	..	..	..
Jaipur	2,089	2,130	778	625	64,421	58,317	..	..	64,339	58,224	1	..	81	93	2,071	1,970	..	..	..	..	..	..
Jaisalmer	149	158	..	..	365	307	..	..	365	307	..	..	..	..	..	..	6,251	5,616	6,247	5,614	4	2
Jhalawar	229	214	17	14	993	1,011	..	..	991	1,008	2	3	..	..	41	48	48	72	48	72	..	..
Karauli	28	5	42	38	828	734	..	..	825	733	..	..	3	1	39	39	..	..	..	..	..	..
Kishangarh	42	28	14	..	2,146	1,911	1	..	2,144	1,911	..	..	1	..	28	7	..	..	..	..	..	..
Kotah	1,071	938	866	572	21,594	21,076	1	..	21,590	21,067	..	2	3	7	111	88	146	196	146	196	..	..
Kushalgarh (Chiefship)	24	15	3	4	3	2	..	..	3	2	..	..	..	..	2	1	..	..	..	..	..	..
Lawa (Estate)	..	..	..	..	75	64	..	..	75	64	..	..	..	..	..	..	..	..	..	..	..	..
Marwar	287	262	20	16	26,888	24,969	60	62	26,709	24,896	..	1	20	10	566	518	22,023	20,127	22,023	20,127	..	..
Mewar	544	502	5,084	5,058	9,710	9,349	..	..	9,702	9,340	3	1	5	8	86	61	115	117	115	117	..	..
Partabgarh	403	325	2,259	2,059	274	274	..	..	274	274	..	..	..	..	2	..	..	..	..	..	..	..
Shahpura (Chiefship)	..	1	..	..	1,140	1,047	..	..	1,140	1,047	..	..	..	..	7	12	..	..	..	..	..	..
Sirohi	415	366	12	11	2,556	2,261	..	..	2,556	2,261	..	..	..	..	12	6	21	18	21	18	..	..
Tonk	229	167	891	885	4,256	3,883	..	..	4,256	3,883	..	..	..	..	143	142	..	..	..	..	..	..
Ajmer-Merwara	229	183	121	59	7,490	6,841	7	5	7,482	6,825	..	1	10	10	54	39	..	1	..	1	..	..
Ajmer	226	182	119	57	6,599	6,047	7	5	6,585	6,035	..	1	7	6	38	30	..	1	..	1	..	..
Merwara	3	1	2	2	900	791	..	..	897	790	..	..	3	4	16	9	..	..	..	..	..	..

* Includes Bāghbān. † Includes Musalman Churigar and Lakhera.

TABLE XIII.—Caste, Tribe, or Race. Part II.—By States or Districts, and Religions—*contd.*

Province; and State or District.	MEHTAR.								MEO (MEWĀTI).								MER.						MERĀT GORĀT.		MERĀT KATHĀT.	
	Total.		Animist.		Hindu.		Musalman.		Total.		Arya.		Hindu.		Musalman.		Total.		Hindu.		Musalman.		Hindu.		Musalman.	
	M.	F.	M.	F.	M.	F.	M.	F.	M.	F.	M.	F.	M.	F.	M.	F.	M.	F.	M.	F.	M.	F.	M.	F.	M.	F.
1	629	630	631	632	633	634	635	636	637	638	639	640	641	642	643	644	645	646	647	648	649	650	651	652	653	654
Rajputana	*3,124*	*3,027*	3	..	3,120	3,025	1	2	*87,347*	*78,343*	1	..	73	73	87,273	78,270	*7,156*	*6,556*	7,127	6,531	29	25	*16*	*10*	*1,263*	*987*
Alwar	*73*	*76*	..	..	73	76	..	..	*59,704*	*53,845*	..	..	3	17	59,701	53,828	*1*	*1*	..	1	1	..	..	..	..	..
Banswara	..	..	..	..	..	..	..	..	*3*	*4*	..	..	..	..	3	4	..	..	..	..	..	..	..	..	..	..
Bharatpur	..	..	..	..	..	..	..	..	*25,578*	*22,642*	..	..	..	..	25,578	22,642	*2*	..	2	..	..	..	..	..	..	..
Bikaner	*59*	*55*	..	..	58	55	1	..	..	..	..	..	..	..	..	..	*1*	..	1	..	..	..	..	..	..	..
Bundi	*7*	*6*	..	..	7	6	..	..	*7*	*7*	..	..	..	..	7	7	*222*	*254*	222	254	..	..	..	..	..	..
Dholpur	*19*	*14*	..	..	19	14	..	..	*27*	*25*	..	..	..	..	27	25	..	..	..	..	..	..	..	..	..	..
Dungarpur	..	..	..	..	..	..	..	..	..	..	..	..	..	..	..	..	..	..	..	..	..	..	..	..	..	..
Jaipur	*1,001*	*906*	..	..	1,001	906	..	..	*332*	*301*	..	..	63	54	269	247	*11*	*10*	2	..	9	10	..	2	..	..
Jaisalmer	*2*	*1*	..	..	2	1	..	..	..	..	..	..	..	..	..	..	..	..	..	..	..	..	..	..	..	..
Jhalawar	..	..	..	..	..	..	..	..	*52*	*56*	..	..	..	..	52	56	*144*	*200*	144	200	..	..	..	..	..	..
Karauli	..	..	..	..	..	..	..	..	*1*	..	..	..	..	..	1	..	..	..	..	..	..	..	..	..	..	..
Kishangarh	*192*	*190*	..	..	192	188	..	2	..	..	..	..	..	..	..	..	*207*	*169*	207	169	..	..	..	..	..	..
Kotah	*11*	*23*	..	..	11	23	..	..	*707*	*612*	1	..	4	..	702	612	*3,000*	*3,003*	3,000	3,003	..	..	..	..	..	..
Kushalgarh (Chiefship)	..	..	..	..	..	..	..	..	..	..	..	..	..	..	..	..	..	..	..	..	..	..	..	..	..	..
Lawa (Estate)	..	*1*	..	..	..	1	..	..	..	..	..	..	..	..	..	..	..	..	..	..	..	..	..	..	..	..
Marwar	*488*	*479*	..	..	488	479	..	..	*11*	*29*	..	..	..	..	11	29	*450*	*317*	431	311	19	6	*4*	*7*	*980*	*783*
Mewar	*1,005*	*1,001*	..	..	1,005	1,001	..	..	*442*	*389*	..	..	3	2	439	387	*3,010*	*2,554*	3,010	2,554	..	..	*11*	*1*	*194*	*159*
Partabgarh	..	..	..	..	..	..	..	..	*67*	*53*	..	..	..	..	67	53	..	..	..	..	..	..	..	..	..	..
Shahpura (Chiefship)	*120*	*125*	..	..	120	125	..	..	..	..	..	..	..	..	..	..	*2*	*1*	2	1	..	..	..	..	..	..
Sirohi	*147*	*150*	3	..	144	150	..	..	*28*	*12*	..	..	..	..	28	12	*106*	*38*	106	38	..	..	*1*	..	*89*	*45*
Tonk	..	..	..	..	..	..	..	..	*388*	*368*	..	..	..	..	388	368	..	..	..	..	..	..	..	..	..	..
Ajmer-Merwara	*449*	*389*	3	3	446	386	..	..	*94*	*79*	..	..	2	4	92	75	*11,634*	*10,169*	11,623	10,151	11	18	*1,300*	*725*	*9,651*	*7,975*
Ajmer	*394*	*344*	..	..	394	344	..	..	*89*	*77*	..	..	2	4	87	73	*10,818*	*9,452*	10,812	9,438	6	14	*121*	*78*	*2,104*	*1,741*
Merwara	*55*	*45*	3	3	52	42	..	..	*5*	*2*	..	..	..	..	5	2	*816*	*717*	811	713	5	4	*1,179*	*647*	*7,547*	*6,234*

TABLE XIII.—Caste, Tribe, or Race. Part II.—By States or Districts, and Religions—*contd.*

Province; and State or District.	MINĀ. Total. M.	F.	Animist. M.	F.	Arya. M.	F.	Hindu. M.	F.	Musalman. M.	F.	MIRĀSI.* Musalman. M.	F.	MOCHI. Total. M.	F.	Animist. M.	F.	Hindu. M.	F.	Musalman. M.	F.	MOGHAL. Musalman. M.	F.	MOGHIĀ. Total. M.	F.	Animist. M.	F.
1	655	656	657	658	659	660	661	662	663	664	665	666	667	668	669	670	671	672	673	674	675	676	677	678	679	680
Rajputana	*296,205*	*262,484*	23,730	22,314	..	..	272,411	240,095	64	75	*11,200*	*10,529*	*8,101*	*7,397*	..	..	7,496	6,784	605	543	*7,460*	*6,653*	*2,211*	*2,103*	46	25
Alwar	*26,839*	*24,301*	..	..	..	..	26,780	24,237	59	67	*997*	*900*	*99*	*74*	..	..	99	74	..	..	*569*	*503*	..	..	..	..
Banswara	..	..	..	..	..	..	..	..	..	..	*2*	*2*	*54*	*43*	..	..	54	43	..	..	*24*	*28*	*37*	*39*	..	..
Bharatpur	*6,092*	*5,317*	..	..	..	..	6,092	5,317	..	..	*718*	*635*	*25*	*22*	..	..	25	22	..	..	*427*	*379*	..	..	..	..
Bikaner	*708*	*588*	..	..	..	..	706	587	2	1	*2,840*	*2,516*	*1,009*	*975*	..	..	850	826	159	149	*332*	*288*	..	..	..	..
Bundi	*16,056*	*13,936*	2	2	..	..	16,054	13,934	..	..	*68*	*62*	*90*	*110*	..	..	90	110	..	..	*43*	*46*	*22*	*19*	..	..
Dholpur	*6,246*	*5,129*	..	..	..	..	6,246	5,129	..	..	*10*	*9*	*36*	*31*	..	..	36	31	..	..	*117*	*83*	*5*	*10*	..	..
Dungarpur	..	..	..	..	..	..	..	..	..	..	*17*	*15*	*136*	*147*	..	..	136	147	..	..	*1*	..	..	..	..	..
Jaipur	*133,412*	*118,076*	..	..	..	..	133,410	118,074	2	2	*2,090*	*2,080*	*1,211*	*1,109*	..	..	1,142	1,053	69	56	*1,617*	*1,562*	*25*	*22*	..	..
Jaisalmer	..	..	..	..	..	..	..	..	..	..	*761*	*659*	*76*	*59*	..	..	29	22	47	37	*123*	*67*	..	..	..	..
Jhalawar	*201*	*161*	..	..	..	..	201	161	..	..	*13*	*10*	*137*	*110*	..	..	137	110	..	..	*118*	*118*	*9*	*6*	..	..
Karauli	*16,803*	*13,909*	..	..	..	..	16,803	13,909	..	..	*13*	*19*	*20*	*13*	..	..	20	13	..	..	*117*	*101*	*76*	*59*	..	..
Kishangarh	*169*	*159*	..	..	..	..	169	159	..	..	*72*	*73*	*47*	*38*	..	..	47	38	..	..	*49*	*37*	..	..	..	..
Kotah	*30,055*	*27,415*	..	..	..	..	30,055	27,415	..	..	*237*	*234*	*235*	*206*	..	..	207	189	28	17	*395*	*385*	*1,194*	*1,155*	..	..
Kushalgarh (Chiefship)	..	..	..	..	..	..	..	..	..	..	*6*	*7*	..	..	..	..	..	..	..	..	..	..	..	..	..	..
Lawa (Estate)	*66*	*59*	..	..	..	..	66	59	..	..	..	..	*1*	*3*	..	..	1	3	..	..	..	..	..	..	..	..
Marwar	*9,689*	*8,249*	160	145	..	..	9,529	8,100	..	4	*3,075*	*2,994*	*3,314*	*2,898*	..	..	3,123	2,724	191	174	*2,829*	*2,428*	..	..	..	..
Mewar	*37,357*	*34,432*	23,345	22,002	..	..	14,011	12,429	1	1	*215*	*227*	*1,117*	*1,013*	..	..	1,008	904	109	109	*296*	*250*	*541*	*510*	..	..
Partabgarh	*81*	*86*	..	..	..	..	81	86	..	..	..	*2*	*46*	*46*	..	..	46	46	..	..	*14*	*11*	*143*	*135*	..	..
Shahpura (Chiefship)	*429*	*336*	..	..	..	..	429	336	..	..	*5*	*5*	*28*	*19*	..	..	28	19	..	..	..	..	..	..	..	..
Sirohi	*3,387*	*2,624*	223	165	..	..	3,164	2,459	..	..	*5*	*3*	*285*	*249*	..	..	284	248	1	1	*44*	*38*	*49*	*35*	..	..
Tonk	*8,615*	*7,614*	..	..	..	..	8,615	7,614	..	..	*56*	*77*	*135*	*162*	..	..	134	162	1	..	*354*	*331*	*117*	*113*	46	25
Ajmer-Merwara	*2,442*	*1,781*	1	..	2	..	2,436	1,781	3	..	*252*	*254*	*810*	*801*	4	..	794	790	12	11	*778*	*637*	..	..	..	..
Ajmer	*2,418*	*1,764*	1	..	2	..	2,412	1,764	3	..	*223*	*225*	*722*	*708*	4	..	713	705	5	3	*727*	*606*	..	..	..	..
Merwara	*24*	*17*	..	..	..	..	24	17	..	..	*29*	*29*	*88*	*93*	..	..	81	85	7	8	*51*	*31*	..	..	..	..

* Includes Musalman Dārhi, Dhādi, Dholi, Nagārchi.

TABLE XIII.—Caste, Tribe, or Race. Part II.—By States or Districts, and Religions—*contd.*

Province; and State or District.	Moghiā—*contd.* Hindu. M.	Moghiā—*contd.* Hindu. F.	Nāi. Total. M.	Nāi. Total. F.	Nāi. Arya. M.	Nāi. Arya. F.	Nāi. Hindu. M.	Nāi. Hindu. F.	Nāi. Jain. M.	Nāi. Jain. F.	Nāi. Musalman. M.	Nāi. Musalman. F.	Nāi. Sikh. M.	Nāi. Sikh. F.
1	681	682	683	684	685	686	687	688	689	690	691	692	693	694
Rajputana	2,165	2,078	84,866	77,597	3	2	80,078	73,039	1	..	4,767	4,551	17	4
Alwar	..	..	6,758	6,315	..	..	5,645	5,225	..	..	1,113	1,090	..	..
Banswara	37	30	93	117	..	..	87	103	..	..	11	14	..	..
Bharatpur	..	..	5,086	4,205	..	..	4,165	3,409	..	..	921	797	..	..
Bikaner	..	..	8,643	7,535	..	..	7,914	6,851	1	..	714	681	14	3
Bundi	22	19	1,845	1,712	..	..	1,817	1,686	..	..	23	26	..	..
Dholpur	6	10	2,581	2,110	..	..	2,563	2,100	..	..	17	10	1	..
Dungarpur	..	..	129	151	..	..	129	151	..	..	..	..	..	..
Jaipur	25	22	22,114	20,535	..	..	20,912	19,362	..	..	1,202	1,173	..	..
Jaisalmer	..	..	771	610	..	..	754	596	..	..	17	14	..	..
Jhalawar	9	8	901	818	1	..	891	808	..	..	9	10	..	..
Karauli	70	60	1,123	950	..	..	1,056	883	..	..	67	67	..	..
Kishangarh	..	..	753	670	..	..	728	646	..	..	25	24	..	..
Kotah	1,194	1,155	5,480	5,188	..	..	5,413	5,123	..	..	65	64	2	1
Kushalgarh (Chiefship)	..	..	25	16	..	..	25	16	..	..	..	..	..	..
Lawa (Estate)	..	..	21	25	..	..	21	25	..	..	..	..	..	..
Marwar	..	..	16,201	15,092	2	3	15,789	14,659	..	..	410	430	..	..
Mewar	541	510	8,780	8,297	..	..	8,749	8,261	..	..	31	36	..	..
Partabgarh	143	135	352	337	..	..	352	337	..	..	..	..	..	..
Shahpura (Chiefship)	..	..	434	399	..	..	434	399	..	..	..	..	..	..
Sirohi	48	35	139	106	..	..	125	102	..	..	14	4	..	..
Tonk	71	88	2,632	2,410	..	..	2,509	2,299	..	..	123	111	..	..
Ajmer-Merwara	..	..	3,297	3,206	4	6	3,181	3,097	..	..	108	103	4	..
Ajmer	..	..	2,614	2,586	1	3	2,515	2,475	..	..	94	88	4	..
Merwara	..	..	683	640	3	3	666	622	..	..	14	15	..	..

Province; and State or District.	Nāik (Nāyak). Total. M.	Nāik (Nāyak). Total. F.	Nāik (Nāyak). Animist. M.	Nāik (Nāyak). Animist. F.	Nāik (Nāyak). Hindu. M.	Nāik (Nāyak). Hindu. F.	Nāik (Nāyak). Musalman. M.	Nāik (Nāyak). Musalman. F.	Nat. Total. M.	Nat. Total. F.	Nat. Animist. M.	Nat. Animist. F.	Nat. Hindu. M.	Nat. Hindu. F.	Nat. Musalman. M.	Nat. Musalman. F.
1	695	696	697	698	699	700	701	702	703	704	705	706	707	708	709	710
Rajputana	22,111	20,380	..	..	22,041	20,326	70	54	4,392	4,055	57	61	3,703	3,408	632	586
Alwar	539	539	..	..	537	538	2	1	292	211	..	..	157	91	135	120
Banswara	2	..	..	..	..	..	2	..	15	16	..	..	15	16	..	..
Bharatpur	3	..	..	..	3	..	..	..	498	450	..	..	388	327	110	123
Bikaner	6,029	5,232	..	..	6,028	5,231	1	1	143	77	..	..	123	61	20	16
Bundi	457	394	..	..	457	394	..	..	85	93	..	1	85	92	..	..
Dholpur	8	9	..	..	8	9	..	..	165	143	..	..	129	116	36	27
Dungarpur	..	..	..	..	..	..	..	..	7	6	..	..	7	6	..	..
Jaipur	8,488	7,810	..	..	8,474	7,803	14	7	1,301	1,186	3	2	1,043	961	255	223
Jaisalmer	..	..	..	..	..	..	..	..	..	..	..	..	..	..	..	..
Jhalawar	105	96	..	..	105	96	..	..	106	115	50	53	30	35	26	27
Karauli	..	..	..	..	..	..	..	..	46	37	..	..	46	37	..	..
Kishangarh	245	214	..	..	244	214	1	..	47	57	..	..	47	57	..	..
Kotah	1,879	1,826	..	..	1,879	1,826	..	..	197	209	..	..	181	194	16	15
Kushalgarh (Chiefship)	..	..	..	..	..	..	..	..	..	..	..	..	..	..	..	..
Lawa (Estate)	15	17	..	..	15	17	..	..	..	..	..	..	..	..	..	..
Marwar	948	890	..	..	934	880	14	10	908	886	..	..	908	886	..	..
Mewar	2,441	2,393	..	..	2,405	2,358	36	35	408	406	..	..	393	400	15	6
Partabgarh	83	62	..	..	83	62	..	..	..	3	..	..	..	..	..	3
Shahpura (Chiefship)	312	286	..	..	312	286	..	..	19	10	..	..	19	10	..	..
Sirohi	2	2	..	..	2	2	..	..	28	34	..	..	20	22	8	12
Tonk	555	510	..	..	555	510	..	..	124	116	4	5	112	97	8	14
Ajmer-Merwara	1,298	1,199	3	..	1,295	1,199	..	..	479	441	..	..	479	439	..	2
Ajmer	1,133	1,065	3	..	1,130	1,065	..	..	421	385	..	..	421	385	..	..
Merwara	165	134	..	..	165	134	..	..	58	56	..	..	58	54	..	2

TABLE XIII.—Caste, Tribe, or Race. Part II.—By States or Districts, and Religions—*contd.*

Province; and State or District.	OD (ODH.)*						PĀRSI.		PATEL.						PATHĀN.		PINĀRĀ.†		PORTUGUESE.		PROHIT.					
	Total.		Hindu.		Musalman.		Total.		Total.		Hindu.		Jain.		Musalman.		Musalman.		Christian.		Total.		Arya.		Hindu.	
	M.	F.	M.	F.	M.	F.	M.	F.	M.	F.	M.	F.	M.	F.	M.	F.	M.	F.	M.	F.	M.	F.	M.	F.	M.	F.
1	711	712	713	714	715	716	717	718	719	720	721	722	723	724	725	726	727	728	729	730	731	732	733	734	735	736
Rajputana	4,150	3,680	3,795	3,400	364	280	191	151	27,751	28,047	27,750	28,047	1	..	57,505	50,786	7,388	7,010	25	20	19,130	17,813	2	1	19,128	17,811
Alwar	10	8	..	1	10	7	2	1	1	2	1	2	..	..	2,710	2,545	245	236	6	6	20	29	..	..	20	29
Banswara	19	20	10	20	..	..	4	..	6,732	7,037	6,732	7,037	..	..	639	651	42	53	..	..	..	..	..	..	..	..
Bharatpur	34	25	20	16	14	9	3	4	..	..	..	..	..	..	2,258	1,856	273	220	2	..	..	..	..	..	..	..
Bikaner	781	700	670	509	214	191	1	3	..	..	..	..	..	..	950	712	104	102	..	..	646	600	..	..	646	600
Bundi	151	120	132	108	19	12	6	2	..	..	..	..	..	..	1,125	1,046	411	380	..	..	..	..	..	..	..	..
Dholpur	110	55	60	30	50	25	3	3	..	..	..	..	..	..	2,715	2,597	..	..	..	..	..	..	..	..	..	..
Dungarpur	12	..	12	..	..	..	..	..	9,627	10,331	9,627	10,331	..	..	635	507	6	1	..	..	..	..	..	..	..	..
Jaipur	107	93	88	74	19	19	16	12	1	..	1	..	..	..	16,165	13,975	975	947	13	8	2,580	2,350	..	..	2,586	2,350
Jaisalmer	153	123	158	123	..	..	..	..	..	..	..	..	..	..	106	89	..	..	..	..	..	..	..	..	..	..
Jhalawar	97	82	97	82	..	..	2	..	1	1	1	1	..	..	1,352	1,346	215	224	..	..	..	..	..	..	..	..
Karauli	11	10	11	10	..	..	..	..	1	2	1	2	..	..	1,047	976	28	19	..	..	..	..	..	..	..	..
Kishangarh	16	16	16	16	..	..	4	3	..	..	..	..	..	..	675	582	102	84	..	..	65	64	..	..	65	64
Kotah	264	274	254	270	10	4	10	10	4	1	4	1	..	..	6,566	5,865	1,056	1,037	2	..	..	..	..	..	..	..
Kushalgarh (Chiefship)	..	..	..	..	..	..	1	..	6	6	6	6	..	..	60	71	2	5	..	..	2	4	..	..	2	4
Lawa (Estate)	..	..	..	..	..	..	..	..	..	..	..	..	..	..	56	33	..	..	..	..	..	..	..	..	..	..
Marwar	1,199	1,042	1,173	1,032	26	10	41	28	10,433	9,820	10,433	9,820	..	..	5,607	4,556	1,809	1,675	..	1	15,741	14,720	2	1	15,739	14,710
Mewar	1,093	1,031	1,003	1,031	..	..	13	9	931	839	930	839	1	..	5,857	5,030	1,729	1,722	1	..	69	45	..	..	69	45
Partabgarh	4	4	4	4	..	..	4	1	..	..	..	..	..	..	489	428	56	54	..	..	..	..	..	..	..	..
Shahpura (Chiefship)	13	4	13	4	..	..	2	..	1	..	1	..	..	..	137	165	99	95	..	..	..	..	..	..	..	..
Sirohi	33	32	33	32	..	..	79	75	13	8	13	8	..	..	707	536	136	150	1	5	..	..	..	..	..	..
Tonk	41	41	42	38	2	3	..	..	..	..	..	..	..	..	7,749	7,220	..	..	..	..	1	..	..	..	1	..
Ajmer-Merwara	183	160	183	160	..	..	134	128	4	2	4	2	..	..	6,176	5,244	555	451	20	9	90	88	..	..	90	88
Ajmer	71	56	71	56	..	..	128	118	3	2	3	2	..	..	5,567	4,766	461	378	20	9	87	86	..	..	87	86
Merwara	112	104	112	104	..	..	6	10	1	..	1	..	..	..	609	478	94	73	..	..	3	2	..	..	3	2

* Includes Beldar.

† Includes Musalman Dhunia and Kanders.

TABLE XIII.—Caste, Tribe, or Race. Part II.—By States or Districts, and Religions—*contd.*

Province; and State or District.	Raigar. Total. M.	Raigar. Total. F.	Raigar. Animist. M.	Raigar. Animist. F.	Raigar. Hindu. M.	Raigar. Hindu. F.	Raigar. Musalman. M.	Raigar. Musalman. F.	Rajput.* Total. M.	Rajput.* Total. F.	Rajput.* Arya. M.	Rajput.* Arya. F.	Rajput.* Brahmo. M.	Rajput.* Brahmo. F.	Rajput.* Hindu. M.	Rajput.* Hindu. F.	Rajput.* Jain. M.	Rajput.* Jain. F.	Rajput.* Musalman. M.	Rajput.* Musalman. F.	Rajput.* Sikh. M.	Rajput.* Sikh. F.	Rana. Total. M.	Rana. Total. F.	Rana. Hindu. M.	Rana. Hindu. F.	Rana. Musalman. M.	Rana. Musalman. F.
1	737	738	739	740	741	742	743	744	745	746	747	748	749	750	751	752	753	754	755	756	757	758	759	760	761	762	763	764
Rajputana	*41,626*	*39,942*	..	..	**41,622**	**39,935**	**4**	**7**	*383,194*	*302,168*	**168**	**99**	**3**	**2**	**335,559**	**277,954**	**13**	**15**	**29,368**	**24,034**	**79**	**64**	*5,967*	*5,841*	**4,979**	**4,770**	**988**	**1,071**
Alwar	*956*	*961*	..	..	953	959	3	2	*16,272*	*13,555*	..	..	..	..	13,711	11,180	..	..	2,561	2,375	..	..	*949*	*1,005*	506	525	443	480
Banswara	..	..	..	..	..	..	..	..	*1,874*	*1,734*	..	..	..	..	1,874	1,734	..	..	..	..	..	..	..	..	..	..	..	..
Bharatpur	*299*	*279*	..	..	299	279	..	..	*6,493*	*4,910*	19	10	..	..	6,353	4,825	..	..	121	75	..	..	*19*	*12*	15	9	4	3
Bikaner	*2,056*	*1,999*	..	..	2,056	1,999	..	..	*49,423*	*37,243*	8	3	..	..	31,095	21,833	12	13	18,306	15,394	2	..	*35*	*29*	30	26	5	3
Bundi	*65*	*33*	..	..	65	33	..	..	*2,909*	*2,139*	..	..	..	..	2,909	2,139	..	..	..	..	..	..	..	..	..	..	..	..
Dholpur	..	..	..	..	..	..	..	..	*15,202*	*11,262*	..	..	2	2	15,192	11,258	..	..	1	..	7	2	..	..	..	..	..	..
Dungarpur	..	..	..	..	..	..	..	..	*5,068*	*5,021*	1	..	..	..	5,063	5,019	..	..	..	..	4	2	..	..	..	..	..	..
Jaipur	*26,643*	*25,579*	..	..	26,643	25,576	..	3	*68,660*	*49,297*	50	19	..	..	67,754	48,352	..	..	801	874	52	52	*4,839*	*4,702*	4,303	4,110	536	583
Jaisalmer	..	..	..	..	..	..	..	..	*19,503*	*14,605*	..	..	..	..	12,577	9,005	..	..	6,926	5,600	..	..	..	..	..	..	..	..
Jhalawar	..	..	..	..	..	..	..	..	*1,775*	*1,551*	..	1	..	..	1,772	1,549	..	..	..	..	3	1	..	..	..	..	..	..
Karauli	..	..	..	..	..	..	..	..	*3,482*	*2,610*	..	..	..	..	3,482	2,610	..	..	..	..	..	..	*50*	*36*	50	36	..	..
Kishangarh	*2,020*	*2,055*	..	..	2,020	2,055	..	..	*2,545*	*2,229*	6	5	..	..	2,490	2,157	..	..	49	67	..	..	*12*	*11*	12	11	..	..
Kotah	*66*	*80*	..	..	66	80	..	..	*7,921*	*6,826*	2	1	..	..	7,910	6,822	..	..	5	1	4	2	*1*	..	1	..	..	..
Kushalgarh (Chiefship)	..	..	..	..	..	..	..	..	*299*	*345*	..	..	..	..	299	345	..	..	..	..	..	..	..	..	..	..	..	..
Lawa (Estate)	*29*	*19*	..	..	29	19	..	..	*46*	*46*	..	..	..	..	46	46	..	..	..	..	..	..	*1*	..	1	..	..	..
Marwar	*6,623*	*6,091*	..	..	6,622	6,089	1	2	*109,734*	*85,995*	64	37	..	..	109,461	85,835	1	1	211	117	7	5	*47*	*25*	47	23	..	..
Mewar	*899*	*921*	..	..	899	921	..	..	*58,088*	*48,795*	..	..	..	..	57,895	48,676	..	..	193	119	..	..	..	*7*	..	5	..	2
Partabgarh	..	..	..	..	..	..	..	..	*1,662*	*1,509*	1	6	..	..	1,657	1,502	..	..	4	1	..	..	..	..	..	..	..	..
Shahpura (Chiefship)	*732*	*732*	..	..	732	732	..	..	*869*	*768*	12	1	..	..	857	767	..	..	..	..	..	..	..	..	..	..	..	..
Sirohi	*50*	*44*	..	..	50	44	..	..	*8,009*	*6,701*	..	..	..	..	7,942	6,680	..	1	67	11	..	..	..	*1*	..	1	..	..
Tonk	*1,145*	*1,149*	..	..	1,145	1,149	..	..	*5,299*	*4,427*	9	10	1	..	5,289	4,411	..	..	..	..	..	..	*14*	*13*	14	13	..	..
Ajmer-Merwara	*10,148*	*9,710*	**13**	**11**	**10,135**	**9,699**	..	..	*8,225*	*6,077*	**43**	**15**	..	..	**8,096**	**6,038**	**1**	**1**	**79**	**21**	**6**	**2**	*9*	*5*	**9**	**5**	..	..
Ajmer	*8,172*	*7,856*	*13*	*11*	8,159	7,845	..	..	*7,548*	*5,644*	35	12	..	..	7,437	5,611	1	..	72	21	3	..	*9*	*5*	9	5	..	..
Merwara	*1,976*	*1,854*	..	..	1,976	1,854	..	..	*677*	*433*	8	3	..	..	659	427	..	1	7	..	3	2	..	..	..	..	..	..

* Details of the various Rajput clans will be found in the subsidiary Tables in the Report Volume.

TABLE XIII.—Caste, Tribe, or Race. Part II.—By States or Districts, and Religions—*contd.*

Province; and State or District.	RANGREZ.*		RÃO.						RÃWAT.										REBÃRI.								RUSSIAN.		SÃD.†			
	Musalman.		Total.		Hindu.		Musalman.		Total.		Animist.		Hindu.		Jain.		Musalman.		Total.		Animist		Hindu.		Musalman.		Christian.		Total.		Animist.	
	M.	F.	M.	F.	M.	F.	M.	F.	M.	F.	M.	F.	M.	F.	M.	F.	M.	F.	M.	F.	M.	F.	M.	F.	M.	F.	M.	F.	M.	F.	M.	F.
1	765	766	767	768	769	770	771	772	773	774	775	776	777	778	779	780	781	782	783	784	785	786	787	788	789	790	791	792	793	794	795	796
Rajputana	*8,049*	*7,436*	*6,335*	*6,236*	**6,328**	**6,228**	**7**	**8**	*7,580*	*6,174*	**11**	**4**	**7,565**	**6,168**	..	..	**4**	**2**	*67,760*	*62,158*	**1**	..	**67,754**	**62,157**	**5**	**1**	..	..	*15,573*	*12,971*	**4**	**2**
Alwar	*846*	*763*	*246*	*259*	246	259	..	..	*4*	*5*	..	..	4	5	..	..	..	..	*585*	*683*	..	..	585	683	..	..	..	..	..	..	..	..
Banswara	*10*	*17*	*5*	*8*	5	8	..	..	..	..	..	..	..	..	..	..	..	..	*462*	*566*	..	..	462	566	..	..	..	..	..	..	..	..
Bharatpur	*421*	*326*	..	..	..	..	..	..	..	..	..	..	..	..	..	..	..	..	*181*	*204*	..	..	181	204	..	..	..	..	*262*	*215*	..	..
Bikaner	*752*	*672*	*2*	*1*	2	1	..	..	*5*	*1*	..	..	5	1	..	..	..	..	*897*	*840*	..	..	897	840	..	..	..	..	..	..	..	..
Bundi	*297*	*301*	*419*	*402*	419	402	..	..	..	..	..	..	..	..	..	..	..	..	*691*	*747*	..	..	691	747	..	..	..	..	..	..	..	..
Dholpur	*141*	*123*	..	..	..	..	..	..	*1*	..	..	..	1	..	..	..	..	..	*35*	*29*	..	..	35	29	..	..	..	..	..	..	..	..
Dungarpur	..	..	..	*6*	..	6	..	..	*4*	..	..	..	4	..	..	..	..	..	*450*	*609*	..	..	450	609	..	..	..	..	..	..	..	..
Jaipur	*2,638*	*2,390*	*1,573*	*1,462*	1,573	1,462	..	..	*13*	*5*	..	..	13	5	..	..	..	..	*1,474*	*1,396*	1	..	1,468	1,395	5	1	..	..	..	..	..	..
Jaisalmer	..	..	..	..	..	..	..	..	..	..	..	..	..	..	..	..	..	..	*103*	*75*	..	..	103	75	..	..	..	..	..	..	..	..
Jhalawar	*79*	*92*	*72*	*67*	72	67	..	..	*4*	*2*	..	..	4	2	..	..	..	..	*99*	*71*	..	..	99	71	..	..	..	..	..	..	..	..
Karauli	*182*	*97*	*79*	*49*	79	49	..	..	..	..	..	..	..	..	..	..	..	..	*83*	*31*	..	..	83	31	..	..	..	..	..	..	..	..
Kishangarh	*27*	*26*	*98*	*97*	98	97	..	..	*3*	*3*	..	..	3	3	..	..	..	..	*124*	*132*	..	..	124	132	..	..	..	..	..	..	..	..
Kotah	*653*	*646*	*1,673*	*1,589*	1,673	1,589	..	..	*40*	*24*	..	..	40	24	..	..	..	..	*1,577*	*1,695*	..	..	1,577	1,695	..	..	..	..	..	..	..	..
Kushalgarh (Chiefship)	*1*	..	..	..	..	..	..	..	..	..	..	..	..	..	..	..	..	..	..	..	..	..	..	..	..	..	..	..	..	..	..	..
Lawa (Estate)	*2*	..	..	..	..	..	..	..	..	..	..	..	..	..	..	..	..	..	..	..	..	..	..	..	..	..	..	..	..	..	..	..
Marwar	*851*	*843*	*397*	*427*	397	427	..	..	*4,681*	*3,873*	..	..	4,677	3,872	..	..	4	1	*48,144*	*43,078*	..	..	48,144	43,078	..	..	..	..	*15,311*	*12,756*	4	2
Mewar	*765*	*741*	*1,706*	*1,809*	1,699	1,801	7	8	*2,813*	*2,253*	11	4	2,802	2,248	..	..	..	1	*4,812*	*4,901*	..	..	4,812	4,901	..	..	..	..	..	..	..	..
Partabgarh	*21*	*20*	*42*	*38*	42	38	..	..	..	..	..	..	..	..	..	..	..	..	*10*	*7*	..	..	10	7	..	..	..	..	..	..	..	..
Shahpura (Chiefship)	*102*	*81*	*13*	*15*	13	15	..	..	..	..	..	..	..	..	..	..	..	..	*103*	*86*	..	..	103	86	..	..	..	..	..	..	..	..
Sirohi	*42*	*32*	*5*	*2*	5	2	..	..	..	..	..	..	..	..	..	..	..	..	*7,760*	*6,844*	..	..	7,760	6,844	..	..	..	..	..	..	..	..
Tonk	*279*	*266*	*5*	*5*	5	5	..	..	*12*	*8*	..	..	12	8	..	..	..	..	*167*	*164*	..	..	167	164	..	..	..	..	..	..	..	..
Ajmer-Merwara	*338*	*263*	*178*	*146*	**178**	**146**	..	..	*24,963*	*22,942*	..	..	**24,953**	**22,908**	**1**	..	**9**	**34**	*1,085*	*948*	..	..	**1,085**	**948**	..	..	*1*	..	..	..	..	..
Ajmer	*318*	*226*	*173*	*140*	173	140	..	..	*487*	*363*	..	..	481	363	1	..	2	..	*1,018*	*892*	..	..	1,018	892	..	..	*1*	..	..	..	..	..
Merwara	*40*	*37*	*5*	*6*	5	6	..	..	*24,476*	*22,579*	..	..	24,469	22,545	..	..	7	34	*67*	*56*	..	..	67	56	..	..	..	..	..	..	..	..

* Includes Musalman Nilgar.

† Includes Sādh (Bharatpur and Marwar).

TABLE XIII.—CASTE, TRIBE, OR RACE. PART II.—BY STATES OR DISTRICTS, AND RELIGIONS—*contd.*

Province; and State or District.	*SĀD—contd.				†SĀDHU.										SAHAR.								SAIYAD.		SANJOGI.		SĀNSI (SĀNSIĀ, SĀNSRI).							
	ARYA.		HINDU.		TOTAL.		ARYA.		HINDU.		JAIN.		SIKH.		TOTAL.		ANIMIST.		HINDU.		MUSALMAN.		MUSALMAN.		HINDU.		TOTAL.		ANIMIST.		HINDU.		MUSALMAN.	
	M.	F.	M.	F.	M.	F.	M.	F.	M.	F.	M.	F.	M.	F.	M.	F.	M.	F.	M.	F.	M.	F.	M.	F.	M.	F.	M.	F.	M.	F.	M.	F.	M.	F.
1	797	798	799	800	801	802	803	804	805	806	807	808	809	810	811	812	813	814	815	816	817	818	819	820	821	822	823	824	825	826	827	828	829	830
Rajputana	**41**	**45**	**15,528**	**12,916**	***6,451***	***4,068***	**2**	**2**	**6,259**	**3,663**	**180**	**396**	**10**	**7**	***6,998***	***6,803***	**807**	**787**	**6,189**	**6,016**	**3**	..	***15,843***	***13,712***	***5,327***	***4,581***	***2,127***	***2,362***	**133**	**93**	**1,993**	**2,269**	**1**	..
Ajwar	..	..	..	..	*44*	*27*	..	..	44	27	..	..	..	..	..	..	..	..	..	..	..	..	*1,449*	*1,415*	*1,034*	*930*	..	..	..	..	..	..	..	..
Banswara	..	..	..	..	*7*	*9*	..	..	7	9	..	..	..	..	..	..	..	..	..	..	..	..	*71*	*94*	..	..	..	..	..	..	..	..	..	..
Bharatpur	..	..	262	216	..	..	..	..	..	..	..	..	..	..	..	..	..	..	..	..	..	..	*1,627*	*1,479*	..	..	..	..	..	..	..	..	..	..
Bikaner	..	..	..	..	*397*	*146*	..	..	375	130	14	9	8	7	..	..	..	..	..	..	..	..	*857*	*687*	..	..	..	..	..	..	..	..	..	..
Bundi	..	..	..	..	*71*	*49*	..	..	68	49	3	..	..	..	..	..	..	..	..	..	..	..	*152*	*179*	..	..	*952*	*883*	..	..	951	883	1	..
Dholpur	..	..	..	..	..	..	..	..	..	..	..	..	..	..	..	..	..	..	..	..	..	..	*531*	*496*	..	..	..	..	..	..	..	..	..	..
Dungarpur	..	..	..	..	*10*	*1*	..	..	8	1	2	..	..	..	..	..	..	..	..	..	..	..	*46*	*48*	..	..	..	..	..	..	..	..	..	..
Jaipur	..	..	..	..	*422*	*60*	..	..	417	58	5	2	..	..	*3*	*3*	..	..	3	3	..	..	*4,179*	*3,677*	*4,037*	*3,425*	*194*	*482*	72	48	122	434	..	..
Jaisalmer	..	..	..	..	*95*	*81*	..	..	92	81	3	..	..	..	..	..	..	..	..	..	..	..	*36*	*29*	..	..	..	..	..	..	..	..	..	..
Jhalawar	..	..	..	..	*7*	*1*	..	..	4	..	3	1	..	..	..	..	..	..	..	..	..	..	*261*	*230*	..	..	*39*	*31*	39	31	..	..	..	..
Karauli	..	..	..	..	*2*	..	..	..	2	..	..	..	..	..	..	..	..	..	..	..	..	..	*205*	*180*	*249*	*224*	..	..	..	..	..	..	..	..
Kishangarh	..	..	..	..	*379*	*315*	..	..	379	306	..	9	..	..	..	..	..	..	..	..	..	..	*170*	*138*	..	..	..	..	..	..	..	..	..	..
Kotah	..	..	..	..	*105*	*19*	..	..	101	11	4	8	..	..	*6,996*	*6,800*	807	787	6,184	6,013	3	..	*1,173*	*1,123*	*7*	*1*	*507*	*530*	..	..	507	530	..	..
Kushalgarh (Chiefship)	..	..	..	..	*30*	*25*	..	..	30	25	..	..	..	..	..	..	..	..	..	..	..	..	*4*	*4*	..	..	..	..	..	..	..	..	..	..
Lawa (Estate)	..	..	..	..	*1*	..	..	..	1	..	..	..	..	..	..	..	..	..	..	..	..	..	..	*1*	..	..	..	..	..	..	..	..	..	..
Marwar	41	45	15,266	12,700	*1,909*	*1,225*	..	..	1,805	941	104	284	..	..	..	..	..	..	..	..	..	..	*1,719*	*1,467*	..	*1*	*395*	*419*	10	9	385	410	..	..
Mewar	..	..	..	..	*1,725*	*1,328*	1	..	1,705	1,265	17	63	2	..	..	..	..	..	..	..	..	..	*812*	*717*	..	..	*23*	*10*	5	..	18	10	..	..
Partabgarh	..	..	..	..	*12*	*8*	..	..	12	8	..	..	..	..	..	..	..	..	..	..	..	..	*51*	*36*	..	..	*2*	..	..	..	2	..	..	..
Shahpura (Chiefship)	..	..	..	..	*522*	*185*	1	2	515	181	6	2	..	..	..	..	..	..	..	..	..	..	*48*	*47*	..	..	*4*	*2*	..	..	4	2	..	..
Sirohi	..	..	..	..	*697*	*579*	..	..	678	561	19	18	..	..	..	..	..	..	..	..	..	..	*189*	*132*	..	..	..	..	..	..	..	..	..	..
Tonk	..	..	..	..	*16*	*10*	..	..	16	10	..	..	..	..	..	..	..	..	..	..	..	..	*1,662*	*1,533*	..	..	*11*	*5*	7	5	4	..	..	..
Ajmer-Merwara	..	..	..	..	***2,552***	***2,086***	..	..	**2,523**	**2,061**	**29**	**25**	..	..	..	..	..	..	..	..	..	..	***2,823***	***2,376***	..	..	***149***	***176***	**61**	**82**	**88**	**94**	..	..
Ajmer	..	..	..	..	*2,290*	*1,859*	..	..	2,282	1,845	8	14	..	..	..	..	..	..	..	..	..	..	*2,701*	*2,295*	..	..	*133*	*150*	59	78	74	72	..	..
Merwara	..	..	..	..	*262*	*227*	..	..	241	216	21	11	..	..	..	..	..	..	..	..	..	..	*122*	*81*	..	..	*16*	*26*	2	4	14	22	..	..

*Includes Sadh (Bharatpur and Marwar).

†Includes Sādh (Bikaner, Jaisalmer and Sirohi).

TABLE XIII.—CASTE, TRIBE, OR RACE. PART II.—BY STATES OR DISTRICTS, AND RELIGIONS—*contd.*

Province; State or District.	SARGARA.						SCOTCH.		SEVAG.*						SHEKH.		SILÁWAT.						SINDHI.		SIRVI.	
	TOTAL.		ANIMIST.		HINDU.		CHRISTIAN.		TOTAL.		HINDU.		JAIN.		MUSALMAN.		TOTAL.		HINDU.		MUSALMAN.		MUSALMAN.		HINDU.	
	M.	F.	M.	F.	M.	F.	M.	F.	M.	F.	M.	F.	M.	F.	M.	F.	M.	F.	M.	F.	M.	F.	M.	F.	M.	F.
1	831	832	833	834	835	836	837	838	839	840	841	842	843	844	845	846	847	848	849	850	851	852	853	854	855	856
Rajputana	*13,865*	*12,655*	48	43	13,823	12,612	*80*	*64*	*4,863*	*5,312*	4,796	5,163	67	49	*96,788*	*85,231*	*3,929*	*3,936*	830	982	3,099	2,954	*17,775*	*15,502*	*26,651*	*24,344*
Alwar	..	..	..	..	..	..	..	..	..	..	..	..	..	..	*4,872*	*4,343*	*1*	..	1	..	..	..	..	..	..	..
Banswara	*302*	*321*	..	..	302	321	..	..	*21*	*22*	21	22	..	..	*315*	*307*	*138*	*137*	63	65	75	72	*60*	*52*	..	..
Bharatpur	..	..	..	..	..	..	*1*	*4*	..	..	..	..	..	..	*6,449*	*5,471*	..	..	..	..	..	..	..	..	..	..
Bikaner	*1*	..	..	..	1	..	..	..	*1,137*	*1,202*	1,130	1,202	7	..	*4,059*	*3,258*	*64*	*63*	..	..	64	63	..	..	..	..
Bundi	..	..	..	..	..	..	..	..	..	..	..	..	..	..	*727*	*630*	*48*	*39*	48	39	..	..	..	..	..	..
Dholpur	..	..	..	..	..	..	..	*1*	..	..	..	..	..	..	*4,184*	*3,827*	..	..	..	..	..	..	..	..	..	..
Dungarpur	*58*	*59*	..	..	58	50	..	..	*17*	..	17	..	..	..	*537*	*520*	..	..	..	..	..	..	..	..	..	..
Jaipur	*2*	*1*	..	..	2	1	*28*	*24*	..	..	..	..	..	..	*33,501*	*30,609*	*545*	*711*	544	709	1	2	..	..	*3*	*6*
Jaisalmer	..	..	..	..	..	..	..	..	*10*	*17*	10	17	..	..	*3,924*	*2,553*	..	..	..	..	..	..	..	..	..	..
Jhalawar	..	..	..	..	..	..	..	*1*	*2*	*3*	..	..	2	3	*1,130*	*1,113*	*66*	*78*	66	78	..	..	..	..	..	..
Karauli	..	..	..	..	..	..	..	..	..	..	..	..	..	..	*1,104*	*840*	..	..	..	..	..	..	..	..	..	..
Kishangarh	*22*	*28*	..	..	22	28	..	..	*51*	*59*	49	50	2	..	*1,098*	*966*	..	..	..	..	..	..	..	..	..	..
Kotah	..	..	..	..	..	..	*3*	*2*	..	..	..	..	..	..	*5,056*	*4,663*	*84*	*67*	54	47	30	20	..	..	..	*2*
Kushalgarh (Chiefship)	..	..	..	..	..	..	..	..	*6*	*5*	4	..	2	5	*30*	*29*	..	..	..	..	..	..	..	..	..	..
Lawa (Estate)	..	..	..	..	..	..	..	..	..	..	..	..	..	..	*1*	..	..	..	..	..	..	..	..	..	..	..
Marwar	*9,882*	*9,004*	..	..	9,882	9,004	*4*	*3*	*1,723*	*2,141*	1,716	2,137	8	4	*18,142*	*15,180*	*2,887*	*2,748*	42	34	2,845	2,714	*17,663*	*15,416*	*26,319*	*24,035*
Mewar	*727*	*662*	..	..	727	662	*3*	*6*	*1,687*	*1,565*	1,656	1,539	31	26	*5,600*	*5,059*	*12*	*17*	..	..	12	17	..	..	*54*	*59*
Partabgarh	*3*	*1*	..	..	3	1	..	..	*2*	*2*	2	2	..	..	*554*	*547*	..	..	..	..	..	..	..	..	..	..
Shahpura (Chiefship)	*6*	*12*	..	..	6	12	..	..	*93*	*91*	93	91	..	..	*314*	*291*	*23*	*36*	..	..	23	36	..	..	..	..
Sirohi	*2,827*	*2,526*	18	15	2,809	2,511	*41*	*23*	*86*	*62*	71	51	15	11	*1,367*	*940*	*54*	*40*	12	10	42	30	*52*	*31*	*275*	*242*
Tonk	*35*	*41*	24	28	11	13	..	..	*28*	*43*	28	43	..	..	*3,822*	*4,076*	..	..	..	..	..	..	..	..	..	..
Ajmer-Merwara	*434*	*400*	..	..	424	400	*66*	*49*	*137*	*117*	135	115	2	2	*13,380*	*11,750*	..	..	..	..	..	..	..	..	*7*	*3*
Ajmer	*275*	*240*	..	..	275	240	*66*	*48*	*125*	*105*	123	104	2	1	*12,504*	*11,067*	..	..	..	..	..	..	..	..	..	..
Merwara	*149*	*160*	..	..	149	160	..	*1*	*12*	*12*	12	11	..	1	*876*	*683*	..	..	..	..	..	..	..	..	*7*	*3*

*Includes Bhojak.

TABLE XIII.—CASTE, TRIBE, OR RACE. PART II.—BY STATES OR DISTRICTS, AND RELIGIONS—*contd.*

Province; and State or District.	SONDHIĀ.		SPANIARD.		SUNĀR.												SUTĀR.										SWĀMI.	
	HINDU.		CHRISTIAN.		TOTAL.		ARYA.		HINDU.		JAIN.		MUSALMAN.		SIKH.		TOTAL.		ARYA.		HINDU.		JAIN.		SIKH.		TOTAL.	
	M.	F.	M.	F.	M.	F.	M.	F.	M.	F.	M.	F.	M.	F.	M.	F.	M.	F.	M.	F.	M.	F.	M.	F.	M.	F.	M.	F.
1	857	858	859	860	861	862	863	864	865	866	867	868	869	870	871	872	873	874	875	876	877	878	879	880	881	882	883	884
Rajputana	*17,018*	*14,675*	*1*	*1*	*35,569*	*33,465*	7	3	35,527	33,434	7	6	16	16	13	6	*23,699*	*23,249*	..	4	23,697	23,241	1	1	4	3	*19,890*	*13,407*
Alwar	..	..	..	..	*1,318*	*1,156*	..	..	1,318	1,156	..	..	..	..	..	..	*5*	..	..	..	5	..	..	..	..	..	*1,330*	*1,125*
Banswara	..	..	..	..	*256*	*265*	..	..	256	265	..	..	..	..	..	..	*544*	*549*	..	..	544	549	..	..	..	..	..	..
Bharatpur	..	..	..	..	*803*	*762*	..	..	803	762	..	..	..	..	..	..	..	..	..	..	..	..	..	..	..	..	..	..
Bikaner	..	..	..	..	*4,317*	*4,055*	7	3	4,290	4,036	..	1	10	11	10	4	*4,092*	*3,584*	..	..	4,088	3,580	..	1	4	3	*78*	*113*
Bundi	*41*	*56*	..	..	*578*	*532*	..	..	578	532	..	..	..	..	..	..	..	..	..	..	..	..	..	..	..	..	*44*	..
Dholpur	..	..	..	..	*608*	*535*	..	..	605	533	..	..	..	..	3	2	..	..	..	..	..	..	..	..	..	..	..	..
Dungarpur	..	..	..	..	*134*	*145*	..	..	134	145	..	..	..	..	..	..	*807*	*836*	..	..	807	836	..	..	..	..	..	..
Jaipur	..	..	..	..	*8,027*	*7,430*	..	..	8,026	7,429	..	..	1	1	..	..	*2*	*1*	..	..	2	1	..	..	..	..	*9,924*	*5,595*
Jaisalmer	..	..	..	..	*415*	*417*	..	..	415	417	..	..	..	..	..	..	*1,258*	*1,296*	..	..	1,258	1,296	..	..	..	..	*305*	*241*
Jhalawar	*13,281*	*11,264*	*1*	..	*469*	*433*	..	..	469	433	..	..	..	..	..	..	..	..	..	..	..	..	..	..	..	..	..	..
Karauli	..	..	..	..	*410*	*359*	..	..	410	359	..	..	..	..	..	..	..	..	..	..	..	..	..	..	..	..	..	..
Kishangarh	..	..	..	..	*297*	*302*	..	..	297	302	..	..	..	..	..	..	..	..	..	..	..	..	..	..	..	..	*512*	*447*
Kotah	*401*	*268*	..	..	*1,798*	*1,532*	..	..	1,708	1,532	..	..	..	..	..	..	*90*	*111*	..	..	90	111	..	..	..	..	*1*	*1*
Kushalgarh (Chiefship)	..	..	..	..	*33*	*35*	..	..	33	35	..	..	..	..	..	..	*12*	*3*	..	..	12	3	..	..	..	..	..	..
Lawa (Estate)	..	..	..	..	*11*	*5*	..	..	11	5	..	..	..	..	..	..	..	..	..	..	..	..	..	..	..	..	*3*	*2*
Marwar	..	..	..	*1*	*9,707*	*9,529*	..	..	9,697	9,523	6	2	4	4	..	..	*8,946*	*8,272*	..	4	8,946	8,268	..	..	..	..	*6,958*	*5,230*
Mewar	..	..	..	..	*4,241*	*3,868*	..	..	4,240	3,866	1	2	..	..	..	..	*5,890*	*5,662*	..	..	5,889	5,662	1	..	..	..	*246*	*222*
Partabgarh	..	..	..	..	*151*	*168*	..	..	151	168	..	..	..	..	..	..	*457*	*460*	..	..	457	460	..	..	..	..	..	..
Shahpura (Chiefship)	..	..	..	..	*128*	*120*	..	..	128	120	..	..	..	..	..	..	..	..	..	..	..	..	..	..	..	..	*36*	*23*
Sirohi	..	..	..	..	*903*	*941*	..	..	903	940	..	1	..	..	..	..	*1,589*	*1,475*	..	..	1,589	1,475	..	..	..	..	*453*	*358*
Tonk	*3,292*	*3,087*	..	..	*965*	*876*	..	..	965	876	..	..	..	..	..	..	..	..	..	..	..	..	..	..	..	..	..	..
Ajmer-Merwara	..	..	*1*	..	*1,674*	*1,526*	7	8	1,663	1,515	..	..	..	..	4	3	*1*	..	..	..	1	..	..	..	..	..	*169*	*163*
Ajmer	..	..	*1*	..	*1,313*	*1,209*	2	3	1,307	1,203	..	..	..	..	4	3	*1*	..	..	..	1	..	..	..	..	..	*160*	*156*
Merwara	..	..	..	..	*361*	*317*	5	5	356	312	..	..	..	..	..	..	..	..	..	..	..	..	..	..	..	..	*9*	*7*

TABLE XIII.—Caste, Tribe, or Race. Part II.—By States or Districts, and Religions—*contd.*

Province; and State or District.	SWĀMI—*concld.*				SWISS.		TELI.								THORI.		WELSH.		WEST AFRICAN.		MINOR CASTES.					
	Hindu.		Jain.		Christian.		Total.		Arya.		Hindu.		Musalman.		Hindu.		Christian.		Christian.		Total.		Animist.		Arya.	
	M.	F.	M.	F.	M.	F.	M.	F.	M.	F.	M.	F.	M.	F.	M.	F.	M.	F.	M.	F.	M.	F.	M.	F.	M.	F.
1	885	886	887	888	889	890	891	892	893	894	895	896	897	898	899	900	901	902	903	904	905	906	907	908	909	910
Rajputana	**19,871**	**13,336**	**19**	**71**	..	*1*	*40,698*	*37,863*	**3**	**3**	**24,071**	**22,540**	**16,624**	**15,319**	*13,167*	*13,246*	*3*	*1*	..	*1*	*96,141*	*90,951*	**1,952**	**2,021**	**32**	**22**
Alwar	1,330	1,125	..	..	..	..	*2,703*	*2,333*	..	..	617	494	2,086	1,839	..	..	..	..	..	..	*5,338*	*5,136*	16	14	12	13
Banswara	..	..	..	..	..	..	*365*	*349*	..	..	194	209	171	140	*61*	*57*	..	..	..	..	*1,227*	*1,169*	..	..	..	..
Bharatpur	..	..	..	..	..	..	*2,296*	*1,916*	..	..	412	396	1,704	1,520	..	..	..	..	..	..	*5,809*	*5,283*	..	..	1	..
Bikaner	50	42	10	71	..	..	*2,091*	*2,053*	..	..	7	11	2,084	2,042	*5,554*	*7,674*	..	..	..	..	*6,920*	*6,231*	..	..	1	..
Bundi	44	..	..	..	..	..	*1,979*	*1,822*	..	..	1,784	1,638	195	184	..	..	..	..	..	..	*2,451*	*2,314*	16	..	..	..
Dholpur	..	..	..	..	..	..	*1,382*	*1,139*	..	..	670	564	712	575	..	..	..	..	..	..	*2,401*	*2,302*	..	..	..	..
Dungarpur	..	..	..	..	..	..	*205*	*181*	..	..	205	184	..	..	..	..	..	..	..	..	*1,485*	*1,446*	..	..	..	..
Jaipur	9,924	5,595	..	..	..	..	*6,827*	*6,473*	..	..	2,454	2,241	4,373	4,232	..	*1*	*1*	..	..	..	*11,222*	*13,550*	40	42	3	..
Jaisalmer	305	241	..	..	..	..	*31*	*41*	..	..	..	..	34	41	..	..	..	..	..	..	*210*	*225*	..	..	..	..
Jhalawar	..	..	..	..	..	..	*918*	*894*	..	..	918	856	30	38	*44*	*16*	..	..	..	..	*871*	*914*	24	18	..	..
Karauli	..	..	..	..	..	..	*646*	*596*	..	..	261	227	385	360	..	..	..	..	..	..	*1,555*	*1,420*	2	..	..	..
Kishangarh	512	447	..	..	..	..	*311*	*276*	..	..	268	237	43	30	..	..	..	..	..	..	*823*	*993*	..	..	..	..
Kotah	1	1	..	..	..	..	*4,319*	*4,084*	..	..	4,209	3,993	110	91	*25*	*23*	..	..	..	..	*7,644*	*7,397*	..	..	1	..
Kushalgarh (Chiefship)	..	..	..	..	..	..	*23*	*33*	..	..	23	33	..	..	*19*	*17*	..	..	..	..	*540*	*521*	..	..	..	..
Lawa (Estate)	3	2	..	..	..	..	*8*	*10*	..	..	8	10	..	..	..	..	..	..	..	..	*30*	*43*	..	..	..	..
Marwar	6,058	5,280	..	..	..	*1*	*5,049*	*4,620*	..	..	581	546	4,468	4,033	*6,110*	*5,414*	*1*	..	..	..	*12,276*	*11,263*	..	..	..	..
Mewar	246	222	..	..	..	..	*8,024*	*7,500*	..	..	8,011	7,492	13	8	*27*	*21*	..	..	..	..	*12,808*	*11,686*	173	144	..	..
Partabgarh	..	..	..	..	..	..	*536*	*494*	..	..	536	494	..	..	*20*	*18*	..	..	..	..	*2,036*	*2,342*	..	..	..	..
Shahpura (Chiefship)	36	23	..	..	..	..	*322*	*316*	3	3	318	311	1	2	..	..	..	..	..	..	*872*	*807*	..	..	12	9
Sirohi	433	358	..	..	..	..	*44*	*43*	..	..	7	9	37	34	..	..	*1*	*1*	..	*1*	*4,846*	*4,532*	..	..	2	..
Tonk	..	..	..	..	..	..	*2,076*	*2,077*	..	..	2,568	2,505	88	82	*4*	*5*	..	..	..	..	*11,776*	*11,377*	1,681	1,803	..	..
Ajmer-Merwara	**169**	**163**	..	..	..	*3*	*2,281*	*2,122*	..	**1**	**2,038**	**1,897**	**246**	**224**	*24*	*15*	*6*	*2*	..	..	*6,922*	*5,972*	**56**	**42**	**12**	**17**
Ajmer	160	156	..	..	..	*3*	*1,851*	*1,683*	..	1	1,673	1,320	181	162	*4*	*2*	*6*	*2*	..	..	*5,644*	*4,987*	56	42	11	14
Merwara	9	7	..	..	..	..	*430*	*439*	..	..	365	377	65	62	*20*	*13*	..	..	..	..	*1,278*	*985*	..	..	1	3

TABLE XIII.—Caste, Tribe, or Race. Part II.—By States or Districts, and Religions—*concld.*

Province; State or District.	Minor Castes—*concld.* Buddhist.		Hindu.		Jain.		Musalman.		Sikh.		Unspecified. Total.		Animist.		Arya.		Hindu.		Jain.		Musalman.		Sikh.	
	M.	F.	M.	F.	M.	F.	M.	F.	M.	F.	M.	F.	M.	F.	M.	F.	M.	F.	M.	F.	M.	F.	M.	F.
1	911	912	913	914	915	916	917	918	919	920	921	922	923	924	925	926	927	928	929	930	931	932	933	934
Rajputana	1	..	70,971	67,033	790	367	32,908	21,236	387	272	190	124	40	28	1	..	9	12	28	19	63	34	58	31
Alwar	..	..	2,904	2,714	..	..	2,316	2,396	..	2	12	8	..	..	..	..	..	..	2	1	..	1	10	6
Banswara	..	..	1,133	1,056	..	..	94	118	..	..	..	..	..	..	..	..	..	..	..	..	..	..	..	..
Bharatpur	..	..	3,250	3,007	..	..	2,558	2,276	..	..	2	..	..	..	..	..	..	..	..	..	2	..	..	..
Bikaner	..	..	2,830	2,438	103	61	3,601	3,467	395	270	1	..	..	..	..	..	1	..	..	..	..	..	..	..
Bundi	..	..	1,399	1,731	7	1	529	582	..	..	1	..	..	..	..	..	..	..	..	..	1	..	..	..
Dholpur	..	..	2,255	2,139	..	..	146	103	..	..	29	18	..	..	..	..	..	..	..	..	24	15	5	3
Dungarpur	..	..	1,434	1,370	3	..	48	76	..	..	..	..	..	..	..	..	..	..	..	..	..	..	..	..
Jaipur	..	..	11,234	10,473	18	1	2,926	3,084	1	..	112	77	40	28	1	..	8	12	25	18	5	5	33	14
Jaisalmer	..	..	83	90	8	..	119	135	..	..	2	..	..	..	..	..	..	..	1	..	..	..	1	..
Jhalawar	..	..	707	701	3	6	137	180	..	..	..	..	..	..	..	..	..	..	..	..	..	..	..	..
Karauli	..	..	1,414	1,284	5	..	134	136	..	..	..	..	..	..	..	..	..	..	..	..	..	..	..	..
Kishangarh	..	..	660	829	2	..	152	164	..	..	..	..	..	..	..	..	..	..	..	..	..	..	..	..
Kotah	..	..	7,023	6,757	8	..	611	640	1	..	8	7	..	..	..	..	..	..	..	..	..	..	8	7
Kushalgarh (Chiefship)	..	..	423	405	..	..	117	116	..	..	..	..	..	..	..	..	..	..	..	..	..	..	..	..
Lawa (Estate)	..	..	29	41	..	..	1	2	..	..	..	..	..	..	..	..	..	..	..	..	..	..	..	..
Marwar	..	..	7,613	7,377	388	175	4,275	3,711	..	..	..	..	..	..	..	..	..	..	..	..	..	..	..	..
Mewar	..	..	11,180	10,247	172	105	1,284	1,190	..	..	30	13	..	..	..	..	..	..	..	..	29	12	1	1
Partabgarh	..	..	1,999	2,324	..	..	37	18	..	..	..	..	..	..	..	..	..	..	..	..	..	..	..	..
Shahpura (Chiefship)	..	..	769	714	5	5	86	70	..	..	..	..	..	..	..	..	..	..	..	..	..	..	..	..
Sirohi	1	..	4,469	4,232	68	11	300	280	..	..	2	1	..	..	..	..	..	..	..	..	2	1	..	..
Tonk	..	..	7,564	7,100	..	2	2,531	2,463	..	..	..	..	..	..	..	..	..	..	..	..	..	..	..	..
Ajmer-Merwara	..	..	3,621	3,225	100	129	3,088	2,538	45	21	116	47	..	..	..	..	51	23	..	..	35	8	30	16
Ajmer	..	..	2,850	2,653	75	99	2,608	2,158	44	21	115	44	..	..	..	..	51	23	..	..	34	5	30	16
Merwara	..	..	771	572	25	30	480	380	1	..	1	3	..	..	..	..	..	..	..	..	1	3	..	..

APPENDIX TO TABLE XIII.—(SEE EXPLANATORY NOTE ON TITLE PAGE.)

[A=Animist. Ar=Arya. Br=Brahmo. H=Hindu. J=Jain. M=Musalman. P=Parsi. S=Sikh. Castes with no letter after them include Hindus only.]
(Where a State or District is given after a name in column 2 the classification is peculiar to that locality.)

Caste in Table XIII in which entries in column 2 are included.	Entries in census schedules.
1	2
Ahir. (Ar. H. J. M.)	Goala (H. J.), Hir, Ir.
Bagri. (A. H. M.) .	Bagar, Bagaria, Bagria (A. H.)
Bairagi. (A. Ar. H. J. S.)	Baba (A. H.), Ogar, Oghar baba, Ramawat.
Balai. (H. M.) .	Balahi, Barahi, Parai, Bhalai, Brahi, Kamar Falai, Kotwal (Alwar).
Bambhi.	Bhabi, Bhambhi, Bhami, Bhobi, Kabar, Kamar Bambhi, Kamariya (Marwar), Kanbat, Kobariya.
Panjara. (A. Ar. H. M. S.)	Baladiya, Banara, Banjar, Binjara (M), Dudya (M), Gunwar, Maghar, Shekh Mukeri (M).
Barhai. (Ar. H.)	Badhai, Fadhi, Farhi.
Bauri. (A. Ar. H. M. S.)	Bhawri.
Bhangi. (A. H. M. S.)	Chandal (Mewar), Chuhra (H. M. S.), Hati, Rathi, Hela (M), Jharukas, Khakrob, Khakrot (H. S.), Khatka, Lalbegi (A. H.), Lalpos.
Bhat. (A. H. M.) .	Bamniya Bhat, Bayti (A. H.), Biram, Hansori, Jaga (M), Maru Bhat, Palti, Rai (H. M.), Rao, Rawa (H. M).
Bhil. (A. Ar. H. M.)	Bhilat, Boya (A), Chuwan (A), Dahana (A), Gameti (A), Giraya (A), Matha, Tedwa (A).
Bhishti. (H. M.) .	Saqqa (H. M.), Sikka (M).
Bhoi. (H. M.) .	Poi.
Bishnoi. (Ar. H.) .	Thapan.
Bohra. (A. J. M.) .	Fadora (M), Bedara (M), Daud (M).
Brahman. (Ar. H. J. M. S.)	Achar, Acharaj, Achari, Ahwasi, Antarbedi, Asari, Badwa, Dara Chobisa, Barara, Bhat Gujrati, Bohra Nandwania, Biyas Parasar, Bohru Palliwal, Bohra Tikkiwal, Brahma Bhat (Kotah), Brahmanachari (Marwar), Byas, Chaube, Chota Chobisa, Chorasi Cammod (S), Dakhni, Dakshni, Dasora, Dayama, Desai, Girinama, Godi, Hawasi, Hiroi, Joshi, Jotshi, Katya, Kartiya, Maha Brahman, Mathuria Danotia, Ojha, Panda, Pandit (Kashmiri), Parasari, Pinda, Rajgar, Sanaid, Shrimali, Surya Duj, Tamrayat.
Chakar. (Ar. H. J. M.)	Chela, Dawada, Gola, Gola Purab (H. J.), Ghulam (H. M.), Hazuri (Ar. H. J. M.), Kanijak (H. J.), Khanezad (H. J. M.), Khawaswal* (except Alwar, Jaipur, and Karauli), Pasban (Kotah), Paswania* (Mewar), Vazir (H. M)
Chamar. (Ar. H. M. S.)	Begari, Bola (M), Chamriya, Chand, Chatarban, Dhedpatia, Jasia, Jaswara, Jatia, Kamar Chamar, Matang, Samar.
Charan. (Ar. H. J.)	Baret, Barot, Dhola (Bundi), Kabiya, Saran.
Chhipa. (Ar. H. J. M. S.)	Bhawsar, Chhapara, Chepa, Chimba, Dagarwal, Nilgar, Rampurwa, Rangara, Rangrez, Saraswar, Sipa.
Dakot. . . .	Bharara, Chhani Chhariya, Desantri, Distari, Garura (J) (Jaipur), Jotgi, Sawni, Thawriya.
Daroga. (Ar. H. J. M.)	Badaran, Badari, Chela (Jaipur), Khanezad (Jaipur), Khawaswal* (Jaipur), Pasban* (Jaipur), Rawnaa ke Sath,* Rayna ke Sath.*
Darzi. (Ar. H. J. M.)	Khayat, Suji.
Deswali (M). .	Ajmeri (M), Deswar (M).
Dhanak, Dhanuk, Dhanka, Dhankia, (A. H. M.)	Gokhi.
Dhed. . . .	Tilangi.
Dholi. (A. H.) .	Damami, Darhi, Dhadi, Dhola, Doli, Gormat, Jachak, Kalarchi, Manganhar, Manguiya, Mirasi, Nagarchi.
Fakir. (H. M.) .	Chishti (M), Durre (M), Durves(M), Khaki Baba (M), Khungar (M), Saha (M), Sain (M), Sauhi (M), Sanyi (M), Suthra (M).
Gadaria (Gadri). (H. M.)	Gari, Gayari.
Garoda (Garodia). .	Bhanbhiyan ro Sad, Gahi, Garura, Garu, Ghuria, Gulia, Gurda, Guroda, Gurrah.
Gosain. (Ar. H. M.)	Bharti, Jobai, Josai, Niranjani, Puri, Radha Balabhi, Saraswati.
Gujar. (Ar. H J.) .	Bagri (Kishangarh), Dhabhai, Ghosi, Gohja, Kataria (A).
Jat. (Ar. H. J. M. S.)	Chodhari, Faujdar, Ghoroi, Godara, Jaitwala, Khar, Kheri, Ramgarhia (S), Ramiya (H. S.), Sidh (H. J. S.), Sinsinwar.
Jogi. (A. Ar. H. M.)	Ayas, Baba Nath, Balaiyon ka Kamar, Dai (H. M.), Jagam, Jogan, Kamar Baba, Nath (H. M).
Julaha. (H. M.) .	Jalawa, Julawa, Koli (M) (Jaisalmer), Mehman (M), Meman (H. M.), Moman, Nurbaf, Nurwaf, Paoli (M), Safed baf (M).
Kahar. (Ar. H. M. S.)	Dhimar (except Karauli), Dhiwar, Kar, Mahri (M).
Kalal. (Ar. H. J. M.)	Kalar, Kaldar, Kalwar, Palledar.
Kandera (Karera) .	Dhunia, Karair, Pinara, Pindara, Pinjara.
Kasai (M).	Beopari (M), Kasab (M), Khatik (M).
Kayastha (Ar. Br. H. S.)	Kayath, Mathur (Ar. H.), Pancholi.
Kharol.	Agar, Agri, Barad, Khaior.
Khati. (Ar. H. S.) .	Karigar, Kharad, Khairati, Kheradi, Mistri, Najjar.
Khatri. (Ar. H. J. M. S.)	Arora (S), Kaira, Kapur, Kshatri, Modi (Bikaner), Siali, Sodi.
Khawaswal. .	Suretwal.
Koli. (A. Ar. H. M.)	Binodiya, Bomjadia, Chunad, Gharami, Kori, Koria (Bharatpur), Kushti.
Kumhar. (A. Ar. H. J. M. S.)	Bhatgar, Bhasunda, Chejara, Kabar, Karya (H. M.), Karigar (Jaipur), Kumawat, Kubar, Kumbar, Memar (H. M.), Mohlia (M), Moyala (M), Raj Kumhar (A. Ar. H).
Kunbi. (Ar. H.) .	Kaibi, Kulbi, Kulmi, Kurmi (Ar. H.).
Lakhera. (Ar. H. J.)	Churigar, Lakara, Manihar.
Loda.	Lodha (Kotah).
Lohar. (Ar. H. J. M.)	Ahangar (M.), Banduka (M), Gadeti (M), Jaradi, Lawar, Lawariya, Lowar, Luar, Luhar, Luwar, Nagauri (M), Ojha (Ajmer).
Mahajan Agarwal. (Ar. H. J. S.)	Andara, Deshwali, Kandoi, Nagori.
Mahajan Bijabargi. (Ar. H. J.)	Gandhi.
Mahajan Hamar (Humbad) (H. J.)	Ham, Huhumawar, Humad, Humar, Humri, Huwar.
Mahajan Khandelwal (Ar. H. J.)	Sonkhia.
Mahajan Maheshri. (Ar. H. J.)	Bagria (H. J.), Bedbargi, Gandi, Masri, Mawesuri, Mochhar, Mundra, Ratigi, Saretwal, Somani, Soni.
Mahajan Mawar (Mahawar) (Ar. H J.)	Dalliwal.
Mahajan Oswal. (Ar. H. J.)	Arora, Deswal, Dugar (J), Loda (J), Matheran (H. J.), Parakh, Parik (H. J.), Bora, Samaigi (J), Sirmari, Srimali (H. J.).
Mahajan Saraogi. (H. J.)	Barang (J).
Mali. (Ar. H. J. M.)	Bagban (H. M.), Bharai, Chowdri, Khadola, Sunkar.
Manihar. (M). .	Churigar (M), Maniyar, Lakhera (M), Sisgar (M).
Merat. (M). .	Maherat (M).
Mirasi. (M). .	Alaya (M), Damami (M), Darhi or Dhadi (M), Dholi (M), Dhori (M), Deora (M), Gormat (M), Manganhar (M), Nagarchi (M).
Mochi (A. H. M). .	Miyangar.
Moghal (M). .	Chhapgar (M), Mirza (M).
Nai (Ar. H. J. M. S.)	Hajjam (H. M.), Jarrah (H. M), Khalipha (M), Khawas (H. M), Nagi, Nau, Nayan, Nawi, Neogi, Padiyar.
Nat. (A. H. M.) .	Kabutra (H. M.), Kakhera, Natiya.
Od or Odh (H. M.) .	Bhatphoda, Beldar (H. M.).
Parsi (P.) . .	Nausherwani, Shahanshahi, Shamsher.
Patel . . .	Patidar.
Pathan (M.) . .	Agwana (M), Balki (M), Belim (M) (Sirohi), Bohdai (M), Khilchi (M), Mian (M), Sameja (M), Thai (M).
Pinara (M.) . .	Dhunia (M), Kandera (M), Karera (M), Naddaph (M), Nayta (M), Pindara (M.), Pinjara (M).
Prohit (Ar. H.) .	Parot.
Rana. (H. M.) .	Jagra.
Rangrez. (M.) .	Nilgar (M), Rangara (M).
Rawat. (A. H. J. M.)	Apat, Baraha, Bharad, Lora.
Robari. (H. M.) .	Raika.
Sadhu. (Ar. H. J. S.)	Arjiyan (J), Brahmchari, Khaki, Mahant, Muniraj (J), Ramanandi, Ramsanehi (H. J.), Sadh (Bikaner, Jaisalmer, Sirohi), Sanei, Sant, Sid Mehta, Suthra (S).
Saiyad. (M.) .	Gair Mehdi or Mehdavi (M), Mir (M).
Sargara. .	Sagra.
Sevag. . .	Bhojak, Bhosak, Sewak.
Shekh. (M.) . .	Babarchi (M), Bara Hazari (M), Binjawar (M), Chaijara (M), Chandur (M), Diwan (M), Ilahiya (M), Jadechi (M), Juneja (M), Karigar (M), Mahore (M), Merabi (M), Namadgar (M), Namani (M), Nankar (M), Pitiyara (M), Sankandral (M).
Sirvi.	Gibar, Janbi.
Sunar. (Ar. H. J. M. S.)	Jargar (H. S.), Soni, Subrankar, Sundar, Zargar (H. S).
Sutar. (H. J. S.) .	Banag, Banayak, Binak.
Swami. (H. J.). .	Bagrot, Kamaria, Kugar, Monisar, Nimawat, Paogiri, Patasar, Samawat, Shami (H. J), Syami, Tarung.
Teli. (Ar. H. M.) .	Belim (M) (Marwar).

*Wrongly included as they are generally illegitimates of Rajputs only, forming a separate caste.

TABLE XIV.

Civil Condition by Age for Selected Castes, Tribes or Races.

Explanatory Note.

The castes selected for this Table are the same as those for Table IX, and a reference should be made to the Explanatory Note to that Table. But the totals of the following castes, *viz.*, Ahir, Bairagi, Balai, Bhangi, Bhil, Brahman, Chamar, Chhipa, Darzi, Dhobi, Fakir, Jat, Kaimkhani, Kalal, Kayastha, Khati, Kumhar, Lohar, Mahajan, Mali, Nai, Naik, Rajput, Rangrez, Sevag, Sunar, Sutar do not agree with those in Table IX because, in this Table, they do not include figures for the Nandwas and Gangapur parganas of Indore and Gwalior in the Mewar Agency, which were not abstracted in the Central India Office.

In this Table, unlike Table IX, separate details by religion have only been given for those religions numbering 500 and over in a caste. The caste *totals*, however, include *all* religions. So, too, no separate details have been given for Ajmer-Merwara for castes totalling less than 500.

TABLE XIV.—Civil Condition by Age for Selected Castes, Tribes or Races.

[In column 3, A.=Animist C.=Christian. H.=Hindu. J.=Jain. M.=Musalman. S.=Sikh.]

Caste, Tribe, or Race.	Locality.	Religion.	Sex.	Population dealt with.	Unmarried.							Married.							Widowed.						
					Total.	0-4.	5-11.	12-14.	15-19.	20-39.	40 and over.	Total.	0-4.	5-11.	12-14.	15-19.	20-39.	40 and over.	Total.	0-4.	5-11.	12-14.	15-19.	20-39.	40 and over.
1	2	3	4	5	6	7	8	9	10	11	12	13	14	15	16	17	18	19	20	21	22	23	24	25	26
Ahir	Rajputana	Total	M.	90,982	43,561	11,297	15,372	4,913	5,546	5,282	1,151	40,659	14	524	1,096	4,667	20,765	13,593	6,768	1	34	32	161	1,691	4,843
			F.	77,806	25,239	11,630	11,591	1,541	335	106	36	41,149	16	1,584	2,695	5,873	22,391	8,590	11,418	..	17	42	139	2,236	8,984
		H.	M.	90,973	43,556	11,296	15,370	4,913	5,545	5,281	1,151	40,655	14	524	1,096	4,667	20,768	13,591	6,768	1	34	32	161	1,691	4,843
			F.	77,802	25,237	11,629	11,591	1,540	335	106	36	41,147	16	1,584	2,695	5,873	22,390	8,589	11,418	..	17	42	139	2,235	8,984
	Ajmer-Merwara	Total	M.	999	416	93	133	40	61	79	10	478	1	9	5	23	275	165	105	..	..	2	3	36	64
			F.	756	184	79	77	12	4	10	2	421	2	16	24	62	235	82	151	..	1	1	2	43	104
		H.	M.	997	415	93	132	40	61	79	10	477	1	9	5	23	274	165	105	..	..	2	3	36	64
			F.	755	184	79	77	12	4	10	2	421	2	16	24	62	235	82	150	..	1	1	2	42	104
Bairagi	Rajputana	Total	M.	29,159	14,740	3,927	3,859	1,227	1,820	2,620	1,287	11,945	6	92	226	730	6,828	4,063	2,474	..	6	64	126	790	1,488
			F.	24,793	7,748	4,006	3,043	374	193	105	27	12,014	9	319	618	1,649	7,253	2,166	5,031	..	13	13	167	1,337	3,501
		H.	M.	29,158	14,740	3,927	3,859	1,227	1,820	2,620	1,287	11,944	6	92	226	730	6,828	4,062	2,474	..	6	64	126	790	1,488
			F.	24,787	7,746	4,005	3,042	374	193	105	27	12,012	9	319	618	1,649	7,252	2,165	5,029	..	13	13	167	1,336	3,500
Balai	Rajputana	Total	M.	100,733	46,008	15,579	15,374	3,735	5,871	5,040	409	49,432	28	512	571	2,804	28,444	17,073	5,293	1	17	27	112	1,748	3,388
			F.	96,061	29,980	16,335	11,919	1,081	408	186	51	50,819	59	1,814	2,175	6,439	31,156	9,176	15,262	2	34	45	125	3,011	12,045
		H.	M.	100,716	46,000	15,577	15,371	3,735	5,871	5,038	408	49,425	28	512	571	2,801	28,440	17,070	5,291	1	17	27	112	1,748	3,386
			F.	96,058	29,979	16,335	11,919	1,081	407	186	51	50,818	59	1,814	2,175	6,439	31,156	9,175	15,261	2	34	45	125	3,011	12,044
	Ajmer-Merwara	Total	M.	12,234	5,359	1,909	1,514	429	651	833	23	6,054	16	90	79	283	3,614	1,972	821	..	3	8	27	314	469
			F.	11,539	3,489	1,949	1,297	160	52	17	14	6,141	35	200	236	745	3,958	967	1,909	1	8	4	21	378	1,497
		H.	M.	12,221	5,353	1,907	1,513	429	649	832	23	6,051	16	90	79	283	3,613	1,971	820	..	3	8	27	314	468
			F.	11,535	3,489	1,949	1,297	160	52	17	14	6,137	35	200	236	744	3,955	967	1,909	1	8	4	21	375	1,497
Bambhi	Rajputana	H.	M.	69,940	34,973	11,391	10,148	3,652	4,929	4,846	207	31,854	102	639	480	1,544	18,770	10,119	3,313	3	25	24	56	989	2,216
			F.	63,886	22,214	11,418	8,001	2,036	625	119	16	31,912	295	1,215	1,209	6,429	17,794	4,970	9,760	1	15	27	167	2,080	7,457
	Ajmer-Merwara	H.	M.	1,305	591	211	170	44	73	89	4	631	6	9	7	24	378	207	83	..	..	1	3	33	46
			F.	1,245	359	214	117	15	9	4	..	690	1	24	33	60	457	115	196	..	2	..	1	47	146
Bhangi	Rajputana	Total	M.	42,403	20,289	6,376	7,239	2,049	2,349	1,997	279	19,747	9	356	494	1,541	10,842	6,505	2,367	1	14	18	109	762	1,463
			F.	40,349	14,138	6,527	6,080	966	420	112	28	21,435	33	635	973	3,002	12,620	4,172	4,774	1	3	19	117	975	3,659
		H.	M.	41,951	20,045	6,282	7,163	2,010	2,326	1,977	278	19,362	9	354	493	1,525	10,742	6,439	2,341	1	14	18	107	755	1,449
			F.	39,923	13,962	6,445	6,006	957	416	110	28	21,230	33	632	967	2,974	12,404	4,130	4,731	1	3	19	116	965	3,627
		M.	M.	318	170	67	52	21	14	15	1	128	..	2	1	15	67	43	20	..	..	..	2	7	11
			F.	291	114	55	52	5	1	1	..	140	..	2	6	22	85	25	37	..	..	..	1	10	26
	Ajmer-Merwara	Total	M.	2,697	1,248	374	426	123	159	130	36	1,286	2	6	18	77	794	389	163	..	..	2	9	59	93
			F.	2,401	809	398	339	50	13	7	2	1,302	2	34	48	195	818	205	290	..	1	..	4	58	227
		H.	M.	2,671	1,234	371	422	120	157	128	36	1,274	2	6	18	77	787	384	163	..	..	2	9	59	93
			F.	2,399	809	398	339	50	13	7	2	1,300	2	34	48	194	817	205	290	..	1	..	4	58	227
Bhil	Rajputana	Total	M.	229,060	120,330	46,917	40,028	8,966	12,659	11,344	416	101,895	42	389	709	4,196	66,796	29,763	6,835	2	22	33	162	2,906	3,710
			F.	279,454	92,036	48,678	33,088	5,737	2,987	1,278	268	165,660	97	1,195	2,538	11,756	75,126	14,948	21,758	2	25	18	136	3,892	17,685
		A.	M.	196,212	104,667	41,113	34,763	7,659	10,934	9,853	335	85,886	30	318	605	3,525	56,422	24,986	5,659	2	20	27	130	2,467	3,023
			F.	169,661	81,208	42,735	29,004	5,232	2,790	1,200	247	89,718	75	959	2,080	9,885	64,202	12,507	18,735	2	22	15	115	3,321	15,260
		H.	M.	32,816	15,663	5,801	5,265	1,307	1,725	1,482	80	16,007	12	71	104	671	10,372	4,777	1,146	..	2	6	32	419	687
			F.	29,792	10,827	5,942	4,084	505	197	78	21	15,948	22	236	456	1,921	10,804	2,441	3,023	..	3	8	21	671	2,425

TABLE XIV.—CIVIL CONDITION BY AGE FOR SELECTED CASTES, TRIBES OR RACES—*contd.*

[In column 3, A.=Animist. C.=Christian. H.=Hindu. J.=Jain. M.=Musalman. S.=Sikh.]

Caste, Tribe, or Race.	Locality.	Religion.	Sex.	Population dealt with.	UNMARRIED.							MARRIED.							WIDOWED.						
					TOTAL.	0-4.	5-11.	12-14.	15-19.	20-39.	40 and over.	Total.	0-4.	5-11.	12-14.	15-19.	20-39.	40 and over.	Total.	0-4	5-11.	12-14.	15-19.	20-39.	40 and over.
1	2	3	4	5	6	7	8	9	10	11	12	13	14	15	16	17	18	19	20	21	22	23	24	25	26
Bhil	Ajmer-Merwara	Total	M.	3,287	1,495	593	515	88	155	140	4	1,634	2	19	13	70	1,082	448	158	..	..	..	3	72	83
			F.	3,217	1,088	650	401	21	10	5	1	1,745	6	62	52	222	1,165	238	384	..	1	1	1	56	325
		A.	M.	1,658	762	300	201	42	82	74	3	807	1	10	5	29	537	225	89	..	..	..	2	45	42
			F.	1,681	570	338	214	11	3	4	..	895	1	25	28	119	599	123	216	..	1	1	1	21	192
		H.	M.	1,629	733	293	254	46	73	66	1	827	1	9	8	41	545	223	69	..	..	..	1	27	41
			F.	1,536	518	312	187	10	7	1	1	850	5	37	24	103	566	115	168	..	..	..	..	85	133
Bishnoi	Rajputana	H.	M.	28,491	13,054	4,384	3,812	1,238	1,660	1,847	113	13,346	81	674	501	1,059	7,341	3,689	2,093	3	13	22	65	743	1,246
			F.	24,386	7,029	4,020	2,446	394	139	25	5	14,006	220	1,227	992	1,890	7,686	1,990	3,352	..	9	13	57	740	2,533
Brahman	Rajputana	Total	M.	474,549	234,089	55,181	70,330	22,624	29,534	43,286	13,125	195,398	73	1,423	3,315	13,126	104,157	73,304	45,071	3	71	133	597	11,637	32,630
			F.	445,654	121,578	56,175	58,873	6,197	1,495	626	212	206,762	143	6,035	11,585	29,805	118,342	40,852	117,314	4	219	429	2,248	33,098	81,316
		H.	M.	474,279	233,962	55,150	70,295	22,613	29,519	43,264	13,121	195,268	73	1,422	3,313	13,115	104,083	73,262	45,049	3	71	133	597	11,628	32,617
			F.	445,443	121,507	56,140	56,846	6,190	1,493	626	212	206,654	143	6,032	11,578	29,763	118,284	40,834	117,252	4	219	429	2,246	33,093	81,291
	Ajmer-Merwara	Total	M.	12,884	5,627	1,320	1,615	548	775	1,092	277	5,931	2	35	88	402	3,492	1,912	1,326	..	2	8	20	435	861
			F.	11,152	2,667	1,274	1,251	95	21	19	7	5,348	5	154	288	847	3,114	940	3,137	..	3	13	61	988	2,072
		H.	M.	12,659	5,518	1,293	1,582	529	757	1,083	274	5,821	2	33	86	389	3,428	1,883	1,320	..	2	8	19	435	856
			F.	11,000	2,617	1,253	1,229	88	21	19	7	5,264	5	154	286	829	3,065	925	3,119	..	3	13	61	983	2,059
Chakar	Rajputana	Total	M.	16,679	8,424	2,564	2,380	683	1,184	1,448	165	7,260	1	48	49	353	4,548	2,261	995	..	7	5	27	374	582
			F.	18,158	5,474	2,618	1,960	320	252	255	69	8,769	3	182	298	1,200	5,741	1,345	3,915	..	6	6	58	1,050	2,785
		H.	M.	16,616	8,391	2,552	2,373	677	1,183	1,441	165	7,231	1	48	49	353	4,528	2,255	991	..	7	4	27	374	579
			F.	18,086	5,451	2,608	1,958	318	251	252	69	8,733	3	181	296	1,103	5,719	1,341	3,902	..	6	6	58	1,045	2,777
Chamar	Rajputana	Total	M.	373,139	166,936	53,602	59,006	18,484	20,001	14,481	1,362	184,847	54	2,695	4,809	14,567	103,816	58,906	21,376	6	125	260	664	6,060	14,261
			F.	351,631	111,970	55,830	47,182	6,247	1,887	666	158	188,261	103	7,748	12,048	27,187	109,577	31,538	51,400	3	98	285	695	11,008	39,371
		H.	M.	373,063	166,891	53,590	58,991	18,478	19,991	14,480	1,361	184,808	54	2,695	4,808	14,567	103,785	58,899	21,364	6	125	260	664	6,057	14,252
			F.	351,340	111,932	55,812	47,166	6,245	1,886	665	158	186,158	103	7,748	12,047	27,175	109,540	31,536	51,450	3	98	285	695	11,006	39,363
	Ajmer-Merwara	Total	M.	6,810	2,867	1,058	926	237	351	284	11	3,547	5	48	49	231	2,234	980	396	..	6	3	18	160	209
			F.	6,527	1,963	1,106	741	67	22	21	6	3,556	13	137	177	544	2,161	524	1,008	..	5	7	18	196	782
		H.	M.	6,809	2,867	1,058	926	237	351	284	11	3,546	5	48	49	231	2,233	980	396	..	6	3	18	160	209
			F.	6,527	1,963	1,106	741	67	22	21	6	3,556	13	137	177	544	2,161	524	1,008	..	5	7	18	196	782
Chhipa	Rajputana	Total	M.	19,605	8,488	2,451	2,713	834	977	1,243	270	9,397	7	126	193	816	5,024	3,431	1,720	..	3	7	46	490	1,174
			F.	18,270	5,076	2,521	2,144	244	124	36	7	9,836	20	363	494	1,277	5,651	2,031	3,358	..	3	16	43	683	2,613
		H.	M.	15,905	6,892	1,941	2,158	675	782	1,081	255	7,527	2	65	135	475	4,021	2,829	1,486	..	1	8	43	434	1,002
			F.	14,954	4,059	2,018	1,713	183	104	35	6	7,976	7	244	398	1,019	4,645	1,663	2,919	..	2	15	38	622	2,242
		M.	M.	3,699	1,596	510	555	159	195	162	15	1,869	5	61	58	141	1,003	601	234	..	2	1	3	56	172
			F.	3,316	1,017	503	431	61	20	1	1	1,860	13	119	96	258	1,006	368	439	..	1	1	5	61	371
	Ajmer-Merwara	Total	M.	1,414	593	193	202	46	61	77	14	674	..	15	15	39	393	212	147	..	2	1	4	46	92
			F.	1,234	337	172	153	10	2	..	..	676	3	40	39	78	404	112	221	..	1	1	2	54	163
		H.	M.	972	397	129	124	32	37	63	12	460	..	4	10	31	275	140	115	..	..	1	4	40	70
			F.	830	211	112	95	3	1	..	..	450	2	24	16	47	297	64	169	..	..	1	3	45	121
		M.	M.	442	196	64	78	14	24	14	2	214	..	11	5	8	118	72	32	..	2	..	..	8	22
			F.	404	126	60	58	7	1	..	..	226	1	16	23	31	107	48	52	..	1	..	..	9	43

TABLE XIV.—Civil Condition by Age for Selected Castes, Tribes or Races—*contd.*

[In column 3, A.=Animist. C.=Christian. H.=Hindu. J.=Jain. M.=Musalman. S.=Sikh.]

Caste, Tribe, or Race.	Locality.	Religion.	Sex.	Population dealt with.	Unmarried. Total.	0-4.	5-11.	12-14.	15-19.	20-39.	40 and over.	Married. Total.	0-4.	5-11.	12-14.	15-19.	20-39.	40 and over.	Widowed. Total.	0-4.	5-11.	12-14.	15-19.	20-39.	40 and over.
1	2	3	4	5	6	7	8	9	10	11	12	13	14	15	16	17	18	19	20	21	22	23	24	25	26
Christian	Rajputana	Total	M.	2,288	1,355	286	341	167	203	333	25	864	..	1	5	12	558	288	69	..	..	..	3	29	37
			F.	1,804	853	309	216	67	119	123	19	801	..	6	2	83	584	126	150	..	2	1	2	28	117
(a) Indian.		C.	M.	1,308	739	174	173	105	156	126	5	521	..	1	5	12	357	146	48	..	..	..	3	22	23
			F.	1,077	471	191	102	41	72	61	4	505	..	6	2	74	353	70	101	..	2	1	2	20	76
(b) Others.		C.	M.	980	616	112	108	62	47	207	20	343	..	..	..	..	201	142	21	..	..	..	..	7	14
			F.	721	382	118	114	26	47	62	15	290	..	..	..	9	231	56	49	..	..	..	..	8	41
	Ajmer-Merwara.	Total	M.	3,090	2,261	269	256	163	289	1,261	33	752	..	..	2	12	483	255	77	..	..	..	1	22	54
			F.	2,105	1,221	253	313	119	321	178	37	740	..	3	6	104	477	150	144	..	..	..	1	41	102
(a) Indian		C.	M.	1,309	850	162	157	118	224	148	11	417	..	..	2	12	298	135	42	..	..	..	1	12	29
			F.	1,421	871	160	107	91	260	114	20	459	..	3	6	91	279	80	91	..	..	..	1	29	61
(b) Others		C.	M.	1,781	1,441	107	99	35	65	1,113	22	305	..	..	..	..	185	120	35	..	..	..	..	10	25
			F.	684	350	84	116	28	41	64	17	281	..	..	..	13	198	70	53	..	..	..	..	12	41
Daroga	Rajputana	Total	M.	53,573	27,622	8,960	7,840	2,602	3,882	5,402	936	22,444	14	373	433	1,198	12,068	8,458	3,507	1	16	16	78	931	2,465
			F.	56,861	15,576	6,948	6,233	1,370	635	275	115	28,790	34	767	1,228	3,918	16,749	6,094	12,495	2	14	22	209	2,739	9,509
		H.	M.	53,560	27,612	6,957	7,839	2,601	3,881	5,401	934	22,441	14	273	433	1,198	12,066	8,457	3,507	1	16	16	78	931	2,465
			F.	56,852	15,574	6,947	6,232	1,370	635	275	115	28,784	34	767	1,228	3,918	16,744	6,093	12,494	2	14	22	209	2,739	9,508
	Ajmer-Merwara.	H.	M.	4,536	1,913	557	539	172	301	299	45	2,273	2	18	28	151	1,423	651	350	..	..	..	10	153	187
			F.	4,398	1,077	575	405	36	27	29	5	2,247	5	63	70	296	1,481	332	1,074	..	2	5	9	218	840
Darzi	Rajputana	Total	M.	23,027	10,554	3,052	3,349	1,146	1,296	1,461	250	10,584	3	78	175	617	5,791	3,920	1,889	1	1	13	39	555	1,280
			F.	22,111	6,444	3,180	2,767	372	93	24	8	11,234	10	369	524	1,518	6,669	2,144	4,433	1	7	10	49	961	3,405
		H.	M.	22,890	10,494	3,042	3,323	1,140	1,285	1,454	250	10,510	3	78	173	610	5,763	3,880	1,880	1	1	13	38	552	1,275
			F.	21,979	6,401	3,165	2,750	360	91	21	8	11,169	10	365	523	1,513	6,632	2,128	4,406	1	7	10	40	952	3,387
	Ajmer-Merwara.	Total	M.	1,225	474	122	143	48	55	88	18	612	..	7	8	39	331	227	139	..	2	1	1	47	88
			F.	1,020	236	127	96	6	..	4	3	543	1	16	30	79	304	113	241	..	3	1	7	57	173
		H.	M.	1,217	471	122	143	48	55	85	18	607	..	7	8	39	328	225	139	..	2	1	1	47	88
			F.	1,018	235	127	96	6	..	4	2	543	1	16	30	79	304	113	240	..	3	1	7	57	172
Dhakar	Rajputana	Total	M.	47,661	22,112	7,020	7,015	2,209	2,424	3,125	319	22,741	9	210	448	1,445	13,754	6,875	2,808	..	10	17	52	998	1,731
			F.	45,700	14,025	7,487	5,742	595	102	56	43	23,622	18	677	1,157	3,033	15,306	3,431	8,053	..	24	13	59	1,729	6,228
		H.	M.	47,660	22,111	7,020	7,015	2,208	2,424	3,125	319	22,741	9	210	448	1,445	13,754	6,875	2,808	..	10	17	52	998	1,731
			F.	45,700	14,025	7,487	5,742	595	102	56	43	23,622	18	677	1,157	3,033	15,306	3,431	8,053	..	24	13	59	1,729	6,228
	Ajmer-Merwara.	H.	M.	321	133	48	38	10	18	18	1	166	..	3	3	11	103	46	22	..	..	..	2	10	10
			F.	305	92	53	32	5	1	1	..	173	1	7	9	17	116	23	40	..	..	..	..	8	32
Dhobi	Rajputana	Total	M.	23,318	10,271	3,273	3,581	1,077	1,240	965	135	11,369	4	169	281	827	6,228	3,860	1,678	1	6	6	52	596	1,087
			F.	22,429	6,721	3,298	2,845	397	125	46	10	11,850	9	440	656	1,644	6,900	2,201	3,858	..	10	11	40	786	3,011
		H.	M.	20,275	8,810	2,845	3,031	915	1,061	846	112	9,998	4	155	246	718	5,523	3,352	1,461	1	4	5	40	461	930
			F.	19,370	5,753	2,869	2,417	319	102	38	8	10,265	7	376	579	1,383	6,047	1,873	3,352	..	8	10	36	679	2,619
		M.	M.	3,043	1,461	428	550	162	179	119	23	1,371	..	14	35	100	705	508	211	..	2	1	6	45	157
			F.	3,059	968	429	428	78	23	8	2	1,585	2	61	77	261	853	328	506	..	2	1	4	107	302
	Ajmer-Merwara.	Total	M.	1,479	677	254	219	56	90	55	3	692	1	5	19	46	424	197	110	..	..	1	4	42	63
			F.	1,403	467	248	180	24	12	2	1	697	3	21	32	109	417	115	239	..	..	..	5	56	178
		H.	M.	1,278	587	216	192	49	79	48	3	599	..	3	17	42	367	170	92	..	..	1	4	35	52
			F.	1,191	490	299	157	21	10	2	1	597	2	17	28	93	359	98	200	..	..	..	5	45	150

TABLE XIV.—CIVIL CONDITION BY AGE FOR SELECTED CASTES, TRIBES OR RACES—*contd.*

[In column 3, A.=Animist. C.=Christian. H.=Hindu. J.=Jain. M.=Musalman. S.=Sikh.]

Caste, Tribe, or Race.	Locality.	Religion.	Sex.	Population dealt with.	UNMARRIED.							MARRIED.							WIDOWED.						
					TOTAL.	0-4.	5-11.	12-14.	15-19.	20-39.	40 and over.	Total.	0-4.	5-11.	12-14.	15-19.	20-39.	40 and over.	Total.	0-4.	5-11.	12-14.	15-19.	20-39.	40 and over.
1	2	3	4	5	6	7	8	9	10	11	12	13	14	15	16	17	18	19	20	21	22	23	24	25	26
Fakir	Rajputana	Total	M.	29,013	12,733	3,916	4,749	1,729	1,735	1,210	394	13,206	3	156	272	1,103	7,012	4,660	2,073	..	13	9	50	522	1,479
			F.	26,179	9,176	4,056	3,949	788	292	59	32	13,655	14	473	754	1,971	7,673	2,770	3,348	..	13	6	39	634	2,656
		M.	M.	28,873	13,451	3,897	4,736	1,724	1,723	1,194	375	13,114	3	156	272	1,100	6,982	4,631	2,058	..	13	9	50	510	1,407
			F.	26,063	9,139	4,036	3,939	786	292	59	27	13,583	13	471	751	1,961	7,634	2,753	3,341	..	13	6	39	634	2,649
	Ajmer-Merwara	Total	M.	921	415	122	125	36	44	67	21	406	..	7	8	22	235	134	100	..	..	3	2	25	70
			F.	830	263	140	97	17	11	4	..	433	3	18	24	50	264	74	128	..	..	..	3	18	107
		M.	M.	913	409	121	123	35	44	65	21	401	..	7	8	22	234	133	100	..	..	3	2	25	70
			F.	806	260	137	92	17	11	3	..	422	3	18	24	48	258	71	124	..	..	..	3	18	103
Goanese	Rajputana	C.	M.	121	48	4	4	2	8	30	..	69	..	..	..	..	40	29	4	..	..	..	..	..	4
			F.	43	18	10	4	..	1	2	1	23	..	..	..	..	21	2	1	..	..	..	..	..	1
	Ajmer-Merwara	C.	M.	168	81	6	10	5	25	33	2	84	..	..	1	1	46	36	3	..	..	..	..	1	2
			F.	69	30	13	8	2	3	3	1	36	..	..	..	5	24	7	3	..	..	..	..	1	2
Gola Purab	Rajputana	H.	M.	5,957	2,755	562	861	265	346	555	166	2,553	..	41	88	238	1,383	803	649	..	..	3	14	194	438
			F.	5,440	1,579	613	671	87	66	103	39	2,698	1	107	185	421	1,500	484	1,163	..	5	7	17	337	797
Gujar	Rajputana	Total	M.	270,413	132,191	34,899	42,801	13,590	17,364	20,421	3,116	119,234	68	1,684	2,567	8,196	65,038	41,681	18,987	2	101	88	377	6,145	12,274
			F.	228,195	70,258	34,218	31,030	3,439	1,064	402	115	121,901	180	5,671	7,009	16,546	70,207	22,288	36,036	3	67	115	324	7,009	28,518
		H.	M.	270,399	132,186	34,897	42,798	13,590	17,364	20,421	3,116	119,226	68	1,684	2,566	8,195	65,034	41,679	18,987	2	101	88	377	6,145	12,274
			F.	228,189	70,254	34,215	31,030	3,430	1,054	401	115	121,899	180	5,671	7,009	16,540	70,205	22,288	36,036	3	67	114	324	7,009	28,518
	Ajmer-Merwara	H.	M.	18,415	7,918	2,635	2,547	705	806	1,082	143	8,783	26	298	244	653	5,048	2,514	1,714	..	15	16	56	727	900
			F.	16,279	4,981	2,690	1,933	177	75	18	8	8,782	95	561	420	1,133	5,217	1,356	2,596	..	14	13	23	524	2,022
Jat	Rajputana	Total	M.	499,508	241,278	65,040	75,989	24,722	31,965	37,509	6,053	219,049	201	3,908	5,307	17,036	119,115	73,482	39,181	9	117	171	774	11,737	26,373
			F.	424,974	127,529	61,726	54,994	7,806	2,388	494	121	225,854	668	10,307	13,631	31,759	126,937	42,552	71,591	6	208	318	887	14,836	55,538
		H.	M.	495,744	239,133	64,612	75,437	24,450	31,580	37,046	5,999	217,638	201	3,893	5,201	16,968	118,391	72,895	38,972	9	117	171	774	11,675	26,226
			F.	422,799	126,617	61,352	54,633	7,713	2,345	484	120	224,766	667	10,291	13,610	31,635	126,272	42,291	71,356	6	208	318	886	14,000	55,366
		S.	M.	3,681	2,113	416	547	266	372	459	53	1,369	..	14	13	67	703	572	202	..	..	..	..	59	143
			F.	2,111	869	369	356	92	43	10	..	1,050	1	11	20	114	619	255	192	..	..	..	1	31	160
	Ajmer-Merwara	Total	M.	16,517	6,792	2,167	2,015	479	710	1,277	144	8,004	20	298	275	690	4,704	2,017	1,721	1	26	18	57	730	889
			F.	13,969	3,516	1,895	1,456	120	35	9	1	7,671	79	492	413	939	4,675	1,073	2,782	3	11	14	47	732	1,975
		H.	M.	15,850	6,366	2,150	2,003	475	617	982	138	7,795	20	298	272	676	4,531	1,998	1,690	1	26	18	55	703	887
			F.	13,881	3,491	1,878	1,448	120	35	9	1	7,610	79	492	412	933	4,622	1,072	2,780	3	11	14	47	732	1,073
		S.	M.	664	426	17	12	4	93	295	5	207	..	..	3	13	172	19	31	..	..	..	2	27	2
			F.	87	25	17	8	..	..	..	..	61	..	..	1	6	53	1	1	..	..	..	..	..	1
Jew	Rajputana	Jewish	M.	15	7	3	1	1	1	1	..	8	..	..	..	1	3	4	..	..	..	..	..	..	..
			F.	16	9	2	5	2	..	..	..	7	..	..	1	1	5	..	..	..	..	..	..	..	..
	Ajmer-Merwara	Jewish	M.	19	8	1	1	1	3	2	..	4	..	..	..	..	2	2	..	..	..	..	..	..	..
			F.	13	5	2	3	..	..	..	..	6	..	..	..	1	4	1	2	..	..	..	..	1	1

TABLE XIV.—Civil Condition by Age for Selected Castes, Tribes or Races—*contd.*

(In column 3, A.=Animist, C.=Christian, H.=Hindu, J.=Jain, M.=Musalman, S.=Sikh.)

Caste, Tribe or Race.	Locality.	Religion.	Sex.	Population dealt with.	Unmarried. Total.	Unmarried. 0-4.	Unmarried. 5-11.	Unmarried. 12-14.	Unmarried. 15-19.	Unmarried. 20-39.	Unmarried. 40 and over.	Married. Total.	Married. 0-4.	Married. 5-11.	Married. 12-14.	Married. 15-19.	Married. 20-39.	Married. 40 and over.	Widowed. Total.	Widowed. 0-4.	Widowed. 5-11.	Widowed. 12-14.	Widowed. 15-19.	Widowed. 20-39.	Widowed. 40 and over.
1	2	3	4	5	6	7	8	9	10	11	12	13	14	15	16	17	18	19	20	21	22	23	24	25	26
Kachhi	Rajputana	H.	M.	31,734	13,855	4,275	5,211	1,546	1,345	1,292	186	15,628	12	250	611	1,612	8,333	4,810	2,251	1	5	16	43	715	1,471
			F.	28,896	9,030	4,452	4,055	366	86	53	18	15,951	14	765	1,254	2,411	8,661	2,846	3,915	..	9	22	64	894	2,926
Kaimkhani	Rajputana	M.	M.	14,823	7,779	2,023	2,421	853	1,222	1,111	149	6,328	2	29	55	291	3,196	2,755	716	..	1	1	8	125	581
			F.	13,514	4,108	1,852	1,830	295	103	23	5	6,519	3	143	317	937	3,750	1,369	2,887	..	5	16	46	734	2,086
	Ajmer-Merwara	M.	M.	306	146	47	41	16	23	17	2	144	..	1	1	4	91	47	16	..	..	..	1	3	12
			F.	236	78	38	35	3	2	..	..	113	..	1	6	26	71	9	45	..	..	..	..	13	32
Kalal	Rajputana	Total	M.	20,325	9,578	2,909	3,039	954	1,194	1,321	171	9,416	15	126	161	653	5,466	2,995	1,331	1	2	6	25	478	819
			F.	19,515	6,091	3,072	2,524	344	105	36	10	9,638	17	367	478	1,341	5,841	1,594	3,786	..	6	6	36	847	2,891
		H.	M.	18,517	8,679	2,643	2,747	841	1,007	1,216	135	8,596	15	95	133	594	5,053	2,706	1,242	1	2	5	24	461	749
			F.	17,843	5,520	2,793	2,200	299	91	31	7	8,761	13	304	423	1,222	5,370	1,423	3,559	..	4	6	34	804	2,711
		M.	M.	1,808	899	266	292	113	87	105	36	820	..	31	28	59	413	289	89	..	..	1	1	17	70
			F.	1,672	571	279	225	45	14	5	3	874	4	63	55	119	462	171	227	..	2	..	2	43	180
	Ajmer-Merwara	Total	M.	695	286	92	99	16	28	46	5	355	..	6	4	32	200	113	54	..	..	..	2	24	28
			F.	646	182	91	75	9	1	4	2	336	2	9	15	49	202	59	128	1	1	..	2	18	106
		H.	M.	674	280	92	95	16	27	45	5	341	..	6	4	27	196	108	53	..	..	..	2	23	28
			F.	634	181	91	74	9	1	4	2	329	2	7	15	49	199	57	124	1	1	..	2	17	103
Kasai	Rajputana	M.	M.	14,577	6,971	2,077	2,673	829	782	558	52	6,899	6	264	310	604	3,516	2,199	707	..	3	6	20	209	469
			F.	14,001	4,669	2,066	2,000	381	170	37	15	7,730	44	628	487	1,033	4,049	1,489	1,602	..	11	6	19	294	1,272
	Ajmer-Merwara	M.	M.	549	255	95	76	34	24	22	4	248	..	5	5	22	136	80	46	..	..	..	1	18	27
			F.	539	167	73	71	13	9	1	..	298	1	11	12	47	174	53	74	..	..	..	1	17	56
Kayastha	Rajputana	Total	M.	12,826	5,671	1,323	1,757	644	686	953	308	5,785	1	38	86	449	3,104	2,107	1,370	..	..	6	16	359	989
			F.	10,747	3,136	1,262	1,574	251	44	5	..	5,334	2	145	305	839	2,947	1,096	2,277	..	2	5	28	617	1,625
		H.	M.	12,630	5,582	1,302	1,724	629	675	944	308	5,690	1	38	86	445	3,043	2,077	1,358	..	..	6	16	356	980
			F.	10,592	3,079	1,242	1,543	249	40	5	..	5,254	2	144	303	827	2,901	1,077	2,259	..	2	5	28	613	1,611
	Ajmer-Merwara	Total	M.	1,320	576	139	209	66	75	71	16	628	..	7	18	57	335	211	116	..	1	1	2	32	80
			F.	1,119	343	170	135	28	7	2	1	594	..	17	33	103	319	122	182	..	..	..	4	36	142
		H.	M.	1,296	567	138	203	66	74	70	16	616	..	7	18	54	329	208	113	..	..	1	2	31	79
			F.	1,101	335	164	134	27	7	2	1	587	..	17	32	102	314	122	179	..	..	..	4	36	139
Khati	Rajputana	Total	M.	69,086	33,116	9,726	11,054	3,291	4,124	4,131	790	30,957	23	310	541	2,140	16,242	11,701	5,013	2	14	11	106	1,436	3,444
			F.	65,574	19,948	9,880	8,580	1,028	258	160	42	34,309	39	1,314	1,842	4,562	19,652	6,900	11,317	5	22	30	149	2,232	8,879
		H.	M.	69,040	33,087	9,723	11,044	3,290	4,120	4,120	790	30,942	23	310	541	2,139	16,233	11,696	5,011	2	14	11	106	1,436	3,442
			F.	65,550	19,943	9,878	8,578	1,027	258	160	42	34,293	39	1,314	1,842	4,556	19,644	6,898	11,314	5	22	30	149	2,231	8,877
	Ajmer-Merwara	H.	M.	3,601	1,467	483	443	119	194	210	18	1,824	..	33	40	130	1,064	557	310	1	6	1	17	122	163
			F.	3,205	843	452	342	28	6	8	7	1,746	8	72	91	223	1,076	276	616	..	2	..	9	138	467

TABLE XIV.—CIVIL CONDITION BY AGE FOR SELECTED CASTES, TRIBES OR RACES—*contd.*

[In column 3. A.=Animist. C.=Christian. H.=Hindu. J.=Jain. M.=Musalman. S.=Sikh.]

Caste, Tribe, or Race.	Locality.	Religion.	Sex.	Population dealt with.	Unmarried.							Married.							Widowed.						
					Total.	0-4.	5-11.	12-14.	15-19.	20-39.	40 and over.	Total.	0-4.	5-11.	12-14.	15-19.	20-39.	40 and over.	Total.	0-4.	5-11.	12-14.	15-19.	20-39.	40 and over.
1	2	3	4	5	6	7	8	9	10	11	12	13	14	15	16	17	18	19	20	21	22	23	24	25	26
Khatik	Rajputana	H.	M.	26,370	11,807	3,721	4,537	1,221	1,309	902	117	12,986	12	321	420	1,195	7,160	3,878	1,577	..	11	20	59	467	1,020
			F.	24,889	8,386	4,009	3,703	501	119	43	11	13,266	19	701	874	1,960	7,465	2,247	3,237	..	11	17	38	736	2,435
	Ajmer-Merwara	H.	M.	1,790	751	236	292	68	84	65	6	925	..	28	24	82	527	264	114	..	3	..	5	42	64
			F.	1,753	508	260	224	15	6	3	..	955	5	74	56	134	522	164	290	..	1	2	6	72	209
Koli	Rajputana	Total	M.	53,499	23,251	6,841	8,369	2,639	2,943	2,217	242	26,214	12	272	506	1,974	14,275	9,175	4,034	..	11	29	128	1,147	2,719
			F.	50,548	15,986	7,512	7,063	945	337	104	25	26,788	14	851	1,416	3,944	15,857	4,706	7,774	..	10	38	142	1,745	5,839
		H.	M.	53,494	23,248	6,840	8,368	2,639	2,943	2,217	241	26,212	12	272	506	1,974	14,274	9,174	4,034	..	11	29	128	1,147	2,710
			F.	50,539	15,984	7,512	7,062	945	336	104	25	26,783	14	851	1,415	3,941	15,856	4,706	7,772	..	10	38	142	1,745	5,837
	Ajmer-Merwara	H.	M.	3,476	1,424	433	473	150	201	147	20	1,877	1	9	99	49	1,183	536	175	..	..	3	1	65	106
			F.	3,078	892	380	440	46	17	7	2	1,739	1	52	95	328	1,037	228	447	..	2	2	14	106	323
Kumbar	Rajputana	Total	M.	150,518	73,499	23,790	24,157	7,278	9,479	8,004	793	76,049	56	1,013	1,423	5,271	42,145	26,141	9,970	4	34	68	272	3,115	6,477
			F.	149,419	47,288	24,332	19,288	2,519	834	242	73	78,112	206	2,858	4,213	11,149	45,309	14,317	24,012	2	41	59	315	4,779	18,816
		H.	M.	155,665	71,469	23,176	23,552	7,023	9,199	7,743	776	74,398	56	1,006	1,409	5,177	41,196	25,554	9,798	4	34	68	272	3,064	6,356
			F.	146,054	45,924	23,711	18,760	2,389	734	237	73	76,500	204	2,836	4,155	10,946	44,341	14,018	23,630	2	41	56	311	4,715	18,505
		M.	M.	3,665	1,922	591	567	238	264	246	16	1,579	..	6	13	88	913	559	164	..	..	..	..	47	117
			F.	3,233	1,308	591	505	124	77	5	..	1,548	2	20	57	194	988	287	373	..	..	3	4	63	303
	Ajmer-Merwara	Total	M.	7,206	2,952	1,050	977	233	346	321	25	3,708	3	73	63	285	2,194	1,090	546	..	3	6	17	188	332
			F.	6,900	1,866	1,036	709	78	24	18	1	3,769	21	182	176	487	2,302	601	1,265	..	5	3	9	281	967
		H.	M.	7,177	2,938	1,046	970	231	345	321	25	3,693	3	73	63	284	2,183	1,085	546	..	3	6	17	188	332
			F.	6,871	1,854	1,030	706	77	24	17	1	3,754	21	182	176	487	2,288	600	1,265	..	5	3	0	280	966
Lodha	Rajputana	Total	M.	24,526	10,999	3,603	3,745	1,108	1,159	1,246	138	11,689	1	136	334	957	6,499	3,762	1,838	..	10	9	52	607	1,160
			F.	22,487	7,353	3,550	3,285	390	95	27	6	11,784	1	495	708	1,731	6,970	1,879	3,350	..	5	12	42	737	2,554
		H.	M.	24,520	10,997	3,601	3,743	1,108	1,159	1,246	138	11,685	1	136	334	957	6,496	3,761	1,838	..	10	9	52	607	1,160
			F.	22,483	7,352	3,550	3,284	390	95	27	6	11,781	1	494	706	1,731	6,968	1,879	3,350	..	5	12	42	737	2,554
	Ajmer-Merwara	H.	M.	566	271	89	88	26	38	27	3	257	1	..	7	11	163	75	38	..	..	..	..	16	22
			F.	555	184	98	77	5	2	1	1	271	..	8	15	36	162	50	100	..	..	..	..	21	79
Lohar	Rajputana	Total	M.	41,196	20,167	6,485	6,501	1,838	2,587	2,521	235	18,595	17	300	338	1,069	10,406	6,465	2,434	2	12	13	44	762	1,601
			F.	39,526	13,609	6,714	5,497	925	363	92	18	19,961	51	737	915	2,427	12,055	3,776	5,956	2	16	14	58	1,169	4,697
		H.	M.	32,302	16,039	5,074	5,054	1,458	2,132	2,132	189	14,371	12	132	193	744	8,215	5,075	1,892	2	3	6	35	610	1,227
			F.	30,275	10,623	5,218	4,287	723	301	79	15	14,785	26	379	618	1,777	9,169	2,810	4,864	2	11	10	48	1,011	3,782
		M.	M.	8,894	4,128	1,411	1,447	380	455	389	46	4,224	5	168	145	325	2,191	1,390	542	..	9	7	9	143	374
			F.	9,251	2,986	1,496	1,210	202	62	13	3	5,173	25	358	297	650	2,886	957	1,092	..	5	4	10	158	915
	Ajmer-Merwara	Total	M.	2,255	928	317	310	97	97	100	7	1,157	2	39	22	83	608	403	170	..	3	5	7	66	89
			F.	1,957	604	326	218	30	22	6	2	1,062	8	40	40	126	648	200	291	..	..	1	6	60	224
		H.	M.	1,320	563	200	179	53	61	66	4	670	2	8	9	37	361	253	87	..	2	1	4	35	44
			F.	1,157	365	206	128	16	13	4	1	616	2	19	19	63	396	117	176	..	..	..	1	33	142
		M.	M.	935	365	117	131	44	36	34	3	487	..	31	13	46	247	150	83	..	1	4	3	30	45
			F.	800	239	118	95	14	9	2	1	446	6	21	21	63	252	83	115	..	..	1	5	27	82

TABLE XIV.—CIVIL CONDITION BY AGE FOR SELECTED CASTES, TRIBES OR RACES—*contd.*

[In column 3, A.=Animist, C.=Christian. H.=Hindu. J.=Jain. M.=Musalman. S.=Sikh.]

Caste, Tribe, or Race.	Locality.	Religion.	Sex.	Population dealt with.	UNMARRIED.							MARRIED.							WIDOWED.						
					TOTAL.	0-4.	5-11.	12-14.	15-19.	20-39.	40 and over.	Total.	0-4.	5-11.	12-14.	15-19.	20-39.	40 and over.	Total.	0-4.	5-11.	12-14.	15-19.	20-39.	40 and over.
1	2	3	4	5	6	7	8	9	10	11	12	13	14	15	16	17	18	19	20	21	22	23	24	25	26
Mahajan or Baniya	Rajputana .	Total .	M.	359,570	178,439	43,988	57,375	17,605	18,945	29,935	10,591	140,081	45	775	2,613	11,328	77,309	47,951	34,110	4	53	89	459	8,822	24,683
			F.	353,960	104,986	43,758	51,366	7,764	1,485	433	192	157,243	77	2,827	8,944	25,325	90,708	29,362	91,719	7	119	267	1,679	28,671	60,976
		H.	M.	192,181	95,787	22,770	31,441	9,718	9,648	15,788	6,427	77,132	27	567	1,969	7,356	40,824	26,380	19,262	..	28	60	344	4,890	13,940
			F.	184,744	53,928	22,607	27,551	2,976	502	188	104	85,177	45	1,916	5,706	13,585	46,923	17,008	45,639	..	78	168	963	13,497	30,933
		J.	M.	160,278	82,593	21,205	25,917	7,874	9,284	14,151	4,162	62,845	18	207	642	3,968	36,455	21,555	14,840	4	25	29	115	3,928	10,739
			F.	169,148	51,045	21,138	23,807	4,784	963	245	88	72,033	32	911	3,237	11,734	43,765	12,354	46,076	7	41	99	716	15,171	30,036
	Ajmer-Merwara	Total .	M.	18,410	8,951	2,023	2,517	836	1,142	1,927	506	7,504	1	22	89	549	4,444	2,399	1,966	..	2	3	19	660	1,271
			F.	16,057	4,387	1,964	2,042	243	50	29	9	7,384	8	84	389	1,148	4,468	1,187	4,436	..	8	13	73	1,520	2,822
		H.	M.	7,646	3,459	783	1,076	324	413	676	188	3,379	..	13	47	285	1,919	1,115	808	..	..	1	12	257	538
			F.	6,656	1,722	791	840	70	8	9	4	3,170	5	52	197	517	1,862	587	1,758	..	5	5	34	574	1,140
		J.	M.	10,659	5,461	1,232	1,482	502	722	1,246	317	4,068	1	9	41	256	2,493	1,268	1,140	..	2	2	7	400	729
			F.	9,331	2,591	1,165	1,192	168	41	20	6	4,071	3	31	159	622	2,580	646	2,669	..	3	8	39	945	1,674
Mali . .	Rajputana .	Total .	M.	174,755	81,778	24,453	27,555	8,712	10,698	9,351	1,009	82,547	61	795	1,239	5,158	45,861	29,433	10,430	2	33	49	229	2,991	7,126
			F.	161,695	50,906	24,640	22,122	2,874	882	361	67	84,020	146	2,791	4,159	11,766	49,600	15,558	26,740	2	41	87	316	5,824	20,479
		H.	M.	174,426	81,819	24,405	27,485	8,701	10,685	9,335	1,008	82,393	61	790	1,235	5,150	45,792	29,385	10,414	2	33	49	229	2,985	7,116
			F.	161,346	50,504	24,591	22,070	2,863	855	350	66	83,853	146	2,782	4,150	11,733	49,516	15,526	26,685	2	41	87	312	5,812	20,435
		M.	M.	251	120	38	52	8	7	14	1	118	..	5	4	7	48	54	13	..	..	..	..	3	10
			F.	278	103	45	41	9	6	1	1	132	..	8	7	18	72	27	43	..	..	..	1	7	35
	Ajmer-Merwara	Total .	M.	7,499	3,095	995	970	313	406	386	25	3,846	..	47	81	258	2,245	1,215	551	..	4	6	17	198	327
			F.	6,836	1,706	953	652	73	10	14	3	3,691	16	173	166	526	2,208	602	1,439	..	7	3	21	342	1,066
		H.	M.	7,482	3,092	993	960	313	406	386	25	3,840	..	47	81	258	2,242	1,212	550	..	4	5	17	197	327
			F.	6,825	1,702	951	651	73	10	14	3	3,685	16	173	166	525	2,208	602	1,438	..	7	3	21	342	1,065
Meghwal .	Rajputana .	Total .	M.	30,003	15,896	4,931	4,849	1,812	2,224	1,985	91	12,682	12	89	132	593	7,481	4,375	1,421	..	6	7	18	419	981
			F.	27,328	9,996	4,851	3,986	881	229	46	5	12,948	32	293	563	1,886	8,075	2,089	4,382	..	6	14	43	1,003	3,316
		H.	M.	30,001	15,889	4,931	4,847	1,812	2,224	1,984	91	12,681	12	89	132	593	7,481	4,374	1,431	..	6	7	18	419	981
			F.	27,326	9,997	4,851	3,985	881	229	46	5	12,947	32	293	563	1,886	8,074	2,090	4,382	..	6	14	43	1,003	3,316
Meo or Mewati.	Rajputana .	Total .	M.	87,346	43,887	10,970	15,076	6,887	6,541	3,794	619	37,683	4	211	767	3,299	19,752	13,650	5,776	..	21	40	145	1,891	3,879
			F.	78,343	39,164	10,968	12,795	3,849	1,356	157	39	38,533	2	564	1,971	6,018	21,727	8,251	10,646	..	16	32	110	2,073	8,415
		M.	M.	87,273	43,861	10,965	15,068	6,882	6,534	3,793	619	37,643	4	210	767	3,298	19,731	13,638	5,764	..	21	39	144	1,887	3,873
			F.	78,270	39,148	10,960	12,787	3,849	1,356	157	39	38,491	..	563	1,970	6,014	21,699	8,245	10,631	..	16	32	110	2,071	8,402
Mer . .	Rajputana .	Total .	M.	7,156	3,212	1,099	908	197	411	556	42	3,487	1	21	15	197	2,206	1,047	456	..	3	..	7	189	257
			F.	6,556	2,115	1,210	787	85	24	7	2	3,509	3	53	87	406	2,443	517	932	1	2	2	16	271	640
		H.	M.	7,127	3,197	1,095	905	194	400	552	42	3,475	1	21	15	197	2,200	1,041	455	..	3	..	7	188	257
			F.	6,531	2,104	1,206	785	80	24	7	2	3,497	3	53	87	406	2,433	515	930	1	2	2	16	270	639
	Ajmer-Merwara.	Total .	M.	11,634	6,097	1,685	1,728	618	848	1,122	96	4,856	1	20	34	126	2,815	1,860	681	1	1	..	13	218	448
			F.	10,169	3,788	1,699	1,540	352	144	44	3	4,906	7	42	121	617	3,195	926	1,479	1	3	..	5	235	1,235
		H.	M.	11,623	6,095	1,685	1,728	618	847	1,121	96	4,850	1	20	34	125	2,811	1,850	678	1	1	..	13	217	446
			F.	10,151	3,712	1,699	1,540	352	144	44	3	4,803	7	42	121	615	3,189	919	1,476	1	3	..	5	235	1,232

TABLE XIV.—Civil Condition by Age for Selected Castes, Tribes or Races—*contd.*

[In column 3, A.=Animist, C.=Christian, H.=Hindu, J.=Jain, M.=Musalman, S.=Sikh.]

Caste, Tribe, or Race.	Locality.	Religion.	Sex.	Population dealt with.	Unmarried. Total.	Unmarried. 0-4.	Unmarried. 5-11.	Unmarried. 12-14.	Unmarried. 15-19.	Unmarried. 20-39.	Unmarried. 40 and over.	Married. Total.	Married. 0-4.	Married. 5-11.	Married. 12-14.	Married. 15-19.	Married. 20-39.	Married. 40 and over.	Widowed. Total.	Widowed. 0-4.	Widowed. 5-11.	Widowed. 12-14.	Widowed. 15-19.	Widowed. 20-39.	Widowed. 40 and over.
1	2	3	4	5	6	7	8	9	10	11	12	13	14	15	16	17	18	19	20	21	22	23	24	25	26
Merat	Rajputana	Total	M.	1,190	684	170	212	53	95	147	7	469	1	3	4	17	240	204	37	..	..	..	1	4	32
			F.	953	356	182	132	27	12	3	..	465	1	4	14	54	319	73	131	..	1	..	6	14	110
	Ajmer-Merwara	Total	M.	3,149	1,689	524	488	129	239	300	9	1,349	2	5	10	42	838	452	111	..	..	..	..	31	80
			F.	2,060	991	505	383	63	34	5	1	887	..	14	23	120	596	134	182	..	..	..	1	33	148
(a) Gorat	Rajputana	H.	M.	16	10	3	1	..	1	5	..	6	..	..	..	..	2	4	..	..	..	..	..	..	..
			F.	10	2	1	1	..	..	..	..	7	..	..	..	2	4	1	1	..	..	..	..	..	1
	Ajmer-Merwara	H.	M.	1,257	673	205	189	55	93	128	3	536	2	3	2	17	313	199	48	..	..	..	..	13	35
			F.	688	418	213	164	27	12	2	..	230	..	5	8	47	162	8	40	..	..	..	..	5	35
(b) Kathat	Rajputana	M.	M.	1,174	674	167	211	53	94	142	7	463	1	3	4	17	238	200	37	..	..	..	1	4	32
			F.	949	354	181	131	27	12	3	..	458	1	4	14	52	315	72	130	..	1	..	6	14	109
	Ajmer-Merwara	M.	M.	1,899	1,016	319	299	74	146	172	6	813	..	2	8	25	525	253	63	..	..	..	..	18	46
			F.	1,379	573	292	219	36	22	3	1	657	..	9	15	73	434	126	142	..	..	..	1	28	113
Mina	Rajputana	Total	M.	396,905	148,724	40,881	48,943	15,730	18,701	21,466	3,003	131,275	35	1,079	2,280	7,841	72,611	47,429	18,206	..	25	52	263	4,530	11,336
			F.	262,482	87,897	41,199	38,642	5,836	1,622	478	120	134,541	72	2,800	6,485	16,962	81,700	26,502	40,044	5	42	131	346	7,471	32,049
		A.	M.	23,730	13,158	5,324	4,137	892	1,254	1,489	62	9,786	5	29	45	314	6,264	3,129	786	..	1	2	16	306	461
			F.	22,314	9,739	5,479	3,430	458	253	98	15	10,059	5	64	190	886	7,213	1,741	2,476	..	1	3	4	359	2,109
		H.	M.	272,411	135,528	35,548	44,790	14,832	17,442	19,975	2,941	121,463	30	1,050	2,235	7,524	66,335	44,289	15,420	..	24	50	247	4,224	10,875
			F.	240,093	78,127	35,708	35,190	5,375	1,369	380	105	124,399	67	2,734	6,294	16,081	74,467	24,756	37,567	5	41	128	342	7,112	29,939
	Ajmer-Merwara	Total	M.	2,440	1,186	383	331	77	122	252	21	1,103	2	6	6	26	711	352	151	..	1	..	1	58	91
			F.	1,781	583	298	237	36	6	3	3	931	1	7	28	95	646	154	267	1	..	..	1	48	217
		H.	M.	2,436	1,185	383	331	77	122	251	21	1,100	2	6	6	26	709	351	151	..	1	..	1	58	91
			F.	1,781	583	298	237	36	6	3	3	931	1	7	28	95	646	154	267	1	..	..	1	48	217
Moghal	Rajputana	M.	M.	7,406	3,768	943	1,197	405	459	651	113	3,181	..	14	37	144	1,583	1,403	457	..	..	2	10	101	344
			F.	6,593	2,417	1,016	998	255	114	34	5	3,143	3	55	131	431	1,846	677	1,033	..	..	4	21	206	802
	Ajmer-Merwara	M.	M.	778	367	78	110	41	62	68	8	359	1	4	5	12	189	148	52	..	2	..	3	15	32
			F.	637	231	94	86	22	9	3	7	323	2	8	10	40	173	90	93	..	..	..	2	21	70
Nai	Rajputana	Total	M.	84,686	39,778	10,873	12,690	4,046	5,260	6,038	871	38,136	13	310	597	2,421	20,797	13,998	6,772	..	24	26	137	2,029	4,556
			F.	77,400	23,185	11,426	9,965	1,233	387	146	28	39,644	45	1,133	1,885	5,500	23,374	7,707	14,571	3	32	31	174	2,916	11,415
		H.	M.	79,944	37,537	10,242	11,931	3,784	4,940	5,823	817	35,973	11	285	554	2,238	19,651	13,233	6,435	..	24	25	130	1,922	4,334
			F.	72,889	21,610	10,759	9,301	1,088	304	134	24	37,325	44	1,079	1,774	5,150	22,061	7,217	13,945	3	32	27	168	2,794	10,922
		M.	M.	4,739	2,239	631	759	262	320	213	54	2,163	2	25	43	183	1,145	765	337	..	..	1	7	107	222
			F.	4,517	1,573	866	663	145	83	12	4	2,318	1	54	111	350	1,312	490	686	1	..	4	6	122	493
	Ajmer-Merwara	Total	M.	3,293	1,367	433	426	105	150	228	25	1,656	1	25	34	107	991	498	270	..	..	1	10	112	147
			F.	3,206	674	469	359	33	9	3	1	1,636	6	61	49	211	1,040	269	696	..	1	2	6	153	534
		H.	M.	3,181	1,325	419	418	98	141	224	25	1,590	1	25	31	101	952	480	266	..	..	1	9	110	146
			F.	3,097	834	447	344	31	8	3	1	1,582	6	61	47	200	1,008	260	681	..	1	2	8	150	922

TABLE XIV.—CIVIL CONDITION BY AGE FOR SELECTED CASTES, TRIBES OR RACES—*contd.*

[In column 3, A.=Animist. C.=Christian. H.=Hindu. J.=Jain. M.=Musalman. S.=Sikh.]

Caste, Tribe, or Race.	Locality.	Religion.	Sex.	Population dealt with.	Unmarried. Total.	0-4.	5-11.	12-14.	15-19.	20-39.	40 and over.	Married. Total.	0-4.	5-11.	12-14.	15-19.	20-39.	40 and over.	Widowed. Total.	0-4.	5-11.	12-14.	15-19.	20-39.	40 and over.
1	2	3	4	5	6	7	8	9	10	11	12	13	14	15	16	17	18	19	20	21	22	23	24	25	26
Naik or Nayak	Rajputana	Total	M.	22,080	10,396	3,269	3,288	997	1,437	1,241	164	10,372	11	60	111	549	5,771	3,870	1,312	..	1	2	22	386	901
			F.	20,243	6,707	3,495	2,712	355	100	35	10	10,696	22	247	441	1,396	6,421	2,169	2,839	..	6	5	28	491	2,309
		H.	M.	22,010	10,367	3,264	3,278	995	1,433	1,233	164	10,338	11	60	109	547	5,751	3,860	1,306	..	1	2	22	384	896
			F.	20,188	6,701	3,492	2,710	354	100	35	10	10,664	22	246	438	1,393	6,404	2,162	2,823	..	6	5	23	488	2,296
	Ajmer-Merwara	H.	M.	1,293	586	214	184	38	73	72	5	606	..	5	5	28	358	210	103	..	2	..	4	48	49
			F.	1,190	362	211	135	11	3	1	1	657	1	21	19	71	449	96	180	..	2	..	3	32	143
Parsi	Rajputana	Parsi	M.	191	103	15	22	15	10	39	2	79	..	..	..	..	34	45	9	..	..	..	..	2	7
			F.	151	81	11	27	14	19	10	..	61	..	..	1	7	31	22	9	..	..	..	..	1	8
	Ajmer-Merwara	Parsi	M.	134	75	18	17	8	11	21	..	57	..	..	..	..	30	27	2	..	..	..	..	..	2
			F.	128	71	16	21	8	18	8	..	47	..	..	..	..	34	13	10	..	..	..	..	..	10
Patel	Rajputana	H.	M.	27,750	13,350	4,469	4,074	1,392	1,832	1,500	83	13,158	10	167	307	1,041	8,274	3,359	1,942	..	3	5	31	431	772
			F.	28,047	9,017	4,507	3,289	802	327	83	9	13,508	33	537	725	1,931	8,611	1,671	5,522	..	7	13	46	1,297	4,159
Pathan	Rajputana	M.	M.	57,471	26,346	6,818	8,178	2,936	3,568	4,333	513	27,261	10	171	284	1,188	14,382	11,226	3,864	..	6	4	75	1,148	2,631
			F.	50,754	16,960	6,911	7,021	1,541	512	212	63	25,864	16	582	1,023	3,288	15,407	5,348	8,930	..	16	12	111	1,744	6,947
	Ajmer-Merwara	M.	M.	6,176	2,806	841	818	307	433	543	64	2,904	..	30	36	122	1,625	1,091	466	..	4	5	13	158	286
			F.	5,244	1,701	700	733	133	66	51	18	2,660	4	64	127	359	1,602	504	883	..	2	4	9	166	702
Prohit	Rajputana	Total	M.	19,130	10,067	2,479	2,606	1,013	1,483	2,179	328	7,459	..	31	46	255	4,073	3,054	1,584	..	3	1	14	387	1,179
			F.	17,812	5,271	2,450	2,218	466	115	20	2	7,707	10	114	244	980	4,960	1,399	4,834	..	4	15	95	1,413	3,307
		H.	M.	19,128	10,086	2,479	2,605	1,013	1,482	2,179	328	7,458	..	31	46	255	4,072	3,054	1,584	..	3	1	14	387	1,179
			F.	17,811	5,271	2,450	2,218	466	115	20	2	7,706	10	114	244	980	4,959	1,399	4,834	..	4	15	95	1,413	3,307
Raigar	Rajputana	Total	M.	41,626	19,042	5,936	6,956	2,092	2,313	1,583	162	20,444	11	203	437	1,521	11,502	6,770	2,140	..	5	10	52	532	1,541
			F.	39,949	13,546	6,478	5,990	741	220	63	54	21,015	15	733	1,217	3,276	12,019	3,755	5,381	4	26	21	84	1,235	4,011
		H.	M.	41,622	19,039	5,936	6,955	2,091	2,313	1,583	161	20,444	11	203	437	1,521	11,502	6,770	2,139	..	5	10	52	532	1,540
			F.	39,935	13,544	6,477	5,989	741	220	63	54	21,013	15	733	1,217	3,276	12,018	3,754	5,378	4	26	21	84	1,234	4,009
	Ajmer-Merwara	H.	M.	10,133	4,704	1,710	1,575	446	577	388	8	4,892	3	22	60	294	3,059	1,454	539	..	2	1	19	172	346
			F.	9,699	3,294	1,748	1,265	202	60	12	7	4,962	6	92	194	766	3,163	761	1,423	..	5	6	17	834	1,061
Rajput	Rajputana	Total	M.	372,484	215,558	43,227	55,023	20,389	30,854	52,481	13,584	133,412	46	580	897	4,844	70,819	56,226	23,514	5	46	77	232	5,659	17,495
			F.	291,354	84,016	36,105	37,118	6,955	2,677	886	275	131,416	102	2,064	4,981	17,766	82,073	24,424	75,928	5	134	219	1,079	19,308	56,183
		H.	M.	355,318	206,017	40,994	52,197	19,272	29,551	50,677	13,320	126,886	45	550	835	4,320	67,770	53,366	22,445	5	43	64	217	5,428	16,088
			F.	276,878	78,751	33,980	34,810	6,463	2,433	803	253	124,695	99	1,873	4,678	16,836	78,140	23,065	73,432	5	131	202	1,039	18,797	53,258
		M.	M.	16,890	9,408	2,214	2,794	1,078	1,282	1,785	255	6,431	1	29	61	512	3,006	2,825	1,048	..	3	13	13	223	796
			F.	14,300	5,208	2,100	2,271	490	242	83	22	6,627	3	189	303	919	3,870	1,343	2,465	..	3	17	39	507	1,890

TABLE XIV.—Civil Condition by Age for Selected Castes, Tribes or Races—*contd.*

[In column 3, A.=Animist. C.=Christian. H.=Hindu. J.=Jain. M.=Musalman. S.=Sikh.]

Caste, Tribe, or Race.	Locality.	Religion.	Sex.	Population dealt with.	Unmarried. Total.	0-4.	5-11.	12-14.	15-19.	20-39.	40 and over.	Married. Total.	0-4.	5-11.	12-14.	15-19.	20-39.	40 and over.	Widowed. Total.	0-4.	5-11.	12-14.	15-19.	20-39.	40 and over.
1	2	3	4	5	6	7	8	9	10	11	12	13	14	15	16	17	18	19	20	21	22	23	24	25	26
Rajput .	Ajmer-Merwara	Total .	M.	8,324	4,309	777	967	400	844	1,244	277	3,344	2	19	34	110	1,925	1,254	571	..	1	2	14	179	375
			F.	6,077	1,642	692	731	124	76	13	6	2,770	..	35	102	349	1,851	433	1,665	..	2	2	25	467	1,169
		H.	M.	8,096	4,246	768	955	393	835	1,220	275	3,282	2	18	34	108	1,881	1,239	568	..	1	2	14	176	375
			F.	6,038	1,630	686	725	124	76	13	6	2,746	..	35	102	348	1,831	430	1,662	..	2	2	25	467	1,166
Rangrez .	Rajputana .	M.	M.	8,043	3,874	1,036	1,279	390	408	387	74	3,813	2	74	101	275	1,954	1,407	656	..	3	1	15	210	427
			F.	7,434	2,468	1,149	1,077	174	49	14	5	3,937	8	186	215	520	2,198	810	1,029	..	6	3	14	181	825
	Ajmer-Merwara	M.	M.	358	164	51	43	16	28	26	2	170	..	8	2	10	83	67	24	..	..	..	..	12	12
			F.	263	85	34	39	10	2	..	..	145	1	5	8	11	84	36	33	..	..	..	..	7	26
Rawat .	Rajputana .	Total .	M.	7,544	4,107	1,278	1,095	307	517	863	47	3,094	4	21	12	75	1,732	1,250	343	..	..	..	6	111	226
			F.	6,133	2,318	1,219	911	110	50	24	4	3,088	7	32	73	330	2,055	591	747	..	1	1	6	107	632
		H.	M.	7,529	4,099	1,274	1,093	305	515	863	47	3,088	4	21	12	75	1,730	1,246	342	..	..	..	6	110	226
			F.	6,147	2,317	1,218	911	110	50	24	4	3,084	7	32	73	330	2,051	591	740	..	1	1	6	107	631
	Ajmer-Merwara	Total .	M.	24,969	13,901	4,472	3,790	979	1,640	2,886	134	9,916	7	27	20	217	5,460	4,185	1,145	..	..	2	17	299	827
			F.	22,943	8,373	4,476	3,143	421	262	50	21	11,398	19	99	227	1,163	7,826	2,064	3,171	..	3	2	11	398	2,757
		H.	M.	24,953	13,896	4,471	3,790	978	1,638	2,885	134	9,912	7	27	20	217	5,458	4,183	1,145	..	..	2	17	299	827
			F.	22,908	8,371	4,475	3,143	421	261	50	21	11,374	19	90	227	1,161	7,810	2,058	3,163	..	3	2	11	398	2,749
Rebari .	Rajputana .	Total .	M.	67,759	33,869	10,136	10,669	3,450	4,410	4,727	477	29,792	61	1,067	828	1,996	16,131	9,709	4,098	2	22	27	97	1,367	2,583
			F.	62,158	19,589	9,603	7,794	1,529	517	121	25	30,647	292	1,882	1,608	4,041	17,879	4,947	11,922	5	17	28	125	2,586	9,161
		H.	M.	67,731	33,867	10,135	10,669	3,449	4,410	4,727	477	29,790	61	1,067	828	1,996	16,131	9,707	4,097	2	22	27	97	1,367	2,582
			F.	62,137	19,589	9,603	7,794	1,529	517	121	25	30,626	292	1,882	1,605	4,041	17,879	4,947	11,922	5	17	28	125	2,586	9,161
	Ajmer-Merwara	H.	M.	1,083	490	143	150	41	64	70	12	516	5	29	24	46	273	139	87	..	1	1	3	26	56
			F.	948	236	105	112	10	8	..	1	463	14	46	21	73	259	50	249	..	1	..	2	76	170
Sadhu .	Rajputana .	Total .	M.	6,361	3,880	605	604	208	424	1,107	932	1,830	..	35	38	112	1,003	642	651	..	1	7	32	170	341
			F.	3,969	1,271	565	469	78	33	77	49	1,724	3	58	57	226	1,044	336	974	1	..	3	15	285	670
		H.	M.	6,072	3,732	600	597	202	407	1,051	875	1,816	..	35	38	111	907	635	524	..	1	6	32	162	333
			F.	3,564	1,120	558	448	59	21	23	11	1,667	3	58	50	222	1,020	314	777	1	..	3	8	177	588
		J.	M.	179	143	5	6	8	16	56	54	12	..	..	..	1	5	6	21	..	..	1	..	7	16
			F.	396	146	4	19	19	12	54	38	51	..	..	7	3	22	22	190	..	..	..	7	108	81
	Ajmer-Merwara	Total .	M.	2,559	1,237	282	337	109	145	242	122	1,097	4	18	30	61	635	349	218	..	..	1	5	77	135
			F.	2,083	563	288	221	19	7	17	11	1,058	3	44	47	141	654	169	462	1	1	2	2	131	325
		H.	M.	2,523	1,214	282	336	108	145	230	113	1,095	4	18	30	61	663	349	214	..	..	1	5	73	135
			F.	2,058	555	285	210	19	7	15	10	1,049	3	44	47	140	647	168	454	1	1	2	2	128	320

TABLE XIV.

TABLE XIV.—CIVIL CONDITION BY AGE FOR SELECTED CASTES, TRIBES OR RACES—*concld.*

(In column 3, A.=Animist, C.=Christian, H.=Hindu, J.=Jain, M.=Musalman, S.=Sikh.)

Caste, Tribe, or Race.	Locality.	Religion.	Sex.	Population dealt with.	UNMARRIED.							MARRIED.							WIDOWED.						
					TOTAL.	0-4.	5-11.	12-14.	15-19.	20-39.	40 and over.	Total.	0-4.	5-11.	12-14.	15-19.	20-39.	40 and over.	Total.	0-4.	5-11.	12-14.	15-19.	20-39.	40 and over.
1	2	3	4	5	6	7	8	9	10	11	12	13	14	15	16	17	18	19	20	21	22	23	24	25	26
Saiyad	Rajputana	M.	M.	15,249	7,209	1,758	2,231	893	1,070	1,098	159	7,033	2	54	80	308	3,656	2,933	1,000	..	3	6	10	256	725
			F.	13,719	4,670	1,891	2,093	417	186	70	13	6,768	3	115	216	934	4,077	1,423	2,274	..	5	5	22	486	1,756
	Ajmer-Merwara	M.	M.	2,823	1,352	335	383	183	219	208	24	1,252	..	6	12	40	664	530	219	..	2	..	1	86	130
			F.	2,376	867	343	340	95	51	25	13	1,128	2	25	34	146	696	225	381	..	..	1	6	88	286
Savag	Rajputana	Total	M.	4,861	2,321	739	740	189	270	342	41	2,166	2	10	26	118	1,280	730	374	..	..	2	7	117	248
			F.	5,207	1,456	660	676	84	25	8	3	2,373	..	45	129	373	1,383	443	1,378	1	4	5	17	368	983
		H.	M.	4,791	2,291	732	731	188	263	337	40	2,131	2	10	26	118	1,252	723	369	..	..	2	7	115	245
			F.	5,158	1,445	653	673	83	25	8	3	2,351	..	44	128	368	1,374	437	1,362	1	4	5	17	362	973
Shekh	Rajputana	M.	M.	96,638	46,388	11,922	14,665	5,570	6,170	7,054	1,007	43,613	12	453	705	2,577	23,124	16,742	6,637	4	29	35	141	1,878	4,550
			F.	85,066	28,601	11,663	12,567	2,466	1,059	627	219	42,434	34	1,417	1,862	5,844	24,951	8,326	14,031	1	35	39	173	2,826	10,957
	Ajmer-Merwara	M.	M.	13,380	6,028	1,658	1,942	669	805	854	100	6,324	3	75	135	404	3,453	2,254	1,030	..	10	7	28	371	614
			F.	11,750	3,967	1,623	1,683	281	160	159	61	5,972	16	211	311	856	3,440	1,138	1,811	..	8	13	29	364	1,397
Sunar	Rajputana	Total	M.	35,510	16,928	4,726	5,799	1,605	1,972	2,322	504	15,919	8	127	286	1,271	8,635	5,592	2,663	..	15	12	52	761	1,823
			F.	33,415	10,055	4,764	4,591	494	135	52	19	16,685	15	553	955	2,419	9,488	3,255	6,675	3	16	18	111	1,622	4,905
		H.	M.	35,481	16,913	4,723	5,797	1,602	1,969	2,320	502	15,907	8	127	284	1,271	8,629	5,588	2,661	..	15	12	52	761	1,821
			F.	33,391	10,046	4,762	4,585	494	134	52	19	16,671	15	553	953	2,416	9,482	3,252	6,674	3	16	18	111	1,622	4,904
	Ajmer-Merwara	Total	M.	1,670	729	201	195	63	105	141	24	782	..	20	16	50	424	272	159	..	..	1	5	47	106
			F.	1,523	407	191	188	21	4	2	1	785	2	50	33	102	447	151	331	..	1	..	6	91	233
		H.	M.	1,663	725	200	194	63	104	140	24	780	..	20	16	50	423	271	158	..	..	1	5	46	106
			F.	1,516	404	191	185	21	4	2	1	783	2	50	33	102	446	150	328	..	1	..	6	90	231
Sutar	Rajputana	Total	M.	23,685	11,803	3,599	3,568	1,135	1,675	1,692	134	10,364	10	95	106	570	6,089	3,494	1,518	..	2	7	38	510	961
			F.	22,241	7,060	3,688	2,824	403	106	31	8	10,742	16	302	470	1,571	6,790	1,593	4,439	..	5	13	52	1,110	3,259
		H.	M.	23,684	11,802	3,599	3,568	1,135	1,675	1,691	134	10,364	10	95	106	570	6,089	3,494	1,518	..	2	7	38	510	961
			F.	22,237	7,058	3,687	2,823	403	106	31	8	10,740	16	302	470	1,570	6,789	1,593	4,439	..	5	13	52	1,110	3,259
Teli	Rajputana	Total	M.	40,628	18,250	5,984	6,299	1,728	1,982	2,009	248	19,306	16	358	523	1,522	10,741	6,146	3,072	4	20	19	96	1,058	1,875
			F.	37,799	11,770	5,995	4,912	602	169	66	26	19,990	48	908	1,141	2,845	11,590	3,458	6,039	..	8	15	97	1,280	4,639
		H.	M.	24,001	10,650	3,677	3,497	868	1,126	1,325	157	11,389	10	180	297	823	6,589	3,490	1,962	3	8	11	63	747	1,130
			F.	22,477	6,944	3,677	2,825	303	89	35	15	11,592	28	481	599	1,579	7,047	1,858	3,941	..	5	9	77	901	2,949
		M.	M.	16,624	7,599	2,307	2,801	860	856	684	91	7,915	6	178	226	699	4,150	2,656	1,110	1	12	8	33	311	745
			F.	15,319	4,824	2,316	2,087	299	80	31	11	8,397	20	427	542	1,266	4,542	1,600	2,098	..	3	6	20	379	1,690
	Ajmer-Merwara	Total	M.	2,284	962	322	293	82	112	123	30	1,118	2	22	29	80	659	326	204	..	2	3	6	91	102
			F.	2,121	533	298	198	27	6	2	2	1,167	9	59	66	159	676	198	421	..	2	..	6	104	309
		H.	M.	2,038	876	312	255	69	101	109	30	981	2	17	24	70	584	284	181	..	2	3	6	79	91
			F.	1,897	472	261	181	21	5	2	2	1,044	8	50	59	137	622	168	381	..	2	..	4	91	284

TABLE XV-A.

Occupation or Means of Livelihood.

Explanatory Note.

This table is divided into two parts. Part I is a Provincial Summary. Part II shows by States or Districts the occupations or means of livelihood which were returned in the schedules as the *principal* means of support. The subsidiary means of support of the agricultural classes only are dealt with in Table XV-B.

Separate figures for Cities are given in Part II, but these are included also in the State and District figures. Jodhpur City includes Jodhpur suburbs which have been shown in Tables IV and V under the name of Jodhpur Town.

To facilitate comparison with the statistics of occupations in other countries the method of classification in the Census of 1901 has been abandoned, and Monsieur Bertillon's scheme, modified where necessary to suit the local conditions of India, has been adopted. Occupations are arranged in 4 Classes, A, B, C, D. The Classes are sub-divided into 12 Sub-classes, which in their turn are sub-divided into 55 Orders. Within the Orders are 169 Groups. For ready reference an Appendix has been added to the Table showing how the groups of the 1901 Table have been amalgamated in the new groups.

Group 29 (persons occupied with feathers), Group 94 (Harbour works, dockyards, and pilots), and Order 43, Group 141 (Navy), have been omitted from Part II of the Table, as there were no occupations returned under these heads.

To meet local requirements certain groups in the standard scheme have been sub-divided as follows :—

Group 2 (ordinary cultivators) into 2 (Actual cultivators [rent payers]) and 2 (*a*) (Unpaid helpers in cultivation) ; Group 142 (Police) into 142 (Police Imperial) and 142 (*a*) (Police Native States) ; Group 145 (Service of Native and Foreign States) into 145 (*a*) (Rulers of Native States and their families), and 145 (*b*) (Native States' administrative officials and menials).

So, too, owing to the difficulty in distinguishing between dyers of textiles and dyers of made-up clothes, Group 30 has been sub-divided into 30 (Bleaching, printing, preparation and sponging of textiles), and 30 (*a*) (Dyeing of textiles), and Group 71 into 71 (Washing and cleaning of clothes) and 71 (*a*) (Dyeing of made-up articles of clothing). The dyeing industry is thus represented by the combination of groups 30 (*a*) and 71 (*a*).

TABLE XV-A.—Occupation or Means of Livelihood.
Part I.—Provincial Summary.

Class, Sub-Class and Order.*	Group.*	Total workers and dependants (both sexes). Rajputana.	Ajmer-Merwara.
1	2	3	4
Population	Total .	10,530,432	501,395
CLASS A. .	Total .	6,832,939	276,327
Sub-Class I.	Total .	6,819,629	275,632
Order 1 .	Total .	6,818,961	275,594
	1	580,907	10,647
	2	3,788,813	145,323
	2(a)	1,513,514	81,873
	3	23,758	456
	4	864,970	30,297
	5	4	1
	6	8,123	891
	7	2,686	152
	8	24,425	979
	9	65,133	828
	10	48,198	632
	11	2,883	1
	12	95,524	3,714
	13	26	..
Order 2 .	Total .	668	38
	14	78	3
	15	590	35
Sub-Class II	Total .	13,310	695
Order 3 .	Total .	357	..
	16	236	..
	17	121	..
Order 4 .	18	5,576	691
Order 5 .	Total .	7,377	4
	19	6,908	4
	20	469	..
CLASS B. .	Total .	2,486,020	161,795
Sub-Class III	Total .	1,547,057	84,701
Order 6 .	Total .	390,522	19,216
	21	30,732	7,979
	22	306,930	9,138
	23	6	11
	24	2,710	343
	25	960	..
	26	5,658	385
	27	24	..
	28	1,843	..
	29	..	..
	30	16,208	404
	30(a)	24,873	892
	31	579	64
Order 7 .	Total .	94,932	5,150
	32	60,818	1,307
	33	32,977	3,835
	34	208	..
	35	929	8
Order 8 .	Total .	144,390	4,998
	36	119,565	4,140
	37	24,825	858
Order 9 .	Total .	67,420	4,171
	38	5	..
	39	302	95
	40	1,343	3
	41	58,275	3,239
	42	6,447	655
	43	916	179
	44	132	..
Order 10 .	Total .	136,964	5,605
	45	391	..
	46	10	..
	47	135,036	5,516
	48	1,518	89
	49	9	..
Order 11 .	Total .	46,446	2,558
	50	1,400	34
	51	73	260
	52	983	74
	53	43,410	2,188
	54	367	1
	55	213	1
Order 12 .	Total .	64,449	3,530
	56	20,372	1,437
	57	401	159
	58	4,462	301
	59	21,016	981
	60	66	..
	61	129	1
	62	220	1
	63	8,998	616
	64	8,570	14
	65	14	..
	66	201	..
Order 13 .	Total .	334,507	13,230
	67	274	..
	68	52,999	3,273
	69	125,501	5,095
	70	980	14
	71	35,968	2,532
	71(a)	10,388	2,495
	72	108,191	4,810
	73	206	11
Order 14 .	Total .	228	..
	74	182	..
	75	46	..
Order 15 .	Total .	89,039	7,188
	76	2,952	285
	77	8,245	4
	78	74,625	6,345
	79	3,217	554
Order 16 .	Total .	427	12
	80	61	3
	81	364	9
	82	2	..
Order 17 .	83	543	35
Order 18 .	Total .	91,692	7,800
	84	518	546
	85	..	2
	86	224	47
	87	81	1
	88	318	65
	89	68,841	5,848
	90	21,188	1,235
	91	352	6
	92	172	50
Order 19 .	93	85,499	6,298
Sub-Class IV	Total .	110,202	34,630
Order 20 .	Total .	1,343	95
	94	..	..
	95	100	2
	96	745	93
	97	498	..
Order 21 .	Total .	73,772	5,784
	98	10,293	760
	99	15,216	2,690
	100	781	69
	101	32,130	600
	102	15,352	1,665
Order 22 .	Total .	31,319	27,809
	103	29,351	27,580
	104	1,968	229
Order 23 .	105	3,768	942
Sub-Class V	Total .	828,761	42,464
Order 24 .	106	185,988	7,191
Order 25 .	107	14,894	1,545
Order 26 .	108	73,855	3,262
Order 27 .	109	18,284	1,150
Order 28 .	110	3,118	93
Order 29 .	111	961	41
Order 30 .	112	221	..
Order 31 .	113	876	39
Order 32 .	Total .	15,752	612
	114	14,658	467
	115	1,094	145
Order 33 .	Total .	395,869	20,194
	116	60	25
	117	236,205	11,359
	118	17,118	1,999
	119	18,015	1,668
	120	24,079	1,564
	121	43,523	1,075
	122	4,277	579
	123	9,258	1,455
	124	43,334	470
Order 34 .	125	9,087	436
Order 35 .	Total .	2,564	283
	126	778	219
	127	1,786	64
Order 36 .	128	2,398	7
Order 37 .	129	8,758	1,250
Order 38 .	130	37,677	2,720
Order 39 .	Total .	15,814	389
	131	1,659	31
	132	13,708	306
	133	447	52
Order 40 .	134	4	..
Order 41 .	Total .	42,811	3,252
	135	29,725	2,244
	136	9,814	658
	137	1,779	252
	138	1,493	98
CLASS C. .	Total .	738,112	35,022
Sub-Class VI	Total .	149,019	8,865
Order 42 .	Total .	86,458	6,447
	139	3,307	6,307
	140	83,151	140
Order 43	141	..	..
Order 44	Total .	62,561	2,418
	142	1,586	1,894
	142(a)	23,864	23
	143	37,111	501
Sub-Class VII	Total .	153,636	4,728
Order 45 .	Total .	153,636	4,728
	144	1,165	2,521
	145(a)	487	11
	145(b)	10,102	763
	146	2,530	937
	147	39,342	496
Sub-Class VIII.	Total .	388,899	19,005
Order 46 .	Total .	277,851	10,109
	148	90,209	1,906
	149	170,135	6,421
	150	4,414	157
	151	13,093	1,625
Order 47 .	Total .	6,501	443
	152	5,060	231
	153	1,441	212
Order 48 .	Total .	14,908	1,102
	154	5,691	540
	155	9,217	562
Order 49 .	156	8,041	1,696
Order 50	Total .	81,598	5,655
	157	122	1
	158	4,776	348
	159	10,260	159
	160	66,440	5,147
Sub-Class IX	Total .	46,558	2,424
Order 51 .	161	46,558	2,424
CLASS D. .	Total .	472,361	28,251
Sub-Class X	Total .	224,700	14,738
Order 52 .	Total .	224,700	14,738
	162	208,595	13,173
	163	16,105	1,565
Sub-Class XI	Total .	92,517	5,152
Order 53 .	Total .	92,517	5,152
	164	448	303
	165	20,058	552
	166	40	..
	167	71,971	4,297
Sub-Class XII	Total .	155,144	8,361
Order 54 .	168	5,219	445
Order 55 .	169	150,925	7,916

*The names of the occupations included in the groups, etc., whose numbers are given in columns 1 and 2, will be found in Part II of the Table.

TABLE XV-A.—OCCUPATION OR MEANS OF LIVELIHOOD. PART II.—BY STATE OR DISTRICT, AND CITY.

Province; and State, District, or City.	Population. Males.	Population. Females.	Total of Classes A, B, C and D. Total workers and dependants. Both sexes.	Total of Classes A, B, C and D. Actual workers. Total. Males.	Total of Classes A, B, C and D. Actual workers. Total. Females.	Total of Classes A, B, C and D. Actual workers. Partially agriculturists. Males.	Total of Classes A, B, C and D. Actual workers. Partially agriculturists. Females.	Total of Classes A, B, C and D. Dependants. Both sexes.	Class A.—Production of Raw Materials. Total Class A. Total workers and dependants. Both sexes.	Total Class A. Actual workers. Total. Males.	Total Class A. Actual workers. Total. Females.	Total Class A. Actual workers. Partially agriculturists. Males.	Total Class A. Actual workers. Partially agriculturists. Females.	Total Class A. Dependants. Both sexes.	Sub-class I.—Exploitation of the surface of the earth. Total Sub-class 1. Total workers and dependants. Both sexes.	Total Sub-class 1. Actual workers. Total. Males.	Total Sub-class 1. Actual workers. Total. Females.	Total Sub-class 1. Actual workers. Partially agriculturists. Males.	Total Sub-class 1. Actual workers. Partially agriculturists. Females.	Total Sub-class 1. Dependants. Both sexes.
1	2	3	4	5	6	7	8	9	10	11	12	13	14	15	16	17	18	19	20	21
Rajputana	5,515,275	5,015,157	10,530,432	3,787,701	2,336,358	212,267	21,387	4,406,373	6,332,939	2,434,749	1,742,435	14,669	1,656	2,655,755	6,319,629	2,429,605	1,739,266	13,550	1,575	2,650,758
Alwar	413,659	378,029	791,688	280,707	186,823	17 596	2,809	324,158	620,294	183,324	144,289	262	29	192,681	519 901	183,181	144,245	344	28	192 475
Banswara	81,620	83,843	165,463	49,224	42,909	2,705	262	73,330	133,096	38,565	38,046	33	..	56,485	133 096	38,565	38,046	33	..	56,485
Bharatpur	302,254	256,531	558,785	217,852	131,743	14,612	2,364	209,190	389,383	152,242	106,144	614	49	131,997	388,957	152 036	105,128	559	49	131,793
Bikaner	371,489	329,494	700,983	256,411	145,287	14 021	2,486	299,305	506,224	188,780	118,483	380	22	193,961	505 279	188,424	118 404	375	19	198 451
Bundi	113,211	105,519	218,730	73,542	39,138	2,117	96	106,050	149,590	48,773	30,181	143	9	70,636	149,567	48,766	30,180	143	9	70,621
Dholpur	144,244	118,944	263,188	102,704	43,241	5,252	587	117,243	190,496	75,512	33,370	256	21	81,614	190,343	75,380	33,339	941	21	81 515
Dungarpur	79,105	80,087	159,192	47,475	38,108	2,737	268	73,608	114,840	33,330	32,406	44	1	49,104	114,840	33 330	32 406	44	1	49,104
Jaipur	1,385,750	1,250,897	2,636,647	988,002	634,315	40,894	6,062	1,014,330	1,547,477	580,297	434,609	640	215	532,571	1,544,368	579,024	433,946	548	204	531,398
Jaisalmer	48,500	39,811	88,311	28,450	5,753	5,834	114	54,108	55,931	18,815	1,734	2,722	64	35,382	55,006	18,808	1,734	2,720	64	35 364
Jhalawar	50,034	46,237	96,271	34,978	15,648	1,225	248	45,645	59,630	21,539	10,989	39	32	27,102	59,462	21,485	10,962	30	23	27,015
Karauli	80,081	66,506	146,587	57,867	35,952	3,488	316	52,768	99,037	38,767	28,378	119	..	31,892	98,940	38 728	28 378	108	..	31,840
Kishangarh	45,718	41,473	87,191	32,449	19,800	2,391	302	34,942	52,135	18,817	14,209	218	54	19,165	51 872	18 674	14 147	197	54	19 031
Kotah	330,324	308,765	639,089	227,239	160,741	10,747	1,332	251,109	413,654	144,429	116,577	627	34	152,578	413 160	144,308	116,487	620	34	152 365
Kushalgarh (Chiefship)	10,956	11,049	22,005	6,362	5,717	71	1	9,926	18,279	5,150	5,225	..	..	7,904	18 274	5,148	5,225	..	..	7,901
Lawa (Estate)	1,302	1,262	2,564	924	681	28	8	959	1,667	564	494	1	..	609	1,667	564	494	1	..	609
Marwar	1,075,269	982,284	2,057,553	734,276	449,534	52,938	7,361	873,743	1,350,763	479,610	351,574	5,098	515	519,579	1,345,193	477,490	349,865	4,935	460	517,838
Mewar	670,750	623,026	1,293,776	439,677	237,325	33,502	5,486	616,774	846,132	274,781	166,111	2,387	528	404,337	845,150	274 464	166 073	2,376	526	404 613
Partabgarh	31,735	30,969	62,704	20,874	16,027	862	145	25,803	44,748	14,200	13,447	68	20	17,101	44 748	14 200	13 447	66	20	17 101
Shahpura (Chiefship)	24,595	22,802	47,397	16,437	11,515	3,046	291	19,445	32,315	10,541	9,544	161	29	12,230	32,315	10 541	9,544	161	29	12 230
Sirohi	98,289	90,838	189,127	63,436	38,719	1,401	183	86,972	105,975	35,494	26,242	126	13	44,239	103 397	35 263	26 133	121	13	44 001
Tonk	156,390	146,791	303,181	108,815	77,402	3,751	646	116,964	201,293	71,222	61,083	135	21	68,988	201,288	71,217	61,083	135	21	68,988
Ajmer-Merwara	266,198	235,197	501,395	184,143	109,669	11,434	1,610	207,583	276,327	96,485	82,030	308	51	97,812	275,632	96,187	81,967	296	50	97,478
Ajmer	201,911	178,473	380,384	140,567	79,959	8,891	1,285	159,858	195,025	68,708	58,214	287	30	68,103	194 431	68,447	58,182	276	29	67,802
Merwara	64,287	56,724	121,011	43,576	29,710	2,543	325	47,725	81,302	27,777	23,816	21	21	29,709	81,201	27,740	23,785	20	21	29,676
CITIES.																				
Rajputana	233,262	214,487	447,749	165,466	62,283	2,123	128	220,060	37,561	15,037	5,060	102	4	17,464	36,385	14,680	4,700	98	3	16,996
Alwar	22,254	19,051	41,305	16,041	4,992	193	45	20,272	5,518	1,913	898	27	4	2,707	5 430	1,903	869	26	3	2 658
Bharatpur	18,803	15,115	33,918	13,417	3,634	409	41	16,867	2,648	1,258	331	54	..	1,059	2 631	1 237	331	54	..	1,043
Bikaner	28,275	27,551	55,826	19,261	6,353	922	7	30,212	2,831	1,309	118	5	..	1,404	2,765	1,278	118	4	..	1,369
Jaipur	70,846	66,252	137,098	51,679	20,235	128	9	65,184	8,305	3,249	1,222	1	..	3,731	8,179	3 235	1,217	1	..	3,720
Jodhpur	41,838	37,918	79,756	28,961	11,215	178	13	39,580	6,443	3,037	531	2	..	2,875	6,348	3,004	525	2	..	2,819
Kotah	16,949	15,804	32,753	12,450	5,288	200	5	15,015	1,944	762	220	5	..	962	1,924	760	217	5	..	947
Tonk	16,837	17,027	33,864	11,382	5,993	75	8	16,489	4,978	1,641	1,029	..	..	2,308	4,075	1,638	1,029	..	..	2 308
Udaipur	17,460	15,769	33,229	12,215	4,573	18	..	16,441	4,994	1,868	711	8	..	2,415	4,140	1,605	403	6	..	2,132
Ajmer-Merwara—																				
Ajmer	47,354	38,868	86,222	32,674	6,852	1,059	13	46,696	4,511	1,826	486	10	..	2,199	4,435	1,799	480	10	..	2,156

TABLE XV-A.—Occupation or Means of Livelihood. Part II.—By State or District, and City—*continued.*

CLASS A.—PRODUCTION OF RAW MATERIALS—*continued.*

SUB-CLASS I.—EXPLOITATION OF THE SURFACE OF THE EARTH—*continued.*

Order 1.—Pasture and Agriculture.

Province; and State, District, or City.	Total Order 1. Total workers and dependants. Both sexes.	Total Order 1. Actual workers. Total. Males.	Total Order 1. Actual workers. Total. Females.	Total Order 1. Actual workers. Partially agriculturists. Males.	Total Order 1. Actual workers. Partially agriculturists. Females.	Total Order 1. Dependants. Both sexes.	(a) Ordinary Cultivation. Total (a). Total workers and dependants. Both sexes.	Total (a). Actual workers. Total. Males.	Total (a). Actual workers. Total. Females.	Total (a). Actual workers. Partially agriculturists. Males.	Total (a). Actual workers. Partially agriculturists. Females.	Total (a). Dependants. Both sexes.	1.—Income from rent of agricultural land (landlords). Total workers and dependants. Both sexes.	1.—Actual workers. Total. Males.	1.—Actual workers. Total. Females.	1.—Dependants. Both sexes.	2.—Ordinary cultivators (rent payers). Total workers and dependants. Both sexes.	2.—Actual workers. Total. Males.	2.—Actual workers. Total. Females.	2.—Dependants. Both sexes.
1	22	23	24	25	26	27	28	29	30	31	32	33	34	35	36	37	38	39	40	41
Rajputana	**6,818,961**	**2,429,268**	**1,739,246**	**13,496**	**1,578**	**2,650,447**	**6,571,967**	**2,313,161**	**1,709,930**	**660**	**11**	**2,548,926**	**580,907**	**215,481**	**19,497**	**345,929**	**3,783,613**	**1,614,452**	**174,695**	**1,999,666**
Alwar	519,877	183,163	144,245	244	28	192,469	511,322	178,826	143,138	..	..	189,358	15,243	5,160	681	9,404	324,492	147,676	13,429	163,487
Banswara	133,096	38,565	38,046	33	..	56,485	132,136	38,032	37,919	16	..	56,185	5,151	1,515	162	3,474	70,836	21,083	1,228	47,925
Bharatpur	388,904	151,998	105,128	548	49	131,778	380,923	146,461	104,371	..	..	130,091	87,247	37,400	2,772	47,066	189,418	60,815	5,612	72,991
Bikaner	505,279	188,424	116,404	275	19	198,451	499,608	185,789	118,277	3	..	195,542	84,036	13,339	880	10,817	349,663	168,729	6,666	174,268
Bundi	149,523	48,746	30,178	141	9	70,599	141,008	45,293	29,708	..	..	66,007	2,114	546	104	1,464	80,821	25,258	1,375	54,188
Dholpur	190,281	75,385	33,339	339	21	81,507	187,274	73,758	32,996	2	..	80,490	18,494	6,398	414	11,682	118,384	48,951	6,343	63,070
Dungarpur	114,831	33,326	32,406	42	1	49,099	114,328	33,087	32,347	..	..	48,894	2,887	819	225	1,843	66,387	21,905	1,672	42,810
Jaipur	1,544,274	578,968	433,937	545	202	531,369	1,509,222	560,951	425,722	22	..	522,549	100,395	35,756	4,225	60,414	917,341	429,194	76,644	411,503
Jaisalmer	55,906	18,808	1,734	2,720	64	35,364	33,410	10,569	1,250	..	..	21,591	6,996	2,292	113	4,591	25,427	8,097	308	16,032
Jhalawar	59,461	21,484	10,962	30	23	27,015	56,386	19,922	10,460	1	..	26,004	2,424	789	67	1,568	34,366	12,737	503	21,126
Karauli	98,802	38,666	28,378	76	..	31,758	96,794	37,375	28,182	3	..	31,237	4,897	1,426	121	3,350	46,280	19,158	1,066	26,062
Kishangarh	51,852	18,664	14,144	107	54	19,044	47,857	16,692	13,525	..	..	17,640	4,340	1,329	149	2,862	24,655	10,746	1,385	12,524
Kotah	412,950	144,205	116,483	603	34	152,262	389,490	129,470	115,008	144	..	145,012	11,703	3,785	738	7,180	176,454	62,750	3,943	109,761
Kushalgarh (Chiefship)	18,274	5,148	5,225	..	..	7,901	18,047	5,093	5,138	..	..	7,816	99	26	3	70	12,067	4,206	183	7,678
Lawa (Estate)	1,662	560	494	..	..	608	1,605	526	492	..	..	587	57	14	5	38	815	361	14	440
Marwar	1,845,180	477,486	849,865	4,934	460	517,829	1,270,871	445,753	843,679	174	..	481,439	206,863	78,520	6,064	122,279	639,200	288,660	15,147	335,393
Mewar	845,145	274,461	166,072	2,376	526	404,612	823,033	264,209	162,373	291	11	396,451	62,326	21,018	2,316	38,992	580,389	211,499	34,424	334,666
Partabgarh	44,748	14,200	13,447	66	20	17,101	43,569	13,634	13,230	..	..	16,725	2,370	765	90	1,515	24,595	10,724	386	13,485
Shahpura (Chiefship)	32,315	10,541	9,544	161	20	12,230	31,441	10,177	9,449	1	..	11,815	1,993	697	51	1,245	19,441	8,950	262	10,229
Sirohi	105,377	35,255	26,132	121	18	43,990	88,071	29,342	22,154	2	..	36,575	9,563	3,472	220	5,862	50,389	20,769	724	28,896
Tonk	201,274	71,215	61,083	135	21	68,976	195,542	68,112	60,512	1	..	66,918	1,707	406	88	1,213	87,207	31,684	3,291	52,232
Ajmer-Merwara	**275,594**	**96,174**	**81,967**	**293**	**50**	**97,453**	**266,596**	**92,602**	**81,243**	**21**	..	**94,751**	**10,647**	**3,430**	**869**	**6,339**	**145,323**	**60,860**	**4,411**	**80,052**
Ajmer	194,397	68,436	58,182	273	29	67,779	186,114	65,275	57,527	21	..	65,312	9,447	3,100	653	5,694	93,485	38,472	2,901	52,112
Merwara	81,197	27,738	23,785	20	21	29,674	80,482	27,327	23,716	..	..	29,439	1,200	330	216	645	51,838	22,388	1,510	27,940
CITIES.																				
Rajputana	**36,256**	**14,611**	**4,709**	**97**	**3**	**16,936**	**29,039**	**11,447**	**3,969**	**7**	..	**12,633**	**8,542**	**2,961**	**355**	**5,106**	**14,272**	**6,555**	**1,193**	**6,524**
Alwar	5,422	1,901	869	36	3	2,652	4,018	1,296	719	..	..	2,003	334	100	23	211	2,897	1,015	316	1,567
Bharatpur	2,596	1,231	331	53	..	1,034	1,700	739	264	..	..	697	303	89	30	184	1,112	556	59	497
Bikaner	2,765	1,278	118	4	..	1,369	2,494	1,149	117	..	..	1,228	640	167	10	343	1,500	844	40	625
Jaipur	8,172	3,235	1,217	1	..	3,720	6,859	2,776	1,001	..	..	3,082	3,055	902	93	1,970	2,668	1,426	394	848
Jodhpur	6,348	3,004	525	2	..	2,819	5,156	2,447	468	..	..	2,241	1,654	929	35	690	2,840	1,282	182	1,376
Kotah	1,853	721	217	5	..	914	1,277	449	178	1	..	650	411	100	57	254	531	219	43	269
Tonk	4,961	1,636	1,029	..	..	2,296	4,218	1,324	899	..	..	1,995	734	140	46	548	1,908	810	102	996
Udaipur	4,140	1,605	403	6	..	2,132	3,317	1,267	323	6	..	1,727	1,411	444	61	906	807	403	58	346
Ajmer-Merwara—																				
Ajmer	4,428	1,798	480	10	..	2,150	3,465	1,350	440	1	..	1,695	898	296	67	533	2,094	868	230	1,001

TABLE XV-A.—OCCUPATION OR MEANS OF LIVELIHOOD. PART II.—BY STATE OR DISTRICT, AND CITY—*continued.*

CLASS A.—PRODUCTION OF RAW MATERIALS—*continued.*

SUB-CLASS I.—EXPLOITATION OF THE SURFACE OF THE EARTH—*continued.*

Order I.—Pasture and Agriculture—*continued.*

Province; and State, District, or City.	(a) Ordinary Cultivation—*continued.* 2 (e) Unpaid helpers in cultivation. Total workers and dependants.	Actual workers. Total		Dependants.	3.—Agents, managers (not planters), clerks, rent collectors, and other employés on landed estates. Total workers and dependants.	Actual workers. Total.		Partially agriculturists.		Dependants.	4.—Paid field labourers and farm servants. Total workers and dependants.	Actual workers. Total.		Dependants.	(b) Growers of special products and market gardening. Total (b). Total workers and dependants.	Actual workers. Total.		Partially agriculturists.		Dependants.	5.—Tea, coffee, cinchona, and indigo plantations. Total workers and dependants.	Actual workers. Total.		Dependants.
	Both sexes.	Males.	Females.	Both sexes.	Both sexes.	Males.	Females.	Males.	Females.	Both sexes.	Both sexes.	Males.	Females.	Both sexes.	Both sexes.	Males.	Females.	Males.	Females.	Both sexes.		Males.	Females.	Both sexes.
1	42	43	44	45	46	47	48	49	50	51	52	53	54	55	56	57	58	59	60	61	62	63	64	65
Rajputana	**1,813,814**	**497,812**	**1,290,886**	**25,116**	**23,753**	**10,541**	**469**	**660**	**11**	**12,742**	**664,970**	**265,115**	**294,383**	**105,472**	**8,127**	**3,929**	**575**	**237**	**11**	**3,623**	**4**	**1**	..	**3**
Alwar	125,504	11,161	112,641	1,792	54	21	..	..	..	33	45,937	14,908	16,387	14,642	1,210	530	60	35	1	630	..	..	..	..
Banswara	43,290	10,979	32,256	55	370	132	1	16	..	237	12,489	3,723	4,272	4,494	43	21	3	2	..	19	..	..	..	..
Bharatpur	119,908	34,984	83,955	1,019	..	..	..	..	..	..	34,350	13,303	12,032	9,015	852	475	18	47	..	350	..	..	..	..
Bikaner	111,104	880	110,224	..	283	90	..	3	..	198	4,522	2,751	507	1,264	226	121	2	1	..	103	..	..	..	..
Bundi	26,541	9,904	16,329	248	..	..	..	..	..	..	31,532	9,525	11,900	10,107	506	208	96	7	..	207	..	..	..	..
Dholpur	33,886	11,866	21,298	734	262	134	..	2	..	128	16,268	6,439	4,953	4,876	238	138	8	17	1	92	..	..	..	..
Dungarpur	34,725	7,168	27,267	190	62	18	..	..	..	44	10,267	3,177	3,083	4,007	12	3	..	..	..	9	..	..	..	..
Jaipur	334,914	46,004	275,087	13,873	1,300	389	..	22	..	911	155,272	49,608	69,816	35,848	1,369	627	109	7	1	633	..	..	..	..
Jaisalmer	831	93	712	16	44	13	7	..	..	44	102	74	20	8	125	61	8	7	..	56	..	..	..	..
Jhalawar	5,042	2,076	2,909	57	35	11	..	1	..	24	14,519	4,309	6,081	3,229	237	112	7	1	1	118	..	..	..	..
Karauli	37,840	14,218	23,622	..	93	65	..	3	..	28	7,678	2,508	3,373	1,797	577	279	70	47	..	228	..	..	..	..
Kishangarh	11,131	2,311	8,570	250	7	3	2	..	..	3	7,724	2,304	3,419	2,001	40	21	3	..	..	16	..	..	..	..
Kotah	97,485	30,305	66,352	828	2,886	1,204	20	144	..	1,662	100,962	31,426	43,055	25,581	695	380	20	19	..	295	..	..	..	..
Kushalgarh (Chiefship)	5,764	838	4,881	45	9	1	..	..	..	8	108	22	71	15	..	..	..	..	..	..	..	..	..	..
Lawa (Estate)	285	9	275	1	..	..	..	..	..	..	448	142	198	108	11	3	..	..	..	8	..	..	..	..
Marwar	321,664	47,269	273,154	1,241	8,124	4,234	..	174	..	3,890	95,020	27,070	49,314	18,636	652	276	76	10	7	300	..	..	..	..
Mewar	105,007	13,962	87,163	3,972	9,629	4,071	439	291	11	5,119	65,392	13,659	38,031	13,702	790	412	83	80	..	295	3	1	..	2
Partabgarh	9,084	187	8,825	72	..	..	..	..	..	..	7,540	1,958	3,029	1,653	11	5	..	..	..	6	..	..	..	..
Shahpura (Chiefship)	8,641	133	8,508	..	30	13	..	1	..	17	1,336	384	628	324	83	13	3	2	..	17	..	..	..	..
Sirohi	20,507	2,002	18,225	280	34	33	..	2	..	51	7,528	3,066	2,076	1,486	191	87	3	5	..	101	1	..	..	1
Tonk	60,191	21,153	38,595	443	461	110	..	1	..	351	45,976	14,759	18,538	12,679	309	182	10	..	..	131	..	..	..	..
Ajmer-Merwara	**81,873**	**18,977**	**61,609**	**1,287**	**456**	**170**	**6**	**21**	..	**280**	**30,297**	**9,156**	**14,348**	**6,793**	**892**	**438**	**34**	**10**	**2**	**420**	**1**	**1**	..	..
Ajmer	57,033	15,300	40,741	992	448	166	6	21	..	276	27,701	8,237	13,226	6,238	850	422	34	7	2	394	1	1	..	..
Merwara	24,840	3,677	20,868	295	8	4	..	..	..	4	2,596	919	1,122	555	42	16	..	3	..	26	..	..	..	..
CITIES.																								
Rajputana	**1,983**	**460**	**1,520**	**54**	**1,830**	**636**	**4**	**7**	..	**1,190**	**2,512**	**866**	**897**	**749**	**3,579**	**1,747**	**212**	**35**	**1**	**1,620**	..	..	..	..
Alwar	183	11	172	..	1	..	..	..	..	1	603	170	209	224	931	415	43	21	1	473	..	..	..	..
Bharatpur	237	69	167	1	..	..	..	..	..	..	48	25	8	15	506	295	9	8	..	202	..	..	..	..
Bikaner	67	..	67	..	149	38	..	..	..	111	329	80	..	149	150	75	..	..	..	75	..	..	..	..
Jaipur	284	88	270	26	200	68	..	..	..	132	562	202	244	106	606	273	50	1	..	283	..	..	..	..
Jodhpur	342	91	247	4	264	104	..	..	..	160	56	41	4	11	417	188	30	2	..	199	..	..	..	..
Kotah	55	12	43	..	187	87	..	1	..	100	98	31	35	27	323	162	12	3	..	149	..	..	..	..
Tonk	570	122	432	16	388	80	..	..	..	308	618	172	319	127	217	120	12	..	..	85	..	..	..	..
Udaipur	145	16	122	7	641	259	4	6	..	378	313	145	78	90	429	219	56	..	..	154	..	..	..	..
Ajmer-Merwara—																								
Ajmer	63	19	40	4	71	28	3	1	..	40	359	148	100	111	543	278	12	3	..	253	1	1	..	..

TABLE XV-A.—Occupation or Means of Livelihood. Part II.—By State or District, and City—*continued*.

Province; and State, City.	CLASS A.—PRODUCTION OF RAW MATERIALS—*continued*. SUB-CLASS I.—EXPLOITATION OF THE SURFACE OF THE EARTH—*continued*. Order 1.—Pasture and Agriculture—*continued*. (b) Growers of special products and market gardening—*continued*. (6) Fruit, flower, vegetable, betel, vine, areca nut, etc., growers. Total workers and dependants. Both sexes.	Actual workers. Total. Males.	Actual workers. Total. Females.	Actual workers. Partially agriculturists. Males.	Actual workers. Partially agriculturists. Females.	Dependants. Both sexes.	(c) Forestry. Total (c). Total workers and dependants. Both sexes.	Actual workers. Total. Males.	Actual workers. Total. Females.	Actual workers. Partially agriculturists. Males.	Actual workers. Partially agriculturists. Females.	Dependants. Both sexes.	7.—Forest officers, rangers, guards, etc. Total workers and dependants. Both sexes.	Actual workers. Total. Males.	Actual workers. Total. Females.	Actual workers. Partially agriculturists. Males.	Actual workers. Partially agriculturists. Females.	Dependants. Both sexes.	8.—Wood-cutters; fire-wood, lac, catechu, rubber, grass, etc., collectors, and charcoal burners. Total workers and dependants. Both sexes.	Actual workers. Total. Males.	Actual workers. Total. Females.	Actual workers. Partially agriculturists. Males.	Actual workers. Partially agriculturists. Females.	Dependants. Both sexes.
1	66	67	68	69	70	71	72	73	74	75	76	77	78	79	80	81	82	83	84	85	86	87	88	89
Rajputana	**8,123**	**3,928**	**575**	**237**	**11**	**3,620**	**27,111**	**8,480**	**10,109**	**1,592**	**725**	**8,522**	**2,686**	**1,174**	**4**	**88**	..	**1,508**	**24,425**	**7,306**	**10,105**	**1,504**	**725**	**7,014**
Alwar	1,210	530	50	35	1	630	1,307	545	302	28	5	460	402	186	..	16	..	216	905	359	302	12	5	244
Banswara	43	21	3	2	..	19	188	74	34	7	..	80	74	30	..	5	..	44	114	44	34	4	..	36
Bharatpur	852	475	18	47	..	359	625	287	187	92	19	151	38	29	..	..	..	9	587	258	187	92	19	142
Bikaner	226	121	2	1	..	103	66	15	12	2	..	39	..	..	..	..	..	..	66	15	12	2	..	39
Bundi	506	203	96	7	..	207	299	65	120	5	..	114	53	22	..	3	..	31	246	43	120	2	..	83
Dholpur	238	128	8	17	1	92	487	177	104	18	5	206	184	67	..	2	..	117	303	110	104	11	5	89
Dungarpur	12	3	..	..	..	9	36	15	2	..	..	19	34	15	..	..	..	19	2	..	2	..	..	..
Jaipur	1,369	627	109	7	1	633	6,442	1,403	3,554	72	143	1,485	395	152	..	22	..	243	6,047	1,251	3,554	50	143	1,242
Jaisalmer	125	61	8	7	..	56	291	117	40	11	2	134	4	3	..	..	..	1	287	114	40	11	2	133
Jhalawar	237	112	7	1	1	118	918	260	374	9	18	284	27	10	1	1	..	16	891	250	373	8	18	268
Karauli	577	279	70	47	..	228	199	109	..	16	..	90	141	51	..	15	..	90	58	58	..	..	..	..
Kishangarh	40	21	3	..	..	16	122	55	19	8	..	48	45	24	1	1	..	20	77	31	18	2	..	28
Kotah	695	380	20	10	..	295	3,071	1,067	854	89	23	1,150	460	186	..	15	..	274	2,611	881	854	74	23	876
Kushalgarh (Chiefship)	..	..	..	..	..	..	184	38	82	..	..	64	..	..	..	..	..	..	184	38	82	..	..	64
Lawa (Estate)	11	3	..	..	..	8	..	..	..	..	..	..	..	..	..	..	..	..	..	..	..	..	..	..
Marwar	652	276	76	10	7	300	3,646	1,298	1,017	276	50	1,331	410	221	..	1	..	180	3,236	1,077	1,017	275	50	1,142
Mewar	787	411	83	30	..	293	6,028	1,963	2,281	812	408	1,784	249	115	2	6	..	132	5,779	1,848	2,279	806	403	1,652
Partabgarh	11	5	..	..	..	6	452	186	140	39	18	126	21	11	..	..	..	10	431	175	140	39	18	116
Shahpura (Chiefship)	33	13	3	2	..	17	318	108	80	84	29	130	..	..	..	..	..	..	318	108	80	84	29	130
Sirohi	190	87	3	5	..	100	1,498	413	609	25	2	476	61	15	..	..	..	46	1,437	398	609	25	2	430
Tonk	309	162	16	..	..	131	934	285	298	10	8	351	88	37	..	3	..	51	846	248	298	7	8	300
Ajmer-Merwara	**891**	**437**	**34**	**10**	**2**	**420**	**1,131**	**422**	**231**	**89**	**10**	**478**	**152**	**77**	**2**	**4**	..	**73**	**979**	**345**	**229**	**85**	**10**	**405**
Ajmer	849	421	34	7	2	394	1,035	371	227	85	10	437	79	31	1	..	..	47	956	340	226	85	10	390
Merwara	42	16	..	3	..	26	96	51	4	4	..	41	73	40	1	4	..	26	23	5	3	..	..	15
CITIES.																								
Rajputana	**3,579**	**1,747**	**212**	**35**	**1**	**1,620**	**1,665**	**553**	**407**	**47**	..	**705**	**561**	**268**	..	**4**	..	**293**	**1,104**	**285**	**407**	**43**	..	**412**
Alwar	931	415	43	21	1	473	323	121	79	3	..	123	157	78	..	3	..	79	166	43	79	..	..	44
Bharatpur	506	295	9	8	..	202	172	78	46	42	..	48	2	1	..	..	..	1	170	77	46	42	..	47
Bikaner	150	75	..	..	..	75	37	10	1	..	..	26	..	..	..	..	..	..	37	10	1	..	..	26
Jaipur	606	273	50	1	..	283	396	93	146	..	..	157	61	25	..	..	..	36	335	68	146	..	..	121
Jodhpur	417	188	30	2	..	199	266	130	..	..	..	136	205	121	..	..	..	84	61	9	..	..	..	52
Kotah	323	162	12	3	..	149	137	45	25	1	..	67	53	19	..	1	..	34	84	26	25	..	..	33
Tonk	217	120	12	..	..	85	256	54	108	..	..	94	22	5	..	..	..	17	234	49	108	..	..	77
Udaipur	429	219	56	..	..	154	78	22	2	..	..	54	61	19	..	..	..	42	17	3	2	..	..	12
Ajmer-Merwara—																								
Ajmer	542	277	12	3	..	253	161	53	8	1	..	100	28	7	..	..	..	21	133	46	8	1	..	79

TABLE XV-A.—Occupation or Means of Livelihood. Part II.—By State or District, and City—*continued.*

CLASS A.—PRODUCTION OF RAW MATERIALS—*continued.*
SUB-CLASS I.—EXPLOITATION OF THE SURFACE OF THE EARTH—*continued.*
Order 1.—Pasture and Agriculture—*continued.*
(d) Raising of farm stock.

Province; and State, District, or City.	Total (d). Total workers and dependants. Both sexes.	Total (d). Actual workers. Total. Males.	Total (d). Actual workers. Total. Females.	Total (d). Actual workers. Partially agriculturists. Males.	Total (d). Actual workers. Partially agriculturists. Females.	Total (d). Dependants. Both sexes.	9.—Cattle and buffalo breeders and keepers. Total workers and dependants. Both sexes.	9. Actual workers. Total. Males.	9. Actual workers. Total. Females.	9. Actual workers. Partially agriculturists. Males.	9. Actual workers. Partially agriculturists. Females.	9. Dependants. Both sexes.
1	90	91	92	93	94	95	96	97	98	99	100	101
Rajputana	211,740	183,756	13,619	10,907	321	88,365	65,133	26,705	5,233	4,050	139	33,195
Alwar	6,038	3,262	755	181	22	2,021	1,078	408	172	46	11	498
Banswara	729	438	90	8	..	201	..	..	..	..	..	..
Bharatpur	6,504	4,775	552	409	30	1,177	123	48	41	26	..	34
Bikaner	5,379	2,400	113	269	19	2,767	1,381	487	33	5	..	862
Bundi	7,710	3,185	254	129	9	4,271	2,319	892	151	67	8	1,276
Dholpur	2,232	1,282	231	207	15	719	24	5	8	1	..	11
Dungarpur	455	221	67	42	1	177	42	15	6	9	..	21
Jaipur	27,238	15,985	4,558	444	58	6,701	921	532	121	24	..	268
Jaisalmer	22,060	8,061	436	2,702	62	13,383	19,810	6,191	408	2,656	62	13,211
Jhalawar	1,920	1,190	131	19	4	609	274	74	96	6	3	104
Karauli	1,232	903	128	11	..	203	49	34	1	..	..	14
Kishangarh	3,833	1,896	597	194	54	1,340	1,367	564	224	63	18	579
Kotah	19,694	13,288	601	351	11	5,805	7,094	5,181	178	171	8	1,735
Kushalgarh (Chiefship)	43	17	5	..	..	21	..	..	..	..	..	..
Lawa (Estate)	46	31	2	..	..	13	..	..	..	..	..	..
Marwar	70,011	30,159	5,093	4,474	408	34,759	13,563	5,641	381	806	13	7,541
Mewar	15,271	7,877	1,322	1,243	107	6,072	716	345	100	5	3	273
Partabgarh	696	375	77	27	3	244	7	2	..	..	..	5
Shahpura (Chiefship)	633	243	12	74	..	268	5	1	2	..	..	2
Sirohi	15,617	5,413	3,366	89	11	6,838	13,297	4,306	3,198	45	11	5,793
Tonk	4,489	2,656	257	124	13	1,576	3,061	1,979	114	30	2	968
Ajmer-Merwara	4,975	2,712	459	173	35	1,604	698	289	146	42	25	273
Ajmer	4,398	2,368	394	160	17	1,436	420	122	108	35	6	190
Merwara	577	344	65	13	21	168	208	87	38	7	19	83
CITIES.												
Rajputana	1,973	864	121	8	3	980	571	278	31	..	1	262
Alwar	150	69	28	2	2	53	11	6	5	..	1	..
Bharatpur	218	110	12	2	..	87	..	..	..	..	..	..
Bikaner	84	44	..	4	..	40	..	..	..	..	..	..
Jaipur	311	93	20	..	..	198	24	11	8	..	..	10
Jodhpur	509	239	27	..	..	243	186	102	..	..	..	84
Kotah	115	65	2	..	..	48	29	24	..	..	..	5
Tonk	270	138	10	..	..	122	205	100	9	..	..	96
Udaipur	316	97	22	..	..	197	110	35	14	..	..	67
Ajmer-Merwara—												
Ajmer	229	117	20	5	..	102	50	11	4	4	..	35

Province; and State, District, or City.	10.—Sheep, goat, and pig breeders. Total workers and dependants. Both sexes.	10. Actual workers. Total. Males.	10. Actual workers. Total. Females.	10. Actual workers. Partially agriculturists. Males.	10. Actual workers. Partially agriculturists. Females.	10. Dependants. Both sexes.	11.—Breeders of other animals (horses, mules, camels, asses, etc.) Total workers and dependants. Both sexes.	11. Actual workers. Total. Males.	11. Actual workers. Total. Females.	11. Actual workers. Partially agriculturists. Males.	11. Actual workers. Partially agriculturists. Females.	11. Dependants. Both sexes.
1	102	103	104	105	106	107	108	109	110	111	112	113
Rajputana	48,196	18,830	3,346	3,029	265	26,232	2,885	1,892	86	80	12	1,707
Alwar	532	190	110	11	1	232	19	7	1	1	..	11
Banswara	..	..	..	..	..	..	..	..	..	..	..	..
Bharatpur	181	64	25	24	5	92	9	4	5	..	..	..
Bikaner	1,354	362	7	17	..	965	24	11	..	..	..	18
Bundi	2,429	799	50	42	..	1,580	785	239	16	6	..	580
Dholpur	27	12	1	1	..	14	12	5	..	..	..	7
Dungarpur	18	7	..	..	..	11	27	12	..	8	..	15
Jaipur	1,201	496	126	37	9	579	221	71	10	2	..	140
Jaisalmer	..	..	..	..	..	..	..	..	..	..	..	..
Jhalawar	..	..	..	..	..	..	12	5	..	..	..	7
Karauli	1	1	..	..	..	..	6	3	..	..	..	3
Kishangarh	160	60	29	28	3	71	1	1	..	..	..	..
Kotah	2,166	1,203	117	32	1	848	475	186	5	..	..	284
Kushalgarh (Chiefship)	..	..	..	..	..	..	8	2	..	..	..	6
Lawa (Estate)	5	3	..	..	..	3	..	..	..	..	..	..
Marwar	38,399	14,651	2,747	2,555	240	21,001	152	60	1	7	..	91
Mewar	918	407	91	196	8	418	1,029	428	36	55	12	565
Partabgarh	20	8	..	2	..	12	6	1	2	..	..	3
Shahpura (Chiefship)	282	110	1	59	..	171	10	3	..	..	..	7
Sirohi	65	23	12	1	..	30	33	13	9	..	..	11
Tonk	440	235	30	24	1	175	56	41	1	1	..	14
Ajmer-Merwara	632	257	34	41	2	341	1	1	..	..	..	..
Ajmer	562	234	29	38	..	299	1	1	..	..	..	..
Merwara	70	23	5	3	2	42	..	..	..	..	..	..
CITIES.												
Rajputana	173	57	3	..	..	113	300	61	2	..	..	217
Alwar	..	..	..	..	..	..	3	2	..	..	..	1
Bharatpur	..	..	..	..	..	..	..	..	..	..	..	..
Bikaner	4	..	..	..	..	4	18	7	..	..	..	11
Jaipur	105	12	2	..	..	94	65	23	..	..	..	42
Jodhpur	..	..	..	..	..	..	36	9	..	..	..	27
Kotah	18	16	..	..	..	2	17	5	..	..	..	12
Tonk	43	29	1	..	..	13	9	3	..	..	..	6
Udaipur	..	..	..	..	..	..	152	32	2	..	..	118
Ajmer-Merwara—												
Ajmer	11	..	..	..	..	11	..	..	..	..	..	..

TABLE XV-A.—Occupation or Means of Livelihood. Part II.—By State or District, and City—*continued.*

Province; and State, District, or City.	CLASS A.—PRODUCTION OF RAW MATERIALS—*continued.* SUB-CLASS I.—EXPLOITATION OF THE SURFACE OF THE EARTH—*continued.* Order 1.—Pasture and Agriculture—*concluded.* (d) Raising of farm stock—*concluded.* 12. Herdsmen, shepherds, goatherds, swineherds, etc. Total workers and dependants. Both sexes.	Actual workers. Total. Males.	Actual workers. Total. Females.	Partially agriculturists. Males.	Partially agriculturists. Females.	Dependants. Both sexes.	Total (e) Raising of small animals. 13. Birds, bees, silkworms, poultry, etc. Total workers and dependants. Both sexes.	Actual workers. Total. Males.	Actual workers. Total. Females.	Partially agriculturists. Males.	Partially agriculturists. Females.	Dependants. Both sexes.	Order 2.—Fishing and Hunting. Total Order 2. Total workers and dependants. Both sexes.	Actual workers. Total. Males.	Actual workers. Total. Females.	Partially agriculturists. Males.	Partially agriculturists. Females.	Dependants. Both sexes.	14. Fishing. Total workers and dependants. Both sexes.	Actual workers. Total. Males.	Actual workers. Total. Females.	Partially agriculturists. Males.	Partially agriculturists. Females.	Dependants. Both sexes.
1	114	115	116	117	118	119	120	121	122	123	124	125	126	127	128	129	130	131	132	133	134	135	136	137
Rajputana	95,524	57,239	9,054	3,838	402	28,241	26	2	13	..	5	11	668	337	20	64	2	311	78	32	5	15	..	41
Alwar	4,409	2,657	472	123	19	1,280	..	..	..	..	..	..	24	18	..	..	..	6	..	..	..	..	..	..
Banswara	729	438	90	8	..	201	..	..	..	..	..	..	..	..	..	..	..	..	..	..	..	..	..	..
Bharatpur	6,191	4,659	481	359	25	1,051	..	..	..	..	..	..	53	38	..	4	..	15	1	1	..	1	..	..
Bikaner	2,620	1,639	74	247	19	907	..	..	..	..	..	..	..	..	..	..	..	..	..	..	..	..	..	..
Bundi	2,177	1,255	37	14	1	885	..	..	..	..	..	..	44	20	2	2	..	22	18	6	..	2	..	12
Dholpur	2,169	1,260	222	205	15	687	..	..	..	..	..	..	12	4	..	2	..	8	2	1	..	..	..	1
Dungarpur	368	187	51	25	1	130	..	..	..	..	..	..	9	4	..	2	..	5	3	..	..	..	..	3
Jaipur	24,895	14,886	4,295	381	40	5,714	3	2	..	..	..	1	94	56	9	3	2	29	1	1	..	..	..	..
Jaisalmer	2,270	1,870	28	46	..	372	..	..	..	..	..	..	..	..	..	..	..	..	..	..	..	..	..	..
Jhalawar	1,634	1,111	25	13	1	498	..	..	..	..	..	..	1	1	..	..	..	..	..	..	..	..	..	..
Karauli	1,176	865	125	11	..	186	..	..	..	..	..	..	144	62	..	32	..	82	..	..	..	..	..	..
Kishangarh	2,305	1,271	344	108	33	690	..	..	..	..	..	..	20	10	3	..	..	7	1	..	..	..	..	1
Kotah	9,957	6,718	301	148	2	2,938	..	..	..	..	..	..	210	103	4	17	..	103	40	18	4	12	..	18
Kushalgarh (Chiefship)	35	15	5	..	..	15	..	..	..	..	..	..	..	..	..	..	..	..	..	..	..	..	..	..
Lawa (Estate)	41	29	2	..	..	10	..	..	..	..	..	..	5	4	..	1	..	1	..	..	..	..	..	..
Marwar	17,897	9,807	1,964	1,016	150	6,125	..	..	..	..	..	..	13	4	..	1	..	9	..	..	..	..	..	..
Mewar	12,606	6,607	1,095	987	84	4,816	23	..	13	..	5	10	5	3	1	..	..	1	..	..	..	..	..	..
Partabgarh	663	364	75	25	2	224	..	..	..	..	..	..	..	..	..	..	..	..	..	..	..	..	..	..
Shahpura (Chiefship)	226	129	9	15	..	88	..	..	..	..	..	..	..	..	..	..	..	..	..	..	..	..	..	..
Sirohi	2,222	1,071	147	43	..	1,004	..	..	..	..	..	..	20	8	1	..	..	11	12	5	1	..	..	6
Tonk	932	401	112	60	10	419	..	..	..	..	..	..	14	2	..	..	..	12	..	..	..	..	..	..
Ajmer-Merwara	3,714	2,245	279	90	11	1,190	..	..	..	..	..	..	38	13	..	3	..	25	3	3	..	..	..	..
Ajmer	3,415	2,011	257	87	11	1,147	..	..	..	..	..	..	34	11	..	3	..	23	3	3	..	..	..	..
Merwara	299	234	22	3	..	43	..	..	..	..	..	..	4	2	..	..	..	2	..	..	..	..	..	..
CITIES.																								
Rajputana	929	448	85	8	2	396	..	..	..	..	..	..	129	69	..	1	..	60	..	..	..	..	..	..
Alwar	136	61	23	2	1	52	..	..	..	..	..	..	8	2	..	..	..	6	..	..	..	..	..	..
Bharatpur	218	119	12	2	..	57	..	..	..	..	..	..	35	26	..	1	..	9	..	..	..	..	..	..
Bikaner	62	37	..	4	..	25	..	..	..	..	..	..	..	..	..	..	..	..	..	..	..	..	..	..
Jaipur	114	47	15	..	..	52	..	..	..	..	..	..	..	..	..	..	..	..	..	..	..	..	..	..
Jodhpur	287	128	27	..	..	132	..	..	..	..	..	..	..	..	..	..	..	..	..	..	..	..	..	..
Kotah	51	20	2	..	..	29	..	..	..	..	..	..	72	39	..	..	..	33	..	..	..	..	..	..
Tonk	13	6	..	..	..	7	..	..	..	..	..	..	14	2	..	..	..	12	..	..	..	..	..	..
Udaipur	48	30	6	..	..	12	..	..	..	..	..	..	..	..	..	..	..	..	..	..	..	..	..	..
Ajmer-Merwara—																								
Ajmer	178	106	16	1	..	56	..	..	..	..	..	..	7	1	..	..	..	6	..	..	..	..	..	..

TABLE XV-A.—OCCUPATION OR MEANS OF LIVELIHOOD. PART II.—BY STATE OR DISTRICT, AND CITY—*continued.*

Province; and State, District, or City.	CLASS A.—PRODUCTION OF RAW MATERIALS—*continued.*																							
	SUB-CLASS I.—EXPLOITATION OF THE SURFACE OF THE EARTH—*concluded.*						SUB-CLASS II.—EXTRACTION OF MINERALS.																	
	Order 2.—Fishing and Hunting—*concluded.*						Total Sub-Class II.						Order 3.—Mines.											
	15.—Hunting.												Total Order 3.						16.—Coal mines and petroleum wells.					
	Total workers and dependants.	Actual workers. Total.		Actual workers. Partially agriculturists.		Dependants.	Total workers and dependants.	Actual workers. Total.		Actual workers. Partially agriculturists.		Dependants.	Total workers and dependants.	Actual workers. Total.		Actual workers. Partially agriculturists.		Dependants.	Total workers and dependants.	Actual workers. Total.		Actual workers. Partially agriculturists.		Dependants.
	Both sexes.	Males.	Females.	Males.	Females.	Both sexes.	Both sexes.	Males.	Females.	Males.	Females.	Both sexes.	Both sexes.	Males.	Females.	Males.	Females.	Both sexes.	Both sexes.	Males.	Females.	Males.	Females.	Both sexes.
1	138	139	140	141	142	143	144	145	146	147	148	149	150	151	152	153	154	155	156	157	158	159	160	161
Rajputana	590	305	15	49	2	270	13,310	5,144	3,169	519	81	4,997	357	141	9	30	..	207	236	92	8	19	..	136
Alwar	24	18	..	..	..	6	393	143	44	13	1	206	14	8	..	..	..	6	14	8	..	..	..	6
Banswara	..	..	..	..	..	..	..	..	..	..	..	..	..	..	..	..	..	..	..	..	..	..	..	..
Bharatpur	52	37	..	3	..	15	426	206	16	63	..	204	..	..	..	..	..	..	..	..	..	..	..	..
Bikaner	..	..	..	..	..	..	945	356	79	105	3	510	193	76	5	19	..	112	193	76	5	19	..	112
Bundi	26	14	2	..	..	10	23	7	1	..	..	15	..	..	..	..	..	..	..	..	..	..	..	..
Dholpur	10	3	..	2	..	7	253	123	31	13	..	99	..	..	..	..	..	..	..	..	..	..	..	..
Dungarpur	6	4	..	2	..	2	..	..	..	..	..	..	..	..	..	..	..	..	..	..	..	..	..	..
Jaipur	93	55	9	3	2	29	3,109	1,273	663	92	11	1,173	35	10	4	..	..	21	18	4	3	..	..	11
Jaisalmer	..	..	..	..	..	..	25	7	..	2	..	18	..	..	..	..	..	..	..	..	..	..	..	..
Jhalawar	1	1	..	..	..	..	168	54	27	9	9	87	6	2	..	..	..	4	..	..	..	..	..	..
Karauli	144	62	..	32	..	82	91	32	..	11	..	59	91	39	..	11	..	52	..	..	..	..	..	..
Kishangarh	19	10	3	..	..	6	313	137	62	21	..	114	4	1	..	..	..	3	..	..	..	..	..	..
Kotah	170	85	..	5	..	85	424	121	90	7	..	213	3	1	..	..	..	2	..	..	..	..	..	..
Kushalgarh (Chiefship)	..	..	..	..	..	..	5	2	..	..	..	3	..	..	..	..	..	..	..	..	..	..	..	..
Lawa (Estate)	5	4	..	1	..	1	..	..	..	..	..	..	..	..	..	..	..	..	..	..	..	..	..	..
Marwar	13	4	..	1	..	9	5,570	2,120	1,709	163	55	1,741	..	..	..	..	..	..	..	..	..	..	..	..
Mewar	5	3	1	..	..	1	989	320	338	11	2	334	10	4	..	..	..	6	10	4	..	..	..	6
Partabgarh	..	..	..	..	..	..	..	..	..	..	..	..	..	..	..	..	..	..	..	..	..	..	..	..
Shahpura (Chiefship)	..	..	..	..	..	..	..	..	..	..	..	..	..	..	..	..	..	..	..	..	..	..	..	..
Sirohi	8	3	..	..	..	5	578	231	109	5	..	238	1	..	..	..	..	1	1	..	..	..	..	1
Tonk	14	2	..	..	..	12	5	5	..	..	..	..	..	..	..	..	..	..	..	..	..	..	..	..
Ajmer-Merwara	35	10	..	3	..	25	693	296	63	12	1	334	..	..	..	..	..	..	..	..	..	..	..	..
Ajmer	31	8	..	3	..	23	594	261	32	11	1	301	..	..	..	..	..	..	..	..	..	..	..	..
Merwara	4	2	..	..	..	2	101	37	31	1	..	33	..	..	..	..	..	..	..	..	..	..	..	..
CITIES.																								
Rajputana	129	69	..	1	..	60	1,176	357	351	4	1	468	14	5	1	..	..	8	8	4	..	..	..	4
Alwar	8	2	..	..	..	6	88	10	29	1	1	49	..	..	..	..	..	..	..	..	..	..	..	..
Bharatpur	35	26	..	1	..	9	17	1	..	..	..	16	..	..	..	..	..	..	..	..	..	..	..	..
Bikaner	..	..	..	..	..	..	66	31	..	1	..	35	..	..	..	..	..	..	..	..	..	..	..	..
Jaipur	..	..	..	..	..	..	33	14	5	..	..	14	5	3	..	..	..	2	5	3	..	..	..	2
Jodhpur	..	..	..	..	..	..	95	33	6	..	..	56	9	2	1	..	..	6	3	1	..	..	..	2
Kotah	72	39	..	..	..	33	20	2	3	..	..	15	..	..	..	..	..	..	..	..	..	..	..	..
Tonk	14	2	..	..	..	12	3	3	..	..	..	..	..	..	..	..	..	..	..	..	..	..	..	..
Udaipur	..	..	..	..	..	..	854	263	308	2	..	283	..	..	..	..	..	..	..	..	..	..	..	..
Ajmer-Merwara—																								
Ajmer	7	1	..	..	..	6	76	27	6	..	..	43	..	..	..	..	..	..	..	..	..	..	..	..

TABLE XV-A.—OCCUPATION OR MEANS OF LIVELIHOOD. PART II.—BY STATE OR DISTRICT, AND CITY—*continued.*

Province; and State, District, or City.	CLASS A.—PRODUCTION OF RAW MATERIALS—*continued.* SUB-CLASS II.—EXTRACTION OF MINERALS—*continued.* Order 3.—Mines—*concluded.* 17.—Mines and metallic minerals (gold, iron, manganese, etc.) Total workers and dependants.	Actual workers. Total.		Partially agriculturists.		Dependants.	Total Order 4.—Quarries of hard rocks. 18.—Other minerals (jade, diamonds, limestone, mica, etc.) Total workers and dependants.	Actual workers. Total.		Partially agriculturists.		Dependants.	Order 5.—Salt, etc. Total Order 5. Total workers and dependants.	Actual workers. Total.		Partially agriculturists.		Dependants.	19.—Rock, sea, and marsh salt. Total workers and dependants.	Actual workers. Total.		Partially agriculturists.		Dependants.
	Both sexes.	Males.	Females.	Males.	Females.	Both sexes.	Both sexes.	Males.	Females.	Males.	Females.	Both sexes.	Both sexes.	Males.	Females.	Males.	Females.	Both sexes.	Both sexes.	Males.	Females.	Males.	Females.	Both sexes.
1	162	163	164	165	166	167	168	169	170	171	172	173	174	175	176	177	178	179	180	181	182	183	184	185
Rajputana	**121**	**49**	**1**	**11**	..	**71**	**5,576**	**1,952**	**1,146**	**241**	**17**	**2,478**	**7,377**	**3,051**	**2,014**	**248**	**64**	**2,312**	**6,908**	**2,857**	**1,969**	**214**	**59**	**2,082**
Alwar	..	..	..	..	..	..	373	134	44	17	1	195	6	1	..	1	..	5	..	..	..	..	..	..
Banswara	..	..	..	..	..	..	..	..	..	..	..	..	..	..	..	..	..	..	..	..	..	..	..	..
Bharatpur	..	..	..	..	..	..	329	151	10	45	..	168	97	55	6	17	..	36	..	..	..	..	..	..
Bikaner	..	..	..	..	..	..	439	166	22	70	..	241	323	114	52	16	3	157	53	13	21	11	3	9
Bundi	..	..	..	..	..	..	5	1	..	..	..	4	18	6	1	..	..	11	14	5	1	..	..	8
Dholpur	..	..	..	..	..	..	237	117	30	9	..	90	16	6	1	4	..	9	..	..	..	..	..	..
Dungarpur	..	..	..	..	..	..	..	..	..	..	..	..	..	..	..	..	..	..	..	..	..	..	..	..
Jaipur	17	6	1	..	..	10	1,179	477	139	49	5	563	1,895	786	520	43	6	589	1,894	785	520	43	6	589
Jaisalmer	..	..	..	..	..	..	..	..	..	..	..	..	25	7	..	2	..	18	25	7	..	2	..	18
Jhalawar	6	2	..	..	..	4	162	52	27	9	9	83	..	..	..	..	..	..	..	..	..	..	..	..
Karauli	91	39	..	11	..	52	..	..	..	..	..	..	..	..	..	..	..	..	..	..	..	..	..	..
Kishangarh	4	1	..	..	..	3	307	134	62	21	..	111	2	2	..	..	..	..	..	..	..	..	..	..
Kotah	3	1	..	..	..	2	365	94	82	5	..	189	56	26	8	2	..	22	56	26	8	2	..	22
Kushalgarh (Chiefship)	..	..	..	..	..	..	5	2	..	..	..	3	..	..	..	..	..	..	..	..	..	..	..	..
Lawa (Estate)	..	..	..	..	..	..	..	..	..	..	..	..	..	..	..	..	..	..	..	..	..	..	..	..
Marwar	..	..	..	..	..	..	634	73	283	..	..	278	4,936	2,047	1,426	163	55	1,463	4,863	2,020	1,409	156	50	1,434
Mewar	..	..	..	..	..	..	972	316	338	11	2	218	..	..	..	..	..	..	..	..	..	..	..	..
Partabgarh	..	..	..	..	..	..	..	..	..	..	..	..	..	..	..	..	..	..	..	..	..	..	..	..
Shahpura (Chiefship)	..	..	..	..	..	..	..	..	..	..	..	..	..	..	..	..	..	..	..	..	..	..	..	..
Sirohi	..	..	..	..	..	..	574	230	109	5	..	235	3	1	..	..	..	2	3	1	..	..	..	2
Tonk	..	..	..	..	..	..	5	5	..	..	..	..	..	..	..	..	..	..	..	..	..	..	..	..
Ajmer-Merwara	..	..	..	..	..	..	**691**	**298**	**59**	**12**	**1**	**334**	**4**	..	**4**	..	..	..	**4**	..	**4**	..	..	..
Ajmer	..	..	..	..	..	..	590	261	28	11	1	301	4	..	4	..	..	..	4	..	4	..	..	..
Merwara	..	..	..	..	..	..	101	37	31	1	..	33	..	..	..	..	..	..	..	..	..	..	..	..
CITIES.																								
Rajputana	**6**	**1**	**1**	..	..	**4**	**1,136**	**344**	**346**	**4**	**1**	**446**	**26**	**8**	**4**	..	..	**14**	**25**	**7**	**4**	..	..	**14**
Alwar	..	..	..	..	..	..	88	10	29	1	1	49	..	..	..	..	..	..	..	..	..	..	..	..
Bharatpur	..	..	..	..	..	..	16	..	..	..	..	16	1	1	..	..	..	..	..	..	..	..	..	..
Bikaner	..	..	..	..	..	..	61	28	..	1	..	33	..	..	..	..	..	..	..	..	..	..	..	..
Jaipur	6	1	1	..	..	4	15	11	..	..	..	4	9	1	4	..	..	4	9	1	4	..	..	4
Jodhpur	..	..	..	..	..	..	79	27	6	..	..	46	16	6	..	..	..	10	16	6	..	..	..	10
Kotah	..	..	..	..	..	..	20	2	3	..	..	15	..	..	..	..	..	..	..	..	..	..	..	..
Tonk	..	..	..	..	..	..	3	3	..	..	..	..	..	..	..	..	..	..	..	..	..	..	..	..
Udaipur	..	..	..	..	..	..	854	263	308	2	..	283	..	..	..	..	..	..	..	..	..	..	..	..
Ajmer-Merwara—																								
Ajmer	..	..	..	..	..	..	76	27	6	..	..	43	..	..	..	..	..	..	..	..	..	..	..	..

TABLE XV-A.—OCCUPATION OR MEANS OF LIVELIHOOD. PART II.—BY STATE OR DISTRICT, AND CITY—*continued.*

Province; and State, District, or City.	CLASS A.—PRODUCTION OF RAW MATERIALS—*concluded.* SUB-CLASS II.—EXTRACTION OF MINERALS—*concluded.* Order 5.—Salt, etc.—*concluded.* 20.—Extraction of saltpetre, alum and other substances soluble in water.						CLASS B.—PREPARATION AND SUPPLY OF MATERIAL SUBSTANCES. TOTAL CLASS B.						SUB-CLASS III.—INDUSTRY. Total Sub-Class III.					
	Total workers and dependants.	Actual workers. Total.		Actual workers. Partially agriculturists.		Dependants.	Total workers and dependants.	Actual workers. Total.		Actual workers. Partially agriculturists.		Dependants.	Total workers and dependants.	Actual workers. Total.		Actual workers. Partially agriculturists.		Dependants.
	Both sexes.	Males.	Females.	Males.	Females.	Both sexes.	Both sexes.	Males.	Females.	Males.	Females.	Both sexes.	Both sexes.	Males.	Females.	Males.	Females.	Both sexes.
1	186	187	188	189	190	191	192	193	194	195	196	197	198	199	200	201	202	203
Rajputana	**469**	**194**	**45**	**34**	**5**	**230**	**2,486,020**	**875,663**	**416,223**	**150,069**	**23 655**	**1,194,134**	**1,547,057**	**554,308**	**322,460**	**121,266**	**16,966**	**669,789**
Alwar	6	1	..	1	..	5	173,135	60,047	31,511	10,513	2,066	81,567	116,634	40,172	27,643	7,826	1,762	48,819
Banswara	..	..	..	..	..	..	22,617	7,467	3,057	2,183	194	12,093	12,984	4,191	2,257	1,719	157	6,536
Bharatpur	97	55	6	17	..	36	115,024	42,983	22,129	10,313	2,000	49,912	73,299	27,281	16,319	7,878	1,529	29,699
Bikaner	270	101	21	5	..	148	129,241	41,746	15,406	10,337	1,956	72,089	69,910	25,882	12,996	8,605	1,730	31,032
Bundi	4	1	..	..	..	3	46,932	15,927	6,151	1,526	63	24,854	32,410	10,801	4,705	1,171	57	16,904
Dholpur	16	6	1	4	..	9	47,749	17,876	7,482	3,904	478	22,391	30,080	11,308	5,673	2,934	410	13,099
Dungarpur	..	..	..	..	..	..	31,263	9,817	3,792	2,193	198	17,654	15,473	4 994	2 031	1,418	119	8,448
Jaipur	1	1	..	..	..	..	694,747	246,990	144,766	25,069	4,401	303,081	460,079	162 910	120,920	20,187	3,765	176,049
Jaisalmer	..	..	..	..	..	..	25,406	7,345	3,428	2,364	44	14,633	19,164	5,119	3,130	2,646	37	10,915
Jhalawar	..	..	..	..	..	..	22,639	8,230	3,272	845	161	11,137	14,109	5,096	2,558	685	141	6,455
Karauli	..	..	..	..	..	..	31,133	12,380	5,932	2,433	277	12,821	17,675	6,676	4,427	1,306	203	6,572
Kishangarh	2	2	..	..	..	..	22,167	8,395	3,651	1,621	158	10,121	14 689	5,643	3,014	1,266	140	5,945
Kotah	..	..	..	..	..	..	145,502	51,247	30,516	7,299	1,106	63,739	93,569	32,746	20,994	5,439	888	39,829
Kushalgarh (Chiefship)	..	..	..	..	..	..	2,228	729	217	55	..	1,282	1,311	414	186	53	..	711
Lawa (Estate)	..	..	..	..	..	..	592	233	123	19	8	236	400	133	99	16	7	148
Marwar	73	27	17	7	5	20	498,531	175,809	59,266	38,734	5,487	263,456	302,909	114,353	46,456	35,076	4,642	141,400
Mewar	..	..	..	..	..	..	329,501	116,991	51,696	24,391	4,173	160,814	186 683	67,171	31,624	18,222	2,503	87,888
Partabgarh	..	..	..	..	..	..	12,012	4,408	1,441	548	70	6,163	5,608	2,092	912	433	30	2,604
Shahpura (Chiefship)	..	..	..	..	..	..	10,111	3,823	1,147	1,497	203	5,141	6,694	2,500	979	1,180	131	3,215
Sirohi	..	..	..	..	..	..	62,219	20,284	9,407	1,061	134	32,528	29,553	9,989	5,389	901	96	14,175
Tonk	..	..	..	..	..	..	63,281	23,026	11,833	2,654	488	28,422	44,538	16,017	10,068	2,282	458	18,453
Ajmer-Merwara	..	..	..	..	..	..	**161,795**	**61,033**	**19,606**	**6,955**	**1,234**	**81,156**	**84,701**	**31,673**	**16,024**	**4,778**	**988**	**37,004**
Ajmer	..	..	..	..	..	..	130,413	48,605	14,847	5,024	1,031	66,961	64,869	24,005	12,010	3,687	838	28,847
Merwara	..	..	..	..	..	..	31,382	12,428	4,759	1,931	203	14,195	19,839	7,668	4,014	1,091	150	8,157
CITIES.																		
Rajputana	**1**	**1**	..	..	..	..	**213,063**	**73,094**	**37,476**	**628**	**112**	**102,433**	**124,651**	**43,493**	**27,292**	**360**	**65**	**53,866**
Alwar	..	..	..	..	..	..	17,599	6,155	3,094	61	38	8,350	11,663	4,116	2,280	39	10	5,267
Bharatpur	1	1	..	..	..	..	14,277	5,306	2,542	189	39	6,429	8,070	2,903	1,735	145	30	3,412
Bikaner	..	..	..	..	..	..	32,871	10,346	3,949	199	7	18,576	17,495	6,153	3,050	110	1	8,293
Jaipur	..	..	..	..	..	..	64,300	23,657	12,738	25	5	27,905	40,333	14,768	10,062	13	5	15,503
Jodhpur	..	..	..	..	..	..	38,054	12,661	5,555	56	13	19,838	21,100	7,105	3,431	20	13	10,550
Kotah	..	..	..	..	..	..	16,736	5,610	3,744	62	4	7,382	9,429	3,260	2,249	30	..	3,918
Tonk	..	..	..	..	..	..	13,510	4,463	3,461	36	6	5,586	8,280	2,789	2,963	10	6	3,228
Udaipur	..	..	..	..	..	..	15,656	4,896	2,393	..	..	8,367	7,575	2,391	1,489	..	..	3,695
Ajmer-Merwara—																		
Ajmer	..	..	..	..	..	..	69,979	22,170	4,326	162	11	33,483	21,728	7,844	3,212	101	10	10,672

TABLE XV-A.—OCCUPATION OR MEANS OF LIVELIHOOD. PART II.—BY STATE OR DISTRICT, AND CITY—*continued.*

CLASS B.—PREPARATION AND SUPPLY OF MATERIAL SUBSTANCES—*continued.*

SUB-CLASS III.—INDUSTRY—*continued.*

Order 6.—Textiles.

Province; and State, District, or City.	Total order 6. Total workers and dependants. Both sexes.	Total order 6. Actual workers. Total. Males.	Total order 6. Actual workers. Total. Females.	Total order 6. Actual workers. Partially agriculturists. Males.	Total order 6. Actual workers. Partially agriculturists. Females.	Total order 6. Dependants. Both sexes.	21.—Cotton ginning, cleaning, carding, and pressing. Total workers and dependants. Both sexes.	21. Actual workers. Total. Males.	21. Actual workers. Total. Females.	21. Actual workers. Partially agriculturists. Males.	21. Actual workers. Partially agriculturists. Females.	21. Dependants. Both sexes.
1	204	205	206	207	208	209	210	211	212	213	214	215
Rajputana	**390,522**	**121,730**	**138,064**	**25,375**	**7,518**	**130,728**	**30,732**	**10,376**	**8,671**	**1,944**	**489**	**11,685**
Alwar	32,373	10,337	11,075	1,550	572	10,961	2,287	834	498	209	50	955
Banswara	2,264	702	481	318	56	1,081	72	15	16	3	..	41
Bharatpur	16,562	5,683	5,462	1,492	603	5,417	1,953	739	443	242	31	771
Bikaner	10,060	3,076	3,501	1,362	480	3,483	329	93	48	33	4	188
Bundi	6,353	1,759	1,924	77	16	2,670	864	239	233	21	2	392
Dholpur	5,584	2,099	1,454	535	155	2,031	686	256	110	63	15	320
Dungarpur	2,054	704	246	220	36	1,104	6	3	..	..	..	3
Jaipur	141,260	41,356	60,695	3,192	1,255	39,209	9,611	3,360	3,053	282	40	3,198
Jaisalmer	8,995	2,030	2,541	1,144	20	4,424	598	151	7	69	1	440
Jhalawar	2,207	708	604	95	59	895	385	140	96	19	..	149
Karauli	6,216	2,164	2,355	374	118	1,697	661	278	168	38	9	215
Kishangarh	4,304	1,638	1,221	239	66	1,445	397	116	136	23	16	145
Kotah	20,411	5,787	8,075	533	166	6,549	2,085	699	598	106	32	788
Kushalgarh (Chiefship)	20	8	6	..	..	6	7	1	3	..	..	3
Lawa (Estate)	216	72	63	3	7	81	5	2	2	..	..	1
Marwar	75,468	26,488	20,388	10,680	2,600	28,592	4,204	1,428	1,001	500	104	1,775
Mewar	41,623	12,607	12,975	2,957	1,107	16,041	4,493	1,316	1,562	217	63	1,615
Partabgarh	375	127	88	32	4	160	44	12	9	2	..	23
Shahpura (Chiefship)	1,302	422	337	193	20	543	270	89	64	35	10	117
Sirohi	3,650	1,100	1,111	40	22	1,439	292	96	62	5	4	134
Tonk	9,225	2,863	3,462	349	170	2,900	1,483	500	462	77	30	521
Ajmer-Merwara	**19,216**	**6,933**	**5,760**	**719**	**269**	**6,523**	**7,979**	**3,337**	**1,942**	**216**	**78**	**2,700**
Ajmer	11,502	3,898	3,629	561	244	3,975	2,778	1,024	961	120	68	793
Merwara	7,714	3,035	2,131	158	25	2,548	5,201	2,313	981	96	10	1,907
CITY.												
Rajputana	**24,572**	**7,714**	**9,430**	**12**	**7**	**7,428**	**1,364**	**398**	**440**	**3**	**6**	**526**
Alwar	3,066	1,164	780	1	..	1,122	266	98	52	1	..	116
Bharatpur	942	378	261	1	1	303	94	40	21	1	1	33
Bikaner	1,813	531	617	3	1	665	117	38	32	..	..	47
Jaipur	11,004	3,597	4,474	..	..	2,933	243	54	94	..	..	95
Jodhpur	1,794	656	442	4	..	696	197	49	57	..	..	91
Kotah	1,912	415	999	2	..	498	76	25	26	1	..	25
Tonk	3,192	720	1,664	1	5	808	315	82	140	..	5	93
Udaipur	859	263	193	..	..	403	56	12	18	..	..	26
Ajmer-Merwara—												
Ajmer	1,559	554	301	1	..	704	110	32	27	..	..	51

Province; and State, District, or City.	22.—Cotton spinning, sizing, and weaving. Total workers and dependants. Both sexes.	22. Actual workers. Total. Males.	22. Actual workers. Total. Females.	22. Actual workers. Partially agriculturists. Males.	22. Actual workers. Partially agriculturists. Females.	22. Dependants. Both sexes.	23.—Jute spinning, pressing, and weaving. Total workers and dependants.	23. Actual workers. Total. Males.	23. Actual workers. Total. Females.	23. Dependants. Both sexes.
1	216	217	218	219	220	221	222	223	224	225
Rajputana	**306,939**	**98,746**	**114,230**	**21,772**	**6,397**	**99,954**	**6**	**5**	..	**1**
Alwar	25,927	8,031	9,482	1,194	462	8,414	..	..	..	..
Banswara	2,054	648	434	304	56	972	1	1	..	..
Bharatpur	13,317	4,535	4,559	1,136	526	4,223	..	..	..	..
Bikaner	6,042	1,968	1,966	1,120	424	2,108	..	..	..	..
Bundi	4,812	1,263	1,598	53	14	1,951	..	..	..	..
Dholpur	4,600	1,720	1,265	436	140	1,615	..	..	..	..
Dungarpur	1,914	670	200	220	36	1,044	..	..	..	..
Jaipur	111,796	30,588	51,900	2,675	1,123	29,308	..	..	..	..
Jaisalmer	7,251	1,519	2,395	944	18	3,337	..	..	..	..
Jhalawar	1,354	389	400	76	37	565	..	..	..	..
Karauli	4,590	1,510	1,890	287	102	1,190	..	..	..	..
Kishangarh	3,672	1,438	1,016	215	50	1,218	..	..	..	..
Kotah	14,993	4,053	6,276	350	114	4,664	..	..	..	..
Kushalgarh (Chiefship)	2	2	..	..	..	..	..	..	..	..
Lawa (Estate)	143	38	43	3	7	62	..	..	..	..
Marwar	60,773	21,283	16,752	9,602	2,242	22,738	..	..	..	..
Mewar	32,162	9,603	9,861	2,661	677	12,698	5	4	..	1
Partabgarh	258	90	61	29	4	107	..	..	..	..
Shahpura (Chiefship)	981	315	257	166	9	409	..	..	..	..
Sirohi	2,083	840	988	34	18	1,146	..	..	..	..
Tonk	7,306	2,225	2,896	266	138	2,185	..	..	..	..
Ajmer-Merwara	**9,138**	**2,931**	**3,140**	**488**	**189**	**3,067**	**11**	**4**	**5**	**2**
Ajmer	7,032	2,279	2,273	427	174	2,480	..	..	..	..
Merwara	2,106	652	867	61	15	587	11	4	5	2
CITY.										
Rajputana	**16,784**	**4,966**	**7,258**	**7**	..	**4,560**	..	..	..	..
Alwar	2,508	970	684	..	..	854	..	..	..	..
Bharatpur	699	281	190	..	..	228	..	..	..	..
Bikaner	493	197	122	3	..	174	..	..	..	..
Jaipur	7,694	2,299	3,529	..	..	1,866	..	..	..	..
Jodhpur	701	250	194	2	..	257	..	..	..	..
Kotah	1,753	362	946	1	..	445	..	..	..	..
Tonk	2,670	576	1,471	1	..	623	..	..	..	..
Udaipur	326	91	122	..	..	113	..	..	..	..
Ajmer-Merwara—										
Ajmer	281	87	68	1	..	126	..	..	..	..

TABLE XV-A.—OCCUPATION OR MEANS OF LIVELIHOOD. PART II.- BY STATE OR DISTRICT, AND CITY—*continued.*

CLASS B.—PREPARATION AND SUPPLY OF MATERIAL SUBSTANCES—*continued.*

SUB-CLASS III.—INDUSTRY—*continued.*

Order 6.—Textiles—*continued.*

Province; and State, District, or City.	24.—Rope, twine, and string. Total workers and dependants. Both sexes.	Actual workers. Total. Males.	Actual workers. Total. Females.	Partially agriculturists. Males.	Partially agriculturists. Females.	Dependants. Both sexes.
1	226	227	228	229	230	231
Rajputana	**2,710**	**1,096**	**764**	**145**	**51**	**820**
Alwar	439	170	114	47	25	155
Banswara	..	..	..	..	..	..
Bharatpur	333	117	108	58	9	108
Bikaner	7	4	1	..	..	2
Bundi	3	1	2	..	..	..
Dholpur	..	..	..	..	..	..
Dungarpur	..	..	..	..	..	..
Jaipur	1,330	527	329	7	2	474
Jaisalmer	..	..	..	..	..	..
Jhalawar	18	5	5	..	..	8
Karauli	98	34	44	10	6	20
Kishangarh	58	25	11	..	..	22
Kotah	230	65	88	13	8	77
Kushalgarh (Chiefship)	..	..	..	..	..	..
Lawa (Estate)	2	..	2	..	..	..
Marwar	131	47	42	10	1	42
Mewar	14	11	..	..	..	3
Partabgarh	..	..	..	..	..	..
Shahpura (Chiefship)	10	4	3	..	..	3
Sirohi	1	1	..	..	..	..
Tonk	36	15	15	..	..	6
Ajmer-Merwara	**343**	**107**	**129**	**2**	..	**107**
Ajmer	341	105	129	2	..	107
Merwara	2	2	..	..	..	..
CITIES. Rajputana	**142**	**27**	**53**	..	..	**62**
Alwar	35	..	16	..	..	10
Bharatpur	6	3	1	..	..	2
Bikaner	..	..	..	..	..	..
Jaipur	74	13	24	..	..	37
Jodhpur	..	..	..	..	..	..
Kotah	13	2	9	..	..	2
Tonk	14	9	3	..	..	2
Udaipur	..	..	..	..	..	..
Ajmer-Merwara— Ajmer	9	7	..	..	..	2

Province; and State, District, or City.	25.—Other fibres (coconut, aloes, flax, hemp, straw, etc.) Total workers and dependants. Both sexes.	Actual workers. Total. Males.	Actual workers. Total. Females.	Partially agriculturists. Males.	Partially agriculturists. Females.	Dependants. Both sexes.
1	232	233	234	235	236	237
Rajputana	**960**	**384**	**241**	**109**	**9**	**335**
Alwar	..	..	..	..	..	..
Banswara	92	29	14	11	..	49
Bharatpur	1	..	1	..	1	..
Bikaner	6	..	4	..	..	2
Bundi	..	..	..	..	..	..
Dholpur	35	4	24	..	..	7
Dungarpur	..	..	..	..	..	..
Jaipur	113	24	76	2	..	13
Jaisalmer	..	..	..	..	..	..
Jhalawar	..	..	..	..	..	..
Karauli	28	19	1	16	..	8
Kishangarh	..	..	..	..	..	..
Kotah	204	89	48	10	7	67
Kushalgarh (Chiefship)	2	2	..	..	..	..
Lawa (Estate)	..	..	..	..	..	..
Marwar	479	227	73	70	..	179
Mewar	..	..	..	..	..	..
Partabgarh	..	..	..	..	..	..
Shahpura (Chiefship)	..	..	..	..	..	..
Sirohi	..	..	..	..	..	..
Tonk	..	..	..	..	..	..
Ajmer-Merwara	..	..	..	..	..	..
Ajmer	..	..	..	..	..	..
Merwara	..	..	..	..	..	..
CITIES. Rajputana	**8**	**1**	**4**	..	..	**3**
Alwar	..	..	..	..	..	..
Bharatpur	..	..	..	..	..	..
Bikaner	..	..	..	..	..	..
Jaipur	6	..	4	..	..	2
Jodhpur	2	1	..	..	..	1
Kotah	..	..	..	..	..	..
Tonk	..	..	..	..	..	..
Udaipur	..	..	..	..	..	..
Ajmer-Merwara— Ajmer	..	..	..	..	..	..

Province; and State, District, or City.	26.—Wool carders and spinners, weavers of woollen blankets, carpets, etc. Total workers and dependants. Both sexes.	Actual workers. Total. Males.	Actual workers. Total. Females.	Partially agriculturists. Males.	Partially agriculturists. Females.	Dependants. Both sexes.
1	238	239	240	241	242	243
Rajputana	**5,653**	**934**	**2,973**	**100**	**106**	**1,786**
Alwar	236	28	170	..	3	38
Banswara	22	..	11	..	..	11
Bharatpur	276	38	159	21	24	79
Bikaner	958	32	796	2	19	130
Bundi	119	47	14	..	..	58
Dholpur	13	6	4	4	..	3
Dungarpur	105	21	46	..	..	38
Jaipur	2,040	360	1,010	28	46	670
Jaisalmer	81	7	68	..	..	6
Jhalawar	18	..	15	..	1	3
Karauli	101	30	25	9	..	46
Kishangarh	26	4	15	..	..	7
Kotah	208	86	75	16	1	137
Kushalgarh (Chiefship)	..	..	..	..	..	..
Lawa (Estate)	..	..	..	..	..	..
Marwar	402	40	224	4	6	138
Mewar	603	153	253	10	7	197
Partabgarh	67	23	18	1	..	26
Shahpura (Chiefship)	14	3	3	..	..	8
Sirohi	3	..	3	..	..	..
Tonk	271	76	64	5	1	131
Ajmer-Merwara	**385**	**75**	**235**	**7**	..	**75**
Ajmer	52	19	5	6	..	28
Merwara	333	56	230	1	..	47
CITIES. Rajputana	**645**	**92**	**391**	..	**1**	**162**
Alwar	6	..	6	..	..	..
Bharatpur	35	3	25	..	..	7
Bikaner	291	16	237	..	1	38
Jaipur	141	46	41	..	..	54
Jodhpur	56	6	44	..	..	6
Kotah	23	6	9	..	..	8
Tonk	91	15	28	..	..	48
Udaipur	2	..	1	..	..	1
Ajmer-Merwara— Ajmer	12	5	..	..	..	7

Province; and State, District, or City.	27.—Silk spinners, and weavers. Total workers and dependants. Both sexes.	Actual workers. Total. Males.	Actual workers. Total. Females.	Dependants. Both sexes.
1	244	245	246	247
Rajputana	**24**	**7**	**2**	**15**
Alwar	..	..	..	..
Banswara	..	..	..	..
Bharatpur	11	3	..	8
Bikaner	..	..	..	..
Bundi	7	2	2	3
Dholpur	..	..	..	..
Dungarpur	..	..	..	..
Jaipur	..	..	..	..
Jaisalmer	..	..	..	..
Jhalawar	..	..	..	..
Karauli	..	..	..	..
Kishangarh	..	..	..	..
Kotah	..	..	..	..
Kushalgarh (Chiefship)	..	..	..	..
Lawa (Estate)	..	..	..	..
Marwar	..	..	..	..
Mewar	..	..	..	..
Partabgarh	6	2	..	4
Shahpura (Chiefship)	..	..	..	..
Sirohi	..	..	..	..
Tonk	..	..	..	..
Ajmer-Merwara	..	..	..	..
Ajmer	..	..	..	..
Merwara	..	..	..	..
CITIES. Rajputana	**11**	**3**	..	**8**
Alwar	..	..	..	..
Bharatpur	11	3	..	8
Bikaner	..	..	..	..
Jaipur	..	..	..	..
Jodhpur	..	..	..	..
Kotah	..	..	..	..
Tonk	..	..	..	..
Udaipur	..	..	..	..
Ajmer-Merwara— Ajmer	..	..	..	..

Province; and State, District, or City.	28.—Hair, camel and horse hair, bristles work, brush makers, etc. Total workers and dependants. Both sexes.	Actual workers. Total. Males.	Actual workers. Total. Females.	Partially agriculturists. Males.	Partially agriculturists. Females.	Dependants. Both sexes.
1	248	249	250	251	252	253
Rajputana	**1,843**	**691**	**317**	**236**	**51**	**835**
Alwar	..	..	..	..	..	..
Banswara	..	..	..	..	..	..
Bharatpur	..	..	..	..	..	..
Bikaner	75	42	8	31	6	25
Bundi	5	3	2	..	..	..
Dholpur	..	..	..	..	..	..
Dungarpur	..	..	..	..	..	..
Jaipur	16	6	1	..	..	9
Jaisalmer	628	217	8	94	1	403
Jhalawar	..	..	..	..	..	..
Karauli	..	..	..	..	..	..
Kishangarh	..	..	..	..	..	..
Kotah	..	..	..	..	..	..
Kushalgarh (Chiefship)	..	..	..	..	..	..
Lawa (Estate)	1	1	..	..	..	..
Marwar	996	384	271	110	43	341
Mewar	2	..	2	..	..	..
Partabgarh	..	..	..	..	..	..
Shahpura (Chiefship)	..	..	..	..	..	..
Sirohi	5	1	1	..	..	3
Tonk	115	37	24	1	1	54
Ajmer-Merwara	..	..	..	..	..	..
Ajmer	..	..	..	..	..	..
Merwara	..	..	..	..	..	..
CITIES. Rajputana	**137**	**49**	**33**	**2**	..	**55**
Alwar	..	..	..	..	..	..
Bharatpur	..	..	..	..	..	..
Bikaner	..	..	..	..	..	..
Jaipur	8	1	1	..	..	6
Jodhpur	37	16	11	2	..	10
Kotah	..	..	..	..	..	..
Tonk	92	32	21	..	..	39
Udaipur	..	..	..	..	..	..
Ajmer-Merwara— Ajmer	..	..	..	..	..	..

TABLE XV-A.—Occupation or Means of Livelihood. Part II.—By State or District, and City—*continued.*

CLASS B.—PREPARATION AND SUPPLY OF MATERIAL SUBSTANCES—*continued.*

SUB-CLASS III.—INDUSTRY—*continued.*

Order 6.—Textiles—*concluded.*

Province; and State, District, or City.	30.—Bleaching, printing, preparation, and sponging of textiles. Total workers and dependants.	Actual workers. Total.		Partially agriculturists.		Dependants.	30(a).—Dyeing of textiles. Total workers and dependants.	Actual workers. Total.		Partially agriculturists.		Dependants.	31.—Other (lace, crape, gold and silver braid, embroideries, fringes, etc.) and insufficiently described textile industries. Total workers and dependants.	Actual workers. Total.		Partially agriculturists.		Dependants.	Total Order 7. Total workers and dependants.	Actual workers. Total.		Partially agriculturists.		Dependants.
	Both sexes.	Males.	Females.	Males.	Females.	Both sexes.	Both sexes.	Males.	Females.	Males.	Females	Both sexes.	Both sexes.	Males.	Females.	Males.	Females.	Both sexes.	Both sexes.	Males.	Females.	Males.	Females.	Both sexes.
1	254	255	256	257	258	259	260	261	262	263	264	265	266	267	268	269	270	271	272	273	274	275	276	277
Rajputana	**16,963**	**5,623**	**4,694**	**327**	**223**	**5,836**	**24,873**	**9,800**	**5,843**	**742**	**158**	**9,230**	**579**	**168**	**320**	..	**33**	**151**	**94,932**	**37,735**	**9,892**	**11,758**	**1,401**	**47,396**
Alwar	628	205	189	5	1	224	2,799	1,067	576	95	19	1,156	57	2	46	..	3	9	4,061	1,612	425	563	19	2,094
Banswara	23	9	6	..	..	8	..	..	..	..	..	..	..	..	..	..	..	..	1,230	441	13	295	2	785
Bharatpur	495	209	121	22	2	165	175	41	71	13	10	63	1	1	..	..	..	..	2,304	1,005	218	648	84	1,081
Bikaner	433	152	104	17	3	177	2,136	759	571	159	30	823	54	26	..	..	..	28	2,680	1,009	301	427	130	1,370
Bundi	460	101	67	..	..	222	93	43	6	1	..	44	..	..	..	..	..	..	3,579	1,175	139	154	6	2,265
Dholpur	..	..	..	..	..	..	241	104	51	22	..	86	..	..	..	..	..	..	362	168	50	77	18	149
Dungarpur	7	4	..	..	..	3	..	..	..	..	..	..	22	6	..	..	..	16	249	53	8	7	1	188
Jaipur	3,174	1,211	945	24	7	1,018	13,113	5,255	3,378	174	28	4,480	67	25	8	..	..	30	23,541	9,688	3,620	2,582	452	10,333
Jaisalmer	437	136	63	37	..	238	..	..	..	..	..	..	..	..	..	..	..	..	98	26	1	7	1	71
Jhalawar	29	9	3	..	1	17	403	156	85	..	..	162	..	..	..	..	..	..	1,214	549	64	164	13	601
Karauli	738	293	227	14	1	218	..	..	..	..	..	..	..	..	..	..	..	..	240	140	29	55	19	161
Kishangarh	33	17	4	..	..	12	54	16	14	1	..	24	64	22	25	..	..	17	897	294	76	157	10	427
Kotah	2,163	645	896	16	3	622	438	150	94	13	1	194	..	..	..	..	..	..	10,624	3,976	1,266	1,246	176	5,362
Kushalgarh (Chiefship)	4	1	1	..	..	2	5	2	2	..	..	1	..	..	..	..	..	..	5	1	..	..	..	4
Lawa (Estate)	..	..	..	..	..	..	65	31	16	..	..	18	..	..	..	..	..	..	16	9	2	5	..	5
Marwar	3,222	1,020	880	121	43	1,313	5,011	2,047	925	263	60	2,030	250	12	211	..	30	27	21,536	8,759	1,435	2,210	134	11,342
Mewar	4,290	1,509	1,167	69	160	1,614	8	7	..	..	..	1	46	4	30	..	..	12	15,463	6,206	1,030	2,625	259	6,227
Partabgarh	..	..	..	..	..	..	..	..	..	..	..	..	..	..	..	..	..	..	494	238	14	87	4	242
Shahpura (Chiefship)	6	4	2	2	..	..	17	7	4	..	1	6	4	..	4	..	..	..	929	358	..	231	..	571
Sirohi	71	38	10	..	..	23	295	115	47	1	..	133	..	..	..	..	..	..	1,490	462	368	26	12	840
Tonk	..	..	..	..	..	..	..	..	..	..	..	..	14	10	1	..	..	3	3,811	1,471	693	292	61	1,647
Ajmer-Merwara	**404**	**149**	**121**	**5**	**2**	**134**	**892**	**325**	**133**	**1**	..	**434**	**64**	**5**	**55**	..	..	**4**	**5,150**	**2,139**	**339**	**692**	**85**	**2,672**
Ajmer	403	148	121	5	2	134	878	319	128	1	..	431	18	4	12	..	..	2	3,401	1,469	180	479	40	1,752
Merwara	1	1	..	..	..	..	14	6	5	..	..	3	46	1	43	..	..	2	1,749	670	159	219	36	920
CITIES.																								
Rajputana	**1,886**	**676**	**517**	..	..	**693**	**3,482**	**1,456**	**732**	..	..	**1,295**	**113**	**47**	**2**	..	..	**4**	**2,443**	**853**	**370**	**11**	**3**	**1,320**
Alwar	6	..	3	..	..	4	235	86	20	..	..	120	..	..	..	..	..	..	247	87	5	1	..	155
Bharatpur	96	47	24	..	..	25	..	..	..	..	..	..	1	1	..	..	..	..	192	51	25	8	3	56
Bikaner	300	107	79	..	..	114	612	207	143	..	..	262	54	26	..	..	..	28	76	40	..	..	..	36
Jaipur	891	325	314	..	..	252	1,911	851	470	..	..	590	42	8	1	..	..	33	527	173	71	..	..	283
Jodhpur	71	17	37	..	..	17	724	311	99	..	..	814	6	6	..	..	..	..	802	241	63	..	..	498
Kotah	47	20	9	..	..	18	..	..	..	..	..	..	..	..	..	..	..	..	195	77	25	..	..	93
Tonk	..	..	..	..	..	..	..	..	..	..	..	..	10	6	1	..	..	3	394	136	78	2	..	120
Udaipur	475	160	52	..	..	263	..	..	..	..	..	..	..	..	..	..	..	..	130	48	3	..	..	79
Ajmer-Merwara—																								
Ajmer	321	109	96	..	..	116	821	310	110	..	..	401	5	4	..	..	..	1	101	35	9	..	..	57

TABLE XV-A.—OCCUPATION OR MEANS OF LIVELIHOOD. PART II.—BY STATE OR DISTRICT, AND CITY—*continued*.

CLASS B.—PREPARATION AND SUPPLY OF MATERIAL SUBSTANCES—*continued*.

SUB-CLASS III.—INDUSTRY—*continued*.

Order 7.—Hides, skins and hard materials from the animal kingdom.

Province; and State, District, or City.	32.—Tanners, curriers, leather dressers and dyers, etc. Total workers and dependants. Both sexes.	32. Actual workers. Total. Males.	32. Actual workers. Total. Females.	32. Actual workers. Partially agriculturists. Males.	32. Actual workers. Partially agriculturists. Females.	32. Dependants. Both sexes.	33.—Makers of leather articles, such as trunks, water bags, sword sheaths, etc., embroiderers on leather. Total workers and dependants. Both sexes.	33. Actual workers. Total. Males.	33. Actual workers. Total. Females.	33. Actual workers. Partially agriculturists. Males.	33. Actual workers. Partially agriculturists. Females.	33. Dependants. Both sexes.	34.—Furriers. Total workers and dependants. Both sexes.	34. Actual workers. Total. Males.	34. Actual workers. Total. Females.	34. Actual workers. Partially agriculturists. Males.	34. Actual workers. Partially agriculturists. Females.	34. Dependants. Both sexes.	35.—Bone, ivory, horn, shell, etc., workers. Total workers and dependants. Both sexes.	35. Actual workers. Total. Males.	35. Actual workers. Total. Females.	35. Actual workers. Partially agriculturists. Males.	35. Actual workers. Partially agriculturists. Females.	35. Dependants. Both sexes.
1	278	279	280	281	282	283	284	285	286	287	288	289	290	291	292	293	294	295	296	297	298	299	300	301
Rajputana	**69,818**	**23,409**	**7,349**	**6,949**	**1,107**	**39,060**	**32,977**	**13,790**	**2,416**	**4,616**	**294**	**16,771**	**208**	**145**	..	**54**	..	**63**	**929**	**391**	**37**	**139**	..	**501**
Alwar	3,912	1,572	399	560	19	1,941	140	40	24	3	..	83	..	..	..	..	..	..	..	..	..	..	..	..
Banswara	82	29	2	9	..	51	1,157	412	11	286	2	734	..	..	..	..	..	..	..	..	..	..	..	..
Bharatpur	2,116	920	191	526	83	1,005	169	70	27	22	1	72	..	..	..	..	..	..	19	15	..	..	..	4
Bikaner	2,635	998	293	427	130	1,344	18	1	8	..	..	9	..	..	..	..	..	..	27	10	..	..	..	17
Bundi	2,978	971	116	140	4	1,891	601	204	23	14	2	374	..	..	..	..	..	..	..	..	..	..	..	..
Dholpur	342	152	50	77	18	140	20	11	..	..	..	9	..	..	..	..	..	..	..	..	..	..	..	..
Dungarpur	249	53	8	7	1	188	..	..	..	..	..	..	..	..	..	..	..	..	..	..	..	..	..	..
Jaipur	17,278	6,801	2,673	1,579	355	7,804	5,908	2,678	947	863	97	2,283	4	2	..	1	..	2	351	207	..	139	..	144
Jaisalmer	98	26	1	7	1	71	..	..	..	..	..	..	..	..	..	..	..	..	..	..	..	..	..	..
Jhalawar	298	122	52	21	6	124	916	427	12	143	7	477	..	..	..	..	..	..	..	..	..	..	..	..
Karauli	332	134	39	55	19	159	8	6	..	..	..	2	..	..	..	..	..	..	..	..	..	..	..	..
Kishangarh	476	192	37	60	2	247	414	200	36	97	8	178	..	..	..	..	..	..	7	2	3	..	..	2
Kotah	4,997	1,976	710	470	103	2,311	5,621	1,997	576	776	73	3,048	..	..	..	..	..	..	6	3	..	..	..	3
Kushalgarh (Chiefship)	..	..	..	..	..	..	5	1	..	..	..	4	..	..	..	..	..	..	..	..	..	..	..	..
Lawa (Estate)	16	9	2	5	..	5	..	..	..	..	..	..	..	..	..	..	..	..	..	..	..	..	..	..
Marwar	10,403	3,959	1,032	1,075	89	5,412	10,799	4,706	403	1,135	45	5,690	2	..	..	..	..	2	332	94	..	..	..	238
Mewar	10,290	4,042	784	1,627	209	5,464	4,916	2,000	240	945	50	2,676	202	143	..	53	..	59	55	21	6	..	..	28
Partabgarh	280	121	13	41	4	146	214	117	1	46	..	96	..	..	..	..	..	..	..	..	..	..	..	..
Shahpura (Chiefship)	349	129	..	84	..	220	580	229	..	147	..	351	..	..	..	..	..	..	..	..	..	..	..	..
Sirohi	1,236	375	342	20	7	519	203	68	46	6	5	89	..	..	..	..	..	..	51	19	..	..	..	32
Tonk	2,451	828	605	159	57	1,018	1,279	623	60	133	4	596	..	..	..	..	..	..	81	20	28	..	..	33
Ajmer-Merwara	**1,307**	**543**	**88**	**198**	**23**	**676**	**3,835**	**1,594**	**251**	**494**	**62**	**1,990**	..	..	..	..	..	..	**8**	**2**	..	..	..	**6**
Ajmer	1,147	472	84	167	22	591	2,249	996	96	306	27	1,157	..	..	..	..	..	..	5	1	..	..	..	4
Merwara	160	71	4	31	1	85	1,586	598	155	188	35	833	..	..	..	..	..	..	3	1	..	..	..	2
CITIES.																								
Rajputana	**2,041**	**706**	**264**	**11**	**3**	**1,071**	**236**	**99**	**2**	..	..	**135**	..	..	..	..	..	..	**166**	**48**	**4**	..	..	**114**
Alwar	173	67	5	1	..	101	74	20	..	..	..	54	..	..	..	..	..	..	..	..	..	..	..	..
Bharatpur	124	45	25	5	3	54	8	6	..	..	..	2	..	..	..	..	..	..	..	..	..	..	..	..
Bikaner	..	..	..	..	..	..	50	31	..	..	..	19	..	..	..	..	..	..	26	9	..	..	..	17
Jaipur	454	152	70	..	..	232	38	11	1	..	..	26	..	..	..	..	..	..	35	10	..	..	..	25
Jodhpur	667	197	62	..	..	408	58	28	1	..	..	29	..	..	..	..	..	..	77	16	..	..	..	61
Kotah	190	76	25	..	..	89	5	1	..	..	..	4	..	..	..	..	..	..	..	..	..	..	..	..
Tonk	319	130	74	2	..	115	3	2	..	..	..	1	..	..	..	..	..	..	12	4	4	..	..	4
Udaipur	114	39	3	..	..	72	..	..	..	..	..	..	..	..	..	..	..	..	16	9	..	..	..	7
Ajmer-Merwara—																								
Ajmer	63	20	9	..	..	34	34	15	..	..	..	19	..	..	..	..	..	..	4	..	..	..	..	4

TABLE XV-A.—OCCUPATION OR MEANS OF LIVELIHOOD. PART II.—BY STATE OR DISTRICT, AND CITY—*continued.*

CLASS B.—PREPARATION AND SUPPLY OF MATERIAL SUBSTANCES—*continued.*

SUB-CLASS III.—INDUSTRY—*continued.*

Order 8.—Wood.

Province; and State, District, or City.	Total Order 8. Total workers and dependants. Both sexes.	Total Order 8. Total workers. Total. Males.	Total Order 8. Total workers. Total. Females.	Total Order 8. Total workers. Partially agriculturists. Males.	Total Order 8. Total workers. Partially agriculturists. Females.	Total Order 8. Dependants. Both sexes.	36.—Sawyers, carpenters, turners, and joiners, etc. Total workers and dependants. Both sexes.	36. Actual workers. Total. Males.	36. Actual workers. Total. Females.	36. Actual workers. Partially agriculturists. Males.	36. Actual workers. Partially agriculturists. Females.	36. Dependants. Both sexes.
1	302	303	304	305	306	307	308	309	310	311	312	313
Rajputana	**144,390**	**56,466**	**11,554**	**19,545**	**794**	**76,376**	**119,565**	**48,738**	**2,666**	**17,750**	**182**	**68,161**
Alwar	11,819	4,290	725	1,146	63	6,874	10,061	3,638	166	1,075	16	6,257
Banswara	1,365	467	200	155	6	698	743	290	2	135	..	451
Bharatpur	6,482	2,698	594	1,202	64	3,190	4,736	2,094	7	977	..	2,635
Bikaner	6,593	2,996	245	1,619	47	3,350	5,165	2,410	21	1,318	1	2,734
Bundi	3,685	1,264	333	404	7	2,088	3,197	1,170	68	400	..	1,061
Dholpur	2,978	1,182	203	426	24	1,593	2,120	879	..	357	..	1,241
Dungarpur	1,535	541	71	206	4	923	1,324	481	8	204	4	835
Jaipur	42,743	16,168	4,479	3,542	215	22,096	35,309	14,107	1,152	3,118	56	20,140
Jaisalmer	1,720	536	34	308	2	1,150	1,360	427	22	271	2	911
Jhalawar	1,374	484	190	66	16	700	979	397	..	61	..	582
Karauli	1,498	601	155	168	..	742	1,139	476	31	159	..	632
Kishangarh	1,109	490	43	207	..	576	1,062	479	25	205	..	558
Kotah	8,456	3,122	1,408	713	96	3,926	4,078	2,119	65	593	4	2,794
Kushalgarh (Chiefship)	137	48	29	..	..	60	15	11	..	..	..	4
Lawa (Estate)	12	7	..	2	..	5	12	7	..	2	..	5
Marwar	29,045	12,614	775	6,207	107	15,656	26,635	11,611	255	5,787	39	14,669
Mewar	16,043	6,107	1,377	2,475	97	8,559	14,377	5,031	719	2,455	56	8,027
Partabgarh	581	242	30	79	..	309	463	200	1	79	..	262
Shahpura (Chiefship)	414	180	19	130	..	215	377	169	..	130	..	208
Sirohi	2,667	967	89	167	2	1,611	2,522	918	40	164	..	1,564
Tonk	4,134	1,524	555	328	44	2,055	3,001	1,224	56	271	4	1,691
Ajmer-Merwara	**4,998**	**2,210**	**322**	**720**	**22**	**2,466**	**4,140**	**1,912**	**57**	**713**	**7**	**2,171**
Ajmer	3,873	1,692	266	553	15	1,915	3,185	1,469	34	549	3	1,682
Merwara	1,125	518	56	167	7	551	955	443	23	164	4	489
CITIES.												
Rajputana	**5,979**	**2,378**	**556**	**11**	**7**	**3,045**	**4,713**	**2,060**	**53**	**16**	..	**2,600**
Alwar	528	176	104	..	2	248	282	119	3	..	..	160
Bharatpur	467	186	95	4	..	186	248	112	..	3	..	136
Bikaner	855	363	..	5	..	492	847	365	..	5	..	402
Jaipur	1,688	700	197	..	5	789	1,339	599	80	..	..	710
Jodhpur	1,024	470	22	..	..	532	977	456	5	..	..	516
Kotah	684	241	11	2	..	432	521	226	..	2	..	295
Tonk	231	74	45	..	..	112	151	66	..	..	..	85
Udaipur	504	168	82	..	..	254	348	127	15	..	..	206
Ajmer-Merwara—												
Ajmer	809	352	43	..	..	414	698	317	7	..	..	374

Province; and State, District, or City.	37.—Basket makers, cane and bamboo chair makers and other industries of woody material including leaves. Total workers and dependants. Both sexes.	37. Actual workers. Total. Males.	37. Actual workers. Total. Females.	37. Actual workers. Partially agriculturists. Males.	37. Actual workers. Partially agriculturists. Females.	37. Dependants. Both sexes.	Total Order 9. Total workers and dependants. Both sexes.	Total Order 9. Actual workers. Total. Males.	Total Order 9. Actual workers. Total. Females.	Total Order 9. Actual workers. Partially agriculturists. Males.	Total Order 9. Actual workers. Partially agriculturists. Females.	Total Order 9. Dependants. Both sexes.
1	314	315	316	317	318	319	320	321	322	323	324	325
Rajputana	**24,825**	**7,722**	**8,388**	**1,795**	**612**	**8,215**	**87,420**	**35,597**	**4,258**	**5,793**	**299**	**37,565**
Alwar	1,759	582	550	71	47	617	2,822	1,114	103	306	8	1,605
Banswara	622	177	198	20	6	247	1,741	584	145	316	2	1,012
Bharatpur	1,746	604	587	225	64	555	2,618	1,010	178	302	26	1,430
Bikaner	1,428	588	224	303	46	616	3,298	1,253	337	241	28	1,708
Bundi	488	94	267	4	7	127	2,155	767	37	57	..	1,351
Dholpur	858	303	203	69	24	352	890	309	4	33	..	577
Dungarpur	211	60	63	2	..	88	1,850	625	133	293	8	1,092
Jaipur	7,344	2,061	3,327	424	159	1,956	11,577	4,403	1,093	383	34	6,081
Jaisalmer	360	109	12	32	..	239	231	92	7	12	..	132
Jhalawar	395	87	190	5	16	118	952	345	13	36	2	594
Karauli	359	125	124	18	..	110	508	201	22	48	4	285
Kishangarh	47	11	18	2	..	18	447	158	47	24	4	242
Kotah	3,478	1,003	1,343	120	92	1,132	4,706	1,831	408	320	13	2,472
Kushalgarh (Chiefship)	122	37	29	..	..	56	159	57	7	30	..	95
Lawa (Estate)	..	..	..	..	..	..	8	4	1	..	..	3
Marwar	2,510	1,003	520	420	66	987	16,003	6,223	1,021	1,332	100	8,759
Mewar	1,666	476	658	20	41	532	13,318	5,114	429	1,753	67	7,775
Partabgarh	118	42	29	..	..	47	431	161	12	40	2	258
Shahpura (Chiefship)	37	11	19	..	..	7	301	116	13	69	..	172
Sirohi	145	49	49	3	2	47	1,828	645	163	85	4	1,030
Tonk	1,133	300	469	57	40	364	1,567	585	90	113	2	692
Ajmer-Merwara	**858**	**298**	**265**	**7**	**15**	**295**	**4,171**	**1,555**	**329**	**234**	**15**	**2,287**
Ajmer	688	223	232	4	12	233	3,156	1,176	214	183	11	1,766
Merwara	170	75	33	3	3	62	1,015	379	115	51	4	521
CITIES.												
Rajputana	**1,266**	**318**	**503**	**1**	**7**	**445**	**5,399**	**2,099**	**259**	**3**	..	**3,041**
Alwar	246	57	101	..	2	88	341	153	5	1	..	183
Bharatpur	219	74	95	1	..	50	230	77	4	..	..	158
Bikaner	8	8	..	..	..	..	813	277	33	..	..	503
Jaipur	347	101	107	..	5	79	1,992	841	168	..	..	983
Jodhpur	47	14	17	..	..	16	704	252	19	..	..	433
Kotah	163	15	11	..	..	137	436	185	15	1	..	236
Tonk	80	8	45	..	..	27	288	108	3	1	..	177
Udaipur	156	41	67	..	..	48	586	206	12	..	..	368
Ajmer-Merwara—												
Ajmer	111	35	36	..	..	40	1,106	425	25	2	1	656

TABLE XV-A.—OCCUPATION OR MEANS OF LIVELIHOOD. PART II.—BY STATE OR DISTRICT, AND CITY—*continued.*

CLASS B.—PREPARATION AND SUPPLY OF MATERIAL SUBSTANCES—*continued.*

SUB-CLASS III.—INDUSTRY—*continued.*

Order 9.—Metals.

Province; and State, District, or City.	38.—Forging and rolling of iron and other metals.				39.—Plough and agricultural implement makers.						40.—Makers of arms, guns, etc.						41.—Other workers in iron and makers of implement and tools, principally or exclusively of iron.						42.—Workers in brass, copper, and bell metal.					
	Total workers and dependants.	Actual workers. Total.		Dependants.	Total workers and dependants.	Actual workers. Total.		Actual workers. Partially agriculturists.		Dependants.	Total workers and dependants.	Actual workers. Total.		Actual workers. Partially agriculturists.		Dependants.	Total workers and dependants.	Actual workers. Total.		Actual workers. Partially agriculturists.		Dependants.	Total workers and dependants.	Actual workers. Total.		Actual workers. Partially agriculturists.		Dependants.
	Both sexes.	Males.	Females.	Both sexes.	Both sexes.	Males.	Females.	Males.	Females.	Both sexes.	Both sexes.	Males.	Females.	Males.	Females.	Both sexes.	Both sexes.	Males.	Females.	Males.	Females.	Both sexes.	Both sexes.	Males.	Females.	Males.	Females.	Both sexes.
1	326	327	328	329	330	331	332	333	334	335	336	337	338	339	340	341	342	343	344	345	346	347	348	349	350	351	352	353
Rajputana	**5**	**4**	..	**1**	**302**	**107**	**4**	**47**	..	**191**	**1,343**	**497**	**106**	**83**	..	**740**	**58,275**	**22,080**	**3,858**	**5,611**	**298**	**30,237**	**6,447**	**2,509**	**167**	**46**	**1**	**3,771**
Alwar	..	..	..	..	..	..	..	..	..	..	..	..	..	..	..	..	2,731	1,063	102	302	8	1,564	56	35	..	4	..	21
Banswara	..	..	..	..	72	26	1	18	..	45	361	115	84	54	..	165	1,180	400	45	244	2	732	98	29	13	..	..	56
Bharatpur	..	..	..	..	..	..	..	..	..	..	49	12	..	..	..	37	2,336	905	178	298	26	1,252	131	51	..	3	..	80
Bikaner	..	..	..	..	..	..	..	..	..	..	24	7	4	4	..	13	2,838	1,085	327	235	28	1,426	417	153	6	..	..	258
Bundi	..	..	..	..	..	..	..	..	..	..	15	5	..	..	..	10	1,944	683	33	57	..	1,228	101	78	4	..	..	109
Dholpur	..	..	..	..	..	..	..	..	..	..	27	9	..	2	..	18	652	220	..	23	..	432	211	80	4	8	..	127
Dungarpur	..	..	..	..	..	..	..	..	..	..	105	37	..	11	..	68	1,557	543	120	282	3	891	184	40	10	..	..	114
Jaipur	..	..	..	..	85	37	2	7	..	46	170	39	7	1	..	74	9,300	3,444	1,036	361	33	4,820	1,827	746	44	14	1	1,097
Jaisalmer	..	..	..	..	..	..	..	..	..	..	6	2	..	..	..	4	216	87	7	12	..	122	9	3	..	..	..	6
Jhalawar	..	..	..	..	..	..	..	..	..	..	2	..	2	..	..	..	746	275	11	34	2	400	158	59	..	2	..	99
Karauli	..	..	..	..	..	..	..	..	..	..	13	5	..	..	..	8	875	146	22	43	4	207	114	45	..	5	..	69
Kishangarh	..	..	..	..	..	..	..	..	..	..	48	16	..	..	..	32	852	122	47	23	4	183	47	20	..	1	..	27
Kotah	..	..	..	..	21	7	1	3	..	13	29	9	..	1	..	20	4,140	1,573	364	314	13	2,203	461	230	31	2	..	208
Kushalgarh (Chiefship)	..	..	..	..	..	..	..	..	..	..	..	..	..	..	..	..	136	50	4	30	..	82	14	4	3	..	..	7
Lawa (Estate)	..	..	..	..	..	..	..	..	..	..	..	..	..	..	..	..	5	3	1	..	..	1	3	1	..	..	..	2
Marwar	5	4	..	1	..	..	..	..	..	..	187	85	1	5	..	101	11,138	5,400	1,011	1,323	100	7,637	1,464	569	9	4	..	886
Mewar	..	..	..	..	112	84	..	17	..	78	190	64	4	2	..	122	12,070	4,682	388	1,732	67	7,000	821	286	35	1	..	500
Partabgarh	..	..	..	..	..	..	..	..	..	..	..	..	..	..	..	..	389	147	6	40	2	237	15	3	6	..	..	5
Shahpura (Chiefship)	..	..	..	..	..	..	..	..	..	..	..	..	..	..	..	..	273	107	18	68	..	159	28	9	..	1	..	19
Sirohi	..	..	..	..	..	..	..	..	..	..	70	27	4	3	..	39	1,005	555	151	82	4	806	107	36	2	..	..	69
Tonk	..	..	..	..	12	3	..	2	..	9	44	15	..	..	..	29	1,286	488	90	110	2	708	108	32	..	1	..	76
Ajmer-Merwara	..	..	..	..	**95**	**34**	**9**	**23**	**6**	**58**	**3**	**2**	..	**1**	..	**1**	**3,239**	**1,181**	**302**	**209**	**8**	**1,756**	**655**	**266**	**14**	**1**	**1**	**375**
Ajmer	..	..	..	..	91	33	9	22	6	40	3	2	..	1	..	1	2,314	839	195	150	5	1,280	583	237	6	1	..	340
Merwara	..	..	..	..	4	1	..	1	..	3	..	..	..	..	..	..	925	342	107	50	3	476	72	20	8	..	1	35
CITIES.																												
Rajputana	..	..	..	..	..	..	..	..	..	..	**133**	**62**	..	..	..	**71**	**3,256**	**1,201**	**214**	**3**	..	**1,843**	**1,588**	**672**	**41**	..	..	**875**
Alwar	..	..	..	..	..	..	..	..	..	..	..	..	..	..	..	..	312	138	4	1	..	170	5	4	..	..	..	1
Bharatpur	..	..	..	..	..	..	..	..	..	..	9	1	..	..	..	8	162	51	4	..	..	107	33	14	..	..	..	19
Bikaner	..	..	..	..	..	..	..	..	..	..	5	1	..	..	..	4	430	145	27	..	..	264	364	127	6	..	..	231
Jaipur	..	..	..	..	..	..	..	..	..	..	47	35	..	..	..	12	944	355	141	..	..	448	878	393	27	..	..	458
Jodhpur	..	..	..	..	..	..	..	..	..	..	37	15	..	..	..	22	427	149	19	..	..	259	132	53	..	..	..	79
Kotah	..	..	..	..	..	..	..	..	..	..	..	..	..	..	..	..	318	134	5	1	..	179	101	46	7	..	..	48
Tonk	..	..	..	..	..	..	..	..	..	..	35	10	..	..	..	25	190	75	3	1	..	112	..	..	..	..	..	..
Udaipur	..	..	..	..	..	..	..	..	..	..	..	..	..	..	..	..	469	154	11	..	..	304	75	35	1	..	..	39
Ajmer-Merwara—																												
Ajmer	..	..	..	..	..	..	..	..	..	..	..	..	..	..	..	..	676	239	21	2	1	416	343	147	3	..	..	193

TABLE XV-A.—OCCUPATION OR MEANS OF LIVELIHOOD. PART II.—BY STATE OR DISTRICT, AND CITY—*continued.*

CLASS B.—PREPARATION AND SUPPLY OF MATERIAL SUBSTANCES—*continued.*

SUB-CLASS III.—INDUSTRY—*continued.*

Order 9.—Metals—*concluded.*

Province; and State, District, or City.	43.—Workers in other metals (tin, zinc, lead, quick-silver, etc.). Total workers and dependants.	Actual workers. Total.		Partially agriculturists.		Dependants.	44.—Workers in mints, die-sinkers, etc. Total workers and dependants.	Actual workers. Total.		Dependants.
	Both sexes.	Males.	Females.	Males.	Females.	Both sexes.	Both sexes.	Males.	Females.	Both sexes.
1	354	355	356	357	358	359	360	361	362	363
Rajputana	916	350	23	6	..	543	132	50	..	82
Alwar	35	14	1	..	..	20	..	..	..	..
Banswara	21	5	2	..	..	14	..	..	..	..
Bharatpur	102	41	..	8	..	61	..	..	..	..
Bikaner	19	8	..	2	..	11	..	..	..	..
Bundi	5	1	..	..	..	4	..	..	..	..
Dholpur	..	..	..	..	..	..	..	..	..	..
Dungarpur	24	5	3	..	..	16	..	..	..	..
Jaipur	113	52	4	..	..	57	82	35	..	47
Jaisalmer	..	..	..	..	..	..	..	..	..	..
Jhalawar	46	11	..	..	..	35	..	..	..	..
Karauli	6	5	..	..	..	1	..	..	..	..
Kishangarh	..	..	..	..	..	..	..	..	..	..
Kotah	52	12	7	..	..	33	..	..	..	..
Kushalgarh (Chiefship)	9	3	..	..	..	6	..	..	..	..
Lawa (Estate)	..	..	..	..	..	..	..	..	..	..
Marwar	159	60	..	..	..	99	50	15	..	35
Mewar	125	48	2	1	..	75	..	..	..	..
Partabgarh	27	11	1	..	..	15	..	..	..	..
Shahpura (Chiefship)	..	..	..	..	..	..	..	..	..	..
Sirohi	56	27	3	..	..	26	..	..	..	..
Tonk	117	47	..	..	..	70	..	..	..	..
Ajmer-Merwara	179	72	4	..	..	103	..	..	..	..
Ajmer	165	65	4	..	..	96	..	..	..	..
Merwara	14	7	..	..	..	7	..	..	..	..
CITIES.										
Rajputana	293	118	4	..	..	171	127	46	..	81
Alwar	24	11	1	..	..	12	..	..	..	..
Bharatpur	35	11	..	..	..	24	..	..	..	..
Bikaner	8	4	..	..	..	4	..	..	..	..
Jaipur	46	27	..	..	..	19	77	31	..	46
Jodhpur	58	20	..	..	..	38	50	15	..	35
Kotah	17	5	3	..	..	9	..	..	..	..
Tonk	63	23	..	..	..	40	..	..	..	..
Udaipur	42	17	..	..	..	25	..	..	..	..
Ajmer-Merwara—										
Ajmer	87	39	1	..	..	47	..	..	..	..

Order 10.—Ceramics.

Province; and State, District, or City.	Total Order 10. Total workers and dependants.	Actual workers. Total.		Partially agriculturists.		Dependants.	45.—Makers of glass and crystal ware. Total workers and dependants.	Actual workers. Total.		Partially agriculturists.		Dependants.	46.—Makers of porcelain and crockery. Total workers and dependants.	Actual workers. Total.		Dependants.
	Both sexes.	Males.	Females.	Males.	Females.	Both sexes.	Both sexes.	Males.	Females.	Males.	Females.	Both sexes.	Both sexes.	Males.	Females.	Both sexes.
1	364	365	366	367	368	369	370	371	372	373	374	375	376	377	378	379
Rajputana	136,964	52,196	27,666	13,383	2,530	57,102	391	175	43	50	5	173	10	7	..	3
Alwar	12,919	4,410	3,237	1,174	326	5,272	2	1	..	..	..	1	..	..	..	..
Banswara	1,189	368	367	86	6	454	..	..	..	..	..	..	..	..	..	..
Bharatpur	7,876	3,091	1,619	1,064	190	3,166	268	116	33	44	5	119	..	..	..	..
Bikaner	3,935	1,580	711	845	217	1,644	..	..	..	..	..	..	..	..	..	..
Bundi	2,901	995	526	85	15	1,380	..	..	..	..	..	..	..	..	..	..
Dholpur	2,629	1,009	597	310	72	1,023	45	29	..	6	..	16	..	..	..	..
Dungarpur	1,558	508	327	105	6	723	..	..	..	..	..	..	..	..	..	..
Jaipur	38,631	15,456	8,682	2,940	533	14,493	5	4	..	..	..	1	3	2	..	1
Jaisalmer	981	320	123	188	5	538	..	..	..	..	..	..	..	..	..	..
Jhalawar	1,216	422	801	58	18	493	..	..	..	..	..	..	..	..	..	..
Karauli	1,485	582	392	171	18	511	..	..	..	..	..	..	..	..	..	..
Kishangarh	1,182	508	242	169	28	432	18	6	5	..	..	5	..	..	..	..
Kotah	7,441	2,652	1,640	408	75	3,149	40	13	5	..	..	22	..	..	..	..
Kushalgarh (Chiefship)	137	41	21	..	..	75	..	..	..	..	..	..	..	..	..	..
Lawa (Estate)	27	8	9	2	..	10	..	..	..	..	..	..	..	..	..	..
Marwar	26,216	10,783	3,707	3,573	609	11,726	5	4	..	..	..	1	..	..	..	..
Mewar	18,330	6,568	3,077	1,692	321	8,691	8	..	..	..	..	8	..	..	..	..
Partabgarh	474	165	107	31	2	202	..	..	..	..	..	..	..	..	..	..
Shahpura (Chiefship)	507	200	44	125	19	263	..	..	..	..	..	..	..	..	..	..
Sirohi	3,707	1,247	924	150	19	1,536	..	..	..	..	..	..	..	..	..	..
Tonk	3,628	1,289	1,013	207	42	1,321	..	..	..	..	..	..	7	5	..	2
Ajmer-Merwara	5,665	2,061	1,478	691	331	2,046	..	..	..	..	..	..	..	..	..	..
Ajmer	4,423	1,631	1,185	537	281	1,607	..	..	..	..	..	..	..	..	..	..
Merwara	1,182	450	293	154	50	439	..	..	..	..	..	..	..	..	..	..
CITIES.																
Rajputana	2,625	883	694	30	..	1,048	1	1	..	..	..	..	..	..	..	..
Alwar	305	101	65	..	..	139	1	1	..	..	..	..	..	..	..	..
Bharatpur	498	193	87	9	..	218	..	..	..	..	..	..	..	..	..	..
Bikaner	314	112	48	17	..	154	..	..	..	..	..	..	..	..	..	..
Jaipur	553	225	179	..	..	149	..	..	..	..	..	..	..	..	..	..
Jodhpur	342	129	42	4	..	171	..	..	..	..	..	..	..	..	..	..
Kotah	228	75	58	..	..	95	..	..	..	..	..	..	..	..	..	..
Tonk	175	65	50	..	..	60	..	..	..	..	..	..	..	..	..	..
Udaipur	210	83	65	..	..	62	..	..	..	..	..	..	..	..	..	..
Ajmer-Merwara—																
Ajmer	367	125	99	12	7	143	..	..	..	..	..	..	..	..	..	..

TABLE XV-A.—Occupation or Means of Livelihood. Part II—By State or District, and City—*continued.*

CLASS B.—PREPARATION AND SUPPLY OF MATERIAL SUBSTANCES—*continued.* SUB-CLASS III.—INDUSTRY—*continued.*

Province; and State, District, or City.	Order 10.—Ceramics—*concluded.* 47.—Potters, and earthen pipe and bowl makers. Total workers and dependants. Both sexes.	47. Actual workers. Total. Males.	47. Actual workers. Total. Females.	47. Actual workers. Partially agriculturists. Males.	47. Actual workers. Partially agriculturists. Females.	47. Dependants. Both sexes.	48.—Brick and tile makers. Total workers and dependants. Both sexes.	48. Actual workers. Total. Males.	48. Actual workers. Total. Females.	48. Actual workers. Partially agriculturists. Males.	48. Actual workers. Partially agriculturists. Females.	48. Dependants. Both sexes.	49.—Other (mosaic, talc, mica, alabaster, etc.) workers. Total workers and dependants. Both sexes.	49. Actual workers. Total. Males.	49. Actual workers. Total. Females.	49. Dependants. Both sexes.	Order 11.—Chemical products properly so called, and analogous. Total Order 11. Total workers and dependants. Both sexes.	Total Order 11. Actual workers. Total. Males.	Total Order 11. Actual workers. Total. Females.	Total Order 11. Actual workers. Partially agriculturists. Males.	Total Order 11. Actual workers. Partially agriculturists. Females.	Total Order 11. Dependants. Both sexes.	50.—Manufacture of matches and explosive materials. Total workers and dependants. Both sexes.	50. Actual workers. Total. Males.	50. Actual workers. Total. Females.	50. Actual workers. Partially agriculturists. Males.	50. Actual workers. Partially agriculturists. Females.	50. Dependants. Both sexes.
1	380	381	382	383	384	385	386	387	388	389	390	391	392	393	394	395	396	397	398	399	400	401	402	403	404	405	406	407
Rajputana	135,036	51,440	27,415	13,212	2,520	56,181	1,518	569	208	121	5	741	9	5	..	4	46,446	17,493	7,168	5,940	754	21,786	1,406	478	160	56	7	768
Alwar	12,869	4,405	3,232	1,173	326	5,231	48	3	5	1	..	40	..	..	..	..	3,154	1,137	424	281	53	1,593	87	35	..	1	..	52
Banswara	1,143	354	248	66	6	441	46	14	19	..	..	13	..	..	..	..	524	157	132	109	34	235	7	1	2	..	..	4
Bharatpur	7,499	2,938	1,578	1,009	191	2,983	103	35	8	11	2	60	6	2	..	4	3,700	1,362	778	539	98	1,560	140	53	10	7	3	77
Bikaner	3,353	1,341	677	758	217	1,335	582	239	34	87	..	309	..	..	..	..	1,531	572	122	310	42	837	18	4	1	..	..	13
Bundi	2,808	904	524	85	15	1,380	3	1	2	..	..	..	..	..	..	..	2,064	736	126	96	1	1,202	32	5	12	2	..	15
Dholpur	2,584	980	597	304	72	1,007	..	..	..	..	..	..	..	..	..	..	1,905	798	258	309	10	849	171	71	18	11	..	82
Dungarpur	1,558	508	327	105	6	723	..	..	..	..	..	..	..	..	..	..	788	228	132	109	11	426	13	4	..	..	..	9
Jaipur	38,453	15,880	8,679	2,932	533	14,394	170	70	3	7	..	97	..	..	..	..	8,776	3,362	1,556	551	68	3,858	218	69	18	4	..	131
Jaisalmer	981	320	123	188	5	538	..	..	..	..	..	..	..	..	..	..	47	15	..	11	..	32	1	1	..	..	..	..
Jhalawar	1,216	422	301	58	18	493	..	..	..	..	..	..	..	..	..	..	276	113	28	22	..	135	6	2	..	..	..	4
Karauli	1,485	582	392	171	18	511	..	..	..	..	..	..	..	..	..	..	396	160	70	73	5	166	87	29	24	3	..	34
Kishangarh	1,164	600	237	160	28	427	..	..	..	..	..	..	..	..	..	..	406	150	47	59	4	209	31	8	5	2	..	18
Kotah	7,355	2,626	1,621	406	75	3,108	46	13	14	..	..	19	..	..	..	..	3,205	1,172	527	271	40	1,506	31	13	1	3	..	17
Kushalgarh (Chiefship)	130	37	21	..	..	72	7	4	..	..	..	3	..	..	..	..	56	15	9	..	..	32	..	..	..	..	..	..
Lawa (Estate)	27	8	9	2	..	10	..	..	..	..	..	..	..	..	..	..	5	1	2	..	..	2	..	..	..	..	..	..
Marwar	26,109	10,741	3,692	3,563	609	11,676	102	38	15	10	..	49	..	..	..	..	8,099	3,392	639	1,671	176	4,068	192	63	23	3	1	106
Mewar	18,111	6,489	3,026	1,687	319	8,596	208	70	51	5	2	87	3	3	..	..	7,830	2,819	1,376	1,122	158	3,635	276	84	31	12	3	161
Partabgarh	423	148	94	31	2	181	51	17	13	..	..	21	..	..	..	..	313	109	52	30	2	152	2	1	..	..	..	1
Shahpura (Chiefship)	507	200	44	125	19	263	..	..	..	..	..	..	..	..	..	..	256	106	32	82	18	118	12	5	3	2	..	4
Sirohi	3,565	1,188	881	150	19	2,496	142	59	43	..	..	40	..	..	..	..	709	231	242	43	8	236	..	..	..	..	..	..
Tonk	3,606	1,278	1,012	207	42	1,316	10	6	1	..	..	3	..	..	..	..	2,408	867	616	151	31	925	76	30	12	..	..	34
Ajmer-Merwara	5,516	2,050	1,472	691	331	1,994	89	31	6	..	..	52	..	..	..	..	2,558	1,040	509	397	98	1,009	34	12	5	1	..	17
Ajmer	4,339	1,600	1,181	537	281	1,558	84	31	4	..	..	49	..	..	..	..	2,006	836	401	344	84	769	30	11	5	1	..	14
Merwara	1,177	450	291	154	50	436	5	..	2	..	..	3	..	..	..	..	552	204	108	53	14	240	4	1	..	..	..	3
CITIES.																												
Rajputana	2,462	929	575	23	..	958	156	51	19	7	..	86	6	2	..	4	2,477	880	203	15	13	1,394	167	57	9	..	..	101
Alwar	297	100	63	..	..	134	7	..	2	..	..	5	..	..	..	..	250	80	20	..	..	150	51	20	..	..	..	31
Bharatpur	412	163	87	2	..	162	80	28	..	7	..	52	6	2	..	4	337	82	29	3	..	126	44	10	..	..	..	34
Bikaner	311	110	48	17	..	153	3	2	..	..	..	1	..	..	..	..	389	129	23	..	..	237	..	..	..	..	..	..
Jaipur	553	225	179	..	..	149	..	..	..	..	..	..	..	..	..	..	443	171	37	..	..	235	9	4	..	..	..	5
Jodhpur	342	129	42	4	..	171	..	..	..	..	..	..	..	..	..	..	589	188	36	8	13	365	30	10	3	..	..	17
Kotah	184	63	44	..	..	77	44	12	14	..	..	18	..	..	..	..	191	94	5	4	..	92	2	1	..	..	..	1
Tonk	166	60	49	..	..	57	9	5	1	..	..	3	..	..	..	..	270	102	44	..	..	124	15	7	6	..	..	2
Udaipur	197	79	63	..	..	55	13	4	2	..	..	7	..	..	..	..	108	34	9	..	..	65	16	5	..	..	..	11
Ajmer-Merwara— Ajmer	302	101	98	12	7	103	65	24	1	..	..	40	..	..	..	..	613	281	85	85	3	247	20	7	4	..	..	9

TABLE XV-A.—OCCUPATION OR MEANS OF LIVELIHOOD. PART II.—BY STATE OR DISTRICT, AND CITY—*continued.*

CLASS B.—PREPARATION AND SUPPLY OF MATERIAL SUBSTANCES—*continued.*

SUB-CLASS III.—INDUSTRY.—*continued*

Order 11.—Chemical products properly so called, and analogous—*continued.*

Province; and State, District, or City.	51.—Manufacture of aerated and mineral waters.						52.—Manufactures of dyes, paint, and ink.						53.—Manufacture and refining of vegetable and mineral oils.						54.—Manufacture of paper cardboard and papier maché.					
	Total workers and dependants.	Actual workers. Total.		Actual workers. Partially agriculturists.		Dependants.	Total workers and dependants.	Actual workers. Total.		Actual workers. Partially agriculturists.		Dependants.	Total workers and dependants.	Actual workers. Total.		Actual workers. Partially agriculturists.		Dependants.	Total workers and dependants.	Actual workers. Total.		Actual workers. Partially agriculturists.		Dependants.
	Both sexes.	Males.	Females.	Males.	Females.	Both sexes.	Both sexes.	Males.	Females.	Males.	Females.	Both sexes.	Both sexes.	Males.	Females.	Males.	Females.	Both sexes.	Both sexes.	Males.	Females.	Males.	Females.	Both sexes.
1	408	409	410	411	412	413	414	415	416	417	418	419	420	421	422	423	424	425	426	427	428	429	430	431
Rajputana	**73**	**31**	**6**	..	..	**36**	**963**	**206**	**434**	**7**	**4**	**343**	**43,410**	**16,602**	**6,474**	**5,775**	**742**	**20,334**	**367**	**106**	**76**	**7**	..	**191**
Alwar	..	..	..	..	..	..	70	22	1	..	..	47	2,071	1,074	423	280	53	1,474	26	6	..	..	..	20
Banswara	..	..	..	..	..	..	..	..	..	..	..	..	517	156	130	109	34	231	..	..	..	..	..	..
Bharatpur	..	..	..	..	..	..	..	..	..	..	..	..	3,546	1,303	768	532	95	1,175	..	..	..	..	..	..
Bikaner	..	..	..	..	..	..	1	1	..	..	..	..	1,488	560	121	316	42	807	..	..	..	..	..	..
Bundi	..	..	..	..	..	..	2	..	2	..	..	..	2,028	780	112	94	1	1,186	..	..	..	..	..	..
Dholpur	1	1	..	..	..	..	27	17	..	6	..	10	1,706	709	240	292	10	757	..	..	..	..	..	..
Dungarpur	..	..	..	..	..	..	..	..	..	..	..	..	773	224	132	100	11	417	..	..	..	..	..	..
Jaipur	1	..	1	..	..	..	267	80	47	1	1	140	8,000	3,160	1,421	646	67	3,470	101	35	68	..	..	88
Jaisalmer	..	..	..	..	..	..	..	..	..	..	..	..	46	14	..	11	..	32	..	..	..	..	..	..
Jhalawar	..	..	..	..	..	..	..	..	..	..	..	..	260	107	27	23	..	120	1	..	..	..	..	1
Karauli	..	..	..	..	..	..	4	..	..	..	..	4	300	126	46	70	5	128	5	5	..	..	..	..
Kishangarh	..	..	..	..	..	..	..	..	..	..	..	..	345	130	39	57	4	176	21	9	3	..	..	12
Kotah	38	17	..	..	..	21	26	13	6	..	..	7	2,999	1,081	516	261	40	1,402	100	40	4	7	..	56
Kushalgarh (Chiefship)	..	..	..	..	..	..	..	..	..	..	..	..	56	15	9	..	..	32	..	..	..	..	..	..
Lawa (Estate)	..	..	..	..	..	..	..	..	..	..	..	..	5	1	2	..	..	2	..	..	..	..	..	..
Marwar	20	12	..	..	..	8	111	35	..	..	..	76	7,701	3,250	606	1,668	175	3,812	..	..	..	..	..	..
Mewar	11	..	5	..	..	6	333	6	289	..	3	38	7,202	2,728	1,051	1,110	147	3,123	1	..	..	..	..	1
Partabgarh	..	..	..	..	..	..	1	1	..	..	..	..	291	102	51	30	2	138	10	5	1	..	..	13
Shahpura (Chiefship)	..	..	..	..	..	..	..	..	..	..	..	..	211	101	29	80	18	111	..	..	..	..	..	..
Sirohi	2	1	..	..	..	1	96	16	75	..	..	5	573	109	161	42	7	210	..	..	..	..	..	..
Tonk	..	..	..	..	..	..	45	15	14	..	..	16	2,285	821	500	151	51	874	..	..	..	..	..	..
Ajmer-Merwara	**260**	**162**	..	**34**	..	**98**	**74**	**22**	**17**	..	..	**35**	**2,188**	**843**	**487**	**362**	**98**	**856**	**1**	**1**	..	..	..	..
Ajmer	260	162	..	34	..	98	45	12	16	..	..	17	1,669	650	380	300	84	630	1	1	..	..	..	..
Merwara	..	..	..	..	..	..	20	10	1	..	..	18	510	193	107	53	14	210	..	..	..	..	..	..
CITIES.																								
Rajputana	**58**	**29**	..	..	..	**29**	**362**	**114**	**30**	..	..	**218**	**1,726**	**620**	**159**	**11**	**13**	**947**	**109**	**39**	**5**	**4**	..	**65**
Alwar	..	..	..	..	..	..	38	7	..	..	..	31	151	53	20	..	..	78	10	..	..	..	..	10
Bharatpur	..	..	..	..	..	..	..	..	..	..	..	..	165	60	29	3	..	87	..	..	..	..	..	..
Bikaner	..	..	..	..	..	..	..	..	..	..	..	..	365	122	23	..	..	220	..	..	..	..	..	..
Jaipur	..	..	..	..	..	..	168	53	15	..	..	100	250	100	21	..	..	129	6	4	1	..	..	1
Jodhpur	20	12	..	..	..	8	98	30	..	..	..	68	430	133	33	8	13	264	..	..	..	..	..	..
Kotah	38	17	..	..	..	21	13	9	1	..	..	3	36	26	..	..	..	10	93	35	4	1	..	54
Tonk	..	..	..	..	..	..	45	15	14	..	..	16	208	70	21	..	..	105	..	..	..	..	..	..
Udaipur	..	..	..	..	..	..	..	..	..	..	..	..	92	29	9	..	..	54	..	..	..	..	..	..
Ajmer-Merwara—																								
Ajmer	260	162	..	34	..	98	30	4	11	..	..	10	301	107	65	51	2	129	1	1	..	..	..	..

TABLE XV-A.—OCCUPATION, OR MEANS OF LIVELIHOOD. PART II.—BY STATE OR DISTRICT, AND CITY—*continued.*

CLASS B.—PREPARATION AND SUPPLY OF MATERIAL SUBSTANCES—*continued.* SUB-CLASS III.—INDUSTRY—*continued.*

Order 11.—Chemical products properly so called and analogous—*concluded.* 55.—Others (soap, candles, lac, cutch, perfumes, and miscellaneous drugs). Order 12.—Food-Industries.

Province; and State, District, or City.	55.—Total workers and dependants. Both sexes.	55.—Actual workers. Total. Males.	55.—Actual workers. Total. Females.	55.—Partially agriculturists. Males.	55.—Partially agriculturists. Females.	55.—Dependants. Both sexes.	Total Order 12. Total workers and dependants. Both sexes.	Total Order 12. Actual workers. Total. Males.	Total Order 12. Actual workers. Total. Females.	Total Order 12. Partially agriculturists. Males.	Total Order 12. Partially agriculturists. Females.	Total Order 12. Dependants. Both sexes.	56.—Rice pounders and huskers and flour grinders. Total workers and dependants. Both sexes.	56.—Actual workers. Total. Males.	56.—Actual workers. Total. Females.	56.—Partially agriculturists. Males.	56.—Partially agriculturists. Females.	56.—Dependants. Both sexes.	57.—Bakers and biscuit makers. Total workers and dependants. Both sexes.	57.—Actual workers. Total. Males.	57.—Actual workers. Total. Females.	57.—Partially agriculturists. Males.	57.—Partially agriculturists. Females.	57.—Dependants. Both sexes.
1	432	433	434	435	436	437	438	439	440	441	442	443	444	445	446	447	448	449	450	451	452	453	454	455
Rajputana	213	75	18	1	1	120	64,449	16,497	20,712	1,839	544	27,329	20,372	415	16,040	8	253	3,917	401	109	16	29	..	216
Alwar	..	..	..	..	..	..	3,903	1,095	1,143	131	25	1,665	1,166	33	881	..	17	252	..	..	..	..	..	..
Banswara	..	..	..	..	..	..	460	22	330	..	4	108	408	3	326	..	4	79	..	..	..	..	..	..
Bharatpur	14	6	..	..	..	8	3,763	641	1,872	107	112	1,250	2,199	50	1,652	5	77	407	50	18	..	..	..	38
Bikaner	24	7	..	..	..	17	2,818	421	1,499	216	92	898	1,052	14	1,304	..	9	334	..	..	..	..	..	..
Bundi	2	1	..	..	..	1	1,345	349	843	10	5	653	334	..	281	..	4	53	..	..	..	..	..	..
Dholpur	..	..	..	..	..	..	1,784	318	777	31	9	689	827	1	670	..	7	156	38	9	..	..	..	20
Dungarpur	..	..	..	..	..	..	2,802	771	486	230	24	1,545	326	3	235	..	..	88	..	..	..	..	..	..
Jaipur	33	12	1	..	..	20	20,989	6,241	5,568	455	70	9,180	4,404	157	3,511	1	18	820	193	109	4	29	..	79
Jaisalmer	..	..	..	..	..	..	375	38	218	3	1	110	272	4	218	..	1	50	..	..	..	..	..	..
Jhalawar	9	4	1	..	..	4	659	100	364	4	21	195	386	5	339	..	19	42	2	..	2	..	..	..
Karauli	..	..	..	..	..	..	650	210	180	1	3	200	198	..	168	..	3	30	..	..	..	..	..	..
Kishangarh	6	3	..	..	..	3	312	67	125	3	1	120	145	1	114	..	1	30	..	..	..	..	..	..
Kotah	11	8	..	..	..	3	3,633	899	1,324	76	23	1,410	1,255	28	1,037	2	18	190	7	4	..	..	..	3
Kushalgarh (Chiefship)	..	..	..	..	..	..	291	78	69	4	..	144	51	..	42	..	..	9	..	..	..	..	..	..
Lawa (Estate)	..	..	..	..	..	..	6	3	2	..	..	1	..	..	..	..	..	..	..	..	..	..	..	..
Marwar	72	26	10	..	..	36	7,338	1,662	2,187	85	32	3,489	2,325	48	1,771	..	17	506	21	8	..	..	..	13
Mewar	7	1	..	..	..	6	8,762	2,457	2,598	420	94	3,707	2,401	33	2,057	..	48	401	38	9	10	..	..	19
Partabgarh	..	..	..	..	..	..	467	86	178	..	..	204	221	..	171	..	..	50	..	..	..	..	..	..
Shahpura (Chiefship)	..	..	..	..	..	..	179	69	18	5	1	92	18	..	17	..	1	1	..	..	..	..	..	..
Sirohi	33	6	6	1	1	21	1,557	201	897	1	9	450	1,069	31	835	..	9	203	47	12	..	..	..	35
Tonk	2	1	..	..	..	1	2,356	679	535	33	2	1,142	535	4	411	..	..	130	..	..	..	..	..	..
Ajmer-Merwara	1	..	..	..	..	1	3,530	880	1,176	10	8	1,474	1,457	42	1,053	..	6	362	159	67	21	..	..	71
Ajmer	1	..	..	..	..	1	3,175	827	1,005	10	7	1,343	1,271	34	911	..	5	323	141	66	7	..	..	68
Merwara	..	..	..	..	..	..	355	53	171	..	1	131	186	8	139	..	1	39	18	1	14	..	..	3
CITIES.																								
Rajputana	55	21	..	..	..	34	11,206	2,360	4,519	9	8	4,320	4,898	57	3,986	..	6	855	121	37	13	..	..	71
Alwar	..	..	..	..	..	..	1,033	251	374	..	6	408	447	12	340	..	6	86	..	..	..	..	..	..
Bharatpur	8	3	..	..	..	5	897	116	451	3	2	330	569	5	437	..	..	127	56	18	..	..	..	38
Bikaner	24	7	..	..	..	17	822	55	509	..	..	258	602	3	480	..	..	119	..	..	..	..	..	..
Jaipur	1	1	..	..	..	..	3,790	1,001	1,249	2	..	1,540	1,392	20	1,081	..	..	281	9	2	3	..	..	4
Jodhpur	11	3	..	..	..	8	1,554	317	498	..	..	739	532	10	404	..	..	118	12	5	..	..	..	7
Kotah	9	6	..	..	..	3	1,015	246	474	2	..	295	493	4	428	..	..	61	7	4	..	..	..	3
Tonk	2	1	..	..	..	1	954	241	330	2	..	383	311	2	258	..	..	51	..	..	..	..	..	..
Udaipur	..	..	..	..	..	..	1,143	142	634	..	..	367	662	1	540	..	..	112	37	8	10	..	..	19
Ajmer-Merwara— Ajmer	1	..	..	..	..	1	2,032	573	564	..	..	895	734	23	525	..	..	187	68	47	5	..	..	16

TABLE XV-A.—OCCUPATION OR MEANS OF LIVELIHOOD. PART II.—BY STATE OR DISTRICT, AND CITY—*continued*.

Province; and State, District, or City.	CLASS B.—PREPARATION AND SUPPLY OF MATERIAL SUBSTANCES—*continued*. SUB-CLASS III.—INDUSTRY—*continued*. Order 12.—Food-Industries—*continued*.																							
	58.—Grain parchers, etc.						59.—Butchers.						60.—Fish curers.						61.—Butter, cheese, and ghee makers.					
	Total workers and dependants.	Actual workers. Total.		Actual workers. Partially agriculturists.		Dependants.	Total workers and dependants.	Actual workers. Total.		Actual workers. Partially agriculturists.		Dependants.	Total workers and dependants.	Actual workers. Total.		Actual workers. Partially agriculturists.		Dependants.	Total workers and dependants.	Actual workers. Total.		Actual workers. Partially agriculturists.		Dependants.
	Both sexes.	Males.	Females.	Males.	Females.	Both sexes.	Both sexes.	Males.	Females.	Males.	Females.	Both sexes.	Both sexes.	Males.	Females.	Males.	Females.	Both sexes.	Both sexes.	Males.	Females.	Males.	Females.	Both sexes.
1	456	457	458	459	460	461	462	463	464	465	466	467	468	469	470	471	472	473	474	475	476	477	478	479
Rajputana	**4,462**	**1,659**	**1,093**	**223**	**55**	**1,716**	**21,016**	**6,912**	**2,238**	**904**	**172**	**11,866**	**66**	**32**	**4**	**19**	..	**30**	**129**	**35**	**62**	**3**	..	**32**
Alwar	641	238	174	45	7	229	1,050	309	74	76	11	613	..	..	..	..	..	..	1	..	..	..	..	1
Banswara	..	..	..	..	..	..	26	8	..	..	..	18	..	..	..	..	..	..	..	..	..	..	..	..
Bharatpur	839	340	206	80	35	294	505	145	3	9	..	357	..	..	..	..	..	..	1	1	..	..	..	..
Bikaner	167	53	64	16	3	50	909	287	127	159	80	495	..	..	..	..	..	..	2	..	1	..	..	1
Bundi	66	24	6	..	..	36	758	231	50	15	1	477	..	..	..	..	..	..	2	..	..	..	..	2
Dholpur	390	129	100	27	2	161	310	88	3	4	..	219	..	..	..	..	..	..	..	..	..	..	..	..
Dungarpur	16	..	..	..	..	16	246	73	4	..	..	169	..	..	..	..	..	..	..	..	..	..	..	..
Jaipur	1,384	514	365	32	3	455	8,538	2,830	1,212	267	44	4,496	..	..	..	..	..	..	44	10	11	..	..	23
Jaisalmer	13	8	..	3	..	10	46	13	..	..	..	33	..	..	..	..	..	..	..	..	..	..	..	..
Jhalawar	38	8	11	..	..	17	120	43	11	4	2	75	..	..	..	..	..	..	..	..	..	..	..	..
Karauli	12	6	1	..	..	5	76	32	8	1	..	36	..	..	..	..	..	..	..	..	..	..	..	..
Kishangarh	62	26	3	1	..	33	45	16	2	1	..	27	..	..	..	..	..	..	..	..	..	..	..	..
Kotah	158	54	33	5	1	71	1,503	472	180	30	4	851	..	..	..	..	..	..	25	15	10	3	..	..
Kushalgarh (Chiefship)	1	..	..	..	..	1	12	2	2	..	..	8	..	..	..	..	..	..	..	..	..	..	..	..
Lawa (Estate)	5	2	2	..	..	1	..	..	..	..	..	..	..	..	..	..	..	..	..	..	..	..	..	..
Marwar	481	160	81	10	4	231	3,156	945	297	68	9	1,014	..	..	..	..	..	..	5	4	..	..	..	1
Mewar	89	33	13	3	..	43	2,496	952	170	255	19	1,365	..	..	..	..	..	..	2	1	..	..	..	1
Partabgarh	20	8	2	..	..	10	39	14	..	..	..	25	..	..	..	..	..	..	..	..	..	..	..	..
Shahpura (Chiefship)	1	..	1	..	..	..	34	12	..	2	..	22	..	..	..	..	..	..	..	..	..	..	..	..
Sirohi	29	12	2	..	..	15	167	51	5	..	..	111	..	..	..	..	..	..	46	3	40	..	..	3
Tonk	102	40	29	1	..	33	965	329	81	13	2	555	66	32	4	19	..	30	1	1	..	..	..	..
Ajmer-Merwara	**301**	**104**	**69**	**4**	**2**	**128**	**961**	**305**	**27**	**4**	..	**649**	..	..	..	..	..	..	**1**	..	..	..	..	**1**
Ajmer	260	90	54	4	2	116	881	275	25	4	..	581	..	..	..	..	..	..	1	..	..	..	..	1
Merwara	41	14	15	..	..	12	100	30	2	..	..	68	..	..	..	..	..	..	..	..	..	..	..	..
CITIES.																								
Rajputana	**468**	**165**	**108**	**2**	**2**	**195**	**3,106**	**887**	**368**	**4**	..	**1,856**	..	..	..	..	..	..	**12**	**5**	..	..	..	**7**
Alwar	46	15	10	..	..	21	167	54	9	..	..	104	..	..	..	..	..	..	..	..	..	..	..	..
Bharatpur	43	16	11	2	2	18	181	49	..	1	..	132	..	..	..	..	..	..	1	1	..	..	..	..
Bikaner	38	7	15	..	..	16	172	37	14	..	..	121	..	..	..	..	..	..	..	..	..	..	..	..
Jaipur	160	60	39	..	..	61	1,055	323	101	1	..	632	..	..	..	..	..	..	7	..	..	..	..	7
Jodhpur	59	19	8	..	..	32	683	164	79	..	..	440	..	..	..	..	..	..	..	..	..	..	..	..
Kotah	30	12	5	..	..	18	296	94	40	..	..	162	..	..	..	..	..	..	4	4	..	..	..	..
Tonk	69	25	15	..	..	29	313	105	55	2	..	153	..	..	..	..	..	..	..	..	..	..	..	..
Udaipur	23	11	5	..	..	7	239	68	65	..	..	112	..	..	..	..	..	..	..	..	..	..	..	..
Ajmer-Merwara—																								
Ajmer	122	32	22	..	..	68	505	132	7	..	..	366	..	..	..	..	..	..	..	..	..	..	..	..

TABLE XV-A.—Occupation or Means of Livelihood. Part II.—By State or District, and City—*continued.*

CLASS B.—PREPARATION AND SUPPLY OF MATERIAL SUBSTANCES—*continued.*

Sub-Class III.—Industry—*continued.*

Order 12.—Food-Industries—*concluded.*

Province; and State, District, or City.	62.—Makers of sugar, molasses, and gur. Total workers and dependants. Both sexes.	62. Actual workers. Total. Males.	62. Actual workers. Total. Females.	62. Actual workers. Partially agriculturists. Males.	62. Actual workers. Partially agriculturists. Females.	62. Dependants. Both sexes.	63.—Sweetmeat makers, preparers of jam and condiments, etc. Total workers and dependants. Both sexes.	63. Actual workers. Total. Males.	63. Actual workers. Total. Females.	63. Actual workers. Partially agriculturists. Males.	63. Actual workers. Partially agriculturists. Females.	63. Dependants. Both sexes.	64.—Brewers and distillers. Total workers and dependants. Both sexes.	64. Actual workers. Total. Males.	64. Actual workers. Total. Females.	64. Actual workers. Partially agriculturists. Males.	64. Actual workers. Partially agriculturists. Females.	64. Dependants. Both sexes.	65.—Toddy drawers. Total workers and dependants. Both sexes.	65. Actual workers. Total. Males.	65. Actual workers. Total. Females.	65. Dependants. Both sexes.	66.—Manufacturer of tobacco, opium and ganja. Total workers and dependants. Both sexes.	66. Actual workers. Total. Males.	66. Actual workers. Total. Females.	66. Actual workers. Partially agriculturists. Males.	66. Actual workers. Partially agriculturists. Females.	66. Dependants. Both sexes.
1	480	481	482	483	484	485	486	487	488	489	490	491	492	493	494	495	496	497	498	499	500	501	502	503	504	505	506	507
Rajputana	220	73	52	1	..	95	8,998	3,875	151	78	2	4,972	8,570	3,114	1,046	565	62	4,410	14	12	..	2	201	111	11	8	..	79
Alwar	..	..	..	..	..	..	1,039	455	14	10	..	570	..	..	..	..	..	..	..	..	..	..	..	..	..	..	..	..
Banswara	..	..	..	..	..	..	25	10	4	..	..	11	1	1	..	..	..	..	..	..	..	..	..	..	..	..	..	..
Bharatpur	50	25	8	1	..	17	70	41	3	6	..	26	3	..	..	..	..	3	..	..	..	..	40	21	..	6	..	19
Bikaner	..	..	..	..	..	..	23	7	3	..	..	13	65	60	..	41	..	5	..	..	..	..	..	..	..	..	..	..
Bundi	..	..	..	..	..	..	132	71	..	3	..	61	50	22	4	1	..	24	..	..	..	..	3	1	2	..	..	..
Dholpur	40	16	..	..	..	24	158	66	1	..	..	91	21	9	3	..	..	9	..	..	..	..	..	..	..	..	..	..
Dungarpur	..	..	..	..	..	..	..	..	..	..	..	..	2,214	695	247	236	24	1,272	..	..	..	..	..	..	..	..	..	..
Jaipur	..	..	..	..	..	..	4,037	1,746	49	41	..	2,242	2,328	859	412	85	11	1,057	14	12	..	2	8	4	4	..	..	..
Jaisalmer	..	..	..	..	..	..	44	18	..	..	..	26	..	..	..	..	..	..	..	..	..	..	..	..	..	..	..	..
Jhalawar	..	..	..	..	..	..	77	36	1	..	..	40	21	6	..	..	..	15	..	..	..	..	8	2	..	..	..	6
Karauli	..	..	..	..	..	..	363	171	3	..	..	180	1	1	..	..	..	..	..	..	..	..	..	..	..	..	..	..
Kishangarh	..	..	..	..	..	..	26	6	5	1	..	15	34	18	1	..	..	15	..	..	..	..	..	..	..	..	..	..
Kotah	1	1	..	..	..	..	213	135	11	5	..	67	389	129	53	29	..	207	..	..	..	..	82	61	..	2	..	21
Kushalgarh (Chiefship)	..	..	..	..	..	..	25	9	1	..	..	15	202	67	24	4	..	111	..	..	..	..	..	..	..	..	..	..
Lawa (Estate)	..	..	..	..	..	..	..	..	..	..	..	..	1	1	..	..	..	..	..	..	..	..	..	..	..	..	..	..
Marwar	..	..	..	..	..	..	1,103	412	23	1	2	668	239	75	12	6	..	152	..	..	..	..	8	1	3	..	..	4
Mewar	71	..	41	..	..	30	693	298	8	2	..	387	2,870	1,126	290	160	27	1,454	..	..	..	..	12	5	..	..	..	7
Partabgarh	..	..	..	..	..	..	159	53	5	..	..	101	..	..	..	..	..	..	..	..	..	..	28	11	..	..	..	17
Shahpura (Chiefship)	..	..	..	..	..	..	85	39	..	..	..	46	41	18	..	3	..	23	..	..	..	..	..	..	..	..	..	..
Sirohi	58	31	3	..	..	24	125	54	10	1	..	61	4	2	..	..	..	2	..	..	..	..	12	5	2	..	..	5
Tonk	..	..	..	..	..	..	601	248	10	..	..	343	86	25	..	..	..	61	..	..	..	..	..	..	..	..	..	..
Ajmer-Merwara	1	1	..	..	..	..	616	353	5	1	..	258	14	8	1	1	..	5	..	..	..	..	..	..	..	..	..	..
Ajmer	1	1	..	..	..	..	606	353	4	1	..	249	14	8	1	1	..	5	..	..	..	..	..	..	..	..	..	..
Merwara	..	..	..	..	..	..	10	..	1	..	..	9	..	..	..	..	..	..	..	..	..	..	..	..	..	..	..	..
CITIES.																												
Rajputana	14	6	..	..	..	8	2,072	1,021	39	1	..	1,012	322	125	6	..	..	191	..	..	..	..	95	66	4	2	..	25
Alwar	..	..	..	..	..	..	373	170	6	..	..	197	..	..	..	..	..	..	..	..	..	..	..	..	..	..	..	..
Bharatpur	14	6	..	..	..	8	24	16	3	..	..	5	..	..	..	..	..	..	..	..	..	..	9	5	..	..	..	4
Bikaner	..	..	..	..	..	..	..	..	..	..	..	..	10	8	..	..	..	2	..	..	..	..	..	..	..	..	..	..
Jaipur	..	..	..	..	..	..	1,119	559	20	1	..	540	51	35	1	..	..	15	..	..	..	..	7	3	4	..	..	..
Jodhpur	..	..	..	..	..	..	268	119	7	..	..	142	..	..	..	..	..	..	..	..	..	..	..	..	..	..	..	..
Kotah	..	..	..	..	..	..	92	63	1	..	..	28	14	7	..	..	..	7	..	..	..	..	79	58	..	2	..	21
Tonk	..	..	..	..	..	..	195	94	2	..	..	99	66	15	..	..	..	51	..	..	..	..	..	..	..	..	..	..
Udaipur	..	..	..	..	..	..	1	..	..	..	..	1	181	60	5	..	..	116	..	..	..	..	..	..	..	..	..	..
Ajmer-Merwara—																												
Ajmer	1	1	..	..	..	..	571	339	4	..	..	228	1	..	1	..	..	..	..	..	..	..	..	..	..	..	..	..

TABLE XV-A.—OCCUPATION OR MEANS OF LIVELIHOOD. PART II.—BY STATE OR DISTRICT, AND CITY.—*continued.*

CLASS B.—PREPARATION AND SUPPLY OF MATERIAL SUBSTANCES—*continued.*

SUB-CLASS III.—INDUSTRY—*continued.*

Order 13.—Industries of dress and the toilet.

Province; and State, District, or City.	Total Order 13.						67—Hat, cap, and turban makers.						68.—Tailors, milliners, dress makers, darners, embroiderers on linen.						69.—Shoe, boot and sandal makers, and embroiderers on shoes.					
	Total workers and dependants.	Actual workers.				Dependants.	Total workers and dependants.	Actual workers.				Dependants.	Total workers and dependants.	Actual workers.				Dependants.	Total workers and dependants.	Actual workers.				Dependants.
		Total.		Partially agriculturists.				Total.		Partially agriculturists.				Total.		Partially agriculturists.				Total.		Partially agriculturists.		
	Both sexes.	Males.	Females.	Males.	Females.	Both sexes.	Both sexes.	Males.	Females.	Males.	Females.	Both sexes.	Both sexes.	Males.	Females.	Males.	Females.	Both sexes.	Both sexes.	Males.	Females.	Males.	Females.	Both sexes.
1	508	509	510	511	512	513	514	515	516	517	518	519	520	521	522	523	524	525	526	527	528	529	530	531
Rajputana	**334,507**	**130,417**	**56,235**	**31,316**	**3,843**	**147,855**	**274**	**61**	**73**	**4**	..	**140**	**52,999**	**18,953**	**15,232**	**2,416**	**619**	**18,814**	**125,561**	**47,943**	**18,345**	**12,278**	**1,297**	**59,213**
Alwar	24,350	8,651	5,455	2,159	577	10,244	213	35	62	4	..	116	2,653	907	785	82	20	961	13,213	4,505	3,307	1,146	387	5,311
Banswara	2,737	930	438	367	43	1,369	..	..	..	..	..	..	905	323	321	60	17	351	724	245	77	168	26	402
Bharatpur	16,265	6,317	2,504	2,142	249	7,354	..	..	..	..	..	..	2,139	751	649	135	33	749	3,888	1,110	526	484	56	1,952
Bikaner	15,884	6,217	3,150	2,458	516	6,517	..	..	..	..	..	..	2,808	1,025	841	145	41	1,032	4,576	1,854	706	631	96	1,926
Bundi	6,116	2,271	682	259	7	3,163	..	..	..	..	..	..	845	309	223	11	..	313	1,358	487	93	73	..	778
Dholpur	8,013	3,410	1,474	1,077	119	3,720	..	..	..	..	..	..	827	332	187	57	3	308	1,130	458	166	125	7	515
Dungarpur	3,345	1,133	511	236	34	1,701	..	..	..	..	..	..	1,204	425	420	100	33	446	531	101	54	77	1	283
Jaipur	94,070	37,371	18,670	5,272	700	38,029	15	4	3	..	..	8	10,234	3,770	3,182	127	38	3,273	40,031	15,634	8,596	2,259	454	16,401
Jaisalmer	5,258	1,586	85	671	8	3,587	..	..	..	..	..	..	960	296	40	96	1	624	3,302	946	81	620	6	2,325
Jhalawar	3,299	1,344	619	195	16	1,436	6	1	..	..	..	5	774	293	167	13	..	314	1,100	493	77	105	1	530
Karauli	3,295	1,370	550	332	36	1,375	..	..	..	..	..	..	281	111	87	7	1	83	804	325	146	74	8	333
Kishangarh	3,373	1,240	725	345	20	1,408	..	..	..	..	..	..	453	154	154	18	2	145	663	254	44	137	5	365
Kotah	20,186	7,737	3,518	1,592	222	8,931	1	1	..	..	..	..	2,588	955	702	92	19	841	6,071	2,414	416	564	28	3,241
Kushalgarh (Chiefship)	339	115	33	18	..	191	..	..	..	..	..	..	69	20	18	..	..	31	216	73	11	10	..	132
Lawa (Estate)	49	24	6	4	..	19	4	1	3	..	..	..	10	5	1	..	..	4	3	1	..	..	..	2
Marwar	64,320	25,476	9,573	7,791	696	29,271	12	6	..	..	..	4	14,835	5,208	4,270	1,102	332	5,258	22,307	8,823	2,335	2,512	137	11,239
Mewar	40,759	16,641	4,846	4,726	337	19,272	..	..	..	..	..	..	6,417	2,310	1,856	208	54	2,251	16,810	6,675	713	2,610	59	9,422
Partabgarh	1,423	582	235	115	18	606	21	9	5	..	..	7	554	190	149	21	4	206	183	76	20	17	7	87
Shahpura (Chiefship)	1,842	714	348	274	55	780	..	..	..	..	..	..	207	69	55	10	3	83	325	152	1	81	..	172
Sirohi	8,123	2,988	960	356	13	4,175	2	2	..	..	..	..	1,617	553	431	22	1	630	4,080	1,587	311	237	9	2,188
Tonk	10,861	4,300	1,863	727	92	4,698	..	..	..	..	..	..	2,349	836	602	44	8	911	3,406	1,337	532	322	12	1,597
Ajmer-Merwara	**18,230**	**6,954**	**2,791**	**1,090**	**141**	**8,485**	..	..	..	..	..	..	**3,273**	**1,251**	**832**	**74**	**15**	**1,190**	**5,095**	**2,000**	**285**	**274**	**4**	**2,810**
Ajmer	14,937	5,727	2,206	876	132	7,004	..	..	..	..	..	..	2,700	1,031	626	56	11	1,040	4,250	1,684	211	239	4	2,355
Merwara	3,293	1,227	585	214	9	1,481	..	..	..	..	..	..	573	217	206	18	4	150	845	316	74	35	..	456
CITIES.																								
Rajputana	**22,970**	**8410**	**5,519**	**51**	**3**	**9,041**	**173**	**14**	**54**	..	..	**105**	**6,161**	**2,207**	**1,828**	..	**1**	**2,126**	**7,446**	**2,810**	**1,534**	**26**	**3**	**3,102**
Alwar	2,010	801	481	11	2	1,238	158	10	51	..	..	97	423	152	85	..	..	186	1,252	437	218	5	2	597
Bharatpur	1,624	619	343	21	..	662	..	..	..	..	..	..	371	136	94	..	..	144	308	135	60	11	..	173
Bikaner	3,190	1,079	769	9	..	1,342	..	..	..	..	..	..	1,082	356	338	..	..	388	922	335	170	..	..	417
Jaipur	6,760	2,717	1,705	4	..	2,338	15	4	3	..	..	8	1,664	617	520	..	..	527	2,623	1,057	579	4	..	987
Jodhpur	4,471	1,424	1,244	1	..	1,803	..	..	..	..	..	..	1,322	484	382	..	..	456	1,174	398	287	..	..	489
Kotah	1,461	578	312	1	..	571	..	..	..	..	..	..	408	155	101	..	..	152	371	150	60	..	..	143
Tonk	1,644	637	372	4	1	635	..	..	..	..	..	..	445	141	151	..	1	153	506	210	93	3	..	203
Udaipur	1,210	465	293	..	..	452	..	..	..	..	..	..	443	166	157	..	..	120	230	70	58	..	..	93
Ajmer-Merwara—																								
Ajmer	4,727	1,704	610	..	..	2,413	..	..	..	..	..	..	1,206	480	203	..	..	583	1,187	428	79		..	680

TABLE XV-A.—OCCUPATION, OR MEANS OF LIVELIHOOD. PART II.—BY STATE OR DISTRICT, AND CITY.—*continued*

CLASS B.—PREPARATION AND SUPPLY OF MATERIAL SUBSTANCES—*continued*.

SUB-CLASS III.—INDUSTRY—*continued*.

Order 13.—Industries of dress and the toilet—*continued*.

Province; and State, District, or City.	70.—Other industries pertaining to dress, gloves, socks, gaiters, belts, buttons, umbrellas, canes, tinsel, etc.						71.—Washing and cleaning of clothes.						71.—(a) Dyeing of made up articles of clothing.						72.—Barbers, hairdressers, and wig makers.					
	Total workers and dependants.	Actual workers. Total.		Actual workers. Partially agriculturists.		Dependants.	Total workers and dependants.	Actual workers. Total.		Actual workers. Partially agriculturists.		Dependants.	Total workers and dependants.	Actual workers. Total		Actual workers. Partially agriculturists.		Dependants.	Total workers and dependants	Actual workers. Total.		Actual workers. Partially agriculturists.		Dependants.
	Both sexes.	Males.	Females.	Males.	Females.	Both sexes.	Both sexes.	Males.	Females.	Males.	Females.	Both sexes.	Both sexes.	Males.	Females.	Males.	Females.	Both sexes.	Both sexes.	Males.	Females.	Males.	Females.	Both sexes.
1	532	533	534	535	536	537	538	539	540	541	542	543	544	545	546	547	548	549	550	551	552	553	554	555
Rajputana	**980**	**347**	**206**	**30**	**16**	**427**	**35,968**	**12,534**	**10,900**	**2,761**	**992**	**12,534**	**10,386**	**2,980**	**3,795**	**356**	**73**	**3,602**	**108,191**	**47,552**	**7,569**	**13,470**	**856**	**53,670**
Alwar	24	5	8	3	4	11	3,293	1,018	1,053	290	143	1,222	..	..	..	..	..	..	4,973	2,181	140	634	14	2,623
Banswara	..	..	..	..	..	..	65	18	20	1	..	27	100	31	20	1	..	46	853	310	..	131	..	543
Bharatpur	3	1	..	..	..	2	2,565	876	785	240	81	904	1,114	459	204	77	12	451	6,555	2,810	440	1,197	67	3,206
Bikaner	..	..	..	..	..	..	708	245	108	46	7	355	..	..	..	..	..	..	7,642	3,003	1,345	1,636	372	3,204
Bundi	23	10	6	..	..	7	1,202	441	257	26	6	504	152	19	75	..	..	50	2,536	1,006	28	149	1	1,502
Dholpur	..	..	..	..	..	..	2,933	1,046	883	305	103	1,004	514	174	113	39	1	227	3,200	1,400	125	401	5	1,675
Dungarpur	6	2	..	..	..	4	136	39	21	..	..	76	130	42	11	..	..	74	1,248	428	2	59	..	818
Jaipur	25	11	4	..	..	10	9,757	3,620	3,127	637	206	3,010	1,828	177	1,338	..	27	263	31,511	14,114	2,364	2,240	65	15,033
Jaisalmer	..	..	..	..	..	..	48	11	10	..	..	27	..	..	..	..	..	..	948	333	4	155	1	611
Jhalawar	..	..	..	..	..	..	257	77	101	12	5	79	..	..	..	..	..	..	1,153	480	174	65	10	499
Karauli	3	1	1	..	..	1	735	275	229	90	20	231	..	..	..	..	..	..	1,472	658	87	161	..	727
Kishangarh	..	..	..	..	..	..	187	60	60	20	4	67	977	275	408	33	7	294	1,003	407	59	137	2	537
Kotah	32	1	22	..	..	9	2,991	916	1,026	189	110	1,049	1,566	610	408	45	2	548	6,933	2,839	854	682	63	3,240
Kushalgarh (Chiefship)	..	..	..	..	..	..	26	6	4	..	..	16	..	..	..	..	..	..	28	16	..	2	..	12
Lawa (Estate)	..	..	..	..	..	..	4	2	2	..	..	..	..	..	..	..	..	..	28	15	..	4	..	13
Marwar	533	214	79	24	..	240	2,869	936	849	140	53	1,084	2,423	635	772	106	7	1,016	21,251	9,562	1,259	3,838	167	10,430
Mewar	278	87	84	2	12	107	5,871	2,223	1,582	503	151	2,066	2	1	..	..	..	1	11,245	5,341	503	1,402	61	5,401
Partabgarh	..	..	..	..	..	..	14	7	3	..	..	4	237	81	58	9	2	95	414	207	..	68	..	207
Shahpura (Chiefship)	53	15	2	1	..	36	188	63	60	29	16	65	476	178	124	28	9	174	593	237	106	115	27	250
Sirohi	..	..	..	..	..	..	401	102	115	4	1	184	291	90	90	2	2	111	1,723	654	7	91	..	1,062
Tonk	..	..	..	..	..	..	1,658	553	545	121	67	560	576	212	121	6	4	243	2,812	1,362	63	234	1	1,387
Ajmer-Merwara	**14**	**5**	**4**	..	..	**5**	**2,532**	**993**	**539**	**154**	**53**	**1,010**	**2,495**	**777**	**694**	**46**	**13**	**1,024**	**4,810**	**1,921**	**447**	**542**	**56**	**2,442**
Ajmer	7	2	2	..	..	3	1,942	683	475	120	52	784	2,104	768	476	46	13	860	3,923	1,549	416	406	52	1,958
Merwara	7	3	2	..	..	2	590	310	54	25	1	226	391	9	218	..	..	164	887	372	31	136	4	484
CITIES.																								
Rajputana	**85**	**26**	**26**	..	..	**33**	**2,929**	**1,013**	**903**	**7**	..	**1 013**	**1,599**	**268**	**794**	**1**	..	**537**	**4,563**	**2,066**	**380**	**17**	..	**2,117**
Alwar	..	..	..	..	..	..	457	151	123	3	..	183	..	..	..	..	..	..	320	141	4	3	..	175
Bharatpur	..	..	..	..	..	..	291	104	97	1	..	90	175	74	36	1	..	65	416	170	56	5	..	190
Bikaner	..	..	..	..	..	..	284	81	74	1	..	129	..	..	..	..	..	..	902	307	187	8	..	408
Jaipur	..	..	..	..	..	..	873	320	290	..	..	264	356	49	260	..	..	47	1,215	655	63	..	..	497
Jodhpur	77	26	18	..	..	33	312	111	102	..	..	99	691	19	410	..	..	262	895	386	45	1	..	464
Kotah	8	..	8	..	..	..	202	71	70	1	..	61	208	65	52	..	..	91	264	128	12	..	..	124
Tonk	..	..	..	..	..	..	275	97	92	1	..	86	169	61	36	..	..	72	249	128	..	..	..	121
Udaipur	..	..	..	..	..	..	235	69	65	..	..	101	..	..	..	..	..	..	302	151	13	..	..	138
Ajmer-Merwara—																								
Ajmer	..	..	..	..	..	..	743	238	174	..	..	331	667	212	84	..	..	371	864	346	70	..	..	448

TABLE XV-A.—Occupation or Means of Livelihood. Part II.—By State or District, and City—*continued.*

Province; and State, District, or City.	CLASS B.—PREPARATION AND SUPPLY OF MATERIAL SUBSTANCES—*continued.*																							
	SUB-CLASS III.—INDUSTRY—*continued.*																							
	Order 13.—Industries of dress and the toilet—*concluded.*						Order 14.—Furniture Industries.																	
	73.—Other industries connected with the toilet (tattooers, shampooers, bath houses, etc.)						Total Order 14.						74.—Cabinet makers, carriage painters, and makers of all kinds of furniture (except of cane and bamboo).						75.—Upholsterers, tent makers, etc.					
	Total workers and dependants.	Actual workers.				Dependants.	Total workers and dependants.	Actual workers.				Dependants.	Total workers and dependants.	Actual workers.				Dependants.	Total workers and dependants.	Actual workers.				Dependants.
		Total.		Partially agriculturists.				Total.		Partially agriculturists.				Total.		Partially agriculturists.				Total.		Partially agriculturists.		
	Both sexes.	Males.	Females.	Males.	Females.	Both sexes.	Both sexes.	Males.	Females.	Males.	Females.	Both sexes.	Both sexes.	Males.	Females.	Males.	Females.	Both sexes.	Both sexes.	Males.	Females.	Males.	Females.	Both sexes.
1	556	557	558	559	560	561	562	563	564	565	566	567	568	569	570	571	572	573	574	575	576	577	578	579
Rajputana	208	38	115	1	..	55	228	94	16	4	..	118	182	81	14	3	..	87	46	13	2	1	..	31
Alwar	1	..	1	..	..	..	5	2	..	..	..	3	5	2	..	..	..	3	..	..	..	..	..	..
Banswara	..	..	..	..	..	..	2	2	..	..	..	..	2	2	..	..	..	..	..	..	..	..	..	..
Bharatpur	1	1	..	..	..	..	6	5	..	..	..	1	4	4	..	..	..	..	2	1	..	..	..	1
Bikaner	..	..	..	..	..	..	16	7	..	..	..	9	9	7	..	..	..	2	7	..	..	..	..	7
Bundi	..	..	..	..	..	..	7	4	..	..	..	3	7	4	..	..	..	3	..	..	..	..	..	..
Dholpur	..	..	..	..	..	..	..	..	..	..	..	..	..	..	..	..	..	..	..	..	..	..	..	..
Dungarpur	..	..	..	..	..	..	..	..	..	..	..	..	..	..	..	..	..	..	..	..	..	..	..	..
Jaipur	69	32	6	..	..	31	43	14	10	1	..	19	29	3	10	..	..	16	14	11	..	1	..	3
Jaisalmer	..	..	..	..	..	..	..	..	..	..	..	..	..	..	..	..	..	..	..	..	..	..	..	..
Jhalawar	..	..	..	..	..	..	5	1	..	..	..	4	5	1	..	..	..	4	..	..	..	..	..	..
Karauli	..	..	..	..	..	..	3	2	1	..	..	..	3	2	1	..	..	..	..	..	..	..	..	..
Kishangarh	..	..	..	..	..	..	..	..	..	..	..	..	..	..	..	..	..	..	..	..	..	..	..	..
Kotah	1	1	..	..	..	..	48	25	4	..	..	19	46	25	2	..	..	19	2	..	2	..	..	..
Kushalgarh (Chiefship)	..	..	..	..	..	..	..	..	..	..	..	..	..	..	..	..	..	..	..	..	..	..	..	..
Lawa (Estate)	..	..	..	..	..	..	..	..	..	..	..	..	..	..	..	..	..	..	..	..	..	..	..	..
Marwar	..	..	..	..	..	..	7	3	..	..	..	4	7	3	..	..	..	4	..	..	..	..	..	..
Mewar	136	4	108	1	..	24	31	6	..	3	..	25	10	5	..	3	..	5	21	1	..	..	..	20
Partabgarh	..	..	..	..	..	..	..	..	..	..	..	..	..	..	..	..	..	..	..	..	..	..	..	..
Shahpura (Chiefship)	..	..	..	..	..	..	1	1	..	..	..	..	1	1	..	..	..	..	..	..	..	..	..	..
Sirohi	..	..	..	..	..	..	47	20	1	..	..	26	47	20	1	..	..	26	..	..	..	..	..	..
Tonk	..	..	..	..	..	..	7	2	..	..	..	5	7	2	..	..	..	5	..	..	..	..	..	..
Ajmer-Merwara	11	7	..	..	..	4	..	..	..	..	..	..	..	..	..	..	..	..	..	..	..	..	..	..
Ajmer	11	7	..	..	..	4	..	..	..	..	..	..	..	..	..	..	..	..	..	..	..	..	..	..
Merwara	..	..	..	..	..	..	..	..	..	..	..	..	..	..	..	..	..	..	..	..	..	..	..	..
CITIES.																								
Rajputana	14	6	..	..	..	8	94	32	13	..	..	49	85	32	11	..	..	42	9	..	2	..	..	7
Alwar	..	..	..	..	..	..	5	2	..	..	..	3	5	2	..	..	..	3	..	..	..	..	..	..
Bharatpur	..	..	..	..	..	..	2	2	..	..	..	..	2	2	..	..	..	..	..	..	..	..	..	..
Bikaner	..	..	..	..	..	..	16	7	..	..	..	9	9	7	..	..	..	2	7	..	..	..	..	7
Jaipur	14	6	..	..	..	8	29	3	10	..	..	16	29	3	10	..	..	16	..	..	..	..	..	..
Jodhpur	..	..	..	..	..	..	5	2	..	..	..	3	5	2	..	..	..	3	..	..	..	..	..	..
Kotah	..	..	..	..	..	..	30	14	3	..	..	13	28	14	1	..	..	13	2	..	2	..	..	..
Tonk	..	..	..	..	..	..	7	2	..	..	..	5	7	2	..	..	..	5	..	..	..	..	..	..
Udaipur	..	..	..	..	..	..	..	..	..	..	..	..	..	..	..	..	..	..	..	..	..	..	..	..
Ajmer-Merwara—																								
Ajmer	..	..	..	..	..	..	..	..	..	..	..	..	..	..	..	..	..	..	..	..	..	..	..	..

TABLE XV-A.—Occupation or Means of Livelihood. Part II.—By State or District, and City—*continued.*

CLASS B.—PREPARATION AND SUPPLY OF MATERIAL SUBSTANCES—*continued.*

SUB-CLASS III.—INDUSTRY—*continued.*

Order 15.—Building Industries.

Province; and State, District, or City.	Total Order 15.						76.—Lime burners, cement workers.						77.—Excavators, plinth builders, and well sinkers.						78.—Stone and marble workers, masons, and bricklayers.					
	Total workers and dependants.	Actual workers.				Dependants.	Total workers and dependants.	Actual workers.				Dependants.	Total workers and dependants.	Actual workers.				Dependants.	Total workers and dependants.	Actual workers.				Dependants.
		Total.		Partially agriculturists.				Total.		Partially agriculturists.				Total.		Partially agriculturists.				Total.		Partially agriculturists.		
	Both sexes.	Males.	Females.	Males.	Females.	Both sexes.	Both sexes.	Males.	Females.	Males.	Females.	Both sexes.	Both sexes.	Males.	Females.	Males.	Females.	Both sexes.	Both sexes.	Males.	Females.	Males.	Females.	Both sexes.
1	580	581	582	583	584	585	586	587	588	589	590	591	592	593	594	595	596	597	598	599	600	601	602	603
Rajputana	**89,639**	**33,577**	**12,729**	**2,309**	**471**	**42,733**	**2,952**	**963**	**663**	**70**	**14**	**1,326**	**8,245**	**2,437**	**3,416**	**133**	**178**	**2,392**	**74,685**	**29,137**	**8,289**	**2,475**	**243**	**37,199**
Alwar	5,007	1,964	470	220	7	2,553	111	47	3	1	..	61	424	170	140	4	..	105	4,041	1,626	309	203	7	2,106
Banswara	433	175	..	53	..	258	..	..	..	..	..	..	..	..	..	..	..	..	433	175	..	53	..	258
Bharatpur	3,726	1,832	389	297	61	1,705	90	43	3	10	..	53	..	..	..	..	..	..	3,050	1,414	240	220	38	1,396
Bikaner	11,461	4,709	1,781	507	61	4,971	201	62	166	6	..	63	1,407	514	450	11	9	443	9,427	3,903	1,152	482	52	4,282
Bundi	1,113	414	69	8	..	630	67	17	7	..	..	43	146	44	39	..	..	63	732	352	14	8	..	366
Dholpur	2,165	844	171	55	..	1,150	124	17	85	..	..	22	304	130	51	2	..	114	1,542	605	21	49	..	916
Dungarpur	453	156	41	5	..	256	..	..	..	..	..	..	..	..	..	..	..	..	428	140	41	5	..	247
Jaipur	26,948	9,403	5,547	802	246	11,998	184	63	28	9	1	93	2,943	543	1,701	11	140	609	23,072	8,538	3,652	755	94	10,882
Jaisalmer	607	216	91	46	..	300	..	..	..	..	..	..	264	108	55	13	..	101	314	107	11	32	..	196
Jhalawar	830	291	120	27	13	419	17	6	..	..	..	11	11	..	11	..	..	..	802	285	109	27	13	408
Karauli	765	280	45	46	..	440	2	2	..	..	..	..	9	5	..	..	..	4	727	259	44	46	..	424
K'shangarh	994	371	282	10	..	791	39	15	6	..	..	18	..	..	..	..	..	..	946	356	226	10	..	364
Kotah	4,347	1,957	393	86	7	1,997	110	39	19	2	1	61	4	4	..	..	..	..	4,135	1,866	370	76	6	1,897
Kushalgarh (Chiefship)	67	21	6	1	..	40	..	..	..	..	..	..	1	1	..	..	..	..	66	20	6	1	..	40
Lawa (Estate)	4	3	1	..	..	..	..	..	..	..	..	..	..	..	..	..	..	..	3	2	1	..	..	..
Marwar	18,025	6,565	1,654	378	38	9,806	991	340	205	3	..	446	1,523	522	417	38	14	584	15,269	5,636	1,030	335	24	8,601
Mewar	7,494	2,681	1,148	167	29	3,665	612	215	87	30	11	310	936	223	424	11	14	309	5,681	2,170	610	125	4	2,901
Partabgarh	276	108	55	10	3	113	..	..	..	..	..	..	22	13	..	5	..	9	246	92	52	5	3	102
Shahpura (Chiefship)	245	110	16	50	3	119	..	..	..	..	..	..	92	55	9	36	1	28	146	50	6	12	2	90
Sirohi	2,446	1,009	257	15	..	1,180	189	65	22	4	..	102	78	58	5	..	..	15	2,126	861	226	10	..	1,089
Tonk	1,633	648	243	26	1	742	107	32	32	5	1	43	61	29	24	2	..	8	1,439	586	169	19	..	684
Ajmer-Merwara	**7,188**	**2,729**	**808**	**54**	**1**	**3,651**	**285**	**69**	**47**	**1**	**..**	**169**	**4**	**4**	**..**	**2**	**..**	**..**	**6,345**	**2,459**	**726**	**47**	**1**	**3,160**
Ajmer	6,270	2,308	741	41	1	3,221	268	68	45	1	..	155	4	4	..	2	..	..	5,487	2,058	671	34	1	2,758
Merwara	918	421	67	13	..	430	17	1	2	..	..	14	..	..	..	..	..	..	858	401	55	13	..	402
CITIES.																								
Rajputana	**23,666**	**9,214**	**2,136**	**215**	**24**	**11,736**	**1,196**	**355**	**357**	**1**	**..**	**484**	**309**	**96**	**107**	**..**	**..**	**104**	**20,121**	**8,240**	**1,534**	**156**	**19**	**10,347**
Alwar	1,961	778	110	18	..	1,078	40	..	..	..	..	40	16	7	..	..	..	9	1,735	716	104	15	..	915
Bharatpur	1,863	771	237	96	24	875	41	18	1	..	..	22	..	..	..	..	..	..	1,436	614	138	48	19	684
Bikaner	5,[illegible]73	2,205	643	76	..	2,525	206	26	159	..	..	21	..	..	..	..	..	..	4,682	2,069	472	76	..	2,341
Jaipur	4,[illegible]74	1,890	432	6	..	2,052	32	11	3	..	..	16	55	31	9	..	..	15	3,995	1,716	409	6	..	1,870
Jodhpur	5,608	1,998	527	3	..	3,083	769	279	166	1	..	324	194	42	75	..	..	77	4,435	1,630	286	1	..	2,519
Kotah	1,845	843	47	16	..	955	4	..	2	..	..	2	..	..	..	..	..	..	1,702	800	45	10	..	917
Tonk	750	289	121	..	..	340	60	9	25	..	..	26	36	19	15	..	..	3	642	262	70	..	..	310
Udaipur	1,293	445	19	..	..	828	44	12	1	..	..	31	8	..	8	..	..	..	1,234	433	10	..	..	791
Ajmer-Merwara—																								
Ajmer	3,943	1,416	452	..	..	2,075	211	43	41	..	..	127	..	..	..	..	..	..	3,442	1,278	388	..	..	1,776

TABLE XV-A.—OCCUPATION OR MEANS OF LIVELIHOOD. PART II.—BY STATE OR DISTRICT, AND CITY—*continued.*

CLASS B.—PREPARATION AND SUPPLY OF MATERIAL SUBSTANCES—*continued.*
SUB-CLASS III.—INDUSTRY—*continued.*

Province; and State, District, or City.	Order 15.—Building Industries—concluded. 79.—Others (thatchers, building contractors, house painters, tilers, plumbers, locksmiths, etc.) Total workers and dependants. Both sexes.	79. Actual workers. Total. Males.	79. Actual workers. Total. Females.	79. Actual workers. Partially agriculturists. Males.	79. Actual workers. Partially agriculturists. Females.	79. Dependants. Both sexes.	Order 16.—Construction of means of transport. Total Order 16. Total workers and dependants. Both sexes.	Total Order 16. Actual workers. Total. Males.	Total Order 16. Actual workers. Total. Females.	Total Order 16. Actual workers. Partially agriculturists. Males.	Total Order 16. Actual workers. Partially agriculturists. Females.	Total Order 16. Dependants. Both sexes.	80.—Cart, carriage, palki, etc., makers and wheelwrights. Total workers and dependants. Both sexes.	80. Actual workers. Total. Males.	80. Actual workers. Total. Females.	80. Dependants. Both sexes.	81.—Saddlers, harness makers, whip and lash makers. Total workers and dependants. Both sexes.	81. Actual workers. Total. Males.	81. Actual workers. Total. Females.	81. Actual workers. Partially agriculturists. Males.	81. Actual workers. Partially agriculturists. Females.	81. Dependants. Both sexes.	82.—Ship and boat builders. Total workers and dependants. Both sexes.	82. Actual workers. Total. Males.	82. Actual workers. Total. Females.
1	604	605	606	607	608	609	610	611	612	613	614	615	616	617	618	619	620	621	622	623	624	625	626	627	628
Rajputana	**3,217**	**1,040**	**361**	**131**	**36**	**1,816**	**427**	**177**	**27**	**9**	..	**223**	**61**	**24**	**1**	**36**	**364**	**151**	**26**	**9**	..	**187**	**2**	**2**	..
Alwar	431	132	18	12	..	281	26	13	2	1	..	11	..	..	..	..	26	13	2	1	..	11	..	..	..
Banswara	..	..	..	..	..	..	..	..	..	..	..	..	..	..	..	..	..	..	..	..	..	..	..	..	..
Bharatpur	577	175	146	67	23	256	32	14	1	1	..	17	2	1	..	1	30	13	1	1	..	16	..	..	..
Bikaner	336	140	13	8	..	183	8	4	..	..	..	4	8	4	..	4	..	..	..	..	..	..	..	..	..
Bundi	168	1	9	..	..	158	20	12	..	..	..	8	1	1	..	..	19	11	..	..	..	8	..	..	..
Dholpur	195	83	14	4	..	98	21	6	..	..	..	15	..	..	..	..	21	6	..	..	..	15	..	..	..
Dungarpur	25	16	..	..	..	9	..	..	..	..	..	..	..	..	..	..	..	..	..	..	..	..	..	..	..
Jaipur	740	250	76	27	13	414	108	43	12	4	..	53	15	6	..	9	91	35	12	4	..	44	2	2	..
Jaisalmer	29	1	25	1	..	3	..	..	..	..	..	..	..	..	..	..	..	..	..	..	..	..	..	..	..
Jhalawar	..	..	..	..	..	..	28	11	2	..	..	15	..	..	..	..	28	11	2	..	..	15	..	..	..
Karauli	27	14	1	..	..	12	11	8	..	3	..	3	2	1	..	1	9	7	..	3	..	2	..	..	..
K'shangarh	9	..	..	..	..	9	..	..	..	..	..	..	..	..	..	..	..	..	..	..	..	..	..	..	..
Kotah	89	46	4	6	..	39	97	40	8	..	..	49	..	..	..	..	97	40	8	..	..	49	..	..	..
Kushalgarh (Chiefship)	..	..	..	..	..	..	..	..	..	..	..	..	..	..	..	..	..	..	..	..	..	..	..	..	..
Lawa (Estate)	1	1	..	..	..	..	4	1	..	..	..	3	..	..	..	..	4	1	..	..	..	3	..	..	..
Marwar	242	65	2	2	..	175	27	7	..	..	..	20	27	7	..	20	..	..	..	..	..	..	..	..	..
Mewar	245	73	27	1	..	145	9	2	..	..	..	7	..	..	..	..	9	2	..	..	..	7	..	..	..
Partabgarh	8	3	3	..	..	2	2	1	1	..	..	..	..	..	..	..	2	1	1	..	..	..	..	..	..
Shahpura (Chiefship)	7	5	1	2	..	1	..	..	..	..	..	..	..	..	..	..	..	..	..	..	..	..	..	..	..
Sirohi	53	25	4	1	..	24	11	5	1	..	..	5	6	4	1	1	5	1	..	..	..	4	..	..	..
Tonk	26	1	18	..	..	7	23	10	..	..	..	13	..	..	..	..	23	10	..	..	..	13	..	..	..
Ajmer-Merwara	**554**	**197**	**35**	**4**	..	**322**	**12**	**7**	**1**	..	..	**4**	**3**	**1**	..	**2**	**9**	**6**	**1**	..	..	**2**	..	..	..
Ajmer	511	178	25	4	..	308	12	7	1	..	..	4	3	1	..	2	9	6	1	..	..	2	..	..	..
Merwara	43	19	10	..	..	14	..	..	..	..	..	..	..	..	..	..	..	..	..	..	..	..	..	..	..
CITIES.																									
Rajputana	**1,460**	**521**	**138**	**58**	**5**	**801**	**139**	**49**	**14**	..	..	**76**	**42**	**16**	..	**26**	**97**	**33**	**14**	..	..	**50**	..	..	..
Alwar	170	50	6	3	..	114	..	..	..	..	..	..	..	..	..	..	..	..	..	..	..	..	..	..	..
Bharatpur	406	139	98	48	5	169	17	7	..	..	..	10	..	..	..	..	17	7	..	..	..	10	..	..	..
Bikaner	285	110	12	..	..	163	8	4	..	..	..	4	8	4	..	4	..	..	..	..	..	..	..	..	..
Jaipur	292	132	11	..	..	149	49	21	9	..	..	19	11	6	..	5	38	15	9	..	..	14	..	..	..
Jodhpur	210	47	..	1	..	163	23	6	..	..	..	17	23	6	..	17	..	..	..	..	..	..	..	..	..
Kotah	79	43	..	6	..	36	37	11	5	..	..	21	..	..	..	..	37	11	5	..	..	21	..	..	..
Tonk	12	..	11	..	..	1	..	..	..	..	..	..	..	..	..	..	..	..	..	..	..	..	..	..	..
Udaipur	6	..	..	..	..	6	5	..	..	..	..	5	..	..	..	..	5	..	..	..	..	5	..	..	..
Ajmer Merwara—																									
Ajmer	290	95	23	..	..	172	5	2	1	..	..	2	3	1	..	2	2	1	1	..	..	..	..	..	..

TABLE XV-A.—OCCUPATION OR MEANS OF LIVELIHOOD. PART II.—BY STATE OR DISTRICT AND CITY—*continued.*

CLASS B.—PREPARATION AND SUPPLY OF MATERIAL SUBSTANCES—*continued.*

SUB-CLASS III.—INDUSTRY—*continued.*

Province; and State, District, or City.	Total Order 17.—Production and transmission of physical forces (heat, light, electricity, motive power, etc.) — 83.—Gas works, electric light, and ice factories — Total workers and dependants — Both sexes.	83.— Actual workers. Total. Males.	83.— Actual workers. Total. Females.	83.— Dependants. Both sexes.	Order 18.—Industries of luxuries and those pertaining to literature and the arts and sciences. — Total Order 18. — Total workers and dependants. Both sexes.	Total Order 18. Actual workers. Total. Males.	Total Order 18. Actual workers. Total. Females.	Total Order 18. Actual workers. Partially agriculturists. Males.	Total Order 18. Actual workers. Partially agriculturists. Females.	Total Order 18. Dependants. Both sexes.	84.—Printers, lithographers, engravers, etc. Total workers and dependants. Both sexes.	84.— Actual workers. Total. Males.	84.— Actual workers. Total. Females.	84.— Actual workers. Partially agriculturists. Males.	84.— Actual workers. Partially agriculturists. Females.	84.— Dependants. Both sexes.	85.—Newspaper and magazine managers and editors, journalists, etc. Total workers and dependants. Both sexes.	85.— Dependants. Both sexes.	86.—Bookbinders, and stitchers, envelope-makers, etc. Total workers and dependants. Both sexes.	86.— Actual workers. Total. Males.	86.— Actual workers. Total. Females.	86.— Actual workers. Partially agriculturists. Males.	86.— Actual workers. Partially agriculturists. Females.	86.— Dependants. Both sexes.
1	629	630	631	632	633	634	635	636	637	638	639	640	641	642	643	644	645	646	647	648	649	650	651	652
Rajputana	542	243	..	299	91,692	32,880	6,729	2,575	161	52,083	518	226	..	1	..	292	..	..	224	81	5	11	..	138
Alwar	2	..	..	2	3,380	1,236	275	121	9	1,869	7	2	..	..	..	5	..	..	14	6	..	..	..	8
Banswara	..	..	..	..	855	281	94	17	4	480	1	1	..	..	..	..	..	..	7	1	..	..	..	6
Bharatpur	..	..	..	..	2,324	928	150	133	8	1,246	34	16	..	..	..	18	..	..	12	3	..	..	..	9
Bikaner	209	112	..	97	8,126	2,901	323	502	37	4,902	118	52	..	..	..	66	..	..	6	5	..	..	..	1
Bundi	13	4	..	9	1,338	502	47	12	..	789	29	10	..	..	..	19	..	..	..	..	..	..	..	..
Dholpur	10	9	..	1	1,126	398	50	42	..	678	42	12	..	1	..	30	..	..	3	3	..	..	..	..
Dungarpur	..	..	..	..	615	198	20	1	..	397	..	..	..	..	..	..	..	..	..	..	..	..	..	..
Jaipur	226	96	..	130	26,322	9,615	2,975	302	22	13,732	28	10	..	..	..	18	..	..	47	13	..	..	..	34
Jaisalmer	..	..	..	..	814	244	15	61	..	555	1	1	..	..	..	..	..	..	..	..	..	..	..	..
Jhalawar	..	..	..	..	1,169	434	59	13	..	676	5	2	..	..	..	3	..	..	..	..	..	..	..	..
Karauli	..	..	..	..	1,015	391	88	31	..	536	..	..	..	..	..	..	..	..	..	..	..	..	..	..
Kishangarh	..	..	..	..	809	310	68	44	2	431	1	1	..	..	..	..	..	..	1	1	..	..	..	..
Kotah	10	2	..	8	4,560	1,780	367	147	5	2,413	38	19	..	..	..	19	..	..	27	10	2	2	..	15
Kushalgarh (Chiefship)	..	..	..	..	87	25	2	..	..	60	..	..	..	..	..	..	..	..	..	..	..	..	..	..
Lawa (Estate)	..	..	..	..	16	7	1	..	..	8	..	..	..	..	..	..	..	..	..	..	..	..	..	..
Marwar	63	16	..	47	22,740	7,778	1,043	840	33	13,919	128	63	..	..	..	65	..	..	22	10	2	..	..	10
Mewar	..	..	..	..	10,910	3,925	782	243	25	6,203	36	13	..	..	..	23	..	..	70	24	1	9	..	45
Partabgarh	..	..	..	..	506	180	49	3	..	277	11	4	..	..	..	7	..	..	..	..	..	..	..	..
Shahpura (Chiefship)	..	..	..	..	307	100	26	10	9	181	..	..	..	..	..	..	..	..	..	..	..	..	..	..
Sirohi	..	..	..	..	2,145	708	84	8	6	1,353	25	14	..	..	..	11	..	..	1	1	..	..	..	..
Tonk	9	4	..	5	2,528	939	211	45	1	1,378	14	6	..	..	..	8	..	..	14	4	..	..	..	10
Ajmer-Merwara	35	20	..	15	7,800	2,908	867	164	15	4,025	546	260	3	..	..	283	2	2	47	19	1	..	..	27
Ajmer	35	20	..	15	6,696	2,485	795	104	11	3,416	526	251	2	..	..	273	2	2	42	18	1	..	..	23
Merwara	..	..	..	..	1,104	423	72	60	4	609	20	9	1	..	..	10	..	..	5	1	..	..	..	4
CITIES.																								
Rajputana	501	225	..	276	14,608	5,414	952	3	..	8,242	374	166	..	..	..	208	..	..	112	36	1	..	..	75
Alwar	..	..	..	..	300	120	19	..	..	161	4	..	..	..	..	4	..	..	14	6	..	..	..	8
Bharatpur	..	..	..	..	532	204	17	..	..	311	27	12	..	..	..	15	..	..	12	3	..	..	..	9
Bikaner	202	111	..	91	2,575	922	109	..	..	1,544	117	52	..	..	..	65	..	..	6	5	..	..	..	1
Jaipur	225	95	..	130	6,185	2,402	581	1	..	3,202	27	9	..	..	..	18	..	..	36	8	..	..	..	28
Jodhpur	56	13	..	43	2,739	953	99	..	..	1,687	126	61	..	..	..	65	..	..	9	3	..	..	..	6
Kotah	9	2	..	7	696	261	68	2	..	367	34	17	..	..	..	17	..	..	13	7	..	..	..	6
Tonk	9	4	..	5	510	182	43	..	..	285	12	4	..	..	..	8	..	..	14	4	..	..	..	10
Udaipur	..	..	..	..	1,071	370	16	..	..	685	27	11	..	..	..	16	..	..	8	..	1	..	..	7
Ajmer-Merwara—																								
Ajmer	35	20	..	15	4,421	1,612	590	1	..	2,219	502	248	1	..	..	259	2	2	30	12	1	..	..	17

TABLE XV-A.—OCCUPATION OR MEANS OF LIVELIHOOD. PART II.—BY STATE OR DISTRICT, AND CITY—*continued.*

CLASS B.—PREPARATION AND SUPPLY OF MATERIAL SUBSTANCES—*continued.*

SUB-CLASS III.—INDUSTRY—*continued.*

Order 18.—Industries of luxuries and those pertaining to literature and the arts and sciences—*continued.*

Province; and State, District, or City.	87.—Makers of musical instruments. Total workers and dependants. Both sexes.	87. Actual workers. Total. Males.	87. Actual workers. Total. Females.	87. Actual workers. Partially agriculturists. Males.	87. Actual workers. Partially agriculturists. Females.	87. Dependants. Both sexes.	88.—Makers of watches, clocks, and optical, photographic, and surgical instruments. Total workers and dependants. Both sexes.	88. Actual workers. Total. Males.	88. Actual workers. Total. Females.	88. Dependants. Both sexes.	89.—Workers in precious stones and metals, enamellers, imitation jewellery makers, gilders, etc. Total workers and dependants. Both sexes.	89. Actual workers. Total. Males.	89. Actual workers. Total. Females.	89. Actual workers. Partially agriculturists. Males.	89. Actual workers. Partially agriculturists. Females.	89. Dependants. Both sexes.	90.—Makers of bangles (materials not specified elsewhere), rosaries, bead and other necklaces, spangles, lingams, sacred threads, and artificial flowers. Total workers and dependants. Both sexes.	90. Actual workers. Total. Males.	90. Actual workers. Total. Females.	90. Actual workers. Partially agriculturists. Males.	90. Actual workers. Partially agriculturists. Females.	90. Dependants. Both sexes.
1	653	654	655	656	657	658	659	660	661	662	663	664	665	666	667	668	669	670	671	672	673	674
Rajputana	81	33	5	1	..	43	318	116	..	302	66,941	24,752	1,251	1,913	11	42,833	21,186	7,452	5,362	644	150	8,372
Alwar	4	1	..	..	..	3	12	7	..	5	2,433	897	19	78	..	1,517	888	314	255	41	9	319
Banswara	..	..	..	..	..	..	2	1	..	1	512	180	8	3	..	324	333	98	86	14	4	149
Bharatpur	31	16	1	..	..	14	5	2	..	3	1,465	540	5	38	1	920	763	345	144	96	7	274
Bikaner	..	..	..	..	..	..	46	18	..	28	6,621	2,330	24	410	5	4,267	1,295	480	294	92	32	521
Bundi	2	1	1	..	..	..	5	2	..	3	1,123	425	11	11	..	687	174	61	35	1	..	78
Dholpur	2	1	..	1	..	1	1	..	..	1	925	350	1	30	..	574	116	22	41	..	..	53
Dungarpur	..	..	..	..	..	..	..	..	..	..	606	195	20	1	..	391	7	3	..	..	..	4
Jaipur	19	5	3	..	..	11	103	44	..	50	16,770	6,973	795	202	1	11,001	7,236	2,515	2,130	100	21	2,582
Jaisalmer	..	..	..	..	..	..	6	1	..	5	720	224	3	50	..	493	87	18	12	2	..	57
Jhalawar	..	..	..	..	..	..	10	5	..	5	936	351	16	12	..	569	213	73	43	1	..	97
Karauli	2	..	..	..	..	2	10	2	..	8	631	241	..	26	..	410	345	142	86	5	..	115
Kishangarh	..	..	..	..	..	..	14	..	..	14	582	219	5	21	..	358	211	89	63	23	2	59
Kotah	3	1	..	..	..	2	13	5	..	8	3,274	1,267	71	122	2	1,930	1,158	450	200	22	3	418
Kushalgarh (Chiefship)	..	..	..	..	..	..	..	..	..	..	66	18	..	..	..	48	21	7	2	..	..	12
Lawa (Estate)	..	..	..	..	..	..	..	..	..	..	13	6	..	..	..	7	3	1	1	..	..	1
Marwar	14	8	..	..	..	6	41	12	..	29	18,345	6,237	123	674	..	11,965	4,119	1,426	891	166	33	1,802
Mewar	1	..	..	..	..	1	13	6	..	7	7,777	2,877	106	170	2	4,794	2,970	997	669	55	23	1,304
Partabgarh	..	..	..	..	..	..	4	1	..	3	328	115	4	3	..	209	109	42	31	..	..	36
Shahpura (Chiefship)	..	..	..	..	..	..	..	..	..	..	218	81	..	10	..	137	76	13	25	..	9	38
Sirohi	..	..	..	..	..	..	..	..	..	..	1,767	572	15	..	..	1,180	320	99	69	8	6	152
Tonk	3	..	..	..	..	3	33	10	..	23	1,709	654	24	27	..	1,031	742	257	184	18	1	301
Ajmer-Merwara	1	1	..	..	..	..	65	26	..	39	5,848	2,153	591	119	..	3,104	1,235	420	272	44	15	543
Ajmer	1	1	..	..	..	..	60	24	..	36	5,031	1,819	585	69	..	2,627	979	344	207	34	11	428
Merwara	..	..	..	..	..	..	5	2	..	3	817	334	6	50	..	477	256	76	65	10	4	115
CITIES.																						
Rajputana	44	14	1	..	..	29	230	84	..	146	11,675	4,361	523	3	..	6,791	2,019	713	372	..	..	834
Alwar	4	1	..	..	..	3	7	5	..	2	208	86	..	..	..	122	48	15	18	..	..	15
Bharatpur	8	8	..	..	..	5	4	1	..	3	404	156	..	..	..	248	70	28	17	..	..	25
Bikaner	..	..	..	..	..	..	36	11	..	25	1,072	718	8	..	..	1,246	424	128	100	..	..	196
Jaipur	12	1	1	..	..	10	98	40	..	58	5,206	2,017	400	1	..	2,791	750	322	145	..	..	283
Jodhpur	14	8	..	..	..	6	40	11	..	29	2,152	734	63	..	..	1,355	310	120	19	..	..	207
Kotah	3	1	..	..	..	2	6	2	..	4	549	205	39	2	..	305	91	29	29	..	..	33
Tonk	3	..	..	..	..	3	33	10	..	23	302	127	5	..	..	170	140	34	37	..	..	69
Udaipur	..	..	..	..	..	..	6	4	..	2	880	318	8	..	..	554	150	37	7	..	..	106
Ajmer-Merwara—																						
Ajmer	1	1	..	..	..	..	52	10	..	33	3,503	1,216	562	1	..	1,725	296	105	26	..	..	168

TABLE XV-A.—OCCUPATION OR MEANS OF LIVELIHOOD. PART II.—BY STATE OR DISTRICT, AND CITY—*continued.*

CLASS B.—PREPARATION AND SUPPLY OF MATERIAL SUBSTANCES—*continued.*

SUB-CLASS III.—INDUSTRY—*concluded.*

Order 18.—Industries of luxuries and those pertaining to literature and the arts and sciences—*concluded.*

Province; and State, District, or City.	91.—Toy, kite, cage, fishing tackle, picture frames, etc., makers, taxidermists, etc. — Total workers and dependants. Both sexes.	91 — Actual workers. Total. Males.	91 — Actual workers. Total. Females.	91 — Actual workers. Partially agriculturists. Males.	91 — Actual workers. Partially agriculturists. Females.	91 — Dependants. Both sexes.	92.—Others, including managers, and persons (other than performers) employed in theatres and other places of public entertainment, employés of public societies, race-course service, huntsmen. — Total workers and dependants. Both sexes.	92 — Actual workers. Total. Males.	92 — Actual workers. Total. Females.	92 — Actual workers. Partially agriculturists. Males.	92 — Actual workers. Partially agriculturists. Females.	92 — Dependants. Both sexes.
1	675	676	677	678	679	680	681	682	683	684	685	686
Rajputana	**352**	**135**	**93**	**3**	..	**124**	**172**	**85**	**13**	**2**	..	**74**
Alwar	15	7	1	..	..	7	7	2	..	2	..	5
Banswara	..	..	..	..	..	..	..	..	..	..	..	..
Bharatpur	12	5	..	1	..	7	2	1	..	..	..	1
Bikaner	..	..	..	..	..	..	40	16	5	..	..	19
Bundi	4	2	..	..	..	2	1	1	..	..	..	..
Dholpur	37	10	8	1	..	19	..	..	..	..	..	..
Dungarpur	1	..	..	..	..	1	1	..	..	..	..	1
Jaipur	117	54	37	..	..	26	2	1	..	..	..	1
Jaisalmer	..	..	..	..	..	..	..	..	..	..	..	..
Jhalawar	..	..	..	..	..	..	5	3	..	..	..	2
Karauli	..	..	..	..	..	..	7	6	..	..	..	1
Kishangarh	..	..	..	..	..	..	..	..	..	..	..	..
Kotah	18	13	..	1	..	5	29	15	4	..	..	10
Kushalgarh (Chiefship)	..	..	..	..	..	..	..	..	..	..	..	..
Lawa (Estate)	..	..	..	..	..	..	..	..	..	..	..	..
Marwar	59	14	27	..	..	18	12	8	..	..	..	4
Mewar	22	6	4	..	..	12	21	2	2	..	..	17
Partabgarh	54	18	14	..	..	23	..	..	..	..	..	..
Shahpura (Chiefship)	6	2	1	..	..	3	7	4	..	..	..	3
Sirohi	1	1	..	..	..	..	31	21	..	..	..	10
Tonk	6	3	1	..	..	2	7	5	2	..	..	..
Ajmer-Merwara	**6**	**3**	..	..	..	**3**	**50**	**26**	..	**1**	..	**24**
Ajmer	6	3	..	..	..	3	40	25	..	1	..	24
Merwara	..	..	..	..	..	..	1	1	..	..	..	..
CITIES.												
Rajputana	**124**	**27**	**54**	..	..	**43**	**30**	**13**	**1**	..	..	**16**
Alwar	15	7	1	..	..	7	..	..	..	..	..	..
Bharatpur	5	..	..	..	..	5	2	1	..	..	..	1
Bikaner	..	..	..	..	..	..	20	8	1	..	..	11
Jaipur	54	5	35	..	..	14	..	..	..	..	..	..
Jodhpur	44	12	17	..	..	15	8	4	..	..	..	4
Kotah	..	..	..	..	..	..	..	..	..	..	..	..
Tonk	6	3	1	..	..	2	..	..	..	..	..	..
Udaipur	..	..	..	..	..	..	..	..	..	..	..	..
Ajmer-Merwara—												
Ajmer	3	1	..	..	..	2	29	16	..	..	..	13

Province; and State, District, or City.	Total Order 19.—Industries concerned with refuse matters. 93.—Sweepers, scavengers, dust and sweeping contractors — Total workers and dependants. Both sexes.	93 — Actual workers. Total. Males.	93 — Actual workers. Total. Females.	93 — Actual workers. Partially agriculturists. Males.	93 — Actual workers. Partially agriculturists. Females.	93 — Dependants. Both sexes.	SUB-CLASS IV.—TRANSPORT. Total Sub-Class IV. — Total workers and dependants. Both sexes.	IV — Actual workers. Total. Males.	IV — Actual workers. Total. Females.	IV — Actual workers. Partially agriculturists. Males.	IV — Actual workers. Partially agriculturists. Females.	IV — Dependants. Both sexes.
1	687	688	689	690	691	692	693	694	695	696	697	698
Rajputana	**85,499**	**29,503**	**27,490**	**1,028**	**490**	**28,197**	**110,202**	**47,196**	**9,353**	**3,226**	**436**	**53,653**
Alwar	12,819	4,361	4,309	174	93	4,143	*5,734*	*2,478*	*156*	*258*	*5*	*3,120*
Banswara	175	62	57	3	..	56	*613*	*266*	*104*	*18*	*4*	*503*
Bharatpur	7,634	2,895	2,464	51	25	2,275	*7,369*	*3,465*	*703*	*309*	*37*	*3,194*
Bikaner	3,291	1,023	1,026	118	74	1,242	*5,437*	*3,539*	*147*	*271*	..	*3,751*
Bundi	1,721	549	479	..	..	693	*2,354*	*958*	*147*	*22*	..	*1,249*
Dholpur	2,013	763	635	49	3	615	*2,678*	*1,179*	*155*	*100*	..	*1,344*
Dungarpur	226	77	56	..	..	93	*843*	*364*	*19*	*98*	..	*460*
Jaipur	24,845	8,994	8,013	161	72	7,838	*27,268*	*12,262*	*1,088*	*692*	*36*	*13,918*
Jaisalmer	38	16	15	..	..	7	*770*	*373*	*83*	*30*	*2*	*178*
Jhalawar	880	294	294	4	3	292	*1,333*	*628*	*37*	*41*	*1*	*668*
Karauli	1,499	567	530	4	..	396	*1,504*	*902*	*64*	*101*	..	*538*
Kishangarh	849	317	268	9	5	264	*804*	*472*	*33*	*26*	*1*	*389*
Kotah	5,845	1,766	2,041	67	65	2,038	*11,889*	*4,805*	*1,595*	*205*	*21*	*5,489*
Kushalgarh (Chiefship)	13	5	4	..	..	4	*50*	*30*	..	..	..	*20*
Lawa (Estate)	37	14	12	..	..	11	*4*	*3*	..	..	..	*1*
Marwar	13,322	4,587	4,034	309	117	4,701	*22,641*	*8,854*	*3,329*	*380*	*276*	*10,458*
Mewar	6,111	2,044	1,986	39	14	2,081	*5,988*	*3,831*	*601*	*429*	*5*	*4,556*
Partabgarh	266	93	91	8	..	82	*272*	*129*	*5*	*6*	..	*138*
Shahpura (Chiefship)	411	124	126	11	6	161	*276*	*96*	*71*	*17*	*38*	*109*
Sirohi	1,168	416	272	10	1	475	*7,142*	*2,350*	*936*	*96*	*5*	*3,656*
Tonk	2,353	836	787	11	12	730	*2,115*	*870*	*140*	*48*	*5*	*1,105*
Ajmer-Merwara	**6,208**	**2,217**	**1,644**	**7**	**3**	**2,347**	**34,630**	**13,961**	**389**	**211**	**13**	**20,280**
Ajmer	5,376	1,929	1,387	5	3	2,060	*32,645*	*12,952*	*303*	*140*	*8*	*19,390*
Merwara	832	288	257	2	..	287	*1,985*	*1,009*	*86*	*62*	*5*	*890*
CITIES.												
Rajputana	**8,550**	**2,873**	**2,827**	..	..	**2,850**	**29,131**	**8,178**	**1,443**	**123**	**4**	**10,516**
Alwar	1,027	328	317	..	..	382	*964*	*406*	*22*	*16*	*1*	*536*
Bharatpur	600	217	206	..	..	177	*1,333*	*666*	*78*	*14*	*2*	*791*
Bikaner	1,049	317	299	..	..	433	*1,903*	*809*	*83*	*56*	..	*1,011*
Jaipur	2,716	932	950	..	..	834	*5,288*	*2,381*	*252*	*5*	..	*2,655*
Jodhpur	1,395	456	459	..	..	480	*5,940*	*2,323*	*246*	..	..	*3,369*
Kotah	690	227	220	..	..	243	*2,492*	*794*	*368*	*17*	*1*	*1,130*
Tonk	616	229	213	..	..	174	*786*	*331*	*64*	*15*	..	*391*
Udaipur	457	167	163	..	..	127	*1,223*	*466*	*180*	..	..	*637*
Ajmer-Merwara—												
Ajmer	2,010	745	433	..	..	832	*28,537*	*11,046*	*216*	*41*	*1*	*17,275*

TABLE XV-A.—OCCUPATION OR MEANS OF LIVELIHOOD. PART II.—BY STATE OR DISTRICT, AND CITY—*continued*.

CLASS B.—PREPARATION AND SUPPLY OF MATERIAL SUBSTANCES—*continued*.

SUB-CLASS IV.—TRANSPORT—*continued*.

Order 20.—Transport by water.

Province; and State, District, or City.	Total Order 20.						95.—Ship owners and their employés, ship brokers, ships' officers, engineers, mariners, and firemen.						96.—Persons employed on the maintenance of streams, irrigation, tanks, rivers and canals (including construction).						97.—Boat owners, boat men, and towmen.					
	Total workers and dependants.	Actual workers. Total.		Actual workers. Partially agriculturists.		Dependants.	Total workers and dependants.	Actual workers. Total.		Actual workers. Partially agriculturists.		Dependants.	Total workers and dependants.	Actual workers. Total.		Actual workers. Partially agriculturists.		Dependants.	Total workers and dependants.	Actual workers. Total.		Actual workers. Partially agriculturists.		Dependants.
	Both sexes.	Males.	Females.	Males.	Females.	Both sexes.	Both sexes.	Males.	Females.	Males.	Females.	Both sexes.	Both sexes.	Males.	Females.	Males.	Females.	Both sexes.	Both sexes.	Males.	Females.	Males.	Females.	Both sexes.
1	699	700	701	702	703	704	705	706	707	708	709	710	711	712	713	714	715	716	717	718	719	720	721	722
Rajputana	**1,343**	**640**	**185**	**84**	**33**	**518**	**100**	**43**	**6**	**8**	..	**51**	**745**	**418**	**112**	**10**	**33**	**215**	**498**	**179**	**67**	**66**	..	**252**
Alwar	30	4	..	1	..	26	13	..	..	..	..	13	17	4	..	1	..	13	..	..	..	..	..	..
Banswara	..	..	..	..	..	..	..	..	..	..	..	..	..	..	..	..	..	..	..	..	..	..	..	..
Bharatpur	38	13	7	1	..	18	1	1	..	..	..	..	33	10	7	1	..	16	4	2	..	..	..	2
Bikaner	9	6	..	..	..	3	..	..	..	..	..	..	9	6	..	..	..	3	..	..	..	..	..	..
Bundi	68	28	..	11	..	40	..	..	..	..	..	..	..	..	..	..	..	..	68	28	..	11	..	40
Dholpur	82	40	..	11	..	42	..	..	..	..	..	..	6	4	..	..	..	2	76	36	..	11	..	40
Dungarpur	..	..	..	..	..	..	..	..	..	..	..	..	..	..	..	..	..	..	..	..	..	..	..	..
Jaipur	123	53	5	10	2	65	43	23	..	6	..	20	80	30	5	4	2	46	..	..	..	..	..	..
Jaisalmer	16	1	15	..	..	..	..	..	..	..	..	..	16	1	15	..	..	..	..	..	..	..	..	..
Jhalawar	..	..	..	..	..	..	..	..	..	..	..	..	..	..	..	..	..	..	..	..	..	..	..	..
Karauli	..	..	..	..	..	..	..	..	..	..	..	..	..	..	..	..	..	..	..	..	..	..	..	..
Kishangarh	5	2	..	..	..	3	..	..	..	..	..	..	3	1	..	..	..	2	2	1	..	..	..	1
Kotah	279	124	5	45	..	150	1	1	..	..	..	..	36	23	..	1	..	13	242	100	5	44	..	137
Kushalgarh (Chiefship)	..	..	..	..	..	..	..	..	..	..	..	..	..	..	..	..	..	..	..	..	..	..	..	..
Lawa (Estate)	..	..	..	..	..	..	..	..	..	..	..	..	..	..	..	..	..	..	..	..	..	..	..	..
Marwar	441	308	45	..	..	88	..	..	..	..	..	..	441	308	45	..	..	88	..	..	..	..	..	..
Mewar	85	32	6	..	..	47	24	5	6	..	..	13	36	15	..	..	..	21	25	12	..	..	..	13
Partabgarh	..	..	..	..	..	..	..	..	..	..	..	..	..	..	..	..	..	..	..	..	..	..	..	..
Shahpura (Chiefship)	68	16	40	3	31	12	..	..	..	..	..	..	68	16	40	3	31	12	..	..	..	..	..	..
Sirohi	81	..	62	..	..	19	..	..	..	..	..	..	..	..	..	..	..	..	81	..	62	..	..	19
Tonk	18	13	..	2	..	5	18	13	..	2	..	5	..	..	..	..	..	..	..	..	..	..	..	..
Ajmer-Merwara	**95**	**54**	..	**8**	..	**41**	**2**	**2**	..	..	..	..	**93**	**52**	..	**8**	..	**41**	..	..	..	..	..	..
Ajmer	82	46	..	8	..	36	..	..	..	..	..	..	82	46	..	8	..	36	..	..	..	..	..	..
Merwara	13	8	..	..	..	5	2	2	..	..	..	..	11	6	..	..	..	5	..	..	..	..	..	..
CITIES.																								
Rajputana	**114**	**66**	**1**	**9**	..	**47**	**12**	**7**	..	**2**	..	**5**	**37**	**25**	..	**1**	..	**12**	**65**	**34**	**1**	**6**	..	**30**
Alwar	2	1	..	1	..	1	..	..	..	..	..	..	2	1	..	1	..	1	..	..	..	..	..	..
Bharatpur	1	1	..	..	..	..	1	1	..	..	..	..	..	..	..	..	..	..	..	..	..	..	..	..
Bikaner	..	..	..	..	..	..	..	..	..	..	..	..	..	..	..	..	..	..	..	..	..	..	..	..
Jaipur	7	..	..	..	..	7	..	..	..	..	..	..	7	..	..	..	..	7	..	..	..	..	..	..
Jodhpur	28	24	..	..	..	4	..	..	..	..	..	..	28	24	..	..	..	4	..	..	..	..	..	..
Kotah	54	26	1	6	..	27	1	1	..	..	..	..	..	..	..	..	..	..	53	25	1	6	..	27
Tonk	10	5	..	2	..	5	10	5	..	2	..	5	..	..	..	..	..	..	..	..	..	..	..	..
Udaipur	12	9	..	..	..	3	..	..	..	..	..	..	..	..	..	..	..	..	12	9	..	..	..	3
Ajmer-Merwara—																								
Ajmer	12	3	..	..	..	9	..	..	..	..	..	..	12	3	..	..	..	9	..	..	..	..	..	..

TABLE XV-A.—Occupation or Means of Livelihood. Part II.—By State or District, and City—*continued.*

CLASS B.—PREPARATION AND SUPPLY OF MATERIAL SUBSTANCES—*continued.*

Sub-Class IV.—Transport—*continued.*

Order 21.—Transport by road.

Province; and State, District, or City.	Total Order 21. Total workers and dependants. Both sexes.	Total Order 21. Actual workers. Total. Males.	Total Order 21. Actual workers. Total. Females.	Total Order 21. Actual workers. Partially agriculturists. Males.	Total Order 21. Actual workers. Partially agriculturists. Females.	Total Order 21. Dependants. Both sexes.	98.—Persons employed on the construction and maintenance of roads and bridges. Total workers and dependants. Both sexes.	98. Actual workers. Total. Males.	98. Actual workers. Total. Females.	98. Actual workers. Partially agriculturists. Males.	98. Actual workers. Partially agriculturists. Females.	98. Dependants. Both sexes.	99.—Cart and carriage owners, hirers, and drivers, coachmen, stable boys, tramway, mail carriage, etc., managers and employés (excluding private servants). Total workers and dependants. Both sexes.	99. Actual workers. Total. Males.	99. Actual workers. Total. Females.	99. Actual workers. Partially agriculturists. Males.	99. Actual workers. Partially agriculturists. Females.	99. Dependants. Both sexes.	100.—Palki, etc., bearers and owners. Total workers and dependants. Both sexes.	100. Actual workers. Total. Males.	100. Actual workers. Total. Females.	100. Actual workers. Partially agriculturists. Males.	100. Actual workers. Partially agriculturists. Females.	100. Dependants. Both sexes.
1	723	724	725	726	727	728	729	730	731	732	733	734	735	736	737	738	739	740	741	742	743	744	745	746
Rajputana	**73,772**	**31,176**	**8,838**	**2,665**	**401**	**33,758**	**10,293**	**2,949**	**5,921**	**85**	**287**	**2,430**	**15,216**	**7,882**	**150**	**531**	**6**	**7,244**	**781**	**365**	**15**	**36**	**1**	**401**
Alwar	4,307	1,889	143	215	5	2,275	192	113	22	5	1	57	965	470	6	40	..	489	40	40	..	..	..	..
Banswara	578	188	104	16	4	286	81	8	46	..	..	7	110	68	..	4	..	42	..	..	..	..	..	..
Bharatpur	5,608	2,551	685	351	37	3,372	1,721	739	498	50	10	489	1,396	831	5	128	..	560	9	5	..	..	..	4
Bikaner	3,325	1,404	113	220	..	1,808	277	104	79	..	..	94	593	232	..	47	..	361	22	9	..	..	..	13
Bundi	1,824	700	140	10	..	975	61	10	42	..	..	9	146	89	2	..	..	55	23	12	..	..	..	11
Dholpur	1,932	829	150	85	..	953	244	81	96	2	..	65	339	181	4	6	..	154	15	4	..	1	..	11
Dungarpur	783	347	19	28	..	417	..	..	..	..	..	..	204	178	7	1	..	24	..	..	..	..	..	..
Jaipur	16,916	8,076	1,055	595	33	7,785	330	166	47	1	..	117	2,792	1,427	48	48	..	1,317	80	55	..	3	..	25
Jaisalmer	737	562	8	27	2	167	..	..	..	..	..	..	82	56	1	1	..	5	..	..	..	..	..	..
Jhalawar	954	454	25	26	1	475	81	37	19	..	..	25	433	216	2	18	..	215	19	10	..	3	..	9
Karauli	1,401	834	59	101	..	508	27	14	1	..	..	12	364	233	1	22	..	130	60	20	..	6	..	30
Kishangarh	649	249	33	22	1	267	27	13	11	..	..	3	316	220	2	15	1	94	6	6	..	..	..	..
Kotah	8,631	3,254	1,413	129	20	3,964	2,143	609	874	10	13	600	1,988	989	31	46	1	968	109	58	..	6	..	51
Kushalgarh (Chiefship)	47	26	..	..	..	21	..	..	..	..	..	..	48	24	..	..	..	19	..	..	..	..	..	..
Lawa (Estate)	4	3	..	..	..	1	..	..	..	..	..	..	..	..	..	..	..	..	..	..	..	..	..	..
Marwar	12,498	4,133	3,280	218	276	5,085	3,107	292	2,437	2	258	378	1,833	830	3	38	..	1,000	26	15	..	..	..	11
Mewar	7,340	3,163	578	466	5	3,599	63	4	34	..	..	25	1,745	949	22	42	..	774	230	36	15	7	1	159
Partabgarh	281	116	5	6	..	110	1	1	..	..	..	..	40	35	..	1	..	11	..	..	..	..	..	..
Shahpura (Chiefship)	199	74	31	14	7	94	4	..	4	..	..	..	47	23	..	1	..	24	..	..	..	..	..	..
Sirohi	4,155	1,545	857	91	5	1,753	1,672	526	729	9	5	417	1,409	624	12	64	..	773	58	20	..	..	..	20
Tonk	1,653	670	140	45	5	843	282	185	85	..	..	72	385	152	4	9	4	220	94	46	..	10	..	48
Ajmer-Merwara	**5,704**	**2,741**	**274**	**142**	**12**	**2,769**	**760**	**334**	**155**	**14**	**9**	**271**	**2,690**	**1,293**	**23**	**182**	**2**	**1,374**	**69**	**34**	**2**	**3**	..	**33**
Ajmer	4,304	1,938	191	84	7	2,175	618	288	96	13	6	234	2,022	932	9	58	..	1,081	69	34	2	3	..	33
Merwara	1,480	803	83	58	5	594	142	46	59	1	3	37	668	361	14	44	2	293	..	..	..	..	..	..
CITIES.																								
Rajputana	**13,355**	**5,440**	**1,429**	**82**	**4**	**6,486**	**1,871**	**572**	**706**	**15**	**3**	**593**	**4,084**	**1,309**	**36**	**25**	..	**2,239**	**274**	**157**	..	**11**	..	**117**
Alwar	755	318	21	13	1	416	..	..	..	..	..	..	378	157	3	5	..	218	..	..	..	..	..	..
Bharatpur	1,103	428	71	13	2	594	364	154	71	8	2	139	280	94	..	3	..	180	9	5	..	..	..	4
Bikaner	1,575	664	83	31	..	828	203	63	74	..	..	66	422	160	..	11	..	253	22	9	..	..	..	13
Jaipur	4,358	2,050	248	4	..	2,060	57	33	4	..	..	15	1,504	782	17	1	..	705	67	45	..	..	..	22
Jodhpur	1,598	596	246	..	..	756	140	87	15	..	..	38	235	94	..	..	..	141	14	9	..	..	..	5
Kotah	2,195	669	567	9	1	959	809	136	490	7	1	278	617	272	3	1	..	342	47	33	..	1	..	14
Tonk	701	299	64	12	..	338	208	94	52	..	..	62	188	61	..	2	..	127	94	46	..	10	..	48
Udaipur	1,070	406	129	..	..	535	..	..	..	..	..	..	480	180	13	..	..	287	21	10	..	..	..	11
Ajmer-Merwara—																								
Ajmer	1,696	727	107	5	..	862	324	141	40	..	..	134	646	254	9	1	..	383	69	34	2	3	..	33

TABLE XV-A.—OCCUPATION OR MEANS OF LIVELIHOOD. PART II.—BY STATE OR DISTRICT, AND CITY—*continued.*

CLASS B.—PREPARATION AND SUPPLY OF MATERIAL SUBSTANCES—*continued.* SUB-CLASS IV.—TRANSPORT—*continued.*

Order 21.—Transport by road—*concluded.*

Province; and State, District, or City.	101.—Pack elephant, camel, mule, ass, and bullock owners and drivers. Total workers and dependants. Both sexes.	Actual workers. Total. Males.	Actual workers. Total. Females.	Partially agriculturists. Males.	Partially agriculturists. Females.	Dependants. Both sexes.	102.—Porters and messengers. Total workers and dependants. Both sexes.	Actual workers. Total. Males.	Actual workers. Total. Females.	Partially agriculturists. Males.	Partially agriculturists. Females.	Dependants. Both sexes.
1	747	748	749	750	751	752	753	754	755	756	757	758
Rajputana	38,130	13,840	2,415	1,659	78	15,875	15,252	6,307	1,237	354	29	7,806
Alwar	2,008	809	73	116	3	1,126	1,102	457	42	54	1	603
Banswara	392	105	58	12	4	234	15	7	5	..	..	3
Bharatpur	1,025	487	126	122	27	462	1,457	539	61	51	..	857
Bikaner	1,570	685	19	137	..	866	863	374	15	36	..	474
Bundi	1,127	398	71	8	..	663	467	205	25	2	..	237
Dholpur	790	317	16	65	..	457	544	246	32	11	..	266
Dungarpur	215	53	12	4	..	150	364	121	..	23	..	243
Jaipur	9,310	4,537	631	466	8	4,142	4,404	1,891	329	77	25	2,184
Jaisalmer	579	472	4	23	1	103	96	84	3	3	1	69
Jhalawar	141	59	4	1	1	78	280	132	..	4	..	148
Karauli	618	390	26	59	..	202	342	177	31	14	..	134
Kishangarh	170	64	2	6	..	110	124	46	18	1	..	60
Kotah	3,488	1,274	403	57	6	1,811	903	324	106	4	..	474
Kushalgarh (Chiefship)	4	2	..	..	..	2	..	..	..	..	..	..
Lawa (Estate)	..	..	..	..	..	..	4	3	..	..	..	1
Marwar	5,754	2,345	541	150	16	2,868	1,778	651	299	28	2	828
Mewar	3,855	1,509	326	394	4	2,015	1,449	645	181	23	..	623
Partabgarh	69	34	5	5	..	30	115	46	..	..	..	69
Shahpura (Chiefship)	73	14	27	5	7	32	75	37	..	8	..	38
Sirohi	548	219	87	3	..	292	468	147	79	15	..	242
Tonk	390	122	39	26	1	229	502	225	12	..	..	265
Ajmer-Merwara	600	295	38	7	1	273	1,665	785	62	16	..	818
Ajmer	527	249	24	2	1	254	1,068	435	60	3	..	573
Merwara	73	46	8	5	..	19	597	350	2	8	..	245
CITIES.												
Rajputana	1,376	584	21	20	..	771	5,750	2,318	666	11	1	2,766
Alwar	30	17	..	..	..	13	347	144	16	8	1	185
Bharatpur	6	5	..	..	..	1	444	180	..	..	..	264
Bikaner	480	213	..	20	..	267	448	210	9	..	..	220
Jaipur	263	111	2	..	..	150	2,467	1,074	225	3	..	1,108
Jodhpur	436	157	15	..	..	251	773	240	216	..	..	308
Kotah	119	58	4	..	..	57	513	170	70	..	..	273
Tonk	10	5	..	..	..	5	201	93	12	..	..	96
Udaipur	32	18	..	..	..	14	557	198	116	..	..	243
Ajmer-Merwara—												
Ajmer	135	73	..	..	..	62	522	225	47	1	..	250

Order 22.—Transport by rail.

Province; and State, District, or City.	Total Order 22. Total workers and dependants. Both sexes.	Actual workers. Total. Males.	Actual workers. Total. Females.	Partially agriculturists. Males.	Partially agriculturists. Females.	Dependants. Both sexes.	103.—Railway employés of all kinds other than construction coolies. Total workers and dependants. Both sexes.	Actual workers. Total. Males.	Actual workers. Total. Females.	Partially agriculturists. Males.	Partially agriculturists. Females.	Dependants. Both sexes.
1	759	760	761	762	763	764	765	766	767	768	769	770
Rajputana	31,319	13,767	323	417	2	17,229	29,351	12,662	97	384	1	16,598
Alwar	1,213	491	13	35	..	709	1,190	482	13	34	..	695
Banswara	..	..	..	..	..	..	..	..	..	..	..	..
Bharatpur	1,536	827	11	46	..	698	1,184	634	..	38	..	550
Bikaner	1,754	980	34	46	..	731	1,125	540	..	33	..	586
Bundi	408	198	7	1	..	203	394	193	5	1	..	196
Dholpur	556	274	5	11	..	277	545	266	5	11	..	274
Dungarpur	4	..	..	..	..	4	4	..	..	..	..	4
Jaipur	9,262	3,729	28	66	1	5,505	9,252	3,727	27	66	1	5,498
Jaisalmer	1	..	..	..	..	1	1	..	..	..	..	1
Jhalawar	274	123	12	14	..	139	191	83	6	13	..	102
Karauli	85	57	5	..	..	23	57	38	1	..	..	18
Kishangarh	195	102	..	4	..	93	195	102	..	4	..	93
Kotah	2,633	1,284	172	26	1	1,177	1,890	934	16	16	..	940
Kushalgarh (Chiefship)	..	..	..	..	..	..	..	..	..	..	..	..
Lawa (Estate)	..	..	..	..	..	..	..	..	..	..	..	..
Marwar	9,029	4,084	4	157	..	4,941	9,029	4,084	4	157	..	4,941
Mewar	1,329	544	15	7	..	770	1,329	544	15	7	..	770
Partabgarh	6	2	..	..	..	4	6	2	..	..	..	4
Shahpura (Chiefship)	..	..	..	..	..	..	..	..	..	..	..	..
Sirohi	2,776	944	17	4	..	1,815	2,711	922	5	4	..	1,784
Tonk	258	119	..	..	..	139	248	111	..	..	..	137
Ajmer-Merwara	27,869	10,835	115	57	1	16,858	27,580	10,767	111	54	1	16,762
Ajmer	27,422	10,682	112	54	1	16,628	27,224	10,672	108	51	1	16,544
Merwara	387	153	3	3	..	231	356	135	3	3	..	218
CITIES.												
Rajputana	5,815	2,350	13	30	..	3,452	5,720	2,309	6	24	..	3,405
Alwar	152	59	1	2	..	92	152	59	1	2	..	92
Bharatpur	374	201	7	1	..	166	307	174	..	1	..	133
Bikaner	208	100	..	25	..	108	187	92	..	19	..	95
Jaipur	651	241	4	..	..	406	651	241	4	..	..	406
Jodhpur	4,203	1,657	..	..	..	2,546	4,203	1,657	..	..	..	2,546
Kotah	141	61	..	2	..	80	134	55	..	2	..	79
Tonk	6	2	..	..	..	4	6	2	..	..	..	4
Udaipur	80	29	1	..	..	50	80	29	1	..	..	50
Ajmer-Merwara—												
Ajmer	26,195	10,111	109	36	1	15,975	26,183	10,108	107	36	1	15,968

TABLE XV-A.—Occupation or Means of Livelihood. Part II.—By State or District, and City—*continued.*

Province; and State, District, or City.	CLASS B.—PREPARATION AND SUPPLY OF MATERIAL SUBSTANCES—*continued.*																							
	SUB-CLASS IV.—TRANSPORT—*concluded.*												SUB-CLASS V.—TRADE.											
	Order 22.—Transport by rail—*concluded.*						Total Order 23.—Post office, telegraph and telephone services.						Total Sub-Class V.						Total order 24.—Banks, establishments of credit, exchange and insurance.					
	104.—Labourers employed on railway construction.						105.—Post office, telegraph and telephone services.												106.—Bank managers, money lenders, exchange and insurance agents, money changers and brokers in shares and stocks and their employés.					
	Total workers and dependants	Actual workers.				Dependants.	Total workers and dependants.	Actual workers.				Dependants.	Total workers and dependants.	Actual workers.				Dependants.	Total workers and dependants.	Actual workers.				Dependants.
		Total.		Partially agriculturists.				Total.		Partially agriculturists.				Total.		Partially agriculturists.				Total.		Partially agriculturists.		
	Both sexes.	Males.	Females.	Males.	Females.	Both sexes.	Both sexes.	Males.	Females.	Males.	Females.	Both sexes.	Both sexes.	Males.	Females.	Males.	Females.	Both sexes.	Both sexes.	Males.	Females.	Males.	Females.	Both sexes.
1	771	772	773	774	775	776	777	778	779	780	781	782	783	784	785	786	787	788	789	790	791	792	793	794
Rajputana	**1,968**	**1,105**	**226**	**33**	**1**	**637**	**3,768**	**1,613**	**7**	**60**	..	**2,148**	**798,761**	**273,659**	**54,410**	**25,575**	**6,414**	**470,692**	**185,988**	**54,837**	**5,955**	**4,447**	**113**	**125,196**
Alwar	23	9	..	1	..	14	204	94	..	7	..	110	50,737	17,397	3,712	2,429	289	29,628	9,819	2,878	215	571	6	6,726
Banswara	..	..	..	..	..	..	35	18	..	2	..	17	9,030	3,070	606	440	33	5,354	4,459	1,563	167	113	9	2,729
Bharatpur	352	193	11	8	..	148	190	74	..	1	..	106	34,370	12,237	5,107	2,036	434	17,026	2,927	828	88	242	3	2,011
Bikaner	629	449	34	13	..	146	349	140	..	5	..	209	53,894	13,325	2,263	1,461	226	38,306	8,786	1,823	306	122	1	6,657
Bundi	14	5	2	..	..	7	54	23	..	..	..	31	12,168	4,168	1,299	333	6	6,701	1,433	439	24	86	1	970
Dholpur	11	8	..	..	..	3	108	36	..	2	..	72	14,991	5,389	1,654	861	68	7,948	1,601	470	29	123	2	1,102
Dungarpur	..	..	..	..	..	..	56	17	..	..	..	39	14,947	4,459	1,742	747	79	8,746	1,412	457	85	28	1	870
Jaipur	10	2	1	..	..	7	967	404	..	21	..	563	207,400	72,428	22,758	4,190	600	112,214	27,183	8,410	921	781	39	17,852
Jaisalmer	..	..	..	..	..	..	22	12	..	3	..	10	5,466	1,651	275	188	5	3,540	3,126	871	94	106	3	2,161
Jhalawar	83	40	6	1	..	37	105	51	..	1	..	54	7,197	2,506	677	119	19	4,014	1,298	438	27	17	..	833
Karauli	28	19	4	..	..	5	18	11	..	..	..	7	11,954	4,802	1,441	1,026	74	5,711	1,622	485	43	85	1	1,094
Kishangarh	..	..	..	..	..	..	45	19	..	..	..	26	6,591	2,280	524	329	17	3,787	1,658	535	59	116	2	1,064
Kotah	743	350	156	10	1	237	346	143	5	5	..	198	40,044	13,696	7,927	1,635	197	18,421	2,432	766	82	159	4	1,584
Kushalgarh (Chiefship)	..	..	..	..	..	..	12	4	..	..	..	8	858	285	31	2	..	542	109	29	3	..	..	77
Lawa (Estate)	..	..	..	..	..	..	..	..	..	..	..	..	188	77	24	3	1	87	15	7	..	..	..	8
Marwar	..	..	..	..	..	..	673	329	..	5	..	344	173,681	52,602	9,481	3,278	569	111,598	78,725	21,868	2,848	841	26	54,009
Mewar	..	..	..	..	..	..	234	92	2	6	..	140	133,830	45,989	19,471	5,600	1,665	68,370	27,486	9,660	592	925	13	17,234
Partabgarh	..	..	..	..	..	..	35	11	..	..	..	24	6,132	2,187	524	107	40	3,421	1,357	444	15	30	1	898
Shahpura (Chiefship)	..	..	..	..	..	..	9	6	..	..	..	3	3,141	1,227	97	300	34	1,817	750	272	3	44	1	475
Sirohi	65	22	12	..	..	31	130	61	..	1	..	69	25,524	7,745	3,082	64	33	14,697	8,153	2,034	330	1	1	5,789
Tonk	10	8	..	..	..	2	186	68	..	1	..	118	16,628	6,139	1,625	334	25	8,864	1,637	565	24	62	..	1,048
Ajmer-Merwara	**229**	**128**	**4**	**3**	..	**97**	**942**	**331**	..	**4**	..	**611**	**40,464**	**15,399**	**3,193**	**1,966**	**233**	**21,872**	**7,191**	**2,455**	**143**	**443**	**13**	**4,593**
Ajmer	198	110	4	3	..	84	837	286	..	3	..	551	30,906	11,648	2,534	1,188	185	16,724	5,981	1,938	115	355	10	3,928
Merwara	31	18	..	..	..	13	105	45	..	1	..	60	9,558	3,751	659	778	48	5,148	1,210	517	28	88	3	665
CITIES.																								
Rajputana	**95**	**41**	**7**	**6**	..	**47**	**847**	**322**	..	**2**	..	**525**	**66,221**	**21,423**	**6,741**	**145**	**43**	**38,057**	**10,908**	**2,938**	**486**	**14**	..	**7,484**
Alwar	..	..	..	..	..	..	55	28	..	..	..	27	4,972	1,633	792	13	27	2,547	304	87	19	2	..	198
Bharatpur	67	27	7	..	..	33	57	26	..	..	..	31	4,672	1,737	709	30	7	2,226	363	104	20	3	..	239
Bikaner	21	8	..	6	..	13	120	45	..	..	..	75	13,473	3,385	816	33	6	9,272	4,575	991	190	3	..	3,394
Jaipur	..	..	..	..	..	..	272	90	..	1	..	182	18,679	6,508	2,424	7	..	9,747	1,957	651	88	3	..	1,218
Udaipur	..	..	..	..	..	..	111	48	..	..	..	63	11,008	3,331	1,858	36	..	5,819	2,130	546	143	1	..	1,441
Kotah	7	6	..	..	..	1	102	38	..	..	..	64	4,815	1,547	934	15	3	2,334	381	124	17	2	..	240
Tonk	..	..	..	..	..	..	69	25	..	1	..	44	3,744	1,343	434	11	..	1,967	433	172	..	..	..	261
Jodhpur	..	..	..	..	..	..	61	22	..	..	..	39	6,858	2,039	774	..	..	4,045	765	263	9	..	..	493
Ajmer-Merwara—																								
Ajmer	12	3	2	..	..	7	634	205	..	..	..	429	9,714	3,280	898	20	..	5,536	1,277	433	39	3	..	805

TABLE XV-A.—OCCUPATION OR MEANS OF LIVELIHOOD. PART II.—BY STATE OR DISTRICT, AND CITY—*continued.*

CLASS B.—PREPARATION AND SUPPLY OF MATERIAL SUBSTANCES—*continued.*

SUB-CLASS V.—TRADE—*continued.*

Province; and State, District, or City.	Total Order 25.—Brokerage, commission and export. 107.—Brokers in merchandise, etc., commission agents, commercial travellers, warehouse owners and employés. Total workers and dependants. Both sexes.	Actual workers. Total. Males.	Actual workers. Total. Females.	Actual workers. Partially agriculturists. Males.	Actual workers. Partially agriculturists. Females.	Dependants. Both sexes.	Total Order 26.—Trade in textiles. 108.—Trade in piece goods, wool, cotton, silk, hair and other textiles. Total workers and dependants. Both sexes.	Actual workers. Total. Males.	Actual workers. Total. Females.	Actual workers. Partially agriculturists. Males.	Actual workers. Partially agriculturists. Females.	Dependants. Both sexes.	Total Order 27.—Trade in skins, leather and furs. 109.—Trade in skins, leather, furs, feathers, horn, ivory, shell, etc. Total workers and dependants. Both sexes.	Actual workers. Total. Males.	Actual workers. Total. Females.	Actual workers. Partially agriculturists. Males.	Actual workers. Partially agriculturists. Females.	Dependants. Both sexes.	Total Order 28.—Trade in wood. 110.—Trade in wood (not firewood) cork, bark, etc. Total workers and dependants. Both sexes.	Actual workers. Total. Males.	Actual workers. Total. Females.	Actual workers. Partially agriculturists. Males.	Actual workers. Partially agriculturists. Females.	Dependants. Both sexes.
1	795	796	797	798	799	800	801	802	803	804	805	806	807	808	809	810	811	812	813	814	815	816	817	818
Rajputana	**14,894**	**3,317**	**19**	**80**	..	**10,958**	**73,855**	**20,700**	**1,896**	**861**	**90**	**51,259**	**18,234**	**7,074**	**1,142**	**2,548**	**204**	**10,068**	**3,116**	**1,048**	**872**	**57**	**3**	**1,198**
Alwar	241	93	1	3	..	147	1,937	659	131	41	14	1,147	3,640	1,009	145	430	42	1,426	200	54	25	2	..	121
Banswara	16	7	..	..	..	9	427	137	2	7	..	298	739	268	6	194	2	465	1	..	1	..	..	..
Bharatpur	233	93	1	9	..	139	3,096	806	26	33	7	1,264	410	154	22	40	5	234	74	31	13	3	1	30
Bikaner	2,830	648	1	17	..	2,181	30,487	4,040	69	283	4	16,378	311	112	6	16	2	193	4	..	..	..	..	4
Bundi	155	64	..	..	..	91	508	164	10	9	..	334	60	16	1	1	..	43	11	4	5	..	1	2
Dholpur	42	23	..	1	..	19	782	277	..	23	..	505	143	49	1	4	..	99	172	78	25	39	..	69
Dungarpur	7	5	..	..	..	3	1,232	322	11	11	2	809	2,509	889	40	461	15	1,571	..	..	..	..	..	..
Jaipur	5,873	1,469	..	13	..	4,404	16,998	5,369	446	128	10	11,183	4,295	1,659	431	502	90	2,145	353	116	154	..	..	83
Jaisalmer	26	9	..	..	..	17	264	88	5	7	..	171	13	5	..	..	..	8	..	..	..	..	..	..
Jhalawar	166	75	..	..	..	91	451	167	9	1	..	275	200	81	9	6	..	110	30	4	1	..	..	31
Karauli	11	7	..	..	..	4	653	267	4	10	..	382	1,160	576	72	415	28	512	..	..	..	..	..	..
Kishangarh	45	25	..	..	..	20	454	171	15	6	..	268	114	50	5	17	4	59	1	..	1	..	..	..
Kotah	368	162	6	6	..	200	2,323	887	150	64	1	1,286	1,001	425	50	171	7	517	108	41	34	2	..	33
Kushalgarh (Chiefship)	3	2	..	..	..	1	71	23	..	..	..	48	11	3	..	..	..	8	..	..	..	..	..	..
Lawa (Estate)	..	..	..	..	..	..	14	9	..	1	..	5	62	22	14	..	..	26	..	..	..	..	..	..
Marwar	3,134	621	..	16	..	2,513	13,299	3,672	66	66	1	9,661	2,663	1,021	187	133	7	1,455	561	220	..	9	..	341
Mewar	912	321	7	9	..	584	8,337	2,646	819	185	50	4,872	1,350	468	104	80	2	778	1,260	336	568	3	1	356
Partabgarh	178	55	2	1	..	131	610	235	23	3	1	352	124	35	0	10	..	83	305	154	40	9	..	111
Shahpura (Chiefship)	20	8	..	4	..	13	196	74	..	3	..	133	5	2	..	1	..	3	9	2	1	1	..	6
Sirohi	208	67	1	1	..	140	2,325	675	24	..	..	1,626	205	74	..	2	..	131	23	8	4	..	..	11
Tonk	426	163	..	..	..	263	391	122	86	..	..	183	329	102	25	15	..	202	..	..	..	..	..	..
Ajmer-Merwara	**1,545**	**597**	**9**	**11**	..	**939**	**3,263**	**1,178**	**84**	**33**	**5**	**2,000**	**1,150**	**407**	**25**	**90**	**5**	**718**	**93**	**32**	**39**	**4**	**1**	**22**
Ajmer	449	182	5	2	..	262	2,400	867	48	23	3	1,485	758	259	17	59	3	482	89	29	39	4	1	21
Merwara	1,096	415	4	9	..	677	862	311	36	9	2	515	392	148	8	21	2	236	4	3	..	..	..	1
CITIES.																								
Rajputana	**2,936**	**1,030**	**5**	..	..	**1,911**	**7,199**	**2,136**	**150**	**6**	..	**4,869**	**889**	**354**	**69**	**2**	..	**566**	**249**	**72**	**32**	..	..	**145**
Alwar	87	35	..	..	..	52	384	149	5	..	..	230	59	1	3	..	..	56	83	26	4	..	..	53
Bharatpur	33	15	..	..	..	18	367	149	3	1	..	315	39	8	..	..	..	21	12	5	..	..	..	7
Bikaner	721	164	..	..	..	557	2,303	459	..	3	..	1,844	144	45	..	..	..	99	..	..	..	..	..	..
Jaipur	1,247	486	..	..	..	761	1,745	665	80	1	..	1,000	305	95	33	..	..	177	59	17	25	..	..	17
Jodhpur	162	44	..	..	..	118	938	308	6	..	..	624	171	51	26	..	..	94	71	20	..	..	..	51
Kotah	146	62	..	..	..	84	408	161	14	1	..	233	38	12	..	..	..	26	5	4	1	..	..	..
Tonk	178	70	..	..	..	108	197	49	41	..	..	107	104	26	5	2	..	73	..	..	..	..	..	..
Udaipur	362	144	5	..	..	213	857	240	1	..	..	616	39	16	3	..	..	30	19	..	2	..	..	17
Ajmer-Merwara—																								
Ajmer	246	110	2	1	..	134	1,068	413	16	3	..	639	83	27	3	..	..	53	35	4	21	..	..	10

TABLE XV-A.—Occupation or Means of Livelihood. Part II.—By State or District, and City—*continued.*

CLASS B.—PREPARATION AND SUPPLY OF MATERIAL SUBSTANCES—*continued.*

SUB-CLASS V.—TRADE—*continued.*

Province; and State, District, or City.	Total Order 29.—Trade in metals. 111.—Trade in metals; machinery, knife, tool, etc., sellers. Total workers and dependants. Both sexes.	Actual workers. Total. Males.	Actual workers. Total. Females.	Actual workers. Partially agriculturists. Males.	Actual workers. Partially agriculturists. Females.	Dependants. Both sexes.	Total Order 30.—Trade in pottery. 112.—Trade in pottery. Total workers and dependants. Both sexes.	Actual workers. Total. Males.	Actual workers. Total. Females.	Actual workers. Partially agriculturists. Males.	Actual workers. Partially agriculturists. Females.	Dependants. Both sexes.	Total Order 31.—Trade in chemical products. 113.—Trade in chemical products (drugs, dyes, paints, petroleum, matches, explosives, etc.) Total workers and dependants. Both sexes.	Actual workers. Total. Males.	Actual workers. Total. Females.	Actual workers. Partially agriculturists. Males.	Actual workers. Partially agriculturists. Females.	Dependants. Both sexes.	Order 32.—Hotels, cafés, restaurants, etc. Total Order 32. Total workers and dependants. Both sexes.	Actual workers. Total. Males.	Actual workers. Total. Females.	Actual workers. Partially agriculturists. Males.	Actual workers. Partially agriculturists. Females.	Dependants. Both sexes.
1	819	820	821	822	823	824	825	826	827	828	829	830	831	832	833	834	835	836	837	838	839	840	841	842
Rajputana	961	347	19	4	..	595	221	47	73	1	..	101	676	267	34	5	2	375	15,752	5,633	2,214	947	131	7,905
Alwar	20	8	..	..	..	12	1	1	..	..	..	..	42	13	1	..	..	28	658	218	81	44	7	359
Banswara	..	..	..	..	..	..	..	..	..	..	..	..	..	..	..	..	..	..	249	124	1	10	1	124
Bharatpur	..	..	..	..	..	..	38	11	8	1	..	19	51	14	..	..	..	37	351	143	54	45	4	154
Bikaner	44	15	..	..	..	29	..	..	..	..	..	..	81	22	3	..	..	56	593	220	26	15	..	347
Bundi	..	..	..	..	..	..	..	..	..	..	..	..	11	5	..	..	..	6	381	124	67	14	..	190
Dholpur	109	44	..	..	..	65	3	..	1	..	..	2	63	33	1	1	..	29	123	37	17	4	1	69
Dungarpur	6	1	..	..	..	5	..	..	..	..	..	..	43	8	..	..	..	35	10	3	..	..	..	7
Jaipur	246	102	7	3	..	137	41	1	30	..	..	10	139	60	4	..	..	75	3,537	1,326	619	102	19	1,592
Jaisalmer	5	1	..	..	..	4	..	..	..	..	..	..	9	4	..	..	..	5	13	4	1	..	..	8
Jhalawar	..	..	..	..	..	..	..	..	..	..	..	..	31	14	1	..	..	16	133	53	16	3	1	64
Karauli	67	52	..	..	..	15	..	..	..	..	..	..	7	6	..	..	..	1	49	14	18	2	..	17
Kishangarh	..	..	..	..	..	..	..	..	..	..	..	..	..	..	..	..	..	..	147	56	18	8	2	73
Kotah	2	..	1	..	..	1	46	6	24	..	..	16	18	11	..	..	..	7	1,039	326	154	72	8	559
Kushalgarh (Chiefship)	..	..	..	..	..	..	..	..	..	..	..	..	..	..	..	..	..	..	94	41	4	2	..	49
Lawa (Estate)	..	..	..	..	..	..	..	..	..	..	..	..	..	..	..	..	..	..	3	1	..	..	..	2
Marwar	306	67	6	..	..	233	..	..	..	..	..	..	100	33	14	2	3	53	1,307	480	73	36	5	754
Mewar	50	20	..	1	..	30	1	1	..	..	..	..	34	18	3	2	..	13	6,043	2,114	999	560	75	2,930
Partabgarh	..	..	..	..	..	..	..	..	..	..	..	..	12	8	..	..	..	4	130	56	2	4	..	72
Shahpura (Chiefship)	14	4	..	..	..	10	..	..	..	..	..	..	..	..	..	..	..	..	19	8	3	6	3	8
Sirohi	35	18	..	..	..	17	75	20	3	..	..	52	35	18	7	..	..	10	543	170	19	5	..	354
Tonk	57	15	5	..	..	37	16	7	7	..	..	2	..	..	..	..	..	..	330	115	42	15	5	173
Ajmer-Merwara	41	11	..	..	..	30	..	..	..	..	..	..	39	13	..	..	..	26	612	220	38	15	..	354
Ajmer	39	11	..	..	..	28	..	..	..	..	..	..	34	10	..	..	..	24	487	175	28	10	..	284
Merwara	2	..	..	..	..	2	..	..	..	..	..	..	5	3	..	..	..	2	125	45	10	5	..	70
CITIES.																								
Rajputana	272	103	5	..	..	164	25	8	1	1	..	16	162	50	4	..	..	108	1,682	539	152	8	..	991
Alwar	4	2	..	..	..	2	..	..	..	..	..	..	20	4	..	..	..	16	132	42	17	..	..	73
Bharatpur	..	..	..	..	..	..	19	4	1	1	..	14	43	11	..	..	..	32	100	40	15	1	..	45
Bikaner	9	3	..	..	..	6	..	..	..	..	..	..	34	9	3	..	..	22	492	171	19	7	..	302
Jaipur	140	67	..	..	..	73	..	..	..	..	..	..	39	13	1	..	..	25	514	183	35	..	..	296
Jodhpur	67	20	..	..	..	47	..	..	..	..	..	..	15	7	..	..	..	8	143	46	12	..	..	85
Kotah	..	..	..	..	..	..	..	..	..	..	..	..	8	5	..	..	..	3	125	28	20	..	..	77
Tonk	34	9	5	..	..	20	6	4	..	..	..	2	..	..	..	..	..	..	43	16	..	..	..	27
Udaipur	18	2	..	..	..	16	..	..	..	..	..	..	3	1	..	..	..	2	133	13	34	..	..	86
Ajmer-Merwara—																								
Ajmer	..	..	..	..	..	..	..	..	..	..	..	..	13	9	..	..	..	4	118	46	2	1	..	70

TABLE XV-A.—OCCUPATION OR MEANS OF LIVELIHOOD. PART II.—BY STATE OR DISTRICT, AND CITY—*continued.*

CLASS B.—PREPARATION AND SUPPLY OF MATERIAL SUBSTANCES—*continued.*

SUB-CLASS V.—TRADE—*continued.*

Order 32.—Hotels, cafés, restaurants, etc.—*concluded.*

Province; and State, District, or City.	114.—Vendors of wine, liquors, aerated waters, ice, etc.						115.—Owners and managers of hotels, cookshops, sarais, etc., and their employés.					
	Total workers and dependants.	Actual workers. Total.		Actual workers. Partially agriculturists.		Dependants.	Total workers and dependants.	Actual workers. Total.		Actual workers. Partially agriculturists.		Dependants.
	Both sexes.	Males.	Females.	Males.	Females.	Both sexes.	Both sexes.	Males.	Females.	Males.	Females.	Both sexes.
1	843	844	845	846	847	848	849	850	851	852	853	854
Rajputana	**14,658**	**5,274**	**2,072**	**874**	**120**	**7,312**	**1,094**	**350**	**142**	**73**	**11**	**593**
Alwar	219	84	7	7	..	128	439	134	74	37	7	221
Banswara	249	124	1	10	1	124	..	..	..	..	..	..
Bharatpur	164	72	13	12	..	79	187	71	41	33	4	75
Bikaner	543	207	23	15	..	313	50	13	3	..	..	84
Bundi	381	124	67	14	..	190	..	..	..	..	..	..
Dholpur	45	19	1	3	1	25	78	18	16	1	..	44
Dungarpur	..	..	..	..	..	..	10	3	..	..	..	7
Jaipur	3,385	1,274	618	102	19	1,495	152	52	3	..	..	97
Jaisalmer	13	4	1	..	..	8	..	..	..	..	..	..
Jhalawar	132	53	15	3	1	64	1	..	1	..	..	..
Karauli	49	14	18	2	..	17	..	..	..	..	..	..
Kishangarh	144	53	18	8	2	73	3	3	..	..	..	..
Kotah	1,029	322	154	72	8	563	10	4	..	..	..	6
Kushalgarh (Chiefship)	94	41	4	2	..	49	..	..	..	..	..	..
Lawa (Estate)	3	1	..	..	..	2	..	..	..	..	..	..
Marwar	1,236	455	70	36	5	711	71	25	3	..	..	43
Mewar	6,030	2,112	999	560	75	2,919	13	2	..	..	..	11
Partabgarh	130	56	2	4	..	72	..	..	..	..	..	..
Shahpura (Chiefship)	19	8	3	6	3	8	..	..	..	..	..	..
Sirohi	493	148	18	3	..	327	60	22	1	2	..	27
Tonk	300	103	42	15	5	155	30	12	..	..	..	18
Ajmer-Merwara	**467**	**167**	**35**	**13**	..	**265**	**145**	**53**	**3**	**2**	..	**89**
Ajmer	370	132	25	9	..	213	117	43	3	1	..	71
Merwara	97	35	10	4	..	52	28	10	..	1	..	18
CITIES.												
Rajputana	**1,305**	**431**	**120**	**8**	..	**754**	**377**	**108**	**33**	..	..	**237**
Alwar	11	9	..	..	..	2	121	33	17	..	..	71
Bharatpur	54	20	3	1	..	31	46	20	12	..	..	14
Bikaner	444	158	16	7	..	270	48	13	3	..	..	32
Jaipur	400	157	35	..	..	208	114	26	..	..	..	58
Jodhpur	142	45	12	..	..	85	1	1	..	..	..	..
Kotah	121	27	20	..	..	74	4	1	..	..	..	3
Tonk	13	4	..	..	..	9	30	13	..	..	..	18
Udaipur	120	11	34	..	..	75	13	2	..	..	..	11
Ajmer-Merwara—												
Ajmer	78	30	1	..	..	47	40	10	1	1	..	23

Order 33.—Other trade in food stuffs.

Province; and State, District, or City.	Total Order 33.						116.—Fish dealers.			
	Total workers and dependants.	Actual workers. Total.		Actual workers. Partially agriculturists.		Dependants.	Total workers and dependants.	Actual workers. Total.		Dependants.
	Both sexes.	Males.	Females.	Males.	Females.	Both sexes.	Both sexes.	Males.	Females.	Both sexes.
1	855	856	857	858	859	860	861	862	863	864
Rajputana	**395,869**	**139,395**	**48,668**	**13,310**	**2,831**	**207,806**	**60**	**19**	**1**	**40**
Alwar	29,324	10,416	2,229	1,074	195	16,679	..	..	..	..
Banswara	2,611	841	411	101	13	1,359	..	..	..	..
Bharatpur	20,215	7,176	3,472	1,152	247	9,567	37	12	..	25
Bikaner	16,501	5,177	1,006	779	139	10,318	..	..	..	..
Bundi	7,0/6	2,563	558	196	1	3,955	..	..	..	..
Dholpur	7,205	2,594	1,086	396	65	3,525	..	..	..	..
Dungarpur	7,059	2,046	1,408	136	55	3,605	..	..	..	..
Jaipur	107.885	40,169	11,649	2,141	259	56,067	..	..	..	..
Jaisalmer	1,576	523	119	64	3	934	..	..	..	..
Jhalawar	4,311	1,493	570	83	18	2,248	..	..	..	..
Karauli	7,056	2,818	961	453	39	3,277	..	..	..	..
Kishangarh	3,187	1,149	239	162	4	1,799	..	..	..	..
Kotah	25,747	8,919	5,226	1,026	127	11,602	..	..	..	..
Kushalgarh (Chiefship)	564	184	24	..	..	356	..	..	..	..
Lawa (Estate)	89	38	7	2	1	44	..	..	..	..
Marwar	60,858	20,751	3,535	1,779	297	36,572	..	..	..	..
Mewar	70.370	24,136	13,404	3,311	1,336	32,830	..	..	..	..
Partabgarh	2,904	1,077	220	42	11	1,607	..	..	..	..
Shahpura (Chiefship)	1,576	656	12	182	..	9^8	..	..	..	..
Sirohi	9,354	2,669	1,521	16	19	5,164	12	4	1	7
Tonk	10,401	4,000	1,011	216	2	5,390	11	3	..	8
Ajmer-Merwara	**20,194**	**7,634**	**1,345**	**1,031**	**31**	**11,215**	**25**	**7**	..	**18**
Ajmer	16,011	6,017	9°9	588	12	9,005	23	5	..	18
Merwara	4,183	1,617	356	443	19	2,210	2	2	..	..
CITIES.										
Rajputana	**30,456**	**10,111**	**5,239**	**92**	**33**	**15,106**	**48**	**15**	..	**33**
Alwar	2,591	818	419	2	23	1,294	..	..	..	..
Bharatpur	2,920	1,007	635	21	7	1,278	37	12	..	25
Bikaner	4,175	1,318	338	17	1	2,519	..	..	..	..
Jaipur	7,570	2,770	1,375	1	..	3,425	..	..	..	..
Jodhpur	5,427	1,718	943	35	..	2,766	..	..	..	..
Kotah	2,632	820	616	11	2	1,196	..	..	..	..
Tonk	1,793	688	337	5	..	868	11	3	..	6
Udaipur	3,408	972	676	..	..	1,760	..	..	..	..
Ajmer-Merwara—										
Ajmer	4,655	1,449	614	10	..	3,592	23	5	..	18

TABLE XV-A.—OCCUPATION OR MEANS OF LIVELIHOOD. PART II.—BY STATE OR DISTRICT, AND CITY—*continued.*

CLASS B.—PREPARATION AND SUPPLY OF MATERIAL SUBSTANCES—*continued.*

SUB-CLASS V.—TRADE—*continued.*

Order 33.—Other trade in food stuffs—*continued.*

Province; and State, District, or City.	117.—Grocers and sellers of vegetable oil, salt and other condiments.						118.—Sellers of milk, butter, ghee, poultry, eggs, etc.						119.—Sellers of sweetmeats, sugar, gur, and molasses.						120.—Cardamom, betel-leaf, vegetables, fruit, and areca nut sellers.					
	Total workers and dependants.	Actual workers. Total.		Actual workers. Partially agriculturists.		Dependants.	Total workers and dependants.	Actual workers. Total.		Actual workers. Partially agriculturists.		Dependants.	Total workers and dependants.	Actual workers. Total.		Actual workers. Partially agriculturists.		Dependants.	Total workers and dependants.	Actual workers. Total.		Actual workers. Partially agriculturists.		Dependants.
	Both sexes.	Males.	Females.	Males.	Females.	Both sexes.	Both sexes.	Males.	Females.	Males.	Females.	Both sexes.	Both sexes.	Males.	Females.	Males.	Females.	Both sexes.	Both sexes.	Males.	Females.	Males.	Females.	Both sexes.
1	865	866	867	868	869	870	871	872	873	874	875	876	877	878	879	880	881	882	883	884	885	886	887	888
Rajputana	**236,306**	**92,854**	**7,748**	**8,441**	**206**	**136,103**	**17,118**	**5,004**	**4,495**	**475**	**205**	**7,619**	**16,615**	**6,865**	**611**	**428**	**10**	**10,539**	**24,079**	**4,447**	**13,871**	**426**	**945**	**5,761**
Alwar	22,270	8,412	519	818	12	13,339	657	189	131	48	14	337	263	108	3	5	..	152	2,338	437	1,275	47	152	626
Banswara	1,061	428	12	47	1	621	86	9	42	3	5	35	24	11	6	..	..	7	13	5	8	..	..	..
Bharatpur	9,778	3,912	393	760	19	5,473	837	277	227	40	5	333	2,770	1,187	63	89	..	1,520	2,760	478	1,799	82	173	483
Bikaner	7,981	2,521	264	512	45	5,196	1,628	502	213	89	31	913	1,610	491	70	3	..	1,049	1,129	318	370	17	61	441
Bundi	5,533	2,135	104	186	..	3,294	52	14	9	2	..	29	134	41	4	..	..	89	339	63	162	4	..	114
Dholpur	3,004	1,090	369	245	28	1,545	176	64	37	2	..	75	1,658	646	84	68	1	928	638	185	248	40	25	205
Dungarpur	2,544	848	154	50	4	1,542	33	13	10	5	..	10	85	36	8	..	..	41	144	51	26	10	..	67
Jaipur	74,214	30,712	2,375	1,725	65	41,127	3,581	1,089	1,132	45	26	1,359	4,141	1,677	35	103	..	2,429	7,292	1,071	4,832	47	99	1,389
Jaisalmer	641	228	18	24	..	395	373	117	18	12	..	237	140	45	4	1	1	91	178	37	76	25	2	65
Jhalawar	2,457	935	164	59	9	1,358	45	15	15	2	..	15	188	83	..	..	..	105	470	101	259	4	5	110
Karauli	4,389	1,853	237	344	7	2,299	376	150	89	6	2	137	37	19	..	..	..	15	368	113	168	43	22	87
Kishangarh	2,292	933	27	146	..	1,332	55	20	7	1	..	28	474	104	76	5	3	294	102	10	76	..	1	16
Kotah	13,978	5,614	1,367	891	29	6,997	4,675	1,164	1,577	147	57	1,934	1,043	445	86	33	1	512	1,799	376	985	28	19	438
Kushalgarh (Chiefship)	127	46	7	..	..	74	11	4	6	..	..	2	7	1	..	..	..	6	3	1	..	..	..	2
Lawa (Estate)	80	34	4	2	1	42	4	2	2	..	..	..	4	2	..	..	..	2	1	..	1	..	..	..
Marwar	42,778	15,128	641	1,377	8	27,007	2,439	779	371	42	2	1,289	3,230	1,111	89	53	3	2,030	2,584	208	1,745	27	259	491
Mewar	30,218	12,663	591	1,136	11	16,974	864	242	252	6	63	370	1,813	713	79	60	1	1,021	2,409	395	1,396	27	109	708
Partabgarh	1,648	658	65	32	5	930	177	58	30	2	..	89	90	45	3	..	..	51	149	41	66	2	2	42
Shahpura (Chiefship)	1,337	563	3	163	..	771	24	15	1	9	..	8	56	20	..	1	..	36	32	12	7	4	..	13
Sirohi	4,039	1,310	117	2	..	2,662	417	102	164	1	..	151	205	72	1	..	..	132	293	69	145	7	16	79
Tonk	5,788	2,346	317	122	2	3,125	609	179	162	13	..	268	34	8	..	..	..	26	998	386	227	12	..	385
Ajmer-Merwara	**11,359**	**4,658**	**154**	**908**	**9**	**6,547**	**1,999**	**637**	**248**	**32**	**2**	**1,114**	**1,668**	**642**	**22**	**15**	**2**	**1,004**	**1,564**	**409**	**613**	**9**	**2**	**542**
Ajmer	8,713	3,601	97	502	..	5,015	1,805	574	199	19	1	1,032	1,325	484	22	14	2	819	1,347	356	515	9	2	476
Merwara	2,646	1,057	57	406	9	1,532	194	63	49	13	1	82	343	158	..	1	..	185	217	53	98	..	..	66
CITIES.																								
Rajputana	**8,923**	**3,332**	**586**	**22**	..	**5,063**	**3,917**	**1,254**	**848**	**15**	..	**1,817**	**2,768**	**1,096**	**123**	**4**	..	**1,549**	**5,337**	**1,212**	**3,543**	**7**	**28**	**1,562**
Alwar	994	390	43	1	..	561	145	50	19	..	..	76	7	3	..	..	..	4	669	138	304	..	22	247
Bharatpur	510	203	8	1	..	299	292	110	67	3	..	115	578	254	6	2	..	318	709	183	358	6	3	168
Bikaner	1,426	439	81	..	..	906	838	265	139	..	..	454	727	215	63	..	..	449	294	103	36	..	1	155
Jaipur	2,400	988	162	..	..	1,250	954	303	257	..	..	394	404	226	2	1	..	176	1,204	342	523	..	..	339
Jodhpur	1,721	606	110	14	..	1,005	1,105	355	214	9	..	536	334	113	28	..	..	193	869	131	503	..	..	235
Kotah	803	239	72	6	..	442	251	84	65	..	..	162	249	119	12	1	..	118	568	106	317	1	2	145
Tonk	721	315	32	..	..	374	244	75	74	3	..	95	9	5	..	..	..	4	282	96	80	..	..	106
Udaipur	348	102	..	..	..	246	68	12	11	..	..	45	460	161	12	..	..	297	722	113	422	..	..	187
Ajmer-Merwara—																								
Ajmer	1,251	453	31	8	..	767	878	254	77	1	..	547	550	162	3	..	..	335	1,073	265	431	..	..	377

TABLE XV-A.—Occupation or Means of Livelihood. Part II.—By State or District, and City—*continued.*

Province; and State, District, or City.	CLASS B.—PREPARATION AND SUPPLY OF MATERIAL SUBSTANCES—*continued.* Sub-Class V.—Trade—*continued.* Order 33.—Other trade in food stuffs—*concluded.* 121.—Grain and pulse dealers. Total workers and dependants. Both sexes.	121. Actual workers. Total. Males.	121. Actual workers. Total. Females.	121. Actual workers. Partially agriculturists. Males.	121. Actual workers. Partially agriculturists. Females.	121. Dependants. Both sexes.	122.—Tobacco, opium, ganja, etc., sellers. Total workers and dependants. Both sexes.	122. Actual workers. Total. Males.	122. Actual workers. Total. Females.	122. Actual workers. Partially agriculturists. Males.	122. Actual workers. Partially agriculturists. Females.	122. Dependants. Both sexes.	123.—Dealers in sheep, goats, and pigs. Total workers and dependants. Both sexes.	123. Actual workers. Total. Males.	123. Actual workers. Total. Females.	123. Actual workers. Partially agriculturists. Males.	123. Actual workers. Partially agriculturists. Females.	123. Dependants. Both sexes.	124.—Dealers in hay, grass, and fodder. Total workers and dependants. Both sexes.	124. Actual workers. Total. Males.	124. Actual workers. Total. Females.	124. Actual workers. Partially agriculturists. Males.	124. Actual workers. Partially agriculturists. Females.	124. Dependants. Both sexes.
1	889	890	891	892	893	894	895	896	897	898	899	900	901	902	903	904	905	906	907	908	909	910	911	912
Rajputana	43,523	14,650	1,580	1,057	23	27,173	4,277	1,581	152	38	4	2,544	9,258	3,403	673	427	26	5,182	43,334	10,872	19,617	2,020	1,852	12,845
Alwar	1,820	588	28	80	..	1,204	126	46	8	2	..	72	1,331	477	52	58	..	802	519	159	213	16	17	147
Banswara	738	248	20	19	1	470	10	4	..	..	..	6	111	28	4	23	..	79	568	108	319	9	6	141
Bharatpur	2,261	892	88	121	8	1,281	167	68	..	..	..	99	200	60	15	13	..	125	1,405	290	887	47	42	228
Bikaner	3,178	861	44	43	2	2,273	183	56	2	..	..	125	363	245	6	37	..	112	429	183	37	78	..	209
Bundi	211	77	1	2	..	133	42	16	1	..	..	25	111	24	61	..	..	26	654	108	216	2	1	245
Dholpur	856	341	12	19	..	503	79	39	2	..	..	38	204	54	..	15	..	150	590	175	334	6	11	81
Dungarpur	2,060	663	125	47	2	1,272	115	30	15	..	..	61	53	13	4	9	1	36	2,025	383	1,066	15	48	576
Jaipur	11,221	3,653	475	132	..	7,093	762	267	18	..	..	477	1,949	621	280	33	2	1,048	4,725	1,079	2,501	56	47	1,143
Jaisalmer	172	60	1	1	..	121	17	7	..	..	..	10	..	..	..	..	..	..	56	39	2	1	..	15
Jhalawar	760	249	29	17	..	482	239	84	12	1	..	143	1	1	..	..	..	..	151	25	91	..	4	35
Karauli	730	263	23	29	..	444	68	39	..	..	..	29	108	47	1	1	1	60	980	334	443	30	7	203
Kishangarh	196	70	16	10	..	110	3	1	..	..	..	2	5	3	..	..	..	2	60	8	37	..	..	15
Kotah	1,120	452	20	57	..	848	291	96	27	7	3	168	190	82	9	2	..	99	2,651	690	1,155	56	18	806
Kushalgarh (Chiefship)	416	132	12	..	..	272	..	..	..	..	..	..	..	..	..	..	..	..	..	..	..	..	..	..
Lawa (Estate)	..	..	..	..	..	..	..	..	..	..	..	..	..	..	..	..	..	..	..	..	..	..	..	..
Marwar	4,747	1,508	130	42	..	3,109	803	313	6	..	..	484	3,376	1,349	187	222	21	1,840	953	265	366	16	4	322
Mewar	8,810	3,385	311	378	9	5,114	910	344	50	28	1	516	384	105	38	5	1	241	24,872	6,299	10,687	1,671	1,141	7,836
Partabgarh	614	224	8	5	1	382	118	36	..	..	..	82	14	6	2	1	..	6	85	14	46	..	3	25
Shahpura (Chiefship)	78	30	..	5	..	48	38	10	..	..	..	28	10	6	..	..	..	4	1	..	1	..	..	..
Sirohi	1,933	528	44	2	..	1,361	133	59	3	..	..	71	244	60	5	2	..	170	2,028	456	1,041	2	3	531
Tonk	1,602	636	113	48	..	853	173	57	8	..	..	108	604	213	9	6	..	382	582	172	175	15	..	235
Ajmer-Merwara	1,075	400	46	8	..	629	578	235	34	3	..	310	1,455	505	42	28	1	908	470	141	186	28	15	143
Ajmer	911	322	33	8	..	556	422	171	21	2	..	231	1,315	464	42	26	1	809	149	40	60	8	6	49
Merwara	164	78	13	..	..	73	156	64	13	1	..	79	140	41	..	2	..	99	321	101	126	20	9	94
CITIES.																								
Rajputana	5,070	1,814	211	3	..	3,045	1,156	385	41	1	..	730	515	161	6	1	..	348	2,722	842	961	39	5	919
Alwar	446	170	6	..	..	270	57	21	5	..	..	31	120	30	2	..	..	88	73	16	40	1	1	17
Bharatpur	386	143	2	..	..	241	77	31	..	..	..	46	31	9	..	..	..	22	300	62	194	9	4	44
Bikaner	557	177	17	..	..	363	106	30	2	..	..	74	27	8	..	..	..	19	180	81	..	17	..	99
Jaipur	1,196	443	147	..	..	606	306	116	14	..	..	176	221	64	1	..	..	156	885	288	269	..	..	328
Jodhpur	905	348	20	..	..	537	232	74	2	..	..	156	22	11	..	..	..	11	239	80	66	12	..	93
Kotah	300	104	4	2	..	192	191	52	14	1	..	125	..	..	..	..	..	..	270	66	132	..	..	72
Tonk	298	111	7	1	..	180	47	21	3	..	..	23	94	39	3	1	..	52	87	23	38	..	..	26
Udaipur	962	818	8	..	..	656	140	40	1	..	..	99	..	..	..	..	..	..	668	226	222	..	..	240
Ajmer-Merwara—																								
Ajmer	632	151	23	1	..	258	214	96	11	..	..	107	160	51	..	..	..	109	74	12	38	..	..	24

TABLE XV-A.—OCCUPATION OR MEANS OF LIVELIHOOD. PART II.—BY STATE OR DISTRICT, AND CITY—*continued.*

Province; and State, District, or City.	CLASS B.—PREPARATION AND SUPPLY OF MATERIAL SUBSTANCES—*continued.* SUB-CLASS V.—TRADE—*continued.* Total Order 34.—Trade in clothing and toilet articles. 125.—Trade in ready made clothing and other articles of dress and the toilet (hats, umbrellas, socks, ready made shoes, perfumes, etc.). Total workers and dependants.	Actual workers. Total.		Partially agriculturists.		Dependants.	Order 35.—Trade in Furniture. Total Order 35. Total workers and dependants.	Actual workers. Total.		Partially agriculturists.		Dependants.	126.—Trade in furniture, carpets, curtains, and beddings. Total workers and dependants.	Actual workers. Total.		Partially agriculturists.		Dependants.	127.—Hardware, cooking utensils, porcelain, crockery, glassware, bottles, articles for gardening and the cellar, etc. Total workers and dependants.	Actual workers. Total.		Partially agriculturists.		Dependants.
	Both sexes.	Males.	Females.	Males.	Females.	Both sexes.	Both sexes.	Males.	Females.	Males.	Females.	Both sexes.	Both sexes.	Males.	Females.	Males.	Females.	Both sexes.	Both sexes.	Males.	Females.	Males.	Females.	Both sexes.
1	913	914	915	916	917	918	919	920	921	922	923	924	925	926	927	928	929	930	931	932	933	934	935	936
Rajputana	9,067	3,255	571	139	23	5,261	2,564	980	237	46	7	1,347	778	285	182	23	7	331	1,786	605	75	24	..	1,016
Alwar	54	22	13	1	4	19	20	3	9	..	..	8	9	..	9	..	..	..	11	3	..	..	..	8
Banswara	10	5	..	..	..	5	..	..	..	..	..	..	..	..	..	..	..	..	..	..	..	..	..	..
Bharatpur	507	204	2	11	..	301	333	158	..	17	..	175	24	12	..	..	..	12	309	146	..	17	..	163
Bikaner	147	62	8	6	..	77	147	51	..	..	..	98	12	3	..	..	..	9	135	48	..	..	..	87
Bundi	31	10	..	..	..	21	87	22	29	..	..	36	59	15	29	..	..	15	28	7	..	..	..	21
Dholpur	174	67	1	1	..	106	45	12	5	..	..	28	6	..	5	..	..	1	39	12	..	..	..	27
Dungarpur	128	26	..	1	..	102	126	28	1	..	..	97	126	23	1	..	..	97	..	..	..	..	..	..
Jaipur	4,108	1,545	359	62	10	2,204	604	260	21	7	..	323	75	22	18	..	..	29	629	232	3	7	..	294
Jaisalmer	..	..	..	..	..	..	..	..	..	..	..	..	..	..	..	..	..	..	..	..	..	..	..	..
Jhalawar	58	18	..	..	..	40	99	37	2	7	..	60	21	16	..	7	..	15	68	21	2	..	..	45
Karauli	60	33	..	..	..	27	32	24	..	..	..	8	..	..	..	..	..	..	32	24	..	..	..	6
Kishangarh	2	2	..	..	..	..	21	10	..	..	..	11	..	..	..	..	..	..	21	10	..	..	..	11
Kotah	475	129	34	16	..	312	310	121	79	14	7	110	304	117	79	14	7	108	6	4	..	..	..	2
Kushalgarh (Chiefship)	1	1	..	..	..	..	..	..	..	..	..	..	..	..	..	..	..	..	..	..	..	..	..	..
Lawa (Estate)	..	..	..	..	..	..	..	..	..	..	..	..	..	..	..	..	..	..	..	..	..	..	..	..
Marwar	490	197	53	1	9	249	257	76	..	..	..	181	..	..	..	..	..	..	257	76	..	..	..	181
Mewar	1,683	534	53	29	..	1,096	387	146	87	1	..	154	126	63	19	1	..	44	261	83	68	..	..	110
Partabgarh	46	16	8	..	..	24	39	13	3	..	..	23	5	3	2	..	..	..	34	10	1	..	..	23
Shahpura (Chiefship)	10	1	2	..	..	7	..	..	..	..	..	..	..	..	..	..	..	..	..	..	..	..	..	..
Sirohi	46	16	9	..	..	21	32	8	1	..	..	23	..	..	..	..	..	..	32	8	1	..	..	23
Tonk	1,046	367	29	1	..	650	25	11	..	..	..	14	1	..	..	..	..	1	24	11	..	..	..	13
Ajmer-Merwara	436	189	4	1	..	263	283	76	42	..	..	165	219	67	41	..	..	111	64	9	1	..	..	54
Ajmer	374	191	4	1	..	239	283	76	42	..	..	165	219	67	41	..	..	111	64	9	1	..	..	54
Merwara	62	38	..	..	..	24	..	..	..	..	..	..	..	..	..	..	..	..	..	..	..	..	..	..
CITIES.																								
Rajputana	2,832	934	43	2	..	1,855	422	146	1	..	..	275	31	16	1	..	..	14	391	130	..	..	..	261
Alwar	12	12	..	..	..	..	4	..	..	..	..	4	..	..	..	..	..	..	4	..	..	..	..	4
Bharatpur	149	70	..	1	..	79	80	35	..	..	..	45	5	3	..	..	..	2	75	32	..	..	..	43
Bikaner	52	18	..	..	..	34	118	31	..	..	..	87	12	3	..	..	..	9	106	28	..	..	..	78
Jaipur	1,031	360	28	1	..	643	109	41	..	..	..	68	2	2	..	..	..	..	107	30	..	..	..	66
Jodhpur	235	109	..	..	..	126	31	12	..	..	..	19	..	..	..	..	..	..	31	12	..	..	..	19
Kotah	147	22	3	..	..	123	12	8	1	..	..	3	12	8	1	..	..	3	..	..	..	..	..	..
Tonk	388	129	9	..	..	250	13	5	..	..	..	8	..	..	..	..	..	..	13	5	..	..	..	8
Udaipur	818	214	4	..	..	600	55	14	..	..	..	41	..	..	..	..	..	..	55	14	..	..	..	41
Ajmer-Merwara—																								
Ajmer	349	123	4	..	..	222	116	39	37	..	..	40	110	39	37	..	..	40	..	..	..	..	..	..

TABLE XV-A.—OCCUPATION OR MEANS OF LIVELIHOOD. PART II.—BY STATE OR DISTRICT, AND CITY—*continued.*

Province; and State, District, or City.	B.—PREPARATION AND SUPPLY OF MATERIAL SUBSTANCES—*continued*. SUB-CLASS V.—TRADE—*continued*. Total Order 36.—Trade in building materials. 128.—Trade in building materials (stones, bricks, plaster, cement, sand, tiles, thatch, etc.)						Total Order 37.—Trade in means of transport. 129.—Dealers in elephants, camels, horses, cattle, asses, mules, etc., sellers (not makers) of carriages, saddlery, etc.						Total Order 38.—Trade in fuel. 130.—Dealers in firewood, charcoal, coal, cowdung, etc.						Order 39.—Trade in articles of luxury and those pertaining to letters and the arts and sciences. Total Order 39.					
	Total workers and dependants.	Actual workers. Total.		Actual workers. Partially agriculturists.		Dependants.	Total workers and dependants.	Actual workers. Total.		Actual workers. Partially agriculturists.		Dependants.	Total workers and dependants.	Actual workers. Total.		Actual workers. Partially agriculturists.		Dependants.	Total workers and dependants.	Actual workers. Total.		Actual workers. Partially agriculturists.		Dependants.
	Both sexes.	Males.	Females.	Males.	Females.	Both sexes.	Both sexes.	Males.	Females.	Males.	Females.	Both sexes.	Both sexes.	Males.	Females.	Males.	Females.	Both sexes.	Both sexes.	Males.	Females.	Males.	Females.	Both sexes.
1	937	938	939	940	941	942	943	944	945	946	947	948	949	950	951	952	953	954	955	956	957	958	959	960
Rajputana	**2,398**	**774**	**656**	**41**	**16**	**988**	**8,788**	**3,577**	**231**	**577**	**12**	**4,980**	**37,677**	**9,532**	**17,257**	**1,007**	**847**	**10,888**	**15,814**	**5,352**	**2,512**	**377**	**92**	**7,950**
Alwar	94	33	1	9	..	60	676	292	40	98	..	344	1,777	528	603	24	11	646	565	207	149	31	8	209
Banswara	29	10	10	..	..	9	70	23	..	15	..	47	145	28	83	4	7	34	42	13	14	2	1	15
Bharatpur	449	181	156	6	10	182	1,762	623	3	178	1	1,136	1,776	560	798	117	115	418	990	346	286	89	28	358
Bikaner	371	80	158	16	..	133	173	77	8	4	..	88	656	63	399	4	65	174	841	231	128	52	14	482
Bundi	176	76	36	..	..	64	281	116	8	2	1	157	1,317	362	469	13	1	486	411	128	85	7	1	198
Dholpur	..	..	..	..	..	..	173	83	2	10	..	88	380	94	204	6	..	82	530	204	114	33	..	212
Dungarpur	20	5	3	..	..	12	422	158	14	86	5	255	176	25	106	..	1	45	1,462	387	64	29	..	1,011
Jaipur	435	156	119	4	3	160	2,844	1,321	123	111	3	1,400	11,620	2,726	6,082	78	130	2,812	4,307	1,448	811	54	23	2,050
Jaisalmer	..	..	..	..	..	..	79	36	..	1	..	43	201	42	48	4	..	111	17	6	1	..	..	10
Jhalawar	..	..	..	..	..	..	38	17	1	1	..	20	26	5	15	..	..	6	235	67	16	..	..	152
Karauli	29	18	1	..	..	10	69	25	1	..	..	43	710	275	292	44	6	143	15	7	6	..	..	2
Kishangarh	62	20	10	1	3	28	12	9	..	..	..	3	181	26	129	2	2	26	141	40	..	1	..	101
Kotah	502	185	127	3	..	190	333	150	13	4	..	170	3,144	694	1,465	61	41	985	1,178	421	345	12	2	412
Kushalgarh (Chiefship)	..	..	..	..	..	..	..	..	..	..	..	..	..	..	..	..	..	..	1	..	..	..	..	1
Lawa (Estate)	..	..	..	..	..	..	..	..	..	..	..	..	..	..	..	..	..	..	5	..	3	..	..	2
Marwar	188	41	23	1	..	124	884	309	..	29	..	575	4,842	1,091	2,484	214	216	1,267	1,819	589	113	3	5	1,117
Mewar	2	..	..	..	..	2	772	278	18	25	2	478	6,410	1,673	2,358	353	171	2,388	2,683	1,047	331	48	9	1,305
Partabgarh	..	..	..	..	..	..	17	5	..	1	..	12	315	61	197	6	27	57	68	25	7	..	..	36
Shahpura (Chiefship)	1	1	..	..	..	..	106	30	..	6	..	76	153	45	58	29	30	50	84	44	11	16	..	29
Sirohi	25	10	2	1	..	13	64	23	..	4	..	41	2,962	954	1,130	33	13	878	348	112	18	..	..	218
Tonk	15	8	1	..	..	6	13	7	..	..	..	6	677	260	337	15	11	280	72	32	10	..	1	30
Ajmer-Merwara	**7**	..	**5**	..	..	**2**	**1,250**	**323**	**69**	**33**	..	**858**	**2,720**	**769**	**1,064**	**94**	**168**	**887**	**389**	**112**	**97**	**3**	**1**	**180**
Ajmer	7	..	5	..	..	2	1,181	297	65	30	..	819	2,023	522	884	67	152	617	378	105	97	3	1	176
Merwara	..	..	..	..	..	..	69	26	4	3	..	39	697	247	180	27	16	270	11	7	..	..	..	4
CITIES.																								
Rajputana	**679**	**188**	**170**	**3**	..	**321**	**484**	**224**	**20**	..	..	**240**	**4,730**	**1,059**	**2,057**	**15**	**9**	**1,614**	**2,124**	**728**	**209**	..	**1**	**1,187**
Alwar	73	20	1	1	..	52	24	12	..	..	..	12	909	320	311	8	4	368	35	8	9	..	..	18
Bharatpur	178	72	2	1	..	104	45	32	..	..	..	13	104	60	20	..	..	24	49	17	11	..	..	21
Bikaner	166	5	90	1	..	71	27	10	8	..	..	9	293	42	157	2	5	94	158	50	6	..	..	102
Jaipur	200	68	59	..	..	73	303	126	9	..	..	168	1,413	285	568	..	..	560	1,101	368	64	..	..	669
Jodhpur	47	14	18	..	..	15	19	8	..	..	..	11	1,010	121	677	..	..	212	367	112	29	..	..	226
Kotah	15	9	..	..	..	6	39	25	..	..	..	14	508	110	192	1	..	206	260	113	70	..	1	67
Tonk	..	..	..	..	..	..	9	6	..	..	..	3	290	79	121	4	..	90	13	8	..	..	..	5
Udaipur	..	..	..	..	..	..	18	5	3	..	..	10	113	42	11	..	..	60	121	52	20	..	..	49
Ajmer-Merwara—																								
Ajmer	6	..	5	..	..	1	258	73	47	..	..	138	393	118	35	1	..	240	160	30	54	..	..	76

TABLE XV-A.—Occupation or Means of Livelihood. Part II—By State or District, and City—*continued*.

B.—PREPARATION AND SUPPLY OF MATERIAL SUBSTANCES—*continued*.

SUB-CLASS V.—TRADE—*continued*.

Province; and State, District, or City.	Order 39.—Trade in articles of luxury and those pertaining to letters and the arts and sciences—*concluded*. 131.—Dealers in precious stones, jewellery (real and imitation), clocks, optical instruments, etc. Total workers and dependants.	Actual workers. Total.		Partially agriculturists.		Dependants.	132.—Dealers in common bangles, bead necklaces, fans, small articles, toys, hunting and fishing tackle, flowers, etc. Total workers and dependants.	Actual workers. Total.		Partially agriculturists.		Dependants.	133.—Publishers, booksellers, stationers, dealers in music, pictures, musical instruments, and curiosities. Total workers and dependants.	Actual workers. Total.		Partially agriculturists.		Dependants.	Order 40.—Trade in refuse matter. 134.—Dealers in rags, stable refuse, etc. Total workers and dependants.	Actual workers. Total.		Partially agriculturists.		Dependants.
	Both sexes.	Males.	Females.	Males.	Females.	Both sexes.	Both sexes.	Males.	Females.	Males.	Females.	Both sexes.	Both sexes.	Males.	Females.	Males.	Females.	Both sexes.	Both sexes.	Males.	Females.	Males.	Females.	Both sexes.
1	961	962	963	964	965	966	967	968	969	970	971	972	973	974	975	976	977	978	979	980	981	982	983	984
Rajputana	1,659	464	37	1	3	1,158	13,768	4,655	2,473	374	89	6,586	447	233	2	2	..	212	4	3	..	..	..	1
Alwar	..	..	..	..	..	..	562	206	149	81	8	207	3	1	..	..	..	2	..	..	..	..	..	..
Banswara	4	1	..	..	..	3	38	12	14	3	1	12	..	..	..	..	..	..	..	..	..	..	..	..
Bharatpur	..	..	..	..	..	..	974	342	286	89	28	846	16	4	..	..	..	12	4	3	..	..	..	1
Bikaner	208	40	2	..	..	186	615	184	128	52	14	805	18	7	..	..	..	11	..	..	..	..	..	..
Bundi	..	..	..	..	..	..	407	126	85	7	1	196	4	2	..	..	..	2	..	..	..	..	..	..
Dholpur	18	6	..	..	..	12	511	197	114	32	..	200	1	1	..	1	..	..	..	..	..	..	..	..
Dungarpur	..	..	..	..	..	..	1,445	382	64	29	..	999	17	5	..	..	..	12	..	..	..	..	..	..
Jaipur	956	269	33	1	3	654	3,090	1,026	778	52	20	1,286	261	151	..	1	..	110	..	..	..	..	..	..
Jaisalmer	10	3	..	..	..	7	7	3	1	..	..	3	..	..	..	..	..	..	..	..	..	..	..	..
Jhalawar	29	12	..	..	..	17	206	55	16	..	..	135	..	..	..	..	..	..	..	..	..	..	..	..
Karauli	..	..	..	..	..	..	11	3	6	..	..	2	4	4	..	..	..	..	..	..	..	..	..	..
Kishangarh	91	24	..	..	..	67	47	15	..	1	..	32	3	1	..	..	..	2	..	..	..	..	..	..
Kotah	10	4	2	..	..	4	1,156	406	343	12	2	405	12	9	..	..	..	3	..	..	..	..	..	..
Kushalgarh (Chiefship)	..	..	..	..	..	..	1	..	..	..	..	1	..	..	..	..	..	..	..	..	..	..	..	..
Lawa (Estate)	..	..	..	..	..	..	5	..	3	..	..	2	..	..	..	..	..	..	..	..	..	..	..	..
Marwar	134	43	..	..	..	91	1,654	535	113	3	5	1,006	31	11	..	..	..	20	..	..	..	..	..	..
Mewar	75	34	..	..	..	41	2,569	997	329	46	9	1,243	39	16	2	..	..	21	..	..	..	..	..	..
Partabgarh	4	4	..	..	..	..	64	21	7	..	..	36	..	..	..	..	..	..	..	..	..	..	..	..
Shahpura (Chiefship)	..	..	..	..	..	..	84	44	11	10	..	29	..	..	..	..	..	..	..	..	..	..	..	..
Sirohi	119	23	..	..	..	96	225	85	18	..	..	122	4	4	..	..	..	..	..	..	..	..	..	..
Tonk	1	1	..	..	..	..	37	14	10	..	1	13	34	17	..	..	..	17	..	..	..	..	..	..
Ajmer-Merwara	31	4	15	1	..	12	306	92	81	2	1	133	52	16	1	..	..	35	..	..	..	..	..	..
Ajmer	31	4	15	1	..	12	302	88	81	2	1	133	45	13	1	..	..	31	..	..	..	..	..	..
Merwara	..	..	..	..	..	..	4	4	..	..	..	..	7	3	..	..	..	4	..	..	..	..	..	..
CITIES.																								
Rajputana	907	276	10	..	..	621	1,024	379	198	..	1	447	188	73	1	..	..	119	4	3	..	..	..	1
Alwar	..	..	..	..	..	..	32	7	9	..	..	16	3	1	..	..	..	2	..	..	..	..	..	..
Bharatpur	..	..	..	..	..	..	40	15	11	..	..	14	9	2	..	..	..	7	4	3	..	..	..	1
Bikaner	93	20	2	..	..	71	49	25	4	..	..	20	16	5	..	..	..	11	..	..	..	..	..	..
Jaipur	773	242	8	..	..	523	219	86	56	..	..	77	109	40	..	..	..	69	..	..	..	..	..	..
Jodhpur	39	12	..	..	..	27	304	90	29	..	..	185	24	10	..	..	..	14	..	..	..	..	..	..
Kotah	1	1	..	..	..	..	271	107	70	..	1	94	8	6	..	..	..	8	..	..	..	..	..	..
Tonk	1	1	..	..	..	..	11	6	..	..	..	5	1	1	..	..	..	..	..	..	..	..	..	..
Udaipur	..	..	..	..	..	..	98	43	19	..	..	36	23	9	1	..	..	13	..	..	..	..	..	..
Ajmer Merwara—																								
Ajmer	24	..	15	..	..	9	95	21	38	..	..	96	41	9	1	..	..	31	..	..	..	..	..	..

TABLE XV-A.—Occupation or Means of Livelihood. Part II.—By State or District, and City—*continued.*

CLASS B.—PREPARATION AND SUPPLY OF MATERIAL SUBSTANCES—*continued.*

SUB-CLASS V.—TRADE—*continued.*

Order 41.—Trade of other sorts.

Province ; and State, District, or City.	Total Order 41. Total workers and dependants. Both sexes.	Total Order 41. Actual workers. Total. Males.	Total Order 41. Actual workers. Total. Females.	Total Order 41. Actual workers. Partially agriculturists. Males.	Total Order 41. Actual workers. Partially agriculturists. Females.	Total Order 41. Dependants. Both sexes.	135.—Shopkeepers otherwise unspecified. Total workers and dependants. Both sexes.	135. Actual workers. Total. Males.	135. Actual workers. Total. Females.	135. Partially agriculturists. Males.	135. Partially agriculturists. Females.	135. Dependants. Both sexes.	136.—Itinerant traders, pedlars, hawkers, etc., of miscellaneous or unspecified articles. Total workers and dependants. Both sexes.	136. Actual workers. Total. Males.	136. Actual workers. Total. Females.	136. Partially agriculturists. Males.	136. Partially agriculturists. Females.	136. Dependants. Both sexes.	137.—Conjurors, acrobats, fortunetellers, reciters, exorcists, exhibitors of curiosities and wild animals. Total workers and dependants. Both sexes.	137. Actual workers. Total. Males.	137. Actual workers. Total. Females.	137. Partially agriculturists. Males.	137. Partially agriculturists. Females.	137. Dependants. Both sexes.
1	985	986	987	988	989	990	991	992	993	994	995	996	997	998	999	1000	1001	1002	1003	1004	1005	1006	1007	1008
Rajputana	**42,811**	**16,921**	**2,054**	**1,121**	**43**	**23,836**	**29,735**	**10,900**	**1,625**	**790**	**37**	**17,200**	**9,814**	**4,336**	**220**	**310**	..	**5,258**	**1,779**	**633**	**176**	**19**	**6**	**970**
Alwar	2,669	903	69	51	2	1,697	2,015	615	55	38	2	1,345	603	259	14	13	..	330	2	2	..	..	..	..
Banswara	222	61	1	..	..	160	6	6	..	..	..	..	208	50	..	..	..	158	8	5	1	..	..	2
Bharatpur	2,154	956	178	94	13	1,020	1,426	596	147	83	13	683	284	173	9	8	..	102	444	187	22	3	..	235
Bikaner	1,922	684	145	147	1	1,093	1,226	446	60	132	1	720	473	155	51	12	..	267	223	83	34	3	..	106
Bundi	230	75	7	5	..	148	51	13	..	2	..	38	116	32	..	3	..	84	60	29	7	..	..	24
Dholpur	3,446	1,330	168	231	..	1,948	1,339	467	68	83	..	804	1,960	815	81	139	..	1,064	147	48	19	9	..	60
Dungarpur	335	104	1	..	..	230	289	96	1	..	..	192	32	5	..	..	..	27	10	3	..	..	..	7
Jaipur	16,992	6,293	982	204	14	9,717	10,073	5,821	946	199	14	9,306	707	428	22	3	..	347	107	40	10	2	..	57
Jaisalmer	137	62	7	6	..	68	136	62	7	6	..	67	1	..	..	..	..	1	..	..	..	..	..	..
Jhalawar	115	42	10	1	..	63	20	3	5	..	..	12	21	10	..	..	..	11	44	18	4	1	..	22
Karauli	414	195	43	17	..	176	284	136	31	17	..	117	71	37	..	..	..	34	58	22	11	..	..	25
Kishangarh	506	187	39	16	..	840	492	160	22	14	..	810	29	18	1	2	..	10	34	4	16	..	..	14
Kotah	1,018	453	128	25	..	437	758	306	124	25	..	828	..	..	..	..	..	..	107	50	..	..	..	57
Kushalgarh (Chiefship)	4	2	..	..	..	2	..	..	..	..	..	..	..	..	..	..	..	..	..	..	..	..	..	..
Lawa (Estate)	..	..	..	..	..	..	..	..	..	..	..	..	..	..	..	..	..	..	..	..	..	..	..	..
Marwar	4,239	1,666	70	148	1	2,494	2,928	1,042	69	118	1	1,817	1,144	561	..	30	..	583	114	40	10	..	..	64
Mewar	6,041	2,591	128	158	6	3,322	2,078	850	68	62	6	1,160	8,548	1,629	33	95	..	1,886	231	32	8	1	..	191
Partabgarh	25	3	1	1	..	21	17	1	1	..	..	15	..	..	..	..	..	..	..	..	..	..	..	..
Shahpura (Chiefship)	198	80	7	6	..	111	145	57	1	2	..	87	48	22	4	4	..	22	..	..	..	..	..	..
Sirohi	1,091	869	13	1	..	209	107	65	10	..	..	32	13	5	3	..	..	5	..	..	..	..	..	..
Tonk	993	365	48	10	6	580	335	158	10	9	..	167	406	137	2	1	..	327	100	70	34	..	6	86
Ajmer-Merwara	**3,252**	**1,403**	**239**	**219**	**9**	**1,620**	**2,244**	**1,018**	**89**	**211**	**7**	**1,137**	**658**	**266**	**54**	**8**	**2**	**338**	**252**	**92**	**67**	..	..	**93**
Ajmer	2,412	1,029	196	46	3	1,187	1,529	674	77	38	2	778	584	249	49	8	1	286	223	83	57	..	..	83
Merwara	840	374	33	173	6	433	715	344	12	173	5	359	74	17	5	..	1	52	20	9	10	..	..	10
CITIES.																								
Rajputana	**2,168**	**866**	**96**	**2**	..	**1,204**	**1,384**	**533**	**71**	**1**	..	**780**	**477**	**303**	**2**	..	..	**273**	**216**	**96**	**23**	**1**	..	**97**
Alwar	231	97	5	..	..	119	91	33	5	..	..	53	114	53	..	..	..	56	2	2	..	..	..	..
Bharatpur	177	105	2	1	..	70	65	34	2	..	..	29	91	68	..	..	..	33	21	13	..	1	..	8
Bikaner	206	69	5	..	..	132	80	10	4	..	..	16	153	50	..	..	..	103	23	9	1	..	..	13
Jaipur	946	313	59	1	..	574	885	293	49	1	..	543	5	2	..	..	..	3	48	16	10	..	..	22
Jodhpur	175	95	4	..	..	76	113	76	4	..	..	33	..	..	..	..	..	..	25	7	..	..	..	18
Kotah	71	44	1	..	..	26	19	9	1	..	..	9	..	..	..	..	..	..	52	35	..	..	..	17
Tonk	243	82	16	..	..	145	92	38	2	..	..	52	111	34	..	..	..	77	38	10	12	..	..	16
Udaipur	129	61	6	..	..	62	89	40	4	..	..	45	3	1	2	..	..	..	7	4	..	..	..	3
Ajmer-Merwara—																								
Ajmer	937	406	19	1	..	512	616	250	16	..	..	350	305	151	3	1	..	151	4	2	..	..	..	2

TABLE XV-A.—OCCUPATION OR MEANS OF LIVELIHOOD. PART II.—BY STATE OR DISTRICT, AND CITY—*continued*.

Province; and State, District, or City.	CLASS B.—PREPARATION AND SUPPLY OF MATERIAL SUBSTANCES—*concluded*. Sub-Class V.—Trade—*concluded*. Order 41.—Trade of other sorts—*concluded*. 138.—Other trades (including farmers of pounds, tolls, and markets).						CLASS C.—PUBLIC ADMINISTRATION AND LIBERAL ARTS. Total Class C.						Sub-Class VI.—Public Force. Total Sub-Class VI.						Order 42.—Army. Total Order 42.					
	Total workers and dependants.	Actual workers. Total.		Actual workers. Partially agriculturists.		Dependants.	Total workers and dependants.	Actual workers. Total.		Actual workers. Partially agriculturists.		Dependants.	Total workers and dependants.	Actual workers. Total.		Actual workers. Partially agriculturists.		Dependants.	Total workers and dependants.	Actual workers. Total.		Actual workers. Partially agriculturists.		Dependants.
	Both sexes.	Males.	Females.	Males.	Females.	Both sexes.	Both sexes.	Males.	Females.	Males.	Females.	Both sexes.	Both sexes.	Males.	Females.	Males.	Females.	Both sexes.	Both sexes.	Males.	Females.	Males.	Females.	Both sexes.
1	1009	1010	1011	1012	1013	1014	1015	1016	1017	1018	1019	1020	1021	1022	1023	1024	1025	1026	1027	1028	1029	1030	1031	1032
Rajputana	**1,493**	**1,052**	**33**	**2**	..	**408**	**738,112**	**296,108**	**68,115**	**41,496**	**3,681**	**373,889**	**149,019**	**72,370**	**211**	**11,624**	**5**	**76,438**	**86,458**	**44,953**	**197**	**3,689**	**5**	**41,308**
Alwar	49	27	..	..	..	22	48,330	18,029	3,593	3,361	259	26,708	11,790	5,309	..	826	..	6,497	7,372	3,518	..	101	..	3,854
Banswara	..	..	..	..	..	..	7,233	2,480	838	447	45	3,915	898	349	..	23	..	549	34	21	..	..	..	13
Bharatpur	..	..	..	..	..	..	41,052	17,042	1,857	2,889	124	22,153	9,081	4,293	..	559	..	4,788	6,566	3,146	..	176	..	3,420
Bikaner	..	..	..	..	..	..	33,983	12,513	4,302	2,495	281	17,168	3,389	2,052	..	769	..	1,337	1,716	1,101	..	680	..	625
Bundi	3	1	..	..	..	2	10,790	4,442	656	306	13	5,692	3,600	1,764	4	124	..	1,832	3,111	1,517	2	116	..	1,592
Dholpur	..	..	..	..	..	..	16,733	6,267	951	860	39	9,515	4,113	1,676	..	109	..	2,437	2,702	1,094	..	96	..	1,608
Dungarpur	4	..	..	..	..	4	8,779	3,016	812	412	36	4,951	1,172	472	2	13	..	698	450	202	2	3	..	255
Jaipur	15	4	4	..	..	7	234,853	97,626	20,366	12,122	911	116,861	50,555	25,642	2	5,064	..	24,911	27,897	15,926	1	921	..	11,970
Jaisalmer	..	..	..	..	..	..	5,827	1,874	387	230	4	3,566	438	173	..	15	..	265	360	153	..	14	..	207
Jhalawar	30	11	1	..	..	18	8,727	3,119	517	204	9	5,091	2,910	826	9	29	..	1,391	1,376	463	2	7	..	911
Karauli	1	..	1	..	..	..	11,948	4,941	698	739	77	6,309	3,252	1,309	..	149	..	1,943	2,740	1,064	..	135	..	1,676
Kishangarh	11	5	..	..	..	6	8,816	3,911	746	499	41	4,159	2,280	1,136	35	95	..	1,109	1,819	918	32	48	..	869
Kotah	153	97	4	..	..	52	37,917	15,723	2,217	1,797	101	19,977	12,863	6,146	..	675	..	6,717	6,153	2,995	..	116	..	3,158
Kushalgarh (Chiefship)	4	2	..	..	..	2	628	200	39	7	1	389	279	88	..	..	..	184	..	..	..	..	..	..
Lawa (Estate)	..	..	..	..	..	..	198	89	32	7	..	77	13	7	..	1	..	6	7	5	..	1	..	2
Marwar	53	23	..	..	..	30	138,715	55,259	17,601	8,437	1,093	65,852	13,509	7,154	..	1,547	..	6,355	4,128	3,020	..	168	..	1,108
Mewar	184	80	10	..	..	85	82,221	31,130	9,330	5,665	582	38,761	17,150	9,089	160	1,397	5	7,901	13,890	7,512	152	1,081	5	6,226
Partabgarh	8	2	..	1	..	6	3,327	1,298	480	159	40	1,510	593	269	..	17	..	324	170	81	..	..	..	89
Shahpura (Chiefship)	5	1	2	..	..	2	3,603	1,672	251	323	23	1,680	513	231	..	33	..	282	234	101	..	18	..	133
Sirohi	971	799	..	1	..	172	15,305	5,476	1,845	165	13	7,984	3,284	1,241	6	16	..	2,037	1,224	378	6	..	..	840
Tonk	2	..	2	..	..	..	19,124	7,001	621	374	12	11,502	8,036	3,161	..	187	..	4,875	4,500	1,648	..	8	..	2,852
Ajmer-Merwara	**98**	**27**	**19**	..	..	**52**	**35,022**	**15,430**	**2,827**	**3,627**	**180**	**16,765**	**8,865**	**5,557**	**14**	**2,287**	**1**	**3,294**	**6,447**	**4,331**	**12**	**2,208**	**1**	**2,104**
Ajmer	76	23	13	..	..	40	30,199	13,605	2,332	3,238	121	14,262	8,282	5,294	4	2,268	1	2,984	6,269	4,272	4	2,206	1	1,993
Merwara	22	4	6	..	..	12	4,823	1,825	495	389	59	2,503	583	263	10	19	..	310	178	59	8	2	..	111
CITIES.																								
Rajputana	**91**	**34**	**2**	..	..	**55**	**132,115**	**50,473**	**7,214**	**1,857**	**9**	**74,428**	**38,653**	**19,583**	**18**	**936**	..	**19,052**	**33,423**	**16,888**	**14**	**893**	..	**15,521**
Alwar	14	4	..	..	..	10	13,159	5,651	498	83	3	7,010	5,877	3,166	..	97	..	2,711	5,173	2,843	..	27	..	2,330
Bharatpur	..	..	..	..	..	..	14,013	5,526	373	154	2	8,114	5,545	2,661	..	80	..	2,884	4,791	2,312	..	53	..	2,479
Bikaner	..	..	..	..	..	..	12,000	4,291	1,083	699	..	6,626	2,000	1,314	..	678	..	686	1,525	1,084	..	677	..	441
Jaipur	8	2	..	..	..	6	44,056	16,528	2,128	75	3	25,400	10,465	4,907	1	7	..	5,557	9,352	4,469	..	6	..	4,883
Jodhpur	37	12	..	..	..	25	20,659	7,660	1,813	95	..	11,186	3,333	2,190	..	86	..	1,143	1,980	1,636	..	85	..	344
Kotah	..	..	..	..	..	..	9,501	3,941	496	117	1	5,064	3,432	1,764	..	43	..	1,668	2,985	1,558	..	39	..	1,427
Tonk	2	..	2	..	..	..	9,709	3,146	267	29	..	6,296	4,577	1,643	..	6	..	2,934	3,956	1,421	..	6	..	2,535
Udaipur	30	16	..	..	..	14	8,988	3,730	556	6	..	4,702	3,494	1,038	17	..	..	1,469	2,061	1,565	14	..	..	1,082
Ajmer-Merwara—																								
Ajmer	12	3	..	..	..	9	11,335	4,313	642	821	2	6,380	2,598	1,355	3	676	1	1,240	1,628	821	3	672	1	804

TABLE XV-A.—Occupation or Means of Livelihood. Part II.—By State or District, and City—*continued.*

CLASS C.—PUBLIC ADMINISTRATION AND LIBERAL ARTS—*continued.*

SUB-CLASS VI.—PUBLIC FORCE—*continued.*

Province; and State, District, or City.	Order 42.—Army—*concluded.* 139.—Army (Imperial). Total workers and dependants. Both sexes.	139. Actual workers. Total. Males.	139. Actual workers. Total. Females.	139. Partially agriculturists. Males.	139. Partially agriculturists. Females.	139. Dependants. Both sexes.	140.—Army (Native States including Imperial Service Troops). Total workers and dependants. Both sexes.	140. Actual workers. Total. Males.	140. Actual workers. Total. Females.	140. Partially agriculturists. Males.	140. Partially agriculturists. Females.	140. Dependants. Both sexes.	Order 44.—Police. Total Order 44. Total workers and dependants. Both sexes.	Total Order 44. Actual workers. Total. Males.	Total Order 44. Actual workers. Total. Females.	Total Order 44. Partially agriculturists. Males.	Total Order 44. Partially agriculturists. Females.	Total Order 44. Dependants. Both sexes.	142.—Police (Imperial). Total workers and dependants. Both sexes.	142. Actual workers. Total. Males.	142. Actual workers. Total. Females.	142. Partially agriculturists. Males.	142. Partially agriculturists. Females.	142. Dependants. Both sexes.
1	1033	1034	1035	1036	1037	1038	1039	1040	1041	1042	1043	1044	1045	1046	1047	1048	1049	1050	1051	1052	1053	1054	1055	1056
Rajputana	**3,307**	**1,596**	**41**	**648**	..	**1,740**	**83,151**	**43,427**	**156**	**3,041**	**5**	**39,568**	**62,561**	**27,417**	**14**	**7,935**	..	**35,130**	**1,586**	**758**	**5**	**42**	..	**823**
Alwar	304	71	..	20	..	233	7,068	3,447	..	81	..	3,621	4,427	1,784	..	725	..	2,643	25	14	..	..	..	11
Banswara	14	14	..	..	..	..	20	7	..	..	..	13	864	328	..	23	..	536	30	23	..	1	..	7
Bharatpur	105	43	..	3	..	62	6,461	3,103	..	173	..	3,358	2,515	1,147	..	383	..	1,368	54	11	..	..	..	43
Bikaner	62	41	..	3	..	21	1,654	1,150	..	677	..	504	1,673	861	..	82	..	812	3	1	..	..	..	2
Bundi	16	7	..	..	..	9	3,095	1,510	2	116	..	1,583	489	247	2	8	..	240	..	..	..	..	..	..
Dholpur	27	12	..	1	..	15	2,675	1,062	..	95	..	1,503	1,411	582	..	66	..	829	5	3	..	..	..	2
Dungarpur	..	..	..	..	..	..	459	202	2	3	..	255	713	270	..	10	..	443	5	5	..	1	..	..
Jaipur	563	212	..	11	..	351	27,334	15,714	1	910	..	11,619	22,658	9,716	1	4,143	..	12,941	635	273	1	17	..	361
Jaisalmer	..	..	..	..	..	..	380	153	..	14	..	207	78	20	..	1	..	58	1	1	..	..	..	..
Jhalawar	..	..	..	..	..	..	1,376	463	2	7	..	911	643	363	..	22	..	480	4	3	..	3	..	1
Karauli	8	1	..	..	..	7	2,732	1,063	..	135	..	1,669	512	245	..	14	..	267	..	..	..	..	..	..
Kishangarh	..	..	..	..	..	..	1,819	918	32	48	..	869	451	206	3	47	..	240	13	6	..	..	..	7
Kotah	15	15	..	..	..	..	6,138	2,980	..	116	..	3,158	6,710	3,151	..	559	..	3,559	41	20	..	..	..	21
Kushalgarh (Chiefship)	..	..	..	..	..	..	..	..	..	..	..	..	272	88	..	..	..	184	..	..	..	..	..	..
Lawa (Estate)	..	..	..	..	..	..	7	5	..	1	..	2	6	2	..	..	..	4	..	..	..	..	..	..
Marwar	305	143	..	3	..	162	3,823	2,877	..	165	..	946	9,381	4,134	..	1,379	..	5,247	139	76	..	7	..	63
Mewar	1,059	753	35	607	..	271	13,831	6,759	117	474	5	5,955	3,260	1,577	8	246	..	1,675	566	281	4	13	..	261
Partabgarh	..	..	..	..	..	..	170	81	..	..	..	89	423	166	..	17	..	235	..	..	..	..	..	..
Shahpura (Chiefship)	..	..	..	..	..	..	234	101	..	18	..	133	279	130	..	15	..	149	..	..	..	..	..	..
Sirohi	813	210	6	..	..	597	411	168	..	..	..	243	2,060	863	..	16	..	1,187	65	41	..	..	..	24
Tonk	16	4	..	..	..	12	4,484	1,644	..	8	..	2,840	3,536	1,513	..	179	..	2,023	..	..	..	..	..	..
Ajmer-Merwara	**6,307**	**4,220**	**11**	**2,197**	**1**	**2,076**	**140**	**111**	**1**	**11**	..	**28**	**2,418**	**1,226**	**2**	**79**	..	**1,190**	**1,894**	**900**	**2**	**19**	..	**902**
Ajmer	6,136	4,166	3	2,195	1	1,967	133	106	1	11	..	26	2,013	1,022	..	62	..	991	1,559	812	..	12	..	747
Merwara	171	54	8	2	..	109	7	5	..	..	..	2	405	204	2	17	..	199	335	178	2	7	..	155
CITIES.																								
Rajputana	**138**	**105**	..	..	..	**33**	**32,265**	**16,783**	**14**	**893**	..	**15,466**	**6,230**	**2,695**	**4**	**43**	..	**3,531**	**118**	**60**	**1**	..	..	**57**
Alwar	11	2	..	..	..	9	5,162	2,841	..	27	..	2,321	704	323	..	..	..	381	19	11	..	..	..	8
Bharatpur	1	1	..	..	..	..	4,790	2,311	..	53	..	2,479	754	349	..	36	..	405	37	10	..	..	..	27
Bikaner	..	..	..	..	..	..	1,325	1,084	..	677	..	441	475	230	..	1	..	245	..	..	..	..	..	..
Jaipur	35	23	..	..	..	12	9,317	4,446	..	6	..	4,671	1,113	438	1	1	..	674	54	33	1	..	..	20
Jodhpur	21	17	..	..	..	4	1,959	1,619	..	85	..	340	1,353	554	..	1	..	799	6	5	..	..	..	2
Kotah	15	15	..	..	..	..	2,970	1,543	..	39	..	1,427	447	206	..	4	..	241	..	..	..	..	..	..
Tonk	11	4	..	..	..	7	3,945	1,417	..	6	..	2,528	621	222	..	..	..	399	..	..	..	..	..	..
Udaipur	44	43	..	..	..	1	2,617	1,522	14	..	..	1,061	763	373	3	..	..	387	..	..	..	..	..	..
Ajmer-Merwara—																								
Ajmer	1,587	785	3	661	1	799	41	36	..	11	..	5	970	534	..	4	..	436	962	531	..	4	..	431

TABLE XV-A.—Occupation or Means of Livelihood. Part II.—By State or District, and City—*continued*.

Province; and State; District, or City.	CLASS C.—PUBLIC ADMINISTRATION AND LIBERAL ARTS—*continued*.																							
	Sub-Class VI.—Public force—*concluded*.												Sub-Class VII.—Public Administration.											
	Order 44.—Police—*concluded*.												Total Sub-class VII.						Order 45.—Public Administration.					
	142 (a).—Police (Native States).						143.—Village watchmen.						Total Order 45.						144.—Government Service.					
	Total workers and dependants.	Actual workers.				Dependants.	Total workers and dependants.	Actual workers.				Dependants.	Total workers and dependants.	Actual workers.				Dependants.	Total workers and dependants.	Actual workers.				Dependants.
		Total.		Partially agriculturists.				Total.		Partially agriculturists.				Total.		Partially agriculturists.				Total.		Partially agriculturists.		
	Both sexes.	Males.	Females.	Males.	Females.	Both sexes.	Both sexes.	Males.	Females.	Males.	Females.	Both sexes.	Both sexes.	Males.	Females.	Males.	Females.	Both sexes.	Both sexes.	Males.	Females.	Males.	Females.	Both sexes.
1	1057	1058	1059	1060	1061	1062	1063	1064	1065	1066	1067	1068	1069	1070	1071	1072	1073	1074	1075	1076	1077	1078	1079	1080
Rajputana	23,864	10,968	9	430	..	12,887	37,111	15,691	..	7,463	..	21,420	153,636	58,020	5,844	5,635	714	89,772	1,165	526	2	11	..	637
Alwar	1,470	624	..	13	..	846	2,932	1,146	..	712	..	1,786	*14,941*	*5,194*	*1,379*	*797*	*105*	*8,368*	53	11	..	2	..	42
Banswara	786	291	..	20	..	495	48	14	..	2	..	34	*968*	*336*	*1*	*26*	..	*631*	19	18	..	..	..	1
Bharatpur	1,409	665	..	59	..	744	1,052	471	..	324	..	581	*10,414*	*3,720*	*39*	*293*	..	*6,655*	77	23	..	..	..	54
Bikaner	1,282	712	..	7	..	570	388	148	..	75	..	240	*6,485*	*2,565*	*61*	*428*	*45*	*3,859*	16	4	..	..	..	12
Bundi	453	229	2	7	..	222	36	18	..	1	..	18	*3,018*	*1,206*	*27*	*72*	..	*1,785*	..	..	..	..	..	..
Dholpur	794	316	..	16	..	478	612	263	..	50	..	349	*4,289*	*1,380*	..	*110*	..	*2,909*	9	5	..	..	..	..
Dungarpur	590	221	..	3	..	369	118	44	..	7	..	74	*1,673*	*625*	*53*	*30*	*5*	*995*	..	..	..	..	..	6
Jaipur	2,399	1,069	..	100	..	1,830	19,624	8,374	..	4,026	..	11,250	*55,037*	*21,319*	*3,479*	*2,076*	*494*	*30,239*	193	81	..	..	..	112
Jaisalmer	77	19	..	1	..	58	..	..	..	..	..	..	*738*	*224*	*8*	*20*	..	*506*	..	..	..	..	..	..
Jhalawar	783	328	..	12	..	455	56	32	..	7	..	24	*2,877*	*998*	*4*	*94*	*2*	*1,875*	..	..	..	..	..	..
Karauli	508	241	..	14	..	267	4	4	..	..	..	..	*2,489*	*1,001*	..	*97*	..	*1,488*	2	2	..	..	..	..
Kishangarh	216	89	3	3	..	124	222	113	..	44	..	109	*1,826*	*764*	*24*	*61*	..	*1,038*	24	5	..	..	..	19
Kotah	3,586	1,755	..	96	..	1,831	3,083	1,376	..	463	..	1,707	*12,196*	*4,632*	*470*	*546*	*50*	*7,094*	52	19	..	..	..	33
Kushalgarh (Chiefship)	272	88	..	..	..	184	..	..	..	..	..	..	*163*	*58*	*1*	*1*	..	*104*	..	..	..	..	..	..
Lawa (Estate)	..	..	..	..	..	..	6	2	..	..	..	4	*57*	*31*	..	..	..	*26*	..	..	..	..	..	..
Marwar	3,382	1,724	..	45	..	1,658	5,860	2,334	..	1,327	..	3,526	*16,176*	*6,191*	*67*	*450*	*5*	*9,918*	328	191	..	..	..	137
Mewar	1,310	674	4	3	..	632	1,384	622	..	230	..	762	*9,837*	*3,847*	*163*	*262*	*1*	*5,827*	176	68	1	6	..	107
Partabgarh	256	123	..	..	..	133	167	65	..	17	..	102	*913*	*380*	*19*	*43*	*2*	*514*	..	..	..	..	..	..
Shahpura (Chiefship)	269	123	..	13	..	146	10	7	..	2	..	3	*743*	*299*	*2*	*53*	*3*	*442*	10	5	..	..	..	5
Sirohi	1,927	788	..	15	..	1,139	68	34	..	1	..	34	*1,918*	*769*	*45*	*42*	*2*	*1,104*	193	92	1	3	..	100
Tonk	2,095	889	..	4	..	1,206	1,441	624	..	175	..	817	*6,898*	*2,491*	*2*	*134*	..	*4,405*	13	4	..	..	..	9
Ajmer-Merwara	23	17	..	1	..	6	501	219	..	59	..	282	4,728	1,802	22	176	1	2,904	2,521	939	2	78	..	1,580
Ajmer	8	5	..	..	..	3	446	205	..	50	..	241	*3,911*	*1,464*	*20*	*144*	*1*	*2,427*	1,989	706	2	63	..	1,281
Merwara	15	12	..	1	..	3	55	14	..	9	..	41	*817*	*338*	*2*	*32*	..	*477*	532	233	..	15	..	299
CITIES																								
Rajputana	6,047	2,599	3	42	..	3,445	65	36	..	1	..	29	44,189	14,059	816	159	1	29,314	444	170	1	..	..	273
Alwar	684	311	..	..	..	373	1	1	..	..	..	..	*4,247*	*1,409*	*334*	*30*	..	*2,504*	6	..	..	..	..	6
Bharatpur	717	339	..	36	..	378	..	..	..	..	..	..	*4,461*	*1,454*	*26*	*28*	..	*2,981*	67	23	..	..	..	44
Bikaner	472	228	..	1	..	244	3	2	..	..	..	1	*2,127*	*740*	*1*	*7*	..	*1,386*	16	4	..	..	..	12
Jaipur	1,059	405	..	1	..	654	..	..	..	..	..	..	*18,276*	*5,956*	*356*	*34*	*1*	*11,964*	130	53	..	..	..	77
Jodhpur	1,337	544	..	..	..	793	8	4	..	1	..	4	*7,047*	*1,930*	..	*8*	..	*5,117*	58	28	..	..	..	30
Kotah	397	180	..	4	..	217	50	26	..	..	..	24	*2,633*	*924*	*58*	*35*	..	*1,651*	45	15	..	..	..	30
Tonk	621	222	..	..	..	399	..	..	..	..	..	..	*2,967*	*885*	..	*15*	..	*2,082*	5	..	..	..	..	5
Udaipur	760	370	3	..	..	387	3	3	..	..	..	..	*2,431*	*768*	*51*	*2*	..	*1,612*	117	47	1	..	..	69
Ajmer-Merwara—																								
Ajmer	6	3	..	..	..	3	2	..	..	..	..	2	*2,384*	*781*	*10*	*42*	..	*1,593*	1,523	469	1	36	..	1,053

TABLE XV-A.—OCCUPATION OR MEANS OF LIVELIHOOD. PART II.—BY STATE OR DISTRICT, AND CITY—*continued.*

CLASS C.—PUBLIC ADMINISTRATION AND LIBERAL ARTS—*continued.*

SUB-CLASS VII.—PUBLIC ADMINISTRATION—*concluded.*

Order 45.—Public Administration—*concluded.*

Province; and State, District, or City.	145 (a).—Rulers of Native States and their families. Total workers and dependants. Both sexes.	Actual workers. Total. Males.	Actual workers. Total. Males.	Partially agriculturists. Males.	Partially agriculturists. Females.	Dependants. Both sexes.	145 (b).—Native States' administrative officials and menials. Total workers and dependants. Both sexes.	Actual workers. Total. Males.	Actual workers. Total. Females.	Partially agriculturists. Males.	Partially agriculturists. Females.	Dependants. Both sexes.
1	1081	1082	1083	1084	1085	1086	1087	1088	1089	1090	1091	1092
Rajputana	**497**	**22**	**6**	..	..	**469**	**110,102**	**40,988**	**1,198**	**1,912**	**18**	**67,916**
Alwar	4	1	3	..	..	..	9,091	3,258	396	275	3	6,337
Banswara	36	1	..	..	..	35	735	256	..	11	..	499
Bharatpur	6	1	..	..	..	5	9,593	3,355	..	192	..	6,238
Bikaner	20	1	..	..	..	28	5,056	2,030	1	49	..	3,025
Bundi	11	1	..	..	..	10	2,506	1,016	22	38	..	1,558
Dholpur	30	1	..	..	..	29	4,215	1,363	..	107	..	2,852
Dungarpur	9	1	3	..	..	5	710	287	14	4	..	418
Jaipur	21	1	..	..	..	20	32,950	13,030	640	441	13	10,280
Jaisalmer	3	1	..	..	..	2	731	221	8	10	..	502
Jhalawar	2	1	..	..	..	2	2,608	376	1	52	..	1,731
Karauli	1	1	..	..	..	..	2,300	913	..	76	..	1,396
Kishangarh	3	1	..	..	..	2	1,663	706	24	53	..	933
Kotah	7	4	..	..	..	3	9,002	3,414	13	222	..	5,575
Kushalgarh (Chiefship)	11	1	..	..	..	10	150	56	1	1	..	93
Lawa (Estate)	4	1	..	..	..	3	51	29	..	..	..	22
Marwar	14	..	..	..	..	14	12,542	4,440	..	120	..	6,102
Mewar	204	1	..	..	..	293	6,021	2,401	47	66	..	3,573
Partabgarh	..	..	..	..	..	..	670	209	16	70	..	385
Shahpura (Chiefship)	7	1	..	..	..	6	693	281	1	44	2	411
Sirohi	3	1	..	..	..	2	1,208	521	12	17	..	765
Tonk	1	1	..	..	..	..	6,480	2,266	2	115	..	4,221
Ajmer-Merwara	**11**	**1**	..	..	..	**10**	**763**	**306**	**7**	**22**	..	**450**
Ajmer	11	1	..	..	..	10	721	297	7	22	..	417
Merwara	..	..	..	..	..	..	42	9	..	..	..	33
CITIES.												
Rajputana	**74**	**5**	..	..	..	**69**	**41,695**	**13,130**	**693**	**151**	**1**	**27,872**
Alwar	..	..	..	..	..	..	3,975	1,281	321	25	..	2,373
Bharatpur	6	1	..	..	..	5	4,073	1,300	..	24	..	2,773
Bikaner	29	1	..	..	..	28	2,014	705	1	7	..	1,308
Jaipur	21	1	..	..	..	20	17,321	5,622	334	34	1	11,365
Jodhpur	14	..	..	..	..	14	6,965	1,864	..	8	..	6,041
Kotah	3	1	..	..	..	2	2,382	845	11	33	..	1,526
Tonk	1	1	..	..	..	..	2,814	835	..	15	..	1,979
Udaipur	..	..	..	..	..	..	2,211	678	26	2	..	1,507
Ajmer-Merwara—												
Ajmer	6	1	..	..	..	5	270	100	2	3	..	168

Province; and State, District, or City.	146.—Municipal and other local (not village) service. Total workers and dependants. Both sexes.	Actual workers. Total. Males.	Actual workers. Total. Females.	Partially agriculturists. Males.	Partially agriculturists. Females.	Dependants. Both sexes.	147.—Village officials and servants other than watchmen. Total workers and dependants. Both sexes.	Actual workers. Total. Males.	Actual workers. Total. Females.	Partially agriculturists. Males.	Partially agriculturists. Females.	Dependants. Both sexes.
1	1093	1094	1095	1096	1097	1098	1099	1100	1101	1102	1103	1104
Rajputana	**2,530**	**1,116**	**61**	**14**	..	**1,353**	**39,342**	**15,368**	**4,577**	**3,698**	**696**	**19,397**
Alwar	423	198	6	4	..	219	4,470	1,726	974	518	102	1,770
Banswara	16	6	..	..	..	10	132	45	1	15	..	86
Bharatpur	394	184	28	2	..	182	344	157	11	99	..	176
Bikaner	141	57	..	2	..	84	1,243	473	60	377	45	710
Bundi	67	42	..	..	..	25	344	147	5	34	..	192
Dholpur	5	2	..	..	..	3	30	11	..	3	..	19
Dungarpur	85	35	1	..	..	49	860	302	35	26	5	523
Jaipur	502	183	..	..	..	319	21,361	8,024	2,839	1,635	481	10,498
Jaisalmer	..	..	..	..	..	..	4	2	..	1	..	2
Jhalawar	57	23	1	..	..	33	209	98	2	42	2	109
Karauli	101	51	..	2	..	50	76	34	..	19	..	42
Kishangarh	30	16	..	..	..	14	106	36	..	8	..	70
Kotah	201	123	..	3	..	138	2,674	1,072	457	321	50	1,346
Kushalgarh (Chiefship)	2	1	..	..	..	1	..	..	..	..	..	..
Lawa (Estate)	..	..	..	..	..	..	2	1	..	..	..	1
Marwar	111	63	..	..	..	48	3,181	1,497	67	330	5	1,617
Mewar	107	51	24	..	..	32	3,239	1,326	91	190	1	1,822
Partabgarh	45	16	..	1	..	29	198	95	3	32	2	100
Shahpura (Chiefship)	..	..	..	..	..	..	33	12	1	9	1	20
Sirohi	15	8	1	..	..	6	409	147	31	22	2	231
Tonk	168	57	..	..	..	111	227	163	..	19	..	64
Ajmer-Merwara	**937**	**344**	**6**	**9**	..	**587**	**496**	**212**	**7**	**67**	**1**	**277**
Ajmer	795	292	6	8	..	497	395	168	5	51	1	222
Merwara	142	52	..	1	..	90	101	44	2	16	..	55
CITIES.												
Rajputana	**1,544**	**631**	**52**	**6**	..	**861**	**432**	**123**	**70**	**2**	..	**239**
Alwar	203	110	2	2	..	142	3	2	1	..	..	..
Bharatpur	302	125	26	2	..	151	13	5	..	2	..	8
Bikaner	68	30	..	..	..	38	..	..	..	..	..	..
Jaipur	484	178	..	..	..	306	320	102	22	..	..	106
Jodhpur	66	37	..	..	..	29	4	1	..	..	..	3
Kotah	133	57	..	2	..	76	70	6	47	..	..	17
Tonk	143	48	..	..	..	95	4	1	..	..	..	3
Udaipur	85	37	24	..	..	24	18	6	..	..	..	12
Ajmer-Merwara—												
Ajmer	565	207	6	3	..	352	20	4	1	1	..	15

TABLE XV-A.—OCCUPATION OR MEANS OF LIVELIHOOD. PART II.—BY STATE OR DISTRICT, AND CITY—*continued.*

CLASS C.—PUBLIC ADMINISTRATION AND LIBERAL ARTS—*continued.*

SUB-CLASS VIII.—PROFESSION AND LIBERAL ARTS.

Province; and State, District, or City.	Total Sub-Class VIII. Total workers and dependants. Both sexes.	Total Sub-Class VIII. Actual workers. Total. Males.	Total Sub-Class VIII. Actual workers. Total. Females.	Total Sub-Class VIII. Actual workers. Partially agriculturists. Males.	Total Sub-Class VIII. Actual workers. Partially agriculturists. Females.	Total Sub-Class VIII. Dependants. Both sexes.	Order 46.—Religion. Total Order 46. Total workers and dependants. Both sexes.	Total Order 46. Actual workers. Total. Males.	Total Order 46. Actual workers. Total. Females.	Total Order 46. Actual workers. Partially agriculturists. Males.	Total Order 46. Actual workers. Partially agriculturists. Females.	Total Order 46. Dependants. Both sexes.	148.—Priests, ministers, etc. Total workers and dependants. Both sexes.	148. Actual workers. Total. Males.	148. Actual workers. Total. Females.	148. Actual workers. Partially agriculturists. Males.	148. Actual workers. Partially agriculturists. Females.	148. Dependants. Both sexes.	149.—Religious mendicants, inmates of monasteries, etc. Total workers and dependants. Both sexes.	149. Actual workers. Total. Males.	149. Actual workers. Total. Females.	149. Actual workers. Partially agriculturists. Males.	149. Actual workers. Partially agriculturists. Females.	149. Dependants. Both sexes.
1	1105	1106	1107	1108	1109	1110	1111	1112	1113	1114	1115	1116	1117	1118	1119	1120	1121	1122	1123	1124	1125	1126	1127	1128
Rajputana	**386,899**	**153,776**	**49,653**	**23,177**	**2,769**	**185,468**	**277,851**	**115,867**	**28,980**	**19,650**	**1,844**	**135,004**	**90,209**	**36,164**	**4,266**	**7,308**	**323**	**49,779**	**170,135**	**72,493**	**22,106**	**11,979**	**1,393**	**75,536**
Alwar	19,658	6,906	1,949	1,660	147	10,810	12,809	4,664	812	1,440	89	7,333	12,241	4,428	752	1,415	87	7,061	34	14	4	4	..	16
Banswara	5,070	1,760	693	398	44	2,623	4,255	1,490	519	363	31	2,246	867	295	23	91	4	549	3,279	1,148	494	264	27	1,637
Bharatpur	19,154	8,333	1,458	1,935	114	9,463	14,444	6,518	1,077	1,787	90	6,849	3,741	1,704	114	548	20	1,923	9,766	4,410	935	1,213	70	4,412
Bikaner	20,390	7,236	2,803	1,260	237	10,331	11,981	4,249	993	1,034	140	6,739	9,447	3,266	767	716	104	5,414	1,310	491	206	127	32	613
Bundi	3,977	1,419	561	108	19	1,997	1,837	711	40	83	3	1,077	1,717	671	34	82	2	1,012	7	1	..	..	..	6
Dholpur	7,497	2,983	762	571	38	3,752	5,841	2,438	447	528	21	2,956	2,164	872	71	283	4	1,221	3,020	1,330	376	171	17	1,314
Dungarpur	5,638	1,890	580	360	31	3,168	5,096	1,710	527	335	29	2,859	1,345	481	30	160	4	834	3,718	1,220	407	173	25	2,001
Jaipur	108,666	44,647	19,577	4,411	314	51,449	85,553	36,723	8,653	3,971	256	40,177	32,045	13,733	1,114	2,173	47	17,198	50,444	21,787	7,330	1,601	208	21,377
Jaisalmer	4,362	1,452	229	195	2	2,681	2,642	893	127	161	2	1,622	1,183	446	43	102	..	694	1,215	381	76	44	1	758
Jhalawar	2,657	1,031	327	63	5	1,300	1,200	508	35	50	2	657	808	314	22	47	2	472	3	1	..	..	..	2
Karauli	5,864	2,518	572	482	77	2,774	4,513	2,020	359	346	2	2,134	1,471	648	9	175	..	814	2,424	1,137	349	136	2	938
Kishangarh	4,316	1,976	553	340	40	1,787	3,348	1,599	375	312	39	1,374	31	10	5	3	..	16	2,815	1,350	338	284	38	1,127
Kotah	11,455	4,588	1,347	558	54	5,520	5,298	2,417	208	420	14	2,678	3,940	1,737	160	376	14	2,043	175	116	5	10	..	54
Kushalgarh (Chiefship)	181	54	28	6	1	99	129	39	17	6	1	73	69	19	5	6	1	45	52	18	12	..	..	22
Laws (Estate)	116	48	25	6	..	43	69	32	5	6	..	32	33	13	2	3	..	18	16	11	3	..	..	2
Marwar	101,098	40,407	14,489	6,326	1,071	46,202	74,849	31,057	9,101	5,081	671	34,691	12,626	4,928	884	459	11	6,814	60,676	25,557	8,195	4,633	660	26,924
Mewar	53,270	20,607	8,496	4,675	872	24,167	34,063	14,663	2,656	3,330	218	16,744	5,008	1,983	179	553	17	2,846	23,272	10,253	2,323	2,170	103	10,696
Partabgarh	1,622	606	386	99	37	630	923	397	128	75	16	398	306	141	12	32	4	153	543	219	116	39	12	208
Shahpura (Chiefship)	2,269	1,119	233	233	20	917	1,608	929	115	205	12	654	172	71	2	40	1	99	1,499	850	111	153	11	538
Sirohi	8,543	3,290	1,121	99	11	4,202	6,607	2,533	759	83	7	3,315	618	247	19	12	..	352	5,843	2,216	736	67	7	2,891
Tonk	3,090	1,088	471	48	12	1,531	696	277	23	28	1	396	377	157	19	22	1	201	24	24	..	..	..	..
Ajmer-Merwara	**19,005**	**7,542**	**2,523**	**1,087**	**175**	**8,940**	**10,109**	**4,419**	**1,107**	**646**	**50**	**4,583**	**1,906**	**763**	**153**	**31**	..	**991**	**6,421**	**2,964**	**885**	**500**	**48**	**2,572**
Ajmer	15,861	6,406	2,066	776	117	7,389	9,109	4,052	932	584	48	4,125	1,704	687	141	18	..	876	5,664	2,688	724	453	46	2,252
Merwara	3,144	1,136	457	311	58	1,551	1,000	367	175	62	2	458	202	76	12	13	..	115	757	276	161	47	2	320
CITIES.																								
Rajputana	**38,128**	**13,817**	**3,640**	**126**	**4**	**20,671**	**19,709**	**7,964**	**1,879**	**71**	**4**	**9,866**	**11,300**	**4,317**	**480**	**54**	**3**	**6,503**	**5,522**	**2,457**	**1,299**	**1**	**1**	**1,766**
Alwar	2,239	785	93	16	2	1,361	812	300	42	6	2	464	684	227	35	6	2	422	7	6	1	..	..	..
Bharatpur	2,069	990	118	20	..	1,561	981	434	59	10	..	488	408	167	17	7	..	224	270	126	35	1	..	100
Bikaner	6,363	1,926	528	10	..	3,809	4,028	1,244	236	6	..	2,548	3,595	1,106	195	6	..	2,294	130	38	40	..	..	52
Jaipur	11,913	4,649	890	33	1	6,374	6,318	2,789	521	21	1	3,008	3,777	1,578	111	20	..	2,088	1,832	917	375	..	1	540
Jodhpur	8,215	3,031	1,247	1	..	3,937	4,649	1,969	782	..	..	1,898	1,860	819	66	..	..	975	2,575	1,051	716	..	..	808
Kotah	2,730	1,076	234	37	1	1,420	1,133	534	67	24	1	532	467	193	44	12	1	230	17	17	..	..	..	..
Tonk	1,190	382	138	5	..	670	272	109	7	1	..	156	76	31	7	..	..	38	24	24	..	..	..	..
Udaipur	2,909	978	392	4	..	1,539	1,516	579	165	3	..	772	433	196	5	3	..	232	607	278	132	..	..	257
Ajmer-Merwara—																								
Ajmer	5,142	1,883	488	89	..	2,771	2,432	996	277	69	..	1,159	444	221	53	3	..	170	1,282	563	219	37	..	500

TABLE XV-A.—Occupation or Means of Livelihood. Part II.—By State or District, and City—*continued.*

CLASS C.—PUBLIC ADMINISTRATION AND LIBERAL ARTS—*continued.*

SUB-CLASS VIII.—PROFESSION AND LIBERAL ARTS—*continued.*

Province; and State, District, or City.	Order 46.—Religion—*concluded.* 150.—Catechists, readers, church and mission service, reciters of sacred books (of any religion). Total workers and dependants.	Actual workers. Total.		Partially agriculturists.		Dependants.	151.—Temple, burial or burning ground service, pilgrim conductors, circumcisers. Total workers and dependants.	Actual workers. Total.		Partially agriculturists.		Dependants.	Order 47.—Law. Total Order 47. Total workers and dependants.	Actual workers. Total.		Partially agriculturists.		Dependants.	152.—Lawyers of all kinds including Kazis, law agents, and Mukhtiars. Total workers and dependants.	Actual workers. Total.		Partially agriculturists.		Dependants.
	Both sexes.	Males.	Females.	Males.	Females.	Both sexes.	Both sexes.	Males.	Females.	Males.	Females.	Both sexes.	Both sexes.	Males.	Females.	Males.	Females.	Both sexes.	Both sexes.	Males.	Females.	Males.	Females.	Both sexes.
1	1129	1130	1131	1132	1133	1134	1135	1136	1137	1138	1139	1140	1141	1142	1143	1144	1145	1146	1147	1148	1149	1150	1151	1152
Rajputana	4,414	1,544	47	133	..	2,823	13,033	5,606	561	1,630	18	6,866	6,501	1,883	..	79	..	4,618	5,060	1,372	..	64	..	3,688
Alwar	96	29	1	3	..	66	438	193	55	24	2	190	496	157	..	17	..	339	254	80	..	14	..	174
Banswara	96	41	..	8	..	55	18	6	2	..	..	5	8	1	..	..	..	7	8	1	..	..	..	7
Bharatpur	300	124	8	7	..	168	687	271	20	19	..	346	344	100	..	9	..	244	150	42	..	4	..	108
Bikaner	374	117	1	11	..	256	850	375	19	181	4	466	605	169	..	7	..	436	474	129	..	7	..	345
Bundi	7	3	..	..	..	4	106	36	15	1	1	55	19	6	..	..	..	13	19	6	..	..	..	13
Dholpur	644	229	..	74	..	415	13	7	..	..	..	6	110	37	..	4	..	73	72	20	..	3	..	52
Dungarpur	10	3	..	..	..	7	23	6	..	2	..	17	12	4	..	..	..	8	12	4	..	..	..	8
Jaipur	871	262	19	11	..	590	2,193	991	190	96	1	1,012	2,230	647	..	18	..	1,592	1,871	495	..	18	..	1,376
Jaisalmer	118	28	3	1	..	87	126	38	5	14	1	83	23	7	..	..	..	16	16	5	..	..	..	11
Jhalawar	106	43	3	2	..	60	283	150	10	1	..	123	84	28	..	3	..	56	63	18	..	3	..	45
Karauli	457	158	..	30	..	299	161	77	1	5	..	83	37	15	..	1	..	22	28	10	..	1	..	18
Kishangarh	28	11	..	2	..	17	474	228	32	23	1	214	37	17	..	1	..	20	25	11	..	1	..	14
Kotah	179	73	..	6	..	106	1,004	491	33	26	..	475	424	126	..	10	..	298	229	58	..	6	..	171
Kushalgarh (Chiefship)	..	..	..	..	..	..	8	2	..	..	..	6	..	..	..	..	..	..	..	..	..	..	..	..
Lawa (Estate)	5	2	..	2	..	3	15	6	..	1	..	9	..	..	..	..	..	..	..	..	..	..	..	..
Marwar	424	141	1	7	..	282	1,123	431	21	62	..	671	1,372	348	..	5	..	1,024	1,370	346	..	4	..	1,024
Mewar	468	222	9	15	..	237	5,315	2,205	145	592	8	2,965	398	123	..	1	..	275	398	123	..	1	..	275
Partabgarh	3	3	..	..	..	..	71	34	..	4	..	37	37	14	..	1	..	23	36	13	..	1	..	23
Shahpura (Chiefship)	26	8	1	3	..	17	1	..	1	..	..	..	15	5	..	1	..	10	12	4	..	1	..	8
Sirohi	14	5	1	..	..	8	132	65	3	4	..	64	28	9	..	..	..	19	21	7	..	..	..	14
Tonk	168	42	..	1	..	146	107	54	4	5	..	49	213	70	..	1	..	143	2	..	..	..	..	2
Ajmer-Merwara	157	55	6	9	..	96	1,625	638	63	106	2	924	443	113	..	6	..	330	231	49	..	2	..	182
Ajmer	131	47	5	8	..	79	1,610	630	62	105	2	918	372	98	..	4	..	274	212	47	..	1	..	165
Merwara	26	8	1	1	..	17	15	8	1	1	..	6	71	15	..	2	..	56	19	2	..	1	..	17
CITIES.																								
Rajputana	617	197	6	1	..	414	2,270	993	94	15	..	1,183	3,835	1,009	..	11	..	2,826	3,156	790	..	10	..	2,366
Alwar	4	..	..	..	..	4	117	73	6	..	..	38	186	63	..	2	..	123	60	25	..	2	..	35
Bharatpur	197	81	4	..	..	112	106	60	3	2	..	43	144	36	..	3	..	108	58	15	..	2	..	43
Bikaner	178	46	..	..	..	132	125	54	1	..	..	70	286	60	..	..	..	226	247	49	..	..	..	198
Jaipur	70	17	..	..	..	53	639	277	35	1	..	327	1,549	420	..	3	..	1,129	1,283	319	..	3	..	964
Jodhpur	31	18	..	..	..	13	183	81	..	..	..	102	1,088	265	..	..	..	823	1,088	265	..	..	..	823
Kotah	24	12	..	..	..	12	625	312	23	12	..	290	180	47	..	2	..	133	129	30	..	2	..	99
Tonk	104	19	..	1	..	85	68	35	..	..	..	33	109	31	..	1	..	78	..	..	..	..	..	..
Udaipur	9	4	2	..	..	3	407	101	26	..	..	280	293	87	..	..	..	206	293	87	..	..	..	206
Ajmer-Merwara—																								
Ajmer	4	2	..	..	..	2	702	210	5	30	..	487	330	86	..	3	..	244	212	47	..	1	..	165

TABLE XV-A.—OCCUPATION OR MEANS OF LIVELIHOOD. PART II.—BY STATE OR DISTRICT, AND CITY—*continued.*

Province; and State, District, or City.	CLASS C.—PUBLIC ADMINISTRATION AND LIBERAL ARTS—*continued.*																						
	SUB-CLASS VIII.—PROFESSION AND LIBERAL ARTS—*continued.*																						
	Order 47.—Law—*concluded.*						Order 48.—Medicine.																
	153.—Lawyers' clerks, petition writers, etc.						Total Order 48.						154.—Medical practitioners of all kinds including dentists, oculists and veterinary surgeons.						155.—Midwives, vaccinators, compounders, nurses, masseurs, etc.						
	Total workers and dependants.	Actual workers. Total.		Actual workers. Partially agriculturists.		Dependants.	Total workers and dependants.	Actual workers. Total.		Actual workers. Partially agriculturists.		Dependants.	Total workers and dependants.	Actual workers. Total.		Actual workers. Partially agriculturists.		Dependants.	Total workers and dependants.	Actual workers. Total.		Actual workers. Partially agriculturists.		Dependants.
	Both sexes.	Males.	Females.	Males.	Females.	Both sexes.	Both sexes.	Males.	Females.	Males.	Females.	Both sexes.	Both sexes.	Males.	Females.	Males.	Females.	Both sexes.	Both sexes.	Males.	Females.	Males.	Females.	Both sexes.
1	1153	1154	1155	1156	1157	1158	1159	1160	1161	1162	1163	1164	1165	1166	1167	1168	1169	1170	1171	1172	1173	1174	1175	1176
Rajputana	**1,441**	**511**	..	**15**	..	**930**	**14,908**	**2,957**	**5,703**	**160**	**339**	**6,248**	**5,691**	**1,854**	**99**	**120**	..	**3,738**	**9,217**	**1,103**	**5,604**	**40**	**339**	**2,510**
Alwar	242	77	..	3	..	165	732	157	201	18	15	374	291	103	2	16	..	186	441	54	199	2	15	188
Banswara	..	..	..	..	..	..	64	18	25	..	2	21	16	9	..	..	..	7	48	9	25	..	2	14
Bharatpur	194	58	..	5	..	136	660	176	130	4	7	354	227	68	1	4	..	158	433	108	129	..	7	196
Bikaner	131	40	..	..	..	91	736	208	132	9	16	396	409	133	3	2	..	273	327	75	129	7	16	123
Bundi	..	..	..	..	..	..	364	106	99	8	1	159	126	50	..	3	..	76	238	56	99	5	1	83
Dholpur	38	17	..	1	..	21	221	58	41	1	..	122	111	37	2	1	..	72	110	21	39	..	..	50
Dungarpur	..	..	..	..	..	..	58	16	18	..	1	24	18	9	..	..	..	9	40	7	18	..	1	15
Jaipur	368	152	..	..	..	216	3,444	933	569	38	9	1,942	2,136	644	33	38	..	1,459	1,308	289	536	..	9	483
Jaisalmer	7	2	..	..	..	5	34	8	5	..	..	21	12	3	..	..	..	9	22	5	5	..	..	12
Jhalawar	21	10	..	..	..	11	159	34	34	..	..	91	57	19	1	..	..	37	102	15	33	..	..	54
Karauli	9	5	..	..	..	4	174	53	38	6	2	83	87	33	..	3	..	54	87	20	38	3	2	29
Kishangarh	12	6	..	..	..	6	173	47	26	7	..	100	145	46	5	7	..	94	28	1	21	..	..	6
Kotah	195	68	..	4	..	127	1,391	347	453	20	21	591	355	115	16	3	..	224	1,036	232	437	17	21	367
Kushalgarh (Chiefship)	..	..	..	..	..	..	11	3	4	..	..	4	5	1	..	..	..	4	6	2	4	..	..	..
Lawa (Estate)	..	..	..	..	..	..	8	3	2	..	..	3	7	3	1	..	..	3	1	..	1	..	..	..
Marwar	2	2	..	1	..	..	2,117	346	1,034	3	66	737	784	262	..	3	..	522	1,333	84	1,034	..	66	215
Mewar	..	..	..	..	..	..	3,787	289	2,597	32	180	901	511	189	18	29	..	304	3,276	100	2,579	3	180	597
Partabgarh	1	1	..	..	..	..	185	20	121	1	15	44	45	14	3	1	..	28	140	6	118	..	15	16
Shahpura (Chiefship)	3	1	..	..	..	2	103	23	23	8	1	57	68	18	3	6	..	47	35	5	20	2	1	10
Sirohi	7	2	..	..	..	5	159	48	31	2	..	80	98	35	1	1	..	62	61	13	30	1	..	18
Tonk	211	70	..	1	..	141	328	64	120	3	3	144	183	63	10	3	..	110	145	1	110	..	3	34
Ajmer-Merwara	**212**	**64**	..	**4**	..	**148**	**1,102**	**298**	**199**	**8**	**7**	**605**	**540**	**168**	**12**	**4**	..	**360**	**562**	**130**	**187**	**4**	**7**	**245**
Ajmer	160	51	..	3	..	109	983	263	180	7	6	540	473	145	11	4	..	317	510	118	169	3	6	223
Merwara	52	13	..	1	..	39	119	35	19	1	1	65	67	23	1	..	..	43	52	12	18	1	1	22
CITIES.																								
Rajputana	**677**	**219**	..	**1**	..	**458**	**2,977**	**812**	**484**	**9**	..	**1,681**	**1,606**	**481**	**34**	**7**	..	**1,091**	**1,371**	**331**	**450**	**2**	..	**590**
Alwar	126	38	..	..	..	88	153	32	17	..	..	104	49	17	..	..	..	32	104	15	17	..	..	72
Bharatpur	86	21	..	..	..	65	236	61	22	..	..	153	80	17	1	..	..	62	156	44	21	..	..	91
Bikaner	39	11	..	..	..	28	347	90	45	2	..	212	217	61	3	..	..	153	130	29	42	2	..	59
Jaipur	266	101	..	..	..	165	910	308	63	2	..	539	558	171	11	2	..	376	352	137	52	..	..	163
Jodhpur	..	..	..	..	..	..	520	150	95	..	..	275	299	99	..	..	..	200	221	51	95	..	..	75
Kotah	51	17	..	..	..	34	315	84	64	2	..	167	152	50	10	2	..	92	163	34	54	..	..	75
Tonk	109	31	..	1	..	78	168	36	49	3	..	83	110	36	8	3	..	66	58	..	41	..	..	17
Udaipur	..	..	..	..	..	..	328	51	129	..	..	148	141	30	1	..	..	110	187	21	128	..	..	38
Ajmer-Merwara—																								
Ajmer	118	39	..	2	..	79	539	150	55	..	3	334	314	90	9	1	..	215	225	60	46	2	..	119

TABLE XV-A.—Occupation or Means of Livelihood. Part II.—By State or District, and City—*continued.*

Province; and State, District, or City.	CLASS C.—PUBLIC ADMINISTRATION AND LIBERAL ARTS—*continued.* Sub-Class. VIII.—Profession and Liberal Arts—*continued.* Total Order 49.—Instruction. 156.—Professors and teachers of all kinds (except law, medicine, music, dancing, and drawing), and clerks and servants connected with education. Total workers and dependants. Both sexes.	Actual workers. Total. Males.	Actual workers. Total. Females.	Actual workers. Partially agriculturists. Males.	Actual workers. Partially agriculturists. Females.	Dependants. Both sexes.	Order 50.—Letters and arts and sciences. Total Order 50. Total workers and dependants. Both sexes.	Actual workers. Total. Males.	Actual workers. Total. Females.	Actual workers. Partially agriculturists. Males.	Actual workers. Partially agriculturists. Females.	Dependants. Both sexes.	157. Public scribes, stenographers, etc. Total workers and dependants. Both sexes.	Actual workers. Total. Males.	Actual workers. Total. Females.	Dependants. Both sexes.	158.—Architects, surveyors, engineers, and their employés. Total workers and dependants. Both sexes.	Actual workers. Total. Males.	Actual workers. Total. Females.	Actual workers. Partially agriculturists. Males.	Actual workers. Partially agriculturists. Females.	Dependants. Both sexes.
1	1177	1178	1179	1180	1181	1182	1183	1184	1185	1186	1187	1188	1189	1190	1191	1192	1193	1194	1195	1196	1197	1198
Rajputana	6,041	3,061	160	81	..	4,820	61,596	30,010	16,816	3,207	786	34,778	122	28	..	94	4,776	1,846	119	36	..	2,811
Alwar	700	234	4	16	..	462	4,921	1,694	925	163	43	2,302	..	..	..	..	641	221	..	7	..	420
Danswara	88	33	..	..	..	55	661	216	149	35	11	294	..	..	..	..	150	38	55	1	..	57
Bharatpur	708	294	6	12	..	408	2,998	1,145	245	117	17	1,608	14	3	..	11	1,100	409	..	15	..	691
Bikaner	502	176	7	6	..	319	6,566	2,434	1,671	204	71	2,461	18	3	..	15	431	188	..	1	..	243
Bundi	118	45	1	..	..	72	1,630	551	412	17	8	676	..	..	..	..	42	20	..	..	..	22
Dholpur	196	84	3	1	..	109	1,129	366	271	37	17	492	4	3	..	1	163	79	..	2	..	84
Dungarpur	89	38	2	..	..	49	383	122	33	25	1	228	..	..	..	..	97	45	4	..	..	48
Jaipur	2,335	886	46	15	..	1,403	15,095	5,458	3,309	369	49	6,328	82	17	..	65	919	345	..	5	..	574
Jaisalmer	30	14	..	1	..	16	1,633	530	97	33	..	1,006	..	..	..	..	25	5	..	..	..	20
Jhalawar	133	65	5	1	..	63	1,081	386	253	9	3	442	..	..	..	..	41	9	..	..	..	32
Karauli	108	27	1	1	..	80	1,032	403	174	128	13	455	..	..	..	..	50	18	..	1	..	32
Kishangarh	103	49	2	2	..	52	655	264	150	18	1	241	..	..	..	..	29	15	..	..	..	14
Kotah	501	193	21	8	..	287	3,841	1,505	670	100	19	1,666	..	..	..	..	439	181	..	3	..	258
Kushalgarh (Chiefship)	11	2	1	..	..	8	30	10	6	..	..	14	..	..	..	..	..	..	..	..	..	..
Lawa (Estate)	1	1	..	..	..	..	38	12	18	..	..	8	..	..	..	..	1	1	..	..	..	..
Marwar	1,078	416	6	6	..	656	21,682	8,240	4,348	1,231	334	9,004	4	2	..	2	82	24	..	..	..	58
Mewar	581	252	18	8	..	311	14,441	5,280	3,225	654	174	5,936	..	..	..	..	192	76	15	..	..	101
Partabgarh	64	26	3	..	..	35	413	149	134	22	6	130	..	..	..	..	22	15	..	..	..	7
Shahpura (Chiefship)	66	26	1	2	..	39	367	136	94	17	7	157	..	..	..	..	27	6	5	1	..	16
Sirohi	168	68	14	2	..	86	1,561	562	317	12	4	702	..	..	..	..	149	72	2	..	..	75
Tonk	461	132	19	..	..	310	1,392	545	306	16	8	598	..	..	..	..	176	79	38	..	..	59
Ajmer-Merwara	1,696	560	87	22	..	1,049	5,655	2,152	1,130	405	118	2,373	1	..	..	1	348	127	5	..	..	216
Ajmer	1,458	485	73	20	..	900	3,939	1,508	881	161	63	1,550	..	..	..	..	207	101	5	..	..	191
Merwara	238	75	14	2	..	149	1,716	644	240	244	55	823	1	..	..	1	51	26	..	..	..	25
CITIES.																						
Rajputana	2,675	880	81	8	..	1,714	8,932	3,152	1,196	27	..	4,584	38	8	..	31	2,613	880	40	10	..	1,693
Alwar	211	76	..	3	..	135	877	308	34	5	..	535	..	..	..	..	546	176	..	4	..	370
Bharatpur	279	91	3	3	..	185	1,029	368	34	4	..	627	8	2	..	6	623	219	..	4	..	404
Bikaner	273	84	6	1	..	183	1,329	448	241	1	..	640	..	..	..	..	328	128	..	..	..	200
Jaipur	778	286	23	1	..	469	2,358	846	283	6	..	1,229	20	6	..	23	530	152	..	1	..	378
Jodhpur	448	145	4	..	..	299	1,510	502	366	1	..	642	2	..	..	2	52	15	..	..	..	37
Kotah	199	59	20	..	..	120	903	352	83	9	..	468	..	..	..	..	248	74	..	1	..	174
Tonk	295	71	11	..	..	213	346	135	71	..	..	140	..	..	..	..	173	76	38	..	..	59
Udaipur	192	68	14	..	..	110	580	193	84	1	..	303	..	..	..	..	113	40	2	..	..	71
Ajmer-Merwara—																						
Ajmer	926	306	43	8	..	577	915	345	113	6	..	457	..	..	..	..	243	73	2	..	..	168

TABLE XV-A.—OCCUPATION OR MEANS OF LIVELIHOOD. PART II.—BY STATE OR DISTRICT, AND CITY—*continued.*

Province; and State, District, or City.	CLASS C.—PUBLIC ADMINISTRATION AND LIBERAL ARTS—*concluded.*																		CLASS D.—MISCELLANEOUS.					
	SUB-CLASS VIII.—PROFESSIONS AND LIBERAL ARTS—*concluded.*												TOTAL SUB-CLASS IX.—PERSONS LIVING PRINCIPALLY ON THEIR PRIVATE INCOME.						Total Class D.					
	Order 50.—Letters and arts and sciences—*concluded.*												Total Order 51.—Persons living principally on their private income.											
	159.—Others (authors, photographers, artists, sculptors, astronomers, meteorologists, botanists, astrologers, poets, etc.)						160. Music composers and masters, players on all kinds of musical instruments (not military), singers, actors, bards and dancers.						161.—Proprietors (other than of agricultural land), holders of funds investments and scholarships, and pensioners.											
	Total workers and dependants.	Actual workers.				Dependants.	Total workers and dependants.	Actual workers.				Dependants.	Total workers and dependants.	Actual workers.				Dependants.	Total workers and dependants.	Actual workers.				Dependants.
		Total.		Partially agriculturists.				Total.		Partially agriculturists.				Total.		Partially agriculturists.				Total.		Partially agriculturists.		
	Both sexes.	Males.	Females.	Males.	Females.	Both sexes.	Both sexes.	Males.	Females.	Males.	Females.	Both sexes.	Both sexes.	Males.	Females.	Males.	Females.	Both sexes.	Both sexes.	Males.	Females.	Males.	Females.	Both sexes.
1	1199	1200	1201	1202	1203	1204	1205	1206	1207	1208	1209	1210	1211	1212	1213	1214	1215	1216	1217	1218	1219	1220	1221	1222
Rajputana	**10,260**	**3,685**	**305**	**548**	**57**	**6,270**	**96,449**	**24,451**	**16,396**	**2,623**	**729**	**25,603**	**46,558**	**11,940**	**12,407**	**1,062**	**193**	**22,211**	**473,361**	**181,181**	**109,585**	**12,631**	**2,375**	**182,595**
Alwar	343	123	17	33	3	203	3,937	1,330	908	123	40	1,679	1,939	697	979	78	7	1,033	49,939	19,307	7,430	3,460	465	23,202
Banswara	51	14	..	3	..	37	480	166	94	31	11	200	301	45	144	..	1	112	2,517	712	968	42	23	837
Bharatpur	42	16	1	4	..	25	1,842	717	241	98	17	861	2,403	796	360	108	14	1,247	13,326	5,685	2,613	797	187	5,128
Bikaner	304	81	2	2	..	218	5,813	2,159	1,669	201	71	1,985	3,719	660	1,438	45	9	1,621	31,535	13,372	7,076	809	227	11,087
Bundi	70	24	4	2	..	42	1,527	507	408	15	8	612	195	53	64	2	1	78	11,418	4,400	2,150	142	11	4,868
Dholpur	5	3	1	..	..	1	957	281	270	35	17	406	867	298	109	17	1	447	8,177	3,049	1,435	234	49	3,693
Dungarpur	131	31	..	14	..	100	155	46	29	11	1	80	296	29	177	9	..	90	4,310	1,312	1,098	88	33	1,900
Jaipur	2,028	641	29	94	2	1,358	12,066	4,455	3,280	270	47	4,331	20,605	6,018	4,308	571	133	10,279	159,570	63,179	34,574	3,063	505	61,817
Jaisalmer	70	23	1	..	..	46	1,538	502	96	33	..	940	289	25	150	..	2	114	1,147	416	204	18	2	527
Jhalawar	78	28	1	..	..	49	902	349	252	9	3	361	974	274	184	18	2	516	5,275	2,090	870	137	46	2,315
Karauli	214	84	4	72	2	126	768	301	170	55	11	297	313	113	96	11	..	104	4,499	1,779	974	197	22	1,746
Kishangarh	30	12	2	3	..	16	596	237	148	15	1	211	404	45	134	3	1	225	4,023	1,332	1,194	53	49	1,497
Kotah	293	133	..	13	..	160	3,109	1,191	670	84	10	1,248	1,403	357	400	18	..	646	42,086	15,840	11,431	1,024	88	14,815
Kushalgarh (Chiefship)	2	2	..	..	..	..	28	8	6	..	..	14	12	..	10	..	..	2	870	283	236	9	..	351
Lawa (Estate)	..	..	..	..	..	..	37	11	18	..	..	8	12	3	7	..	..	2	107	38	32	1	..	37
Marwar	3,030	1,095	1	70	..	1,934	18,560	7,119	4,347	1,161	334	7,100	7,932	1,507	3,048	114	17	3,377	69,544	23,598	21,090	717	266	24,856
Mewar	3,280	1,275	237	236	50	1,777	10,960	3,929	2,973	418	124	4,058	1,964	587	511	51	4	866	35,922	13,772	9,888	1,059	203	12,262
Partabgarh	9	5	..	..	..	4	382	129	134	22	6	119	199	43	75	..	1	81	2,617	968	659	89	16	990
Shahpura (Chiefship)	62	25	2	..	..	35	298	105	87	16	7	106	78	23	16	4	..	39	1,368	401	573	65	36	394
Sirohi	136	39	3	2	..	94	1,296	451	312	10	4	533	1,560	246	673	8	..	641	5,628	2,182	1,225	49	23	2,221
Tonk	73	28	..	..	..	45	1,143	438	271	16	8	434	1,100	261	148	5	..	691	19,483	7,566	3,865	573	125	8,052
Ajmer-Merwara	**159**	**61**	**2**	**3**	..	**96**	**5,147**	**1,964**	**1,123**	**402**	**118**	**2,060**	**2,424**	**529**	**268**	**77**	**3**	**1,627**	**28,251**	**11,195**	**5,206**	**544**	**145**	**11,859**
Ajmer	142	57	2	3	..	83	3,500	1,350	874	158	63	1,276	2,145	441	242	50	2	1,462	24,747	9,049	4,566	342	103	10,532
Merwara	17	4	..	..	..	13	1,647	614	249	244	55	784	279	88	26	27	1	165	3,504	1,546	640	202	42	1,318
CITIES.																								
Rajputana	**1,616**	**582**	**7**	**13**	..	**1,027**	**4,664**	**1,682**	**1,149**	**4**	..	**1,833**	**11,145**	**3,014**	**2,740**	**36**	**4**	**5,391**	**65,070**	**26,802**	**12,533**	**136**	**3**	**25,735**
Alwar	91	28	2	1	..	61	240	104	32	..	..	104	796	298	81	10	1	417	5,029	2,322	502	22	..	2,205
Bharatpur	30	8	1	..	..	21	368	139	33	..	..	196	1,368	421	229	17	2	718	2,950	1,327	388	19	..	1,235
Bikaner	264	67	2	..	..	195	737	253	239	1	..	245	1,610	311	554	3	..	745	8,121	3,315	1,203	20	..	3,006
Jaipur	467	180	1	3	..	286	1,332	508	282	2	..	542	3,402	1,016	881	1	1	1,505	20,537	8,245	4,147	27	1	8,145
Jodhpur	292	116	..	1	..	176	1,104	371	306	..	..	427	2,064	509	566	..	..	989	14,600	5,603	3,316	25	..	5,681
Kotah	193	94	..	8	..	99	462	184	83	..	..	195	706	177	204	2	..	325	4,572	2,137	828	16	..	1,607
Tonk	34	12	..	..	..	22	139	47	33	..	..	59	975	236	129	3	..	610	5,667	2,132	1,236	10	2	2,299
Udaipur	245	77	1	..	..	167	222	76	81	1	..	65	224	46	96	..	..	82	3,591	1,721	913	4	..	957
Ajmer-Merwara—																								
Ajmer	100	41	..	..	..	59	572	231	111	6	..	230	1,121	204	141	14	1	776	10,397	4,365	1,398	66	..	4,634

TABLE XV-A.—Occupation or Means of Livelihood. Part II.—By State or District, and City—*continued.*

CLASS D.—MISCELLANEOUS—*continued.*

Province; and State, District, or City.	Sub-Class X.—Domestic Service. Total Sub-Class X. Total Order 52. Total workers and dependants. Both sexes.	Actual workers. Total. Males.	Actual workers. Total. Females.	Actual workers. Partially agriculturists. Males.	Actual workers. Partially agriculturists. Females.	Dependants. Both sexes.	Order 52.—Domestic Service. 162.—Cooks, water carriers, doorkeepers, watchmen, and other indoor servants. Total workers and dependants. Both sexes.	Actual workers. Total. Males.	Actual workers. Total. Females.	Actual workers. Partially agriculturists. Males.	Actual workers. Partially agriculturists. Females.	Dependants. Both sexes.	163.—Private grooms, coachmen, chauffeurs, dog boys and attendants on other animals, etc. Total workers and dependants. Both sexes.	Actual workers. Total. Males.	Actual workers. Total. Females.	Actual workers. Partially agriculturists. Males.	Actual workers. Partially agriculturists. Females.	Dependants. Both sexes.	Sub-Class XI.—Insufficiently described occupations. Total Sub-Class XI. Total Order 53.—General terms which do not indicate a definite occupation. Total workers and dependants. Both sexes.	Actual workers. Total. Males.	Actual workers. Total. Females.	Actual workers. Partially agriculturists. Males.	Actual workers. Partially agriculturists. Females.	Dependants. Both sexes.
1	1223	1224	1225	1226	1227	1228	1229	1230	1231	1232	1233	1234	1235	1236	1237	1238	1239	1240	1241	1242	1243	1244	1245	1246
Rajputana	**224,700**	**83,160**	**54,705**	**5,012**	**1,235**	**86,835**	**208,595**	**74,978**	**54,665**	**4,712**	**1,235**	**78,952**	**16,105**	**8,182**	**40**	**300**	..	**7,883**	**92,517**	**29,358**	**29,621**	**969**	**293**	**33,538**
Alwar	21,708	7,827	3,796	1,269	278	10,085	19,511	6,785	3,792	1,224	278	8,934	2,197	1,042	4	45	..	1,161	2,668	868	792	31	19	1,008
Banswara	2,265	602	885	31	15	778	2,103	531	885	29	15	687	162	71	..	2	..	91	80	27	41	..	..	12
Bharatpur	7,002	2,709	1,321	410	112	2,972	6,293	2,321	1,321	400	112	2,631	709	388	..	10	..	321	3,270	1,364	838	181	51	1,068
Bikaner	13,386	5,248	3,118	239	75	5,020	12,285	4,655	3,118	232	75	4,512	1,101	593	..	7	..	508	2,547	1,068	396	41	5	1,083
Bundi	4,535	1,610	1,105	7	1	1,820	4,320	1,521	1,104	6	1	1,695	215	89	1	1	..	125	1,354	471	301	8	..	582
Dholpur	4,740	1,653	689	115	17	2,398	4,052	1,356	689	112	17	2,007	688	297	..	8	..	391	1,563	594	408	42	7	561
Dungarpur	3,541	1,083	924	84	26	1,534	3,404	1,005	924	61	20	1,475	137	78	..	23	..	59	541	116	137	1	7	288
Jaipur	81,672	32,616	15,631	1,740	255	33,425	77,156	30,352	15,631	1,640	255	31,173	4,516	2,264	..	100	..	2,252	32,301	10,248	10,738	225	80	11,315
Jaisalmer	667	260	127	14	2	280	518	209	123	6	2	186	149	51	4	8	..	94	106	26	36	..	..	44
Jhalawar	2,092	667	460	13	24	895	1,762	539	460	12	24	763	260	128	..	1	..	132	430	173	36	3	..	221
Karauli	2,874	1,017	716	123	18	1,141	2,662	931	716	121	18	1,015	212	86	..	2	..	126	332	137	62	..	1	133
Kishangarh	1,601	503	573	16	21	525	1,438	415	569	11	21	454	163	88	4	5	..	71	1,136	354	380	13	24	402
Kotah	6,690	2,578	1,714	102	16	2,398	5,707	2,036	1,713	91	16	1,958	983	542	1	11	..	440	19,671	6,058	7,997	152	5	5,616
Kushalgarh (Chiefship)	426	124	159	1	..	143	402	111	150	1	..	132	24	13	..	..	..	11	151	50	22	..	..	79
Lawa (Estate)	81	25	26	1	..	30	80	25	26	1	..	29	1	..	..	..	..	1	..	..	..	..	..	..
Marwar	39,147	13,575	13,219	363	205	12,353	37,221	12,527	13,210	334	205	11,475	1,926	1,048	..	29	..	878	19,103	5,042	5,347	61	21	8,714
Mewar	19,181	6,416	6,998	303	87	5,767	17,905	5,700	6,981	278	87	5,234	1,276	716	17	25	..	543	4,333	1,833	955	182	50	1,545
Partabgarh	1,589	513	529	20	6	547	1,489	472	521	25	6	496	100	41	8	4	..	51	106	56	8	..	..	48
Shahpura (Chiefship)	798	231	301	40	18	266	714	194	301	22	18	219	84	37	..	18	..	47	463	104	264	13	18	95
Sirohi	3,317	1,306	616	25	14	1,395	2,971	1,142	615	24	14	1,214	346	164	1	1	..	181	952	300	354	8	4	292
Tonk	7,458	2,597	1,798	87	45	3,063	6,602	2,151	1,798	82	45	2,653	856	446	..	5	..	410	1,410	463	509	8	..	438
Ajmer-Merwara	**14,732**	**6,172**	**2,195**	**203**	**63**	**6,371**	**13,173**	**5,409**	**2,191**	**194**	**63**	**5,573**	**1,565**	**763**	**4**	**9**	..	**798**	**5,152**	**1,609**	**1,491**	**17**	**10**	**2,052**
Ajmer	13,812	5,743	2,016	197	61	6,060	12,314	5,012	2,012	188	61	5,290	1,505	731	4	9	..	770	4,732	1,433	1,383	11	10	1,916
Merwara	919	429	179	6	2	311	859	397	179	6	2	283	60	32	..	..	..	28	420	176	108	6	..	136
CITIES.																								
Rajputana	**46,335**	**17,666**	**9,529**	**112**	**3**	**19,205**	**38,354**	**13,690**	**9,518**	**82**	**3**	**15,146**	**7,981**	**3,918**	**4**	**30**	..	**4,059**	**8,436**	**3,063**	**1,399**	**19**	..	**3,974**
Alwar	3,200	1,299	257	17	..	1,644	1,882	760	257	7	..	865	1,318	539	..	10	..	779	315	122	64	9	..	129
Bharatpur	2,241	967	305	11	..	969	1,598	624	305	8	..	669	643	343	..	3	..	300	407	184	32	1	..	191
Bikaner	5,350	1,948	859	17	..	2,543	4,490	1,542	859	15	..	2,089	860	406	..	2	..	454	432	190	25	1	..	217
Jaipur	15,502	5,965	2,924	27	1	6,613	13,327	4,998	2,924	27	1	5,405	2,175	967	..	..	..	1,208	2,929	998	850	..	..	1,081
Jodhpur	10,574	3,968	2,816	18	..	3,790	9,396	3,281	2,816	14	..	3,299	1,178	687	..	4	..	491	2,987	951	273	7	..	1,763
Kotah	2,698	1,054	660	9	..	984	2,032	690	659	3	..	683	666	364	1	6	..	301	817	419	95	7	..	378
Tonk	4,086	1,435	896	9	2	1,755	3,278	1,019	896	4	2	1,363	808	416	..	5	..	392	457	171	100	1	..	186
Udaipur	2,684	972	805	4	..	907	2,351	776	802	4	..	773	333	196	3	..	..	134	92	28	30	..	..	34
Ajmer-Merwara—																								
Ajmer	6,829	3,113	775	62	..	2,941	6,089	2,696	771	61	..	2,622	740	417	4	1	..	319	2,015	612	373	3	..	1,030

TABLE XV-A.—OCCUPATION OR MEANS OF LIVELIHOOD. PART II.—BY STATE OR DISTRICT, AND CITY—*continued.*

CLASS D.—MISCELLANEOUS—*continued.*

SUB-CLASS XI.—INSUFFICIENTLY DESCRIBED OCCUPATIONS—*concluded.*

Order 53.—General terms which do not indicate a definite occupation—*concluded.*

Province; and State, District, or City.	164.—Manufacturers, business men, and contractors, otherwise unspecified. Total workers and dependants.	Actual workers. Total.		Partially agriculturists.		Dependants.	165.—Cashiers, accountants, book-keepers, clerks, and other employés in unspecified offices, warehouses, and shops; private secretaries. Total workers and dependants.	Actual workers. Total.		Partially agriculturists.		Dependants.	166.—Mechanics otherwise unspecified. Total workers and dependants.	Actual workers. Total.		Dependants.	167.—Labourers and workmen otherwise unspecified. Total workers and dependants.	Actual workers. Total.		Partially agriculturists.		Dependants.
	Both sexes.	Males.	Females.	Males.	Females.	Both sexes.	Both sexes.	Males.	Females.	Males.	Females.	Both sexes.	Both sexes.	Males.	Females.	Both sexes.	Both sexes.	Males.	Females.	Males.	Females.	Both sexes.
1	1247	1248	1249	1250	1251	1252	1253	1254	1255	1256	1257	1258	1259	1260	1261	1262	1263	1264	1265	1266	1267	1268
Rajputana	448	139	16	6	1	291	20,058	6,707	104	198	7	13,187	40	13	..	27	71,971	22,439	20,409	765	234	20,058
Alwar	24	9	4	..	..	13	187	61	2	5	..	124	..	..	..	..	2,455	708	788	26	19	871
Banswara	..	..	..	..	..	..	..	..	..	..	..	..	..	..	..	..	80	27	41	..	..	12
Bharatpur	48	12	..	1	..	36	228	81	..	2	..	147	..	..	..	..	2,994	1,271	838	178	51	385
Bikaner	..	..	..	..	..	..	794	180	..	7	..	614	37	13	..	24	1,716	875	396	34	5	445
Bundi	2	1	..	..	..	1	614	256	3	8	..	355	..	..	..	..	738	214	298	..	..	226
Dholpur	72	13	..	..	..	59	185	118	5	2	..	62	..	..	..	..	1,306	468	402	40	7	440
Dungarpur	11	1	..	..	..	10	171	67	14	1	7	90	..	..	..	..	359	48	123	..	..	188
Jaipur	190	68	9	3	..	113	4,299	1,420	..	39	..	2,879	3	..	..	8	27,809	8,760	10,729	183	80	8,320
Jaisalmer	..	..	..	..	..	..	5	3	..	..	..	2	..	..	..	..	101	23	36	..	..	42
Jhalawar	..	..	..	..	..	..	356	151	1	3	..	204	..	..	..	..	74	22	35	..	..	17
Karauli	2	..	2	..	1	..	152	70	..	..	..	82	..	..	..	..	178	67	60	..	..	51
Kishangarh	..	..	..	..	..	..	296	102	8	3	..	186	..	..	..	..	840	252	372	10	24	216
Kotah	13	5	1	..	..	7	3,688	1,719	40	102	..	1,829	..	..	..	..	15,970	4,334	7,956	50	5	3,080
Kushalgarh (Chiefship)	..	..	..	..	..	..	115	45	2	..	..	68	..	..	..	..	36	5	20	..	..	11
Lawa (Estate)	..	..	..	..	..	..	..	..	..	..	..	..	..	..	..	..	..	..	..	..	..	..
Marwar	..	..	..	..	..	..	7,992	2,036	..	15	..	5,956	..	..	..	..	11,111	3,006	5,247	46	21	2,758
Mewar	1	1	..	..	..	..	690	312	13	9	..	365	..	..	..	..	3,842	1,520	942	173	50	1,180
Partabgarh	15	2	..	..	..	13	68	47	1	..	..	20	..	..	..	..	23	7	7	..	..	9
Shahpura (Chiefship)	..	..	..	..	..	..	2	2	..	..	..	..	..	..	..	..	461	102	264	13	18	95
Sirohi	38	20	2	2	..	16	92	58	1	2	..	38	..	..	..	..	822	233	351	4	4	238
Tonk	30	7	..	..	..	23	124	44	14	..	..	66	..	..	..	..	1,256	412	495	8	..	349
Ajmer-Merwara	303	73	2	3	..	228	552	216	7	3	..	329	..	..	..	..	4,297	1,320	1,482	11	10	1,495
Ajmer	272	63	2	..	..	207	495	190	7	2	..	298	..	..	..	..	3,965	1,180	1,374	9	10	1,411
Merwara	31	10	..	3	..	21	57	26	..	1	..	31	..	..	..	..	332	140	108	2	..	84
CITIES.																						
Rajputana	65	15	..	..	..	50	4,158	1,625	..	7	..	2,533	38	13	..	25	4,175	1,410	1,390	12	..	1,366
Alwar	3	1	..	..	..	2	27	12	..	..	..	15	..	..	..	..	285	109	64	2	..	112
Bharatpur	31	6	..	..	..	25	129	33	..	..	..	96	..	..	..	..	247	145	32	1	..	70
Bikaner	..	..	..	..	..	..	144	53	..	..	..	91	37	13	..	24	251	124	25	1	..	102
Jaipur	8	4	..	..	..	4	811	394	..	..	..	417	1	..	..	1	2,109	600	850	..	..	659
Jodhpur	..	..	..	..	..	..	2,167	672	..	..	..	1,495	..	..	..	..	820	279	273	7	..	268
Kotah	2	..	..	..	..	2	761	406	..	7	..	355	..	..	..	..	54	13	25	..	..	16
Tonk	21	4	..	..	..	17	85	40	..	..	..	45	..	..	..	..	351	127	100	1	..	124
Udaipur	..	..	..	..	..	..	34	15	..	..	..	19	..	..	..	..	68	13	30	..	..	15
Ajmer-Merwara—																						
Ajmer	151	27	2	..	..	122	339	112	3	2	..	224	..	..	..	..	1,625	473	368	1	..	664

TABLE XV-A.—OCCUPATION OR MEANS OF LIVELIHOOD. PART II.—BY STATE OR DISTRICT, AND CITY—*concluded.*

Province; and State, District, or City.	CLASS D.—MISCELLANEOUS—*concluded.* Sub-Class XII.—Unproductive. Total Sub-Class XII. Total workers and dependants. Both sexes.	Total Sub-Class XII. Actual workers. Total. Males.	Total Sub-Class XII. Actual workers. Total. Females.	Total Sub-Class XII. Actual workers. Partially agriculturists. Males.	Total Sub-Class XII. Actual workers. Partially agriculturists. Females.	Total Sub-Class XII. Dependants. Both sexes.	Total Order 54.—Inmates of jails, asylums and hospitals. 168.—Inmates of jails, asylums, hospitals and orphanages. Total workers and dependants. Both sexes.	168. Actual workers. Total. Males.	168. Actual workers. Total. Females.	168. Actual workers. Partially agriculturists. Males.	168. Actual workers. Partially agriculturists. Females.	168. Dependants. Both sexes.	Total Order 55.—Beggars, vagrants, prostitutes. 169.—Beggars, vagrants, procurers, prostitutes, receivers of stolen goods, cattle poisoners. Total workers and dependants. Both sexes.	169. Actual workers. Total. Males.	169. Actual workers. Total. Females.	169. Actual workers. Partially agriculturists. Males.	169. Actual workers. Partially agriculturists. Females.	169. Dependants. Both sexes.
1	1269	1270	1271	1272	1273	1274	1275	1276	1277	1278	1279	1280	1281	1282	1283	1284	1285	1286
Rajputana	156,144	68,663	25,259	6,650	848	62,232	5,219	4,630	360	5	7	229	150,925	64,033	24,890	6,645	841	61,998
Alwar	25,563	10,612	2,849	2,160	168	12,109	565	513	20	1	..	32	24,998	10,099	2,822	2,159	168	12,077
Banswara	179	83	42	11	8	47	47	47	..	..	..	..	125	36	42	11	8	47
Bharatpur	3,054	1,519	454	206	24	1,088	279	250	26	..	..	3	2,775	1,262	428	206	24	1,085
Bikaner	15,609	7,056	3,562	529	147	4,984	365	354	..	1	..	11	15,237	6,702	3,562	528	147	4,973
Bundi	5,539	2,319	744	127	10	2,466	112	86	20	..	..	6	5,417	2,233	724	127	10	2,460
Dholpur	1,874	802	338	77	25	734	128	128	..	..	..	..	1,746	674	338	77	25	734
Dungarpur	228	113	37	3	..	78	55	50	1	..	..	4	173	63	36	3	..	74
Jaipur	45,597	20,315	8,205	1,098	170	17,077	1,161	967	96	1	..	98	44,436	19,348	8,109	1,097	170	16,979
Jaisalmer	374	130	41	4	..	203	27	27	..	..	..	..	347	103	41	4	..	203
Jhalawar	2,823	1,250	374	121	22	1,199	53	53	..	..	..	..	2,770	1,197	374	121	22	1,190
Karauli	1,293	628	196	74	3	479	70	58	11	..	..	1	1,223	567	185	74	3	471
Kishangarh	1,286	475	241	24	4	570	67	55	8	..	..	4	1,219	420	233	24	4	566
Kotah	15,725	7,204	1,720	770	67	6,801	398	354	39	..	..	5	15,327	6,850	1,681	770	67	6,796
Kushalgarh (Chiefship)	293	109	55	8	..	129	15	15	..	..	..	..	278	94	55	8	..	129
Lawa (Estate)	26	13	6	..	..	7	..	..	..	..	..	..	26	13	6	..	..	7
Marwar	11,294	4,987	2,524	293	40	3,789	540	485	32	..	..	23	10,754	4,496	2,492	293	40	3,768
Mewar	12,408	5,523	1,935	574	66	4,950	1,062	937	86	2	7	39	11,346	4,586	1,849	572	59	4,911
Partabgarh	922	399	129	60	9	401	33	26	7	..	..	..	889	373	115	60	9	401
Shahpura (Chiefship)	107	66	8	12	..	33	21	21	..	..	..	..	86	45	8	12	..	33
Sirohi	1,359	570	255	16	5	534	73	70	3	..	..	..	1,286	500	252	16	5	594
Tonk	10,615	4,506	1,558	483	80	4,551	148	134	11	..	..	3	10,467	4,372	1,547	483	80	4,548
Ajmer-Merwara	8,361	3,414	1,520	324	72	3,427	445	19	16	..	..	410	7,916	3,395	1,504	324	72	3,017
Ajmer	6,196	2,473	1,167	134	32	2,556	315	6	6	..	..	303	5,881	2,467	1,161	134	32	2,253
Merwara	2,165	941	353	190	40	871	130	13	10	..	..	107	2,035	928	343	190	40	764
CITIES.																		
Rajputana	10,299	6,131	1,612	5	..	2,556	3,792	3,493	271	..	..	116	6,507	2,728	1,341	5	..	2,438
Alwar	1,514	901	181	3	..	439	550	508	19	..	..	32	955	393	162	3	..	400
Bharatpur	302	176	51	..	..	75	105	81	22	..	..	2	197	96	29	..	..	73
Bikaner	2,342	1,177	319	2	..	846	316	305	..	..	..	11	2,026	872	319	2	..	835
Jaipur	2,106	1,382	373	..	..	451	1,021	892	86	..	..	43	1,085	390	287	..	..	408
Jodhpur	1,039	684	227	..	..	128	536	483	32	..	..	21	503	201	195	..	..	107
Kotah	1,057	664	143	..	..	250	394	351	38	..	..	5	663	313	105	..	..	245
Tonk	1,194	586	240	..	..	358	130	119	10	..	..	1	994	407	230	..	..	357
Udaipur	815	721	78	..	..	16	731	664	64	..	..	3	84	57	14	..	..	13
Ajmer-Merwara—																		
Ajmer	1,553	640	250	1	..	663	245	6	5	..	..	234	1,308	634	245	1	..	429

APPENDIX TO TABLE XV-A.—(See EXPLANATORY NOTE ON TITLE PAGE.)

Statement showing the Groups in Table XV-A under which those of the last Census have been included.

[*N. B.*—Where old groups have been split up into two or more new groups the specific portions included in each group have been named, where possible, in column 2.]

Group in XV-A.	Groups of last census included in each group.
1	2
1	36.
2	37*a*, 37*b*, 40.
2*a*	37*c*.
3	54, 55 Agricultural experts, 56, 57.
4	38, 39.
5	41, 42, 43, 44, 45, 46, 47, 48.
6	49, 50, 51, 52, 53.
7	58, 59.
8	83, 150 Firewood and charcoal collectors, 346 Wood cutters, 349*a* Pith and bark collectors, 354, 356, 358, 360.
9	26 Cattle breeders and Commissariat farm establishments, 78 Cow and buffalo keepers.
10	30 Sheep and goat breeders, 32 Pig breeders.
11	25 Horse, mule and ass breeders and attendants, 29 Camel breeders and attendants, 34, 35*a*.
12	27, 31, 32 Swine-herds.
13	259.
14	79 Fishermen, 319.
15	28 Elephant catchers, 35, 492.
16	146, 147, 148 Colliery managers, 503.*
17	309, 310, 310*a*, 373 Antimony preparers, 503.*
18	311, 311*a*, 503.*
19	127.
20	365, 370.
21	263, 264, 271.
22	265, 266, 267, 268, 272, 273, 275, 279, 301 Muslin makers.
23	283, 284, 285, 286.
24	287, 288, 29*c* Rope and net makers.
25	292, 290 Sacking makers.
26	248, 249, 250 Pashm workers, 251 Persons occupied with blankets, woollen cloth, yarn and natural wool, 252.
27	255, 256, 257, 258, 260.
28	250 Felt workers, 382, 383, 390 Workers of bristles.
29	251 Persons occupied with feathers.
30	277.
30*a*	253,* 262,* 278.*
31	301 Lace makers and embroiderers, 316 Gold and silver braid makers.
32	384 Tanneries—owners, managers and superior staff, 385 Tanneries—operatives and other subordinates, 386, 388, 390 Workers of hides.
33	384 Leather factories—owners, managers, etc., 385 Leather factories—operatives, etc., 391.
34	251 Persons occupied with fur.
35	195, 380, 381, 390 Workers of horns and bones.
36	194, 196 Cotton stamp makers, 197 Turners, 231 Loom and loom comb makers, 340, 341, 342, 343, 344, 316 Sawyers.
37	347 Basket, mat, fan, screen, broom, etc., makers, 348 Tooth stick makers, 349 Leafplate makers, 349*a* Pith and bark workers, 349*b* Palmyra leaf umbrella makers.
38	326, 327.
39	230, 234.
40	235 Arms factories—superior staff, 236 Arms factories—operatives, etc., 237, 238, 241, 242, 243 Gun makers and menders, 246.
41	33 Farriers, etc., 225, 226, 227, 229, 328.
42	320, 321, 322.
43	199, 314 Electroplaters, 323*a* Aluminium workers, 324.
44	198, 307, 308.
45	210, 330, 331, 332 Makers of glassware other than bangles.
46	332 Makers of chinaware.
47	334, 335, 336.
48	151, 152, 153.
49	200 Mica, flint and talc workers, 201 Mosaic and alabaster workers.
50	138, 139, 145 Match makers, 235 Ammunition factories—superior staff, 236 Ammunition factories—operatives, etc., 239, 240, 244.
51	107, 108.
52	367, 368, 374 Madder-saffron and logwood workers, 375 Ink makers, 379.
53	89, 90, 100, 140, 141, 143.
54	179, 180, 181 Paper makers, 204 Papier maché workers.
55	145 Makers of torches, and candles, 350, 351, 352, 353, 361, 362, 363, 364, 376, 378.
56	87, 88, 91, 92, 96, 102.
57	95, 85, 86.
58	98.
59	76.
60	79 Fish curers.
61	77 Cheese makers, 82 Ghee preparers.
62	93, 94, 99 Makers of sugar, molasses and gur by hand.
63	103.
64	109, 110, 111, 112, 133.
65	131.
66	113, 114, 119, 120, 125, 129.
67	302 Hat, cap and turban makers and binders.
68	306.
69	305, 387.
70	224 Walking stick makers, 296, 297, 298, 299, 300*a*, 348 Comb makers.
71	65.
71*a*	253,* 262,* 278.*
72	60.
73	67, 70 Bath house, (etc.)—owners and managers, 486.
74	145 Lamp, lantern makers, 173, 197 Lacquerers, 218, 219, 220.
75	269, 270, 281.
76	157, 160, 161.
77	500, 501.
78	153, 154, 163, 166, 338.
79	162, 164, 165.
80	167 Tramway factories—superior staff, 168 Tramway factories—operatives, etc. 169, 170, 171, 174 Palki, dandi and rickshaw makers.
81	222 Harness (not leather) makers, 223 Saddle cloth makers and embroiderers, 224 Whip, goad makers.
82	175, 176, 178.
83	115, 116, 136, 137, 137*a*, 137*b*.
84	183, 184, 185.
85	188 Newspaper proprietors, managers, etc., 454 Editors, journalists, etc., 455 Reporters.
86	181 Palm leaf binders, 186.
87	206, 489.
88	190, 193 Other scientific instrument makers and menders.
89	212, 312, 313, 314 Gilders, 318 Gold and silver wire-drawers, 317.
90	208, 214, 216 Flower garland makers, 217 Makers of spangles, lingams and sacred threads.
91	202 Toy, kite and cage makers, 203 Hukka stem makers.
92	458, 491, 493, 494, 495, 497.
93	74, 75, 150 Cowdung collectors.
94	426, 427, 430, 432.
95	423, 424, 428.
96	431, 502 Canal labourers.
97	425, 429.
98	502 Road labourers.
99	416, 417, 419.
100	420.
201	421, 422.
102	441.
103	167 Railway factories—superior staff, 168 Railway factories—operatives, etc., 409, 410, 411, 412, 413, 414, 415.
104	502 Railway labourers.
105	433, 434, 435, 436, 437, 438.
106	392, 393, 394, 395.
107	148 Coal brokers, 402, 403 Auctioneers, auditors, etc., 406, 439, 440, 442.
108	254 Dealers in woollen goods, 261, 270*a*, 276, 280, 289, 291, 293 Bag sellers, 304, 390 Sellers of bristles.
109	254 Dealers in fur and feathers, 390 Sellers of hides, horns and bones, 389 Sellers of manufactured leather goods.
110	345, 347 Basket sellers, 349 Leaf plate sellers, 349*a* Pith and bark sellers, 377 Sandal wood sellers.
111	228, 233, 243 Gun sellers, 247.
112	337.
113	142, 145 Match sellers and sellers of candles, torches, 245, 355, 357, 359, 366, 369, 371, 373 Antimony sellers, 374 Madder, saffron and log-wood dealers, 377 Manure sellers.
114	132, 134, 135, 405 Farmers of liquor.
115	69, 70 Rest house, serai owners and managers, 71.
116	80.
117	101, 117, 118, 124, 128, 144.
118	77 Cheese sellers, 78 Milk and butter sellers, 81, 82 Ghee sellers, 84.
119	99 Sellers of sugar, molasses and gur, 104.
120	123, 105, 106.
121	97.
122	126, 130, 405 Farmers of opium.
123	30 Sheep and goat dealers, 32 Pig dealers.
124	149.
125	294, 295, 303, 300, 302 Hat, cap and turban sellers, 303 Hosiers, 348 Comb and tooth stick sellers, 349*b* Palmyra leaf umbrella sellers, 372, 377 Perfume sellers, 399 Sellers of foot wear.
126	221, 274, 293 Fibre matting sellers, 347 Mat, screen, broom, etc., sellers.
127	145 Lamp, lantern sellers, 323, 323*a* Aluminium sellers, 325, 329, 333.
128	156, 158, 159, 282.
129	25 Horse, mule and ass dealers, 26 Cattle dealers, 28 Elephant dealers, 29 Camel dealers, 172, 174 Palki, dandi and rickshaw sellers, 222 Harness (not leather) sellers, 223 Saddle cloth sellers, 418.
130	148 Coal dealers, 150 Fire-wood, charcoal and cow-dung sellers.
131	191, 192, 193 Other scientific instrument sellers, 213, 315, 318.
132	200 Mica, flint and talc sellers, 201 Mosaic and alabaster sellers, 202 Toy, kite and cage sellers, 203 Hukka stem sellers, 204 Papier maché sellers, 209, 211, 215, 216 Flower garland sellers, 217 Sellers of spangles, lingams and sacred threads, 347 Fan sellers, 398*a*.
133	181 Paper sellers, 182, 187, 188 Newspaper sellers, 189, 205, 207, 375 Ink sellers, 456 Almanac sellers.
134	....
135	396, 398.
136	401.
137	449 Diviners, 496, 498, 499.
138	177, 196 Cotton stamp sellers, 231 Looms and Loom comb sellers, 339, 404, 465, 447 Undertakers.
139	11, 12, 13, 14, 16.
140	16*a*, 16*b*, 23, 24.
141	17, 18, 19.
142	4 Constables, 15 Military Police, etc.
142*a*	4*b*.*
143	10 Watchmen.
144	1, 2, 3, 4 Messengers, warders, and unspecified.
145*a*	4*a*.
145*b*	*4*b*, 20, 21, 22.
146	5, 6, 7, 73, 121, 122.
147	8, 9, 10 Other village servants.
148	444.
149	446.
150	445, 447 Church service.
151	447 Temple, burial or burning ground service, pilgrim conductors, etc., 448.
152	403 Notaries public, 459, 460, 461, 462.
153	463, 464.
154	33 Veterinary surgeons, 72, 466, 467, 468, 469, 470.
155	472, 471, 473.
156	483 Superintendents of Schools of Art, etc., 451 Administrative and inspecting officials, 452, 453.
157	455 Shorthand writers, etc., 457 Public scribes.
158	474, 475, 476, 477, 478.
159	55 Agricultural chemists, 334*a*, 403 Actuaries, 449 Astrologers, horoscope makers, etc., 450 Almanac makers, 454 Authors, 479, 480, 481, 482, 483 Painters, 484, 485.
160	487, 488, 490.
161	503,* 510, 511, 512, 514, 515, 516.
162	61, 62, 64, 66, 68, 68*a*, 443.
163	63.
164	407.
165	397, 399, 400, 408, 450, 457 Copyists, 506.*
166	232, 505.*
167	504.
168	517, 518, 519, 520.
169	505,* 536, 507, 508, 609, 513.

* Part only.

TABLE XV-B.

Subsidiary Occupations of Agriculturists.

Explanatory Note.

This Table shows, by States or Districts, the most important subsidiary occupations of the four main classes of Agriculturists (workers only), *viz.* :—

(1) Rent Receivers (Landlords).

(2) Rent Payers (Ordinary Cultivators).

(3) Unpaid Helpers in Cultivation.

(4) Paid Field Labourers and Farm Servants.

The occupation headings given in the Table are necessarily brief and condensed. But the numbers in brackets indicate the groups in Table XV-A. which have been included in the occupations classified in this Table.

TABLE XV-B.—SUBSIDIARY OCCUPATIONS OF AGRICULTURISTS.—(ACTUAL WORKERS ONLY.)

(1) RENT RECEIVERS (LANDLORDS).

Province; and State or District.	Total number of rent receivers. (Actual workers).		Number of actual workers who returned subsidiary occupations.		Details of Subsidiary Occupations Returned. Rent payers (ordinary cultivators). (2).		Unpaid helpers in cultivation. (2 a).		Paid field labourers and farm servants. (4).		Cotton ginning, cleaning, and pressing. (21).		Cotton spinning, sizing, and weaving. (22).		Carpenters, sawyers, turners, joiners, etc. (36).		General workers in iron (41).		Potters, and earthen pipe and bowl makers (47).		Boot and shoe makers, and embroiderers on shoes (69).		Money-lenders, bank managers, etc. (106).	
	M.	F.	M.	F.	M.	F.	M.	F.	M.	F.	M.	F.	M.	F.	M.	F.	M.	F.	M.	F.	M.	F.	M.	F.
1	2	3	4	5	6	7	8	9	10	11	12	13	14	15	16	17	18	19	20	21	22	23	24	25
Rajputana	*215,481*	*19,497*	45,276	2,173	22,792	628	408	181	1,739	275	35	8	167	227	123	...	34	...	60	21	87	8	866	28
Alwar	*5,160*	*691*	1,818	268	1,105	40	...	51	9	2	5	...	...	6	...	...	...	...	...	...	...	...	24	4
Banswara	*1,515*	*162*	297	6	28	...	...	...	28	3	...	...	...	...	...	...	...	...	...	...	1	...	8	1
Bharatpur	*37,409*	*2,772*	11,782	537	7,322	293	61	1	1,083	112	...	...	9	28	23	...	7	...	4	...	1	...	446	12
Bikaner	*13,339*	*880*	1,498	45	479	3	2	...	1	...	...	...	8	1	8	...	...	...	1	...	14	...	11	...
Bundi	*546*	*104*	186	5	66	2	2	...	3	1	...	...	...	1	...	...	...	...	...	...	...	...	4	...
Dholpur	*6,398*	*414*	1,711	81	1,460	40	19	8	2	...	1	...	...	...	...	...	...	...	...	...	...	...	47	1
Dungarpur	*819*	*225*	116	17	19	1	...	...	...	...	...	...	...	...	...	...	...	...	...	...	...	...	...	...
Jaipur	*35,756*	*4,225*	7,412	390	4,191	97	96	34	79	18	2	...	2	68	7	...	2	...	2	...	3	2	160	5
Jaisalmer	*2,292*	*113*	1,832	33	3	1	...	...	...	...	...	...	1	...	5	...	...	...	2	...	1	...	5	...
Jhalawar	*789*	*67*	245	15	96	3	...	...	11	3	...	...	...	...	...	...	...	...	...	...	...	...	3	...
Karauli	*1,426*	*131*	222	3	53	...	1	...	2	...	...	...	...	2	...	...	...	...	...	...	...	...	10	...
Kishangarh	*1,829*	*149*	405	18	243	6	5	...	11	5	1	...	1	...	...	...	...	...	...	...	...	...	2	...
Kotah	*3,785*	*738*	1,830	95	702	24	9	7	42	20	...	...	...	9	1	...	3	...	3	...	1	2	8	2
Kushalgarh (Chiefship)	*96*	*8*	11	...	...	...	...	...	...	...	...	...	...	...	...	...	...	...	...	...	...	...	...	...
Lawa (Estate)	*14*	*5*	2	...	...	...	...	...	...	...	...	...	...	...	...	...	...	...	...	...	...	...	...	...
Marwar	*78,520*	*6,064*	11,916	510	4,979	79	208	73	415	74	15	6	114	86	31	...	6	...	...	2	19	...	125	3
Mewar	*21,018*	*2,316*	3,049	212	1,499	15	4	6	40	33	11	3	30	30	48	...	15	...	40	19	43	4	11	1
Partabgarh	*765*	*90*	275	6	185	8	1	...	4	1	...	...	1	...	...	...	...	...	...	...	...	...	...	...
Shahpura (Chiefship)	*697*	*51*	215	5	68	...	...	...	1	2	...	...	1	1	...	...	...	...	...	...	...	...	3	...
Sirohi	*3,472*	*229*	377	16	215	7	...	1	5	3	...	...	...	...	...	...	...	...	...	...	4	...	...	...
Tonk	*406*	*88*	86	...	59	...	...	...	...	...	...	...	...	...	...	...	1	...	...	...	...	...	...	...
Ajmer-Merwara	*3,439*	*869*	1,343	110	458	27	8	...	38	46	1	...	2	8	18	...	5	...	1	...	3	...	38	1
Ajmer	*3,100*	*653*	1,088	80	456	27	8	...	33	30	1	...	1	6	6	...	1	...	...	...	...	...	19	1
Merwara	*339*	*216*	255	30	2	...	...	...	5	16	...	...	1	2	12	...	4	...	1	...	3	...	19	...

TABLE XV-B.—Subsidiary Occupations of Agriculturists.—(Actual Workers Only.)

(1) Rent Receivers (Landlords)—concluded.

Details of Subsidiary Occupations Returned—contd.

Province; and State or District.	Grain and pulse dealers. (121). M.	F.	Other traders of all kinds. (107-120; 122-136.) M.	F.	Army (Imperial). (139). M.	F.	Army (Native States, including Imperial Service Troops). (140). M.	F.	Government service. (144). M.	F.	Native States' administrative officials and menials. (145b). M.	F.	Priests, ministers, etc. (148). M.	F.	Medical practitioners of all kinds, including compounders, vaccinators, midwives, veterinary surgeons, etc. (154 and 155). M.	F.	Professors, school masters, and teachers of all kinds (except law, medicine, music, dancing and drawing). (156). M.	F.	Clerks of all kinds, cashiers, accountants, etc. (excluding Government or Native State employés). M.	F.	Beggars (not religious), prostitutes, receivers of stolen goods, etc. (169). M.	F.	Others. M.	F.
1	26	27	28	29	30	31	32	33	34	35	36	37	38	39	40	41	42	43	44	45	46	47	48	49
Rajputana	41	1	521	24	73	...	526	...	38	...	642	10	2,143	76	40	14	45	...	322	1	1,668	68	12,906	608
Alwar	1	...	4	1	3	...	7	...	4	...	18	6	201	28	...	1	3	...	1	...	102	24	331	40
Banswara	...	...	7	...	...	...	...	...	...	...	2	...	35	...	...	...	...	...	...	...	...	...	193	5
Bharatpur	17	...	218	21	14	...	22	...	9	...	47	...	114	6	1	...	3	...	...	...	18	...	2,363	64
Bikaner	...	...	11	...	...	...	13	...	...	...	30	...	186	8	6	...	...	...	2	...	151	5	570	28
Bundi	...	...	4	1	...	...	19	...	...	...	20	...	25	...	2	...	...	...	...	...	12	...	12	...
Dholpur	...	...	20	1	...	...	10	...	1	...	16	...	16	...	2	...	1	...	7	...	12	1	97	1
Dungarpur	...	1	3	...	...	...	3	...	...	...	21	...	15	...	...	...	...	...	32	...	...	...	23	15
Jaipur	13	...	33	...	4	...	116	...	8	...	82	1	578	11	12	1	9	...	5	...	415	21	1,593	137
Jaisalmer	...	...	...	...	...	...	2	...	...	...	5	...	...	...	...	...	...	...	...	...	...	...	1,808	32
Jhalawar	1	...	1	...	...	...	...	...	...	...	11	...	15	...	...	...	4	...	...	...	85	5	18	4
Karauli	...	...	25	...	1	...	36	...	...	...	22	...	20	...	...	...	1	...	...	...	3	...	48	1
Kishangarh	...	...	3	...	...	...	12	...	...	...	14	...	8	...	...	...	1	...	5	...	...	...	99	1
Kotah	2	...	14	...	...	...	18	...	1	...	26	...	190	9	2	...	4	...	27	...	537	7	241	15
Kushalgarh (Chiefship)	...	...	...	...	...	...	...	...	...	...	4	...	4	...	1	...	...	...	...	...	...	...	2	...
Lawa (Estate)	...	...	...	...	...	...	...	...	...	...	1	...	...	...	...	...	...	...	...	...	...	...	1	...
Marwar	5	...	129	...	46	...	224	...	10	...	237	1	537	8	12	12	8	...	233	1	132	4	4,405	162
Mewar	2	...	41	...	5	...	36	...	5	...	61	2	114	5	2	...	6	...	7	...	188	1	828	94
Partabgarh	...	...	...	...	...	...	1	...	...	...	11	...	38	1	...	...	3	...	...	...	7	...	24	1
Shahpura (Chiefship)	...	...	1	...	...	...	4	...	...	...	7	...	12	...	...	...	2	...	2	...	1	...	114	2
Sirohi	...	...	5	...	...	...	...	...	...	...	2	...	12	...	...	...	...	...	1	...	...	...	133	6
Tonk	...	...	2	...	...	...	3	...	...	...	6	...	3	...	...	...	...	...	...	...	5	...	8	...
Ajmer-Merwara	...	...	99	4	14	...	...	...	15	...	13	...	18	...	3	...	9	...	5	...	14	...	581	24
Ajmer	...	...	17	1	...	...	...	...	1	...	10	...	17	...	3	...	8	...	5	...	13	...	489	15
Merwara	...	...	82	3	14	...	...	...	14	...	3	...	1	...	...	...	1	...	...	...	1	...	92	9

TABLE XV-B.—SUBSIDIARY OCCUPATIONS OF AGRICULTURISTS.—(ACTUAL WORKERS ONLY.)

(2) RENT PAYERS (ORDINARY CULTIVATORS).

Province ; and State or District.	Total number of rent payers. (Actual workers).		Number of actual workers who returned subsidiary occupations.		Details of Subsidiary Occupations Returned. Rent receivers (landlords). (1).		Unpaid helpers in cultivation. (3 d).		Paid field labourers and farm servants. (4).		Cotton ginning, cleaning, and pressing. (21).		Cotton spinning, sizing, and weaving. (22).		Carpenters, sawyers, turners, joiners, etc. (35).		General workers in iron. (41).		Potters, and earthen pipe and bowl makers. (47).		Boot and shoe makers, and embroiderers on shoes. (60).		Barbers. (73).	
	M.	F.	M.	F.	M.	F.	M.	F.	M.	F.	M.	F.	M.	F.	M.	F.	M.	F.	M.	F.	M.	F.	M.	F.
1	2	3	4	5	6	7	8	9	10	11	12	13	14	15	16	17	18	19	20	21	22	23	24	25
Rajputana	1,614,452	174,695	143,635	9,576	6,152	314	880	319	19,143	3,193	1,172	63	7,566	646	5,207	62	1,035	44	2,416	62	5,033	70	3,019	64
Alwar	147,576	13,429	11,296	1,493	1,403	59	20	15	2,329	622	62	2	151	69	116	17	21	3	187	29	475	6	98	4
Banswara	21,683	1,228	3,046	93	26	...	...	...	199	19	5	...	50	...	22	...	67	...	5	1	36	...	13	...
Bharatpur	60,815	5,612	15,961	1,161	1,078	42	104	22	7,299	701	15	...	58	40	130	...	58	...	108	1	223	1	169	8
Bikaner	168,729	6,666	16,575	442	170	6	2	3	361	3	69	...	1,402	70	1,008	5	82	3	484	3	832	4	969	10
Bundi	25,258	1,375	1,222	34	38	...	...	...	47	6	6	...	10	...	44	1	22	...	26	...	87	...	51	1
Dholpur	48,951	6,343	3,114	251	230	9	87	4	518	63	13	...	54	12	52	...	1	...	19	...	67	3	76	...
Dungarpur	21,905	1,672	558	38	...	...	...	...	4	3	...	...	3	...	17	...	27	...	12	...	1	...	10	2
Jaipur	429,194	76,644	22,844	2,551	1,277	104	447	179	2,300	354	91	15	567	279	319	5	38	2	280	15	1,205	45	161	19
Jaisalmer	8,097	398	5,300	101	...	...	...	...	2	...	29	...	367	14	104	...	...	...	27	...	144	...	47	...
Jhalawar	12,787	508	1,058	36	378	11	...	...	78	4	5	...	11	...	26	...	31	1	15	...	21	...	42	...
Karauli	19,158	1,066	1,674	51	8	2	...	...	184	16	4	...	17	...	19	...	10	2	16	...	40	...	22	...
Kishangarh	10,746	1,885	1,430	85	61	...	11	...	105	31	2	...	53	7	12	...	4	...	42	...	51	...	12	...
Kotah	63,750	3,943	8,000	305	316	5	96	10	1,258	130	23	...	70	6	242	...	106	1	90	1	319	1	187	4
Kushalgarh (Chiefship)	4,206	183	23	...	...	...	...	...	3	...	...	...	...	...	...	...	...	...	...	...	...	...	...	...
Lawa (Estate)	361	14	46	...	1	...	...	...	11	...	...	...	...	...	6	...	4	...	...	...	...	...	2	...
Marwar	288,660	15,147	28,686	1,753	630	66	77	66	3,500	1,128	754	26	4,101	111	1,678	5	205	...	654	10	1,510	6	706	7
Mewar	211,499	34,424	14,706	987	311	7	33	16	329	52	65	18	425	28	1,156	27	283	31	285	2	677	4	239	12
Partabgarh	10,724	386	2,400	52	33	3	...	...	107	7	...	...	8	...	16	...	8	...	6	...	8	...	14	...
Shahpura (Chiefship)	8,950	262	2,043	41	61	...	...	...	116	14	17	1	97	1	68	1	10	1	63	...	150	1	31	...
Sirohi	20,769	724	1,154	36	19	...	...	4	19	1	4	...	19	...	26	...	15	...	47	...	41	...	15	...
Tonk	31,684	3,291	2,433	66	103	...	3	...	206	30	8	1	13	...	137	1	43	...	50	...	96	...	95	2
Ajmer-Merwara	60,860	4,411	7,582	216	225	24	41	1	641	60	149	10	205	10	219	...	77	2	223	3	224	...	164	2
Ajmer	38,472	2,901	5,233	145	212	24	38	1	513	43	75	7	120	5	171	...	56	2	169	1	190	...	122	2
Merwara	22,388	1,510	2,349	71	13	...	3	...	128	17	74	3	85	5	48	...	21	...	54	2	34	...	42	...

TABLE XV-B.—SUBSIDIARY OCCUPATIONS OF AGRICULTURISTS.—(ACTUAL WORKERS ONLY.)

(2). RENT PAYERS (ORDINARY CULTIVATORS)—*concluded.*

Province; and State or District.	DETAILS OF SUBSIDIARY OCCUPATIONS RETURNED—*concld.* Money-lenders, bank managers, etc. (106).		Breeders and keepers of cattle, sheep, goats, pigs, etc. (9 and 10), and sellers of milk, butter, ghi, etc. (118).		Grain and pulse dealers. (121).		Other traders of all kinds. (107-117, 119, 120, 122-138).		Army (Imperial). (139).		Army (Native States, including Imperial Service Troops). (140).		Village watchmen. (143).		Government Service. (144).		Native States' administrative officials and menials. (145).		Priests, ministers, etc. (148).		Beggars (not religious), prostitutes, receivers of stolen goods, etc. (169).		Others.	
	M.	F.	M.	F.	M.	F.	M.	F.	M.	F.	M.	F.	M.	F.	M.	F.	M.	F.	M.	F.	M.	F.	M.	F.
1	26	27	28	29	30	31	32	33	34	35	36	37	38	39	40	41	42	43	44	45	46	47	48	49
Rajputana	2,402	57	12,244	274	474	10	6,983	576	135	2	377	2	3,240	...	181	2	1,100	12	3,013	120	4,003	177	57,010	3,498
Alwar	294	8	265	25	64	...	387	152	6	...	13	...	378	...	31	1	57	4	534	72	609	56	3,786	340
Banswara	33	8	17	3	105	1	640	18	...	...	...	...	6	...	...	...	1	...	105	10	13	8	1,702	30
Bharatpur	251	7	200	17	23	...	1,013	168	6	...	10	...	230	...	9	...	21	...	361	5	98	4	3,689	141
Bikaner	64	..	1,024	21	32	5	591	7	17	...	6	...	156	...	9	...	41	...	498	14	690	27	7,978	261
Bundi	38	1	212	14	2	...	154	5	1	...	37	...	2	...	...	...	55	...	49	2	109	...	283	4
Dholpur	126	2	148	...	6	...	406	29	...	...	10	...	15	...	...	...	12	...	140	8	16	2	1,019	120
Dungarpur	...	..	2	...	1	...	201	21	26	...	14	...	16	...	17	...	9	...	21	...	...	...	172	12
Jaipur	631	11	514	15	50	...	232	31	41	...	98	...	925	...	80	...	110	1	500	2	843	48	11,757	1,426
Jaisalmer	44	1	4,073	82	...	...	42	...	...	...	...	...	...	...	...	...	5	...	25	...	8	...	392	4
Jhalawar	11	...	11	...	6	...	76	7	...	...	3	...	15	...	...	...	...	...	24	...	124	3	181	5
Karauli	80	3	282	6	10	...	419	15	1	...	8	...	6	...	1	...	4	...	53	...	21	...	460	7
Kishangarh	34	..	321	9	...	...	74	18	...	...	12	...	29	...	...	...	6	...	1	...	6	2	504	18
Kotah	273	5	689	25	84	4	390	10	1	...	17	2	116	...	2	...	617	5	206	2	542	5	3,336	80
Kushalgarh (Chiefship)	...	...	...	...	...	...	2	...	...	...	...	...	...	...	...	...	...	...	...	...	8	...	10	...
Lawa (Estate)	1	..	...	...	...	...	2	...	...	...	...	...	4	...	...	...	2	...	...	...	...	...	13	...
Marwar	249	6	3,054	24	45	...	1,433	67	2	...	35	...	974	...	22	1	66	2	135	8	150	4	8,037	216
Mewar	212	5	554	7	23	...	315	18	34	2	101	...	103	...	10	...	32	...	294	5	426	13	8,799	740
Partabgarh	6	...	...	2	3	...	24	...	...	...	...	...	27	...	...	...	...	...	12	...	38	...	2,180	40
Shahpura (Chiefship)	14	..	440	4	...	...	162	2	...	...	1	...	6	...	...	...	16	...	12	...	4	...	766	16
Sirohi	1	..	261	16	...	...	235	8	...	...	...	...	2	...	...	...	2	...	8	...	2	...	438	7
Tonk	31	...	78	4	9	...	45	...	...	...	3	...	230	...	...	...	44	...	35	1	296	5	908	22
Ajmer-Merwara	112	6	640	17	13	1	681	13	10	...	...	...	67	...	29	2	8	...	6	...	140	6	3,708	59
Ajmer	88	6	478	10	18	...	520	12	3	...	...	...	59	...	7	...	8	...	4	...	66	4	2,315	28
Merwara	24	...	162	7	...	1	155	1	7	...	...	...	8	...	22	2	...	...	2	..	74	2	1,393	31

TABLE XV-B.—SUBSIDIARY OCCUPATIONS OF AGRICULTURISTS.—(ACTUAL WORKERS ONLY.)

(3) UNPAID HELPERS IN CULTIVATION.

Province; and State or District.	Total number of unpaid helpers in cultivation. (Actual workers).		Number of actual workers who returned subsidiary occupations.		Details of Subsidiary Occupations Returned.																			
					Agricultural rent receivers (landlords). (1).		Rent payers (ordinary cultivators). (2).		Paid field labourers and farm servants. (4).		Cotton ginning, cleaning, and pressing. (21).		Cotton spinning, sizing, and weaving. (22).		Carpenters, sawyers, turners, joiners etc. (38).		General workers in iron. (41).		Potters, and earthen pipe and bowl makers. (47).		Boot and shoe makers and embroiderers on shoes. (69).		Barbers. (72)	
	M.	F.	M.	F.	M.	F.	M.	F.	M.	F.	M.	F.	M.	F.	M.	F.	M.	F.	M.	F.	M.	F.	M.	F.
1	2	3	4	5	6	7	8	9	10	11	12	13	14	15	16	17	18	19	20	21	22	23	24	25
Rajputana	267,512	1,930,886	8,209	20,957	302	68	188	412	2,337	6,275	62	172	289	1,791	169	28	54	53	114	353	231	171	151	169
Alwar	11,161	112,641	539	1,789	11	7	3	4	106	782	...	6	4	229	2	3	4	...	10	54	4	27	4	5
Banswara	10,979	82,256	195	383	...	...	...	...	13	68	...	...	...	...	...	...	7	...	1	2	3	...	4	...
Bharatpur	34,934	83,955	2,462	2,899	11	2	38	24	1,308	1,475	5	2	4	116	18	...	4	2	26	40	15	14	24	16
Bikaner	880	110,224	71	1,996	...	5	...	4	1	1	...	...	3	440	...	4	...	4	2	118	2	33	4	86
Bundi	9,964	16,329	98	23	1	...	4	...	3	4	2	...	...	1	4	...	7	1	4	7	1	...	10	...
Dholpur	11,866	21,286	344	425	...	...	6	...	108	108	...	...	10	13	8	...	...	...	3	4	...	...	7	...
Dungarpur	7,168	27,367	370	560	...	...	...	...	28	147	...	1	1	...	1	...	10	...	3	3	...	...	4	...
Jaipur	46,004	275,037	1,063	3,897	42	18	95	287	335	1,344	13	48	9	106	7	3	1	18	13	81	39	68	8	12
Jaisalmer	93	712	8	1	...	...	...	...	...	...	...	...	1	...	...	...	...	...	...	...	...	...	...	...
Jhalawar	2,076	2,909	21	95	...	...	...	...	...	15	...	...	...	2	6	...	...	...	...	...	3	...	...	...
Karauli	14,218	23,622	386	397	10	1	4	...	70	106	...	...	2	3	1	...	1	2	1	1	6	...	2	...
Kishangarh	2,311	8,570	54	236	1	2	3	2	11	212	...	...	8	8	...	2	...	...	...	1	...	1	...	...
Kotah	30,305	66,352	796	1,448	14	13	19	62	108	734	2	19	5	25	37	...	6	7	14	14	46	7	38	22
Kushalgarh (Chiefship)	838	4,881	1	6	...	...	...	...	...	...	...	...	...	...	...	...	...	...	...	...	...	...	...	...
Lawa (Estate)	9	275	...	5	...	...	...	...	...	1	...	...	...	...	...	...	...	...	...	...	...	...	...	...
Marwar	47,269	278,154	1,577	4,352	212	20	15	28	108	897	35	73	241	819	79	16	7	18	29	60	106	17	32	19
Mewar	13,962	87,163	6	706	...	...	...	...	...	...	...	...	...	...	...	...	...	...	...	...	...	...	...	...
Partabgarh	187	8,825	30	865	...	...	...	1	1	70	...	...	...	3	...	...	...	...	...	2	...	...	...	...
Shahpura (Chiefship)	138	8,508	3	370	...	...	...	...	1	97	...	23	...	14	...	...	...	1	...	3	...	1	...	6
Sirohi	2,002	18,225	27	263	...	...	...	...	7	31	...	...	1	3	2	...	1	...	...	7	3	3	...	1
Tonk	21,153	38,595	221	286	...	...	1	...	39	93	5	...	...	...	4	...	6	...	8	6	3	...	14	2
Ajmer-Merwara	18,077	61,609	819	1,474	2	4	9	4	185	543	23	67	14	29	38	...	9	9	30	47	41	...	39	8
Ajmer	15,300	40,741	698	1,104	2	4	9	4	175	494	23	65	13	15	35	...	9	9	25	34	38	...	27	8
Merwara	3,677	20,868	127	370	...	...	...	...	7	49	...	2	1	14	3	...	...	...	5	13	3	...	12	...

TABLE XV-B.—SUBSIDIARY OCCUPATIONS OF AGRICULTURISTS.—(ACTUAL WORKERS ONLY.)

(3) UNPAID HELPERS IN CULTIVATION—*concluded.*

Province; and State or District.	Details of Subsidiary Occupations Returned.—*contd.* Money lenders, bank managers, etc. (106).		Breeders and keepers of cattle, sheep, goats (9 and 10), and sellers of milk, butter, ghi, etc. (118).		Grain and pulse dealers. (121).		Other traders of all kinds. (107-117, 119, 120, 122-136).		Army (Imperial). (138).		Army (Native States, including Imperial Service Troops). (140).		Village watchmen. (143).		Government service. (144).		Native States' administrative officials and menials. (145 b).		Priests, ministers, etc. (146).		Beggars (not religious), prostitutes, receivers of stolen goods, etc. (169).		Others.	
	M.	F.	M.	F.	M.	F.	M.	F.	M.	F.	M.	F.	M.	F.	M.	F.	M.	F.	M.	F.	M.	F.	M.	F.
1	26	27	28	29	30	31	32	33	34	35	36	37	38	39	40	41	42	43	44	45	46	47	48	49
Rajputana	78	26	236	500	41	1	635	3,621	2	...	22	...	63	...	166	18	34	4	83	148	332	217	2,620	6,930
Alwar	7	2	14	19	2	1	69	337	...	...	2	...	12	...	164	1	...	...	10	37	31	25	80	250
Banswara	1	...	...	30	...	...	66	214	...	...	...	...	2	...	...	...	...	...	9	...	...	1	80	67
Bharatpur	34	9	55	96	13	...	160	490	2	...	3	...	15	...	1	...	3	...	19	15	10	5	625	584
Bikaner	...	...	1	45	...	...	3	75	...	...	...	...	...	...	...	...	...	...	4	73	...	107	52	902
Bundi	5	...	3	...	...	...	10	3	...	...	2	...	...	...	...	...	1	...	4	...	8	...	23	12
Dholpur	2	...	2	...	1	...	44	105	...	...	...	...	...	...	...	...	...	...	7	...	1	...	145	105
Dungarpur	...	...	...	...	...	...	72	338	...	...	...	...	...	...	...	...	...	...	2	...	...	...	249	71
Jaipur	8	3	18	39	13	...	3	113	...	...	12	...	20	...	...	...	12	...	5	6	47	18	363	1,783
Jaisalmer	...	...	2	1	...	...	...	...	...	...	...	...	...	...	...	...	...	...	...	...	...	...	...	...
Jhalawar	...	...	...	1	1	...	...	45	...	...	...	...	...	...	...	...	...	...	...	...	7	10	4	22
Karauli	10	1	31	14	6	...	114	187	...	...	...	...	...	...	...	...	2	...	8	...	4	...	116	82
Kishangarh	1	...	8	1	...	...	3	6	...	...	1	...	...	...	...	...	...	...	...	...	...	...	18	51
Kotah	6	2	43	60	2	...	28	95	...	...	...	...	3	...	...	...	12	2	12	1	81	7	231	378
Kushalgarh (Chiefship)	...	...	...	...	...	...	...	...	...	...	...	...	...	...	...	...	...	...	...	...	...	6	1	...
Lawa (Estate)	...	...	...	...	...	...	...	1	...	...	...	...	...	...	...	...	...	...	...	...	...	...	...	3
Marwar	1	9	49	115	8	...	30	1,341	...	...	2	...	8	...	1	17	2	2	3	16	108	81	497	854
Mewar	...	...	...	...	...	...	1	16	...	...	...	...	...	...	...	...	...	...	...	...	...	...	5	690
Partabgarh	...	...	...	...	...	...	...	2	...	...	...	...	...	...	...	...	...	...	...	...	...	1	29	786
Shahpura (Chiefship)	...	...	...	...	...	...	...	152	...	...	...	...	...	...	...	...	...	...	...	...	...	...	2	73
Sirohi	...	...	3	79	...	...	6	100	...	...	...	...	...	...	...	...	...	...	...	...	...	1	4	38
Tonk	3	...	8	...	...	...	3	1	...	...	...	...	3	...	...	...	2	...	...	...	35	5	87	179
Ajmer-Merwara	4	...	49	110	...	...	75	372	1	...	...	...	3	...	...	...	...	1	1	1	13	19	283	251
Ajmer	3	...	43	86	...	...	45	227	...	...	...	...	1	...	...	...	...	1	1	1	7	11	228	145
Merwara	1	...	1	33	...	...	30	145	1	...	...	...	2	...	...	...	...	...	...	...	6	8	55	106

TABLE XV-B.—SUBSIDIARY OCCUPATIONS OF AGRICULTURISTS.—(ACTUAL WORKERS ONLY.)

(4) PAID FIELD LABOURERS AND FARM SERVANTS.

Province, and State or District.	Total number of paid field labourers and farm servants. (Actual workers).		Number of actual workers who returned subsidiary occupations.		Details of Subsidiary Occupations Returned. Rent receivers (landlords). (1).		Rent payers (ordinary cultivators). (2).		Unpaid helpers in cultivation. (5a).		Woodcutters, grass cutters, charcoal burners, etc. (8).		Herdsmen, shepherds, goatherds, swineherds (12).		Cotton ginning, cleaning, and pressing. (21).		Cotton spinning, sizing, and weaving. (22).		Dyeing, bleaching, printing, etc., of fabrics (30 & 30a).		Tanners, curriers, leather dyers and dressers. (33).		Carpenters, sawyers, turners, joiners, etc. (36).	
	M.	F.	M.	F.	M.	F.	M.	F.	M.	F.	M.	F.	M.	F.	M.	F.	M.	F.	M.	F.	M.	F.	M.	F.
1	2	3	4	5	6	7	8	9	10	11	12	13	14	15	16	17	18	19	20	21	22	23	24	25
Rajputana	205,115	294,383	12,629	8,780	316	63	5,065	770	386	1,522	408	467	153	32	159	116	500	658	19	8	116	13	18	29
Alwar	14,908	16,387	2,318	1,372	38	1	1,176	211	53	504	...	1	4	1	57	6	229	126	1	1	5	...	...	...
Banswara	3,723	4,272	141	150	7	...	4	1	...	...	57	3	...	...	...	...	...	...	...	...	...	...	...	...
Bharatpur	18,303	12,032	2,565	1,065	55	5	1,730	184	202	414	...	4	14	1	1	1	26	52	...	...	...	...	4	...
Bikaner	2,751	507	146	...	1	...	124	...	...	...	...	...	...	...	...	...	...	...	2	...	...	...	...	...
Bundi	9,525	11,900	112	36	3	...	25	2	...	2	18	1	...	...	1	...	9	...	5	...	4	...	1	...
Dholpur	6,439	4,953	198	71	1	2	80	6	2	10	5	...	...	...	...	...	3	...	...	...	...	2	...	...
Dungarpur	8,177	3,083	105	146	...	...	2	...	1	...	1	...	1	...	...	...	...	...	...	...	...	...	...	...
Jaipur	49,608	69,816	1,973	1,237	37	12	619	121	56	132	19	67	31	5	67	74	92	148	...	...	56	5	1	2
Jaisalmer	74	20	2	1	...	...	...	...	...	...	...	...	...	...	...	...	...	1	...	...	...	...	...	...
Jhalawar	4,809	6,981	257	196	25	7	20	1	2	4	24	65	2	...	11	5	15	33	...	...	7	...	1	...
Karauli	2,508	3,378	96	21	...	...	43	3	6	1	...	...	...	...	...	...	...	...	...	...	...	...	...	...
Kishangarh	2,304	3,419	155	116	2	..	56	28	3	21	1	3	1	...	1	1	1	10	1	...	6	...	...	...
Kotah	31,426	43,955	1,651	1,070	19	6	883	86	27	178	69	131	14	4	3	6	15	38	1	...	3	5	3	4
Kushalgarh (Chiefship)	22	71	1	5	...	...	...	...	...	...	...	...	...	...	...	...	...	...	...	...	...	...	...	...
Lawa (Estate)	142	195	1	1	...	...	1	...	...	...	...	...	...	1	...	...	...	...	...	...	...	...	...	...
Marwar	27,070	49,314	877	1,054	39	12	135	83	10	155	12	14	11	13	14	8	61	183	3	...	11	...	6	21
Mewar	13,659	39,031	1,322	1,341	82	14	63	31	14	58	184	154	66	5	1	15	29	47	6	2	13	1	2	2
Partabgarh	1,958	3,929	82	196	1	1	16	1	...	1	9	22	3	1	...	...	1	1	...	...	1	...	...	...
Shahpura (Chiefship)	384	628	57	18	3	1	12	2	...	9	2	1	1	...	1	1	4	...	...	...	5	...	...	...
Sirohi	3,066	2,976	106	100	2	...	5	1	3	14	7	1	5	1	...	...	3	10	...	...	...	...	...	...
Tonk	14,759	18,538	469	164	1	2	62	9	5	19	...	...	...	...	2	4	12	9	...	...	5	...	...	...
Ajmer-Merwara	9,156	14,348	507	264	46	15	70	14	8	40	16	4	16	1	2	17	28	20	1	2	8	3	1	...
Ajmer	8,237	13,226	443	228	42	12	51	11	8	31	14	4	14	1	2	16	27	18	1	2	8	2	1	...
Merwara	919	1,122	64	36	4	3	19	3	...	9	2	...	2	...	...	1	1	2	...	...	...	1	...	...

TABLE XV-B.—SUBSIDIARY OCCUPATIONS OF AGRICULTURISTS.—(ACTUAL WORKERS ONLY.)

(4) PAID FIELD LABOURERS AND FARM SERVANTS—*concluded.*

Province; and State or District.	DETAILS OF SUBSIDIARY OCCUPATIONS RETURNED—*contd.*																							
	General workers in iron. (41).		Potters, and earthen pipe and bowl makers. (47).		Oil pressers. (53).		Boot and shoe makers, and embroiderers on shoes. (69).		Washing, cleaning, and dyeing, of clothes. (71 & 71a).		Barbers. (72).		Other traders of all kinds. (107-117, 119-135, 137, 138).		Breeders and keepers of cattle, sheep, goats, pigs (9 & 10), sellers of milk, butter, ghi, etc. (118).		Itinerant traders, pedlars. (136).		Village watchmen. (143).		General labourers. (167).		Others.	
	M.	F.	M.	F.	M.	F.	M.	F.	M.	F.	M.	F.	M.	F.	M.	F.	M.	F.	M.	F.	M.	F.	M.	F.
1	26	27	28	29	30	31	32	33	34	35	36	37	38	39	40	41	42	43	44	45	46	47	48	49
Rajputana	15	48	41	52	31	9	630	168	43	42	43	30	674	817	80	130	9	5	113	...	158	121	3,652	3,685
Alwar	...	...	5	4	...	...	214	121	1	3	9	...	25	26	5	...	...	...	5	...	36	69	455	298
Banswara	...	...	...	...	...	...	2	...	...	...	...	...	64	131	...	...	..	..	...	...	...	...	7	15
Bharatpur	...	...	2	6	...	...	22	...	2	...	6	...	177	235	5	3	...	...	2	...	12	2	305	159
Bikaner	...	...	1	...	...	...	2	...	...	...	...	...	...	...	...	...	...	...	1	...	2	...	13	...
Bundi	...	...	...	...	...	...	3	...	...	...	1	...	3	5	6	2	...	...	...	...	...	...	33	24
Dholpur	...	...	...	...	...	...	8	...	...	...	...	...	68	45	...	...	5	1	1	...	2	...	17	5
Dungarpur	...	...	...	...	...	3	...	...	...	...	...	...	93	126	...	...	...	...	...	...	...	...	7	17
Jaipur	1	...	13	3	...	1	187	24	2	5	3	6	...	...	9	2	1	4	16	...	46	12	715	614
Jaisalmer	...	...	1	...	...	...	...	...	...	...	...	...	...	...	...	...	...	...	...	...	...	...	1	...
Jhalawar	2	1	...	1	1	...	9	1	3	2	...	...	3	9	...	2	...	...	3	...	...	...	120	55
Karauli	...	...	...	...	1	...	...	...	...	...	...	...	20	11	...	...	...	...	..	...	...	...	26	6
Kishangarh	...	...	1	2	...	...	24	...	2	...	...	...	2	...	6	2	...	...	1	...	3	1	44	48
Kotah	2	2	3	5	3	1	32	3	9	30	6	6	139	30	14	8	..	...	2	...	34	12	370	525
Kushalgarh (Chiefship)	...	...	...	...	...	...	...	...	...	3	...	...	...	...	...	...	...	...	...	...	...	...	1	2
Lawa (Estate)	...	...	...	...	...	...	...	...	...	...	...	...	...	...	...	...	...	...	...	...	...	...	...	..
Marwar	...	33	8	28	1	3	61	13	5	4	14	8	49	143	14	30	...	...	23	...	11	15	389	293
Mewar	10	11	7	3	22	...	27	5	14	5	3	9	...	2	8	78	3	...	14	...	8	7	747	1,393
Partabgarh	...	1	...	..	1	...	1	...	...	...	...	...	1	3	...	...	...	...	1	...	...	...	47	95
Shahpura (Chiefship)	...	...	...	...	...	...	2	...	1	...	...	...	2	2	...	...	...	...	...	.	...	...	24	2
Sirohi	...	...	...	..	1	1	9	...	...	...	1	...	27	49	2	2	...	...	1	...	2	..	38	21
Tonk	...	...	...	1	1	...	27	1	4	...	...	2	1	...	11	1	...	...	43	...	2	3	293	113
Ajmer-Merwara	1	1	4	1	1	...	28	...	3	3	1	5	54	53	14	5	1	...	6		1	1	107	79
Ajmer	1	1	4	1	1	...	28	...	3	3	1	4	49	48	12	5	...	...	5	...	1	1	170	68
Merwara	...	...	...	...	...	...	...	...	...	...	...	1	5	5	2	...	1	...	1	...	...	...	27	11

TABLE XV-E.

Statistics of Industries.

Explanatory Note.

This Table classifies the information about industries which was collected in a special Industrial Schedule filled in by the owners, managers, or agents of factories, etc., in which at least 20 persons were employed on March 10th, 1911. The Table is divided into four parts.

Part I is a Provincial Summary showing the number of persons employed in each industry dealt with.

Part II shows, for each State or District, the number of persons employed in each class of industries.

Parts III and IV give the castes or nationalities of the owners and managers, respectively, of the Cotton factories, presses, and mills in the two Provinces.

TABLE XV-E. — STATISTICS OF INDUSTRIES. PART I.—PROVINCIAL SUMMARY (RAJPUTANA).

Serial number of class of industry.	Description of factory, mine, etc.	Classification of factory, etc., according to number of persons employed (including management).	Number of factories.	Total number of persons employed.		CLASSIFICATION OF PERSONS EMPLOYED. Direction, supervision, and clerical work. Europeans and Anglo-Indians.		Indians.		Skilled workmen. Europeans and Anglo-Indians.		Indians.		Unskilled labourers. Age 14 and over.		Age under 14.		Power.	State of business :— (1) Much brisker than usual. (2) Brisker than usual. (3) Somewhat brisker than usual. (4) Normal. (5) Somewhat slacker than usual. (6) Slacker than usual. (7) Much slacker than usual.	Remarks.
				Males.	Females.	Males.	Females.	Males.	Females.	Males.	Females.	Males.	Females.	Males.	Females.	Males.	Females.			
1	2	3	4	5	6	7	8	9	10	11	12	13	14	15	16	17	18	19	20	21
	Rajputana . . .	**Total** .	44	*4,948*	*792*	21	...	245	...	24	...	1,580	...	2,857	752	221	40	Steam . 31 Steam and electricity . 1 Gas . . 1 Hand . . 11	(1) . . 3 (2) . . 2 (3) . . 5 (4) . . 28 (5) . . 2 (6) . . 5	
1	MINES . . . . . Collieries— Mechanical . .	TOTAL . 100—200	*1*	111	12	...	...	*8*	...	...	...	*12*	...	*87*	*9*	*4*	*3*	Steam . 1	(3) . . 1	
2	QUARRIES OF HARD ROCKS . Lime Stone and Marble Quarries— Non-mechanical .	TOTAL . 400 and over .	*1*	400	151	*3*	...	*3*	...	...	...	*11*	...	*368*	*138*	*15*	*13*	Hand . 1	(4) . . 1	
3	TEXTILE INDUSTRIES .	TOTAL .	*22*	1,751	585	*2*	...	*120*	...	*23*	...	*199*	...	*1,231*	*563*	*176*	*22*	Steam . 19 Hand . 3	(2) . . 1 (3) . . 3 (4) . . 13 (5) . . 2 (6) . . 3	
	(1) Cotton . . .	Total .	19	*1,515*	585	2	...	112	...	23	...	141	...	1,186	563	51	22	Steam . 19	(2) . . 1 (3) . . 3 (4) . . 10 (5) . . 2 (6) . . 3	
	(a) Cotton ginning, cleaning and pressing mills . . .	*Total* .	*18*	1,099	471	*2*	...	*94*	...	*23*	...	*122*	...	*813*	*449*	*45*	*22*	Steam . 18	(2) . . 1 (3) . . 3 (4) . . 10 (5) . . 1 (6) . . 3	
	Mechanical . .	20— 50	*7	237	26	...	...	29	...	...	...	39	...	159	24	10	2	Steam . 7	(3) . . 2 (4) . . 1 (5) . . 1 (6) . . 3	* One of these falls also under "Wool Presses."
		50—100	8	427	182	...	...	41	...	...	...	74	...	200	108	13	14	Steam . 8	(2) . . 1 (3) . . 1 (4) . . 6	
		100—200	1	114	54	...	...	6	...	...	...	...	...	108	54	...	...	Steam . 1	(4) . . 1	
		200—400	2	321	209	2	...	18	...	23	...	9	...	247	203	22	6	Steam . 2	(4) . . 2	
	(b) Cotton spinning, weaving and other mills— Mechanical . .	400 and over	†*1*	416	114	...	...	*18*	...	...	...	*19*	...	*373*	*114*	*6*	...	Steam . 1	(5) . . 1	† Falls also under "Cotton ginning, cleaning and pressing mills."
	(2) Wool, Carpet, Blanket and Shawl Factories	Total .	3	*236*	...	...	...	8	...	...	...	58	...	45	...	125	...	Hand . 3	(4) . . 3	
	Non-mechanical .	20—50	1	39	...	...	...	2	...	...	...	32	...	...	...	5	...	Hand . 1	(4) . . 1	
		50—100	1	95	...	...	...	4	...	...	...	1	...	25	...	65	...	Hand . 1	(4) . . 1	
		100—200	1	102	...	...	...	2	...	...	...	25	...	20	...	55	...	Hand . 1	(4) . . 1	

TABLE XV-E.—STATISTICS OF INDUSTRIES. PART I.—PROVINCIAL SUMMARY (RAJPUTANA)—*concluded.*

Serial number of class of industry.	Description of factory, mine, etc.	Classification of factory, etc., according to number of persons employed (including management).	Number of factories.	Total number of persons employed. Males.	Total number of persons employed. Females.	Direction, supervision, and clerical work. Europeans and Anglo-Indians. Males.	Direction, supervision, and clerical work. Europeans and Anglo-Indians. Females.	Direction, supervision, and clerical work. Indians. Males.	Direction, supervision, and clerical work. Indians. Females.	Skilled workmen. Europeans and Anglo-Indians. Males.	Skilled workmen. Europeans and Anglo-Indians. Females.	Skilled workmen. Indians. Males.	Skilled workmen. Indians. Females.	Unskilled labourers. Age 14 and over. Males.	Unskilled labourers. Age 14 and over. Females.	Unskilled labourers. Age under 14. Males.	Unskilled labourers. Age under 14. Females.	Power.	State of business:— (1) Much brisker than usual. (2) Brisker than usual. (3) Somewhat brisker than usual. (4) Normal. (5) Somewhat slacker than usual. (6) Slacker than usual. (7) Much slacker than usual.	Remarks.
1	2	3	4	5	6	7	8	9	10	11	12	13	14	15	16	17	18	19	20	21
4	METAL INDUSTRIES. Machinery and Engineering Workshops	TOTAL	*5*	616	31	*2*	...	*32*	...	...	...	*448*	...	*123*	*31*	*11*	...	Steam . 1; Steam and electricity 1; Hand . 3	(3) . 1; (4) . 4	
	Mechanical	100—200	2	251	1	1	...	14	...	...	...	202	...	34	1	...	...	Steam . 1; Steam and electricity 1	(3) . 1; (4) . 1	
	Non-mechanical	20—50	2	71	...	1	...	4	...	...	...	30	...	20	...	1	...	Hand . 2	(4) . 2	
		200-400	1	294	30	...	...	14	...	...	...	210	...	60	30	10	...	Hand . 1	(4) . 1	
5	FOOD INDUSTRIES	TOTAL	*5*	245	13	*2*	...	*25*	...	...	...	*46*	...	*159*	*11*	*13*	*2*	Steam . 5	(1) . 1; (2) . 1; (4) . 3	
	(1) Sugar factories—Mechanical	50—100	1	*51*	7	...	...	6	...	...	...	7	...	32	6	6	1	Steam . 1	(2) . 1	
	(2) Breweries and distilleries	Total	2	*82*	...	...	...	16	...	...	...	15	...	48	...	3	...	Steam . 2	(1) . 1; (4) . 1	
	Mechanical	20—50	1	27	...	...	...	5	...	...	...	1	...	20	...	1	...	Steam . 1	(4) . 1	
		50—100	1	55	...	...	...	11	...	...	...	14	...	28	...	2	...	Steam . 1	(1) . 1	
	(3) Water Works—Mechanical	50—100	1	*53*	*2*	2	...	2	...	...	...	20	...	29	2	...	...	Steam . 1	(4) . 1	
	(4) Forage Presses—Mechanical	50—100	1	*59*	*4*	...	...	1	...	...	...	4	...	50	3	4	1	Steam . 1	(4) . 1	
6	CONSTRUCTION OF MEANS OF TRANSPORT	TOTAL	*3*	1,466	...	*7*	...	*27*	...	*1*	...	*740*	...	*691*	...	...	...	Steam . 2; Hand . 1	(4) . 3	
	(1) Railway Workshops	Total	2	*1,405*	...	7	...	25	...	1	...	682	...	690	...	...	...	Steam . 2	(4) . 2	
	Mechanical	50-100	1	66	...	1	...	1	...	...	[illegible]	38	...	26	...	...	...	Steam . 1	(4) . 1	
		400 and over	1	1,339	...	6	...	24	...	1	...	644	...	664	...	...	...	Steam . 1	(4) . 1	
	(2) Coach Building Factories—Non-mechanical	50—100	1	*61*	...	...	...	2	...	...	...	58	...	1	...	...	...	Hand . 1	(4) . 1	
7	PRODUCTION AND TRANSMISSION OF PHYSICAL FORCES	TOTAL	*4*	168	...	*5*	...	*15*	...	...	...	*37*	...	*109*	...	*2*	...	Steam . 3; Gas . 1	(4) . 3; (6) . 1	
	(1) Ice Factories—Mechanical	20—50	2*	*43*	...	2	...	6	...	...	...	16	...	18	...	1	...	Steam . 2	(4) . 1; (6) . 1	* Falls also under "Industries connected with chemical products (Aerated Water factories)."
	(2) Gas and Electric Light Works	Total	2	*125*	...	3	...	9	...	...	...	21	...	91	...	1	...	Steam . 1; Gas . 1	(4) . 2	
	Mechanical	20—50	1	33	...	1	...	3	...	...	...	8	...	20	...	1	...	Steam . 1	(4) . 1	
		50—100	1	92	...	2	...	6	...	...	...	13	...	71	...	...	...	Gas . 1	(4) . 1	
8	INDUSTRIES OF LUXURY. Printing Presses	TOTAL	*3*	191	...	...	...	*15*	...	...	...	*87*	...	*89*	...	...	...	Hand . 3	(1) . 1; (4) . 1; (6) . 1	
	Non-mechanical	20—50	1	24	...	...	...	2	...	...	...	17	...	5	...	...	...	Hand . 1	(6) . 1	
		50—100	1	64	...	...	...	5	...	...	...	9	...	50	...	...	...	Hand . 1	(1) . 1	
		100—200	1	103	...	...	...	8	...	...	...	61	...	34	...	...	...	Hand . 1	(4) . 1	

TABLE XV-E.—STATISTICS OF INDUSTRIES. PART I.—PROVINCIAL SUMMARY (AJMER-MERWARA).

Serial number of class of industry.	Description of factory, mine, etc.	Classification of factory, etc., according to number of persons employed (including management).	Number of factories.	Total number of persons employed.		Classification of persons employed. Direction, supervision, and clerical work. Europeans and Anglo-Indians.		Direction, supervision, and clerical work. Indians.		Skilled workmen. Europeans and Anglo-Indians.		Skilled workmen. Indians.		Unskilled labourers. Age 14 and over.		Unskilled labourers. Age under 14.		Power.	State of business :— (1) Much brisker than usual. (2) Brisker than usual. (3) Somewhat brisker than usual. (4) Normal. (5) Somewhat slacker than usual. (6) Slacker than usual. (7) Much slacker than usual.	Remarks.
				Males.	Females.	Males.	Females.	Males.	Females.	Males.	Females.	Males.	Females.	Males	Females.	Males.	Females.			
1	2	3	4	5	6	7	8	9	10	11	12	13	14	15	16	17	18	19	20	21
	Ajmer-Merwara	**Total**	20	*11,115*	*1,048*	72	...	341	...	302	...	7,037	84	3,128	894	235	70	Steam . 12 Electricity 1 Steam and electricity. 1 Oil . 1 Hand . 5	(1) . . 1 (2) . . 4 (3) . . 2 (4) . . 9 (6) . . 2 (7) . . 2	
1	MINES Mica Mines— Non-mechanical	TOTAL 50—100	*2*	103	11	...	...	*5*	...	...	...	*46*	*8*	*44*	*3*	*8*	...	Hand . 2	(4) . . 2	
2	TEXTILE INDUSTRIES Cotton	TOTAL	*9*	2,300	1,033	*5*	...	*75*	...	*3*	...	*1,116*	*72*	*982*	*891*	*119*	*70*	Steam . 9	(1) . . 1 (2) . . 2 (4) . . 3 (6) . . 2 (7) . . 1	
	(a) Cotton ginning, cleaning and pressing mills	*Total*	8	1,301	843	*8*	..	*39*	...	*1*	...	493	85	665	739	*100*	70	Steam . 8	(1) . . 1 (2) . . 1 (4) . . 3 (6) . . 2 (7) . . 1	
	Mechanical	20—50	1*	20	20	1	...	1	...	1	...	2	...	10	20	5	...	Steam . 1	(7) . . 1	* Falls also under "Food Industries (Flour and rice mills)."
		50—100	3†	130	100	...	...	6	...	...	...	29	...	86	96	9	4	Steam . 3	(2) . . 1 (6) . . 2	† One of these falls also under "Wool Presses."
		100—200	2†	186	121	...	...	5	...	...	...	26	...	143	107	12	14	Steam . 2	(4) . . 2	
		400 and over	2‡	965	602	2	...	27	...	...	...	436	35	426	515	74	52	Steam . 2	(1) . . 1 (4) . . 1	‡ One of these falls also under "Cotton spinning, weaving and other mills" and the other under "Wool Presses."
	(b) Cotton spinning, weaving and other mills— Mechanical	400 and over	*1*	999	190	*2*	...	*36*	...	*2*	...	*623*	*37*	*317*	*153*	*19*	...	Steam . 1	(2) . . 1	

TABLE XV-E.—STATISTICS OF INDUSTRIES. PART I.—PROVINCIAL SUMMARY (AJMER-MERWARA)—*concluded.*

Serial number of class of industry.	Description of factory, mine, etc.	Classification of factory, etc., according to number of persons employed (including management).	Number of factories.	Total number of persons employed.		CLASSIFICATION OF PERSONS EMPLOYED.												Power.	State of business :— (1) Much brisker than usual. (2) Brisker than usual. (3) Somewhat brisker than usual. (4) Normal. (5) Somewhat slacker than usual. (6) Slacker than usual. (7) Much slacker than usual.	REMARKS.
						DIRECTION, SUPERVISION, AND CLERICAL WORK.				SKILLED WORKMEN.				UNSKILLED LABOURERS.						
						Europeans and Anglo-Indians.		Indians.		Europeans and Anglo-Indians.		Indians.		Age 14 and over.		Age under 14.				
				Males.	Females.	Males	Females.	Males.	Females.	Males.	Females.	Males.	Females.	Males.	Females.	Males.	Females.			
1	2	3	4	5	6	7	8	9	10	11	12	13	14	15	16	17	18	19	20	21
3	FOOD INDUSTRIES Breweries and Distilleries— Non-mechanical	TOTAL 20—50	*1*	21	...	...	...	*1*	...	...	...	*1*	...	*19*	...	...	...	Hand . 1	(4) . . 1	
4	CONSTRUCTION OF MEANS OF TRANSPORT Railway workshops	TOTAL	*3*	8,373	4	*65*	...	*237*	...	*299*	...	*5,659*	*4*	*2,027*	...	*86*	...	Electricity . 1 Steam . 1 Steam and electricity. 1	(2) . . 1 (4) . . 2	
	Mechanical	200—400	1	236	...	6	...	21	...	12	...	105	...	84	...	8	...	Electricity . 1	(4) . . 1	
		400 and over	2	8,137	4	59	...	216	...	287	...	5,554	4	1,943	...	78	...	Steam . 1 Steam and electricity. 1	(2) . . 1 (4) . . 1	
5	PRODUCTION AND TRANSMISSION OF PHYSICAL FORCES Ice Factories— Mechanical	TOTAL 20—50	*1**	44	...	...	...	*2*	...	...	...	*19*	...	*17*	...	*6*	...	Steam . 1	(7) . . 1	* Falls also under the following heads :— (1) Metal Industries (iron and brass foundry). (2) Industries connected with chemical products (aerated water). (3) Food Industries (Flour Mill).
6	INDUSTRIES OF LUXURY Printing Presses	TOTAL	*4*	274	...	*2*	...	*21*	...	...	...	*196*	...	*39*	...	*16*	...	Steam . 1 Oil . 1 Hand . 2	(2) . . 1 (3) . . 2 (4) . . 1	
	Mechanical	20—50	1	46	...	...	...	5	...	...	...	21	...	10	...	10	...	Steam . 1	(2) . . 1	
		100—200	1	147	...	2	...	6	...	...	...	117	...	22	...	...	...	Oil . 1	(3) . . 1	
	Non-mechanical	20—50	2	81	...	...	...	10	...	...	...	58	...	7	...	6	...	Hand . 2	(3) . . 1 (4) . . 1	

TABLE XV-E.—STATISTICS OF INDUSTRIES. PART II.—DISTRIBUTION BY STATES OR DISTRICTS.

Province; and State or District.	Description of industry, etc.	Number of factories, etc.	Total number of persons employed.		Classification of persons employed. Direction, supervision, and clerical work. Europeans and Anglo-Indians.		Indians.		Skilled workmen. Europeans and Anglo-Indians.		Indians.		Unskilled labourers. Age 14 and over.		Age under 14.		Remarks.
			Males.	Females.	Males.	Females.	Males.	Females.	Males.	Females.	Males.	Females.	Males.	Females.	Males.	Females.	
1	2	3	4	5	6	7	8	9	10	11	12	13	14	15	16	17	18
Rajputana†	**Total**	44	*4,948*	*792*	21	...	245	...	24	...	1,580	...	2,857	752	221	40	
Alwar	*Total*	*3*	308	54	*1*	...	*12*	...	...	...	*118*	...	*177*	*54*	...	...	
	Textile Industries	2	165	54	...	...	7	...	...	...	...	...	158	54	...	...	
	Metal Industries	1	143	...	1	...	5	...	...	...	118	...	19	...	...	...	
Banswara	Food Industries	*1*	55	...	...	...	*11*	...	...	...	*14*	...	*28*	...	*2*	...	
Bharatpur	*Total*	*4*	253	5	...	...	*17*	...	...	...	*110*	...	*122*	*4*	*4*	*1*	
	Textile Industries	1	22	...	...	...	2	...	...	...	13	...	7	...	...	...	
	Metal Industries	1	108	1	...	...	9	...	...	...	84	...	15	1	...	...	
	Food Industries	1	59	4	...	...	1	...	...	...	4	...	50	3	4	1	
	Industries of Luxury	1	64	...	...	...	5	...	...	...	9	...	50	...	...	...	
Bikaner	*Total*	*2*	150	12	...	...	*10*	...	...	...	*44*	...	*87*	*9*	*9*	*3*	
	Mines	1	111	12	...	...	8	...	...	...	12	...	87	9	4	3	
	Textile Industries	1	39	...	...	...	2	...	...	...	32	...	...	...	5	...	
Bundi	Textile Industries	*1*	40	6	...	...	*6*	...	...	...	*3*	...	*28*	*4*	*3*	*2*	
Jaipur	*Total*	*6*	535	169	*6*	...	*27*	...	...	...	*78*	...	*293*	*165*	*131*	*4*	
	Textile Industries	4	390	167	2	...	19	...	...	...	45	...	193	163	131	4	
	Food Industries	1	53	2	2	...	2	...	...	...	20	...	29	2	...	...	
	Production and transmission of physical forces.	1	92	...	2	...	6	...	...	...	13	...	71	...	...	...	
Jhalawar	Textile Industries	*2*	104	29	...	...	*6*	...	...	...	*16*	...	*75*	*25*	*7*	*4*	
Karauli	Textile Industries	*1*	39	1	...	...	*8*	...	...	...	*4*	...	*24*	*1*	*3*	...	
Kishangarh	Textile Industries	*3*	486	130	...	...	*22*	...	...	...	*26*	...	*429*	*130*	*9*	...	
Kotah	*Total*	*6*	225	48	*1*	...	*31*	...	...	...	*71*	...	*119*	*47*	*3*	*1*	
	Textile Industries	3	147	48	...	...	23	...	...	...	18	...	104	47	2	1	
	Metal Industries	1	34	...	...	...	3	...	...	...	25	...	6	...	...	...	
	Production and transmission of physical forces.	*1	20	...	1	...	3	...	...	...	11	...	4	...	1	...	* Falls also under "Industries connected with chemical products (Ice factories)."
	Industries of Luxury	1	24	...	...	...	2	...	...	...	17	...	5	...	...	...	

† Dholpur, Dungarpur, Jaisalmer, Kushalgarh, Lawa, Partabgarh, are omitted as they contain no industries.

TABLE XV-E.—STATISTICS OF INDUSTRIES. PART II.—DISTRIBUTION BY STATES OR DISTRICTS—*concluded.*

Province; and State or District.	Description of industry, etc.	Number of factories, etc.	Total number of persons employed.		Classification of persons employed. Direction, supervision, and clerical work. Europeans and Anglo-Indians.		Indians.		Skilled workmen. Europeans and Anglo-Indians.		Indians.		Unskilled labourers. Age 14 and over.		Age under 14.		Remarks.
			Males.	Females.	Males.	Females.	Males.	Females.	Males.	Females.	Males.	Females.	Males.	Females.	Males.	Females.	
1	2	3	4	5	6	7	8	9	10	11	12	13	14	15	16	17	18
Rajputana—*concld.* §																	
Marwar	***Total***	*7*	1,996	151	*12*	...	*44*	...	*1*	...	*798*	...	*1,124*	*138*	*17*	*13*	
	Quarries of hard rocks	1	400	151	3	...	3	...	...	...	11	...	368	138	15	13	
	Metal Industries	1	37	...	1	...	1	...	...	...	11	...	23	...	1	...	
	Construction of means of transport	2	1,400	...	6	...	26	...	1	...	702	...	665	...	...	...	
	Production and transmission of physical forces.	*2	56	...	2	...	6	...	...	...	13	...	34	...	1	...	*One of these falls also under "Industries connected with chemical products. (See Factories)."
	Industries of Luxury	1	103	...	...	...	8	...	...	...	61	...	34	...	...	...	
Mewar	***Total***	*3*	505	114	...	...	*29*	...	*23*	...	*221*	...	*206*	*108*	*26*	*6*	
	Textile Industries	2	211	84	...	...	15	...	23	...	11	...	146	78	16	6	
	Metal Industries	1	294	30	...	...	14	...	...	...	210	...	60	30	10	...	
Shahpura	Textile Industries	*1*	66	14	...	...	*5*	...	...	...	*16*	...	*45*	*14*	...	...	
Sirohi	***Total***	*3*	144	7	*1*	...	*12*	...	...	...	*46*	...	*78*	*6*	*7*	*1*	
	Food Industries	2	78	7	...	...	11	...	...	...	8	...	52	6	7	1	
	Construction of means of transport	1	66	...	1	...	1	...	...	...	38	...	26	...	...	...	
Tonk	Textile Industries	*1*	42	52	...	...	*5*	...	...	...	*15*	...	*22*	*47*	...	*5*	
Ajmer-Merwara	**Total**	20	*11,115*	*1,048*	72	...	341	...	302	...	7,037	84	3,128	894	235	70	
Ajmer	***Total***	*13*	8,911	124	*68*	...	*270*	...	*300*	...	*5,914*	*4*	*2,237*	*116*	*122*	*4*	
	Textile Industries	†4	199	120	1	...	9	...	1	...	39	...	135	116	14	4	†Includes one falling also under "Food Industries."
	Food Industries	1	21	...	...	...	1	...	...	...	1	...	19	...	...	...	
	Construction of means of transport	3	8,373	4	65	...	237	...	290	...	5,659	4	2,027	...	86	...	
	Production and transmission of physical forces.	‡1	44	...	...	...	2	...	...	...	19	...	17	...	6	...	‡Falls also under the following heads:— (1) Metal Industries. (2) Industries connected with chemical products. (3) Food Industries.
	Industries of Luxury	4	274	...	2	...	21	...	...	...	106	...	39	...	16	...	
Merwara	***Total***	*7*	2,204	924	*4*	...	*71*	...	*2*	...	*1,123*	*80*	*891*	*778*	*113*	*66*	
	Mines	2	103	11	...	...	5	...	...	...	46	8	44	3	8	...	
	Textile Industries	5	2,101	913	4	...	66	...	2	...	1,077	72	847	775	105	66	

§ Dholpur, Dungarpur, Jaisalmer, Kushalgarh, Lawa, Partabgarh, are omitted as they contain no industries.

TABLE XV-E.—Statistics of Industries (Cotton Factories, Mills, and Presses only). Part III.—Caste or Race of Directors and Owners of Factories, etc.

Description of factories, etc.	Province.	Number of factories, etc.	Number owned by Companies of which the Directors are			Number privately owned by					
			Europeans and Anglo-Indians.	Indians.	Of both races.	European and Anglo-Indians.	Indians.				
							Total.	Bhargava.	Mahajan.	Musalman.	Rajput.
1	2	3	4	5	6	7	8	9	10	11	12
TEXTILE INDUSTRIES.											
Cotton	Rajputana . . .	19	...	4	...	...	15	...	6	2	7
	Ajmer-Merwara . . .	9	2	4	...	...	3*	1	2	2	...

* Figures in columns 9, 10, 11 do not agree with total in column 8 as one of the factories is owned by persons of different castes.

TABLE XV-E.—Statistics of Industries (Cotton Factories, Mills, and Presses only). Part IV.—Caste or Race of Managers of Factories, etc.

Description of factories, etc.	Province.	Number of factories, etc.	Number managed by							
			Europeans and Anglo-Indians.	Indians.						
				Total.	Brahman.	Hindu unspecified.	Kayastha.	Mahajan.	Musalman.	Rajput.
1	2	3	4	5	6	7	8	9	10	11
TEXTILE INDUSTRIES.										
Cotton	Rajputana	19	...	19	3	...	1	11	1	3
	Ajmer-Merwara . . .	9	1	8	...	1	...	5	2	...

TABLE XV-F.

Principal Castes supported mainly by Agriculture.

Explanatory Note.

This Table has been compiled especially for these provinces. Its purpose is to show which of the most important castes depend mainly upon agriculture, in some form or other, for their means of support, whether principal or subsidiary. Column 16 shows the percentage of the caste (including dependants) supported in *some* way by agriculture. Column 17 shows the percentage of the caste (excluding dependants) supported *principally* by agriculture.

The Table shows separate figures for four localities (*viz.*, the three natural divisions of Rajputana, and Ajmer-Merwara) and for rural and urban areas within each locality. The 'Total' figures include both Provinces. Separate figures for localities and for areas, however, have not been given where they contain less than 1,000 and 500, respectively, of the caste; but the figures for such are included in the 'Total' figures for the caste.

The Table does not include figures for Alwar, Bundi, Tonk (Eastern Division) and Kushalgarh (Southern Division), as it was not compiled by these States.

The castes shown in the Table are:—

(*a*) all those selected for Table IX, the percentage in which, in column 16, is 50 or over in rural areas in any of the four localities;

(*b*) all those in Table XIII the percentage in which, in column 16, is 80 or over in rural areas in any of the four localities;

(*c*) a few others of special interest.

The figures for Caste Totals in columns 4, 5, 6 correspond to the Totals in Table XIII, *minus* the omitted States noted above.

In column 1 is shown what is generally considered to be the traditional or original occupation of each caste, thus helping to show how far non-agricultural castes have supplemented or replaced their traditional occupations with agriculture, and how far the original cultivating castes still depend upon agriculture for their main support.

TABLE XV-F.—PRINCIPAL CASTES SUPPORTED MAINLY BY AGRICULTURE.

Caste and traditional occupation.	Locality.	Area (Rural or Urban).	Total population of caste in area in column 3.			Number in caste supported by Agriculture.									Percentage of column 13 to column 4.	Percentage of columns 7 and 8 to column 4.
						Principal occupation.		Subsidiary occupation.		Dependants.		Total.				
			P.	M.	F.	M.	F.	M.	F.	M.	F.	P.	M.	F		
1	2	3	4	5	6	7	8	9	10	11	12	13	14	15	16	17
Ahir Graziers and dairymen.	**Total**	R.	88,085	48,327	40,758	31,422	22,608	142	19	18,913	16,100	84,204	45,477	38,727	94	60
		U.	5,006	2,836	2,186	685	353	57	6	265	390	1,756	1,007	749	35	20
	Rajputana Eastern Division.	R.	*77,843*	*42,435*	*35,408*	27,964	20,823	128	12	12,102	12,969	74,018	40,194	33,824	95	62
		U.	*3,505*	*1,921*	*1,584*	579	309	23	3	232	301	1,447	834	613	41	25
	Southern Division.	R.	*8,543*	*4,401*	*4,142*	2,586	1,179	5	2	1,406	2,627	7,805	3,997	3,808	91	44
	Western Division.	R.	*1,832*	*1,045*	*837*	612	381	7	5	288	370	1,663	907	755	88	52
	Ajmer-Merwara.	R.	*817*	*446*	*371*	260	225	2	..	117	114	718	379	339	87	59
		U.	*943*	*557*	*386*	31	21	12	1	3	16	84	46	38	8	5
Bagri Huntsmen, fowlers, etc.	**Total**	R.	8,580	4,377	4,203	2,135	1,495	60	18	1,017	1,227	5,962	3,212	2,740	69	42
	Rajputana Eastern Division.	R.	*3,749*	*1,793*	*1,956*	1,096	687	27	16	418	550	2,794	1,541	1,253	74	47
	Southern Division.	R.	*1,585*	*824*	*761*	127	85	12	1	71	66	362	210	152	22	13
	Western Division.	R.	*2,712*	*1,474*	*1,238*	782	630	5	..	463	519	2,390	1,250	1,149	88	52
Bairagi Devotees.	**Total**	R.	46,694	24,924	21,700	8,142	6,971	2,161	162	3,333	5,239	26,508	14,136	12,372	56	32
		U.	4,811	2,821	1,990	272	167	36	3	99	190	757	407	350	15	9
	Rajputana. Eastern Division.	R.	*15,633*	*8,509*	*7,129*	2,705	2,317	824	64	1,158	1,719	8,787	4,687	4,100	56	32
		U.	*1,469*	*945*	*524*	78	43	12	1	26	48	208	116	92	14	8
	Southern Division.	R.	*19,856*	*10,404*	*9,452*	2,036	2,105	1,079	65	1,414	1,866	8,565	4,529	4,036	43	20
		U.	*1,037*	*578*	*459*	39	45	14	..	26	36	100	79	81	15	8
	Western Division	R.	*10,643*	*5,787*	*4,856*	3,319	2,445	248	28	1,229	1,590	8,859	4,796	4,063	83	54
		U.	*2,305*	*1,298*	*1,007*	155	79	10	2	47	96	389	212	177	16	10
Balai Village watchmen and menials.	**Total**	R.	189,219	96,928	92,291	32,133	34,099	6,963	1,526	15,229	22,163	112,113	54,325	57,788	59	35
		U.	11,585	6,047	5,538	440	388	144	67	168	196	1,401	752	649	12	7
	Rajputana. Eastern Division.	R.	*88,703*	*45,453*	*43,250*	16,190	16,512	2,026	476	6,407	7,241	48,852	24,623	24,229	53	36
		U.	*5,670*	*2,939*	*2,731*	254	232	102	46	84	115	833	440	393	14	8
	Southern Division.	R.	*59,991*	*30,949*	*29,042*	7,807	8,390	3,631	740	5,024	10,538	35,930	16,262	19,668	59	26
		U.	*2,372*	*1,242*	*1,130*	59	77	23	6	29	43	237	111	126	10	5
	Western Division.	R.	*19,292*	*9,608*	*9,684*	4,055	4,542	399	74	1,980	2,323	13,573	6,634	6,939	70	44
		U.	*1,003*	*550*	*453*	65	48	6	..	31	14	164	102	62	16	11
	Ajmer-Merwara.	R.	*21,233*	*10,918*	*10,315*	4,281	4,655	707	236	1,818	2,061	13,758	6,806	6,952	64	42
		U.	*2,540*	*1,316*	*1,224*	62	28	13	15	24	27	167	99	68	6	5
Bambhi Leather workers.	**Total**	R.	131,116	68,514	62,602	21,197	28,267	10,717	1,823	10,178	11,369	83,552	42,093	41,459	63	37
		U.	4,835	2,518	2,317	215	312	192	41	85	100	946	492	454	19	10
	Rajputana. Southern Division.	R.	*2,318*	*1,203*	*1,115*	112	313	51	33	44	71	624	207	417	26	18
	Western Division.	R.	*126,179*	*65,975*	*60,204*	20,742	27,516	10,617	1,786	9,952	11,312	81,725	41,311	40,414	64	38
		U.	*4,708*	*2,472*	*2,236*	201	296	191	41	81	95	905	473	432	19	10
	Ajmer-Merwara.	R.	*2,449*	*1,262*	*1,187*	327	402	40	2	172	171	1,114	539	575	45	29
Banjara Carriers.	**Total**	R.	19,491	10,464	9,027	3,092	2,382	400	23	1,461	1,687	9,025	4,933	4,092	46	22
		U.	874	429	445	19	2	4	..	7	10	42	30	12	4	2
	Rajputana. Eastern Division.	R.	*9,977*	*5,599*	*4,373*	1,524	1,167	202	20	721	719	4,353	2,447	1,906	43	27
	Southern Division.	R.	*9,018*	*4,602*	*4,416*	1,562	1,207	196	3	719	963	4,652	2,477	2,175	51	30
Bauri Hunters and fowlers.	**Total**	R.	29,692	15,557	14,135	7,344	7,145	1,160	12	4,177	4,537	24,365	12,681	11,684	82	46
		U.	1,401	769	632	398	316	60	2	173	184	1,043	541	502	74	44
	Rajputana. Eastern Division.	R.	*2,151*	*1,158*	*993*	156	149	28	1	89	98	521	273	248	24	14
	Western Division.	R.	*26,327*	*14,037*	*12,790*	7,018	6,858	1,124	11	3,966	4,268	23,245	12,108	11,137	86	51
		U.	*1,306*	*705*	*601*	295	305	53	..	164	173	990	512	478	75	45
Bhil Forest and hill tribe.	**Total**	R.	420,729	214,498	206,231	114,688	96,146	4,513	2,107	76,671	86,604	380,129	195,872	184,257	90	56
		U.	9,010	5,262	3,748	819	434	716	38	430	457	2,894	1,965	929	32	13
	Rajputana. Eastern Division.	R.	*24,951*	*12,719*	*12,232*	6,174	5,978	397	75	3,578	3,924	20,126	10,149	9,977	80	48
	Southern Division.	R.	*337,213*	*170,532*	*166,681*	91,895	77,017	2,890	1,604	63,815	72,470	309,691	158,600	151,091	91	50
		U.	*6,622*	*3,941*	*2,681*	477	260	644	8	249	272	1,910	1,370	540	28	11
	Western Division.	R.	*52,129*	*28,016*	*24,113*	15,088	11,594	1,093	318	8,467	8,803	45,363	24,648	20,715	87	51
		U.	*1,848*	*1,001*	*847*	288	153	31	9	173	167	821	492	329	44	23
	Ajmer-Merwara.	R.	*6,436*	*3,231*	*3,205*	1,531	1,557	133	110	811	807	4,949	2,475	2,474	76	48
Bhoi Fishermen and palki bearers.	**Total**	R.	5,257	2,654	2,603	1,255	972	62	19	766	1,014	4,088	2,083	2,005	77	42
		U.	3,219	1,550	1,669	383	177	31	12	224	347	1,184	648	536	36	17
	Rajputana. Eastern Division.	R.	*760*	*371*	*389*	118	100	10	1	46	78	353	174	179	46	28
		U.	*678*	*344*	*334*	49	10	9	1	26	36	131	84	47	19	8
	Southern Division.	R.	*4,259*	*2,171*	*2,118*	1,115	850	41	17	694	918	3,635	1,850	1,785	84	45
		U.	*2,455*	*1,153*	*1,302*	344	167	22	11	190	311	1,045	556	489	42	20

TABLE XV-F.—Principal Castes supported mainly by Agriculture.

Caste and traditional occupation.	Locality.	Area (Rural or Urban.)	Total population of caste in area in column 3. P.	M.	F.	Number in caste supported by Agriculture. Principal occupation. M.	F.	Subsidiary occupation. M.	F.	Dependants. M.	F.	Total. P.	M.	F.	Percentage of column 13 to column 4.	Percentage of columns 7 and 8 to column 4.
1	2	3	4	5	6	7	8	9	10	11	12	13	14	15	16	17
Bishnoi	**Total**	R.	50,695	27,297	23,398	17,753	13,483	41	4	9,927	9,558	49,866	26,821	23,045	98	61
Cultivators.		U.	2,187	1,197	990	725	518	6	..	289	296	1,834	1,020	814	83	56
	Rajputana. Southern Division.	R.	*588*	*320*	*268*	156	156	..	..	79	88	459	235	224	78	53
		U.	*537*	*259*	*278*	84	47	5	..	44	65	245	133	112	45	24
	Western Division.	R.	*50,101*	*26,973*	*23,128*	17,597	13,327	41	4	8,948	9,400	49,407	26,586	22,821	98	61
		U.	*1,650*	*938*	*712*	641	471	1	..	245	231	1,589	887	702	96	67
Brahman	**Total**	R.	682,669	349,687	332,982	180,277	115,043	14,897	5,247	74,497	126,006	516,477	269,581	246,896	75	42
Priests.		U.	167,588	83,670	83,918	10,114	4,187	1,916	150	4,795	10,245	31,467	16,885	14,582	18	8
	Rajputana Eastern Division.	R.	*390,408*	*201,173*	*189,235*	101,569	61,203	5,917	447	37,384	63,663	270,163	144,850	125,313	69	41
		U.	*89,470*	*45,152*	*44,318*	8,294	2,358	1,225	73	2,899	6,218	19,067	10,418	8,649	21	9
	Southern Division.	R.	*125,423*	*63,517*	*61,906*	33,471	21,628	6,088	4,432	16,906	30,434	112,979	56,465	56,514	90	43
		U.	*15,227*	*7,724*	*7,503*	1,126	582	227	13	570	1,149	3,667	1,923	1,744	24	11
	Western Division.	R.	*153,319*	*78,027*	*75,292*	42,387	30,509	2,566	348	18,900	29,919	124,629	63,853	60,776	81	47
		U.	*52,368*	*24,877*	*27,491*	2,555	1,177	386	62	1,253	2,738	8,171	4,194	3,977	15	7
	Ajmer-Merwara.	R.	*13,519*	*6,970*	*6,549*	2,850	2,303	326	20	1,237	1,970	8,706	4,413	4,293	64	38
		U.	*10,523*	*5,917*	*4,606*	139	70	78	2	73	140	502	290	212	4	2
Chakar	**Total**	R.	47,680	23,439	24,241	10,557	6,381	393	118	5,140	8,300	30,813	16,090	14,723	64	35
Domestic servants		U.	8,587	3,776	4,811	240	152	68	5	122	244	831	430	401	9	4
	Rajputana Eastern Division.	R.	*14,704*	*7,468*	*7,236*	4,370	1,907	56	19	1,709	3,385	11,536	6,135	5,401	78	43
		U.	*2,011*	*779*	*1,232*	57	62	18	3	24	60	224	99	125	11	5
	Southern Division.	R.	*26,090*	*12,444*	*13,646*	4,619	3,475	247	81	2,650	3,887	14,965	7,522	7,443	57	31
		U.	*3,472*	*1,522*	*1,950*	88	58	11	2	44	91	294	143	151	8	4
	Western Division.	R.	*6,721*	*3,448*	*3,273*	1,529	796	90	13	758	1,012	4,198	2,377	1,821	62	34
		U.	*2,999*	*1,425*	*1,574*	92	32	39	..	54	93	310	185	125	10	4
Chamar	**Total**	R.	575,029	297,527	277,502	149,397	142,930	16,481	2,752	63,961	73,305	448,756	229,769	218,987	78	50
Leather workers.		U.	32,393	16,474	15,919	2,743	2,758	1,014	190	1,118	1,569	9,339	4,875	4,457	29	17
	Rajputana Eastern Division.	R.	*447,598*	*230,841*	*216,757*	120,278	114,481	10,289	2,186	49,493	55,584	352,311	180,060	172,251	77	52
		U.	*20,585*	*10,511*	*10,074*	2,085	1,955	726	166	860	1,114	6,015	3,680	3,235	33	19
	Southern Division.	R.	*50,088*	*25,407*	*24,681*	6,107	9,181	4,011	189	4,011	5,950	29,429	14,129	15,300	58	30
		U.	*2,084*	*1,038*	*1,046*	88	135	81	1	40	82	427	209	218	20	10
	Western Division.	R.	*68,701*	*36,777*	*31,924*	20,541	16,760	1,892	388	9,421	10,628	59,630	31,854	27,776	86	54
		U.	*5,015*	*2,605*	*2,410*	503	626	179	20	194	280	1,802	876	926	35	22
	Ajmer-Merwara.	R.	*8,642*	*4,502*	*4,140*	2,381	2,508	289	9	1,056	1,143	7,386	3,726	3,660	85	56
		U.	*4,709*	*2,320*	*2,389*	67	42	28	3	15	33	188	110	78	4	2
Charan	**Total**	R.	34,162	17,690	16,472	9,960	2,058	197	38	4,461	11,317	27,871	14,458	13,413	81	34
Poets and bards.		U.	1,015	628	387	151	55	16	..	105	97	426	274	152	42	29
	Rajputana Eastern Division.	R.	*10,070*	*5,048*	*5,022*	1,856	378	36	11	803	2,400	5,483	2,694	2,789	54	22
	Southern Division.	R.	*3,872*	*1,927*	*1,945*	970	369	25	2	613	1,294	3,279	1,614	1,665	84	34
	Western Division.	R.	*19,943*	*10,566*	*9,377*	6,963	1,302	134	24	2,935	7,320	18,687	10,032	8,655	94	41
		U.	*518*	*344*	*172*	101	50	12	..	91	58	312	204	108	60	29
Dangi	**Total**	R.	32,036	16,325	15,711	10,554	6,950	3	..	5,737	8,633	31,877	16,294	15,583	99	54
Cultivators.	*Rajputana.* Eastern Division.	R.	*825*	*444*	*381*	305	223	1	..	133	150	812	439	373	98	64
	Southern Division.	R.	*31,210*	*15,880*	*15,330*	10,249	6,727	2	..	5,604	8,483	31,065	15,855	15,210	99	54
Daroga	**Total**	R.	103,537	50,801	52,736	21,450	16,277	722	196	9,077	11,934	59,656	31,249	28,407	57	36
Domestic servants		U.	16,062	7,408	8,654	646	433	185	13	256	447	1,979	1,086	893	12	6
	Rajputana Eastern Division.	R.	*35,748*	*16,945*	*18,803*	6,417	4,841	305	53	2,601	3,895	18,202	9,413	8,789	50	31
		U.	*6,564*	*2,701*	*3,863*	202	142	114	6	82	154	700	398	302	10	5
	Southern Division.	R.	*7,469*	*3,607*	*3,862*	1,372	1,039	46	18	804	1,070	4,349	2,222	2,127	58	32
	Western Division.	R.	*53,286*	*26,803*	*26,483*	12,188	8,965	314	100	5,017	6,199	32,783	17,519	15,264	61	39
		U.	*7,084*	*3,344*	*3,740*	401	253	31	4	161	272	1,122	593	529	15	9
	Ajmer-Merwara.	R.	*7,034*	*3,446*	*3,588*	1,473	1,432	57	25	565	770	4,322	2,095	2,227	61	41
		U.	*1,918*	*1,104*	*814*	10	7	38	3	..	8	72	54	18	3	1
Deswali	**Total**	R.	6,619	3,611	3,008	1,968	1,374	34	..	1,035	1,124	5,535	3,037	2,498	83	50
Cultivators.		U.	1,527	767	760	266	196	18	1	106	172	759	388	371	49	30
	Rajputana Eastern Division.	R.	*939*	*529*	*410*	268	215	16	..	101	121	721	385	336	76	51
		U.	*1,268*	*635*	*633*	228	197	11	1	99	130	666	338	328	52	33
	Western Division.	R.	*2,951*	*1,535*	*1,416*	819	627	8	..	454	540	2,448	1,281	1,167	83	49
	Ajmer-Merwara.	R.	*2,328*	*1,351*	*977*	778	423	7	..	422	400	2,029	1,207	822	87	51
Dhakar	**Total**	R.	77,796	39,640	38,065	25,274	20,345	37	4	12,338	16,140	74,138	37,649	36,489	95	58
Cultivators.		U.	1,619	854	765	482	230	7	1	166	336	1,224	655	569	75	44
	Rajputana Eastern Division.	R.	*53,147*	*27,114*	*26,033*	17,556	14,962	34	3	8,048	10,010	50,612	25,637	24,975	96	61
		U.	*1,623*	*891*	*722*	481	230	6	1	161	338	1,217	648	569	79	46
	Southern Division.	R.	*24,018*	*12,250*	*11,768*	7,526	5,219	3	1	4,274	6,033	22,996	11,743	11,253	95	53

TABLE XV-F.—Principal Castes supported mainly by Agriculture.

Caste and traditional occupation.	Locality.	Area (Rural or Urban).	Total population of caste in area in column 3.			Number in caste supported by agriculture.									Percentage of column 13 to column 4.	Percentage of columns 7 and 8 to column 4.
						Principal occupation.		Subsidiary occupation.		Dependants.		Total.				
			P.	M.	F.	M.	F.	M.	F.	M.	F.	P.	M.	F.		
1	2	3	4	5	6	7	8	9	10	11	12	13	14	15	16	17
Dhanak	**Total**	R.	**18,650**	**9,492**	**9,158**	**3,523**	**3,537**	**312**	**190**	**1,526**	**1,692**	**10,642**	**5,363**	**5,279**	**57**	**37**
Labourers.		U.	**2,916**	**1,495**	**1,421**	**31**	**40**	**15**	**9**	**19**	**25**	**139**	**65**	**74**	**4**	**2**
	Rajputana Eastern Division.	R.	*13,043*	*6,568*	*6,475*	1,874	2,056	196	94	758	826	5,804	2,828	2,976	44	30
		U.	*1,579*	*764*	*815*	15	33	11	8	11	14	92	37	55	5	3
	Western Division.	R.	*5,205*	*2,721*	*2,484*	1,605	1,435	113	26	749	770	4,608	2,467	2,231	90	58
	Ajmer-Merwara.	U.	*1,092*	*600*	*492*	1	..	1	..	..	..	2	2	..	..	..
Gadaria	**Total**	R.	**59,976**	**30,994**	**28,982**	**15,699**	**10,124**	**1,541**	**147**	**9,466**	**14,263**	**51,240**	**26,706**	**24,534**	**85**	**43**
Graziers.		U.	**1,887**	**1,030**	**857**	**242**	**106**	**36**	..	**137**	**203**	**726**	**415**	**311**	**38**	**18**
	Rajputana Eastern Division.	R.	*14,517*	*7,623*	*6,894*	3,393	2,532	405	67	1,815	2,465	10,767	5,703	5,064	74	40
		U.	*1,336*	*713*	*623*	130	57	29	..	83	124	423	242	181	31	14
	Southern Division.	R.	*45,419*	*23,346*	*22,073*	12,306	7,592	1,046	80	7,651	11,798	40,473	21,003	19,470	89	43
		U.	*500*	*292*	*217*	111	51	7	..	54	77	300	172	128	58	31
Ghanchi	**Total**	R.	**14,224**	**7,620**	**6,604**	**3,883**	**3,396**	**686**	**89**	**1,836**	**1,967**	**11,851**	**6,399**	**5,452**	**83**	**51**
Basket makers and oil pressers		U.	**5,131**	**2,593**	**2,538**	**601**	**701**	**106**	**5**	**400**	**460**	**2,467**	**1,301**	**1,166**	**48**	**29**
	Rajputana Southern Division.	R.	*4,950*	*2,702*	*2,248*	1,323	1,054	94	20	714	776	3,981	2,131	1,850	80	48
		U.	*1,174*	*600*	*574*	118	73	55	4	85	108	443	258	185	37	16
	Western Division.	R.	*9,273*	*4,917*	*4,356*	2,559	2,342	592	60	1,116	1,101	7,860	4,267	3,602	84	53
		U.	*3,954*	*1,992*	*1,962*	683	628	45	1	315	352	2,024	1,043	981	51	33
Grassia	**Total.**	R.	**17,295**	**8,841**	**8,454**	**5,122**	**4,550**	**13**	**10**	**3,198**	**3,078**	**15,971**	**8,333**	**7,638**	**92**	**55**
Cultivators.	*Rajputana* Southern Division.	R.	*14,347*	*7,373*	*6,974*	4,235	3,761	12	10	2,633	2,404	13,055	6,880	6,175	91	55
	Western Division.	R.	*2,948*	*1,468*	*1,480*	887	789	1	..	565	674	2,916	1,453	1,463	98	56
Gujars	**Total**	R.	**431,894**	**234,043**	**197,851**	**142,759**	**105,148**	**1,900**	**235**	**62,611**	**74,091**	**386,144**	**206,670**	**179,474**	**89**	**57**
Graziers and dairy men.		U.	**17,185**	**9,666**	**7,519**	**2,231**	**1,333**	**309**	**28**	**617**	**1,316**	**6,034**	**3,357**	**2,677**	**35**	**20**
	Rajputana Eastern Division.	R.	*308,455*	*168,366*	*140,089*	105,352	78,702	1,128	195	42,131	47,559	275,157	148,611	126,546	89	59
		U.	*11,590*	*6,497*	*5,093*	1,610	989	130	12	572	834	4,147	2,312	1,835	35	22
	Southern Division.	R.	*68,912*	*36,705*	*32,207*	21,385	11,878	266	14	12,285	18,567	64,395	33,036	30,459	93	48
		U.	*1,726*	*928*	*798*	168	100	10	1	86	173	544	270	274	31	15
	Western Division.	R.	*21,568*	*11,616*	*9,952*	5,455	5,022	358	16	2,362	2,732	15,945	8,175	7,770	73	48
		U.	*1,769*	*988*	*781*	241	151	47	8	91	161	690	379	320	39	22
	Ajmer-Merwara.	R.	*32,959*	*17,356*	*15,603*	10,567	9,456	148	10	5,233	5,233	30,847	15,948	14,609	93	60
		U.	*2,100*	*1,253*	*847*	212	93	116	7	68	148	644	398	248	30	14
Jat	**Total**	R.	**890,993**	**480,095**	**410,898**	**316,629**	**243,590**	**872**	**114**	**134,561**	**157,706**	**853,472**	**452,062**	**401,410**	**95**	**62**
Cultivators.		U.	**21,456**	**13,153**	**8,303**	**5,043**	**2,898**	**997**	**4**	**1 639**	**2,149**	**12,730**	**7,679**	**5,061**	**59**	**37**
	Rajputana Eastern Division.	R.	*383,951*	*208,194*	*175,757*	141,045	105,750	501	60	58,450	65,407	372,253	200,956	171,307	97	64
		U.	*10,409*	*6,281*	*4,128*	2,542	1,371	161	3	752	1,178	6,007	3,435	2,552	57	37
	Southern Division.	R.	*70,122*	*36,226*	*33,896*	13,900	12,142	29	2	7,205	20,419	53,787	21,224	32,563	76	37
	Western Division.	R.	*408,749*	*220,876*	*187,873*	150,668	116,786	251	49	64,888	67,577	400,219	215,807	184,412	97	65
		U.	*8,283*	*4,900*	*3,383*	2,191	1,293	88	1	789	849	5,181	3,038	2,143	62	42
	Ajmer-Merwara.	R.	*28,171*	*14,799*	*13,372*	10,026	8,912	31	3	4,018	4,213	27,263	14,075	13,128	96	67
		U.	*2,326*	*1,727*	*599*	233	187	740	..	103	84	1,347	1,076	271	57	18
Jogi	**Total**	R.	**55,101**	**29,103**	**25,998**	**7,967**	**7,334**	**2,124**	**272**	**3,735**	**5,338**	**26,770**	**13,826**	**12,944**	**48**	**27**
Priests and devotees.		U.	**3,767**	**2,011**	**1,756**	**115**	**129**	**33**	**7**	**49**	**97**	**430**	**197**	**233**	**11**	**6**
	Rajputana Eastern Division	R.	*33,774*	*17,904*	*15,870*	4,039	4,259	1,384	155	1,719	2,501	14,057	7,142	6,915	41	24
		U.	*1,331*	*676*	*655*	57	61	18	7	21	40	204	96	108	15	8
	Southern Division.	R.	*11,027*	*5,619*	*5,408*	1,473	1,160	407	81	942	1,318	3,671	2,012	2,759	51	23
			8,204	*4,465*	*3,739*	1,056	1,472	161	28	849	1,052	5,318	2,966	2,352	67	41
	Western Division.	R.	*1,744*	*925*	*819*	32	47	6	..	19	51	155	57	98	8	4
		U.	*2,096*	*1,115*	*981*	490	443	82	8	223	207	1,524	806	718	72	44
	Ajmer-Merwara	R.														
Kachhi	**Total**	R.	**44,901**	**23,888**	**21,013**	**16,095**	**12,221**	**163**	**116**	**6,602**	**7,493**	**42,690**	**22,860**	**19,830**	**95**	**63**
Cultivators.		U.	**5,795**	**3,012**	**2,783**	**1,596**	**1,158**	**123**	**22**	**575**	**845**	**4,321**	**2,296**	**2,025**	**74**	**47**
	Rajputana Eastern Division.	R.	*44,743*	*23,798*	*20,945*	16,061	12,218	163	116	6,372	7,446	42,566	22,786	19,780	95	63
		U.	*5,718*	*2,971*	*2,747*	1,595	1,158	122	22	573	843	4,313	2,290	2,023	75	48
Kahar	**Total.**	R.	**11,188**	**5,736**	**5,452**	**2,809**	**2,229**	**329**	**48**	**1,419**	**1,636**	**8,470**	**4,557**	**3,913**	**75**	**45**
Palki bearers.		U.	**4,238**	**2,355**	**1,883**	**333**	**259**	**117**	**23**	**113**	**173**	**1,017**	**563**	**454**	**24**	**14**
	Rajputana. Eastern Division.	R.	*8,473*	*4,359*	*4,114*	2,012	1,476	302	47	989	1,117	5,943	3,303	2,640	70	41
		U.	*2,930*	*1,669*	*1,261*	264	208	96	19	100	135	822	460	362	28	16
	Ajmer-Merwara.	R.	*1,982*	*1,017*	*965*	605	612	1	1	337	327	1,943	1,009	940	98	64
		U.	*1,061*	*563*	*498*	66	51	21	3	13	38	192	100	92	18	11
Kaimkhani	**Total**	R.	**19,815**	**10,243**	**9,572**	**4,906**	**405**	**113**	**12**	**2,791**	**6,796**	**15,023**	**7,810**	**7,213**	**75**	**36**
Agricultural land-holders.		U.	**8,544**	**4,599**	**3,945**	**1,863**	**99**	**266**	**14**	**590**	**1,421**	**3,473**	**1,939**	**1,534**	**40**	**13**
	Rajputana. Eastern Division.	R.	*10,665*	*5,481*	*5,184*	2,520	177	73	9	1,434	3,577	7,790	4,027	3,763	73	25
		U.	*3,812*	*1,975*	*1,837*	234	64	203	13	111	253	878	548	330	23	7
	Western Division.	R.	*8,210*	*4,229*	*3,981*	2,160	167	34	3	1,246	2,976	6,586	3,440	3,146	80	28
		U.	*4,529*	*2,499*	*2,030*	847	35	43	1	477	1,157	2,560	1,367	1,193	5	19

TABLE XV-F.—PRINCIPAL CASTES SUPPORTED MAINLY BY AGRICULTURE.

Caste and traditional occupation.	Locality.	Area (Rural or Urban).	Total population of caste to area in column 3. P.	M.	F.	Number in caste supported by Agriculture. Principal occupation. M.	F.	Subsidiary occupation. M.	F.	Dependants. M.	F.	Total. P.	M.	F.	Percentage of column 13 to column 4.	Percentage of columns 7 and 8 to column 4.
1	2	3	4	5	6	7	8	9	10	11	12	13	14	15	16	17
Khanzada	**Total**	R.	**1,387**	**675**	**662**	**390**	**155**	**7**	**2**	**194**	**414**	**1,162**	**591**	**571**	**86**	**40**
		U.	**125**	**63**	**62**	**17**	..	**1**	..	**2**	**3**	**23**	**20**	**3**	**18**	**13**
Domestic servants.	*Rajputana*. Eastern Division.	R.	*1,325*	*665*	*660*	390	155	7	2	194	414	1,162	591	571	87	41
Kharol	**Total**	R.	**8,621**	**4,419**	**4,202**	**2,031**	**1,959**	**76**	**9**	**1,125**	**1,658**	**7,458**	**3,832**	**3,626**	**86**	**53**
		U.	**392**	**205**	**187**	**89**	**73**	**14**	..	**27**	**46**	**249**	**130**	**119**	**63**	**41**
Salt workers.	*Rajputana*. Eastern Division.	R.	*2,597*	*1,297*	*1,300*	817	601	22	2	340	455	2,237	1,179	1,058	86	54
	Southern Division.	R.	*3,716*	*1,861*	*1,854*	1,007	720	44	5	494	866	3,138	1,545	1,593	84	46
	Ajmer-Merwara.	R.	*1,665*	*878*	*787*	624	494	10	2	227	264	1,621	861	760	97	67
Khati	**Total**	R.	**108,309**	**55,472**	**52,837**	**8,848**	**17,615**	**11,032**	**206**	**4,376**	**6,215**	**48,292**	**24,256**	**24,036**	**44**	**24**
		U.	**11,672**	**5,297**	**5,175**	**189**	**486**	**408**	**6**	**95**	**175**	**1,359**	**692**	**667**	**12**	**6**
Carpenters.	*Rajputana* Eastern Division.	R.	*60,488*	*30,671*	*29,817*	3,508	7,794	4,828	104	1,765	2,478	20,477	10,101	10,376	33	18
		U.	*6,000*	*3,188*	*2,812*	35	170	173	3	20	53	454	228	226	7	3
	Southern Division.	R.	*11,282*	*5,871*	*5,411*	1,064	1,452	1,331	41	698	1,383	5,969	3,003	2,876	52	22
		U.	*461*	*246*	*213*	10	38	33	1	5	9	96	48	48	20	10
	Western Division.	R.	*31,370*	*16,266*	*15,104*	3,680	7,115	4,198	44	1,636	2,000	18,682	9,523	9,159	59	34
		U.	*2,941*	*1,507*	*1,434*	142	271	188	2	67	109	776	397	382	26	14
	Ajmer-Merwara.	R.	*5,169*	*2,664*	*2,505*	567	1,254	675	17	277	354	3,184	1,539	1,625	61	35
		U.	*1,670*	*956*	*714*	2	7	14	..	3	4	30	19	11	1	..
Khatik	**Total**	R.	**36,291**	**18,683**	**17,608**	**3,917**	**4,101**	**976**	**203**	**1,948**	**2,871**	**14,010**	**6,835**	**7,175**	**38**	**22**
		U.	**11,192**	**5,748**	**5,450**	**303**	**431**	**306**	**124**	**149**	**233**	**1,636**	**848**	**788**	**14**	**6**
Butchers.	*Rajputana* Eastern Division.	R.	*21,021*	*10,817*	*10,204*	1,623	2,010	450	96	714	951	5,844	2,787	3,057	27	17
		U.	*5,874*	*3,082*	*2,792*	118	265	282	109	66	81	911	456	455	15	5
	Southern Division.	R.	*9,795*	*5,006*	*4,789*	1,614	1,276	329	68	964	1,549	5,800	2,907	2,893	59	29
		U.	*1,473*	*718*	*755*	82	72	24	9	43	79	309	149	160	21	10
	Western Division.	R.	*3,415*	*1,794*	*1,621*	310	397	148	28	114	183	1,165	572	613	34	20
		U.	*2,353*	*1,215*	*1,138*	84	90	67	6	43	50	340	194	146	14	7
	Ajmer-Merwara.	R.	*2,060*	*1,066*	*994*	370	418	43	11	156	183	1,181	569	612	57	38
		U.	*1,492*	*727*	*765*	19	4	23	..	7	22	76	49	27	5	1
Kir	**Total**	R.	**16,190**	**8,453**	**7,737**	**4,334**	**3,142**	**236**	**60**	**2,291**	**2,360**	**12,923**	**6,861**	**6,062**	**79**	**46**
		U.	**1,037**	**503**	**534**	**255**	**203**	**24**	**11**	**129**	**170**	**792**	**408**	**384**	**76**	**44**
Cultivators.	*Rajputana* Eastern Division.	R.	*8,979*	*4,719*	*4,260*	2,174	1,735	212	56	1,062	1,139	6,378	3,448	2,930	71	43
		U.	*602*	*322*	*280*	128	96	18	8	53	66	369	199	170	61	37
	Southern Division.	R.	*5,701*	*2,947*	*2,754*	1,676	1,027	18	4	993	1,438	5,156	2,687	2,469	90	47
Kirar	**Total**	R.	**11,380**	**5,900**	**5,480**	**3,504**	**2,968**	**11**	**1**	**1,981**	**2,299**	**10,764**	**5,496**	**5,268**	**94**	**56**
Cultivators.	*Rajputana* Eastern Division.	R.	*11,344*	*5,891*	*5,453*	3,504	2,968	11	1	1,981	2,299	10,764	5,496	5,268	94	57
Koli	**Total**	R.	**67,901**	**34,894**	**33,007**	**4,116**	**4,096**	**2,373**	**871**	**2,018**	**2,330**	**16,398**	**8,561**	**7,897**	**24**	**13**
		U.	**21,848**	**11,530**	**10,318**	**179**	**253**	**516**	**261**	**62**	**120**	**1,385**	**751**	**634**	**6**	**2**
Weavers, and cultivators.	*Rajputana* Eastern Division.	R.	*61,554*	*31,580*	*29,974*	2,516	3,293	2,367	870	933	1,258	11,237	5,816	5,421	18	9
		U.	*14,683*	*7,777*	*6,906*	172	240	482	252	59	115	1,320	713	607	9	2
	Southern Division.	R.	*5,045*	*2,630*	*2,415*	1,392	1,211	4	1	944	989	4,491	2,340	2,151	89	51
		U.	*1,021*	*493*	*528*	7	12	27	9	3	5	63	37	26	6	1
	Ajmer-Merwara	U.	*6,146*	*3,269*	*2,876*	..	2	1	..	..	..	2	1	1	..	..
Kumhar	**Total**	R.	**260,920**	**135,357**	**125,563**	**42,931**	**39,569**	**12,772**	**2,818**	**20,108**	**25,194**	**143,332**	**75,811**	**67,521**	**54**	**31**
		U.	**32,055**	**16,163**	**15,893**	**2,656**	**2,292**	**904**	**204**	**1,254**	**1,545**	**8,855**	**4,814**	**4,041**	**27**	**15**
Potters.	*Rajputana* Eastern Division.	R.	*109,480*	*56,557*	*52,923*	13,718	14,433	5,379	1,065	5,435	6,300	46,530	24,532	21,998	42	25
		U.	*14,510*	*7,199*	*7,311*	540	546	479	110	175	299	2,148	1,193	955	14	7
	Southern Division.	R.	*52,614*	*27,033*	*25,581*	8,602	5,923	2,084	312	5,112	7,919	29,952	15,798	14,154	56	27
		U.	*3,382*	*1,724*	*1,658*	135	141	18	3	63	91	451	216	235	13	8
	Western Division.	R.	*86,584*	*45,494*	*41,090*	18,189	16,616	4,607	1,110	8,575	9,606	58,703	31,371	27,334	67	40
		U.	*12,285*	*6,295*	*5,990*	1,961	1,594	390	84	1,006	1,147	6,182	3,357	2,825	50	28
	Ajmer-Merwara.	R.	*12,242*	*6,273*	*5,969*	2,422	2,537	702	331	986	1,187	8,145	4,110	4,035	66	40
		U.	*1,378*	*945*	*933*	20	11	18	7	10	8	74	48	26	3	1
Kunbi	**Total**	R.	**43,496**	**22,439**	**21,059**	**14,617**	**12,257**	**11**	**2**	**7,353**	**8,160**	**42,400**	**21,981**	**20,419**	**97**	**61**
Cultivators.	*Rajputana* Eastern Division.	R.	*3,011*	*1,581*	*1,430*	982	650	6	..	405	625	2,668	1,393	1,275	88	54
	Southern Division.	R.	*11,504*	*5,979*	*5,525*	3,923	3,000	3	1	1,933	2,196	11,064	5,858	5,206	96	60
	Western Division.	R.	*28,643*	*14,721*	*13,922*	9,628	8,505	2	1	4,972	5,292	28,400	14,602	13,798	99	63
Labhana	**Total**	R.	**4,591**	**2,373**	**2,218**	**1,346**	**1,084**	..	..	**716**	**858**	**4,004**	**2,062**	**1,942**	**87**	**53**
Carriers.	*Rajputana* Western Division.	R.	*4,033*	*2,058*	*1,945*	1,346	1,084	..	..	716	858	4,004	2,062	1,942	99	60

TABLE XV-F.—Principal Castes supported mainly by Agriculture.

Caste and traditional occupation.	Locality.	Area (Rural or Urban).	Total population of caste in area in column 3. P.	M.	F.	Number in caste supported by Agriculture. Principal occupation. M.	F.	Subsidiary occupation. M.	F.	Dependants. M.	F.	Total. P.	M.	F.	Percentage of column 13 to column 4.	Percentage of columns 7 and 8 to column 4.
1	2	3	4	5	6	7	8	9	10	11	12	13	14	15	16	17
Loda . .	**Total** .	R.	**7,713**	**4,105**	**3,608**	**2,512**	**2,042**	**6**	..	**1,528**	**1,528**	**7,616**	**4,046**	**3,570**	**98**	**59**
Cultivators.	*Rajputana* Eastern Division.	R.	*7,600*	*4,056*	*3,544*	2,479	1,997	6	..	1,512	1,511	7,505	3,997	3,508	98	58
Lodha . .	**Total** .	R.	**41,672**	**21,787**	**19,885**	**14,513**	**11,157**	**35**	**5**	**6,437**	**8,283**	**40,430**	**20,985**	**19,445**	**97**	**61**
Cultivators.		U.	**1,900**	**992**	**908**	**379**	**260**	**31**	**7**	**146**	**190**	**1,016**	**550**	**466**	**53**	**34**
	Rajputana Eastern Division.	R.	*40,262*	*21,069*	*19,193*	14,068	10,699	35	5	6,238	8,079	39,124	20,341	18,783	97	61
		U.	*1,394*	*756*	*638*	377	269	31	7	140	188	1,012	548	464	72	46
	Ajmer-Merwara.	R.	*728*	*381*	*347*	257	228	..	..	114	119	718	371	347	98	66
Mali . .	**Total** .	R.	**290,230**	**115,364**	**104,866**	**73,383**	**55,826**	**691**	**639**	**33,406**	**37,250**	**201,195**	**107,480**	**93,715**	**91**	**58**
Cultivators.		U.	**75,701**	**38,504**	**37,197**	**17,266**	**11,075**	**505**	**326**	**7,390**	**8,945**	**45,441**	**25,095**	**20,346**	**60**	**37**
	Rajputana Eastern Division.	R.	*151,246*	*79,261*	*71,985*	51,002	39,663	279	228	22,576	24,459	138,207	73,857	64,350	91	59
		U.	*43,357*	*22,041*	*21,316*	10,508	7,096	282	146	4,403	4,905	27,340	15,193	12,147	63	40
	Southern Division.	R.	*21,175*	*10,918*	*10,257*	6,582	3,745	59	110	3,629	5,127	19,252	10,270	8,982	91	48
		U.	*3,600*	*1,792*	*1,808*	841	505	26	16	438	622	2,448	1,305	1,143	68	37
	Western Division.	R.	*39,497*	*20,880*	*18,617*	12,942	9,811	332	293	6,056	6,473	35,907	19,330	16,577	90	57
		U.	*22,716*	*11,477*	*11,239*	5,094	3,135	121	156	2,172	2,810	13,488	7,387	6,101	59	36
	Ajmer-Merwara.	R.	*8,312*	*4,305*	*4,007*	2,857	2,607	21	8	1,145	1,191	7,829	4,023	3,806	94	65
		U.	*6,028*	*3,194*	*2,834*	757	339	76	8	377	608	2,165	1,210	955	35	18
Meghwal .	**Total** .	R.	**53,486**	**28,008**	**25,478**	**9,647**	**9,627**	**3,773**	**426**	**5,101**	**6,064**	**34,638**	**18,521**	**16,117**	**64**	**35**
Leather workers.		U.	**3,968**	**2,045**	**1,923**	**165**	**256**	**222**	**25**	**90**	**110**	**870**	**477**	**393**	**21**	**10**
	Rajputana Western Division.	R.	*52,959*	*27,766*	*25,193*	9,540	9,404	3,763	425	5,041	5,986	34,229	18,344	15,885	64	35
		U.	*3,761*	*1,957*	*1,804*	164	255	222	25	89	110	865	475	390	23	11
Meo or Mewati Cultivators.	**Total** .	R.	**51,120**	**27,086**	**24,034**	**17,960**	**14,914**	**51**	**9**	**8,269**	**8,467**	**49,670**	**26,280**	**23,390**	**97**	**64**
	Rajputana Eastern Division.	R.	*50,146*	*26,584*	*23,562*	17,806	14,806	46	6	8,166	8,295	49,125	26,018	23,107	98	65
Mer . . .	**Total** .	R.	**33,392**	**17,603**	**15,789**	**10,495**	**8,280**	**107**	**23**	**4,886**	**6,481**	**30,272**	**15,488**	**14,784**	**89**	**56**
Forest and hill tribe.		U.	**1,645**	**964**	**681**	**161**	**42**	**396**	**1**	**50**	**49**	**639**	**547**	**92**	**38**	**8**
	Rajputana Eastern Division.	R.	*6,140*	*3,075*	*3,065*	1,094	1,694	67	6	456	802	4,119	1,617	2,502	67	45
	Southern Division.	R.	*5,698*	*3,109*	*2,589*	1,834	444	5	..	1,073	2,066	5,422	2,912	2,510	95	40
	Ajmer-Merwara	R.	*20,809*	*10,991*	*9,818*	7,300	5,949	32	17	3,220	3,494	20,021	10,561	9,460	95	63
		U.	*994*	*643*	*351*	71	31	395	..	32	45	574	498	76	57	10
Merat . .	**Total** .	R.	**21,093**	**11,679**	**9,414**	**7,211**	**5,290**	**28**	**1**	**4,054**	**3,900**	**20,484**	**11,293**	**9,191**	**97**	**59**
Forest and hill tribe.		U.	**834**	**551**	**283**	**26**	**3**	**288**	**1**	**3**	**10**	**331**	**317**	**14**	**39**	**3**
	Rajputana Western Division.	R.	*1,774*	*984*	*790*	620	386	1	..	318	290	1,615	939	676	91	56
	Ajmer-Merwara.	R.	*18,822*	*10,400*	*8,422*	6,451	4,764	27	1	3,678	3,596	18,517	10,156	8,361	98	59
		U.	*829*	*551*	*278*	26	3	288	1	3	10	331	317	14	39	3
Mina . .	**Total** .	R.	**451,234**	**238,718**	**212,516**	**139,318**	**117,063**	**5,638**	**1,098**	**59,994**	**68,961**	**392,972**	**204,950**	**187,122**	**86**	**56**
Forest and hill tribe.		U.	**14,314**	**8,419**	**5,895**	**2,881**	**2,126**	**581**	**10**	**1,070**	**1,311**	**7,919**	**4,472**	**3,447**	**55**	**34**
	Rajputana Eastern Division.	R.	*354,079*	*187,742*	*166,337*	120,392	102,477	4,307	237	48,363	51,981	327,757	173,062	154,695	92	62
		U.	*10,045*	*5,731*	*4,314*	2,303	1,751	235	9	838	1,056	6,192	3,376	2,816	61	40
	Southern Division.	R.	*75,155*	*39,090*	*36,065*	12,261	9,647	1,209	858	8,419	13,346	45,740	21,889	23,851	60	29
		U.	*2,812*	*1,735*	*1,077*	356	250	13	1	166	163	949	535	414	33	21
	Western Division.	R.	*18,360*	*9,896*	*8,464*	5,395	3,831	117	3	2,579	3,110	15,035	8,091	6,944	81	50
		U.	*874*	*501*	*373*	144	95	24	..	85	90	418	233	185	47	27
	Ajmer-Merwara.	R.	*3,640*	*1,990*	*1,650*	1,270	1,108	5	..	633	524	3,540	1,908	1,632	97	65
		U.	*583*	*452*	*131*	18	30	309	..	1	2	360	328	32	61	8
Moghal . .	**Total** .	R.	**8,716**	**4,657**	**4,059**	**2,179**	**1,226**	**61**	**3**	**1,093**	**1,743**	**6,305**	**3,333**	**2,972**	**72**	**39**
(No traditional occupation).		U.	**4,975**	**2,624**	**2,351**	**158**	**21**	**127**	**2**	**96**	**197**	**595**	**375**	**220**	**12**	**3**
	Rajputana Eastern Division.	R.	*2,537*	*1,316*	*1,221*	317	88	29	2	208	448	1,092	554	538	43	16
		U.	*2,968*	*1,524*	*1,444*	105	16	119	1	52	106	399	276	123	13	4
	Western Division.	R.	*5,022*	*2,747*	*2,275*	1,636	1,038	16	1	792	1,064	4,547	2,444	2,103	90	53
		U.	*1,045*	*537*	*508*	45	3	4	..	32	76	160	81	79	15	4
	Ajmer-Merwara.	R.	*673*	*342*	*331*	195	81	3	..	77	191	547	275	272	81	41
		U.	*742*	*436*	*306*	7	2	2	1	2	11	25	11	14	3	1
Moghia . .	**Total** .	R.	**3,772**	**1,984**	**1,838**	**514**	**473**	**121**	**81**	**354**	**379**	**1,922**	**989**	**933**	**51**	**26**
Hunters and fowlers.	*Rajputana* Eastern Division	R.	*2,416*	*1,228*	*1,188*	195	193	111	75	115	125	814	421	393	33	16
	Southern Division.	R.	*1,356*	*706*	*650*	319	280	10	6	239	254	1,108	568	540	81	44

TABLE XV-F.—Principal Castes supported mainly by Agriculture.

Caste and traditional occupation.	Locality.	Area (Rural or Urban).	Total population of caste in area in column 3.			Number in caste supported by Agriculture.									Percentage of column 13 to column 4.	Percentage of columns 7 and 8 to column 4.
						Principal occupation.		Subsidiary occupation.		Dependants.		Total.				
			P.	M.	F.	M.	F.	M.	F.	M.	F.	P.	M.	F.		
1	2	3	4	5	6	7	8	9	10	11	12	13	14	15	16	17
Nai	**Total**	R.	125,738	66,053	59,685	7,975	11,943	12,123	1,408	3,786	5,047	41,572	23,874	17,698	33	15
Barbers.		U.	21,473	10,808	10,665	293	312	659	74	143	231	1,711	1,094	617	8	2
	Rajputana Eastern Division.	R.	*63,254*	*33,312*	*29,942*	2,631	3,755	4,924	515	1,159	1,590	14,574	8,714	5,860	23	10
		U.	*10,138*	*5,181*	*4,957*	72	67	252	25	34	82	532	358	174	5	1
	Southern Division.	R.	*16,563*	*8,537*	*8,026*	631	636	1,466	282	400	687	4,113	2,508	1,605	24	7
		U.	*1,943*	*961*	*982*	11	16	61	1	22	26	137	94	43	7	1
	Western Division.	R.	*40,946*	*21,708*	*19,238*	4,316	6,197	5,202	546	2,023	2,533	20,817	11,541	9,276	50	25
		U.	*7,906*	*3,907*	*3,999*	202	228	327	48	85	123	1,013	614	399	12	5
	Ajmer-Merwara.	R.	*5,017*	*2,538*	*2,479*	397	655	519	65	195	237	2,068	1,111	957	41	20
		U.	*1,486*	*759*	*727*	7	1	19	..	2	..	29	28	1	2	1
Nayak	**Total**	R.	36,706	19,056	17,650	8,860	7,912	629	86	4,373	5,055	26,915	13,862	12,053	73	45
Village watchmen and menials.		U.	5,188	2,802	2,386	333	240	136	33	140	144	1,028	611	417	19	11
	Rajputana Eastern Division.	R.	*17,301*	*8,882*	*8,419*	3,128	3,243	346	60	1,413	1,627	9,822	4,887	4,935	56	36
		U.	*4,012*	*2,173*	*1,839*	95	117	124	33	55	63	480	274	215	12	5
	Southern Division.	R.	*4,866*	*2,453*	*2,413*	1,199	893	122	10	714	1,002	3,940	2,035	1,905	81	43
	Western Division.	R.	*12,299*	*6,520*	*5,779*	3,910	3,192	144	12	1,935	2,119	11,312	5,989	5,323	92	57
		U.	*800*	*457*	*343*	208	111	10	..	76	70	475	294	181	59	39
	Ajmer-Merwara.	R.	*2,240*	*1,201*	*1,039*	623	579	17	4	311	307	1,841	951	890	82	53
Patel	**Total**	R.	55,333	27,509	27,824	17,914	17,134	34	2	9,001	10,074	54,159	26,949	27,210	97	63
Cultivators.	*Rajputana.* Southern Division.	R.	*35,106*	*17,092*	*18,014*	10,605	10,544	1	2	6,202	7,192	34,546	16,808	17,738	98	60
	Western Division.	R.	*20,215*	*10,409*	*9,806*	7,309	6,590	32	..	2,709	2,882	19,612	10,140	9,472	97	68
Pathan	**Total**	R.	47,679	25,980	21,699	6,045	2,363	637	128	3,153	5,901	19,830	10,438	9,392	41	21
(No traditional occupation.)		U.	49,506	26,057	23,449	1,191	439	454	9	499	1,197	3,789	2,144	1,645	7	3
	Rajputana. Eastern Division.	R.	*28,906*	*15,501*	*13,195*	4,758	2,043	405	35	2,195	3,990	13,426	7,358	6,068	46	23
		U.	*29,370*	*15,170*	*14,200*	804	291	300	6	336	847	2,584	1,440	1,144	8	3
	Southern Division.	R.	*10,034*	*5,462*	*4,572*	604	506	122	82	333	1,015	2,662	1,059	1,603	26	11
		U.	*5,345*	*27,656*	*2,580*	109	104	64	1	60	114	452	233	219	8	4
	Western Division.	R.	*5,946*	*3,357*	*2,589*	1,197	756	105	11	572	845	3,486	1,874	1,612	58	32
		U.	*6,074*	*3,306*	*2,768*	186	23	50	2	72	197	535	308	227	8	3
	Ajmer-Merwara.	R.	*2,703*	*1,360*	*1,343*	89	58	5	..	53	51	256	147	109	9	5
		U.	*8,717*	*4,816*	*3,901*	92	16	40	..	31	39	218	163	55	2	1
Prohit	**Total**	R.	35,521	18,368	17,153	12,591	5,360	80	17	4,800	10,635	33,492	17,480	16,012	94	50
Priests.		U.	1,543	829	714	236	76	6	..	33	194	569	319	270	38	19
	Rajputana. Eastern Division.	R.	*4,149*	*2,173*	*1,976*	1,225	204	40	3	465	1,271	3,208	1,730	1,478	77	34
		U.	*916*	*478*	*438*	80	9	2	..	38	112	241	120	121	26	9
	Western Division.	R.	*31,081*	*16,036*	*15,045*	11,311	5,134	42	13	4,314	9,206	30,110	15,667	14,443	96	53
		U.	*626*	*351*	*275*	150	67	4	..	45	82	349	199	149	55	34
Raigar	**Total**	R.	83,078	42,442	40,636	8,856	10,614	2,565	454	3,498	4,833	30,620	14,919	15,701	36	23
Leather workers		U.	14,036	7,163	6,873	809	749	237	34	270	362	2,281	1,116	1,145	16	9
	Rajputana. Eastern Division.	R.	*51,491*	*26,235*	*25,256*	6,926	8,077	1,157	214	2,639	3,218	22,231	10,722	11,509	43	29
		U.	*7,042*	*3,554*	*3,488*	411	523	138	19	159	199	1,449	708	741	20	13
	Southern Division.	R.	*1,914*	*949*	*965*	315	315	132	8	175	271	1,216	622	594	63	32
	Western Division.	R.	*13,324*	*6,910*	*6,414*	1,430	1,850	1,069	193	602	1,022	6,166	3,101	3,065	46	24
		U.	*3,435*	*1,809*	*1,676*	104	152	80	14	54	75	479	238	241	13	7
	Ajmer-Merwara.	R.	*16,349*	*8,348*	*8,001*	185	372	207	39	82	122	1,007	474	533	6	3
		U.	*3,509*	*1,800*	*1,709*	94	74	19	1	67	88	333	170	163	9	4
Rajput	**Total**	R.	616,339	343,789	274,550	197,320	38,520	4,236	206	98,746	196,788	530,816	295,302	235,514	85	38
Agricultural land holders.		U.	37,419	24,790	12,629	4,582	460	1,543	22	1,566	3,025	11,198	7,691	3,507	29	13
	Rajputana Eastern Division.	R.	*171,454*	*97,299*	*74,155*	56,397	4,098	1,126	23	26,267	59,166	147,677	83,790	63,887	86	35
		U.	*15,038*	*9,694*	*5,344*	1,669	208	273	6	735	1,487	4,378	2,677	1,701	29	12
	Southern Division.	R.	*133,127*	*71,520*	*61,607*	34,050	12,804	273	77	18,382	33,465	99,051	52,705	46,346	74	35
		U.	*5,334*	*3,181*	*2,153*	468	103	79	14	152	379	1,195	699	496	22	10
	Western Division.	R.	*302,842*	*169,028*	*133,814*	103,280	20,533	2,794	104	47,529	100,083	274,323	153,603	120,720	90	40
		U.	*13,661*	*9,632*	*4,029*	2,284	138	829	2	566	1,128	4,917	3,649	1,268	36	17
	Ajmer-Merwara.	R.	*10,916*	*5,942*	*4,974*	3,593	485	43	2	1,568	4,074	9,765	5,204	4,561	89	37
		U.	*3,386*	*2,283*	*1,103*	211	11	362	..	93	31	798	666	42	20	5
Rawat	**Total**	R.	66,904	32,052	28,852	20,386	17,464	109	14	16,658	10,930	59,483	31,075	28,408	97	62
Cultivators.		U.	726	475	251	190	21	35	..	29	48	228	159	69	31	16
	Rajputana Southern Division.	R.	*4,888*	*2,685*	*2,203*	1,559	980	34	2	818	1,079	4,472	2,411	2,061	91	51
	Western Division.	R.	*8,361*	*4,611*	*3,770*	2,907	2,302	5	..	1,446	1,412	8,162	4,448	3,714	97	63
	Ajmer-Merwara.	R.	*47,540*	*24,695*	*22,845*	15,738	14,171	69	12	8,385	6,430	46,800	24,187	22,613	98	62
Rebar	**Total**	R.	126,946	66,319	60,627	11,999	18,220	4,756	485	5,877	7,283	48,795	22,632	26,073	38	23
Graziers.		U.	1,965	1,080	885	60	200	36	..	19	17	332	115	217	16	13
	Rajputana Eastern Division.	R.	*7,222*	*3,609*	*3,613*	463	745	111	15	227	282	1,843	801	1,042	25	16
	Southern Division.	R.	*26,310*	*13,426*	*12,884*	1,862	2,283	408	35	1,265	2,049	7,902	3,535	4,367	30	15
	Western Division.	R.	*91,391*	*48,208*	*43,183*	9,400	14,845	4,223	414	4,235	4,784	37,901	17,858	20,043	41	26
		U.	*1,746*	*936*	*810*	45	197	27	..	17	17	303	89	214	17	13
	Ajmer-Merwara.	R.	*2,023*	*1,076*	*947*	274	447	14	21	150	153	1,059	438	621	52	35

TABLE XV-F.—Principal Castes supported mainly by Agriculture.

Caste and traditional occupation.	Locality.	Area (Rural or Urban).	Total population of caste in area in column 3. P.	M.	F.	Number in caste supported by Agriculture. Principal occupation. M.	F.	Subsidiary occupation. M.	F.	Dependants. M.	F.	Total. P.	M.	F.	Percentage of column 13 to column 4.	Percentage of columns 7 and 8 to column 4.
1	2	3	4	5	6	7	8	9	10	11	12	13	14	15	16	17
Sad . . .	**Total** .	R.	**25,588**	**13,823**	**11,765**	**3,986**	**4,094**	**1,391**	**162**	**1,730**	**2,631**	**13,904**	**7,107**	**6,887**	**54**	**31**
		U.	**2,956**	**1,750**	**1,206**	**133**	**133**	**22**	**4**	**38**	**110**	**440**	**193**	**247**	**14**	**9**
Devotees.	*Rajputana* Western Division.	R.	*25,111*	*13,561*	*11,550*	3,839	4,044	1,391	162	1,640	2,483	13,559	6,870	6,689	54	31
		U.	*2,956*	*1,750*	*1,206*	133	133	22	4	38	110	440	193	247	14	9
Sadhu . .	**Total** .	R.	**12,146**	**6,927**	**5,219**	**1,231**	**1,426**	**469**	**37**	**664**	**867**	**4,694**	**2,364**	**2,330**	**38**	**21**
		U.	**2,739**	**1,915**	**824**	**91**	**29**	**65**	**2**	**30**	**27**	**244**	**186**	**58**	**8**	**4**
Devotees.	*Rajputana* Eastern Division.	R.	*1,818*	*1,319*	*499*	135	161	71	2	85	99	553	291	262	30	16
	Southern Division.	R.	*4,003*	*2,214*	*1,789*	324	476	197	8	216	304	1,525	737	788	38	20
	Western Division.	R.	*2,508*	*1,353*	*1,155*	163	85	43	5	58	95	449	264	185	17	9
		U.	*1,345*	*1,048*	*297*	59	10	50	..	21	5	145	130	15	10	5
	Ajmer-Merwara.	R.	*3,817*	*2,041*	*1,776*	609	704	158	22	305	369	2,167	1,072	1,095	56	34
		U.	*821*	*511*	*310*	7	4	5	..	3	2	21	15	6	2	1
Saiyad . .	**Total** .	R.	**10,833**	**5,951**	**4,882**	**1,284**	**479**	**168**	**25**	**662**	**1,382**	**4,100**	**2,214**	**1,886**	**37**	**17**
		U.	**16,922**	**8,847**	**8,075**	**638**	**82**	**304**	**9**	**403**	**1,016**	**2,452**	**1,345**	**1,107**	**14**	**4**
(No traditional occupation.)	*Rajputana* Eastern Division.	R.	*6,572*	*3,590*	*2,982*	709	243	134	16	358	755	2,215	1,201	1,014	33	14
		U.	*8,993*	*4,604*	*4,389*	471	35	170	9	266	726	1,677	907	770	18	5
	Southern Division.	R.	*1,200*	*649*	*551*	62	37	11	..	19	40	160	92	77	14	8
		U.	*996*	*520*	*476*	12	12	7	..	11	22	64	30	34	6	2
	Western Division.	R.	*1,809*	*1,044*	*765*	318	130	14	3	137	258	860	469	391	47	24
		U.	*2,986*	*1,568*	*1,418*	85	12	12	..	44	130	283	141	142	9	3
	Ajmer-Merwara.	R.	*1,252*	*668*	*584*	295	69	9	6	148	329	856	452	404	68	29
		U.	*3,947*	*2,165*	*1,792*	70	23	115	..	82	138	428	267	161	10	2
Sansi . .	**Total** .	R.	**4,584**	**2,154**	**2,430**	**325**	**372**	**54**	**22**	**168**	**202**	**1,143**	**547**	**596**	**25**	**15**
Vagrants and thieves.	*Rajputana* Eastern Division.	R.	*1,759*	*726*	*1,033*	177	238	33	7	81	92	628	291	337	35	23
	Western Division.	R.	*2,574*	*1,323*	*1,251*	138	110	21	12	83	103	476	242	234	18	10
Shekh . .	**Total**	R.	**86,688**	**47,948**	**38,740**	**12,454**	**7,739**	**1,954**	**282**	**5,835**	**8,656**	**36,911**	**20,243**	**16,668**	**42**	**23**
		U.	**101,923**	**52,769**	**49,154**	**2,124**	**1,039**	**682**	**48**	**1,102**	**2,169**	**7,164**	**3,908**	**3,256**	**7**	**3**
(No traditional occupation.)	*Rajputana* Eastern Division.	R.	*45,026*	*24,323*	*20,703*	4,383	2,618	1,145	220	2,019	3,731	14,116	7,547	6,569	31	15
		U.	*55,593*	*28,516*	*27,077*	961	379	466	26	516	1,070	3,418	1,943	1,475	6	2
	Southern Division.	R.	*8,042*	*4,402*	*3,640*	540	434	137	26	296	471	1,904	973	931	23	12
		U.	*7,704*	*3,971*	*3,733*	86	71	41	2	58	122	380	185	195	4	2
	Western Division.	R.	*29,931*	*17,265*	*12,666*	7,114	4,402	590	26	3,307	4,124	19,563	11,011	8,552	65	38
		U.	*17,185*	*8,860*	*8,325*	996	561	120	19	490	879	3,065	1,606	1,459	17	9
	Ajmer-Merwara.	R.	*3,689*	*1,953*	*1,731*	417	276	82	10	213	330	1,328	712	616	36	18
		U.	*21,441*	*11,422*	*10,019*	81	28	55	1	38	98	301	174	127	1	..
Sirvi . . .	**Total** .	R.	**45,631**	**23,840**	**21,781**	**16,160**	**13,515**	**28**	**2**	**7,516**	**8,089**	**45,310**	**23,704**	**21,606**	**99**	**65**
		U.	**5,384**	**2,818**	**2,566**	**1,769**	**1,409**	**2**	**6**	**973**	**922**	**5,061**	**2,744**	**2,337**	**94**	**59**
Cultivators .	*Rajputana* Western Division.	R.	*44,992*	*23,513*	*21,479*	15,973	13,333	4	2	7,419	7,995	44,726	23,396	21,330	99	65
		U.	*5,362*	*2,806*	*2,556*	1,767	1,401	2	6	972	922	5,070	2,741	2,329	94	59
Sondhia . . Cultivators .	**Total** . *Rajputana* Eastern Division.	R.	**25,195**	**13,668**	**11,527**	**9,849**	**1,063**	**8**	**7**	**3,831**	**10,358**	**24,556**	**13,188**	**11,368**	**97**	**41**
Sutar . .	**Total** .	R.	**41,110**	**21,233**	**19,877**	**4,859**	**7,225**	**6,493**	**89**	**2,705**	**3,796**	**23,107**	**11,987**	**11,120**	**56**	**29**
		U.	**4,812**	**2,443**	**2,369**	**38**	**117**	**144**	**4**	**14**	**31**	**346**	**196**	**152**	**7**	**3**
Carpenters.	*Rajputana* Southern Division.	R.	*17,052*	*8,675*	*8,377*	1,241	2,176	1,816	32	826	1,449	7,540	3,883	3,657	44	20
		U.	*1,217*	*612*	*605*	8	16	10	..	5	10	49	23	26	4	2
	Western Division.	R.	*23,853*	*12,465*	*11,388*	3,570	5,009	2,590	57	1,862	2,327	15,415	8,022	7,393	64	36
		U.	*3,595*	*1,831*	*1,764*	30	101	134	4	9	21	299	173	126	8	3
Teli . . .	**Total** .	R.	**55,062**	**28,677**	**26,385**	**6,325**	**6,218**	**4,144**	**547**	**3,151**	**4,597**	**24,982**	**13,620**	**11,362**	**45**	**22**
		U.	**13,658**	**6,924**	**6,734**	**757**	**890**	**890**	**193**	**412**	**542**	**3,684**	**2,059**	**1,625**	**27**	**12**
Oil pressers.	*Rajputana* Eastern Division.	R.	*27,753*	*14,406*	*13,347*	2,484	2,427	1,718	214	1,003	1,402	9,248	5,205	4,043	33	17
		U.	*4,920*	*2,563*	*2,357*	126	172	334	73	66	98	869	526	343	18	6
	Southern Division.	R.	*15,848*	*8,233*	*7,615*	2,253	1,742	1,169	151	1,432	2,368	9,115	4,854	4,261	57	25
		U.	*1,896*	*941*	*955*	122	117	108	39	77	113	576	307	269	30	12
	Western Division.	R.	*8,514*	*4,481*	*4,033*	1,062	1,461	1,012	115	466	565	4,681	2,540	2,141	55	29
		U.	*5,383*	*2,693*	*2,690*	467	571	314	50	250	307	1,959	1,031	928	36	19
	Ajmer-Merwara	R.	*2,947*	*1,557*	*1,390*	526	588	245	67	250	262	1,938	1,021	917	65	37
		U.	*1,459*	*727*	*732*	42	30	134	31	19	24	280	195	85	19	4
Thori .	**Total** .	R.	**26,642**	**14,269**	**12,373**	**7,765**	**6,322**	**534**	**82**	**3,874**	**4,283**	**22,830**	**12,133**	**10,697**	**85**	**52**
		U.	**1,765**	**899**	**866**	**133**	**149**	**58**	**4**	**68**	**105**	**506**	**259**	**249**	**28**	**15**
Hunters and fowlers	*Rajputana* Western Division.	R.	*26,290*	*14,066*	*12,224*	7,658	6,306	554	79	3,858	4,265	22,720	12,070	10,650	86	53
		U.	*1,762*	*898*	*864*	132	140	58	4	68	105	507	258	249	28	15

TABLE XVI.

Occupations of Europeans and Allied Races, Armenians, and Anglo-Indians.

Explanatory Note.

This Table has been prepared only for Europeans and allied races, Anglo-Indians, and Armenians. It shows, under heads corresponding mainly to the Sub-classes of Table XV-A, the occupations or means of support of actual workers only.

"Anglo-Indian" includes all persons hitherto known as Eurasians, and is not confined to those of partially British origin.

TABLE XVI.—OCCUPATIONS OF EUROPEANS AND ALLIED RACES, ARMENIANS, AND ANGLO-INDIANS.

Race.	Sex.	Population dealt with: Actual workers.	Population dealt with: Dependants.	Income from rent of agricultural land.	Cultivators of all kinds.	Planters and forest officers, and their clerks; rent collectors, agents, and managers and other employés on landed estates, etc.	Extraction of minerals: Owners, managers, clerks, etc.	Extraction of minerals: Labourers.	Industries: Owners, managers, clerks, etc., (excluding contractors).	Industries: Artisans and other workmen.	Transport: Owners, managers, etc., connected with transport: Post office and Telegraph officials, and clerks.	Transport: Labourers, boatmen, carters, palki bearers, etc., Post office and Telegraph employés below clerks.	Trade.	Public force: Commissioned and gazetted officers.	Public force: Others.	Public administration: Gazetted officers.	Public administration: Others.	Arts and professions: Religious.	Arts and professions: Lawyers, doctors and teachers.	Arts and professions: Others.	Persons living on their private income, pensioners, etc.	Domestic service.	Unspecified or insufficiently described occupations.
1	2	3	4	5	6	7	8	9	10	11	12	13	14	15	16	17	18	19	20	21	22	23	24
Rajputana	Total	695	1,013	5	2	3	14	..	3	7	289	..	12	31	89	14	15	27	58	37	73	15	1
	Males	597	383	4	2	3	14	..	3	7	289	..	12	31	89	14	15	16	27	30	38	2	1
	Females	98	630	1	..	..	..	..	..	..	..	..	..	..	..	..	..	11	31	7	35	13	..
Europeans and allied races.	Total	539	638	5	1	3	10	..	..	5	191	..	11	29	87	13	11	23	41	31	66	11	1
	Males	465	252	4	1	3	10	..	..	5	191	..	11	29	87	13	11	15	21	25	36	2	1
	Females	74	386	1	..	..	..	..	..	..	..	..	..	..	..	..	..	8	20	6	30	9	..
Armenians	Total	2	..	..	..	..	..	..	..	..	..	..	..	..	..	..	..	1	..	..	1	..	..
	Males	..	..	..	..	..	..	..	..	..	..	..	..	..	..	..	..	..	..	..	..	..	..
	Females	2	..	..	..	..	..	..	..	..	..	..	..	..	..	..	..	1	..	..	1	..	..
Anglo-Indians	Total	154	375	..	1	..	4	..	3	2	98	..	1	2	2	1	4	3	17	6	6	4	..
	Males	132	131	..	1	..	4	..	3	2	98	..	1	2	2	1	4	1	6	5	2	..	..
	Females	22	244	..	..	..	..	..	..	..	..	..	..	..	..	..	..	2	11	1	4	4	..
Ajmer-Merwara	Total	1,580	885	..	1	..	..	..	6	2	408	..	4	61	948	8	3	55	34	16	32	2	..
	Males	1,512	269	..	..	..	..	..	6	..	408	..	4	61	948	8	3	28	23	3	18	2	..
	Females	68	616	..	1	..	..	..	..	2	..	..	..	..	..	..	..	27	11	13	14	..	..
European and allied races	Total	1,334	421	..	1	..	..	..	6	2	193	..	3	61	945	8	2	51	26	13	21	2	..
	Males	1,285	117	..	..	..	..	..	6	..	193	..	3	61	945	8	2	28	22	2	13	2	..
	Females	49	304	..	1	..	..	..	..	2	..	..	..	..	..	..	..	23	4	11	8	..	..
Anglo-Indians	Total	246	464	..	..	..	..	..	..	..	215	..	1	..	3	..	1	4	8	3	11	..	..
	Males	227	152	..	..	..	..	..	..	..	215	..	1	..	3	..	1	..	1	1	5	..	..
	Females	19	312	..	..	..	..	..	..	..	..	..	..	..	..	..	..	4	7	2	6	..	..

TABLE XVII.

Territorial Distribution of Christians by Sect and Race.

Explanatory Note.

This Table gives figures, by States or Districts, for the most important sects of Christianity. Christians have been divided into three main racial groups, *viz.*, Europeans and allied races (including Armenians), Anglo-Indians, and Indians. Indians have been sub-divided into Goanese and "others." The term "Anglo-Indian" includes all persons hitherto known as Eurasians, and is not confined to those of partially British origin.

At the end of the Table will be found an Appendix showing the method of classification of the smaller sects of Christianity likely to be found in Rajputana and Ajmer-Merwara, which was adopted at this Census.

Banswara, Bundi, Jaisalmer, Kushalgarh, Lawa, and Partabgarh are omitted from the Table, as they contain no Christians.

TABLE XVII.—Territorial Distribution of Christians by Sect and Race.

Province; and State or District.	All Denominations. Total.			Europeans and allied races.		Anglo-Indians.		Indians. Total.		Goanese.		‡Others.		Anglican Communion. Total.			Europeans and allied races.		Anglo-Indians.		Indians.	
	P.	M.	F.	M.	F.	M.	F.	M.	F.	M.	F.	M.	F.	P.	M.	F.	M.	F.	M.	F.	M.	F.
1	2	3	4	5	6	7	8	9	10	11	12	13	14	15	16	17	18	19	20	21	22	23
Rajputana	4,256	2,409	1,847	717	*468	263	260	1,429	1,119	121	42	1,308	1,077	1,186	688	498	460	300	137	136	91	62
Alwar	92	50	42	21	†14	4	8	25	20	4	...	21	20	18	10	8	8	5	...	...	2	3
Bharatpur	566	315	251	8	13	12	11	295	227	3	3	292	224	70	32	38	5	13	6	7	21	18
Bikaner	151	97	54	10	10	4	...	83	44	7	...	76	44	20	10	10	8	10	1	...	1	...
Dholpur	41	26	15	8	5	5	5	13	5	1	...	12	5	15	12	3	5	1	...	...	7	2
Dungarpur	2	1	1	...	...	...	...	1	1	...	...	1	1	...	...	...	...	...	...	...	...	...
Jaipur	1,326	689	637	235	166	128	156	326	315	19	7	307	308	406	211	195	133	104	62	72	16	19
Jhalawar	26	18	8	8	5	1	...	9	3	5	1	4	2	2	1	1	1	1	...	...	...	...
Karauli	28	15	13	1	...	...	...	14	13	...	...	14	13	1	1	...	1	...	...	...	...	...
Kishangarh	23	8	15	...	...	...	...	8	15	1	4	7	11	...	...	...	...	...	...	...	...	...
Kotah	507	274	233	17	14	8	8	249	211	7	...	242	211	37	18	19	13	12	1	5	4	2
Marwar	440	235	205	42	37	31	33	162	135	8	5	154	130	99	50	49	24	20	20	22	6	7
Mewar	237	152	85	21	17	2	...	129	68	17	3	112	65	56	41	15	10	9	2	...	29	6
Shahpura (Chiefship)	1	1	...	...	...	...	...	1	...	1	...	...	...	...	...	...	...	...	...	...	...	...
Sirohi	804	522	282	344	†181	68	45	110	56	47	19	63	37	459	302	157	252	125	45	30	5	2
Tonk	12	6	6	2	...	...	...	4	6	1	...	3	6	3	...	3	...	...	...	...	...	3
Ajmer-Merwara	5,432	3,258	2,174	1,409	353	379	331	1,477	1,490	168	69	1,309	1,421	1,689	1,271	418	1,003	197	180	153	88	68
Ajmer	4,910	2,996	1,914	1,393	347	373	325	1,230	1,242	166	69	1,064	1,173	1,669	1,260	409	999	195	175	148	86	66
Merwara	522	262	260	9	6	6	6	247	248	2	...	245	248	20	11	9	4	2	5	5	2	2

* Includes two Armenians.
† Includes one Armenian.

TABLE XVII.—Territorial Distribution of Christians by Sect and Race—*continued*.

Province; and State or District.	Baptist. Total.			Baptist. Europeans and allied races.		Baptist. Anglo-Indians.		Baptist. Indians.		Congregationalist. Total.			Congregationalist. Europeans and allied races.		Greek. Total.			Greek. Europeans and allied races.	
	P.	M.	F.	M.	F.	M.	F.	M.	F.	P.	M.	F.	M.	F.	P.	M.	F.	M.	F.
1	24	25	26	27	28	29	30	31	32	33	34	35	36	37	38	39	40	41	42
Rajputana	31	18	13	7	6	3	1	8	6	8	5	3	5	3	...	...	...	...	...
Alwar	...	...	...	...	...	...	...	...	...	...	...	...	...	...	...	...	...	...	...
Bharatpur	...	...	...	...	...	...	...	...	...	...	...	...	...	...	...	...	...	...	...
Bikaner	1	1	...	...	...	...	...	1	...	...	...	...	...	...	...	...	...	...	...
Dholpur	12	5	7	1	3	...	1	4	3	...	...	...	...	...	...	...	...	...	...
Dungarpur	...	...	...	...	...	...	...	...	...	...	...	...	...	...	...	...	...	...	...
Jaipur	6	5	3	4	3	1	...	...	...	...	...	...	...	...	...	...	...	...	...
Jhalawar	...	...	...	...	...	...	...	...	...	...	...	...	...	...	...	...	...	...	...
Karauli	...	...	...	...	...	...	...	...	...	...	...	...	...	...	...	...	...	...	...
Kishangarh	...	...	...	...	...	...	...	...	...	...	...	...	...	...	...	...	...	...	...
Kotah	...	...	...	...	...	...	...	...	...	...	...	...	...	...	...	...	...	...	...
Marwar	3	2	1	...	...	...	...	2	1	1	1	...	1	...	...	...	...	...	...
Mewar	...	...	...	...	...	...	...	...	...	...	...	...	...	...	...	...	...	...	...
Shahpura (Chiefship)	...	...	...	...	...	...	...	...	...	...	...	...	...	...	...	...	...	...	...
Sirohi	7	5	2	2	...	2	...	1	2	7	4	3	4	3	...	...	...	...	...
Tonk	...	...	...	...	...	...	...	...	...	...	...	...	...	...	...	...	...	...	...
Ajmer-Merwara	20	9	11	6	9	...	...	3	2	2	1	1	1	1	2	2	...	2	..
Ajmer	20	9	11	6	9	...	...	3	2	2	1	1	1	1	1	1	...	1	...
Merwara	...	...	...	...	...	...	...	...	...	...	...	...	...	...	1	1	...	1	...

Province; and State or District.	Lutheran. Total.			Lutheran. Europeans and allied races.		Lutheran. Anglo-Indians.		Lutheran. Indians.		Methodist. Total.			Methodist. Europeans and allied races.		Methodist. Anglo-Indians.		Methodist. Indians.	
	P.	M.	F.	M.	F.	M.	F.	M.	F.	P.	M.	F.	M.	F.	M.	F.	M.	F.
1	43	44	45	46	47	48	49	50	51	52	53	54	55	56	57	58	59	60
Rajputana	14	9	5	2	3	1	...	6	2	988	523	465	16	10	5	3	502	452
Alwar	...	...	...	...	...	...	...	...	...	...	...	...	...	...	...	...	...	...
Bharatpur	...	...	...	...	...	...	...	...	...	423	240	183	...	...	4	1	236	182
Bikaner	...	...	...	...	...	...	...	...	...	109	70	39	1	...	...	...	69	39
Dholpur	...	...	...	...	...	...	...	...	...	3	1	2	1	...	...	2	...	...
Dungarpur	...	...	...	...	...	...	...	...	...	...	...	...	...	...	...	...	...	...
Jaipur	2	1	1	1	1	...	...	...	...	397	185	212	7	6	...	...	178	206
Jhalawar	...	...	...	...	...	...	...	...	...	...	...	...	...	...	...	...	...	...
Karauli	...	...	...	...	...	...	...	...	...	...	...	...	...	...	...	...	...	...
Kishangarh	...	...	...	...	...	...	...	...	...	13	4	9	...	...	...	...	4	9
Kotah	...	...	...	...	...	...	...	...	...	1	1	...	...	...	...	...	1	...
Marwar	...	...	...	...	...	...	...	...	...	26	12	14	2	2	1	...	9	12
Mewar	...	...	...	...	...	...	...	...	...	...	...	...	...	...	...	...	...	...
Shahpura (Chiefship)	...	...	...	...	...	...	...	...	...	...	...	...	...	...	...	...	...	...
Sirohi	12	8	4	1	2	1	...	6	2	16	10	6	5	2	...	...	5	4
Tonk	...	...	...	...	...	...	...	...	...	...	...	...	...	...	...	...	...	...
Ajmer-Merwara	...	...	...	...	...	...	...	...	...	565	271	294	48	12	9	9	214	273
Ajmer	...	...	...	...	...	...	...	...	...	563	271	292	48	12	9	9	214	271
Merwara	...	...	...	...	...	...	...	...	...	2	...	2	...	...	...	...	...	2

TABLE XVII.—TERRITORIAL DISTRIBUTION OF CHRISTIANS BY SECT A D RACE—*continued.*

Province; and State or District.	MINOR PROTESTANT DENOMINATIONS.							PRESBYTERIAN.													PROTESTANT, UNSECTARIAN OR SECT UNSPECIFIED.												
	Total.			Anglo-Indians.		Indians.		Total.			Europeans and allied races.		Anglo-Indians.		Indians.						Total.			Europeans and allied races.		Anglo-Indians.		Indians.					
															Total.		Goanese.		Others.									Total.		Goanese.		Others.	
	P.	M.	F.	M.	F.	M.	F.	P.	M.	F.	M.	F.	M.	F.	M.	F.	M.	F.	M.	F.	P.	M.	F.	M.	F.	M.	F.	M.	F.	M.	F.	M.	F.
1	61	62	63	64	65	66	67	68	69	70	71	72	73	74	75	76	77	78	79	80	81	82	83	84	85	86	87	88	89	90	91	92	93
Rajputana	6	5	1	1	...	4	1	1,008	553	455	58	41*	11	8	484	406	2	...	482	406	170	91	79	15	11	2	2	74	66	4	...	70	66
Alwar	...	...	...	...	...	...	...	33	17	16	...	...	...	...	17	16	...	...	17	16	4	2	2	2	2	...	...	...	...	...	...	...	...
Bharatpur	1	1	...	1	...	...	...	6	3	3	...	...	...	...	3	3	...	...	3	3	53	32	21	1	...	...	1	31	20	...	...	31	20
Bikaner	...	...	...	...	...	...	...	10	5	5	...	...	...	...	5	5	...	...	5	5	1	1	...	...	...	1	...	...	...	...	...	...	...
Dholpur	...	...	...	...	...	...	...	...	...	...	...	...	...	...	...	...	...	...	...	...	...	...	...	...	...	...	...	...	...	...	...	...	...
Dungarpur	...	...	...	...	...	...	...	2	1	1	...	...	...	...	1	1	...	...	1	1	...	...	...	...	...	...	...	...	...	...	...	...	...
Jaipur	...	...	...	...	...	...	...	72	43	29	23	14	5	4	15	11	...	...	15	11	99	49	50	8	7	...	...	41	43	4	...	37	43
Jhalawar	...	...	...	...	...	...	...	...	...	...	...	...	...	...	...	...	...	...	...	...	...	...	...	...	...	...	...	...	...	...	...	...	...
Karauli	...	...	...	...	...	...	...	...	...	...	...	...	...	...	...	...	...	...	...	...	...	...	...	...	...	...	...	...	...	...	...	...	...
Kishangarh	...	...	...	...	...	...	...	...	...	...	...	...	...	...	...	...	...	...	...	...	...	...	...	...	...	...	...	...	...	...	...	...	...
Kotah	...	...	...	...	...	...	...	451	239	212	2	2	5	3	232	207	...	...	232	207	...	...	...	...	...	...	...	...	...	...	...	...	...
Marwar	5	4	1	...	...	4	1	205	111	94	3	3	1	...	107	91	...	...	107	91	4	3	1	1	...	1	1	1	...	...	...	1	...
Mewar	...	...	...	...	...	...	...	144	86	58	3	2	...	...	83	56	2	...	81	56	5	3	2	3	2	...	...	...	...	...	...	...	...
Shahpura (Chiefship)	...	...	...	...	...	...	...	...	...	...	...	...	...	...	...	...	...	...	...	...	...	...	...	...	...	...	...	...	...	...	...	...	...
Sirohi	...	...	...	...	...	...	...	85	48	37	27	20*	...	1	21	16	...	...	21	16	...	...	...	...	...	...	...	...	...	...	...	...	...
Tonk	...	...	...	...	...	...	...	...	...	...	...	...	...	...	...	...	...	...	...	...	4	1	3	...	...	...	...	1	3	...	...	1	3
Ajmer-Merwara	...	...	...	...	...	...	...	1,943	922	1,021	62	46	9	6	831	969	1	3	850	966	1	1	...	1	...	...	...	...	...	...	...	...	...
Ajmer	...	...	...	...	...	...	...	1,453	678	775	61	45	9	5	608	725	1	3	607	722	...	...	...	...	...	...	...	...	...	...	...	...	...
Merwara	...	...	...	...	...	...	...	490	244	246	1	1	...	1	243	244	...	...	243	244	1	1	...	1	...	...	...	...	...	...	...	...	...

* Includes one Armenian.

TABLE XVII.—TERRITORIAL DISTRIBUTION OF CHRISTIANS BY SECT AND RACE—*concluded.*

Province; and State or District.	Quaker. Total. P.	Quaker. Total. M.	Quaker. Total. F.	Quaker. Europeans and allied races. M.	Quaker. Europeans and allied races. F.	Quaker. Anglo-Indians. M.	Quaker. Anglo-Indians. F.	Roman Catholic. Total. P.	Roman Catholic. Total. M.	Roman Catholic. Total. F.	Roman Catholic. Europeans and allied races. M.	Roman Catholic. Europeans and allied races. F.	Roman Catholic. Anglo-Indians. M.	Roman Catholic. Anglo-Indians. F.	Roman Catholic. Indians. Total. M.	Roman Catholic. Indians. Total. F.	Roman Catholic. Indians. Goanese. M.	Roman Catholic. Indians. Goanese. F.	Roman Catholic. Indians. Others. M.	Roman Catholic. Indians. Others. F.
1	94	95	96	97	98	99	100	101	102	103	104	105	106	107	108	109	110	111	112	113
Rajputana	*1*	*1*	...	1	...	...	...	*837*	*510*	*327*	148	88*	103	116	259	123	*115*	*42*	*144*	*81*
Alwar	*1*	*1*	...	1	...	...	...	*36*	*20*	*16*	10	7*	4	8	6	1	*4*	...	*2*	*1*
Bharatpur	...	...	...	...	...	...	...	*13*	*7*	*6*	2	..	1	2	4	4	*3*	*3*	*1*	*1*
Bikaner	...	...	...	...	...	...	...	*10*	*10*	...	1	...	2	...	7	...	*7*	...	...	...
Dholpur	...	...	...	...	...	...	...	*11*	*8*	*3*	1	1	5	2	2	...	*1*	...	*1*	...
Dungarpur	...	...	...	...	...	...	...	...	...	...	...	...	...	...	...	...	...	...	...	...
Jaipur	...	...	...	...	...	...	...	*389*	*193*	*146*	57	31	60	80	76	35	*15*	*7*	*61*	*28*
Jhalawar	...	...	...	...	...	...	...	*24*	*17*	*7*	7	4	1	...	9	3	*5*	*1*	*4*	*2*
Karauli	...	...	...	...	...	...	...	*27*	*14*	*13*	...	...	...	...	14	13	...	...	*14*	*13*
Kishangarh	...	...	...	...	...	...	...	*10*	*4*	*6*	...	...	...	...	4	6	*1*	*4*	*3*	*2*
Kotah	...	...	...	...	...	...	...	*18*	*16*	*2*	2	...	2	...	12	2	*7*	...	*5*	*2*
Marwar	...	...	...	...	...	...	...	*96*	*51*	*45*	10	12	8	10	33	23	*8*	*5*	*25*	*18*
Mewar	...	...	...	...	...	...	...	*81*	*21*	*10*	4	4	...	...	17	6	*15*	*3*	*2*	*3*
Shahpura (Chiefship)	...	...	...	...	...	...	...	*1*	*1*	...	...	...	...	...	1	...	*1*	...	...	...
Sirohi	...	...	...	...	...	...	...	*218*	*145*	*73*	53	29	20	14	72	30	*47*	*19*	*25*	*11*
Tonk	...	...	...	...	...	...	...	*3*	*3*	...	1	...	...	...	2	...	*1*	...	*1*	...
Ajmer-Merwara	*2*	...	*2*	...	1	...	1	*1,190*	*772*	*427*	275	87	180	162	317	178	*167*	*66*	*150*	*112*
Ajmer	*2*	...	*2*	...	1	...	1	*1,191*	*767*	*424*	273	84	179	162	315	178	*155*	*66*	*150*	*112*
Merwara	...	...	...	...	...	...	...	*8*	*5*	*3*	2	3	1	...	2	...	*2*	...	...	...

Province; and State or District.	Salvationist. Total. P.	Salvationist. Total. M.	Salvationist. Total. F.	Salvationist. Europeans and allied races. M.	Salvationist. Europeans and allied races. F.	Salvationist. Indians. M.	Salvationist. Indians. F.	Sect not returned. Total. P.	Sect not returned. Total. M.	Sect not returned. Total. F.	Sect not returned. Europeans and allied races. M.	Sect not returned. Europeans and allied races. F.	Sect not returned. Indians. M.	Sect not returned. Indians. F.	Indefinite beliefs. Total. P.	Indefinite beliefs. Total. M.	Indefinite beliefs. Total. F.	Indefinite beliefs. Europeans and allied races. M.	Indefinite beliefs. Europeans and allied races. F.	Indefinite beliefs. Anglo-Indians. M.	Indefinite beliefs. Anglo-Indians. F.
1	114	115	116	117	118	119	120	121	122	123	124	125	126	127	128	129	130	131	132	133	134
Rajputana	*2*	*2*	...	1	...	1	...	*3*	*2*	*1*	2	...	...	1	*2*	*2*	...	2	...	...	...
Alwar	...	...	...	...	...	...	...	...	...	...	...	...	...	...	...	...	...	...	...	...	...
Bharatpur	...	...	...	...	...	...	...	...	...	...	...	...	...	...	...	...	...	...	...	...	...
Bikaner	...	...	...	...	...	...	...	...	...	...	...	...	...	...	...	...	...	...	...	...	...
Dholpur	...	...	...	...	...	...	...	...	...	...	...	...	...	...	...	...	...	...	...	...	...
Dungarpur	...	...	...	...	...	...	...	...	...	...	...	...	...	...	...	...	...	...	...	...	...
Jaipur	...	...	...	...	...	...	...	*2*	*1*	*1*	1	...	...	1	*1*	*1*	...	1	...	...	...
Jhalawar	...	...	...	...	...	...	...	...	...	...	...	...	...	...	...	...	...	...	...	...	...
Karauli	...	...	...	...	...	...	...	...	...	...	...	...	...	...	...	...	...	...	...	...	...
Kishangarh	...	...	...	...	...	...	...	...	...	...	...	...	...	...	...	...	...	...	...	...	...
Kotah	...	...	...	...	...	...	...	...	...	...	...	...	...	...	...	...	...	...	...	...	...
Marwar	...	...	...	...	...	...	...	*1*	*1*	...	1	...	...	...	...	...	...	...	...	...	...
Mewar	...	...	...	...	...	...	...	...	...	...	...	...	...	...	*1*	*1*	...	1	...	...	...
Shahpura (Chiefship)	...	...	...	...	...	...	...	...	...	...	...	...	...	...	...	...	...	...	...	...	...
Sirohi	...	...	...	...	...	...	...	...	...	...	...	...	...	...	...	...	...	...	...	...	...
Tonk	*2*	*2*	...	1	...	1	...	...	...	...	...	...	...	...	...	...	...	...	...	...	...
Ajmer-Merwara	*1*	*1*	...	1	...	...	...	*4*	*4*	...	...	...	4	...	*4*	*4*	...	3	...	1	...
Ajmer	*1*	*1*	...	1	...	...	...	*4*	*4*	...	...	...	4	...	*4*	*4*	...	3	...	1	...
Merwara	...	...	...	...	...	...	...	...	...	...	...	...	...	...	...	...	...	...	...	...	...

* Includes one Armenian.

APPENDIX TO TABLE XVII.—(SEE EXPLANATORY NOTE.)

Main Sects in Table.	**Smaller Sects included in Main Sects.*
Anglican Communion . .	. Catholic Anglican. Church Missionary Society. Church of England. Church of Ireland. Episcopal Church of America. Episcopalian. High Church. Scotch Episcopal Mission. Society for the Propagation of the Gospel.
Baptist	. American Baptist. Canadian Baptist.
Congregationalist . .	. Independent.
Lutheran	. American Lutheran. German Church. Moravian.
Methodist	. American Episcopal Methodist. American Methodist. Methodist Episcopalian. Primitive Methodist. Wesleyan. Wesleyan Methodist.
Minor Protestant Denominations	. Church of India. Evangelical. Plymouth Brethren.
Presbyterian	. American Presbyterian. Calvinist. Canadian Presbyterian. Church of Scotland. Free Church of Scotland. Irish Presbyterian. Reformed Church. United Free Church. United Presbyterian.
Protestant Unsectarian or Sect unspecified.	Church of America. Dissenter. Nonconformist. Protestant. Undenominational. Zenana Bible Mission.
Quaker	. Friend.
Roman Catholic	. Catholic. Church of Rome.
Indefinite Beliefs . . .	. Agnostic. Atheist. Freethinker. Positivist. Rationalist. Theist. Theosophist. Unitarian.

*It is not certain that all these sects were actually returned in the Census Schedules.

TABLE XVIII.

Europeans and Allied Races, Armenians, and Anglo-Indians, by Age.

Explanatory Note.

This Table gives statistics by age, and by State or District, for all Europeans and allied races, Armenians, and Anglo-Indians. To save space, figures for Armenians have been included among those for Europeans.

The term "Anglo-Indian" includes all persons hitherto known as Eurasians, and is not confined to those of partially British origin.

Europeans have been subdivided into "British subjects" and "others." For this purpose the term "British subjects" embraces (*a*) all British races (including Colonials, etc.), and (*b*) all other Europeans and allied races born in Great Britain or in a British Colony or Dependency.

The Table gives separate statistics for Cities, but these are included also in the State and District figures. Jodhpur City includes Jodhpur suburbs, which have been shown in Tables III and IV under the name of Jodhpur Town.

Banswara, Bundi, Dungarpur, Jaisalmer, Kishangarh, Kushalgarh, Lawa, Partabgarh, Shahpura are omitted from the Table, as they contain no Christians.

TABLE XVIII.—Europeans and Allied Races, Armenians, and Anglo-Indians, by Age.

Province; and State, District, or City.	TOTAL.			Europeans and Allied Races (including Armenians): British Subjects: All ages.			0-11.		12-14.		15-29.		30-49.		50 & over.	
	P.	M.	F.	P.	M.	F.	M.	F.	M.	F.	M.	F.	M.	F.	M.	F.
1	2	3	4	5	6	7	8	9	10	11	12	13	14	15	16	17
Rajputana.	1,708	980	728	1,127	682	445	197	131	37	20	187	124	220	152	41	18
Alwar	47	25	22	30	19	11	4	3	1	..	5	4	6	4	3	..
Bharatpur	44	20	24	19	6	13	1	3	..	..	2	1	3	9	..	..
Bikaner	24	14	10	20	10	10	2	2	..	..	..	3	5	5	3	..
Dholpur	23	13	10	11	7	4	3	..	1	..	..	..	2	4	1	..
Jaipur	685	363	322	384	223	161	85	56	6	5	50	40	69	51	13	9
Jhalawar	14	9	5	3	1	2	..	..	..	..	..	..	1	2	..	..
Karauli	1	1	...	1	1	..	..	..	..	..	..	..	1	..	..	..
Kotah	47	25	22	29	15	14	1	3	1	..	3	3	8	7	2	1
Marwar	143	73	70	74	39	35	4	6	..	..	11	10	18	16	6	3
Mewar	40	23	17	38	21	17	4	2	..	1	3	7	9	7	5	..
Sirohi	638	412	226	516	338	178	113	56	28	14	113	57	76	46	8	5
Tonk	2	2	...	2	2	..	..	..	..	..	..	..	2	..	..	..
Ajmer Merwara	2,465	1,781	684	1,702	1,369	333	99	104	11	5	995	96	226	106	38	22
Ajmer	2,438	1,766	672	1,688	1,361	327	98	102	11	5	993	94	222	105	37	21
Merwara	27	15	12	14	8	6	1	2	..	..	2	2	4	1	1	1
CITIES.																
Rajputana.	309	160	149	190	98	92	20	14	1	1	17	20	44	47	16	10
Alwar	29	14	15	15	10	5	..	..	..	..	3	2	4	3	3	..
Bharatpur	41	18	23	18	5	13	1	3	..	..	1	1	3	9	..	..
Bikaner	18	10	8	15	7	8	..	1	..	..	..	2	5	5	2	..
Jaipur	116	68	48	76	44	32	14	4	..	1	8	6	15	13	7	8
Jodhpur	70	32	38	34	14	20	1	3	..	..	5	5	7	10	1	2
Kotah	15	6	9	12	6	6	..	1	1	..	..	1	4	4	1	..
Tonk	2	2	...	2	2	..	..	..	..	..	..	..	2	..	..	..
Udaipur	18	10	8	18	10	8	4	2	..	..	..	3	4	3	2	..
Ajmer-Merwara—																
Ajmer	1,297	718	579	569	329	240	64	61	11	5	108	84	114	70	32	20

Province; and State, District, or City.	Europeans and Allied Races (including Armenians): Others: All ages.			0-11.		12-14.		15-29.		30-49.		50 & over.	
	P.	M.	F.	M.	F.	M.	F.	M.	F.	M.	F.	M.	F.
1	18	19	20	21	22	23	24	25	26	27	28	29	30
Rajputana.	52*	35	17*	1	..	1	..	6	2	13	8†	14	7†
Alwar	5†	2	3†	..	..	..	..	..	..	..	1	2	2†
Bharatpur	2	2	..	..	..	..	..	..	..	1	..	1	..
Bikaner	..	..	..	..	..	..	..	..	..	..	..	..	..
Dholpur	2	1	1	..	..	..	..	..	..	1	1	..	..
Jaipur	17	12	5	..	..	..	..	3	..	4	3	5	2
Jhalawar	10	7	3	..	..	..	..	..	1	4	1	3	1
Karauli	..	..	..	..	..	..	..	..	..	..	..	..	..
Kotah	2	2	..	..	..	..	..	2	..	..	..	..	..
Marwar	5	3	2	1	..	..	..	..	..	1	1	1	1
Mewar	..	..	..	..	..	..	..	..	..	..	..	..	..
Sirohi	9†	6	3†	..	..	1	..	1	1	2	1†	2	1
Tonk	..	..	..	..	..	..	..	..	..	..	..	..	..
Ajmer Merwara	53	33	20	3	2	..	..	4	3	25	14	1	1
Ajmer	52	32	20	3	2	..	..	4	3	24	14	1	1
Merwara	1	1	..	..	..	..	..	..	..	1	..	..	..
CITIES.													
Rajputana.	19†	13	6†	..	..	..	..	3	..	3	2	7	4†
Alwar	3†	1	2†	..	..	..	..	..	..	..	..	1	2†
Bharatpur	1	1	..	..	..	..	..	..	..	..	..	1	..
Bikaner	..	..	..	..	..	..	..	..	..	..	..	..	..
Jaipur	15	11	4	..	..	..	..	3	..	3	2	5	2
Jodhpur	..	..	..	..	..	..	..	..	..	..	..	..	..
Kotah	..	..	..	..	..	..	..	..	..	..	..	..	..
Tonk	..	..	..	..	..	..	..	..	..	..	..	..	..
Udaipur	..	..	..	..	..	..	..	..	..	..	..	..	..
Ajmer-Merwara—													
Ajmer	44	24	20	3	2	..	..	3	3	18	14	..	1

Province; and State, District, or City.	Anglo-Indians: All ages.			0-11.		12-14.		15-29.		30-49.		50 & over.	
	P.	M.	F.	M.	F.	M.	F.	M.	F.	M.	F.	M.	F.
1	31	32	33	34	35	36	37	38	39	40	41	42	43
Rajputana.	529	263	266	90	92	16	15	67	72	73	64	17	23
Alwar	12	4	8	..	1	..	1	..	2	4	2	..	2
Bharatpur	23	12	11	3	4	..	..	4	4	2	3	3	..
Bikaner	4	4	..	..	..	..	..	1	..	3	..	..	..
Dholpur	10	5	5	3	2	..	..	..	2	1	1	1	..
Jaipur	284	128	156	50	57	5	9	33	43	30	31	10	16
Jhalawar	1	1	..	..	..	..	..	1	..	..	..	..	..
Karauli	..	..	..	..	..	..	..	..	..	..	..	..	..
Kotah	16	8	8	2	4	..	..	4	1	2	3	..	..
Marwar	64	31	33	9	12	1	1	7	11	13	6	1	3
Mewar	2	2	..	..	..	..	..	2	..	..	..	..	..
Sirohi	113	68	45	23	12	10	4	15	9	17	18	3	2
Tonk	..	..	..	..	..	..	..	..	..	..	..	..	..
Ajmer Merwara	710	379	331	104	94	23	23	135	115	95	71	22	28
Ajmer	698	373	325	103	91	23	23	134	115	91	69	22	27
Merwara	12	6	6	1	3	..	..	1	..	4	2	..	1
CITIES.													
Rajputana.	100	49	51	13	15	1	2	12	14	18	11	5	9
Alwar	11	3	8	..	1	..	1	..	2	3	2	..	2
Bharatpur	22	12	10	3	4	..	..	4	4	3	2	2	..
Bikaner	3	3	..	..	..	..	..	1	..	2	..	..	..
Jaipur	25	13	12	2	1	..	..	6	3	3	3	2	5
Jodhpur	36	18	18	8	8	1	1	1	5	7	2	1	2
Kotah	3	..	3	..	1	..	..	..	..	..	2	..	..
Tonk	..	..	..	..	..	..	..	..	..	..	..	..	..
Udaipur	..	..	..	..	..	..	..	..	..	..	..	..	..
Ajmer-Merwara—													
Ajmer	684	365	319	100	88	23	22	130	114	90	68	22	27

* Includes 2 Armenians. † Includes 1 Armenian.

TABLE XIX.

Immigration by Age-periods, and Selected Birthplaces, Castes, and Occupations, for Ajmer City.

Explanatory Note.

This Table has been prepared for Ajmer City only, to show the most important or interesting occupations or means of support and the birthplaces of immigrants, among certain selected castes or races, which have been chosen either for their numerical importance or their local interest.

It also shows the ages of all immigrants under three periods, namely 0 to 14, 15 to 39, and 40 and over.

Details by occupations have not been abstracted nor shown in columns 12 to 33 against "other" castes, nor have figures for age combined with birthplace been given against "others" in columns 6 to 11 under the different birthplaces. For this reason, (1) the figures in columns 12 to 15 against " All castes" in the entries for "Total immigrants," and (2) the figures in, columns 6 to 11 and 12 to 15 against "Totals" in the entries under the various birthplaces, will not work up in either case to the totals in columns 3 to 5.

The figures for immigrants exclude immigrants from Ajmer District into the City, figures for such not being available.

TABLE XIX.—Immigration by Age, and Selected Birthplaces, Castes, and Occupations. (Ajmer City).

Birthplace.	Caste.	Total number of immigrants.			Age-periods. 0—14.		15—39.		40 and over.		All Occupations. Workers.		Dependants.	
		P.	M.	F.	M.	F.	M.	F.	M.	F.	M.	F.	M.	F.
1	2	3	4	5	6	7	8	9	10	11	12	13	14	15
Population	*Ajmer City*	*86,222*	*47,354*	*38,868*	*13,859*	*13,442*	*23,082*	*17,698*	*10,413*	*8,728*	*32,674*	*6,553*	*14,680*	*32,015*
Total Immigrants.	**All castes**	**40,694**	**22,604**	**18,090**	**4,205**	**3,534**	**13,599**	**10,715**	**4,800**	**3,841**	**10,688**	**1,505**	**2,690**	**9,133**
	Brahman	4,588	2,587	2,001	491	386	1,581	1,180	515	435	2,062	189	525	1,812
	Kayastha	762	344	418	92	96	177	234	75	88	214	7	130	411
	Koli	3,124	1,631	1,493	257	299	1,122	967	252	207	1,382	238	249	1,255
	Mahajan	2,475	1,175	1,300	273	210	649	755	253	335	911	155	264	1,145
	Christian (Indian)	742	471	271	100	64	300	160	71	47	340	45	131	226
	Christian (Others)	1,057	608	449	131	131	365	223	112	95	460	47	148	402
	Pathan	3,184	1,907	1,277	340	241	1,115	767	452	269	1,543	181	364	1,096
	Rajput	1,263	907	356	170	75	597	213	140	68	716	65	191	291
	Saiyad	916	583	333	107	67	343	199	133	67	467	69	110	284
	Shekh	5,905	3,165	2,740	621	579	1,842	1,606	702	555	2,593	509	572	2,231
	Others	16,678	9,226	7,452	1,623	1,386	5,508	4,391	2,095	1,075				
I.—Countries in India.	**Total**	40,307	22,317	17,990	2,564	2,128	7,945	6,276	2,662	2,143	10,508	1,480	2,663	9,067
Ajmer-Merwara.														
Merwara	**Total**	1,804	1,147	657	27	28	63	78	10	23	83	18	26	111
	Brahman	23	12	11	3	1	6	7	3	3	8	..	4	11
	Kayastha	9	6	3	4	..	2	1	..	2	2	..	4	3
	Koli	12	7	5	1	1	3	2	3	2	5	..	2	5
	Mahajan	49	21	28	10	6	10	19	1	3	15	1	6	27
	Christian (Indian)	30	6	24	2	4	2	16	2	4	5	11	1	13
	Christian (Others)	3	1	2	..	..	..	2	1	..	1	..	..	2
	Pathan	27	13	14	2	1	10	9	1	4	12	3	1	11
	Rajput	6	6	..	..	..	6	..	..	..	4	..	2	..
	Saiyad	3	1	2	..	1	1	1	..	..	1	1	..	1
	Shekh	76	36	40	5	14	23	21	8	5	30	2	6	38
	Others	1,566	1,038	528									FIGURES NOT AVAILABLE.	

Selected Occupations (and group number in Table XV-A) of actual workers.

Birthplace.	Caste.	2.—Ordinary cultivators (rent-payers).		78.—Stone and marble workers, masons and brick-layers.		89.—Workers in precious stones and metals, enamellers, imitation jewelry makers, gilders, etc.		103.—Railway employés of all kinds other than construction coolies.		106.—Bank managers, money lenders, exchange and insurance agents, money changers, and brokers in shares and stocks, and their employés.		149.—Religious mendicants, inmates of monasteries, etc.		161.—Proprietors (other than of agricultural land), holders of funds, investments and scholarships, and pensioners.		162.—Cooks, water carriers, door-keepers, watchmen, and other indoor servants.		169.—Beggars, vagrants, procurers, prostitutes, receivers of stolen goods, cattle poisoners.	
		M.	F.	M.	F.	M.	F.	M.	F.	M.	F.	M.	F.	M.	F.	M.	F.	M.	F.
1	2	16	17	18	19	20	21	22	23	24	25	26	27	28	29	30	31	32	33
Population	*Ajmer City*	*863*	*230*	*1,278*	*388*	*1,216*	*562*	*10,108*	*107*	*433*	*39*	*563*	*219*	*294*	*141*	*2,096*	*771*	*634*	*245*
Total Immigrants.	**All castes**	**99**	**12**	**168**	**23**	**420**	**138**	**4,922**	**60**	**106**	**8**	**157**	**22**	**124**	**57**	**1,034**	**305**	**186**	**74**
	Brahman	14	2	20	1	16	..	1,138	5	20	..	140	22	54	11	232	95	..	..
	Kayastha	5	3	..	..	..	..	81	1	1	1	..	..	7	1	6	..	..	..
	Koli	..	..	4	6	..	..	1,195	16	..	..	..	..	..	..	48	38	10	8
	Mahajan	4	..	..	..	53	7	156	9	63	3	2	..	15	21	57	16	1	..
	Christian (Indian)	..	..	..	..	..	..	205	..	..	..	..	..	4	4	43	6	..	1
	Christian (Others)	..	..	..	..	..	..	328	..	..	..	..	..	18	12	7	2	..	..
	Pathan	13	2	54	2	129	32	531	10	5	..	7	..	11	3	176	30	36	9
	Rajput	33	2	10	3	3	1	261	5	1	..	..	..	4	1	124	18	4	2
	Saiyad	6	..	13	3	53	16	127	7	1	..	6	..	3	..	42	12	36	2
	Shekh	24	3	58	8	166	82	900	7	17	4	2	..	8	4	299	88	90	52
	Others			FIGURES NOT AVAILABLE.															
I.—Countries in India.	**Total**	97	12	168	23	419	138	4,831	60	106	8	157	22	114	51	1,032	305	185	74
Ajmer-Merwara.																			
Merwara	**Total**	2	..	2	..	2	1	29	..	..	..	..	..	4	1	4	3	3	2
	Brahman	..	..	..	..	..	..	2	..	..	..	..	..	1	..	2	..	..	..
	Kayastha	..	..	..	..	..	..	1	..	..	..	..	..	..	..	..	..	..	..
	Koli	..	..	..	..	..	..	5	..	..	..	..	..	..	..	..	..	..	..
	Mahajan	..	..	..	..	2	..	..	..	..	..	..	..	1	..	1	..	..	..
	Christian (Indian)	..	..	..	..	..	..	4	..	..	..	..	..	..	..	..	3	..	..
	Christian (Others)	..	..	..	..	..	..	1	..	..	..	..	..	..	..	..	..	..	..
	Pathan	1	..	..	..	..	..	5	..	..	..	..	..	1	1	..	..	1	1
	Rajput	1	..	..	..	..	..	2	..	..	..	..	..	..	..	..	..	..	..
	Saiyad	..	..	..	..	..	1	1	..	..	..	..	..	..	..	..	..	..	..
	Shekh	..	..	2	..	..	..	8	..	..	..	..	..	1	..	1	..	2	1
	Others																		

TABLE XIX.—Immigration by Age, and Selected Birthplaces, Castes and Occupations. (Ajmer City)—*continued.*

Birthplace.	Caste.	Total number of immigrants.			Age-Periods. 0—14.		15—39.		40 and over.		All Occupations. Workers.		Dependants.		Selected Occupations (and group number in Table XV-A) of actual workers. 2.—Ordinary cultivators (rent-payers).		78.—Stone and marble workers, masons and brick-layers.		89.—Workers in precious stones and metals, enamellers, imitation jewelry makers, gilders, etc.		103.—Railway employés of all kinds other than construction coolies.		106.—Bank managers, money lenders, exchange and insurance agents, money changers, and brokers in shares and stocks, and their employés.		149.—Religious mendicants, inmates of monasteries, etc.		161.—Proprietors (other than of agricultural land), holders of funds, investments and scholarships, and pensioners.		162.—Cooks, water carriers, door-keepers, watchmen and other indoor servants.		169.—Beggars, vagrants, procurers, prostitutes, receivers of stolen goods, and cattle poisoners.	
		P.	M.	F.	M.	F.	M.	F.	M.	F.	M.	F.	M.	F.	M.	F.	M.	F.	M.	F.	M.	F.	M.	F.	M.	F.	M.	F.	M.	F.	M.	F.
1	2	3	4	5	6	7	8	9	10	11	12	13	14	15	16	17	18	19	20	21	22	23	24	25	26	27	28	29	30	31	32	33
Rajputana .	Total .	22,360	11,904	10,456	1,224	1,029	4,062	3,492	1,130	1,182	5,177	958	1,239	4,745	54	4	127	15	177	69	1,960	29	80	6	82	15	60	32	581	175	73	44
Jaipur . .	*Total* .	*9,151*	*4,934*	*4,917*	*512*	*493*	*1,861*	*1,483*	*407*	*391*	*2,373*	*435*	*507*	*1,039*	*17*	*1*	*36*	*3*	*77*	*34*	*1,154*	*14*	*26*	..	*39*	*8*	*5*	*6*	*192*	*65*	*37*	*38*
	Brahman . .	591	322	269	71	49	206	171	45	49	255	55	67	214	3	..	2	..	..	..	91	..	5	..	32	8	..	1	64	29	..	..
	Kayastha . .	127	55	72	21	23	26	40	8	9	25	1	30	71	..	..	..	..	..	..	..	..	..	..	..	..	1	1	1	..	..	..
	Koli . .	2,005	1,063	942	181	196	759	642	123	104	910	182	153	760	..	..	2	3	..	..	823	11	..	..	..	..	..	..	15	16	9	8
	Mahajan . .	552	291	261	40	37	193	153	58	71	237	87	54	224	..	..	..	..	7	3	18	..	18	..	..	..	4	4	7	4	..	..
	Christian (Indians)	59	35	24	13	5	17	16	5	3	12	3	23	21	..	..	..	..	..	..	9	..	..	..	..	..	..	..	1	1	..	..
	Christian (Others)	34	18	16	5	7	13	8	..	1	11	1	7	15	..	..	..	..	..	..	10	..	..	..	..	..	..	..	..	..	..	..
	Pathan . .	558	324	234	73	46	197	144	54	44	257	18	67	216	1	..	22	..	35	5	76	..	..	..	7	..	..	..	11	1	1	..
	Rajput . .	247	183	64	23	20	140	30	20	14	153	9	30	65	12	1	4	..	2	1	49	..	..	..	..	..	..	..	27	3	..	..
	Saiyad . .	77	45	32	9	5	28	22	8	5	39	9	6	23	..	..	..	..	5	1	8	..	1	..	..	..	..	..	6	..	3	..
	Shekh . .	897	444	453	76	105	282	257	86	91	374	120	70	333	1	..	6	..	23	24	70	3	..	..	..	..	..	..	60	11	14	15
	Othe s . .	4,004	2,154	1,850									FIGURES	NOT AV	AILA	BLE.																
Marwar .	*Total* .	*5,309*	*2,634*	*2,668*	*276*	*188*	*616*	*771*	*239*	*319*	*852*	*196*	*272*	*1,083*	*9*	..	*47*	*4*	*51*	*9*	*97*	..	*29*	*9*	*16*	*5*	*10*	*9*	*139*	*41*	*13*	*10*
	Brahman . .	500	221	279	45	39	139	160	37	80	176	45	45	234	2	..	22	1	7	..	3	..	7	..	15	5	2	..	59	28	..	..
	Kayastha . .	131	43	88	12	24	22	41	9	23	32	..	11	88	..	..	..	..	..	..	8	..	..	..	..	..	3	..	..	..	..	..
	Koli . .	40	22	18	8	5	9	10	5	3	14	1	8	17	..	..	..	..	..	..	9	..	..	..	..	..	..	..	1	1	..	..
	Mahajan . .	542	216	326	65	45	98	191	58	90	154	39	62	287	1	..	..	..	22	2	6	..	22	2	1	..	4	4	10	4	..	..
	Christian (Indians)	21	10	11	1	3	8	4	1	4	9	2	1	9	..	..	..	..	..	..	6	..	..	..	..	..	..	..	1	..	..	..
	Christian (Others)	19	8	11	5	6	2	3	1	..	1	..	7	11	..	..	..	..	..	..	..	..	..	..	..	..	..	..	..	..	..	..
	Pathan . .	159	72	87	12	6	44	64	16	17	59	9	13	78	..	..	..	..	3	..	13	..	..	..	..	..	..	2	9	..	1	3
	Rajput . .	297	206	91	45	14	120	57	41	20	160	26	46	65	4	..	5	5	..	..	19	..	..	..	..	..	..	1	45	3	4	2
	Saiyad . .	68	30	38	8	6	16	25	6	7	23	18	7	25	..	..	..	..	..	..	5	..	..	..	..	..	..	..	1	1	1	..
	Shekh . .	625	296	329	75	38	158	216	63	75	224	61	72	268	2	..	30	..	19	7	28	..	..	..	..	..	1	2	6	4	7	5
	Others . .	2,900	1,510	1,390									FIGURES	NOT AV	AILA	BLE.																

TABLE XIX.

TABLE XIX.—Immigration by Age, and Selected Birthplaces, Castes, and Occupations. (Ajmer City)—*continued.*

Birthplace.	Caste.	Total number of immigrants.			Age-periods. 0—14.		15—39.		40 and over.		All Occupations. Workers.		Dependants.	
		P.	M.	F.	M.	F.	M.	F.	M.	F.	M.	F.	M.	F.
1	2	3	4	5	6	7	8	9	10	11	12	13	14	15
Other States	*Total*	*7,907*	*4,336*	*3,571*	*436*	*348*	*1,585*	*1,938*	*491*	*472*	*2,052*	*337*	*460*	*1,731*
	Brahman	693	428	265	62	37	283	157	83	71	365	41	83	224
	Kayastha	117	43	74	10	14	29	48	4	12	28	..	15	74
	Koli	629	340	289	37	45	225	191	78	53	292	29	48	260
	Mahajan	616	256	359	41	54	152	196	63	109	210	50	46	309
	Christian (Indians)	155	107	48	26	6	77	42	4	..	80	13	27	35
	Christian (Others)	32	19	13	9	9	10	2	..	2	6	2	13	11
	Pathan	773	449	324	82	59	279	184	88	81	371	57	78	307
	Rajput	298	228	70	49	13	118	47	31	10	174	14	54	56
	Saiyad	136	77	59	14	13	46	32	17	14	63	6	14	53
	Shekh	1,122	565	557	106	98	336	330	123	120	463	115	102	442
	Others	3,337	1,324	1,513									Figures	not available.
Bombay Presidency,	Total	1,105	668	497	106	92	260	166	80	52	333	32	119	278
	Brahman	241	141	100	32	31	72	51	37	18	98	8	43	92
	Kayastha	24	14	10	4	3	8	5	2	2	7	1	7	9
	Koli	12	1	11	..	2	1	6	..	3	1	1	..	10
	Mahajan	70	42	28	8	9	29	12	5	7	32	5	10	23
	Christian (Indians)	41	24	17	4	8	17	7	3	2	19	3	5	14
	Christian (Others)	137	91	46	26	12	52	28	13	6	66	3	25	43
	Pathan	56	26	30	5	9	14	16	7	5	21	2	5	28
	Rajput	29	18	11	5	3	10	4	3	4	11	2	7	9
	Saiyad	26	21	5	4	..	15	4	2	1	20	..	1	5
	Shekh	126	74	52	18	15	42	33	14	4	58	7	16	45
	Others	403	216	187									Figures	not available.

Selected Occupations (and group number in Table XV-A) of actual workers.

Birthplace.	Caste.	2.—Ordinary cultivators (rent-payers).		78.—Stone and marble workers, masons and brick-layers.		89.—Workers in precious stones and metals, enamellers, imitation jewelry makers, gilders, etc.		103.—Railway employés of all kinds other than construction coolies.		106.—Bank managers, money lenders, exchange and insurance agents, money changers, and brokers in shares and stocks, and their employés.		149.—Religious mendicants, inmates of monasteries, etc.		151.—Proprietors (other than of agricultural land), holders of funds, investments and scholarships, and pensioners.		162.—Cooks, water carriers, door-keepers, watchmen, and other indoor servants.		169.—Beggars, vagrants, procurers, prostitutes, receivers of stolen goods, and cattle poisoners.	
		M.	F.	M.	F.	M.	F.	M.	F.	M.	F.	M.	F.	M.	F.	M.	F.	M.	F.
1	2	16	17	18	19	20	21	22	23	24	25	26	27	28	29	30	31	32	33
Other States	*Total*	*28*	*3*	*44*	*8*	*49*	*36*	*729*	*15*	*27*	*4*	*27*	*9*	*45*	*17*	*257*	*69*	*33*	*11*
	Brahman	5	1	5	..	4	..	132	1	3	..	27	2	33	7	59	15	..	..
	Kayastha	..	..	..	..	..	..	11	..	..	..	..	..	..	..	..	..	..	..
	Koli	..	..	1	3	..	..	245	5	..	..	..	..	..	..	7	6	1	..
	Mahajan	2	..	..	..	18	2	20	1	15	..	..	..	3	10	21	5	..	..
	Christian (Indians)	..	..	..	..	..	..	32	..	..	..	..	..	..	..	7	..	..	..
	Christian (Others)	..	..	..	..	..	..	6	..	..	..	..	..	..	..	..	..	..	..
	Pathan	1	..	14	1	6	8	112	3	1	..	..	..	4	..	56	12	5	2
	Rajput	11	1	1	..	..	..	40	3	1	..	..	..	3	..	34	6	..	..
	Saiyad	1	..	1	..	6	2	16	..	..	..	..	..	..	..	5	..	6	2
	Shekh	8	1	22	4	15	14	115	2	7	4	..	..	2	..	88	25	21	7
	Others	Figures not available.																	
Bombay Presidency,	Total	4	..	1	1	4	..	174	2	3	..	4	1	8	4	24	9	8	2
	Brahman	..	..	..	..	1	..	67	1	..	..	3	1	3	2	3	4	..	..
	Kayastha	..	..	..	..	..	..	5	1	..	..	..	..	..	..	..	..	..	..
	Koli	..	..	..	..	..	..	1	..	..	..	..	..	..	..	..	1	..	..
	Mahajan	..	..	..	..	2	..	4	..	2	..	..	..	1	1	4	..	..	..
	Christian (Indians)	..	..	..	..	..	..	11	..	..	..	..	..	1	..	3	..	..	..
	Christian (Others)	..	..	..	..	..	..	52	..	..	..	..	..	1	1	1	..	..	..
	Pathan	..	..	1	..	..	..	9	..	1	..	..	..	1	..	2	2	..	..
	Rajput	2	..	..	..	..	..	2	..	..	..	..	..	..	..	2	2	..	..
	Saiyad	..	..	..	..	1	..	2	..	..	..	..	..	..	..	1	..	2	..
	Shekh	2	..	..	1	..	..	21	..	..	..	1	..	1	..	8	..	6	2
	Others	Figures not available.																	

TABLE XIX.—IMMIGRATION BY AGE, AND SELECTED BIRTHPLACES, CASTES, AND OCCUPATIONS (AJMER CITY)—*continued.*

Birthplace.	Caste.	Total number of immigrants.			Age-periods.						All Occupations.				Selected Occupations (and group number in Table XV-A) of actual workers.																	
					0—14.		15—39.		40 and over.		Workers.		Dependants.		2.—Ordinary cultivators (rent-payers).		73.—Stone and marble workers, masons and brick-layers.		69.—Workers in precious stones and metals, enamellers, imitation jewelry makers, gilders, etc.		103.—Railway employés of all kinds other than construction coolies.		106.—Bank managers, money lenders, exchange and insurance agents, money changers, and brokers in shares and stocks, and their employés.		149.—Religious mendicants, inmates of monasteries, etc.		151.—Proprietors (other than of agricultural land), holders of funds, investments and scholarships, and pensioners.		162.—Cooks, water carriers, door-keepers, watchmen, and other indoor servants.		169.—Beggars, vagrants, procurers, prostitutes, receivers of stolen goods, and cattle poisoners.	
		P.	M.	F.	M.	F.	M.	F.	M.	F.	M.	F.	M.	F.	M.	F.	M.	F.	M.	F.	M.	F.	M.	F.	M.	F.	M.	F.	M.	F.	M.	F.
1	2	3	4	5	6	7	8	9	10	11	12	13	14	15	16	17	18	19	20	21	22	23	24	25	26	27	28	29	30	31	32	33
Central India	Total .	1,265	638	627	109	84	286	237	69	61	325	65	139	317	5*	..	5	..	6	3	127	1	1	1	3	1	3	..	32	21	6	10
	Brahman . .	129	72	57	23	18	45	33	4	6	41	7	31	50	..	..	..	..	..	..	14	..	..	..	3	1	2	..	5	6	..	..
	Kayastha . .	20	9	11	2	1	6	7	1	3	6	..	3	11	..	..	..	..	..	..	1	..	..	..	..	..	..	..	..	..	..	..
	Koli . .	18	7	11	1	4	4	6	2	1	6	3	1	8	..	..	1	..	..	..	3	..	..	..	..	..	..	..	1	1	..	..
	Mahajan . .	101	43	58	12	13	24	36	7	9	26	3	17	55	..	..	..	..	1	..	5	..	1	1	..	..	..	..	2	1	..	..
	Christian (Ind ans)	47	28	19	12	7	14	11	2	1	13	..	15	19	..	..	..	..	..	..	11	..	..	..	..	..	1	..	..	..	..	..
	Christian (Others)	35	22	13	6	4	15	7	1	2	16	1	6	12	..	..	..	..	..	..	15	..	..	..	..	..	..	..	..	3	3	2
	Pathan . .	109	63	46	8	10	40	31	15	5	51	8	12	38	1	..	1	..	1	..	14	..	..	..	..	..	..	..	9	2	..	..
	Rajput . .	53	44	9	7	1	30	6	7	2	31	4	13	5	..	..	..	..	..	..	21	1	..	..	..	..	..	..	4	..	..	..
	Saiyad . .	51	33	18	5	2	21	15	7	1	22	1	11	17	2	..	1	..	..	..	9	..	..	..	..	..	..	..	..	..	2	..
	Shekh . .	283	143	140	33	24	87	85	23	31	113	38	30	102	2	..	2	..	4	3	34	..	..	..	..	..	..	..	11	8	1	8
	Others . .	419	174	245	FIGURES NOT AVAILABLE.																											
Panjab .	Total .	2,009	1,240	769	151	120	508	269	197	102	691	79	160	412	13	4	5	..	137	29	224	3	5	1	14	1	7	3	45	20	24	1
	Brahman . .	201	120	81	26	20	69	44	25	17	98	7	22	74	..	1	..	..	1	..	32	..	3	..	14	1	3	..	11	5	..	..
	Kayastha . .	61	27	34	8	10	11	14	8	10	14	1	13	33	1	..	..	..	..	..	9	..	..	1	..	..	1	..	1	..	..	..
	Koli . .	8	3	5	1	1	2	4	..	..	2	..	1	5	..	..	..	..	..	..	..	..	..	..	..	..	..	..	..	..	..	..
	Mahajan . .	72	47	25	13	5	22	17	12	3	35	1	12	24	..	..	..	..	..	..	15	..	2	..	..	..	1	1	..	..	1	..
	Christian (Ind ans)	45	28	17	5	6	21	7	2	4	23	3	5	14	..	..	..	..	..	..	19	..	..	..	..	..	..	1	..	..	..	..
	Christian (Others)	71	35	36	12	12	17	15	6	9	25	5	10	31	..	..	..	..	..	..	16	..	..	..	..	..	..	1	1	2	..	..
	Pathan . .	293	198	95	33	16	121	62	44	17	162	18	36	77	4	2	1	..	47	9	43	2	..	..	..	..	1	..	8	1	6	..
	Rajput . .	43	33	10	4	3	25	2	4	5	29	1	4	9	2	..	..	..	1	..	14	..	..	..	..	..	..	..	3	..	..	..
	Saiyad . .	132	87	45	9	9	59	31	19	5	75	12	12	33	1	..	..	..	38	11	19	1	..	..	..	..	1	..	1	..	2	..
	Shekh . .	416	273	143	40	38	156	73	77	32	228	31	45	112	5	1	4	..	50	9	57	..	..	..	..	..	..	..	20	12	15	1
	Others . .	667	389	278	FIGURES NOT AVAILABLE.																											

TABLE XIX.—IMMIGRATION BY AGE, AND SELECTED BIRTHPLACES, CASTES, AND OCCUPATIONS (AJMER CITY)—*continued.*

Birthplace.	Caste.	Total number of immigrants.			AGE-PERIODS.						ALL OCCUPATIONS.				SELECTED OCCUPATIONS (AND GROUP NUMBER IN TABLE XV-A) OF ACTUAL WORKERS.																	
					0—14.		15—39.		40 and over.		Workers.		Dependants.		2.—Ordinary cultivators (rent-payers).		78.—Stone and marble workers, masons and brick-layers.		89.—Workers in precious stones and metals, enamellers, imitation jewelry makers, gilders, etc.		108.—Railway employés of all kinds other than construction coolies.		106.—Bank managers, money lenders, exchange and insurance agents, money changers, and brokers in shares and stocks and their employés.		149.—Religious mendicants, inmates of monasteries, etc.		161.—Proprietors (other than of agricultural land), holders of funds, investments and scholarships, and pensioners.		162.—Cooks, water carriers, door-keepers, watchmen and other indoor servants.		169.—Beggars, vagrants, procurers, prostitutes, receivers of stolen goods, and cattle poisoners.	
		P.	M.	F.	M.	F.	M.	F.	M.	F.	M.	F.	M.	F.	M.	F.	M.	F.	M.	F.	M.	F.	M.	F.	M.	F.	M.	F.	M.	F.	M.	F.
1	2	3	4	5	6	7	8	9	10	11	12	13	14	15	16	17	18	19	20	21	22	23	24	25	26	27	28	29	30	31	32	33
United Provinces.	Total	10,339	5,895	4,444	832	661	2,364	1,806	1,006	621	3,374	261	838	2,827	16	1	27	6	90	36	3,025	19	13	..	48	3	18	7	287	61	55	8
	Brahman	2,060	1,184	876	210	180	714	519	260	177	958	20	226	856	4	..	..	..	2	..	776	3	2	..	40	3	6	1	22	6	..	..
	Kayastha	232	132	100	26	16	67	86	39	18	91	..	41	100	4	..	..	..	..	..	41	..	..	..	..	..	2	..	3	..	..	..
	Koli	386	183	203	28	43	114	120	41	40	147	21	36	183	..	..	..	..	..	..	104	..	..	..	..	..	..	..	24	13	..	..
	Mahajan	413	229	184	78	32	103	112	48	40	177	16	52	168	1	..	..	..	..	..	87	3	1	..	1	..	..	1	8	..	..	..
	Christian (Indians)	108	63	45	15	10	36	22	12	13	44	6	19	39	..	..	..	..	..	..	23	..	..	..	..	..	1	2	5	..	..	..
	Christian (Others)	163	76	87	23	21	35	41	18	25	50	5	28	82	..	..	..	..	..	..	40	..	..	..	..	..	..	2	1	..	..	..
	Pathan	1,070	659	411	115	84	339	240	205	87	540	58	119	353	..	..	14	1	36	10	239	1	2	..	..	..	4	..	74	9	13	1
	Rajput	262	172	90	30	14	110	64	32	12	140	3	32	87	1	..	..	..	..	..	111	1	..	..	..	..	1	..	9	2	..	..
	Saiyad	373	246	126	52	30	129	65	65	31	186	23	60	103	2	..	11	3	2	1	53	4	..	..	6	..	2	..	27	10	16	..
	Shekh	2,224	1,258	966	255	231	717	557	286	178	1,041	100	217	857	4	1	2	2	50	25	546	2	8	..	1	..	2	1	114	21	26	7
	Others	3,049	1,693	1,356							FIGURES NOT AVAILABLE																					
Other Provinces and States of India.	Total	1,365	825	540	115	114	407	228	155	102	525	67	152	377	3	3	1	1	3	..	272	6	4	..	6	1	14	4	59	16	16	7
	Brahman	150	87	63	19	11	47	38	21	14	63	6	24	57	..	..	..	..	1	..	21	..	..	..	6	1	4	..	7	2	..	..
	Kayastha	41	15	26	5	5	6	12	4	9	9	4	6	22	..	2	..	..	..	..	5	..	1	..	..	..	..	..	1	..	..	..
	Koli	14	5	9	..	2	5	6	..	1	5	1	..	8	..	..	..	..	..	..	5	..	..	..	..	..	..	..	..	..	..	..
	Mahajan	61	30	31	6	9	18	19	6	3	25	3	5	28	..	..	..	..	1	..	1	..	2	..	..	..	1	..	4	2	..	..
	Christian (Indians)	235	170	65	22	15	108	34	40	16	135	4	35	61	..	..	..	..	..	..	85	..	..	..	..	..	1	1	26	2	..	1
	Christian (Others)	313	177	136	33	39	106	70	38	27	136	5	41	131	..	..	..	..	..	..	101	..	..	..	..	..	7	2	4	..	..	..
	Pathan	114	78	36	10	10	50	17	18	9	53	8	25	28	3	..	1	..	1	..	20	4	1	..	..	..	..	..	7	2	6	..
	Rajput	28	17	11	7	7	8	3	2	1	14	6	3	5	..	..	..	..	..	..	3	..	..	..	..	..	..	..	..	..	..	..
	Saiyad	41	33	8	1	1	23	4	9	3	32	4	1	4	..	..	..	..	..	..	12	2	..	..	..	..	..	..	1	1	4	..
	Shekh	124	65	59	12	15	36	25	17	19	53	26	12	33	..	..	..	1	..	..	19	..	..	..	..	..	1	1	8	7	6	6
	Others	244	148	96							FIGURES NOT AVAILABLE																					

TABLE XIX.—Immigration by Age, and Selected Birthplaces, Castes, and Occupations (Ajmer City)—*concluded*.

Birthplace.	Caste.	Total number of immigrants.			Age-periods.						All Occupations.				Selected Occupations (and group number in Table XV-A) of actual workers.																	
					0—14		15—39.		40 and over.		Workers.		Dependants.		2.—Ordinary cultivators (rent-payers).		78.—Stone and marble workers, masons and brick-layers.		89.—Workers in precious stones and metals, enamellers, imitation jewelry makers, gilders, etc.		103.—Railway employés of all kinds other than construction coolies.		106.—Bank managers, money lenders, exchange and insurance agents, money changers, and brokers in shares and stocks, and their employés.		149.—Religious mendicants, inmates of monasteries, etc.		151.—Proprietors (other than of agricultural land), holders of funds, investments and scholarships, and pensioners.		162.—Cooks, water carriers, door keepers, watchmen, and other indoor servants.		169.—Beggars, vagrants, procurers, prostitutes, receivers of stolen goods, and cattle poisoners.	
		P.	M.	F.	M.	F.	M.	F.	M.	F.	M.	F.	M.	F.	M.	F.	M.	F.	M.	F.	M.	F.	M.	F.	M.	F.	M.	F.	M.	F.	M.	F.
1	2	3	4	5	6	7	8	9	10	11	12	13	14	15	16	17	18	19	20	21	22	23	24	25	26	27	28	29	30	31	32	33
II.—Asiatic Countries Outside India.	Total	139	127	·12	3	1	33	2	11	..	37	..	10	3	2	..	..	..	1	..	3	..	2	..	..	..	..	..	2	..	1	..
	Brahman	..	..	..	..	..	..	..	..	..	..	..	..	..	..	..	..	..	..	..	..	..	..	..	..	..	..	..	..	..	..	..
	Kayastha	..	..	..	..	..	..	..	..	..	..	..	..	..	..	..	..	..	..	..	..	..	..	..	..	..	..	..	..	..	..	..
	Koli	..	..	..	..	..	..	..	..	..	..	..	..	..	..	..	..	..	..	..	..	..	..	..	..	..	..	..	..	..	..	..
	Mahajan	..	..	..	..	..	..	..	..	..	..	..	..	..	..	..	..	..	..	..	..	..	..	..	..	..	..	..	..	..	..	..
	Christian (Indians)	..	..	..	..	..	..	..	..	..	..	..	..	..	..	..	..	..	..	..	..	..	..	..	..	..	..	..	..	..	..	..
	Christian (Others)	8	5	3	..	1	3	2	2	..	5	..	..	3	..	..	..	..	..	..	4	..	..	..	..	..	..	..	..	..	..	..
	Pathan	25	25	..	..	..	21	..	4	..	17	..	8	..	2	..	..	..	..	..	..	..	..	..	..	..	..	..	..	..	..	..
	Rajput	..	..	..	..	..	..	..	..	..	..	..	..	..	..	..	..	..	..	..	..	..	..	..	..	..	..	..	..	..	..	..
	Saiyad	8	8	..	3	..	5	..	..	..	6	..	2	..	..	..	..	..	1	..	2	..	..	..	..	..	..	..	..	..	..	..
	Shekh	9	9	..	..	..	4	..	5	..	9	..	..	..	..	..	..	..	..	..	2	..	2	..	..	..	..	..	2	..	1	..
	Others	89	80	9									Figures not available																			
III.—Non-Asiatic Countries.	Total	248	160	86	15	19	113	46	32	23	143	25	17	63	..	..	..	..	..	..	83	..	..	..	..	..	10	6	..	..	..	..
	Brahman	..	..	..	..	..	..	..	..	..	..	..	..	..	..	..	..	..	..	..	..	..	..	..	..	..	..	..	..	..	..	..
	Kayastha	..	..	..	..	..	..	..	..	..	..	..	..	..	..	..	..	..	..	..	..	..	..	..	..	..	..	..	..	..	..	..
	Koli	..	..	..	..	..	..	..	..	..	..	..	..	..	..	..	..	..	..	..	..	..	..	..	..	..	..	..	..	..	..	..
	Mahajan	..	..	..	..	..	..	..	..	..	..	..	..	..	..	..	..	..	..	..	..	..	..	..	..	..	..	..	..	..	..	..
	Christian (Indians)	1	..	1	..	..	..	1	..	..	..	..	..	1	..	..	..	..	..	..	..	..	..	..	..	..	..	..	..	..	..	..
	Christian (Others)	242	156	86	12	18	112	45	32	23	143	25	13	61	..	..	..	..	..	..	83	..	..	..	..	..	10	6	..	..	..	..
	Pathan	..	..	..	..	..	..	..	..	..	..	..	..	..	..	..	..	..	..	..	..	..	..	..	..	..	..	..	..	..	..	..
	Rajput	..	..	..	..	..	..	..	..	..	..	..	..	..	..	..	..	..	..	..	..	..	..	..	..	..	..	..	..	..	..	..
	Saiyad	2	2	..	2	..	..	..	..	..	..	..	2	..	..	..	..	..	..	..	..	..	..	..	..	..	..	..	..	..	..	..
	Shekh	3	2	1	1	1	1	..	..	..	..	..	2	1	..	..	..	..	..	..	..	..	..	..	..	..	..	..	..	..	..	..
	Others	..	..	..	..	..	..	..	..	..	..	..	..	..	..	..	..	..	..	..	..	..	..	..	..	..	..	..	..	..	..	..

PROVINCIAL TABLE I.

Area, Houses, and Population of Administrative Units.

Explanatory Note.

The two Provincial Tables in this volume give statistics for the various administrative units in the States and Districts, *e.g.*, for Tahsils, Nizamats, Parganas, Towns, or whatever the local unit may be called.

This Table shows for each such unit its area, number of towns and villages and of houses in rural and urban areas, population (urban and rural) of 1911, density of population per square mile, population of 1901, and percentage of variation for 1891-1901 and 1901-1911.

The units have been arranged so far as possible in alphabetical order, except that the capitals of States and Districts have been printed first in each case, and towns whose areas are shown as included in that of some Pargana, etc., have been printed immediately next to such Pargana.

Many of the units have been completely changed since 1901. The figures in columns 14 to 16, therefore, will not always agree with those in the Tables of previous censuses. In some such cases, owing to the impossibility of adjusting the population, these columns have been left blank.

In some cases towns have been taken out of the Parganas, etc., in which they were included in the 1901 Tables, and are shown separately.

Very many of the areas given in column 3 for the administrative units are merely approximate, being based on the rough revenue records of the States.

Compared with the Imperial Tables differences will be found in this Table—

(1) in the areas of Rajputana, Alwar, Dholpur, Jaipur, Karauli, Marwar, Tonk, Ajmer-Merwara, Ajmer, and Merwara, owing to the Imperial Table figures being based on the Imperial Survey, and those in this Table on the latest revenue records;

(2) in all the figures (except urban) for (*a*) Rajputana, Marwar, Mewar, Ajmer-Merwara, and Merwara, owing to the inclusion in this Table, in the 1911 figures for Rajputana, Marwar, and Mewar, of the villages belonging to these States which are situated in Merwara; (*b*) Rajputana, Dholpur, and Mewar, through the inclusion of Nimrol village (shown in the Central India Imperial Tables) in Dholpur, and the exclusion from Mewar of the Parganas * of Nandwas of Indore and Gangapur of Gwalior (shown in the Central India Provincial Tables). The figures for Nimrol appear to have been omitted from the Provincial Tables of 1901, and the village is said to have escaped the census of 1891 altogether;

(3) in the 1901 figures for Alwar and Kotah Cities, as this Table gives the adjusted figures.

* For details of these Parganas see foot-note to Imperial Table I.

PROVINCIAL TABLE I.—AREA, HOUSES, AND POPULATION OF ADMINISTRATIVE UNITS.

State or District.	Administrative Unit (Pargana, Tahsil, Town, etc.)	Approximate area in square miles.	Inhabited towns.	Inhabited villages.	Occupied houses in Towns.	Occupied houses in Villages.	Population 1911. Persons in Towns.	Persons in Villages.	Males in Towns.	Males in Villages.	Females in Towns.	Females in Villages.	Population 1901 both sexes.	Percentage of variation 1901-1911.	Percentage of variation 1891-1901.	Number of persons per square mile in 1911.	REMARKS.
1	2	3	4	5	6	7	8	9	10	11	12	13	14	15	16	17	18
	Rajputana	**1,282,616**	**133**	**32,342**	**337,125**	**2,109,916**	**1,343,095**	**9,221,975**	**688,936**	**4,844,912**	**654,159**	**4,377,063**	**9,842,482***	**+ 6·9***	**− 19·1***	**82**	* Excludes Merwara villages belonging to Marwar and Mewar.
Alwar.	*Alwar State*	*3,210*	*7*	*1,765*	*10,380*	*137,114*	*74,604*	*717,084*	*39,185*	*374,474*	*35,419*	*342,610*	*898,487*	*− 4·4*	*+ 7·9†*	*247*	† Includes Railway and European figures for 1891; these are excluded from the figures for units in the 1891 Tables.
	Alwar City	14	1	..	11,407	..	41,305	..	22,254	..	19,051	..	58,113	− 28·9	+ 11·5	2,950	
	Alwar Tahsil	525	..	224	..	10,607	..	90,017	..	46,789	..	43,228	92,448	− 2·6	+ 12·1	171	
	Bahadurpur Town	10	1	..	942	..	4,236	..	2,098	..	2,138	..	4,087	+ 3·6	− 3·9	424	
	Bahror Tahsil	237	..	132	..	14,003	..	67,023	..	34,660	..	32,363	65,542	+ 2·3	+ 2·9	283	
	Bahror Town	6	1	..	1,158	..	5,253	..	2,685	..	2,568	..	5,540	− 5·2	− 3·1	876	
	Bansur Tahsil	338	..	140	..	15,452	..	71,282	..	37,119	..	34,163	72,566	− 1·8	+ 11·3	211	
	Govindgarh Tahsil	46	..	50	..	3,421	..	15,195	..	7,983	..	7,212	15,714	− 3·3	− 4·5	330	
	Govindgarh Town	2	1	..	882	..	3,879	..	1,993	..	1,886	..	4,932	− 21·4	− 5·9	1,040	
	Katumbar Tahsil	143	..	79	..	9,005	..	40,787	..	21,887	..	18,900	41,152	− ·9	+ 5·6	285	
	Kishangarh Tahsil	221	..	158	..	14,510	..	65,213	..	34,123	..	31,090	68,713	− 5·1	+ 11·4	295	
	Lachhmangarh Tahsil	243	..	175	..	13,285	..	63,883	..	33,396	..	30,487	61,727	+ 3·5	+ 2·1	263	
	Mandawar Tahsil	221	..	133	..	14,132	..	65,135	..	34,161	..	30,974	66,214	− 1·6	+ 11·9	295	
	Rajgarh Tahsil	433	..	203	..	16,922	..	76,170	..	39,351	..	36,819	79,108	− 3·7	+ ·6	176	
	Rajgarh Town	6	1	..	2,388	..	9,865	..	4,954	..	4,911	..	11,008	− 10·4	+ 6·9	1,644	
	Ramgarh Tahsil	169	..	118	..	10,903	..	46,047	..	23,894	..	22,153	48,864	− 5·8	+ 14·1	272	
	Ramgarh Town	2	1	..	689	..	3,505	..	1,860	..	1,645	..	5,179	− 32·3	+ 1·6	1,753	
	Thanaghazi Tahsil	309	..	142	..	12,055	..	50,614	..	26,281	..	24,333	51,955	− 2·6	− 4·8	164	
	Tijara Tahsil	255	..	192	..	11,849	..	56,986	..	30,130	..	26,856	59,042	− 3·5	+ 29·7	223	
	Tijara Town	5	1	..	1,614	..	6,561	..	3,341	..	3,220	..	7,784	− 15·7	+ 10·4	1,312	
	Nimrana Thikana	25	..	19	..	1,730	..	8,732	..	4,700	..	4,032	8,799	− ·8	+ 10·9	349	
Banswara.	*Banswara State*	*1,606*	*1*	*1,070*	*2,104*	*35,544*	*7,665*	*157,798*	*3,729*	*77,891*	*3,936*	*79,907*	*149,128*	*+ 11·0*	*− 17·3*	*103*	
	Banswara Town	‡	1	..	2,104	..	7,665	..	3,729	..	3,936	..	7,038	+ 8·9	− 14·5	‡	‡ Details of areas for units not available.
	Khalsa villages		..	392	..	16,087	..	70,483	..	34,666	..	35,817	142,090§	+ 11·1§	− 17·4§		§ Units have been changed since 1901 and no comparison by separate rural units is possible.
	Jagir and other villages		..	678	..	19,457	..	87,315	..	43,225	..	44,090					
Bharatpur.	*Bharatpur State*	*1,982*	*7*	*1,285*	*20,480*	*113,788*	*77,590*	*481,265*	*42,069*	*260,185*	*35,451*	*221,080*	*626,665*	*− 10·8*	*− 2·7‖*	*282*	‖ Includes Railway figures for 1891; these are excluded from the figures for units in the 1891 Tables.
	Bharatpur City	7	1	..	9,319	..	33,918	..	18,803	..	15,115	..	43,601	− 22·2	− 35·5	4,845	
	Bharatpur Tahsil	191·1	..	140	..	10,790	..	44,948	..	24,662	..	20,286	51,408	− 12·6	+ 27·1	235	
	Bhusawar Sub-Tahsil	82·7	..	51	..	5,173	..	22,040	..	11,822	..	10,218	¶	¶	¶	318	¶ Included in Wer Tahsil.
	Bhusawar Town		1	..	1,158	..	4,300	..	2,252	..	2,057	..	6,690	− 35·6	− 9·8		
	Biana Tahsil	311·6	..	156	..	15,044	..	60,830	..	33,010	..	27,820	64,438	− 5·6	− 3·9	218	
	Biana Town		1	..	1,910	..	7,029	..	3,714	..	3,315	..	6,867	+ 2·4	− 15·1		
	Dig Tahsil	195·6	..	107	..	9,624	..	42,030	..	23,214	..	18,816	46,042	− 9·9	− 1·9	282	
	Dig Town		1	..	3,217	..	13,147	..	7,076	..	6,071	..	15,409	− 14·7	+ 1·6		
	Kaman Tahsil	136·1	..	108	..	7,182	..	31,264	..	16,769	..	14,495	36,086	− 13·4	+ 10·5	295	
	Kaman Town		1	..	2,289	..	8,912	..	4,867	..	4,045	..	12,083	− 26·2	+ 5·8		
	Kumher Tahsil	185·0	..	109	..	9,311	..	40,857	..	22,558	..	18,299	46,116	− 11·4	+ 3·6	248	
	Kumher Town		1	..	1,238	..	5,075	..	2,679	..	2,396	..	6,240	− 18·7	− 6·3		
	Nagar Tahsil	181·7	..	156	..	12,018	..	50,358	..	26,678	..	23,680	51,646	− 2·5	+ 1·0	277	
	Nandbai Tahsil**	171·8	..	110	..	11,274	..	50,230	..	27,141	..	23,089	59,433	− 15·5	+ 30·1	292	** Called Akhegarh in 1901.
	Pahari Tahsil	149	..	123	..	10,117	..	41,979	..	22,123	..	19,856	45,911	− 8·6	+ 11·1	282	
	Rupbas Tahsil	150·3	..	92	..	10,072	..	42,325	..	23,029	..	19,296	66,826	− 7·2	− 14·5	282	
	Uchain Sub-Tahsil	64·8	..	42	..	4,867	..	19,481	..	10,443	..	9,038				301	
	Wer Tahsil	155·1	..	91	..	8,366	..	34,923	..	18,736	..	16,187	61,758††	− 7·8††	− 9·7††	256	†† Includes Bhusawar Sub-Tahsil.
	Wer Town		1	..	1,349	..	5,130	..	2,678	..	2,452	..	5,711	− 10·2	− 16·3		

PROVINCIAL TABLE I.—AREA, HOUSES, AND POPULATION OF ADMINISTRATIVE UNITS—*continued*.

State or District.	Administrative Unit (Pargana, Tahsil, Town, etc.)	Approximate area in square miles.	Inhabited towns.	Inhabited villages.	Occupied houses in Towns.	Occupied houses in Villages.	Population 1911. Persons in Towns.	Persons in Villages.	Males in Towns.	Males in Villages.	Females in Towns.	Females in Villages.	1901 both sexes.	Percentage of variation 1901-1911.	Percentage of variation 1891-1901.	Number of persons per square mile in 1911.	Remarks.
1	2	3	4	5	6	7	8	9	10	11	12	13	14	15	16	17	18
Bikaner.	***Bikaner State***	***23,315***	***9***	***2,177***	***28,710***	***124,063***	***127,489***	***573,501***	***63,245***	***308,244***	***64,237***	***265,257***	***584,755****	***+ 19·9****	***— 29·7****	***30***	* Includes villages transferred from Punjab since 1901.
	Bikaner City	4	1	..	13,269	..	55,826	..	28,275	..	27,551	..	53,075	+ 5·2	+ 5·1	13,957	
	Bikaner Nizamat	**9,775**	..	**512**	..	**31,464**	..	**139,975**	..	**74,284**	..	**65,691**	**128,269**	**+ 9·1**	**— 39·2**	**14**	
	Bikaner Tahsil	3,435	..	150	..	9,762	..	42,525	..	22,171	..	20,354	38,925‡	+ 9·2	— 28·2	12	
	Lunkaransar Tahsil	3,115	..	154	..	7,038	..	31,583	..	17,039	..	14,544	29,365‡	+ 7·6	— 47·9	10	
	Magra Sub-Tahsil†	1,613	..	94	..	4,706	..	20,711	..	11,078	..	9,633	16,572	+ 25·0	— 39·0	13	
	Surpura Sub-Tahsil	1,612	..	114	..	9,958	..	45,156	..	23,996	..	21,160	43,407‡	+ 4·0	— 40·4	28	† Formed since 1901 out of Bikaner and Surpura Tahsils.
	Reni Nizamat	**4,757·7**	**4**	**638**	**6,972**	**34,171**	**31,601**	**161,926**	**15,446**	**87,829**	**16,155**	**74,097**	**172,363**	**+ 12·3**	**— 32·1**	**41**	
	Bahadran Tahsil	732·7	..	110	..	7,689	..	36,553	..	19,925	..	16,628	32,065‡	+ 13·9	— 32·8	50	
	Churu Tahsil	647	..	91	..	6,178	..	28,888	..	15,332	..	13,556	24,621‡	+ 17·3	— 32·3	45	
	Churu Town	24	1	..	3,490	..	16,038	..	7,793	..	8,245	..	15,657‡	+ 2·4	+ 11·7	668	
	Nohar Tahsil	1,831	..	172	..	9,538	..	43,499	..	23,748	..	19,751	38,677‡	+ 12·8	— 44·7	24	
	Nohar Town	19	1	..	1,067	..	5,133	..	2,518	..	2,615	..	4,696	+ 9·3	— 16·9	270	
	Rajgarh Tahsil	991	..	188	..	7,980	..	39,438	..	21,463	..	17,975	35,227‡	+ 12·0	— 33·5	40	
	Rajgarh Town	21	1	..	1,082	..	4,526	..	2,262	..	2,264	..	4,136	+ 9·4	— 11·6	216	
	Reni Sub-Tahsil	477	..	77	..	2,796	..	13,548	..	7,361	..	6,187	11,617‡	+ 16·6	— 28·1	28	‡ Figures differ from 1901 owing to changes in boundaries.
	Reni Town	15	1	..	1,304	..	5,904	..	2,873	..	3,031	..	5,745	+ 2·8	— 12·3	394	
	Sujangarh Nizamat.	**3,705**	**3**	**478**	**7,851**	**34,186**	**37,264**	**158,508**	**18,034**	**80,485**	**19,230**	**73,023**	**162,966**	**+ 17·1**	**— 30·2**	**51**	
	Dungargarh Sub-Tahsil	453	..	87	..	7,457	..	32,611	..	16,952	..	15,659	31,000‡	+ 5·2	— 28·9	72	
	Ratangarh Tahsil	346	..	89	..	7,106	..	32,564	..	17,120	..	15,444	25,506‡	+ 27·7	— 30·8	94	
	Ratangarh Town	50	1	..	2,705	..	12,803	..	6,078	..	6,725	..	11,744	+ 9·0	+ 11·5	256	
	Sardarshahar Tahsil	1,780	..	154	..	8,221	..	37,338	..	19,763	..	17,575	31,179‡	+ 19·8	— 48·5	21	
	Sardarshahar Town	15	1	..	2,655	..	12,375	..	6,008	..	6,367	..	10,052	+ 23·1	+ 9·3	825	
	Sujangarh Tahsil	1,045	..	148	..	11,402	..	50,995	..	26,650	..	24,345	43,721	+ 16·6	— 30·4	49	
	Sujangarh Town	16	1	..	2,491	..	12,086	..	5,948	..	6,138	..	9,762	+ 23·8	— ·2	755	
	Suratgarh Nizamat	**5,073·3**	**1**	**549**	**618**	**24,242**	**2,791**	**118,092**	**1,490**	**65,646**	**1,301**	**52,446**	**68,082**	**+ 77·6**	**— 18·5**	**24**	
	Anupgarh Sub-Tahsil	1,450	..	83	..	2,462	..	12,512	..	6,837	..	5,675	7,497	+ 66·9	— 24·0	9	
	Hanumangarh Tahsil	1,066	..	139	..	8,706	..	41,519	..	23,447	..	18,072	20,165	+ 105·9	— 30·2	39	
	Mirzawala Tahsil	1,312	..	145	..	6,199	..	31,311	..	17,204	..	14,107	14,272	+ 119·4	+ 37·6	24	
	Suratgarh Tahsil	923	..	144	..	4,556	..	21,197	..	11,699	..	9,498	15,565	+ 36·2	— 30·0	23	
	Suratgarh Town	25	1	..	618	..	2,791	..	1,490	..	1,301	..	2,398	+ 16·4	— 0·8	112	
	Tibi Sub-Tahsil	297·3	..	38	..	2,319	..	11,553	..	6,459	..	5,094	8,185‡	+ 41·1	+ 56·7	39	
Bundi.	***Bundi State***	***2,220***	***2***	***793***	***6,508***	***44,314***	***24,558***	***194,173***	***12,314***	***100,897***	***12,244***	***93,375***	***171,997***	***+ 27·7***	***— 42·1***	***99***	
	Bundi Town	7	1	..	5,195	..	19,598	..	9,805	..	9,793	..	10,313	+ 1·5	— 14·3	2,800	
	Arila Pargana	70	..	32	..	2,099	..	10,120	..	5,336	..	4,793	7,078	+ 27·0	— 30·8	145	
	Arnola Pargana	43	..	17	..	1,391	..	6,217	..	3,227	..	2,990	5,886	+ 5·6	— 18·1	145	
	Barundhan Pargana	408	..	107	..	4,740	..	20,943	..	10,879	..	10,064	15,226	+ 37·5	— 49·1	51	
	Deji Pargana	201	..	91	..	4,840	..	20,778	..	10,811	..	9,967	15,415	+ 34·8	— 44·4	103	
	Gotra Pargana	217	..	66	..	4,103	..	18,047	..	9,478	..	8,569	12,110	+ 49·0	— 52·8	83	
	Gundowali Pargana	202	..	91	..	5,047	..	22,474	..	11,635	..	10,839	18,696	+ 20·2	— 30·0	111	
	Hindoli Pargana	333	..	111	..	6,631	..	27,237	..	14,168	..	13,069	18,521	+ 47·1	— 59·5	82	

PROVINCIAL TABLE I.—AREA, HOUSES, AND POPULATION OF ADMINISTRATIVE UNITS—*continued*.

State or District.	Administrative Unit (Pargana, Tahsil, Town, etc.)	Approximate area in square miles.	Inhabited towns.	Inhabited villages.	Occupied houses in Towns.	Occupied houses in Villages.	Population 1911 Persons in Towns.	Population 1911 Persons in Villages.	Population 1911 Males in Towns.	Population 1911 Males in Villages.	Population 1911 Females in Towns.	Population 1911 Females in Villages.	Population 1901 both sexes.	Percentage of variation 1901-1911.	Percentage of variation 1891-1901.	Number of persons per square mile in 1911.	Remarks.
1	2	3	4	5	6	7	8	9	10	11	12	13	14	15	16	17	18
Bundi—contd.	Karwar Pargana	168	..	54	..	3,341	..	15,198	..	7,792	..	7,406	12,457	+ 23·0	— 34·7	90	* Included in Gotra Pargana in 1901. † 1891 figures not available.
	Lakheri Pargana	141	..	44	..	2,828	..	12,132	..	6,324	..	5,808	9,136	+ 32·8	— 38·5	86	
	Naenwa Pargana*	60	..	32	..	1,902	..	8,201	..	4,278	..	3,923	6,376	+ 28·6	†	137	
	Naenwa Town	9	1	..	1,313	..	4,960	..	2,509	..	2,451	..	4,501	+ 10·2	— 26·1	551	
	Patan Pargana	82	..	34	..	3,221	..	14,479	..	7,519	..	6,960	13,247	+ 9·3	— 18·1	177	
	Selore Pargana	194	..	79	..	3,150	..	13,702	..	7,028	..	6,674	9,298	+ 47·4	— 59·8	71	
	Talwas Pargana	85	..	34	..	1,021	..	4,635	..	2,422	..	2,213	3,065	+ 51·2	— 48·8	55	
Dholpur.	*Dholpur State*	*1,200*	*3*	*520*	*8,648*	*48,151*	*37,713*	*225,880*	*20,065*	*124,390*	*17,648*	*101,490*	*271,496‡*	— *2·9*	— *3·0*	*220*	‡ Includes Nimrol in Central India (523), excluded from 1901 Tables. § Included in Gird Tahsil in 1901.
	Dholpur Town	5·3	1	..	4,580	..	19,922	..	10,783	..	9,139	..	19,310§	+ 3·2	+ 13·4	3,759	
	Bari Tahsil	278·7	..	106	..	8,593	..	40,877	..	22,633	..	18,244	43,396	— 5·8	+ 2·2	147	
	Bari Town	9·3	1	..	2,680	..	11,401	..	5,755	..	5,646	..	11,603	— 1·7	— 4·0	1,226	
	Baseri Tahsil	193	..	80	..	9,819	..	43,446	..	23,819	..	19,627	50,825	— 14·5	+ 4·3	225	
	Gird Tahsil	237·8	..	146	..	10,695	..	50,055	..	27,564	..	22,491	48,516‡	+ 3·2	— 18·8	210	
	Kolari Tahsil	122	..	74	..	9,164	..	45,447	..	24,653	..	20,794	43,697	+ 4·0	— 6·7	373	
	Rajakhera Tahsil	144·6	..	75	..	5,884	..	30,290	..	16,979	..	13,311	27,689	+ 9·4	— ·2	209	
	Rajakhera Town	11·3	1	..	1,388	..	6,390	..	3,527	..	2,863	..	6,609	— 3·3	— 2·6	565	
	Sarmathra and Rajboni Jagirs.	198	..	39	..	3,996	..	15,765	..	8,742	..	7,023	19,851	— 20·6	+ 7·5	80	
Dungarpur.	*Dungarpur State*	*1,447*	*3*	*713*	*3,523*	*34,577*	*14,883*	*144,309*	*7,190*	*71,915*	*7,693*	*72,394*	*100,103*	+ *59·0*	+ *1·7*	*110*	‖ Units changed since 1901. ¶ Areas of zillas not available. ** Figures for 1891 and 1901 not available.
	Dungarpur Town ‖	·4	1	..	1,747	..	6,470	..	3,116	..	3,354	..	6,094	+ 6·2	— 5·2	16,175	
	Dungarpur Zilla	¶	..	410	..	16,553	..	70,009	..	35,134	..	34,875	**	**	**	¶	
	Galiakot Town	·2	1	..	506	..	3,914	..	1,965	..	1,949	..	1,989	+ 96·8	+ 34·5	19,570	
	Sagwara Zilla	¶	..	303	..	18,024	..	74,300	..	36,781	..	37,519	**	**	**	¶	
	Sagwara Town.	·3	1	..	1,270	..	4,499	..	2,109	..	2,390	..	4,084	+ 11·5	— 1·2	14,997	
Jaipur.	*Jaipur State*	*14,537·8*	*37*†	*5,765*	*97,333*	*501,000*	*411,757*	*2,224,890*	*210,890*	*1,174,860*	*200,867*	*1,050,030*	*2,658,666*	— *·8*	— *5·9*	*181*	
	Jaipur City	3	1	..	34,656	..	137,098	..	70,846	..	66,252	..	160,167	— 14·4	+ ·9	45,699	
	Bandikui Nizamat and Tahsil.	††	..	8	..	2,604	..	9,499	..	5,116	..	4,383	9,262	+ 2·6	+ 115·5	††	†† Included in Baswa Tahsil.
	Dausa Nizamat	1,068‡‡	3	790	4.294	68,518	17,420	295,078	8,792	153,290	8,628	141,788	328,175	— 3·3	— 1·5	296‡‡	‡‡ Includes Bandikui Nizamat.
	Baswa Tahsil	236·8‡‡ (Baswa Tahsil and Town)	..	171	..	14,622	..	66,065	..	33,616	..	32,449	64,076	+ 3·1	+ 1·4	342‡‡ (Baswa Tahsil and Town)	
	Baswa Town		1	..	1,345	..	5,532	..	2,820	..	2,712	..	5,906	— 6·4	— 3·4		
	Dausa Tahsil	547·7 (Dausa Tahsil and Town)	..	310	..	26,494	..	112,102	..	58,171	..	53,931	117,704	— 4·8	— 2·9	214 (Dausa Tahsil and Town)	
	Dausa Town		1	..	1,242	..	5,191	..	2,672	..	2,519	..	7,540	— 31·2	— 10·4		
	Lalsot Tahsil	210·3 (Lalsot Tahsil and Town)	..	242	..	20,206	..	86,362	..	45,554	..	40,808	88,698	— 2·6	— 5·8	448 (Lalsot Tahsil and Town)	
	Lalsot Town		1	..	1,707	..	6,697	..	3,300	..	3,397	..	8,131	— 17·6	— 4·0		
	Sikrai Tahsil	93·2	..	67	..	7,196	..	30,549	..	15,949	..	14,600	31,118	— 1·8	+ 17·1	328	

PROVINCIAL TABLE I.—Area, Houses, and Population of Administrative Units—*continued.*

State or District.	Administrative Unit (Pargana, Tahsil, Town, etc.)	Approximate area in square miles.	Inhabited towns.	Inhabited villages.	Occupied houses in Towns.	Occupied houses in Villages.	Population 1911 Persons in Towns.	Population 1911 Persons in Villages.	Population 1911 Males in Towns.	Population 1911 Males in Villages.	Population 1911 Females in Towns.	Population 1911 Females in Villages.	1901 both sexes.	Percentage of variation 1901-1911.	Percentage of variation 1891-1901.	Number of persons per square mile in 1911.	Remarks.
1	2	3	4	5	6	7	8	9	10	11	12	13	14	15	16	17	18
Jaipur—contd.	**Gangapur Nizamat**	**277**	**2**	**155**	**2,674**	**15,581**	**10,072**	**62,013**	**5,428**	**32,905**	**4,644**	**29,108**	**74,175**	**— 2·8**	**— 8·7**	**260**	
	Bamanawas Tahsil	38·5	..	27	..	1,744	..	6,607	..	3,425	..	3,182	7,352	— 10·1	— 8·2	283	
	Bamanawas Town		1	..	1,022	..	4,202	..	2,229	..	2,063	..	5,294	— 18·6	— 8·8		
	Gangapur Tahsil	161·5	..	97	..	8,583	..	34,755	..	18,544	..	16,211	34,311	+ 1·3	— 11·0	251	
	Gangapur Town		1	..	1,552	..	5,780	..	3,199	..	2,581	..	5,155	+ 12·1	— 12·3		
	Wazirpur Tahsil	77	..	81	..	5,254	..	20,651	..	10,936	..	9,715	22,063	— 6·4	— 2·9	268	
	Hindaun Nizamat	**674**	**2**	**411**	**4,376**	**39,448**	**17,526**	**167,719**	**9,256**	**89,819**	**8,270**	**77,900**	**185,113**	**+ ·1**	**— ·7**	**275**	
	Ghonsla Tahsil	47·5	..	39	..	3,866	..	16,618	..	9,184	..	7,434	15,913	+ 4·4	+ 7·1	350	
	Hindaun Tahsil	183	..	83	..	9,430	..	40,685	..	21,800	..	18,885	39,802	+ 2·2	+ 6·1	280	
	Hindaun Town		1	..	2,717	..	10,640	..	5,737	..	4,903	..	11,038	— 10·9	— 8·1		
	Mahwa Tahsil	167·5	..	92	..	8,025	..	32,877	..	17,206	..	15,671	35,569	— 7·6	— 4·4	196	
	Ratanzila Tahsil	107	..	30	..	4,220	..	17,262	..	9,282	..	7,980	17,116	+ ·9	+ 15·2	161	
	Toda Bhim Tahsil	85·5	..	102	..	8,085	..	35,847	..	18,958	..	16,889	36,279	— 1·2	— ·5	500	
	Toda Bhim Town		1	..	1,650	..	6,886	..	3,519	..	3,367	..	6,629	+ 3·9	— 6·0		
	Weighat Tahsil	83·5	..	66	..	5,822	..	24,430	..	13,389	..	11,041	21,867	+ 11·7	— 14·3	293	
	Jaipur Nizamat	**2,392**	**5**	**1,518**	**4,353**	**105,945**	**18,979**	**465.045**	**9,693**	**243,992**	**9,286**	**221,053**	**534,117**	**— 9·4**	**— 4·9**	**202**	
	Chaksu Tahsil	460·5	..	330	..	16,322	..	70,924	..	37,605	..	33,319	81,917	— 13·4	— 21·9	163	
	Chaksu Town		1	..	1,023	..	3,949	..	2,099	..	1,850	..	4,902	— 19·4	— 37·7		
	Jaipur Tahsil	965	..	580	..	38,940	..	168,637	..	88,601	..	80,036	182,811	— 7·8	+ 2·3	184	
	Chaumun Town		1	..	1,844	..	6,497	..	3,225	..	3,272	..	9,300	— 30·1	+ 8·5		
	Samod Town		1	..	649	..	2,806	..	1,381	..	1,425	..	3,257	— 13·8	— 50·5		
	Jamwa Ramgarh Tahsil	536·8	..	358	..	28,230	..	123,780	..	64,377	..	59,403	133,046	— 7·6	— 3·0	241	
	Manoharpur Town		1	..	163	..	2,094	..	1,084	..	1,010	..	5,032	— 58·4	+ 8·4		
	Shahpura Town		1	..	674	..	3,633	..	1,904	..	1,729	..	5,245	— 30·7	+ 14·3		
	Kalegh Tahsil	429·7	..	250	..	21,953	..	101,704	..	53,409	..	48,295	107,707	— 5·6	+ ·2	237	
	Kot Kasim Nizamat and Tahsil.	**62·8**	..	**53**	..	**4,094**	..	**18,267**	..	**9,560**	..	**8,707**	**20,827**	**— 12·3**	**+ 22·1**	**291**	
	Madhopur Nizamat	**(b) 1,774**	**1**	**553**	**3,259**	**46,932**	**11,166**	**195,221**	**5,900**	**103,073**	**5,266**	**92,148**	**199,008**	**+ 3·7**	**— 18·0**	†	* Included in figures for Bonli and Malarna Tahsils. (a) Includes portions of Barwara and Isarda Thikanas. (b) Includes portions of Uniara Thikana.
	Barwara Thikana	*	..	25	..	2,388	..	9,918	..	5,114	..	4,804	8,871	+ 11·8	— 27·7		
	Bonli Tahsil	(a) 977·8	..	144	..	12,211	..	51,511	..	27,190	..	24,321	50,209	+ 2·6	— 27·7		
	Isarda Thikana	*	..	39	..	2,868	..	11,925	..	6,208	..	5,717	11,729	+ 1·7	— 13·0		
	Khundar Tahsil	210·5	..	86	..	7,864	..	30,811	..	16,377	..	14,434	31,131	— 1·0	— 7·1		
	Malarna Tahsil	(a) 293	..	136	..	11,124	..	45,013	..	24,392	..	21,521	45,739	+ ·4	— 14·5		
	Sawai Madhopur Tahsil	292·7	..	123	..	10,677	..	45,143	..	23,792	..	21,351	41,001	+ 10·1	— 12·1		
	Sawai Madhopur Town		1	..	3,259	..	11,166	..	5,900	..	5,266	..	10,328	+ 8·1	— 26·1		
	Malpura Nizamat	**(b) 1,460**	**3**	**326**	**3,698**	**27,555**	**15,302**	**120,153**	**8,402**	**63,513**	**6,900**	**56,640**	**123,728**	**+ 9·5**	**— 31·0**		
	Malpura Tahsil	663·5	..	130	..	12,046	..	53,079	..	28,187	..	24,892	49,023	+ 8·3	— 28·2		† Figures not available owing to inclusion of portions of Uniara Thikana in Madhopur and Malpura Nizamats.
	Malpura Town		1	..	1,522	..	6,140	..	3,230	..	2,910	..	6,502	— 5·6	— 22·1		
	Newai Tahsil	186·2	..	79	..	5,480	..	23,003	..	12,154	..	10,849	22,886	+ ·5	— 32·3		
	Newai Town		1	..	1,068	..	4,730	..	2,851	..	1,879	..	4,432	+ 6·7	— 24·0		
	Toda Rai Singh Tahsil	610·3	..	117	..	10,029	..	44,071	..	23,172	..	20,899	37,088	+ 19·0	— 35·3		
	Toda Rai Singh Town		1	..	1,088	..	4,432	..	2,321	..	2,111	..	3,847	+ 15·2	— 31·9		

PROVINCIAL TABLE I.—AREA, HOUSES, AND POPULATION OF ADMINISTRATIVE UNITS—*continued.*

State or District.	Administrative Unit (Pargana, Tahsil, Town, etc.)	Approximate area in square miles.	Inhabited towns.	Inhabited villages.	Occupied houses in Towns.	Occupied houses in Villages.	Population 1911. Persons in Towns.	Persons in Villages.	Males in Towns.	Males in Villages.	Females in Towns.	Females in Villages.	1901 both sexes.	Percentage of variation 1901-1911.	Percentage of variation 1891-1901.	Number of persons per square mile in 1911.	Remarks.
1	2	3	4	5	6	7	8	9	10	11	12	13	14	15	16	17	18
Jaipur—concld.	**Sambhar Nizamat**	1,597	2½	324	4,057	34,131	17,476	154,992	9,619	82,413	7,857	72,579	171,618	+ ·5	— 6·9	108	
	Danta Ramgarh Tahsil	444·8	..	100	..	16,621	..	78,605	..	41,674	..	36,931	84,266	— 6·7	+ 9·4	102	
	Sri Madhopur Town		1	..	1,527	..	6,738	..	3,367	..	3,371	..	6,892	— 2·2	+ 12·4		
	Mauzamabad Tahsil	176	..	56	..	6,034	..	27,565	..	14,495	..	13,070	25,800	+ 0·8	— 23·8	137	
	Naraina Tahsil	883·2	..	81	..	5,570	..	23,941	..	13,049	..	10,892	22,472	+ 6·5	— 20·0		
	Naraina Town		1	..	1,003	..	5,190	..	3,255	..	1,935	..	5,266	— 1·4	+ 3·8		
	Sambhar Tahsil		..	6	..	480	..	2,024	..	1,076	..	948	2,002	+ 1·1	— 6·0	33	
	Sambhar Town		½	..	1,625	..	5,548	..	2,997	..	2,551	..	5,437	+ 2·0	— 12·0		
	Phagi Tahsil	93	..	71	..	5,426	..	22,857	..	12,119	..	10,738	19,453	+ 17·3	— 24·6	240	
	Shekhawati Nizamat	3,696	7	437	12,326	47,241	58,702	231,355	29,249	123,179	29,453	108,176	263,755	+ 10·0	— 3·2	78	
	Bisau Town	(a) 3,468·8	1	..	1,514	..	6,838	..	3,203	..	3,635	..	7,726	— 11·5	— 3·9		
	Jhunjhnu Tahsil		..	367	..	35,273	..	174,098	..	92,308	..	81,790	152,129	+ 14·4	— 5·2		
	Jhunjhnu Town		1	..	2,565	..	13,266	..	6,575	..	6,691	..	12,279	+ 8·0	+ ·1		
	Mandawa Town		1	..	1,128	..	5,536	..	2,754	..	2,782	..	5,165	+ 7·2	+ 4·5		
	Nawalgarh Town		1	..	2,967	..	14,050	..	6,874	..	7,185	..	13,315	+ 14·2	— 2·0	*	* Figures not available owing to inclusion of portion of Khetri and Sikar Thikanas in Jhunjhnu Tahsil and Torawati Nizamat
	Singhana Town		1	..	1,132	..	5,268	..	2,422	..	2,846	..	5,176	+ 1·8	— 12·3		
	Surajgarh Town		1	..	1,156	..	5,992	..	2,962	..	3,030	..	5,243	+ 14·3	— 5·7		
	Udaipur Tahsil	227·2	..	70	..	11,968	..	57,257	..	30,871	..	26,386	35,084	+ 3·9	+ 5·1	286	
	Udaipur Town		1	..	1,824	..	7,743	..	4,459	..	3,284	..	8,838	— 10·4	— 16·5		
	Torawati Nizamat	(a) 1,504	3	368	4,502	49,919	19,425	226,020	9,835	119,535	9,590	106,485	260,410	— 5·7	+ 4·4		(a) Includes portions of Khetri and Sikar Thikanas.
	Bairath Tahsil	250·5	..	66	..	10,981	..	49,456	..	25,743	..	23,713	52,480	— 5·8	+ ·10		
	Bairath Town		1	..	1,228	..	5,273	..	2,549	..	2,724	..	5,637	— 6·5	— 1·9		
	Khandela Tahsil	435·5	..	136	..	12,070	..	57,030	..	30,401	..	26,629	63,074	— 9·6	+ 8·1	§	
	Khandela Town		1	..	1,921	..	8,206	..	3,995	..	4,211	..	9,156	— 10·4	— 9·0		
	Nimka Thana Town		1	..	1,446	..	5,946	..	3,201	..	2,655	..	6,741	— 11·8	+ 17·6		
	Sawai Ramgarh Tahsil	318	..	166	..	26,868	..	119,534	..	63,391	..	56,143	123,313	— 2·1	+ 1·2		
	Khetri Thikana	†	3	269	4,892	23,751	21,983	112,004	11,052	58,910	10,931	53,094	131,913	+ 1·6	+ 2·1		† Included in figures for Torawati Nizamat and Jhunjhnu Tahsil.
	Chirawa Town		1	..	1,611	..	7,979	..	3,891	..	4,088	..	7,065	+ 12·9	+ 5·4		
	Khetri Tahsil		..	269	..	23,751	..	112,004	..	58,910	..	53,094	107,872	+ 3·8	+ 1·3	‡	‡ Included in figures for Malpura and Madhopur Nizamats.
	Khetri Town		1	..	1,706	..	7,125	..	3,718	..	3,407	..	8,537	— 16·5	+ 1·4		
	Kot Putli Town		1	..	1,575	..	6,870	..	3,443	..	3,436	..	8,439	— 18·5	+ 11·2		
	Sikar Thikana	†	4	429	13,133	28,756	61,905	138,429	30,465	74,147	31,530	64,282	173,485	+ 15·5	— 3·3		§ Figures not available owing to inclusion of portion of Khetri and Sikar Thikanas in Jhunjhnu Tahsil and Torawati Nizamat.
	Fatehpur Town		1	..	3,691	..	17,294	..	8,280	..	9,014	..	16,303	+ 5·5	— 1·1		
	Lachhmangarh Town		1	..	2,236	..	10,828	..	5,024	..	5,804	..	10,176	+ 6·4	+ 7·0		
	Ramgarh Town		1	..	2,683	..	11,556	..	5,657	..	5,899	..	11,023	+ 4·8	— 9·6	§	
	Sikar Tahsil		..	429	..	28,756	..	138,429	..	74,147	..	64,282	114,370	+ 21·0	— 5·6		
	Sikar Town		1	..	4,523	..	22,317	..	11,501	..	10,816	..	21,523	+ 3·7	+ 8·2		
	Uniara Thikana	‡	1	124	1,123	6,526	4,613	29,095	2,353	15,408	2,260	13,687	27,913	+ 20·8	— 35·7		‖ Figures not available owing to inclusion of portion of Uniara Thikana in Madhopur and Malpura Nizamats.
	Uniara Tahsil		..	124	..	6,525	..	29,095	..	15,408	..	13,687	23,452	+ 24·1	— 37·7	‖	
	Uniara Town		1	..	1,123	..	4,613	..	2,353	..	2,260	..	4,461	+ 3·4	— 22·1		

PROVINCIAL TABLE I.—AREA, HOUSES, AND POPULATION OF ADMINISTRATIVE UNITS—*continued.*

State or District.	Administrative Unit (Pargana, Tahsil, Town, etc.)	Approximate area in square miles.	Inhabited towns.	Inhabited villages.	Occupied houses in Towns.	Occupied houses in Villages.	Population 1911. Persons in Towns.	Population 1911. Persons in Villages.	Population 1911. Males in Towns.	Population 1911. Males in Villages.	Population 1911. Females in Towns.	Population 1911. Females in Villages.	Population 1901 both sexes.	Percentage of variation 1901-1911.	Percentage of variation 1891-1901.	Number of persons per square mile in 1911.	Remarks.
1	2	3	4	5	6	7	8	9	10	11	12	13	14	15	16	17	18
Jaisalmer.	***Jaisalmer State***	16,062	*1*	*479*	*2,068*	*18,869*	*7,420*	*80,891*	3,667	44,833	3,753	36,058	78,370	+ 20·4	— 36·6	5	
	Jaisalmer Town	·4	1	..	2,068	..	7,420	..	3,667	..	3,753	..	7,137	+ 4·0	— 32·1	18,650	
	Bap Pargana	700	..	24	..	2,461	..	10,501	..	5,897	..	4,604	7,791	+ 34·8	— 44·8	15	
	Barawa Bu li Pargana	700	..	9	..	275	..	1,156	..	644	..	512	1,124	+ 2·8	— 15·2	2	
	Devikot Pargana	800	..	38	..	1,821	..	8,297	..	4,673	..	3,624	4,725	+ 75·6	— 63·1	10	
	Dewa Pargana	1,200	..	30	..	732	..	3,097	..	1,667	..	1,430	3,063	+ 1·1	— 5·4	3	
	Fatehgarh Pargana	700	..	37	..	1,497	..	6,263	..	3,386	..	2,877	5,679	+ 10·3	— 25·2	9	
	Jaisalmer Pargana	1,199·6	..	55	..	1,400	..	5,800	..	3,187	..	2,613	5,653	+ 2·6	— 31·3	5	
	Khuiala Pargana	1,000	..	15	..	604	..	3,068	..	1,747	..	1,321	3,787	— 19·0	— 18·9	3	
	Kishangarh Pargana	400	..	1	..	136	..	875	..	574	..	301	403	+ 117·1	— 30·3	2	
	Lakhan Pargana	282	..	17	..	954	..	4,224	..	2,282	..	1,942	3,031	+ 8·9	— 30·1	16	
	Mayaj lar Pargana	800	..	9	..	611	..	2,544	..	1,433	..	1,111	2,226	+ 14·3	— 31·6	3	
	Mohangarh Nachna Pargana.	2,200	..	20	..	1,480	..	6,387	..	3,660	..	2,727	5,021	+ 27·2	— 25·2	3	
	Nokh Pargana	2,100	..	72	..	4,046	..	17,062	..	9,465	..	7,597	11,803	+ 44·6	— 51·4	8	
	Ramgarh Pargana	400	..	9	..	569	..	2,344	..	1,188	..	1,156	2,112	+ 11·0	— 32·1	6	
	Shahgarh Ghotra Pargana	1,600	..	100	..	880	..	3,547	..	1,893	..	1,654	3,734	— 5·0	— 20·1	2	
	Shamkhaba Pargana	1,700	..	35	..	1,260	..	5,270	..	2,870	..	2,400	4,650	+ 13·3	— 30·9	3	
	Tanot Pargana	300	..	1	..	125	..	456	..	267	..	189	511	— 10·8	— 45·1	2	
Jhalawar.	***Jhalawar***	*810*	*9*	*408*	*5,755*	*18,010*	*18,664*	*77,607*	*9,144*	*40,890*	*9,520*	*36,717*	*90,175*	+ 6·8	— 40·3	*119*	
	Jhalrapatan Chhaoni*	·9	1	..	3,584	..	11,474	..	5,597	..	5,877	..	14,315	— 19·8	— 38·7	12,749	*In Patan Tahsil in 1901.
	Awar Tahsil	80	..	42	..	2,304	..	9,741	..	5,259	..	4,482	9,240	+ 5·4	— 41·4	122	
	Dag Tahsil	168	..	70	..	4,137	..	18,139	..	9,469	..	8,670	16,167	+ 12·2	— 38·8	108	
	Gangadhar Tahsil	187	..	113	..	5,006	..	22,165	..	11,675	..	10,490	18,439	+ 20·2	— 40·2	119	
	Pachpahar Tahsil	131	..	63	..	2,600	..	10,988	..	5,739	..	5,259	9,313	+ 18·1	— 48·8	84	
	Patan Tahsil	169·7	..	92	..	2,727	..	11,457	..	6,037	..	5,420	10,234	+ 12·0	— 41·5	68	
	Patan Town*	·4	1	..	2,171	..	7,100	..	3,547	..	3,643	..	7,955	— 9·6	— 26·2	17,975	
	Srichhatarpur Tahsil*	73	..	28	..	1,238	..	5,107	..	2,711	..	2,396	4,512	+ 13·2	— 46·8	70	
Karauli.	***Karauli State***	*1,239*	*1*	*439*	*5,319*	*30,693*	*19,803*	*120,784*	*10,548*	*69,533*	*9,255*	*57,251*	*156,786*	— 6·5	+ ·1	*118*	
	Karauli Town.	228 (with Hazur Tahsil)	1	..	5,312	..	19,803	..	10,548	..	9,255	..	23,482	— 15·7	+ 1·5	277 (with Hazur Tahsil)	
	Hazur Tahsil		..	135	..	10,345	..	43,460	..	23,012	..	19,548	44,099	— 1·4	+ 10·6		
	Machilpur Tahsil	253	..	81	..	5,158	..	20,241	..	11,321	..	8,920	24,015	— 15·7	— 3·9	80	
	Mandrail Tahsil	226	..	57	..	4,460	..	18,443	..	10,123	..	8,320	19,665	— 6·2	— 15·0	82	
	Sapotra Tahsil†	190	..	87	..	7,773	..	32,716	..	17,444	..	15,272	32,646	+ ·2	+ 3·3	172	†Called Jirota in 1901.
	Utgir Tahsil	342	..	79	..	2,957	..	11,924	..	6,733	..	5,191	12,879	— 7·4	— 19·1	35	
Kishangarh.	***Kishangarh State***	*858*	*3*	*226*	*5,051*	*16,283*	*17,824*	*60,367*	*9,180*	*36,538*	*8,644*	*32,829*	*90,970*	— 4·2	— 27·5	*109*	
	Kishangarh Town	1	1	..	3,097	..	10,418	..	5,443	..	4,975	..	12,663	— 17·7	— 18·1	10,418	
	Kishangarh Pargana	258	..	66	..	4,526	..	19,144	..	10,002	..	9,052	22,992	— 16·7	— 28·7	74	
	Arain Pargana	144	..	46	..	3,675	..	15,435	..	8,201	..	7,144	17,994	— 14·2	— 25·9	107	
	Fatehgarh Pargana‡	157	..	22	..	1,495	..	6,358	..	3,401	..	2,957	‡	‡	‡	40	‡In Sarwar Pargana in 1901 and 1891.
	Rupnagar Pargana	152	..	50	..	3,867	..	16,785	..	8,732	..	8,053	13,733	+ 22·2	— 30·1	110	
	Rupnagar Town	1	1	..	800	..	2,088	..	1,510	..	1,449	..	3,676	— 18·7	— 26·6	2,088	
	Sarwar Pargana	144	..	42	..	2,698	..	11,645	..	6,022	..	5,623	15,302	— 17·0	— 32·9	81	
	Sarwar Town	1	1	..	1,154	..	4,418	..	2,218	..	2,200	..	4,520	— 2·3	— 23·4	4,418	

PROVINCIAL TABLE I.—Area, Houses, and Population of Administrative Units—*continued.*

State or District.	Administrative Unit (Pargana, Tahsil, Town, etc.)	Approximate area in square miles.	Inhabited towns.	Inhabited villages.	Occupied houses in Towns.	Occupied houses in Villages.	Population 1911. Persons in Towns.	Persons in Villages.	Males in Towns.	Males in Villages.	Females in Towns.	Females in Villages.	1901 both sexes.	Percentage of variation 1901-1911.	Percentage of variation 1891-1901.	Number of persons per square mile in 1911.	Remarks.
1	2	3	4	5	6	7	8	9	10	11	12	13	14	15	16	17	18
Kotah.	***Kotah State***	*5,684*	*4*	*2,554*	*15,659*	*141,477*	*52,592*	*586,497*	*27,118*	*303,206*	*25,474*	*283,291*	*544,879*	*+ 17·3*	*− 24·2*	*112*	
	Kotah City	4·2	1	..	10,394	..	32,753	..	16,949	..	15,804	..	32,146*	+ 1·9	− 12·9	7,798	*Adjusted owing to change of boundaries.
	Nizamats Total	**5,423·8**	**3**	**2,395**	**5,265**	**129,572**	**19,839**	**538,501**	**10,169**	**278,458**	**9,670**	**260,043**	**468,120**	**+ 19·3**	**− 25·0**	**103**	
	Akiera	212	..	197	..	7,675	..	33,135	..	17,254	..	15,881	26,091†	+ 27·0	− 20·4	137	†Figures differ from 1901 owing to changes in constitution of units.
	Anta	201	..	79	..	6,874	..	27,968	..	14,145	..	13,823	23,658	+ 18·2	− 27·9	139	
	Aasnawar	115	..	85	..	2,596	..	10,779	..	5,595	..	5,184	8,243†	+ 30·8	− 36·1	94	
	Bakani	216	..	191	..	6,519	..	29,509	..	15,404	..	14,105	22,640	+ 30·3	− 19·7	137	
	Baran	188	..	82	..	6,796	..	27,629	..	14,051	..	13,578	24,404	+ 13·2	− 20·9	198	
	Baran Town		1	..	2,647	..	9,507	..	4,973	..	4,534	..	7,892	+ 20·5	+ 11·7		
	Barod	158	..	73	..	4,478	..	18,903	..	9,695	..	9,208	15,977	+ 18·3	− 31·6	120	
	Chechat	304	..	139	..	7,774	..	30,543	..	15,733	..	14,810	26,565†	+ 18·1	− 37·7	99	
	Chhipa Barod	327	..	164	..	7,929	..	33,585	..	17,227	..	16,358	27,396	+ 22·6	− 20·0	103	
	Digod	159	..	76	..	4,875	..	20,123	..	10,360	..	9,763	17,494	+ 15·0	− 20·7	127	
	Etawah	148	..	61	..	5,054	..	20,871	..	10,750	..	10,121	18,019	+ 15·8	− 22·0	141	
	Kanwas	289	..	99	..	5,389	..	21,430	..	11,192	..	10,238	17,554	+ 22·1	− 36·4	74	
	Khanpur	354	..	188	..	10,885	..	43,967	..	22,553	..	21,414	36,754†	+ 19·6	− 34·4	123	
	Kishanganj	600	..	153	..	6,333	..	25,842	..	13,523	..	12,319	21,265†	+ 21·5	− 26·7	43	
	Kunjer	136	..	64	..	4,709	..	19,229	..	10,021	..	9,208	15,692	+ 22·5	− 27·3	141	
	Ladpura	558·8	..	170	..	10,398	..	41,771	..	21,746	..	20,025	35,938†	+ 16·2	− 31·7	75	
	Mangrol	179	..	74	..	5,679	..	23,897	..	12,152	..	11,745	22,317	+ 7·1	− 15·0	100	
	Mangrol Town		1	..	1,207	..	4,789	..	2,429	..	2,360	..	5,156	− 7·1	− 9·8		
	Manoharthana	248	..	180	..	7,772	..	34,930	..	18,202	..	16,728	27,086	+ 29·2	− 2·6	141	
	Sango	197	..	112	..	5,489	..	23,316	..	11,979	..	11,337	19,463	+ 19·8	− 29·3	148	
	Sangod Town		1	..	1,411	..	5,543	..	2,767	..	2,776	..	4,369	+ 26·9	− 13·4		
	Shahabad	590	..	129	..	6,276	..	27,296	..	14,241	..	13,055†	22,739†	+ 20.0	− 15·5	46	
	Shergarh	210	..	79	..	5,870	..	24,220	..	12,575	..	11,645†	21,408†	+ 13·1	− 24·4	115	
	Kotris Total	**256**	..	**159**	..	**11,905**	..	**47,996**	..	**24,748**	..	**23,248**	**44,613**	**+ 7·6**	**− 19·9**	**187**	
	Antarda	20	..	7	..	656	..	2,935	..	1,502	..	1,433	2,538	+ 15·6	− 39·8	147	
	Balwan	34	..	21	..	723	..	3,446	..	1,794	..	1,652	2,622	+ 31·4	− 9·2	101	
	Farera (Sub-Kotri)	1·5	..	1	..	42	..	166	..	83	..	83	177	− 6·2	− 9·7	111	
	Gainta	32	..	5	..	1,079	..	4,107	..	2,047	..	2,060	3,820	+ 7·5	− 19·2	128	
	Indargarh	60	..	84	..	5,044	..	22,589	..	11,681	..	10,908	21,046	+ 7·3	− 19·7	376	
	Karwar	12	..	5	..	492	..	1,978	..	1,024	..	954	1,854	+ 6·7	− 26·6	165	
	Khatoli	48	..	21	..	1,799	..	7,162	..	3,682	..	3,480	7,105	+ ·8	− 10·0	149	
	Kherli (Sub-Kotri)	2·5	..	1	..	85	..	332	..	154	..	178	325	+ 2·2	‡	133	‡ 1891 figures not available.
	Phusod	14	..	6	..	195	..	752	..	406	..	346	756	− ·5	− 19·7	54	
	Pipalda Mustarka	6	..	1	..	823	..	3,091	..	1,612	..	1,479	3,135	− 1·4	− 22·0	515	
	Pipalda Thikana	26	..	7	..	367	..	1,443	..	768	..	675	1,235	+ 16·4	− 41·5	55	
Kushalgarh.	***Kushalgarh Chiefship***	*340*	*1*	*285*	*696*	*3,940*	*2,594*	*19,411*	*1,276*	*9,680*	*1,318*	*9,731*	*16,222*	*+ 35·6*	*+ 180·9*	*65*	
	Kushalgarh Town §	·3	1	..	696	..	2,594	..	1,276	..	1,318	..	2,838	− 8·6	+ ·7	8,647	§ In Kushalgarh Tahsil in 1901.
	Dungra Tahsil (including Thanbesar Jagir.) ‖	88	..	86	..	1,486	..	7,016	..	3,475	..	3,541	‖	‖	‡	80	‖ In Patan Tahsil in 1901.
	Mayad Tahsil §	135·7	..	107	..	1,309	..	6,771	..	3,375	..	3,396	3,929	+ 72·3		50	
	Patan Tahsil (including Chudibar Jagir.)	116	..	92	..	1,145	..	5,624	..	2,830	..	2,794	9,455¶	+ 33·7¶		48	¶ Includes Dungra Tahsil.
Lawa.	***Lawa Estate***	*19*	..	*7*	..	*647*	..	*2,564*	..	*1,202*	..	*1,362*	*2,671*	*− 4·0*	*− 20·5*	*135*	

PROVINCIAL TABLE I.—AREA, HOUSES, AND POPULATION OF ADMINISTRATIVE UNITS—*continued*.

State or District.	Administrative Unit (Pargana, Tahsil, Town, etc.)	Approximate area in square miles.	Inhabited towns.	Inhabited villages.	Occupied houses in Towns.	Occupied houses in Villages.	Population 1911 Persons in Towns.	Population 1911 Persons in Villages.	Population 1911 Males in Towns.	Population 1911 Males in Villages.	Population 1911 Females in Towns.	Population 1911 Females in Villages.	Population 1901 both sexes.	Percentage of variation 1901-1911.	Percentage of variation 1891-1901.	Number of persons per square mile in 1911.	Remarks.
1	2	3	4	5	6	7	8	9	10	11	12	13	14	15	16	17	18
Marwar.	***Marwar State***	***34,986***	***25½***	***4,088***	***63,556***	***400,456***	***252,863***	***1,811,899***	***128,593***	***950,569***	***124,270***	***861,330***	***1,935,565****	+ ***0·3****	— ***23·4****	***59***	* Excludes Merwara villages.
	Jodhpur City	1·9	1	..	14,697	..	50,262	..	20,351	..	29,011	..	50,437	— 1·9	— 2·1	31,191	
	Jodhpur Town or Suburbs.	·8	1	..	5,111	..	20,494	..	12,487	..	8,007	..	18,672	+ 9·8	+ ·1	25,618	
	Bali Pargana	834	..	150	..	22,949	..	95,716	..	48,879	..	46,837	91,008	+ 5·2	— 56·1	121	
	Bali Town		1	..	1,360	..	5,593	..	2,732	..	2,861	..	5,186	+ 7·8	— 3·1		
	Bilara Pargana	792	..	117	..	13,638	..	58,967	..	30,808	..	28,159	42,314	+ 39·4	— 35·3	95	
	Bilara Town		1	..	2,190	..	8,606	..	4,453	..	4,153	..	8,095	— 1·0	— 23·6		
	Pipar Town		1	..	1,784	..	7,556	..	3,796	..	3,760	..	6,785	+ 11·4	— 16·3		
	Desuri Pargana	710	..	139	..	14,620	..	64,412	..	33,501	..	31,361	61,143	+ 5·3	†	97	† 1891 figures not available.
	Sadri Town		1	..	1,154	..	4,742	..	2,389	..	2,353	..	6,621	— 28·4	— 12·8		
	Didwana Pargana	1,136	..	230	..	16,419	..	77,470	..	39,806	..	37,664	27,168	+ 185·2	— 23·5	86	
	Didwana Town		1	..	2,126	..	10,122	..	5,438	..	4,684	..	9,410	+ 7·6	— 17·3		
	Ladnun Town		1	..	1,992	..	9,685	..	4,574	..	5,111	..	8,064	+ 20·1	+ 8·9		
	Jaitaran Pargana	860	..	117	..	20,279	..	90,014	..	46,888	..	43,126	59,596	+ 51·0	— 27·2	116	
	Jaitaran Town		1	..	1,046	..	4,371	..	2,108	..	2,263	..	4,033	+ 8·4	†		
	Nimaj Town		1	..	1,111	..	5,015	..	2,520	..	2,495	..	4,104	+ 22·2	— 28·6		
	Jalor Pargana	1,552	..	223	..	30,268	..	133,719	..	69,293	..	64,426	133,437	+ ·2	— 17·0	91	
	Jalor Town		1	..	2,125	..	7,624	..	3,791	..	3,833	..	7,443	+ 2·4	— 22·9		
	Jaswantpura Pargana	1,360	..	212	..	21,739	..	99,348	..	52,037	..	47,311	78,825	+ 26·0	— 25·5	77	
	Bhinmal Town		1	..	1,343	..	5,214	..	2,598	..	2,616	..	4,545	+ 14·7	— 20·8		
	Jodhpur Pargana	2,893·3	..	371	..	28,819	..	129,415	..	68,996	..	60,419	156,352	— 17·2	— 36·7	45	
	Mallani Pargana	5,760	..	462	..	33,631	..	162,047	..	86,912	..	75,135	166,266	— 2·5	— 22·9	29	
	Barmer Town		1	..	1,513	..	6,380	..	3,285	..	3,095	..	6,064	+ 5·2	+ 8·1		
	Maroth Pargana	368	..	107	..	12,376	..	56,075	..	29,713	..	26,362	44,124	+ 27·1	+ ·3	178	
	Kuchaman Town		1	..	2,262	..	9,605	..	4,754	..	4,851	..	10,749	— 10·6	— 16·1		
	Merta Pargana	1,615·3	..	320	..	28,891	..	129,454	..	67,370	..	62,084	138,493	— 6·5	— 30·3	80	
	Merta Town	·7	1	..	1,252	..	4,397	..	2,283	..	2,114	..	4,361	+ ·8	— 38·9	628	
	Nagaur Pargana	2,608	..	308	..	27,369	..	123,672	..	64,371	..	59,301	149,261	— 17·1	— 35·1	54	
	Nagaur Town		1	..	3,311	..	12,960	..	6,442	..	6,518	..	13,377	— 3·1	— 22·3		
	Mundwa Town		1	..	1,249	..	5,027	..	2,473	..	2,554	..	5,121	— 1·8	— 1·8		
	Nawa Pargana	192	..	11	..	1,778	..	7,586	..	4,039	..	3,547	10,320	— 60·7	— 26·9	60	
	Nawa Town		1	..	1,336	..	5,657	..	2,963	..	2,694	..	5,640	+ ·3	+ 10·0		
	Pachbhadra Pargana	856	..	96	..	6,036	..	25,791	..	13,521	..	12,270	31,115	— 17·1	— 26·5	39	
	Pachbhadra Town		1	..	657	..	2,158	..	1,098	..	1,060	..	3,194	— 32·4	— 37·7		
	Balotra Town		1	..	1,438	..	5,408	..	2,902	..	2,506	..	5,118	+ 5·7	— 5·8		
	Pali Pargana	1,024	..	141	..	11,073	..	50,716	..	26,464	..	24,252	31,216	+ 62·5	— 24·4	62	
	Pali Town		1	..	3,620	..	12,939	..	6,580	..	6,359	..	12,673	+ 2·1	— 26·1		
	Parbatsar Pargana	840	..	199	..	22,002	..	105,305	..	54,687	..	50,618	87,127	+ 20·9	— 17·0	125	
	Phalodi Pargana	2,624	..	101	..	12,144	..	58,578	..	31,516	..	27,062	40,373	+ 45·1	— 27·8	29	
	Phalodi Town		1	..	3,330	..	13,825	..	6,375	..	7,450	..	13,924	— ·7	+ 32·6		
	Lohawat Town		1	..	968	..	4,814	..	2,472	..	2,342	..	5,322	— 9·5	— ·8		
	Sachor Pargana	1,776	..	225	..	16,708	..	80,230	..	42,530	..	37,700	70,401	+ 14·0	— 26·6	45	
	Sambhar Pargana	80	..	7	..	505	..	2,097	..	1,116	..	981	2,002	+ 4·7	— 6·0	96	
	Sambhar Town		½	..	1,523	..	5,546	..	2,995	..	2,551	..	5,436	+ 2·0	— 12·1		
	Sankra Pargana	1,264	..	51	..	4,216	..	19,416	..	10,745	..	8,671	16,835	+ 3·1	+ 764·4	20	
	Pokaran Town		½	..	1,532	..	5,814	..	2,863	..	2,951	..	7,125	— 18·4	— 9·8		
	Sheo Pargana	2,406	..	66	..	7,189	..	31,411	..	17,396	..	14,015	24,405	+ 28·7	— 19·4	13	
	Shergarh Pargana	1,456	..	80	..	11,711	..	58,027	..	31,075	..	26,952	56,921	+ 1·9	— 19·7	40	
	Siwana Pargana	760	..	83	..	9,494	..	40,854	..	21,008	..	19,846	53,931	— 24·2	— 16·7	54	
	Sojat Pargana	1,172	..	211	..	23,997	..	104,370	..	54,455	..	49,915	98,726	+ 5·7	— 23·6	98	
	Sojat Town		1	..	2,528	..	10,049	..	4,971	..	5,078	..	11,107	— 9·5	— 12·0		
	Villages in Merwara District	50	..	21	..	1,711	..	7,209	..	3,893	..	3,316	‡	‡	‡	144	‡ 1891 and 1901 figures not available.

PROVINCIAL TABLE I.—Area, Houses, and Population of Administrative Units—*continued.*

State or District.	Administrative Unit (Pargana, Tahsil, Town, etc.).	Approximate area in square miles.	Inhabited towns.	Inhabited villages.	Occupied houses in Towns.	Occupied houses in Villages.	Population 1911. Persons in Towns.	Persons in Villages.	Males in Towns.	Males in Villages.	Females in Towns.	Females in Villages.	1901 both sexes.	Percentage of variation. 1901-1911.	1891-1901.	Number of persons per square mile in 1911.	Remarks.
1	2	3	4	5	6	7	8	9	10	11	12	13	14	15	16	17	18
Mewar.	*Mewar State*	*12,914·8*	*14*	*7,341*	*26,318*	*302,709*	*93,812*	*1,226,988*	*48,807*	*636,412*	*45,005*	*590,576*	*1,018,805**	+ *23·8**	− *40·4**	*109*	* Excludes Merwara villages.
	Udaipur City	..	1	..	9,453	..	33,220	..	17,460	..	15,760	..	45,978	− 27·7	− 1·5	..	
	Amet Thikana	..	..	86	..	2,763	..	11,005	..	5,905	..	5,100	8,616	+ 28·8	− 47·8	..	
	Asind Thikana	..	..	66	..	3,596	..	15,658	..	8,094	..	7,564	12,528	+ 25·0	− 41·5	..	
	Badnor Thikana	..	..	124	..	4,840	..	21,592	..	11,475	..	10,117	15,242	+ 41·7	− 44·6	..	
	Bagor Tahsil	..	..	29	..	2,326	..	8,800	..	4,573	..	4,227	7,482	+ 17·6	− 40·5	..	
	Banera Thikana	..	..	106	..	5,249	..	22,474	..	11,638	..	10,836	18,530	+ 21·2	− 40·3	..	
	Banera Town	..	1	..	1,056	..	4,335	..	2,144	..	2,191	..	4,261	+ 1·7	− 26·0	..	
	Bansi Thikana	..	..	57	..	1,451	..	6,403	..	3,289	..	3,114	5,736	+ 11·6	+ 24·2	..	
	Bari Sadri Thikana	..	..	117	..	3,407	..	14,363	..	7,267	..	7,096	10,599	+ 35·5	− 35·8	..	
	Bedla Thikana	..	..	120	..	4,152	..	16,469	..	8,478	..	7,991	12,866	+ 28·0	− 46·2	..	
	Begun Thikana	..	..	130	..	3,013	..	12,452	..	6,518	..	5,934	8,880	+ 40·2	− 64·4	..	
	Begun Town	..	1	..	1,381	..	4,385	..	2,204	..	2,181	..	3,625	+ 21·0	− 38·4	..	
	Bhainsrorgarh Thikana	..	..	94	..	3,668	..	14,330	..	7,318	..	7,012	12,270	+ 16·8	− 47·8	..	
	Bhilwara Thikana	..	..	227	..	15,167	..	62,260	..	32,507	..	29,753	51,721	+ 20·4	− 34·8	..	
	Bhilwara Town	..	1	..	2,211	..	8,763	..	4,613	..	4,150	..	10,340	− 15·3	+ ·02	..	
	Bhindar Thikana	..	..	112	..	2,736	..	11,023	..	5,527	..	5,496	7,925	+ 39·1	− 56·2	..	
	Bhindar Town	..	1	..	1,336	..	4,630	..	2,345	..	2,285	..	5,172	− 10·5	− 23·8	..	
	Bijolia Thikana	..	..	68	..	2,553	..	11,112	..	5,702	..	5,410	7,678	+ 44·8	− 48·7	..	
	Chhoti Sadri Thikana	..	..	211	..	7,551	..	30,695	..	15,607	..	15,088	26,612	+ 15·3	− 37·7	..	
	Chhoti Sadri Town	..	1	..	1,246	..	4,576	..	2,344	..	2,232	..	5,050	− 9·4	− 5·9	..	
	Chitorgarh Thikana	..	..	429	..	20,430	..	80,044	..	41,073	..	38,971	58,411	+ 37·0	− 53·4	..	
	Chitorgarh Town	..	1	..	2,157	..	7,332	..	3,939	..	3,393	..	7,593	− 3·4	− 18·8	..	
	Delwara Thikana	..	..	168	..	5,450	..	21,689	..	11,160	..	10,529	16,235	+ 33·4	− 40·0	..	
	Deogarh Thikana	..	..	207	..	7,437	..	29,855	..	15,798	..	14,057	19,762	+ 51·1	− 59·8	..	
	Deogarh Town	..	1	..	1,499	..	5,461	..	2,638	..	2,823	..	5,384	+ 1·4	− 27·2	..	
	Devasthan Thikana	..	..	108	..	6,910	..	27,103	..	14,030	..	13,165	23,622	+ 15·1	− 43·3	..	
	Girwa (including Dharinvad) Thikana	..	..	512	..	23,004	..	93,126	..	48,016	..	45,110	70,271	+ 32·5	− 29·4	..	
	Gogunda Thikana	..	..	96	..	2,475	..	9,447	..	4,797	..	4,650	7,708	+ 22·6	− 44·3	..	
	Hurra Thikana	..	..	188	..	10,096	..	45,561	..	23,830	..	21,731	35,799	+ 27·3	− 33·7	..	
	Jahazpur Thikana	..	..	315	..	13,532	..	55,159	..	29,134	..	26,025	38,751	+ 42·3	− 51·9	..	
	Jahazpur Town	..	1	..	1,331	..	3,986	..	2,105	..	1,881	..	3,390	+ 17·8	− 33·4	..	
	Kachola (Shahpura) Thikana	..	..	84	..	4,005	..	16,549	..	8,637	..	7,912	12,515	+ 32·2	− 52·3	..	
	Kankroli Thikana	..	..	34	..	1,787	..	6,932	..	3,553	..	3,379	4,995	+ 38·8	− 39·8	..	
	Kanor Thikana	..	..	116	..	3,319	..	12,962	..	6,609	..	6,353	11,249	+ 15·2	− 28·7	..	
	Kapasin Thikana	..	..	157	..	8,901	..	36,566	..	19,168	..	17,398	28,371	+ 28·9	− 45·8	..	
	Kargali Thikana	..	..	20	..	823	..	3,381	..	1,741	..	1,640	2,222	+ 52·2	− 57·9	..	
	Khamnor Thikana	..	..	258	..	6,853	..	26,673	..	13,901	..	12,772	20,810	+ 28·2	− 30·2	..	
	Kherwara Bhumat	..	..	205	..	5,648	..	24,086	..	12,120	..	11,966	17,558	+ 37·2	+ 36·7	..	
	Kherwara Cantonment	..	1	..	551	..	2,016	..	1,295	..	721	..	2,289	− 11·9	+ 253·2	..	
	Kotharia Thikana	..	..	76	..	2,304	..	9,052	..	4,742	..	4,310	8,053	+ 12·4	− 47·6	..	
	Kotra Bhumat	..	..	412	..	4,937	..	20,480	..	10,708	..	9,772	16,738	+ 22·4	+ 105·5	..	
	Kotra Cantonment	..	1	..	202	..	746	..	461	..	285	..	903	− 17·4	+ 502·0	..	
	Kumbhalgarh Thikana	..	..	458	..	9,483	..	37,584	..	19,766	..	17,818	28,003	+ 34·2	− 45·9	..	
	Kurabar Thikana	..	..	65	..	4,049	..	15,404	..	7,670	..	7,734	12,643	+ 21·8	− 50·3	..	
	Magra (Sarara) Thikana	..	..	404	..	18,460	..	68,537	..	34,860	..	33,677	48,460	+ 41·4	− 22·9	..	
	Mandalgarh Thikana	..	..	203	..	12,340	..	49,947	..	26,016	..	23,931	33,619	+ 48·6	− 60·2	..	
	Moja Thikana	..	..	16	..	960	..	3,729	..	1,934	..	1,795	3,216	+ 16·0	− 36·9	..	
	Nathdwara Thikana	..	..	40	..	2,342	..	9,077	..	4,751	..	4,326	7,246	+ 25·3	− 41·2	..	
	Nathdwara Town	..	1	..	1,348	..	5,424	..	2,906	..	2,518	..	8,591	− 36·9	− 7·0	..	
	Parsoli Thikana	..	..	42	..	1,216	..	5,175	..	2,772	..	2,403	3,388	+ 52·7	− 60·0	..	† Included in Bhilwara Thikana in 1901.
	Pur Town †	..	1	..	1,303	..	4,423	..	2,209	..	2,214	..	4,498	− 1·7	+ 33·9	..	

PROVINCIAL TABLE I.—AREA, HOUSES, AND POPULATION OF ADMINISTRATIVE UNITS—*continued*.

State or District.	Administrative Unit (Pargana, Tahsil, Town, etc.)	Approximate area in square miles.	Inhabited towns.	Inhabited villages.	Occupied houses in Towns.	Occupied houses in Villages.	Population 1911. Persons in Towns.	Population 1911. Persons in Villages.	Males in Towns.	Males in Villages.	Females in Towns.	Females in Villages.	1901 both sexes.	Percentage of variation 1901-1911.	Percentage of variation 1891-1901.	Number of persons per square mile in 1911.	Remarks.
1	2	3	4	5	6	7	8	9	10	11	12	13	14	15	16	17	18
Mewar—*concld.*	Rajnagar Thikana	..	..	124	..	7,098	..	28,977	..	15,070	..	13,907	22,064	+ 31·3	— 44·6	..	
	Rasmi Thikana	..	..	96	..	8,130	..	33,560	..	17,517	..	16,043	26,897	+ 24·8	— 42·5	..	
	Saharan District (including Sheopur).	..	..	294	..	17,607	..	73,642	..	38,448	..	35,194	54,683	+ 34·7	— 46·0	..	
	Saira Thikana	..	..	136	..	4,504	..	17,953	..	9,176	..	8,777	12,989	+ 38·2	— 44·8	..	
	Salumbar Thikana	..	..	194	..	7,816	..	30,839	..	15,743	..	15,096	20,366	+ 17·0	— 46·2	..	
	Salumbar Town	..	1	..	1,244	..	4,506	..	2,144	..	2,362	..	4,602	— 4·0	— 22·2	..	
	Sardargarh Thikana	..	..	28	..	1,039	..	4,264	..	2,212	..	2,052	3,340	+ 27·7	— 40·3	..	
	Shivrati Thikana	..	..	25	..	1,521	..	6,453	..	3,307	..	3,146	4,898	+ 31·7	— 48·4	..	
	Udaipur Tahsil *	..	..	102	..	6,296	..	24,848	..	13,323	..	11,525	19,435	+ 27·9	— 27·3	..	* Included in Udaipur City in 1901.
	Villages in Merwara District.	221·3	..	92	..	9,558	..	39,516	..	20,932	..	18,584	†	†	†	179	† 1891 and 1901 figures not available.
Partabgarh.	*Partabgarh State*	*886*	*1*	*617*	*2,342*	*13,745*	*8,329*	*54,375*	*4,186*	*27,549*	*4,143*	*26,826*	*52,025*	*+ 20·5*	*— 40·9*	*71*	
	Partabgarh Town	6	1	..	2,342	..	8,329	..	4,186	..	4,143	..	9,819	— 15·2	— 33·7	1,388	‡ Includes Bairangarh, Kanora and Partabgarh Zillas (excluding Partabgarh Town) of 1901.
	Hathunia Zilla‡	348	..	240	..	7,006	..	27,576	..	13,920	..	13,656	22,347	+ 23·4	} §	79	§ Figures not available.
	Magra Zilla	274	..	133	..	1,791	..	6,856	..	3,572	..	3,284	5,846	+ 17·3		25	
	Sagthali Zilla	238	..	244	..	4,948	..	19,943	..	10,057	..	9,886	14,013	+ 42·3		77	
Shahpura.	*Shahpura Chiefship*	*405*	*1*	*133*	*2,163*	*9,128*	*7,929*	*39,468*	*4,074*	*20,321*	*3,855*	*18,847*	*42,676*	*+ 11·1*	*— 32·9*	*117*	
	Shahpura Town	18	1	..	2,163	..	7,929	..	4,074	..	3,855	..	8,074	— 11·6	— 23·4	441	
	Shahpura Tahsil	26	..	18	..	638	..	3,000	..	1,622	..	1,378	2,554	+ 17·5	+ 35·5	115	
	Amli Tahsil	34	..	8	..	725	..	2,975	..	1,500	..	1,415	2,486	+ 19·7	— 68·3	88	
	Dhikola Tahsil	79	..	28	..	1,762	..	7,530	..	3,964	..	3,566	6,308	+ 18·2	— 40·2	95	
	Kanechan Tahsil	65	..	16	..	1,158	..	4,622	..	2,410	..	2,212	4,246	+ 8·9	— 51·8	71	
	Kothian Tahsil	60	..	20	..	1,063	..	7,546	..	3,875	..	3,671	5,428	+ 39·0	— 10·4	109	
	Phulia Tahsil	67	..	21	..	1,937	..	8,580	..	4,417	..	4,163	6,028	+ 23·8	— 39·7	128	
	Sangaria Tahsil	47	..	22	..	1,225	..	5,215	..	2,673	..	2,542	5,602	— 6·4	+ 9·7	111	
Sirohi.	*Sirohi State*	*1,964*	*5*	*409*	*6,947*	*39,437*	*24,124*	*165,003*	*13,106*	*85,183*	*11,018*	*79,820*	*134,544*	*+ 22·4*	*— 11·8*	*96*	
	Sirohi Town	‖	1	..	1,866	..	6,615	..	3,272	..	3,343	..	5,631	+ 17·1	— 0·0	‖	‖ Included in Sirohi Tahsil.
	Abu Tahsil	135·18	..	15	..	698	..	2,494	..	1,356	..	1,138	1,752	+ 42·4	— 24·9	18	
	Anadra Tahsil	(a)	..	11	..	1,618	..	6,690	..	3,422	..	3,268	5,431	+ 23·2	— 31·0	(a)	(a) Included in Pamera Tahsil.
	Bhakhar Tahsil	96	..	21	..	564	..	2,329	..	1,194	..	1,135	1,681	+ 38·5	§	24	
	Erinpura Cantonment	1	1	..	1,108	..	3,033	..	1,856	..	1,177	..	8,206	— 5·4	— 7·5	3,033	
	Jhora Tahsil	308	..	29	..	4,957	..	21,109	..	10,791	..	10,318	17,488	+ 21·1	— 14·1	101	
	Madar Tahsil	276	..	63	..	4,341	..	18,816	..	9,840	..	8,976	13,950	+ 34·9	— 25·7	68	
	Magra Tahsil	200	..	37	..	5,415	..	22,806	..	11,687	..	11,119	19,925	+ 14·5	— 15·6	114	
	Mt. Abu Town	·82	1	..	941	..	3,286	..	2,083	..	1,203	..	3,488	— 5·8	+ 34·0	4,007	
	(1) *Bazar*	} §	{ ..	..	*454*	..	*1,675*	..	*995*	..	*680*	..	*1,954*	— *14·3*	+ *52·7*	} §	
	(2) *Civil limits*		..	..	*400*	..	*1,158*	..	*753*	..	*405*	..	*1,330*	— *13·5*	+ *10·4*		
	(3) *Military limits*		..	..	*87*	..	*453*	..	*335*	..	*118*	..	*195*	+ *132·3*	+ *112·0*		
	Pamera Tahsil	(b) 228	..	49	..	4,585	..	18,864	..	9,585	..	9,279	18,959	+ 35·1	— 27·4	112(b)	(b) Includes Anadra Tahsil.
	Pindwara Tahsil	212	..	51	..	4,306	..	18,902	..	10,047	..	8,855	15,381	+ 22·9	— 25·6	89	
	Posalia Tahsil	} 239	{ ..	15	..	6,144	..	21,544	..	11,196	..	10,348	19,411	+ 11·0	— 23·7	} 107	
	Sheoganj Town		1	..	1,064	..	4,010	..	1,888	..	2,122	..	4,361	— 8·0	+ 171·4		
	Rohera Tahsil	192	..	36	..	4,248	..	16,556	..	8,251	..	8,305	12,249	+ 35·2	— 32·0	86	
	Santpura Tahsil	} 132	{ ..	45	..	3,258	..	13,609	..	7,105	..	6,504	8,900	+ 52·9	— 22·1	} 157	
	Kherari Town (Abu Road).		1	..	1,968	..	7,180	..	4,007	..	3,173	..	6,661	+ 7·8	+ 50·1		
	Sirohi Tahsil	(c) 44	..	7	..	808	..	1,284	..	709	..	575	1,100	+ 16·7	+ 18·4	(c) 180	(c) Includes Sirohi Town.

PROVINCIAL TABLE I.—AREA, HOUSES, AND POPULATION OF ADMINISTRATIVE UNITS—*concluded.*

State or District.	Administrative Unit (Pargana, Tahsil, Town, etc.)	Approximate area in square miles.	Inhabited towns.	Inhabited villages.	Occupied houses in Towns.	Occupied houses in Villages.	Population 1911, Persons in Towns.	Population 1911, Persons in Villages.	Males in Towns.	Males in Villages.	Females in Towns.	Females in Villages.	1901 both sexes.	Percentage of variation 1901-1911.	Percentage of variation 1891-1901.	Number of persons per square mile in 1911.	Remarks.
1	2	3	4	5	6	7	8	9	10	11	12	13	14	15	16	17	18
Tonk.	*Tonk State*	*2,586*	*5*	*1,273*	*15,570*	*55,978*	*60,959*	*242,222*	*30,550*	*125,840*	*30,409*	*116,382*	*273,367**	+ *10·9*	− *28·1*	*117*	* Includes 66 Railway figures omitted in 1901 Table.
	Tonk City	16	1	..	8,600	..	33,864	..	16,837	..	17,027	..	38,750	− 12·6	− 15·6	2,117	
	Aligarh Pargana	157	..	85	..	3,559	..	16,288	..	8,503	..	7,785	17,063	− 4·5	− 13·0	104	
	Chhabra Pargana	308	..	182	..	7,764	..	33,270	..	17,405	..	15,865	29,388*	+ 13·2	− 24·7	108	
	Chhabra Town	5	1	..	1,589	..	6,164	..	3,108	..	3,056	..	6,724	− 8·3	− 9·5	1,233	
	Nimbahera Pargana	379	..	187	..	10,217	..	40,412	..	20,568	..	19,844	35,053	+ 15·3	− 41·1	107	
	Nimbahera Town	7	1	..	1,479	..	4,278	..	2,260	..	2,018	..	5,446	− 21·4	− ·7	611	
	Pitawa Pargana	268	..	116	..	5,827	..	24,830	..	13,045	..	11,785	20,515	+ 21·0	− 41·7	93	
	Pitawa Town	3	1	..	1,222	..	4,562	..	2,262	..	2,300	..	4,771	− 4·4	− 15·2	1,521	
	Sironj Pargana	881	1	451	2,680	16,664	12,091	76,728	6,083	39,567	6,008	37,161	68,539	+ 29·6	− 27·0	101	
	(1) *Lahri Tahsil*	*336*	..	*180*	..	*6,311*	..	*28,561*	..	*14,729*	..	*13,832*	*58,122* (1 and 2)	+ *32·0* (1 and 2)	− *29·2* (1 and 2)	*74*	
	(2) *Sialpur and Sadar Tahsil*	*483*	..	*271*	..	*10,353*	..	*48,167*	..	*24,838*	..	*23,329*				*100*	
	(3) *Sironj Town*	*12*	*1*	..	*2,680*	..	*12,091*	..	*6,083*	..	*6,008*	..	*10,417*	+ *16·1*	− *11·2*	*1,008*	
	Tonk Pargana	562	..	252	..	11,947	..	50,694	..	26,752	..	23,942	47,009	+ 7·8	− 31·2	90	
	(1) *Bagri Tahsil*	*352*	..	*134*	..	*6,798*	..	*29,093*	..	*15,300*	..	*13,793*	*47,009* (1 and 2)	+ *7·8* (1 and 2)	− *31·2* (1 and 2)	*83*	
	(2) *Chandlai Tahsil*	*210*	..	*118*	..	*5,149*	..	*21,601*	..	*11,452*	..	*10,149*				*103*	
Ajmer.	**AJMER-MERWARA.**	**2,609·4**	**5**	**630**	**37,712**	**73,851**	**140,394**	**314,276**	**77,177**	**164,196**	**63,217**	**150,080**	**476,912†**	+ **5·1†**	− **12·1†**	**174**	† Includes figures for Marwar and Mewar villages shown above under those States.
	Ajmer District	*2,135·3*	*4*	*425*	*31,585*	*61,977*	*117,594*	*262,790*	*64,849*	*137,062*	*52,745*	*125,728*	*367,453*	+ *3·5*	− *13·0*	*178*	
	Ajmer City	27	1	..	23,571	..	86,222	..	47,354	..	38,868	..	73,839	+ 16·8	+ 7·8	3,193	
	Ajmer Istimrari area	427·8	..	73	..	12,100	..	51,525	..	27,057	..	24,408	259,970‡ (Istimrari and Khalsa)	+ 1·1‡ (Istimrari and Khalsa)	− 18·6‡ (Istimrari and Khalsa)	120	‡ Includes Kekri Istimrari area.
	Ajmer Khalsa area	851	..	193	..	27,722	..	116,039	..	60,842	..	55,107				136	
	Deoli Town	1	1	..	1,791	..	5,205	..	3,071	..	2,134	..	4,007	+ 27·0	− 22·5	5,205	
	(1) *Agency Bazar*	§ (1 to 3)	..	..	*330*	..	*1,293*	..	*698*	..	*595*	..	§ (1 to 3)	§	§	§	§ Figures not available.
	(2) *Sadar Bazar*		..	..	*596*	..	*2,497*	..	*1,302*	..	*1,195*	..					
	(3) *Cantonment*		..	..	*865*	..	*1,415*	..	*1,071*	..	*344*	..					
	Kekri Istimrari area	819·2	..	159	..	22,155	..	95,226	..	49,163	..	46,063	‖	‖	‖	116	‖ Included in Ajmer Khalsa area.
	Kekri Town	·7	1	..	1,490	..	5,926	..	3,126	..	2,800	..	7,053	− 16·0	− ·7	8,466	
	Nasirabad Town	8·6	1	..	4,733	..	20,241	..	11,298	..	8,943	..	22,494	− 10·0	+ 3·6	2,342	
	(1) *Civil limits*	§ (1 and 2)	..	..	*3,981*	..	*16,144*	..	*8,135*	..	*8,009*	..	§ (1 and 2)	§	§	§	
	(2) *Military limits*		..	..	*752*	..	*4,097*	..	*3,163*	..	*934*	..					
Merwara.	*Merwara District*	*474·1*	*1*	*205*	*6,127*	*11,874*	*22,800*	*51,486*	*12,328*	*27,134*	*10,472*	*24,352*	*109,459†*	+ *10·6†*	− *8·8†*	*157*	
	Beawar Town	2·8	1	..	6,127	..	22,800	..	12,328	..	10,472	..	21,928	+ 4·0	+ 4·5	8,142	
	Beawar Tahsil (British villages)	256·4	..	182	..	9,605	..	42,174	..	22,218	..	19,956	§ (both Tahsils)	§	§	164	
	Todgarh Tahsil (British villages)	214·9	..	23	..	2,269	..	9,312	..	4,916	..	4,396				43	

PROVINCIAL TABLE II.

Administrative Units by Religion and Education.

Explanatory Note.

This Table gives, for administrative units, details of religion for Animists, Christians, Hindus, Jains, Musalmans, and Sikhs, the remaining religions being amalgamated under the head " others, " and of education by the three age periods 0 to 14, 15 to 19, and 20 and over.

Discrepancies will be apparent between the figures in this Table and Imperial Tables VI and VIII in the case of Rajputana, Dholpur, Marwar, Ajmer-Merwara, and Merwara. The reasons for these discrepancies are given in the Explanatory Note to Provincial Table I, to which a reference should be made.

PROVINCIAL TABLE II.—ADMINISTRATIVE UNITS BY RELIGION AND EDUCATION.

State or District.	Administrative Unit (Pargana, Tahsil, Town, etc.)	Total Population. M.	Total Population. F.	Distribution by Religion. Hindu. M.	Hindu. F.	Jain. M.	Jain. F.	Sikh. M.	Sikh. F.	Musalman. M.	Musalman. F.	Animist. M.	Animist. F.	Christian. M.	Christian. F.	Others. M.	Others. F.	Number of Literate Persons. 0—14. M.	0—14. F.	15—19. M.	15—19. F.	20 and over. M.	20 and over. F.
1	2	3	4	5	6	7	8	9	10	11	12	13	14	15	16	17	18	19	20	21	22	23	24
	RAJPUTANA	**5,533,848**	**5,031,292**	**4,615,253**	**4,165,058**	**162,739**	**171,336**	**5,491**	**3,471**	**519,890**	**470,043**	**226,849**	**218,478**	**2,420**	**1,857**	**1,235**	**969**	**25,618**	**1,408**	**35,668**	**1,518**	**268,622**	**9,598**
	Alwar State	***413,659***	***378,039***	***307,493***	***280,805***	***2,158***	***1,953***	***16***	***13***	***103,079***	***95,177***	***17***	***14***	***50***	***49***	***21***	***25***	***1,592***	***60***	***1,991***	***57***	***16,669***	***384***
Alwar.	Alwar City	22,254	19,051	15,711	13,533	289	199	7	8	6,207	5,277	1	..	33	29	6	5	140	16	180	4	3,071	91
	Alwar Tahsil	46,789	43,228	28,686	26,919	56	46	..	..	17,840	16,255	..	..	5	6	1	2	111*	2*	162*	3*	1,454*	21*
	Bahadurpur Town	2,098	2,138	1,367	1,232	13	10	..	..	818	896	..	..	..	..	..	..						
	Behror Tahsil	34,660	32,363	33,108	30,772	..	..	..	..	1,492	1,501	..	..	..	..	..	..	295*	4*	304*	8*	1,877*	32*
	Behror Town	2,685	2,568	2,096	1,957	51	50	..	..	637	657	..	..	..	..	1	4						
	Bansur Tahsil	37,119	34,163	35,522	32,531	23	28	..	..	1,572	1,601	..	..	..	..	2	3	212	9	215	2	1,417	37
	Govindgarh Tahsil	7,983	7,212	3,219	2,982	..	..	..	..	4,764	4,280	..	..	..	..	..	..	31*	1*	51*	5*	314*	11*
	Govindgarh Town	1,993	1,886	1,343	1,247	52	55	..	..	597	684	..	..	..	..	1	..						
	Katumbar Tahsil	21,887	18,900	19,770	17,146	223	221	..	..	1,894	1,583	..	..	..	..	..	..	60	7	79	8	632	31
	Kishangarh Tahsil	34,123	31,090	16,148	14,621	33	25	..	2	17,937	16,487	..	..	..	..	5	5	54	3	92	3	926	11
	Lachhmangarh Tahsil	33,396	30,487	26,567	24,117	463	453	2	1	6,364	5,916	..	..	..	..	..	..	112	3	154	6	1,243	40
	Mandawar Tahsil	34,161	30,974	28,104	25,221	41	36	..	..	5,995	5,704	12	10	6	3	3	..	144	7	169	7	1,122	22
	Rajgarh Tahsil	39,351	36,819	37,619	35,158	155	131	2	1	1,575	1,529	..	..	..	..	..	..	148*	4*	215*	2*	1,826*	17*
	Rajgarh Town	4,934	4,911	4,092	3,995	67	48	2	..	788	864	..	..	5	4	..	..						
	Ramgarh Tahsil	23,894	22,153	8,050	7,430	293	271	..	..	15,651	14,452	..	..	..	..	..	..	62*	5*	76*	5*	759*	20*
	Ramgarh Town	1,860	1,645	1,346	1,198	97	87	..	..	417	300	..	..	..	..	..	..						
	Thanaghazi Tahsil	26,281	24,333	25,264	23,524	113	104	1	..	901	699	..	..	..	..	2	6	134	7	179	4	1,291	39
	Tijara Tahsil	30,130	26,856	12,952	11,618	7	11	..	..	17,167	15,223	4	4	..	..	..	..	41*	..	70*	..	547*	6*
	Tijara Town	3,341	3,220	1,858	1,755	182	178	2	1	1,209	1,286	..	..	..	..	..	..						
	Nimrana Thikana	4,700	4,032	4,443	3,899	..	..	..	..	257	133	..	..	..	..	..	..	30	1	27	..	100	5
	Banswara State	***81,620***	***83,843***	***29,611***	***30,728***	***2,196***	***2,200***	***1***	***..***	***2,483***	***2,403***	***47,323***	***48,511***	***..***	***..***	***6***	***1***	***231***	***9***	***400***	***20***	***3,157***	***167***
Banswara.	Banswara Town	3,729	3,936	2,061	2,190	141	127	1	..	1,041	1,186	479	432	..	..	6	1	65	7	94	8	720	94
	Khalsa villages	34,666	35,817	12,201	12,712	1,202	1,209	..	..	790	658	20,464	21,238	..	..	..	..	98	1	157	2	1,303	19
	Jagir and other villages	43,225	44,090	15,349	15,826	853	864	..	..	643	559	26,380	26,841	..	..	..	..	68	1	149	10	1,134	54
	Bharatpur State	***303,254***	***256,531***	***245,735***	***206,995***	***1,474***	***1,946***	***28***	***24***	***54,550***	***47,899***	***..***	***..***	***313***	***251***	***152***	***116***	***2,146***	***149***	***2,831***	***133***	***19,986***	***593***
Bharatpur.	Bharatpur City	18,803	15,115	12,784	10,014	296	239	19	17	5,328	4,540	..	..	271	223	108	82	394	85	451	66	2,807	271
	Bharatpur Tahsil	24,662	20,286	23,406	19,375	40	46	5	4	1,209	861	..	..	1	..	1	..	158	5	150	11	883	42
	Bhusawar Sub-Tahsil	11,822	10,218	11,334	9,790	55	50	..	..	430	377	..	..	1	..	2	1	66	1	58	3	424	5
	Bhusawar Town	2,252	2,057	1,625	1,438	2	1	1	1	621	612	..	..	..	..	3	5	22	3	22	..	212	7
	Biana Tahsil	33,010	27,820	31,197	26,247	19	14	..	..	1,793	1,559	..	..	1	..	..	..	105	4	102	2	778	12
	Biana Town	3,714	3,315	2,806	2,470	95	84	..	..	810	757	..	..	..	..	3	4	47	2	57	1	422	5
	Dig Tahsil	23,214	18,816	20,266	16,327	70	59	..	..	2,678	2,430	..	..	..	..	..	..	55	..	144	..	353	0
	Dig Town	7,076	6,071	5,660	4,802	127	102	..	..	1,273	1,067	..	..	6	6	10	4	151	8	300	4	743	24
	Kaman Tahsil	16,769	14,495	9,245	7,880	81	96	..	..	7,438	6,515	..	..	..	..	5	4	111	1	148	6	381	8
	Kaman Town	4,867	4,045	4,067	3,309	94	85	..	..	702	646	..	..	..	..	3	5	69	11	102	18	542	28
	Kumher Tahsil	22,558	18,299	21,579	17,522	60	40	1	..	907	731	..	..	10	6	1	..	149	..	251	3	448	4
	Kumher Town	2,679	2,396	2,038	1,829	35	28	2	2	580	525	..	..	15	12	..	..	42	5	60	1	234	12
	Nagar Tahsil	26,678	23,680	15,547	13,647	50	47	..	..	11,068	9,975	..	..	6	3	7	8	162	2	280	6	635	23
	Nandbai Tahsil	27,141	23,089	25,116	21,188	226	191	..	..	1,789	1,706	..	..	4	1	6	3	212	4	301	4	861	20
	Pahari Tahsil	22,123	19,856	8,364	7,507	61	34	..	..	13,708	12,315	..	..	..	..	..	..	78	2	103	3	481	5
	Rupbas Tahsil	23,029	19,296	20,953	17,716	19	21	..	..	2,054	1,559	..	..	..	..	3	..	134	1	106	1	914	12
	Uchain Sub-Tahsil	10,443	9,038	9,665	8,385	18	14	..	..	755	639	..	..	..	..	5	..	64	2	61	..	384	6
	Wer Tahsil	18,736	16,187	17,982	15,529	91	69	..	..	663	589	..	..	..	..	..	..	59	..	91	..	562	7
	Wer Town	2,678	2,452	2,101	1,930	43	26	..	..	534	496	..	..	..	..	..	..	68	6	42	4	222	17

*Details of literacy for Tahsils and Towns separately are not available.

PROVINCIAL TABLE II.—Administrative Units by Religion and Education—*continued.*

State or District.	Administrative Unit (Pargana, Tahsil, Town, etc).	Total Population.		Distribution by Religion. Hindu.		Jain.		Sikh.		Musalman.		Animist.		Christian.		Others.		Number of Literate Persons. 0—14.		15—19.		20 and over.	
		M.	F.	M.	F.	M.	F.	M.	F.	M.	F.	M.	F.	M.	F.	M.	F.	M.	F.	M.	F.	M.	F.
1	2	3	4	5	6	7	8	9	10	11	12	13	14	15	16	17	18	19	20	21	22	23	24
Bikaner.	***Bikaner State***	***371,489***	***329,494***	***306,659***	***269,040***	***10,255***	***14,603***	***5,034***	***3,160***	***49,347***	***43,583***	..	..	***97***	***54***	***77***	***55***	***1,468***	***59***	***2,339***	***94***	***15,960***	***655***
	Bikaner City	28,275	27,551	20,522	19,949	1,610	2,200	141	27	5,887	5,312	..	..	87	49	28	14	441	25	683	51	4,920	294
	Bikaner Nizamat	**74,284**	**65,691**	**64,408**	**56,199**	**2,970**	**3,959**	**7**	..	**6,888**	**5,525**	..	..	**6**	**3**	**5**	**5**	**122**	**1**	**207**	**1**	**1,884**	**42**
	Bikaner Tahsil	22,171	20,354	16,871	15,189	1,367	1,929	4	..	3,919	3,228	..	..	6	3	4	5	90	1	107	..	878	17
	Lunkaransar Tahsil	17,039	14,544	14,731	12,481	422	555	..	..	1,885	1,508	..	..	..	..	1	..	18	..	49	..	468	..
	Magra Sub-Tahsil	11,078	9,633	10,242	8,680	285	332	..	..	571	421	..	..	..	..	..	..	3	..	11	..	183	4
	Surpura Sub-Tahsil	23,996	21,160	22,564	19,649	916	1,143	3	..	513	368	..	..	..	..	..	..	11	..	40	1	405	21
	Reni Nizamat	**103,275**	**90,252**	**92,166**	**79,459**	**1,293**	**1,703**	**20**	**3**	**9,773**	**9,071**	..	..	**1**	..	**22**	**17**	**379**	**11**	**591**	**16**	**3,709**	**111**
	Bahadran Tahsil	19,925	16,628	18,230	15,035	167	231	4	..	1,324	1,362	..	..	..	..	..	..	33	..	78	1	587	6
	Churu Tahsil	15,332	13,556	14,021	12,409	32	39	..	..	1,279	1,108	..	..	..	..	..	..	41	1	40	2	279	6
	Churu Town	7,793	8,245	5,269	5,438	308	496	2	..	2,108	2,300	..	..	1	..	15	11	133	9	224	11	993	38
	Nohar Tahsil	23,748	19,751	22,152	18,491	33	24	10	1	1,552	1,233	..	..	..	..	1	..	16	1	30	1	497	14
	Nohar Town	2,518	2,615	1,803	1,884	96	147	2	1	615	580	..	..	..	..	2	3	42	..	68	..	314	15
	Rajgarh Tahsil	21,463	17,975	20,358	17,087	187	242	..	..	923	646	..	..	..	..	..	..	20	..	37	..	372	8
	Rajgarh Town	2,282	2,204	1,262	1,172	149	193	1	..	850	809	..	..	..	..	..	..	68	..	49	..	267	11
	Reni Sub-Tahsil	7,361	6,187	6,925	5,781	13	16	..	..	423	300	..	..	..	..	..	..	3	..	4	..	60	6
	Reni Town	2,873	3,031	2,151	2,162	218	316	1	..	499	551	..	..	..	..	4	3	23	..	61	1	331	7
	Sujangarh Nizamat	**98,519**	**92,253**	**87,403**	**79,849**	**4,232**	**6,621**	**3**	**2**	**6,861**	**5,765**	..	..	..	..	**20**	**16**	**442**	**15**	**680**	**19**	**4,044**	**186**
	Dungargarh Sub-Tahsil	16,952	15,659	15,670	14,280	659	991	..	..	623	388	..	..	..	..	..	..	24	..	67	2	456	9
	Ratangarh Tahsil	17,120	15,444	15,782	13,912	484	823	..	..	854	709	..	..	..	..	..	..	44	..	49	..	270	21
	Ratangarh Town	6,078	6,725	4,849	5,200	198	339	2	..	1,228	1,186	..	..	..	..	1	..	89	8	155	3	807	26
	Sardarshahar Tahsil	19,763	17,575	18,856	16,761	181	246	..	..	726	568	..	..	..	..	..	..	15	..	25	..	335	17
	Sardarshahar Town	6,008	6,367	3,740	3,578	1,122	1,808	1	2	1,144	979	..	..	..	..	1	..	74	2	125	1	843	12
	Sujangarh Tahsil	26,650	24,345	24,702	22,074	944	1,443	..	..	1,094	828	..	..	..	..	..	..	49	..	111	9	683	70
	Sujangarh Town	5,946	6,138	4,004	4,044	644	971	..	..	1,282	1,107	..	..	..	..	18	16	147	5	148	4	650	31
	Suratgarh Nizamat	**67,136**	**53,747**	**42,160**	**33,584**	**150**	**120**	**4,883**	**3,129**	**19,938**	**16,909**	..	..	**3**	**2**	**2**	**3**	**84**	**7**	**171**	**7**	**1,403**	**22**
	Anupgarh Sub-Tahsil	6,837	5,675	2,583	2,086	1	..	120	78	4,133	3,511	..	..	..	..	..	..	4	..	13	2	165	1
	Hanumangarh Tahsil	23,447	18,072	15,358	11,894	106	81	2,819	1,851	5,162	4,243	..	..	..	..	2	3	41	3	82	2	564	8
	Mirza wala Tahsil	17,204	14,107	9,010	7,210	1	..	1,685	1,081	6,508	5,786	..	..	..	..	..	..	3	1	22	..	188	3
	Suratgarh Tahsil	11,699	9,498	9,836	8,050	18	23	181	70	1,664	1,355	..	..	..	..	..	..	9	..	15	..	186	..
	Suratgarh Town	1,490	1,301	1,194	1,094	12	11	1	..	280	194	..	..	3	2	..	..	25	2	30	2	212	9
	Tibi Sub-Tahsil	6,459	5,094	4,179	3,220	12	5	77	49	2,191	1,820	..	..	..	..	..	..	2	1	9	1	88	1
Bundi.	***Bundi State***	***113,211***	***105,519***	***102,046***	***94,879***	***3,475***	***3,139***	***1***	..	***5,414***	***5,249***	***9,275***	***9,257***	..	..	***6***	***2***	***211***	***12***	***380***	***13***	***4,301***	***123***
	Bundi Town	9,806	9,793	6,040	6,891	470	424	..	..	2,317	2,416	74	60	..	..	4	2	86	12	109	11	1,519	95
	Arila Pargana	5,336	4,793	4,928	4,430	118	105	..	..	288	256	2	2	..	..	..	..	4	..	14	..	189	3
	Arneta Pargana	3,227	2,990	3,198	2,968	6	4	..	..	20	14	3	4	..	..	..	..	1	..	6	..	63	..
	Barundhan Pargana	10,879	10,084	9,095	8,380	203	183	..	..	293	246	1,288	1,255	..	..	..	..	5	..	17	1	232	5
	Deji Pargana	10,811	9,967	10,072	9,281	439	391	..	..	280	267	20	28	..	..	..	..	5	..	12	..	231	1
	Gotra Pargana	9,478	8,569	8,812	7,996	294	287	1	..	301	216	69	71	..	..	..	..	25	..	18	..	247	..
	Gundowali Pargana	11,635	10,839	11,209	10,417	242	233	..	..	80	76	104	118	..	..	..	..	11	..	16	..	315	1

PROVINCIAL TABLE II.

PROVINCIAL TABLE II.—ADMINISTRATIVE UNITS BY RELIGION AND EDUCATION—*continued*.

State or District.	Administrative Unit (Pargana, Tahsil, Town, etc.)	Total Population.		Distribution by Religion.														Number of Literate Persons.					
				Hindu.		Jain.		Sikh.		Musalman.		Animist.		Christian.		Others.		0—14.		15—19.		20 and over.	
		M.	F.	M.	F.	M.	F.	M.	F.	M.	F.	M.	F.	M.	F.	M.	F.	M.	F.	M.	F.	M.	F.
1	2	3	4	5	6	7	8	9	10	11	12	13	14	15	16	17	18	19	20	21	22	23	24
Bundi—concld.	Hindoli Pargana	14,168	13,069	12,861	11,887	400	368	..	..	498	406	315	321	..	..	..	..	8	..	24	..	288	2
	Karwar Pargana	7,702	7,406	7,070	6,766	458	390	..	..	262	247	2	3	..	..	..	..	10	..	18	..	221	3
	Lakheri Pargana	6,324	5,808	6,031	5,558	122	99	..	..	168	149	3	2	..	..	..	..	13	..	24	..	240	1
	Naenwa Pargana	4,278	3,923	4,028	3,696	101	83	..	..	72	68	77	76	..	..	..	..	..	..	8	..	78	..
	Naenwa Town	2,309	2,451	1,766	1,716	373	377	..	..	368	358	..	..	..	..	2	..	7	..	17	..	221	..
	Patan Pargana	7,519	6,960	7,049	6,530	124	95	..	..	332	318	14	17	..	..	..	..	27	..	29	1	303	10
	Selore Pargana	7,028	6,674	6,531	6,209	70	67	..	..	121	100	297	298	..	..	..	..	6	..	5	..	91	1
	Taiwan Pargana	2,422	2,213	2,349	2,155	46	38	..	..	30	13	7	7	..	..	..	..	8	..	3	..	53	..
Dholpur.	*Dholpur State*	*144,455*	*119,138*	*133,617*	*109,503*	*1,176*	*858*	*56*	*39*	*9,569*	*8,709*	..	..	*96*	*15*	*11*	*14*	*616*	*45*	*614*	*51*	*3,958*	*185*
	Dholpur Town	10,798	9,139	7,428	6,153	30	17	81	36	3,242	2,909	..	..	23	14	9	10	248	38	249	42	1,458	125
	Bari Tahsil	22,633	18,244	21,994	17,767	..	..	..	..	639	477	..	..	..	..	..	..	14	1	18	..	153	..
	Bari Town	5,755	5,646	4,167	3,778	5	6	..	..	1,581	1,867	..	..	1	..	1	..	48	2	61	..	441	12
	Baseri Tahsil	23,819	19,627	23,017	18,965	1	..	..	..	801	662	..	..	..	..	..	..	42	..	47	..	842	6
	Gird Tahsil	27,564	22,401	26,256	21,413	284	204	..	..	1,023	873	..	..	1	1	..	..	75	..	70	4	472	11
	Kolari Tahsil	24,653	20,704	23,497	19,821	6	8	..	..	1,150	970	..	..	..	..	..	..	96	..	74	1	418	6
	Rajakhera Tahsil	16,970	13,311	16,037	12,598	396	438	3	1	342	270	..	..	..	..	1	4	28	1	25	2	213	13
	Rajakhera Town	3,527	2,863	2,957	2,391	252	190	..	..	317	282	..	..	1	..	..	..	25	2	19	..	151	4
	Sarmathra and Rajhoni Jagirs.	8,742	7,023	8,264	6,622	2	..	2	2	474	399	..	..	..	..	..	..	40	1	51	2	315	8
Dungarpur.	*Dungarpur State*	*79,105*	*80,087*	*35,540*	*37,138*	*2,703*	*3,807*	*4*	*2*	*3,390*	*3,383*	*37,593*	*36,758*	*1*	*1*	*5*	*4*	*274*	*24*	*399*	*35*	*3,456*	*151*
	Dungarpur Town	3,116	3,354	1,694	1,801	325	320	3	2	821	975	273	247	..	..	..	..	72	13	117	22	706	86
	Dungarpur Zilla	35,134	34,875	12,506	12,779	580	586	..	..	557	428	21,485	21,080	..	..	..	..	38	2	76	3	749	19
	Galiakot Town	1,965	1,949	491	469	110	124	..	..	1,115	1,170	248	183	1	1	..	..	38	4	89	3	409	14
	Sagwara Zilla	36,781	37,519	19,856	20,985	1,478	1,562	1	..	395	242	15,048	14,730	..	..	1	..	99	4	183	5	1,197	25
	Sagwara Town	2,109	2,390	1,000	1,096	204	204	..	..	432	566	469	516	..	..	4	4	27	1	34	2	393	7
Jaipur.	*Jaipur State*	*1,385,750*	*1,250,897*	*1,169,980*	*1,136,600*	*20,995*	*18,113*	*89*	*68*	*101,925*	*94,535*	*955*	*894*	*689*	*637*	*917*	*190*	*6,401*	*840*	*9,310*	*876*	*68,940*	*9,337*
	Jaipur City	70,846	66,252	45,962	44,508	3,863	3,640	80	58	19,773	17,891	..	..	139	103	49	52	1,044	129	1,423	124	11,002	629
	Bandikui Nizamat and Tahsil.	5,116	4,383	3,966	3,389	82	82	..	..	880	723	1	1	172	171	15	17	81	80	77	15	588	109
	Dausa Nizamat	162,082	150,416	157,330	145,982	1,217	1,084	..	..	3,534	3,348	..	..	1	2	..	..	483*	14*	671*	15*	5,551*	144*
	Baswa Tahsil	33,616	32,449	32,884	31,761	223	170	..	..	509	518	..	..	..	..	..	..	..	..	..	..	..	..
	Baswa Town	2,820	2,712	2,560	2,433	50	53	..	..	209	224	..	..	1	2	..	..	..	..	..	..	..	..
	Dausa Tahsil	58,171	53,931	56,674	52,371	587	653	..	..	910	807	..	..	..	..	..	..	..	..	..	..	..	..
	Dausa Town	2,672	2,519	2,151	1,983	43	29	..	..	478	327	..	..	..	..	..	..	..	..	..	..	..	..
	Lalsot Tahsil	45,554	40,808	44,431	39,792	246	227	..	..	877	789	..	..	..	..	..	..	..	..	..	..	..	..
	Lalsot Town	3,300	3,397	3,019	3,134	43	39	..	..	238	224	..	..	..	..	..	..	..	..	..	..	..	..
	Sikrai Tahsil	15,949	14,600	15,611	14,328	25	13	..	..	313	259	..	..	..	..	..	..	..	..	..	..	..	..

* Details of literacy for Tahsils and Towns, etc., are not available.

PROVINCIAL TABLE II.—ADMINISTRATIVE UNITS BY RELIGION AND EDUCATION—*continued.*

State or District.	Administrative Unit (Pargana, Tahsil, Town, etc.)	Total Population.		Distribution by Religion. Hindu.		Jain.		Sikh.		Musalman.		Animist.		Christian.		Others.		Number of Literate Persons. 0–14.		15–19.		20 and over.	
		M.	F.	M.	F.	M.	F.	M.	F.	M.	F.	M.	F.	M.	F.	M.	F.	M.	F.	M.	F.	M.	F.
1	2	3	4	5	6	7	8	9	10	11	12	13	14	15	16	17	18	19	20	21	22	23	24
Jaipur—*continued.*	**Gangapur Nisamat**	**38,333**	**33,752**	**35,483**	**31,470**	**222**	**187**	..	..	**2,544**	**2,026**	**2**	**2**	**79**	**67**	**3**	**1**	**82***	**12***	**134***	**12***	**1,343***	**57***
	Bamanwas Tahsil	3,425	3,182	3,287	3,064	28	19	..	..	110	99	..	..	..	..	..	..	..	..	..	..	..	..
	Bamanwas Town	2,229	2,063	2,105	1,936	30	25	..	..	94	82	..	..	..	..	..	..	..	..	..	..	..	..
	Gangapur Tahsil	18,544	16,211	17,650	15,456	60	58	..	..	833	696	..	..	..	..	1	1	..	..	..	..	..	..
	Gangapur Town	3,199	2,581	2,527	2,111	33	26	..	..	558	376	..	1	79	67	2	..	..	..	..	..	..	..
	Wazirpur Tahsil	10,936	9,715	9,914	8,883	71	59	..	..	949	772	2	1	..	..	..	..	..	..	..	..	..	..
	Hindaun Nisamat	**99,075**	**86,170**	**92,285**	**80,187**	**852**	**670**	..	..	**5,926**	**5,302**	..	..	**5**	**5**	**7**	**6**	**275***	**5***	**371***	**8***	**3,063***	**83***
	Ghonsla Tahsil	9,184	7,434	8,703	7,026	87	83	..	..	394	325	..	..	..	..	..	..	..	..	..	..	..	..
	Hindaun Tahsil	21,800	18,985	20,575	17,882	296	228	..	..	929	775	..	..	..	..	..	..	..	..	..	..	..	..
	Hindaun Town	5,737	4,903	4,517	3,783	68	60	..	..	1,146	1,053	..	..	4	5	2	2	..	..	..	..	..	..
	Mahwa Tahsil	17,206	15,671	16,150	14,811	151	114	..	..	895	746	..	..	1	..	..	..	..	..	..	..	..	..
	Ratanzila Tahsil	9,282	7,980	8,641	7,426	81	62	..	..	555	488	..	..	..	..	5	4	..	..	..	..	..	..
	Toda Bhim Tahsil	18,958	16,889	18,021	16,050	63	45	..	..	874	794	..	..	..	..	..	..	..	..	..	..	..	..
	Toda Bhim Town	3,519	3,367	2,980	2,775	20	15	..	..	519	577	..	..	..	..	..	..	..	..	..	..	..	..
	Waighat Tahsil	13,389	11,041	12,689	10,424	86	63	..	..	614	544	..	..	..	..	..	..	..	..	..	..	..	..
	Jaipur Nisamat	**253,685**	**230,339**	**241,189**	**219,489**	**3,760**	**3,216**	**7**	**1**	**8,602**	**7,603**	**36**	**15**	**3**	**1**	**88**	**14**	**961***	**43***	**1,305***	**34***	**10,701***	**268***
	Chaksu Tahsil	37,605	33,810	35,892	31,918	979	783	..	..	722	610	12	8	..	..	..	..	..	..	..	..	..	..
	Chaksu Town	2,099	1,850	1,628	1,381	80	67	7	1	383	400	..	..	..	..	1	1	..	..	..	..	..	..
	Chaumun Town	3,223	3,272	2,735	2,723	68	65	..	..	422	484	..	..	..	..	..	..	..	..	..	..	..	..
	Jaipur Tahsil	88,601	80,080	85,202	77,407	918	765	..	..	2,460	1,852	6	4	1	..	14	8	..	..	..	..	..	..
	Jamwa Ramgarh Tahsil	64,377	59,408	62,354	57,681	143	106	..	..	1,880	1,066	..	..	..	..	..	..	..	..	..	..	..	..
	Kalegh Tahsil	53,409	48,295	49,582	44,824	1,568	1,428	..	..	2,166	2,034	18	3	2	1	73	5	..	..	..	..	..	..
	Manoharpur Town	1,084	1,010	917	815	..	..	..	..	167	195	..	..	..	..	..	..	..	..	..	..	..	..
	Sanod Town	1,381	1,425	1,202	1,256	4	2	..	..	175	167	..	..	..	..	..	..	..	..	..	..	..	..
	Shahpura Town	1,904	1,729	1,677	1,534	..	..	..	..	227	195	..	..	..	..	..	..	..	..	..	..	..	..
	Kot Kasim Nisamat and Tahsil	**9,560**	**8,707**	**8,374**	**7,582**	**29**	**21**	..	..	**1,157**	**1,104**	..	..	..	..	..	..	**50***	..	**60***	**5***	**398***	**5***
	Madhopur Nisamat	**108,973**	**97,414**	**98,602**	**88,323**	**2,293**	**1,977**	**12**	**2**	**8,049**	**7,092**	**7**	**15**	**8**	**5**	**2**	..	**270***	**10***	**430***	**11***	**4,283***	**108***
	Barwara Thikana	5,114	4,804	4,488	4,214	270	253	..	..	350	324	6	13	..	..	..	..	..	..	..	..	..	..
	Bonli Tahsil	27,190	24,321	25,246	22,637	668	566	..	..	1,279	1,117	1	1	..	..	1	..	..	..	..	..	..	..
	Isarda Thikana	6,208	5,717	5,809	5,380	191	150	..	..	203	183	..	1	5	3	..	..	..	..	..	..	..	..
	Khundar Tahsil	16,377	14,434	16,052	14,175	103	99	..	..	222	160	..	..	..	..	..	..	..	..	..	..	..	..
	Malarna Tahsil	24,392	21,521	21,737	19,304	276	210	1	2	2,378	1,996	..	..	..	..	..	..	..	..	..	..	..	..
	Sawai Madhopur Tahsil	23,792	21,351	21,024	18,924	438	382	..	..	2,308	2,043	..	..	3	2	..	..	..	..	..	..	..	..
	Sawai Madhopur Town	5,900	5,206	4,216	3,689	332	308	11	..	1,309	1,269	..	..	1	..	1	..	..	..	..	..	..	..
	Malpura Nisamat	**71,915**	**63,540**	**65,562**	**58,285**	**2,397**	**2,005**	..	..	**3,305**	**2,662**	**651**	**588**	..	..	..	..	**300***	**7***	**249***	**10***	**3,377***	**51***
	Malpura Tahsil	28,187	24,802	26,024	23,151	773	653	..	..	1,020	745	370	342	..	..	..	..	..	..	..	..	..	..
	Malpura Town	3,230	2,910	2,244	2,043	183	142	..	..	790	709	13	16	..	..	..	..	..	..	..	..	..	..
	Newai Tahsil	12,154	10,849	11,568	10,331	289	227	..	..	288	236	9	5	..	..	..	..	..	..	..	..	..	..
	Newai Town	2,851	1,879	2,371	1,490	224	206	..	..	256	183	..	..	..	..	..	..	..	..	..	..	..	..
	Toda Rai Singh Tahsil	23,172	20,809	21,605	19,661	714	565	..	..	604	453	249	220	..	..	..	..	..	..	..	..	..	..
	Toda Rai Singh Town	2,321	2,111	1,750	1,609	214	212	..	..	347	286	10	4	..	..	..	..	..	..	..	..	..	..

*Details of literacy for Tahsils and Towns are not available.

PROVINCIAL TABLE II.—ADMINISTRATIVE UNITS BY RELIGION AND EDUCATION—*continued.*

State or District.	Administrative Unit (Pargana, Tahsil, Town, etc.)	TOTAL POPULATION.		DISTRIBUTION BY RELIGION.														NUMBER OF LITERATE PERSONS.					
				HINDU.		JAIN.		SIKH.		MUSALMAN.		ANIMIST.		CHRISTIAN.		OTHERS.		0—14		15—19.		20 and over.	
		M.	F.	M.	F.	M.	F.	M.	F.	M.	F.	M.	F.	M.	F.	M.	F.	M.	F.	M.	F.	M.	F.
1	2	3	4	5	6	7	8	9	10	11	12	13	14	15	16	17	18	19	20	21	22	23	24
Jaipur—concluded.	**Sambhar Nizamat**	**92,032**	**80,436**	**83,060**	**72,788**	**2,656**	**2,281**	**7**	**3**	**5,927**	**5,004**	**77**	**60**	**280**	**280**	**25**	**20**	**604***	**40***	**738***	**74***	**5,679**	**296***
	Danta Ramgarh Tahsil	41,674	36,931	39,270	34,659	805	793	..	..	1,588	1,478	2	1	..	..	..	..	..	..	..	..	..	..
	Mauzamabad Tahsil	14,495	13,070	12,800	11,623	524	426	..	..	1,021	835	8	6	142	180	..	..	..	..	..	..	..	..
	Naraina Tahsil	13,049	10,802	11,200	9,455	509	427	5	..	1,159	882	42	28	111	80	23	20	..	..	..	..	..	..
	Naraina Town	3,255	1,935	2,763	1,510	64	61	..	..	425	361	..	..	3	3	..	..	..	..	..	..	..	..
	Phagi Tahsil	12,119	10,738	11,039	9,900	690	518	..	..	368	286	25	25	..	..	2	..	..	..	..	..	..	..
	Sambhar Tahsil	1,076	948	1,032	915	3	2	..	..	41	31	..	..	..	..	..	..	..	..	..	..	..	..
	Sambhar Town	2,997	2,551	1,989	1,711	40	31	..	..	948	798	..	..	20	11	..	..	..	..	..	..	..	..
	Sri Madhopur Town	3,367	3,371	2,958	3,006	21	23	2	3	382	333	..	..	4	6	..	..	..	..	..	..	..	..
	Shekhawati Nizamat	**152,428**	**137,629**	**136,081**	**120,540**	**392**	**422**	..	..	**15,906**	**16,638**	**46**	**29**	..	..	**3**	..	**560***	**16***	**1,173***	**18***	**6,436***	**194***
	Bisau Town	3,203	3,635	3,180	2,501	12	11	..	..	1,011	1,123	..	..	..	..	..	..	..	..	..	..	..	..
	Jhunjhnu Tahsil	92,306	81,790	84,667	74,074	260	270	..	..	7,346	7,424	34	22	..	..	1	..	..	..	..	..	..	..
	Jhunjhnu Town	6,575	6,691	3,770	3,590	76	101	..	..	2,715	2,984	12	7	..	..	2	..	..	..	..	..	..	..
	Mandawa Town	2,754	2,782	2,328	2,367	5	2	..	..	421	413	..	..	..	..	..	..	..	..	..	..	..	..
	Nawalgarh Town	6,874	7,185	5,704	5,969	23	20	..	..	1,147	1,196	..	..	..	..	..	..	..	..	..	..	..	..
	Singhana Town	2,422	2,846	1,412	1,465	7	11	..	..	1,003	1,370	..	..	..	..	..	..	..	..	..	..	..	..
	Surajgarh Town	2,962	3,030	2,318	2,372	2	..	..	..	642	658	..	..	..	..	..	..	..	..	..	..	..	..
	Udaipur Tahsil	30,871	26,386	29,647	25,271	5	4	..	..	1,219	1,111	..	..	..	..	..	..	..	..	..	..	..	..
	Udaipur Town	4,459	3,284	4,055	2,922	2	3	..	..	402	359	..	..	..	..	..	..	..	..	..	..	..	..
	Torawati Nizamat	**129,370**	**116,075**	**123,031**	**109,972**	**630**	**679**	..	..	**5,699**	**5,419**	**3**	**5**	..	..	**7**	..	**761***	**13***	**923***	**18***	**6,320***	**147***
	Bairath Tahsil	25,743	23,713	24,902	22,950	16	20	..	..	825	743	..	..	..	..	..	..	..	..	..	..	..	..
	Bairath Town	2,549	2,724	2,004	2,079	182	210	..	..	363	435	..	..	..	..	..	..	..	..	..	..	..	..
	Khandela Tahsil	30,401	26,629	29,292	25,564	335	330	..	..	774	715	..	..	..	..	..	..	..	..	..	..	..	..
	Khandela Town	3,995	4,211	2,855	2,869	64	68	..	..	1,059	1,274	..	..	..	..	7	..	..	..	..	..	..	..
	Nimka Thana Town	3,291	2,655	2,803	2,302	12	11	..	..	476	342	..	..	..	..	..	..	..	..	..	..	..	..
	Sawai Ramgarh Tahsil	63,391	56,143	61,165	54,206	21	20	..	..	2,202	1,910	3	5	..	..	..	..	..	..	..	..	..	..
	Khetri Thikana	**69,962**	**64,025**	**64,516**	**58,597**	**17**	**20**	..	..	**5,391**	**5,375**	**30**	**28**	..	..	**8**	**5**						
	Chirawa Town	3,891	4,088	3,282	3,516	6	8	..	..	603	564	..	..	..	..	..	..						
	Khetri Tahsil	58,910	53,094	55,724	49,875	1	..	..	..	3,155	3,191	30	28	..	..	..	..						
	Khetri Town	3,718	3,407	2,751	2,485	10	12	..	..	949	905	..	..	..	..	8	5						
	Kot Putli Town	3,443	3,436	2,759	2,721	..	..	..	..	684	715	..	..	..	..	..	..						
	Sikar Thikana	**104,612**	**95,812**	**89,678**	**80,859**	**1,115**	**1,234**	**3**	**4**	**13,804**	**13,707**	..	..	**2**	**3**	**10**	**5**						
	Fatehpur Town	8,280	9,014	5,667	6,158	263	328	..	..	2,343	2,528	..	..	..	..	7	2	1,030*	21*	1,656*	32*	10,204*	246*
	Lachhmangarh Town	5,024	5,804	4,070	4,810	24	20	..	..	930	974	..	..	..	..	..	..						
	Ramgarh Town	5,657	5,899	4,354	4,434	50	61	..	..	1,253	1,402	..	..	..	1	..	1						
	Sikar Tahsil	74,147	64,282	68,871	59,495	394	371	..	..	4,881	4,414	..	..	1	2	..	..						
	Sikar Town	11,504	10,813	6,716	5,962	384	454	3	4	4,397	4,391	..	..	1	..	3	2						
	Uniara Thikana	**17,761**	**15,947**	**16,161**	**14,629**	**770**	**595**	..	..	**728**	**642**	**102**	**81**	..	..	..	..						
	Uniara Tahsil	15,408	13,687	14,289	12,855	607	433	..	..	410	318	102	81	..	..	..	..						
	Uniara Town	2,353	2,260	1,872	1,774	163	162	..	..	318	324	..	..	..	..	..	..						

* Details of literacy for Thikanas, Tahsils and Towns are not available.

PROVINCIAL TABLE II.—Administrative Units by Religion and Education—*continued*.

State or District.	Administrative Unit (Pargana, Tahsil, Town, etc.)	Total Population. M.	Total Population. F.	Hindu. M.	Hindu. F.	Jain. M.	Jain. F.	Sikh. M.	Sikh. F.	Musalman. M.	Musalman. F.	Animist. M.	Animist. F.	Christian. M.	Christian. F.	Others. M.	Others. F.	Literate 0—14. M.	Literate 0—14. F.	Literate 15—19. M.	Literate 15—19. F.	Literate 20 and over. M.	Literate 20 and over. F.
1	2	3	4	5	6	7	8	9	10	11	12	13	14	15	16	17	18	19	20	21	22	23	24
Jaisalmer.	***Jaisalmer State***	***48,500***	***39,811***	***33,198***	***27,753***	***549***	***553***	***1***	..	***12,506***	***9,593***	***9,946***	***1,812***	..	..	..	..	***250***	***3***	***297***	***10***	***2,180***	***83***
	Jaisalmer Town	3,667	3,753	2,968	3,052	60	121	..	..	518	474	128	106	..	..	..	..	163	8	144	7	1,017	55
	Bap Pargana	5,897	4,604	4,942	3,771	2	..	..	..	595	581	358	302	..	..	..	..	14	..	18	1	112	7
	Barawa Bulli Pargana	644	512	423	344	..	..	..	..	319	168	2	..	..	..	..	..	..	..	..	..	1	..
	Devikot Pargana	4,673	3,624	3,302	2,617	83	45	..	..	1,137	818	151	149	..	..	..	..	5	..	16	..	128	..
	Dewa Pargana	1,667	1,430	1,376	1,218	..	..	..	..	207	146	84	66	..	..	..	..	4	..	4	..	32	1
	Fatehgarh Pargana	3,386	2,877	2,530	2,223	111	108	..	..	547	357	198	189	..	..	..	..	5	..	11	..	90	1
	Jaisa mer Pargana	3,187	2,613	2,433	1,990	31	82	..	..	525	404	195	187	..	..	..	..	6	..	6	..	107	..
	Kuslala Pargana	1,747	1,321	418	419	3	..	..	..	1,248	850	78	52	..	..	..	..	4	..	3	..	15	..
	Kishangarh Pargana	574	301	116	53	1	..	..	..	426	225	31	23	..	..	..	..	..	..	..	..	2	..
	Lalkhan Pargana	2,282	1,942	1,704	1,464	215	196	..	..	296	222	67	60	..	..	..	..	7	..	16	..	125	4
	Mayajilar Pargana	1,433	1,111	1,081	879	20	18	..	..	237	152	95	62	..	..	..	..	8	..	7	..	44	1
	Mohangarh Nachna Pargana	3,060	2,727	1,804	1,301	..	..	..	..	1,672	1,260	184	166	..	..	..	..	1	..	15	1	102	4
	Nokh Pargana	9,465	7,597	7,219	5,863	21	31	..	..	1,731	1,308	494	395	..	..	..	..	24	..	40	1	243	8
	Ramgarh Pargana	1,188	1,156	1,012	989	2	2	..	..	149	143	25	22	..	..	..	..	2	..	4	..	22	1
	Shahgarh Ghotra Pargana	1,893	1,654	193	153	..	..	1	..	1,656	1,468	43	33	..	..	..	..	8	..	4	..	65	3
	Shamkhaba Pargana	2,870	2,400	1,621	1,382	..	..	..	..	1,143	931	106	87	..	..	..	..	4	..	9	..	72	..
	Tanot Pargana	267	180	61	35	..	..	..	..	197	141	9	13	..	..	..	..	..	..	..	..	8	..
Jhalawar.	***Jhalawar State***	***50,034***	***46,237***	***44,137***	***40,448***	***1,312***	***1,170***	***32***	***21***	***4,265***	***4,360***	***228***	***192***	***18***	***8***	***43***	***32***	***268***	***32***	***378***	***31***	***2,810***	***195***
	Jhalrapatan Chhaoni Town	3,597	5,877	3,649	3,817	88	84	22	16	1,783	1,080	8	4	17	8	30	18	73	23	103	20	810	115
	Awar Tahsil	3,259	4,482	4,849	4,152	240	171	7	5	168	154	..	..	..	..	..	..	29	..	23	1	162	2
	Dag Tahsil	9,460	8,670	8,806	8,010	269	241	2	..	391	414	..	..	..	..	1	5	37	2	41	1	325	12
	Gangdhar Tahsil	11,675	10,490	10,887	9,745	807	267	..	..	480	478	..	..	1	..	..	..	30	2	61	1	451	12
	Pachpahar Tahsil	5,730	5,259	5,197	4,746	131	134	..	..	407	377	2	2	..	..	2	..	31	1	41	..	318	8
	Patan Tahsil	6,037	5,420	5,780	5,220	5	2	..	..	161	124	90	74	..	..	..	..	11	..	15	..	67	..
	Patan Town	3,547	3,643	2,514	2,562	265	276	..	..	766	805	1	..	..	..	1	..	46	4	83	8	585	45
	Srichhatarpur Tahsil	2,711	2,396	2,455	2,196	6	1	1	..	114	78	127	112	..	..	8	9	11	..	11	..	92	1
Karauli.	***Karauli State***	***80,081***	***66,506***	***75,485***	***62,504***	***225***	***169***	..	..	***4,345***	***3,818***	***6***	***2***	***15***	***13***	***5***	***3***	***262***	***22***	***357***	***18***	***3,153***	***106***
	Karauli Town	10,548	9,255	8,102	6,909	158	132	..	..	2,275	2,190	2	..	13	12	4	3	134	20	159	17	1,747	73
	Hasur Tahsil	23,912	19,548	23,202	19,021	29	14	..	..	681	513	..	..	..	..	..	..	36	1	57	..	456	8
	Machilpur Tahsil	11,321	8,020	10,951	8,647	6	1	..	..	364	272	..	..	..	..	..	..	8	..	20	..	133	2
	Mandrail Tahsil	10,123	8,320	9,855	8,084	4	..	..	..	264	236	..	..	..	..	..	..	41	..	36	1	193	10
	Sapotra Tahsil	17,444	15,272	16,745	14,695	32	22	..	..	660	552	4	2	2	1	1	..	27	1	60	..	498	11
	Utgir Tahsil	6,733	5,191	6,630	5,148	2	..	..	..	101	43	..	..	..	..	..	..	16	..	25	..	131	2
Kishangarh.	***Kishangarh State***	***45,718***	***41,473***	***40,171***	***36,471***	***1,680***	***1,496***	***4***	..	***3,577***	***3,908***	***263***	***272***	***8***	***15***	***15***	***11***	***347***	***18***	***424***	***30***	***2,995***	***151***
	Kishangarh Town	5,143	4,975	3,610	3,255	442	407	4	..	1,459	1,282	7	7	6	13	15	11	123	13	172	23	1,116	97
	Kishangarh Pargana	10,092	9,052	9,095	8,178	250	199	..	..	741	669	6	8	..	..	..	..	47	..	67	2	418	21
	Arain Pargana	8,291	7,144	7,795	6,743	302	258	..	..	180	133	14	15	..	..	..	..	32	1	45	1	356	12
	Fatehgarh Pargana	3,401	2,957	3,072	2,663	126	104	..	..	105	95	98	95	..	..	..	..	22	1	14	2	161	9
	Rupnagar Pargana	8,732	8,053	8,311	7,667	145	128	..	..	276	258	..	..	..	..	..	..	38	..	31	1	305	6
	Rupnagar Town	1,510	1,469	1,123	1,084	121	134	..	..	273	240	..	..	2	2	..	..	44	3	36	1	201	5
	Sarwar Pargana	6,022	5,623	5,674	5,345	170	138	..	..	97	49	81	91	..	..	..	..	12	..	21	..	186	1
	Sarwar Town	2,218	2,200	1,591	1,536	124	133	..	..	446	473	57	53	..	..	..	..	29	..	38	..	252	..

PROVINCIAL TABLE II.—Administrative Units by Religion and Education—*continued*.

State or District.	Administrative Unit (Pargana, Tahsil, Town, etc.)	Total Population. M.	Total Population. F.	Distribution by Religion. Hindu. M.	Hindu. F.	Jain. M.	Jain. F.	Sikh. M.	Sikh. F.	Musalman. M.	Musalman. F.	Animist. M.	Animist. F.	Christian. M.	Christian. F.	Others. M.	Others. F.	Number of Literate Persons. 0–14. M.	0–14. F.	15–19. M.	15–19. F.	20 and over. M.	20 and over. F.
1	2	3	4	5	6	7	8	9	10	11	12	13	14	15	16	17	18	19	20	21	22	23	24
Kotah.	*Kotah State*	*330,324*	*308,765*	*301,657*	*283,480*	*3,460*	*2,939*	*109*	*107*	*23,163*	*21,406*	*1,558*	*1,517*	*274*	*233*	*103*	*70*	*1,303*	*99*	*1,828*	*106*	*15,009*	*596*
	Kotah City	18,040	15,804	11,389	10,447	517	459	12	10	4,942	4,801	18	18	33	46	38	28	227	35	385	45	2,721	207
	Nizamats Total	288,627	269,713	267,903	250,879	2,323	1,968	96	96	16,476	15,046	1,528	1,498	236	184	65	42	992	48	1,324	52	11,277	345
	Akiera	17,254	15,881	16,334	15,078	171	142	..	..	747	661	..	..	..	..	2	..	47	3	49	2	415	10
	Anta	14,145	13,823	13,143	12,846	25	16	6	..	970	956	..	..	..	..	1	5	59	3	67	3	558	21
	Annawar	6,595	5,184	6,376	4,986	22	13	4	8	193	177	..	..	..	..	..	..	13	1	14	1	122	6
	Bakani	15,404	14,105	14,581	13,314	150	136	..	..	663	643	8	12	..	..	..	..	33	1	52	1	462	18
	Baran	14,051	13,578	13,565	13,185	29	20	..	..	409	333	47	40	1	..	..	..	47	4	48	4	575	10
	Baran Town	4,973	4,584	3,745	3,349	156	105	..	..	1,060	1,072	..	..	..	..	12	8	58	1	83	..	572	18
	Barod	9,695	9,208	9,168	8,673	64	59	..	..	463	476	..	..	..	..	..	..	21	1	49	..	394	5
	Chechat	15,738	14,310	14,653	13,378	180	110	2	1	842	773	51	43	1	2	4	3	69	2	79	4	764	9
	Chhipa Barod	17,227	16,358	16,198	15,400	74	71	..	..	922	861	33	28	..	..	..	..	73	6	72	3	628	19
	Digod	10,380	9,763	9,630	9,116	117	108	..	..	532	514	13	13	..	..	18	14	16	1	28	2	370	4
	Etawah	10,750	10,121	10,248	9,635	144	122	..	..	355	361	..	..	..	..	3	3	28	1	58	3	381	9
	Kanwas	11,192	10,238	10,606	9,717	90	71	..	..	495	450	..	..	..	..	1	..	19	2	41	1	484	6
	Khanpur	22,553	21,414	21,255	20,226	253	235	..	..	927	828	115	124	2	3	1	..	71	2	81	2	787	14
	Kishanganj	13,523	12,310	12,586	11,410	43	25	18	13	417	415	429	456	..	..	..	..	50	8	48	2	440	14
	Kunjer	10,021	9,206	9,378	8,656	93	87	..	..	343	299	..	..	203	163	4	1	67	5	95	14	844	100
	Ladpura	21,746	20,025	18,506	17,119	372	321	65	74	2,278	2,019	483	473	29	16	13	3	92	5	134	6	1,068	46
	Mangrol	12,152	11,745	11,515	11,201	46	38	..	..	587	505	4	1	..	..	..	..	57	4	84	3	555	3
	Mangrol Town	2,429	2,360	1,769	1,674	50	42	..	..	606	639	..	..	..	..	4	5	89	1	34	1	209	10
	Manoharthana	18,282	16,728	16,078	15,715	82	47	..	..	1,202	966	..	..	..	..	..	..	39	..	38	..	410	2
	Sangod	11,079	11,337	11,243	10,734	23	16	..	..	678	559	35	28	..	..	..	..	37	..	28	..	394	19
	Sangod Town	2,767	2,776	2,223	2,204	65	61	..	..	479	510	..	1	..	..	..	..	30	..	38	..	301	..
	Shahabad	14,241	13,056	13,441	12,372	51	33	1	..	441	352	307	278	..	..	..	..	14	2	61	..	300	1
	Shergarh	12,575	11,645	11,712	10,891	73	72	..	..	785	679	3	3	..	..	2	..	38	..	43	..	360	1
	Kotris Total	24,748	23,248	22,365	21,154	620	525	1	1	1,745	1,559	12	6	5	3	..	..	84	9	119	9	1,004	44
	Antarda	1,502	1,433	1,374	1,314	66	70	..	..	60	46	2	3	..	..	..	..	1	..	2	..	38	..
	Balwan	1,794	1,652	1,662	1,539	29	26	..	..	103	87	..	..	..	..	..	..	3	..	2	..	39	..
	Farera (Sub-Kotri)	83	83	78	76	..	..	..	..	5	7	..	..	..	..	..	..	..	..	..	..	5	1
	Gainta	2,047	2,060	1,907	1,945	25	23	..	..	115	92	..	..	..	..	..	..	3	4	11	1	114	2
	Indargarh	11,681	10,906	10,325	9,726	437	358	1	1	903	817	10	3	5	3	..	..	57	1	67	5	458	19
	Karwar	1,024	954	908	840	21	18	..	..	95	96	..	..	..	..	..	..	1	..	2	..	22	..
	Khatoli	3,682	3,460	3,358	3,203	32	23	..	..	292	254	..	..	..	..	..	..	9	4	7	3	144	17
	K otri (Sub-Kotri)	154	178	150	173	..	..	..	..	4	5	..	..	..	..	..	..	..	..	..	..	3	1
	Phusod	406	346	382	328	..	..	..	..	24	18	..	..	..	..	..	..	..	..	..	..	4	..
	Pipalda Mustarka	1,612	1,479	1,475	1,355	10	7	..	..	127	117	..	..	..	..	..	..	10	..	27	..	165	4
	Pipalda Thikana	768	676	746	655	..	..	..	..	17	20	..	..	..	..	..	..	..	..	1	..	12	..
Kushalgarh.	*Kushalgarh Chiefship*	*10,956*	*11,049*	*1,848*	*1,840*	*270*	*243*	..	..	*349*	*348*	*8,488*	*8,619*	..	..	*1*	..	*78*	*3*	*51*	*3*	*357*	*27*
	Kushalgarh Town	1,276	1,318	616	666	258	239	..	..	203	201	199	212	..	..	..	..	54	3	42	3	296	23
	Dungra Tahsil (including Thanb sar Jagir)	3,475	3,541	578	574	5	1	..	..	69	62	2,823	2,904	..	..	..	..	1	..	5	..	58	4
	Mayad Tahsil	3,375	3,396	310	283	..	..	..	..	33	30	3,031	3,083	..	..	1	..	13	..	2	..	5	..
	Patan Tahsil (including Chudibar Jagir)	2,330	2,794	344	323	7	3	..	..	44	55	2,435	2,413	..	..	..	..	10	..	2	..	3	..
Lawa.	*Lawa Estate*	*1,309*	*1,269*	*1,143*	*1,139*	*75*	*67*	..	..	*83*	*56*	..	..	..	..	*1*	..	*9*	*1*	*6*	*1*	*89*	*19*

PROVINCIAL TABLE II.—Administrative Units by Religion and Education—*continued*.

State or District.	Administrative Unit (Pargana, Tahsil, Town, etc.).	Total Population.		Distribution by Religion.																Number of Literate Persons.					
				Hindu.		Jain.		Sikh.		Musalman.		Animist.		Christian.		Others.		0—14.		15—19.		20 and over.	
		M.	F.	M.	F.	M.	F.	M.	F.	M.	F.	M.	F.	M.	F.	M.	F.	M.	F.	M.	F.	M.	F.
1	2	3	4	5	6	7	8	9	10	11	12	13	14	15	16	17	18	19	20	21	22	23	24
Marwar.	***Marwar State***	***1,079,162***	***985,600***	***902,010***	***812,433***	***61,300***	***70,749***	***84***	***14***	***88,917***	***79,221***	***26,966***	***22,719***	***236***	***205***	***319***	***366***	***6,629****	***273****	***3,284****	***280****	***60,622****	***2,242****
	Jodhpur City	29,351	29,911	19,542	20,121	2,067	2,077	6	6	7,647	7,603	7	4	22	17	40	23	783	40	996	47	6,801	818
	Jodhpur Town or Suburbs	12,487	8,007	10,088	5,277	723	208	7	2	1,033	1,316	17	22	96	95	103	87	167	41	202	19	1,602	186
	Bali Pargana	48,879	46,837	42,496	38,248	5,319	7,701	..	..	749	619	289	251	28	23	..	..	427	7	476	15	3,207	112
	Bali Town	2,732	2,801	1,771	1,616	655	931	..	..	306	294	..	..	..	..	..	..	74	..	51	..	386	3
	Balotra Town	2,802	2,606	2,016	1,784	412	490	1	2	371	329	..	..	2	1	..	..	73	2	78	..	589	22
	Barmer Town	3,285	3,095	2,398	2,163	471	524	..	..	401	398	9	3	..	..	6	7	63	2	90	1	556	10
	Bhinmal Town	2,598	2,616	1,585	1,491	627	846	..	..	147	101	238	178	..	..	1	..	44	..	59	9	409	4
	Bilara Pargana	30,808	28,159	28,033	25,512	1,498	1,531	1	..	1,228	1,003	16	20	..	..	2	3	111	1	156	1	1,096	20
	Bilara Town	4,453	4,153	3,837	3,552	288	290	..	..	328	311	..	..	..	..	..	..	23	1	40	2	282	17
	Desuri Pargana	33,051	31,361	29,684	26,150	3,410	4,309	..	..	796	663	150	143	7	5	4	1	230	6	251	7	2,257	56
	Didwana Pargana	39,806	37,664	36,011	33,580	278	334	..	..	3,402	3,636	17	10	..	..	96	104	92	3	157	3	1,235	77
	Didwana Town	5,438	4,884	4,006	3,140	81	114	..	..	1,343	1,422	..	..	8	8	..	..	91	6	146	1	1,018	22
	Jaitaran Pargana	46,888	43,126	41,503	38,138	2,450	2,481	..	..	2,025	2,490	7	8	1	..	2	..	255	10	272	10	2,187	104
	Jaitaran Town	2,108	2,263	1,481	1,505	235	300	..	..	392	458	..	..	..	..	..	..	33	..	38	..	223	14
	Jalor Pargana	69,293	64,425	57,496	51,291	7,821	9,760	..	..	1,366	1,066	2,610	2,300	..	..	..	..	608	18	539	23	4,325	157
	Jalor Town	3,791	3,833	2,572	2,355	684	888	..	..	371	425	184	165	..	..	..	..	39	2	71	1	534	14
	Jaswantpura Pargana	52,037	47,311	41,592	37,409	3,867	4,240	..	..	1,436	1,103	5,141	4,499	..	..	1	..	234	2	271	1	2,251	21
	Jodhpur Pargana	68,996	60,419	63,558	55,338	2,366	2,433	..	..	2,059	1,612	989	834	1	2	3	..	355	24	381	23	2,040	140
	Kuchaman Town	4,754	4,851	3,548	3,575	242	294	..	..	963	982	..	..	1	..	..	..	86	1	121	2	642	21
	Ladnun Town	4,574	5,111	2,309	2,375	819	1,298	..	..	1,440	1,443	..	..	..	..	..	..	27	2	77	4	438	22
	Lohawat Town	2,472	2,342	2,000	1,784	307	496	..	..	48	32	27	30	..	..	..	..	31	1	29	..	137	7
	Mallani Pargana	86,912	75,135	66,581	58,063	3,067	2,515	..	..	12,023	10,118	5,237	4,433	4	4	..	..	185	9	337	3	2,234	58
	Maroth Pargana	29,713	20,362	27,856	24,788	1,092	925	..	..	754	646	..	..	4	3	..	..	87	4	99	6	853	69
	Merta Pargana	67,370	62,084	62,902	56,971	1,884	1,978	..	..	3,472	3,123	9	10	3	2	..	..	227	10	351	8	2,531	76
	Merta Town	2,283	2,114	1,515	1,400	118	108	..	..	650	597	..	..	..	..	..	..	8	..	36	..	290	..
	Mundwa Town	2,473	2,554	2,106	2,185	22	18	..	..	345	340	..	..	..	2	..	..	33	..	40	1	861	3
	Nagaur Pargana	64,371	59,301	58,813	52,829	1,748	2,254	5	2	3,788	4,203	17	13	..	..	..	..	149	11	252	18	2,123	89
	Nagaur Town	6,442	6,518	3,488	3,623	506	678	3	1	2,350	2,209	..	..	4	1	5	6	113	1	104	5	1,251	21
	Nawa Pargana	4,030	3,547	3,605	3,236	165	133	..	..	268	174	..	..	4	4	..	..	23	..	24	2	247	8
	Nawa Town	2,903	2,694	2,233	1,905	129	154	..	..	590	520	..	..	9	10	2	6	17	1	38	1	252	6
	Nimal Town	2,520	2,495	2,129	2,074	150	168	..	..	241	253	..	..	..	..	..	..	20	1	20	1	148	5
	Pachbhadra Pargana	13,521	12,270	11,067	9,965	984	909	..	..	1,217	1,132	253	204	..	..	..	..	71	1	100	..	414	..
	Pachbhadra Town	1,096	1,060	721	634	290	340	..	..	21	19	66	67	..	..	..	..	20	6	38	2	258	12
	Pali Pargana	26,464	24,252	24,065	21,841	1,579	1,753	..	..	521	414	296	241	..	..	3	3	145	0	167	9	1,216	40
	Pali Town	6,580	6,359	3,478	3,356	1,047	1,099	..	..	2,051	1,001	4	3	..	..	..	..	58	5	160	4	1,317	46
	Parbatsar Pargana	54,687	50,618	49,545	45,806	887	927	..	..	4,237	3,875	..	..	10	7	8	3	392	7	330	10	2,379	84
	Phalodi Pargana	31,516	27,062	26,711	22,800	948	1,063	..	..	2,485	2,027	1,372	1,172	..	..	..	..	18	2	40	..	475	12
	Phalodi Town	6,375	7,450	4,461	5,173	857	1,348	..	..	984	869	73	69	..	..	..	..	92	1	218	7	1,012	47
	Pipar Town	3,796	3,760	2,491	2,357	469	530	..	..	631	868	..	..	..	..	5	5	52	..	67	..	361	24
	Pokaran Town	2,863	2,911	2,248	2,406	30	35	..	..	400	440	95	70	..	..	..	..	39	..	84	..	479	3
	Sachor Pargana	42,530	37,700	30,336	27,209	1,454	1,337	..	..	5,701	4,673	4,898	4,281	1	..	..	..	152	1	175	5	1,283	43
	Sadri Town	2,329	2,353	1,947	1,890	340	392	..	..	88	61	12	8	..	..	4	2	25	2	27	2	271	10
	Sambhar Pargana	1,116	981	1,065	945	4	1	..	..	42	34	..	..	..	..	6	1	..	..	2	..	8	..
	Sambhar Town	2,993	2,551	1,988	1,711	40	31	..	..	947	799	..	..	20	10	..	..	20	2	50	4	341	13
	Sankra Pargana	10,745	8,671	6,981	5,706	6	1	..	..	3,086	2,402	672	562	..	..	..	..	2	..	5	..	70	2
	Sheo Pargana	17,396	14,015	9,006	8,046	324	291	..	..	5,084	4,729	1,162	949	..	..	..	..	23	..	53	..	406	..
	Shergarh Pargana	31,075	26,952	26,980	23,281	1,152	1,163	..	..	1,503	1,275	1,350	1,233	..	..	..	..	144	2	123	1	1,116	24
	Siwana Pargana	21,008	19,846	16,793	15,490	2,746	3,131	..	..	479	341	990	884	..	..	..	..	178	6	290	2	1,482	10
	Sojat Pargana	54,455	49,915	48,343	43,548	4,354	4,860	1	1	1,708	1,447	27	26	12	11	10	2	409	10	420	19	3,325	124
	Sojat Town	4,971	5,078	3,460	3,428	683	804	..	..	781	883	..	..	..	..	16	13	72	2	87	7	740	31
	Villages in Merwara District	3,893	3,316	2,875	2,069	76	73	..	..	1,428	1,165	12	9	1	..	..	..	5	..	6	3	150	8

* These totals exceed the actual totals of the details, as they include figures for certain minor religions which were not sorted for administrative units.

PROVINCIAL TABLE II.—ADMINISTRATIVE UNITS BY RELIGION AND EDUCATION—*continued.*

State or District.	Administrative Unit (Pargana, Tahsil, Town, etc).	Total Population.		Distribution by Religion. Hindu.		Jain.		Sikh.		Musalman.		Animist.		Christian.		Others.		Number of Literate Persons. 0—14.		15—19.		20 and over.	
		M.	F.	M.	F.	M.	F.	M.	F.	M.	F.	M.	F.	M.	F.	M.	F.	M.	F.	M.	F.	M.	F.
1	2	3	4	5	6	7	8	9	10	11	12	13	14	15	16	17	18	19	20	21	22	23	24
	Mewar State	***685,219***	***635,581***	***542,449***	***502,909***	***33,447***	***32,783***	***8***	***6***	***23,003***	***22,178***	***83,114***	***77,573***	***169***	***95***	***43***	***35***	***9,002***	***97***	***3,777***	***136***	***34,209***	***973***
Mewar.	Udaipur City	17,400	15,769	10,401	9,736	1,883	1,680	1	..	3,911	3,663	1,107	634	69	38	8	9	140	9	410	21	3,373	102
	Amet Thikana	5,905	5,190	4,781	4,205	615	514	..	..	151	130	315	330	..	..	1	..	50	4	61	1	471	10
	Asind Thikana	8,094	7,584	6,001	6,442	390	355	..	..	303	201	497	476	..	..	..	..	18	..	21	..	298	3
	Badnor Thikana	11,475	10,117	9,752	8,358	471	361	..	..	400	382	702	783	..	..	..	..	19	3	43	1	412	15
	Bagor Tahsil	4,573	4,227	4,125	3,842	176	150	..	..	101	95	167	150	..	..	..	..	13	..	22	..	208	1
	Banera Thikana	11,638	10,830	10,566	9,610	144	110	..	..	405	357	715	755	..	..	8	4	2	..	10	..	136	..
	Banera Town	2,144	2,101	1,644	1,707	125	111	..	..	375	373	..	..	..	..	..	..	14	1	36	3	345	10
	Bansi Thikana	3,289	3,114	1,630	1,560	51	42	2	..	66	61	1,504	1,442	..	..	..	..	4	..	10	..	92	3
	Bari Sadri Thikana	7,257	7,094	4,560	4,471	476	441	..	..	361	352	1,861	1,829	..	..	..	..	32	..	73	3	517	18
	Bedla Thikana	8,478	7,091	7,693	7,217	179	101	..	..	110	135	455	471	..	..	2	3	16	2	32	..	313	10
	Begun Thikana	6,518	5,934	5,738	5,288	103	17	..	..	101	67	572	532	..	..	..	..	..	..	8	1	123	7
	Begun Town	2,204	2,181	1,571	1,583	188	204	..	..	413	359	2	2	..	..	..	..	4	1	17	1	176	8
	Bhainsrorgarh Thikana	7,318	7,012	5,536	5,364	140	100	..	..	215	183	1,388	1,302	..	..	..	..	12	..	16	..	270	1
	Bhilwara Thikana	32,307	29,734	29,010	27,043	672	574	..	..	1,151	1,014	1,182	1,072	..	..	3	1	73	4	118	2	1,172	50
	Bhilwara Town	6,413	4,150	3,143	3,058	350	337	..	..	[illegible]	739	10	4	1	2	..	..	95	2	114	..	927	22
	Bhindar Thikana	5,527	5,106	4,364	4,332	180	154	..	..	107	88	858	922	..	..	..	..	6	..	14	..	119	..
	Bhindar Town	2,345	2,265	1,565	1,622	359	312	..	..	402	342	18	9	..	..	..	..	7	..	33	..	358	1
	Bijolia Thikana	5,702	5,410	4,743	4,450	120	181	..	..	117	97	662	682	..	..	..	..	32	..	35	1	292	14
	Chhoti Sadri Thikana	15,007	13,098	14,536	11,167	332	230	..	..	355	287	381	374	..	..	..	..	28	3	42	1	366	14
	Chhoti Sadri Town	2,344	2,232	1,722	1,620	234	242	..	..	373	365	2	4	..	..	..	..	40	7	65	7	384	33
	Chitorgarh Thikana	41,073	38,971	36,853	31,934	800	720	..	..	1,013	1,012	2,304	2,298	2	..	11	7	78	5	167	5	1,685	25
	Chitorgarh Town	3,039	3,338	2,781	2,444	260	243	..	..	752	680	93	24	11	4	2	..	45	..	114	2	802	14
	Delwara Thikana	11,160	10,320	8,632	8,145	515	479	..	..	159	136	1,854	1,770	..	..	..	..	26	..	58	2	400	6
	Deogarh Thikana	15,708	14,037	13,910	12,456	1,041	847	..	..	211	212	500	522	..	..	..	..	50	10	175	8	1,711	32
	Deogarh Town	2,638	2,823	1,827	1,931	493	498	..	..	252	350	30	34	..	..	..	..	61	..	50	3	500	18
	Devasthan Thikana	14,040	13,185	10,853	10,177	929	912	..	..	151	94	2,115	1,080	..	..	..	..	67	2	86	1	806	34
	Girwa (including Dhariavad) Thikana.	48,016	45,110	20,525	27,852	3,256	2,555	..	..	912	802	14,291	13,515	2	2	..	..	141	7	251	11	2,110	47
	Gogunda Thikana	4,797	4,650	3,053	2,870	444	532	..	..	69	82	1,231	1,168	..	..	..	..	26	..	35	1	252	7
	Hurra Thikana	23,830	21,731	20,419	18,651	1,274	1,082	..	..	742	617	1,302	1,147	..	..	3	4	69	3	120	8	1,027	29
	Jahazpur Thikana	29,134	26,025	26,089	23,298	713	511	..	..	501	473	1,700	1,710	3	1	..	..	41	1	80	1	971	45
	Jahazpur Town	2,105	1,881	1,540	1,312	18	7	..	..	531	542	16	..	..	..	..	..	22	..	25	1	302	10
	Kachola (Shahpura) Thikana.	8,637	7,012	7,842	7,225	188	139	..	..	137	125	470	421	..	..	..	..	10	..	21	..	260	6
	Kankroli Thikana	3,553	3,379	2,950	2,794	181	227	..	..	162	139	251	219	..	..	..	..	10	..	12	..	168	5
	Kanor Thikana	6,009	6,353	4,825	4,208	453	422	..	..	211	210	1,617	1,509	..	..	..	..	27	2	64	4	488	16
	Kapasan Thikana	10,168	17,398	16,308	14,874	733	739	..	..	855	723	1,110	1,053	..	..	..	..	32	1	98	3	1,044	32
	Kariah Thikana	1,741	1,640	1,490	1,397	33	31	..	..	13	8	215	204	..	..	..	..	2	..	..	..	28	2
	Khamnor Thikana	13,901	12,772	10,894	9,955	1,142	1,102	..	..	90	73	1,775	1,642	..	..	..	..	25	4	26	4	278	34
	Kherwara Bhumat	12,129	11,066	4,568	4,506	281	309	..	..	181	189	7,084	6,923	2	..	..	..	17	..	39	1	304	2
	Kherwara Cantonment	1,205	721	1,047	531	10	4	1	1	201	175	..	..	33	10	..	..	24	1	48	2	281	17
	Kotharia Thikana	4,742	4,310	3,987	3,625	212	170	..	..	42	51	501	464	..	..	..	..	9	..	35	2	271	3
	Kotra Bhumat	10,708	9,772	3,742	3,351	307	240	..	..	[illegible]	121	6,453	6,051	..	..	..	..	22	..	30	1	333	6
	Kotra Cantonment	401	255	161	137	6	7	..	..	67	39	236	102	2	..	..	..	3	..	4	..	56	1

PROVINCIAL TABLE II.—Administrative Units by Religion and Education—*continued.*

State or District.	Administrative Unit (Pargana, Tahsil, Town, etc.)	Total Population. M.	Total Population. F.	Hindu. M.	Hindu. F.	Jain. M.	Jain. F.	Sikh. M.	Sikh. F.	Musalman. M.	Musalman. F.	Animist. M.	Animist. F.	Christian. M.	Christian. F.	Others. M.	Others. F.	Literate 0—14. M.	Literate 0—14. F.	Literate 15—19. M.	Literate 15—19. F.	Literate 20 and over. M.	Literate 20 and over. F.
1	2	3	4	5	6	7	8	9	10	11	12	13	14	15	16	17	18	19	20	21	22	23	24
Mewar,—concluded.	Kumbhalgarh Thikana	19,738	17,818	15,363	13,594	1,682	1,648	..	..	202	166	2,510	2,410	..	..	..	..	19	3	51	..	486	28
	Kurabar Thikana	7,670	7,731	5,502	5,540	718	749	..	..	172	111	1,318	1,384	..	..	..	..	31	..	34	..	309	8
	Magra (Sarara) Thikana	34,860	33,677	30,710	29,676	2,171	2,279	..	..	671	465	1,313	1,255	2	2	..	..	62	1	118	4	1,181	20
	Mandalgarh Thikana	26,016	23,931	22,000	20,163	907	763	..	..	1,060	1,046	2,056	1,955	..	..	3	4	27	..	65	..	807	19
	Meja Thikana	1,934	1,795	1,740	1,623	10	16	..	..	53	41	122	115	..	..	..	..	..	..	9	..	53	2
	Nathdwara Thikana	4,751	4,326	3,068	3,375	237	218	..	..	25	16	608	717	..	..	..	..	5	2	11	1	110	6
	Nathdwara Town	2,906	2,518	2,533	2,219	61	37	..	..	214	170	93	80	5	3	..	..	7	..	21	..	317	3
	Parsoli Thikana	2,772	2,403	2,555	2,193	61	54	..	..	32	40	104	114	..	..	..	..	5	1	10	1	105	2
	Pur Town	2,209	2,214	1,687	1,681	257	289	..	..	218	230	17	14	..	..	..	..	12	2	26	3	226	12
	Rajnagar Thikana	15,070	13,907	12,602	11,777	813	754	..	..	201	276	1,154	1,100	..	..	..	..	22	1	33	2	324	10
	Rasmi Thikana	17,517	16,043	15,164	14,076	964	747	..	..	611	528	775	692	..	..	..	..	91	..	121	3	844	12
	Sahran District (including Sheopur).	38,448	35,194	32,770	30,045	2,783	2,153	1	3	991	904	1,900	1,785	3	2	..	..	96	7	178	10	1,560	53
	Saira Thikana	9,176	8,777	6,223	5,736	977	1,166	..	..	44	35	1,927	1,818	1	2	..	..	33	..	67	2	492	10
	Salumbar Thikana	15,743	15,006	9,434	9,097	930	905	..	..	290	219	3,089	4,874	..	..	..	..	30	..	78	..	725	..
	Salumbar Town	2,144	2,362	1,496	1,585	177	238	..	..	372	410	100	100	..	..	..	..	25	..	28	..	275	2
	Sardargarh Thikana	2,212	2,052	1,771	1,637	200	235	..	..	54	45	127	112	..	..	..	..	13	..	10	..	127	..
	Shivrati Thikana	3,307	3,146	2,810	2,663	175	163	..	..	17	17	305	303	..	..	..	..	2	..	5	..	38	..
	Udaipur Tahsil	13,323	11,325	8,449	7,204	460	468	1	..	492	247	3,009	3,527	16	19	..	..	32	8	67	8	595	51
	Villages in Merwara District	20,932	18,581	18,222	16,265	1,110	1,008	2	2	1,103	849	474	427	10	10	2	3	72	..	125	..	1,034	13
Partabgarh.	*Partabgarh State*	*31,735*	*30,969*	*17,077*	*16,771*	*2,339*	*2,079*	*1*	*1*	*1,830*	*1,795*	*10,530*	*10,309*	..	..	*12*	*14*	*194*	*10*	*288*	*16*	*2,279*	*95*
	Partabgarh Town	4,186	4,143	2,189	2,199	1,103	1,077	1	1	859	848	28	14	..	..	9	4	121	6	152	10	1,106	50
	Hathunia Zilla	18,920	13,656	9,349	9,194	520	440	..	..	624	583	3,424	3,189	..	..	1	..	29	1	67	5	480	25
	Magra Zilla	3,572	3,284	845	603	77	89	..	..	90	41	2,754	2,572	..	..	..	..	11	..	16	..	125	2
	Sagthali Zilla	10,057	9,886	4,804	4,776	502	473	..	..	275	253	4,321	4,374	..	..	2	10	33	3	63	1	568	18
Shahpura.	*Shahpura Chiefship*	*24,395*	*22,803*	*21,381*	*19,868*	*885*	*734*	..	..	*1,236*	*1,171*	*989*	*963*	*1*	..	*103*	*66*	*128*	*11*	*221*	*6*	*1,839*	*60*
	Shahpura Town	4,074	3,855	2,964	2,806	265	211	..	..	770	748	40	41	1	..	72	49	62	10	105	6	846	30
	Amli Tahsil	1,560	1,415	1,441	1,329	57	42	..	..	21	12	41	32	..	..	..	..	2	..	10	..	68	3
	Dhikola Tahsil	3,964	3,566	3,690	3,317	65	56	..	..	77	58	142	140	..	..	..	..	12	..	14	..	140	3
	Kanechan Tahsil	2,410	2,212	2,195	2,019	50	41	..	..	28	23	121	129	..	..	..	..	2	..	6	..	163	..
	Kotdan Tahsil	3,875	3,071	3,313	3,142	216	205	..	..	179	157	105	109	..	..	..	..	25	1	37	..	247	14
	Phulia Tahsil	4,417	4,153	3,889	3,704	118	99	..	..	113	94	250	240	..	..	31	17	15	..	22	..	210	5
	Sargaria Tahsil	2,673	2,542	2,403	2,308	100	80	..	..	75	82	83	72	..	..	..	..	7	..	7	..	24	3
	Shahpura Tahsil	1,622	1,378	1,490	1,243	..	..	..	..	7	4	125	131	..	..	..	..	3	..	20	..	74	2
Sirohi.	*Sirohi State*	*98,289*	*90,638*	*83,887*	*75,519*	*7,990*	*9,698*	*63*	*13*	*4,124*	*3,116*	*2,308*	*2,123*	*322*	*282*	*95*	*87*	*1,153*	*127*	*960*	*76*	*7,079*	*438*
	Sirohi Town	3,272	3,343	2,497	2,474	447	651	1	..	310	213	..	..	10	4	1	1	2	..	1	..	10	..
	Abu Tahsil	1,356	1,138	1,177	1,014	63	61	..	..	114	71	..	..	2	2	..	..	10	3	13	3	108	5
	Anadra Tahsil	3,422	3,208	3,051	2,855	248	325	..	..	120	88	..	..	..	..	..	..	31	1	21	..	185	8
	Bhakhar Tahsil	1,191	1,135	1,167	1,117	..	..	..	..	27	18	..	..	..	..	..	..	..	..	..	..	..	..
	Erinpura Cantonment	1,856	1,177	1,250	845	13	11	58	12	501	259	7	1	10	8	3	2	21	..	59	2	424	12
	Jhora Tahsil	10,791	10,118	9,351	8,542	961	1,378	..	..	127	95	352	303	..	..	..	..	96	4	86	4	555	24
	Kharari Town (Abu Road)	4,037	3,173	2,508	2,012	104	74	2	..	1,010	867	13	11	186	146	55	43	132	48	120	28	761	142
	Madar Tahsil	9,840	8,976	8,273	7,338	821	710	..	..	241	320	662	608	..	..	..	..	87	5	50	3	438	33
	Magra Tahsil	11,687	11,119	9,595	8,653	1,307	1,827	..	..	157	124	628	611	..	..	..	..	127	1	119	..	834	29

PROVINCIAL TABLE II.—ADMINISTRATIVE UNITS BY RELIGION AND EDUCATION—*concluded.*

State or District.	Administrative Unit (Pargana, Tahsil, Town, etc).	Total Population.		Distribution by Religion.														Number of Literate Persons.					
				Hindu.		Jain.		Sikh.		Musalman.		Animist.		Christian.		Others.		0—14.		15—19.		20 and over.	
		M.	F.	M.	F.	M.	F.	M.	F.	M.	F.	M.	F.	M.	F.	M.	F.	M.	F.	M.	F.	M.	F.
1	2	3	4	5	6	7	8	9	10	11	12	13	14	15	16	17	18	19	20	21	22	23	24
Sirohi—concld.	Mt. Abu Town	2,083	1,203	1,288	763	27	10	2	1	360	208	93	73	294	113	31	35	147	40	74	10	492	77
	(1) Bazar	*995*	*680*	*736*	*494*	*27*	*10*	*2*	*1*	*210*	*117*	..	..	*7*	*6*	*13*	*22*	*29*	*4*	*37*	*8*	*238*	*12*
	(2) Civil limits	*753*	*405*	*379*	*225*	..	..	..	..	*113*	*56*	*81*	*64*	*132*	*47*	*13*	*13*	*68*	*5*	*29*	*6*	*125*	*48*
	(3) Military limits	*335*	*118*	*153*	*44*	..	..	..	..	*13*	*5*	*14*	*9*	*165*	*60*	..	..	*50*	*31*	*8*	*5*	*129*	*17*
	Pamera Tahsil	9,565	9,279	8,739	8,237	638	887	..	..	123	86	65	69	..	..	..	..	79	1	48	..	443	9
	Pindwara Tahsil	10,047	8,855	8,962	7,927	826	796	..	..	257	132	2	..	..	..	..	..	91	1	97	1	700	23
	Posalia Tahsil	11,106	10,348	9,913	8,610	1,022	1,518	..	..	83	59	167	132	11	9	..	..	113	5	71	2	525	7
	Rohera Tahsil	8,251	8,305	7,472	7,208	447	719	..	..	147	133	184	185	..	..	1	..	69	..	74	1	471	6
	Santpura Tahsil	7,195	6,304	6,688	6,122	58	33	..	..	223	208	132	130	..	..	4	6	17	..	20	2	181	2
	Sheoganj Town	1,888	2,122	1,191	1,222	481	601	..	..	215	209	1	..	..	..	..	..	48	2	40	2	419	21
	Sirohi Tahsil	709	575	695	570	7	2	..	..	7	3	..	..	..	..	..	..	83	16	56	9	517	40
Tonk.	***Tonk State***	***136,300***	***146,791***	***127,001***	***119,245***	***4,163***	***3,738***	..	***3***	***20,516***	***19,916***	***3,751***	***3,835***	***6***	***6***	***51***	***48***	***263***	***20***	***540***	***17***	***5,219***	***93***
	Tonk City	16,837	17,027	7,589	7,310	520	489	..	2	8,720	9,218	1	1	6	6	1	..	80	10	184	12	1,563	50
	Aligarh Pargana	8,503	7,785	7,193	6,711	457	377	..	..	797	634	56	63	..	..	..	..	15	1	22	..	226	4
	Chhabra Pargana	17,405	15,865	15,575	13,956	7	5	..	..	615	603	1,208	1,201	..	..	..	..	3	..	12	1	100	..
	Chhabra Town	3,108	3,056	2,280	2,199	132	119	..	..	693	738	1	..	..	..	..	..	29	3	32	1	350	17
	Nimbahera Pargana	20,568	19,844	17,810	17,364	936	814	..	..	890	761	931	905	..	..	1	..	35	1	69	..	690	12
	Nimbahera Town	2,240	2,018	1,310	1,222	254	216	..	..	645	537	19	16	..	..	32	27	18	..	58	2	368	..
	Pirawa Pargana	13,045	11,785	12,001	10,823	144	94	..	..	358	204	542	572	..	..	..	..	..	..	..	..	101	..
	Pirawa Town	2,202	2,300	1,128	1,138	355	392	..	..	779	770	..	..	..	..	..	..	30	..	44	..	345	..
	Sironj Pargana	45,650	43,169	35,558	34,297	725	694	..	..	5,683	5,317	767	700	..	..	17	21	31	4	73	1	818	8
	(1) Latiri Tahsil	*14,729*	*13,832*	*12,999*	*12,230*	*172*	*184*	..	..	*1,116*	*983*	*440*	*435*	..	..	*2*	..	*7*	..	*11*	..	*139*	..
	(2) Sironj and Sadar Tahsil.	*24,838*	*23,329*	*21,835*	*20,480*	*360*	*352*	..	..	*2,301*	*2,112*	*327*	*355*	..	..	*15*	*21*	*9*	*3*	*18*	*1*	*259*	*2*
	(3) Sironj Town	*6,083*	*6,008*	*3,724*	*3,578*	*193*	*158*	..	..	*2,166*	*2,272*	..	..	..	..	..	..	*15*	*1*	*11*	..	*420*	*6*
	Tonk Pargana	26,732	23,012	24,457	22,213	635	538	..	..	1,434	904	226	107	..	..	..	..	18	1	46	..	641	2
	(1) Bagri Tahsil	*15,300*	*13,793*	*14,073*	*12,843*	*455*	*401*	..	..	*715*	*498*	*57*	*51*	..	..	..	..	*10*	..	*32*	..	*457*	..
	(2) Chandlai Tahsil	*11,432*	*10,149*	*10,384*	*9,370*	*180*	*137*	..	..	*719*	*496*	*169*	*146*	..	..	..	..	*3*	*1*	*11*	..	*184*	*2*
	AJMER-MERWARA.	**241,373**	**213,307**	**184,958**	**165,342**	**9,614**	**8,412**	**781**	**137**	**41,302**	**35,188**	**1,501**	**1,556**	**3,247**	**2,144**	**670**	**498**	**2,895**	**569**	**3,534**	**671**	**25,216**	**1,914**
	Ajmer District	***201,911***	***178,473***	***155,993***	***140,083***	***7,654***	***6,659***	***779***	***137***	***32,585***	***27,880***	***1,308***	***1,370***	***2,996***	***1,914***	***596***	***430***	***2,547***	***524***	***2,972***	***620***	***21,680***	***1,669***
Ajmer.	Ajmer City	47,354	38,669	27,187	22,021	1,440	1,252	61	26	16,635	14,019	52	49	1,450	1,132	520	369	1,168	324	1,442	317	8,610	1,006
	Ajmer Istimrari area	27,057	24,468	21,993	19,071	1,443	1,309	2	4	3,141	2,708	435	448	41	33	..	..	227	11	206	14	1,706	60
	Ajmer Khalsa area	60,842	55,197	51,416	46,799	1,446	1,185	3	8	7,248	6,410	485	529	223	256	21	15	530	27	640	75	3,798	100
	Deoli Town	3,011	2,134	2,467	1,736	29	15	86	29	440	336	1	..	38	18	1	..	42	5	64	8	629	30
	(1) Sadar Bazar	*1,302*	*1,195*	*1,078*	*1,008*	*23*	*10*	..	..	*191*	*169*	..	..	*7*	*8*	..	..						
	(2) Agency Bazar	*638*	*595*	*531*	*458*	*6*	*5*	..	..	*155*	*128*	..	..	*5*	*4*	*1*	..	†39	†5	†55	†3	†313	†20
	(3) Cantonment	*1,071*	*344*	*858*	*270*	..	..	*86*	*29*	*100*	*39*	*1*	..	*26*	*6*	..	..	*3*	..	*9*	..	*286*	*10*
	Kekri Istimrari area	49,103	46,063	44,421	41,813	2,939	2,018	1	..	1,547	1,342	211	280	8	9	6	1	338	14	438	20	3,740	127
	Kekri Town	3,126	2,800	2,280	2,151	204	162	..	..	637	486	..	..	4	2	1	..	59	6	54	4	531	18
	Nasirabad Town	11,298	8,943	6,229	5,592	151	118	626	75	2,928	2,585	94	64	1,223	464	47	45	183	137	228	187	2,627	148
	(1) Civil limits	*8,135*	*8,009*	*5,282*	*5,291*	*146*	*117*	*8*	*4*	*2,598*	*2,494*	..	..	*59*	*61*	*42*	*42*	*129*	*19*	*145*	*19*	*1,125*	*61*
	(2) Military limits	*3,163*	*934*	*947*	*301*	*5*	*1*	*618*	*71*	*330*	*91*	*94*	*64*	*1,161*	*403*	*5*	*3*	*54*	*113*	*83*	*168*	*1,502*	*87*
Merwara.	***Merwara District***	***39,462***	***34,834***	***28,965***	***25,259***	***1,960***	***1,733***	***9***	..	***8,717***	***7,308***	***193***	***186***	***251***	***230***	***74***	***68***	***348***	***45***	***562***	***51***	***3,536***	***245***
	Beawar Town	12,328	10,472	8,397	7,136	1,236	1,130	1	..	2,417	1,030	8	5	196	203	73	68	261	41	434	42	2,560	222
	Beawar Tahsil*	22,218	19,956	15,389	14,131	494	427	..	..	6,248	6,315	55	60	31	23	1	..	71	1	93	4	723	17
	Todgarh Tahsil*	4,916	4,306	4,479	3,992	230	196	1	..	52	63	130	121	24	24	..	..	16	3	35	5	253	6

* Excluding Marwar and Mewar villages.

† Details of literacy for the 2 bazars separately are not available.